6년간 아무도 깨지 못한 기록

합격자 수 1위
에듀윌

KRI 한국기록원 2016, 2017, 2019년 공인중개사 최다 합격자 배출 공식 인증 (2022년 현재까지 업계 최고 기록)

에듀윌을 선택한 이유는 분명합니다

합격자 수 수직 상승
1,800%

명품 강의 만족도
99%

베스트셀러 1위
46개월 (3년 10개월)

4년 연속 공무원 교육
1위

에듀윌 공무원을 선택하면 합격은 현실이 됩니다.

* 2017/2021 에듀윌 공무원 과정 최종 환급자 수 기준
* 7·9급공무원 대표 교수진 2021년 7월 강의 만족도 평균(배영표/성정혜/신형철/윤세훈/강성민)
* YES24 수험서 자격증 공무원 베스트셀러 1위 (2017년 3월, 2018년 4월~6월, 8월, 2019년 4월, 6월~12월, 2020년 1월~12월, 2021년 1월~12월, 2022년 1월~9월 월별 베스트, 매월 1위 교재는 다름)
* 2022, 2021 대한민국 브랜드만족도 7·9급공무원 교육 1위 (한경비즈니스) / 2020, 2019 한국브랜드만족지수 7·9급공무원 교육 1위 (주간동아, G밸리뉴스)

합격자 수 1,800%[*] 수직 상승!
매년 놀라운 성장

에듀윌 공무원은 '합격자 수'라는 확실한 결과로 증명하며
지금도 기록을 만들어 가고 있습니다.

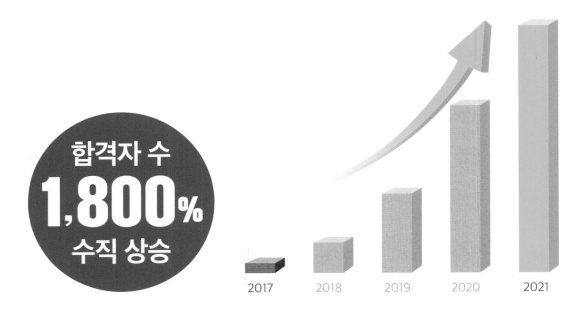

합격자 수
1,800%
수직 상승

2017 2018 2019 2020 2021

합격자 수를 폭발적으로 증가시킨 독한 평생패스

합격 시 수강료 평생 0원 최대 300% 환급 (최대 402만 원 환급)	합격할 때까지 전 강좌 무제한 수강	합격생 & 독한 교수진 1:1 학습관리

※ 환급내용은 상품페이지 참고. 상품은 변경될 수 있음.

상품
페이지

강의 만족도 99%[*]
명품 강의

에듀윌 공무원 전문 교수진!
합격의 차이를 직접 경험해 보세요

합격자 수 1,800%[*] 수직 상승으로 증명된 합격 커리큘럼

독한 시작		독한 회독		독한 기출요약		독한 문풀		독한 파이널
기초 + 기본이론	▶	심화이론 완성	▶	핵심요약 + 기출문제 파악	▶	단원별 문제풀이	▶	동형모의고사 + 파이널

독한 에듀윌 공무원 노량진학원
GRAND OPEN

공무원학원 1위*
합격자 수 1,800%* 수직 상승!

앞줄 왼쪽부터
배영표(국어), 임지혜(국어), 조은아(국어), 성정혜(영어), 손재석(영어), 이원일(영어), 이지훈(영어), 신형철(한국사), 이종길(한국사), 서익환(한국사), 한유진(한국사), 윤세훈(행정학), 김시동(행정학), 강성민(행정법), 김용철(행정법), 고세훈(교육학), 권구현(교육학), 홍형철(형사소송법), 이나경(민법, 민사소송법), 신현식(형법), 한진희(헌법), 김윤경(세법), 최정연(회계학), 손용근(사회복지학), 김준휘(관세법), 박도준(경영학), 장성국(토목설계, 응용역학), 손승호(컴퓨터일반, 정보보호론), 최승윤(건축계획), 안병관(건축구조), 김영복(전기이론), 김지호(전기기기), 조현(기계일반, 기계설계), 이영주(보건행정, 공중보건), 한수지(간호관리, 지역사회 간호), 김소영(면접), 이승찬(면접), 헤더진(G-TELP)

2021 공무원 수석 합격자* 배출!
합격생들의 진짜 합격스토리

 에듀윌 강의·교재·학습시스템의 우수성을
2021년도에도 입증하였습니다!

에듀윌 커리큘럼을 따라가며 기출 분석을 반복한 결과 7.5개월 만에 합격

권○혁 지방직 9급 일반행정직 최종 합격

샘플 강의를 듣고 맘에 들었는데, 가성비도 좋아 에듀윌을 선택하게 되었습니다. 특히, 공부에 집중하기 좋은 깔끔한 시설과 교수님께 바로 질문할 수 있는 환경이 좋았습니다. 학원을 다니면서 에듀윌에서 무료로 제공하는 온라인 강의를 많이 활용했습니다. 늦게 시작했기 때문에 처음에는 진도를 따라가기 위해서 활용했고, 그 후에는 기출 분석을 복습하기 위해 활용했습니다. 마지막에 반복했던 기출 분석은 합격에 중요한 영향을 미쳤던 것 같습니다.

고민없이 에듀윌을 선택, 온라인 강의 반복 수강으로 합격 완성

박○은 국가직 9급 일반농업직 최종 합격

공무원 시험은 빨리 준비할수록 더 좋다고 생각해서 상담 후 바로 고민 없이 에듀윌을 선택했습니다. 과목별 교재가 동일하기 때문에 한 과목당 세 교수님의 강의를 모두 들었습니다. 심지어 전년도 강의까지 포함하여 강의를 무제한으로 들었습니다. 덕분에 중요한 부분을 알게 되었고 그 부분을 집중적으로 먼저 외우며 공부할 수 있었습니다. 우울할 때에는 내용을 아는 활기찬 드라마를 틀어놓고 공부하며 위로를 받았는데 집중도 잘되어 좋았습니다.

체계가 잘 짜여진 에듀윌은 합격으로 가는 최고의 동반자

김○욱 국가직 9급 출입국관리직 최종 합격

에듀윌은 체계가 굉장히 잘 짜여져 있습니다. 만약, 공무원이 되고 싶은데 아무것도 모르는 초시생이라면 묻지 말고 에듀윌을 선택하시면 됩니다. 에듀윌은 기초·기본이론부터 심화이론, 기출문제, 단원별 문제, 모의고사, 그리고 면접까지 다 챙겨주는, 시작부터 필기합격 후 끝까지 전부 관리해 주는 최고의 동반자입니다. 저는 체계적인 에듀윌의 커리큘럼과 하루에 한 페이지라도 집중해서 디테일을 외우려고 노력하는 습관 덕분에 합격할 수 있었습니다.

다음 합격의 주인공은 당신입니다!

더 많은
합격스토리

eduwill

회원 가입하고
100% 무료 혜택 받기

가입 즉시, 공무원 공부에 필요한 모든 걸 드립니다!

혜택1 출제경향을 반영한 과목별 테마특강 제공

※ 에듀윌 홈페이지 ⋯ 직렬 사이트 선택
⋯ 상단 '무료특강' 메뉴를 통해 수강

혜택2 초보 수험생 필수 기초강의 제공

※ 에듀윌 홈페이지 ⋯ '합격필독서 무료증정' 선택
⋯ '9급공무원 합격교과서' 신청 후 '나의 강의실'에서 확인
(7일 수강 가능)

혜택3 전 과목 기출문제 해설강의 제공

※ 에듀윌 홈페이지 ⋯ 직렬 사이트 선택
⋯ 상단 '학습자료' 메뉴를 통해 수강
(최신 3개년 주요 직렬 기출문제 해설강의 제공)

* 배송비 별도 / 비매품

기초학습 합격 입문서+기초강의

무료배포
선착순 100명

무료배포
이벤트

친구 추천하고
한 달 만에 920만원 받았어요

2021년 2월 1달간 실제로 리워드 금액을 받아가신
*a*o*h**** 고객님의 실제사례입니다.

1초 합격예측
모바일 성적분석표

1초 안에 '클릭' 한 번으로 성적을 확인하실 수 있습니다!

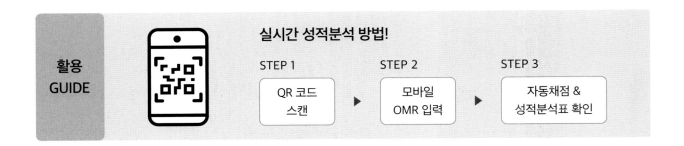

활용 GUIDE

실시간 성적분석 방법!

STEP 1
QR 코드 스캔

▶

STEP 2
모바일 OMR 입력

▶

STEP 3
자동채점 & 성적분석표 확인

STEP 1

QR 코드 스캔

- 교재의 QR 코드를 모바일로 스캔 후 에듀윌 회원 로그인
- QR 코드 하단의 바로가기 주소로도 접속 가능

STEP 2

모바일 OMR 입력

- 회차 확인 후 '응시하기' 클릭
- 모바일 OMR에 답안 입력
- 문제풀이 시간까지 측정 가능

STEP 3

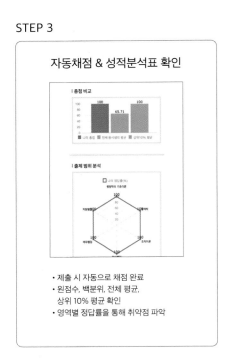

자동채점 & 성적분석표 확인

- 제출 시 자동으로 채점 완료
- 원점수, 백분위, 전체 평균, 상위 10% 평균 확인
- 영역별 정답률을 통해 취약점 파악

처음에는 당신이 원하는 곳으로
갈 수는 없겠지만,
당신이 지금 있는 곳에서
출발할 수는 있을 것이다.

– 작자 미상

1 에듀윌 합격앱 접속하기

또는

QR코드
스캔하기

에듀윌 합격앱
다운받기

2 기출OX 퀴즈 무료로 이용하기

| 하단 딱풀 메뉴에서 기출OX 선택 | ▶ | 과목과 PART 선택 | ▶ | 퀴즈 풀기 |

• 틀린 문제는 기출오답노트(기출 OX)에서 다시 확인할 수 있습니다.

3 교재 구매 인증하기

• 무료이용 후 7일이 지나면 교재 구매 인증을 해야 합니다(최초 1회 인증 필요).
• 교재 구매 인증화면에서 정답을 입력하면 기간 제한 없이 기출OX 퀴즈를 무료로 이용할 수 있습니다(정답은 교재에서 찾을 수 있음).

※에듀윌 합격앱 어플에서 회원 가입 후 이용하실 수 있는 서비스입니다.
※스마트폰에서만 이용 가능하며, 일부 단말기에서는 서비스가 지원되지 않을 수 있습니다.
※해당 서비스는 추후 다른 서비스로 변경될 수 있습니다.

설문조사에 참여하고 스타벅스 아메리카노를 받아가세요!

에듀윌 9급공무원 7개년 기출문제집을 선택한 이유는 무엇인가요?

소중한 의견을 주신 여러분들에게 더욱더 완성도 있는 교재로 보답하겠습니다.

참여 방법	QR코드 스캔 ▶ 설문조사 참여(1분만 투자하세요!)
이벤트 기간	2022년 9월 21일~2023년 8월 31일
추첨 방법	매월 6명 추첨 후 당첨자 개별 연락
경품	스타벅스 아메리카노(tall)

2023

에듀윌 9급공무원

7개년 기출문제집

영어

당신의 미래를 응원합니다

기출을 넘어 기적을 만듭니다.

"공시에서 가장 중요한 것이 무엇인가요?"
수험생들이 '가장 중요한 것', 즉 '핵심이 무엇인가'를 묻는 것은 어쩌면 당연한 일입니다.
정답은 바로 '기출문제'입니다.
기출문제는 출제자에게 Bible이며, 수험생에게도 또한 마찬가지입니다.

"그럼 그 기출을 어떻게 공부해야 하나요?" 라는 질문이 바로 이어집니다.
저는 이렇게 답합니다.
"기출, 그 이상을 만들어 줄 수 있는 교재로 공부하세요."
이미 기출제된 문항인 '기출'을 통해서 출제 개념은 필수적으로 체화해야 하며, 이를 넘어서 앞으로의 문항의 방향성과, 관련된 상위 개념에 대한 경쟁력을 구축하는 것 또한 제대로 된 기출 분석을 통해서만 가능합니다.

〈에듀윌 9급공무원 7개년 기출문제집〉은 기출문제를 정확하게 수록하였고, 미시적인 단계적 분석과 거시적인 문제 접근을 통해 현재의 문제뿐만 아니라 다른 문제로의 적용이 가능하도록 설계되었습니다.

공시 준비생은 강의를 듣는 시간보다 자습하는 시간에 훨씬 더 많은 시간을 씁니다. 강의를 듣는 시간뿐만 아니라, 개인 학습 시간 활용이 무엇보다 중요합니다. 자습하는 그 수많은 시간 동안만큼은 제가 여러분과 함께 할 수 없기에 이 책을 통해 여러분을 만나고자 합니다. 자습을 통해 강의를 듣는 만큼의 지식을 얻고 적용할 수 있도록 문항별 카테고리, 〈1초 합격예측 서비스〉의 실제 누적 데이터에 기반을 둔 문항별 오답률과 선지별 선택률 등 여러 요소를 디테일하게 배치하였습니다.
하나의 요소마다 새겨진 의도와 방향성을 이해하여 원하시는 합격의 점수를 만들어 내시기를 바랍니다.

책의 머리말을 차분히 읽는 독자들은 많지 않습니다. 하지만 이 글을 지금 마주하고 계신 여러분이라면, 기출의 본질을 정확히 파악하여, 지금 앉으신 곳에서 반드시 성공을 이뤄낼 것을 믿습니다.
수험생 여러분께 경의를 표합니다.
건승을 바랍니다.

성정혜

기출문제가 학습의 기준이 되는 이유

☑ 주요 빈출 개념은 반드시 반복 출제된다.

☑ 매년 출제되는 문제 유형은 정해져 있다.

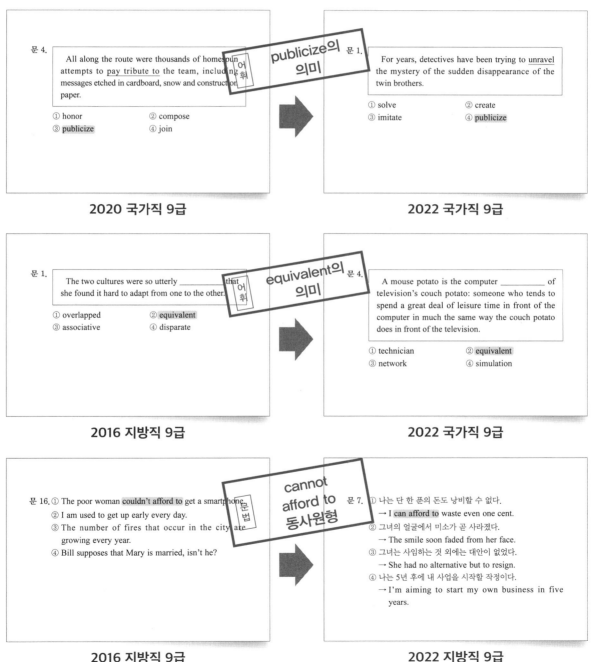

문 4.
All along the route were thousands of homespun attempts to pay tribute to the team, including messages etched in cardboard, snow and construction paper.

① honor
② compose
③ publicize
④ join

2020 국가직 9급

publicize의 의미

문 1.
For years, detectives have been trying to unravel the mystery of the sudden disappearance of the twin brothers.

① solve
② create
③ imitate
④ publicize

2022 국가직 9급

문 1.
The two cultures were so utterly _____ that she found it hard to adapt from one to the other.

① overlapped
② equivalent
③ associative
④ disparate

2016 지방직 9급

equivalent의 의미

문 4.
A mouse potato is the computer _____ of television's couch potato: someone who tends to spend a great deal of leisure time in front of the computer in much the same way the couch potato does in front of the television.

① technician
② equivalent
③ network
④ simulation

2022 국가직 9급

문 16. ① The poor woman couldn't afford to get a smartphone.
② I am used to get up early every day.
③ The number of fires that occur in the city are growing every year.
④ Bill supposes that Mary is married, isn't he?

2016 지방직 9급

cannot afford to 동사원형

문 7. ① 나는 단 한 푼의 돈도 낭비할 수 없다.
→ I can afford to waste even one cent.
② 그녀의 얼굴에서 미소가 곧 사라졌다.
→ The smile soon faded from her face.
③ 그녀는 사임하는 것 외에는 대안이 없었다.
→ She had no alternative but to resign.
④ 나는 5년 후에 내 사업을 시작할 작정이다.
→ I'm aiming to start my own business in five years.

2022 지방직 9급

이 책의 구성

기출
문제편

2022~2016년도 7개년 기출문제 32회분

❶ 1초 합격예측 서비스
회차별 QR 코드 스캔 후, 모바일 OMR을 이용하여 기출문제를 실전처럼 풀이한다.

해설편

직렬별 기출분석 REPORT

수준&약점 체크 가능한 해설

❶ 출제 Point & 대비전략
과년도 기출의 핵심 내용과 2023년도
기출을 대비할 전략을 한눈에 파악한다.

❷ 최근 7개년 출제경향 & 출제비중
파트, 챕터가 어떤 식으로 얼마나 출제되
었는지 확인한다.

❶ 합격예상 체크 & 취약영역 체크
나의 점수로 합격, 불합격을 미리 예상해 보고,
영역별 틀린 문제 수로 나의 취약영역을 체크한다.

❷ 정답해설 + 오답해설
문제의 핵심을 짚는 해설로 틀린 문제까지 완전
히 내 것으로 만든다.

❸ 문항별 오답률 + 선택지 선택률
경쟁자들의 선택과 내 선택을 비교하여 현재 나
의 위치를 파악한다.

에듀윌 기출문제집의 자신감

완벽한 학습을 도와줄 무료 합격팩

1

최신기출 해설특강

최신 3개년 주요 직렬 해설강의 무료제공

· 수강방법: 에듀윌 도서몰(book.eduwill.net) 접속 → 동영상강의실
→ 공무원 → '[해설특강] 9급공무원 기출문제집 영어' →
수강 또는 좌측 QR코드를 통해 바로 접속

2

기출OX APP

기출OX 문제풀이 APP 무료제공

· 본인의 취약 파트를 빠르게 풀어볼 수 있는 기출OX 퀴즈 제공
· 7일 무료이용 후 교재 구매 인증을 통해 계속 이용 가능
· 에듀윌 합격앱 또는 좌측 QR코드를 통해 바로 접속

3

1초 합격예측 서비스

1초 합격예측! 모바일 성적분석표 발급 서비스

· 회차별 QR 스캔 후 모바일 OMR 자동채점으로 점수 확인
· 모바일 성적분석표 즉시 발급(전체&상위 10% 평균, 백분위, 영역별
정답률 등)
※ 자세한 내용은 앞광고 마지막 페이지를 확인하세요!

4

지역인재 기출문제 특별부록

최근 2개년 지역인재 기출문제

· 2021~2020년도 지역인재 9급 기출문제와 해설(2회분)
· 기출 유형 연습과 실전훈련이 가능한 연습문제

5

OMR 카드 + 빠른 정답표

실전 연습을 위한 OMR 카드 + 빠른 정답표

· 여러 번 사용할 수 있는 특수 OMR 카드로 실전처럼 마킹하며
문제풀이와 회독 가능
· 한 장으로 제공되는 정답표를 활용하여 빠른 채점 가능

※ 1~3 서비스는 에듀윌 회원가입 후 이용하실 수 있습니다.

이 책의 차례

특별부록

지역인재 기출문제 2회분(정답과 해설 포함)

OMR 카드

※특별부록은 교재의 본문 시작 전에 수록되어 있습니다.

국가직 9급

지방직 9급

서울시 9급		기출문제편	해설편
	2019 서울시 9급	96	108
	2018 서울시 9급	100	113
	2018 서울시 기술직 9급	104	118
	2017 서울시 9급	108	123
	2016 서울시 9급	112	128

법원직 9급		기출문제편	해설편
	2022 법원직 9급	118	136
	2021 법원직 9급	128	145
	2020 법원직 9급	136	154
	2019 법원직 9급	143	163
	2018 법원직 9급	151	171
	2017 법원직 9급	158	179
	2016 법원직 9급	165	186

교육 행정직 9급		기출문제편	해설편
	2018 교육행정직 9급	174	196
	2017 교육행정직 9급	179	202
	2016 교육행정직 9급	184	207
	2015 교육행정직 9급	189	212

국가직 9급 공개경쟁채용 필기시험

응 시 번 호	
성 명	

문 제 책 형

【시 험 과 목】

제1과목	국 어	제2과목	영 어	제3과목	한 국 사
제4·5과목	행정법총론, 행정학개론				

응시자 주의사항

1. **시험 시작 전**에 시험문제를 열람하는 행위나 **시험 종료 후** 답안을 작성하는 행위를 한 사람은 「지방공무원 임용령」 제65조 등 관련 법령에 의거 **부정행위자**로 처리됩니다.

2. 시험 시작 즉시 **과목편철 순서, 문제누락 여부, 인쇄상태 이상 유무 및 표지와 개별과목의 문제책형 일치 여부 등을 확인**한 후 문제책 표지에 응시번호, 성명을 기재합니다.

3. 반드시 본인의 **응시표에 인쇄된 시험과목 순서에 따라** 제4과목과 제5과목의 **답안을 표기**하여야 합니다. 과목 순서를 바꾸어 표기한 경우에도 **본인의 응시표에 기재된 과목 순서대로 채점**되므로 반드시 유의하시기 바랍니다.

4. 시험이 시작되면 문제를 주의 깊게 읽은 후, **문항의 취지에 가장 적합한 하나의 정답만을 고르며**, 문제 내용에 관한 질문은 받지 않습니다.

5. **시험시간 관리의 책임**은 전적으로 응시자 본인에게 있습니다.

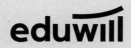

2022

4월 2일 시행
국가직 9급

| 풀이 시간: ____:____ ~ ____:____ / 점수: ____점

※ 밑줄 친 부분의 의미와 가장 가까운 것을 고르시오.

[문 1 ~ 문 3]

문 1.

> For years, detectives have been trying to unravel the mystery of the sudden disappearance of the twin brothers.

① solve
② create
③ imitate
④ publicize

문 2.

> Before the couple experienced parenthood, their four-bedroom house seemed unnecessarily opulent.

① hidden
② luxurious
③ empty
④ solid

문 3.

> The boss hit the roof when he saw that we had already spent the entire budget in such a short period of time.

① was very satisfied
② was very surprised
③ became extremely calm
④ became extremely angry

※ 밑줄 친 부분에 들어갈 말로 가장 적절한 것을 고르시오.

[문 4 ~ 문 5]

문 4.

> A mouse potato is the computer _____ of television's couch potato: someone who tends to spend a great deal of leisure time in front of the computer in much the same way the couch potato does in front of the television.

① technician
② equivalent
③ network
④ simulation

문 5.

> Mary decided to _____ her Spanish before going to South America.

① brush up on
② hear out
③ stick up for
④ lay off

문 6. 어법상 옳은 것은?

① A horse should be fed according to its individual needs and the nature of its work.

② My hat was blown off by the wind while walking down a narrow street.

③ She has known primarily as a political cartoonist throughout her career.

④ Even young children like to be complimented for a job done good.

문 7. 다음 글의 내용과 일치하지 않는 것은?

Umberto Eco was an Italian novelist, cultural critic and philosopher. He is widely known for his 1980 novel *The Name of the Rose*, a historical mystery combining semiotics in fiction with biblical analysis, medieval studies and literary theory. He later wrote other novels, including *Foucault's Pendulum* and *The Island of the Day Before*. Eco was also a translator: he translated Raymond Queneau's book *Exercices de style* into Italian. He was the founder of the Department of Media Studies at the University of the Republic of San Marino. He died at his Milanese home of pancreatic cancer, from which he had been suffering for two years, on the night of February 19, 2016.

① *The Name of the Rose* is a historical novel.
② Eco translated a book into Italian.
③ Eco founded a university department.
④ Eco died in a hospital of cancer.

문 8. 밑줄 친 부분 중 어법상 옳지 않은 것은?

To find a good starting point, one must return to the year 1800 during ① which the first modern electric battery was developed. Italian Alessandro Volta found that a combination of silver, copper, and zinc ② were ideal for producing an electrical current. The enhanced design, ③ called a Voltaic pile, was made by stacking some discs made from these metals between discs made of cardboard soaked in sea water. There was ④ such talk about Volta's work that he was requested to conduct a demonstration before the Emperor Napoleon himself.

문 9. 다음 글의 제목으로 가장 적절한 것은?

Lasers are possible because of the way light interacts with electrons. Electrons exist at specific energy levels or states characteristic of that particular atom or molecule. The energy levels can be imagined as rings or orbits around a nucleus. Electrons in outer rings are at higher energy levels than those in inner rings. Electrons can be bumped up to higher energy levels by the injection of energy — for example, by a flash of light. When an electron drops from an outer to an inner level, "excess" energy is given off as light. The wavelength or color of the emitted light is precisely related to the amount of energy released. Depending on the particular lasing material being used, specific wavelengths of light are absorbed (to energize or excite the electrons) and specific wavelengths are emitted (when the electrons fall back to their initial level).

① How Is Laser Produced?
② When Was Laser Invented?
③ What Electrons Does Laser Emit?
④ Why Do Electrons Reflect Light?

문 10. 다음 글의 흐름상 가장 어색한 문장은?

Markets in water rights are likely to evolve as a rising population leads to shortages and climate change causes drought and famine. ① But they will be based on regional and ethical trading practices and will differ from the bulk of commodity trade. ② Detractors argue trading water is unethical or even a breach of human rights, but already water rights are bought and sold in arid areas of the globe from Oman to Australia. ③ Drinking distilled water can be beneficial, but may not be the best choice for everyone, especially if the minerals are not supplemented by another source. ④ "We strongly believe that water is in fact turning into the new gold for this decade and beyond," said Ziad Abdelnour. "No wonder smart money is aggressively moving in this direction."

※ 밑줄 친 부분에 들어갈 말로 가장 적절한 것을 고르시오.

[문 11 ~ 문 12]

문 11.

A: I heard that the university cafeteria changed their menu.
B: Yeah, I just checked it out.
A: And they got a new caterer.
B: Yes. Sam's Catering.
A: _____?
B: There are more dessert choices. Also, some sandwich choices were removed.

① What is your favorite dessert
② Do you know where their office is
③ Do you need my help with the menu
④ What's the difference from the last menu

문 12.

A: Hi there. May I help you?
B: Yes, I'm looking for a sweater.
A: Well, this one is the latest style from the fall collection. What do you think?
B: It's gorgeous. How much is it?
A: Let me check the price for you. It's $120.
B: _____.
A: Then how about this sweater? It's from the last season, but it's on sale for $50.
B: Perfect! Let me try it on.

① I also need a pair of pants to go with it
② That jacket is the perfect gift for me
③ It's a little out of my price range
④ We are open until 7 p.m. on Saturdays

※ 우리말을 영어로 잘못 옮긴 것을 고르시오.

[문 13 ~ 문 14]

문 13. ① 우리가 영어를 단시간에 배우는 것은 결코 쉬운 일이 아니다.
→ It is by no means easy for us to learn English in a short time.
② 우리 인생에서 시간보다 더 소중한 것은 없다.
→ Nothing is more precious as time in our life.
③ 아이들은 길을 건널 때 아무리 조심해도 지나치지 않다.
→ Children cannot be too careful when crossing the street.
④ 그녀는 남들이 말하는 것을 쉽게 믿는다.
→ She easily believes what others say.

문 14. ① 커피 세 잔을 마셨기 때문에, 그녀는 잠을 이룰 수 없다.
→ Having drunk three cups of coffee, she can't fall asleep.
② 친절한 사람이어서, 그녀는 모든 이에게 사랑받는다.
→ Being a kind person, she is loved by everyone.
③ 모든 점이 고려된다면, 그녀가 그 직위에 가장 적임인 사람이다.
→ All things considered, she is the best-qualified person for the position.
④ 다리를 꼰 채로 오랫동안 앉아 있는 것은 혈압을 상승시킬 수 있다.
→ Sitting with the legs crossing for a long period can raise blood pressure.

문 15. 밑줄 친 (A), (B)에 들어갈 말로 가장 적절한 것은?

Beliefs about maintaining ties with those who have died vary from culture to culture. For example, maintaining ties with the deceased is accepted and sustained in the religious rituals of Japan. Yet among the Hopi Indians of Arizona, the deceased are forgotten as quickly as possible and life goes on as usual. _____(A)_____, the Hopi funeral ritual concludes with a break-off between mortals and spirits. The diversity of grieving is nowhere clearer than in two Muslim societies — one in Egypt, the other in Bali. Among Muslims in Egypt, the bereaved are encouraged to dwell at length on their grief, surrounded by others who relate to similarly tragic accounts and express their sorrow. _____(B)_____, in Bali, bereaved Muslims are encouraged to laugh and be joyful rather than be sad.

	(A)	(B)
①	However	Similarly
②	In fact	By contrast
③	Therefore	For example
④	Likewise	Consequently

문 16. 밑줄 친 부분에 들어갈 말로 가장 적절한 것은?

Scientists have long known that higher air temperatures are contributing to the surface melting on Greenland's ice sheet. But a new study has found another threat that has begun attacking the ice from below: Warm ocean water moving underneath the vast glaciers is causing them to melt even more quickly. The findings were published in the journal *Nature Geoscience* by researchers who studied one of the many "ice tongues" of the Nioghalvfjerdsfjorden Glacier in northeast Greenland. An ice tongue is a strip of ice that floats on the water without breaking off from the ice on land. The massive one these scientists studied is nearly 50 miles long. The survey revealed an underwater current more than a mile wide where warm water from the Atlantic Ocean is able to flow directly towards the glacier, bringing large amounts of heat into contact with the ice and _____ the glacier's melting.

① separating
② delaying
③ preventing
④ accelerating

문 17. 다음 글의 제목으로 가장 적절한 것은?

Do people from different cultures view the world differently? A psychologist presented realistic animated scenes of fish and other underwater objects to Japanese and American students and asked them to report what they had seen. Americans and Japanese made about an equal number of references to the focal fish, but the Japanese made more than 60 percent more references to background elements, including the water, rocks, bubbles, and inert plants and animals. In addition, whereas Japanese and American participants made about equal numbers of references to movement involving active animals, the Japanese participants made almost twice as many references to relationships involving inert, background objects. Perhaps most tellingly, the very first sentence from the Japanese participants was likely to be one referring to the environment, whereas the first sentence from Americans was three times as likely to be one referring to the focal fish.

① Language Barrier Between Japanese and Americans
② Associations of Objects and Backgrounds in the Brain
③ Cultural Differences in Perception
④ Superiority of Detail-oriented People

문 18. 주어진 문장이 들어갈 위치로 가장 적절한 곳은?

Thus, blood, and life-giving oxygen, are easier for the heart to circulate to the brain.

People can be exposed to gravitational force, or g-force, in different ways. It can be localized, affecting only a portion of the body, as in getting slapped on the back. It can also be momentary, such as hard forces endured in a car crash. A third type of g-force is sustained, or lasting for at least several seconds. (①) Sustained, body wide g-forces are the most dangerous to people. (②) The body usually withstands localized or momentary g-force better than sustained g-force, which can be deadly because blood is forced into the legs, depriving the rest of the body of oxygen. (③) Sustained g-force applied while the body is horizontal, or lying down, instead of sitting or standing tends to be more tolerable to people, because blood pools in the back and not the legs. (④) Some people, such as astronauts and fighter jet pilots, undergo special training exercises to increase their bodies' resistance to g-force.

문 19. 다음 글의 요지로 가장 적절한 것은?

　　If someone makes you an offer and you're legitimately concerned about parts of it, you're usually better off proposing all your changes at once. Don't say, "The salary is a bit low. Could you do something about it?" and then, once she's worked on it, come back with "Thanks. Now here are two other things I'd like..." If you ask for only one thing initially, she may assume that getting it will make you ready to accept the offer (or at least to make a decision). If you keep saying "and one more thing...," she is unlikely to remain in a generous or understanding mood. Furthermore, if you have more than one request, don't simply mention all the things you want A, B, C, and D; also signal the relative importance of each to you. Otherwise, she may pick the two things you value least, because they're pretty easy to give you, and feel she's met you halfway.

① Negotiate multiple issues simultaneously, not serially.
② Avoid sensitive topics for a successful negotiation.
③ Choose the right time for your negotiation.
④ Don't be too direct when negotiating salary.

문 20. 주어진 글 다음에 이어질 글의 순서로 가장 적절한 것은?

　　Today, Lamarck is unfairly remembered in large part for his mistaken explanation of how adaptations evolve. He proposed that by using or not using certain body parts, an organism develops certain characteristics.

(A) There is no evidence that this happens. Still, it is important to note that Lamarck proposed that evolution occurs when organisms adapt to their environments. This idea helped set the stage for Darwin.

(B) Lamarck thought that these characteristics would be passed on to the offspring. Lamarck called this idea *inheritance of acquired characteristics.*

(C) For example, Lamarck might explain that a kangaroo's powerful hind legs were the result of ancestors strengthening their legs by jumping and then passing that acquired leg strength on to the offspring. However, an acquired characteristic would have to somehow modify the DNA of specific genes in order to be inherited.

① (A) − (C) − (B)
② (B) − (A) − (C)
③ (B) − (C) − (A)
④ (C) − (A) − (B)

2021

4월 17일 시행
국가직 9급

| 풀이 시간: ____:____ ~ ____:____ / 점수: ____점

※ 밑줄 친 부분의 의미와 가장 가까운 것을 고르시오.

[문 1 ~ 문 3]

문 1.

> Privacy as a social practice shapes individual behavior in conjunction with other social practices and is therefore central to social life.

① in combination with   ② in comparison with
③ in place of   ④ in case of

문 2.

> The influence of Jazz has been so pervasive that most popular music owes its stylistic roots to jazz.

① deceptive   ② ubiquitous
③ persuasive   ④ disastrous

문 3.

> This novel is about the vexed parents of an unruly teenager who quits school to start a business.

① callous   ② annoyed
③ reputable   ④ confident

문 4. 밑줄 친 부분에 들어갈 말로 가장 적절한 것은?

> A group of young demonstrators attempted to _____ the police station.

① line up   ② give out
③ carry on   ④ break into

문 5. 다음 글의 내용과 일치하는 것은?

> The most notorious case of imported labor is of course the Atlantic slave trade, which brought as many as ten million enslaved Africans to the New World to work the plantations. But although the Europeans may have practiced slavery on the largest scale, they were by no means the only people to bring slaves into their communities: earlier, the ancient Egyptians used slave labor to build their pyramids, early Arab explorers were often also slave traders, and Arabic slavery continued into the twentieth century and indeed still continues in a few places. In the Americas some native tribes enslaved members of other tribes, and slavery was also an institution in many African nations, especially before the colonial period.

① African laborers voluntarily moved to the New World.
② Europeans were the first people to use slave labor.
③ Arabic slavery no longer exists in any form.
④ Slavery existed even in African countries.

문 6. 어법상 옳은 것은?

① This guide book tells you where should you visit in Hong Kong.
② I was born in Taiwan, but I have lived in Korea since I started work.
③ The novel was so excited that I lost track of time and missed the bus.
④ It's not surprising that book stores don't carry newspapers any more, doesn't it?

문 7. 다음 글의 제목으로 가장 적절한 것은?

> Warming temperatures and loss of oxygen in the sea will shrink hundreds of fish species — from tunas and groupers to salmon, thresher sharks, haddock and cod — even more than previously thought, a new study concludes. Because warmer seas speed up their metabolisms, fish, squid and other water-breathing creatures will need to draw more oxygen from the ocean. At the same time, warming seas are already reducing the availability of oxygen in many parts of the sea. A pair of University of British Columbia scientists argue that since the bodies of fish grow faster than their gills, these animals eventually will reach a point where they can't get enough oxygen to sustain normal growth. "What we found was that the body size of fish decreases by 20 to 30 percent for every 1 degree Celsius increase in water temperature," says author William Cheung.

① Fish Now Grow Faster than Ever
② Oxygen's Impact on Ocean Temperatures
③ Climate Change May Shrink the World's Fish
④ How Sea Creatures Survive with Low Metabolism

문 8. 밑줄 친 부분 중 어법상 옳지 않은 것은?

> Urban agriculture (UA) has long been dismissed as a fringe activity that has no place in cities; however, its potential is beginning to ① be realized. In fact, UA is about food self-reliance: it involves ② creating work and is a reaction to food insecurity, particularly for the poor. Contrary to ③ which many believe, UA is found in every city, where it is sometimes hidden, sometimes obvious. If one looks carefully, few spaces in a major city are unused. Valuable vacant land rarely sits idle and is often taken over — either formally, or informally — and made ④ productive.

문 9. 주어진 문장이 들어갈 위치로 가장 적절한 것은?

> For example, the state archives of New Jersey hold more than 30,000 cubic feet of paper and 25,000 reels of microfilm.

> Archives are a treasure trove of material: from audio to video to newspapers, magazines and printed material — which makes them indispensable to any History Detective investigation. While libraries and archives may appear the same, the differences are important. (①) An archive collection is almost always made up of primary sources, while a library contains secondary sources. (②) To learn more about the Korean War, you'd go to a library for a history book. If you wanted to read the government papers, or letters written by Korean War soldiers, you'd go to an archive. (③) If you're searching for information, chances are there's an archive out there for you. Many state and local archives store public records — which are an amazing, diverse resource. (④) An online search of your state's archives will quickly show you they contain much more than just the minutes of the legislature — there are detailed land grant information to be found, old town maps, criminal records and oddities such as peddler license applications.

> *treasure trove: 귀중한 발굴물(수집물)
> **land grant: (대학·철도 등을 위해) 정부가 주는 땅

문 10. 다음 글의 흐름상 가장 어색한 문장은?

The term burnout refers to a "wearing out" from the pressures of work. Burnout is a chronic condition that results as daily work stressors take their toll on employees. ① The most widely adopted conceptualization of burnout has been developed by Maslach and her colleagues in their studies of human service workers. Maslach sees burnout as consisting of three interrelated dimensions. The first dimension — emotional exhaustion — is really the core of the burnout phenomenon. ② Workers suffer from emotional exhaustion when they feel fatigued, frustrated, used up, or unable to face another day on the job. The second dimension of burnout is a lack of personal accomplishment. ③ This aspect of the burnout phenomenon refers to workers who see themselves as failures, incapable of effectively accomplishing job requirements. ④ Emotional labor workers enter their occupation highly motivated although they are physically exhausted. The third dimension of burnout is depersonalization. This dimension is relevant only to workers who must communicate interpersonally with others (e.g. clients, patients, students) as part of the job.

※ 밑줄 친 부분에 들어갈 말로 가장 적절한 것을 고르시오.

[문 11 ~ 문 12]

문 11.

A: Were you here last night?
B: Yes. I worked the closing shift. Why?
A: The kitchen was a mess this morning. There was food spattered on the stove, and the ice trays were not in the freezer.
B: I guess I forgot to go over the cleaning checklist.
A: You know how important a clean kitchen is.
B: I'm sorry. _____

① I won't let it happen again.
② Would you like your bill now?
③ That's why I forgot it yesterday.
④ I'll make sure you get the right order.

문 12.

A: Have you taken anything for your cold?
B: No, I just blow my nose a lot.
A: Have you tried nose spray?
B: _____
A: It works great.
B: No, thanks. I don't like to put anything in my nose, so I've never used it.

① Yes, but it didn't help.
② No, I don't like nose spray.
③ No, the pharmacy was closed.
④ Yeah, how much should I use?

문 13. 다음 글의 내용과 일치하지 않는 것은?

Deserts cover more than one-fifth of the Earth's land area, and they are found on every continent. A place that receives less than 25 centimeters (10 inches) of rain per year is considered a desert. Deserts are part of a wider class of regions called drylands. These areas exist under a "moisture deficit," which means they can frequently lose more moisture through evaporation than they receive from annual precipitation. Despite the common conceptions of deserts as hot, there are cold deserts as well. The largest hot desert in the world, northern Africa's Sahara, reaches temperatures of up to 50 degrees Celsius (122 degrees Fahrenheit) during the day. But some deserts are always cold, like the Gobi Desert in Asia and the polar deserts of the Antarctic and Arctic, which are the world's largest. Others are mountainous. Only about 20 percent of deserts are covered by sand. The driest deserts, such as Chile's Atacama Desert, have parts that receive less than two millimeters (0.08 inches) of precipitation a year. Such environments are so harsh and otherworldly that scientists have even studied them for clues about life on Mars. On the other hand, every few years, an unusually rainy period can produce "super blooms," where even the Atacama becomes blanketed in wildflowers.

① There is at least one desert on each continent.
② The Sahara is the world's largest hot desert.
③ The Gobi Desert is categorized as a cold desert.
④ The Atacama Desert is one of the rainiest deserts.

※ 우리말을 영어로 가장 잘 옮긴 것을 고르시오.
[문 14 ~ 문 15]

문 14. ① 나는 너의 답장을 가능한 한 빨리 받기를 고대한다.
→ I look forward to receive your reply as soon as possible.
② 그는 내가 일을 열심히 했기 때문에 월급을 올려 주겠다고 말했다.
→ He said he would rise my salary because I worked hard.
③ 그의 스마트 도시 계획은 고려할 만했다.
→ His plan for the smart city was worth considered.
④ Cindy는 피아노 치는 것을 매우 좋아했고 그녀의 아들도 그랬다.
→ Cindy loved playing the piano, and so did her son.

문 15. ① 당신이 부자일지라도 당신은 진실한 친구들을 살 수는 없다.
→ Rich as if you may be, you can't buy sincere friends.
② 그것은 너무나 아름다운 유성 폭풍이어서 우리는 밤새 그것을 보았다.
→ It was such a beautiful meteor storm that we watched it all night.
③ 학위가 없는 것이 그녀의 성공을 방해했다.
→ Her lack of a degree kept her advancing.
④ 그는 사형이 폐지되어야 하는지 아닌지에 대한 에세이를 써야 한다.
→ He has to write an essay on if or not the death penalty should be abolished.

※ 밑줄 친 부분에 들어갈 말로 가장 적절한 것을 고르시오.
[문 16 ~ 문 17]

문 16.

Social media, magazines and shop windows bombard people daily with things to buy, and British consumers are buying more clothes and shoes than ever before. Online shopping means it is easy for customers to buy without thinking, while major brands offer such cheap clothes that they can be treated like disposable items — worn two or three times and then thrown away. In Britain, the average person spends more than £1,000 on new clothes a year, which is around four percent of their income. That might not sound like much, but that figure hides two far more worrying trends for society and for the environment. First, a lot of that consumer spending is via credit cards. British people currently owe approximately £670 per adult to credit card companies. That's 66 percent of the average wardrobe budget. Also, not only are people spending money they don't have, they're using it to buy things _____. Britain throws away 300,000 tons of clothing a year, most of which goes into landfill sites.

① they don't need
② that are daily necessities
③ that will be soon recycled
④ they can hand down to others

문 17.

Excellence is the absolute prerequisite in fine dining because the prices charged are necessarily high. An operator may do everything possible to make the restaurant efficient, but the guests still expect careful, personal service: food prepared to order by highly skilled chefs and delivered by expert servers. Because this service is, quite literally, manual labor, only marginal improvements in productivity are possible. For example, a cook, server, or bartender can move only so much faster before she or he reaches the limits of human performance. Thus, only moderate savings are possible through improved efficiency, which makes an escalation of prices _____. (It is an axiom of economics that as prices rise, consumers become more discriminating.) Thus, the clientele of the fine-dining restaurant expects, demands, and is willing to pay for excellence.

① ludicrous
② inevitable
③ preposterous
④ inconceivable

문 18. 주어진 글 다음에 이어질 글의 순서로 가장 적절한 것은?

> To be sure, human language stands out from the decidedly restricted vocalizations of monkeys and apes. Moreover, it exhibits a degree of sophistication that far exceeds any other form of animal communication.

> (A) That said, many species, while falling far short of human language, do nevertheless exhibit impressively complex communication systems in natural settings.
> (B) And they can be taught far more complex systems in artificial contexts, as when raised alongside humans.
> (C) Even our closest primate cousins seem incapable of acquiring anything more than a rudimentary communicative system, even after intensive training over several years. The complexity that is language is surely a species-specific trait.

① (A) − (B) − (C)   ② (B) − (C) − (A)
③ (C) − (A) − (B)   ④ (C) − (B) − (A)

문 19. 다음 글의 주제로 가장 적절한 것은?

> During the late twentieth century socialism was on the retreat both in the West and in large areas of the developing world. During this new phase in the evolution of market capitalism, global trading patterns became increasingly interlinked, and advances in information technology meant that deregulated financial markets could shift massive flows of capital across national boundaries within seconds. 'Globalization' boosted trade, encouraged productivity gains and lowered prices, but critics alleged that it exploited the low-paid, was indifferent to environmental concerns and subjected the Third World to a monopolistic form of capitalism. Many radicals within Western societies who wished to protest against this process joined voluntary bodies, charities and other non-governmental organizations, rather than the marginalized political parties of the left. The environmental movement itself grew out of the recognition that the world was interconnected, and an angry, if diffuse, international coalition of interests emerged.

① The affirmative phenomena of globalization in the developing world in the past
② The decline of socialism and the emergence of capitalism in the twentieth century
③ The conflict between the global capital market and the political organizations of the left
④ The exploitative characteristics of global capitalism and diverse social reactions against it

문 20. 다음 글에 나타난 Johnbull의 심경으로 가장 적절한 것은?

> In the blazing midday sun, the yellow egg-shaped rock stood out from a pile of recently unearthed gravel. Out of curiosity, sixteen-year-old miner Komba Johnbull picked it up and fingered its flat, pyramidal planes. Johnbull had never seen a diamond before, but he knew enough to understand that even a big find would be no larger than his thumbnail. Still, the rock was unusual enough to merit a second opinion. Sheepishly, he brought it over to one of the more experienced miners working the muddy gash deep in the jungle. The pit boss's eyes widened when he saw the stone. "Put it in your pocket," he whispered. "Keep digging." The older miner warned that it could be dangerous if anyone thought they had found something big. So Johnbull kept shoveling gravel until nightfall, pausing occasionally to grip the heavy stone in his fist. Could it be?

① thrilled and excited
② painful and distressed
③ arrogant and convinced
④ detached and indifferent

해설편 ▶ P.11

2020
7월 11일 시행
국가직 9급

| 풀이 시간: ____:____ ~ ____:____ / 점수: ____점

※ 밑줄 친 부분의 의미와 가장 가까운 것을 고르시오.
[문 1 ~ 문 4]

문 1.

> Extensive lists of microwave oven models and styles along with candid customer reviews and price ranges are available at appliance comparison websites.

① frank
② logical
③ implicit
④ passionate

문 2.

> It had been known for a long time that Yellowstone was volcanic in nature and the one thing about volcanoes is that they are generally conspicuous.

① passive
② vaporous
③ dangerous
④ noticeable

문 3.

> He's the best person to tell you how to get there because he knows the city inside out.

① eventually
② culturally
③ thoroughly
④ tentatively

문 4.

> All along the route were thousands of homespun attempts to pay tribute to the team, including messages etched in cardboard, snow and construction paper.

① honor
② compose
③ publicize
④ join

문 5. 어법상 옳은 것은?

① The traffic of a big city is busier than those of a small city.
② I'll think of you when I'll be lying on the beach next week.
③ Raisins were once an expensive food, and only the wealth ate them.
④ The intensity of a color is related to how much gray the color contains.

문 6. 우리말을 영어로 가장 잘 옮긴 것은?

① 몇 가지 문제가 새로운 회원들 때문에 생겼다.
  → Several problems have raised due to the new members.
② 그 위원회는 그 건물의 건설을 중단하라고 명했다.
  → The committee commanded that construction of the building cease.
③ 그들은 한 시간에 40마일이 넘는 바람과 싸워야 했다.
  → They had to fight against winds that will blow over 40 miles an hour.
④ 거의 모든 식물의 씨앗은 혹독한 날씨에도 살아남는다.
  → The seeds of most plants are survived by harsh weather.

문 7. 우리말을 영어로 잘못 옮긴 것은?

① 인간은 환경에 자신을 빨리 적응시킨다.
  → Human beings quickly adapt themselves to the environment.
② 그녀는 그 사고 때문에 그녀의 목표를 포기할 수밖에 없었다.
  → She had no choice but to give up her goal because of the accident.
③ 그 회사는 그가 부회장으로 승진하는 것을 금했다.
  → The company prohibited him from promoting to vice-president.
④ 그 장난감 자동차를 조립하고 분리하는 것은 쉽다.
  → It is easy to assemble and take apart the toy car.

문 8. 다음 글의 요지로 가장 적절한 것은?

Listening to somebody else's ideas is the one way to know whether the story you believe about the world — as well as about yourself and your place in it — remains intact. We all need to examine our beliefs, air them out and let them breathe. Hearing what other people have to say, especially about concepts we regard as foundational, is like opening a window in our minds and in our hearts. Speaking up is important. Yet to speak up without listening is like banging pots and pans together: even if it gets you attention, it's not going to get you respect. There are three prerequisites for conversation to be meaningful: 1. You have to know what you're talking about, meaning that you have an original point and are not echoing a worn-out, hand-me-down or pre-fab argument; 2. You respect the people with whom you're speaking and are authentically willing to treat them courteously even if you disagree with their positions; 3. You have to be both smart and informed enough to listen to what the opposition says while handling your own perspective on the topic with uninterrupted good humor and discernment.

① We should be more determined to persuade others.
② We need to listen and speak up in order to communicate well.
③ We are reluctant to change our beliefs about the world we see.
④ We hear only what we choose and attempt to ignore different opinions.

문 9. 다음 글의 제목으로 가장 적절한 것은?

The future may be uncertain, but some things are undeniable: climate change, shifting demographics, geopolitics. The only guarantee is that there will be changes, both wonderful and terrible. It's worth considering how artists will respond to these changes, as well as what purpose art serves, now and in the future. Reports suggest that by 2040 the impacts of human-caused climate change will be inescapable, making it the big issue at the centre of art and life in 20 years' time. Artists in the future will wrestle with the possibilities of the post-human and post-Anthropocene — artificial intelligence, human colonies in outer space and potential doom. The identity politics seen in art around the #MeToo and Black Lives Matter movements will grow as environmentalism, border politics and migration come even more sharply into focus. Art will become increasingly diverse and might not 'look like art' as we expect. In the future, once we've become weary of our lives being visible online for all to see and our privacy has been all but lost, anonymity may be more desirable than fame. Instead of thousands, or millions, of likes and followers, we will be starved for authenticity and connection. Art could, in turn, become more collective and experiential, rather than individual.

① What will art look like in the future?
② How will global warming affect our lives?
③ How will artificial intelligence influence the environment?
④ What changes will be made because of political movements?

문 10. 다음 글의 내용과 일치하지 않는 것은?

The Second Amendment of the U.S. Constitution states: "A well-regulated Militia, being necessary to the security of a free State, the right of the people to keep and bear Arms, shall not be infringed." Supreme Court rulings, citing this amendment, have upheld the right of states to regulate firearms. However, in a 2008 decision confirming an individual right to keep and bear arms, the court struck down Washington, D.C. laws that banned handguns and required those in the home to be locked or disassembled. A number of gun advocates consider ownership a birthright and an essential part of the nation's heritage. The United States, with less than 5 percent of the world's population, has about 35~50 percent of the world's civilian-owned guns, according to a 2007 report by the Switzerland-based Small Arms Survey. It ranks number one in firearms per capita. The United States also has the highest homicide-by-firearm rate among the world's most developed nations.

But many gun-rights proponents say these statistics do not indicate a cause-and-effect relationship and note that the rates of gun homicide and other gun crimes in the United States have dropped since highs in the early 1990's.

① In 2008, the U.S. Supreme Court overturned Washington, D.C. laws banning handguns.

② Many gun advocates claim that owning guns is a natural-born right.

③ Among the most developed nations, the U.S. has the highest rate of gun homicides.

④ Gun crimes in the U.S. have steadily increased over the last three decades.

문 11. 두 사람의 대화 중 가장 <u>어색한</u> 것은?

① A: When is the payment due?
   B: You have to pay by next week.

② A: Should I check this baggage in?
   B: No, it's small enough to take on the plane.

③ A: When and where shall we meet?
   B: I'll pick you up at your office at 8:30.

④ A: I won the prize in a cooking contest.
   B: I couldn't have done it without you.

문 12. 밑줄 친 부분에 들어갈 말로 가장 적절한 것은?

A: Thank you for calling the Royal Point Hotel Reservations Department. My name is Sam. How may I help you?
B: Hello, I'd like to book a room.
A: We offer two room types: the deluxe room and the luxury suite.
B: _____?
A: For one, the suite is very large. In addition to a bedroom, it has a kitchen, living room and dining room.
B: It sounds expensive.
A: Well, it's $200 more per night.
B: In that case, I'll go with the deluxe room.

① Do you need anything else

② May I have the room number

③ What's the difference between them

④ Are pets allowed in the rooms

문 13. 밑줄 친 (A), (B)에 들어갈 말로 가장 적절한 것은?

Advocates of homeschooling believe that children learn better when they are in a secure, loving environment. Many psychologists see the home as the most natural learning environment, and originally the home was the classroom, long before schools were established. Parents who homeschool argue that they can monitor their children's education and give them the attention that is lacking in a traditional school setting. Students can also pick and choose what to study and when to study, thus enabling them to learn at their own pace. _____(A)_____, critics of homeschooling say that children who are not in the classroom miss out on learning important social skills because they have little interaction with their peers. Several studies, though, have shown that the home-educated children appear to do just as well in terms of social and emotional development as other students, having spent more time in the comfort and security of their home, with guidance from parents who care about their welfare. _____(B)_____, many critics of homeschooling have raised concerns about the ability of parents to teach their kids effectively.

	(A)	(B)
①	Therefore	Nevertheless
②	In contrast	In spite of this
③	Therefore	Contrary to that
④	In contrast	Furthermore

문 14. 다음 글의 주제로 가장 적절한 것은?

For many people, work has become an obsession. It has caused burnout, unhappiness and gender inequity, as people struggle to find time for children or passions or pets or any sort of life besides what they do for a paycheck. But increasingly, younger workers are pushing back. More of them expect and demand flexibility — paid leave for a new baby, say, and generous vacation time, along with daily things, like the ability to work remotely, come in late or leave early, or make time for exercise or meditation. The rest of their lives happens on their phones, not tied to a certain place or time — why should work be any different?

① ways to increase your paycheck
② obsession for reducing inequity
③ increasing call for flexibility at work
④ advantages of a life with long vacations

문 15. 주어진 글 다음에 이어질 글의 순서로 가장 적절한 것은?

Past research has shown that experiencing frequent psychological stress can be a significant risk factor for cardiovascular disease, a condition that affects almost half of those aged 20 years and older in the United States.

(A) Does this mean, though, that people who drive on a daily basis are set to develop heart problems, or is there a simple way of easing the stress of driving?

(B) According to a new study, there is. The researchers noted that listening to music while driving helps relieve the stress that affects heart health.

(C) One source of frequent stress is driving, either due to the stressors associated with heavy traffic or the anxiety that often accompanies inexperienced drivers.

① (A) − (C) − (B)   ② (B) − (A) − (C)
③ (C) − (A) − (B)   ④ (C) − (B) − (A)

문 16. 다음 글의 흐름상 가장 어색한 문장은?

When the brain perceives a threat in the immediate surroundings, it initiates a complex string of events in the body. It sends electrical messages to various glands, organs that release chemical hormones into the bloodstream. Blood quickly carries these hormones to other organs that are then prompted to do various things. ① The adrenal glands above the kidneys, for example, pump out adrenaline, the body's stress hormone. ② Adrenaline travels all over the body doing things such as widening the eyes to be on the lookout for signs of danger, pumping the heart faster to keep blood and extra hormones flowing, and tensing the skeletal muscles so they are ready to lash out at or run from the threat. ③ The whole process is called the fight-or-flight response, because it prepares the body to either battle or run for its life. ④ Humans consciously control their glands to regulate the release of various hormones. Once the response is initiated, ignoring it is impossible, because hormones cannot be reasoned with.

문 17. 주어진 문장이 들어갈 위치로 가장 적절한 것은?

It was then he remembered his experience with the glass flask, and just as quickly, he imagined that a special coating might be applied to a glass windshield to keep it from shattering.

In 1903 the French chemist, Edouard Benedictus, dropped a glass flask one day on a hard floor and broke it. (①) However, to the astonishment of the chemist, the flask did not shatter, but still retained most of its original shape. (②) When he examined the flask he found that it contained a film coating inside, a residue remaining from a solution of collodion that the flask had contained. (③) He made a note of this unusual phenomenon, but thought no more of it until several weeks later when he read stories in the newspapers about people in automobile accidents who were badly hurt by flying windshield glass. (④) Not long thereafter, he succeeded in producing the world's first sheet of safety glass.

문 18. 다음 글의 내용과 일치하지 않는 것은?

Dubrovnik, Croatia, is a mess. Because its main attraction is its seaside Old Town surrounded by 80-foot medieval walls, this Dalmatian Coast town does not absorb visitors very well. And when cruise ships are docked here, a legion of tourists turn Old Town into a miasma of tank-top-clad tourists marching down the town's limestone-blanketed streets. Yes, the city of Dubrovnik has been proactive in trying to curb cruise ship tourism, but nothing will save Old Town from the perpetual swarm of tourists. To make matters worse, the lure of making extra money has inspired many homeowners in Old Town to turn over their places to Airbnb, making the walled portion of town one giant hotel. You want an "authentic" Dubrovnik experience in Old Town, just like a local? You're not going to find it here. Ever.

① Old Town은 80피트 중세 시대 벽으로 둘러싸여 있다.
② 크루즈 배가 정박할 때면 많은 여행객이 Old Town 거리를 활보한다.
③ Dubrovnik 시는 크루즈 여행을 확대하려고 노력해 왔다.
④ Old Town에서는 많은 집이 여행객 숙소로 바뀌었다.

문 19. 밑줄 친 (A), (B)에 들어갈 말로 가장 적절한 것은?

When an organism is alive, it takes in carbon dioxide from the air around it. Most of that carbon dioxide is made of carbon-12, but a tiny portion consists of carbon-14. So the living organism always contains a very small amount of radioactive carbon, carbon-14. A detector next to the living organism would record radiation given off by the carbon-14 in the organism. When the organism dies, it no longer takes in carbon dioxide. No new carbon-14 is added, and the old carbon-14 slowly decays into nitrogen. The amount of carbon-14 slowly ____(A)____ as time goes on. Over time, less and less radiation from carbon-14 is produced. The amount of carbon-14 radiation detected for an organism is a measure, therefore, of how long the organism has been ____(B)____. This method of determining the age of an organism is called carbon-14 dating. The decay of carbon-14 allows archaeologists to find the age of once-living materials. Measuring the amount of radiation remaining indicates the approximate age.

	(A)	(B)
①	decreases	dead
②	increases	alive
③	decreases	productive
④	increases	inactive

문 20. 밑줄 친 부분에 들어갈 말로 가장 적절한 것은?

All creatures, past and present, either have gone or will go extinct. Yet, as each species vanished over the past 3.8-billion-year history of life on Earth, new ones inevitably appeared to replace them or to exploit newly emerging resources. From only a few very simple organisms, a great number of complex, multicellular forms evolved over this immense period. The origin of new species, which the nineteenth-century English naturalist Charles Darwin once referred to as "the mystery of mysteries," is the natural process of speciation responsible for generating this remarkable _____ with whom humans share the planet. Although taxonomists presently recognize some 1.5 million living species, the actual number is possibly closer to 10 million. Recognizing the biological status of this multitude requires a clear understanding of what constitutes a species, which is no easy task given that evolutionary biologists have yet to agree on a universally acceptable definition.

① technique of biologists
② diversity of living creatures
③ inventory of extinct organisms
④ collection of endangered species

해설편 ▶ P.18

2019

4월 6일 시행
국가직 9급

| 풀이 시간: _____:_____ ~ _____:_____ / 점수: _____ 점

※ 밑줄 친 부분의 의미와 가장 가까운 것을 고르시오.

[문 1 ~ 문 2]

문 1.

> *Natural Gas World* subscribers will receive accurate and reliable key facts and figures about what is going on in the industry, so they are fully able to <u>discern</u> what concerns their business.

① distinguish
② strengthen
③ undermine
④ abandon

문 2.

> Ms. West, the winner of the silver in the women's 1,500m event, <u>stood out</u> through the race.

① was overwhelmed
② was impressive
③ was depressed
④ was optimistic

문 3. 두 사람의 대화 중 가장 <u>어색한</u> 것은?

① A: I'm traveling abroad, but I'm not used to staying in another country.
　B: Don't worry. You'll get accustomed to it in no time.

② A: I want to get a prize in the photo contest.
　B: I'm sure you will. I'll keep my fingers crossed!

③ A: My best friend moved to Sejong City. I miss her so much.
　B: Yeah. I know how you feel.

④ A: Do you mind if I talk to you for a moment?
　B: Never mind. I'm very busy right now.

문 4. 밑줄 친 부분에 들어갈 말로 가장 적절한 것은?

> A: Would you like to try some dim sum?
> B: Yes, thank you. They look delicious. What's inside?
> A: These have pork and chopped vegetables, and those have shrimps.
> B: And, um, _____?
> A: You pick one up with your chopsticks like this and dip it into the sauce. It's easy.
> B: Okay. I'll give it a try.

① how much are they
② how do I eat them
③ how spicy are they
④ how do you cook them

※ 우리말을 영어로 잘못 옮긴 것을 고르시오.　　[문 5 ~ 문 6]

문 5. ① 제가 당신께 말씀드렸던 새로운 선생님은 원래 페루 출신입니다.
　→ The new teacher I told you about is originally from Peru.
② 나는 긴급한 일로 자정이 5분이나 지난 후 그에게 전화했다.
　→ I called him five minutes shy of midnight on an urgent matter.
③ 상어로 보이는 것이 산호 뒤에 숨어 있었다.
　→ What appeared to be a shark was lurking behind the coral reef.
④ 그녀는 일요일에 16세의 친구와 함께 산 정상에 올랐다.
　→ She reached the mountain summit with her 16-year-old friend on Sunday.

문 6. ① 개인용 컴퓨터를 가장 많이 가지고 있는 나라는 종종 바뀐다.
　→ The country with the most computers per person changes from time to time.
② 지난여름 나의 사랑스러운 손자에게 일어난 일은 놀라웠다.
　→ What happened to my lovely grandson last summer was amazing.
③ 나무 숟가락은 아이들에게 매우 좋은 장난감이고 플라스틱 병 또한 그렇다.
　→ Wooden spoons are excellent toys for children, and so are plastic bottles.
④ 나는 은퇴 후부터 내내 이 일을 해 오고 있다.
　→ I have been doing this work ever since I retired.

※ 밑줄 친 부분 중 어법상 옳지 않은 것을 고르시오.

[문 7 ~ 문 8]

문 7.

Domesticated animals are the earliest and most effective 'machines' ① available to humans. They take the strain off the human back and arms. ② Utilizing with other techniques, animals can raise human living standards very considerably, both as supplementary foodstuffs (protein in meat and milk) and as machines ③ to carry burdens, lift water, and grind grain. Since they are so obviously ④ of great benefit, we might expect to find that over the centuries humans would increase the number and quality of the animals they kept. Surprisingly, this has not usually been the case.

문 8.

A myth is a narrative that embodies — and in some cases ① helps to explain — the religious, philosophical, moral, and political values of a culture. Through tales of gods and supernatural beings, myths ② try to make sense of occurrences in the natural world. Contrary to popular usage, myth does not mean "falsehood." In the broadest sense, myths are stories — usually whole groups of stories — ③ that can be true or partly true as well as false; regardless of their degree of accuracy, however, myths frequently express the deepest beliefs of a culture. According to this definition, the *Iliad* and the *Odyssey*, the Koran, and the Old and New Testaments can all ④ refer to as myths.

문 9. 다음 글의 제목으로 가장 적절한 것은?

Mapping technologies are being used in many new applications. Biological researchers are exploring the molecular structure of DNA ("mapping the genome"), geophysicists are mapping the structure of the Earth's core, and oceanographers are mapping the ocean floor. Computer games have various imaginary "lands" or levels where rules, hazards, and rewards change. Computerization now challenges reality with "virtual reality," artificial environments that simulate special situations, which may be useful in training and entertainment. Mapping techniques are being used also in the realm of ideas. For example, relationships between ideas can be shown using what are called concept maps. Starting from a general or "central" idea, related ideas can be connected, building a web around the main concept. This is not a map by any traditional definition, but the tools and techniques of cartography are employed to produce it, and in some ways it resembles a map.

① Computerized Maps vs. Traditional Maps
② Where Does Cartography Begin?
③ Finding Ways to DNA Secrets
④ Mapping New Frontiers

문 10. 다음 글의 요지로 가장 적절한 것은?

When giving performance feedback, you should consider the recipient's past performance and your estimate of his or her future potential in designing its frequency, amount, and content. For high performers with potential for growth, feedback should be frequent enough to prod them into taking corrective action, but not so frequent that it is experienced as controlling and saps their initiative. For adequate performers who have settled into their jobs and have limited potential for advancement, very little feedback is needed because they have displayed reliable and steady behavior in the past, knowing their tasks and realizing what needs to be done. For poor performers — that is, people who will need to be removed from their jobs if their performance doesn't improve — feedback should be frequent and very specific, and the connection between acting on the feedback and negative sanctions such as being laid off or fired should be made explicit.

① Time your feedback well.
② Customize negative feedback.
③ Tailor feedback to the person.
④ Avoid goal-oriented feedback.

문 11. 다음 글의 내용과 일치하지 <u>않는</u> 것은?

> Langston Hughes was born in Joplin, Missouri, and graduated from Lincoln University, in which many African-American students have pursued their academic disciplines. At the age of eighteen, Hughes published one of his most well-known poems, "Negro Speaks of Rivers." Creative and experimental, Hughes incorporated authentic dialect in his work, adapted traditional poetic forms to embrace the cadences and moods of blues and jazz, and created characters and themes that reflected elements of lower-class black culture. With his ability to fuse serious content with humorous style, Hughes attacked racial prejudice in a way that was natural and witty.

① Hughes는 많은 미국 흑인들이 다녔던 대학교를 졸업하였다.
② Hughes는 실제 사투리를 그의 작품에 반영하였다.
③ Hughes는 하층 계급 흑인들의 문화적 요소를 반영한 인물을 만들었다.
④ Hughes는 인종편견을 엄숙한 문체로 공격하였다.

문 12. 밑줄 친 부분 중 글의 흐름상 가장 <u>어색한</u> 것은?

> In 2007, our biggest concern was "too big to fail." Wall Street banks had grown to such staggering sizes, and had become so central to the health of the financial system, that no rational government could ever let them fail. ① Aware of their protected status, banks made excessively risky bets on housing markets and invented ever more complicated derivatives. ② New virtual currencies such as bitcoin and ethereum have radically changed our understanding of how money can and should work. ③ The result was the worst financial crisis since the breakdown of our economy in 1929. ④ In the years since 2007, we have made great progress in addressing the too-big-to-fail dilemma. Our banks are better capitalized than ever. Our regulators conduct regular stress tests of large institutions.

문 13. 다음 글의 주제로 가장 적절한 것은?

> Imagine that two people are starting work at a law firm on the same day. One person has a very simple name. The other person has a very complex name. We've got pretty good evidence that over the course of their next 16 plus years of their career, the person with the simpler name will rise up the legal hierarchy more quickly. They will attain partnership more quickly in the middle parts of their career. And by about the eighth or ninth year after graduating from law school the people with simpler names are about seven to ten percent more likely to be partners — which is a striking effect. We try to eliminate all sorts of other alternative explanations. For example, we try to show that it's not about foreignness because foreign names tend to be harder to pronounce. But even if you look at just white males with Anglo-American names — so really the true in-group, you find that among those white males with Anglo names they are more likely to rise up if their names happen to be simpler. So simplicity is one key feature in names that determines various outcomes.

① the development of legal names
② the concept of attractive names
③ the benefit of simple names
④ the roots of foreign names

※ 밑줄 친 부분의 의미와 가장 가까운 것을 고르시오.
[문 14 ~ 문 15]

문 14.

> Schooling is <u>compulsory</u> for all children in the United States, but the age range for which school attendance is required varies from state to state.

① complementary
② systematic
③ mandatory
④ innovative

문 15.

> Although the actress experienced much turmoil in her career, she never <u>disclosed</u> to anyone that she was unhappy.

① let on
② let off
③ let up
④ let down

문 16. 밑줄 친 (A), (B)에 들어갈 말로 가장 적절한 것은?

Visionaries are the first people in their industry segment to see the potential of new technologies. Fundamentally, they see themselves as smarter than their opposite numbers in competitive companies — and, quite often, they are. Indeed, it is their ability to see things first that they want to leverage into a competitive advantage. That advantage can only come about if no one else has discovered it. They do not expect, _____(A)_____, to be buying a well-tested product with an extensive list of industry references. Indeed, if such a reference base exists, it may actually turn them off, indicating that for this technology, at any rate, they are already too late. Pragmatists, _____(B)_____, deeply value the experience of their colleagues in other companies. When they buy, they expect extensive references, and they want a good number to come from companies in their own industry segment.

	(A)	(B)
①	therefore	on the other hand
②	however	in addition
③	nonetheless	at the same time
④	furthermore	in conclusion

문 17. 주어진 문장이 들어갈 위치로 가장 적절한 것은?

Some of these ailments are short-lived; others may be long-lasting.

For centuries, humans have looked up at the sky and wondered what exists beyond the realm of our planet. (①) Ancient astronomers examined the night sky hoping to learn more about the universe. More recently, some movies explored the possibility of sustaining human life in outer space, while other films have questioned whether extraterrestrial life forms may have visited our planet. (②) Since astronaut Yuri Gagarin became the first man to travel in space in 1961, scientists have researched what conditions are like beyond the Earth's atmosphere, and what effects space travel has on the human body. (③) Although most astronauts do not spend more than a few months in space, many experience physiological and psychological problems when they return to the

Earth. (④) More than two-thirds of all astronauts suffer from motion sickness while traveling in space. In the gravity-free environment, the body cannot differentiate up from down. The body's internal balance system sends confusing signals to the brain, which can result in nausea lasting as long as a few days.

문 18. 밑줄 친 부분에 들어갈 말로 가장 적절한 것은?

Why bother with the history of everything? _____. In literature classes you don't learn about genes; in physics classes you don't learn about human evolution. So you get a partial view of the world. That makes it hard to find *meaning* in education. The French sociologist Emile Durkheim called this sense of disorientation and meaninglessness *anomie*, and he argued that it could lead to despair and even suicide. The German sociologist Max Weber talked of the "disenchantment" of the world. In the past, people had a unified vision of their world, a vision usually provided by the origin stories of their own religious traditions. That unified vision gave a sense of purpose, of meaning, even of enchantment to the world and to life. Today, though, many writers have argued that a sense of meaninglessness is inevitable in a world of science and rationality. Modernity, it seems, means meaninglessness.

① In the past, the study of history required disenchantment from science
② Recently, science has given us lots of clever tricks and meanings
③ Today, we teach and learn about our world in fragments
④ Lately, history has been divided into several categories

문 19. 다음 글의 내용과 일치하지 <u>않는</u> 것은?

The earliest government food service programs began around 1900 in Europe. Programs in the United States date from the Great Depression, when the need to use surplus agricultural commodities was joined to concern for feeding the children of poor families. During and after World War II, the explosion in the number of working women fueled the need for a broader program. What was once a function of the family — providing lunch — was shifted to the school food service system. The National School Lunch Program is the result of these efforts. The program is designed to provide federally assisted meals to children of school age. From the end of World War II to the early 1980s, funding for school food service expanded steadily. Today it helps to feed children in almost 100,000 schools across the United States. Its first function is to provide a nutritious lunch to all students; the second is to provide nutritious food at both breakfast and lunch to underprivileged children. If anything, the role of school food service as a replacement for what was once a family function has been expanded.

① The increase in the number of working women boosted the expansion of food service programs.
② The US government began to feed poor children during the Great Depression despite the food shortage.
③ The US school food service system presently helps to feed children of poor families.
④ The function of providing lunch has been shifted from the family to schools.

문 20. 주어진 문장 다음에 이어질 글의 순서로 가장 적절한 것은?

South Korea boasts of being the most wired nation on earth.

(A) This addiction has become a national issue in Korea in recent years, as users started dropping dead from exhaustion after playing online games for days on end. A growing number of students have skipped school to stay online, shockingly self-destructive behavior in this intensely competitive society.
(B) In fact, perhaps no other country has so fully embraced the Internet.
(C) But such ready access to the Web has come at a price as legions of obsessed users find that they cannot tear themselves away from their computer screens.

① (A) − (B) − (C)   ② (A) − (C) − (B)
③ (B) − (A) − (C)   ④ (B) − (C) − (A)

해설편 ▶ P.25

2018

4월 7일 시행
국가직 9급

┃ 풀이 시간: ___:___ ~ ___:___ / 점수: ___점

1초 합격예측! 모바일 성적분석표

QR 코드로 접속하여 문제 풀이시간을 측정하고,
〈1초 합격예측 & 모바일 성적분석표〉 서비스를 통해
지금 바로! 실력을 점검해 보세요.
http://eduwill.kr/Uqy6

※ 밑줄 친 부분에 들어갈 말로 가장 적절한 것을 고르시오.

[문 1 ~ 문 2]

문 1.

A: Can I ask you for a favor?
B: Yes, what is it?
A: I need to get to the airport for my business trip, but my car won't start. Can you give me a lift?
B: Sure. When do you need to be there by?
A: I have to be there no later than 6：00.
B: It's 4：30 now. _____.
　 We'll have to leave right away.

① That's cutting it close
② I took my eye off the ball
③ All that glitters is not gold
④ It's water under the bridge

문 2.

　Fear of loss is a basic part of being human. To the brain, loss is a threat and we naturally take measures to avoid it. We cannot, however, avoid it indefinitely. One way to face loss is with the perspective of a stock trader. Traders accept the possibility of loss as part of the game, not the end of the game. What guides this thinking is a portfolio approach; wins and losses will both happen, but it's the overall portfolio of outcomes that matters most. When you embrace a portfolio approach, you will be _____ because you know that they are small parts of a much bigger picture.

① less inclined to dwell on individual losses
② less interested in your investments
③ more averse to the losses
④ more sensitive to fluctuations in the stock market

문 3. 다음 글의 제목으로 가장 적절한 것은?

　Over the last years of traveling, I've observed how much we humans live in the past. The past is around us constantly, considering that, the minute something is manifested, it is the past. Our surroundings, our homes, our environments, our architecture, our products are all past constructs. We should live with what is part of our time, part of our collective consciousness, those things that were produced during our lives. Of course, we do not have the choice or control to have everything around us relevant or conceived during our time, but what we do have control of should be a reflection of the time in which we exist and communicate the present. The present is all we have, and the more we are surrounded by it, the more we are aware of our own presence and participation.

① Travel: Tracing the Legacies of the Past
② Reflect on the Time That Surrounds You Now
③ Manifestation of a Hidden Life
④ Architecture of a Futuristic Life

문 4. 밑줄 친 부분 중 어법상 옳지 않은 것은?

　It would be difficult ① to imagine life without the beauty and richness of forests. But scientists warn we cannot take our forest for ② granted. By some estimates, deforestation ③ has been resulted in the loss of as much as eighty percent of the natural forests of the world. Currently, deforestation is a global problem, ④ affecting wilderness regions such as the temperate rainforests of the Pacific.

문 5. 밑줄 친 부분의 의미와 가장 가까운 것은?

　Robert J. Flaherty, a legendary documentary filmmaker, tried to show how indigenous people gathered food.

① native　　　　　　② ravenous
③ impoverished　　　④ itinerant

문 6. 밑줄 친 부분에 들어갈 말로 가장 적절한 것은?

> Listening to music is _____ being a rock star. Anyone can listen to music, but it takes talent to become a musician.

① on a par with
② a far cry from
③ contingent upon
④ a prelude to

문 7. 다음 글의 흐름상 가장 어색한 문장은?

> Biologists have identified a gene that will allow rice plants to survive being submerged in water for up to two weeks — over a week longer than at present. Plants under water for longer than a week are deprived of oxygen and wither and perish. ① The scientists hope their discovery will prolong the harvests of crops in regions that are susceptible to flooding. ② Rice growers in these flood-prone areas of Asia lose an estimated one billion dollars annually to excessively waterlogged rice paddies. ③ They hope the new gene will lead to a hardier rice strain that will reduce the financial damage incurred in typhoon and monsoon seasons and lead to bumper harvests. ④ This is dreadful news for people in these vulnerable regions, who are victims of urbanization and have a shortage of crops. Rice yields must increase by 30 percent over the next 20 years to ensure a billion people can receive their staple diet.

문 8. 밑줄 친 부분에 들어갈 말로 가장 적절한 것은?

> A: Do you know how to drive?
> B: Of course. I'm a great driver.
> A: Could you teach me how to drive?
> B: Do you have a learner's permit?
> A: Yes, I got it just last week.
> B: Have you been behind the steering wheel yet?
> A: No, but I can't wait to _____.

① take a rain check
② get my feet wet
③ get an oil change
④ change a flat tire

문 9. 다음 글의 내용과 일치하는 것은?

> Sharks are covered in scales made from the same material as teeth. These flexible scales protect the shark and help it swim quickly in water. A shark can move the scales as it swims. This movement helps reduce the water's drag. Amy Lang, an aerospace engineer at the University of Alabama, studies the scales on the shortfin mako, a relative of the great white shark. Lang and her team discovered that the mako shark's scales differ in size and in flexibility in different parts of its body. For instance, the scales on the sides of the body are tapered — wide at one end and narrow at the other end. Because they are tapered, these scales move very easily. They can turn up or flatten to adjust to the flow of water around the shark and to reduce drag. Lang feels that shark scales can inspire designs for machines that experience drag, such as airplanes.

① A shark has scales that always remain immobile to protect itself as it swims.
② Lang revealed that the scales of a mako shark are utilized to lessen drag in water.
③ A mako shark has scales of identical size all over its body.
④ The scientific designs of airplanes were inspired by shark scales.

문 10. 밑줄 친 부분 중 어법상 옳지 않은 것은?

> Focus means ① getting stuff done. A lot of people have great ideas but don't act on them. For me, the definition of an entrepreneur, for instance, is someone who can combine innovation and ingenuity with the ability to execute that new idea. Some people think that the central dichotomy in life is whether you're positive or negative about the issues ② that interest or concern you. There's a lot of attention ③ paying to this question of whether it's better to have an optimistic or pessimistic lens. I think the better question to ask is whether you are going to do something about it or just ④ let life pass you by.

문 11. 밑줄 친 부분 중 글의 흐름상 가장 어색한 것은?

Most people like to talk, but few people like to listen, yet listening well is a ① rare talent that everyone should treasure. Because they hear more, good listeners tend to know more and to be more sensitive to what is going on around them than most people. In addition, good listeners are inclined to accept or tolerate rather than to judge and criticize. Therefore, they have ② fewer enemies than most people. In fact, they are probably the most beloved of people. However, there are ③ exceptions to that generality. For example, John Steinbeck is said to have been an excellent listener, yet he was hated by some of the people he wrote about. No doubt his ability to listen contributed to his capacity to write. Nevertheless, the result of his listening didn't make him ④ unpopular.

문 12. 다음 글의 주제로 가장 적절한 것은?

Worry is like a rocking horse. No matter how fast you go, you never move anywhere. Worry is a complete waste of time and creates so much clutter in your mind that you cannot think clearly about anything. The way to learn to stop worrying is by first understanding that you energize whatever you focus your attention on. Therefore, the more you allow yourself to worry, the more likely things are to go wrong! Worrying becomes such an ingrained habit that to avoid it you consciously have to train yourself to do otherwise. Whenever you catch yourself having a fit of worry, stop and change your thoughts. Focus your mind more productively on what you do want to happen and dwell on what's already wonderful in your life so more wonderful stuff will come your way.

① What effects does worry have on life?
② Where does worry originate from?
③ When should we worry?
④ How do we cope with worrying?

문 13. 다음 글의 내용과 일치하지 않는 것은?

Students at Macaulay Honors College (MHC) don't stress about the high price of tuition. That's because theirs is free. At Macaulay and a handful of other service academies, work colleges, single-subject schools and conservatories, 100 percent of the student body receive a full tuition scholarship for all four years. Macaulay students also receive a laptop and $7,500 in "opportunities funds" to pursue research, service experiences, study abroad programs and internships. "The most important thing is not the free tuition, but the freedom of studying without the burden of debt on your back," says Ann Kirschner, university dean of Macaulay Honors College. The debt burden, she says, "really compromises decisions students make in college, and we are giving them the opportunity to be free of that." Schools that grant free tuition to all students are rare, but a greater number of institutions provide scholarships to enrollees with high grades. Institutions such as Indiana University Bloomington offer automatic awards to high-performing students with stellar GPAs and class ranks.

① MHC에서는 모든 학생이 4년간 수업료를 내지 않는다.
② MHC에서는 학생들에게 컴퓨터 구입 비용과 교외활동 비용을 합하여 $7,500를 지급한다.
③ 수업료로 인한 빚 부담이 있으면 학생들이 자유롭게 공부할 수 없다고 Kirschner 학장은 말한다.
④ MHC와 달리 학업 우수자에게만 장학금을 주는 대학도 있다.

※ 밑줄 친 부분의 의미와 가장 가까운 것을 고르시오.

[문 14 ~ 문 15]

문 14.

> The police spent seven months working on the crime case but were never able to determine the identity of the malefactor.

① culprit ② dilettante
③ pariah ④ demagogue

문 15.

> While at first glance it seems that his friends are just leeches, they prove to be the ones he can depend on through thick and thin.

① in no time
② from time to time
③ in pleasant times
④ in good times and bad times

문 16. 주어진 문장이 들어갈 위치로 가장 적절한 것은?

> Some remain intensely proud of their original accent and dialect words, phrases and gestures, while others accommodate rapidly to a new environment by changing their speech habits, so that they no longer "stand out in the crowd."

> Our perceptions and production of speech change with time. (①) If we were to leave our native place for an extended period, our perception that the new accents around us were strange would only be temporary. (②) Gradually, we will lose the sense that others have an accent and we will begin to fit in — to accommodate our speech patterns to the new norm. (③) Not all people do this to the same degree. (④) Whether they do this consciously or not is open to debate and may differ from individual to individual, but like most processes that have to do with language, the change probably happens before we are aware of it and probably couldn't happen if we were.

문 17. 다음 글의 내용과 일치하지 않는 것은?

> Insomnia can be classified as transient, acute, or chronic. Transient insomnia lasts for less than a week. It can be caused by another disorder, by changes in the sleep environment, by the timing of sleep, severe depression, or by stress. Its consequences such as sleepiness and impaired psychomotor performance are similar to those of sleep deprivation. Acute insomnia is the inability to consistently sleep well for a period of less than a month. Acute insomnia is present when there is difficulty initiating or maintaining sleep or when the sleep that is obtained is not refreshing. These problems occur despite adequate opportunity and circumstances for sleep and they can impair daytime functioning. Acute insomnia is also known as short term insomnia or stress related insomnia. Chronic insomnia lasts for longer than a month. It can be caused by another disorder, or it can be a primary disorder. People with high levels of stress hormones or shifts in the levels of cytokines are more likely than others to have chronic insomnia. Its effects can vary according to its causes. They might include muscular weariness, hallucinations, and/or mental fatigue. Chronic insomnia can also cause double vision.
>
> ※ cytokines: groups of molecules released by certain cells of the immune system

① Insomnia can be classified according to its duration.
② Transient insomnia occurs solely due to an inadequate sleep environment.
③ Acute insomnia is generally known to be related to stress.
④ Chronic insomnia patients may suffer from hallucinations.

문 18. 밑줄 친 부분에 들어갈 말로 가장 적절한 것은?

Kisha Padbhan, founder of Everonn Education, in Mumbai, looks at his business as nation-building. India's student-age population of 230million (kindergarten to college) is one of the largest in the world. The government spends $83 billion on instruction, but there are serious gaps. "There aren't enough teachers and enough teacher-training institutes," says Kisha. "What children in remote parts of India lack is access to good teachers and exposure to good-quality content." Everonn's solution? The company uses a satellite network, with two-way video and audio _____. It reaches 1,800 colleges and 7,800 schools across 24 of India's 28 states. It offers everything from digitized school lessons to entrance exam prep for aspiring engineers and has training for job-seekers, too.

① to improve the quality of teacher training facilities
② to bridge the gap through virtual classrooms
③ to get students familiarized with digital technology
④ to locate qualified instructors across the nation

문 19. 주어진 문장 다음에 이어질 글의 순서로 가장 적절한 것은?

A technique that enables an individual to gain some voluntary control over autonomic, or involuntary, body functions by observing electronic measurements of those functions is known as biofeedback.

(A) When such a variable moves in the desired direction (for example, blood pressure down), it triggers visual or audible displays — feedback on equipment such as television sets, gauges, or lights.

(B) Electronic sensors are attached to various parts of the body to measure such variables as heart rate, blood pressure, and skin temperature.

(C) Biofeedback training teaches one to produce a desired response by reproducing thought patterns or actions that triggered the displays.

① (A) − (B) − (C)   ② (B) − (C) − (A)
③ (B) − (A) − (C)   ④ (C) − (A) − (B)

문 20. 우리말을 영어로 잘못 옮긴 것은?

① 그 연사는 자기 생각을 청중에게 전달하는 데 능숙하지 않았다.
  → The speaker was not good at getting his ideas across to the audience.

② 서울의 교통 체증은 세계 어느 도시보다 심각하다.
  → The traffic jams in Seoul are more serious than those in any other city in the world.

③ 네가 말하고 있는 사람과 시선을 마주치는 것은 서양 국가에서 중요하다.
  → Making eye contact with the person you are speaking to is important in western countries.

④ 그는 사람들이 생각했던 만큼 인색하지 않았다는 것이 드러났다.
  → It turns out that he was not so stingier as he was thought to be.

해설편 ▶ P.31

2017

4월 8일 시행
국가직(= 사회복지직) 9급

| 풀이 시간: ____:____ ~ ____:____ / 점수: ____점

※ 밑줄 친 부분과 의미가 가장 가까운 것을 고르시오.

[문 1 ~ 문 2]

문 1.

I absolutely detested the idea of staying up late at night.

① abandoned 　② confirmed
③ abhorred 　④ defended

문 2.

I had an uncanny feeling that I had seen this scene somewhere before.

① odd 　② ongoing
③ obvious 　④ offensive

※ 밑줄 친 부분에 들어갈 말로 가장 적절한 것을 고르시오.

[문 3 ~ 문 4]

문 3.

A: May I help you?
B: I bought this dress two days ago, but it's a bit big for me.
A: _____
B: Then I'd like to get a refund.
A: May I see your receipt, please?
B: Here you are.

① I'm sorry, but there's no smaller size.
② I feel like it fits you perfectly, though.
③ That dress sells really well in our store.
④ I'm sorry, but this purchase can't be refunded.

문 4.

A: Every time I use this home blood pressure monitor, I get a different reading. I think I'm doing it wrong. Can you show me how to use it correctly?
B: Yes, of course. First, you have to put the strap around your arm.
A: Like this? Am I doing this correctly?
B: That looks a little too tight.
A: Oh, how about now?
B: Now it looks a bit too loose. If it's too tight or too loose, you'll get an incorrect reading.
A: _____
B: Press the button now. You shouldn't move or speak.
A: I get it.
B: You should see your blood pressure on the screen in a few moments.

① Should I check out their website?
② Right, I need to read the book.
③ Oh, okay. What do I do next?
④ I didn't see anything today.

문 5. 어법상 옳은 것은?

① They didn't believe his story, and neither did I.
② The sport in that I am most interested is soccer.
③ Jamie learned from the book that World War I had broken out in 1914.
④ Two factors have made scientists difficult to determine the number of species on Earth.

문 6. 어법상 옳지 않은 것은?

① A few words caught in passing set me thinking.
② Hardly did she enter the house when someone turned on the light.
③ We drove on to the hotel, from whose balcony we could look down at the town.
④ The homeless usually have great difficulty getting a job, so they are losing their hope.

① Luxury brands are thriving at Soleil

② Soleil has decided against making bold moves

③ Increasing the online customer base may be the last hope

④ A five-story dragon slide may not be a bad place to start

※ 밑줄 친 부분에 들어갈 말로 가장 적절한 것을 고르시오.

[문 7 ~ 문 9]

문 7.

Why might people hovering near the poverty line be more likely to help their fellow humans? Part of it, Keltner thinks, is that poor people must often band together to make it through tough times — a process that probably makes them more socially astute. He says, "When you face uncertainty, it makes you orient to other people. You build up these strong social networks." When a poor young mother has a new baby, for instance, she may need help securing food, supplies, and childcare, and if she has healthy social times, members of her community will pitch in. But limited income is hardly a prerequisite for developing this kind of empathy and social responsiveness. Regardless of the size of our bank accounts, suffering becomes a conduit to altruism or heroism when our own pain compels us to be _____ other people's needs and to intervene when we see someone in the clutches of the kind of suffering we know so well.

① more indifferent to   ② more attentive to
③ less preoccupied with   ④ less involved in

문 8.

The Soleil department store outlet in Shanghai would seem to have all the amenities necessary to succeed in modern Chinese retail: luxury brands and an exclusive location. Despite these advantages, however, the store's management thought it was still missing something to attract customers. So next week they're unveiling a gigantic, twisting, dragon-shaped slide that shoppers can use to drop from fifth-floor luxury boutiques to first-floor luxury boutiques in death-defying seconds. Social media users are wondering, half-jokingly, whether the slide will kill anyone. But Soleil has a different concern that Chinese shopping malls will go away completely. Chinese shoppers, once seemingly in endless supply, are no longer turning up at brick-and-mortar outlets because of the growing online shopping, and they still go abroad to buy luxury goods. So, repurposing these massive spaces for consumers who have other ways to spend their time and money is likely to require a lot of creativity. _____.

문 9.

It is easy to devise numerous possible scenarios of future developments, each one, on the face of it, equally likely. The difficult task is to know which will actually take place. In hindsight, it usually seems obvious. When we look back in time, each event seems clearly and logically to follow from previous events. Before the event occurs, however, the number of possibilities seems endless. There are no methods for successful prediction, especially in areas involving complex social and technological changes, where many of the determining factors are not known and, in any event, are certainly not under any single group's control. Nonetheless, it is essential to _____. We do know that new technologies will bring both dividends and problems, especially human, social problems. The more we try to anticipate these problems, the better we can control them.

① work out reasonable scenarios for the future

② legitimize possible dividends from future changes

③ leave out various aspects of technological problems

④ consider what it would be like to focus on the present

문 10. 다음 글의 내용과 일치하는 것은?

Taste buds got their name from the nineteenth-century German scientists Georg Meissner and Rudolf Wagner, who discovered mounds made up of taste cells that overlap like petals. Taste buds wear out every week to ten days, and we replace them, although not as frequently over the age of forty-five: our palates really do become jaded as we get older. It takes a more intense taste to produce the same level of sensation, and children have the keenest sense of taste. A baby's mouth has many more taste buds than an adult's, with some even dotting the cheeks. Children adore sweets partly because the tips of their tongues, more sensitive to sugar, haven't yet been blunted by trying to eat hot soup before it cools.

① Taste buds were invented in the nineteenth century.
② Replacement of taste buds does not slow down with age.
③ Children have more sensitive palates than adults.
④ The sense of taste declines by eating cold soup.

문 11. 밑줄 친 부분과 의미가 가장 가까운 것은?

At this company, we will not put up with such behavior.

① evaluate   ② tolerate
③ record   ④ modify

문 12. 밑줄 친 부분 중 의미상 옳지 않은 것은?

① I'm going to take over his former position.
② I can't take on any more work at the moment.
③ The plane couldn't take off because of the heavy fog.
④ I can't go out because I have to take after my baby sister.

문 13. 다음 글의 제목으로 가장 적절한 것은?

Drama is doing. Drama is being. Drama is such a normal thing. It is something that we all engage in every day when faced with difficult situations. You get up in the morning with a bad headache or an attack of depression, yet you face the day and cope with other people, pretending that nothing is wrong. You have an important meeting or an interview coming up, so you talk through the issues with yourself beforehand and decide how to present a confident, cheerful face, what to wear, what to do with your hands, and so on. You've spilt coffee over a colleague's papers, and immediately you prepare an elaborate excuse. Your partner has just run off with your best friend, yet you cannot avoid going in to teach a class of inquisitive students. Getting on with our day-to-day lives requires a series of civilized masks if we are to maintain our dignity and live in harmony with others.

① Dysfunctions of Drama
② Drama in Our Daily Lives
③ Drama as a Theatrical Art
④ Dramatic Changes in Emotions

문 14. 다음 글의 요지로 가장 적절한 것은?

How on earth will it help the poor if governments try to strangle globalization by stemming the flow of trade, information, and capital — the three components of the global economy? That disparities between rich and poor are still too great is undeniable. But it is just not true that economic growth benefits only the rich and leaves out the poor, as the opponents of globalization and the market economy would have us believe. A recent World Bank study entitled "Growth Is Good for the Poor" reveals a one-for-one relationship between income of the bottom fifth of the population and per capita GDP. In other words, incomes of all sectors grow proportionately at the same rate. The study notes that openness to foreign trade benefits the poor to the same extent that it benefits the whole economy.

① Governments must control the flow of trade to revive the economy.
② Globalization can be beneficial regardless of one's economic status.
③ The global economy grows at the expense of the poor.
④ Globalization deepens conflicts between rich and poor.

※ 우리말을 영어로 잘못 옮긴 것을 고르시오.　[문 15 ~ 문 16]

문 15. ① 이 편지를 받는 대로 곧 본사로 와 주십시오.
　　→ Please come to the headquarters as soon as you receive this letter.
② 나는 소년 시절에 독서하는 버릇을 길러 놓았어야만 했다.
　　→ I ought to have formed a habit of reading in my boyhood.
③ 그는 10년 동안 외국에 있었기 때문에 영어를 매우 유창하게 말할 수 있다.
　　→ Having been abroad for ten years, he can speak English very fluently.
④ 내가 그때 그 계획을 포기했었다면 이렇게 훌륭한 성과를 얻지 못했을 것이다.
　　→ Had I given up the project at that time, I should have achieved such a splendid result.

문 16. ① 그 회의 후에야 그는 금융 위기의 심각성을 알아차렸다.
　　→ Only after the meeting did he recognize the seriousness of the financial crisis.
② 장관은 교통문제를 해결하기 위해 강 위에 다리를 건설해야 한다고 주장했다.
　　→ The minister insisted that a bridge be constructed over the river to solve the traffic problem.
③ 비록 그 일이 어려운 것이었지만, Linda는 그것을 끝내기 위해 최선을 다했다.
　　→ As difficult a task as it was, Linda did her best to complete it.
④ 그는 문자 메시지에 너무 정신이 팔려서 제한속도보다 빠르게 달리고 있다는 것을 몰랐다.
　　→ He was so distracted by a text message to know that he was going over the speed limit.

문 17. 빈칸 (A), (B)에 들어갈 말로 가장 적절한 것은?

The amount of information gathered by the eyes as contrasted with the ears has not been precisely calculated. Such a calculation not only involves a translation process, but scientists have been handicapped by lack of knowledge of what to count. A general notion, however, of the relative complexities of the two systems can be obtained by _____(A)_____ the size of the nerves connecting the eyes and the ears to the centers of the brain. Since the optic nerve contains roughly eighteen times as many neurons as the cochlear nerve, we assume it transmits at least that much more information. Actually, in normally alert subjects, it is probable that the eyes may be as much as a thousand times as effective as the ears in _____(B)_____ information.

*cochlear: 달팽이관의

　　　(A)　　　　　　　　(B)
① comparing　　　　　sweeping up
② comparing　　　　　reducing
③ adding　　　　　　disseminating
④ adding　　　　　　clearing up

문 18. 글의 흐름상 가장 어색한 문장은?

Children's book awards have proliferated in recent years; today, there are well over 100 different awards and prizes by a variety of organizations. ① The awards may be given for books of a specific genre or simply for the best of all children's books published within a given time period. An award may honor a particular book or an author for a lifetime contribution to the world of children's literature. ② Most children's book awards are chosen by adults, but now a growing number of children's choice book awards exist. The larger national awards given in most countries are the most influential and have helped considerably to raise public awareness about the fine books being published for young readers. ③ An award ceremony for outstanding services to the publishing industry is put on hold. ④ Of course, readers are wise not to put too much faith in award-winning books. An award doesn't necessarily mean a good reading experience, but it does provide a starting place when choosing books.

문 19. 주어진 문장이 들어갈 가장 적절한 위치는?

> This inequality is corrected by their getting in their turn better portions from kills by other people.

> Let us examine a situation of simple distribution such as occurs when an animal is killed in a hunt. One might expect to find the animal portioned out according to the amount of work done by each hunter to obtain it. (①) To some extent this principle is followed, but other people have their rights as well. (②) Each person in the camp gets a share depending upon his or her relation to the hunters. (③) When a kangaroo is killed, for example, the hunters have to give its main parts to their kinfolk and the worst parts may even be kept by the hunters themselves. (④) The net result in the long run is substantially the same to each person, but through this system the principles of kinship obligation and the morality of sharing food have been emphasized.

문 20. 주어진 글 다음에 이어질 글의 순서로 가장 적절한 것은?

> The most innovative of the group therapy approaches was psychodrama, the brainchild of Jacob L. Moreno. Psychodrama as a form of group therapy started with premises that were quite alien to the Freudian world view that mental illness essentially occurs within the psyche or mind.

(A) But he also believed that creativity is rarely a solitary process but something brought out by social interactions. He relied heavily on theatrical techniques, including role-playing and improvisation, as a means to promote creativity and general social trust.

(B) Despite his theoretical difference from the mainstream viewpoint, Moreno's influence in shaping psychological consciousness in the twentieth century was considerable. He believed that the nature of human beings is to be creative and that living a creative life is the key to human health and well-being.

(C) His most important theatrical tool was what he called role reversal — asking participants to take on another's persona. The act of pretending "as if" one were in another's skin was designed to help bring out the empathic impulse and to develop it to higher levels of expression.

① (A) − (C) − (B)　　② (B) − (A) − (C)
③ (B) − (C) − (A)　　④ (C) − (B) − (A)

해설편 ▶ P.37

2017

10월 21일 시행
국가직 9급 추가

| 풀이 시간: _____:_____ ~ _____:_____ / 점수: _____점

※ 밑줄 친 부분에 들어갈 말로 가장 적절한 것을 고르시오.

[문 1 ~ 문 2]

문 1.

Mary: Hi, James. How's it going?
James: Hello, Mary. What can I do for you today?
Mary: How can I arrange for this package to be delivered?
James: Why don't you talk to Bob in Customer Service?
Mary: _____.

① Sure. I will deliver this package for you.
② OK. Let me take care of Bob's customers.
③ I will see you at the Customs office.
④ I tried calling his number, but no one is answering.

문 2.

A: Wow! Look at the long line. I'm sure we have to wait at least 30 minutes.
B: You're right. _____
A: That's a good idea. I want to ride the roller coaster.
B: It's not my cup of tea.
A: How about the Flume Ride then? It's fun and the line is not so long.
B: That sounds great! Let's go!

① Let's find seats for the magic show.
② Let's look for another ride.
③ Let's buy costumes for the parade.
④ Let's go to the lost and found.

※ 우리말을 영어로 잘못 옮긴 것을 고르시오. [문 3 ~ 문 4]

문 3. ① 그 클럽은 입소문을 통해서 인기를 얻었다.
→ The club became popular by word of mouth.
② 무서운 영화를 좋아한다면 이것은 꼭 봐야 할 영화이다.
→ If you like scary movies, this is a must-see movie.
③ 뒤쪽은 너무 멀어요. 중간에 앉는 걸로 타협합시다.
→ The back is too far away. Let's promise and sit in the middle.
④ 제 예산이 빠듯합니다. 제가 쓸 수 있는 돈은 15달러뿐입니다.
→ I am on a tight budget. I only have fifteen dollars to spend.

문 4. ① 식사가 준비됐을 때, 우리는 식당으로 이동했다.
→ The dinner being ready, we moved to the dining hall.
② 저쪽에 있는 사람이 누구인지 알겠니?
→ Can you tell who that is over there?
③ 이 질병이 목숨을 앗아가는 일은 좀처럼 없다.
→ It rarely happens that this disease proves fatal.
④ 과정을 관리하면서 발전시키는 것이 나의 목표였다.
→ To control the process and making improvement was my objectives.

※ 밑줄 친 부분과 의미가 가장 가까운 것을 고르시오.

[문 5 ~ 문 7]

문 5.

These days, Halloween has drifted far from its roots in pagan and Catholic festivals, and the spirits we appease are no longer those of the dead: needy ghosts have been replaced by costumed children demanding treats.

① assign   ② apprehend
③ pacify   ④ provoke

문 6.

I usually make light of my problems, and that makes me feel better.

① consider something as serious
② treat something as unimportant
③ make an effort to solve a problem
④ seek an acceptable solution

문 7.

A hamburger and French fries became the quintessential American meal in the 1950s, thanks to the promotional efforts of the fast food chains.

① healthiest   ② affordable
③ typical   ④ informal

문 8. 주어진 문장이 들어갈 위치로 가장 적절한 곳은?

Only New Zealand, New Caledonia and a few small islands peek above the waves.

Lurking beneath New Zealand is a long-hidden continent called Zealandia, geologists say. But since nobody is in charge of officially designating a new continent, individual scientists will ultimately have to judge for themselves. (①) A team of geologists pitches the scientific case for the new continent, arguing that Zealandia is a continuous expanse of continental crust covering around 4.9 million square kilometers. (②) That's about the size of the Indian subcontinent. Unlike the other mostly dry continents, around 94 percent of Zealandia hides beneath the ocean. (③) Except those tiny areas, all parts of Zealandia submerge under the ocean. "If we could pull the plug on the world's oceans, it would be quite clear that Zealandia stands out about 3,000 meters above the surrounding ocean crust," says a geologist. (④) "If it wasn't for the ocean level, long ago we'd have recognized Zealandia for what it was — a continent."

문 9. 다음 글의 내용과 일치하지 않는 것은?

The first decades of the 17th century witnessed an exponential growth in the understanding of the Earth and heavens, a process usually referred to as the Scientific Revolution. The older reliance on the philosophy of Aristotle was fast waning in universities. In the Aristotelian system of natural philosophy, the movements of bodies were explained 'causally' in terms of the amount of the four elements (earth, water, air, fire) that they possessed, and objects moved up or down to their 'natural' place depending on the preponderance of given elements of which they were composed. Natural philosophy was routinely contrasted with 'mixed mathematical' subjects such as optics, hydrostatics, and harmonics, where numbers could be applied to measurable external quantities such as length or duration.

① There was an increase in the knowledge of the Earth and heavens in the early 17th century.
② Dependence on the philosophy of Aristotle was on the decline in universities in the 17th century.
③ Natural philosophy proposed four elements to explain the movements of bodies.
④ In natural philosophy, numbers were routinely put to use for measurable external quantities.

문 10. 다음 글의 내용과 가장 일치하는 것은?

Stressful events early in a person's life, such as neglect or abuse, can have psychological impacts into adulthood. New research shows that these effects may persist in their children and even their grandchildren. Larry James and Lorena Schmidt, biochemists at the Tufts School of Medicine, caused chronic social stress in adolescent mice by regularly relocating them to new cages over the course of seven weeks. The researchers then tested these stressed mice in adulthood using a series of standard laboratory measures for rodent anxiety, such as how long the mice spent in open areas of a maze and how frequently they approached mice they had never met before. Female mice showed more anxious behaviors compared with control animals, whereas the males did not. Both sexes' offspring displayed more anxious behaviors, however, and the males who had been stressed as adolescents even transmitted these behavior patterns to their female grandchildren and great-grandchildren.

① Your grandfather's stress when he was an adolescent might make you more anxious.
② Early stressful experiences alleviate anxiety later in life.
③ Constant moving from one place to another can benefit offspring.
④ Chronic social stress cannot be caused by relocation.

문 11. 밑줄 친 부분에 공통으로 들어갈 말로 가장 적절한 것은?

• She's disappointed about their final decision, but she'll _____ it eventually.
• It took me a very long time to _____ the shock of her death.

① get away　　　　　② get down
③ get ahead　　　　　④ get over

문 12. 주어진 글 다음에 이어질 글의 순서로 가장 적절한 것은?

Through the ages, industrious individuals have continuously created conveniences to make life easier. From the invention of the wheel to the lightbulb, inventions have propelled society forward.

(A) In addition, interactive media can be used to question a lecturer or exchange opinions with other students via e-mail. Such computerized lectures give students access to knowledge that was previously unavailable.
(B) One recent modern invention is the computer, which has improved many aspects of people's lives. This is especially true in the field of education. One important effect of computer technology on higher education is the availability of lectures.
(C) As a result of the development of computer networks, students can obtain lectures from many universities in real time. They are now able to sit down in front of a digital screen and listen to a lecture being given at another university.

① (A) － (B) － (C)　　　② (B) － (C) － (A)
③ (C) － (A) － (B)　　　④ (C) － (B) － (A)

※ 어법상 옳은 것을 고르시오.　　　　　[문 13 ~ 문 14]

문 13. ① Undergraduates are not allowed to using equipments in the laboratory.
② The extent of Mary's knowledge on various subjects astound me.
③ If she had been at home yesterday, I would have visited her.
④ I regret to inform you that your loan application has not approved.

문 14. ① My father was in the hospital during six weeks.
② The whole family is suffered from the flu.
③ She never so much as mentioned it.
④ She would like to be financial independent.

※ 밑줄 친 부분에 들어갈 말로 가장 적절한 것을 고르시오.
[문 15 ~ 문 17]

문 15.

As a middle-class Jew growing up in an ethnically mixed Chicago neighborhood, I was already in danger of being beaten up daily by rougher working-class boys. Becoming a bookworm would only have given them a decisive reason for beating me up. Reading and studying were more permissible for girls, but they, too, had to be careful not to get too _____, lest they acquire the stigma of being 'stuck up.'

① athletic   ② intellectual
③ hospitable   ④ inexperienced

문 16.

You asked us, "What keeps satellites from falling out of the sky?" Over the last half-century, more than 2,500 satellites have followed the first one into space. What keeps them all afloat? It is a delicate balance between a satellite's speed and the pull of gravity. Satellites are _____.
Crazy, right? They fall at the same rate that the curve of the Earth falls away from them if they're moving at the right speed. Which means instead of racing farther out into space or spiraling down to Earth, they hang out in orbit around the planet. Corrections are often needed to keep a satellite on the straight and narrow. Earth's gravity is stronger in some places than others. Satellites can get pulled around by the sun, the moon and even the planet Jupiter.

① created to shut off once they are in orbit
② designed to intensify the Earth's gravity
③ theoretically pulling other planets
④ basically continuously falling

문 17.

Rosberg observed that color advertisements in the trade publication Industrial Marketing produced more attention than black and white advertisements. It is an interesting historical sidelight to note that the color advertisements in Rosberg's study were considerably more expensive to run than corresponding black and white advertisements. Although the color advertisements did produce more attention, they did not attract as many readers per dollar as the black and white advertisements. Today, the technology, economy, and efficiency of printing has progressed to the point where color advertisements are no longer so rare. As a result, color advertisements may no longer be an 'exception.' In some color, glossy magazines, or on television, color advertisements may be so common that the rare black and white advertisement now attracts attention due to _____.

① contrast   ② hostility
③ deportation   ④ charity

문 18. 다음 글의 흐름상 가장 어색한 문장은?

Researchers have developed a new model they said will provide better estimates about the North Atlantic right whale population, and the news isn't good. ① The model could be critically important to efforts to save the endangered species, which is in the midst of a year of high mortality, said Peter Corkeron, who leads the large whale team for the National Oceanic and Atmospheric Administration's Northeast Fisheries Science Center. ② The agency said the analysis shows the probability the population has declined since 2010 is nearly 100 percent. ③ "One problem was, are they really going down or are we not seeing them? They really have gone down, and that's the bottom line," Corkeron said. ④ The new research model has successfully demonstrated that the number of right whales has remained intact despite the worrisome, widening population gap between whale males and females.

문 19. 다음 글의 내용과 일치하지 않는 것은?

When the gong sounds, almost every diner at Beijing restaurant Duck de Chine turns around. That's because one of the city's greatest culinary shows is about to begin — the slicing of a Peking duck. Often voted by local guides in China as the best Peking duck in the city, the skin on Duck de Chine's birds is crispy and caramelized, its meat tender and juicy. "Our roasted duck is a little different than elsewhere," says An Ding, manager of Duck de Chine. "We use jujube wood, which is over 60 years old, and has a strong fruit scent, giving the duck especially crispy skin and a delicious flavor." The sweet hoisin sauce, drizzled over sliced spring onions and cucumbers and encased with the duck skin in a thin pancake, is another highlight. "The goal of our service is to focus on the details," says Ding. "It includes both how we present the roasted duck, and the custom sauces made for our guests." Even the plates and the chopsticks holders are duck-shaped. Duck de Chine also boasts China's first Bollinger Champagne Bar. Though Peking duck is the star, there are plenty of other worthy dishes on the menu. The restaurant serves both Cantonese and Beijing cuisine, but with a touch of French influence.

① The restaurant presents a culinary performance.
② The restaurant is highly praised in Beijing.
③ The restaurant features a special champagne bar.
④ The restaurant only serves dishes from the Beijing region.

문 20. 밑줄 친 부분에 들어갈 말로 가장 적절한 것은?

Since dog baths tend to be messy, time-consuming and not a whole lot of fun for everyone involved, it's natural to wonder, "How often should I bathe my dog?" As is often the case, the answer is "_____." "Dogs groom themselves to help facilitate the growth of hair follicles and to support skin health," says Dr. Adam Denish of Rhawnhurst Animal Hospital. "However, bathing is needed for most dogs to supplement the process. But bathing too often can be detrimental to your pet as well. It can irritate the skin, damage hair follicles, and increase the risk of bacterial or fungal infections." Dr. Jennifer Coates, veterinary advisor with petMD, adds, "the best bath frequency depends on the reason behind the bath. Healthy dogs who spend most of their time inside may only need to be bathed a few times a year to control natural 'doggy odors.' On the other hand, frequent bathing is a critical part of managing some medical conditions, like allergic skin disease."

① It depends
② Just once
③ Bathing is never necessary
④ When the bath is detrimental to your dog

해설편 ▶ P.43

① Nobody mentioned that to me.
② Where is the price tag?
③ What's the problem with it?
④ I got a good deal on it.

2016

4월 9일 시행
국가직 9급

┃ 풀이 시간: _____:_____ ~ _____:_____ / 점수: _____점

문 1. 밑줄 친 부분에 들어갈 말로 가장 적절한 것은?

> The campaign to eliminate pollution will prove
> _____ unless it has the understanding
> and full cooperation of the public.

① enticing　② enhanced　③ fertile　④ futile

문 2. 밑줄 친 부분과 의미가 가장 가까운 것은?

> Up to now, newspaper articles have only
> scratched the surface of this tremendously complex
> issue.

① superficially dealt with
② hit the nail on the head of
③ seized hold of
④ positively followed up on

※ 밑줄 친 부분에 들어갈 말로 가장 적절한 것을 고르시오.
[문 3 ~ 문 4]

문 3.

> A: I'd like to get a refund for this tablecloth I
> 　bought here yesterday.
> B: Is there a problem with the tablecloth?
> A: It doesn't fit our table and I would like to return
> 　it. Here is my receipt.
> B: I'm sorry, but this tablecloth was a final sale
> 　item, and it cannot be refunded.
> A: _____
> B: It's written at the bottom of the receipt.

문 4.

> A: Hello? Hi, Stephanie. I'm on my way to the
> 　office. Do you need anything?
> B: Hi, Luke. Can you please pick up extra paper
> 　for the printer?
> A: What did you say? Did you say to pick up ink
> 　for the printer? Sorry, _____
> B: Can you hear me now? I said I need more paper
> 　for the printer.
> A: Can you repeat that, please?
> B: Never mind. I'll text you.
> A: Okay. Thanks, Stephanie. See you soon.

① my phone has really bad reception here.
② I couldn't pick up more paper.
③ I think I've dialed the wrong number.
④ I'll buy each item separately this time.

문 5. 우리말을 영어로 잘못 옮긴 것은?

① 나의 이모는 파티에서 그녀를 만난 것을 기억하지 못했다.
　→ My aunt didn't remember meeting her at the
　　party.
② 나의 첫 책을 쓰는 데 40년이 걸렸다.
　→ It took me 40 years to write my first book.
③ 학교에서 집으로 걸어오고 있을 때 강풍에 내 우산이 뒤
　집혔다.
　→ A strong wind blew my umbrella inside out as I
　　was walking home from school.
④ 끝까지 생존하는 생물은 가장 강한 생물도, 가장 지적인
　생물도 아니고, 변화에 가장 잘 반응하는 생물이다.
　→ It is not the strongest of the species, nor the most
　　intelligent, or the one most responsive to change
　　that survives to the end.

문 6. 글의 제목으로 가장 적절한 것은?

> After analyzing a mass of data on job interview results, a research team discovered a surprising reality. Did the likelihood of being hired depend on qualifications? Or was it work experience? In fact, it was neither. It was just one important factor: did the candidate appear to be a pleasant person. Those candidates who had managed to ingratiate themselves were very likely to be offered a position; they had charmed their way to success. Some had made a special effort to smile and maintain eye contact. Others had praised the organization. This positivity had convinced the interviewers that such pleasant and socially skilled applicants would fit well into the workplace, and so should be offered a job.

① To Get a Job, Be a Pleasant Person
② More Qualifications Bring Better Chances
③ It Is Ability That Counts, Not Personality
④ Show Yourself As You Are at an Interview

문 7. 글의 내용과 일치하지 않는 것은?

> Most writers lead double lives. They earn good money at legitimate professions, and carve out time for their writing as best they can: early in the morning, late at night, weekends, vacations. William Carlos Williams and Louis-Ferdinand Céline were doctors. Wallace Stevens worked for an insurance company. T.S. Elliot was a banker, then a publisher. Don DeLilo, Peter Carey, Salman Rushdie, and Elmore Leonard all worked for long stretches in advertising. Other writers teach. That is probably the most common solution today, and with every major university and college offering so-called creative writing courses, novelists and poets are continually scratching and scrambling to land themselves a spot. Who can blame them? The salaries might not be big, but the work is steady and the hours are good.

① Some writers struggle for teaching positions to teach creative writing courses.
② As a doctor, William Carlos Williams tried to find the time to write.
③ Teaching is a common way for writers to make a living today.
④ Salman Rushdie worked briefly in advertising with great triumph.

문 8. 글의 흐름상 가장 어색한 문장은?

> One of the largest celebrations of the passage of young girls into womanhood occurs in Latin American and Hispanic cultures. This event is called La Quinceañera, or the fifteenth year. ① It acknowledges that a young woman is now of marriageable age. The day usually begins with a Mass of Thanksgiving. ② By comparing the rites of passage of one culture with those of another, we can assess differences in class status. The young woman wears a full-length white or pastel-colored dress and is attended by fourteen friends and relatives who serve as maids of honor and male escorts. ③ Her parents and godparents surround her at the foot of the altar. When the Mass ends, other young relatives give small gifts to those who attended, while the Quinceañera herself places a bouquet of flowers on the altar of the Virgin. ④ Following the Mass is an elaborate party, with dancing, cake, and toasts. Finally, to end the evening, the young woman dances a waltz with her favorite escort.

문 9. 주어진 문장이 들어갈 위치로 가장 적절한 곳은?

> He dismally fails the first two, but redeems himself in the concluding whale episode, where he does indeed demonstrate courage, honesty, and unselfishness.

> Disney's work draws heavily from fairy tales, myths, and folklore, which are profuse in archetypal elements. (①) *Pinocchio* is a good example of how these elements can be emphasized rather than submerged beneath a surface realism. (②) Early in the film, the boy/puppet Pinocchio is told that in order to be a "real boy," he must show that he is "brave, truthful, and unselfish." (③) The three principal episodes of the movie represent ritualistic trials, testing the youth's moral fortitude. (④) As such, like most of Disney's works, the values in *Pinocchio* are traditional and conservative, an affirmation of the sanctity of the family unit, the importance of a Higher Power in guiding our destinies, and the need to play by society's rules.

문 10. 글의 내용과 일치하지 않는 것은?

> Stanislavski was fortunate in many ways. He was the son of a wealthy man who could give him the advantages of a broad education, the opportunity to see the greatest exponents of theatre art at home and abroad. He acquired a great reputation because he had set high goals and never faltered along the hard road leading to them. His personal integrity and inexhaustible capacity for work contributed to making him a professional artist of the first rank. Stanislavski was also richly endowed by nature with a handsome exterior, fine voice and genuine talent. As an actor, director and teacher, he was destined to influence and inspire the many who worked with him and under him or who had the privilege of seeing him on the stage.

① Stanislavski was born with attractive features.
② Stanislavski remained uninfluential on his colleagues throughout his life.
③ Stanislavski's father was affluent enough to support his education.
④ Stanislavski became a top-ranked artist by the aid of his upright character and untiring competence.

※ 밑줄 친 부분과 의미가 가장 가까운 것을 고르시오.
　　　　　　　　　　　　　　　　　　　 [문 11 ~ 문 12]

문 11.

> It was personal. Why did you have to stick your nose in?

① hurry　　　　　　　② interfere
③ sniff　　　　　　　④ resign

문 12.

> Newton made unprecedented contributions to mathematics, optics, and mechanical physics.

① mediocre　　　　　　② suggestive
③ unsurpassed　　　　　④ provocative

문 13. 어법상 옳은 것은?

① Jessica is a much careless person who makes little effort to improve her knowledge.
② But he will come or not is not certain.
③ The police demanded that she not leave the country for the time being.
④ The more a hotel is expensiver, the better its service is.

문 14. 글의 제목으로 가장 적절한 것은?

> Character is a respect for human beings and the right to interpret experience differently. Character admits self-interest as a natural trait, but pins its faith on man's hesitant but heartening instinct to cooperate. Character is allergic to tyranny, irritable with ignorance and always open to improvement. Character is, above all, a tremendous humility before the facts — an automatic alliance with truth even when that truth is bitter medicine.

① Character's Resistance to Truth
② How to Cooperate with Characters
③ The Ignorance of Character
④ What Character Means

문 15. 글의 주제로 가장 적절한 것은?

> Children who under-achieve at school may just have poor working memory rather than low intelligence. Researchers from a university surveyed more than 3,000 primary school children of all ages and found that 10% of them suffer from poor working memory, which seriously impedes their learning. Nationally, this equates to almost 500,000 children in primary education being affected. The researchers also found that teachers rarely identify poor working memory and often describe children with this problem as inattentive or less intelligent.

① children's identification with teachers at school
② low intelligence of primary school children
③ influence of poor working memory on primary school children
④ teachers' efforts to solve children's working-memory problem

문 16. 글의 내용과 일치하는 것은?

> A new study by Harvard researchers may provide a compelling reason to remove canned soup and juice from your dining table. People who ate one serving of canned food daily over the course of five days, the study found, had significantly elevated levels — more than a tenfold increase — of bisphenol-A, or BPA, a substance that lines most food and drink cans. Public health officials in the United States have come under increasing pressure to regulate it. Some of the research on BPA shows that it is linked to a higher risk of cancer, heart disease, and obesity. Some researchers, though, counter that its reputation as a health threat to people is exaggerated. The new study published in *The Journal of the American Medical Association* is the first to measure the amounts of BPA that are ingested when people eat food that comes directly out of a can.

① 하버드의 새로운 연구가 통조림 음식의 안전성을 입증하였다.

② 비스페놀 A와 암, 심장병, 비만의 연관성이 과장되었다는 데에 모든 학자들이 동의한다.

③ 통조림 음식으로부터 사람의 몸에 유입된 비스페놀 A의 양이 아직 측정되지 않았다.

④ 미국의 보건 관리들은 비스페놀 A를 규제하라는 압력을 점점 더 받고 있다.

문 17. 주어진 글 다음에 이어질 글의 순서로 가장 적절한 것은?

> All animals have the same kind of brain activation during sleep as humans. Whether or not they dream is another question, which can be answered only by posing another one: Do animals have consciousness?

> (A) These are three of the key aspects of consciousness, and they could be experienced whether or not an animal had verbal language as we do. When the animal's brain is activated during sleep, why not assume that the animal has some sort of perceptual, emotional, and memory experience?
>
> (B) Many scientists today feel that animals probably do have a limited form of consciousness, quite different from ours in that it lacks language and the capacity for propositional or symbolic thought.
>
> (C) Animals certainly can't report dreams even if they do have them. But which pet owner would doubt that his or her favourite animal friend has perception, memory, and emotion?

① (A) − (B) − (C) ② (A) − (C) − (B)
③ (B) − (C) − (A) ④ (C) − (B) − (A)

문 18. 밑줄 친 부분 중 어법상 옳은 것은?

> ① <u>As the old saying go</u>, you are what you eat. The foods you eat ② <u>obvious affect your body's performance</u>. They may also influence how your brain handles tasks. If your brain handles them well, you think more clearly, and you are more emotionally stable. The right food can ③ <u>help you being concentrated</u>, keep you motivated, sharpen your memory, speed your reaction time, reduce stress, and perhaps ④ <u>even prevent your brain from aging</u>.

※ 밑줄 친 부분에 들어갈 말로 가장 적절한 것을 고르시오.
[문 19 ~ 문 20]

문 19.

There's a knock at your door. Standing in front of you is a young man who needs help. He's injured and is bleeding. You take him in and help him, make him feel comfortable and safe and phone for an ambulance. This is clearly the right thing to do. But if you help him just because you feel sorry for him, according to Immanuel Kant, _____. Your sympathy is irrelevant to the morality of your action. That's part of your character, but nothing to do with right and wrong. Morality for Kant wasn't just about what you do, but about why you do it. Those who do the right thing don't do it simply because of how they feel: the decision has to be based on reason, reason that tells you what your duty is, regardless of how you happen to feel.

① that wouldn't be a moral action at all
② your action is founded on reason
③ then you're exhibiting ethical behavior
④ you're encouraging him to be an honest person

문 20.

A group of tribes and genera of hopping reptiles, small creatures of the dinosaur type, seem to have been pushed by competition and the pursuit of their enemies towards the alternatives of extinction or adaptation to colder conditions in the higher hills or by the sea. Among these distressed tribes there was developed a new type of scale — scales that were elongated into quill-like forms and that presently branched into the crude beginnings of feathers. These quill-like scales lay over one another and formed a heat-retaining covering more efficient than any reptilian covering that had hitherto existed. So they permitted an invasion of colder regions that were otherwise uninhabited. Perhaps simultaneously with these changes there arose in these creatures a greater solicitude for their eggs. Most reptiles are apparently quite careless about their eggs, which are left for sun and season to hatch. But some of the varieties upon this new branch of the tree of life were acquiring a habit of guarding their eggs and _____. With these adaptations to cold, other internal modifications were going on that made these creatures, the primitive birds, warm-blooded and independent of basking.

① hatching them unsuccessfully
② leaving them under the sun on their own
③ keeping them warm with the warmth of their bodies
④ flying them to scaled reptiles

해설편 ▶ P.49

오랫동안 꿈을 그리는 사람은
마침내 그 꿈을 닮아간다.

– 앙드레 말로(Andre Malraux)

2022~2016년 시행

지방직 9급 공개경쟁채용 필기시험

응 시 번 호	
성　　　명	

문 제 책 형

【시 험 과 목】

제1과목	국　　어	제2과목	영　　어	제3과목	한 국 사
제4·5과목	행정법총론, 행정학개론				

응시자 주의사항

1. **시험 시작 전**에 시험문제를 열람하는 행위나 **시험 종료 후** 답안을 작성하는 행위를 한 사람은 「지방공무원 임용령」 제65조 등 관련 법령에 의거 **부정행위자**로 처리됩니다.

2. 시험 시작 즉시 **과목편철 순서, 문제누락 여부, 인쇄상태 이상 유무 및 표지와 개별과목의 문제책형 일치 여부 등을 확인**한 후 문제책 표지에 응시번호, 성명을 기재합니다.

3. 반드시 본인의 **응시표에 인쇄된 시험과목 순서에 따라** 제4과목과 제5과목의 **답안을 표기**하여야 합니다. 과목 순서를 바꾸어 표기한 경우에도 **본인의 응시표에 기재된 과목 순서대로 채점**되므로 반드시 유의하시기 바랍니다.

4. 시험이 시작되면 문제를 주의 깊게 읽은 후, **문항의 취지에 가장 적합한 하나의 정답만을 고르며**, 문제 내용에 관한 질문은 받지 않습니다.

5. **시험시간 관리의 책임**은 전적으로 응시자 본인에게 있습니다.

| 풀이 시간: ___:___ ~ ___:___ / 점수: ___점

※ 밑줄 친 부분의 의미와 가장 가까운 것을 고르시오.
[문 1 ~ 문 3]

문 1.
School teachers have to be <u>flexible</u> to cope with different ability levels of the students.

① strong　　　　② adaptable
③ honest　　　　④ passionate

문 2.
Crop yields <u>vary</u>, improving in some areas and falling in others.

① change　　　　② decline
③ expand　　　　④ include

문 3.
I don't feel inferior to anyone <u>with respect to</u> my education.

① in danger of　　　② in spite of
③ in favor of　　　④ in terms of

문 4. 밑줄 친 부분에 들어갈 말로 가장 적절한 것은?

Sometimes we _____ money long before the next payday.

① turn into　　　　② start over
③ put up with　　　④ run out of

※ 어법상 옳지 않은 것을 고르시오. [문 5 ~ 문 6]

문 5. ① He asked me why I kept coming back day after day.
② Toys children wanted all year long has recently discarded.
③ She is someone who is always ready to lend a helping hand.
④ Insects are often attracted by scents that aren't obvious to us.

문 6. ① You can write on both sides of the paper.
② My home offers me a feeling of security, warm, and love.
③ The number of car accidents is on the rise.
④ Had I realized what you were intending to do, I would have stopped you.

※ 우리말을 영어로 잘못 옮긴 것을 고르시오. [문 7 ~ 문 8]

문 7. ① 나는 단 한 푼의 돈도 낭비할 수 없다.
→ I can afford to waste even one cent.
② 그녀의 얼굴에서 미소가 곧 사라졌다.
→ The smile soon faded from her face.
③ 그녀는 사임하는 것 외에는 대안이 없었다.
→ She had no alternative but to resign.
④ 나는 5년 후에 내 사업을 시작할 작정이다.
→ I'm aiming to start my own business in five years.

문 8. ① 식사를 마치자마자 나는 다시 배고프기 시작했다.

→ No sooner I have finishing the meal than I started feeling hungry again.

② 그녀는 조만간 요금을 내야만 할 것이다.

→ She will have to pay the bill sooner or later.

③ 독서와 정신의 관계는 운동과 신체의 관계와 같다.

→ Reading is to the mind what exercise is to the body.

④ 그는 대학에서 의학을 공부했으나 결국 회계 회사에서 일하게 되었다.

→ He studied medicine at university but ended up working for an accounting firm.

문 9. 두 사람의 대화 중 가장 어색한 것은?

① A: I like this newspaper because it's not opinionated.

B: That's why it has the largest circulation.

② A: Do you have a good reason for being all dressed up?

B: Yeah, I have an important job interview today.

③ A: I can hit the ball straight during the practice but not during the game.

B: That happens to me all the time, too.

④ A: Is there any particular subject you want to paint on canvas?

B: I didn't do good in history when I was in high school.

문 10. 밑줄 친 부분에 들어갈 말로 가장 적절한 것은?

A: Hey! How did your geography test go?

B: Not bad, thanks. I'm just glad that it's over! How about you? How did your science exam go?

A: Oh, it went really well. _____. I owe you a treat for that.

B: It's my pleasure. So, do you feel like preparing for the math exam scheduled for next week?

A: Sure. Let's study together.

B: It sounds good. See you later.

① There's no sense in beating yourself up over this

② I never thought I would see you here

③ Actually, we were very disappointed

④ I can't thank you enough for helping me with it

문 11. 주어진 글 다음에 이어질 글의 순서로 가장 적절한 것은?

For people who are blind, everyday tasks such as sorting through the mail or doing a load of laundry present a challenge.

(A) That's the thinking behind Aira, a new service that enables its thousands of users to stream live video of their surroundings to an on-demand agent, using either a smartphone or Aira's proprietary glasses.

(B) But what if they could "borrow" the eyes of someone who could see?

(C) The Aira agents, who are available 24/7, can then answer questions, describe objects or guide users through a location.

① (A) − (B) − (C)　　② (A) − (C) − (B)

③ (B) − (A) − (C)　　④ (C) − (A) − (B)

문 12. 주어진 문장이 들어갈 위치로 가장 적절한 곳은?

> The comparison of the heart to a pump, however, is a genuine analogy.

An analogy is a figure of speech in which two things are asserted to be alike in many respects that are quite fundamental. Their structure, the relationships of their parts, or the essential purposes they serve are similar, although the two things are also greatly dissimilar. Roses and carnations are not analogous. (①) They both have stems and leaves and may both be red in color. (②) But they exhibit these qualities in the same way; they are of the same genus. (③) These are disparate things, but they share important qualities: mechanical apparatus, possession of valves, ability to increase and decrease pressures, and capacity to move fluids. (④) And the heart and the pump exhibit these qualities in different ways and in different contexts.

문 13. 다음 글의 제목으로 가장 적절한 것은?

One of the areas where efficiency can be optimized is the work force, through increasing individual productivity — defined as the amount of work (products produced, customers served) an employee handles in a given time. In addition to making sure you have invested in the right equipment, environment, and training to ensure optimal performance, you can increase productivity by encouraging staffers to put an end to a modern-day energy drain: multitasking. Studies show it takes 25 to 40 percent longer to get a job done when you're simultaneously trying to work on other projects. To be more productive, says Andrew Deutscher, vice president of business development at consulting firm The Energy Project, "do one thing, uninterrupted, for a sustained period of time."

① How to Create More Options in Life
② How to Enhance Daily Physical Performance
③ Multitasking is the Answer for Better Efficiency
④ Do One Thing at a Time for Greater Efficiency

문 14. 글의 흐름상 가장 어색한 문장은?

The skill to have a good argument is critical in life. But it's one that few parents teach to their children. ① We want to give kids a stable home, so we stop siblings from quarreling and we have our own arguments behind closed doors. ② Yet if kids never get exposed to disagreement, we may eventually limit their creativity. ③ Children are most creative when they are free to brainstorm with lots of praise and encouragement in a peaceful environment. ④ It turns out that highly creative people often grow up in families full of tension. They are not surrounded by fistfights or personal insults, but real disagreements. When adults in their early 30s were asked to write imaginative stories, the most creative ones came from those whose parents had the most conflict a quarter-century earlier.

※ 다음 글의 내용과 일치하지 않는 것을 고르시오.
[문 15 ~ 문 16]

문 15.

Christopher Nolan is an Irish writer of some renown in the English language. Brain damaged since birth, Nolan has had little control over the muscles of his body, even to the extent of having difficulty in swallowing food. He must be strapped to his wheelchair because he cannot sit up by himself. Nolan cannot utter recognizable speech sounds. Fortunately, though, his brain damage was such that Nolan's intelligence was undamaged and his hearing was normal; as a result, he learned to understand speech as a young child. It was only many years later, though, after he had reached 10 years, and after he had learned to read, that he was given a means to express his first words. He did this by using a stick which was attached to his head to point to letters. It was in this 'unicorn' manner, letter-by-letter, that he produced an entire book of poems and short stories, *Dam-Burst of Dreams*, while still a teenager.

① Christopher Nolan은 뇌 손상을 갖고 태어났다.
② Christopher Nolan은 음식을 삼키는 것도 어려웠다.
③ Christopher Nolan은 청각 장애로 인해 들을 수 없었다.
④ Christopher Nolan은 10대일 때 책을 썼다.

문 16.

In many Catholic countries, children are often named after saints; in fact, some priests will not allow parents to name their children after soap opera stars or football players. Protestant countries tend to be more free about this; however, in Norway, certain names such as Adolf are banned completely. In countries where infant mortality is very high, such as in Africa, tribes only name their children when they reach five years old, the age in which their chances of survival begin to increase. Until that time, they are referred to by the number of years they are. Many nations in the Far East give their children a unique name which in some way describes the circumstances of the child's birth or the parents' expectations and hopes for the child. Some Australian aborigines can keep changing their name throughout their life as the result of some important experience which has in some way proved their wisdom, creativity or determination. For example, if one day, one of them dances extremely well, he or she may decide to re-name him/herself 'supreme dancer' or 'light feet'.

① Children are frequently named after saints in many Catholic countries.

② Some African children are not named until they turn five years old.

③ Changing one's name is totally unacceptable in the culture of Australian aborigines.

④ Various cultures name their children in different ways.

문 17. 다음 글의 요지로 가장 적절한 것은?

In one study, done in the early 1970s when young people tended to dress in either "hippie" or "straight" fashion, experimenters donned hippie or straight attire and asked college students on campus for a dime to make a phone call. When the experimenter was dressed in the same way as the student, the request was granted in more than two-thirds of the instances; when the student and requester were dissimilarly dressed, the dime was provided less than half the time. Another experiment showed how automatic our positive response to similar others can be. Marchers in an antiwar demonstration were found to be more likely to sign the petition of a similarly dressed requester and to do so without bothering to read it first.

① People are more likely to help those who dress like themselves.

② Dressing up formally increases the chance of signing the petition.

③ Making a phone call is an efficient way to socialize with other students.

④ Some college students in the early 1970s were admired for their unique fashion.

문 18. (A)와 (B)에 들어갈 말로 가장 적절한 것은?

Duration shares an inverse relationship with frequency. If you see a friend frequently, then the duration of the encounter will be shorter. Conversely, if you don't see your friend very often, the duration of your visit will typically increase significantly. _____(A)_____, if you see a friend every day, the duration of your visits can be low because you can keep up with what's going on as events unfold. If, however, you only see your friend twice a year, the duration of your visits will be greater. Think back to a time when you had dinner in a restaurant with a friend you hadn't seen for a long period of time. You probably spent several hours catching up on each other's lives. The duration of the same dinner would be considerably shorter if you saw the person on a regular basis. _____(B)_____, in romantic relationships the frequency and duration are very high because couples, especially newly minted ones, want to spend as much time with each other as possible. The intensity of the relationship will also be very high.

	(A)	(B)
①	For example	Conversely
②	Nonetheless	Furthermore
③	Therefore	As a result
④	In the same way	Thus

문 19.

One of the most frequently used propaganda techniques is to convince the public that the propagandist's views reflect those of the common person and that he or she is working in their best interests. A politician speaking to a blue-collar audience may roll up his sleeves, undo his tie, and attempt to use the specific idioms of the crowd. He may even use language incorrectly on purpose to give the impression that he is "just one of the folks." This technique usually also employs the use of glittering generalities to give the impression that the politician's views are the same as those of the crowd being addressed. Labor leaders, businesspeople, ministers, educators, and advertisers have used this technique to win our confidence by appearing to be _____.

① beyond glittering generalities
② just plain folks like ourselves
③ something different from others
④ better educated than the crowd

문 20.

As a roller coaster climbs the first lift hill of its track, it is building potential energy — the higher it gets above the earth, the stronger the pull of gravity will be. When the coaster crests the lift hill and begins its descent, its potential energy becomes kinetic energy, or the energy of movement. A common misperception is that a coaster loses energy along the track. An important law of physics, however, called the law of conservation of energy, is that energy can never be created nor destroyed. It simply changes from one form to another. Whenever a track rises back uphill, the cars' momentum — their kinetic energy — will carry them upward, which builds potential energy, and roller coasters repeatedly convert potential energy to kinetic energy and back again. At the end of a ride, coaster cars are slowed down by brake mechanisms that create _____ between two surfaces. This motion makes them hot, meaning kinetic energy is changed to heat energy during braking. Riders may mistakenly think coasters lose energy at the end of the track, but the energy just changes to and from different forms.

① gravity   ② friction
③ vaccum   ④ acceleration

해설편 ▶ P.58

2021

6월 5일 시행
지방직(= 서울시) 9급

| 풀이 시간: ____:____ ~ ____:____ / 점수: ____점

문 1. 밑줄 친 부분의 의미와 가장 가까운 것은?

> For many compulsive buyers, the act of purchasing, rather than what they buy, is what leads to gratification.

① liveliness
② confidence
③ tranquility
④ satisfaction

※ 밑줄 친 부분에 들어갈 말로 가장 적절한 것을 고르시오.
[문 2 ~ 문 4]

문 2.

> Globalization leads more countries to open their markets, allowing them to trade goods and services freely at a lower cost with greater _____.

① extinction
② depression
③ efficiency
④ caution

문 3.

> We're familiar with the costs of burnout: Energy, motivation, productivity, engagement, and commitment can all take a hit, at work and at home. And many of the _____ are fairly intuitive: Regularly unplug. Reduce unnecessary meetings. Exercise. Schedule small breaks during the day. Take vacations even if you think you can't afford to be away from work, because you can't afford not to be away now and then.

① fixes
② damages
③ prizes
④ complications

문 4.

> The government is seeking ways to soothe salaried workers over their increased tax burdens arising from a new tax settlement system. During his meeting with the presidential aides last Monday, the President _____ those present to open up more communication channels with the public.

① fell on
② called for
③ picked up
④ turned down

문 5. 밑줄 친 부분의 의미와 가장 가까운 것은?

> In studying Chinese calligraphy, one must learn something of the origins of Chinese language and of how they were originally written. However, except for those brought up in the artistic traditions of the country, its aesthetic significance seems to be very difficult to apprehend.

① encompass
② intrude
③ inspect
④ grasp

※ 우리말을 영어로 잘못 옮긴 것을 고르시오. [문 6 ~ 문 7]

문 6. ① 그의 소설들은 읽기가 어렵다.
→ His novels are hard to read.
② 학생들을 설득하려고 해 봐야 소용없다.
→ It is no use trying to persuade the students.
③ 나의 집은 5년마다 페인트칠된다.
→ My house is painted every five years.
④ 내가 출근할 때 한 가족이 위층에 이사 오는 것을 보았다.
→ As I went out for work, I saw a family moved in upstairs.

문 7. ① 경찰 당국은 자신의 이웃을 공격했기 때문에 그 여성을 체포하도록 했다.
→ The police authorities had the woman arrested for attacking her neighbor.
② 네가 내는 소음 때문에 내 집중력을 잃게 하지 말아라.
→ Don't let me distracted by the noise you make.
③ 가능한 한 빨리 제가 결과를 알도록 해 주세요.
→ Please let me know the result as soon as possible.
④ 그는 학생들에게 모르는 사람들에게 전화를 걸어 성금을 기부할 것을 부탁하도록 시켰다.
→ He had the students phone strangers and ask them to donate money.

문 8. 어법상 옳은 것은?

① My sweet-natured daughter suddenly became unpredictably.

② She attempted a new method, and needless to say had different results.

③ Upon arrived, he took full advantage of the new environment.

④ He felt enough comfortable to tell me about something he wanted to do.

문 9. 다음 글의 제목으로 가장 적절한 것은?

The definition of 'turn' casts the digital turn as an analytical strategy which enables us to focus on the role of digitalization within social reality. As an analytical perspective, the digital turn makes it possible to analyze and discuss the societal meaning of digitalization. The term 'digital turn' thus signifies an analytical approach which centers on the role of digitalization within a society. If the linguistic turn is defined by the epistemological assumption that reality is constructed through language, the digital turn is based on the assumption that social reality is increasingly defined by digitalization. Social media symbolize the digitalization of social relations. Individuals increasingly engage in identity management on social networking sites(SNS). SNS are polydirectional, meaning that users can connect to each other and share information.

*epistemological: 인식론의

① Remaking Identities on SNS

② Linguistic Turn Versus Digital Turn

③ How to Share Information in the Digital Age

④ Digitalization Within the Context of Social Reality

문 10. 주어진 글 다음에 이어질 글의 순서로 가장 적절한 것은?

Growing concern about global climate change has motivated activists to organize not only campaigns against fossil fuel extraction consumption, but also campaigns to support renewable energy.

(A) This solar cooperative produces enough energy to power 1,400 homes, making it the first large-scale solar farm cooperative in the country and, in the words of its members, a visible reminder that solar power represents "a new era of sustainable and 'democratic' energy supply that enables ordinary people to produce clean power, not only on their rooftops, but also at utility scale."

(B) Similarly, renewable energy enthusiasts from the United States have founded the Clean Energy Collective, a company that has pioneered "the model of delivering clean power-generation through medium-scale facilities that are collectively owned by participating utility customers."

(C) Environmental activists frustrated with the UK government's inability to rapidly accelerate the growth of renewable energy industries have formed the Westmill Wind Farm Co-operative, a community-owned organization with more than 2,000 members who own an onshore wind farm estimated to produce as much electricity in a year as that used by 2,500 homes. The Westmill Wind Farm Co-operative has inspired local citizens to form the Westmill Solar Co-operative.

① (C) − (A) − (B) ② (A) − (C) − (B)

③ (B) − (C) − (A) ④ (C) − (B) − (A)

문 11. 밑줄 친 부분에 들어갈 말로 가장 적절한 것은?

A: Did you have a nice weekend?

B: Yes, it was pretty good. We went to the movies.

A: Oh! What did you see?

B: *Interstellar*. It was really good.

A: Really? _____

B: The special effects. They were fantastic. I wouldn't mind seeing it again.

① What did you like the most about it?

② What's your favorite movie genre?

③ Was the film promoted internationally?

④ Was the movie very costly?

문 12. 두 사람의 대화 중 가장 어색한 것은?

① A: I'm so nervous about this speech that I must give today.

　B: The most important thing is to stay cool.

② A: You know what? Minsu and Yujin are tying the knot!

　B: Good for them! When are they getting married?

③ A: A two-month vacation just passed like one week. A new semester is around the corner.

　B: That's the word. Vacation has dragged on for weeks.

④ A: How do you say 'water' in French?

　B: It is right on the tip of my tongue, but I can't remember it.

문 13. 다음 글의 내용과 일치하지 않는 것은?

Women are experts at gossiping, and they always talk about trivial things, or at least that's what men have always thought. However, some new research suggests that when women talk to women, their conversations are far from frivolous, and cover many more topics (up to 40 subjects) than when men talk to other men. Women's conversations range from health to their houses, from politics to fashion, from movies to family, from education to relationship problems, but sports are notably absent. Men tend to have a more limited range of subjects, the most popular being work, sports, jokes, cars, and women. According to Professor Petra Boynton, a psychologist who interviewed over 1,000 women, women also tend to move quickly from one subject to another in conversation, while men usually stick to one subject for longer periods of time. At work, this difference can be an advantage for men, as they can put other matters aside and concentrate fully on the topic being discussed. On the other hand, it also means that they sometimes find it hard to concentrate when several things have to be discussed at the same time in a meeting.

① 남성들은 여성들의 대화 주제가 항상 사소한 것들이라고 생각해 왔다.

② 여성들의 대화 주제는 건강에서 스포츠에 이르기까지 매우 다양하다.

③ 여성들은 대화하는 중에 주제의 변환을 빨리한다.

④ 남성들은 회의 중 여러 주제가 논의될 때 집중하기 어렵다.

문 14. 다음 글의 흐름상 적절하지 않은 문장은?

There was no divide between science, philosophy, and magic in the 15th century. All three came under the general heading of 'natural philosophy'. ① Central to the development of natural philosophy was the recovery of classical authors, most importantly the work of Aristotle. ② Humanists quickly realized the power of the printing press for spreading their knowledge. ③ At the beginning of the 15th century Aristotle remained the basis for all scholastic speculation on philosophy and science. ④ Kept alive in the Arabic translations and commentaries of Averroes and Avicenna, Aristotle provided a systematic perspective on mankind's relationship with the natural world. Surviving texts like his *Physics*, *Metaphysics*, and *Meteorology* provided scholars with the logical tools to understand the forces that created the natural world.

문 15. 어법상 옳지 않은 것은?

① Fire following an earthquake is of special interest to the insurance industry.

② Word processors were considered to be the ultimate tool for a typist in the past.

③ Elements of income in a cash forecast will be vary according to the company's circumstances.

④ The world's first digital camera was created by Steve Sasson at Eastman Kodak in 1975.

※ 밑줄 친 부분에 들어갈 말로 가장 적절한 것을 고르시오. [문 16 ~ 문 17]

문 16.

The slowing of China's economy from historically high rates of growth has long been expected to _____ growth elsewhere. "The China that had been growing at 10 percent for 30 years was a powerful source of fuel for much of what drove the global economy forward", said Stephen Roach at Yale. The growth rate has slowed to an official figure of around 7 percent. "That's a concrete deceleration", Mr. Roach added.

① speed up　　　　② weigh on

③ lead to　　　　 ④ result in

문 17.

As more and more leaders work remotely or with teams scattered around the nation or the globe, as well as with consultants and freelancers, you'll have to give them more _____. The more trust you bestow, the more others trust you. I am convinced that there is a direct correlation between job satisfaction and how empowered people are to fully execute their job without someone shadowing them every step of the way. Giving away responsibility to those you trust can not only make your organization run more smoothly but also free up more of your time so you can focus on larger issues.

① work ② rewards
③ restrictions ④ autonomy

문 18. 다음 글의 요지로 가장 적절한 것은?

"In Judaism, we're largely defined by our actions," says Lisa Grushcow, the senior rabbi at Temple Emanu-El-Beth Sholom in Montreal. "You can't really be an armchair do-gooder." This concept relates to the Jewish notion of tikkun olam, which translates as "to repair the world." Our job as human beings, she says, "is to mend what's been broken. It's incumbent on us to not only take care of ourselves and each other but also to build a better world around us." This philosophy conceptualizes goodness as something based in service. Instead of asking "Am I a good person?" you may want to ask "What good do I do in the world?" Grushcow's temple puts these beliefs into action inside and outside their community. For instance, they sponsored two refugee families from Vietnam to come to Canada in the 1970s.

① We should work to heal the world.
② Community should function as a shelter.
③ We should conceptualize goodness as beliefs.
④ Temples should contribute to the community.

문 19. (A)와 (B)에 들어갈 말로 가장 적절한 것은?

Ancient philosophers and spiritual teachers understood the need to balance the positive with the negative, optimism with pessimism, a striving for success and security with an openness to failure and uncertainty. The Stoics recommended "the premeditation of evils," or deliberately visualizing the worst-case scenario. This tends to reduce anxiety about the future: when you soberly picture how badly things could go in reality, you usually conclude that you could cope. _____(A)_____, they noted, imagining that you might lose the relationships and possessions you currently enjoy increases your gratitude for having them now. Positive thinking, _____(B)_____, always leans into the future, ignoring present pleasures.

	(A)	(B)
①	Nevertheless	in addition
②	Furthermore	for example
③	Besides	by contrast
④	However	in conclusion

문 20. 주어진 문장이 들어갈 위치로 가장 적절한 것은?

And working offers more than financial security.

Why do workaholics enjoy their jobs so much? Mostly because working offers some important advantages. (①) It provides people with paychecks — a way to earn a living. (②) It provides people with self-confidence; they have a feeling of satisfaction when they've produced a challenging piece of work and are able to say, "I made that". (③) Psychologists claim that work also gives people an identity; they work so that they can get a sense of self and individualism. (④) In addition, most jobs provide people with a socially acceptable way to meet others. It could be said that working is a positive addiction; maybe workaholics are compulsive about their work, but their addiction seems to be a safe — even an advantageous — one.

해설편 ▶ P.65

2020

6월 13일 시행

지방직(= 서울시) 9급

| 풀이 시간: ____:____ ~ ____:____ / 점수: ____점

문 1. 밑줄 친 부분에 들어갈 말로 가장 적절한 것은?

> The issue with plastic bottles is that they're not _____, so when the temperatures begin to rise, your water will also heat up.

① sanitary   ② insulated
③ recyclable   ④ waterproof

※ 밑줄 친 부분의 의미와 가장 가까운 것을 고르시오.

[문 2 ~ 문 4]

문 2.

> The cruel sights touched off thoughts that otherwise wouldn't have entered her mind.

① looked after   ② gave rise to
③ made up for   ④ kept in contact with

문 3.

> Strategies that a writer adopts during the writing process may alleviate the difficulty of attentional overload.

① complement   ② accelerate
③ calculate   ④ relieve

문 4.

> The school bully did not know what it was like to be shunned by the other students in the class.

① avoided   ② warned
③ punished   ④ imitated

문 5. 어법상 옳은 것은?

① Of the billions of stars in the galaxy, how much are able to hatch life?
② The Christmas party was really excited and I totally lost track of time.
③ I must leave right now because I am starting work at noon today.
④ They used to loving books much more when they were younger.

문 6. 밑줄 친 부분의 의미와 가장 가까운 것은?

> After Francesca made a case for staying at home during the summer holidays, an uncomfortable silence fell on the dinner table. Robert was not sure if it was the right time for him to tell her about his grandiose plan.

① objected to
② dreamed about
③ completely excluded
④ strongly suggested

문 7. 우리말을 영어로 잘못 옮긴 것은?

① 보증이 만료되어서 수리는 무료가 아니었다.
   → Since the warranty had expired, the repairs were not free of charge.
② 설문지를 완성하는 누구에게나 선물카드가 주어질 예정이다.
   → A gift card will be given to whomever completes the questionnaire.
③ 지난달 내가 휴가를 요청했더라면 지금 하와이에 있을 텐데.
   → If I had asked for a vacation last month, I would be in Hawaii now.
④ 그의 아버지가 갑자기 작년에 돌아가셨고, 설상가상으로 그의 어머니도 병에 걸리셨다.
   → His father suddenly passed away last year, and, what was worse, his mother became sick.

문 8. 밑줄 친 부분 중 어법상 옳지 않은 것은?

Elizabeth Taylor had an eye for beautiful jewels and over the years amassed some amazing pieces, once ① declaring "a girl can always have more diamonds." In 2011, her finest jewels were sold by Christie's at an evening auction ② that brought in $115.9 million. Among her most prized possessions sold during the evening sale ③ were a 1961 bejeweled timepiece by Bulgari. Designed as a serpent to coil around the wrist, with its head and tail ④ covered with diamonds and having two hypnotic emerald eyes, a discreet mechanism opens its fierce jaws to reveal a tiny quartz watch.

문 9. 밑줄 친 (A), (B)에 들어갈 말로 가장 적절한 것은?

Assertive behavior involves standing up for your rights and expressing your thoughts and feelings in a direct, appropriate way that does not violate the rights of others. It is a matter of getting the other person to understand your viewpoint. People who exhibit assertive behavior skills are able to handle conflict situations with ease and assurance while maintaining good interpersonal relations.   (A)   , aggressive behavior involves expressing your thoughts and feelings and defending your rights in a way that openly violates the rights of others. Those exhibiting aggressive behavior seem to believe that the rights of others must be subservient to theirs.   (B)   , they have a difficult time maintaining good interpersonal relations. They are likely to interrupt, talk fast, ignore others, and use sarcasm or other forms of verbal abuse to maintain control.

	(A)	(B)
①	In contrast	Thus
②	Similarly	Moreover
③	However	On one hand
④	Accordingly	On the other hand

문 10. 다음 글의 주제로 가장 적절한 것은?

The e-book applications available on tablet computers employ touchscreen technology. Some touchscreens feature a glass panel covering two electronically-charged metallic surfaces lying face-to-face. When the screen is touched, the two metallic surfaces feel the pressure and make contact. This pressure sends an electrical signal to the computer, which translates the touch into a command. This version of the touchscreen is known as a resistive screen because the screen reacts to pressure from the finger. Other tablet computers feature a single electrified metallic layer under the glass panel. When the user touches the screen, some of the current passes through the glass into the user's finger. When the charge is transferred, the computer interprets the loss in power as a command and carries out the function the user desires. This type of screen is known as a capacitive screen.

① how users learn new technology
② how e-books work on tablet computers
③ how touchscreen technology works
④ how touchscreens have evolved

문 11. 밑줄 친 부분에 들어갈 말로 가장 적절한 것은?

A: Oh, another one! So many junk emails!
B: I know. I receive more than ten junk emails a day.
A: Can we stop them from coming in?
B: I don't think it's possible to block them completely.
A: _____?
B: Well, you can set up a filter on the settings.
A: A filter?
B: Yeah. The filter can weed out some of the spam emails.

① Do you write emails often
② Isn't there anything we can do
③ How did you make this great filter
④ Can you help me set up an email account

문 12. 두 사람의 대화 중 가장 자연스러운 것은?

① A: Do you know what time it is?

　 B: Sorry, I'm busy these days.

② A: Hey, where are you headed?

　 B: We are off to the grocery store.

③ A: Can you give me a hand with this?

　 B: OK. I'll clap for you.

④ A: Has anybody seen my purse?

　 B: Long time no see.

문 13. 우리말을 영어로 잘못 옮긴 것은?

① 나는 네 열쇠를 잃어버렸다고 네게 말한 것을 후회한다.

　 → I regret to tell you that I lost your key.

② 그 병원에서의 그의 경험은 그녀의 경험보다 더 나빴다.

　 → His experience at the hospital was worse than hers.

③ 그것은 내게 지난 24년의 기억을 상기시켜준다.

　 → It reminds me of the memories of the past 24 years.

④ 나는 대화할 때 내 눈을 보는 사람들을 좋아한다.

　 → I like people who look me in the eye when I have a conversation.

문 14. 다음 글의 제목으로 가장 적절한 것은?

Louis XIV needed a palace worthy of his greatness, so he decided to build a huge new house at Versailles, where a tiny hunting lodge stood. After almost fifty years of labor, this tiny hunting lodge had been transformed into an enormous palace, a quarter of a mile long. Canals were dug to bring water from the river and to drain the marshland. Versailles was full of elaborate rooms like the famous Hall of Mirrors, where seventeen huge mirrors stood across from seventeen large windows, and the Salon of Apollo, where a solid silver throne stood. Hundreds of statues of Greek gods such as Apollo, Jupiter, and Neptune stood in the gardens; each god had Louis's face!

① True Face of Greek Gods

② The Hall of Mirrors vs. the Salon of Apollo

③ Did the Canal Bring More Than Just Water to Versailles?

④ Versailles: From a Humble Lodge to a Great Palace

문 15. 글의 흐름상 가장 어색한 문장은?

Philosophers have not been as concerned with anthropology as anthropologists have with philosophy. ① Few influential contemporary philosophers take anthropological studies into account in their work. ② Those who specialize in philosophy of social science may consider or analyze examples from anthropological research, but do this mostly to illustrate conceptual points or epistemological distinctions or to criticize epistemological or ethical implications. ③ In fact, the great philosophers of our time often drew inspiration from other fields such as anthropology and psychology. ④ Philosophy students seldom study or show serious interest in anthropology. They may learn about experimental methods in science, but rarely about anthropological fieldwork.

문 16. 밑줄 친 부분에 들어갈 말로 가장 적절한 것은?

All of us inherit something: in some cases, it may be money, property or some object — a family heirloom such as a grandmother's wedding dress or a father's set of tools. But beyond that, all of us inherit something else, something _____, something we may not even be fully aware of. It may be a way of doing a daily task, or the way we solve a particular problem or decide a moral issue for ourselves. It may be a special way of keeping a holiday or a tradition to have a picnic on a certain date. It may be something important or central to our thinking, or something minor that we have long accepted quite casually.

① quite unrelated to our everyday life

② against our moral standards

③ much less concrete and tangible

④ of great monetary value

문 17. 다음 글의 요지로 가장 적절한 것은?

> Evolutionarily, any species that hopes to stay alive has to manage its resources carefully. That means that first call on food and other goodies goes to the breeders and warriors and hunters and planters and builders and, certainly, the children, with not much left over for the seniors, who may be seen as consuming more than they're contributing. But even before modern medicine extended life expectancies, ordinary families were including grandparents and even great-grandparents. That's because what old folk consume materially, they give back behaviorally — providing a leveling, reasoning center to the tumult that often swirls around them.

① Seniors have been making contributions to the family.
② Modern medicine has brought focus to the role of old folk.
③ Allocating resources well in a family determines its prosperity.
④ The extended family comes at a cost of limited resources.

문 18. 주어진 글 다음에 이어질 글의 순서로 가장 적절한 것은?

> Nowadays the clock dominates our lives so much that it is hard to imagine life without it. Before industrialization, most societies used the sun or the moon to tell the time.

(A) For the growing network of railroads, the fact that there were no time standards was a disaster. Often, stations just some miles apart set their clocks at different times. There was a lot of confusion for travelers.

(B) When mechanical clocks first appeared, they were immediately popular. It was fashionable to have a clock or a watch. People invented the expression "of the clock" or "o'clock" to refer to this new way to tell the time.

(C) These clocks were decorative, but not always useful. This was because towns, provinces, and even neighboring villages had different ways to tell the time. Travelers had to reset their clocks repeatedly when they moved from one place to another. In the United States, there were about 70 different time zones in the 1860s.

① (A) − (B) − (C)
② (B) − (A) − (C)
③ (B) − (C) − (A)
④ (C) − (A) − (B)

문 19. 주어진 문장이 들어갈 위치로 가장 적절한 것은?

> But there is also clear evidence that millennials, born between 1981 and 1996, are saving more aggressively for retirement than Generation X did at the same ages, 22 ~ 37.

> Millennials are often labeled the poorest, most financially burdened generation in modern times. Many of them graduated from college into one of the worst labor markets the United States has ever seen, with a staggering load of student debt to boot. (①) Not surprisingly, millennials have accumulated less wealth than Generation X did at a similar stage in life, primarily because fewer of them own homes. (②) But newly available data providing the most detailed picture to date about what Americans of different generations save complicates that assessment. (③) Yes, Gen Xers, those born between 1965 and 1980, have a higher net worth. (④) And that might put them in better financial shape than many assume.

문 20. 다음 글의 내용과 일치하지 않는 것은?

> Carbonate sands, which accumulate over thousands of years from the breakdown of coral and other reef organisms, are the building material for the frameworks of coral reefs. But these sands are sensitive to the chemical make-up of sea water. As oceans absorb carbon dioxide, they acidify — and at a certain point, carbonate sands simply start to dissolve. The world's oceans have absorbed around one-third of human-emitted carbon dioxide. The rate at which the sands dissolve was strongly related to the acidity of the overlying seawater, and was ten times more sensitive than coral growth to ocean acidification. In other words, ocean acidification will impact the dissolution of coral reef sands more than the growth of corals. This probably reflects the corals' ability to modify their environment and partially adjust to ocean acidification, whereas the dissolution of sands is a geochemical process that cannot adapt.

① The frameworks of coral reefs are made of carbonate sands.

② Corals are capable of partially adjusting to ocean acidification.

③ Human-emitted carbon dioxide has contributed to the world's ocean acidification.

④ Ocean acidification affects the growth of corals more than the dissolution of coral reef sands.

해설편 ▶ P.71

2019

6월 15일 시행
지방직 9급

| 풀이 시간: ____:____ ~ ____:____ / 점수: ____점

※ 밑줄 친 부분의 의미와 가장 가까운 것을 고르시오.

[문 1 ~ 문 2]

문 1.

> I came to see these documents as relics of a sensibility now dead and buried, which needed to be excavated.

① exhumed
② packed
③ erased
④ celebrated

문 2.

> Riding a roller coaster can be a joy ride of emotions: the nervous anticipation as you're strapped into your seat, the questioning and regret that comes as you go up, up, up, and the sheer adrenaline rush as the car takes that first dive.

① utter
② scary
③ occasional
④ manageable

문 3. 두 사람의 대화 중 가장 어색한 것은?

① A: What time are we having lunch?
　B: It'll be ready before noon.
② A: I called you several times. Why didn't you answer?
　B: Oh, I think my cell phone was turned off.
③ A: Are you going to take a vacation this winter?
　B: I might. I haven't decided yet.
④ A: Hello. Sorry I missed your call.
　B: Would you like to leave a message?

문 4. 밑줄 친 부분에 들어갈 말로 가장 적절한 것은?

> A: Hello. I need to exchange some money.
> B: Okay. What currency do you need?
> A: I need to convert dollars into pounds. What's the exchange rate?
> B: The exchange rate is 0.73 pounds for every dollar.
> A: Fine. Do you take a commission?
> B: Yes, we take a small commission of 4 dollars.
> A: _____?
> B: We convert your currency back for free. Just bring your receipt with you.

① How much does this cost
② How should I pay for that
③ What's your buy-back policy
④ Do you take credit cards

문 5. 밑줄 친 부분 중 어법상 옳지 <u>않은</u> 것은?

> Each year, more than 270,000 pedestrians ① lose their lives on the world's roads. Many leave their homes as they would on any given day never ② to return. Globally, pedestrians constitute 22% of all road traffic fatalities, and in some countries this proportion is ③ as high as two thirds of all road traffic deaths. Millions of pedestrians are non-fatally ④ injuring — some of whom are left with permanent disabilities. These incidents cause much suffering and grief as well as economic hardship.

문 6. 어법상 옳은 것은?

① The paper charged her with use the company's money for her own purposes.
② The investigation had to be handled with the utmost care lest suspicion be aroused.
③ Another way to speed up the process would be made the shift to a new system.
④ Burning fossil fuels is one of the lead cause of climate change.

문 7. 주어진 글 다음에 이어질 글의 순서로 가장 적절한 것은?

There is a thought that can haunt us: since everything probably affects everything else, how can we ever make sense of the social world? If we are weighed down by that worry, though, we won't ever make progress.

(A) Every discipline that I am familiar with draws caricatures of the world in order to make sense of it. The modern economist does this by building *models*, which are deliberately stripped down representations of the phenomena out there.

(B) The economist John Maynard Keynes described our subject thus: "Economics is a science of thinking in terms of models joined to the art of choosing models which are relevant to the contemporary world."

(C) When I say "stripped down," I really mean stripped down. It isn't uncommon among us economists to focus on one or two causal factors, exclude everything else, hoping that this will enable us to understand how just those aspects of reality work and interact.

① (A) − (B) − (C) ② (A) − (C) − (B)
③ (B) − (C) − (A) ④ (B) − (A) − (C)

문 8. 다음 글의 내용과 일치하는 것은?

Prehistoric societies some half a million years ago did not distinguish sharply between mental and physical disorders. Abnormal behaviors, from simple headaches to convulsive attacks, were attributed to evil spirits that inhabited or controlled the afflicted person's body. According to historians, these ancient peoples attributed many forms of illness to demonic possession, sorcery, or the behest of an offended ancestral spirit. Within this system of belief, called *demonology*, the victim was usually held at least partly responsible for the misfortune. It has been suggested that Stone Age cave dwellers may have treated behavior disorders with a surgical method called *trephining*, in which part of the skull was chipped away to provide an opening through which the evil spirit could escape.

People may have believed that when the evil spirit left, the person would return to his or her normal state. Surprisingly, trephined skulls have been found to have healed over, indicating that some patients survived this extremely crude operation.

※ convulsive: 경련의, behest: 명령

① Mental disorders were clearly differentiated from physical disorders.
② Abnormal behaviors were believed to result from evil spirits affecting a person.
③ An opening was made in the skull for an evil spirit to enter a person's body.
④ No cave dwellers survived trephining.

문 9. 다음 글의 주제로 가장 적절한 것은?

As the digital revolution upends newsrooms across the country, here's my advice for all the reporters. I've been a reporter for more than 25 years, so I have lived through a half dozen technological life cycles. The most dramatic transformations have come in the last half dozen years. That means I am, with increasing frequency, making stuff up as I go along. Much of the time in the news business, we have no idea what we are doing. We show up in the morning and someone says, "Can you write a story about (pick one) tax policy/immigration/climate change?" When newspapers had once-a-day deadlines, we said a reporter would learn in the morning and teach at night — write a story that could inform tomorrow's readers on a topic the reporter knew nothing about 24 hours earlier. Now it is more like learning at the top of the hour and teaching at the bottom of the same hour. I'm also running a political podcast, for example, and during the presidential conventions, we should be able to use it to do real-time interviews anywhere. I am just increasingly working without a script.

① a reporter as a teacher
② a reporter and improvisation
③ technology in politics
④ fields of journalism and technology

문 10. 글의 흐름상 가장 <u>어색한</u> 문장은?

Children's playgrounds throughout history were the wilderness, fields, streams, and hills of the country and the roads, streets, and vacant places of villages, towns, and cities. ① The term *playground* refers to all those places where children gather to play their free, spontaneous games. ② Only during the past few decades have children vacated these natural playgrounds for their growing love affair with video games, texting, and social networking. ③ Even in rural America few children are still roaming in a free-ranging manner, unaccompanied by adults. ④ When out of school, they are commonly found in neighborhoods digging in sand, building forts, playing traditional games, climbing, or playing ball games. They are rapidly disappearing from the natural terrain of creeks, hills, and fields, and like their urban counterparts, are turning to their indoor, sedentary cyber toys for entertainment.

※ 밑줄 친 부분의 의미와 가장 가까운 것을 고르시오.

[문 11 ~ 문 12]

문 11.

Time does seem to slow to a trickle during a boring afternoon lecture and race when the brain is <u>engrossed in</u> something highly entertaining.

① enhanced by　　　② apathetic to
③ stabilized by　　　④ preoccupied with

문 12.

These daily updates were designed to help readers <u>keep abreast of</u> the markets as the government attempted to keep them under control.

① be acquainted with　　② get inspired by
③ have faith in　　　　④ keep away from

※ 밑줄 친 (A), (B)에 들어갈 말로 가장 적절한 것을 고르시오.
[문 13 ~ 문 14]

문 13.

In the 1840s, the island of Ireland suffered famine. Because Ireland could not produce enough food to feed its population, about a million people died of _____(A)_____; they simply didn't have enough to eat to stay alive. The famine caused another 1.25 million people to _____(B)_____; many left their island home for the United States; the rest went to Canada, Australia, Chile, and other countries. Before the famine, the population of Ireland was approximately 6 million. After the great food shortage, it was about 4 million.

	(A)	(B)
①	dehydration	be deported
②	trauma	immigrate
③	starvation	emigrate
④	fatigue	be detained

문 14.

Today the technology to create the visual component of virtual-reality (VR) experiences is well on its way to becoming widely accessible and affordable. But to work powerfully, virtual reality needs to be about more than visuals. _____(A)_____ what you are hearing convincingly matches the visuals, the virtual experience breaks apart. Take a basketball game. If the players, the coaches, the announcers, and the crowd all sound like they're sitting midcourt, you may as well watch the game on television — you'll get just as much of a sense that you are "there." _____(B)_____, today's audio equipment and our widely used recording and reproduction formats are simply inadequate to the task of re-creating convincingly the sound of a battlefield on a distant planet, a basketball game at courtside, or a symphony as heard from the first row of a great concert hall.

	(A)	(B)
①	If	By contrast
②	Unless	Consequently
③	If	Similarly
④	Unless	Unfortunately

문 15. 주어진 문장이 들어갈 위치로 가장 적절한 것은?

> The same thinking can be applied to any number of goals, like improving performance at work.

The happy brain tends to focus on the short term. (①) That being the case, it's a good idea to consider what short-term goals we can accomplish that will eventually lead to accomplishing long-term goals. (②) For instance, if you want to lose thirty pounds in six months, what short-term goals can you associate with losing the smaller increments of weight that will get you there? (③) Maybe it's something as simple as rewarding yourself each week that you lose two pounds. (④) By breaking the overall goal into smaller, shorter-term parts, we can focus on incremental accomplishments instead of being overwhelmed by the enormity of the goal in our profession.

문 16. 우리말을 영어로 잘못 옮긴 것은?

① 혹시 내게 전화하고 싶은 경우에 이게 내 번호야.
   → This is my number just in case you would like to call me.

② 나는 유럽 여행을 준비하느라 바쁘다.
   → I am busy preparing for a trip to Europe.

③ 그녀는 남편과 결혼한 지 20년 이상 되었다.
   → She has married to her husband for more than two decades.

④ 나는 내 아들이 읽을 책을 한 권 사야 한다.
   → I should buy a book for my son to read.

※ 다음 글의 내용과 일치하지 않는 것을 고르시오.
[문 17 ~ 문 18]

문 17.

In the nineteenth century, the most respected health and medical experts all insisted that diseases were caused by "miasma," a fancy term for bad air. Western society's system of health was based on this assumption: to prevent diseases, windows were kept open or closed, depending on whether there was more miasma inside or outside the room; it was believed that doctors could not pass along disease because gentlemen did not inhabit quarters with bad air. Then the idea of germs came along. One day, everyone believed that bad air makes you sick. Then, almost overnight, people started realizing there were invisible things called microbes and bacteria that were the real cause of diseases. This new view of disease brought sweeping changes to medicine, as surgeons adopted antiseptics and scientists invented vaccines and antibiotics. But, just as momentously, the idea of germs gave ordinary people the power to influence their own lives. Now, if you wanted to stay healthy, you could wash your hands, boil your water, cook your food thoroughly, and clean cuts and scrapes with iodine.

① In the nineteenth century, opening windows was irrelevant to the density of miasma.

② In the nineteenth century, it was believed that gentlemen did not live in places with bad air.

③ Vaccines were invented after people realized that microbes and bacteria were the real cause of diseases.

④ Cleaning cuts and scrapes could help people to stay healthy.

문 18.

Followers are a critical part of the leadership equation, but their role has not always been appreciated. For a long time, in fact, "the common view of leadership was that leaders actively led and subordinates, later called followers, passively and obediently followed." Over time, especially in the last century, social change shaped people's views of followers, and leadership theories gradually recognized the active and important role that followers play in the leadership process. Today it seems natural to accept the important role followers play. One aspect of leadership is particularly worth noting in this regard: Leadership is a social influence process shared among all members of a group. Leadership is not restricted to the influence exerted by someone in a particular position or role; followers are part of the leadership process, too.

① For a length of time, it was understood that leaders actively led and followers passively followed.
② People's views of subordinates were influenced by social change.
③ The important role of followers is still denied today.
④ Both leaders and followers participate in the leadership process.

※ 밑줄 친 부분에 들어갈 말로 가장 적절한 것을 고르시오.
[문 19 ~ 문 20]

문 19.

Language proper is itself double-layered. Single noises are only occasionally meaningful: mostly, the various speech sounds convey coherent messages only when combined into an overlapping chain, like different colors of ice-cream melting into one another. In birdsong also, _____: the sequence is what matters. In both humans and birds, control of this specialized sound-system is exercised by one half of the brain, normally the left half, and the system is learned relatively early in life. And just as many human languages have dialects, so do some bird species: in California, the white-crowned sparrow has songs so different from area to area that Californians can supposedly tell where they are in the state by listening to these sparrows.

① individual notes are often of little value
② rhythmic sounds are important
③ dialects play a critical role
④ no sound-system exists

문 20.

Nobel Prize-winning psychologist Daniel Kahneman changed the way the world thinks about economics, upending the notion that human beings are rational decision-makers. Along the way, his discipline-crossing influence has altered the way physicians make medical decisions and investors evaluate risk on Wall Street. In a paper, Kahneman and his colleagues outline a process for making big strategic decisions. Their suggested approach, labeled as "Mediating Assessments Protocol," or MAP, has a simple goal: To put off gut-based decision-making until a choice can be informed by a number of separate factors. "One of the essential purposes of MAP is basically to _____ intuition," Kahneman said in a recent interview with *The Post*. The structured process calls for analyzing a decision based on six to seven previously chosen attributes, discussing each of them separately and assigning them a relative percentile score, and finally, using those scores to make a holistic judgment.

① improve   ② delay
③ possess   ④ facilitate

해설편 ▶ P.77

2018
5월 19일 시행
지방직 9급

| 풀이 시간: ___:___ ~ ___:___ / 점수: ___점

※ 밑줄 친 부분의 의미와 가장 가까운 것을 고르시오.
[문 1 ~ 문 2]

문 1.

The <u>paramount</u> duty of the physician is to do no harm. Everything else — even healing — must take second place.

① chief
② sworn
③ successful
④ mysterious

문 2.

It is not unusual that people <u>get cold feet</u> about taking a trip to the North Pole.

① become ambitious
② become afraid
③ feel exhausted
④ feel saddened

문 3. 밑줄 친 부분 중 어법상 옳지 않은 것은?

I am writing in response to your request for a reference for Mrs. Ferrer. She has worked as my secretary ① <u>for the last three years</u> and has been an excellent employee. I believe that she meets all the requirements ② <u>mentioned</u> in your job description and indeed exceeds them in many ways. I have never had reason ③ <u>to doubt</u> her complete integrity. I would, therefore, recommend Mrs. Ferrer for the post ④ <u>what</u> you advertise.

문 4. 우리말을 영어로 잘못 옮긴 것은?

① 모든 정보는 거짓이었다.
→ All of the information was false.
② 토마스는 더 일찍 사과했어야 했다.
→ Thomas should have apologized earlier.
③ 우리가 도착했을 때 영화는 이미 시작했었다.
→ The movie had already started when we arrived.
④ 바깥 날씨가 추웠기 때문에 나는 차를 마시려 물을 끓였다.
→ Being cold outside, I boiled some water to have tea.

문 5. 밑줄 친 부분의 의미와 가장 가까운 것은?

The student who finds the state-of-the-art approach <u>intimidating</u> learns less than he or she might have learned by the old methods.

① humorous
② friendly
③ convenient
④ frightening

문 6. 밑줄 친 부분에 들어갈 말로 가장 적절한 것은?

Since the air-conditioners are being repaired now, the office workers have to _____ electric fans for the day.

① get rid of
② let go of
③ make do with
④ break up with

문 7. 어법상 옳은 것은?

① Please contact to me at the email address I gave you last week.
② Were it not for water, all living creatures on earth would be extinct.
③ The laptop allows people who is away from their offices to continue to work.
④ The more they attempted to explain their mistakes, the worst their story sounded.

문 8. 우리말을 영어로 옳게 옮긴 것은?

① 그는 며칠 전에 친구를 배웅하기 위해 역으로 갔다.
→ He went to the station a few days ago to see off his friend.

② 버릇없는 그 소년은 아버지가 부르는 것을 못 들은 체했다.
→ The spoiled boy made it believe he didn't hear his father calling.

③ 나는 버팔로에 가본 적이 없어서 그곳에 가기를 고대하고 있다.
→ I have never been to Buffalo, so I am looking forward to go there.

④ 나는 아직 오늘 신문을 못 읽었어. 뭐 재미있는 것 있니?
→ I have not read today's newspaper yet. Is there anything interested in it?

문 9. 다음 글의 흐름상 가장 <u>어색한</u> 문장은?

The Renaissance kitchen had a definite hierarchy of help who worked together to produce the elaborate banquets. ① At the top, as we have seen, was the *scalco*, or steward, who was in charge of not only the kitchen, but also the dining room. ② The dining room was supervised by the butler, who was in charge of the silverware and linen and also served the dishes that began and ended the banquet — the cold dishes, salads, cheeses, and fruit at the beginning and the sweets and confections at the end of the meal. ③ This elaborate decoration and serving was what in restaurants is called "the front of the house." ④ The kitchen was supervised by the head cook, who directed the undercooks, pastry cooks, and kitchen help.

문 10. 다음 글의 요지로 가장 적절한 것은?

My students often believe that if they simply meet more important people, their work will improve. But it's remarkably hard to engage with those people unless you've already put something valuable out into the world. That's what piques the curiosity of advisers and sponsors. Achievements show you have something to give, not just something to take. In life, it certainly helps to know the right people. But how hard they go to bat for you, how far they stick their necks out for you, depends on what you have to offer. Building a powerful network doesn't require you to be an expert at networking. It just requires you to be an expert at something. If you make great connections, they might advance your career. If you do great work, those connections will be easier to make. Let your insights and your outputs — not your business cards — do the talking.

① Sponsorship is necessary for a successful career.

② Building a good network starts from your accomplishments.

③ A powerful network is a prerequisite for your achievement.

④ Your insights and outputs grow as you become an expert at networking.

문 11. 밑줄 친 부분에 들어갈 말로 가장 적절한 것은?

A: My computer just shut down for no reason. I can't even turn it back on again.
B: Did you try charging it? It might just be out of battery.
A: Of course, I tried charging it.
B: _____
A: I should do that, but I'm so lazy.

① I don't know how to fix your computer.

② Try visiting the nearest service center then.

③ Well, stop thinking about your problems and go to sleep.

④ My brother will try to fix your computer because he's a technician.

문 12. 다음 글에 나타난 화자의 심경으로 가장 적절한 것은?

My face turned white as a sheet. I looked at my watch. The tests would be almost over by now. I arrived at the testing center in an absolute panic. I tried to tell my story, but my sentences and descriptive gestures got so confused that I communicated nothing more than a very convincing version of a human tornado. In an effort to curb my distracting explanation, the proctor led me to an empty seat and put a test booklet in front of me. He looked doubtfully from me to the clock, and then he walked away. I tried desperately to make up for lost time, scrambling madly through analogies and sentence completions. "Fifteen minutes remain," the voice of doom declared from the front of the classroom. Algebraic equations, arithmetic calculations, geometric diagrams swam before my eyes. "Time! Pencils down, please."

① nervous and worried   ② excited and cheerful
③ calm and determined   ④ safe and relaxed

문 13. 주어진 문장 다음에 이어질 글의 순서로 가장 적절한 것은?

Devices that monitor and track your health are becoming more popular among all age populations.

(A) For example, falls are a leading cause of death for adults 65 and older. Fall alerts are a popular gerotechnology that has been around for many years but have now improved.

(B) However, for seniors aging in place, especially those without a caretaker in the home, these technologies can be lifesaving.

(C) This simple technology can automatically alert 911 or a close family member the moment a senior has fallen.

※gerotechnology: 노인을 위한 양로 기술

① (B) - (C) - (A)   ② (B) - (A) - (C)
③ (C) - (A) - (B)   ④ (C) - (B) - (A)

※ 밑줄 친 부분에 들어갈 말로 가장 적절한 것을 고르시오.
[문 14 ~ 문 15]

문 14.

A: Where do you want to go for our honeymoon?
B: Let's go to a place that neither of us has been to.
A: Then, why don't we go to Hawaii?
B: _____

① I've always wanted to go there.
② Isn't Korea a great place to live?
③ Great! My last trip there was amazing!
④ Oh, you must've been to Hawaii already.

문 15.

The secret of successful people is usually that they are able to concentrate totally on one thing. Even if they have a lot in their head, they have found a method that the many commitments don't impede each other, but instead they are brought into a good inner order. And this order is quite simple: _____. In theory, it seems to be quite clear, but in everyday life it seems rather different. You might have tried to decide on priorities, but you have failed because of everyday trivial matters and all the unforeseen distractions. Separate off disturbances, for example, by escaping into another office, and not allowing any distractions to get in the way. When you concentrate on the one task of your priorities, you will find you have energy that you didn't even know you had.

① the sooner, the better
② better late than never
③ out of sight, out of mind
④ the most important thing first

문 16. 다음 글의 제목으로 가장 적절한 것은?

With the help of the scientist, the commercial fishing industry has found out that its fishing must be done scientifically if it is to be continued. With no fishing pressure on a fish population, the number of fish will reach a predictable level of abundance and stay there. The only fluctuation would be due to natural environmental factors, such as availability of food, proper temperature, and the like. If a fishery is developed to take these fish, their population can be maintained if the fishing harvest is small. The mackerel of the North Sea is a good example. If we increase the fishery and take more fish each year, we must be careful not to reduce the population below the ideal point where it can replace all of the fish we take out each year. If we fish at this level, called the *maximum sustainable* yield, we can maintain the greatest possible yield, year after year. If we catch too many, the number of fish will decrease each year until we fish ourselves out of a job. Examples of severely overfished animals are the blue whale of the Antarctic and the halibut of the North Atlantic. Fishing just the correct amount to maintain a maximum annual yield is both a science and an art. Research is constantly being done to help us better understand the fish population and how to utilize it to the maximum without depleting the population.

① Say No to Commercial Fishing
② Sea Farming Seen As a Fishy Business
③ Why Does the Fishing Industry Need Science?
④ Overfished Animals: Cases of Illegal Fishing

문 17. 밑줄 친 (A), (B)에 들어갈 말로 가장 적절한 것은?

Does terrorism ever work? 9/11 was an enormous tactical success for al Qaeda, partly because it involved attacks that took place in the media capital of the world and the actual capital of the United States, ____(A)____ ensuring the widest possible coverage of the event. If terrorism is a form of theater where you want a lot of people watching, no event in human history was likely ever seen by a larger global audience than the 9/11 attacks. At the time, there was much discussion about how 9/11 was like the attack on Pearl Harbor. They were

indeed similar since they were both surprise attacks that drew America into significant wars. But they were also similar in another sense. Pearl Harbor was a great tactical success for Imperial Japan, but it led to a great strategic failure: Within four years of Pearl Harbor the Japanese empire lay in ruins, utterly defeated. ____(B)____, 9/11 was a great tactical success for al Qaeda, but it also turned out to be a great strategic failure for Osama bin Laden.

	(A)	(B)
①	thereby	Similarly
②	while	Therefore
③	while	Fortunately
④	thereby	On the contrary

문 18. 다음 글의 내용과 일치하지 않는 것은?

We entered a new phase as a species when Chinese scientists altered a human embryo to remove a potentially fatal blood disorder — not only from the baby, but all of its descendants. Researchers call this process "germline modification." The media likes the phrase "designer babies." But we should call it what it is, "eugenics." And we, the human race, need to decide whether or not we want to use it. Last month, in the United States, the scientific establishment weighed in. A National Academy of Sciences and National Academy of Medicine joint committee endorsed embryo editing aimed at genes that cause serious diseases when there is "no reasonable alternative." But it was more wary of editing for "enhancement," like making already-healthy children stronger or taller. It recommended a public discussion, and said that doctors should "not proceed at this time." The committee had good reason to urge caution. The history of eugenics is full of oppression and misery.

※ eugenics: 우생학

① Doctors were recommended to immediately go ahead with embryo editing for enhancement.
② Recently, the scientific establishment in the U.S. joined a discussion on eugenics.
③ Chinese scientists modified a human embryo to prevent a serious blood disorder.
④ "Designer babies" is another term for the germline modification process.

문 19. 주어진 문장이 들어갈 위치로 가장 적절한 것은?

> If neither surrendered, the two exchanged blows until one was knocked out.

The ancient Olympics provided athletes an opportunity to prove their fitness and superiority, just like our modern games. (①) The ancient Olympic events were designed to eliminate the weak and glorify the strong. Winners were pushed to the brink. (②) Just as in modern times, people loved extreme sports. One of the favorite events was added in the 33rd Olympiad. This was the pankration, or an extreme mix of wrestling and boxing. The Greek word *pankration* means "total power." The men wore leather straps with metal studs, which could make a terrible mess of their opponents. (③) This dangerous form of wrestling had no time or weight limits. In this event, only two rules applied. First, wrestlers were not allowed to gouge eyes with their thumbs. Secondly, they could not bite. Anything else was considered fair play. The contest was decided in the same manner as a boxing match. Contenders continued until one of the two collapsed. (④) Only the strongest and most determined athletes attempted this event. Imagine wrestling "Mr. Fingertips," who earned his nickname by breaking his opponents' fingers!

문 20. 밑줄 친 부분에 들어갈 말로 가장 적절한 것은?

In our time it is not only the law of the market which has its own life and rules over man, but also the development of science and technique. For a number of reasons, the problems and organization of science today are such that a scientist does not choose his problems; the problems force themselves upon the scientist. He solves one problem, and the result is not that he is more secure or certain, but that ten other new problems open up in place of the single solved one. They force him to solve them; he has to go ahead at an ever-quickening pace. The same holds true for industrial techniques. The pace of science forces the pace of technique. Theoretical physics forces atomic energy on us; the successful production of the fission bomb forces upon us the manufacture of the hydrogen bomb. We do not choose our problems, we do not choose our products; we are pushed, we are forced — by what? By a system which has no purpose and goal transcending it, and which _____.

① makes man its appendix
② creates a false sense of security
③ inspires man with creative challenges
④ empowers scientists to control the market laws

해설편 ▶ P.83

2017

| 풀이 시간: ____:____ ~ ____:____ / 점수: ____점

1초 합격예측! 모바일 성적분석표

QR 코드로 접속하여 문제 풀이시간을 측정하고,
〈1초 합격예측 & 모바일 성적분석표〉 서비스를 통해
지금 바로! 실력을 점검해 보세요.

http://eduwill.kr/Viy6

※ 밑줄 친 부분에 들어갈 말로 가장 적절한 것을 고르시오.

[문 1 ~ 문 2]

문 1.

> A: I just received a letter from one of my old high school buddies.
> B: That's nice!
> A: Well, actually it's been a long time since I heard from him.
> B: To be honest, I've been out of touch with most of my old friends.
> A: I know. It's really hard to maintain contact when people move around so much.
> B: You're right. _____.
> But you're lucky to be back in touch with your buddy again.

① The days are getting longer
② People just drift apart
③ That's the funniest thing I've ever heard of
④ I start fuming whenever I hear his name

문 2.

> A: What are you getting Ted for his birthday? I'm getting him a couple of baseball caps.
> B: I've been _____ trying to think of just the right gift. I don't have an inkling of what he needs.
> A: Why don't you get him an album? He has a lot of photos.
> B: That sounds perfect! Why didn't I think of that? Thanks for the suggestion!

① contacted by him
② sleeping all day
③ racking my brain
④ collecting photo albums

※ 밑줄 친 부분의 의미와 가장 가까운 것을 고르시오.

[문 3 ~ 문 5]

문 3.

> Some of the newest laws authorize people to appoint a surrogate who can make medical decisions for them when necessary.

① proxy   ② sentry
③ predecessor   ④ plunderer

문 4.

> A: He thinks he can achieve anything.
> B: Yes, he needs to keep his feet on the ground.

① live in a world of his own
② relax and enjoy himself
③ be brave and confident
④ remain sensible and realistic about life

문 5.

> She is on the fence about going to see the Mona Lisa at the Louvre Museum.

① anguished   ② enthusiastic
③ apprehensive   ④ undecided

문 6. 어법상 옳지 않은 것은?

① You might think that just eating a lot of vegetables will keep you perfectly healthy.
② Academic knowledge isn't always that leads you to make right decisions.
③ The fear of getting hurt didn't prevent him from engaging in reckless behaviors.
④ Julie's doctor told her to stop eating so many processed foods.

문 7. 어법상 옳은 것은?

① The oceans contain many forms of life that has not yet been discovered.
② The rings of Saturn are so distant to be seen from Earth without a telescope.
③ The Aswan High Dam has been protected Egypt from the famines of its neighboring countries.
④ Included in this series is "The Enchanted Horse," among other famous children's stories.

문 8. 다음 글의 내용과 일치하는 것은?

Soils of farmlands used for growing crops are being carried away by water and wind erosion at rates between 10 and 40 times the rates of soil formation, and between 500 and 10,000 times soil erosion rates on forested land. Because those soil erosion rates are so much higher than soil formation rates, that means a net loss of soil. For instance, about half of the top soil of Iowa, the state whose agriculture productivity is among the highest in the U.S., has been eroded in the last 150 years. On my most recent visit to Iowa, my hosts showed me a churchyard offering a dramatically visible example of those soil losses. A church was built there in the middle of farmland during the 19th century and has been maintained continuously as a church ever since, while the land around it was being farmed. As a result of soil being eroded much more rapidly from fields than from the churchyard, the yard now stands like a little island raised 10 feet above the surrounding sea of farmland.

① A churchyard in Iowa is higher than the surrounding farmland.
② Iowa's agricultural productivity has accelerated its soil formation.
③ The rate of soil formation in farmlands is faster than that of soil erosion.
④ Iowa has maintained its top soil in the last 150 years.

문 9. 다음 글의 흐름상 가장 어색한 문장은?

Whether you've been traveling, focusing on your family, or going through a busy season at work, 14 days out of the gym takes its toll — not just on your muscles, but your performance, brain, and sleep, too. ① Most experts agree that after two weeks, you're in trouble if you don't get back in the gym. "At the two week point without exercising, there are a multitude of physiological markers that naturally reveal a reduction of fitness level," says Scott Weiss, a New York-based exercise physiologist and trainer who works with elite athletes. ② After all, despite all of its abilities, the human body (even the fit human body) is a very sensitive system and physiological changes (muscle strength or a greater aerobic base) that come about through training will simply disappear if your training load dwindles, he notes. Since the demand of training isn't present, your body simply slinks back toward baseline. ③ More protein is required to build more muscles at a rapid pace in your body. ④ Of course, how much and how quickly you'll decondition depends on a slew of factors like how fit you are, your age, and how long sweating has been a habit. "Two to eight months of not exercising at all will reduce your fitness level to as if you never exercised before," Weiss notes.

문 10. 다음 글의 내용과 일치하지 않는 것은?

Before the fifteenth century, all four characteristics of the witch (night flying, secret meetings, harmful magic, and the devil's pact) were ascribed individually or in limited combination by the church to its adversaries, including Templars, heretics, learned magicians, and other dissident groups. Folk beliefs about the supernatural emerged in peasant confessions during witch trials. The most striking difference between popular and learned notions of witchcraft lay in the folk belief that the witch had innate supernatural powers not derived from the devil. For learned men, this bordered on heresy. Supernatural powers were never human in origin, nor could witches derive their craft from the tradition of learned magic, which required a scholarly training at the university, a masculine preserve at the time. A witch's power necessarily came from the pact she made with the devil.

① The folk and learned men had different views on the source of the witch's supernatural powers.
② According to the folk belief, supernatural powers belonged to the essential nature of the witch.
③ Four characteristics of the witch were attributed by the church to its dissident groups.
④ Learned men believed that the witch's power came from a scholarly training at the university.

문 11. 주어진 문장이 들어갈 위치로 가장 적절한 것은?

> Fortunately, however, the heavy supper she had eaten caused her to become tired and ready to fall asleep.

> Various duties awaited me on my arrival. I had to sit with the girls during their hour of study. (①) Then it was my turn to read prayers; to see them to bed. Afterwards I ate with the other teachers. (②) Even when we finally retired for the night, the inevitable Miss Gryce was still my companion. We had only a short end of candle in our candlestick, and I dreaded lest she should talk till it was all burnt out. (③) She was already snoring before I had finished undressing. There still remained an inch of candle. (④) I now took out my letter; the seal was an initial F. I broke it; the contents were brief.

문 12. 다음 글의 제목으로 가장 적절한 것은?

> Fear and its companion pain are two of the most useful things that men and animals possess, if they are properly used. If fire did not hurt when it burnt, children would play with it until their hands were burnt away. Similarly, if pain existed but fear did not, a child would burn himself again and again, because fear would not warn him to keep away from the fire that had burnt him before. A really fearless soldier — and some do exist — is not a good soldier, because he is soon killed; and a dead soldier is of no use to his army. Fear and pain are therefore two guards without which human beings and animals might soon die out.

① Obscurity of Fear and Pain in Soldiers
② Indispensability of Fear and Pain
③ Disapproval of Fear and Pain
④ Children's Association with Fear and Pain

※ 우리말을 영어로 잘못 옮긴 것을 고르시오.   [문 13 ~ 문 14]

문 13. ① 나는 매달 두세 번 그에게 전화하기로 규칙을 세웠다.
→ I made it a rule to call him two or three times a month.
② 그는 나의 팔을 붙잡고 도움을 요청했다.
→ He grabbed me by the arm and asked for help.
③ 폭우로 인해 그 강은 120cm만큼 상승했다.
→ Owing to the heavy rain, the river has risen by 120cm.
④ 나는 눈 오는 날 밖에 나가는 것보다 집에 있는 것을 더 좋아한다.
→ I prefer to staying home than to going out on a snowy day.

문 14. ① 그를 당황하게 한 것은 그녀의 거절이 아니라 그녀의 무례함이었다.
→ It was not her refusal but her rudeness that perplexed him.
② 부모는 아이들 앞에서 그들의 말과 행동에 대해 아무리 신중해도 지나치지 않다.
→ Parents cannot be too careful about their words and actions before their children.
③ 환자들과 부상자들을 돌보기 위해 더 많은 의사가 필요했다.
→ More doctors were required to tend sick and wounded.
④ 설상가상으로, 또 다른 태풍이 곧 올 것이라는 보도가 있다.
→ To make matters worse, there is a report that another typhoon will arrive soon.

※ 밑줄 친 부분에 들어갈 말로 가장 적절한 것을 고르시오.
[문 15 ~ 문 16]

문 15.

Our main dish did not have much flavor, but I made it more _____ by adding condiments.

① palatable
② dissolvable
③ potable
④ susceptible

문 16.

London taxi drivers have to undertake years of intense training known as "the knowledge" to gain their operating license, including learning the layout of over twenty-five thousand of the city's streets. A researcher and her team investigated the taxi drivers and the ordinary people. The two groups were asked to watch videos of routes unfamiliar to them through a town in Ireland. They were then asked to take a test about the video that included sketching out routes, identifying landmarks, and estimating distances between places. Both groups did well on much of the test, but the taxi drivers did significantly better on identifying new routes. This result suggests that the taxi drivers' mastery can be _____ to new and unknown areas. Their years of training and learning through deliberate practice prepare them to take on similar challenges even in places they do not know well or at all.

① confined
② devoted
③ generalized
④ contributed

문 17. 주어진 글 다음에 이어질 글의 순서로 가장 적절한 것은?

I remember the day Lewis discovered the falls. They left their camp at sunrise and a few hours later they came upon a beautiful plain and on the plain were more buffalo than they had ever seen before in one place.

(A) A nice thing happened that afternoon, they went fishing below the falls and caught half a dozen trout, good ones, too, from sixteen to twenty-three inches long.

(B) After a while the sound was tremendous and they were at the great falls of the Missouri River. It was about noon when they got there.

(C) They kept on going until they heard the faraway sound of a waterfall and saw a distant column of spray rising and disappearing. They followed the sound as it got louder and louder.

① (A) − (B) − (C)
② (B) − (C) − (A)
③ (C) − (A) − (B)
④ (C) − (B) − (A)

문 18. 다음 글의 요지로 가장 적절한 것은?

Novelty-induced time expansion is a well-characterized phenomenon which can be investigated under laboratory conditions. Simply asking people to estimate the length of time they are exposed to a train of stimuli shows that novel stimuli simply seem to last longer than repetitive or unremarkable ones. In fact, just being the first stimulus in a moderately repetitive series appears to be sufficient to induce subjective time expansion. Of course, it is easy to think of reasons why our brain has evolved to work like this — presumably novel and exotic stimuli require more thought and consideration than familiar ones, so it makes sense for the brain to allocate them more subjective time.

① Response to stimuli is an important by−product of brain training.
② The intensity of stimuli increases with their repetition.
③ Our physical response to stimuli influences our thoughts.
④ New stimuli give rise to subjective time expansion.

※ 밑줄 친 부분에 들어갈 말로 가장 적절한 것을 고르시오.

[문 19 ~ 문 20]

문 19.

One of the tricks our mind plays is to highlight evidence which confirms what we already believe. If we hear gossip about a rival, we tend to think "I knew he was a nasty piece of work"; if we hear the same about our best friend, we're more likely to say "that's just a rumour." Once you learn about this mental habit — called confirmation bias — you start seeing it everywhere. This matters when we want to make better decisions. Confirmation bias is OK as long as we're right, but all too often we're wrong, and we only pay attention to the deciding evidence when it's too late. How _____ depends on our awareness of why, psychologically, confirmation bias happens. There are two possible reasons. One is that we have a blind spot in our imagination and the other is we fail to ask questions about new information.

① we make our rivals believe us
② our blind spot helps us make better decisions
③ we can protect our decisions from confirmation bias
④ we develop exactly the same bias

문 20.

For many big names in consumer product brands, exporting and producing overseas with local labor and for local tastes have been the right thing to do. In doing so, the companies found a way to improve their cost structure, to grow in the rapidly expanding consumer markets in emerging countries. But, Sweets Co. remains stuck in the domestic market. Even though its products are loaded with preservatives, which means they can endure long travel to distant markets, Sweets Co. _____, let alone produce overseas. The unwillingness or inability to update its business strategy and products for a changing world is clearly damaging to the company.

① is intent on importing
② does very little exporting
③ has decided to streamline operations
④ is expanding into emerging markets

해설편 ▶ P.89

2017
12월 16일 시행
지방직 9급 추가

| 풀이 시간: ____:____ ~ ____:____ / 점수: ____점

※ 밑줄 친 부분과 의미가 가장 가까운 것을 고르시오.
[문 1 ~ 문 3]

문 1.

> During both World Wars, government subsidies and demands for new airplanes vastly improved techniques for their design and construction.

① financial support   ② long-term planning
③ technical assistance   ④ non-restrictive policy

문 2.

> Tuesday night's season premiere of the TV show seemed to be trying to strike a balance between the show's convoluted mythology and its more human, character-driven dimension.

① ancient   ② unrelated
③ complicated   ④ otherworldly

문 3.

> By the time we wound up the conversation, I knew that I would not be going to Geneva.

① initiated   ② resumed
③ terminated   ④ interrupted

문 4. 밑줄 친 부분에 들어갈 말로 가장 적절한 것은?

> A police sergeant with 15 years of experience was dismayed after being _____ for promotion in favor of a young officer.

① run over   ② asked out
③ carried out   ④ passed over

문 5. 밑줄 친 부분 중 어법상 옳은 것은?

> Last week I was sick with the flu. When my father ① heard me sneezing and coughing, he opened my bedroom door to ask me ② that I needed anything. I was really happy to see his kind and caring face, but there wasn't ③ anything he could do it to ④ make the flu to go away.

문 6. 어법상 옳은 것은?

① A week's holiday has been promised to all the office workers.
② She destined to live a life of serving others.
③ A small town seems to be preferable than a big city for raising children.
④ Top software companies are finding increasingly challenging to stay ahead.

※ 밑줄 친 부분에 들어갈 말로 가장 적절한 것을 고르시오
[문 7 ~ 문 8]

문 7.

> A: How do you like your new neighborhood?
> B: It's great for the most part. I love the clean air and the green environment.
> A: Sounds like a lovely place to live.
> B: Yes, but it's not without its drawbacks.
> A: Like what?
> B: For one, it doesn't have many different stores. For example, there's only one supermarket, so food is very expensive.
> A: _____
> B: You're telling me. But thank goodness. The city is building a new shopping center now. Next year, we'll have more options.

① How many supermarkets are there?
② Are there a lot of places to shop there?
③ It looks like you have a problem.
④ I want to move to your neighborhood.

문 8.

> A: So, Mr. Wong, how long have you been living in New York City?
> B: I've been living here for about seven years.
> A: Can you tell me about your work experience?
> B: I've been working at a pizzeria for the last three years.
> A: What do you do there?
> B: I seat the customers and wait on them.
> A: How do you like your job?
> B: It's fine. Everyone's really nice.
> A: _____
> B: It's just that I want to work in a more formal environment.
> A: Okay. Is there anything else you would like to add?
> B: I am really good with people. And I can also speak Italian and Chinese.
> A: I see. Thank you very much. I'll be in touch shortly.
> B: I hope to hear from you soon.

① So, what is the environment like there?
② Then, why are you applying for this job?
③ But are there any foreign languages you are good at?
④ And what qualities do you think are needed to work here?

문 9. 우리말을 영어로 옳게 옮긴 것은?

① 내가 열쇠를 잃어버리지 않았더라면 모든 것이 괜찮았을 텐데.
　→ Everything would have been OK if I haven't lost my keys.
② 그 영화가 너무 지루해서 나는 삼십 분 후에 잠이 들었어.
　→ The movie was so bored that I fell asleep after half an hour.
③ 내가 산책에 같이 갈 수 있는지 네게 알려줄게.
　→ I will let you know if I can accompany with you on your walk.
④ 내 컴퓨터가 작동을 멈췄을 때, 나는 그것을 고치기 위해 컴퓨터 가게로 가져갔어.
　→ When my computer stopped working, I took it to the computer store to get it fixed.

문 10. 우리말을 영어로 잘못 옮긴 것은?

① 예산은 처음 기대했던 것보다 약 25퍼센트 더 높다.
　→ The budget is about 25% higher than originally expecting.
② 시스템 업그레이드를 위해 해야 될 많은 일이 있다.
　→ There is a lot of work to be done for the system upgrade.
③ 그 프로젝트를 완성하는 데 최소 한 달, 어쩌면 더 긴 시간이 걸릴 것이다.
　→ It will take at least a month, maybe longer to complete the project.
④ 월급을 두 배 받는 그 부서장이 책임을 져야 한다.
　→ The head of the department, who receives twice the salary, has to take responsibility.

문 11. 밑줄 친 (A), (B)에 들어갈 말로 가장 적절한 것은?

> The decline in the number of domestic adoptions in developed countries is mainly the result of a falling supply of domestically adoptable children. In those countries, the widespread availability of safe and reliable contraception combined with the pervasive postponement of childbearing as well as with legal access to abortion in most of them has resulted in a sharp reduction of unwanted births and, consequently, in a reduction of the number of adoptable children. _____(A)_____, single motherhood is no longer stigmatized as it once was and single mothers can count on State support to help them keep and raise their children. _____(B)_____, there are not enough adoptable children in developed countries for the residents of those countries wishing to adopt, and prospective adoptive parents have increasingly resorted to adopting children abroad.

	(A)	(B)
①	However	Consequently
②	However	In summary
③	Furthermore	Nonetheless
④	Furthermore	As a consequence

문 12. 글의 흐름상 가장 어색한 것은?

A story that is on the cutting edge of modern science began in an isolated part of northern Sweden in the 19th century. ① This area of the country had unpredictable harvests through the first half of the century. In years that the harvest failed, the population went hungry. However, the good years were very good. ② The same people who went hungry during bad harvests overate significantly during the good years. A Swedish scientist wondered about the long-term effects of these eating patterns. He studied the harvest and health records of the area. He was astonished by what he found. ③ Boys who overate during the good years produced children and grandchildren who died about six years earlier than the children and grandchildren of those who had very little to eat. Other scientists found the same result for girls. ④ Both boys and girls benefited greatly from the harvests of the good years. The scientists were forced to conclude that just one reason of overeating could have a negative impact that continued for generations.

※ 다음 글의 내용과 일치하지 <u>않는</u> 것을 고르시오.

[문 13 ~ 문 14]

문 13.

There is a basic principle that distinguishes a hot medium like radio from a cool one like the telephone, or a hot medium like the movie from a cool one like TV. A hot medium is one that extends one single sense in "high definition." High definition is the state of being well filled with data. A photograph is visually "high definition." A cartoon is "low definition," simply because very little visual information is provided. Telephone is a cool medium, or one of low definition, because the ear is given a meager amount of information. And speech is a cool medium of low definition, because so little is given and so much has to be filled in by the listener. On the other hand, hot media do not leave so much to be filled in or completed by the audience.

① Media can be classified into hot and cool.
② A hot medium is full of data.
③ Telephone is considered high definition.
④ Cool media leave much to be filled in by the audience.

문 14.

December usually marks the start of humpback whale season in Hawaii, but experts say the animals have been slow to return this year. The giant whales are an iconic part of winter on the islands and a source of income for tour operators. But officials at the Humpback Whale Marine Sanctuary said they've been getting reports that the whales have been difficult to spot so far. "One theory was that something like this happened as whales increased. It's a product of their success. With more animals, they're competing against each other for food resources, and it takes an energy of reserve to make the long trip back," said Ed Lyman, a Maui-based resource protection manager and response coordinator for the sanctuary. He was surprised by how few of the animals he saw while responding to a call about a distressed calf on Christmas Eve, saying "We've just seen a handful of whales." It will be a while before officials have hard numbers because the annual whale counts don't take place until the last Saturday of January, February and March, according to former sanctuary co-manager Jeff Walters.

① Humpback whale season in Hawaii normally begins at the end of the year.
② Humpback whales are profitable for tour operators in Hawaii.
③ The drop in the number of humpback whales spotted in Hawaii may be due to their success.
④ The number of humpback whales that have returned to Hawaii this whale season has been officially calculated.

문 15. 주어진 문장이 들어갈 위치로 가장 적절한 곳은?

> However, should understanding not occur, you will find yourself soon becoming drowsy.

> Dictionaries are your most reliable resources for the study of words. Yet the habit of using them needs to be cultivated. Of course, it can feel like an annoying interruption to stop your reading and look up a word. You might tell yourself that if you keep going, you would eventually understand it from the context. (①) Indeed, reading study guides often advise just that. (②) Often it's not the need for sleep that is occurring but a gradual loss of consciousness. (③) The knack here is to recognize the early signs of word confusion before drowsiness takes over when it is easier to exert sufficient willpower to grab a dictionary for word study. (④) Although this special effort is needed, once the meaning is clarified, the perceptible sense of relief makes the effort worthwhile.

문 16. 다음 글의 주제로 가장 적절한 것은?

> It is easy to look at the diverse things people produce and to describe their differences. Obviously a poem is not a mathematical formula, and a novel is not an experiment in genetics. Composers clearly use a different language from that of visual artists, and chemists combine very different things than do playwrights. To characterize people by the different things they make, however, is to miss the universality of how they create. For at the level of the creative process, scientists, artists, mathematicians, composers, writers, and sculptors use a common set of what we call "tools for thinking," including emotional feelings, visual images, bodily sensations, reproducible patterns, and analogies. And all imaginative thinkers learn to translate ideas generated by these subjective thinking tools into public languages to express their insights, which can then give rise to new ideas in others' minds.

① obstacles to imaginative thinking
② the difference between art and science
③ the commonality of the creative process
④ distinctive features of various professions

※ 밑줄 친 부분에 들어갈 말로 가장 적절한 것을 고르시오.

[문 17 ~ 문 19]

문 17.

> There are few simple answers in science. Even seemingly straightforward questions, when probed by people in search of proof, lead to more questions. Those questions lead to nuances, layers of complexity and, more often than we might expect, _____. In the 1990s, researchers asking "How do we fight oxygen-hungry cancer cells?" offered an obvious solution: Starve them of oxygen by cutting off their blood supply. But as Laura Beil describes in "Deflating Cancer," oxygen deprivation actually drives cancer to grow and spread. Scientists have responded by seeking new strategies: Block the formation of collagen highways, for instance, or even, as Beil writes, give the cells "more blood, not less."

① plans that end up unrealized
② conclusions that contradict initial intuition
③ great inventions that start from careful observations
④ misunderstandings that go against scientific progress

문 18.

> Before the lecture began, the speaker of the day distributed photocopies of his paper to each of the audience, and I got one and leafed through it and grasped the main idea of the text. Waiting for him to begin, I prayed in silence that this speaker would not read but speak instead directly to the audience with his own words about what he knew on the subject. But to my great disappointment, he _____. Soon I found I was mechanically following the printed words on the paper in my hand.

① was afraid of making his lecture too formal
② elaborated on his theories without looking at his paper
③ began to read his lengthy and well-prepared paper faithfully
④ made use of lots of humorous gestures to attract the audience

문 19.

In a famous essay on Tolstoy, the liberal philosopher Sir Isaiah Berlin distinguished between two kinds of thinkers by harking back to an ancient saying attributed to the Greek lyric poet Archilochus (seventh century BC): "The fox knows many things, but the hedgehog knows one big thing." Hedgehogs have one central idea and see the world exclusively through the prism of that idea. They overlook complications and exceptions, or mold them to fit into their world view. There is one true answer that fits at all times and all circumstances. Foxes, for whom Berlin had greater sympathy, have a variegated take on the world, which prevents them from _____. They are skeptical of grand theories as they feel the world's complexity prevents generalizations. Berlin thought Dante was a hedgehog while Shakespeare was a fox.

① behaving rationally
② finding multiple solutions
③ articulating one big slogan
④ grasping the complications of the world

문 20. 다음 글에서 Locke의 주장으로 가장 적절한 것은?

In Locke's defense of private property, the significant point is what happens when we mix our labor with God's land. We add value to the land by working it; we make fertile what once lay fallow. In this sense, it is our labor that is the source of the value, or the added value, of the land. This value-creating power of my labor makes it right that I own the piece of land which I have made valuable by clearing it, the well I have made full by digging it, the animals I have raised and fattened. With Locke, *Homo faber* — the man of labor — becomes for the first time in the history of political thought a central rather than peripheral figure. In Locke's world, status and honor still flowed to the aristocrats, who were entitled to vast landholdings but were letting history pass them by precisely because new economic realities were in the process of shifting wealth to a bourgeoisie that actually created value by work. In time, Locke's elevation of the significance of labor was bound to appeal to the rising bourgeoisie.

① Ownership of property comes from labor.
② Labor is the most important ideal to aristocratic society.
③ The accumulation of private property is a source of happiness.
④ A smooth transition to bourgeois society is essential for social progress.

2016

6월 18일 시행

지방직 9급

| 풀이 시간: ____:____ ~ ____:____ / 점수: ____점

※ 밑줄 친 부분에 들어갈 말로 가장 적절한 것을 고르시오.

[문 1 ~ 문 3]

문 1.

The two cultures were so utterly _____ that she found it hard to adapt from one to the other.

① overlapped ② equivalent
③ associative ④ disparate

문 2.

Penicillin can have an _____ effect on a person who is allergic to it.

① affirmative ② aloof
③ adverse ④ allusive

문 3.

Last year, I had a great opportunity to do this performance with the staff responsible for _____ art events at the theater.

① turning into ② doing without
③ putting on ④ giving up

※ 우리말을 영어로 잘못 옮긴 것을 고르시오. [문 4 ~ 문 5]

문 4. ① 오늘 밤 나는 영화 보러 가기보다는 집에서 쉬고 싶다.
→ I'd rather relax at home than going to the movies tonight.
② 경찰은 집안 문제에 대해서는 개입하기를 무척 꺼린다.
→ The police are very unwilling to interfere in family problems.
③ 네가 통제하지 못하는 과거의 일을 걱정해봐야 소용없다.
→ It's no use worrying about past events over which you have no control.
④ 내가 자주 열쇠를 엉뚱한 곳에 두어서 내 비서가 나를 위해 여분의 열쇠를 갖고 다닌다.
→ I misplace my keys so often that my secretary carries spare ones for me.

문 5. ① 그녀가 어리석은 계획을 포기하도록 설득해 줄래요?
→ Can you talk her out of her foolish plan?
② 그녀의 어머니에 대해서는 나도 너만큼 아는 것이 없다.
→ I know no more than you don't about her mother.
③ 그의 군대는 거의 2대 1로 수적 열세였다.
→ His army was outnumbered almost two to one.
④ 같은 나이의 두 소녀라고 해서 반드시 생각이 같은 것은 아니다.
→ Two girls of an age are not always of a mind.

※ 글의 제목으로 가장 적절한 것을 고르시오. [문 6 ~ 문 7]

문 6.

The planet is warming, from North Pole to South Pole, and everywhere in between. Globally, the mercury is already up more than 1 degree Fahrenheit, and even more in sensitive polar regions. And the effects of rising temperatures aren't waiting for some far-flung future. They're happening right now. Signs are appearing all over, and some of them are surprising. The heat is not only melting glaciers and sea ice; it's also shifting precipitation patterns and setting animals on the move.

① Preventive Measures Against Climate Change
② Melting Down of North Pole's Ice Cap
③ Growing Signs of Global Warming
④ Positive Effects of Temperature Rise

문 7.

Few words are tainted by so much subtle nonsense and confusion as *profit*. To my liberal friends the word connotes the proceeds of fundamentally unrespectable and unworthy behaviors: minimally, greed and selfishness; maximally, the royal screwing of millions of helpless victims. *Profit* is the incentive for the most unworthy performance. To my conservative friends, it is a term of highest endearment, connoting efficiency and good sense. To them, *profit is* the ultimate incentive for worthy performance. Both connotations have some small merit, of course, because profit may result from both greedy, selfish activities and from sensible, efficient ones. But overgeneralizations from either bias do not help us in the least in understanding the relationship between profit and human competence.

① Relationship Between Profit and Political Parties
② Who Benefits from Profit
③ Why Making Profit Is Undesirable
④ Polarized Perceptions of Profit

문 8. 글의 내용과 일치하는 것은?

Electric cars were always environmentally friendly, quiet, clean — but definitely not sexy. The Sesta Speedking has changed all that. A battery-powered sports car that sells for $120,000 and has a top speed of 125m.p.h. (200 km/h), the Speedking has excited the clean-tech crowd since it was first announced. Some Hollywood celebrities also joined a long waiting list for the Speedking; magazines like Wired drooled over it. After years of setbacks and shake-ups, the first Sesta Speedkings were delivered to customers this year. Reviews have been ecstatic, but Sesta Motors has been hit hard by the financial crisis. Plans to develop an affordable electric sedan have been put on hold, and Sesta is laying off employees. But even if the Speedking turns out to be a one-hit wonder, it's been an exciting electric ride.

① Speedking is a new electric sedan.
② Speedking has received negative feedback.
③ Sesta is hiring more employees.
④ Sesta has suspended a new car project.

문 9. 콜라비에 대한 설명 중 글의 내용과 일치하지 않는 것은?

Kohlrabi is one of the vegetables many people avoid, mainly because of its odd shape and strange name. However, kohlrabi is delicious, versatile and good for you. Kohlrabi is a member of Brassica, which also includes broccoli and cabbage. Brassica plants are high in antioxidants, and kohlrabi is no exception. Plus kohlrabi contains fiber, useful amounts of vitamin C, together with vitamin B, potassium and calcium. Kohlrabi can be eaten raw: it's delicious when thinly sliced and mixed into salads. You can also roast chunks of it in the oven, or use it as the base for a soup.

* brassica: 배추속(屬)

① 생김새와 이름이 이상하여 사람들이 좋아하지 않는다.
② 브로콜리와 양배추와 함께 배추속에 속한다.
③ 다른 배추속 식물과는 달리 항산화제가 적다.
④ 날것으로 먹거나 오븐에 구워먹을 수 있다.

문 10. 밑줄 친 부분에 들어갈 말로 가장 적절한 것은?

In an early demonstration of the mere exposure effect, participants in an experiment were exposed to a set of alphabets from the Japanese language. As most people know, Japanese alphabets look like drawings and are called ideograms. In the experiment, the duration of exposure to each ideogram was deliberately kept as short as 30 milliseconds. At such short durations of exposure — known as subliminal exposure — people cannot register the stimuli and hence, participants in the experiment were not expected to recall seeing the ideograms. Nevertheless, when participants were shown two sets of alphabets, one to which they had been previously exposed and another to which they hadn't, participants reported greater liking for the former even though they couldn't recall seeing them! These results have been replicated numerous times and across a variety of types of stimuli, so they are robust. What the mere exposure results show is that _____.

① we can learn the Japanese language with extensive exposure

② duration is responsible for the robust results across studies

③ it is impossible to register the stimuli at short durations

④ people develop a liking towards stimuli that are familiar

문 11. 밑줄 친 부분에 공통으로 들어갈 말로 가장 적절한 것은?

- The psychologist used a new test to _____ overall personality development of students.
- Snacks _____ 25% to 30% of daily energy intake among adolescents.

① carry on
② figure out
③ account for
④ depend upon

문 12. 밑줄 친 'your dad's character'를 가장 잘 표현하는 것은?

I began to get a pretty good sense of your father the first time I came to visit you at your house. Before my visit, he asked me some detailed questions about my physical needs. As soon as he learned about my heavy wheelchair, he began planning how he would build a ramp to the front door. The first day I came to the house, the ramp was ready, built with his own hands. Later on, when your dad found out about your younger brother's autism, he said one thing I will never forget. "If Sam can't learn in school," he told me, "I will take a couple of years off work and we will sail around the world. I will teach him everything he needs to know in those two years." That says everything about your dad's character.

* autism: 자폐증

① strict and stern
② funny and humorous
③ lazy and easygoing
④ considerate and thoughtful

문 13. 밑줄 친 부분에 들어갈 말로 가장 적절한 것은?

John: Excuse me. Can you tell me where Namdaemun Market is?
Mira: Sure. Go straight ahead and turn right at the taxi stop over there.
John: Oh, I see. Is that where the market is?
Mira: _____

① That's right. You have to take a bus over there to the market.
② You can usually get good deals at traditional markets.
③ I don't really know. Please ask a taxi driver.
④ Not exactly. You need to go down two more blocks.

문 14. 두 사람의 대화 중 가장 어색한 것은?

① A: Would you like to go to dinner with me this week?
　 B: OK. But what's the occasion?
② A: Why don't we go to a basketball game sometime?
　 B: Sure. Just tell me when.
③ A: What do you do in your spare time?
　 B: I just relax at home. Sometimes I watch TV.
④ A: Could I help you with anything?
　 B: Yes, I would like to. That would be nice.

※ 어법상 옳은 것을 고르시오.　　　　　　[문 15 ～ 문 16]

문 15. ① That place is fantastic whether you like swimming or to walk.
② She suggested going out for dinner after the meeting.
③ The dancer that I told you about her is coming to town.
④ If she took the medicine last night, she would have been better today.

문 16. ① The poor woman couldn't afford to get a smartphone.
② I am used to get up early every day.
③ The number of fires that occur in the city are growing every year.
④ Bill supposes that Mary is married, isn't he?

문 17. 글의 흐름상 가장 어색한 문장은?

Progress is gradually being made in the fight against cancer. ① In the early 1900s, few cancer patients had any hope of long-term survival. ② But because of advances in medical technology, progress has been made so that currently four in ten cancer patients survive. ③ It has been proven that smoking is a direct cause of lung cancer. ④ However, the battle has not yet been won. Although cures for some forms of cancer have been discovered, other forms of cancer are still increasing.

문 18. 주어진 문장이 들어갈 위치로 가장 적절한 곳은?

But the truth is, after you successfully make it through this problem, there will be another problem to face.

Some people are convinced that life is simply a series of problems to be solved. The sooner they get through with the problem they are facing, the sooner they will be happy. (①) And after you overcome that obstacle, there will be something else to overcome and there's always another mountain to climb. (②) That's why it is important to enjoy the journey, not just the destination. (③) In this world, we will never arrive at a place where everything is perfect and we have no more challenges. (④) As admirable as setting goals and reaching them may be, you can't get so focused on accomplishing your goals that you make the mistake of not enjoying where you are right now.

※ 밑줄 친 부분에 들어갈 말로 가장 적절한 것을 고르시오.
[문 19 ~ 문 20]

문 19.

I don't know how it is for women or for other guys, but when I was young, I had a fear of _____. I thought it was a giant step toward death. So I did all I could to resist it because the idea was frightening to me. Then, one day I met Jane while I was shooting my first film. This changed everything. Jane, who was from Kentucky, was waitressing at that time, and I noticed her right away. She was really beautiful, and it took me all day to get up the nerve to ask her out. Just then a makeup man on the film snapped a photo of the two of us. About two years ago he sent it to me, saying, "Here you are asking a local girl for a date." He didn't know that that "local girl" became my wife. I still remember that day vividly.

① death
② marriage
③ making films
④ taking photos

문 20.

One well-known difficulty in finding new things has been termed the 'oasis trap' by the cognitive psychologist David Perkins. Knowledge becomes centered in an 'oasis' of rich findings and it is just too risky and expensive to leave that still productive and well-watered zone. So people stick to _____. This is what happened to a certain extent in China over many centuries. The huge physical distances between centers of knowledge in China and the fact that the distant centers turned out to be little different from one another discouraged exploration.

① what they know
② the undiscovered world
③ their dream and imagination
④ how things are going to change

해설편 ▶ P.101

2019~2016년 시행

서울시 9급 공개경쟁채용 필기시험

응시번호	
성 명	

문제책형

【시험과목】

제1과목	국 어	제2과목	영 어	제3과목	한 국 사
제4·5과목	행정법총론, 행정학개론				

응시자 주의사항

1. **시험 시작 전**에 시험문제를 열람하는 행위나 **시험 종료 후** 답안을 작성하는 행위를 한 사람은 「지방공무원 임용령」 제65조 등 관련 법령에 의거 **부정행위자**로 처리됩니다.

2. 시험 시작 즉시 **과목편철 순서, 문제누락 여부, 인쇄상태 이상 유무 및 표지와 개별과목의 문제책형 일치 여부 등을 확인**한 후 문제책 표지에 응시번호, 성명을 기재합니다.

3. 반드시 본인의 **응시표에 인쇄된 시험과목 순서에 따라** 제4과목과 제5과목의 **답안을 표기**하여야 합니다. 과목 순서를 바꾸어 표기한 경우에도 **본인의 응시표에 기재된 과목 순서대로 채점**되므로 반드시 유의하시기 바랍니다.

4. 시험이 시작되면 문제를 주의 깊게 읽은 후, **문항의 취지에 가장 적합한 하나의 정답만을 고르며**, 문제 내용에 관한 질문은 받지 않습니다.

5. **시험시간 관리의 책임**은 전적으로 응시자 본인에게 있습니다.

2019

6월 15일 시행

서울시 9급

┃ 풀이 시간: ____:____ ~ ____:____ / 점수: ____점

※ 밑줄 친 부분의 의미와 가장 가까운 것은? [문 1 ~ 문 2]

문 1.

> At least in high school she made one decision where she finally saw eye to eye with her parents.

① quarreled ② disputed
③ parted ④ agreed

문 2.

> Justifications are accounts in which one accepts responsibility for the act in question, but denies the pejorative quality associated with it.

① derogatory ② extrovert
③ mandatory ④ redundant

※ 밑줄 친 부분에 들어갈 말로 가장 적절한 것은? [문 3 ~ 문 5]

문 3.

> Tests ruled out dirt and poor sanitation as causes of yellow fever, and a mosquito was the _____ carrier.

① suspected ② uncivilized
③ cheerful ④ volunteered

문 4.

> Generally speaking, people living in 2018 are pretty fortunate when you compare modern times to the full scale of human history. Life expectancy _____ at around 72 years, and diseases like smallpox and diphtheria, which were widespread and deadly only a century ago, are preventable, curable, or altogether eradicated.

① curtails ② hovers
③ initiates ④ aggravates

문 5.

> To imagine that there are concrete patterns to past events, which can provide _____ for our lives and decisions, is to project on to history a hope for a certainty which it cannot fulfill.

① hallucinations ② templates
③ inquiries ④ commotion

문 6. 대화 중 가장 어색한 것은?

① A: What was the movie like on Saturday?
  B: Great. I really enjoyed it.
② A: Hello. I'd like to have some shirts pressed.
  B: Yes, how soon will you need them?
③ A: Would you like a single or a double room?
  B: Oh, it's just for me, so a single is fine.
④ A: What time is the next flight to Boston?
  B: It will take about 45 minutes to get to Boston.

※ 밑줄 친 부분 중 어법상 가장 옳지 않은 것은? [문 7 ~ 문 10]

문 7.

> Inventor Elias Howe attributed the discovery of the sewing machine ① for a dream ② in which he was captured by cannibals. He noticed as they danced around him ③ that there were holes at the tips of spears, and he realized this was the design feature he needed ④ to solve his problem.

문 8.

> By 1955 Nikita Khrushchev ① had been emerged as Stalin's successor in the USSR, and he ② embarked on a policy of "peaceful coexistence" ③ whereby East and West ④ were to continue their competition, but in a less confrontational manner.

문 9.
Squid, octopuses, and cuttlefish are all ① types of cephalopods. ② Each of these animals has special cells under its skin that ③ contains pigment, a colored liquid. A cephalopod can move these cells toward or away from its skin. This allows it ④ to change the pattern and color of its appearance.

문 10.
There is a more serious problem than ① maintaining the cities. As people become more comfortable working alone, they may become ② less social. It's ③ easier to stay home in comfortable exercise clothes or a bathrobe than ④ getting dressed for yet another business meeting!

문 11. 글의 제목으로 가장 적절한 것은?

Economists say that production of an information good involves high fixed costs but low marginal costs. The cost of producing the first copy of an information good may be substantial, but the cost of producing(or reproducing) additional copies is negligible. This sort of cost structure has many important implications. For example, cost-based pricing just doesn't work: a 10 or 20 percent markup on unit cost makes no sense when unit cost is zero. You must price your information goods according to consumer value, not according to your production cost.

① Securing the Copyright
② Pricing the Information Goods
③ Information as Intellectual Property
④ The Cost of Technological Change

문 12. 밑줄 친 부분이 지칭하는 대상이 다른 것은?

Dracula ants get their name for the way they sometimes drink the blood of their own young. But this week, ① the insects have earned a new claim to fame. Dracula ants of the species *Mystrium camillae* can snap their jaws together so fast, you could fit 5,000 strikes into the time it takes us to blink an eye. This means ② the blood-suckers wield the fastest known movement in nature, according to a study published this week in the journal *Royal Society Open Science*. Interestingly, the ants produce their record-breaking snaps simply by pressing their jaws together so hard that ③ they bend. This stores energy in one of the jaws, like a spring, until it slides past the other and lashes out with extraordinary speed and force — reaching a maximum velocity of over 200 miles per hour. It's kind of like what happens when you snap your fingers, only 1,000 times faster. Dracula ants are secretive predators as ④ they prefer to hunt under the leaf litter or in subterranean tunnels.

문 13. 밑줄 친 부분에 들어갈 말로 가장 옳은 것은?

I am writing to you from a train in Germany, sitting on the floor. The train is crowded, and all the seats are taken. However, there is a special class of "comfort customers" who are allowed to make those already seated _____ their seats.

① give up   ② take
③ giving up   ④ taken

※ 글의 흐름상 빈칸에 들어갈 말로 가장 적절한 것은?

[문 14 ~ 문 16]

문 14.

A country's wealth plays a central role in education, so lack of funding and resources from a nation-state can weaken a system. Governments in sub-Saharan Africa spend only 2.4 percent of the world's public resources on education, yet 15 percent of the school-age population lives there. _____, the United States spends 28 percent of all the money spent in the world on education, yet it houses only 4 percent of the school-age population.

① Nevertheless   ② Furthermore
③ Conversely   ④ Similarly

문 15.

"Highly conscientious employees do a series of things better than the rest of us," says University of Illinois psychologist Brent Roberts, who studies conscientiousness. Roberts owes their success to "hygiene" factors. Conscientious people have a tendency to organize their lives well. A disorganized, unconscientious person might lose 20 or 30 minutes rooting through their files to find the right document, an inefficient experience conscientious folks tend to avoid. Basically, by being conscientious, people _____ they'd otherwise create for themselves.

① deal with setbacks   ② do thorough work
③ follow norms   ④ sidestep stress

문 16.

Climate change, deforestation, widespread pollution and the sixth mass extinction of biodiversity all define living in our world today — an era that has come to be known as "the Anthropocene". These crises are underpinned by production and consumption which greatly exceeds global ecological limits, but blame is far from evenly shared. The world's 42 wealthiest people own as much as the poorest 3.7 billion, and they generate far greater environmental impacts. Some have therefore proposed using the term "Capitalocene" to describe this era of ecological devastation and growing inequality, reflecting capitalism's logic of endless growth and _____ _____.

① the better world that is still within our reach
② the accumulation of wealth in fewer pockets
③ an effective response to climate change
④ a burning desire for a more viable future

문 17. 글의 흐름상 빈칸에 들어갈 말로 가장 적절한 것은?

Ever since the time of ancient Greek tragedy, Western culture has been haunted by the figure of the revenger. He or she stands on a whole series of borderlines: between civilization and barbarity, between _____ and the community's need for the rule of law, between the conflicting demands of justice and mercy. Do we have a right to exact revenge against those who have destroyed our loved ones? Or should we leave vengeance to the law or to the gods? And if we do take action into our own hands, are we not reducing ourselves to the same moral level as the original perpetrator of murderous deeds?

① redemption of the revenger from a depraved condition
② divine vengeance on human atrocities
③ moral depravity of the corrupt politicians
④ an individual's accountability to his or her own conscience

문 18. 글의 흐름상 가장 적절하지 <u>않은</u> 문장은?

It seems to me possible to name four kinds of reading, each with a characteristic manner and purpose. The first is reading for information — reading to learn about a trade, or politics, or how to accomplish something. ① <u>We read a newspaper this way, or most textbooks, or directions on how to assemble a bicycle.</u> ② <u>With most of this material, the reader can learn to scan the page quickly, coming up with what he needs and ignoring what is irrelevant to him, like the rhythm of the sentence, or the play of metaphor.</u> ③ <u>We also register a track of feeling through the metaphors and associations of words.</u> ④ <u>Courses in speed reading can help us read for this purpose, training the eye to jump quickly across the page.</u>

문 19. 〈보기〉의 문장이 들어갈 위치로 가장 적절한 것은?

〈보기〉

In this situation, we would expect to find less movement of individuals from one job to another because of the individual's social obligations toward the work organization to which he or she belongs and to the people comprising that organization.

Cultural differences in the meaning of work can manifest themselves in other aspects as well. (①) For example, in American culture, it is easy to think of work simply as a means to accumulate money and make a living. (②) In other cultures, especially collectivistic ones, work may be seen more as fulfilling an obligation to a larger group. (③) In individualistic cultures, it is easier to consider leaving one job and going to another because it is easier to separate jobs from the self. (④) A different job will just as easily accomplish the same goals.

문 20. 글을 문맥에 가장 어울리는 순서대로 배열한 것은?

㉠ To navigate in the dark, a microbat flies with its mouth open, emitting high-pitched squeaks that humans cannot hear. Some of these sounds echo off flying insects as well as tree branches and other obstacles that lie ahead. The bat listens to the echo and gets an instantaneous picture in its brain of the objects in front of it.

㉡ Microbats, the small, insect-eating bats found in North America, have tiny eyes that don't look like they'd be good for navigating in the dark and spotting prey.

㉢ From the use of echolocation, or sonar, as it is also called, a microbat can tell a great deal about a mosquito or any other potential meal. With extreme exactness, echolocation allows microbats to perceive motion, distance, speed, movement, and shape. Bats can also detect and avoid obstacles no thicker than a human hair.

㉣ But, actually, microbats can see as well as mice and other small mammals. The nocturnal habits of bats are aided by their powers of echolocation, a special ability that makes feeding and flying at night much easier than one might think.

① ㉠ - ㉢ - ㉡ - ㉣　　　② ㉡ - ㉣ - ㉠ - ㉢
③ ㉡ - ㉢ - ㉣ - ㉠　　　④ ㉠ - ㉣ - ㉢ - ㉡

해설편 ▶ P.108

① He had a Jewish background.
② He was supervised by his uncle.
③ He had a doctrinaire faith.
④ He was a sociologist with a philosophical background.

2018

6월 23일 시행
서울시 9급

| 풀이 시간: _____:_____ ~ _____:_____ / 점수: _____점

1초 합격예측! 모바일 성적분석표

QR 코드로 접속하여 문제 풀이시간을 측정하고,
〈1초 합격예측 & 모바일 성적분석표〉 서비스를 통해
지금 바로! 실력을 점검해 보세요.
http://eduwill.kr/liy6

문 1. 글의 흐름상 빈칸에 들어갈 단어로 가장 옳은 것은?

Social learning theorists offer a different explanation for the counter-aggression exhibited by children who experience aggression in the home. An extensive research on aggressive behavior and the coercive family concludes that an aversive consequence may also elicit an aggressive reaction and accelerate ongoing coercive behavior. These victims of aggressive acts eventually learn via modeling to _____ aggressive interchanges. These events perpetuate the use of aggressive acts and train children how to behave as adults.

① stop
② attenuate
③ abhor
④ initiate

문 2. 밑줄 친 인물(Marcel Mauss)에 대한 설명으로 가장 옳지 않은 것은?

Marcel Mauss (1872~1950), French sociologist, was born in Épinal (Vosges) in Lorraine, where he grew up within a close-knit, pious, and orthodox Jewish family. Emile Durkheim was his uncle. By the age of 18 Mauss had reacted against the Jewish faith; he was never a religious man. He studied philosophy under Durkheim's supervision at Bordeaux; Durkheim took endless trouble in guiding his nephew's studies and even chose subjects for his own lectures that would be most useful to Mauss. Thus Mauss was initially a philosopher (like most of the early Durkheimians), and his conception of philosophy was influenced above all by Durkheim himself, for whom he always retained the utmost admiration.

문 3. 글의 문맥에 가장 어울리는 순서대로 배열한 것은?

ⓐ Today, however, trees are being cut down far more rapidly. Each year, about 2 million acres of forests are cut down. That is more than equal to the area of the whole of Great Britain.

ⓑ There is not enough wood in these countries to satisfy the demand. Wood companies, therefore, have begun taking wood from the forests of Asia, Africa, South America, and even Siberia.

ⓒ While there are important reasons for cutting down trees, there are also dangerous consequences for life on earth. A major cause of the present destruction is the worldwide demand for wood. In industrialized countries, people are using more and more wood for paper.

ⓓ There is nothing new about people cutting down trees. In ancient times, Greece, Italy, and Great Britain were covered with forests. Over the centuries those forests were gradually cut back. Until now almost nothing is left.

① ⓐ - ⓑ - ⓒ - ⓓ
② ⓓ - ⓐ - ⓑ - ⓒ
③ ⓑ - ⓐ - ⓒ - ⓓ
④ ⓓ - ⓐ - ⓒ - ⓑ

※ 밑줄 친 부분과 의미가 가장 가까운 것은? [문 4 ~ 문 6]

문 4.

Man has continued to be disobedient to authorities who tried to muzzle new thoughts and to the authority of long-established opinions which declared a change to be nonsense.

① express
② assert
③ suppress
④ spread

문 5.

> Don't be pompous. You don't want your writing to be too informal and colloquial, but you also don't want to sound like someone you're not — like your professor or boss, for instance, or the Rhodes scholar teaching assistant.

① presumptuous   ② casual
③ formal   ④ genuine

문 6.

> Surgeons were forced to call it a day because they couldn't find the right tools for the job.

① initiate   ② finish
③ wait   ④ cancel

문 7. 대화 중 가장 어색한 것은?

① A: I'd like to make a reservation for tomorrow, please.
   B: Certainly. For what time?
② A: Are you ready to order?
   B: Yes, I'd like the soup, please.
③ A: How's your risotto?
   B: Yes, we have risotto with mushroom and cheese.
④ A: Would you like a dessert?
   B: Not for me, thanks.

문 8. 밑줄 친 부분 중 어법상 가장 옳지 않은 것은?

> His survival ① over the years since independence in 1961 does not alter the fact that the discussion of real policy choices in a public manner has hardly ② never occurred. In fact, there have always been ③ a number of important policy issues ④ which Nyerere has had to argue through the NEC.

문 9. 밑줄 친 부분 중 어법상 가장 옳은 것은?

> More than 150 people ① have fell ill, mostly in Hong Kong and Vietnam, over the past three weeks. And experts ② are suspected that ③ another 300 people in China's Guangdong province had the same disease ④ begin in mid-November.

문 10. 글의 흐름상 빈칸에 들어갈 가장 적절한 문장은?

> What became clear by the 1980s, however, as preparations were made for the 'Quincentenary Jubilee', was that many Americans found it hard, if not impossible, to see the anniversary as a 'jubilee'. There was nothing to celebrate the legacy of Columbus. _____.

① According to many of his critics, Columbus had been the harbinger not of progress and civilization, but of slavery and the reckless exploitation of the environment.
② The Chicago World's Fair of 1893 reinforced the narrative link between discovery and the power of progress of the United States.
③ This reversal of the nineteenth-century myth of Columbus is revealing.
④ Columbus thus became integrated into Manifest Destiny, the belief that America's progress was divinely ordained.

문 11. 글의 흐름상 빈칸에 들어갈 단어로 가장 옳지 않은 것은?

> Following his father's imprisonment, Charles Dickens was forced to leave school to work at a boot-blacking factory alongside the River Thames. At the run-down, rodent-ridden factory, Dickens earned six shillings a week labeling pots of "blacking," a substance used to clean fireplaces. It was the best he could do to help support his family. Looking back on the experience, Dickens saw it as the moment he said goodbye to his youthful innocence, stating that he wondered "how he could be so easily cast away at such a young age." He felt _____ by the adults who were supposed to take care of him.

① abandoned   ② betrayed
③ buttressed   ④ disregarded

문 12. 글의 내용과 일치하는 것은?

A family hoping to adopt a child must first select an adoption agency. In the United States, there are two kinds of agencies that assist with adoption. Public agencies generally handle older children, children with mental or physical disabilities, or children who may have been abused or neglected. Prospective parents are not usually expected to pay fees when adopting a child from a public agency. Fostering, or a form of temporary adoption, is also possible through public agencies. Private agencies can be found on the Internet. They handle domestic and international adoption.

① Public adoption agencies are better than private ones.
② Parents pay huge fees to adopt a child from a foster home.
③ Children in need cannot be adopted through public agencies.
④ Private agencies can be contacted for international adoption.

문 13. 글의 흐름상 빈칸에 들어갈 표현으로 가장 옳은 것은?

Contemporary art has in fact become an integral part of today's middle class society. Even works of art which are fresh from the studio are met with enthusiasm. They receive recognition rather quickly — too quickly for the taste of the surlier culture critics. _____, not all works of them are bought immediately, but there is undoubtedly an increasing number of people who enjoy buying brand new works of art. Instead of fast and expensive cars, they buy the paintings, sculptures and photographic works of young artists. They know that contemporary art also adds to their social prestige. _____, since art is not exposed to the same wear and tear as automobiles, it is a far better investment.

① Of course − Furthermore
② Therefore − On the other hand
③ Therefore − For instance
④ Of course − For example

문 14. 밑줄 친 부분과 의미가 가장 먼 것은?

As a prerequisite for fertilization, pollination is essential to the production of fruit and seed crops and plays an important part in programs designed to improve plants by breeding.

① crucial   ② indispensable
③ requisite   ④ omnipresent

문 15. 글의 흐름상 빈칸에 들어갈 단어로 가장 옳은 것은?

Mr. Johnson objected to the proposal because it was founded on a _____ principle and also was _____ at times.

① faulty − desirable
② imperative − reasonable
③ conforming − deplorable
④ wrong − inconvenient

※ 밑줄 친 부분 중 어법상 가장 옳지 않은 것은?
[문 16 ~ 문 17]

문 16.

I'm ① pleased that I have enough clothes with me. American men are generally bigger than Japanese men so ② it's very difficult to find clothes in Chicago that ③ fits me. ④ What is a medium size in Japan is a small size here.

문 17.

Blue Planet II, a nature documentary ① produced by the BBC, left viewers ② heartbroken after showing the extent ③ to which plastic ④ affects on the ocean.

문 18. 글의 내용과 가장 부합하는 속담은?

It is one thing to believe that our system of democracy is the best, and quite another to impose it on other countries. This is a blatant breach of the UN policy of non-intervention in the domestic affairs of independent nations. Just as Western citizens fought for their political institutions, we should trust the citizens of other nations to do likewise if they wish to. Democracy is also not an absolute term — Napoleon used elections and referenda to legitimize his hold on power, as do leaders today in West Africa and Southeast Asia. States with partial democracy are often more aggressive than totally unelected dictatorships which are too concerned with maintaining order at home. The differing types of democracy make it impossible to choose which standards to impose. The U.S. and European countries all differ in terms of restraints on government and the balance between consensus and confrontation.

① The grass is always greener on the other side of the fence.
② One man's food is another's poison.
③ There is no rule but has exceptions.
④ When in Rome, do as the Romans do.

문 19. 글의 흐름상 빈칸에 들어갈 단어로 가장 옳은 것은?

Moths and butterflies both belong to the order Lepidoptera, but there are numerous physical and behavioral differences between the two insect types. On the behavioral side, moths are _____ and butterflies are diurnal (active during the day). While at rest, butterflies usually fold their wings back, while moths flatten their wings against their bodies or spread them out in a "jet plane" position.

① nocturnal   ② rational
③ eternal   ④ semi-circular

문 20. 글의 흐름상 빈칸에 들어갈 표현으로 가장 옳은 것은?

The idea of clowns frightening people started gaining strength in the United States. In South Carolina, for example, people reported seeing individuals wearing clown costumes, often hiding in the woods or in cities at night. Some people said that the clowns were trying to lure children into empty homes or the woods. Soon, there were reports of threatening-looking clowns trying to frighten both children and adults. Although there were usually no reports of violence, and many of the reported sightings were later found to be false, this _____.

① benefited the circus industry
② promoted the use of clowns in ads
③ caused a nationwide panic
④ formed the perfect image of a happy clown

해설편 ▶ P.113

2018

3월 24일 시행
서울시 기술직 9급

| 풀이 시간: ____:____ ~ ____:____ / 점수: ____점

1초 합격예측! 모바일 성적분석표

QR 코드로 접속하여 문제 풀이시간을 측정하고,
〈1초 합격예측 & 모바일 성적분석표〉 서비스를 통해
지금 바로! 실력을 점검해 보세요.
http://eduwill.kr/giy6

※ 밑줄 친 부분과 의미가 가장 가까운 것은? [문 1 ~ 문 2]

문 1.

Ethical considerations can be an <u>integral</u> element of biotechnology regulation.

① key
② incidental
③ interactive
④ popular

문 2.

If the area of the brain associated with speech is destroyed, the brain may use <u>plasticity</u> to cause other areas of the brain not originally associated with this speech to learn the skill as a way to make up for lost cells.

① accuracy
② systemicity
③ obstruction
④ suppleness

※ 빈칸에 들어갈 단어로 가장 적절한 것은? [문 3 ~ 문 4]

문 3.

Mephisto demands a signature and contract. No mere _____ contract will do. As Faust remarks, the devil wants everything in writing.

① genuine
② essential
③ reciprocal
④ verbal

문 4.

The company and the union reached a tentative agreement in this year's wage deal as the two sides took the company's _____ operating profits seriously amid unfriendly business environments.

① deteriorating
② enhancing
③ ameliorating
④ leveling

※ 밑줄 친 부분 중 어법상 가장 옳지 않은 것은? [문 5 ~ 문 7]

문 5.

I ① <u>convinced</u> that making pumpkin cake ② <u>from</u> scratch would be ③ <u>even</u> easier than ④ <u>making</u> cake from a box.

문 6.

When you find your tongue ① <u>twisted</u> as you seek to explain to your ② <u>six-year-old</u> daughter why she can't go to the amusement park ③ <u>that</u> has been advertised on television, then you will understand why we find it difficult ④ <u>wait</u>.

문 7.

Lewis Alfred Ellison, a small-business owner and ① <u>a</u> construction foreman, died in 1916 after an operation to cure internal wounds ② <u>suffering</u> after shards from a 100-lb ice block ③ <u>penetrated</u> his abdomen when it was dropped while ④ <u>being loaded</u> into a hopper.

※ 빈칸에 들어갈 것으로 가장 적절한 것은? [문 8 ~ 문 9]

문 8.

A: You don't know about used cars, Ned. Whew! 70,000 miles.
B: Oh, that's a lot of miles! We have to take a close look at the engine, the doors, the tires, everything ...
A: It's too expensive, Ned. _____
B: You have to watch these used car salesmen.

① Let's buy it.
② I'll dust it down.
③ What model do you want?
④ I don't want to get ripped off.

문 9.

The term combines two concepts — "bionic" which means to give a living thing an artificial capability like a bionic arm, and "nano" which _____ particles smaller than 100 nanometers that can be used to imbue the living thing with its new capability.

① breaks in
② refers to
③ originates from
④ lays over

문 10. 어법상 가장 옳은 것은?

① If the item should not be delivered tomorrow, they would complain about it.
② He was more skillful than any other baseball players in his class.
③ Hardly has the violinist finished his performance before the audience stood up and applauded.
④ Bakers have been made come out, asking for promoting wheat consumption.

문 11. 〈보기〉 문장이 들어갈 곳으로 가장 적절한 것은?

〈보기〉

If you are unhappy yourself, you will probably be prepared to admit that you are not exceptional in this.

(①) Animals are happy so long as they have health and enough to eat. Human beings, one feels, ought to be, but in the modern world they are not, at least in a great majority of cases. (②) If you are happy, ask yourself how many of your friends are so. (③) And when you have reviewed your friends, teach yourself the art of reading faces; make yourself receptive to the moods of those whom you meet in the course of an ordinary day. (④)

문 12. 글의 흐름상 가장 적절하지 않은 문장은?

Tighter regulations on cigarette products have spilled over to alcohol, soda and other consumer products, which has restricted consumer choices and made goods more expensive. ① Countries have taken more restrictive measures, including taxation, pictorial health warnings and prohibitions on advertising and promotion, against cigarette products over the past four decades. ② Regulatory measures have failed to improve public health, growing cigarette smuggling. ③ Applying restrictions first to tobacco and then to other consumer products have created a domino effect, or what is called a "slippery slope," for other industries. ④ At the extreme end of the slippery slope is plain packaging, where all trademarks, logos and brand-specific colors are removed, resulting in unintended consequences and a severe infringement of intellectual property rights.

※ 글의 흐름상 빈칸에 들어갈 가장 적절한 것은?

[문 13 ~ 문 14]

문 13.

Language changes when speakers of a language come into contact with speakers of another language or languages. This can be because of migration, perhaps, because they move to more fertile lands, or because they are displaced on account of war or poverty or disease. It can also be because they are invaded. Depending on the circumstances, the home language may succumb completely to the language of the invaders, in which case we talk about replacement. _____, the home language might persist side-by-side with the language of the invaders, and depending on political circumstances, it might become the dominant language.

① Typically
② Consistently
③ Similarly
④ Alternatively

문 14.

The notion that a product tested without branding is somehow being more objectively appraised is entirely _____. In the real world, we no more appraise things with our eyes closed and holding our nose than we do by ignoring the brand that is stamped on the product we purchase, the look and feel of the box it comes in, or the price being asked.

① correct ② reliable
③ misguided ④ unbiased

문 15. 〈보기〉 글의 제목으로 가장 적절한 것은?

─〈보기〉─

Many visitors to the United States think that Americans take their exercise and free time activities too seriously. Americans often schedule their recreation as if they were scheduling business appointments. They go jogging every day at the same time, play tennis two or three times a week, or swim every Thursday. Foreigners often think that this kind of recreation sounds more like work than relaxation. For many Americans, however, their recreational activities are relaxing and enjoyable, or at least worthwhile, because they contribute to health and physical fitness.

① Health and fitness
② Popular recreational activities in the United States
③ The American approach to recreation
④ The definition of recreation

문 16. 〈보기〉 글의 요지로 가장 적절한 것은?

─〈보기〉─

Feelings of pain or pleasure or some quality in between are the bedrock of our minds. We often fail to notice this simple reality because the mental images of the objects and events that surround us, along with the images of the words and sentences that describe them, use up so much of our overburdened attention. But there they are, feelings of myriad emotions and related states, the continuous musical line of our minds, the unstoppable humming of the most universal of melodies that only dies down when we go to sleep, a humming that turns into all-out singing when we are occupied by joy, or a mournful requiem when sorrow takes over.

① Feelings are closely associated with music.
② Feelings are composed of pain and pleasure.
③ Feelings are ubiquitous in our minds.
④ Feelings are related to the mental images of objects and events.

문 17. 〈보기〉 글의 분위기로 가장 적절한 것은?

─〈보기〉─

I go to the local schoolyard, hoping to join in a game. But no one is there. After several minutes of standing around, dejected under the netless basketball hoops and wondering where everybody is, the names of those I expected to find awaiting me start to fill my mind. I have not played in a place like this for years. What was that? What was I thinking of, coming here? When I was a child, a boy, I went to the schoolyard to play. That was a long time ago. No children here will ever know me. Around me the concrete is empty except for pebbles, bottles, and a beer can that I kick, clawing a scary noise out of the pavement.

① calm and peaceful ② festive and merry
③ desolate and lonely ④ horrible and scary

문 18. 글의 흐름상 빈칸에 들어갈 단어를 순서대로 고른 것은?

> Often described as the _____ "rags to riches" tale, the story of steel magnate Andrew Carnegie's rise begins in 1835 in a small one-room home in Dunfermline, Scotland. Born into a family of _____ laborers, Carnegie received little schooling before his family emigrated to America in 1848. Arriving in Pennsylvania, he soon got a job in a textile mill, where he earned only $1.20 per week.

① quintessential − destitute
② exceptive − devout
③ interesting − meticulous
④ deleterious − impoverished

문 19. 〈보기〉 글의 내용과 일치하는 것은?

〈보기〉

> In the American Southwest, previously the Mexican North, Anglo-America ran into Hispanic America. The meeting involved variables of language, religion, race, economy, and politics. The border between Hispanic America and Anglo-America has shifted over time, but one fact has not changed: it is one thing to draw an arbitrary geographical line between two spheres of sovereignty; it is another to persuade people to respect it. Victorious in the Mexican-American War in 1848, the United States took half of Mexico. The resulting division did not ratify any plan of nature. The borderlands were an ecological whole; northeastern Mexican desert blended into southeastern American desert with no prefiguring of nationalism. The one line that nature did provide — the Rio Grande — was a river that ran through but did not really divide continuous terrain.

① The borderlands between America and Mexico signify a long history of one sovereignty.
② While nature did not draw lines, human society certainly did.
③ The Mexican-American War made it possible for people to respect the border.
④ The Rio Grande has been thought of as an arbitrary geographical line.

문 20. 〈보기〉 글을 문맥에 가장 어울리게 순서대로 배열한 것은?

〈보기〉

> ㉠ The trigger for the aggressive driver is usually traffic congestion coupled with a schedule that is almost impossible to meet.
> ㉡ Unfortunately, these actions put the rest of us at risk. For example, an aggressive driver who resorts to using a roadway shoulder to pass may startle other drivers and cause them to take an evasive action that results in more risk or even a crash.
> ㉢ As a result, the aggressive driver generally commits multiple violations in an attempt to make up time.
> ㉣ Aggressive driving is a traffic offense or combination of offenses such as following too closely, speeding, unsafe lane changes, failing to signal intent to change lanes, and other forms of negligent or inconsiderate driving.

① ㉠ − ㉢ − ㉡ − ㉣
② ㉠ − ㉣ − ㉢ − ㉡
③ ㉣ − ㉠ − ㉢ − ㉡
④ ㉣ − ㉡ − ㉢ − ㉠

해설편 ▶ P.118

2017

6월 24일 시행
서울시 9급

| 풀이 시간: ____:____ ~ ____:____ / 점수: ____점

1초 합격예측! 모바일 성적분석표

QR 코드로 접속하여 문제 풀이시간을 측정하고,
〈1초 합격예측 & 모바일 성적분석표〉 서비스를 통해
지금 바로! 실력을 점검해 보세요.

http://eduwill.kr/ziy6

※ 빈칸에 들어갈 가장 적절한 단어는?   [문 1 ~ 문 2]

문 1.

Again and again we light on words used once in a good, but now in an unfavorable sense. Until the late Eighteenth century this word was used to mean serviceable, friendly, very courteous and obliging. But a(n) _____ person nowadays means a busy uninvited meddler in matters which do not belong to him/her.

① servile   ② officious
③ gregarious   ④ obsequious

문 2.

A faint odor of ammonia or vinegar makes one-week-old infants grimace and _____ their heads.

① harness   ② avert
③ muffle   ④ evoke

문 3. 밑줄 친 부분 중 어법상 가장 옳지 않은 것은?

The first coffeehouse in western Europe ① opened not in ② a center of trade or commerce but in the university city of Oxford, ③ in which a Lebanese man ④ naming Jacob set up shop in 1650.

문 4. 다음 문장 중 어법상 가장 옳지 않은 것은?

① John promised Mary that he would clean his room.
② John told Mary that he would leave early.
③ John believed Mary that she would be happy.
④ John reminded Mary that she should get there early.

문 5. 대화의 흐름으로 보아 빈칸에 들어갈 가장 적절한 것은?

A: Why don't you let me treat you to lunch today, Mr. Kim?

B: _____.

① No, I'm not. That would be a good time for me
② Good. I'll put it on my calendar so I don't forget
③ OK. I'll check with you on Monday
④ Wish I could but I have another commitment today

문 6. 글의 흐름으로 보아 빈칸에 들어갈 단어를 순서대로 고른 것은?

For centuries, people gazing at the sky after sunset could see thousands of vibrant, sparkling stars. But these days, you'll be lucky if you can view the Big Dipper. The culprit: electric beams pouring from homes and street lamps, whose brightness obscures the night sky. In the U.S., so-called light pollution has gotten so bad that by one estimate, 8 out of 10 children born today will never encounter a sky _____ enough for them to see the Milky Way. There is hope, however, in the form of astrotourism, a small but growing industry centered on stargazing in the worlds' darkest places. These remote sites, many of them in national parks, offer views for little more than the cost of a campsite. And the people who run them often work to reduce light pollution in surrounding communities. _____ astrotourism may not be as luxurious as some vacations, travelers don't seem to mind.

① dark − Although   ② bright − Because
③ dark − Since   ④ bright − In that

※ 밑줄 친 부분과 의미가 가장 가까운 것은? [문 7 ~ 문 8]

문 7.

Leadership and strength are <u>inextricably</u> bound together. We look to strong people as leaders because they can protect us from threats to our group.

① inseparably　　　② inanimately
③ ineffectively　　　④ inconsiderately

문 8.

Prudence indeed will dictate that governments long established should not be changed for light and <u>transient</u> causes.

① transparent　　　② momentary
③ memorable　　　④ significant

※ 밑줄 친 부분 중 어법상 가장 옳지 <u>않은</u> 것은? [문 9 ~ 문 10]

문 9.

The idea that justice ① <u>in allocating</u> access to a university has something to do with ② <u>the goods</u> that ③ <u>universities properly</u> pursue ④ <u>explain why</u> selling admission is unjust.

문 10.

Strange as ① <u>it may</u> seem, ② <u>the Sahara</u> was once an expanse of grassland ③ <u>supported</u> the kind of animal life ④ <u>associated with</u> the African plains.

문 11. 대화의 흐름으로 보아 빈칸에 들어갈 가장 적절한 것은?

A: Do you think we can get a loan?
B: Well, it depends. Do you own any other property? Any stocks or bonds?
A: No.
B: I see. Then you don't have any _____.
　 Perhaps you could get a guarantor — someone to sign for the loan for you.

① investigation　　　② animals
③ collateral　　　④ inspiration

문 12. 다음 글의 주제로 가장 적절한 것은?

In 1782, J. Hector St. John De Crèvecoeur, a French immigrant who had settled in New York before returning to Europe during the Revolutionary War, published a series of essays about life in the British colonies in North America, *Letters from an American Farmer*. The book was an immediate success in England, France, and the United States. In one of its most famous passages, Crèvecoeur describes the process by which people from different backgrounds and countries were transformed by their experiences in the colonies and asks, "What then is the American?" In America, Crèvecoeur suggests, "individuals of all nations are melted into a new race of men, whose labors and posterity will one day cause great changes in the world." Crèvecoeur was among the first to develop the popular idea of America as that would come to be called "melting pot".

① Crèvecoeur's book became an immediate success in England.
② Crèvecoeur developed the idea of melting pot in his book.
③ Crèvecoeur described and discussed American individualism.
④ Crèvecoeur explained where Americans came from in his book.

문 13. 빈칸에 공통으로 들어갈 가장 적절한 것은?

In some cultures, such as in Korea and Egypt, politeness norms require that when someone is offered something to eat or drink, it must be refused the first time around. However, such a refusal is often viewed as a rejection of someone's hospitality and thoughtlessness in other cultures, particularly when no _____ is made for the refusal. Americans and Canadians, for instance, expect refusals to be accompanied by a reasonable _____.

① role　　　　　② excuse
③ choice　　　　④ situation

문 14. 다음 주어진 문장이 들어갈 가장 적절한 곳은?

> Instead, these employees spoke first of the sincerity of the relationships at work, that their work culture felt like an extension of home, and that their colleagues were supportive.

> (①) There is a clear link between job satisfaction and productivity. However, job satisfaction also depends on the service culture of an organization. (②) This culture comprises the things that make a business distinctive and make the people who work there proud to do so. (③) When employees of the Top 10 Best Companies to Work For were asked by *Fortune* magazine why they loved working for these companies, it was notable that they didn't mention pay, reward schemes, or advancing to a more senior position. (④)

문 15. 다음 글의 내용과 일치하는 것은?

> Why Orkney of all places? How did this scatter of islands off the northern tip of Scotland come to be such a technological, cultural, and spiritual powerhouse? For starters, you have to stop thinking of Orkney as remote. For most of history, Orkney was an important maritime hub, a place that was on the way to everywhere. It was also blessed with some of the richest farming soils in Britain and a surprisingly mild climate, thanks to the effects of the Gulf Stream.

① Orkney people had to overcome a lot of social and natural disadvantages.

② The region was one of the centers of rebellion that ultimately led to the annihilation of the civilization there.

③ Orkney did not make the best of its resources because it was too far from the mainland.

④ Orkney owed its prosperity largely to its geographical advantage and natural resources.

문 16. 다음 글의 제목으로 가장 적절한 것은?

> Initially, papyrus and parchment were kept as scrolls that could be unrolled either vertically or horizontally, depending on the direction of the script. The horizontal form was more common, and because scrolls could be quite long, a scribe would typically refrain from writing a single line across the entire length, but instead would mark off columns of a reasonable width. That way the reader could unroll one side and roll up the other while reading. Nevertheless, the constant need to re-roll the scroll was a major disadvantage to this format, and it was impossible to jump to various places in the scroll the way we skip to a particular page of a book. Moreover, the reader struggled to make notes while reading since both hands (or weights) were required to keep the scroll open.

① The inconvenience of scrolls

② The evolution of the book

③ The development of writing and reading

④ The ways to overcome disadvantages in scrolls

문 17. 다음 글을 문맥에 맞게 순서대로 배열한 것은?

> ㉠ Millions of people suffering from watery and stinging eyes, pounding headaches, sinus issues, and itchy throats, sought refuge from the debilitating air by scouring stores for air filters and face masks.
> ㉡ The outrage among Chinese residents and the global media scrutiny impelled the government to address the country's air pollution problem.
> ㉢ Schools and businesses were closed, and the Beijing city government warned people to stay inside their homes, keep their air purifiers running, reduce indoor activities, and remain as inactive as possible.
> ㉣ In 2013, a state of emergency in Beijing resulting from the dangerously high levels of pollution led to chaos in the transportation system, forcing airlines to cancel flights due to low visibility.

① ㉡ - ㉠ - ㉣ - ㉢　　　② ㉡ - ㉢ - ㉣ - ㉠

③ ㉣ - ㉡ - ㉢ - ㉠　　　④ ㉣ - ㉢ - ㉠ - ㉡

※ 글의 흐름으로 보아 빈칸에 들어갈 가장 적절한 것은?
[문 18 ~ 문 20]

문 18.

Both novels and romances are works of imaginative fiction with multiple characters, but that's where the similarities end. Novels are realistic; romances aren't. In the 19th century, a romance was a prose narrative that told a fictional story dealt with its subjects and characters in a symbolic, imaginative, and nonrealistic way. _____, a romance deals with plots and people that are exotic, remote in time or place from the reader, and obviously imaginary.

① Typically
② On the other hand
③ Nonetheless
④ In some cases

문 19.

Definitions are especially _____ to children. There's an oft-cited 1987 study in which fifth graders were given dictionary definitions and asked to write their own sentences using the words defined. The results were discouraging. One child given the word *erode* wrote "Our family erodes a lot," because the definition given was "eat out, eat away."

① beneficial
② disrespectful
③ unhelpful
④ forgettable

문 20.

Modern banking has its origins in ancient England. In those days people wanting to safeguard their gold had two choices — hide it under the mattress or turn it over to someone else for safekeeping. The logical people to turn to for storage were the local goldsmiths, since they had the strongest vaults. The goldsmiths accepted the gold for storage, giving the owner a receipt stating that the gold could be redeemed at a later date. When a payment was due, the owner went to the goldsmith, redeemed part of the gold and gave it to the payee. After all that, the payee was very likely to turn around and give the gold back to the goldsmith for safekeeping. Gradually, instead of taking the time and effort to physically exchange the gold, business people _____.

① began to exchange the goldsmith's receipts as payment
② saw the potential for profit in this arrangement
③ warned the depositors against redeeming their gold
④ lent the gold to somebody else for a fee

해설편 ▶ P.123

2016

6월 25일 시행
서울시 9급

풀이 시간: ____:____ ~ ____:____ / 점수: ____점

※ 다음 중 밑줄 친 단어와 뜻이 가장 가까운 것은? [문 1 ~ 문 3]

문 1.

Parents must not give up on kids who act <u>rebellious</u> or seem socially awkward; this is a normal stage most youngsters go through and eventually outgrow.

① passive   ② delirious
③ disobedient   ④ sporadic

문 2.

He was born to a wealthy family in New York in 1800's. This circumstance allowed him to lead a <u>prodigal</u> existence for much of his life.

① perjury   ② unstable
③ pernicious   ④ lavish

문 3.

Perhaps the brightest spot in the contemporary landscape of American higher education is the <u>resurgence</u> of interest in engaging students in civic life beyond campus.

① comeback   ② disappearance
③ motivation   ④ paucity

문 4. 밑줄 친 부분 중 어법상 가장 옳지 않은 것은?

He acknowledged that ① <u>the number</u> of Koreans were forced ② <u>into</u> labor ③ <u>under harsh conditions</u> in some of the locations ④ <u>during the 1940's.</u>

문 5. 다음 대화에서 어법상 가장 옳지 않은 것은?

Ann: Your hair ① <u>looks nice.</u>
Tori: I ② <u>had it cut by</u> the tall hairdresser in the new hair salon next to the cafeteria.
Ann: Not that place where I ③ <u>got my head to stick</u> in the drier?
Tori: ④ <u>Must be,</u> I suppose. Yes, that one.
Ann: Huh, and they still let them open.

※ 어법상 빈칸에 들어가기에 가장 적절한 것은? [문 6 ~ 문 7]

문 6.

Creativity is thinking in ways that lead to original, practical and meaningful solutions to problems or _____ new ideas or forms of artistic expression.

① that generate   ② having generated
③ to be generated   ④ being generated

문 7.

It was when I got support across the board politically, from Republicans as well as Democrats, _____ I knew I had done the right thing.

① who   ② whom
③ whose   ④ that

문 8. 문맥상 빈칸에 들어갈 가장 적절한 것은?

Usually several skunks live together; however, adult male striped skunks are _____ during the summer.

① nocturnal   ② solitary
③ predatory   ④ dormant

문 9. 문맥상 빈칸에 들어갈 가장 적절한 것은?

Language and spelling change. Crystal, one of the most prolific writers on English, has helped popularize that truth. If, as internet use suggests, people are now starting to write "rhubarb" as "rubarb", that, he says, may one day become an acceptable _____.

① alternative   ② obligation
③ risk   ④ order

문 10. 다음 빈칸에 들어갈 표현으로 가장 적절한 것은?

The reputation of Genghis Khan as _____ may be worse than the reality. Much of our information comes from chroniclers of the time who often exaggerated the facts. It is possible that they were encouraged by their Mongol employers to exaggerate the tales of cruelty so that the Mongols appeared more frightening to their enemies.

① an exaggerating storyteller
② a courageous emperor
③ an influential figure
④ an utterly ruthless warrior

문 11. 다음 빈칸에 들어갈 가장 적절한 연결어를 고르면?

Our brain processes and stores different kinds of information in different ways. Think about factual knowledge. Fact memory entails learning explicit information, such as names, faces, words and dates. It is related to our conscious thoughts and our ability to manipulate symbols and language. When fact memories are committed to long-term memory, they are usually filed along with the context in which they were learned: _____, when you think of your new friend Joe, you probably picture him at the basketball game where you met him.

① In short   ② For instance
③ Above all   ④ In addition

문 12. 문맥상 빈칸에 들어갈 가장 적절한 것은?

As incredible as it sounds, there are some species of insects that will _____ themselves to protect their nests. When faced with an intruder, the Camponotus cylindricus ant of Borneo will grab onto the invader and squeeze itself until it explodes. The ant's abdomen ruptures, releasing a sticky yellow substance that will be lethal for both the defender and the attacker, permanently sticking them together and preventing the attacker from reaching the nest.

① commit   ② replace
③ expose   ④ sacrifice

문 13. 문맥상 빈칸에 들어갈 가장 적절한 것을 고르면?

E-waste is being produced on a scale never seen before. Computers and other electronic equipment become _____ in just a few years, leaving customers with little choice but to buy newer ones to keep up. Thus, tens of millions of computers, TVs and cell phones are _____ each year.

① efficient − documented
② obsolete − discarded
③ fascinating − reused
④ identical − thrown

문 14. 다음 빈칸에 들어갈 가장 적절한 것을 고르면?

In the last twenty years the amount of time Americans have spent at their jobs has risen steadily. Each year the change is small, amounting to about nine hours, or slightly more than one additional day of work. In any given year such a small increment has probably been _____. But the accumulated increase over two decades is substantial.

① dazzling   ② vulnerable
③ imperceptible   ④ compulsory

※ 다음 빈칸에 들어갈 단어를 순서대로 고르면? [문 15 ~ 문 16]

문 15.

The country with the highest rate of crime in the world is Vatican City, with 1.5 crimes per resident. However, this high ratio is due to the country's tiny population of only around 840 people. It is likely that the vast majority of the crimes, which consist mainly of pick-pocketing and shop-lifting, are _____ by outsiders. The Vatican has a special police force with 130 members responsible for criminal investigation, border control and protection of the pope. There is no prison in Vatican City, with the exception of a few detention cells to hold criminals before trial. The majority of criminals are _____ by Italian courts.

① manipulated − sealed
② dominated − overruled
③ committed − tried
④ conducted − enforced

문 16.

Albert Einstein's general theory of relativity is about to celebrate its 100th anniversary, and his revolutionary hypothesis has _____ the test of time, despite numerous expert attempts to find _____. Einstein changed the way we think about the most basic things, which are space and time. And that opened our eyes to the universe, and how the most interesting things in it work, like black holes.

① withstood − flaws   ② resisted − proofs
③ wasted − examples   ④ squandered − pitfalls

문 17. 다음 글의 목적으로 가장 적절한 것은?

Casa Heiwa is an apartment building where people can learn some important life skills and how to cope with living in a new environment. The building managers run a service that offers many programs to children and adults living in the building. For the children, there is a day-care center that operates from 7 a.m. until 6 p.m. There are also educational programs available for adults including computer processing and English conversation courses.

① to argue for a need for educational programs
② to recruit employees for an apartment building
③ to attract apartment residents toward programs
④ to recommend ways to improve the living standard

문 18. 다음 글을 문맥에 맞게 순서대로 배열한 것은?

㉠ Rosa Parks was arrested, jailed, convicted and fined. She refused to pay. Her experience set off a 382-day boycott of Montgomery city buses.
㉡ According to the segregation laws of the day, Rosa Parks, an African American, was required to sit in the back of the bus. She was accused of encroaching on the whites-only section, and the bus driver tried to convince her to obey the law.
㉢ Instead, Rosa Parks kept both her mien and her seat. At last, the driver warned her that he would send for the police. "Go ahead and call them." Parks answered.
㉣ On December 1, 1955, Rosa Parks took a city bus home from her job at a store in downtown Montgomery, Alabama.

① ㉡ − ㉠ − ㉣ − ㉢   ② ㉣ − ㉢ − ㉠ − ㉡
③ ㉡ − ㉢ − ㉣ − ㉠   ④ ㉣ − ㉡ − ㉢ − ㉠

문 19. 다음 글의 분위기로 가장 어울리는 것은?

As Ryan Cox was waiting to pay for his coffee order at an Indiana, US fast food drive-through, he decided to try something he'd seen on a TV news show — he paid for the coffee order of the driver in the car behind. The small gesture made the young Indianapolis entrepreneur feel great, so he shared his experience on Facebook. An old friend suggested that rather than paying for people's coffee, Ryan put that money towards helping school students pay off their delinquent school lunch accounts. So the following week Ryan visited his nephew's school cafeteria and asked if he could pay off some accounts, and handed over $100.

① gloomy   ② serene
③ touching   ④ boring

문 20. 아래 글 바로 다음에 이어질 문장으로 가장 적절한 것을 고르면?

The moon is different from the earth in many respects. First of all, there is no known life on the moon. And in terms of size, it is much smaller than the earth. You may think both of them have the same spherical shape. But strictly speaking, they are not the same. The moon is almost a perfect sphere; its diameter differs by no more than 1% in any direction. The faster an astronomical object spins, the more it becomes bulged at the equator and flattened at the poles. _____

① So spinning objects undergo some changes of their shape, except for the moon and the earth.
② Since the moon rotates more slowly than the earth, it is more nearly spherical.
③ Moreover, the moon's diameter has been varied for the last hundred years.
④ In fact, the moon's spherical shape is rather unexpected, considering its density and gravity.

해설편 ▶ P.128

ENERGY

모든 꽃이 봄에 피지는 않는다.

– 노먼 프랜시스(Norman Francis)

2022~2016년 시행

법원직 9급 공개경쟁채용 필기시험

응 시 번 호	
성 명	

문 제 책 형

【시 험 과 목】

1교시		헌법, 국어, 한국사, 영어
2교시	법원사무직렬	민법, 민사소송법, 형법, 형사소송법
	등기사무직렬	민법, 민사소송법, 상법(총론·회사편), 부동산등기법

응시자 주의사항

1. **시험 시작 전**에 시험문제를 열람하는 행위나 **시험 종료 후** 답안을 작성하는 행위를 한 사람은 「지방공무원 임용령」 제65조 등 관련 법령에 의거 **부정행위자**로 처리됩니다.

2. 시험 시작 즉시 **과목편철 순서, 문제누락 여부, 인쇄상태 이상 유무 및 표지와 개별과목의 문제책형 일치 여부 등을 확인**한 후 문제책 표지에 응시번호, 성명을 기재합니다.

3. 반드시 본인의 **응시표에 인쇄된 시험과목 순서에 따라** 제4과목과 제5과목의 **답안을 표기**하여야 합니다. 과목 순서를 바꾸어 표기한 경우에도 **본인의 응시표에 기재된 과목 순서대로 채점**되므로 반드시 유의하시 기 바랍니다.

4. 시험이 시작되면 문제를 주의 깊게 읽은 후, **문항의 취지에 가장 적합한 하나의 정답만을 고르며**, 문제 내 용에 관한 질문은 받지 않습니다.

5. **시험시간 관리의 책임**은 전적으로 응시자 본인에게 있습니다.

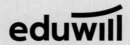

2022

6월 25일 시행
법원직 9급

| 풀이 시간: ____:____ ~ ____:____ / 점수: ____점

문 1. (A), (B), (C)의 각 네모 안에서 어법에 맞는 표현으로 가장 적절한 것은?

The selection of the appropriate protective clothing for any job or task (A) [is / are] usually dictated by an analysis or assessment of the hazards presented. The expected activities of the wearer as well as the frequency and types of exposure, are typical variables that input into this determination. For example, a firefighter is exposed to a variety of burning materials. Specialized multilayer fabric systems are thus used (B) [to meet / meeting] the thermal challenges presented. This results in protective gear that is usually fairly heavy and essentially provides the highest levels of protection against any fire situation. In contrast, an industrial worker who has to work in areas (C) [where / which] the possibility of a flash fire exists would have a very different set of hazards and requirements. In many cases, a flame-resistant coverall worn over cotton work clothes adequately addresses the hazard.

* thermal: 열의

	(A)	(B)	(C)
①	is	to meet	where
②	is	meeting	which
③	are	meeting	where
④	are	to meet	which

문 2. 다음 글의 내용을 한 문장으로 요약하고자 한다. 빈칸 (A), (B)에 들어갈 말로 가장 적절한 것은?

In India, approximately 360 million people — one-third of the population — live in or very close to the forests. More than half of these people live below the official poverty line, and consequently they depend crucially on the resources they obtain from the forests. The Indian government now runs programs aimed at improving their lot by involving them in the commercial management of their forests, in this way allowing them to continue to obtain the food and materials they need, but at the same time to sell forest produce. If the programs succeed, forest dwellers will be more prosperous, but they will be able to preserve their traditional way of life and culture, and the forest will be managed sustainably, so the wildlife is not depleted.

⇒ The Indian government is trying to ____(A)____ the lives of the poor who live near forests without ____(B)____ the forests.

	(A)	(B)
①	improve	ruining
②	control	preserving
③	improve	limiting
④	control	enlarging

문 3. 다음 글의 내용을 한 문장으로 요약하고자 한다. 빈칸 (A), (B)에 들어갈 말로 가장 적절한 것은?

In the absence of facial cues or touch during pandemic, there is a greater need to focus on other aspects of conversation, including more emphasis on tone and inflection, slowing the speed, and increasing loudness without sounding annoying. Many nuances of the spoken word are easily missed without facial expression, so eye contact will assume an even greater importance. Some hospital workers have developed innovative ways to try to solve this problem. One of nurse specialists was deeply concerned that her chronically sick young patients could not see her face, so she printed off a variety of face stickers to get children to point towards. Some hospitals now also provide their patients with 'face-sheets' that permit easier identification of staff members, and it is always useful to reintroduce yourself and colleagues to patients when wearing masks.

*nuance: 미묘한 차이, 뉘앙스

Some hospitals and workers are looking for _____(A)_____ ways to _____(B)_____ conversation with patients during pandemic.

	(A)	(B)
①	alternative	complement
②	bothering	analyze
③	effective	hinder
④	disturbing	improve

문 4. 주어진 글 다음에 이어질 글의 순서로 가장 적절한 것은?

Once they leave their mother, primates have to keep on making decisions about whether new foods they encounter are safe and worth collecting.

(A) By the same token, if the sampler feels fine, it will reenter the tree in a few days, eat a little more, then wait again, building up to a large dose slowly. Finally, if the monkey remains healthy, the other members figure this is OK, and they adopt the new food.

(B) If the plant harbors a particularly strong toxin, the sampler's system will try to break it down, usually making the monkey sick in the process. "I've seen this happen," says Glander. "The other members of the troop are watching with great interest — if the animal gets sick, no other animal will go into that tree. There's a cue being given — a social cue."

(C) Using themselves as experiment tools is one option, but social primates have found a better way. Kenneth Glander calls it "sampling." When howler monkeys move into a new habitat, one member of the troop will go to a tree, eat a few leaves, then wait a day.

① (A) − (B) − (C)　　② (B) − (A) − (C)
③ (C) − (B) − (A)　　④ (C) − (A) − (B)

문 5. 다음 글의 Zainichi에 관한 내용으로 가장 일치하지 않는 것은?

Following Japan's defeat in World War II, the majority of ethnic Koreans (1-1.4 million) left Japan. By 1948, the population of ethnic Koreans settled around 600,000. These Koreans and their descendants are commonly referred to as Zainichi (literally "residing in Japan"), a term that appeared in the immediate postwar years. Ethnic Koreans who remained in Japan did so for diverse reasons. Koreans who had achieved successful careers in business, the imperial bureaucracy, and the military during the colonial period or who had taken advantage of economic opportunities that opened up immediately after the war — opted to maintain their relatively privileged status in Japanese society rather than risk returning to an impoverished and politically unstable post-liberation Korea. Some Koreans who repatriated were so repulsed by the poor conditions they observed that they decided to return to Japan. Other Koreans living in Japan could not afford the train fare to one of the departure ports, and among them who had ethnic Japanese spouses and Japanese-born, Japanese-speaking children, it made more sense to stay in Japan rather than to navigate the cultural and linguistic challenges of a new environment.

* repatriate: 본국으로 송환하다

① 주로 제2차 세계대전 이후에 일본에 남은 한국인들과 후손을 일컫는다.
② 전쟁 후에 경제적인 이득을 취한 사람들도 있었다.
③ 어떤 사람들은 한국에 갔다가 다시 일본으로 돌아왔다.
④ 한국으로 돌아갈 교통비를 마련하지 못한 사람들은 일본인과 결혼했다.

문 6. 다음 빈칸에 들어갈 말로 가장 적절한 것은?

There are a few jobs where people have had to _____. We see referees and umpires using their arms and hands to signal directions to the players — as in cricket, where a single finger upwards means that the batsman is out and has to leave the wicket. Orchestra conductors control the musicians through their movements. People working at a distance from each other have to invent special signals if they want to communicate. So do people working in a noisy environment, such as in a factory where the machines are very loud, or lifeguards around a swimming pool full of school children.

* wicket: (크리켓에서) 삼주문

① support their parents and children
② adapt to an entirely new work style
③ fight in court for basic human rights
④ develop their signing a bit more fully

문 7. 다음 글의 내용과 가장 일치하지 않는 것은?

　　Opponents of the use of animals in research also oppose use of animals to test the safety of drugs or other compounds. Within the pharmaceutical industry, it was noted that out of 19 chemicals known to cause cancer in humans when taken, only seven caused cancer in mice and rats using standards set by the National Cancer Instituted (Barnard and Koufman, 1997). For example, and antidepressant, nomifensin, had minimal toxicity in rats, rabbits, dogs, and monkeys yet caused liver toxicity and anemia in humans. In these and other cases, it has been shown that some compounds have serious adverse reactions in humans that were not predicted by animal testing resulting in conditions in the treated humans that could lead to disability, or even death. And researchers who are calling for an end to animal research state that they have better methods available such as human clinical trials, observation aided by laboratory of autopsy tests.

　　　　　　　　　　　　　　　　* anemia: 빈혈

① 한 기관의 실험 결과 동물과 달리 19개의 발암물질 중에 7개는 인간에게 영향을 미쳤다.
② 어떤 약물은 동물 실험 때와 달리 인간에게 간독성과 빈혈을 일으켰다.
③ 동물 실험에서 나타난 결과가 인간에게는 다르게 작용될 수 있다.
④ 동물 실험을 반대하는 연구자들은 대안적인 방법들을 제시하고 있다.

문 8. 다음 중 문맥상 낱말의 쓰임이 가장 적절하지 않는 것은?

　　Cold showers are any showers with a water temperature below 70°F. They may have health benefits. For people with depression, cold showers can work as a kind of gentle electroshock therapy. The cold water sends many electrical impulses to your brain. They jolt your system to ① increase alertness, clarity, and energy levels. Endorphins, which are sometimes called happiness hormones, are also released. This effect leads to feelings of well-being and ② optimism. For people that are obese, taking a cold shower 2 or 3 times per week may contribute to increased metabolism. It may help fight obesity over time. The research about how exactly cold showers help people lose weight is ③ clear. However, it does show that cold water can even out certain hormone levels and heal the gastrointestinal system. These effects may add to the cold shower's ability to lead to weight loss. Furthermore, when taken regularly, cold showers can make our circulatory system more efficient. Some people also report that their skin looks better as a result of cold showers, probably because of better circulation. Athletes have known this benefit for years, even if we have only ④ recently seen data that supports cold water for healing after a sport injury.

　　* jolt: 갑자기 덜컥 움직이다 ** gastrointestinal: 위장의

문 9. 다음 글의 내용을 한 문장으로 요약하고자 한다. 빈칸 (A), (B)에 들어갈 말로 가장 적절한 것은?

Researchers have been interested in the habitual ways a single individual copes with conflict when it occurs. They've called this approach conflict styles. There are several apparent conflict styles, and each has its pros and cons. The collaborating style tends to solve problems in ways that maximize the chances that the best result is provided for all involved. The pluses of a collaborating style include creating trust, maintaining positive relationship, and building commitment. However, it's time consuming and it takes a lot of energy to collaborate with another during conflict. The competing style may develop hostility in the person who doesn't achieve their goals. However, the competing style tends to resolve a conflict quickly.

The collaborating style might be used for someone who put a great value in _____(A)_____, while a person who prefers _____(B)_____ may choose the competing style.

	(A)	(B)
①	financial ability	interaction
②	saving time	peacefulness
③	mutual understanding	time efficiency
④	effectiveness	consistency

문 10. 주어진 글 다음에 이어질 글의 순서로 가장 적절한 것은?

The historical evolution of Conflict Resolution gained momentum in the 1950s and 1960s, at the height of the Cold War, when the development of nuclear weapons and conflict between the superpowers seemed to threaten human survival.

(A) The combination of analysis and practice implicit in the new ideas was not easy to reconcile with traditional scholarly institutions or the traditions of practitioners such as diplomats and politicians.

(B) However, they were not taken seriously by some. The international relations profession had its own understanding of international conflict and did not see value in the new approaches as proposed.

(C) A group of pioneers from different disciplines saw the value of studying conflict as a general phenomenon, with similar properties, whether it occurs in international relations, domestic politics, industrial relations, communities, or between individuals.

① (B) − (A) − (C) ② (B) − (C) − (A)
③ (C) − (A) − (B) ④ (C) − (B) − (A)

문 11. (A), (B), (C)의 각 네모 안에서 어법에 맞는 표현으로 가장 적절한 것은?

The key to understanding economics is accepting (A) [that / what] there are always unintended consequences. Actions people take for their own good reasons have results they don't envision or intend. The same is true with geopolitics. It is doubtful that the village of Rome, when it started its expansion in the seventh century BC, (B) [had / have] a master plan for conquering the Mediterranean world five hundred years later. But the first action its inhabitants took against neighboring villages set in motion a process that was both constrained by reality and (C) [filled / filling] with unintended consequences. Rome wasn't planned, and neither did it just happen.

* geopolitics: 지정학

	(A)	(B)	(C)
①	that	had	filled
②	what	had	filling
③	what	have	filled
④	that	have	filling

문 12. 다음 빈칸에 들어갈 말로 가장 적절한 것을 고르시오.

Water and civilization go hand-in-hand. The idea of a "hydraulic civilization" argues that water is the unifying context and justification for many large-scale civilizations throughout history. For example, the various multi-century Chinese empires survived as long as they did in part by controlling floods along the Yellow River. One interpretation of the hydraulic theory is that the justification for gathering populations into large cities is to manage water. Another interpretation suggests that large water projects enable the rise of big cities. The Romans understood the connections between water and power, as the Roman Empire built a vast network of aqueducts throughout land they controlled, many of which remain intact. For example, Pont du Gard in southern France stands today as a testament to humanity's investment in its water infrastructure. Roman governors built roads, bridges, and water systems as a way of _____.

* hydraulic: 수력학의 ** aqueduct: 송수로

① focusing on educating young people

② prohibiting free trade in local markets

③ concentrating and strengthening their authority

④ giving up their properties to other countries

문 13. 주어진 글 다음에 이어질 글의 순서로 가장 적절한 것은?

> Ambiguity is so uncomfortable that it can even turn good news into bad. You go to your doctor with a persistent stomachache. Your doctor can't figure out what the reason is, so she sends you to the lab for tests.

> (A) And what happens? Your immediate relief may be replaced by a weird sense of discomfort. You still don't know what the pain was! There's got to be an explanation somewhere.
>
> (B) A week later you're called back to hear the results. When you finally get into her office, your doctor smiles and tells you the tests were all negative.
>
> (C) Maybe it is cancer and they've just missed it. Maybe it's worse. Surely they should be able to find a cause. You feel frustrated by the lack of a definitive answer.

① (B) − (A) − (C)　　② (B) − (C) − (A)
③ (C) − (A) − (B)　　④ (C) − (B) − (A)

문 14. 글의 흐름으로 보아, 주어진 문장이 들어가기에 가장 적절한 곳은?

> The effect, however, was just the reverse.

> How we dress for work has taken on a new element of choice, and with it, new anxieties. (①) The practice of having a "dress-down day" or "casual day," which began to emerge a decade or so ago, was intended to make life easier for employees, to enable them to save money and feel more relaxed at the office. (②) In addition to the normal workplace wardrobe, employees had to create a "workplace casual" wardrobe. (③) It couldn't really be the sweats and T-shirts you wore around the house on the weekend. (④) It had to be a selection of clothing that sustained a certain image — relaxed, but also serious.
>
> * wardrobe: 옷, 의류

문 15. 다음 글의 밑줄 친 부분 중, 어법상 가장 틀린 것은?

> You should choose the research method ① that best suits the outcome you want. You may run a survey online that enables you to question large numbers of people and ② provides full analysis in report format, or you may think asking questions one to one is a better way to get the answers you need from a smaller test selection of people. ③ Whichever way you choose, you will need to compare like for like. Ask people the same questions and compare answers. Look for both similarities and differences. Look for patterns and trends. Deciding on a way of recording and analysing the data ④ are important. A simple self created spreadsheet may well be enough to record some basic research data.

문 16. 다음 글의 요지로 가장 적절한 것은?

> Some criminal offenders may engage in illegal behavior because they love the excitement and thrills that crime can provide. In his highly influential work Seductions of Crime, sociologist Jack Katz argues that there are immediate benefits to criminality that "seduce" people into a life of crime. For some people, shoplifting and *vandalism are attractive because getting away with crime is a thrilling demonstration of personal competence. The need for excitement may counter fear of apprehension and punishment. In fact, some offenders will deliberately seek out especially risky situations because of the added "thrill". The need for excitement is a significant predictor of criminal choice.
>
> * vandalism: 기물 파손

① 범죄를 줄이기 위해서 재소자를 상대로 한 교육이 필요하다.
② 범죄 행위에서 생기는 흥분과 쾌감이 범죄를 유발할 수 있다.
③ 엄격한 형벌 제도와 법 집행을 통해 강력 범죄를 줄일 수 있다.
④ 세밀하고 꼼꼼한 제도를 만들어 범죄 피해자를 도울 필요가 있다.

문 17. 다음 빈칸에 들어갈 말로 가장 적절한 것은?

In one classic study showing the importance of attachment, Wisconsin University psychologists Harry and Margaret Harlow investigated the responses of young monkeys. The infants were separated from their biological mothers, and two surrogate mothers were introduced to their cages. One, the wire mother, consisted of a round wooden head, a mesh of cold metal wires, and a bottle of milk from which the baby monkey could drink. The second mother was a foam-rubber form wrapped in a heated terry-cloth blanket. The infant monkeys went to the wire mother for food, but they overwhelmingly preferred and spent significantly more time with the warm terry-cloth mother. The warm terry-cloth mother provided no food, but did provide _____.

* surrogate: 대리의

① jobs
② drugs
③ comfort
④ education

문 18. 다음 글의 밑줄 친 부분 중, 어법상 가장 틀린 것은?

I was released for adoption by my biological parents and ① spend the first decade of my life in orphanages. I spent many years thinking that something was wrong with me. If my own parents didn't want me, who could? I tried to figure out ② what I had done wrong and why so many people sent me away. I don't get close to anyone now because if I do they might leave me. I had to isolate ③ myself emotionally to survive when I was a child, and I still operate on the assumptions I had as a child. I am so fearful of being deserted ④ that I won't venture out and take even minimal risks. I am 40 years old now, but I still feel like a child.

문 19. 다음 글의 밑줄 친 부분 중 어법상 가장 틀린 것은?

Music can have psychotherapeutic effects that may transfer to everyday life. A number of scholars suggested people ① to use music as psychotherapeutic agent. Music therapy can be broadly defined as being 'the use of music as an adjunct to the treatment or rehabilitation of individuals to enhance their psychological, physical, cognitive or social ② functioning'. Positive emotional experiences from music may improve therapeutic process and thus ③ strengthen traditional cognitive/behavioral methods and their transfer to everyday goals. This may be partially because emotional experiences elicited by music and everyday behaviors ④ share overlapping neurological pathways responsible for positive emotions and motivations.

* psychotherapeutic: 심리 요법의

문 20. 다음 빈칸에 들어갈 말로 가장 적절한 것은?

Cultural interpretations are usually made on the basis of _____ rather than measurable evidence. The arguments tend to be circular. People are poor because they are lazy. How do we "know" they are lazy? Because they are poor. Promoters of these interpretations rarely understand that low productivity results not from laziness and lack of effort but from lack of capital inputs to production. African farmers are not lazy, but they do lack soil nutrients, tractors, feeder roads, irrigated plots, storage facilities, and the like. Stereotypes that Africans work little and therefore are poor are put to rest immediately by spending a day in a village, where backbreaking labor by men and women is the norm.

① statistics
② prejudice
③ appearance
④ circumstances

문 21. 글의 흐름으로 보아, 주어진 문장이 들어가기에 가장 적절한 곳은?

> But the demand for food isn't elastic; people don't eat more just because food is cheap.

The free market has never worked in agriculture and it never will. (①) The economics of a family farm are very different than a firm's: When prices fall, the firm can lay off people and idle factories. (②) Eventually the market finds a new balance between supply and demand. (③) And laying off farmers doesn't help to reduce supply. (④) You can fire me, but you can't fire my land, because some other farmer who needs more cash flow or thinks he's more efficient than I am will come in and farm it.

* elastic: 탄력성 있는

문 22. 다음 글의 주제로 가장 적절한 것은?

Daily training creates special nutritional needs for an athlete, particularly the elite athlete whose training commitment is almost a fulltime job. But even recreational sport will create nutritional challenges. And whatever your level of involvement in sport, you must meet these challenges if you're to achieve the maximum return from training. Without sound eating, much of the purpose of your training might be lost. In the worst-case scenario, dietary problems and deficiencies may directly impair training performance. In other situations, you might improve, but at a rate that is below your potential or slower than your competitors. However, on the positive side, with the right everyday eating plan your commitment to training will be fully rewarded.

① how to improve body flexibility
② importance of eating well in exercise
③ health problems caused by excessive diet
④ improving skills through continuous training

문 23. 다음 글의 주제로 가장 적절한 것은?

A very well-respected art historian called Ernst Gombrich wrote about something called "the beholder's share". It was Gombrich's belief that a viewer "completed" the artwork, that part of an artwork's meaning came from the person viewing it. So you see — there really are no wrong answers as it is you, as the viewer who is completing the artwork. If you're looking at art in a gallery, read the wall text at the side of the artwork. If staff are present, ask questions. Ask your fellow visitors what they think. Asking questions is the key to understanding more — and that goes for anything in life — not just art. But above all, have confidence in front of an artwork. If you are contemplating an artwork, then you are the intended viewer and what you think matters. You are the only critic that counts.

① 미술작품의 가치는 일정 부분 정해져 있다.
② 미술 작품을 제작할 때 대중의 요구를 반영해야 한다.
③ 미술작품은 감상하는 사람으로 인하여 비로소 완성된다.
④ 미술 감상의 출발은 작가의 숨겨진 의도를 파악하는 것이다.

문 24. Argentina에 관한 다음 글의 내용과 가장 일치하지 않는 것은?

Argentina is the world's eighth largest country, comprising almost the entire southern half of South America. Colonization by Spain began in the early 1500s, but in 1816 Jose de San Martin led the movement for Argentine independence. The culture of Argentina has been greatly influenced by the massive European migration in the late nineteenth and early twentieth centuries, primarily from Spain and Italy. The majority of people are at least nominally Catholic, and the country has the largest Jewish population (about 300,000) in South America. From 1880 to 1930, thanks to its agricultural development, Argentina was one of the world's top ten wealthiest nations.

① Jose de San Martin이 스페인으로부터의 독립운동을 이끌었다.
② 북미 출신 이주민들이 그 문화에 많은 영향을 끼쳤다.
③ 남미지역 중에서 가장 많은 유대인들이 살고 있는 곳이다.
④ 농업의 발전으로 한때 부유한 국가였다.

문 25. Sonja Henie에 관한 다음 글의 내용과 가장 일치하지 않는 것은?

Sonja Henie is famous for her skill into a career as one of the world's most famous figure skaters — in the rink and on the screen. Henie, winner of three Olympic gold medals and a Norwegian and European champion, invented a thrillingly theatrical and athletic style of figure skating. She introduced short skirts, white skates, and attractive moves. Her spectacular spins and jumps raised the bar for all competitors. In 1936, Twentieth-Century Fox signed her to star in One in a Million, and she soon became one of Hollywood's leading actresses. In 1941, the movie 'Sun Valley Serenade' received three Academy Award nominations which she played as an actress. Although the rest of Henie's films were less acclaimed, she triggered a popular surge in ice skating. In 1938, she launched extravagant touring shows called Hollywood Ice Revues. Her many ventures made her a fortune, but her greatest legacy was inspiring little girls to skate.

① 피겨 스케이터와 영화배우로서의 업적으로 유명하다.
② 올림픽과 다른 대회들에서 좋은 성적을 거두었다.
③ 출연한 영화가 1941년에 영화제에서 3개 부문에 수상했다.
④ 어린 여자아이들에게 스케이트에 대한 영감을 주었다.

해설편 ▶ P.136

2021

| 풀이 시간: ____:____ ~ ____:____ / 점수: ____점

문 1. 다음 글의 내용을 한 문장으로 요약하고자 한다. 빈칸 (A)와 (B)에 들어갈 말로 가장 적절한 것은?

Microorganisms are not calculating entities. They don't care what they do to you any more than you care what distress you cause when you slaughter them by the millions with a soapy shower. The only time a pathogen cares about you is when it kills you too well. If they eliminate you before they can move on, then they may well die out themselves. This in fact sometimes happens. History, Jared Diamond notes, is full of diseases that "once caused terrifying epidemics and then disappeared as mysteriously as they had come." He cites the robust but mercifully transient English sweating sickness, which raged from 1485 to 1552, killing tens of thousands as it went, before burning itself out. Too much efficiency is not a good thing for any infectious organism.

*pathogen: 병원체

↓

The more _____(A)_____ pathogens are, the faster it is likely to be _____(B)_____.

	(A)	(B)
①	weaker	disappear
②	weaker	spread
③	infectious	spread
④	infectious	disappear

문 2. 밑줄 친 "drains the mind"가 글에서 의미하는 바로 가장 적절한 것은?

If the writing is solid and good, the mood and temper of the writer will eventually be revealed and not at the expense of the work. Therefore, to achieve style, begin by affecting none — that is, draw the reader's attention to the sense and substance of the writing. A careful and honest writer does not need to worry about style. As you become proficient in the use of language, your style will emerge, because you yourself will emerge, and when this happens you will find it increasingly easy to break through the barriers that separate you from other minds and at last, make you stand in the middle of the writing. Fortunately, the act of composition, or creation, disciplines the mind; writing is one way to go about thinking, and the practice and habit of writing drains the mind.

① to heal the mind
② to help to be sensitive
③ to satisfy his/her curiosity
④ to place oneself in the background

문 3. (A), (B), (C)의 각 네모 안에서 어법에 맞는 표현으로 가장 적절한 것은?

Some of our dissatisfactions with self and with our lot in life are based on real circumstances, and some are false and simply (A) [perceive / perceived] to be real. The perceived must be sorted out and discarded. The real will either fall into the changeable or the unchangeable classification. If it's in the latter, we must strive to accept it. If it's in the former, then we have the alternative to strive instead to remove, exchange, or modify it. All of us have a unique purpose in life; and all of us are gifted, just (B) [different / differently] gifted. It's not an argument about whether it's fair or unfair to have been given one, five, or ten talents; it's about what we have done with our talents. It's about how well we have invested (C) [them / those] we have been given. If one holds on to the outlook that their life is unfair, then that's really holding an offense against God.

	(A)	(B)	(C)
①	perceive	different	them
②	perceive	differently	those
③	perceived	different	them
④	perceived	differently	those

문 4. 주어진 글 다음에 이어질 글의 순서로 가장 적절한 것은?

> People assume that, by charging a low price or one lower than their competitors, they will get more customers. This is a common fallacy.

(A) It is, therefore, far better to have lower-volume, higher-margin products and services as you start; you can always negotiate to reduce your price if you are forced to, but it is rare that you will be able to negotiate an increase.

(B) It is because when you charge reduced prices compared to your competition, you attract the lower end of the customer market. These customers want more for less and often take up more time and overhead in your business. They may also be your most difficult customers to deal with and keep happy.

(C) You also, ironically, repel the better customers because they will pay a higher price for a higher level of product or service. We have seen many competitors come into the market and charge day rates that aren't sustainable. They often struggle even to fill their quota, and soon enough they give up and move on to doing something else.

*repel: 쫓아 버리다

① (B) − (A) − (C)   ② (B) − (C) − (A)
③ (C) − (A) − (B)   ④ (C) − (B) − (A)

문 5. 다음 글의 밑줄 친 부분 중, 어법상 가장 틀린 것은?

> Children who enjoy writing are often interested in seeing ① their work in print. One informal approach is to type, print, and post their poetry. Or you can create a photocopied anthology of the poetry of many child writers. But for children who are truly dedicated and ambitious, ② submit a poem for publication is a worthy goal. And there are several web and print resources that print children's original poetry. Help child poets become familiar with the protocol for submitting manuscripts (style, format, and so forth). Let them choose ③ which poems they are most proud of, keep copies of everything submitted, and get parent permission. Then celebrate with them when their work is accepted and appear in print. Congratulate them, ④ publicly showcase their accomplishment, and spread the word. Success inspires success. And, of course, if their work is rejected, offer support and encouragement.
>
> *anthology: 문집, 선집 **protocol: 규약, 의례

문 6. 글의 흐름으로 보아, 주어진 문장이 들어가기에 가장 적절한 곳은?

> With love and strength from the tribe, the tiny seeds mature and grow tall and crops for the people.

> In the Pueblo Indian culture, corn is to the people the very symbol of life. (①) The Corn Maiden "grandmother of the sun and the light" brought this gift, bringing the power of life to the people. (②) As the corn is given life by the sun, the Corn Maiden brings the fire of the sun into the human bodies, giving man many representations of her love and power through nature. (③) Each Maiden brings one seed of corn that is nurtured with love like that given to a child and this one seed would sustain the entire tribe forever. (④) The spirit of the Corn Maidens is forever present with the tribal people.

문 7. 다음 빈칸에 들어갈 말로 가장 적절한 것은?

Beeches, oaks, spruce and pines produce new growth all the time, and have to get rid of the old. The most obvious change happens every autumn. The leaves have served their purpose: they are now worn out and riddled with insect damage. Before the trees bid them adieu, they pump waste products into them. You could say they are taking this opportunity to relieve themselves. Then they grow a layer of weak tissue to separate each leaf from the twig it's growing on, and the leaves tumble to the ground in the next breeze. The rustling leaves that now blanket the ground — and make such a satisfying scrunching sound when you scuffle through them — are basically _____.

① tree toilet paper
② the plant kitchen
③ lungs of the tree
④ parents of insects

문 8. 글의 흐름상 가장 어색한 문장은?

Fiction has many uses and one of them is to build empathy. When you watch TV or see a film, you are looking at things happening to other people. Prose fiction is something you build up from 26 letters and a handful of punctuation marks, and you, and you alone, using your imagination, create a world and live there and look out through other eyes. ① You get to feel things, and visit places and worlds you would never otherwise know. ② Fortunately, in the last decade, many of the world's most beautiful and unknown places have been put in the spotlight. ③ You learn that everyone else out there is a me, as well. ④ You're being someone else, and when you return to your own world, you're going to be slightly changed.

문 9. 다음 빈칸에 들어갈 말로 가장 적절한 것은?

The seeds of willows and poplars are so minuscule that you can just make out two tiny dark dots in the fluffy flight hairs. One of these seeds weighs a mere 0.0001 grams. With such a meagre energy reserve, a seedling can grow only 1–2 millimetres before it runs out of steam and has to rely on food it makes for itself using its young leaves. But that only works in places where there's no competition to threaten the tiny sprouts. Other plants casting shade on it would extinguish the new life immediately. And so, if a fluffy little seed package like this falls in a spruce or beech forest, the seed's life is over before it's even begun. That's why willows and poplars _____.

*minuscule: 아주 작은

① prefer settling in unoccupied territory
② have been chosen as food for herbivores
③ have evolved to avoid human intervention
④ wear their dead leaves far into the winter

문 10. 다음 글의 밑줄 친 부분 중 문맥상 낱말의 쓰임이 가장 적절하지 않은 것은?

Good walking shoes are important. Most major athletic brands offer shoes especially designed for walking. Fit and comfort are more important than style; your shoes should feel ① supportive but not tight or constricting. The uppers should be light, breathable, and flexible, the insole moisture-resistant, and the sole ② shock-absorbent. The heel wedge should be ③ lowered, so the sole at the back of the shoe is two times thicker than at the front. Finally, the toe box should be ④ spacious, even when you're wearing athletic socks.

① supportive   ② shock-absorbent
③ lowered   ④ spacious

문 11. 다음 글의 요지로 가장 알맞은 것은?

If your kids fight every time they play video games, make sure you're close enough to be able to hear them when they sit down to play. Listen for the particular words or tones of voice they are using that are aggressive, and try to intervene before it develops. Once tempers have settled, try to seat your kids down and discuss the problem without blaming or accusing. Give each kid a chance to talk, uninterrupted, and have them try to come up with solutions to the problem themselves. By the time kids are elementary-school age, they can evaluate which of those solutions are win-win solutions and which ones are most likely to work and satisfy each other over time. They should also learn to revisit problems when solutions are no longer working.

① Ask your kids to evaluate their test.
② Make your kids compete each other.
③ Help your kids learn to resolve conflict.
④ Teach your kids how to win an argument.

문 12. 다음 글의 요지로 가장 적절한 것은?

There's a current trend to avoid germs at all cost. We disinfect our bathrooms, kitchens, and the air. We sanitize our hands and gargle with mouthwash to kill germs. Some folks avoid as much human contact as possible and won't even shake your hand for fear of getting germs. I think it's safe to say that some people would purify everything but their minds. Remember the story of "the Boy in the Bubble"? He was born without an immune system and had to live in a room that was completely germ free, with no human contact. Of course, everyone should take prudent measures to maintain reasonable standards of cleanliness and personal hygiene, but in many cases, aren't we going overboard? When we come in contact with most germs, our body destroys them, which in turn strengthens our immune system and its ability to further fight off disease. Thus, these "good germs" actually make us healthier. Even if it were possible to avoid all germs and to live in a sterile environment, wouldn't we then be like "the Boy in the Bubble"?

① 세균에 감염되지 않도록 개인의 위생 환경 조성이 필요하다.
② 면역 능력이 상실된 채로 태어난 유아에 대한 치료가 시급하다.
③ 지역사회의 방역 능력 강화를 위해 국가의 재정 지원이 시급하다.
④ 과도하게 세균을 제거하려고 하는 것이 오히려 면역 능력을 해친다.

문 13. 다음 글의 밑줄 친 부분을 어법상 바르게 고친 것이 아닌 것은?

① Knowing as the Golden City, Jaisalmer, a former caravan center on the route to the Khyber Pass, rises from a sea of sand, its 30-foot-high walls and medieval sandstone fort ② shelters carved spires and palaces that soar into the sapphire sky. With its tiny winding lanes and hidden temples, Jaisalmer is straight out of The Arabian Nights, and so little has life altered here ③ which it's easy to imagine yourself back in the 13th century. It's the only fortress city in India still functioning, with one quarter of its population ④ lived within the walls, and it's just far enough off the beaten path to have been spared the worst ravages of tourism. The city's wealth originally came from the substantial tolls it placed on passing camel caravans.

① Knowing → Known
② shelters → sheltering
③ which → that
④ lived → lives

문 14. 다음 글에서 필자가 주장하는 바로 가장 적절한 것은?

The learned are neither apathetic nor indifferent regarding the world's problems. More books on these issues are being published than ever, though few capture the general public's attention. Likewise, new research discoveries are constantly being made at universities, and shared at conferences worldwide. Unfortunately, most of this activity is self-serving. With the exception of science — and here, too, only selectively — new insights are not trickling down to the public in ways to help improve our lives. Yet, these discoveries aren't simply the property of the elite, and should not remain in the possession of a select few professionals. Each person must make his and her own life's decisions, and make those choices in light of our current understanding of who we are and what is good for us. For that matter, we must find a way to somehow make new discoveries accessible to every person.

*apathetic: 냉담한, 무관심한   **trickle: 흐르다

① 학자들은 연구 논문을 작성할 때 주관성을 배제해야 한다.
② 새로운 연구 결과에 모든 사람이 접근할 수 있게 해야 한다.
③ 소수 엘리트 학자들의 폐쇄성을 극복할 계기를 마련해야 한다.
④ 학자들이 연구 과정에서 겪는 어려움을 극복하도록 도와야 한다.

문 15. 다음 글의 주제로 가장 알맞은 것은?

Language gives individual identity and a sense of belonging. When children proudly learn their language and are able to speak it at home and in their neighborhood, the children will have a high self-esteem. Moreover, children who know the true value of their mother tongue will not feel like they are achievers when they speak a foreign language. With improved self-identity and self-esteem, the classroom performance of a child also improves because such a child goes to school with less worries about linguistic marginalization.

*linguistic marginalization: 언어적 소외감

① the importance of mother tongue in child development
② the effect on children's foreign language learning
③ the way to improve children's self-esteem
④ the efficiency of the linguistic analysis

문 16. 다음 글의 주제로 가장 적절한 것은?

Many animals are not loners. They discovered, or perhaps nature discovered for them, that by living and working together, they could interact with the world more effectively. For example, if an animal hunts for food by itself, it can only catch, kill, and eat animals much smaller than itself — but if animals band together in a group, they can catch and kill animals bigger than they are. A pack of wolves can kill a horse, which can feed the group very well. Thus, more food is available to the same animals in the same forest if they work together than if they work alone. Cooperation has other benefits: The animals can alert each other to danger, can find more food (if they search separately and then follow the ones who succeed in finding food), and can even provide some care to those who are sick and injured. Mating and reproduction are also easier if the animals live in a group than if they live far apart.

① benefits of being social in animals
② drawbacks of cooperative behaviors
③ common traits of animals and humans
④ competitions in mating and reproduction

문 17. 다음 글의 밑줄 친 부분 중, 문맥상 낱말의 쓰임이 가장 적절하지 않은 것은?

My own curiosity had been encouraged by my studies in philosophy at university. The course listed the numerous philosophers that we were supposed to study and I thought at first that our task was to learn and absorb their work as a sort of secular Bible. But I was ① delighted to discover that my tutor was not interested in me reciting their theories but only in helping me to develop my own, using the philosophers of the past as stimulants not authorities. It was the key to my intellectual ② freedom. Now I had official permission to think for myself, to question anything and everything and only agree if I thought it right. A ③ good education would have given me that permission much earlier. Some, alas, never seem to have received it and go on reciting the rules of others as if they were sacrosanct. As a result, they become the unwitting ④ opponents of other people's worlds. Philosophy, I now think, is too important to be left to professional philosophers. We should all learn to think like philosophers, starting at primary school.

*sacrosanct: 신성불가침의   **unwitting: 자신도 모르는

문 18. (A), (B), (C)의 괄호 안에서 어법에 맞는 표현으로 가장 적절한 것은?

Looking back, scientists have uncovered a mountain of evidence (A) [that / what] Mayan leaders were aware for many centuries of their uncertain dependence on rainfall. Water shortages were not only understood but also recorded and planned for. The Mayans enforced conservation during low rainfall years, tightly regulating the types of crops grown, the use of public water, and food rationing. During the first half of their three-thousand-year reign, the Mayans continued to build larger underground artificial lakes and containers (B) [stored / to store] rainwater for drought months. As impressive as their elaborately decorated temples (C) [did / were], their efficient systems for collecting and warehousing water were masterpieces in design and engineering.

*rationing: 배급

	(A)	(B)	(C)
①	that	to store	were
②	what	stored	did
③	that	to store	did
④	what	stored	were

문 19. 주어진 글 다음에 이어질 글의 순서로 가장 적절한 것은?

Religion can certainly bring out the best in a person, but it is not the only phenomenon with that property.

(A) People who would otherwise be self-absorbed or shallow or crude or simply quitters are often ennobled by their religion, given a perspective on life that helps them make the hard decisions that we all would be proud to make.

(B) Having a child often has a wonderfully maturing effect on a person. Wartime, famously, gives people an abundance of occasions to rise to, as do natural disasters like floods and hurricanes.

(C) But for day-in, day-out lifelong bracing, there is probably nothing so effective as religion: it makes powerful and talented people more humble and patient, it makes average people rise above themselves, it provides sturdy support for many people who desperately need help staying away from drink or drugs or crime.

① (B) − (A) − (C)　　② (B) − (C) − (A)

③ (C) − (A) − (B)　　④ (C) − (B) − (A)

문 20. 주어진 글 다음에 이어질 글의 순서로 가장 적절한 것은?

More people require more resources, which means that as the population increases, the Earth's resources deplete more rapidly.

(A) Population growth also results in increased greenhouse gases, mostly from CO2 emissions. For visualization, during that same 20th century that saw fourfold population growth, CO2 emissions increased twelvefold.

(B) The result of this depletion is deforestation and loss of biodiversity as humans strip the Earth of resources to accommodate rising population numbers.

(C) As greenhouse gases increase, so do climate patterns, ultimately resulting in the long-term pattern called climate change.

*deplete: 고갈시키다, 대폭 감소시키다

① (A) − (B) − (C) ② (B) − (A) − (C)
③ (B) − (C) − (A) ④ (C) − (A) − (B)

문 21. 다음 글에서 전체 흐름과 관계 없는 문장은?

Medical anthropologists with extensive training in human biology and physiology study disease transmission patterns and how particular groups adapt to the presence of diseases like malaria and sleeping sickness. ① Because the transmission of viruses and bacteria is strongly influenced by people's diets, sanitation, and other behaviors, many medical anthropologists work as a team with epidemiologists to identify cultural practices that affect the spread of disease. ② Though it may be a commonly held belief that most students enter medicine for humanitarian reasons rather than for the financial rewards of a successful medical career, in developed nations the prospect of status and rewards is probably one incentive. ③ Different cultures have different ideas about the causes and symptoms of disease, how best to treat illnesses, the abilities of traditional healers and doctors, and the importance of community involvement in the healing process. ④ By studying how a human community perceives such things, medical anthropologists help hospitals and other agencies deliver health care services more effectively.

*epidemiologist: 유행[전염]병학자

문 22. 주어진 글 다음에 이어질 글의 순서로 가장 적절한 것은?

Sequoya (1760?-1843) was born in eastern Tennessee, into a prestigious family that was highly regarded for its knowledge of Cherokee tribal traditions and religion.

(A) Recognizing the possibilities writing had for his people, Sequoya invented a Cherokee alphabet in 1821. With this system of writing, Sequoya was able to record ancient tribal customs.

(B) More importantly, his alphabet helped the Cherokee nation develop a publishing industry so that newspapers and books could be printed. School-age children were thus able to learn about Cherokee culture and traditions in their own language.

(C) As a child, Sequoya learned the Cherokee oral tradition; then, as an adult, he was introduced to Euro-American culture. In his letters, Sequoya mentions how he became fascinated with the writing methods European Americans used to communicate.

① (B) − (A) − (C) ② (B) − (C) − (A)
③ (C) − (A) − (B) ④ (C) − (B) − (A)

문 23. Peanut Butter Drive에 관한 다음 안내문의 내용과 가장 일치하지 않는 것은?

SPREAD THE LOVE
Fight Hunger During the Peanut Butter Drive

Make a contribution to our community by helping local families who need a little assistance. We are kicking off our 4th annual area-wide peanut butter drive to benefit children, families and seniors who face hunger in Northeast Louisiana.

Peanut butter is a much needed staple at Food Banks as it is a protein-packed food that kids and adults love. Please donate peanut butter in plastic jars or funds to the Monroe Food Bank by Friday, March 29th at 4:00 pm. Donations of peanut butter can be dropped off at the food bank's distribution center located at 4600 Central Avenue in Monroe on Monday through Friday, 8:00 am to 4:00 pm. Monetary donations can be made here or by calling 427-418-4581.

For other drop-off locations, visit our website at https://www.foodbanknela.org

---

① 배고픈 사람들에게 도움을 주려는 행사이다.
② 토요일과 일요일에도 땅콩버터를 기부할 수 있다.
③ 전화를 걸어 금전 기부를 할 수도 있다.
④ 땅콩버터를 기부하는 장소는 여러 곳이 있다.

문 24. 다음 글에 나타난 화자의 심경으로 가장 적절한 것은?

Our whole tribe was poverty-stricken. Every branch of the Garoghlanian family was living in the most amazing and comical poverty in the world. Nobody could understand where we ever got money enough to keep us with food in our bellies. Most important of all, though, we were famous for our honesty. We had been famous for honesty for something like eleven centuries, even when we had been the wealthiest family in what we liked to think was the world. We put pride first, honest next, and after that we believed in right and wrong. None of us would take advantage of anybody in the world.

*poverty-stricken: 가난에 시달리는

---

① peaceful and calm
② satisfied and proud
③ horrified and feared
④ amazed and astonished

문 25. 다음 글의 내용과 가장 일치하지 않는 것은?

Despite the increasing popularity of consuming raw foods, you can still gain nutrients from cooked vegetables. For example, our body can absorb lycopene more effectively when tomatoes are cooked. (Keep in mind, however, that raw tomatoes are still a good source of lycopene.) Cooked tomatoes, however, have lower levels of vitamin C than raw tomatoes, so if you're looking to increase your levels, you might be better off sticking with the raw. Whether you decide to eat them cooked or raw, it's important not to dilute the health benefits of tomatoes. If you're buying tomato sauce or paste, choose a variety with no salt or sugar added — or better yet, cook your own sauce at home. And if you're eating your tomatoes raw, salt them sparingly and choose salad dressings that are low in calories and saturated fat.

*dilute: 희석하다, 묽게 하다

---

① 토마토를 요리하여 먹었을 때, 우리의 몸은 리코펜을 더 효과적으로 흡수할 수 있다.
② 더 많은 비타민C를 섭취하고 싶다면 생토마토보다 조리된 토마토를 섭취하는 것이 낫다.
③ 토마토 소스를 구입하고자 한다면, 소금이나 설탕이 첨가되지 않은 것으로 골라야 한다.
④ 생토마토를 섭취 시, 소금을 적게 넣거나, 칼로리가 적은 드레싱을 선택하도록 한다.

해설편 ▶ P.145

2020

2월 22일 시행
법원직 9급

| 풀이 시간: ___:___ ~ ___:___ / 점수: ___점

문 1. 다음 밑줄 친 (A), (B), (C)의 각 괄호 안에서 문맥에 맞는
낱말로 가장 적절한 것은?

It's tempting to identify knowledge with facts, but not every fact is an item of knowledge. Imagine shaking a sealed cardboard box containing a single coin. As you put the box down, the coin inside the box has landed either heads or tails: let's say that's a fact. But as long as no one looks into the box, this fact remains unknown; it is not yet within the realm of (A) [fact / knowledge]. Nor do facts become knowledge simply by being written down. If you write the sentence 'The coin has landed heads' on one slip of paper and 'The coin has landed tails' on another, then you will have written down a fact on one of the slips, but you still won't have gained knowledge of the outcome of the coin toss. Knowledge demands some kind of access to a fact on the part of some living subject. (B) [With / Without] a mind to access it, whatever is stored in libraries and databases won't be knowledge, but just ink marks and electronic traces. In any given case of knowledge, this access may or may not be unique to an individual: the same fact may be known by one person and not by others. Common knowledge might be shared by many people, but there is no knowledge that dangles (C) [attached / unattached] to any subject.

	(A)	(B)	(C)
①	fact	With	unattached
②	knowledge	Without	unattached
③	knowledge	With	attached
④	fact	Without	attached

문 2. 다음 빈칸에 들어갈 말로 가장 적절한 것은?

Impressionable youth are not the only ones subject to _____. Most of us have probably had an experience of being pressured by a salesman. Have you ever had a sales rep try to sell you some "office solution" by telling you that 70 percent of your competitors are using their service, so why aren't you? But what if 70 percent of your competitors are idiots? Or what if that 70 percent were given so much value added or offered such a low price that they couldn't resist the opportunity? The practice is designed to do one thing and one thing only — to pressure you to buy. To make you feel you might be missing out on something or that everyone else knows but you.

① peer pressure   ② impulse buying
③ bullying tactics   ④ keen competition

문 3. 다음 밑줄 친 (A), (B), (C)의 각 괄호 안에서 문맥에 맞는
낱말로 가장 적절한 것은?

People with high self-esteem have confidence in their skills and competence and enjoy facing the challenges that life offers them. They (A) [willingly / unwillingly] work in teams because they are sure of themselves and enjoy taking the opportunity to contribute. However, those who have low self-esteem tend to feel awkward, shy, and unable to express themselves. Often they compound their problems by opting for avoidance strategies because they (B) [deny / hold] the belief that whatever they do will result in failure. Conversely, they may compensate for their lack of self-esteem by exhibiting boastful and arrogant behavior to cover up their sense of unworthiness. Furthermore, such individuals account for their successes by finding reasons that are outside of themselves, while those with high self-esteem (C) [attempt / attribute] their success to internal characteristics.

	(A)	(B)	(C)
①	willingly	deny	attempt
②	willingly	hold	attribute
③	unwillingly	hold	attempt
④	unwillingly	deny	attribute

문 4. 다음 글의 제목으로 가장 적절한 것은?

To be sure, no other species can lay claim to our capacity to devise something new and original, from the sublime to the sublimely ridiculous. Other animals do build things — birds assemble their intricate nests, beavers construct dams, and ants dig elaborate networks of tunnels. "But airplanes, strangely tilted skyscrapers and Chia Pets, well, they're pretty impressive," Fuentes says, adding that from an evolutionary standpoint, "creativity is as much a part of our tool kit as walking on two legs, having a big brain and really good hands for manipulating things." For a physically unprepossessing primate, without great fangs or claws or wings or other obvious physical advantages, creativity has been the great equalizer — and more — ensuring, for now, at least, the survival of Homo sapiens.

*sublime: 황당한, (터무니없이) 극단적인

*Chia Pets: 잔디가 머리털처럼 자라나는 피규어

① Where Does Human Creativity Come From?
② What Are the Physical Characteristics of Primates?
③ Physical Advantages of Homo Sapiens over Other Species
④ Creativity: a Unique Trait Human Species Have For Survival

문 5. 다음 글의 요지를 한 문장으로 요약하고자 한다. 빈칸 (A), (B)에 들어갈 말로 가장 적절한 것은?

"Most of bird identification is based on a sort of subjective impression — the way a bird moves and little instantaneous appearances at different angles and sequences of different appearances, and as it turns its head and as it flies and as it turns around, you see sequences of different shapes and angles," Sibley says, "All that combines to create a unique impression of a bird that can't really be taken apart and described in words. When it comes down to being in the fieldland looking at a bird, you don't take time to analyze it and say it shows this, this, and this; therefore it must be this species. It's more natural and instinctive. After a lot of practice, you look at the bird, and it triggers little switches in your brain. It looks right. You know what it is at a glance."

↓

According to Sibley, bird identification is based on ___(A)___ rather than ___(B)___.

	(A)	(B)
①	instinctive impression	discrete analysis
②	objective research	subjective judgements
③	physical appearances	behavioral traits
④	close observation	distant observation

문 6. 주어진 글 다음에 이어질 글의 순서로 가장 적절한 것은?

As cars are becoming less dependent on people, the means and circumstances in which the product is used by consumers are also likely to undergo significant changes, with higher rates of participation in car sharing and short-term leasing programs.

(A) In the not-too-distant future, a driverless car could come to you when you need it, and when you are done with it, it could then drive away without any need for a parking space. Increases in car sharing and short-term leasing are also likely to be associated with a corresponding decrease in the importance of exterior car design.

(B) As a result, the symbolic meanings derived from cars and their relationship to consumer self-identity and status are likely to change in turn.

(C) Rather than serving as a medium for personalization and self-identity, car exteriors might increasingly come to represent a channel for advertising and other promotional activities, including brand ambassador programs, such as those offered by Free Car Media.

① (A) − (C) − (B)
② (B) − (C) − (A)
③ (C) − (A) − (B)
④ (C) − (B) − (A)

문 7. 주어진 글 다음에 이어질 글의 순서로 가장 적절한 것은?

There is a wonderful story of a group of American car executives who went to Japan to see a Japanese assembly line. At the end of the line, the doors were put on the hinges, the same as in America.

(A) But something was missing. In the United States, a line worker would take a rubber mallet and tap the edges of the door to ensure that it fit perfectly. In Japan, that job didn't seem to exist.

(B) Confused, the American auto executives asked at what point they made sure the door fit perfectly. Their Japanese guide looked at them and smiled sheepishly. "We make sure it fits when we design it."

(C) In the Japanese auto plant, they didn't examine the problem and accumulate data to figure out the best solution — they engineered the outcome they wanted from the beginning. If they didn't achieve their desired outcome, they understood it was because of a decision they made at the start of the process.

① (A) − (B) − (C)　　② (A) − (C) − (B)
③ (B) − (A) − (C)　　④ (B) − (C) − (A)

문 8. 다음 글의 빈칸 (A), (B)에 들어갈 말로 가장 적절한 것은?

There has been much research on nonverbal cues to deception dating back to the work of Ekman and his idea of leakage. It is well documented that people use others' nonverbal behaviors as a way to detect lies. My research and that of many others has strongly supported people's reliance on observations of others' nonverbal behaviors when assessing honesty. _____(A)_____, social scientific research on the link between various nonverbal behaviors and the act of lying suggests that the link is typically not very strong or consistent. In my research, I have observed that the nonverbal signals that seem to give one liar away are different than those given by a second liar. _____(B)_____, the scientific evidence linking nonverbal behaviors and deception has grown weaker over time. People infer honesty based on how others nonverbally present themselves, but that has very limited utility and validity.

	(A)	(B)
①	However	What's more
②	As a result	On the contrary
③	However	Nevertheless
④	As a result	For instance

문 9. 다음 글의 밑줄 친 부분 중 어법상 틀린 것은?

As soon as the start-up is incorporated it will need a bank account, and the need for a payroll account will follow quickly. The banks are very competitive in services to do payroll and related tax bookkeeping, ① starting with even the smallest of businesses. These are areas ② where a business wants the best quality service and the most "free" accounting help it can get. The changing payroll tax legislation is a headache to keep up with, especially when a sales force will be operating in many of the fifty states. And the ③ requiring reports are a burden on a company's administrative staff. Such services are often provided best by the banker. The banks' references in this area should be compared with the payroll service alternatives such as ADP, but the future and the long-term relationship should be kept in mind when a decision is ④ being made.

문 10. 다음 글의 밑줄 친 부분 중 어법상 틀린 것은?

Many people refuse to visit animal shelters because they find it too sad or ① depressed. They shouldn't feel so bad because so many lucky animals are saved from a dangerous life on the streets, ② where they're at risk of traffic accidents, attack by other animals or humans, and subject to the elements. Many lost pets likewise ③ are found and reclaimed by distraught owners simply because they were brought into animal shelters. Most importantly, ④ adoptable pets find homes, and sick or dangerous animals are humanely relieved of their suffering.

문 11. 다음 밑줄 친 (A), (B), (C)의 각 괄호 안에서 문맥에 맞는 낱말로 가장 적절한 것은?

EQ testing, when performed with reliable testing methods, can provide you with very useful information about yourself. I've found, having tested thousands of people, that many are a bit surprised by their results. For example, one person who believed she was very socially responsible and often concerned about others came out with an (A) [average / extraordinary] score in that area. She was quite disappointed in her score. It turned out that she had very high standards for social responsibility and therefore was extremely (B) [easy / hard] on herself when she performed her assessment. In reality, she was (C) [more / less] socially responsible than most people, but she believed that she could be much better than she was.

	(A)	(B)	(C)
①	average	easy	less
②	average	hard	more
③	extraordinary	hard	less
④	extraordinary	easy	more

문 12. 다음 빈칸에 들어갈 말로 가장 적절한 것은?

A person may try to _____ by using evidence to his advantage. A mother asks her son, "How are you doing in English this term?" He responds cheerfully, "Oh, I just got a ninety-five on a quiz." The statement conceals the fact that he has failed every other quiz and that his actual average is 55. Yet, if she pursues the matter no further, the mother may be delighted that her son is doing so well. Linda asks Susan, "Have you read much Dickens?" Susan responds, "Oh, *Pickwick Papers* is one of my favorite novels." The statement may disguise the fact that *Pickwick Papers* is the only novel by Dickens that she has read, and it may give Linda the impression that Susan is a great Dickens enthusiast.

① earn extra money
② effect a certain belief
③ hide memory problems
④ make other people feel guilty

문 13. 다음 글의 내용을 한 문장으로 요약하고자 한다. 빈칸 (A), (B)에 들어갈 말로 가장 적절한 것은?

Whether we are complimented for our appearance, our garden, a dinner we prepared, or an assignment at the office, it is always satisfying to receive recognition for a job well done. Certainly, reinforcement theory sees occasional praise as an aid to learning a new skill. However, some evidence cautions against making sweeping generalizations regarding the use of praise in improving performance. It seems that while praise improves performance on certain tasks, on others it can instead prove harmful. Imagine the situation in which the enthusiastic support of hometown fans expecting victory brings about the downfall of their team. In this situation, it seems that praise creates pressure on athletes, disrupting their performance.

⬇

Whether _____(A)_____ helps or hurts a performance depends on _____(B)_____.

	(A)	(B)
①	praise	task types
②	competition	quality of teamwork
③	praise	quality of teamwork
④	competition	task types

문 14. 다음 글의 밑줄 친 부분 중 어법상 틀린 것은?

As we consider media consumption in the context of anonymous social relations, we mean all of those occasions that involve the presence of strangers, such as viewing television in public places like bars, ① going to concerts or dance clubs, or reading a newspaper on a bus or subway. Typically, there are social rules that ② govern how we interact with those around us and with the media product. For instance, it is considered rude in our culture, or at least aggressive, ③ read over another person's shoulder or to get up and change TV channels in a public setting. Any music fan knows what is appropriate at a particular kind of concert. The presence of other people is often crucial to defining the setting and hence the activity of media consumption, ④ despite the fact that the relationships are totally impersonal.

문 15. 다음 글의 밑줄 친 부분 중 어법상 틀린 것은?

Many of us believe that amnesia, or sudden memory loss, results in the inability to recall one's name and identity. This belief may reflect the way amnesia is usually ① portrayed in movies, television, and literature. For example, when we meet Matt Damon's character in the movie *The Bourne Identity*, we learn that he has no memory for who he is, why he has the skills he does, or where he is from. He spends much of the movie ② trying to answer these questions. However, the inability to remember your name and identity ③ are exceedingly rare in reality. Amnesia most often results from a brain injury that leaves the victim unable to form new memories, but with most memories of the past ④ intact. Some movies do accurately portray this more common syndrome; our favorite *Memento*.

문 16. 다음 빈칸에 들어갈 말로 가장 적절한 것은?

Much is now known about natural hazards and the negative impacts they have on people and their property. It would seem obvious that any logical person would avoid such potential impacts or at least modify their behavior or their property to minimize such impacts. However, humans are not always rational. Until someone has a personal experience or knows someone who has such an experience, most people subconsciously believe "It won't happen here" or "It won't happen to me." Even knowledgeable scientists who are aware of the hazards, the odds of their occurrence, and the costs of an event _____.

① refuse to remain silent

② do not always act appropriately

③ put the genetic factor at the top end

④ have difficulty in defining natural hazards

문 17. 다음 글의 주제로 가장 적절한 것은?

The rise of cities and kingdoms and the improvement in transport infrastructure brought about new opportunities for specialization. Densely populated cities provided full-time employment not just for professional shoemakers and doctors, but also for carpenters, priests, soldiers and lawyers. Villages that gained a reputation for producing really good wine, olive oil or ceramics discovered that it was worth their while to specialize nearly exclusively in that product and trade it with other settlements for all the other goods they needed. This made a lot of sense. Climates and soils differ, so why drink mediocre wine from your backyard if you can buy a smoother variety from a place whose soil and climate is much better suited to grape vines? If the clay in your backyard makes stronger and prettier pots, then you can make an exchange.

① how climates and soils influence the local products

② ways to gain a good reputation for local specialties

③ what made people engage in specialization and trade

④ the rise of cities and full-time employment for professionals

문 18. 밑줄 친 the issue가 가리키는 내용으로 가장 적절한 것은?

Nine-year-old Ryan Kyote was eating breakfast at home in Napa, California, when he saw the news: an Indiana school had taken a 6-year-old's meal when her lunch account didn't have enough money. Kyote asked if that could happen to his friends. When his mom contacted the school district to find out, she learned that students at schools in their district had, all told, as much as $25,000 in lunch debt. Although the district says it never penalized students who owed, Kyote decided to use his saved allowance to pay off his grade's debt, about $74 — becoming the face of a movement to end lunch-money debt. When California Governor Gavin Newsom signed a bill in October that banned "lunch shaming," or giving worse food to students with debt, he thanked Kyote for his "empathy and his courage" in raising awareness of the issue. "Heroes," Kyote points out, "come in all ages."

① The governor signed a bill to decline lunch items to students with lunch debt.
② Kyote's lunch was taken away because he ran out of money in his lunch account.
③ The school district with financial burden cut the budget failing to serve quality meals.
④ Many students in the district who could not afford lunch were burdened with lunch debt.

문 19. 청고래에 관한 다음 글의 내용과 일치하지 않는 것은?

The biggest heart in the world is inside the blue whale. It weighs more than seven tons. It's as big as a room. When this creature is born it is 20 feet long and weighs four tons. It is way bigger than your car. It drinks a hundred gallons of milk from its mama every day and gains 200 pounds a day, and when it is seven or eight years old it endures an unimaginable puberty and then it essentially disappears from human ken, for next to nothing is known of the mating habits, travel patterns, diet, social life, language, social structure and diseases. There are perhaps 10,000 blue whales in the world, living in every ocean on earth, and of the largest animal who ever lived we know nearly nothing. But we know this: the animals with the largest hearts in the world generally travel in pairs, and their penetrating moaning cries, their piercing yearning tongue, can be heard underwater for miles and miles.

① 아기 청고래는 매일 100갤런의 모유를 마시고, 하루에 200 파운드씩 체중이 증가한다.
② 청고래는 사춘기를 지나면서 인간의 시야에서 사라져서 청고래에 대해 알려진 것이 많지 않다.
③ 세계에서 가장 큰 심장을 지닌 동물이면서, 몸집이 가장 큰 동물이다.
④ 청고래는 일반적으로 혼자서 이동하고, 청고래의 소리는 물속을 관통하여 수 마일까지 전달될 수 있다.

문 20. 다음 글의 주제로 가장 적절한 것은?

In addition to controlling temperatures when handling fresh produce, control of the atmosphere is important. Some moisture is needed in the air to prevent dehydration during storage, but too much moisture can encourage growth of molds. Some commercial storage units have controlled atmospheres, with the levels of both carbon dioxide and moisture being regulated carefully. Sometimes other gases, such as ethylene gas, may be introduced at controlled levels to help achieve optimal quality of bananas and other fresh produce. Related to the control of gases and moisture is the need for some circulation of air among the stored foods.

① The necessity of controlling harmful gases in atmosphere
② The best way to control levels of moisture in growing plants and fruits
③ The seriousness of increasing carbon footprints every year around the world
④ The importance of controlling certain levels of gases and moisture in storing foods

문 21. 다음 글의 밑줄 친 부분 중 문맥상 낱말의 쓰임이 가장 적절하지 않은 것은?

Even if lying doesn't have any harmful effects in a particular case, it is still morally wrong because, if discovered, lying weakens the general practice of truth telling on which human communication relies. For instance, if I were to lie about my age on grounds of vanity, and my lying were discovered, even though no serious harm would have been done, I would have ① undermined your trust generally. In that case you would be far less likely to believe anything I might say in the future. Thus all lying, when discovered, has indirect ② harmful effects. However, very occasionally, these harmful effects might possibly be outweighed by the ③ benefits which arise from a lie. For example, if someone is seriously ill, lying to them about their life expectancy might probably give them a chance of living longer. On the other hand, telling them the truth could possibly ④ prevent a depression that would accelerate their physical decline.

문 22. 글의 흐름으로 보아 아래 문장이 들어가기에 가장 적절한 곳은?

> Water is also the medium for most chemical reactions needed to sustain life.

> Several common properties of seawater are crucial to the survival and well-being of the ocean's inhabitants. Water accounts for 80-90% of the volume of most marine organisms. (①) It provides buoyancy and body support for swimming and floating organisms and reduces the need for heavy skeletal structures. (②) The life processes of marine organisms in turn alter many fundamental physical and chemical properties of seawater, including its transparency and chemical makeup, making organisms an integral part of the total marine environment. (③) Understanding the interactions between organisms and their marine environment requires a brief examination of some of the more important physical and chemical attributes of seawater. (④) The characteristics of pure water and sea water differ in some respects, so we consider first the basic properties of pure water and then examine how those properties differ in seawater.

문 23. (A), (B), (C)의 각 네모 안에서 문맥에 맞는 낱말로 가장 적절한 것은?

> Here's the even more surprising part: The advent of AI didn't (A) diminish / increase the performance of purely human chess players. Quite the opposite. Cheap, supersmart chess programs (B) discouraged / inspired more people than ever to play chess, at more tournaments than ever, and the players got better than ever. There are more than twice as many grand masters now as there were when Deep Blue first beat Kasparov. The top-ranked human chess player today, Magnus Carlsen, trained with AIs and has been deemed the most computerlike of all human chess players. He also has the (C) highest / lowest human grand master rating of all time.

	(A)	(B)	(B)
①	diminish	discouraged	highest
②	increase	discouraged	lowest
③	diminish	inspired	highest
④	increase	inspired	lowest

문 24. 다음 글의 내용을 요약할 때 빈칸에 들어갈 말로 가장 적절한 것은?

> Aesthetic value in fashion objects, like aesthetic value in fine art objects, is self-oriented. Consumers have the need to be attracted and to surround themselves with other people who are attractive. However, unlike aesthetic value in the fine arts, aesthetic value in fashion is also other-oriented. Attractiveness of appearance is a way of eliciting the reaction of others and facilitating social interaction.

⬇

> Aesthetic value in fashion objects is _____.

① inherently only self-oriented
② just other-oriented unlike the other
③ both self-oriented and other-oriented
④ hard to define regardless of its nature

문 25. 글의 흐름으로 보아 아래 문장이 들어가기에 가장 적절한 곳은?

> The great news is that this is true whether or not we remember our dreams.

> Some believe there is no value to dreams, but it is wrong to dismiss these nocturnal dramas as irrelevant. There is something to be gained in remembering. (①) We can feel more connected, more complete, and more on track. We can receive inspiration, information, and comfort. Albert Einstein stated that his theory of relativity was inspired by a dream. (②) In fact, he claimed that dreams were responsible for many of his discoveries. (③) Asking why we dream makes as much sense as questioning why we breathe. Dreaming is an integral part of a healthy life. (④) Many people report being inspired with a new approach for a problem upon awakening, even though they don't remember the specific dream.

해설편 ▶ P.154

| 풀이 시간: ___:___ ~ ___:___ / 점수: ___점

문 1. 다음 글의 밑줄 친 부분 중 어법상 틀린 것은?

Recent research reveals that some individuals are genetically ① predisposed to shyness. In other words, some people are born shy. Researchers say that between 15 and 20 percent of newborn babies show signs of shyness: they are quieter and more vigilant. Researchers have identified physiological differences between sociable and shy babies ② that show up as early as two months. In one study, two-month-olds who were later identified as shy children ③ reacting with signs of stress to stimuli such as moving mobiles and tape recordings of human voices: increased heart rates, jerky movements of arms and legs, and excessive crying. Further evidence of the genetic basis of shyness is the fact that parents and grandparents of shy children more often say that they were shy as children ④ than parents and grandparents of non-shy children.

문 2. 다음 밑줄 친 (A), (B), (C)에서 문맥에 맞는 낱말로 가장 적절한 것은?

South Korea is one of the only countries in the world that has a dedicated goal to become the world's leading exporter of popular culture. It is a way for Korea to develop its "soft power." It refers to the (A) [tangible / intangible] power a country wields through its image, rather than through military power or economic power. Hallyu first spread to China and Japan, later to Southeast Asia and several countries worldwide. In 2000, a 50-year ban on the exchange of popular culture between Korea and Japan was partly lifted, which

improved the (B) [surge / decline] of Korean popular culture among the Japanese. South Korea's broadcast authorities have been sending delegates to promote their TV programs and cultural contents in several countries. Hallyu has been a blessing for Korea, its businesses, culture and country image. Since early 1999, Hallyu has become one of the biggest cultural phenomena across Asia. The Hallyu effect has been tremendous, contributing to 0.2% of Korea's GDP in 2004, amounting to approximately USD 1.87 billion. More recently in 2014, Hallyu had an estimated USD 11.6 billion (C) [boost / stagnation] on the Korean economy.

	(A)	(B)	(C)
①	tangible	surge	stagnation
②	intangible	decline	boost
③	intangible	surge	boost
④	tangible	decline	stagnation

문 3. 다음 글에서 전체의 흐름과 가장 관계없는 문장은?

The immortal operatically styled single Bohemian Rhapsody by Queen was released in 1975 and proceeded to the top of the UK charts for 9 weeks. ① A song that was nearly never released due to its length and unusual style but which Freddie insisted would be played became the instantly recognizable hit. ② By this time Freddie's unique talents were becoming clear, a voice with a remarkable range and a stage presence that gave Queen its colorful, unpredictable and flamboyant personality. ③ The son of Bomi and Jer Bulsara, Freddie spent the bulk of his childhood in India where he attended St. Peter's boarding school. ④ Very soon Queen's popularity extended beyond the shores of the UK as they charted and triumphed around Europe, Japan and the USA where in 1979 they topped the charts with Freddie's song Crazy Little thing Called Love.

문 4. (A), (B), (C)의 각 부분에서 어법에 맞는 표현으로 가장 적절한 것은?

Mel Blanc, considered by many industry experts to be the inventor of cartoon voice acting, began his career in 1927 as a voice actor for a local radio show. The producers did not have the funds to hire many actors, so Mel Blanc resorted to (A) [create / creating] different voices and personas for the show as needed. He became a regular on The Jack Benny Program, (B) [where / which] he provided voices for many characters — human, animal, and nonliving objects such as a car in need of a tune-up. The distinctive voice he created for Porky Pig fueled his breakout success at Warner Bros. Soon Blanc was closely associated with many of the studio's biggest cartoon stars as well as characters from Hanna-Barbera Studios. His longest running voice-over was for the character Daffy Duck — about 52 years. Blanc was extremely protective of his work — screen credits reading "Voice Characterization by Mel Blanc" (C) [was / were] always under the terms of his contracts.

*personas (극 · 소설 등의) 등장인물

	(A)	(B)	(C)
①	create	where	was
②	create	which	were
③	creating	where	were
④	creating	which	was

문 5. 다음 빈칸에 들어갈 말로 가장 적절한 것은?

With the present plummeting demand market for office buildings, resulting in many vacant properties, we need to develop plans that will enable some future exchange between residential and commercial or office functions. This vacancy has reached a historic level; at present the major towns in the Netherlands have some five million square metres of unoccupied office space, while there is a shortage of 160,000 homes. At least a million of those square metres can be expected to stay vacant, according to the association of Dutch property developers. There is a real threat of 'ghost towns' of empty office buildings springing up around the major cities. In spite of this forecast, office building activities are continuing at full tilt, as these were planned during a period of high returns. Therefore, it is now essential that _____.

① a new design be adopted to reduce costs for the maintenance of buildings
② a number of plans for office buildings be redeveloped for housing
③ residential buildings be converted into commercial buildings
④ we design and deliver as many shops as possible

문 6. 다음 글의 내용과 가장 일치하는 것은?

Child psychologists concentrate their efforts on the study of the individual from birth through age eleven. Developmental psychologists study behavior and growth patterns from the prenatal period through maturity and old age. Many clinical psychologists specialize in dealing with the behavior problems of children. Research in child psychology sometimes helps shed light on work behavior. For example, one study showed that victims of childhood abuse and neglect may suffer long-term consequences. Among them are lower IQs and reading ability, more suicide attempts, and more unemployment and low-paying jobs. Many people today have become interested in the study of adult phases of human development. The work of developmental psychologists has led to widespread interest in the problems of the middle years, such as the mid-life crisis. A job-related problem of interest to developmental psychologists is why so many executives die earlier than expected after retirement.

① 아동심리학의 연구대상은 주로 사춘기 이후의 아동이다.
② 발달심리학자들은 인간의 일생의 행동과 성장을 연구한다.
③ 아동기에 학대 받은 성인의 실업률이 더 낮은 경향이 있다.
④ 임원들의 은퇴 후 조기 사망이 최근 임상심리학의 관심사이다.

문 7. 다음 글의 내용을 한 문장으로 요약하고자 한다. 빈칸 (A), (B)에 들어갈 말로 가장 적절한 것은?

One presentation factor that can influence decision making is the contrast effect. For example, a $70 sweater may not seem like a very good deal initially, but if you learn that the sweater was reduced from $200, all of a sudden it may seem like a real bargain. It is the contrast that "seals the deal." Similarly, my family lives in Massachusetts, so we are very used to cold weather. But when we visit Florida to see my aunt and uncle for Thanksgiving, they urge the kids to wear hats when it is 60 degree outside — virtually bathing suit weather from the kids' perspective! Research even shows that people eat more when they are eating on large plates than when eating from small plates; the same portion simply looks larger on a small plate than a large plate, and we use perceived portion size as a cue that tells us when we are full.

↓

The contrast effect is the tendency to ___(A)___ a stimulus in different ways depending on the salient comparison with ___(B)___.

	(A)	(B)
①	perceive	previous experience
②	provide	predictive future
③	perceive	unexpected events
④	provide	initial impressions

문 8. 다음 글의 밑줄 친 부분 중 문맥상 낱말의 쓰임이 가장 적절하지 <u>않은</u> 것은?

Most of the fatal accidents happen because of over speeding. It is a natural subconscious mind of humans to excel. If given a chance man is sure to achieve infinity in speed. But when we are sharing the road with other users we will always remain behind some or other vehicle. ① <u>Increase</u> in speed multiplies the risk of accident and severity of injury during accident. Faster vehicles are more prone to accident than the slower one and the severity of accident will also be more in case of faster vehicles. ② <u>The higher</u> the speed, the greater the risk. At high speed the vehicle needs greater distance to stop — i.e., braking distance. A slower vehicle comes to halt immediately while faster one takes long way to stop and also skids a ③ <u>short</u> distance because of The First Law of Motion. A vehicle moving on high speed will have greater impact during the crash and hence will cause more injuries. The ability to judge the forthcoming events also gets ④ <u>reduced</u> while driving at faster speed which causes error in judgment and finally a crash.

*severity: 심함

문 9. 다음 글의 요지로 가장 적절한 것은?

It is first necessary to make an endeavor to become interested in whatever it has seemed worth while to read. The student should try earnestly to discover wherein others have found it good. Every reader is at liberty to like or to dislike even a masterpiece but he is not in a position even to have an opinion of it until he appreciates why it has been admired. He must set himself to realize not what is bad in a book, but what is good. The common theory that the critical faculties are best developed by training the mind to detect shortcoming is as vicious as it is false. Any carper can find the faults in a great work; it is only the enlightened who can discover all its merits. It will seldom happen that a sincere effort to appreciate a good book will leave the reader uninterested.

① Give attention to a weakness which can damage the reputation of a book.
② Try to understand the value of the book worthwhile to read before judging it.
③ Read books in which you are not only interested but also uninterested.
④ Until the book is finished, keep a critical eye on the theme.

문 10. 다음 도표의 내용과 가장 일치하지 <u>않는</u> 문장은?

Majority of Americans say organic produce is healthier than conventionally grown produce

% of U.S. adults who say organic fruits and vegetables are _____ than conventionally grown produce

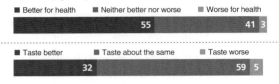

■ Better for health	■ Neither better nor worse	■ Worse for health
55	41	3

■ Taste better	■ Taste about the same	■ Taste worse
32	59	5

Note: Respondents who did not give an answer are not shown.
Source: Survey conducted May 10-June 6. 2016.
"The New Food Fights: U.S. Public Divides Over Food Science"

PEW RESEARCH CENTER

Most Americans are buying organic foods because of health concerns. ① More than half of the public says that organic fruits and vegetables are better for one's health than conventionally grown produce. ② More than forty percent say organic produce is neither better nor worse for one's health and the least number of people say that organic produce is worse for one's health. ③ Fewer Americans say organic produce tastes better than conventionally grown fruits and vegetables. ④ About one-third of U.S. adults say that organic produce tastes better, and over two-thirds of people says that organic and conventionally grown produce taste about the same.

문 11. 밑줄 친 brush them off가 다음 글에서 의미하는 바로 가장 적절한 것은?

Much of the communication between doctor and patient is personal. To have a good partnership with your doctor, it is important to talk about sensitive subjects, like sex or memory problems, even if you are embarrassed or uncomfortable. Most doctors are used to talking about personal matters and will try to ease your discomfort. Keep in mind that these topics concern many older people. You can use booklets and other materials to help you bring up sensitive subjects when talking with your doctor. It is important to understand that problems with memory, depression, sexual function, and incontinence are not necessarily normal parts of aging. A good doctor will take your concerns about these topics seriously and not <u>brush them off</u>. If

you think your doctor isn't taking your concerns seriously, talk to him or her about your feelings or consider looking for a new doctor.

*incontinence: (대소변)실금

① discuss sensitive topics with you
② ignore some concerns you have
③ feel comfortable with something you say
④ deal with uncomfortable subjects seriously

문 12. 다음 빈칸에 들어갈 말로 가장 적절한 것은?

Although we all possess the same physical organs for sensing the world — eyes for seeing, ears for hearing, noses for smelling, skin for feeling, and mouths for tasting — our perception of the world depends to a great extent on the language we speak, according to a famous hypothesis proposed by linguists Edward Sapir and Benjamin Lee Whorf. They hypothesized that language is like a pair of eyeglasses through which we "see" the world in a particular way. A classic example of the relationship between language and perception is the word snow. Eskimo languages have as many as 32 different words for snow. For instance, the Eskimos have different words for falling snow, snow on the ground, snow packed as hard as ice, slushy snow, wind-driven snow, and what we might call "cornmeal" snow. The ancient Aztec languages of Mexico, in contrast, used only one word to mean snow, cold, and ice. Thus, if the Sapir-Whorf hypothesis is correct and we can perceive only things that we have words for, the Aztecs perceived snow, cold, and ice as _____.

① one and the same phenomenon
② being distinct from one another
③ separate things with unique features
④ something sensed by a specific physical organ

문 13. 글의 흐름으로 보아, 주어진 문장이 들어가기에 가장 적절한 곳을 고르시오.

> "Soft power" on the contrary is "the ability to achieve goals through attraction and persuasion, rather than coercion or fee."

The concept of "soft power" was formed in the early 1990s by the American political scientist, deputy defense of the Clinton's administration, Joseph Nye, Jr. The ideas of the American Professor J. Nye allowed to take a fresh look at the interpretation of the concept of "power," provoked scientific debate and stimulated the practical side of international politics. (①) In his works he identifies two types of power: "hard power" and "soft power." (②) He defines "hard power" as "the ability to get others to act in ways that contradict their initial preferences and strategies." (③) The "soft power" of the state is its ability to "charm" other participants in the world political process, to demonstrate the attractiveness of its own culture (in a context it is attractive to others), political values and foreign policy (if considered legitimate and morally justified). (④) The main components of "soft power" are culture, political values and foreign policy.

*contradict: 부인하다, 모순되다

문 14. 다음 글의 주제로 가장 적절한 것은?

> The rapidity of AI deployment in different fields depends on a few critical factors: retail is particularly suitable for a few reasons. The first is the ability to test and measure. With appropriate safeguards, retail giants can deploy AI and test and measure consumer response. They can also directly measure the effect on their bottom line fairly quickly. The second is the relatively small consequences of a mistake. An AI agent landing a passenger aircraft cannot afford to make a mistake because it might kill people. An AI agent deployed in retail that makes millions of decisions every day can afford to make some mistakes, as long as the overall effect is positive. Some smart robot technology is already happening in retail. But many of the most significant changes will come from deployment of AI rather than physical robots or autonomous vehicles.

① dangers of AI agent
② why retail is suited for AI
③ retail technology and hospitality
④ critical factors of AI development

문 15. 다음 빈칸에 들어갈 말로 가장 적절한 것은?

> "_____" is the basic understanding of how karma works. The word karma literally means "activity." Karma can be divided up into a few simple categories — good, bad, individual and collective. Depending on one's actions, one will reap the fruits of those actions. The fruits may be sweet or sour, depending on the nature of the actions performed. Fruits can also be reaped in a collective manner if a group of people together perform a certain activity or activities. Everything we say and do determines what's going to happen to us in the future. Whether we act honestly, dishonestly, help or hurt others, it all gets recorded and manifests as a karmic reaction either in this life or a future life. All karmic records are carried with the soul into the next life and body.

① It never rains but it pours
② A stitch in time saves nine
③ Many hands make light work
④ What goes around comes around

문 16. 다음 글에서 필자가 주장하는 바로 가장 적절한 것은?

Creating a culture that inspires out-of-the-box thinking is ultimately about inspiring people to stretch and empowering them to drive change. As a leader, you need to provide support for those times when change is hard, and that support is about the example you set, the behaviors you encourage and the achievements you reward. First, think about the example you set. Do you consistently model out-of-the-box behaviors yourself? Do you step up and take responsibility and accountability, focus on solutions and display curiosity? Next, find ways to encourage and empower the people who are ready to step out of the box. Let them know that you recognize their efforts; help them refine their ideas and decide which risks are worth taking. And most importantly, be extremely mindful of which achievements you reward. Do you only recognize the people who play it safe? Or, do you also reward the people who are willing to stretch, display out-of-the-box behaviors and fall short of an aggressive goal?

*mindful: 신경을 쓰는, 염두에 두는

① 책임감 있는 리더가 되기 위해서는 보편적 윤리관을 가져야 한다.
② 구성원에 따라 다양한 전략과 전술을 수립하고 적용해야 한다.
③ 팀원들의 근무 환경 개선을 위해 외부의 평가를 받아야 한다.
④ 팀원에게 창의적인 사고를 할 수 있는 토대를 만들어줘야 한다.

※ 다음 글을 읽고 물음에 답하시오.   [문 17 ~ 문 18]

The dictionary defines winning as "achieving victory over others in a competition, receiving a prize or reward for achievement." However, some of the most meaningful wins of my life were not victories over others, nor were there prizes involved. To me, winning means overcoming obstacles.

My first experience of winning occurred in elementary school gym. Nearly every day, after the warm up of push-ups and squat thrusts, we were forced to run relays. Although I suffered from asthma as a child, my team won many races. My chest would burn terribly for several minutes following these races, but it was worth it to feel so proud, not because I'd beaten others, but because I had overcome a handicap. By the way, I (A) "outgrew" my chronic condition by age eleven.

In high school, I had another experience of winning. Although I loved reading about biology, I could not bring myself to dissect a frog in lab. I hated the smell of anything dead, and the idea of cutting open a frog (B) disgusted me. Every time I tried to take the scalpel to the frog, my hands would shake and my stomach would turn. Worst of all, my biology teacher reacted to my futile attempts with contempt. After an (C) amusing couple of weeks, I decided get hold of myself. I realized that I was overreacting. With determination, I swept into my next lab period, walked up to the table, and with one swift stroke, slit open a frog. After that incident, I (D) excelled in biology. I had conquered a fear of the unknown and discovered something new about myself. I had won again.

Through these experiences, I now know that I appreciate life more if have to sacrifice to overcome these impediments. This is a positive drive for me, the very spirit of winning.

*asthma: 천식, dissect: 해부하다, futile: 헛된, 효과 없는

문 17. 윗글의 제목으로 가장 적절한 것은?
① What Winning Is to Me
② The Pursuit of Happiness
③ Winners in the Second Half
④ Narratives of Positive Thinking

문 18. 밑줄 친 (A)~(D) 중에서 문맥상 낱말의 쓰임이 가장 적절하지 않은 것은?
① (A)   ② (B)   ③ (C)   ④ (D)

문 19. 다음 글의 내용을 요약할 때 빈칸 (A), (B)에 들어갈 말로 가장 적절한 것은?

One classic psychology study involved mothers and their twelve-month-old babies. Each mother was with her baby throughout the study, but the mothers were divided into two groups, A and B. Both groups A and B were exposed to the same situation, the only difference being that group B mothers had to positively encourage their baby to continue playing with the thing in front of them, whereas the mothers in group A just had to be themselves in response to what their baby was playing with.

What were these babies playing with? An extremely large but tame python. The study went as follows: the children from group A were placed on the floor so the python could slither among them. As the fear of snakes is innate in humans but isn't activated until approximately the age of two, these babies saw the python as a large toy. As the group A babies started playing with the live python, they looked up to see what their mothers were doing. The mothers, who were told to be themselves, naturally looked horrified. Seeing the fear on their mothers' faces, the babies burst into tears. When it was group B's turn, as instructed the mothers laughed and encouraged their babies to keep playing with the python. As a result these babies were grabbing and chewing on the python, all because their mothers were supportive of their new toy.

*slither: 미끄러져 가다

↓

_____(A)_____ are learned, usually by children watching a parent's _____(B)_____ to certain things.

	(A)	(B)
①	Rules of the game	support
②	Preferences for toys	participation
③	All phobias	reaction
④	Various emotions	encouragement

문 20. 다음 글의 밑줄 친 부분 중, 문맥상 낱말의 쓰임이 가장 적절하지 <u>않은</u> 것은?

According to the modernization theory of aging, the status of older adults declines as societies become more modern. The status of old age was low in hunting-and-gathering societies, but it ① <u>rose</u> dramatically in stable agricultural societies, in which older people controlled the land. With the coming of industrialization, it is said, modern societies have tended to ② <u>revalue</u> older people. The modernization theory of aging suggests that the role and status of older adults are ③ <u>inversely</u> related to technological progress. Factors such as urbanization and social mobility tend to disperse families, whereas technological change tends to devalue the wisdom or life experience of elders. Some investigators have found that key elements of modernization were, in fact, broadly related to the ④ <u>declining</u> status of older people in different societies.

문 21. 다음 글의 밑줄 친 부분 중 어법상 <u>틀린</u> 것은?

Rice stalks lower their heads when they are mature and corn kernels remain on the shoots even when they are ripe. This may not seem strange, but, in reality, these types of rice and corn should not survive in nature. Normally, when they mature, seeds should fall down to the ground in order to germinate. However, rice and corn are mutants, and they have been modified to keep their seeds ① <u>attached</u> for the purpose of convenient and efficient harvesting. Humans have continuously selected and bred such mutants, through breeding technology, in order ② <u>for these phenomena</u> to occur. These mutant seeds have been spread intentionally, ③ <u>which</u> means that the plants have become artificial species not found in nature, ④ <u>having bred</u> to keep their seeds intact. By nurturing these cultivars, the most preferred seeds are produced.

*germinate: 발아하다, cultivar: 품종

문 22. (A), (B), (C)에서 어법에 맞는 표현으로 가장 적절한 것은?

First impression bias means that our first impression sets the mold (A) [which / by which] later information we gather about this person is processed, remembered, and viewed as relevant. For example, based on observing Ann-Chinn in class, Loern may have viewed her as a stereotypical Asian woman and assumed she is quiet, hard working, and unassertive. (B) [Reached / Having reached] these conclusions, rightly or wrongly, he now has a set of prototypes and constructs for understanding and interpreting Ann-Chinn's behavior. Over time, he fits the behavior consistent with his prototypes and constructs into the impression (C) [that / what] he has already formed of her. When he notices her expressing disbelief over his selection of bumper stickers, he may simply dismiss it or view it as an odd exception to her real nature because it doesn't fit his existing prototype.

	(A)	(B)	(C)
①	which	Reached	that
②	which	Having reached	what
③	by which	Having reached	that
④	by which	Reached	what

문 23. 다음 글의 밑줄 친 부분 중, 어법상 틀린 것은?

The wave of research in child language acquisition led language teachers and teacher trainers to study some of the general findings of such research with a view to drawing analogies between first and second language acquisition, and even to ① justifying certain teaching methods and techniques on the basis of first language learning principles. On the surface, it is entirely reasonable to make the analogy. All children, ② given a normal developmental environment, acquire their native languages fluently and efficiently. Moreover, they acquire them "naturally," without special instruction, ③ despite not without significant effort and attention to language. The direct comparisons must be treated with caution, however. There are dozens of salient differences between first and second language learning; the most obvious difference, in the case of adult second language learning, ④ is the tremendous cognitive and affective contrast between adults and children.

문 24. 다음 글의 밑줄 친 부분 중 문맥상 낱말의 쓰임이 가장 적절하지 않은 것은?

The American physiologist Hudson Hoagland saw scientific mysteries everywhere and felt it his calling to solve them. Once, when his wife had a fever, Hoagland drove to the drugstore to get her aspirin. He was quick about it, but when he returned, his normally ① reasonable wife complained angrily that he had been slow as molasses. Hoagland wondered if her fever had ② distorted her internal clock, so he took her temperature, had her estimate the length of a minute, gave her the aspirin, and continued to have her estimate the minutes as her temperature dropped. When her temperature was back to normal he plotted the logarithm and found it was ③ linear. Later, he continued the study in his laboratory, artificially raising and lowering the temperatures of test subjects until he was certain he was right: higher body temperatures make the body clock go faster, and his wife had not been ④ justifiably cranky.

*molasses: 당밀, logarithm: (수학) 로그

문 25. 다음 빈칸에 들어갈 말로 가장 적절한 것은?

Saint Paul said the invisible must be understood by the visible. That was not a Hebrew idea, it was Greek. In Greece alone in the ancient world people were preoccupied with the visible; they were finding the satisfaction of their desires in what was actually in the world around them. The sculptor watched the athletes contending in the games and he felt that nothing he could imagine would be as beautiful as those strong young bodies. So he made his statue of Apollo. The storyteller found Hermes among the people he passed in the street. He saw the god "like a young men at that age when youth is loveliest," as Homer says. Greek artists and poets realized how splendid a man could be, straight and swift and strong. He was the fulfillment of their search for beauty. They had no wish to create some fantasy shaped in their own minds. All the art and all the thought of Greece _____.

① had no semblance of reality
② put human beings at the center
③ were concerned with an omnipotent God
④ represented the desire for supernatural power

해설편 ▶ P.163

문 1. 다음 글의 주제로 가장 적절한 것은?

Short-term stress can boost your productivity and immunity. But when stress lingers, you may find yourself struggling. People show some signs when they suffer from more stress than when they are healthy. First, you can't concentrate. In times of stress, your body goes into fight or flight mode, pouring its efforts into keeping safe from danger. That's why it may be hard to concentrate on a single task, and you're more likely to get distracted. "The brain's response becomes all about survival", says Heidi Hanna, author of *Stressaholic: 5 Steps to Transform Your Relationship with Stress.* "The fear response takes up all the energy of the brain for how to protect yourself." Second, you tend to get pessimistic. Because you're primed for survival, your brain has more circuits to pay attention to negatives than to positives. "When you're feeling overwhelmed by the chaos of life, take time to appreciate everything that's going well. You have to be intentional about practicing positivity", Hanna says.

① Advantages of short-term stress
② Why people keep distracted
③ Dangers of pessimism
④ Signs of excessive stress

문 2. 다음 글의 빈칸 (A), (B)에 들어갈 말로 가장 적절한 것은?

Sometimes, the meaning of analogies may not be obvious. For instance, what comes to mind when you hear the phrase "white elephant" or "black sheep"? The expression "white elephant" comes from Thailand. Long ago, in Thailand, white elephants were very rare. Whenever one was found, it was given to the king. The king would then give

it as a royal "gift" to someone he did not like since the beautiful animal cost a fortune to take care of. Nobody could refuse such a present, but it could financially ruin its owner. Moreover, it was a serious crime to mistreat a present from the king. Even riding it was not allowed, so a white elephant was almost useless. The expression, introduced in England in the 18th century, turned out to be useful for describing ____(A)____ but ____(B)____ public buildings. Today, it is used to refer to anything that might be ____(A)____ and ____(B)____.

	(A)	(B)
①	valuable	unprotected
②	costly	worthless
③	extravagant	appropriate
④	priceless	eco-friendly

문 3. 다음 글의 밑줄 친 부분 중 문맥상 낱말의 쓰임이 적절하지 않은 것은?

When asked, nearly everyone says the proper response to a compliment is "Thank you". But researchers found that when actually given a compliment, only a third of people accept it so ① simply. The difficulty lies in the fact that every compliment ("What a nice sweater!") has two levels: a gift component (accept or reject) and a content component (agree or disagree). The recipient is confronted with a ② dilemma — how to respond simultaneously to both: "I must agree with the speaker and thank him for the gift of a compliment while avoiding self-praise." Interestingly, women and men are both ③ less likely to accept a compliment coming from a man than from a woman. When a man says, "Nice scarf," a woman is more likely to respond ④ affirmatively: "Thanks. My sister knitted it for me." But when one woman tells another, "That's a beautiful sweater," the recipient is likely to disagree or deflect. "It was on sale, and they didn't even have the colour I wanted."

문 4. 다음 글의 빈칸 (A), (B)에 들어갈 말로 가장 적절한 것은?

The chairperson should seek to have a progressive discussion that leads towards a consensus view. As the discussion develops, the chairperson should be searching to find the direction in which the weight of members' views is pointing. If, _____(A)_____, there are five members and the chair senses that two want to follow course A and a third follow course B, the focus should quickly be turned towards the remaining two members. The chair turns to member 4. If he or she wants course A, the chairperson simply has the job of getting first the other neutral (member 5) and then the dissenting member 3 to assent to the fact that course A is the majority view. If, _____(B)_____, member 4 wants course B, then member 5's view is the critical one, which the chairperson must now bring in. And so, very quickly, you can sense where the balance of opinion is pointing, and lead the meeting towards unanimous assent.

*consensus 의견 일치 **unanimous 만장일치의

	(A)	(B)
①	whereas	likewise
②	for example	therefore
③	whereas	for instance
④	for example	on the other hand

문 5. 다음 글의 제목으로 가장 적절한 것은?

As early as 525 BCE, a Greek named Theagenes, who lived in southern Italy, identified myths as scientific analogies or allegories — an attempt to explain natural occurrences that people could not understand. To him, for instance, the mythical stories of gods fighting among themselves were allegories representing the forces of nature that oppose each other, such as fire and water. This is clearly the source of a great many explanatory or "causal" myths, beginning with the accounts found in every society or civilization that explain the creation of the universe, the world, and humanity. These "scientific" myths attempted to explain seasons, the rising and setting of the sun, the course of the stars. Myths like these were, in some ways, the forerunners of science. Old mythical explanations for the workings of nature began to be replaced by

a rational attempt to understand the world, especially in the remarkable era of Greek science and philosophy that began about 500 BCE.

① Myths : Basis of Scientific Inquiry
② Dispelling the Myths about Science
③ How Are Creation Myths Universal
④ How Much Myths Affect Our World Views

문 6. 다음 글의 내용과 일치하는 것은?

Every year in early October, Helsinki's harbor changes into a lively, colorful set for the Baltic Herring Festival, first held in 1743. Fishermen from all over Finland bring their latest catch to Helsinki to take part in one of Finland's oldest festivals. Sellers in bright orange tents line the harbor and sell herring in every imaginable form: fried, pickled, smoked, in bottles, in cans, in soup, on pizza, and in sandwiches. The choices are endless. On the first day of the festival, competitions are held to select the most delicious seasoned herring and the best herring surprise. Herring surprise is a traditional dish made with herring, cheese, and onions. The winner of each competition is awarded a trophy.

① The festival has been held in every second year since 1743.
② Sellers set up orange tents along the harbor and sell herring.
③ The competition of the festival is limited to Helsinki residents.
④ A trophy is only given to the winner of the best herring surprise.

문 7. 다음 글의 밑줄 친 부분 중 문맥상 낱말의 쓰임이 적절하지 않은 것은?

As a youngster I shared a bedroom with my older sister. Although the age difference was slight, in intellect and maturity she viewed me from across the great divide. Her serious academic and cultural pursuits contrasted sharply with my activities of closely monitoring the radio shows. Because of these ① dissimilar interests and the limited resource of one bedroom between us, we frequently had conflict over what constituted disturbing and inconsiderate behavior. For months, there were attempts to ② compromise by "splitting the difference" in our divergent viewpoints or practicing "share and share alike." Even with written schedules and agreements plus parental mediation, the controversy persisted. Ultimately the matter was ③ aggravated when we both came to recognize that considerable time and energy were being wasted as we maneuvered and positioned ourselves for the next mathematical compromise. With recognition of a ④ common interest in solving the problem for our mutual benefit, we were able to think beyond physical resources of space, hours, and materials. The satisfying solution that met both of our needs was the purchase of earphones for the radio.

문 8. 다음 글의 빈칸에 들어갈 말로 가장 적절한 것은?

One of the most popular of computer games in the world is called Age of Empires. For several months my own ten-year-old son was all but addicted to it. Its organizing premise is that the history of the world is the history of imperial conflict. Rival political entities vie with one another to control finite resources: people, fertile land, forests, gold mines and waterways. In their endless struggles the competing empires must strike a balance between the need for economic development and the exigencies of warfare. The player who is too aggressive soon runs out of resources if he has not taken the trouble to cultivate his existing territory, to expand its population and to accumulate gold. The player who focuses too much on getting rich may find himself _____ if he meanwhile neglects his defenses.

*exigencies 긴급 사태

① immune to illness
② tolerant to change
③ vulnerable to invasion
④ addicted to entertainment

문 9. 다음 글에서 전체 흐름과 관계없는 문장은?

Can an old cell phone help save the rainforests? As a matter of fact, it can. Illegal logging in the rainforests has been a problems for years, but not much has been done about it because catching illegal loggers is difficult. ① To help solve this problem, an American engineer, Topher White, invented a device called RFCx with discarded cell phones. ② When the device, which is attached to a tree, picks up the sound of chainsaws, it sends an alert message to the rangers' cell phones. ③ This provides the rangers with the information they need to locate the loggers and stop the illegal logging. ④ Destruction of the rainforest is caused by logging, farming, mining, and other human activities and among these, logging is the main reason for the nature's loss. The device has been tested in Indonesia and has proven to work well. As a result, it is now being used in the rainforests in Africa and South America.

문 10. 다음 글의 제목으로 가장 적절한 것은?

In any symphony, the composer and the conductor have a variety of responsibilities. They must make sure that the brass horns work in synch with the woodwinds, that the percussion instruments don't drown out the violas. But perfecting those relationships — important though it is — is not the ultimate goal of their efforts. What conductors and composers desire is the ability to marshal these relationships into a whole whose magnificence exceeds the sum of its parts. So it is with the high-concept aptitude of Symphony. The boundary crosser, the inventor, and the metaphor maker all understand the importance of relationships. But the Conceptual Age also demands the ability to grasp the relationships between relationships. This meta-ability goes by many names — systems thinking, gestalt thinking, holistic thinking.

*marshal 모으다, 결집시키다

① The Power of Music
② Seeing the Big Picture
③ The Essence of Creativity
④ Collaboration Makes a Difference

문 11. 다음 글의 밑줄 친 부분 중 어법상 옳지 않은 것은?

In criminal cases, the burden of proof is often on the prosecutor to persuade the trier (whether judge or jury) ① that the accused is guilty beyond a reasonable doubt of every element of the crime charged. If the prosecutor fails to prove this, a verdict of not guilty is ② rendered. This standard of proof contrasts with civil cases, ③ where the claimant generally needs to show a defendant is liable on the balance of probabilities (more than 50% probable). In the USA, this is ④ referring to as the preponderance of the evidence.

문 12. 다음 밑줄 친 This system이 의미하는 바로 가장 적절한 것은?

In order to meet the demands of each course, Escoffier modernized meal preparation by dividing his kitchens into five different sections. The first section made cold dishes and organized the supplies for the whole kitchen. The second section took care of soups, vegetables, and desserts. The third dealt with dishes that were roasted, grilled, or fried. The fourth section focused only on sauces, and the last was for making pastries. This allowed restaurant kitchens to make their dishes much more quickly than in the past. If a customer ordered eggs Florentine, for example, one section would cook the eggs, another would make the sauce, and yet another would make the pastry. Then, the head chef would assemble the dish before it was served to the customer. This system was so efficient that it is still used in many restaurants today.

① The competition of the different sections in the kitchen
② The extended room for preparing the necessary ingredients
③ The distribution of the separate dishes to the customer by the head chef
④ The kitchen being divided into different sections to prepare a meal

문 13. 다음 글의 내용을 한 문장으로 요약하고자 한다. 빈칸 (A), (B)에 들어갈 말로 가장 적절한 것은?

McAdams makes an important point about identity: It is a story you tell about yourself to make sense out of what has happened in the past and the kind of person you are now. From this perspective, it is not essential that the story be true. I see myself as culturally adventurous (that is, high on openness). I happen to believe this is true — that is, compared with others, I would be relatively open to trying new things on a menu, taking up new activities, visiting new places, and so on. But, from McAdams's perspective, when we're talking about identity, whether our beliefs about ourselves are true or not is pretty much irrelevant.

⬇

According to McAdams, our identity is a(n) _____(A)_____ that we create, which in itself may or may not be _____(B)_____.

	(A)	(B)
①	adventure	exciting
②	image	visible
③	door	available
④	narrative	factual

문 14. 다음 밑줄 친 단어(어구)가 가리키는 대상이 나머지 셋과 다른 것은?

Watson had been watching ① his companion intently ever since he had sat down to the breakfast table. Holmes happened to look up and catch his eye.

"Well, Watson, what are you thinking about?" he asked.

"About you."

"② Me?"

"Yes, Holmes. I was thinking how superficial are these tricks of yours, and how wonderful it is that the public should continue to show interest in them."

"I quite agree," said Holmes. "In fact, I have a recollection that I have ③ myself made a similar remark."

"Your methods," said Watson severely, "are really easily acquired."

"No doubt", Holmes answered with a smile. "Perhaps you will ④ yourself give an example of this method of reasoning."

문 15. 다음 글의 밑줄 친 부분 중 어법상 옳지 <u>않은</u> 것은?

In the 1860s, the populations of Manhattan and Brooklyn were rapidly increasing, and ① so was the number of the commuters between them. Thousands of people took boats and ferries across the East River every day, but these forms of transport were unstable and frequently stopped by bad weather. Many New Yorkers wanted to have a bridge directly ② connected Manhattan and Brooklyn because it would make their commute quicker and safer. Unfortunately, because of the East River's great width and rough tides, ③ it would be difficult to build anything on it. It was also a very busy river at that time, with hundreds of ships constantly ④ sailing on it.

문 16. 다음 글의 밑줄 친 부분 중 어법상 옳지 <u>않은</u> 것은?

In recent years, peer-peer (P2P) lending has ① become the poster child of the alternative finance industry. In a 2015 report Morgan Stanley predicted that such marketplace lending ② would command $150 billion to $490 billion globally by 2020. P2P lending is the practice of lending money to individuals or businesses through online services that match lenders-investors directly with borrowers, ③ enabled both parties to go around traditional providers such as banks. Lenders typically achieve better rates of return, while borrowers — individuals and SMEs (small and medium-sized enterprises) — get access to flexible and competitively priced loans. For investors, the benefits are attractive. Being ④ matched with a borrower can take anywhere from a few days to a few hours. And where a bank might typically earn under 2% on personal lending, P2P returns can be more than three times that.

문 17. 다음 글에 드러난 "I"의 심경으로 가장 적절한 것은?

So when I stood at the plate in that Old Timers game, staring at a pitcher whose hair was gray, and when he threw what used to be his fastball but what now was just a pitch that floated in toward my chest, and when I swung and made contact and heard the familiar thwock, and I dropped my bat and began to run, convinced that I had done something fabulous, forgetting my old gauges, forgetting that my arms and legs lacked the power they once had, forgetting that you age, the walls get farther away, and when I looked up and saw what I had first thought to be a solid hit, maybe a home run, now coming down just beyond the infield toward the waiting glove of the second baseman, no more than a pop-up, a wet firecracker, a dud, and a voice in my head yelled, "Drop it! Drop it!" as that second baseman squeezed his glove around my final offering to this maddening game.

① jealous ② delighted
③ passionate ④ disappointed

문 18. 다음 글의 밑줄 친 부분 중 문맥상 낱말의 쓰임이 적절하지 <u>않은</u> 것은?

In our daily conscious activity, we generally experience a ① separation between the mind and the body. We think about our bodies and our physical actions. Animals do not experience this division. When we start to learn any skill that has a physical component, this separation becomes even ② less apparent. We have to think about the various actions involved, the steps we have to follow. We are aware of our slowness and of how our bodies respond in an awkward way. At certain points, as we ③ improve, we have glimpses of how this process could function differently, of how it might feel to practice the skill fluidly, with the mind not getting in the way of the body. With such glimpses, we know what to aim for. If we take our practice far enough the skill becomes ④ automatic, and we have the sensation that the mind and the body are operating as one.

문 19. 다음 글의 밑줄 친 부분 중 어법상 옳지 않은 것은?

In 2000, scientists at Harvard University suggested a neurological way of ① explaining Mona Lisa's elusive smile. When a viewer looks at her eyes, the mouth is in peripheral vision, ② which sees in black and white. This accentuates the shadows at the corners of her mouth, making the smile ③ seems broader. But the smile diminishes when you look straight at it. It is the variability of her smile, the fact that it changes when you look away from it, ④ that makes her smile so alive, so mysterious.

문 20. 글의 흐름으로 보아, 주어진 문장이 들어가기에 가장 적절한 곳은?

So around about the time we are two, our brains will already have distinct and individual patterns.

When we are babies our brains develop in relationship with our earliest caregivers. Whatever feelings and thought processes they give to us are mirrored, reacted to and laid down in our growing brains. (①) When things go well, our parents and caregivers also mirror and validate our moods and mental states, acknowledging and responding to what we are feeling. (②) It is then that our left brains mature sufficiently to be able to understand language. (③) This dual development enables us to integrate our two brains, to some extent. (④) We become able to begin to use the left brain to put into language the feelings of the right.

문 21. 글의 흐름으로 보아, 주어진 문장이 들어가기에 가장 적절한 곳은?

Nowadays, it is much easier to find out where you are and which way to go because you have one of the world's greatest inventions at your fingertips.

For thousands of years, humans had difficulty trying to figure out where they were. (①) So, they devoted a great deal of time and effort to resolving this problem. (②) They drew complicated maps, constructed great landmarks to keep themselves on the right path, and even learned to navigate by looking up at the stars. (③) As long as you have a Global Positioning System(GPS) receiver, you never have to worry about taking a wrong turn. (④) Your GPS receiver can tell you your exact location and give you directions to wherever you need to go, no matter where you are on the planet!

문 22. 다음 글의 빈칸에 들어갈 말로 가장 적절한 것은?

A great ad is a wonderful thing; it's why you love advertising. But what you're looking at is only half of what's there, and the part you can't see has more to do with that ad's success than the part you can. Before those surface features (the terrific headline or visual or storyline or characters or voiceover or whatever) can work their wonders, the ad has to have something to say, something that matters. Either it addresses real consumer motives and real consumer problems, or it speaks to no one. To make great ads, then, you have to start where they start: with _____.

① the effective tool
② the invisible part
③ the corporate needs
④ the surface features

문 23. 글의 흐름으로 보아, 주어진 문장이 들어가기에 가장 적절한 곳은?

> Wham-O, the visionary toy company known for its Hula-Hoops bought the rights a year later and renamed the flying disc Frisbee.

Walter Fredrick Morrison and his girlfriend, Lucile Nay, discovered that flying discs were marketable when a stranger asked to buy the metal cake pan they were flipping through the air on a beach in California. (①) By 1938, the couple were selling the 5-cent pans for 25 cents a piece. (②) Later, Morrison tried his hand at developing a flying disc far better than that of a flying cake pan. (③) Together with Franscioni, he created the Pluto Platter. (④) By the mid-1960s it got so popular that you could see a Frisbee stuck on almost every roof of houses.

문 24. 다음 글의 빈칸에 들어갈 말로 가장 적절한 것은?

Paradoxically, the initial discovery of an interest often goes unnoticed by the discoverer. In other words, when you just start to get interested in something, you may not even realize that's what's happening. The emotion of boredom is always self-conscious — you know it when you feel it — but when your attention is attracted to a new activity or experience, you may have very little reflective appreciation of what's happening to you. This means that, at the start of a new endeavor, asking yourself nervously every few days whether you've found your passion is _____.

① relevant
② necessary
③ premature
④ uncommon

문 25. 다음 글의 밑줄 친 부분 중 어법상 옳지 않은 것은?

After lots of trial and error, Richard finally created a system of flashing LED lights, ① powered by an old car battery that was charged by a solar panel. Richard set the lights up along the fence. At night, the lights could be seen from outside the stable and took turns flashing, ② which appeared as if people were moving around with torches. Never again ③ lions crossed Richard's fence. Richard called his system Lion Lights. This simple and practical device did no harm to lions, so human beings, cattle, and lions were finally able to make peace with ④ one another.

해설편 ▶ P.171

2017
2월 25일 시행
법원직 9급

| 풀이 시간: ____:____ ~ ____:____ / 점수: ____점

문 1. 다음 글의 밑줄 친 부분 중 문맥상 낱말의 쓰임이 적절하지 않은 것은?

All living things share basic characteristics. These common threads can be explained by descent from a common ancestor. Many kinds of evidence suggest that life began with ① single cells and that the present rainbow of organisms evolved from this common origin over hundreds of millions of years. In other words, the process of ② evolution explains the unity we observe in living things. The other striking thing about life on earth is its diversity. The same coral reef contains a multitude of animal species. Yet, each body type suits a ③ particular lifestyle. The process of evolution, which involves changes in the genetic material and then physical modifications suited to different environments, explains the ④ unity we observe in living things.

문 2. 다음 글의 빈칸에 들어갈 내용으로 가장 적절한 것은?

A biology teacher cannot teach proteins, carbohydrates, fats, and vitamins, without having understood the basics of organic chemistry. The teacher while teaching the use of a thermometer can discuss various scales of measuring temperature. If he or she says that the body temperature of a healthy human being is 37℃ and a student wants to know the temperature in Kelvin or Fahrenheit, then the teacher can satisfy the student only if he or she knows the process of converting one scale of temperature to another. In the same way, a chemistry teacher when teaching proteins, enzymes, carbohydrates, and fats, etc. should have some understanding of the human digestive system to be able to explain these concepts effectively by relating the topic to the life experiences of the learners. Thus, all branches of science _____.

① cannot be taught and learned in isolation
② converge on knowledge of organic chemistry
③ are interrelated with each learner's experiences
④ should be acquired with the basics of chemistry

문 3. 다음 글에서 밑줄 친 표현의 쓰임이 문맥상 적절하지 않은 것은?

Left alone, Dodge quickly ① lay down on the burnt soil. As the flames approached him, he covered his mouth with a wet handkerchief in order not to ② breathe in the smoke. As the fire surrounded him, Dodge closed his eyes and tried to breathe from the ③ thick layer of oxygen that remained near the ground. Several painful minutes passed, and Dodge survived the fire, unharmed. Sadly, with the ④ exception of two men who found shelter in a small crack in a rock, all of the other men died in the awful fire.

문 4. 글의 흐름으로 보아 아래 문장이 들어가기에 가장 적절한 곳은?

One population of Berwick's swans wintering in England put on fat more rapidly than usual, making them ready to begin their Siberian migration early.

Wherever human light spills into the natural world, some aspect of life — breeding, feeding, migration — is affected. Some birds — blackbirds and nightingales, among others — sing at unnatural hours in the presence of artificial light. (①) Scientists have determined that long artificial days — and artificially short nights — induce early breeding in a wide range of birds. (②) And because a longer day allows for longer feeding, it can also affect migration schedules. (③) The problem with them is that migration, like most other aspects of bird behavior, is a precisely timed biological behavior. (④) Leaving early may mean arriving too soon for nesting conditions to be right.

문 5. (A), (B), (C)의 각 네모 안에서 어법에 맞는 표현으로 가장 적절한 것은?

Once we emerge from childhood, eye contact actually becomes a very unreliable clue to deception. Why? The answer is that eye contact is very easy to control. Much of what happens to us when we feel nervous, such as getting sweaty hands or feeling dry in the mouth, (A) is / being uncontrollable. Most of us, however, have a great deal of control over (B) which / what we're looking at. Thus, many adults have little problem looking others in the eye while lying to them. Moreover, because skilled communicators know that people (C) equate / equating the lack of eye contact with deception, they deliberately maintain normal eye contact when they lie so the other person won't get suspicious. The eyes may be the windows to the soul, as the saying goes, but eye contact is no window to honesty!

	(A)	(B)	(C)
①	is	which	equate
②	being	which	equating
③	is	what	equate
④	being	what	equating

문 6. 다음 갈등해결을 위한 조언으로 빈칸 (A)~(D)에 적절하지 않은 것은?

Tips for Conflict Resolution

(A)

Maintaining and strengthening the relationship, rather than "winning" the argument, should always be your first priority. Be respectful of the other person and his or her viewpoint.

(B)

If you're holding on to old hurts and resentments, your ability to see the reality of the current situation will be impaired. Rather than looking to the past and assigning blame, focus on what you can do right now to solve the problem.

(C)

Conflicts can be draining, so it's important to consider whether the issue is really worthy of your time and energy. Maybe you don't want to yield a parking space if you've been circling for 15 minutes. But if there are dozens of spots, arguing over a single space isn't worth it.

(D)

If you can't come to an agreement, agree to disagree. It takes two people to keep an argument going. If a conflict is going nowhere, you can choose to move on.

① (A) Make the relationship your priority.
② (B) Focus on the present.
③ (C) Weigh your words before speaking.
④ (D) Know when to let something go.

문 7. 다음 글의 빈칸에 들어갈 내용으로 가장 적절한 것은?

By "scarcity," most of us mean that goods are in short supply: there isn't enough of something to go around. While there often is no clear-cut understanding of what constitutes "enough," the simple fact is that there is more than sufficient food to sustain everyone on the planet. The same is true of land and renewable energy. The important question, then, is why the staples of life are so unequally distributed — why, for example, the United States, with a little more than 5 percent of the world's population, uses approximately 40 percent of the world's resources. What appears to be a problem of scarcity usually turns out, on closer inspection, to be a problem of distribution. But mainstream economists ＿＿＿＿＿＿＿＿＿: they talk only about whether a given system is productive or efficient, and it is up to us to ask, "For whom?"

① avert their eyes from this problem
② pay attention to reducing inequality
③ cling to solving distributional issues
④ have no interest in improving efficiency

문 8. 다음 글의 내용을 요약할 때 빈칸 (A), (B)에 들어갈 말로 가장 적절한 것은?

Injuries sometimes occur when people do not take adequate carefulness with everyday activities. Although some such injuries occur because of pure carelessness or misfortune, others happen because the person did not want others to perceive him or her as too careful. For example, many people seem to avoid wearing seat belts in automobiles, helmets on bicycles and motorcycles, and life preservers in boats because such devices convey an impression of excessive carefulness. In addition, many people seem reluctant to wear protective gear (e.g., safety goggles, gloves, and helmets) when operating power tools or dangerous machinery because they will be viewed as nervous or extremely careful. This concern emerges at a young age; anecdotally, children as young as 6 or 7 years old are sometimes unwilling to wear knee pads and helmets when rollerskating because of what other children will think of them.

↓

Why do people get injured?
1. People lack _____(A)_____.
2. People tend to take a risk of danger rather than be viewed as _____(B)_____.

	(A)	(B)
①	vigilance	overcautious
②	inattention	intimidated
③	prudence	audacious
④	heedlessness	vulnerable

문 9. 다음 글의 밑줄 친 부분 중 어법상 쓰임이 적절하지 <u>않은</u> 것은?

Performing from memory is often seen ① to have the effect of boosting musicality and musical communication. It is commonly argued that the very act of memorizing can guarantee a more thorough knowledge of and intimate connection with the music. In addition, memorization can enable use of direct eye contact with an audience ② who is more convincing than reference to the score. Those who "possess" the music in this way often convey the impression that they are spontaneously and sincerely communicating from the heart, and indeed, contemporary evidence suggests that musicians who achieve this ③ are likely to find their audiences more responsive. Moreover, when performers receive and react to visual feedback from the audience, a performance can become truly interactive, ④ involving genuine communication between all concerned.

문 10. 다음 글의 밑줄 친 부분 중 문맥상 낱말의 쓰임이 적절하지 <u>않은</u> 것은?

Even though people seek both social status and affluence, their primary goal is to attain social status. A case can be made, in particular, that their pursuit of affluence is instrumental: they pursue it not for its own sake but because ① increased affluence will enhance their social standing. Why, after all, do they want the clothes, the car, and the house they long for? In large part because ② attaining these things will impress other people. Indeed, if there were no one around to impress, few would feel driven to live a life of ③ frugality, even if they could gain that without having to work for it. Likewise, if wealthy individuals found themselves living in a culture in which people ④ despised rather than admired those who live in luxury, one imagines that they would abandon their mansion and late-model car in favor of a modest home with an old car parked in the driveway.

문 11. 다음 글에서 전체 흐름과 <u>관계없는</u> 문장은?

It is generally believed that primates first appeared on Earth approximately 80 million years ago. Unlike reptiles, they were very sociable animals, creating a large community. ① One of the many ways in which the primates built a network of social support was grooming. ② In most cases, primates have visible folds that they would not have if they had, even lightly, groomed the area. ③ For instance, apes spent a large amount of time grooming each other. ④ Interestingly, in the case of Barbary macaques, the giving of grooming resulted in more stress relief than the receiving of grooming.

문 12. 다음 글에서 전체 흐름과 <u>관계없는</u> 문장은?

Most people agree that Plato was a pretty good teacher. He frequently used stories to teach people how to think. One story Plato used to teach about the limitations of democracy was about a ship in the middle of the ocean. On this ship was a captain who was rather shortsighted and slightly deaf. ① He and his crew followed the principles of majority rule on decisions about navigational direction. ② They had a very skilled navigator who knew how to read the stars on voyages, but the navigator was not very popular and was rather introverted. ③ As you know, it's not easy to communicate with introverted people, in particular, on the ship. ④ In the panic of being lost, the captain and crew made a decision by voting to follow the most charismatic and persuasive of the crew members. They ignored and ridiculed the navigator's suggestions, remained lost, and ultimately starved to death at sea.

문 13. 다음 글의 빈칸 (A), (B)에 들어갈 말로 가장 적절한 것은?

Before the creation of money, people used to exchange something they had for something they needed. This system of exchange is called bartering. People traded things like animal furs, shells, beads for necklaces, and cloth. Later, people realized that some items were easier to trade than others, and those items became more common in bartering. _____(A)_____, people could trade gold for almost any other item because most people knew that it was valuable and that they could easily trade it again if they needed to. After some time, certain goods became the standard goods of exchange, and everyone began to trade with the same items. Eventually, the standard goods became money — one common unit of trade most people accepted and used in business and for their daily lives. _____(B)_____, some people still use the barter system today, especially in developing countries, where people exchange different kinds of food in order to survive.

	(A)	(B)
①	Furthermore	For instance
②	In other words	Besides
③	In contrast	However
④	For example	Nevertheless

문 14. 다음 글의 빈칸 (A), (B)에 들어갈 말로 가장 적절한 것은?

Many people find it difficult to relate to someone who has a physical disability, often because they have not had any personal interaction with anyone with a disability. _____(A)_____, they might be unsure what to expect from a person who has a mobility impairment and uses a wheelchair because they have never spent any time with wheelchair users. This lack of understanding can create additional challenges for people with disabilities. If society responded more adequately to people who have impairments, they would not experience nearly as many challenges and limitations. Consider office workers who happen to use wheelchairs. Provided that there is only one level or there are ramps or elevators between levels, they may need no assistance whatsoever in the workplace. _____(B)_____, in an adapted work environment, they do not have a disability.

	(A)	(B)
①	However	Thus
②	In contrast	Similarly
③	Furthermore	In addition
④	For example	In other words

문 15. 다음 글에 나타난 필자의 심경 변화로 가장 적절한 것은?

I was always mad at Charles even though I couldn't ever put my finger on exactly what he was doing to make me angry. Charles was just one of those people who rubbed me the wrong way. Yet, I was constantly upset. When we began looking at anger in this class, I thought, "What's my primary feeling about Charles?" I almost hate to admit what I found out because it makes me look like I'm a lot more insecure than I feel I really am, but my primary feeling was fear. I was afraid that Charles with his brilliance and sharp tongue was going to make me look stupid in front of the other students. Last week I asked him to stay after class and I just told him how threatened I get when he pins me down on some minor point. He was kind of stunned, and said he wasn't trying to make me look bad, that he was really trying to score brownie points with me. We ended up laughing about it and I'm not threatened by him anymore. When he forgets and pins me down now, I just laugh and say, "Hey, that's another brownie point for you."

*brownie point: 윗사람의 신임 점수

① relieved → irritated
② uneasy → relieved
③ calm → envious
④ frightened → indifferent

문 16. 다음 글의 제목으로 가장 적절한 것은?

Amid the confusion and clutter of the natural environment, predators concentrate their search on telltale signs, ignoring everything else. There is a great benefit to this: When you specialize in searching for specific details, even cryptically colored prey can seem obvious. But there is also a cost to paying too close attention, since you can become blind to the alternatives. When a bird searches intently for caterpillars that look like twigs, it misses nearby moths that look like bark. The benefit of concealing coloration is not that it provides a solid guarantee of survival, but that it consistently yields a small advantage in the chance of living through each successive threatening encounter. At a minimum, even a tiny delay between the approach of a predator and its subsequent attack can help a prey animal escape. And at best, the prey will be completely overlooked.

① Predators in Disguise
② Beauty of Concentration
③ Camouflage: A Slight Edge
④ Merits of Specialized Search

문 17. 글의 흐름으로 보아 아래 문장이 들어가기에 가장 적절한 곳은?

But let us say that the ranger who painted the sign meant to say just the opposite.

An ambiguous term is one which has more than a single meaning and whose context does not clearly indicate which meaning is intended. For instance, a sign posted at a fork in a trail which reads "Bear To The Right" can be understood in two ways. (①) The more probable meaning is that it is instructing hikers to take the right trail, not the left. (②) He was trying to warn hikers against taking the right trail because there is a bear in the area through which it passes. (③) The ranger's language was therefore careless, and open to misinterpretation which could have serious consequences. (④) The only way to avoid ambiguity is to spell things out as explicitly as possible: "Keep left. Do not use trail to the right. Bears in the area."

문 18. 다음 글의 제목으로 가장 적절한 것은?

River otters have webbed toes, short legs, and tapered tails. For this reason, the river otter has a streamlined body, which helps it to move through the water very easily. Sea otters are near-sighted largely because aquatic life is much more important to them than terrestrial life. As a result, the sea otter is not as well-equipped for terrestrial life as for aquatic life.

① What Is Difference Between Aquatic and Terrestrial Life?
② Are Otters Aquatic or Terrestrial Animals?
③ Physical Characteristics of Sea Otters
④ Otter: A Perfect Terrestrial Life

문 19. 밑줄 친 it이 가리키는 대상이 나머지 셋과 <u>다른</u> 하나는?

Black pepper is one of the most widely used spices in the world. At first, it was cultivated in India as a simple ingredient for cooking. However, ① it became a lot more important to some Europeans who also used it for keeping meat from going bad. Until the 15th century, some cities in Italy were the center for trading black pepper. As the Ottoman Empire in the Middle East grew stronger in the 16th century, however, ② it forced the European traders to pay them a high tax. This made black pepper so expensive that only a few rich people could afford ③ it. In some parts of Europe, black pepper was even considered as valuable as gold. The great demand for ④ it caused Europeans to search for new sea routes to India.

문 20. 다음 글의 빈칸 (A), (B)에 들어갈 말로 가장 적절한 것은?

In addition to the problems of individual resources, there are increasing links among energy, food, and water. As a result, problems in one area can spread to another, creating a _____(A)_____ circle. For instance, Uganda experienced a prolonged drought in 2004 and 2005, threatening the food supply. The country was using so much water from massive Lake Victoria that the water level fell by a full meter, and Uganda cut back on hydroelectric power generation at the lake. Electricity prices nearly doubled, so Ugandans began to use more wood for fuel. People cut heavily into forests, which _____(B)_____ the soil. The drought that began as a threat to food sources became an electricity problem and, eventually, an even more profound food problem. Cycles like these can end in political unrest and disasters for whole populations.

	(A)	(B)
①	vicious	fertilized
②	virtuous	deteriorated
③	destructive	degraded
④	constructive	undermined

문 21. 다음 도표의 내용과 일치하는 문장은?

Reading proficiency of boys and girls at age 15 in OECD countries

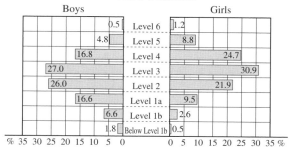

This graph compares the percentages of male and female students in OECD countries who achieved various levels of reading proficiency at age 15. ① The percentage of girls is more than three times the percentage of boys at Below Level 1b. ② The percentage of girls is more than twice the percentage of boys at Level 5. ③ The difference between the percentages of boys and girls is smallest at Level 4 and greatest at Level 6. ④ The percentage of girls is always higher than that of boys at Level 3 and above, whereas the percentage of boys is higher than that of girls at Level 2 and below.

문 22. 다음 글의 주제로 가장 적절한 것은?

Béla Bartók's *Duos for Two Violins* is characterized by dissonance. By employing dissonance in this work, Bartók tries to reveal the rich diversity of sounds. However, dissonance is a relative concept, and it needs to be understood in relation to consonance. Further, the dissonance prevalent in this work does not express disorder. Rather, it tries to evoke subtle harmony among individual sounds. This is mainly because dissonance can be perceived as an expression of harmonious individuality.

① ways of revealing diversity of sounds
② role of consonance in violin performance
③ importance of harmony in *Duos for Two Violins*
④ true meaning of dissonance in Béla Bartók's work

문 23. 글의 흐름으로 보아 아래 문장이 들어가기에 가장 적절한 곳은?

> Nevertheless, Schulz believed in his work and did not change Peanuts.

These dull characters created by Charles Schulz attracted neither cartoon critics nor the people at Walt Disney, who didn't want to buy Peanuts. They said the characters did not inspire people to dream or encourage them to hope. (①) Even after it became popular in many newspapers, critics still thought the comic strip would fail, criticizing it for having uninteresting characters. (②) Some people said that Snoopy, the dog, should be taken out. (③) He even kept Snoopy, who is now one of the most loved cartoon characters of all time. (④)

문 24. 다음 글의 밑줄 친 부분 중 어법상 옳은 것은?

Most of the time journalism cannot possibly offer anything but a fleeting record of events ① compiling in great haste. Many news stories are, at bottom, hypotheses about what happened. Science, of course, works by hypotheses, discarding them when errors are discovered, and it does so, on the whole, without blame, even when a mistake costs lives. The press, ② that lays no claim to scientific accuracy, is not easily forgiven its errors. Admittedly, the press often rushes into print with insufficient information, responding to an occasionally mindless hunger for news. A utopian society might demand that the press ③ print nothing until it had reached absolute certainty. But such a society, while waiting for some ultimate version of events, would be so rife with rumor, alarm, and lies ④ which the errors of our journalism would by comparison seem models of truth.

문 25. 다음 빈칸에 들어갈 내용으로 가장 적절한 것은?

Children often invent novel ways to express desired meanings. In her 1995 article, linguist Clark cited such examples as a 24-month-old saying, "There comes the rat-man" and a 25-month-old saying, "Mommy just fixed this spear-page." The "rat-man" was a colleague of her father's who worked with rats in a psychology laboratory; the "spear-page" was a torn picture of a jungle tribe holding spears that her mother had taped together. Clark also cited the example of a 28-month-old saying, "You're the sworder and I'm the gunner." As these examples suggest, children's innovative uses of language are _____. They reflect rules for forming new words, such as combining words or other components that are meaningful in their own right and that, when put together, have an unambiguous meaning. Such linguistic creativity allows children to express meanings that are well beyond what their limited vocabularies would otherwise allow.

① impromptu
② quite arbitrary
③ far from random
④ results from endless drills

해설편 ▶ P.179

| 풀이 시간: ____:____ ~ ____:____ / 점수: ____점

문 1. 다음 글의 빈칸에 들어갈 말로 가장 적절한 것은?

Anthropologists believe wisdom teeth, or the third set of molars, were the evolutionary answer to our ancestor's early diet of coarse, rough food — like leaves, roots, nuts and meats — which required more chewing power and resulted in excessive wear of the teeth. The modern diet with its softer foods, along with marvels of modern technologies such as forks, spoons and knives, has made the need for wisdom teeth nonexistent. As a result, evolutionary biologists now classify wisdom teeth as vestigial organs, or body parts that have become functionless due to _____.

① dental decay
② evolution
③ hardness
④ their shape

문 2. 주어진 글 다음에 이어질 글의 순서로 가장 적절한 것은?

In today's technology-driven world, almost everyone, at some point in their lives, has either used or had some sort of contact with a microwave oven. Like many of the great inventions of our past, the idea behind the microwave oven was accidentally stumbled upon in 1946.

(A) Shortly after the accidental discovery, engineers at Raytheon went to work on Spencer's new idea, developing and refining it to be of practical use.

(B) Dr. Percy Spencer was working as an engineer with the Raytheon Corporation at the time, when he discovered something very unusual one day while working on a radar-related research project. While testing a new vacuum tube known as a magnetron, he discovered that a candy bar in his pocket had melted.

(C) Intrigued as he was, Spencer decided upon further experimentation. Later on, having pointed the tube at such objects as a bag of popcorn kernels and an egg, with similar results in both experiments (the popcorn popped and the egg exploded), he correctly concluded that the observed effects in each case were all attributed to exposure to low-density microwave energy.

① (A) − (C) − (B)
② (B) − (A) − (C)
③ (B) − (C) − (A)
④ (C) − (B) − (A)

문 3. 다음 글의 밑줄 친 부분 중, 어법상 옳지 않은 것은?

To "win hands down" which means to "win easily" or "win with little or no effort" has ① its origins in horse racing. In a close, photo-finish race, a jockey ② typically strikes his horse with a bat or the reins to force it to maintain or increase speed. When the horse is leading by several lengths and a win is assured, the jockey will usually cease striking the horse or let the reins ③ go loose: In effect, he puts his "hands down." The expression ④ was appeared in the mid-19th century; by the end of the century, it was being used outside of horse racing to mean "with no trouble at all."

문 4. 다음 밑줄 친 (A), (B), (C)에서 문맥에 맞는 낱말로 가장 적절한 것은?

In many ways, the differences between pairs of training shoe are marginal. Mr. Twitchell calls them fungible, "essentially interchangeable." But successive savvy advertising strategies turned a little Oregon sports outfitter into the globally (A) dominant / dormant sports giant Nike. Their swoosh logo is now one of the most recognizable images on the planet, rendering the actual name unnecessary. And while Nike may not have been the first company to seek (B) celebrator / celebrity plugs, its relationship with Michael Jordan is arguably the most successful endorsement in history. The release of the Just Do It motto in 1988 was a (C) transparent / transformative moment for the company, weaving their brand, seemingly forever, with the inspiring and dramatic physicality of sport.

	(A)	(B)	(C)
①	dominant	celebrator	transparent
②	dormant	celebrator	transformative
③	dominant	celebrity	transformative
④	dormant	celebrity	transparent

문 5. 밑줄 친 he[him]가 가리키는 대상이 나머지 셋과 다른 하나는?

"There may be a devilish Indian behind every tree." said Goodman Brown to himself; and ① he glanced fearfully behind him as he added, "What if the devil himself should be at my very elbow!" His head being turned back, ② he passed a crook of the road, and, looking forward again, beheld the figure of a man, in grave and decent attire seated at the foot of an old tree. He arose at Goodman Brown's approach and walked onward side by side with ③ him. "You are late, Goodman Brown," said the man. "My wife kept me back a while," he replied, with a tremor in his voice, caused by the sudden appearance of ④ him, though not wholly unexpected.

문 6. 다음 글의 밑줄 친 부분 중, 문맥상 낱말의 쓰임이 적절하지 않은 것은?

Our "ego" or self-conception could be pictured as a leaking balloon, forever requiring the helium of external love to remain ① inflated, and ever vulnerable to the smallest pinpricks of neglect. There is something at once sobering and absurd in the extent to which we are lifted by the attentions of others and sunk by their ② disregard. Our mood may ③ brighten because a colleague greets us distractedly or our telephone calls go unreturned. And we are capable of thinking life ④ worthy of living because someone remembers our name or sends us a fruit basket.

문 7. 다음 글의 제목으로 가장 적절한 것은?

If a black hole has a non-zero temperature — no matter how small — the most basic and well-established physical principles would require it to emit radiation, much like a glowing poker. But black holes, as everyone knows, are black; they supposedly do not emit anything. This was the case until Hawking, in 1974, discovered something truly amazing. Black holes, Hawking announced, are not completely black. If one ignores quantum mechanics and invokes only the laws of classical general relativity, then as originally found some six decades previously, black holes certainly do not allow anything — not even light — to escape their gravitational grip. But the inclusion of quantum mechanics modifies this conclusion in a profound way, and Hawking found that black holes do emit radiation, quantum mechanically.

① What Happens inside Black Holes?
② Mystery of the Quantum World
③ The Birth of General Relativity
④ Is a Black Hole Really Black?

문 8. 다음 글에서 전체 흐름과 관계없는 문장은?

For the New World as a whole, the Indian population decline in the century or two following Columbus's arrival is estimated to have been as large as 95 percent. The main killers were Old World germs to which Indians had never been exposed, and against which they therefore had neither immune nor genetic resistance. ① Smallpox, measles, influenza, and typhus competed for top rank among the killers. ② For example, in 1837 the Mandan Indian tribe, with one of the most elaborate cultures in our Great Plains, contracted smallpox from a steamboat traveling up the Missouri River from St. Louis. ③ The Mandan survived mainly by hunting, farming and gathering wild plants, though some food came from trade. ④ The population of one Mandan village plummeted from 2,000 to fewer than 40 within a few weeks.

문 9. 다음 글의 빈칸에 들어갈 말로 가장 적절한 것은?

Most of the world's great cities have grown randomly, little by little, in response to the needs of the moment; very rarely is a city planned for the remote future. The evolution of a city is like the evolution of the brain: it develops from a small center and slowly grows and changes, leaving many old parts still functioning. There is no way for evolution to remove _____ and replace it with something of more modern manufacture. The brain must function during the renovation. That is why our brain stem is surrounded by the R-complex, then the limbic system and finally the cerebral cortex. The old parts are in charge of too many fundamental functions for them to be replaced altogether. So they wheeze along, out-of-date and sometimes counterproductive, but a necessary consequence of our evolution.

*R-complex: (두뇌의) R영역
**limbic system: (두뇌의) 변연계
***cerebral cortex: 대뇌피질

① the arrangement of new city streets
② the invasion of an alien substance
③ the advantage of natural selection
④ the ancient interior of the brain

문 10. 주어진 글 다음에 이어질 글의 순서로 가장 적절한 것은?

The "denotation" of a word is what the word literally means. *Blue*, for instance, means "the color of the sky on a sunny day."

(A) Likewise, We would like to have friends who are "true *blue*," to win a "*blue* ribbon", and to own "*blue*-chip stocks". But we might not like being called a "*bluenose*".
(B) As you see above, even a simple word naming a color can have a wide range of possible meanings, depending on how it's used. This is what is meant by connotation, the implied (suggested) meaning of a word.
(C) Beyond the denotation of the word, however, we also can find many other meanings in the name of the color. We usually do not like feeling *blue*, but we may enjoy hearing a great *blues* singer.

① (B) − (A) − (C)   ② (B) − (C) − (A)
③ (C) − (A) − (B)   ④ (C) − (B) − (A)

문 11. 주어진 글 다음에 이어질 글의 순서로 가장 적절한 것은?

> "Begin with the End in Mind" is based on the principle that all things are created twice. There's a mental or first creation, and a physical or second creation to all things.

> (A) If you want a family-centered home, you plan a family room where it would be a natural gathering place. You plan sliding doors and a patio for children to play outside. You work with ideas. You work with your mind until you get a clear image of what you want to build.
>
> (B) Take the construction of a home, for example. You design it in every detail before you ever hammer the first nail into place. You try to get a very clear sense of what kind of house you want.
>
> (C) Then you reduce it to blueprint and develop construction plans. All of this is done before the earth is touched. If not, then in the second creation, the physical creation, you will have to make expensive changes that may double the cost of your home.

① (A) − (C) − (B) ② (B) − (A) − (C)
③ (B) − (C) − (A) ④ (C) − (B) − (A)

문 12. 주어진 글 다음에 이어질 글의 순서로 가장 적절한 것은?

> Observations are not always undertaken with a clear sense of what data may be relevant. On a long and rough sea voyage in 1882, many of the ship's passengers were afflicted with seasickness.

> (A) James speculated that seasickness must be due to some temporary disturbance of the inner ear, a problem to which the deaf mutes were not sensitive at all. Later experimentation, some carried out by James, confirmed this suspicion.
>
> (B) This crucial clue about the causes of seasickness came thanks to James' ability to see the importance of something interesting that others had overlooked.
>
> (C) One who was not was the American philosopher and psychologist, William James. James had the great good fortune to notice that 15 of the passengers, all of whom were deaf and mute, were completely unaffected.

① (A) − (C) − (B)
② (B) − (C) − (A)
③ (C) − (A) − (B)
④ (B) − (A) − (C)

문 13. 다음 글의 내용을 한 문장으로 요약하고자 한다. 빈칸 (A)와 (B)에 들어갈 말로 가장 적절한 것은?

> Umpires and other sports officials are the decision-makers and rulebook enforcers whose word is law on the field of play. Such authority comes with heavy responsibility to match. Sports officials must be unbiased masters of the rules and have thick skins. They must keep control of the conduct of games at all times, be good communicators, and stay cool in situations that can quickly grow heated — both on the field and in the stands. For every winner in sports there is a loser, of course, and the outcome may ride on a few crucial calls. Was that three-and-two pitch a ball or a strike? Was that last-second basket a buzzer-beater or not? While instant replay provides a fallback in professional and big-time college sports, officials at other levels are on their own. The stakes can be higher than just one game. High school athletes may hope for college scholarships, and key calls against them could hurt their chances when scouts are on hand. As one veteran high school official put it, "You never know who's in the stands."

⬇

> The roles of umpires are so (A) that they can have (B) influence on players' individual future plans as well as the play at the field.

	(A)	(B)
①	professional	slight
②	expansive	significant
③	ambiguous	valuable
④	comprehensive	positive

문 14. 다음 글의 빈칸에 들어갈 말로 가장 적절한 것은?

Why would anyone be foolish enough to argue about the money supply? The more money, the merrier, right? Wrong. In slapstick movie, bumbling gangsters drop suitcases filled with bills, and bystanders dive past one another hoping to grab a few. The passer-bys always smile, but the bad guys wail and so do economists. Why do economists cry with the gangsters? A problem does not arise when just a few suitcases burst open. But if lots of luggage were to suddenly flood a town with bills, ＿＿＿＿＿＿ might follow. If the amount of money overwhelms the capacity to produce goods, consumers, with more money to spend, bid up prices. The town is no wealthier than before; more bills do not bring a higher standard of living any more than if everyone added two zeroes to his or her salary.

① recession
② inflation
③ bankruptcy
④ unemployment

문 15. 다음 글의 (A), (B), (C)의 각 밑줄 친 부분 중 어법상 낱말의 쓰임이 적절한 것을 바르게 나열한 것은?

Exactly how, when, why, and where the first maps came to be created is difficult to discover. Much of what was drawn in prehistoric and early historical times (A) [has / have] not survived, so what we find today may not be wholly representative of what was once there. There are other problems for the modern observer. Maps (B) [make / made] in prehistoric times cannot be accompanied by a title that explains the meaning of the drawing or that describes its content. However, we may be sure that in early times, just like today, maps were created for a variety of purposes and (C) [took / taken] a variety of forms. It may also be clear that, contrary to popular belief, of all the purposes to which maps have been put through the ages, the least important single purpose has been to find the way. Sea charts did not come into existence until the European Middle Ages, and topographical maps were not normally carried about by land travelers until the 18th century.

	(A)	(B)	(C)
①	have	make	taken
②	have	made	took
③	has	made	taken
④	has	made	took

문 16. 글의 흐름으로 보아 주어진 문장이 들어가기에 가장 적절한 것은?

Recordings at theaters around the world show that the pattern transcends different cultural habits and that different crowds all follow one universal curve showing how the sound rises over several seconds.

When the curtain closes at any stage theater, the audience bursts into applause. ㉠ It's usually a few clappers who hesitantly start on their own, and then others join in. ㉡ Applause is a funny thing in which each person tries to give credit to the performers, but also tries to blend into the crowd; you don't want to clap before everyone else, or to go on after others have stopped. ㉢ In fact, if you study it, you'll discover there is a pronounced pattern in the way an audience goes from silence to full volume of applause. ㉣ Even more remarkably, this curve is absolutely identical to a curve known from physics that describes how a group of atoms or molecules collectively go from one kind of behavior to another, rapidly and abruptly, because what one does depends very strongly on what others nearby do.

① ㉠
② ㉡
③ ㉢
④ ㉣

문 17. 다음 글의 빈칸 (A), (B)에 들어갈 말로 가장 적절한 것은?

Fifty years ago, bees lived healthy lives in our cities and rural areas because they had plenty of flowers to feed on, fewer insecticides contaminating their floral food and fewer exotic diseases and pests. Wild bees nested successfully in undisturbed soil and twigs. _____(A)_____, bees have trouble finding pollen and nectar sources because of the extensive use of herbicides that kill off so many flowering plants among crops and in ditches, roadsides and lawns. Flowers can be contaminated with insecticides that can kill bees directly or lead to chronic, debilitating effects on their health. _____(B)_____, with the increase in global trade and transportation, blood-sucking parasites, viruses and other bee pathogens have been inadvertently transmitted to bees throughout the world. These parasites and pathogens weaken bees' immune systems, making them even more susceptible to effects of poor nutrition from lack of flowers, particularly in countries with high agricultural intensity and pesticide use.

	(A)	(B)
①	However	As a result
②	However	In addition
③	Thus	By contrast
④	Thus	On the other hand

문 18. 밑줄 친 (A), (B), (C)에서 문맥에 맞는 낱말로 가장 적절한 것은?

Sea foam forms when the ocean is agitated by wind and waves. Each coastal region has (A) differing / diffusing conditions governing the formation of sea foams. Algal blooms are one common source of thick sea foams. When large blooms of algae decay offshore, great amounts of decaying algal matter often wash ashore. Foam forms as this organic matter is churned up by the (B) surface / surf. Most sea foam is not harmful to humans and is often an indication of a productive ocean ecosystem. But when large harmful algal blooms decay near shore,

there are potential for impacts to human health and the environment. Along Gulf coast beaches during blooms of Karenia brevis, for example, popping sea foam bubbles are one way that algal toxins become airborne. The resulting aerosol can (C) irrigate / irritate the eyes of beach goers and poses a health risk for those with asthma or other respiratory conditions.

	(A)	(B)	(C)
①	differing	surface	irrigate
②	diffusing	surface	irritate
③	diffusing	surf	irrigate
④	differing	surf	irritate

문 19. 글의 흐름으로 보아, 주어진 문장이 들어가기에 가장 적절한 것은?

However, elevated levels and/or long term exposure to air pollution can lead to more serious symptoms and conditions affecting human health.

A variety of air pollutants have been known to be or suspected to cause harmful effects on human health and the environment. In most areas of Europe, these pollutants are principally the products of combustion from space heating, power generation or from motor vehicle traffic. ㉠ Pollutants from these sources may not only prove a problem in the immediate vicinity of these sources but can travel long distances. ㉡ Generally if you are young and in a good state of health, moderate air pollution levels are unlikely to have any serious short term effects. ㉢ This mainly affects the respiratory and inflammatory systems, but can also lead to more serious conditions such as heart disease and cancer. ㉣ People with lung or heart conditions may be more susceptible to the effects of airpollution.

① ㉠   ② ㉡   ③ ㉢   ④ ㉣

문 20. 다음 글의 빈칸 (A), (B)에 들어갈 말로 가장 적절한 것은?

Sea snakes are some of the most venomous creatures on Earth. Their venom is far deadlier than the venom of coral snakes, rattlesnakes, or even king cobras. Sea snakes use their venom to kill the fish they eat and to defend themselves against predators. It's not necessarily a good thing, however, for a sea snake to use its venom to defend itself. Venom can take a lot of energy to make-energy that could be used for growing or hunting. _____(A)_____, the more often a sea snake or other venomous animal is attacked, the more likely it is to get hurt-even if it can defend itself. Like coral snakes, many sea snakes solve this problem by warning predators up front. _____(B)_____, the yellow-bellied sea snake has bright, splashy colors that tell predators not to try anything. Over millions of years, predators have evolved to pay attention to this warning. Only a few kinds of sharks and sea eagles dare attack sea snakes. This keeps sea snakes from constantly having to defend themselves and increases their chances of survival.

	(A)	(B)
①	However	In other words
②	Also	By contrast
③	However	In addition
④	Also	For example

문 21. 다음 글의 빈칸에 들어갈 말로 가장 적절한 것은?

Despite what you might think, _____, according to research by psychologist Richard Wiseman. Instead, it's a result of the way lucky people think and act — which means that anyone can learn to be lucky! For instance, Wiseman found that lucky people always take notice of what's going on around them and stay open to new experiences and opportunities. Meanwhile, unlucky people tend to be tenser and too focused on certain tasks, which stops them from noticing opportunities they aren't explicitly looking for. So, next time you're heading to a party, don't go in with a goal in mind(no matter how much you want to attract someone). Instead, take things as they come and you never know what might happen. You could even make some awesome new friends.

① luck isn't matter of fate or destiny
② luck brings you closer relationships
③ luck can't be obtained at any costs
④ luck is the most precious asset for a person

문 22. 다음 글의 빈칸에 들어갈 말로 가장 적절한 것은?

Coral reefs are some of the most diverse and valuable ecosystems on Earth. Coral reefs support more species per unit area than any other marine environment, including about 4,000 species of fish, 800 species of hard corals and hundreds of other species. Scientists estimate that there may be another 1 to 8 million undiscovered species of organisms living in and around reefs. _____ is considered key to finding new medicines for the 21st century. Many drugs are now being developed from coral reef animals and plants as possible cures for cancer, arthritis, human bacterial infections, viruses, and other diseases. Storehouses of immense biological wealth, reefs also provide economic and environmental services to millions of people. Coral reefs may provide goods and services worth $375 billion each year. This is an amazing figure for an environment that covers less than 1 percent of the Earth's surface.

① This biodiversity
② Their beauty
③ Survival skill of coral reefs
④ Food chain

문 23. 다음 글의 목적으로 가장 적절한 것은?

> Dear Charles,
>
>   It was a pleasure having lunch with you yesterday. I am very interested in the new household product you mentioned and how I might work with you develop it. I have seen nothing like it advertised in any of the trade journals, so it may be an original, one-of-a-kind product. If so, you will want to move fast to register it to protect your intellectual property rights in it. Let me know if you want to pursue this and I will have our patent associate contact you with a proposal. Let's get together again soon.
>
> Until then,
> Frank

① 새로 구입한 가정용품을 환불하려고
② 새로 개발한 가정용품 구매를 요청하려고
③ 새로 개발한 가정용품에 대해 표창하려고
④ 새로 개발한 가정용품의 특허등록을 제안하려고

문 24. 다음 글에서 필자가 주장하는 바로 가장 적절한 것은?

>   I have always taught my children that politeness, learning, and order are good things, and that something good is to be desired and developed for its own sake. But at school they learned, and very quickly, that children earn Nature Trail tickets for running the quarter-mile track during lunch recess. Or Lincoln Dollars for picking up trash on the playground or for helping a young child find the bathroom — deeds that used to be called 'good citizenship.' Why is it necessary to buy the minimal cooperation of children with rewards or treats? What disturbs me is the idea that good behavior must be reinforced with incentives. Children must be taught to perform good deeds for their own sake, not in order to receive stickers, stars, and candy bars.

① 아이들은 예절에 관한 교육을 잘 받아야 한다.
② 금전적이거나 물질적인 보상은 아이를 망친다.
③ 아이들이 보상 없이도 선행하도록 교육시켜야 한다.
④ 효과적인 교육을 위해서는 적절한 칭찬을 해주어야 한다.

문 25. 다음 글에서 밑줄 친 낱말의 쓰임이 문맥상 적절하지 않은 것은?

>   Lead is a naturally occurring toxic metal found in the Earth's crust. Its widespread use has resulted ① in extensive environmental contamination, human exposure and significant public health problems in many parts of the world. Young children are particularly vulnerable to the toxic effects of lead and can suffer profound and permanent ② adverse health effects, particularly affecting the development of the brain and nervous system. Lead also causes long-term harm in adults, including ③ decreased risk of high blood pressure and kidney damage. ④ Exposure of pregnant women to high levels of lead can cause miscarriage, stillbirth, premature birth and low birth weight, as well as minor malformations.

해설편 ▶ P.186

2018~2015년 시행

교육행정직 9급 공개경쟁채용 필기시험

응시번호	
성 명	

문제책형

【시 험 과 목】

제1과목	국 어	제2과목	영 어	제3과목	한 국 사
제4·5과목	교육학개론, 행정법총론				

응시자 주의사항

1. **시험 시작 전**에 시험문제를 열람하는 행위나 **시험 종료 후** 답안을 작성하는 행위를 한 사람은 「지방공무원임용령」 제65조 등 관련 법령에 의거 **부정행위자**로 처리됩니다.

2. 시험 시작 즉시 **과목편철 순서, 문제누락 여부, 인쇄상태 이상 유무 및 표지와 개별과목의 문제책형 일치여부 등을 확인**한 후 문제책 표지에 응시번호, 성명을 기재합니다.

3. 반드시 본인의 **응시표에 인쇄된 시험과목 순서에 따라** 제4과목과 제5과목의 **답안을 표기**하여야 합니다. 과목 순서를 바꾸어 표기한 경우에도 **본인의 응시표에 기재된 과목 순서대로 채점**되므로 반드시 유의하시기 바랍니다.

4. 시험이 시작되면 문제를 주의 깊게 읽은 후, **문항의 취지에 가장 적합한 하나의 정답만을 고르며**, 문제 내용에 관한 질문은 받지 않습니다.

5. **시험시간 관리의 책임**은 전적으로 응시자 본인에게 있습니다.

2018

5월 19일 시행
교육행정직 9급

| 풀이 시간: ____:____ ~ ____:____ / 점수: ____점

※ 다음 빈칸에 들어갈 단어로 가장 적절한 것을 고르시오.
　　　　　　　　　　　　　　　　　　　[문 1 ~ 문 3]

문 1.

　　The postmodern is everywhere and nowhere. It has no zero point, no fixed essence. It contains all the traces of everything that has come before. Its dominating logic is that of a _____, never pure, always compromising, not 'either-or', but 'both-and'. The postmodern impulse is playful and paradoxical. It mocks and absorbs historical forms, always having it both ways, always modern and postmodern, nothing escapes its attention.

① reality　　　　　　② hybrid
③ specialty　　　　　④ simulation

문 2.

　　In talking with other people, don't begin by discussing the things on which you differ. Begin by emphasizing — and keep on emphasizing — the things on which you _____. Keep emphasizing, if possible, that you are both striving for the same end and that your only difference is one of method and not of purpose. Get the other person saying "Yes, yes" at the outset. Keep your opponent, if possible, from saying "No."

① live　　　　　　　② agree
③ charge　　　　　　④ doubt

문 3.

　　Under ordinary circumstances, individuals will take significant measures to avoid the huge expense of having a car stolen — parking in safe places, locking the car, using an antitheft device, etc. But once that car is insured for nearly its full replacement value, the driver has significantly less incentive to take such _____.

① discounts　　　　　② rewards
③ risks　　　　　　　④ precautions

문 4. 다음 글의 밑줄 친 부분 중 문맥상 단어의 쓰임이 적절하지 않은 것은?

　　It is important to remember that making and responding to works of art, in many media, are social practices. It is ① inconceivable that these practices are the invention of any distinct individual. Any intention on the part of an individual to make art would be ② meaningful, were there no already going practices of artistic production and response. If there are no shared criteria for artistic success, then the word art cannot be used ③ objectively, as a descriptive term. If I have only myself to go on, then "Whatever is going to seem right to me to call art is ④ right. And that only means that here we can't talk about 'right.'"

※ 다음 빈칸 (A), (B)에 들어갈 표현으로 어법상 가장 적절한 것을 고르시오.　　　　　　　[문 5 ~ 문 6]

문 5.

　　____(A)____ the Wright Brothers' maiden voyage on December 17, 1903, lasted just twelve seconds and covered only 120 feet — "you could have thrown a ball farther" — it displayed the possibility of conquering air itself to the world. The flight proved highly ____(B)____ to the U.S. government, which through the army had given seed money to a similar program under the direction of Samuel P. Langley.

	(A)	(B)
①	Despite	embarrassed
②	Despite	embarrassing
③	Although	embarrassed
④	Although	embarrassing

문 6.

Modern industrial societies and their problems are becoming increasingly complex, and because _____(A)_____ one person today can master all the social sciences, growing emphasis is placed on the interdisciplinary approach to many social problems. The interdisciplinary approach means _____(B)_____ a group of social scientists with different specialties will work together on a certain problem, not all of whose aspects any one of the group fully understands.

(A)	(B)		(A)	(B)
① no	that		② any	that
③ no	what		④ any	what

문 7. 다음 밑줄 친 단어가 가리키는 대상이 나머지 셋과 다른 것은?

Alexander loved sport, and riding more than anything. No one rode better than he. His father once bought a beautiful horse that no one could tame. His name was Bucephalus. Whenever anyone tried to mount ① him they were thrown off. But Alexander worked out why ② he did it: the horse was afraid of his own shadow. So Alexander turned the horse's head towards the sun so that he couldn't see ③ his shadow on the ground. Stroking him gently, ④ he swung himself onto his back and rode round to the applause of the whole court.

※ 다음 밑줄 친 부분 중 어법상 옳지 않은 것을 고르시오.
[문 8 ~ 문 9]

문 8.

In agreement with the Egyptian Supreme Council of Antiquities, Franck Goddio and his team ensured that artifacts ① found in their exploration would remain in the East Port until a decision can be made about the possible creation of an underwater museum at the site. Yet the significance of some of their finds was such that they were unwilling to leave ② them untouched on the seabed without establishing a precise visual record of their appearance that would permit future scholars to study them in detail. The solution lay in temporarily removing some objects from their underwater sites to permit casting and then ③ returning them to the seabed. The replication process ④ overseen by Georges Brocot, a French artist who specializes in molding techniques.

문 9.

Sustainability is a difficult and complex issue, and an elusive one. It is enormously important ① since it has to do with nothing less than the chances of humankind surviving on this planet. At the rate that the human race is using scarce and limited resources it appears that, unless measures are taken now — and if there is still time — the future of civilization, at least as we understand it now, ② is uncertain, to say the least. It follows that such a complex subject has no simple and straightforward treatment, especially ③ considered that sustainability is not a goal but a process. It leads to a better life for the present generation and survival for generations to come, ④ enhancing their ability to cope with the world that they will inherit.

문 10. 다음 대화의 빈칸에 들어갈 말로 가장 적절한 것은?

A: Jenny, have you signed up for the in-service training next week?
B: No, I haven't. How about you?
A: I've already signed up for the Wednesday session.
B: Good for you. But I'm afraid I can't make it on weekdays.
A: No worries. I heard there are weekend programs, too.
B: Really?
A: Yes, but the spaces must be limited.
B: Then, _____.
A: Yeah, you should. You know, first come, first served.

① you should have gone to them
② if I were you, I'd sign up for them
③ I'd better go and sign up right away
④ you should take a rain check this time

문 11. 다음 글의 주제로 가장 적절한 것은?

Cholesterol-lowering drugs are among the most widely used medications in the world. Your body produces cholesterol, and it's found in many foods. But what is it for? Clearly, there is a reason for cholesterol because your liver naturally makes it, but why? You may be surprised to know that your body does need cholesterol as a foundation of good health in many ways. For example, cholesterol is used by the body to make hormones that help your body respond to physical and mental stress. It also is the foundation for the production of sex hormones, contributing to regulation of body actions from puberty to pregnancy, including all aspects of reproductive function.

① the reasons we need cholesterol in our body
② the way cholesterol is produced in the body
③ the mechanism of cholesterol-lowering drugs
④ the reproductive function of cholesterol

문 12. 다음 빈칸에 들어갈 단어로 가장 적절한 것은?

Although the cinema has most often been compared with literature, it really has far more in common with architecture. Both forms are public, collaborative, and above all, _____. In both arts, economic constraints have always dictated the shape of the work produced. By comparison, literature (especially "serious" literature) seems almost a priestly calling: novelists and poets, at least since Romanticism, have (for better or worse) been largely able to write whatever pleased them, without regard for audience or expense.

① artistic   ② expensive
③ sacred   ④ productive

문 13. 다음 빈칸 (A), (B)에 들어갈 말로 가장 적절한 것은?

The motivating concepts that guide disaster management — the reduction of harm to life, property, and the environment — are largely the same throughout the world. _____(A)_____, the capacity to carry out this mission is by no means uniform. Whether due to political, cultural, economic, or other reasons, the unfortunate reality is that some countries and some regions are more capable than others at addressing the problem. But no nation, regardless of its wealth or influence, is advanced enough to be fully immune from disasters' negative effects. _____(B)_____, the emergence of a global economy makes it more and more difficult to contain the consequences of any disaster within one country's borders.

	(A)	(B)
①	However	Furthermore
②	Otherwise	Furthermore
③	However	In contrast
④	Otherwise	In contrast

문 14. Spencer Stanhope에 관한 다음 글의 내용과 일치하지 않는 것은?

Spencer Stanhope came from a middle-class family and was educated at Rugby and Christchurch, Oxford. He began to study art with G. F. Watts in 1850, visiting Italy with him in 1853. He became one of the circle of young artists around the Pre-Raphaelites in the mid-1850s and was particularly friendly with Burne-Jones, who influenced his painting and became a lifelong friend. He first exhibited at the Royal Academy in 1859 and later at the Grosvenor Gallery. Like his artist friends, he had a sympathy for ordinary people and often chose subjects showing them at work, though often in an idealized manner. *Washing Day* in which the women wash the clothes while the men get on with the business of fishing, is typical of Stanhope's work.

① 1853년에 G. F. Watts와 함께 이탈리아를 방문했다.
② Burne-Jones가 그의 그림에 영향을 주었다.
③ 1859년에 Grosvenor Gallery에서 첫 전시회를 열었다.
④ *Washing Day*는 그의 작품의 전형적인 특징을 보여준다.

문 15. 다음 글의 내용과 일치하는 것은?

> The bright butterflies and moths number 140,000 species, exceeded only by the beetles. "Lepidoptera," the order's scientific name, means "scaly-winged," and tiny scales cover the wings and bodies of most adult forms. In size, butterflies and moths vary more than any other insect group. An owlet moth of South America is a foot across; the Eriocranid moth has a quarter-inch wingspan. Some species are even smaller. There are no hard and fast rules for telling a butterfly from a moth. But in general, moths spin cocoons, butterflies do not. When at rest, the moth tends to fold its wings like a tent while the butterfly presses them together overhead.

① Lepidoptera는 모든 성충의 몸이 큰 비늘로 덮여있다는 것을 뜻한다.
② 나비와 나방은 다른 어떤 곤충집단보다 크기가 더 다양하다.
③ Eriocranid 나방은 날개 길이가 2분의 1인치이다.
④ 나비는 쉴 때 텐트처럼 날개를 접는 경향이 있다.

문 16. 다음 글의 제목으로 가장 적절한 것은?

> Archaeological finds come in many forms — as artifacts, food remains, houses, human skeletons, and so on. These finds are usually cleaned, identified, and cataloged in the field before being packed for transport to the laboratory. Once back from the field, these data — including not only finds but also the detailed notes, drawings, and other recorded data acquired in the field — are subjected to analysis. At this stage some specific materials, such as radiocarbon samples and pollen grains, are sent to specialists for analysis. Most laboratory analysis involves detailed artifact classification and study of animal bones and other food remains — the basis for the later interpretation of data.

① Various Laboratory Analyses of Archaeological Finds
② Processing and Analysis of Archaeological Finds
③ Importance of Archaeology in Human History
④ Different Types of Archaeological Finds

문 17. 주어진 글 다음에 이어질 글의 순서로 가장 적절한 것은?

> The metaphors or analogies that we chose to think about ourselves can have different effects on our understandings and our actions.

> (A) For example, Michael White and David Epson explain that if we think that people and relationships are like complex machines, we will probably see their problems as malfunctions in the machinery and the solution would be to repair them, as a mechanic would.
>
> (B) Someone who is guided by this metaphor would probably encourage the person to "vent" and express that anger to release the growing pressure.
>
> (C) An example of this is when we say that anger was building up inside us like steam in a pressure cooker and that the steam has to be let out or the cooker will explode.

① (A) − (C) − (B)
② (B) − (A) − (C)
③ (B) − (C) − (A)
④ (C) − (A) − (B)

문 18. 글의 흐름으로 보아 주어진 문장이 들어가기에 가장 적절한 곳은?

> The closer the individual film came to being described by the first term in each pair, the more its difference from Hollywood films was regarded as "innovative" and hence positive.

> Something in the German films was obviously viewed as "aesthetic," but what was it? (①) In America, the term "German cinema" came to mark out an aesthetic space, if you will, somewhere outside the normative boundaries of conventional Hollywood style. (②) At issue was how far outside, and whether this aesthetic distance from the Hollywood cinema constituted a positive or negative aesthetic difference. (③) Discussions of individual films tended to be framed by three aesthetic criteria, each having both a positive and a negative dimension: spectacular / excessive, complex / elitist, and artistic / self-indulgent. (④) A film defined by the latter terms, however, was seen as too different and hence too "strange."

문 19. 다음 글에서 전체 흐름과 관계 없는 문장은?

Leadership is centered on the communication between leaders and followers rather than on the unique qualities of the leader. ① Thought of as a relationship, leadership becomes a process of collaboration that occurs between leaders and followers. ② A leader affects and is affected by followers, and both leader and followers are affected in turn by the situation that surrounds them. ③ For example, a leader in the fund-raising campaign knows every step and procedure in the fund-raising process and is able to use this knowledge to run an effective campaign. ④ This approach emphasizes that leadership is not a linear one-way event, but rather an interactive event.

문 20. 다음 글의 요지로 가장 적절한 것은?

When the state spends money which it has raised by taxation, it is taking money out of the pockets of the taxpayers to put it into the pockets of those upon whom it is spending. The expenditure may be really an investment: education, for instance, is an investment in the young, and is universally recognised as part of the duty of the state. In such a case, provided the investment is sound, public expenditure is obviously justified: the community would not be ultimately enriched by ceasing to educate its children, nor yet by neglecting harbours, roads, and public works generally.

① The state should inform its taxpayers of its investment plans.
② Reducing public expenditure will make the community richer.
③ Public expenditure can be justified through a proper investment.
④ The state should spend more money on public works than on education.

해설편 ▶ P.196

2017

6월 17일 시행
교육행정직 9급

| 풀이 시간: ____:____ ~ ____:____ / 점수: ____점

※ 다음 빈칸에 들어갈 단어로 가장 적절한 것을 고르시오.

[문 1 ~ 문 3]

문 1.

　　Many times, when it starts raining, there is an arrangement of raindrops visible on the window. Each time it rains the arrangement is different, but they still all look the same (that is, like all the other arrangements of raindrops) because we can't see any patterns in them. There are no patterns there to detect, and our mind becomes _____ to them. That is, we do not notice them.

① alert   ② blind
③ sharp   ④ sensitive

문 2.

　　Conversation is usually _____; thus speakers have to 'think standing up'. They therefore do not have the time to plan out what they want to say, and their grammar is inevitably loosely constructed, often containing rephrasing and repetition.

① grammatical   ② organized
③ spontaneous   ④ manipulative

문 3.

　　In many markets, firms will be competing for the same consumers but will be offering products that are not merely different but that directly _____ each other. Some firms sell cigarettes; others sell products that help you quit smoking. Some firms sell fast food; others sell diet advice.

① approve   ② advertise
③ resemble   ④ oppose

문 4. 다음 글의 밑줄 친 부분 중 문맥상 단어의 쓰임이 적절하지 않은 것은?

　　Problem solving tends to be better when groups are of diverse backgrounds and abilities. When a group can draw on a rich variety of perspectives and experiences, decision making can be of higher quality than if the perspectives and experiences shared by the group members are ① different. Yet, as was the case with creativity and innovation, the most effective problem solving emerges when a ② balance of diversity exists. Diversity without any shared values and goals is likely to break a group ③ apart; however, shared values and goals may lead to what Irving Janis has termed *groupthink*. Groupthink describes what happens when groups ④ converge on a single answer to a problem and, rather than critically evaluate the solution, they convince themselves and each other that the solution they came up with is the best one.

※ 다음 빈칸 (A), (B)에 들어갈 표현으로 어법상 가장 적절한 것을 고르시오.

[문 5 ~ 문 6]

문 5.

　　_____(A)_____ earliest times the lives of humans and animals have been closely related, providing a rich source of symbolism. Animals have been worshipped as gods, linked with good or bad luck, and _____(B)_____ as sources of power and wisdom. Many are symbolically associated with a human quality.

　(A)　　(B)   (A)　　(B)
① Since — see   ② When — seen
③ Since — seen   ④ When — see

문 6.

　　The French arrived in North America about the same time the English _____(A)_____, but France was more interested in the profitable fur trade than in colonization and sent few French settlers; as a result, the population of New France stayed tiny compared with _____(B)_____ of the English colonies to the south.

　(A)　　(B)   (A)　　(B)
① did — that   ② was — this
③ did — this   ④ was — that

문 7. 다음 글의 주제로 가장 적절한 것은?

The personalities of people in groups speaking different languages often can diverge. A study revealed that personality tests taken by English-speaking Americans and Spanish-speaking Mexicans differ reliably: The Americans were found to be more extroverted, more agreeable, and more conscientious than the Mexicans. But why? To see if language might play a role in this difference, the researchers then sought out Spanish-English bilinguals in Texas, California, and Mexico and gave them the personality scale in each language. And in fact, language was a key: Scores of the bilingual participants were more extroverted, agreeable, and conscientious when they took the test in English than when they took it in Spanish.

① the procedure of developing a personality scale
② the influence of language on personality differences
③ test-taking strategies of bilinguals in personality tests
④ the role of environment in language learning

문 8. 다음 밑줄 친 부분 중 어법상 옳지 않은 것을 고르시오.

Some researchers claim that aggressive children simply prefer violent TV and would behave just as violently without that exposure. However, that argument cannot account for the results of numerous studies ① in which children are assigned to watch either a violent or nonviolent video or film. In most of this research, ② those exposed to violence behave more aggressively immediately afterward. In one study, for example, 396 seven-to-nine-year-old boys watched either a violent or nonviolent film and then played indoor hockey. Researchers who did not know which film the boys had seen ③ rating their aggressive acts during the game, looking for moves that are banned in hockey. These included elbowing, kneeing, and tripping opponents. Overall, the boys who saw the violent film ④ were more aggressive.

문 9. 다음 밑줄 친 부분 중 어법상 옳지 않은 것을 고르시오.

From a neurological perspective, every time you encounter something new, your brain tries to record as ① much information as possible. Thousands of neurons are stimulated, which help code and store this information, ultimately ② caused you to feel and notice a lot. But as time goes on, the "new" experience becomes old, and your brain begins to use less and less energy ③ to encode information — simply because it already knows it. If you drive to and from work every day, the drive isn't stimulating your brain ④ nearly as much as the first time you took that route.

문 10. 다음 대화의 빈칸에 들어갈 말로 가장 적절한 것은?

A: Welcome to BW Print Shop. How may I help you?
B: Hi. I'd like to get copies of this flyer.
A: All right. How many copies do you need?
B: I need two hundred and fifty copies.
A: Okay. Would you like them delivered? It's an extra 5,000 won.
B: No, _____. When will they be ready?
A: In about an hour.
B: That's great. I'll be back then.
A: Okay.

① I'd like to know the number of the copies
② I'll pick them up when they're finished
③ please send them to my office
④ I don't want them bound

문 11. 밑줄 친 her[she]가 가리키는 대상이 나머지 셋과 다른 것은?

When Nosipho first heard that they would be discussing ageing in class, she felt a little disappointed. Perhaps this section would be less interesting and less relevant to ① her own life than the material they had covered in the course so far. But after reading a little on the subject Nosipho found her thoughts turning to ② her grandmother who lived out in the rural areas. She only saw ③ her about once a year but her grandmother was still a very important figure in her family's life. Having respect for older people was something her mother had impressed on her right from when ④ she was a young child.

문 12. 다음 빈칸에 들어갈 단어로 가장 적절한 것은?

Humans evolved to detect sharp changes and distinctive events, such as the sudden appearance of a lion or sources of food. We are far less able to detect gradual changes. Ornstein and Ehrlich believe perceptual capacities that aided survival when humans were hunters and gatherers can now be a _____. Many of the threats facing civilization develop very slowly. Examples include the degradation of the environment, global warming, and erosion of the ozone layer. Ornstein and Ehrlich relate the large-scale threats we face to what they call the "boiled frog syndrome." Frogs placed in a pan of water that is slowly heated cannot detect the gradual rise in temperature. They will sit still until they die. Like the doomed frogs, many people seem unable to detect gradual but deadly trends in modern civilization.

① handicap　　　　② relief
③ weapon　　　　④ cure

문 13. 다음 빈칸에 들어갈 말로 가장 적절한 것은?

It is clear that peers value competence in physical activity and sport. That is, one way in which children and youth can achieve better status among their peers is to be perceived as physically competent. _____, a problem that persists in physical education is the inability to provide equitable learning experiences for less-skilled children and youth. Less-skilled students typically get fewer opportunities to practice and have less success than do their more-skilled peers. When games are played, the less-skilled students sometimes get few real opportunities to take part in meaningful play.

① However　　　　② In short
③ For instance　　　④ In other words

문 14. 미국 노동통계국의 조사 결과에 관한 다음 글의 내용과 일치하는 것은?

Settling into a job is not necessarily a permanent situation, as occupational careers are characterized by significant fluidity. According to the U.S. Bureau of Labor Statistics, in 2005, more than 3 percent of employees left their jobs each month, most of them taking a job with another employer. The Bureau of Labor Statistics also determined that at the beginning of 2004, wage and salary workers had put in a median of only 4 years with their current employer. As might be expected, older workers stay at the same job for a longer period than younger ones do. Among workers 45 years of age and older, about half had been with their current employer for 10 years or more. In contrast, only about one-quarter of workers between the ages of 35 and 44 had a tenure of this length.

① 2005년에 피고용인의 3% 미만이 매달 직장을 옮겼다.
② 2004년 초에 모든 임금노동자는 그 당시의 고용주와 4년 이상 근무했다.
③ 젊은 노동자가 나이가 더 많은 노동자보다 같은 직장에 더 오래 머물렀다.
④ 45세 이상 노동자의 약 절반 정도는 그 당시의 고용주와 10년 이상 근무했다.

문 15. Mark Young에 관한 다음 글의 내용과 일치하지 않는 것은?

Mark Young is the head of the painting department in a large hospital and 20 union employees report to him. Prior to coming on board at the hospital, he had worked as an independent contractor. At the hospital he took a position that was newly created because the hospital believed change was needed in how painting services were provided. Upon beginning his job, Mark did a 4-month analysis of the direct and indirect costs of painting services. His findings supported the perceptions of his administrators that painting services were inefficient and costly. As a result, Mark completely reorganized the department, designed a new schedule procedure, and redefined the expected standards of performance.

① 대형 병원 페인팅 부서의 장이다.
② 병원에 오기 전에 독립계약자로 일했다.
③ 병원에서 새로 마련한 직책을 맡았다.
④ 비효율적인 페인팅 서비스를 발견하지 못했다.

문 16. 다음 글의 제목으로 가장 적절한 것은?

Pineapples were brought back from the West Indies by early European explorers during the seventeenth century. From that time on, the pineapple was cultivated in Europe and became the favored fruit to serve to royalty and the elite. The pineapple was later introduced into North America and became a part of North American hospitality as well. Pineapples were displayed at doors or on gateposts, announcing to friends and acquaintances: "The ship is in! Come join us. Food and drink for all!" Since its introduction, the pineapple has been internationally recognized as a symbol of hospitality and a sign of friendliness, warmth, and cheer.

① Pineapples: A Symbol of Hospitality
② Cultivation of Pineapples in the West
③ Pineapple Industry in the West
④ Hospitality: Essence of Humans

문 17. 주어진 글 다음에 이어질 글의 순서로 가장 적절한 것은?

Some organizations do have policies which allow either men or women to take career breaks to look after children.

(A) Indeed, the knowledge of this may well be a cause of the low take-up of such schemes by men.
(B) Organizations, therefore, not only need to establish the structures which allow careers to be more flexible, they also need to change attitudes which typically remain thoroughly traditional.
(C) However, not only have very few fathers actually availed themselves of such opportunities, anecdotal evidence also suggests that if they had done so, their careers would have been 'ruined' for life.

① (A) － (C) － (B)   ② (B) － (A) － (C)
③ (C) － (A) － (B)   ④ (C) － (B) － (A)

문 18. 글의 흐름으로 보아 주어진 문장이 들어가기에 가장 적절한 곳은?

Adolescent clients, however, are too old to play with toys and often too young to be comfortable with a primarily verbal format.

Adult clients are usually comfortable with therapy that involves talking as its primary vehicle. (①) Child clients often do best in play therapy, where they can use toys and other materials to supplement their verbal expressions. (②) This means that working with adolescents requires a creative use of various kinds of structure, both to help the client feel more comfortable and to promote talking, self-exploration, and problem solving. (③) These kinds of structure include the use of more questions, therapist self-disclosure, providing treatment in many different settings, and structured mutual activities, such as going for walks or meeting in a restaurant for lunch. (④) Research suggests that with adolescents "traditional long-term individual psychotherapy is less effective than briefer and more focused psychotherapeutic interventions".

문 19. 다음 글에서 전체 흐름과 관계 없는 문장은?

The functionalist theory holds that inequality is necessary if a society is to motivate its most talented and hard-working members to perform its most important roles. Some roles (including jobs) require more skill and training than do others. ① Ordinarily, the more skill and training required to perform a role, the fewer the number of people qualified to "do the job" and, all else equal, the more valuable their abilities are to the whole group. ② Functionalists argue that unequal rewards are effective ways to recruit the most able individuals into the most socially valuable roles. ③ Inequality offers few benefits to anyone except the elite and, indeed, is harmful to the whole society because of the unnecessary conflicts it creates. ④ Unless there are rewards for those with the talents most of us lack, they will have no incentive to put those talents to work in activities that benefit all of us.

문 20. 다음 글의 요지로 가장 적절한 것은?

Unfortunately, our brain is more affected by negative than positive information. For instance, imagine these two scenarios. In the first you learn that you've won a $500 gift certificate from Saks. You would feel pretty good about that, wouldn't you? In the second scenario, you lose your wallet containing $500. How unhappy would you feel about that? According to the results of risk-taking research, the intensities of your responses to these experiences differ markedly. As the result of what scientists refer to as the brain's negativity bias, the distress you're likely to experience as a result of the loss of $500 will greatly exceed the pleasure you feel at winning that gift certificate.

① People more readily experience pleasure than negative emotions.
② The negativity bias of the human brain is reinforced by positive experiences.
③ Balancing positive and negative emotions is the source of happiness.
④ People are more influenced by negative experiences than positive ones.

해설편 ▶ P.202

2016

| 풀이 시간: ____:____ ~ ____:____ / 점수: ____점

1초 합격예측! 모바일 성적분석표

QR 코드로 접속하여 문제 풀이시간을 측정하고,
〈1초 합격예측 & 모바일 성적분석표〉 서비스를 통해
지금 바로! 실력을 점검해 보세요.
http://eduwill.kr/Xiy6

※ 다음 빈칸에 들어갈 단어로 가장 적절한 것을 고르시오.
[문 1 ～ 문 3]

문 1.

> Agriculture accelerates the loss of biodiversity.
> As we've cleared areas of grassland and forest for
> farms, we've lost crucial habitat, making agriculture
> a major driver of wildlife _____.

① extinction   ② reproduction
③ classification   ④ diversification

문 2.

> *To Free a Family* tells the remarkable story of
> Mary Walker, who in August 1848 fled her owner
> for refuge in the North. Her freedom, like that of
> thousands who _____ from bondage, came
> at a great price — remorse at parting without a
> word, fear for her family's fate.

① escaped   ② differed
③ benefited   ④ originated

문 3.

> Unlike most of us, whose calendars run from January
> through December, and corporations, whose "fiscal
> years" can start and end at whatever month the
> treasurer deems best, concert seasons are usually
> _____ from the fall through the spring.

① entrusted   ② inquired
③ legislated   ④ reckoned

문 4. 다음 글의 밑줄 친 부분 중 문맥상 단어의 쓰임이 적절하지
않은 것은?

> Leaders actively direct some aspects of their own
> development. A systematic plan outlining self-
> improvement goals will help leaders take advantage
> of opportunities they otherwise might ① overlook.
> Developing a systematic plan also will help leaders
> ② prioritize the importance of different goals.
> Leaders who carefully choose which seminars and
> conferences to attend may help themselves ③ lessen
> their contribution to their personal developmental
> goals. Leaders should look for opportunities on the
> job or in volunteer work for responsibilities that
> may ④ further their growth.

※ 다음 빈칸 (A), (B)에 들어갈 표현으로 어법상 가장 적절한 것
을 고르시오.   [문 5 ～ 문 6]

문 5.

> Kids and tickling go together ____(A)____ milk
> and cookies, right? But tickle your newborn and
> she may not so much as crack a smile. Why? It's
> not really the sensation of being tickled that makes
> a child ____(B)____ — in fact, studies show
> most people don't truly enjoy the feeling.

  (A)   (B)   (A)   (B)
① like — laugh   ② like — to laugh
③ alike — laugh   ④ alike — to laugh

문 6.

> ____(A)____ the fact that sport is a salient part
> of our daily lives, it has, until recently, received
> little serious study by sociologists. Accordingly,
> there ____(B)____ few clear and compelling
> definitions and descriptions of sport as a social
> activity.

  (A)   (B)   (A)   (B)
① Although— are   ② Despite — is
③ Despite — are   ④ Although— is

문 7. 다음 대화의 빈칸에 들어갈 말로 가장 적절한 것은?

> A: Did you have fun last weekend at the potluck party?
> B: Absolutely! People brought a lot of delicious dishes.
> A: Really? Which one was your favorite?
> B: Brian's. He made lasagna which tasted so good that there were no leftovers.
> A: I'm sorry I missed it!
> B: _____
> A: Well, I'm a terrible cook. I have no idea what to make.
> B: No worries. You can just bring fruit or beverages instead.
> A: That's a relief. Then let me know when you get together again.

① Let me give it a try.
② Would you like some more?
③ That's not exactly what I mean.
④ How about joining us next time?

※ 다음 밑줄 친 부분 중 어법상 옳지 않은 것을 고르시오.
[문 8 ~ 문 10]

문 8.

> Indeed, it is the nature of men ① that whenever they see profit, they cannot help chasing after ② them, and whenever they see harm, they cannot help running away. To illustrate, when the merchant engages in trade and travels twice the ordinary distance in a day, ③ uses the night to extend the day, and covers a thousand miles without considering it too far, it is ④ because profit lies ahead.

문 9.

> The navigational compass was one of ① the most important inventions in history. It sparked an enormous age of exploration ② which in turn brought great wealth to Europe. This wealth is ③ that fueled later events such as the Enlightenment and the Industrial Revolution. It has been continually simplifying the lives of people around the globe ④ since its introduction to the world.

문 10.

> Fear of speaking, or communication apprehension, is a common condition ① experienced even by seasoned speakers. While its causes are not fully understood, it seems to surface particularly when a speaker is faced with an unfamiliar role in an unfamiliar environment before an unfamiliar audience ② whose reception of the speaker's ideas is highly in question. The control of communication apprehension lies in removing ③ so many of the areas of uncertainty and unfamiliarity as possible. Thorough preparation and practice coupled with a good mental attitude will help ④ guard against the disabling effects of communication apprehension.

문 11. 다음 밑줄 친 단어가 가리키는 대상이 나머지 셋과 다른 것은?

> Have you heard the story of "The Scorpion and the Frog"? A frog comes upon a scorpion and pleads for his life. The scorpion says he will not kill the frog if the frog takes ① him across the river. The frog asks, "How do I know you won't kill ② me as I carry you?" The scorpion replies, "If I were to strike you, we would both surely die." Thinking it over, the frog agrees and halfway across the river the scorpion strikes the frog in the back. As they both start to drown, the frog asks, "Why did ③ you strike me? Now we will both die." The scorpion replies with his last breath, "Because it is in ④ my nature that I cannot control."

문 12. 다음 빈칸에 들어갈 말로 가장 적절한 것은?

> I once attended a seminar where the speaker's slide — a map of North America — was upside down. The speaker quickly said, "This is what North America looks like from the Southern Hemisphere," which got a good laugh. A year or so later, I was speaking and my map of Brazil was backwards, so I said, "Here's what Brazil looks like when seen from the center of the earth." It took them a minute to get it, but they laughed at this one too. Even though you're very careful to get your slides in right, sometimes you screw up, and if you're prepared with one of these stock _____, you can always get the audience on your side.

① maps ② slides ③ proverbs ④ jokes

문 13. 2013년의 차(tea) 생산에 관한 다음 글의 내용과 일치하는 것은?

World tea production increased significantly by 6 percent to 5.07 million tonnes in 2013. Black tea output increased by 5.4 percent in response to continued firm prices while green tea output increased by 5.1 percent. Growth in world output was due to major increases in the major tea producing countries. China remained the largest tea producing country with an output of 1.9 million tonnes, accounting for more than 38 percent of the world total, while production in India, the second largest producer, also increased to reach 1.2 million tonnes. Output also increased in the two largest exporting countries where production reached 436,300 tonnes in Kenya and 343,100 tonnes in Sri Lanka. Apart from the 7.5 percent decline in Vietnam to 185,000 tonnes, production in other major producing countries such as Indonesia, Bangladesh, and Rwanda increased.

① 세계 차 생산량이 감소하였다.
② 인도보다 중국의 차 생산량이 적었다.
③ 케냐와 스리랑카의 차 생산량이 증가하였다.
④ 베트남의 차 생산량이 증가하였다.

문 14. Abby Kelley Foster에 관한 다음 글의 내용과 일치하지 않는 것은?

Born in Massachusetts to a Quaker farm family, Abby Kelley Foster was the seventh daughter in a time when farmers prayed for boys. She was raised in the town of Worcester, completed grammar school, and was one of the rare girls to go on to higher education, at a Quaker school in Providence, Rhode Island. She alternated studying with spells of teaching children to earn her way. Hearing a lecture on slavery by William Lloyd Garrison changed the course of her life. While teaching in Lynn, Massachusetts, she joined the local female antislavery society and soon became a paid lecturer for the Abolition Movement. She married Stephen S. Foster in 1845, and they often traveled together as abolitionist speakers. They worked their farm in Worcester and made it a haven for fugitive slaves.

① 농가의 일곱 번째 딸로 태어났다.
② 중등학교를 마쳤지만 고등 교육을 받지 못하였다.
③ 노예 제도에 관한 강연을 듣고 그녀의 인생이 바뀌었다.
④ Worcester에서 남편과 함께 농장을 운영하였다.

문 15. 다음 빈칸에 들어갈 말로 가장 적절한 것은?

Firms have traditionally focused on the individual transaction with a customer as the fruition of their marketing efforts. But as global markets have become increasingly competitive and volatile, many firms have turned their attention to building a continuing long-term relationship between the organization and the customer as the ultimate objective of a successful marketing strategy. They are taking action to increase lifetime customer value — the present value of a stream of revenue that can be produced by a customer over time. For an automobile manufacturer, _____, the lifetime value of a first-time car buyer who can be kept satisfied and loyal to the manufacturer — buying all future new cars from the same company — is well over a million dollars.

① for instance ② in addition
③ otherwise ④ nonetheless

문 16. 다음 글의 제목으로 가장 적절한 것은?

Uncle Walt couldn't afford to buy all the land he wanted for Disneyland. So, in order to fit everything in, he used movie makers' tricks to make everything look bigger. One trick was to use things that are familiar, but make them smaller than normal. Unless you look carefully and measure with your eyes, you'll assume, for example, that the Disneyland train is normal size. It isn't. It is built to 5/8 scale. Many of the Disney buildings use the same trick, but that's just the beginning. If you look carefully at some of the Disney buildings, you'll notice there's something a little odd about them. They are not only smaller than normal, but their second and third stories are still smaller. By tapering the upper stories, the designers fool your eyes into believing that they are bigger and taller than they really are.

① Movie Making in Disneyland
② Disneyland: Land of Illusions
③ Tricks Do Not Always Work
④ Safety Rules in Disneyland

문 17. 주어진 글 다음에 이어질 글을 순서대로 바르게 배열한 것은?

When we speak of the political organization of a particular cultural system, we frequently are left with the impression that political boundaries and cultural boundaries are the same.

(A) Thus, the term Comanche refers to a people with a common language and culture who never united to carry out common political activities.
(B) But the boundaries of a polity, or politically organized unit, may or may not correspond with the boundaries of a particular way of life.
(C) For example, the Comanche of the Great Plains shared a common language, customs, and ethnic identity, yet politically, they were never organized above the local group.

① (B) − (A) − (C)　　② (B) − (C) − (A)
③ (C) − (A) − (B)　　④ (C) − (B) − (A)

문 18. 다음 글에서 주장하는 바를 한 문장으로 요약할 때, 빈칸 (A), (B)에 들어갈 말로 가장 적절한 것은?

The commons dilemma takes its name from this parable: You are a shepherd in a small village. There is a piece of land, called the commons, that everyone is free to share. Most of the time, your sheep graze on your own land, but when a few of them need a little extra grass, you are free to take them to the commons. There are 50 shepherds in the village, and the commons can support about 50 sheep a day. So if each shepherd takes an average of one sheep per day to the commons, everything works out. Suppose a few shepherds decide to take several sheep per day to the commons to save the grass on their own land. Not to be outdone, other shepherds do the same. Soon the commons is barren and useless to all.

Pursuing ____(A)____ interests only can lead to ____(B)____ effects to the whole.

　　(A)　　　　　(B)
① collective — damaging
② collective — beneficial
③ individual — positive
④ individual — harmful

문 19. 글의 흐름으로 보아 주어진 문장이 들어가기에 가장 적절한 곳은?

> This factor is evident in technology, since most technological advancements are the result of such recombinations.

An innovation may be anything — from new religious beliefs to a technological change — that is internally generated by members of the society. People are constantly changing what they do and how they do it. In most cases these changes are minor, imperceptible, and unconscious. (①) In the telling of a myth a person may delete some part while elaborating another. (②) Individuals may wear their hair differently or paint their faces with a new design. (③) Most innovations consist of the recombining of two or more existing ideas or objects to produce something new. (④) In North America, Fulton took a paddle wheel, a steam engine, and a boat and put them together to create a steamboat.

문 20. 다음 글의 요지로 가장 적절한 것은?

> Similarity can consist of being part of the same group, even if the party in distress is a stranger. In one study, students were made to think about their favorite soccer team, thereby activating their identity as a fan of that team. Each participant was then made to walk to another building. On the way, he encountered a student who was injured and either wearing a shirt of the participant's favorite team, a shirt of a competitor, or a shirt with no team name. The injured student received more help when wearing a shirt of the participant's favorite team than when wearing either of the other kinds of shirts. People who are fans of the same soccer team form an ingroup, and generally speaking, we are more likely to help ingroup rather than outgroup members.

① Social identity is strongly related to people's hobbies.
② Outgroup members regard similarity as a key to friendship.
③ People are likely to mimic one another to get help.
④ Similarity plays a role in likelihood of being helped.

해설편 ▶ P.207

2015

6월 27일 시행
교육행정직 9급

| 풀이 시간: ____:____ ~ ____:____ / 점수: ____ 점

문 1. 빈칸에 들어갈 단어로 가장 적절한 것은?

> If you describe someone as _____, you think that he or she is strange or unusual, often in an unpleasant way.

① peculiar   ② extrovert
③ responsive   ④ submissive

문 2. 밑줄 친 단어와 뜻이 가장 가까운 것은?

> Throughout history, food has had a huge impact on civilization as a catalyst of social change, political organization, geopolitical competition, industrial development, military conflict, and economic expansion.

① trigger   ② deterrent
③ justification   ④ consequence

문 3. 밑줄 친 단어와 뜻이 가장 가까운 것은?

> Most of the characteristics of the early primates are studied from fossils of their teeth and skulls. *Bone fossilization* is the process by which minerals slowly replace the organic content of the bones of a dead animal, resulting in a very detailed stone replica of the original bone. Fossils can be so detailed that they show scratches under a microscope.

① emblem   ② duplicate
③ remnant   ④ craftwork

문 4. 다음 글의 밑줄 친 부분 중 문맥상 단어의 쓰임이 적절하지 않은 것은?

> To the world at large, Ethiopia is practically ① synonymous with famine and desert, to the extent that the Ethiopian Airlines' Johannesburg office regularly receives tactful enquiries about what, if any, food is served on their flights. This widespread ② misconception, regarding a country set in a continent plagued by drought and erratic rainfall, says much about the workings of the mass media. It says rather less about Ethiopia. ③ Contrary to Western myth, the elevated central plateau that covers half of Ethiopia's surface area, and supports the vast majority of its population, is the most extensive contiguous area of fertile land in the eastern side of Africa. The deserts do exist, but they are, as you might expect, ④ densely populated; they have little impact on the life of most Ethiopians — and they are most unlikely to be visited by tourists. To all intents and purposes, the fertile highland plateau is Ethiopia.

문 5. 다음 중 어법상 옳지 않은 것은?

① I saw one of the most impressive government policies in years.
② If I were you, I'd apply for the position just for the experience.
③ That wonderful thought was suddenly occurred after I came to Jeju.
④ I urged in my previous letter that they be treated as his colleagues.

문 6. 다음 빈칸 (A), (B)에 들어갈 표현으로 어법상 가장 적절한 것은?

> Beekeepers in the United States first noticed that their bee colonies ____(A)____ dying off in 2006. Since then, scientists have been desperately ____(B)____ to figure out what's causing the collapse.

	(A)	(B)		(A)	(B)
①	were	tried	②	were	trying
③	have been	tried	④	have been	trying

문 7. 다음 빈칸 (A),(B)에 들어갈 표현으로 어법상 가장 적절한 것은?

> We tend to organize _____(A)_____ we perceive into whole, continuous figures. If the stimulus pattern is incomplete, we most likely will fill in the missing elements. Reading the letters K..O.. ..E..A, Koreans are apt to add the missing letter to form the word KOREA. However, a person from another culture might read the letters _____(B)_____, not unconsciously supplying the letter R and, hence, arriving at an entirely different interpretation of the letters.

　　(A)　　(B)　　　　　　　(A)　　(B)
① what － different　　② what － differently
③ that － different　　④ that － differently

문 8. 밑줄 친 부분 중 어법상 옳지 않은 것은?

> I met a university professor who reported that his daughter ① had sent thirteen thousand text messages to her friends in a single month. If each message took, say, fifteen seconds ② to key in, the father calculated that the daughter spent hours a day texting, a word my spell-checker does not yet recognize. Sending text messages ③ is obviously an addictive and compulsive behavior. My wife and I once drove past a young man ④ rode no hands on a bicycle. In one hand he was thumbing a text message. In the other he held what looked like a three- or four-month-old baby.

문 9. 밑줄 친 부분 중 어법상 옳지 않은 것은?

> As our knowledge of emotional intelligence continues to evolve, ① so does this book on emotional and social intelligence. Just over ten years ② have passed since we wrote the first edition of this book. The previous revised editions were driven by the huge increase in knowledge, both scientific and experiential, ③ that arose on this new topic. The present revision is primarily driven by the first major revision of the most widely used test of emotional intelligence in the world, the Emotional Quotient Inventory, now ④ referring to as the Emotional Quotient Inventory 2.0.

문 10. 다음 대화에서 밑줄 친 부분에 들어갈 말로 가장 적절한 것은?

> A: I'm starving.
> B: Me, too. What are you in the mood for?
> A: Korean food, definitely. You know I'm a huge fan of bulgogi.
> B: Oh, I heard there's a nice Korean restaurant near here.
> A: _____
> B: Good! Do you want to go right now?
> A: Sure. Don't you think we need a reservation?
> B: Probably. I'll call and ask them.

① Then, what are we waiting for?
② Wow, unbelievable! That's a steal!
③ Didn't you know that I don't like meat?
④ I think it just isn't my day.

문 11. 다음 대화에서 밑줄 친 부분에 들어갈 말로 가장 적절한 것은?

> A: Hey. You are late.
> B: Sorry. I was busy helping Jenny with her math homework. She seemed to have problems with some of the questions.
> A: What? Jenny with curly hair?
> B: Yes. Jenny Kim in my class.
> A: _____
> B: What do you mean by that?
> A: She's a math genius. She practically knows everything about math.
> B: Oh, I didn't know that. She never told me she didn't need help.
> A: Jenny is very thoughtful. She probably didn't want to hurt your feelings.

① You taught a fish how to swim.
② Don't bite the hand that feeds you.
③ She just jumped on the bandwagon.
④ You locked the barn door after the horse escaped.

문 12. 주어진 글 다음에 이어질 글의 순서로 가장 적절한 것은?

> For poststructuralist theory the common factor in the analysis of social organization, social meanings, and power and individual consciousness is language.

> (A) Yet it is also the place where our sense of ourselves, our subjectivity, is constructed.
> (B) The assumption that subjectivity is constructed implies that it is not innate, not genetically determined, but socially produced.
> (C) Language is the place where actual and possible forms of social organization and their likely social and political consequences are defined and contested.

① (B) − (A) − (C)　　② (B) − (C) − (A)
③ (C) − (A) − (B)　　④ (C) − (B) − (A)

문 13. 다음 글에서 전체 흐름과 관계없는 문장은?

> When they sailed across the Atlantic in the early 1600s, the Europeans saw the new world through their own cultural lens. They saw a wilderness that was filled with seemingly infinite abundance, but untamed, having no plowed fields, fences, or farm houses. ① The Native Americans they met were considered to be savage peoples, with none of the characteristics of European civilization, nor did they possess true religion according to this view. ② Lacking civilization, however, they lived closer to the natural world, and some Europeans believed this gave them a simple nobility that Europeans themselves lacked. ③ Native Americans understood through long experience that outsiders could bring war, death, and destruction. ④ Thus, they coined the term "noble savage" to describe Native Americans.

문 14. 글의 흐름으로 보아 주어진 글이 들어가기에 가장 적절한 곳은?

> Euathlos reasons a little differently, however. If I lose, he thinks, then I will have lost my first court case, in which event, the original agreement releases me from having to pay any tuition fees.

> Euathlos has learned from Protagoras how to be a lawyer, under a very generous arrangement whereby he doesn't need to pay anything for his tuition until and unless he wins his first court case. (①) Rather to Protagoras' annoyance, however, after giving up hours of his time training Euathlos, the pupil decides to become a musician and never takes any court cases. (②) Protagoras demands that Euathlos pay him for his trouble and, when the musician refuses, decides to sue him in court. (③) Protagoras reasons that if Euathlos loses the case, he, Protagoras, will have won, in which case he will get his money back, and furthermore, that even if he loses, Euathlos will then have won a case and will therefore still have to pay up. (④) And, even if he wins, Protagoras will still have lost the right to enforce the contract, so he will not need to pay anything.

문 15. 밑줄 친 he(his) 중 가리키는 대상이 나머지 셋과 다른 것은?

> On October 21, 1984, President Ronald Reagan and his challenger, former Vice President Walter Mondale, held the second of two nationally televised presidential debates in the run-up to the presidential election. President Reagan remained popular, but his support was softening in light of growing concerns about ① his age (he was 73 at the time of the debate). His poor performance in the previous debate, three weeks earlier, had opened the door to questions about ② his mental fitness. When the moderator asked him if age was a concern in the election, he famously replied that ③ he would not make age an issue of that campaign. Reagan said, "I am not going to exploit, for political purposes, my opponent's youth and inexperience." Mondale, not exactly a spring chicken at fifty-six, later commented that he knew at that very moment ④ he had lost the campaign.

문 16. Lawrence Richard Walters에 관한 다음 글의 내용과 일치하지 않는 것은?

On 2 July 1982, American truck driver Lawrence Richard Walters, nicknamed 'Lawnchair Larry', built a homemade airship. Using his lawn chair, 45 helium weather balloons, a Citizens' Band radio, and a pellet gun, he flew to 15,000 feet over controlled airspace near Los Angeles International Airport. After 45 minutes, aware that he had breached commercial airspace, he shot several balloons and began his descent. He lost his pellet gun overboard and eventually got caught in power lines, causing a twenty-minute blackout in Long Beach. His action and subsequent arrest for breaking federal aviation laws caused a media sensation and spawned a wave of cultural reinterpretations in film, theatre, music, and even video games.

① 비행선을 직접 만들었다.
② 여러 개의 풍선을 터뜨려 하강하였다.
③ Long Beach의 정전 사태를 일으켰다.
④ 위기 상황에서도 연방 항공법을 준수하였다.

문 17. 다음 빈칸 (A), (B)에 들어갈 말로 가장 적절한 것은?

Natural scientists such as chemists or physicists can usually conduct controlled experiments where "all other things" are in fact held constant (or virtually so). They can test with great precision the assumed relationship between two variables. _____(A)_____, they might examine the height from which an object is dropped and the length of time it takes to hit the ground. But economics is not a laboratory science. Economists test their theories using real-world data, which are generated by the actual operation of the economy. In this rather bewildering environment, "other things" do change. Despite the development of complex statistical techniques designed to hold other things equal, control is less than perfect. _____(B)_____, economic principles are less certain and less precise than those of laboratory sciences. That also means they are more open to debate than many scientific theories.

	(A)	(B)
①	For example	Nevertheless
②	For example	As a result
③	In contrast	Conversely
④	In contrast	Therefore

문 18. 빈칸에 공통으로 들어갈 말로 가장 적절한 것은?

Centuries ago, the philosopher Jeremy Bentham wrote, "Pain and pleasure govern us in all we do, in all we say, in all we think." The institutions and incentive structures of society operate largely in accordance with Bentham's claim and thus are missing out on some of the most profound motivators of human behavior. What Bentham and the rest of us typically overlook is that humans are wired with another set of interests that are just as basic as physical pain and pleasure. We are wired to be _____. We are driven by deep motivations to stay connected with friends and family. We are naturally curious about what is going on in the minds of other people. These connections lead to behaviors that violate our expectation of rational self-interest and make sense only if our _____ nature is taken as a starting point for who we are.

① social   ② creative
③ intuitive   ④ egocentric

문 19. 다음 글의 제목으로 가장 적절한 것은?

Throughout history, and in every culture, emotional tears are shed — everyone, everywhere, cries at some time. People weep during funeral rituals, for instance, in every culture except in Bali, and even there people weep in mourning — tearless funerals are made possible only by postponing the rites until two full years after the death. Around the globe, infants cry in hunger and pain and children in frustration and disappointment. However much the rules governing emotional display may vary from time to time and place to place, adults weep for myriad reasons and sometimes, a few claim, for no reason at all. In American culture, even those rare people (usually male) who claim they never cry can remember doing so as children.

① Cultural Benefits of Crying
② Stop Weeping and Start Living
③ Shedding Tears: A Human Universal
④ Diverse Effects of Emotional Crying

문 20. 다음 글의 요지로 가장 적절한 것은?

Foraging is a subsistence strategy based on gathering plants that grow wild in the environment and hunting available animals. In some cases, foraging might not seem like production at all. Walking through the forest, finding a fruit-bearing tree, picking the fruit, and eating it might strike contemporary urbanities as living in Eden, not producing. Most people who live in direct contact with the environment and employ relatively little technology in the acquisition of food actually work harder than simply picking low-hanging fruit, but gathering what grows wild in the environment is a form of production. It is also a key economic strategy of foragers. Production refers to any human action intended to convert resources in the environment into food. Berries growing on a bush are simply seed-carriers for the reproduction of the plant; they do not become "food" until they are identified as edible and taken off the bush. Identifying and picking the fruit, then, is an act of production.

① Productive activities are valued for the survival of human beings.

② Foraging strategies for acquiring food in the wild should be developed.

③ It is necessary to improve the environment to support human survival.

④ We need to understand foraging as an act of production.

해설편 ▶ P.212

삶의 순간순간이
아름다운 마무리이며
새로운 시작이어야 한다.

– 법정 스님

여러분의 작은 소리
에듀윌은 크게 듣겠습니다.

본 교재에 대한 여러분의 목소리를 들려주세요.

공부하시면서 어려웠던 점, 궁금한 점,

칭찬하고 싶은 점, 개선할 점, 어떤 것이라도 좋습니다.

에듀윌은 여러분께서 나누어 주신 의견을

통해 끊임없이 발전하고 있습니다.

에듀윌 도서몰 book.eduwill.net
- 부가학습자료 및 정오표: 에듀윌 도서몰 → 도서자료실
- 교재 문의: 에듀윌 도서몰 → 문의하기 → 교재(내용, 출간) / 주문 및 배송

2023 에듀윌 9급공무원 7개년 기출문제집 영어

발 행 일	2022년 9월 21일 초판
편 저 자	성정혜
펴 낸 이	권대호
펴 낸 곳	(주)에듀윌
등록번호	제25100-2002-000052호
주 소	08378 서울특별시 구로구 디지털로34길 55
	코오롱싸이언스밸리 2차 3층

* 이 책의 무단 인용 · 전재 · 복제를 금합니다.   ISBN 979-11-360-1909-7 (13350)

www.eduwill.net

대표전화 1600-6700

9급공무원 공개경쟁채용 필기시험 답안지

※ 시험감독관 서명
(성명을 정자로 기재할 것)

책형 확인란 사용

성명

자필성명 | 본인 성명 기재

응시직렬

응시지역

시험장소

[필적감정용 기재]
*아래 예시문을 옮겨 적으시오
본인은 ○○○(응시자성명)임을 확인함

기 재 란

생 년 월 일

응 시 번 호

연습용

문번					
1	①	②	③	④	⑤
2	①	②	③	④	⑤
3	①	②	③	④	⑤
4	①	②	③	④	⑤
5	①	②	③	④	⑤
6	①	②	③	④	⑤
7	①	②	③	④	⑤
8	①	②	③	④	⑤
9	①	②	③	④	⑤
10	①	②	③	④	⑤
11	①	②	③	④	⑤
12	①	②	③	④	⑤
13	①	②	③	④	⑤
14	①	②	③	④	⑤
15	①	②	③	④	⑤
16	①	②	③	④	⑤
17	①	②	③	④	⑤
18	①	②	③	④	⑤
19	①	②	③	④	⑤
20	①	②	③	④	⑤

응시자 준수사항

□ 답안지 작성요령

※다음 사항을 준수하지 않을 경우에 발생하는 불이익은 응시자의 귀책사유가 되므로 기재된 내용대로 이행하여 주시기 바랍니다.

1. 특정은 OCR 스캐너 판독결과에 따라 산출합니다. 모든 기재 및 표기사항은 "컴퓨터용 흑색 사인펜"을 사용하여 반드시 〈보기〉의 올바른 표기 방식으로 답안을 작성해야 합니다.

   이를 준수하지 않아 발생하는 불이익(특히 부정확한 필적으로 응시자 본인의 책임이며, 답안을 전부 채우지 않고 점만 찍어 표기한 경우, 번짐 등으로 두 개 이상의 답란에 표기된 경우, 농도가 옅어 컴퓨터용 사인펜을 사용하여 답안을 올바르게 표기한 경우 등에는 불이익(득점 불인정 등)을 받을 수 있으니 유의하시기 바랍니다.

   〈보기〉 올바른 표기: ●   잘못된 표기: ⊗ ◑ ◐ ◍ ⦿ ● ② ③

2. 책색볼펜, 연필, 샤프펜 등 볼의 종류와 상관없이 예비표기를 하여 중복 답안으로 판독된 경우에는 불이익을 받을 수 있으므로 각별히 주의하시기 바랍니다.

3. 답안지를 받으면 상단에 인쇄된 성명, 응시지역, 시험장소, 응시번호, 생년월일이 응시자 정보와 일치하는지 확인하시기 바랍니다.

   가. (책 형) 응시자는 시험 시작 전 감독관 지시에 따라 문제책 앞면의 인쇄된 책형을 확인한 후, 답안지 책형란에 해당 책형(1개)을 "●"로 표기하여야 합니다.

   ※ 책형 및 인적사항을 기재하지 않을 경우 본인의 불이익으로 직접 처리되며 그 불이익은 본인에게 있습니다.

   나. (필적감정용 기재) 예시문과 동일한 내용을 본인의 필적으로 직접 작성해야 합니다.

   다. (자필성명) 본인의 한글성명을 정자로 직접 기재하여야 합니다.

   라. (교체답안지 작성) 답안지를 교체하면 반드시 교체답안지 상단 책형란에 해당 책형(1개)을 "●"로 표기하고, 필적감정용 기재란, 성명, 응시지역, 시험장소, 응시번호, 생년월일을 빠짐없이 작성(표기)해야 하며, 작성한 답안지는 1인 1매만 유효합니다.

4. 시험이 시작되면 문제책 편철과 표지의 과목순서의 일치 여부, 문제 누락·파손 등 문제책 인쇄상태를 반드시 확인하여야 하며, 과목 순서를 바꾸어 표기한 경우에도 문제책 표지의 과목순서대로 채점되므로 각별히 유의하시기 바랍니다.

5. 답안은 반드시 문제책 표지의 과목순서에 맞추어 표기하여야 하며, 과목 순서를 바꾸어 표기한 경우에도 문제책 표지의 과목순서대로 채점되므로 각별히 유의하시기 바랍니다.

---

6. 답안을 잘못 표기하였을 경우에는 답안지를 교체하여 작성하거나 수정할 수 있으며, 수정 시 아래와 같이 진행합니다.

   - 선택과목이 있는 행정직군 응시자는 본인의 응시표에 인쇄된 선택과목 순서에 따라 제1과목부터 제5과목의 답안을 표기하여야 합니다. 원서접수 시 선택한 이외 다른 과목을 선택하여 답안을 채점되므로 유의하시기 바랍니다.

   - 답안을 잘못 표기하였을 경우에는 답안지를 교체하여 작성하거나, 그 숫자에 "●"로 표기해야 하며, 답안을 정정할 경우에는 답안지를 교체하여 작성하거나 교체하여 작성할 수 있습니다.

   - 표기한 답안을 수정하는 경우에는 응시자 본인이 가져온 수정테이프만을 사용하여 해당 부분을 완전히 지우고 부정하지 말아야지 않도록 주의하여 한다(수정액 또는 수정스티커 등은 사용 불가).

7. 답안지는 훼손·오염되거나 구겨지지 않도록 주의해야 하며, 특히 답안지 상단의 타이밍 마크(▮▮▮▮)를 절대 훼손해서는 안됩니다.

□ 부정행위 등 금지

※다음 사항을 위반한 경우에는 공무원임용시험령 제51조(부정행위자 등에 대한 조치)에 따라 그 시험의 정지, 무효, 합격취소, 5년간 공무원임용시험 응시자격정지 등의 불이익 처분을 받게 됩니다.

1. 시험시작 전까지 문제내용을 보아서는 안됩니다.

2. 시험시간 중 일체의 통신기기(휴대폰, 태블릿PC, 스마트시계, 이어폰, 등) 및 전자기기(전자계산기, 전자사전 등)를 소지할 수 없습니다.

3. 응시표를 출력하여 시험과 관련된 내용이 인쇄 또는 메모된 응시표를 시험시간 중 소지하고 있는 경우 답안지 무효 처분을 받을 수 있으며, 특히 부정한 자료로 판단되는 경우에는 5년간 공무원 임용시험 응시자격 정지 처분을 받을 수 있습니다.

4. 시험종료 후에도 계속하여 답안지를 작성하거나, 시험감독관의 답안지 제출 지시에 불응할 경우에는 무효처분을 받게 됩니다.

5. 시험시간 중 시험문제 내용과 관련된 물건을 휴대하거나, 다른 수험자와 주고받는 경우에는 답안지 무효 처분을 받을 수 있습니다.

   - 답안, 책형 및 인적사항 등 모든 기재(표기) 사항 작성 시 누락되는 항목이 없도록 유의하시기 바랍니다.

6. 그 밖에 공고문의 응시자 준수사항이나 시험감독관의 정당한 지시 등을 따르지 않는 경우 부정행위자로 간주될 수 있습니다.

9급공무원 공개경쟁채용 필기시험 답안지

책형

컴퓨터용 흑색사인펜만 사용

[필적감정용 기재]
*아래 예시문을 옮겨 적으시오
본인은 ○○○(응시자성명)임을 확인함

기 재 란

성 명	
직렬성명	본인 성명 기재
응시직렬	
응시지역	
시험장소	

응시번호

생년월일

※시험감독관 서명
(성명을 정자로 기재할 것)

감독관 확인란

문번						연습용
1	①	②	③	④	⑤	
2	①	②	③	④	⑤	
3	①	②	③	④	⑤	
4	①	②	③	④	⑤	
5	①	②	③	④	⑤	
6	①	②	③	④	⑤	
7	①	②	③	④	⑤	
8	①	②	③	④	⑤	
9	①	②	③	④	⑤	
10	①	②	③	④	⑤	
11	①	②	③	④	⑤	
12	①	②	③	④	⑤	
13	①	②	③	④	⑤	
14	①	②	③	④	⑤	
15	①	②	③	④	⑤	
16	①	②	③	④	⑤	
17	①	②	③	④	⑤	
18	①	②	③	④	⑤	
19	①	②	③	④	⑤	
20	①	②	③	④	⑤	

응시자 준수사항

□ 답안지 작성요령

※다음 사항을 준수하지 않을 경우에 발생하는 불이익은 응시자의 귀책사유가 되므로 기재된 내용대로 이행하여 주시기 바랍니다.

1. 답안은 OCR 스캐너 판독결과에 따라 산출합니다. 모든 기재 및 표기사항은 "컴퓨터용 흑색 사인펜"을 사용하여 반드시 〈보기〉의 올바른 표기방식으로 답안을 작성해야 합니다.

   이를 준수하지 않아 발생하는 불이익(득점 불인정 등)은 응시자 본인의 책임입니다.

   특히, 답안을 전부 채우지 않고 점만 찍어 표기한 경우, 번짐 등으로 두 개 이상이 답안에 표기된 경우, 농도가 엷어 컴퓨터용 사인펜을 사용하여 답안을 흐리게 표기한 경우 등에는 불인정 등의 불이익을 받을 수 있으나 유의하시기 바랍니다.

   〈보기〉　올바른 표기: ●　잘못된 표기: ⊗⊙◑◐○◍◔③

2. 작성불가, 연필, 샤프펜 등 펜의 종류와 상관없이 예비표기를 하여 중복 답안으로 판독된 경우에는 불이익을 받을 수 있으므로 각별히 주의하시기 바랍니다.

3. 답안지를 받으면 상단에 인쇄된 성명, 응시직렬, 응시지역, 시험장소, 응시번호, 생년월일이 응시자 본인의 정보와 일치하는지 확인하시기 바랍니다.

   가. (책　형) 응시자는 시험 시작 전 감독관 지시에 따라 문제책 앞면에 인쇄된 책형을 확인한 후, 답안지 책형란에 해당 책형(1개)을 "●"로 표기하여야 합니다.

   ※ 책형 및 인적사항을 기재하지 않을 경우 불이익(답안지 무효 처리 등)을 받을 수 있습니다.

   나. (필적감정용 기재) 예시문을 본인의 필적으로 직접 기재해야 합니다.

   다. (자필성명) 본인의 한글성명을 정자로 직접 기재해야 합니다.

   라. (교체답안지 작성) 답안지를 교체(덧칠한 반드시 교체답안지 상단 책형란에 해당 책형(1개)를 "●" 로 표기하고, 필적감정용 기재란, 성명, 응시직렬, 응시지역, 시험장소, 응시번호, 생년월일을 빠짐없이 직성(표기)해야 하며, 작성한 답안지는 1인 1매만 유효합니다.

4. 시험이 시작되면 문제책 표지의 과목순서와 일치하여야 하며, 과목 순서를 바꾸어 표기한 경우에도 문제책 표지의 과목순서대로 채점되므로 각별히 유의하시기 바랍니다.

5. 답안은 반드시 문제책 표지의 과목순서에 맞추어 표기해야 하며, 과목 순서를 바꾸어 표기한 경우에도 문제책 표지의 과목순서대로 채점되므로 각별히 유의하시기 바랍니다.

6. 그 밖에 공고문의 응시자 준수사항이나 시험감독관의 정당한 지시 등을 따르지 않은 경우 부정행위자로 간주될 수 있습니다.

---

7. 답안지는 훼손·오염되거나 구겨지지 않도록 주의해야 하며, 특히 답안지 상단의 타이밍 마크(▮▮▮▮)를 절대 훼손해서는 안됩니다.

- 선택과목이 있는 행정직군 응시자는 본인이 응시표에 인쇄된 선택과목 순서에 따라 채점되므로 제5회의 답안을 답안을 골라 그 숫자에 "●"로 표기해야 하며, 답안을 잘못 기재하였을 경우에는 답안지를 교체하거나, 현수 경우 선택한 과목이 아닌 다른 과목 순서대로 채점되므로 유의하시기 바랍니다.

- 답안을 잘못 표기하였을 경우에는 답안지를 교체하여 작성하거나 수정테이프만을 사용하여 수정할 수 있습니다(수정액 또는 수정스티커 등은 사용 불가).

- 표기한 답안을 수정하는 경우에는 응시자 본인이 가져온 수정테이프를 사용하여 해당 부분을 완전히 지우고 부정확 수정테이프의 표기가 벗어나거나 남지 않도록 주의해야 합니다(수정한 부분을 마르지 않은 상태에서 문지를 경우 번짐 등으로 채점상의 불이익을 받을 수 있으므로 응시자 본인에게 책임이 있음).

□ 부정행위 등 금지

※다음 사항을 위반한 경우에는 공무원임용시험령 제51조(부정행위자 등에 대한 조치)에 따라 그 시험의 정지, 무효, 합격취소, 5년간 공무원임용시험 응시자격정지 등의 불이익 처분을 받게 됩니다.

1. 시험시작 전까지 문제내용을 보아서는 안됩니다.

2. 시험시간 중 일체의 통신기기(휴대폰, 태블릿PC, 스마트워치, 이어폰, 등) 및 전자기기(전자계산기, 전자사전 등)를 소지할 수 없습니다.

3. 응시표출력사항 외 시험과 관련된 내용이 인쇄 또는 메모된 응시표를 시험시간 중 소지하고 있는 경우 단체시험 무효 처분을 받을 수 있으며, 특히 부정한 자료로 판단되는 경우에는 5년간 공무원임용시험 응시자격 정지 처분을 받을 수 있습니다.

4. 시험종료 후에도 계속하여 답안지를 작성하거나, 시험감독관의 답안지 제출 지시에 응하지 않는 경우 무효처분을 받게 됩니다.

5. 답안, 채점 및 인적사항 등 모든 기재(표기) 사항 작성은 시험종료 후 시험감독관의 지시가 있을 때까지 반드시 답안지 교체 작성 시 누락되는 항목이 없도록 유의하시기 바랍니다.

- 답안, 채점 및 인적사항 등 모든 기재(표기) 사항 작성은 시험종료 후 시험감독관의 지시가 있을 때까지 제출할 수 없으며, 시험종료 후 시험감독관의 정당한 지시를 따르지 않은 경우 부정행위자로 간주될 수 있습니다.

9급공무원 공개경쟁채용 필기시험 답안지

컴퓨터용 흑색사인펜만 사용

※ 시험감독관 서명
(성명을 정자로 기재할 것)

시험감독관 서명

성 명	
자필성명	본인 성명 기재
응시직렬	
응시지역	
시험장소	

생 년 월 일

응 시 번 호

[필적감정용 기재]
*아래 예시문을 옮겨 적으시오
본인은 ○○○(응시자성명)임을 확인함

기 재 란

책	
형	

연습용

문번					
1	①	②	③	④	⑤
2	①	②	③	④	⑤
3	①	②	③	④	⑤
4	①	②	③	④	⑤
5	①	②	③	④	⑤
6	①	②	③	④	⑤
7	①	②	③	④	⑤
8	①	②	③	④	⑤
9	①	②	③	④	⑤
10	①	②	③	④	⑤
11	①	②	③	④	⑤
12	①	②	③	④	⑤
13	①	②	③	④	⑤
14	①	②	③	④	⑤
15	①	②	③	④	⑤
16	①	②	③	④	⑤
17	①	②	③	④	⑤
18	①	②	③	④	⑤
19	①	②	③	④	⑤
20	①	②	③	④	⑤

응시자 준수사항

합격자가 답해주는
에듀윌 지식인

공무원
무엇이든지
궁금하다면
?

접속방법

에듀윌 지식인(king.eduwill.net) 접속

에듀윌 지식인 신규가입회원 혜택
5,000원 쿠폰증정

발급방법 | 에듀윌 지식인 사이트 (king.eduwill.net) 접속 ▶ 신규회원가입 ▶ 자동발급
사용방법 | 에듀윌 온라인 강의 수강 신청 시 타 쿠폰과 중복하여 사용 가능

※ 본 혜택은 예고 없이 다른 혜택으로 대체될 수 있습니다.

에듀윌
지식인

46개월* 베스트셀러 1위
에듀윌 공무원 교재

7·9급공무원 교재
※ 기본서·단원별 기출&예상 문제집은 국어/영어/한국사/행정학/행정법총론/(운전직)사회로 구성되어 있음.

| 기본서(국어) | 기본서(영어) | 기본서(한국사) | 기본서(행정학) | 기본서(운전직 사회) | 단원별 기출&예상 문제집(국어) |

7·9급공무원 교재
※ 기출문제집·실전동형 모의고사는 국어/영어/한국사/행정학/행정법총론/(운전직)사회로 구성되어 있음.

| 기출문제집(국어) | 기출문제집(영어) | 기출문제집(한국사) | 기출문제집(운전직 사회) | 기출PACK 공통과목(국어+영어+한국사) /전문과목(행정법총론+행정학) | 실전동형 모의고사 (행정법총론) |

7·9급공무원 교재

| 봉투모의고사 (일반행정직 대비 필수과목 /국가직·지방직 대비 공통과목 1, 2) | 지방직 합격면접 | PSAT 기본서 (언어논리/상황판단/자료해석) | PSAT 기출문제집 | PSAT 민경채 기출문제집 | 7급 기출문제집 (행정학/행정법/헌법) |

경찰공무원 교재

| 기본서(경찰학) | 기본서(형사법) | 기본서(헌법) | 기출문제집 (경찰학/형사법/헌법) | 실전동형 모의고사 2차 시험 대비 (경찰학/형사법/헌법) | 합격 경찰면접 |

소방공무원 교재

기본서
(소방학개론/소방관계법규
/행정법총론)

기출PACK
(소방학개론+소방관계법규
+행정법총론)

실전동형 모의고사
(한국사/영어/행정법총론
/소방학+관계법규)

봉투모의고사
(한국사+영어+행정법총론
/소방학+관계법규)

군무원 교재

기출문제집
(국어/행정법/행정학)

봉투모의고사
(국어+행정법+행정학)

계리직공무원 교재

※ 단원별 문제집은 한국사/우편상식/금융상식/컴퓨터일반으로 구성되어 있음.

기본서(한국사)

기본서(우편상식)

기본서(금융상식)

기본서(컴퓨터일반)

단원별 문제집(한국사)

기출문제집
(한국사+우편·금융상식+컴퓨터일반)

국어 집중 교재

매일 기출한자(빈출순)

매일 푸는 비문학(4주 완성)

영어 집중 교재

빈출 VOCA

매일 3문 독해
(기본완성/실력완성)

빈출 문법(4주 완성)

단권화 요약노트 교재

국어 문법 단권화 요약노트

영어 단기 공략
(핵심 요약집)

한국사 흐름노트

행정학 단권화 요약노트

행정법 단권화 요약노트

기출판례집(빈출순) 교재

행정법

헌법

형사법

더 많은
공무원 교재

취업, 공무원, 자격증 시험준비의 흐름을 바꾼 화제작!

에듀윌 히트교재 시리즈

에듀윌 교육출판연구소가 만든 히트교재 시리즈!
YES 24, 교보문고, 알라딘, 인터파크, 영풍문고 등 전국 유명 온/오프라인 서점에서 절찬 판매 중!

공인중개사 기초서/기본서/핵심요약집/문제집/기출문제집/실전모의고사 외 12종

주택관리사 기초서/기본서/핵심요약집/문제집/기출문제집/실전모의고사

7·9급공무원 기본서/단원별 기출&예상 문제집/기출문제집/기출팩/실전, 봉투모의고사

공무원 국어 한자·문법·독해/영어 단어·문법·독해/한국사·행정학·행정법 노트/행정법·헌법 판례집/면접

7급공무원 PSAT 기본서/기출문제집

계리직공무원 기본서/문제집/기출문제집

군무원 기출문제집/봉투모의고사

경찰공무원 기본서/기출문제집/모의고사/판례집/면접

소방공무원 기본서/기출문제집/실전, 봉투모의고사

뷰티 미용사/맞춤형화장품

검정고시 고졸/중졸 기본서/기출문제집/실전모의고사/총정리

사회복지사(1급) 기본서/기출문제집/핵심요약집

직업상담사(2급) 기본서/기출문제집

경비 기본서/기출/1차 한권끝장/2차 모의고사

전기기사 필기/실기/기출문제집

전기기능사 필기/실기

2023

에듀윌
9급공무원

해설편

영어

성정혜 편저 / 방재운, 백세레나, 이원일, 이지훈, 장종재 감수

공무원 영어 **베스트셀러 1위**!
쉽고 빠른 합격을 위한 필독서

|국가직|

2016 (②책형)

1	2	3	4	5
④	①	①	④	⑤

6	7	8	9	10
①	②	②	④	②

11	12	13	14	15
④	①	①	①	③

16	17	18	19	20
①	①	①	①	③

2017 국가(④책형)

1	2	3	4	5
④	③	③	④	⑤

6	7	8	9	10
②	④	②	④	②

11	12	13	14	15
④	④	②	④	③

16	17	18	19	20
④	①	④	④	④

2017 (⑮책형)

1	2	3	4	5
③	①	③	④	①

6	7	8	9	10
③	②	②	④	②

11	12	13	14	15
②	④	①	④	②

16	17	18	19	20
③	②	④	①	②

2018 (㉮책형)

1	2	3	4	5
②	②	③	③	①

6	7	8	9	10
①	①	④	④	①

11	12	13	14	15
④	③	②	①	①

16	17	18	19	20
④	②	②	④	④

2019 (㉯책형)

1	2	3	4	5
①	③	④	②	②

6	7	8	9	10
②	④	①	④	③

11	12	13	14	15
④	③	④	③	①

16	17	18	19	20
①	②	②	②	④

2020 (㉮책형)

1	2	3	4	5
③	④	③	①	④

6	7	8	9	10
②	③	③	④	③

11	12	13	14	15
②	③	④	④	②

16	17	18	19	20
②	②	④	①	①

2021 (㉯책형)

1	2	3	4	5
①	②	②	④	④

6	7	8	9	10
②	③	①	①	②

11	12	13	14	15
①	②	④	④	②

16	17	18	19	20
①	②	②	④	①

2022 (㉯책형)

1	2	3	4	5
①	②	④	②	①

6	7	8	9	10
①	④	②	①	④

11	12	13	14	15
①	③	④	④	④

16	17	18	19	20
④	③	②	①	①

|지방직|

2016 (Ⓐ책형)

1	2	3	4	5
④	③	③	④	②

6	7	8	9	10
①	②	③	④	④

11	12	13	14	15
④	②	③	③	③

16	17	18	19	20
③	③	②	④	①

2017 국가(Ⓐ책형)

1	2	3	4	5
④	③	③	④	①

6	7	8	9	10
①	④	②	④	①

11	12	13	14	15
④	④	②	④	③

16	17	18	19	20
③	②	②	②	②

2017 (Ⓑ책형)

1	2	3	4	5
③	③	①	④	④

6	7	8	9	10
③	④	④	③	②

11	12	13	14	15
①	④	③	④	③

16	17	18	19	20
③	④	③	②	②

2018 (Ⓑ책형)

1	2	3	4	5
①	②	④	③	④

6	7	8	9	10
③	③	④	④	①

11	12	13	14	15
②	②	③	④	③

16	17	18	19	20
③	④	①	①	②

2019 (Ⓐ책형)

1	2	3	4	5
①	④	④	②	④

6	7	8	9	10
②	①	②	④	②

11	12	13	14	15
④	③	①	②	①

16	17	18	19	20
③	③	③	①	②

2020 (Ⓓ책형)

1	2	3	4	5
④	③	①	①	④

6	7	8	9	10
②	④	③	①	①

11	12	13	14	15
④	③	①	①	④

16	17	18	19	20
②	②	③	③	③

2021 (Ⓐ책형)

1	2	3	4	5
③	①	①	④	④

6	7	8	9	10
④	④	④	②	④

11	12	13	14	15
③	③	②	④	②

16	17	18	19	20
②	④	②	③	②

2022 (Ⓐ책형)

1	2	3	4	5
②	①	④	④	③

6	7	8	9	10
②	③	④	④	②

11	12	13	14	15
②	①	②	④	②

16	17	18	19	20
③	④	①	②	③

|서울시|

2019 (A책형)

1	②	6	④	11	①	16	②
2	④	7	①	12	①	17	①
3	①	8	①	13	①	18	①
4	④	9	②	14	①	19	②
5	②	10	④	15	④	20	③

2018 (B책형)

1	③	6	④	11	④	16	③
2	①	7	③	12	③	17	④
3	④	8	④	13	④	18	①
4	③	9	④	14	②	19	②
5	③	10	①	15	①	20	③

2018 기술직 (A책형)

1	①	6	①	11	④	16	②
2	④	7	③	12	④	17	③
3	②	8	④	13	①	18	①
4	④	9	①	14	③	19	②
5	①	10	①	15	③	20	③

2017 (B책형)

1	②	6	②	11	①	16	②
2	④	7	①	12	④	17	②
3	④	8	④	13	④	18	②
4	③	9	②	14	④	19	③
5	④	10	④	15	③	20	①

2016 (A책형)

1	①	6	③	11	①	16	②
2	④	7	③	12	④	17	④
3	②	8	①	13	④	18	②
4	①	9	①	14	②	19	②
5	④	10	③	15	②		

|법원직|

2022 (①책형)

1	③	6	①	11	①	16	②	21	②
2	①	7	②	12	③	17	③	22	②
3	①	8	④	13	①	18	①	23	③
4	④	9	①	14	②	19	①	24	①
5	④	10	④	15	④	20	②	25	③

2021 (①책형)

1	④	6	④	11	④	16	④	21	①
2	④	7	④	12	①	17	④	22	④
3	③	8	④	13	②	18	①	23	①
4	④	9	②	14	①	19	③	24	②
5	③	10	④	15	①	20	④	25	②

2020 (①책형)

1	②	6	②	11	②	16	②	21	④
2	③	7	①	12	①	17	①	22	①
3	④	8	④	13	①	18	①	23	④
4	④	9	①	14	④	19	③	24	④
5	④	10	①	15	①	20	④	25	②

2019 (①책형)

1	④	6	③	11	②	16	②	21	④
2	②	7	③	12	④	17	①	22	②
3	③	8	②	13	③	18	④	23	②
4	④	9	④	14	④	19	②	24	④
5	①	10	④	15	④	20	②	25	②

2018 (①책형)

1	①	6	②	11	②	16	②	21	②
2	②	7	②	12	④	17	④	22	④
3	③	8	②	13	④	18	④	23	④
4	④	9	④	14	④	19	①	24	④
5	④	10	①	15	④	20	②	25	③

2017 (①책형)

1	④	6	④	11	②	16	②	21	④
2	②	7	①	12	①	17	③	22	②
3	③	8	①	13	④	18	④	23	③
4	④	9	④	14	④	19	④	24	③
5	④	10	②	15	④	20	②	25	③

2016 (①책형)

1	②	6	②	11	③	16	②	21	①
2	③	7	③	12	④	17	③	22	①
3	④	8	④	13	④	18	②	23	④
4	④	9	④	14	④	19	②	24	③
5	④	10	④	15	④	20	④	25	③

|교육행정직|

2018 (B책형)

1	②	6	②	11	①	16	②
2	④	7	④	12	④	17	②
3	④	8	④	13	①	18	④
4	④	9	③	14	③	19	③
5	④	10	④	15	③	20	③

2017 (A책형)

1	①	6	②	11	③	16	③
2	③	7	③	12	①	17	①
3	④	8	④	13	①	18	①
4	④	9	①	14	②	19	④
5	③	10	③	15	②	20	④

2016 (A책형)

1	①	6	②	11	②	16	②
2	②	7	①	12	④	17	④
3	③	8	④	13	④	18	④
4	④	9	④	14	④	19	④
5	③	10	④	15	①	20	②

2015 (A책형)

1	①	6	①	11	②	16	④
2	①	7	①	12	②	17	②
3	②	8	④	13	④	18	①
4	④	9	④	14	②	19	④
5	③	10	③	15	①	20	④

국가직

국가직 기출 POINT

Point 1 사용 빈도가 낮은 어휘보다는 필수 어휘가 다수 출제되는 경향이 강하다.

Point 2 기존에 출제되었던 문법 기출 포인트가 반복되고 있다.

Point 3 독해 난이도가 이전보다 평이해져 실수가 합격의 당락을 결정할 수 있으므로, 정확한 독해풀이가 요구된다.

2023년 국가직 시험 대비전략

"기출에 대한 정확한 분석"

Point 1 기존에 기출되었던 영역에서 모든 내용이 출제되었다. 기출문제를 정확하게 분석하는 훈련이 필요하다.

Point 2 출제포인트를 숙지한 후에는 기출 출제포인트를 기반으로 제작된 예상문제와 모의고사를 통해 실력 쌓기가 필요하다.

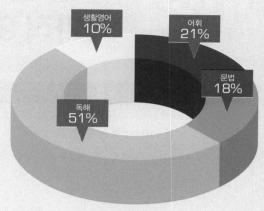

▲ 최근 7개년 평균 출제비중

최근 7개년 출제경향 및 출제비중

연도	총평	어휘	문법	독해	생활영어
2022	**기출에 근거해 평이하게 출제!** · 난이도, 문제 배분 방식, 선택지 배열 방식 등이 기출과 동일해 체감 난이도는 높지 않았음 · 기출의 범위를 정확하게 한정하고 공부했다면 고득점이 가능했음	25% (5문항)	20% (4문항)	45% (9문항)	10% (2문항)
2021	**기본에 충실했다면 고득점 가능!** · 전년도에 비해 문항 출제에 특이점이 없어, 기출을 정확히 분석해 온 수험생들이 고득점을 다수 달성함 · 독해 소재가 평이하고, 문법에서도 기존 출제 포인트가 재출제되면서, 기출 분석만으로도 우위 선점이 가능했음	20% (4문항)	20% (4문항)	50% (10문항)	10% (2문항)
2020	**국가직과 지방직의 확실한 차이가 존재한다!** · 지방직에 비해 평균 점수가 5~10점까지 하락한 경우로, 지문이나 출제 아이템의 난이도보다는 지문 길이로 인한 시간 관리가 관건이었음 · 독해에서 X세대와 밀레니엄 세대를 구분하는 새로운 주제 외에는 평이한 소재임에도 불구하고 지문 길이가 늘어나 체감 난도가 높았음	20% (4문항)	15% (3문항)	55% (11문항)	10% (2문항)
2019	**고른 문항 분포, 핵심 개념을 묻다!** · 기출 개념이 반복 출제되고 있는 경향이 뚜렷함 · 영작형 어법 문항에 까다로운 관용표현인 shy of가 출제되어 체감 난도 상승 · 독해 소재가 무난하여 수험생들의 전략 포인트가 될 수 있는 시험이었음	20% (4문항)	20% (4문항)	50% (10문항)	10% (2문항)
2018	**기본에 충실한 개념을 묻다!** · 기본 개념 인지 후 문제에 적용할 수 있는지를 묻는 개념 적용 문제 중심 · 어휘 또한 문맥상 추론으로 오답 선지 제거 가능 · 독해는 지문 소재가 다양해짐	20% (4문항)	15% (3문항)	55% (11문항)	10% (2문항)
2017	**고득점 기대해 볼 만!** · 평이한 어휘 문제 및 과년도 기출에서 많이 다루었던 패턴의 문법 출제 · put up with, take over 등 노골적인 관용 숙어 제시	20% (4문항)	20% (4문항)	50% (10문항)	10% (2문항)
2017 추가	**문제의 난이도보다는 시간 관리가 관건!** · 문제의 난이도는 평이 · 인공위성 관련 지문은 소재가 까다로웠으나 선택지 매력도가 떨어짐	20% (4문항)	20% (4문항)	50% (10문항)	10% (2문항)
2016	**독해 영역 수준!** · 제목이나 주제 찾기 문제 다수 출제 · 「not A nor B but C」의 등위상관접속사의 응용 표현 제시 · 삽입, 삭제, 배열 총합 3문제 출제	20% (4문항)	15% (3문항)	55% (11문항)	10% (2문항)

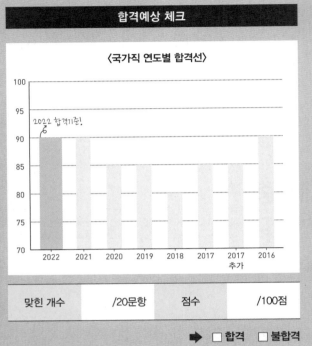

※ 해당 회차는 〈1초 합격예측 서비스〉의 데이터 누적 기간이 충분하지 않아 오답률, 선지 선택률 기재를 생략하였습니다.

| 1 | 어휘 > 유의어 찾기 | 답 ① |

| 해석 | 수년 동안, 형사들은 그 쌍둥이 형제의 갑작스러운 실종에 관한 수수께끼를 풀려고 노력해 오고 있었다.
① 풀다, 해결하다 　　　　② 창조하다, 만들어 내다
③ 모방하다 　　　　　　 ④ 알리다

| 정답해설 | ① unravel은 '(이해하기 어려운 것·미스터리 등을) 풀다'라는 의미로 solve(풀다, 해결하다)와 동의어이다.

어휘

detective 형사, 탐정
unravel (이해하기 어려운 것·미스터리 등을) 풀다
imitate 모방하다, 흉내 내다　　　 publicize 알리다, 광고[홍보]하다

| 2 | 어휘 > 유의어 찾기 | 답 ② |

| 해석 | 그 부부가 부모가 되기 전에, 그들의 침실 4개짜리 집은 쓸데없이 호화로운 것 같았다.
① 숨겨진 　　　　　　　② 호화로운
③ 빈 　　　　　　　　　④ 꽉 찬, 견고한

| 정답해설 | ② opulent는 '호화로운'이라는 의미로 luxurious(호화로운)와 동의어이다.

어휘

parenthood 부모임, 부모의 신분[입장]
opulent 호화로운　　　　　　　 solid 꽉 찬, 견고한, 단단한

| 3 | 어휘 > 유의어 찾기 | 답 ④ |

| 해석 | 사장님은 우리가 그렇게나 짧은 기간에 전체 예산을 이미 다 써버린 것을 보았을 때 격노했다.
① 매우 만족했다 　　　　② 매우 놀랐다
③ 극도로 차분해졌다 　　④ 극도로 화가 났다

| 정답해설 | ④ hit the roof는 '격노하다, 머리끝까지 화가 나다'는 의미이므로 정답은 ④이다.

어휘

hit the roof 격노하다, 머리끝까지 화가 나다
budget 예산

| 4 | 어휘 > 빈칸 완성 | 답 ② |

| 해석 | 마우스 포테이토는 컴퓨터에서 텔레비전의 카우치 포테이토에 ② 상응하는 것으로, 카우치 포테이토가 텔레비전 앞에서 하는 것과 상당 부분 같은 방식으로 여가 시간의 많은 부분을 컴퓨터 앞에서 보내는 경향이 있는 사람이다.
① 기술자 　　　　　　　② 상응하는 것
③ 네트워크 　　　　　　④ 시뮬레이션

| 정답해설 | ② mouse potato는 '컴퓨터 앞에서 시간을 많이 보내는 사람'이라는 의미로, '소파에 앉아 텔레비전만 보며 많은 시간을 보내는 사람'을 일컫는 couch potato와 유사한 말이다. mouse potato는 텔레비전의 couch potato에 '상응하는[동등한] 것'을 나타

내는 표현이므로 빈칸에는 equivalent(상응[대응]하는 것, 등가물) 가 가장 적절하다.

| 오답해설 | 텔레비전 앞에서 시간을 보내는 사람과 컴퓨터 앞에서 시간을 보내는 사람을 일대일로 비교하여 설명하고 있으므로, 나머지 선지는 문맥상 빈칸에 어색하다.

어휘

mouse potato 마우스 포테이토, 컴퓨터 앞에서 시간을 많이 보내는 사람
couch potato 카우치 포테이토, 소파에 앉아 텔레비전만 보며 많은 시간을 보내는 사람
tend to V ~하는 경향이 있다   leisure 여가
equivalent 상응[대응]하는 것, 등가물
simulation 시뮬레이션, 가장, 겉치레

5　어휘 > 빈칸 완성　　　　　　　　　답 ①

| 해석 | Mary는 남미로 가기 전 자신의 스페인어 ① 공부를 다시 하는 것을 결심했다.

① ~의 공부를 다시 하다, 복습하다
② 끝까지 듣다
③ ~을 변호[옹호]하다
④ 해고하다

| 정답해설 | ① 남미에 가기 전에 스페인어를 '다시 공부하기'로 결심했다는 것이 문맥상 가장 자연스러우므로, 정답은 brush up on (~의 공부를 다시 하다, 복습하다)이다.

어휘

brush up on ~의 공부를 다시 하다, 복습하다
hear out 끝까지 듣다   stick up for ~을 변호하다, 옹호하다
lay off 해고하다

6　문법 > 태, 전치사　　　　　　　　답 ①

| 해석 | ① 말은 개별 요구와 일의 성질에 따라 먹이를 공급받아야 한다.
② 내가 좁은 길을 걷고 있을 때, 바람 때문에 모자가 날아갔다.
③ 그녀는 경력 내내 정치 만화가로 주로 알려져 왔다.
④ 어린아이들조차도 잘한 일에 대해서는 칭찬받기를 좋아한다.

| 정답해설 | ① 주어인 A horse는 먹이를 공급받는 대상이므로 수동태 동사인 should be fed가 올바르게 사용되었다. 또한 according to는 전치사구이므로 명사구 its individual needs and the nature of its work를 알맞게 이끌고 있다.

| 오답해설 | ② 주절과 종속절의 주어가 같은 경우 종속절의 주어와 be동사를 생략하고 「접속사 + 분사」 형태로 쓸 수 있으나, 해당 문장에서는 주절의 주어는 My hat이고 종속절의 주어는 I로 서로 다르기 때문에 종속절의 주어와 be동사를 생략할 수 없다. 따라서 My hat was blown off by the wind while I was walking down a narrow street.로 고쳐야 알맞다.
③ 주어인 She는 정치 만화가로 알려져 있는 대상이므로 동사는 수동태로 쓰여야 한다. 따라서 She has been primarily known as ~가 되어야 알맞다.
④ done은 과거분사이므로 부사의 수식을 받아야 한다. good은 형용사이므로 부사인 well로 고쳐야 알맞다.

어휘

nature 특성, 성질   narrow 좁은
primarily 주로   compliment 칭찬하다

7　독해 > Micro Reading > 내용일치/불일치　　답 ④

| 해석 | Umberto Eco는 이탈리아의 소설가이자 문화비평가, 그리고 철학자였다. 그는 그의 1980년작 소설 『The Name of the Rose』로 널리 알려져 있는데, 이는 소설의 기호학을 성경 분석, 중세 연구, 그리고 문학 이론과 결합한 역사 미스터리물이다. 이후 그는 『Foucault's Pendulum』과 『The Island of the Day Before』를 포함한 다른 소설도 집필했다. Eco는 또한 번역가였다. 그는 Raymond Queneau의 저서 『Exercises de style』을 이탈리아어로 번역했다. 그는 산마리노 공화국 대학교 언론학과의 창설자였다. 그는 2016년 2월 19일 밤에 자신의 밀라노 집에서 2년 동안 앓아 오던 췌장암으로 인해 사망했다.

① 『The Name of the Rose』는 역사 소설이다.
② Eco는 책 한 권을 이탈리아어로 번역했다.
③ Eco는 대학의 학과를 창설했다.
④ Eco는 암으로 병원에서 사망했다.

| 정답해설 | ④ 마지막 문장 He died at his Milanese home of pancreatic cancer.에서 Eco가 그의 밀라노 집에서 췌장암으로 사망했다고 진술하고 있으므로, ④는 글의 내용과 일치하지 않는다.

| 오답해설 | ① 두 번째 문장 He is widely known for his 1980 novel ~에서 『The Name of the Rose』가 역사 미스터리물이라고 했으므로 본문 내용과 일치함을 알 수 있다.
② 네 번째 문장 Eco was also a translator ~에서 Eco가 Raymond Queneau의 저서 『Exercises de style』을 이탈리아어로 번역했다고 했으므로 본문 내용과 일치함을 알 수 있다.
③ 다섯 번째 문장 He was the founder of the Department of Media Studies ~에서 Eco가 산마리노 공화국 대학교 언론학과를 창설했다고 했으므로 본문 내용과 일치함을 알 수 있다.

어휘

critic 비평가   semiotics 기호학
fiction 소설, 허구   biblical 성경의
analysis 분석   medieval 중세의
Milanese 밀라노의   pancreatic 췌장의

8　문법 > 일치　　　　　　　　　　답 ②

| 해석 | 좋은 출발점을 찾으려면, 최초의 현대식 전기 배터리가 개발된 해인 1800년으로 되돌아가야 한다. 이탈리아인인 Alessandro Volta는 은, 구리, 그리고 아연의 조합이 전류를 발생시키는 데 이상적이라는 것을 발견했다. 볼타의 전지라고 불리는 향상된 디자인이 이러한 금속으로 만들어진 몇 개의 판을 해수에 담근 판지로 만들어진 판 사이에 쌓아서 만들어졌다. Volta의 연구에 대한 세평이 자자해 그는 직접 나폴레옹 황제 앞에서 시연을 하도록 요청받았다.

| 정답해설 | ② that절의 주어는 a combination으로 단수형이고 of silver, copper, and zinc는 주어를 수식하는 전명구이므로, 동사는 단수형 동사인 was가 되어야 알맞다. 따라서 ② were는 어법상 옳지 않다.

| 오답해설 | ① 선행사는 때를 나타내는 the year 1800이지만 이어

서 전치사 during이 왔으므로 관계대명사 which를 이용하여 수식을 하는 것이 올바르다. 만일 전치사 during이 없다면 관계부사 when를 이용하여 수식할 수 있을 것이다. 관계부사 when은 「전치사 + which」로 대체할 수 있다.

③ 주어 The enhanced design이 수식을 받는 대상이므로 수동의 의미를 갖는 과거분사 called가 알맞게 사용되었다.

④ 원인과 결과를 나타내는 「so/such ~ that …」 구문에서, 형용사/부사를 수식할 때는 so를, 명사를 수식할 때는 such를 쓴다. 이 문장에서 talk는 '세평, (화제의) 소문'이라는 의미의 불가산명사로 사용되었기 때문에 such를 사용했다.

| 더 알아보기 | 수 일치

주어는 전명구, 분사구, 부정사구, 관계사절, 동격절 등의 수식을 받을 수 있다. 주어-동사의 수 일치는 이러한 수식어구를 제외한, 주어로 쓰인 명사에 의해 결정된다. 즉, 문장의 주어로 쓰인 명사가 단수이면 단수 동사를, 복수이면 복수 동사를 사용하는 것이 옳다.

어휘

copper 구리 　　　　　　　　　　　zinc 아연
electrical current 전류 　　　　　　enhance 향상시키다, 발달시키다
Voltaic pile 볼타의 전지 　　　　　stack 쌓다
soak 담그다, 흠뻑 적시다 　　　　　talk 세평, (화제의) 소문
conduct 수행하다, 실시하다 　　　　demonstration 시연

9　　독해 > Macro Reading > 제목　　　　답 ①

| 해석 | 레이저는 빛이 전자와 반응하는 방식으로 인해 발생할 수 있다. 전자는 그 특정한 원자 또는 분자 고유의 특정 에너지 수준 또는 상태로 존재한다. 에너지 수준은 핵 주위의 고리 또는 궤도로 생각해 볼 수 있다. 외부 고리에 있는 전자는 내부 고리의 전자보다 더 높은 에너지 수준에 있다. 전자는, 예를 들어 섬광과 같은 에너지 주입을 통해 더 높은 에너지 수준으로 올라갈 수 있다. 전자가 외부 수준에서 내부 수준으로 떨어질 때, "잉여" 에너지는 빛으로 발산된다. 발산된 빛의 파장 또는 색은 방출된 에너지의 양과 정확히 관련되어 있다. 사용되는 특정한 레이저 물질에 따라, 특정한 빛의 파장이 (전자에 동력을 제공하거나 자극하기 위해) 흡수되고, (전자가 초기 수준으로 다시 떨어질 때) 특정한 파장이 발산된다.
① 레이저는 어떻게 발생하는가?
② 레이저는 언제 발명되었는가?
③ 레이저는 어떤 전자를 발산하는가?
④ 왜 전자는 빛을 반사하는가?

| 정답해설 | ① 첫 번째 문장 Lasers are possible because of the way light interacts with electrons.에서 레이저가 발생될 수 있는 원리를 제시한 후, 이어서 구체적으로 전자(electron)의 특징과 어떻게 전자가 빛에 반응하여 특정한 파장을 방출해 내는지 설명하고 있다. 따라서 전체 글의 제목으로 가장 적절한 것은 ①이다.

| 오답해설 | ②④ 본문에서 언급되지 않은 내용이므로 오답이다.
③ 본문에서는 전자가 레이저를 발생시킨다고 설명하고 있으므로, 레이저가 전자를 발산한다는 진술은 본문과 반대되는 진술이다.

어휘

interact 반응하다 　　　　　　　　electron 전자
characteristic of ~ 고유의, ~에 특유한

---

atom 원자 　　　　　　　　　　molecule 분자
orbit 궤도 　　　　　　　　　　nucleus 핵
bump up 올리다, 인상하다 　　　injection 주입, 투여
excess 초과한, 여분의 　　　　　give off 발산[방출]하다, 뿜다
wavelength 파장 　　　　　　　emit 발산[방출]하다, 내뿜다
precisely 정확히 　　　　　　　release 방출하다
absorb 흡수하다
energize 동력을 제공하다, 작동시키다
excite 자극하다 　　　　　　　　initial 초기의, 처음의
reflect 반사하다

10　　독해 > Logical Reading > 삭제　　　답 ③

| 해석 | 증가하는 인구가 (물) 부족으로 이어지고 기후 변화가 가뭄과 기근을 야기함에 따라 수리권 시장은 변화할 것으로 보인다. 그러나 그것들은 지역 및 도덕적 무역 관행에 기초할 것이며 대량 상품 무역과는 다를 것이다. 반대자들은 물을 거래하는 것이 비도덕적이라거나 심지어 인권 침해라고 주장하지만, 이미 수리권은 오만에서부터 호주에 이르기까지 세계의 건조 지역에서 매매된다. ③ 증류수를 마시는 것은 이로울 수 있지만, 특히 다른 공급원을 통해 미네랄이 보충되지 않는다면, 모든 사람에게 최고의 선택지인 것은 아니다. "우리는 다가올 10년과 그 이후에 실제로 물이 새로운 금으로 변모할 것이라고 굳게 믿는다"라고 Ziad Abdelnour는 말했다. "스마트 머니가 공격적으로 이 방향으로 움직이는 것은 놀라운 일이 아니다."

| 정답해설 | ③ 본문은 '수리권(water rights)'과 관련되어 대두되고 있는 문제점과 점점 더 높아지는 수리권의 중요성에 관해 설명하는 글이다. 그런데 ③에서는 '증류수를 마시는 것'에 있어 주의할 점에 관해 언급하고 있으므로, 수리권과는 거리가 먼 내용이다.

어휘

water right 수리권(수자원을 배타적·독점적으로 사용할 수 있는 권리)
evolve 변하다, 진화하다 　　　　　shortage 부족
drought 가뭄 　　　　　　　　　famine 기근
ethical 윤리적인, 도덕적인 　　　　bulk 대량
commodity 상품
detractor 가치를 깎아내리는[폄하하는] 사람, 비방가, 비평가, 반대자
argue 주장하다 　　　　　　　　　unethical 비윤리적인, 비도덕적인
breach 침해 　　　　　　　　　　arid 건조한
distill 증류하다 　　　　　　　　　beneficial 이로운
supplement 보충하다
smart money 스마트 머니(전문적인 지식을 갖고 투자·투기한 돈)
aggressively 공격적으로, 정력적으로

11　　생활영어 > 회화/관용표현　　　　답 ④

| 해석 | A: 대학교 구내식당의 메뉴가 바뀌었다고 들었어요.
B: 맞아요, 저도 방금 확인했어요.
A: 그리고 새로운 업체를 고용했대요.
B: 그래요. Sam's Catering이에요.
A: ④ 예전 메뉴와 차이점은 무엇인가요?
B: 디저트 메뉴 선택지가 더 많아졌어요. 또 일부 샌드위치 메뉴는 없어졌어요.
① 당신이 제일 좋아하는 디저트는 무엇인가요
② 그들의 사무실이 어딘지 아시나요
③ 메뉴에 관해 제 도움이 필요하신가요
④ 예전 메뉴와 차이점은 무엇인가요

| 정답해설 | ④ 대화 초반에서 구내식당의 메뉴와 업체가 변경되었다고 말하고 있고, 마지막 B의 대답에서는 메뉴에서 추가된 것과 삭제된 것에 관해 언급하고 있으므로, 빈칸에서 A는 예전 메뉴와의 차이점에 관해 질문했을 것이라고 추측할 수 있다.

어휘

cafeteria 구내식당, 카페테리아　　　caterer 음식 공급자

12　생활영어 > 회화/관용표현　　　답 ③

| 해석 | A: 안녕하세요. 도와드릴까요?
B: 네, 저는 스웨터를 찾고 있어요.
A: 음, 이게 가을 컬렉션에 나온 최신 스타일이에요. 어때요?
B: 멋지네요. 얼마죠?
A: 가격을 확인해 볼게요. 120달러예요.
B: ③ 제가 생각한 가격대에 좀 맞지 않아요.
A: 그러면 이 스웨터는 어떠세요? 지난 시즌에 나온 것이지만 50달러로 할인 중이에요.
B: 완벽해요! 입어 볼게요.
① 그것과 어울리는 바지도 필요해요
② 그 재킷은 저를 위한 완벽한 선물이에요
③ 제가 생각한 가격대에 좀 맞지 않아요
④ 토요일에 저희는 7시까지 열어요

| 정답해설 | ③ A가 제품의 가격을 말해 주자 B가 빈칸의 답변을 하고, 이어서 A가 더 저렴한 제품을 추천해 주고 있으므로 B는 처음 제안받은 제품의 가격에 대한 불만족을 말했을 가능성이 있다.

어휘

gorgeous (아주) 멋진　　　　　try on 입어 보다
go with ~와 어울리다　　　　　price range 가격대, 가격 폭

13　문법 > 비교　　　답 ②

| 정답해설 | ② 원급과 비교급을 이용하여 최상급의 의미를 나타낼 수 있다. 원급을 사용할 경우 「부정 주어 + is as[so] ~ as …」로, 비교급을 사용할 경우 「부정 주어 + is more ~ than …」으로 써야 한다. 따라서 ②는 원급과 비교급 중 한 가지를 이용한 표현으로 고쳐야 한다. 즉, Nothing is as[so] precious as time in our life. 또는 Nothing is more previous than time in our life.로 바꿀 수 있다.

| 오답해설 | ① 난이형용사(easy 등)는 to부정사를 진주어로 취하므로 옳게 사용된 문장이며, to부정사의 의미상 주어도 「for + 목적격」으로 알맞게 영작되었다. 여기서 by no means는 '결코 ~이 아닌'이라는 의미의 부사구가 삽입된 것이다.

③ 「cannot be too + 형용사」는 '아무리 ~해도 지나치지 않다'라는 의미의 조동사 관용표현으로 알맞게 사용되었으며, 주절의 주어와 종속절의 주어가 children으로 동일하므로 종속절에서 주어와 be동사를 생략하고 「when + 현재분사」의 구조를 사용한 것도 옳다.

④ what은 선행사를 포함한 관계대명사로 명사절을 이끌어 타동사의 목적어로 사용될 수 있다.

| 더 알아보기 | **최상급 대용 표현**

> 원급과 비교급을 이용해서 다양한 최상급 표현이 가능하다.
> • He is the tallest in the world.
> 　그는 세상에서 가장 키가 크다.
> = No one in the world is as tall as he (is).
> = No one in the world is so tall as he (is).
> = No one in the world is taller than he (is).
> = He is taller than any other person in the world.
> = He is taller than all the other people in the world.
> = He is taller than anyone else in the world.

| 더 알아보기 | **시험에 자주 나오는 관용표현**

> • cannot be too + 형용사 ~: 아무리 ~해도 지나치지 않다
> • cannot but + 동사원형 ~: ~하지 않을 수 없다
> • had better + 동사원형 ~: ~하는 편이 낫다
> • It would be better to + 동사원형 ~: ~하는 것이 낫다
> • don't have to + 동사원형 ~: ~할 필요는 없다

어휘

by no means 결코 ~이 아닌　　　precious 소중한

14　문법 > 분사　　　답 ④

| 정답해설 | ④ with 분사구문은 '~한 채로'라는 의미로 동시 상황을 나타낼 때 사용할 수 있다. 이때 「with + 목적어 + 분사」에서, 목적어와 분사의 관계가 능동이면 현재분사를, 수동이면 과거분사를 써야 하는데, 다리는 '꼬여지는' 대상이므로 수동의 의미가 알맞다. 따라서 crossing을 crossed로 고쳐야 옳은 문장이 된다.

| 오답해설 | ① 커피를 마신 것은 과거의 일이고 그 결과 지금 잠을 이룰 수 없는 것이므로, 완료 분사구문 Having drunk ~가 올바르게 사용되었다.

② 그녀가 친절한 사람인 사실은 변하지 않는 특성이므로, 단순 분사구문 Being ~이 알맞게 사용되었다.

③ 주절과 분사구문의 주어가 다르면 분사구문의 주어를 표시해 주는데, 이를 독립분사구문이라고 한다. 여기서 분사구문의 주어는 All things이고 주절의 주어는 she이므로 각각 표시해 주었고, All things는 고려되는 대상이므로 수동의 의미를 갖는 과거분사 considered가 알맞게 쓰였다. 본래 All things (being) considered에서 being은 생략 가능하므로 considered만 남아 있는 형태이다. 단, considering all things는 '모든 것을 고려하자면'이라는 의미로 해석상의 차이에 주의해야 한다.

| 더 알아보기 | **신체와 관련된 with 분사구문 표현**

> 신체와 관련된 with 분사구문은 「with + one's 신체 부위 + 분사」의 형태로 표현한다.
> • with one's eyes closed 눈을 감고서
> • with one's arms folded 팔짱을 끼고서
> • with one's legs crossed 다리를 꼬고서
> • with one's mouth watering 침을 흘리면서
> • with one's body shaking 몸을 흔들면서

---

15 독해 > Logical Reading > 연결사   답 ②

| 해석 | 망자와 유대를 유지하는 것에 대한 믿음은 문화마다 다르다. 예를 들어, 고인과 유대를 유지하는 것은 일본의 종교 의식에서 받아들여지고 지속된다. 그러나 Arizona의 Hopi 인디언들 사이에서 고인은 가능한 한 빨리 잊혀지고 삶은 평소대로 계속된다. (A) 실제로, Hopi족의 장례 의식은 인간과 영혼의 단절로 마무리된다. 애도의 다양성이 두 무슬림 사회에서보다 더 극명한 곳은 없는데, 하나는 이집트이고 다른 하나는 발리이다. 이집트의 무슬림들 사이에서 유족들은 비극적인 이야기에 유사하게 공감하고 그들의 슬픔을 표현하는 다른 사람들에게 둘러싸여, 자신들의 슬픔을 오래 곱씹는 것이 권장된다. (B) 대조적으로, 발리에서 유족이 된 무슬림들은 슬퍼하기보다는 웃고 즐거워하도록 격려된다.

	(A)	(B)
①	그러나	유사하게
②	실제로	대조적으로
③	그러므로	예를 들어
④	마찬가지로	결과적으로

| 정답해설 | ② (A) 빈칸 이전에서 Hopi 인디언들이 고인을 대하는 태도에 관해 언급하고, 이후에서는 그들의 장례 의식이 마무리되는 방식을 덧붙여 설명하고 있으므로, 빈칸에는 앞서 나온 내용에 대해 첨언할 때 사용할 수 있는 In fact(실제로)가 들어가는 것이 가장 적절하다.

(B) 무슬림 사회에서 죽음을 애도하는 두 가지 방식을 이집트와 발리의 예시를 들어 각각 설명하고 있다. 빈칸 이전에서는 슬픔을 오래 곱씹는 이집트에 관해 언급했고, 빈칸 이후에서는 이와는 반대로 죽음을 웃음과 기쁨으로 승화시키는 발리에 관해 설명하고 있다. 서로 대조되는 예시를 제시하고 있으므로 빈칸에는 By contrast(대조적으로)가 가장 적절하다.

| 오답해설 | ① (A) 전후 내용이 역접 관계가 아니므로 오답이다.
③ (B) 전후 내용이 예시 관계가 아니므로 오답이다.
④ (B) 전후 내용이 인과 관계가 아니므로 오답이다.

| 더 알아보기 | **첨언과 대조를 나타내는 연결사**

- 첨언 연결사: in addition (to), besides, furthermore, moreover 등
- 대조 연결사: however, in contrast, on the other hand, nevertheless, nonetheless 등

---

16 독해 > Reading for Writing > 빈칸 구 완성   답 ④

| 해석 | 과학자들은 더 높아진 대기 온도가 그린란드 대륙 빙하 표면 용해의 원인이 되고 있다는 것을 오랫동안 알고 있었다. 그러나 새로운 연구가 아래로부터 빙하를 공격하기 시작한 또 다른 위협 요소를 발견해 냈다. 거대한 빙하 아래로 이동하는 따뜻한 해수가 훨씬 더 빠르게 빙하를 녹게 하는 원인이 되고 있다. 연구 결과는 북동 그린란드에 있는 Nioghalvfjerdsfjorden Glacier의 많은 "빙설" 중 하나를 연구한 연구원들에 의해 학술지인 *Nature Geoscience*에 게재되었다. 빙설은 육지의 얼음에서 떨어지지 않은 채로 물 위에 떠 있는 긴 얼음 조각이다. 이 과학자들이 연구한 거대한 빙설은 길이가 거의 50마일이다. 연구는 대서양의 따뜻한 해류가 빙하 쪽으로 곧장 흘러가 이로 인해 많은 양의 열이 빙하와 접촉하게 되고 빙하의 용해를 ④ 가속화시키는 폭이 1마일이 넘는 수중 해류를 밝혀냈다.

① 분리하는   ② 늦추는
③ 막는   ④ 가속화시키는

| 정답해설 | ④ 두 번째 문장의 콜론(:) 뒤 Warm ocean water moving underneath the vast glaciers is causing them to melt even more quickly.에서 따뜻한 해수로 인해 거대 빙하가 더 빨리 녹고 있다는 사실을 알 수 있으며, 본문 중후반에는 이와 관련된 구체적인 연구 결과가 제시되고 있다. 따라서 빙하가 더 빨리 녹는 과정을 설명하는 표현이 빈칸에 들어가는 것이 가장 적절하므로, 빈칸에는 ④가 가장 적절하다. 참고로 선지만 비교해 보아도 ①②③의 의미와 ④의 의미가 서로 상반되기 때문에, 이 점에 유의하여 선지를 먼저 확인해 보는 것도 좋다.

---

17 독해 > Macro Reading > 제목   답 ③

| 해석 | 다른 문화의 사람들은 세상을 다르게 바라볼까? 한 심리학자가 실감 나는 물고기 및 기타 수중 물체의 영상을 일본인과 미국인 학생들에게 보여 주었고 그들이 본 것을 보고하도록 요청했다. 미국인들과 일본인들은 중심이 되는 물고기들에 관해서는 거의 동일한 횟수의 언급을 했으나, 일본인들은 물, 돌, 물방울, 그리고 비활성 동물물을 포함한 배경 요소에 관해서는 60% 이상 더 많은 언급을 했다. 게다가, 일본인과 미국인 참가자들이 활동적인 동물들과 관련된 움직임에 관해 거의 비슷한 횟수의 언급을 한 반면, 일본인 참가자들은 비활동적인 배경 물체와 관련된 관계에 관한 언급을 거의 2배 정도 더 많이 했다. 아마 가장 강력한 차이는, 일본인 참가자들이 제일 처음 말한 문장은 환경을 언급하는 것인 반면, 미국인들의 첫 번째 문장은 중심이 되는 물고기를 언급하는 것일 가능성이 3배나 높았다.

① 일본인과 미국인 사이의 언어 장벽
② 뇌에서 물체와 배경의 연상
③ 인식에 있어서의 문화적 차이
④ 꼼꼼한 사람들의 우월성

| 정답해설 | ③ 첫 번째 문장 Do people from different cultures

view the world differently?에서 주제와 관련한 질문을 던진 후, 이에 대한 답변이 되는 실험 결과를 이후에 제시하고 있다. 본문에서는 같은 영상을 본 후, 미국인 학생들과 일본인 학생들이 영상의 내용을 다르게 설명했다는 점을 언급하며, 인식에 있어서의 문화적 차이에 대한 근거를 제시하고 있다.

| 오답해설 | ① 본문에 언어에 관한 내용은 언급되지 않는다.
② 뇌에서 물체와 배경이 어떻게 연상되는지는 본문에 제시되지 않는다.
④ 꼼꼼한 사람들이 더 우수하다는 내용은 본문에 언급되지 않는다.

어휘

reference 언급	focal 중심의, 초점의
inert 비활성의, 비활동적인	tellingly 강력하게
language barrier 언어 장벽	association 연상; 유대; 제휴
perception 인식, 인지, 지각	superiority 우월성, 우수성
detail-oriented 세부적인 것을 중요시하는, 꼼꼼한	

---

18 독해 > Logical Reading > 삽입   답 ④

| 해석 | 사람들은 여러 방식으로 인력, 즉 중력에 노출될 수 있다. 그것은 등을 찰싹 맞을 때처럼 신체의 일부에만 영향을 미치는 국부적인 것일 수도 있다. 그것은 또한 자동차 충돌에서 겪는 강한 힘과 같이 순간적일 수도 있다. 세 번째 유형의 중력은 지속되는데, 다시 말해 적어도 수초 간 이어진다. 지속적이면서 온몸에 미치는 중력은 사람에게 가장 위험하다. 신체는 보통 지속적인 중력보다 국부적이거나 순간적인 중력을 더 잘 견디는데, 혈액이 다리 쪽으로 쏠리게 되어, 신체의 나머지 부분에 산소가 부족해지기 때문에 지속적인 중력은 치명적일 수 있다. 앉거나 서 있는 대신에 신체가 수평으로 되어 있거나 누워 있는 상태에서 적용된 지속적인 중력은 사람들이 더 잘 견딜 수 있는데, 혈액이 다리가 아니라 등에 고이기 때문이다. ④ 따라서, 혈액과 생명을 유지해 주는 산소를 심장이 뇌로 더 쉽게 순환시킬 수 있다. 우주 비행사와 전투기 조종사 같은 일부 사람들은 중력에 대한 신체의 저항을 증가시키기 위해 특수 훈련 연습을 실시한다.

| 정답해설 | ④ 주어진 문장에서는 혈액과 산소가 뇌로 더 쉽게 공급될 수 있는 상황에 대해 설명하고 있다. ③ 이전 문장에서 피가 다리 쪽으로 쏠리면 나머지 신체는 산소가 부족하다고 언급하고, ③ 이후 문장에서 수평으로 있거나 누워 있을 때는 피가 등 쪽에 고여 있어 중력을 더 잘 견딜 수 있다고 설명한다. 이러한 상황에서 피가 뇌 쪽으로 더 잘 순환될 수 있다는 내용이 이어지는 것이 자연스러우므로 주어진 문장은 ④에 들어가는 것이 가장 적절하다.

| 오답해설 | ③ 주어진 문장의 Thus(따라서)로 보아 주어진 문장 이전에 피가 뇌로 더 잘 순환될 수 있는 상황을 제시해 주어야 하는데, ③ 이전 문장에서는 피가 다리 쪽으로 쏠려 신체의 나머지 부분에 산소가 부족해진다고 언급하고 있으므로, 주어진 문장이 결과로 이어지는 것은 문맥상 자연스럽지 않다.

어휘

circulate 순환시키다, 차례로 돌다	gravitational force 중력, 인력
localize 국한시키다, 국부적이 되게 하다	
momentary 순간적인	endure 견디다
sustain 지속[계속]시키다	withstand 견디다, 참다
deadly 치명적인	deprive A of B A에게서 B를 빼앗다
horizontal 가로의, 수평의	tend to V ～하는 경향이 있다

---

tolerable 참을 수 있는, 견딜 수 있는	
pool 모이다, 고이다	astronaut 우주 비행사
undergo 받다, 겪다	resistance 저항

---

19 독해 > Macro Reading > 요지   답 ①

| 해석 | 만일 누군가 당신에게 제안을 했는데, 당신이 그것의 일부가 정당한 이유로 염려스럽다면, 보통 당신은 당신의 모든 변경 조건들을 동시에 제시하는 것이 더 낫다. "급여가 조금 낮네요. 이에 대해 어떻게 해 주실 수 있나요?"라고 말하고, 일단 그녀가 그것을 처리하고 나면 다시 돌아가 "감사합니다. 이제 여기 제가 원하는 두 가지 다른 것들이 있는데…"라고 말하지 말라. 만일 당신이 처음에 단 한 가지만을 요청한다면, 그녀는 그것을 들어주면 당신이 제안을 받아들일 (아니면 적어도 결정을 내릴) 준비가 될 것이라고 생각할 것이다. 만일 당신이 계속 "그리고 한 가지 더…"라고 말한다면 그녀가 인자하거나 이해심 있는 기분으로 계속 있지는 않을 것이다. 게다가, 만일 당신에게 한 가지가 넘는 요구 사항이 있다면, 당신이 원하는 모든 것을 A, B, C, 그리고 D라고 단순히 말하지 마라. 당신에게 있어 각각의 상대적인 중요성에 대해서도 신호를 보내라. 그렇지 않으면 당신에게 제공하기 상당히 쉽다는 이유로 그녀는 당신이 가장 덜 중요하게 생각하는 두 가지를 선택하고 당신과 타협했다고 느낄지도 모르기 때문이다.
① 다수의 사안을 연속적이 아니라 동시에 협상하라.
② 성공적인 협상을 위해 민감한 주제는 피하라.
③ 알맞은 협상 시기를 골라라.
④ 급여 협상 시 너무 단도직입적으로 하지 마라.

| 정답해설 | ① 첫 번째 문장 ～ you're usually better off proposing all your changes at once.에서 한꺼번에 제안에 관한 변경 조건들을 제시할 것을 조언하고 있다. 이어서, 변경 조건들을 하나씩 차례로 말하는 상황을 예시하면서 그로 인해 부정적인 결과가 발생할 수 있음을 암시하고 있다. 따라서 글의 요지로 가장 적절한 것은 ①이다.

| 오답해설 | ② 본문에서는 제안에 대한 이의 제기를 한꺼번에 제시하라고 언급하고 있을 뿐, 그러한 이의의 내용에 관해서는 구체적으로 설명하고 있지 않으므로 오답이다.
③ 협상 시기에 대해서는 본문에 언급되지 않는다.
④ 본문에서는 협상 내용의 한 예시로 급여를 제시한 것일 뿐, 글 전체가 급여 협상에 관한 내용은 아니므로 글의 요지로는 부적절하다.

어휘

legitimately 정당하게, 합법적으로	
concerned about ～을 염려하는	better off ～하는 것이 더 나은
at once 동시에, 한 번에	initially 초기에, 처음에
assume 추정하다, 가정하다	relative 상대적인
otherwise 그렇지 않으면	
meet ～ halfway ～와 타협[절충]하다	
negotiate 협상하다	simultaneously 동시에, 일제히
serially 연속으로	

---

20 독해 > Logical Reading > 배열   답 ③

| 해석 | 오늘날, Lamarck는 어떻게 적응이 발달하느냐에 관한 그의 잘못된 설명으로 인해 대부분 부당하게 기억된다. 그는 특정 신체 부위를 사용 또는 사용하지 않음으로써 생물이 특정 형질을 발달시킨다고 제안했다.

(B) Lamarck는 이러한 형질이 자손에게 이어질 것이라고 생각했다. Lamarck는 이 발상을 획득형질유전이라고 명명했다.

(C) 예를 들면, Lamarck는 캥거루의 강력한 뒷다리는 조상들이 점프를 통해 자신들의 다리를 강화시키고, 그 획득된 다리 힘을 자손에게 물려준 결과라고 설명했다. 그러나, 획득된 형질이 유전되기 위해서는 특정 유전자의 DNA를 어떻게든 변형시켜야 할 것이다.

(A) 이것이 발생한다는 근거는 없다. 그럼에도 불구하고, Lamarck가 생물이 자신들의 환경에 적응할 때 진화가 발생한다는 점을 제안했다는 것에 주목하는 것은 중요하다. 이 발상이 Darwin을 위한 무대를 마련하는 데 도움을 주었다.

| 정답해설 | ③ 주어진 글의 두 번째 문장의 certain characteristics를 (B)의 첫 문장 these characteristics가 직접적으로 가리키고 있으므로, (B)가 주어진 문장에 바로 이어지는 것이 적절하다. 이어서 (B)에서 언급한 this idea에 관한 구체적인 예시가 (C)에서 For example 이하에 나오므로 (C)가 연결되는 것이 자연스럽다. 마지막으로 (A)에서 (C)의 두 번째 문장에서 설명한 '획득형질유전을 위해 DNA가 변형되는 것'을 this로 가리키며, 이것이 발생하는 근거가 없다고 언급하고 있으므로, (A)가 (C)에 이어지는 것이 적절하다. 따라서 올바른 순서는 (B) – (C) – (A)이다.

| 오답해설 | ①② (C)가 (A)에서 제시한 내용의 구체적인 예시가 아니므로 (A) 다음에 (C)가 오는 것은 어색하다.

어휘

unfairly 부당하게, 불공평하게	adaptation 적응, 순응
evolve 진화하다, 발달하다	organism 생물
adapt to ~에 적응하다	
set the stage for ~을 위한 장(場)[무대]을 마련하다	
pass on 넘겨주다, 물려주다, 전달하다	
offspring 자식, 자손, 새끼	inheritance 유전
acquire 획득하다, 얻다	ancestor 조상
somehow 어떻게든	modify 변형하다, 수정하다
gene 유전자	

합격예상 체크

〈국가직 연도별 합격선〉

2021 합격기준 6

맞힌 개수	/20문항	점수	/100점

➡ ☐ 합격 ☐ 불합격

취약영역 체크

문항	정답	영역	문항	정답	영역
1	①	어휘 > 유의어 찾기	11	①	생활영어 > 회화/관용표현
2	②	어휘 > 유의어 찾기	12	②	생활영어 > 회화/관용표현
3	②	어휘 > 유의어 찾기	13	④	독해 > Micro Reading > 내용 일치/불일치
4	④	어휘 > 빈칸 완성	14	④	문법 > 강조와 도치
5	④	독해 > Micro Reading > 내용 일치/불일치	15	②	문법 > 접속사
6	②	문법 > 시제	16	①	독해 > Reading for Writing > 빈칸 절 완성
7	③	독해 > Macro Reading > 제목	17	②	독해 > Reading for Writing > 빈칸 구 완성
8	③	문법 > 관계사	18	③	독해 > Logical Reading > 배열
9	④	독해 > Logical Reading > 삽입	19	④	독해 > Macro Reading > 제목
10	④	독해 > Logical Reading > 삭제	20	①	독해 > Macro Reading > 심경

⬇ 영역별 틀린 개수로 취약영역을 확인하세요!

어휘	/4	문법	/4	독해	/10	생활영어	/2

➡ 나의 취약영역: _____

※ [정답해설]과 [오답해설] 선지의 50% 표시는 〈1초 합격예측 서비스〉를 통해 수집된 선지 선택률을 나타냅니다.

1 어휘 > 유의어 찾기 | 오답률 29% | 답 ①

| 해석 | 사회적 관습으로서의 사적 자유(프라이버시)는 다른 사회적 관습과 함께 개인의 행위를 형성하며, 따라서 사회 생활에 중심이 된다.
① 71% ~와 결합하여　② 19% ~와 비교하여
③ 4% ~ 대신에　④ 6% ~의 경우에

| 정답해설 | ① in conjunction with는 '~와 함께'라는 의미로, in combination with와 의미가 가장 가깝다.

어휘

shape 형성하다, 형태를 주다
in conjunction with ~와 함께
in combination with ~와 결합하여
in comparison with ~와 비교하여
in place of ~ 대신에
in case of ~의 경우에

2 어휘 > 유의어 찾기 | 오답률 36% | 답 ②

| 해석 | 재즈의 영향력은 매우 널리 퍼져 있어서 대부분의 대중음악은 양식상의 뿌리를 재즈에 둔다.
① 12% 사기의　② 64% 편재하는, 어디에나 있는
③ 20% 설득력 있는　④ 4% 비참한, 재해의

| 정답해설 | ② pervasive는 '골고루 미치는, 만연하는, 널리 퍼진'이라는 의미이므로, '편재(遍在)하는, 어디에나 있는'이라는 뜻의 ubiquitous와 가장 의미가 유사하다.

어휘

pervasive 골고루 미치는, 만연하는, 널리 퍼진
owe A to B A에 대하여 B의 은혜[신세]를 지다
deceptive 사기의
ubiquitous 편재하는, 어디에나 있는
persuasive 설득력 있는　disastrous 비참한; 재해의

3 어휘 > 유의어 찾기 | 오답률 45% | 답 ②

| 해석 | 이 소설은 사업을 시작하기 위해 학교를 그만두는 제멋대로인 십대 청소년의 짜증 난 부모에 관한 것이다.
① 13% 무정한, 냉담한　② 55% 짜증 난, 약이 오른
③ 17% 평판 좋은　④ 15% 자신감 있는, 확신하는

| 정답해설 | ② vexed는 '짜증 난, 화난'이라는 의미이므로, '짜증 난, 약이 오른'이라는 의미의 annoyed가 유의어이다.

어휘

vexed 짜증 난, 화난　unruly 제멋대로인, 다루기 힘든
callous 무정한, 냉담한　reputable 평판 좋은

4 어휘 > 빈칸 완성 | 오답률 26% | 답 ④

| 해석 | 한 무리의 젊은 시위자들이 경찰서에 ④ 침입하려고 시도했다.
① 16% ~을 일렬[한 줄]로 세우다[배열하다]
② 3% 나눠 주다

③ 7% 계속하다
④ 74% ~로 침입하다, 난입하다

| **정답해설** | ④ 빈칸 뒤에 '경찰서'라는 장소가 등장하므로, 이와 관련한 시위자들의 행위로 문맥상 가장 적절한 표현은 선지 중 '침입하다, 난입하다'라는 뜻의 break into이다.

어휘
demonstrator 시위자
line up ~을 일렬[한 줄]로 세우다[배열하다]
give out 나눠 주다　　　　carry on 계속하다
break into ~로 침입하다, 난입하다, 몰래 잠입하다

5　독해 > Micro Reading > 내용일치/불일치　오답률 21%　답 ④

| **해석** | 가장 악명 높은 수입 노동력의 사례는 물론 대서양 노예 매매인데, 이것은 농장에서 노동할 천만 명이나 되는 아프리카인 노예들을 신세계(New World)로 이주시켰다. 그러나 비록 유럽인들이 가장 큰 규모로 노예제를 실행했을지 몰라도, 그들이 노예를 자신들의 공동체로 끌어들인 유일한 사람들은 결코 아니었다. 그에 앞서, 고대 이집트인들은 피라미드 건설을 위해 노예 노동력을 이용했고, 초창기 아랍 탐험가들 또한 종종 노예 상인이었으며, 아랍 노예제는 20세기까지 지속되었고, 실제로 아직도 몇몇 장소에서는 지속되고 있다. 아메리카 대륙에서는 일부 원주민 부족이 다른 부족의 구성원을 노예로 삼았으며, 노예제는 또한 많은 아프리카 국가에서도 하나의 사회 제도였는데, 특히 식민지 시대 이전에 그러했다.
① 아프리카 노동자들은 자발적으로 신세계로 이주했다.
② 유럽인들은 노예 노동을 이용한 최초의 사람들이었다.
③ 아랍의 노예제는 어떠한 형태로든 더 이상 존재하지 않는다.
④ 노예제는 심지어 아프리카 국가들에서도 존재했다.

| **정답해설** | ④ 79% 마지막 문장의 후반부에서 노예제는 또한 많은 아프리카 국가에서도 하나의 사회 제도였다고 했으므로 글의 내용과 일치한다.

| **오답해설** | ① 8% 첫 번째 문장에서 농장에서 일할 아프리카인 노예들을 대서양 노예 매매를 통해 신세계로 이주시켰다고 했으므로 그들이 자발적으로 이주했다는 것은 글의 내용과 일치하지 않는다.
② 7% 두 번째 문장에서 유럽인들은 노예를 그들의 공동체로 끌어들인 유일한 사람들이 아니었고, 그 이전에 이집트인들이 피라미드 건설에 이미 노예 노동력을 이용했으며 초창기 아랍 탐험가들 또한 종종 노예 상인이었다고 했으므로, 글의 내용과 일치하지 않는다.
③ 6% 두 번째 문장 후반부에서 아랍의 노예제는 여전히 몇몇 장소에서 지속되고 있음을 진술하고 있으므로 글의 내용과 일치하지 않는다.

어휘
notorious 악명 높은　　　　enslave 노예로 만들다
plantation (대규모) 농장　　　slavery 노예제
by no means 결코 ~이 아닌　　tribe 부족
institution (사회) 제도; 관례, 관습　colonial 식민지의
voluntarily 자발적으로

6　문법 > 시제　오답률 46%　답 ②

| **해석** | ① 이 안내 책자는 홍콩에서 어디를 방문해야 하는지 여러분에게 말해 준다.
② 나는 대만에서 태어났지만, 일을 시작한 이래로 한국에 살고 있다.
③ 그 소설이 너무 재미있어서 나는 시간 가는 줄 몰랐고 버스를 놓쳤다.
④ 서점들이 신문을 더 이상 취급하지 않는다는 것은 놀랍지 않아, 그렇지?

| **정답해설** | ② 54% since는 '~ 이래로'라는 의미로, since절에는 과거시제가, 주절에는 현재완료시제가 쓰인다. 따라서 have lived와 started의 시제는 모두 올바르다.

| **오답해설** | ① 9% 의문사 where가 이끄는 절이 4형식 동사 tell의 직접목적어로 사용되었으므로 where절의 주어와 동사는 의문문 어순으로 바뀌지 않는다. 따라서 where should you는 where you should의 어순이 되어야 한다.
③ 25% 감정형용사가 사람의 감정 상태를 나타낼 때는 과거분사형(-ed)이, 사물의 상태를 나타낼 때는 현재분사형(-ing)이 쓰인다. 여기에서는 사물인 novel의 상태를 서술하므로 excited가 exciting으로 바뀌어야 옳다.
④ 12% 부가의문문은 주절이 긍정형이면 부정형으로, 주절이 부정형이면 긍정형으로 쓰여야 하며, 주절의 동사가 be동사이면 be동사로, 일반동사이면 대동사(do)로 받아야 하고 수와 시제 또한 주절에 일치시켜야 한다. 여기서는 주절의 동사가 is not이므로 부가의문문의 동사는 doesn't가 아닌 is가 되어야 한다.

| **더 알아보기** | 감정형 분사

- 감정 제공 형용사 (현재분사): interesting, exciting, pleasing, amusing, worrying 등
- 감정 상태 형용사 (과거분사): interested, excited, pleased, amused, worried 등

어휘
lose track of time 시간 가는 것을 잊다
carry (가게에서 품목을) 취급하다

7　독해 > Macro Reading > 제목　오답률 31%　답 ③

| **해석** | 바다의 온난화와 산소의 손실은 참치와 농어에서부터 연어, 환도상어, 해덕, 그리고 대구에 이르기까지 수백 가지의 어종을 이전에 생각했던 것보다 훨씬 더 많이 작아지게 할 것이라고 한 새로운 연구는 결론짓는다. 더 따뜻한 바다가 그것들의 신진대사를 촉진시키기 때문에, 어류, 오징어, 그리고 기타 수중 호흡 생물들은 바다로부터 더 많은 산소를 들이마셔야 한다. 동시에, 온도가 상승하는 바다는 이미 바다의 많은 부분에서 산소의 이용 가능성을 감소시키고 있다. British Columbia대학교의 과학자 두 명은 어류의 몸이 그것들의 아가미보다 더 빠르게 자라기 때문에, 이 동물들은 결국 일반적인 성장을 유지하기 위한 충분한 산소를 얻지 못하는 지점에 이르게 될 것이라고 주장한다. "우리가 발견한 것은 수온이 섭씨 1도 상승할 때마다 어류의 몸 크기가 20~30퍼센트 줄어든다는 것이었습니다."라고 저자인 William Cheung은 말한다.
① 현재 어류는 그 어느 때보다 더 빨리 자란다
② 해양 온도에 미치는 산소의 영향
③ 기후 변화는 세계의 어류(의 크기)를 작아지게 할 수도 있다
④ 신진대사가 느린 해양 생물이 생존하는 방법

| 정답해설 | ③ 69% 첫 번째 문장에서 바다의 온난화와 산소의 손실은 수백 가지 어종을 작아지게(shrink) 할 것이라고 설명하며, 마지막 문장에서는 그에 대한 근거로 자세한 수치를 제시하고 있으므로, 글의 제목으로 가장 적절한 것은 ③이다.

| 오답해설 | ① 4% 본문 후반 어류의 몸이 아가미보다 더 빨리 자란다는 내용이 있으나, 이는 어류의 몸과 아가미의 상대적 성장 속도를 비교하는 것이지, 어류 자체가 더 빨리 자란다는 뜻이 아니므로, 글의 제목으로 부적절하다.

② 23% 산소가 해양 온도에 미치는 영향이 아니라 해양 온도가 어류의 산소 흡수량에 미치는 영향을 설명하고 있는 글이다.

④ 4% 글에서 제시되지 않는 내용으로, 제목이 될 수 없다.

어휘

shrink 줄어들게[작아지게] 하다   grouper 농어
thresher shark 환도상어
haddock 해덕(대구와 비슷하나 그보다 작은 바다 고기)
cod 대구   metabolism 신진대사
draw (연기나 공기를) 들이마시다, 빨아들이다
gill 아가미   sustain 유지하다, 지탱하다, 지속하다

오답률 TOP 3

| **8** | 문법 > 관계사 | 오답률 47% | 답 ③ |

| 해석 | 도시 농업(UA)은 오랫동안 도시에서 설 곳이 없는 비주류 활동으로 치부되어 왔다. 그러나 그것의 잠재력이 인식되기 시작하고 있다. 사실, UA는 식량 자립에 관한 것이다. 그것은 일자리 창출을 수반하며, 특히 빈곤한 사람들에게 있어서 식량 불안정에 대한 대응이다. 많은 사람들이 믿는 것과 대조적으로, UA는 모든 도시에서 발견되는데, 그곳에서 그것은 때때로 숨겨져 있거나, 때로는 눈에 잘 띈다. 주의 깊게 살펴보면, 대도시에서 사용되지 않는 공간은 거의 없다. 귀중한 공지는 좀처럼 놀고 있지 않으며, 공식적으로든 비공식적으로든 종종 점유되어 있고, 생산적이 된다.

| 정답해설 | ③ 53% 밑줄 친 which 이후의 many believe에서 many는 주어의 역할을 하는 명사로 사용되었고, 타동사인 believe의 목적어가 없으므로 밑줄 친 which는 believe의 목적어 역할을 하는 목적격 관계대명사로 볼 수 있다. 그러나 관계대명사 which 앞에는 반드시 선행사의 역할을 하는 명사가 존재해야 하나, 밑줄 이전에는 (구)전치사 Contrary to만 존재하므로 옳지 않은 문장이다. 따라서 (구)전치사의 목적어 역할을 함과 동시에 선행사를 포함하는 관계대명사 what이 오는 것이 적절하므로 밑줄 친 which는 what으로 수정해야 한다.

| 오답해설 | ① 7% 주어 its potential과 realize는 의미상 수동의 관계이므로 begin의 목적어로 to부정사의 수동태가 온 것은 적절하다.

② 14% involve는 동명사를 목적어로 취하는 완전타동사이므로 동명사 creating의 쓰임은 적절하다.

④ 26% made 앞에 중복되는 be동사 is가 생략된 수동태 문장으로, 불완전타동사 make가 수동태로 전환될 때, 목적격 보어로 쓰인 형용사는 그대로 동사 뒤에 위치하므로, 형용사 형태인 productive는 적절하다.

어휘

urban 도시의   agriculture 농업
dismiss 묵살하다, 일축하다, 치부하다
fringe 비주류의, 주변의   self-reliance 자립, 자기 의존
insecurity 불안정   obvious 명백한, 눈에 잘 띄는
vacant 빈   idle 비어 있는, 노는
take over 차지하다   productive 생산적인

| **9** | 독해 > Logical Reading > 삽입 | 오답률 26% | 답 ④ |

| 해석 | 기록 보관소는 오디오에서 비디오, 그리고 신문, 잡지, 인쇄물까지 자료의 보고이며, 이것은 그것들을 어떠한 역사 탐구 조사에 있어서도 없어서는 안 될 것으로 만든다. 도서관과 기록 보관소가 동일해 보일지도 모르지만, 차이점들은 중요하다. 기록 보관소 소장품은 거의 항상 1차적인 자료로 구성되어 있지만, 도서관은 2차적인 자료를 포함한다. 한국 전쟁에 대해 더 알고자 한다면, 당신은 역사책을 보기 위해 도서관으로 갈 것이다. 당신이 정부 문서 혹은 한국 전쟁 군인들에 의해 쓰여진 서신을 읽길 원한다면, 당신은 기록 보관소에 갈 것이다. 만일 당신이 정보를 찾고 있다면, 아마 당신을 위한 기록 보관소가 있을 것이다. 많은 주 기록 보관소와 지역 기록 보관소들이 공공 기록을 보관하는데, 이것들은 놀랍고 다양한 자료이다. ④ 예를 들어, New Jersey주의 주립 기록 보관소는 3만 입방피트가 넘는 문서와 2만 5천 릴이 넘는 마이크로필름을 소장하고 있다. 당신이 사는 주의 기록 보관소를 온라인으로 검색하면 당신에게 그것들이 단지 입법부의 회의록보다 훨씬 많은 것을 소장하고 있다는 것을 빠르게 보여 줄 것이다. 거기엔 찾을 수 있는 무상 토지에 대한 상세한 정보, 예전의 도시 지도, 범죄 기록, 그리고 행상인 면허 신청서와 같은 특이한 것들이 있다.

| 정답해설 | ④ 74% 주어진 문장은 For example로 시작하여 New Jersey주의 기록 보관소가 소장하고 있는 자료의 양을 예시하고 있는데, ④ 이전 문장에서 많은 주 기록 보관소와 지역 기록 보관소들이 공공 기록을 보관한다고 언급하고 있으므로, 문맥상 ④에 주어진 문장이 들어가야 알맞다.

어휘

archive 기록 보관소   cubic feet 입방피트
reel (실·밧줄·녹음 테이프·호스 등을 감는) 릴, 감는 틀
treasure trove 보고, 매장물, 귀중한 발굴물[수집물]
indispensable 없어서는 안 되는, 불가결의, 필수적인
investigation 조사, 연구   be made up of ~로 구성되다
secondary 2차적인, 부차적인
chances are 아마 ~일 것이다, ~할 가능성이 충분하다
diverse 다양한   minutes 회의록
legislature 입법부, 입법 기관
land grant (대학·철도의 부지로서) 정부가 주는 땅, 무상으로 불하받은 토지
oddity 이상적인 것[물건]   peddler 행상인
application 신청서, 지원서

| **10** | 독해 > Logical Reading > 삭제 | 오답률 16% | 답 ④ |

| 해석 | 번아웃이라는 용어는 업무의 압박 때문에 "지치는 것"을 일컫는다. 번아웃은 일상의 업무 스트레스 요인이 직원들에게 피해를 주기 때문에 생기는 만성적 질환이다. 가장 널리 받아들여지는 번아웃에 대한 개념화는 Maslach와 그녀의 동료들에 의해 서비스직에 종사하는 사람들에 대한 연구에서 발전되었다. Maslach는 번아웃을 상호 관련된 세 가지 차원으로 구성되어 있는 것으로 생각한다. 감정적 피로라는 첫 번째 차원은 번아웃 현상의 진정한 핵심이다. 근로자들은 그들이 피로하거나, 낙담하거나, 소모되

거나 또는 직장에서 다음 날을 맞이할 수 없음을 느낄 때 감정적 피로를 경험한다. 번아웃의 두 번째 차원은 개인적 성취의 부재이다. 번아웃 현상의 이 양상은 자기 자신을 효율적으로 직무 요구 사항을 수행할 수 없는 패배자라고 생각하는 근로자들을 가리킨다. ④ 감정 노동자들은 그들이 신체적으로 지쳐 있음에도 불구하고 매우 의욕적으로 직업에 입문한다. 번아웃의 세 번째 차원은 비인격화이다. 이 차원은 업무의 일부로 타인(예를 들어 고객, 환자, 학생)과 상호적으로 의사소통을 해야 하는 근로자들하고만 관련이 있다.

| 정답해설 | ④ 84% 번아웃의 정의를 제시한 후, 번아웃이 세 가지 차원으로 구성되어 있다고 생각하는 Maslach의 이론을 설명하고 있는 글이다. ③ 이전 문장에서 번아웃의 두 번째 차원으로 개인적 성취의 부재를 제시하고 있는데, 이에 대한 부연 설명으로 감정 노동자들이 신체적으로 지쳐 있음에도 의욕적으로 직업에 입문한다는 ④의 내용은 앞서 제시된 개인적 성취의 부재와는 상반된다.

어휘

refer to ~을 일컫다, 가리키다	chronic 만성적인
stressor 스트레스 요인	take one's toll 피해를 주다
conceptualization 개념화	consist of ~로 구성되다
dimension 차원, 관점	exhaustion 피로, 지침
phenomenon 현상	fatigued 피로한
frustrated 낙담한, 좌절한	used up 몹시 지친, 소모된
accomplishment 성과, 성취	occupation 직업
motivated 의욕을 가진, 동기가 부여된	
depersonalization 비인격화, 몰인격화	

---

11 생활영어 > 회화/관용표현   오답률 8%   답 ①

| 해석 | A: 어젯밤 여기에 있었나요?
B: 네, 저는 마감조로 일했어요. 왜 그러시죠?
A: 오늘 아침 주방이 엉망이었어요. 음식이 레인지 위에 널려져 있고 얼음 틀은 냉동실에 없었어요.
B: 제가 청소 점검 목록 검토를 깜박한 것 같아요.
A: 청결한 주방이 얼마나 중요한지는 당신도 아시죠.
B: 죄송해요. ① 다시는 그런 일이 생기지 않도록 할게요.
① 다시는 그런 일이 생기지 않도록 할게요.
② 지금 계산서를 드릴까요?
③ 그게 제가 어제 그것을 깜박한 이유예요.
④ 주문한 음식이 제대로 나오게 할게요.

| 정답해설 | ① 92% A가 어젯밤 주방 청소를 제대로 하지 않은 B에게 청결한 주방의 중요성에 대해 말하고 있고, 이에 대해 B가 사과하고 있으므로, 이어지는 빈칸에는 그런 일이 다시 생기지 않게 하겠다고 답하는 것이 가장 자연스럽다.

어휘

closing shift 마감조	spatter 흩뿌리다
go over ~을 검토하다	bill 계산서
order 주문, 주문한 음식[음료]	

---

12 생활영어 > 회화/관용표현   오답률 15%   답 ②

| 해석 | A: 감기약은 드셨나요?
B: 아뇨, 그냥 코를 많이 풀고 있어요.
A: 코 스프레이를 써 보셨어요?

B: ② 아뇨, 저는 코 스프레이를 좋아하지 않아요.
A: 그거 효과가 아주 좋아요.
B: 괜찮아요. 저는 코에 무언가 넣는 걸 좋아하지 않아서, 한 번도 그걸 써 보지 않았어요.
① 네, 그런데 효과가 없었어요.
② 아뇨, 저는 코 스프레이를 좋아하지 않아요.
③ 아뇨, 약국이 닫혀 있었어요.
④ 네, 얼마나 많이 사용해야 하죠?

| 정답해설 | ② 85% 감기에 걸려 코를 많이 푼다는 B에게 A가 코 스프레이를 써 보았는지 묻고 있으므로, 이에 대한 B의 답변으로는 코 스프레이의 사용 여부에 관한 것이 가장 적절하다. 그런데 B가 마지막 진술에서 코에 무언가 넣는 것을 싫어하며, 한 번도 그것을 써 보지 않았다고 답했으므로 빈칸에 가장 적절한 것은 ②이다.

어휘

nose spray 코[비강] 스프레이   pharmacy 약국

---

13 독해 > Micro Reading > 내용일치/불일치   오답률 11%   답 ④

| 해석 | 사막은 지구 육지 영역의 5분의 1을 넘게 차지하며, 모든 대륙에서 찾아볼 수 있다. 연간 25센티미터(10인치) 미만의 비가 내리는 곳은 사막으로 여겨진다. 사막은 건조지라 불리는 더 넓은 지역 구분의 한 부분이다. 이 지역들은 "수분 부족" 상태로 존재하고, 이는 그곳들이 연간 강우를 통해 얻는 것보다 증발을 통해 더 많은 수분을 빈번하게 상실할 수 있다는 것을 의미한다. 사막은 뜨겁다는 일반적인 개념에도 불구하고, 추운 사막 또한 있다. 세계 최대의 뜨거운 사막인 북아프리카의 Sahara는 낮 동안 최대 섭씨 50도(화씨 122도)의 기온에 도달한다. 그러나 아시아의 Gobi 사막과 세계 최대의 사막으로 남극과 북극에 있는 극지방의 사막과 같은 일부 사막은 항상 춥다. 다른 것들은 산지이다. 오직 사막의 20퍼센트만이 모래로 덮여 있다. 칠레의 Atacama 사막과 같이 가장 건조한 사막에는 1년 강우량이 2밀리미터(0.08인치) 미만인 지역들이 있다. 그러한 환경은 너무 혹독하고 비현실적이라서 과학자들은 화성의 생명체에 대한 단서를 찾기 위해 심지어 그것들을 연구해 왔다. 반면, 몇 년에 한 번씩 비정상적인 우기가 "슈퍼 블룸[개화]"을 일으킬 수 있는데, 이때는 Atacama 사막조차도 야생화로 뒤덮이게 된다.
① 각각의 대륙에 적어도 하나의 사막이 있다.
② Sahara 사막은 세계 최대의 뜨거운 사막이다.
③ Gobi 사막은 추운 사막으로 분류된다.
④ Atacama 사막은 비가 가장 많이 내리는 사막 중 하나이다.

| 정답해설 | ④ 89% 본문 중후반 The driest deserts, such as Chile's Atacama Desert, ~의 내용에서 Atacama 사막을 가장 건조한 사막의 대표적인 예로 제시했으므로 글의 내용과 반대된다.

| 오답해설 | ① 6% 첫 번째 문장 they are found on every continent에서 사막은 모든 대륙에서 찾아볼 수 있다고 했으므로 글의 내용과 일치함을 알 수 있다.
② 2% 본문 중반 The largest hot desert in the world, northern Africa's Sahara, ~에서 Sahara 사막을 세계 최대의 뜨거운 사막이라고 언급했으므로 글의 내용과 일치함을 알 수 있다.
③ 3% 본문 중반 But some deserts are always cold, like the Gobi Desert ~에서 Gobi 사막은 극지방의 사막과 더불어 추운 사막으로 예시되었으므로 글의 내용과 일치하는 것을 알 수 있다.

어휘

continent 대륙	moisture 수분
deficit 부족, 결핍	evaporation 증발
precipitation 강우[강수]량	conception 개념, 생각
Celsius 섭씨	Fahrenheit 화씨
Antarctic 남극(의)	Arctic 북극(의)
mountainous 산이 많은, 산지의	otherworldly 비현실적인

produce 일으키다, 야기하다, 생산하다
super bloom 슈퍼 블룸(사막에 일시적으로 들꽃이 많이 피는 현상)
categorize 분류하다

---

14 문법 > 강조와 도치 　　오답률 39%　답 ④

| 정답해설 | ④ 61% so가 '~도 그러하다[마찬가지이다]'라는 뜻으로 사용될 때는 주어, 동사가 의문문 어순으로 도치되어야 한다. and 앞 절의 동사가 일반동사의 과거형인 loved이므로 이를 의문문 어순인 did her son으로 옳게 사용하였다.

| 오답해설 | ① 21% look forward to는 '~을 고대하다'라는 뜻으로, 여기서 to는 전치사이므로 목적어로 (동)명사가 온다. 따라서 동사원형 receive는 동명사 receiving이 되어야 한다.
② 9% rise는 '오르다'라는 뜻의 완전자동사로 목적어를 취할 수 없으므로, '~을 올리다'라는 뜻의 완전타동사인 raise로 고쳐야 옳다.
③ 9% 「be worth -ing」는 '~할 가치가 있다'라는 관용표현으로 worth 뒤에는 동명사가 와야 한다. 따라서 considered는 considering으로 고쳐야 한다.

| 더 알아보기 | 헷갈리는 전치사 to 관용표현

• look forward to + 명사/ing: ~을 고대하다
• object to + 명사/ing: ~을 반대하다
• when it comes to + 명사: ~에 관해서라면
• pay attention to + 명사: ~에 주의를 기울이다
• lead to + 명사: 결국 ~가 되다, ~로 이끌다

---

15 문법 > 접속사 　　오답률 43%　답 ②

| 정답해설 | ② 57% '너무 ~해서 …하다'라는 표현은 「so[such] ~ that …」 구문으로 나타낼 수 있으며, 이때 강조어가 명사를 수식하고 있으므로 such를 올바르게 사용했고, 어순도 「such a + 형용사 + 명사」로 바르게 썼다.

| 오답해설 | ① 15% as if는 '마치 ~인 것처럼'이라는 뜻의 접속사이므로 우리말 해석에 일치하지 않는다. '~일지라도'라는 양보의 의미가 되려면 「형용사/명사 + as + 주어 + 동사」의 어순이 되어야 하므로 if를 삭제하는 것이 옳다. 즉, Rich as you may be ~가 올바르다.
③ 11% 「keep A -ing」는 'A가 계속 ~하게 하다'라는 의미이므로 우리말과 일치하지 않는다. 'A가 B하는 것을 방해하다'라는 표현은 「keep A from B(-ing)」로 해야 한다. 따라서 her 뒤에 from이 삽입되어야 알맞다.

---

④ 17% 접속사 if는 '~인지 아닌지'의 의미로 쓰일 때, 바로 이어서 or not과 함께 쓰일 수 없으며, 전치사의 목적어로도 사용할 수 없다. 따라서 if 대신 whether를 써야 어법에 맞는 문장이 된다.

어휘

sincere 진실한	meteor 유성

advance 전진하다, 나아가다, 진보[향상]하다
abolish 폐지하다

---

16 독해 > Reading for Writing > 빈칸 절 완성 　　오답률 15%　답 ①

| 해석 | 소셜 미디어, 잡지, 그리고 진열장은 매일 사람들에게 살 것들을 퍼붓고 영국 소비자들은 그 어느 때보다 더 많은 옷과 신발을 사고 있다. 온라인 쇼핑은 소비자들이 생각하지 않고 구입하기 쉽다는 것과 동시에, 주요 브랜드들이 두세 번 입고 버려지는 일회용품처럼 취급될 수 있는 매우 저렴한 옷을 제공한다는 것을 의미한다. 영국에서, 보통 사람이 1년에 1천 파운드가 넘는 금액을 새 옷 구매에 지출하는데, 이것은 그들 수입의 약 4퍼센트이다. 그것은 많은 것처럼 들리지 않을지도 모르지만, 그 수치는 사회와 환경에 있어서 두 가지 훨씬 더 걱정스러운 추세를 숨기고 있다. 첫째, 그 소비자 지출의 다수가 신용카드를 통한 것이다. 영국인들은 현재 성인 1인당 약 670파운드를 신용카드 회사에 빚지고 있다. 그것은 평균적인 의류 예산의 66퍼센트이다. 또한, 사람들은 그들이 가지고 있지 않은 돈을 사용할 뿐만 아니라, 그것을 ① 그들이 필요하지 않은 것들을 사기 위해 사용하고 있다. 영국은 연간 30만 톤의 의류를 버리는데, 그것들 중 대부분은 쓰레기 매립지로 보내진다.

① 그들이 필요하지 않은　　② 일상 필수품인
③ 곧 재활용될　　④ 그들이 다른 사람에게 물려줄 수 있는

| 정답해설 | ① 85% 영국인들의 온라인 쇼핑 소비 행태에 대한 글이다. 빈칸에는 이러한 소비 행태로 인해 대두되는 문제점을 설명하는 말이 들어가야 한다. 본문 중반에서 사회와 환경에 두 가지 우려되는 추세를 언급하며, 첫 번째로 사회적 우려인 신용카드 남용을 제시했다. 따라서 빈칸에는 환경적 우려를 낳을 수 있는 행위가 제시되어야 한다. 마지막 문장에서 영국은 연간 30만 톤의 의류를 버린다고 했는데, 버리는 물건이란 그들에게 필요 없는 물건이라는 뜻이므로 빈칸에는 ①이 들어가는 것이 적절하다.

| 오답해설 | ②③④ 6% 6% 3% 환경 문제를 야기할 수 있는 것들에 대한 설명이 아니므로 빈칸에 적절하지 않다.

어휘

bombard 퍼붓다, 쏟아 붓다
disposable 사용 후 버릴 수 있는, 일회용의
figure 수치
via (특정한 사람·시스템 등을) 통하여

approximately 약, 대략	wardrobe 의류; 옷장
landfill 쓰레기 매립지	necessity 필수품

recycle 재활용하다
hand down to ~로 전하다, 물려주다

---

17 독해 > Reading for Writing > 빈칸 구 완성 　　오답률 44%　답 ②

| 해석 | 청구되는 가격이 반드시 높기 때문에 탁월함은 고급 식당에서 절대적인 전제 조건이다. 운영자는 식당을 효율적으로 만들기 위해 가능한 모든 것을 할지도 모르지만, 손님들은 여전히 고도로 숙련된 요리사에 의해

준비되고 전문적인 서버가 나르는 주문 음식과 같은 세심한 개인 서비스를 원한다. 이 서비스가 말 그대로 육체노동이기 때문에, 생산성에 있어서는 오직 미미한 향상만이 가능하다. 예를 들어, 요리사, 서버, 또는 바텐더는 그 또는 그녀가 인간 성능의 한계에 다다르기 전까지 고작 조금 더 빨리 움직일 수 있을 뿐이다. 그러므로, 향상된 효율성을 통해서는 오직 그저 그런 정도의 절약만이 가능한데, 이는 가격의 상승을 ② 불가피하게 만든다. (가격이 상승할수록, 소비자는 안목이 더 높아진다는 것이 경제학의 이치이다.) 따라서, 고급 식당의 고객들은 탁월함을 기대하고, 요구하며, 기꺼이 그에 대한 지불을 한다.

① 터무니없는 　　　　　　　　② 불가피한
③ 터무니없는 　　　　　　　　④ 상상[생각]도 할 수 없는

| 정답해설 | ② 56% 본문 초반에서 고급 식당의 전제 조건으로 탁월함(excellence)을 제시하며, 그 이유로 높은 가격을 언급하고 있다. 이어서 이렇게 가격이 상승할 수밖에 없는 이유를 설명하고 있는데, 이런 탁월함의 바탕에는 요리사, 서버, 바텐더의 육체노동이 있고 인간의 능력은 한계가 있으므로 생산성 향상도 미미할 수밖에 없고 그렇게 향상된 효율성을 통한 절약도 그저 그런 수준이라고 했다. 따라서 고객이 기대하는 탁월함의 유지를 위해서는 가격 상승이 필요할 것이므로 빈칸에 가장 적절한 표현은 inevitable(불가피한)이다.

어휘

absolute 절대적인	prerequisite 전제 조건
fine dining 고급 식당; 고급 식사	efficient 효율적인
skilled 숙련된	server 서버, 웨이터, 웨이트리스
literally 말[글자] 그대로	manual 육체를 쓰는
marginal 미미한	productivity 생산성
only so much 제한된, 고작 이 정도까지인, 한계가 있는	
moderate 그저 그런, 약간의, 중간의	
efficiency 효율성	escalation 증가, 확대, 상승
axiom 자명한 이치, 공리, 격언	
discriminating 안목이 있는, 판단[감식]력이 뛰어난[예리한]	
clientele 고객	ludicrous 터무니없는
inevitable 불가피한	preposterous 터무니없는
inconceivable 상상[생각]도 할 수 없는	

오답률 TOP 1
18 　독해 > Logical Reading > 배열　　　오답률 51%　　답 ③

| 해석 | 확실히, 인간의 언어는 원숭이와 유인원의 명백히 제한적인 발성보다 뛰어나다. 게다가, 그것은 다른 어떤 형태의 동물의 의사소통을 훨씬 능가하는 어느 정도의 정교함을 보여 준다.
(C) 우리의 가장 가까운 계통인 영장류조차도 수년 동안의 집중 훈련 후에도 가장 기초적인 의사소통 체계 이상의 것을 습득하지는 못하는 것처럼 보인다. 언어라는 복잡성은 확실히 종에 특화된 특성이다.
(A) 그렇긴 하지만, 많은 종들이 인간의 언어에는 훨씬 못 미치지만, 그럼에도 불구하고, 자연 환경에서 인상적으로 복잡한 의사소통 체계를 보여 준다.
(B) 그리고 그것들은 인간과 함께 자라는 때와 같은 인위적인 상황에서 훨씬 더 복잡한 체계를 배울 수 있다.

| 정답해설 | ③ 49% 주어진 글에서는 다른 유인원과 비교할 때 인간 언어의 정교함을 설명하고 있다. 이어질 내용으로 가장 적절한 것은, Even(심지어)을 이용하여 인간과 가장 가까운 영장류의 언어를 인간의 언어와 비교하고 있는 (C)이다. (C)의 두 번째 문장에서

언어라는 복잡성은 '종에 특화된(species-specific) 특성'이라고 언급하며 인간에게만 국한된 특성이라는 점을 암시하고 있는데, 이어서 That said(그렇긴 하지만)와 양보의 연결사 nevertheless(그럼에도 불구하고)를 이용해, 인간 외에 다른 많은 종들도 자연 환경에서 복잡한 의사소통을 한다고 글의 내용을 전환하는 (A)가 오는 것이 자연스럽다. 마지막으로 (A)의 many species를 they로 지칭하고 (A)에서 제시된 '자연적 환경(natural settings)'과 대치되는 표현으로 '인위적인 상황(artificial contexts)'을 제시하는 (B)가 (A) 이후에 오는 것이 알맞다. 따라서 (C) − (A) − (B)의 순서가 알맞다.

어휘

stand out 두드러지다, 눈에 띄다, 뛰어나다	
decidedly 확실히, 분명히	vocalization 발성(법)
ape 유인원	exhibit 드러내다, 보여 주다
sophistication 정교함	exceed 능가하다, 넘어서다
that said 그렇긴 하지만	
fall short of (예상되는·필요한 기준인) ~에 미치지 못하다, 미흡하다	
impressively 인상적으로	artificial 인위적인, 인공적인
primate 영장류	acquire 습득하다, 획득하다
rudimentary 가장 기초[기본]적인	intensive 집중적인
complexity 복잡성, 복잡함	
species-specific 종에 특화된, 한 종에만 연관된	
trait 특성, 특징	

오답률 TOP 2
19 　독해 > Macro Reading > 제목　　　오답률 50%　　답 ④

| 해석 | 20세기 후반에, 사회주의는 서구와 많은 지역의 개발도상국들에서 후퇴하고 있었다. 시장 자본주의 진화에서의 이러한 새로운 국면 동안, 세계 무역의 양상은 점점 더 연결되었고, 정보 기술의 발달은 규제가 철폐된 금융 시장이 몇 초 이내에 국경을 가로질러 어마어마한 자본 흐름을 이동시킬 수 있다는 것을 의미했다. '세계화'는 무역을 신장시키고, 생산성 향상을 고취하고, 가격을 낮추었지만, 비평가들은 그것이 저임금 노동자를 착취하고, 환경과 관련된 우려에 무관심했으며, 제3세계를 독점적인 형태의 자본주의에 예속시켰다고 주장했다. 이러한 과정에 저항하길 원했던 서구 사회의 많은 급진주의자들은 소외된 좌파 정당보다는 자원봉사 단체, 자선 단체, 그리고 다른 비정부 기구에 가입했다. 세계가 연결되어 있다는 인식으로부터 환경 운동이 발달했으며, 비록 흩어져 분산되어 있긴 하지만 분노한 국제 이익 연합체가 생겨났다.
① 과거 개발도상국에서의 긍정적인 세계화 현상들
② 20세기 사회주의의 위축과 자본주의의 등장
③ 세계 자본 시장과 좌파 정치 집단의 갈등
④ 세계 자본주의의 착취적인 특성과 그것에 반하는 다양한 사회적 반응

| 정답해설 | ④ 50% 본문 초반에서 사회주의의 후퇴와 자본주의의 확장에 대해 설명한 후, 이로 인한 세계화의 부작용을 제시하고 있다. 이어서 이에 대한 급진주의자의 반응, 환경 운동의 발달 등을 설명하며 세계화의 부작용에 대한 사회 여러 분야의 반응을 제시하고 있다. 따라서 글의 주제로 가장 적절한 것은 ④이다.

| 오답해설 | ① 10% 세계화의 긍정적 역할이 본문 중반에 제시되고 있으나, 글 전체를 아우르는 내용은 아니므로 오답이다.
② 15% 첫 번째 문장에 사회주의의 후퇴와 자본주의의 등장이 언급되어 있으나, 그 이후에 나오는 세계화에 따른 부작용과 그에 반발하는 여러 단체와 운동이 이 글의 주된 내용이므로 글 전체

의 주제로는 적절하지 않다.

③ 25% 본문에 제시되지 않은 내용이다.

| 더 알아보기 | Socialism & Capitalism

> • Socialism(사회주의): 생산 수단을 사회적으로 공유하는 사회 체제를 통해 모든 사람이 평등하게 조화를 이루는 사회를 실현하려는 사상 또는 운동
> • Capitalism(자본주의): 생산 수단을 자본으로서 소유한 자본가가 이윤 획득을 위하여 생산 활동을 하도록 보장하는 사회 경제 체제

어휘

socialism 사회주의	retreat 후퇴, 철수
capitalism 자본주의	interlink 연결하다
deregulate 규제를 철폐하다	globalization 세계화
allege 주장하다	exploit 착취하다
indifferent 무관심한	
subject A to B A를 B에 복종[예속]시키다	
monopolistic 독점적인	radical 급진주의자
protest 저항하다, 반대하다	body 단체, 조직
charity 자선[구호] 단체	
marginalize ~을 (특히 사회의 진보에서) 처지게 하다, 내버려두다	
left 좌파, 좌익	recognition 인식
interconnect 연결하다	diffuse 확산한, 흩어진
coalition 연합(체)	emerge 나타나다, 등장하다
affirmative 긍정적인	
phenomenon 현상(pl. phenomena)	
emergence 등장, 출현	exploitative 착취적인

어휘

blazing 불타는 듯한	stand out 눈에 띄다, 두드러지다
pile 더미	unearth 파다
gravel 자갈	miner 광부
finger 손가락으로 만지다	pyramidal 피라미드형의
plane 면, 평면	find 발견물, 발견한 것
merit (상벌 · 감사 · 비난 등을) 받을 만하다, ~할 가치[자격]이 있다	
second opinion 다른 견해[의견]	sheepishly 소심하게
gash (바위 등의) 갈라진 금[틈]	pit boss (광산의) 현장 감독
shovel 삽으로 파다, 삽질하다	nightfall 해 질 녘, 해거름
thrilled 신난, 몹시 흥분한	distressed 고뇌에 찬
arrogant 거만한, 오만한	convinced 확신하는
detached 무심한, 초연한	indifferent 무관심한

---

20 독해 > Macro Reading > 심경   오답률 20%   답 ①

| 해석 | 불타는 듯한 한낮의 태양 아래, 노란색 계란 모양의 돌이 최근에 파헤쳐진 자갈 더미 사이에서 눈에 띄었다. 호기심에 16세의 광부 Komba Johnbull은 그것을 주워 손가락으로 편평한 피라미드의 면을 만져 보았다. Johnbull은 전에 다이아몬드를 본 적이 없었지만, 그는 커다란 발견물조차도 그의 엄지손톱보다 더 클 리 없다는 것을 이해할 정도는 알고 있었다. 하지만, 그 돌은 다른 견해의 가치가 있을 만큼 충분히 진귀했다. 소심하게, 그는 그것을 정글 깊은 곳에서 진흙투성이 틈 사이에서 작업하고 있는 더 경험이 많은 광부 중 한 명에게 가져갔다. 그 돌을 보았을 때, 그 현장 감독의 눈이 커졌다. "그것을 네 주머니에 넣어라."라고 그가 속삭였다. "계속해서 파." 그 나이 많은 광부는 만일 누군가 그들이 커다란 것을 발견했다고 생각한다면 위험할 수 있다고 경고했다. 그래서 Johnbull은 해 질 녘까지 계속해서 자갈을 삽으로 퍼내며, 이따금씩 그의 주먹으로 그 무거운 돌을 움켜쥐기 위해 멈추었다. 혹시?

① 신나고 들뜬
② 괴롭고 고뇌에 찬
③ 오만하고 확신에 찬
④ 무심하고 무관심한

| 정답해설 | ① 80% 어린 광부인 Johnbull이 가치 있을 것이라 생각되는 돌(아마도 다이아몬드)을 발견하는데, 다른 나이 든 광부의 반응을 통해 해당 돌이 실제로 매우 가치 있는 것일 수 있음을 유추할 수 있다. Johnbull이 그 돌을 만지작거리면서 Could it be?(혹시?)라고 한 것으로 보아 그것이 진짜 다이아몬드일지도 모른다고 기대하고 있음을 알 수 있다. Johnbull의 심경으로 가장 적절한 것은 ①이다.

합격예상 체크

〈국가직 연도별 합격선〉

2020 합격기준!

| 2022 | 2021 | 2020 | 2019 | 2018 | 2017 | 2017 추가 | 2016 |

맞힌 개수	/20문항	점수	/100점

➡ ☐ 합격 ☐ 불합격

취약영역 체크

문항	정답	영역	문항	정답	영역
1	①	어휘 > 유의어 찾기	11	④	생활영어 > 회화/관용표현
2	④	어휘 > 유의어 찾기	12	③	생활영어 > 회화/관용표현
3	③	어휘 > 유의어 찾기	13	②	독해 > Logical Reading > 연결사
4	①	어휘 > 유의어 찾기	14	③	독해 > Macro Reading > 주제
5	④	문법 > 강조와 도치	15	③	독해 > Logical Reading > 배열
6	②	문법 > 조동사	16	④	독해 > Logical Reading > 삭제
7	③	문법 > 태	17	④	독해 > Logical Reading > 삽입
8	②	독해 > Macro Reading > 요지	18	③	독해 > Micro Reading > 내용 일치/불일치
9	①	독해 > Macro Reading > 제목	19	①	독해 > Reading for Writing > 빈칸 구 완성
10	④	독해 > Micro Reading > 내용 일치/불일치	20	②	독해 > Reading for Writing > 빈칸 구 완성

⬇ 영역별 틀린 개수로 취약영역을 확인하세요!

어휘	/4	문법	/3	독해	/11	생활영어	/2

➡ 나의 취약영역:

※ [정답해설]과 [오답해설] 선지의 50% 표시는 〈1초 합격예측 서비스〉를 통해 수집된 선지 선택률을 나타냅니다.

1	어휘 > 유의어 찾기	오답률 33%	답 ①

| 해석 | 전자레인지 모델 및 스타일에 대한 광범위한 목록을 솔직한 소비자 리뷰 및 가격대와 함께 가전제품 비교 웹사이트에서 이용할 수 있다.
① 67% 솔직한
② 10% 논리적인
③ 11% 암시적인
④ 12% 열정적인

| 정답해설 | ① candid는 '솔직한, 정직한'이라는 의미이므로 frank(솔직한)가 정답이다.

| 더 알아보기 | candid의 유의어

frank, outspoken, forthright, straightforward

어휘
extensive 광범위한, 대규모의   price range 가격대
appliance 가전제품, (가정용) 기기

2	어휘 > 유의어 찾기	오답률 46%	답 ④

| 해석 | Yellowstone이 사실상 화산 작용에 의해 만들어졌다는 것이 오랫동안 알려져 있었고, 화산에 대한 한 가지 사실은 그것들이 보통 눈에 잘 띈다는 것이다.
① 6% 수동적인
② 15% 증기가 많은
③ 25% 위험한
④ 54% 눈에 잘 띄는

| 정답해설 | ④ conspicuous는 '눈에 잘 띄는'이라는 의미이므로 noticeable(눈에 띄는)이 정답이다.

어휘
volcanic 화산 작용에 의한, 화산의   in nature 사실상

3	어휘 > 유의어 찾기	오답률 18%	답 ③

| 해석 | 그는 그 도시를 속속들이 알고 있으므로 그곳에 어떻게 가는지 당신에게 말해 줄 적임자이다.
① 3% 결국
② 8% 문화적으로
③ 82% 완전히
④ 7% 시험적으로

| 정답해설 | ③ know ~ inside out은 '~을 속속들이[훤하게] 알다'라는 뜻이며, '그가 길을 알려줄 적임자'라고 설명하고 있으므로 '그가 지리를 잘 알고 있다'는 것을 유추할 수 있다. 따라서 정답은 thoroughly(완전히, 철저하게)이다.

오답률 TOP 1

4	어휘 > 유의어 찾기	오답률 62%	답 ①

| 해석 | 마분지, 눈, 그리고 색판지에 새겨진 메시지들을 포함하여 그 팀에게 경의를 표하기 위한 수많은 소박한 노력들이 그 길 내내 있었다.
① 38% 경의를 표하다
② 24% 구성하다
③ 10% 알리다
④ 28% 합류하다

| 정답해설 | ① pay tribute to는 '~에게 경의를 표하다'라는 의미이므로 이와 가장 유사한 표현은 honor(경의를 표하다, 영예를 주다)이다.

어휘

homespun 소박한, 손으로 만든   attempt 노력, 시도
etch 식각[에칭]하다, 새기다   construction paper 색판지

---

5   문법 > 강조와 도치   오답률 47%   답 ④

| 해석 | ① 대도시의 교통은 소도시의 그것보다 더 혼잡하다.
② 내가 다음 주에 해변에 누워 있을 때 나는 네 생각을 할 거야.
③ 건포도는 한때 값비싼 음식이었고, 오직 부유한 사람들만이 그것들을 먹었다.
④ 색의 명암은 그 색이 얼마나 많은 회색을 포함하고 있는지와 관련된다.

| 정답해설 | ④ 53% how much ~ contains는 문장에서 전치사 to의 목적어 역할을 하고 있으므로 간접의문문의 「의문부사(how) + 형용사(much) + 명사(gray) + 주어(the color) + 동사(contains)」의 어순이 어법상 알맞다.

The intensity of a color is related to
　주어　　　전명구　　　동사　　전치사

　　　　[how much gray the color contains.]
　　　　의문부사+형용사+명사　주어　　　동사
　　　　→ 전치사의 목적어(간접의문문)

| 오답해설 | ① 11% 비교하는 대상이 the traffic으로 단수형이므로 those는 단수 대명사 that으로 바뀌어야 옳다.
② 11% 시간이나 조건을 나타내는 부사절에서는 현재가 미래를 대신하므로 I'll be lying은 I'm lying이 되어야 적절하다.
③ 25% 「the + 형용사」는 '~하는 사람들'이라는 뜻으로 복수 명사 역할을 할 수 있다. 따라서 the wealth가 아니라 the wealthy가 되어야 알맞다.

어휘

raisin 건포도   intensity 명암, 강렬함

오답률 TOP 3

6   문법 > 조동사   오답률 57%   답 ②

| 정답해설 | ② 43% 동사 command(명령하다)의 목적어로 쓰인 that절이 당위의 의미를 가질 때 that절의 동사는 「should + 동사원형」으로 쓰는 것이 원칙이나 조동사 should를 생략하고 동사원형만 쓸 수 있으므로 cease는 적절하다. cease는 '중단되다'라는 뜻의 자동사로 사용되었다.

The committee commanded that
　주어　　　　　동사　　명사절 접속사

　　　construction of the building (should) cease.
　　　　주어　　　전명구　　　조동사 생략 동사원형

| 오답해설 | ① 20% raise는 '일으키다'라는 의미의 타동사이므로 목적어가 필요한데, 동사 뒤에 목적어 없이 전치사구가 나오므로 '(사건 등이) 발생하다'의 의미인 자동사 arise의 능동태 또는 타동사 raise의 수동태가 쓰여야 적절하다. 즉, have arisen 또는 have

been raised가 옳다.
③ 18% 주절의 시제가 had to fight로 과거이므로, 선행사인 winds를 수식하는 관계대명사절의 시제도 과거가 되어야 한다. 따라서 will blow를 blew로 고쳐 써야 한다.
④ 19% survive는 타동사로 쓰일 때 능동태로 사용되어 '~에도 살아남다, 견뎌 내다'의 의미를 나타낼 수 있다. 주어진 우리말 해석이 '~에도 살아남는다'라고 제시되었으므로 수동태로 쓰인 are survived by는 능동태인 survive가 되어야 옳다. 또한 주어진 해석이 '거의 모든'이므로 most를 almost all (the)로 수정하여 The seeds of almost all plants survive harsh weather.가 되어야 한다.

| 더 알아보기 | 당위의 조동사 should 생략

「S + 주장/요구/명령/제안 동사 + (that) + S + (should) + 동사원형」
• 주장, 제안: propose, insist, argue, suggest
• 요구, 명령: require, request, ask, demand, order, command
• 조언, 권고: advise, recommend

어휘

committee 위원회   harsh 혹독한, 가혹한

오답률 TOP 2

7   문법 > 태   오답률 61%   답 ③

| 정답해설 | ③ 39% promote는 '승진시키다'라는 의미의 타동사이며 '그(him)'는 부회장으로 승진되는 대상이므로, 수동태로 써야 한다. 따라서 promoting을 being promoted로 고쳐 써야 한다.

The company prohibited him from being promoted
　주어　　　　　동사　　목적어 전치사 전치사의 목적어(수동태)

　　　　　　　　　　to vice-president.
　　　　　　　　　　전명구

| 오답해설 | ① 14% adapt oneself to는 '~에 적응하다, 자신을 ~에 적응시키다'라는 의미이며, 주어(Human beings)와 목적어가 같은 대상이므로 재귀대명사 themselves가 바르게 사용되었다.
② 31% 「have no choice but to + 동사원형」은 '~할 수밖에 없다'라는 의미의 관용표현이다.
④ 16% 주어가 구 또는 절로 길어질 경우 주어 자리에 가주어 It을 쓰고, 진주어는 뒤로 이동시킨다.

어휘

vice-president 부회장, 부통령   take apart 분해하다

---

8   독해 > Macro Reading > 요지   오답률 7%   답 ②

| 해석 | 타인의 생각을 경청하는 것은 당신 자신과 세상에서의 당신의 위치에 대해서뿐만 아니라, 당신이 세상에 대해 믿는 이야기가 온전한지 알 수 있는 하나의 방법이다. 우리는 모두 우리의 신념을 검토하고, 그것들을 환기시키고 그것들이 숨 쉬도록 해 주어야 한다. 특히 우리가 기본이라고 여기는 개념에 대해 타인의 의견을 듣는 것은 우리의 정신과 마음의 창문을 여는 것과 같다. 대담하게 소신을 말하는 것은 중요하다. 그러나 경청하지 않고 대담하게 소신을 말하는 것은 냄비와 팬을 함께 두드리는 것과 같다. 비록 그것이 당신에게 관심을 가져올지라도, 그것이 당신에게 존중심을 가

져오지는 않을 것이다. 대화가 의미 있어지려면 세 가지 전제 조건이 있다. 1. 당신은 당신이 무엇에 대해 말하고 있는지 알아야 하는데, 이는 당신이 독창적인 논점을 지니고 있고, 진부하거나, 독창성 없거나, 또는 조립식의 (기존의 것들을 짜깁기하는) 논점을 되풀이하지 않는다는 것을 의미한다. 2. 당신은 당신과 대화하고 있는 사람을 존중하고, 비록 당신이 그들의 입장과 다르더라도 진정으로 기꺼이 그들을 예의 바르게 대우한다. 3. 당신은 끊이지 않는 좋은 유머와 안목으로 주제에 대한 당신의 관점을 다루는 동시에 상대가 말하는 것을 경청할 정도로 충분히 현명하고 많이 알아야 한다.

① 우리는 타인을 설득하기 위해 더 단호해져야 한다.
② 우리는 의사소통을 잘하기 위해 경청하고 대담하게 소신을 말해야 한다.
③ 우리는 우리가 보는 세상에 대한 자신의 신념을 바꾸기를 꺼린다.
④ 우리는 오직 우리가 선택한 것만 듣고 다른 의견은 무시하려고 한다.

| 정답해설 | ② [93%] 본문 초반에 대화에서의 '듣기[경청]의 역할'에 대해 언급하고, 본문 중반에서는 내 생각을 말하는 것이 중요하기는 하지만 경청하지 않고 말하는 것은 당신을 존중받게 해 주지 않을 것이라고 하면서, 대화를 할 때 듣기와 말하기의 조화가 중요함을 주장하고 있다.

어휘

intact 완전한, 온전한	foundational 기본의, 기초적인
speak up 대담하게 소신을 말하다	
bang 쾅 하고 치다	prerequisite 전제 조건
echo 그대로 되풀이하다	worn-out 낡은, 진부한
hand-me-down 독창성 없는; 싸구려의; [옷이] 물림인	
pre-fab 조립식의	authentically 확실하게, 진정으로
courteously 예의 바르게, 공손하게	position 입장, 태도
informed 많이 아는	opposition 반대 측, 상대방
handle 다루다, 처리하다	perspective 관점, 시각
uninterrupted 끊이지 않는, 연속된	discernment 안목, 인식력
determined 단호한	
be reluctant to V ~을 주저하다, 망설이다	

---

9   독해 > Macro Reading > 제목   오답률 20%   답 ①

| 해석 | 미래는 불확실할지 모르지만, 기후 변화, 변화하는 인구 통계 및 지정학과 같은 어떠한 것들은 부인할 수 없다. 유일하게 보장할 수 있는 것은 변화가 있을 것이라는 점인데, (그 변화들은) 멋지기도 하고 끔찍하기도 할 것이다. 현재와 미래에 예술이 어떠한 목적을 제공할지뿐만 아니라, 예술가들이 이러한 변화에 어떻게 대응할지 고려해 볼 가치가 있다. 보고서들에 따르면 2040년까지 인간이 유발한 기후 변화의 영향은 피할 수 없게 될 것이며, 20년 후 예술과 삶의 중심에서 중요한 사안이 될 것이라고 말한다. 미래의 예술가들은 포스트 인간과 포스트 인류세의 가능성, 즉 인공 지능, 인간의 우주 식민지, 그리고 잠재적인 파멸과 싸울 것이다. 예술에서 보이는 #Me Too(미투 운동)와 Black Lives Matter 운동(흑인 인권 운동)을 둘러싼 정체성 정치학은 환경 운동, 국경 정치, 이주가 훨씬 더 급격하게 뚜렷해지면서 성장할 것이다. 예술은 점점 더 다양해지고 우리가 예상하는 '예술처럼 보이지' 않을지도 모른다. 미래에, 모든 사람이 볼 수 있도록 온라인에서 보여지는 우리의 삶에 우리가 지치고, 우리의 사생활을 거의 잃게 된다면, 익명성은 명성보다 더욱 바람직하게 될지도 모른다. 수천 또는 수백만의 좋아요와 팔로워 대신에, 우리는 신뢰성과 연결성에 굶주릴 것이다. 결국, 예술은 개인적이기보다는 더욱 집단적이고 실험적이 될 수도 있다.

① 미래의 예술은 어떤 모습일까?
② 지구 온난화는 우리의 삶에 어떻게 영향을 미칠까?
③ 인공 지능은 환경에 어떻게 영향을 미칠까?
④ 정치 운동으로 인해 어떤 변화가 일어날까?

| 정답해설 | ① [80%] 본문 초반에서 미래의 변화에 대한 글이라는 것을 알 수 있으며 세 번째 문장부터는 특히 예술이 어떤 방향으로 변화할지에 대해 서술하고 있다. 뒤이어 미래의 예술의 양상을 예측하고 있으므로 글의 제목으로는 ①이 가장 적절하다.

어휘

undeniable 부인할 수 없는, 명백한	shift 변화하다
demographics 인구 통계	geopolitics 지정학
inescapable 피할 수 없는	wrestle 싸우다, 안간힘을 쓰다
Anthropocene 인류세(Paul Crurzen이 처음 사용한 개념으로 산업혁명 이후 인간의 활동이 지구의 환경과 역사에 영향을 미친 시기를 일컫는 지질학 용어)	
artificial intelligence 인공 지능	doom 멸망, 파멸
identity politics 정체성 정치(학)	environmentalism 환경 보호주의
border 국경, 경계	come into focus 뚜렷해지다
weary of ~에 지친, 싫증 난	all but 거의, 사실상
anonymity 익명성	desirable 바람직한, 호감 가는
fame 명성	authenticity 신뢰성, 확실성
in turn 결국; 차례로	collective 집단적인, 집합적인

---

10   독해 > Micro Reading > 내용일치/불일치   오답률 12%   답 ④

| 해석 | 미국 헌법의 헌법 수정 제2조는 "잘 규율된 민병대는 자유로운 주의 안보에 필요하므로, 사람들이 무기를 소지하고 휴대할 권리는 침해될 수 없다."라고 명시한다. 이 수정 헌법 조항을 인용한 대법원의 판결은 주의 총기 규제 권한을 옹호해 왔다. 그러나, 개인이 무기를 소지하고 휴대할 권리를 확정하는 2008년 판결에서, 법원은 권총을 금지하고 가정에 있는 권총의 잠금 장치를 잠가 놓거나 분해해 놓도록 한 Washington, D.C.의 법을 폐지했다. 수많은 총기 옹호자들은 (총기) 소유권을 생득권이며 국가 유산의 필수 요소라 여긴다. 스위스에 기반을 둔 Small Arms Survey의 2007년 보고서에 따르면, 세계 인구의 5% 미만에 해당하는 미국은 세계의 민간인 소지 권총의 약 35~50%를 가지고 있다. 이는 1인당 총기 보유에서 1위이다. 미국은 또한 세계의 최선진국들 가운데 가장 높은 총기에 의한 살인율을 보유하고 있다. 그러나 많은 총기 권리 옹호자들은 이러한 통계가 인과 관계를 나타내지는 않는다고 말하며 미국의 총기 살인 및 기타 총기 범죄율은 1990년대 초 최고치 이후로 감소해 왔다고 언급한다.

① 2008년, 미국 대법원은 권총을 금지하는 Washington, D.C.의 법을 뒤집었다.
② 많은 총기 옹호자들은 총을 소유하는 것이 타고난 권리라고 주장한다.
③ 최선진국들 사이에서 미국은 가장 높은 총기 살인율을 보유하고 있다.
④ 미국에서 총기 범죄는 지난 30년 동안 꾸준히 증가해 왔다.

| 정답해설 | ④ [88%] 마지막 문장에서 미국의 총기 살인 및 기타 총기 범죄는 1990년대 초 최고치 이후로 감소해 왔다고 언급하고 있으므로, 총기 범죄가 감소하는 추세임을 알 수 있다.

| 오답해설 | ① [3%] 세 번째 문장에서 법원이 권총을 금지한 Washington, D.C.의 법을 폐지했다고 했으므로 ①은 글의 내용과 일치한다.
② [4%] 본문 중반 A number of gun advocates consider ownership a birthright에서 수많은 총기 옹호자들은 (총기) 소유권을 생득권(birthright)이라고 여긴다고 했으므로 ②는 글의 내용과 일치한다.
③ [5%] 본문 후반 The United States also has the highest homicide-by-firearm rate among the world's most developed nations에서 미국은 세계의 최선진국들 가운데 가장

높은 총기에 의한 살인율을 보유하고 있다고 했으므로 ③은 글의 내용과 일치한다.

어휘

constitution 헌법; 구성; 체질	well-regulated 잘 규율된, 잘 정돈된
militia 민병대, 시민군	bear (무기 등을) 몸에 지니다
infringe 침해하다, 어기다	Supreme Court 대법원
ruling 판결	cite 인용하다
uphold 지지하다, 인정하다, 유지하다	regulate 규제하다, 관리하다
firearms (소형 권총 등의) 소형 화기	strike down 폐지하다
disassemble 분해하다	advocate 옹호자, 지지자
birthright 생득권	heritage 유산
per capita 1인당	homicide 살인
proponent 지지자	overturn 뒤집다
cause-and-effect 인과 관계의, 원인과 결과의	
natural-born 타고난, 천부적인	steadily 꾸준히, 끊임없이

11 생활영어 > 회화/관용표현　오답률 16%　답 ④

| 해석 | ① A: 지불 기일이 언제인가요?
B: 당신은 다음 주까지 지불해야 합니다.
② A: 이 짐을 부쳐야 하나요?
B: 아니요, 그것은 기내에 가지고 탈 수 있을 만큼 충분히 작네요.
③ A: 언제 어디서 만날까?
B: 8시 30분에 네 사무실로 데리러 갈게.
④ A: 나는 요리 대회에서 상을 받았어.
B: 네가 없었다면 나는 그것을 할 수 없었을 거야.

| 정답해설 | ④ 84% 요리 대회에서 상을 받은 것은 A인데 B가 상을 받은 것에 대한 감사 표현을 A에게 하는 것은 어색하다.

| 더 알아보기 | '감사합니다'를 뜻하는 표현

- Thanks a lot.
- Thanks a million.
- I can't thank you enough.
- How can I ever thank you?
- I don't know how to thank you (enough).

어휘

check in ~을 부치다

12 생활영어 > 회화/관용표현　오답률 4%　답 ③

| 해석 | A: Royal Point 호텔 예약 부서에 전화해 주셔서 감사합니다. 제 이름은 Sam입니다. 어떻게 도와드릴까요?
B: 안녕하세요, 객실을 예약하고 싶습니다.
A: 저희는 두 가지 객실 타입을 제공하고 있습니다. 디럭스룸과 럭셔리 스위트룸입니다.
B: ③ 그것들의 차이가 뭐죠?
A: 한 가지로, 스위트룸은 매우 넓습니다. 침실 외에도 주방, 거실 그리고 식당을 포함하고 있습니다.
B: 비쌀 것 같네요.
A: 네, 1박에 200달러가 추가됩니다.
B: 그렇다면, 저는 디럭스룸으로 할게요.
① 또 필요한 것이 있으신가요
② 방 번호를 알 수 있을까요
③ 그것들의 차이가 뭐죠
④ 반려동물이 객실에 허용되나요

| 정답해설 | ③ 96% 빈칸 앞에서 A가 디럭스룸과 럭셔리 스위트룸이라는 두 가지 객실 선택 사항을 제시한 후, 빈칸 뒤에서 각 객실의 특징을 설명하고 있으므로 B의 질문으로 가장 적절한 것은 두 객실의 차이를 묻는 ③이다.

어휘

department 부서	book 예약하다

13 독해 > Logical Reading > 연결사　오답률 36%　답 ②

| 해석 | 홈스쿨링 옹호자들은 아이들이 안전하고 애정 어린 환경에 있을 때 더 잘 배운다고 믿는다. 많은 심리학자들은 집을 가장 자연스러운 학습 환경으로 보며, 학교가 설립되기 훨씬 이전에는 본래 집이 교실이었다. 홈스쿨링을 하는 부모들은 자신들이 아이들의 교육을 관리할 수 있고 전통적인 학교 환경에서 부족한 관심을 아이들에게 줄 수 있다고 주장한다. 학생들은 또한 무엇을 공부할지 그리고 언제 공부할지 고르고 선택할 수 있으며, 이는 그들이 자신들만의 속도에 맞추어 배울 수 있도록 해 준다. (A) 그에 반해, 홈스쿨링 비판자들은 교실에 있지 않은 아이들은 자신들의 또래와 상호 작용을 거의 하지 않기 때문에 중요한 사회적 기술 학습을 놓친다고 말한다. 그러나, 몇몇 연구는 아이들의 행복을 신경 쓰는 부모의 지도와 함께 가정의 편안함과 안정감 속에서 더 많은 시간을 보내는 가정 학습을 받은 아이들이 사회적, 감정적 발달 면에서 다른 학생들과 마찬가지로 잘하는 것으로 보인다는 점을 증명했다. (B) 이것에도 불구하고, 많은 홈스쿨링 비판자들은 아이들을 효과적으로 가르칠 수 있는 부모들의 능력에 대한 우려를 제기해 왔다.

	(A)	(B)
①	그러므로	그럼에도 불구하고
②	그에 반해	이것에도 불구하고
③	그러므로	그것에 반하여
④	그에 반해	게다가

| 정답해설 | ② 64% (A) 빈칸 이전에는 홈스쿨링 옹호자들의 의견을 제시하고, 빈칸 이후에는 홈스쿨링 비판자들의 의견을 제시하고 있으므로 '대조'를 나타내는 In contrast(그에 반해)가 빈칸에 알맞다.
(B) 빈칸 이전에는 홈스쿨링을 하는 아이들의 발달에 문제가 없다는 연구 결과를 언급하며, 홈스쿨링의 긍정적인 측면을 제시하고 있으나, 빈칸 이후에는 홈스쿨링을 하는 부모의 교육 능력에 대한 홈스쿨링 비판자들의 염려에 대해 설명하고 있으므로, 양보를 나타내는 Nevertheless(그럼에도 불구하고) 또는 In spite of this(이것에도 불구하고)가 빈칸에 알맞다.

| 오답해설 | ①③ 3% 4% (A) 전후 내용이 인과 관계가 아니므로 Therefore(그러므로)는 빈칸에 적절하지 않다.
④ 29% (B) 전후 내용이 서로 대조적이므로 첨가를 나타내는 Furthermore(게다가)는 빈칸에 적절하지 않다.

어휘

setting 환경, 장소	pace 속도
interaction 상호 작용	peer 또래
in terms of ~ 면에서, ~에 관하여	guidance 지도
welfare 행복, 복지	concern 염려, 걱정

14 독해 > Macro Reading > 주제 | 오답률 22% | 답 ③

| 해석 | 많은 사람들에게, 일은 강박이 되어 왔다. 사람들이 급여를 받기 위해 하는 일 외에 자녀들, 열정, 반려동물, 또는 어떠한 종류의 인생을 위한 시간을 내기 위해 노력함에 따라, 그것(일)은 극도의 피로, 불행 그리고 성 불평등을 유발해 왔다. 그러나 점점, 젊은 근로자들이 반발하고 있다. 그들 중 더 많은 이들이 유연성을 기대하고 요구하는데, 말하자면, 원격으로 일하거나, 늦게 출근 또는 일찍 퇴근하거나, 또는 운동이나 명상을 위한 시간을 낼 수 있는 역량과 같은 일상적인 것들과 더불어, 신생아를 위한 유급 휴가와 넉넉한 휴가 기간 등이다. 그들의 삶의 나머지 부분이 그들의 핸드폰 상에서 일어나고 특정 장소나 시간에 얽매이지 않는데, 일이라고 왜 달라야 하는가?
① 당신의 급료를 인상시키는 방법들
② 불평등을 감소시키려는 강박
③ 직장에서의 유연성에 대한 증가하는 요구
④ 긴 휴가가 있는 삶의 장점들

| 정답해설 | ③ 78% 강박적으로 일에 몰두하던 과거와는 달리, 최근에는 여가 및 업무의 유연성을 중요시한다는 내용이다. 특히 본문 중후반부에 젊은 근로자들이 직장에서의 유연성을 점점 더 많이 기대하고 요구하는 것들의 예가 나열되므로, 글의 주제로 가장 적절한 것은 ③이다.

| 오답해설 | ④ 6% 본문에서 '직장에서의 유연성(flexibility)'에 대한 예시로 '넉넉한 휴가 기간(generous vacation time)'이 제시되기는 하나, 이것의 장점에 대해서는 직접적으로 언급되지 않았다.

어휘
obsession 강박, 집착
struggle 노력하다, 애쓰다, 분투하다
flexibility 유연성, 융통성
ability 능력, 역량
meditation 명상
burnout 극도의 피로, (심신의) 소모
paycheck 급여
paid leave 유급 휴가
remotely 떨어져서, 멀리서
call 요구

15 독해 > Logical Reading > 배열 | 오답률 17% | 답 ③

| 해석 | 과거의 연구는 빈번한 심리적 스트레스를 경험하는 것이 미국의 20세 이상의 사람들 거의 절반에게 발생하는 질환인 심혈관계 질환의 주요 위험 요인이 될 수 있다는 것을 보여 주었다.
(C) 빈번한 스트레스의 한 가지 근본 원인은 운전인데, 그것은 교통 체증과 관련된 스트레스 요인 또는 미숙한 운전자에게 종종 동반되는 불안 때문이다.
(A) 그렇지만, 이것이 매일 운전하는 사람이 심장 문제를 겪을 수밖에 없다는 의미인가, 아니면 운전의 스트레스를 완화하는 간단한 방법이 있는가?
(B) 새로운 연구에 따르면, (방법이) 있다. 연구원들은 운전 중 음악을 듣는 것이 심장 건강에 영향을 미치는 스트레스를 완화하는 데 도움이 된다고 언급했다.

| 정답해설 | ③ 83% 주어진 글에서 스트레스와 심혈관 질환의 관계에 대해 언급하고 있으므로, 빈번한 스트레스의 근본 원인 중 하나인 '운전(driving)'을 최초로 언급하는 (C)가 바로 이어지는 것이 적절하다. 이후 운전과 심장 질환과의 관계와 스트레스 완화 방법의 존재 유무에 대해 질문하는 (A)가 이어지고, 마지막으로 (A)의 질문에 대한 대답을 제시하는 (B)가 이어지는 것이 적절하다.

| 오답해설 | ②④ 5% 9% (A)에서 is there ~?이라고 질문을 하고

있으므로 (B)에서 there is로 답하는 것이 자연스럽다. 따라서 (B)가 (A)보다 이전에 위치하는 것은 어색하다.

어휘
cardiovascular 심혈관계의
affect (질병이) 발생하다, 영향을 미치다
be set to V ~하도록 예정되어 있다
relieve 완화하다
associated with ~와 관련된
inexperienced 미숙한
condition 질환, (건강) 상태
ease 완화시키다
stressor 스트레스 요인
accompany 동반되다, 함께 가다

16 독해 > Logical Reading > 삭제 | 오답률 29% | 답 ④

| 해석 | 뇌가 가까운 환경에서 위협을 인지하면, 그것은 신체에 복잡한 일련의 일들을 발생시킨다. 그것은 화학 호르몬을 혈류로 분비시키는 기관인 다양한 분비선에 전기 메시지를 보낸다. 혈액은 이러한 호르몬을 이후 다양한 일을 하도록 자극받는 다른 기관으로 빠르게 운반한다. 예를 들어, 신장 위쪽에 있는 부신은 신체의 스트레스 호르몬인 아드레날린을 분출한다. 아드레날린은 위험 신호를 지켜보기 위해 눈을 크게 뜨고, 혈액과 추가적인 호르몬이 계속해서 흐르도록 심장을 더 빠르게 펌프질하고, 위협적인 존재를 후려치거나 그것으로부터 도망칠 준비가 되어 있도록 골격근을 긴장시키는 것과 같은 일들을 하며 전신을 순환한다. 전체 과정은 투쟁 도피 반응이라고 불리는데, 왜냐하면 그것이 신체를 싸우거나 필사적으로 도망치도록 준비시키기 때문이다. ④ 인간은 의식적으로 다양한 호르몬 분비를 조절하는 자신의 분비선을 통제할 수 있다. 호르몬은 이치를 따져 타이를 수 없기 때문에 일단 반응이 시작되면, 그것을 무시하는 것은 불가능하다.

| 정답해설 | ④ 71% 본문은 위험 지각 시 뇌의 반응에 관한 내용으로, 특히 호르몬 분비의 과정 및 역할을 설명하고 있다. 본문 초반에서 언급된 내용에 대한 구체적인 예시를 for example을 이용해 ①로 연결하고, ①에서 설명한 아드레날린(Adrenaline)의 역할을 ②에서 설명하고 있으므로 두 문장이 이어지는 것은 자연스럽다. 이후 앞서 설명한 작용 전체를 통틀어 투쟁 도피 반응(fight-or-flight response)이라고 설명하는 ③이 이어지는 것이 자연스럽다. 그런데 마지막 문장에서 호르몬은 이치를 따져 타이를 수 없기 때문에 일단 반응이 시작되면, 그것을 무시하는 것은 불가능하다고 언급하고 있으므로, 상기의 과정은 임의로 조절하는 것이 불가능하다는 것을 알 수 있다. 따라서 인간이 의식적으로 다양한 호르몬 분비를 조절하도록 자신의 분비선을 통제할 수 있다는 ④는 전체 글의 흐름과 맞지 않는다.

어휘
perceive 인지하다
immediate 아주 가까이에 있는; 즉시의, 즉석의
surroundings 환경
gland (분비)선[샘]
bloodstream 혈류
kidney 신장
be on the lookout 지켜보다, 세심히 살피다
tense 긴장시키다
lash out at ~을 후려치다; ~을 맹렬히 비난하다
fight-or-flight response 투쟁 도피 반응
run for one's life 필사적으로 도망치다
consciously 의식적으로, 자각하여
reason with (이치를 따져) ~을 설득하다, 타이르다
initiate 시작하다
organ 기관, 장기
adrenal gland 부신
regulate 규제하다, 조절하다

17 독해 > Logical Reading > 삽입 　 오답률 38% 　 답 ④

| 해석 | 1903년에 프랑스 화학자인 Edouard Benedictus는 어느 날 유리 플라스크를 딱딱한 바닥에 떨어뜨려 깨뜨렸다. 그러나, 놀랍게도, 그 플라스크는 산산조각나지 않았는데, 여전히 본래 모양을 대부분 유지하고 있었다. 그가 플라스크를 살펴보았을 때, 그는 그 플라스크에 담겨 있던 콜로디온 용액의 남은 잔여물로 그것이 필름 코팅되어 있는 것을 발견했다. 그는 이 특이한 현상에 대해 메모를 남겼으나, 몇 주 후 그가 자동차 사고에서 날아오는 전면 유리 파편 때문에 심하게 다친 사람들에 대한 이야기를 신문에서 읽을 때까지 그것에 대해 더 이상 생각하지 않았다. ④ 그가 유리 플라스크와의 경험을 기억해 낸 것은 그때였고, 재빨리 그는 자동차 전면 유리가 산산조각나는 것을 방지하기 위해 특수 코팅이 적용될 수 있을 것이라고 생각했다. 그 후 오래 지나지 않아, 그는 세계 최초의 안전유리 생산에 성공했다.

| 정답해설 | ④ 62% 본문은 안전유리(safety glass)의 발명 경위에 관한 내용이다. 주어진 문장은 과거의 경험을 기억하여 자동차 전면 유리에 특수 코팅을 적용했다는 내용이므로 자동차 사고 때 전면 유리 파편에 다친 사람들에 관한 신문 기사를 읽었다는 문장과 실제로 얼마 지나지 않아 안전유리 생산에 성공했다는 문장 사이인 ④에 들어가야 글의 흐름이 자연스러워진다. 주어진 문장의 then은 ④ 문장 앞에서 언급된 '신문에서 자동차 사고'에 대한 이야기를 읽었을 때를 가리킨다.

어휘

windshield (자동차 앞쪽에 있는 바람막이용) 전면 유리
shatter 부서지다, 산산조각이 나다 　 astonishment 놀람
retain 유지하다, 보유하다 　 residue 잔여물, 찌꺼기
solution 용액 　 phenomenon 현상
thereafter 그 후, 그리고 나서

18 독해 > Micro Reading > 내용일치/불일치 　 오답률 29% 　 답 ③

| 해석 | 크로아티아의 Dubrovnik시는 엉망이다. 그곳의 주요 명소가 80피트의 중세 시대 벽으로 둘러싸인 해변가의 Old Town이기 때문에, 이 Dalmatian Coast 마을은 방문객을 그다지 잘 흡수하지 못한다. 그리고 크루즈 배가 이곳에 정박할 때, 많은 여행객들이 Old Town을 마을의 석회암으로 뒤덮인 거리를 탱크톱을 입고 활보하는 여행객들의 기운으로 바꾸어 놓는다. 그렇다, Dubrovnik시는 크루즈 여행을 억제하기 위해 노력하는 데 적극적이었으나, 끊임없는 여행객 무리로부터 Old Town을 구할 것은 아무것도 없을 것이다. 설상가상으로, 여분의 돈을 벌 수 있다는 유혹은 Old Town의 많은 집주인들이 자신들의 집을 Airbnb로 바꾸도록 자극했고, 마을의 벽으로 둘러싸인 부분을 하나의 거대한 호텔로 만들었다. 당신은 마치 지역 주민처럼 Old Town에서 '진정한' Dubrovnik시를 경험하고 싶은가? 당신은 여기에서 그것을 찾지 못할 것이다. 절대로.

| 정답해설 | ③ 71% 본문 중반부에서 Dubrovnik시는 크루즈 여행을 억제하기 위해 노력하는 데 적극적이었다고 했으므로, ③은 글의 내용과 반대된다.

| 오답해설 | ① 2% 두 번째 문장 Old Town surrounded by 80-foot medieval walls에서 Dubrovnik시의 주요 명소가 80피트의 중세 시대 벽으로 둘러싸인 해변의 Old Town이라고 했으므로 ①은 글의 내용과 일치한다.
② 19% 세 번째 문장에서 크루즈 배가 정박할 때, 많은 여행객들이 Old Town을 마을의 석회암으로 뒤덮인 거리를 탱크톱을 입고 활보하는 여행객들의 기운으로 바꾸어 놓는다고 했으므로 ②는 글의 내용과 일치한다.
④ 8% 본문 후반부의 To make matters worse 이후에 여분의 돈을 벌 수 있다는 유혹은 Old Town의 많은 집주인들이 자신들의 집을 Airbnb로 바꾸도록 만들어, 마을의 벽으로 둘러싸인 부분을 하나의 거대한 호텔로 만들었다고 했으므로 ④는 글의 내용과 일치한다.

어휘

mess 엉망, 혼란	attraction 명소, 관광지
medieval 중세의	absorb 받아들이다, 흡수하다
dock 정박하다	legion 다수, 큰 떼
miasma (지저분한·불쾌한) 공기[기운, 냄새]	
-clad ~(옷)을 입은	limestone 석회석, 석회암
blanket 뒤덮다	proactive 적극적인, 주도적인
curb 억제하다, 제한하다	perpetual 끊임없는
swarm 떼, 무리, 군중	lure 유혹, 매력

19 독해 > Reading for Writing > 빈칸 구 완성 　 오답률 43% 　 답 ①

| 해석 | 유기체가 살아 있을 때, 그것은 주변의 공기로부터 이산화탄소를 흡수한다. 그 이산화탄소 중 대부분은 탄소-12로 이루어져 있으나, 아주 적은 부분은 탄소-14로 구성되어 있다. 따라서 살아 있는 유기체는 늘 매우 적은 양의 방사성 탄소인 탄소-14를 함유하고 있다. 살아 있는 유기체 옆에 있는 검출기는 유기체 내의 탄소-14가 방출하는 방사선을 기록할 것이다. 그 유기체가 죽으면, 그것은 더 이상 이산화탄소를 흡수하지 않는다. 새로운 탄소-14가 추가되지 않으며, 기존의 탄소-14는 서서히 질소로 붕괴한다. 시간이 지남에 따라 탄소-14의 양은 서서히 (A) 감소한다. 시간이 흐르고, 탄소-14로부터 점점 더 적은 방사선이 생산된다. 그러므로, 유기체에서 검출된 탄소-14 방사선의 양은 그 유기체가 얼마나 오래 (B) 죽어 있었는지에 대한 측정이다. 유기체의 연대를 확인하는 이 방법은 방사성 탄소 연대 측정법이라고 불린다. 탄소-14의 붕괴는 고고학자들이 한때 살아 있었던 물질의 연대를 알아내도록 해 준다. 남아 있는 방사선의 양을 측정하는 것은 대략적인 연대를 보여 준다.

① 감소한다 – 죽은
② 증가한다 – 살아 있는
③ 감소한다 – 생산적인
④ 증가한다 – 활동하지 않는

| 정답해설 | ① 57% (A) 빈칸 앞에서 유기체가 죽으면 새로운 탄소-14가 추가되지 않으며 기존의 탄소-14는 서서히 질소로 붕괴한다고 했으므로, 탄소-14의 양이 점점 줄어든다는 것을 알 수 있다. 따라서 빈칸에는 decreases가 알맞다.
(B) 빈칸 이전에 사후 유기체에서 시간의 흐름에 따라 탄소-14의 생산이 점점 줄어든다고 제시하고 있다. 따라서 유기체에 남아 있는 탄소-14 방사선의 양을 측정하여 유기체의 연대를 특정하는 '방사성 탄소 연대 측정법'은 유기체가 얼마나 오랫동안 죽은 상태로 있었는지를 측정하는 방법임을 알 수 있다. 따라서 빈칸에는 dead가 가장 적절하다.

| 오답해설 | ②④ 11% 4% (A) 앞에서 새로운 탄소-14가 추가되지 않는다고 했으므로 탄소-14의 양이 증가하지 않을 것임을 알 수 있다. 따라서 increases는 부적절하다.

③ 28% 본문 중반에서 유기체가 죽은 후 탄소-14의 변화를 설명하고 있다. productive는 '생산적인'이라는 뜻이므로 빈칸에 적절하지 않다.

어휘

organism 유기체, 생물   carbon dioxide 이산화탄소
radioactive carbon 방사성 탄소   radiation 방사선
give off 방출하다, 뿜다
decay (방사성 물질이) 자연 붕괴하다; 부패하다, 썩다
nitrogen 질소   detect 감지하다, 탐지하다
measure 측정   determine 확인하다, 측정하다
carbon-14 dating 방사성 탄소 연대 측정법
archaeologist 고고학자

---

20   독해 > Reading for Writing > 빈칸 구 완성   오답률 27%   답 ②

| 해석 | 과거와 현재의 모든 생물은 사라졌거나 멸종될 것이다. 그러나, 지구 생명체의 지난 38억 년 역사 동안 각각의 종이 사라짐에 따라, 새로운 종들이 필연적으로 그것들을 대체하거나 새로이 출현한 자원을 이용하기 위해 나타났다. 그저 몇 가지의 매우 단순한 유기체로부터, 엄청난 수의 복잡한 다세포 형태가 이 엄청난 기간 동안 진화했다. 19세기 영국의 박물학자 Charles Darwin이 한때 '미스터리 중의 미스터리'라고 칭했던 새로운 종의 기원은 인간이 지구를 공유하는 이 놀라운 ② 생명체의 다양성을 일으키는 원인인 종 분화의 자연적인 과정이다. 분류학자들은 현재 약 150만의 생물 종을 인정하지만, 실제 숫자는 아마도 1천만에 가까울 것이다. 이렇게 많은 수의 생물학적 상태를 인지하는 것은 무엇이 종을 구성하는지에 대한 분명한 이해를 필요로 하는데, 보편적으로 받아들일 수 있는 정의에 진화 생물학자들이 아직 합의하지 못했다는 점을 고려하면 이는 쉬운 작업이 아니다.

① 생물학자들의 기술   ② 생명체의 다양성
③ 멸종 유기체의 목록   ④ 멸종 위기종 모음

| 정답해설 | ② 73% 빈칸 문장 앞 문장인 multicellular forms evolved over this immense period에서 단순한 유기체로부터 엄청난 수의 복잡한 다세포 형태의 유기체로 진화했다고 했고 빈칸 문장 이후에서 살아 있는 종의 수가 거의 천만에 달한다고 설명하고 있으므로 생물의 다양성에 대한 내용이라는 것을 알 수 있다. 따라서 종 분화(speciation)의 결과는 생명체의 다양성이라고 해야 하므로 답은 ②이다.

어휘

multicellular 다세포의   naturalist 박물학자, 동물학자
speciation 종 분화, 종 형성   remarkable 놀라운
taxonomist 분류학자   multitude 다수, 대량
constitute 구성하다   given that ~을 고려하면
universally 보편적으로, 일반적으로   definition 정의, 설명
have yet to V 아직 ~하지 않았다
inventory 목록   endangered 멸종 위기에 처한

합격예상 체크

〈국가직 연도별 합격선〉

2019 합격기준!

	2022	2021	2020	2019	2018	2017	2017 추가	2016

맞힌 개수	/20문항	점수	/100점

➡ ☐ 합격 ☐ 불합격

취약영역 체크

문항	정답	영역	문항	정답	영역
1	①	어휘 > 유의어 찾기	11	④	독해 > Micro Reading > 내용 일치/불일치
2	②	어휘 > 유의어 찾기	12	②	독해 > Logical Reading > 삭제
3	④	생활영어 > 회화/관용표현	13	③	독해 > Macro Reading > 주제
4	②	생활영어 > 회화/관용표현	14	③	어휘 > 유의어 찾기
5	②	문법 > 형용사	15	①	어휘 > 유의어 찾기
6	①	문법 > 형용사	16	①	독해 > Logical Reading > 연결사
7	②	문법 > 분사	17	④	독해 > Logical Reading > 삽입
8	④	문법 > 태	18	③	독해 > Reading for Writing > 빈칸 절 완성
9	④	독해 > Macro Reading > 제목	19	②	독해 > Micro Reading > 내용 일치/불일치
10	③	독해 > Macro Reading > 요지	20	④	독해 > Logical Reading > 배열

⬇ 영역별 틀린 개수로 취약영역을 확인하세요!

어휘	/4	문법	/4	독해	/10	생활영어	/2

➡ 나의 취약영역: _____

※ [정답해설]과 [오답해설] 선지의 50% 표시는 〈1초 합격예측 서비스〉를 통해 수집된 선지 선택률을 나타냅니다.

1	어휘 > 유의어 찾기	오답률 29%	답 ①

| 해석 | *Natural Gas World* 구독자들은 이 업계에서 어떤 일들이 일어나고 있는지에 대해 정확하고 믿을 수 있는 주요한 사실들과 수치들을 얻게 될 것이므로, 그들은 무엇이 그들의 사업과 관계되는지 충분히 **구별할** 수 있다.
① 71% 구별하다, 식별하다 ② 6% 강화하다
③ 12% 약화시키다 ④ 11% 버리다, 포기하다

| 정답해설 | ① 71% discern은 '구별하다'라는 뜻을 가진 동사로, 밑줄 친 단어 전에 잡지 구독자들이 정확한 정보를 얻게 될 것이라고 하였으므로 무엇이 그들의 사업과 관계되는지 충분히 '구별할' 수 있다는 내용으로 유추할 수 있다. 따라서 discern은 distinguish(구별하다, 식별하다)와 의미가 가장 가깝다.

어휘
subscriber 구독자 reliable 믿을 수 있는
figure 수치 concern 관계되다

2	어휘 > 유의어 찾기	오답률 36%	답 ②

| 해석 | 여성 1,500m 대회의 은메달 리스트인 Ms. West는 경기 내내 **돋보였다.**
① 29% 압도되었다 ② 64% 인상적이었다
③ 3% 우울했었다 ④ 4% 긍정적이었다

| 정답해설 | ② 64% stood out은 '눈에 띄었다, 돋보였다'라는 의미로 was impressive(인상적이었다)와 의미가 가장 가깝다.

어휘
winner 우승자

3	생활영어 > 회화/관용표현	오답률 13%	답 ④

| 해석 | ① A: 나는 해외여행을 갈 거야. 하지만 나는 다른 나라에서 머무는 것에 익숙하지 않아.
 B: 걱정하지 마. 너는 금방 그것에 익숙해질 거야.
② A: 나는 사진 대회에서 상을 타고 싶어.
 B: 나는 네가 그럴 거라고 확신해. 행운을 빌게!
③ A: 나의 가장 친한 친구가 세종시로 이사를 갔어. 나는 그녀가 너무 그리워.
 B: 그래. 난 네가 어떤 기분인지 알아.
④ A: 잠깐 이야기를 나눠도 괜찮을까요?
 B: 괜찮아요. 전 지금 매우 바빠요.

| 정답해설 | ④ 87% '꺼리다'라는 뜻의 동사 mind는 Do you mind if ~?의 형태로 정중하게 부탁할 때 사용된다. 이때 mind는 부정적인 의미를 내포하고 있으므로 부정의 대답이 긍정의 의미를 나타낸다. A가 잠깐 이야기를 나누자고 요청했는데 B가 처음에는 괜찮다고 한 뒤 이어서 '전 지금 매우 바빠요.'라고 했으므로 대답으로 적절하지 않다.

| 오답해설 | ① 8% 「be used to + (동)명사」와 「get accustomed to + (동)명사」는 '~에 익숙하다'라는 뜻이다. A가 다른 나라에서 머무는 것이 익숙하지 않다고 걱정하자 B가 곧 익숙해질 거라고 대답하였으므로 적절한 대화이다.

② 3% A가 사진 대회에서 상을 타고 싶다고 하자 B가 행운을 빈다고 했으므로 적절한 대화이다. keep one's fingers crossed는 '행운을 빌다'라는 의미의 관용표현이다.

③ 2% A가 가장 친한 친구가 이사를 가서 그녀가 그립다고 하자 B가 그 기분이 어떤지 안다고 공감하고 있으므로 적절한 대화이다.

어휘

in no time 곧
keep one's fingers crossed 행운을 빌다
mind 꺼리다, 상관하다

---

4 생활영어 > 회화/관용표현   오답률 3%   답 ②

| 해석 | A: 딤섬을 좀 드셔 보시겠어요?
B: 네, 감사합니다. 맛있어 보여요. 안에 무엇이 들어 있나요?
A: 이것들은 돼지고기와 다진 채소가 들어 있고, 저것들은 새우가 들어 있어요.
B: 그리고 음, ② 제가 그것들을 어떻게 먹으면 되나요?
A: 이렇게 젓가락으로 하나를 집어서 소스에 찍으면 돼요. 아주 쉽습니다.
B: 알겠어요. 한 번 해 볼게요.
① 그것들은 얼마인가요
② 제가 그것들을 어떻게 먹으면 되나요
③ 그것들은 얼마나 맵나요
④ 당신은 그것들을 어떻게 요리하나요

| 정답해설 | ② 97% 빈칸 이후에 A가 젓가락으로 집어서 소스에 찍어 먹으라고 하였으므로 빈칸에는 먹는 방법을 물어보는 말이 들어가야 알맞다.

어휘

chopped 다진   dip 살짝 찍다
give it a try 한 번 해 보다

---

5 문법 > 형용사   오답률 35%   답 ②

| 정답해설 | ② 65% shy of는 '~이 모자라는'이라는 뜻이다. 주어진 우리말은 '자정이 5분이나 지난 후'인데 five minutes shy of midnight이라고 하였으므로 맞지 않다. 올바른 문장은 I called him five minutes after midnight on an urgent matter.이다.

| 오답해설 | ① 12% '제가 당신께 말씀드렸던 새로운 선생님'은 관계대명사를 사용하여 The new teacher (who(m)) I told you about으로 옮길 수 있다.

③ 14% appear는 '나타나다, ~처럼 보이다'라는 뜻의 자동사로, '상어로 보이는 것'이라고 하였고 문장의 시제는 과거이므로 What appeared to be a shark는 알맞은 표현이다.

④ 9% reach는 '도착하다, 도달하다'라는 뜻의 타동사이므로 뒤에 전치사를 동반하지 않는다. 따라서 She reached the mountain summit은 올바른 표현이다. 또한 '16세의 친구'처럼 나이가 명사 앞에서 수식하는 형용사가 되는 경우에는 16-years-old가 아

닌 16-year-old로, year를 단수형으로 쓰는 것이 적절하다.

| 더 알아보기 | **appear의 주격 보어**

- appear + 주격 보어[(to be) + 형용사/명사]
- appear + 주격 보어[to부정사/과거분사]

| 더 알아보기 | **주의해야 할 완전타동사의 쓰임**

- reach[arrive in[at], get to] ~에 도착하다
- enter[get into] ~에 들어가다
- greet[bow to] ~에게 인사하다
- resemble[look like] ~을 닮다

어휘

originally 원래   shy of ~이 모자라는, 부족한
urgent 긴급한   lurk 숨어 있다
reef 암초   summit 정상

---

6 문법 > 형용사   오답률 39%   답 ①

| 정답해설 | ① 61% computers per person은 1인당 갖고 있는 컴퓨터를 의미하며 '개인용 컴퓨터를 가장 많이 가지고 있는'의 의미로는 with the largest number of personal computers가 적절한 표현이다.

| 오답해설 | ② 8% happen은 '일어나다'라는 의미의 자동사이므로 능동태로 사용한 것은 알맞다.

③ 15% '~ 또한 그렇다'라는 표현은 「so + 동사 + 주어」로 표현할 수 있다.

④ 16% 과거에서부터 지금까지 진행되고 있는 동작이나 상태는 현재완료나 현재완료진행형으로 표현할 수 있다. '은퇴 후부터 내내' 이 일을 하고 있다고 하였으므로 have been doing this work는 적절한 표현이다.

어휘

from time to time 때때로   retire 은퇴하다

오답률 TOP 2

7 문법 > 분사   오답률 49%   답 ②

| 해석 | 가축화된 동물들은 인간들이 이용할 수 있는 가장 초기의(가장 오래된) 그리고 가장 효과적인 '기계들'이다. 그들은 인간의 등과 팔의 부담을 덜어 준다. 다른 기술들과 함께 이용되면서, 동물들은 보조적인 음식 재료(고기와 우유의 단백질로서) 그리고 짐을 실어 나르고 물을 끌어올리고 곡식을 가는 기계 두 가지로 인간의 생활 수준을 아주 상당히 올릴 수 있다. 그들이 너무나 명백하게 이롭기 때문에, 우리는 아마 수세기 동안 인간들이 그들이 소유했던 동물들의 수와 질을 증가시켰을 것임을 알아낼 것이라고 예상할 수도 있다. 놀랍게도, 이것은 대개 사실이 아니었다.

| 정답해설 | ② 51% 인간이 가축들을 어떻게 이용하여 왔는지 설명하는 글이다. 분사구문 Utilizing with other techniques에 주어가 없으므로 주절의 주어(animals)와 동일한 것을 알 수 있고, utilize는 '~을 이용하다'라는 의미의 타동사이므로 목적어를 수반해야 하는데 Utilizing 이후에 목적어가 없으므로 수동태 분사

구문이 되어야 한다. 또한 해석상으로도 주어 animals는 인간에 의해 이용되는 객체이므로 수동태 분사구문이 사용되어야 한다는 것을 알 수 있다.

As animals are utilized with other techniques ~
→ Being utilized with other techniques ~
→ Utilized with other techniques ~

| 오답해설 | ① 5% 「주격 관계대명사 + be동사」가 생략된 구문으로, 'machines' that are available to humans에서 that are가 생략되어 형용사구 available to humans가 'machines'를 후치 수식하고 있다.

③ 14% 형용사적 용법의 to부정사로 앞의 명사 machines를 수식한다.

④ 30% 「of + 추상명사」는 형용사의 뜻을 가지므로, of great benefit은 greatly beneficial과 같은 의미이다.

| 더 알아보기 | 「of + 추상명사」의 관용적 표현

• of talent	talented(재능이 있는)
• of learning	learned(학식이 있는)
• of use ⇒	useful(유용한)
• of sense	sensible(분별 있는)
• of ability	able(유능한)
• of importance	important(중요한)

어휘

domesticated 가축화된	strain 부담
utilize 이용[활용]하다	considerably 상당하게
supplementary 보충적인, 보조적인	foodstuff 음식 재료
burden 짐, 부담	obviously 명확하게

8　　문법 > 태　　　오답률 37%　　답 ④

| 해석 | 신화는 한 문화의 종교적, 철학적, 도덕적 그리고 정치적인 가치를 구현하고, 어떤 경우에는 설명을 도와주는 이야기이다. 신들과 초자연적 존재들에 관한 이야기들을 통해, 신화는 자연 세계 내의 사건들을 이해하도록 시도한다. 대중적인 용법과 반대로, 신화는 "허구"를 의미하지는 않는다. 가장 넓은 관점에서, 신화는 거짓뿐 아니라 진실이거나 부분적으로 진실일 수 있는 이야기들, 주로 이야기들의 덩어리 전체이다. 그러나 그들의 정확성의 정도와는 상관없이, 신화들은 종종 문화의 가장 심오한 믿음들을 표현한다. 이러한 의미에 따라, 『Iliad』와 『Odyssey』, 코란 그리고 구약과 신약은 모두 신화로 불릴 수 있다.

| 정답해설 | ④ 63% 「refer to + 명사 + as」는 '~을 …라고 부르다, 지칭하다, 일컫다, 언급하다'의 의미로 전치사 to 다음에 목적어가 필요한데, 본문에는 목적어가 없으므로 수동태로 사용되어야 하는 것을 알 수 있다. 따라서 be referred to as로 써야 옳다.

| 오답해설 | ① 19% help는 목적어로 to부정사와 원형부정사 모두 사용할 수 있다.

② 9% 「try + to부정사」는 '~하려고 애쓰다, 노력하다'라는 뜻으로 알맞은 표현이다.

③ 9% 선행사가 stories이므로 관계대명사 that이 이끄는 절로 수식하는 것은 적절하다.

| 더 알아보기 | help의 용례

- help(완전타동사) + 목적어[명사/to부정사/원형부정사]
- help(불완전타동사) + 목적어 + 목적격 보어[to부정사/원형부정사]

어휘

myth 신화, 근거 없는 믿음	narrative 이야기, 서술
embody 구현하다, 상징하다; 담다	religious 종교적인
philosophical 철학적인	moral 도덕적인
tale 이야기	supernatural 초자연적인
being 존재	make sense of ~을 이해하다
occurrence 발생, 사건	contrary to ~와는 대조적으로
falsehood 거짓말, 허구(임)	regardless of ~와 상관없이
Old and New Testament 구약/신약 성서	

9　　독해 > Macro Reading > 제목　　오답률 17%　　답 ④

| 해석 | 지도 제작 기술들은 많은 새로운 응용 분야에서 사용되고 있다. 생물학 연구원들은 DNA의 분자적 구조를 조사하고 있는 중이("게놈을 지도화하는 중")이고, 지구 물리학자들은 지구의 핵의 구조를 지도화하고 있고, 해양학자들은 해저를 지도화하고 있는 중이다. 컴퓨터 게임들은 다양한 가상의 "토지" 혹은 규칙들, 위험, 그리고 보상이 변하는 레벨들을 갖고 있다. 컴퓨터화는 지금 "가상 현실", 즉 특수한 상황들을 시뮬레이션하는 인공적인 환경들과 함께 현실에 도전하는데, 그것들은 훈련과 오락에 유용할지도 모른다. 지도 제작 기술들은 또한 아이디어들의 영역에서 사용되고 있다. 예를 들면, 아이디어들 사이의 관계들은 콘셉트 지도들이라고 불리는 것을 사용하여 보여질 수 있다. 일반적이거나 "중심적인" 아이디어들로부터 시작하여, 연관된 아이디어들은 주요 콘셉트 주변에 망을 구축하면서 연결될 수 있다. 이것은 어떤 전통적인 정의에 의한 지도가 아니지만, 지도 제작의 도구들과 기술들은 그것을 생산하기 위해 이용되며, 어떤 면에서 그것은 지도와 닮았다.

① 컴퓨터화된 지도들 대 전통적인 지도들
② 지도 제작은 어디에서 시작되는가?
③ DNA의 비밀에 다가가는 방법 찾기
④ 새로운 분야들을 지도화하기

| 정답해설 | ④ 83% 본문 첫 문장에서 지도 제작 기술이 많은 새로운 응용 분야에서 사용되고 있다고 언급한 후, 그에 대한 예시를 나열하고 있다. 과거의 전통적 지도 제작 기술들이 새로운 분야에서 사용되고 있다는 내용이며, 또한 전통적인 개념의 지도가 아니지만 닮은 점도 있다고 본문에서 설명하고 있으므로, 글의 제목으로 ④가 알맞다. (참고로, 본문의 simulate는 기출에 stimulate로 출제되었으나, 문맥과 출제 원문에 맞게 simulate로 수정하였다.)

| 오답해설 | ① 10% 컴퓨터화된 지도들과 전통적인 지도들을 비교하고 있는 것은 아니므로 적절하지 않다.

③ 3% 본문에서 DNA는 지도 제작 기술이 응용되는 분야의 한 예로 언급된 것이므로 전체 글의 제목으로는 적절하지 않다.

어휘

mapping 지도 제작	application 응용 (분야)
molecular 분자의	geophysicist 지구 물리학자
core 핵	oceanographer 해양학자
ocean floor 해저	imaginary 가상의, 상상의
hazard 위험 (요소)	virtual reality 가상 현실
realm 영역	cartography 지도 제작

resemble 닮다　　　　　frontier 새로운 분야; 경계

10　독해 > Macro Reading > 요지　　오답률 22%　　답 ③

| 해석 | 성과 피드백을 줄 때, 그것(피드백)의 빈도와 양, 그리고 내용을 설계하는 데 있어서 당신은 (피드백을) 받는 사람의 과거 성과와 그 또는 그녀의 향후 잠재력에 관한 당신의 평가를 고려해야 한다. 성장 잠재력을 가진 고성과자의 경우, 그들이 시정 조치를 취하도록 자극할 만큼 피드백이 충분히 빈번해야 하지만, 이것이 통제로 경험되어 그들의 진취성을 약화시킬 만큼 너무 빈번해서는 안 된다. 자신의 업무에 정착하여 발전 가능성이 제한되어 있는 유능한 성과자들에게는 피드백이 거의 필요하지 않은데, 그들은 자신들의 일을 알고 있고 무슨 일이 행해져야 하는지 인식하고 있기에 과거 신뢰할 만하고 안정된 행동을 보여 왔기 때문이다. 저성과자의 경우, 즉 성과가 향상되지 않으면 직장에서 퇴출되어야 할 사람들은 피드백이 빈번하고 매우 구체적이어야 하며, 피드백에 따라 행동하는 것과 일시적으로 해고되거나 영구적으로 해고되는 것과 같은 부정적인 제재 사이의 연관성이 분명히 나타나도록 해야 한다.
① 타이밍에 맞춰 피드백을 잘하라.
② 부정적인 피드백을 맞춤화하라.
③ 사람마다 피드백을 맞춰 하라.
④ 목적 지향적인 피드백을 피하라.

| 정답해설 | ③ 78% 성장 잠재력이 있는 고성과자, 유능한 성과자 그리고 퇴출 가능성이 있는 저성과자에게 각각 피드백을 어떻게 해야 하는지 설명하고 있으므로 ③이 요지로 알맞다.

어휘
performance 성과, 수행 (능력)　　recipient 수신자, 받는 사람
estimate 평가, 판단; 추정(치)　　frequency 빈도
prod 자극하다, 찌르다　　corrective 교정의
sap 약화시키다　　initiative 진취성, 계획
adequate 적임인, 유능한; 적절한　　sanction 제재; 승인
lay off (일시) 해고하다　　explicit 분명한
time 시간을 맞추다[조절하다]　　customize 맞추다, 주문 제작하다
tailor 맞추다, 조정하다　　goal-oriented 목표 지향적인

11　독해 > Micro Reading > 내용일치/불일치　　오답률 10%　　답 ④

| 해석 | Langston Hughes는 Missouri주 Joplin에서 태어났으며, 많은 아프리카계 미국 학생들이 학문을 닦은 Lincoln대학교를 졸업했다. Hughes는 열여덟 살 때 가장 유명한 시 중 하나인 "Negro Speaks of Rivers"를 출간했다. 창의적이고 실험적이었기에 Hughes는 그의 작품에 진짜 사투리를 접목시켰고, 블루스와 재즈의 억양과 분위기를 담기 위해 전통적인 시 형식에 변화를 주었으며, 하층 계급 흑인 문화의 요소를 반영하는 인물과 주제를 창조했다. 진지한 내용에 익살 맞은 양식을 결합시키는 그의 능력으로, Hughes는 자연스럽고 재치 있는 방법으로 인종 편견을 공격했다.

| 정답해설 | ④ 90% 본문 마지막에 진지한 내용과 익살 맞은 양식을 결합시키는 능력으로 Hughes가 자연스럽고 재치 있게 인종 편견을 공격했다고 했으므로 ④는 글의 내용과 일치하지 않는다.

어휘
discipline 교육, 훈련, 훈육　　experimental 실험적인
incorporate 통합시키다　　authentic 진짜의
dialect 지역 언어　　embrace 수용하다
cadence 억양　　fuse 결합[융합]시키다
prejudice 편견　　witty 위트 있는, 재치 있는

12　독해 > Logical Reading > 삭제　　오답률 26%　　답 ②

| 해석 | 2007년에, 우리의 가장 큰 걱정은 "대마불사(파산하기에는 너무 거대하다)"였다. 월 스트리트의 은행들은 매우 압도적인 규모로 성장했고, 금융 시스템의 건전성에 구심점이 되었기 때문에, 합리적인 정부라면 어떤 정부도 그들을 파산하게 내버려둘 수 없었다. 자신들의 보호받는 지위를 인식하고 있었기에 은행들은 주택 시장에 과도하게 위험한 투자를 했고, 그 어느 때보다도 더 많은 복잡한 파생 상품들을 만들었다. ② bitcoin과 ethereum 같은 새로운 가상 통화는 어떻게 돈이 작용할 수 있고 작용해야 하는지에 대한 우리의 이해를 급진적으로 변화시켰다. 그 결과는 1929년 우리 경제가 붕괴된 이래로 최악의 금융 위기였다. 2007년 이후 몇 년 동안, 우리는 "대마불사" 딜레마를 해결하는 데 큰 진전을 이루었다. 우리 은행들은 그 어느 때보다도 자본화가 잘 되어 있다. 우리의 규제 담당자들은 대형 기관의 정기적인 스트레스 테스트를 수행한다.

| 정답해설 | ② 74% 2007년 월 스트리트의 금융 시스템 붕괴에 대해 설명하는 내용이다. 따라서 돈의 작용 원리를 이해하는 데 있어 가상 통화가 미친 영향을 서술하고 있는 ②는 본문과 관련이 없다.

어휘
fail 실패하다; 파산하다　　staggering 압도적인, 충격적인
financial 금융의, 재정의　　rational 이성적인
aware of ~을 인식하는　　excessively 과도하게
make a bet on ~에 돈을 걸다, 내기하다
derivative 파생 상품　　virtual currency 가상 통화
radically 극단적으로　　breakdown 붕괴
address 다루다　　capitalize 자본화하다
regulator 규제 담당자, 단속 기관　　conduct 수행하다

13　독해 > Macro Reading > 주제　　오답률 2%　　답 ③

| 해석 | 두 사람이 같은 날 한 로펌에서 일을 시작한다고 상상해 보라. 한 사람은 아주 단순한 이름을 가지고 있다. 다른 사람은 아주 복잡한 이름을 가지고 있다. 우리는 그들의 향후 16년 이상의 경력 동안 더 단순한 이름을 가진 사람이 더 빨리 법적 지배 계층에 오를 것이라는 꽤 타당한 증거를 가지고 있다. 그들은 경력 중간에 더 빨리 파트너 지위를 얻을 것이다. 그리고 로스쿨을 졸업한 지 8~9년쯤 되었을 때, 더 단순한 이름을 가진 사람들이 파트너가 될 가능성이 약 7~10% 더 높은데, 이것은 인상적인 결과이다. 우리는 모든 종류의 대안적인 설명들을 없애려고 시도한다. 예를 들어, 우리는 외국 이름이 발음하기가 더 어려운 경향이 있기 때문에 이것이 외래성에 관한 것은 아니라는 것을 보여 주려고 시도한다. 하지만 여러분이 그저 진정한 내집단에 속하는, 영국계 미국 이름을 가진 백인 남성들을 보게 되더라도, 만약 그들의 이름이 더 단순해진다면, 그들이 그런 이름을 가진 백인 남성들 사이에서 더 승진할 가능성이 높다는 것을 알게 된다. 따라서 단순함은 이름에 있어서 다양한 결과를 결정짓는 하나의 핵심적 특징이다.
① 법적 이름의 발전
② 매력적인 이름의 개념
③ 단순한 이름의 이점
④ 외국 이름의 어원

| 정답해설 | ③ 98% 본문 마지막 문장이 주제문으로, 단순함은 이름에 있어서 다양한 결과를 결정짓는 하나의 핵심적 특징이라고 하였다. 또한 본문의 전체 내용을 통해 단순한 이름이 그렇지 않은 이름보다 승진이나 성공을 더 빨리 한다는 것을 알 수 있으므로 ③이 주제로 알맞다.

어휘

over the course of ~ 동안	rise up 올라가다
hierarchy 계층, 계급; (조직 내의) 고위층, 지배층	
striking 인상적인, 현저한	eliminate 제거하다
alternative 대안(의)	foreignness 외래성; 이질성
in-group 내집단	outcome 결과

---

14 어휘 > 유의어 찾기 　　오답률 30%　답 ③

| 해석 | 학교 교육은 미국의 모든 아이들에게 의무적이지만, 학교 출석이 요구되는 연령대는 주마다 다르다.

① 11% 보완적인　　　　② 15% 체계적인
③ 70% 의무적인　　　　④ 4% 혁신적인

| 정답해설 | ③ compulsory는 '강제적인, 의무적인'이란 뜻을 가진 형용사로 비슷한 뜻을 가진 단어는 mandatory(의무적인)이다.

어휘
schooling 학교 교육

오답률 TOP 1

15 어휘 > 유의어 찾기 　　오답률 71%　답 ①

| 해석 | 비록 그 여배우가 그녀의 경력에서 많은 혼란을 겪었지만, 그녀는 어느 누구에게도 절대 자신이 불행하다고 밝힌 적이 없다.

① 29% 말하다, 털어놓다
② 40% (처벌하지 않거나 가벼운 처벌로) ~를 봐주다; (총을) 발사하다; (폭탄 등을) 터뜨리다
③ 10% 약해지다, 누그러지다
④ 21% 실망시키다

| 정답해설 | ① disclose는 '밝히다, 공개하다'라는 뜻을 가진 동사로 이와 비슷한 뜻을 가진 단어는 let on(말하다, 털어놓다)이다.

어휘
turmoil 혼란, 소란
let off (처벌하지 않거나 가벼운 처벌로) ~를 봐주다; (총을) 발사하다; (폭탄 등을) 터뜨리다
let up 약해지다, 누그러지다　　　let down 실망시키다

---

16 독해 > Logical Reading > 연결사 　　오답률 38%　답 ①

| 해석 | 선지자들은 그들의 업계에서 새로운 기술의 잠재력을 알아보는 첫 번째 사람들이다. 근본적으로, 그들은 자신들이 경쟁사에 있는 그들의 상대보다 더 똑똑하다고 여긴다. 그리고 꽤 자주, 그들은 그렇다. 실제로, 그들이 경쟁 우위로 활용하고 싶어 하는 것들을 먼저 보는 것이 그들의 능력이다. 그 우위는 다른 누구도 그것을 발견하지 않았을 때만 생길 수 있다. (A) 따라서, 그들은 업계의 광범위한 참고 자료 목록을 지닌 검증된 제품을 사려고 하지 않는다. 사실, 만약 그러한 참고 자료의 근거가 존재한다면, 이 기술에 대해서는, 어쨌든 그들이 이미 너무 늦었다는 것을 암시하기 때문에 그것은 실제로 그들이 흥미를 잃게 만들 수도 있다. (B) 반면에, 실용주의자들은 다른 기업에 있는 동료들의 경험을 대단히 가치 있게 여긴다. 구매를 할 때, 그들은 광범위한 참고 자료들을 기대하며, 그들 자신의 업계 내 기업들에서 상당히 많은 참고 자료들이 나오기를 원한다.

|　　　　(A)　　　　　　　(B)
① 　　따라서　　　　　　반면에
② 　　그러나　　　　　　게다가
③ 　　그럼에도 불구하고　동시에
④ 　　게다가　　　　　　결과적으로

| 정답해설 | ① 62% (A) 빈칸 이전에서 '선지자들'의 특성을 설명한 후, 빈칸 문장에서 그에 따른 선지자들의 행동적 특징(검증된 제품을 사지 않는 것)에 대해 서술하고 있으므로, 인과 관계를 나타내는 연결사 therefore가 빈칸에 적절하다.
(B) 빈칸 앞까지는 선지자들의 특성을 설명하고 빈칸 뒤부터 실용주의자들에 대해 서술하고 있으므로, 대조의 연결사 on the other hand가 알맞다.

어휘

visionary 선지자	segment 분야, 부분
fundamentally 근본적으로	
opposite number (다른 조직에서 같은 일을 하는) 상대방	
leverage 활용하다, ~에 영향을 주다; 영향력	
competitive advantage 경쟁(상의) 우위	
expect to V (당연한 것으로) ~할 작정이다	
come about 발생하다, 생기다	
extensive 광범위한	well-tested 입증된
indicate 암시하다; 가리키다	reference 참고, 언급
	pragmatist 실용주의자

---

17 독해 > Logical Reading > 삽입 　　오답률 32%　답 ④

| 해석 | 수세기 동안, 인간들은 하늘을 올려다보며 우리 행성의 영역 바깥에 무엇이 존재하는지를 궁금해했다. 고대 천문학자들은 우주에 관해 더 많이 배우기를 희망하며 밤하늘을 조사했다. 보다 최근에, 일부 영화들은 외계 생명체가 우리 행성을 방문했을 수도 있는지를 궁금해했던 반면, 다른 영화들은 우주 공간에서 인간의 삶을 지속시키는 것의 가능성을 탐구했다. 우주 비행사인 Yuri Gagarin이 1961년에 우주를 여행했던 최초의 인간이 된 이후, 과학자들은 지구의 대기권 바깥이 어떤 조건일지, 그리고 우주여행이 인간의 신체에 어떤 영향을 주는지를 연구해 왔다. 대부분의 우주 비행사들이 우주에서 몇 개월 이상을 지내지 않음에도 불구하고, 지구에 복귀할 때는 많은 이들이 생리적·심리적 문제들을 겪는다. ④ 이 질병들 중 일부는 오래 가지 않지만 다른 것들은 오래 지속될 수도 있다. 모든 우주 비행사들 중 2/3 이상은 우주에서 여행하는 동안 멀미로 고생한다. 무중력 환경에서, 신체는 위아래를 구분할 수 없다. 신체의 내부 균형 시스템이 뇌에 혼란스런 신호를 전달하고, 이는 최대 며칠 동안 지속되는 메스꺼움을 초래할 수 있다.

| 정답해설 | ④ 68% 주어진 문장에서 '이 질병들 중 일부는 오래 가지 않지만 다른 것들은 오래 지속될 수도 있다.'라고 서술하고 있으므로 주어진 문장 전후로 질병에 관련된 내용이 언급되는 것이 글의 흐름상 적절하다. 주어진 문장의 these ailments가 physiological and psychological problems를 가리키는 것으로 보는 것이 가장 적절하므로 주어진 문장의 자리로는 ④가 알맞다.

어휘

ailment 질병	short-lived 오래 가지 못하는
long-lasting 오래 지속되는	realm 영역
astronomer 천문학자	sustain 지속시키다, 유지하다
extraterrestrial 외계의	physiological 생리학적인
psychological 심리적인	motion sickness 멀미
differentiate 구별하다	result in ~을 초래하다
nausea 메스꺼움	

| **해석** | 왜 모든 것의 역사에 대해 신경 쓰는가? ③ 오늘날, 우리는 세상에 대해 단편적으로 가르치고 배운다. 문학 수업에서 당신은 유전자에 관해 배우지 않는다. 물리 수업에서 당신은 인간 진화에 관해 배우지 않는다. 따라서 당신은 세상에 대한 부분적인 견해를 얻는다. 그것은 교육에서 '의미'를 찾기 어렵게 만든다. 프랑스 사회학자인 Emile Durkheim은 이 혼란과 무의미함의 느낌을 '아노미(사회적 무질서)'라고 불렀고, 그는 그것이 절망으로, 그리고 심지어는 자살로까지 이끌 수도 있다고 주장했다. 독일 사회학자인 Max Weber는 세상의 "각성"에 관해 이야기했다. 과거에, 사람들은 그들의 세상에 대해 통합된 시각을 지녔고, 이는 보통 그들 자신의 종교적 전통의 기원 설화에 의해 주어지는 시각이었다. 그 통합된 시각은 목적에 대한, 의미에 대한, 심지어 세상에의 현혹에 대한, 그리고 삶에 대한 감각을 제공했다. 그러나 오늘날, 많은 작가들은 무의미함의 느낌은 과학과 이성의 세상에서 필연적이라고 주장해 왔다. 현대성은 무의미함을 의미하는 것처럼 보인다.

① 과거에, 역사 연구는 과학으로부터의 각성을 요구했다
② 최근에, 과학은 우리에게 많은 영리한 속임수들과 의미들을 제공해 왔다
③ 오늘날, 우리는 단편적으로 우리의 세상에 대해 가르치고 배운다
④ 최근에, 역사는 몇 가지 항목으로 나뉘었다

| **정답해설** | ③ 60% 빈칸 다음에 문학 수업에서 유전자에 관해 배우지 않고 물리 수업에서 진화에 관해 배우지 않는다고 하면서 '따라서 당신은 세상에 대한 부분적 견해를 얻는다'고 하였으므로 이와 일치하는 내용이 빈칸에 들어가야 한다. 따라서 빈칸에는 ③이 들어가는 것이 가장 적절하다.

| **오답해설** | ① 17% 빈칸 이후에서 오늘날 행해지는 단편적 교육에 대한 예시를 제시하고 있으므로, 빈칸에 과거의 역사 연구에 관한 내용이 들어가는 것은 문맥상 어색하다.
② 11% 본문 마지막에 '현대성은 무의미함을 의미하는 것처럼 보인다'고 했으므로 빈칸에 적절하지 않다.
④ 12% 본문에서 언급되지 않은 내용이다.

어휘

disorientation 혼란, 방향 감각 상실
anomie 아노미, 사회적 무질서   despair 절망
disenchantment 각성; 환멸   unified 통합된
enchantment 황홀감, 현혹   inevitable 불가피한, 필연적인
rationality 이성, 합리성   modernity 현대성
fragment 조각, 파편

| **해석** | 가장 초기의 정부 급식 프로그램은 유럽에서 1900년경에 시작되었다. 미국의 프로그램은 대공황부터 시작되었는데, 그때 잉여 농산물을 소진할 필요와 빈곤 가정의 아이들에게 음식을 제공하는 것에 대한 관심이 합쳐졌다. 2차 세계 대전 동안과 그 이후에는, 근로 여성 수의 폭발이 더 폭넓은 프로그램에 대한 필요를 자극했다. 한때 가정의 기능이었던 점심 제공은 학교의 급식 시스템으로 이동되었다. National School Lunch Program은 이러한 노력들의 결과이다. 그 프로그램은 연방 정부의 지원을 받는 식사를 학령 아동들에게 제공하기 위해 만들어졌다. 2차 세계 대전 종전부터 1980년대 초까지, 학교 급식을 위한 자금 지원은 꾸준히 확대되었다. 오늘날 그것은 미국 전역에서 거의 10만 개 학교의 아이들에게 급식을 제공하는 것을 돕는다. 그것의 첫 번째 기능은 영양가 높은 점심을 모든 학생들에게 제공하는 것이다. 두 번째는 아침 식사와 점심 식사 때 영양가 높은 음식을 소외 계층 아이들에게 제공하는 것이다. 오히려, 한때 가정의 기능이었던 것의 대체물로서 학교 급식의 역할이 확대되어 왔다.

① 근로 여성 수의 증가가 급식 프로그램의 확대를 촉진시켰다.
② 미국 정부는 식량 부족에도 불구하고 대공황 동안 가난한 아이들에게 음식을 제공하기 시작했다.
③ 미국 학교의 급식 시스템은 현재 빈곤 가정의 아이들에게 음식을 제공하는 것을 돕는다.
④ 점심을 제공하는 기능이 가정에서 학교로 이동되었다.

| **정답해설** | ② 58% 대공황 때 잉여 농작물 소진의 필요성과 빈곤 가정의 아이들에게 음식을 제공하는 것의 필요에 대한 관심이 합쳐졌을 때 급식이 시작되었다고 설명하고 있으므로 ②는 본문과 일치하지 않는다.

어휘

date from ~부터 시작되다   the Great Depression 대공황
surplus 잉여의, 과잉의   agricultural 농업의
commodity 상품   explosion 폭발
fuel 자극하다; 연료를 공급하다   shift 이동시키다
fund 자금을 지원하다; 자금, 기금   nutritious 영양가 높은
underprivileged 혜택을 받지 못한, 가난한
if anything 오히려   boost 밀어 올리다; 후원하다

| **해석** | 대한민국은 지구상에서 인터넷 연결이 가장 잘 되어 있는 국가임을 자랑한다.
(B) 사실, 아마 그 어떤 국가도 인터넷을 그렇게 완전히 수용한 적은 없을 것이다.
(C) 그러나 다수의 강박적 사용자들이 컴퓨터 화면으로부터 자신들을 떼어 놓을 수 없다는 사실을 깨닫게 됨에 따라 웹에 대한 그러한 신속한 접근은 대가를 치르게 되었다.
(A) 사용자들이 며칠 동안 계속해서 온라인 게임을 한 후 탈진으로 급사하기 시작하면서, 이 중독은 최근 몇 년간 한국에서 국가적 이슈가 되었다. 점점 더 많은 학생들이 온라인에 머물기 위해 학교를 가지 않았는데, 이것은 이 극도로 경쟁적인 사회에서 매우 자멸적인 행동이다.

| **정답해설** | ④ 67% 주어진 문장에서 대한민국이 인터넷 연결이 가장 잘 되어 있다고 언급했다. (B)는 첨언 연결사 In fact로 시작되는데 주어진 문장에 이어 다른 국가들과 비교하면서 한국의 인터넷 보급이 최상임을 강조한다. (C)는 역접 연결사 But으로 시작하여 훌륭한 인터넷 보급에 대가가 따른다고 언급하며 부정적 측면이 있음을 지적한다. 특히 강박적 사용자들(obsessed users)이 컴퓨터 사용을 못한다는 (C)의 내용을 (A)에서는 This addiction으로 지칭했다. 따라서 (B) - (C) - (A)의 순서가 알맞다.

어휘

boast of ~을 자랑하다, 뽐내다   wired 컴퓨터 시스템에 연결된
embrace 수용하다; 껴안다   ready 신속한, 즉시의
at a price 상당한 대가를 치르고   legions of 수많은
drop dead 급사하다   exhaustion 탈진
on end 계속하여   self-destructive 자멸적인
intensely 극도로, 강렬하게

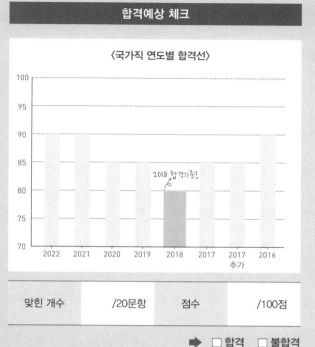

합격예상 체크

〈국가직 연도별 합격선〉

2018 합격기준

맞힌 개수	/20문항	점수	/100점

➡ □ 합격　□ 불합격

취약영역 체크

문항	정답	영역	문항	정답	영역
1	①	생활영어 > 회화/관용표현	11	④	독해 > Logical Reading > 문맥상 다양한 추론
2	①	독해 > Reading for Writing > 빈칸 구 완성	12	④	독해 > Macro Reading > 주제
3	②	독해 > Macro Reading > 제목	13	②	독해 > Micro Reading > 내용 일치/불일치
4	③	문법 > 태	14	①	어휘 > 유의어 찾기
5	①	어휘 > 유의어 찾기	15	④	어휘 > 유의어 찾기
6	②	어휘 > 빈칸 완성	16	④	독해 > Logical Reading > 삽입
7	④	독해 > Logical Reading > 삭제	17	②	독해 > Micro Reading > 내용 일치/불일치
8	②	생활영어 > 회화/관용표현	18	②	독해 > Reading for Writing > 빈칸 구 완성
9	②	독해 > Micro Reading > 내용 일치/불일치	19	③	독해 > Logical Reading > 배열
10	③	문법 > 분사	20	④	문법 > 비교

➡ 영역별 틀린 개수로 취약영역을 확인하세요!

어휘	/4	문법	/3	독해	/11	생활영어	/2

➡ 나의 취약영역:

※ [정답해설]과 [오답해설] 선지의 50% 표시는 〈1초 합격예측 서비스〉를 통해 수집된 선지 선택률을 나타냅니다.

1　생활영어 > 회화/관용표현　오답률 17%　답 ①

| 해석 | A: 부탁 하나만 해도 될까요?
B: 네, 뭐가요?
A: 출장 때문에 공항에 가야 하는데, 차가 시동이 걸리지 않아요. 저 좀 태워 줄 수 있으세요?
B: 물론이죠. 언제까지 그곳에 도착해야 하나요?
A: 늦어도 6시까지는 도착해야 해요.
B: 지금이 4시 30분이에요. ① 아슬아슬하네요. 지금 당장 출발해야겠어요.
① 아슬아슬하네요
② 제가 방심했어요
③ 반짝인다고 다 금은 아니에요
④ 이미 다 지나간 일이에요

| 정답해설 | ① 83% A가 공항에 도착해야 하는 시간은 6시인데, B가 지금 시간은 4시 30분이고 빈칸 이후에 지금 당장 출발해야겠다고 답하고 있으므로 빈칸에 가장 적절한 말은 시간과 관련된 표현인 ①이다.

어휘
no later than 늦어도 ~까지
That's cutting it close (상황이) 아슬아슬하다; 절약하다
take one's eye off the ball 방심하다, 한눈을 팔다
All that glitters is not gold. 반짝인다고 모두 금은 아니다.
water under the bridge 지나간 일

2　독해 > Reading for Writing > 빈칸 구 완성　오답률 26%　답 ①

| 해석 | 손실의 두려움은 인간의 기본적인 부분이다. 뇌에게 손실은 위협이며 우리는 자연적으로 그것을 피하기 위한 조치를 취한다. 그러나, 우리는 그것을 무한히 피할 수는 없다. 손실을 마주하는 한 가지 방법은 주식 투자자의 관점을 가지는 것이다. 투자자들은 손실의 가능성을 게임의 끝으로서가 아니라 게임의 한 부분으로서 받아들인다. 이러한 사고를 이끄는 것은 포트폴리오 접근법이다. 수익과 손실은 둘 다 발생하겠지만, 가장 중요한 것은 결과의 전체적인 포트폴리오이다. 당신이 포트폴리오 접근법을 받아들일 때, 당신은 그것들이 훨씬 더 큰 그림의 작은 부분들임을 알고 있기 때문에 ① 개별적인 손실에 덜 연연하게 될 것이다.
① 개별적인 손실에 덜 연연하게
② 당신의 투자에 관심을 덜 가지게
③ 손실을 더 싫어하게
④ 주식 시장의 변동에 더 민감하게

| 정답해설 | ① 74% 빈칸 뒤의 문장에서 a much bigger picture는 전체적인 포트폴리오를, 그리고 small parts는 개별적인 수익과 손실을 말한다. 즉, 전체적인 결과를 가장 중요시하는 포트폴리오 접근법을 수용하면 작은 부분인 개별적인 손실들에 덜 집착하게 된다는 것을 유추할 수 있다. 따라서 빈칸에 들어갈 말로 가장 적절한 것은 ①이다.

어휘
perspective 관점　　　　　　　stock trader 주식 투자자
embrace 받아들이다　　　　　　dwell on ~을 곱씹다, ~에 연연하다
averse ~을 싫어하는　　　　　　fluctuation 변동, 오르내림

| **3** | 독해 > Macro Reading > 제목 | 오답률 7% | 답 ② |

| **해석** | 지난 수년간의 여행 동안, 나는 우리 인간들이 얼마나 과거 속에서 살고 있는지를 관찰해 왔다. 어떤 것이 나타나자마자 그것이 과거가 된다는 점을 고려할 때 과거는 항상 우리 주변에 존재한다. 우리의 주변, 우리의 집, 우리의 환경, 우리의 건축물, 우리의 생산품들 모두 과거의 구조물이다. 우리는 우리의 시간과 집단 의식의 일부인 것들, 우리가 사는 동안에 생산된 것들과 더불어 살아야 한다. 물론, 우리는 우리가 사는 동안 우리와 관련 있거나 상상했던 우리 주변의 모든 것들에 대한 선택권이나 통제력을 가지고 있지는 않지만, 우리가 통제력을 갖는 것은 우리가 존재하고, 현재와 소통하는 시간의 반영이어야 한다. 현재는 우리가 가진 모든 것이고, 우리가 그것에 더 많이 둘러싸여 있을수록, 우리는 우리 자신의 존재와 참여를 더 자각하게 된다.
① 여행: 과거의 유산을 쫓는 것
② 현재 당신을 에워싼 시간에 대해 깊이 생각해 보라
③ 숨겨진 삶의 표명
④ 초현대적인 삶의 건축

| **정답해설** | ② 93% 글의 중반부 We should live ~부터 우리는 과거의 것이 아닌 현재 우리를 둘러싼 것들과 더불어 살아야 한다는 주장이 드러난다. 현재는 우리가 가진 모든 것이라는 내용으로 글을 마무리하고 있으므로 본문 전체의 내용을 아우를 제목으로 가장 적절한 것은 ②이다.

어휘

the minute ~하자마자	manifest 드러내 보이다; 증명하다
surroundings 인근[주변] 환경	collective 집단의, 공동의
consciousness 자각, 의식	relevant 관련 있는, 적절한
conceive 생각하다, 상상하다	reflection 반영; 숙고, 반성
presence 존재	legacy 유산
reflect on ~을 깊이 생각하다; 반성하다	
manifestation 징후, 표명	futuristic 초현대적인, 미래의

| **4** | 문법 > 태 | 오답률 36% | 답 ③ |

| **해석** | 숲의 아름다움과 풍요로움이 없는 삶을 상상하기는 어렵다. 그러나 과학자들은 우리가 숲을 당연한 것으로 여겨서는 안 된다고 경고한다. 몇몇 추정에 따르면, 삼림 벌채는 전 세계 천연 숲의 80퍼센트에 달하는 손실을 가져왔다. 현재, 삼림 벌채는 세계적인 문제이며, 태평양의 온난한 열대 우림과 같은 원생 지역에 영향을 미치고 있다.

| **정답해설** | ③ 64% result in은 '결과를 낳다, 야기하다'라는 의미로 수동태로 사용하지 않는다. 따라서 has resulted in으로 고치는 것이 옳다.

| **오답해설** | ① 5% to imagine은 진주어로 쓰인 to부정사이다.
② 17% take ~ for granted는 '~을 당연한 것으로 여기다'라는 의미의 구문이다. 해당 문장에서는 our forest가 take의 목적어로 사용되었다.
④ 14% 문장의 주어인 deforestation이 영향을 미치는 능동의 의미이므로 현재분사인 affecting이 적절하게 쓰였다.

| **더 알아보기** | 원인과 결과 관계를 나타내는 동사

- result in ~을 야기하다
- bring about ~을 유발하다
- create ~을 만들어 내다
- result from, stem from, come from ~로부터 비롯되다, 기인하다
- derive from ~로부터 파생되다

어휘

richness 풍부함, 풍요로움
take ~ for granted ~을 당연한 것으로 여기다
deforestation 삼림 벌채
wilderness 자연이 보전되어 있는 지역, 원생 지역
temperate 온난한

| **5** | 어휘 > 유의어 찾기 | 오답률 32% | 답 ① |

| **해석** | 전설적인 다큐멘터리 제작자 Robert J. Flaherty는 어떻게 토착민들이 음식을 모았는지를 보여 주려고 시도했다.
① 68% 토착의, 토종의
② 9% 배가 고파 죽을 지경인, 엄청난
③ 16% 빈곤한, 결핍된
④ 7% 떠돌아다니는, 순회하는

| **정답해설** | ① indigenous는 '토종의, 토착민의'라는 뜻으로 native와 의미가 가장 가깝다.

어휘

filmmaker 영화 제작자, 감독

오답률 TOP2

| **6** | 어휘 > 빈칸 완성 | 오답률 45% | 답 ② |

| **해석** | 음악을 듣는 것은 록 스타가 되는 것과는 ② 거리가 멀다. 누구나 음악을 들을 수 있지만, 음악가가 되기 위해서는 타고난 재능이 필요하다.
① 16% ~와 동등한[같은] ② 55% ~와는 거리가 먼, 전혀 다른
③ 12% ~ 여하에 달린 ④ 17% ~의 서막인

| **정답해설** | ② 두 번째 문장에서 누구나 음악을 들을 수는 있지만 음악가가 되기 위해서는 재능이 필요하다고 말하고 있으므로 음악을 듣는 것과 음악가가 되는 것은 별개의 것임을 알 수 있다. 따라서 빈칸에 가장 적절한 것은 차이가 있음을 나타내는 a far cry from이다.

| **7** | 독해 > Logical Reading > 삭제 | 오답률 35% | 답 ④ |

| **해석** | 생물학자들은 벼가 물에 잠긴 채 현재보다 일주일 더 긴 2주까지 생존할 수 있게 할 유전자를 알아냈다. 일주일 넘게 물 속에 잠긴 식물들은 산소가 결핍되어 시들어 죽는다. 과학자들은 그들의 발견이 홍수에 취약한 지역의 농작물 수확을 연장시키기를 바란다. 아시아의 홍수가 나기 쉬운 이 지역의 벼 재배자들은 과도하게 물에 잠긴 논 때문에 매년 약 10억 달러에 달하는 손실을 입는다. 그들은 새로운 유전자가 더 강한 벼 품종으로 이어져 태풍과 장마철에 일어나는 재정적 손실을 줄이고 풍작으로 이어지길 희망한다. ④ 이는 도시화의 희생자이며 농작물 부족을 겪는 이 취약한 지역들에 사는 사람들에게 끔찍한 소식이다. 벼 생산량은 10억 인구가 그들의 주식을 얻을 수 있도록 보장하기 위해 향후 20년에 걸쳐 30퍼센트까지 증가해야만 한다.

| 정답해설 | ④ 65% 생물학자들이 물에 잠긴 채 더 오래 견딜 수 있는 벼 유전자를 알아냈는데, 그것이 벼 재배자들에게 긍정적인 영향을 줄 것으로 기대된다는 내용이다. 따라서 그러한 발견에 대해 부정적인 시각으로 서술하고 있는 ④는 글의 전체 흐름에 어긋난다.

어휘

identify 확인하다, 알아내다	rice plant 벼
submerge 잠수하다, 물[액체] 속에 넣다	
be deprived of ~을 빼앗기다	wither 시들다
perish 죽다, 소멸되다	prolong 연장시키다, 연장하다
susceptible to ~에 취약한	-prone (좋지 않은 일을) 당하기 쉬운
waterlogged 물에 잠긴	paddy 논
strain 종류, 변형	incur 초래하다, 발생시키다
monsoon 우기, 장마	bumper harvest 풍작

---

8 생활영어 > 회화/관용표현 오답률 37% 답 ②

| 해석 | A: 운전하는 법을 아세요?
B: 물론이죠, 저는 운전을 잘해요.
A: 제게 운전을 가르쳐 줄 수 있으신가요?
B: 임시 운전면허증을 가지고 있나요?
A: 네, 지난주에 취득했어요.
B: 운전을 해 본 적이 있으세요?
A: 아뇨, 그렇지만 어서 ② 발을 담가 보고(해 보고) 싶어서 참을 수가 없어요.
① 다음을 기약하다 　　　　　② 발을 담그다, 처음 해 보다
③ 오일을 교체하다 　　　　　④ 펑크 난 타이어를 교체하다

| 정답해설 | ② 63% A가 B에게 운전을 가르쳐 달라고 요청하고 있는 상황으로 A는 운전을 하고 싶은 의지가 있음을 알 수 있다. can't wait to는 '빨리 ~을 하고 싶다, ~을 하고 싶어서 참을 수 없다'라는 표현이므로 빈칸에는 ②가 가장 적절하다.

어휘

learner's permit 임시 운전면허증

오답률 TOP 3

9 독해 > Micro Reading > 내용일치/불일치 오답률 44% 답 ②

| 해석 | 상어는 이빨과 같은 재질로 만들어진 비늘로 덮여 있다. 이 유연한 비늘은 상어를 보호하고 물속에서 빨리 헤엄칠 수 있도록 돕는다. 상어는 헤엄치면서 비늘들을 움직일 수 있다. 이러한 움직임은 물의 저항력을 감소시키도록 돕는다. Alabama대학교의 항공우주 엔지니어인 Amy Lang은 대백상어 계통인 청상아리의 비늘을 연구한다. Lang과 그녀의 팀은 청상아리의 비늘이 몸의 부위에 따라 크기와 유연성이 다르다는 것을 발견했다. 예를 들어, 옆구리 쪽의 비늘은 점점 가늘어진다. 즉, 한쪽은 넓고 반대쪽은 가늘다. 그것들이 가늘어지기 때문에, 이러한 비늘들은 아주 쉽게 움직인다. 그것들은 상어 주변의 물의 흐름을 따르고 물의 저항력을 감소시키기 위해 치켜세워지거나 납작해질 수도 있다. Lang은 상어의 비늘이 비행기와 같이 저항력을 받는 기계의 디자인에 영감을 줄 수 있다고 생각한다.
① 상어는 헤엄칠 때 자신을 보호하기 위해 항상 움직임 없이 그대로 있는 비늘을 가지고 있다.
② Lang은 청상아리의 비늘이 물속에서 저항력을 낮추기 위해 이용된다는 것을 밝혀 냈다.
③ 청상아리는 몸 전체에 동일한 크기의 비늘을 가지고 있다.
④ 비행기의 과학적인 디자인은 상어 비늘에서 영감을 받았다.

| 정답해설 | ② 56% Lang이 발견한 내용 중 본문 후반 They can turn up or flatten ~ to reduce drag.를 통해 글의 내용과 일치하는 것을 알 수 있다.

| 오답해설 | ① 3% 세 번째 문장에서 상어는 헤엄칠 때 비늘을 움직일 수 있다고 했으므로 글의 내용과 일치하지 않는다.

③ 11% 여섯 번째 문장에서 몸의 부위에 따라 크기가 다른 비늘을 가지고 있다고 했다.

④ 30% 마지막 문장에서 상어의 비늘이 비행기 디자인에 영향을 줄 수 있다는 가능성이 제시되고 있으나 실제로 영향을 주었는지 여부는 본문을 통해서는 알 수 없다.

어휘

scale 비늘	flexible 유연한; 신축성 있는
drag 항력, 끌림	aerospace 항공우주 산업
shortfin mako 청상아리	taper 점점 가늘어지다
flatten 납작해지다	inspire 영감을 주다, 고무시키다
immobile 움직이지 않는	lessen 줄이다

---

10 문법 > 분사 오답률 41% 답 ③

| 해석 | 집중은 어떤 일들을 해내는 것을 의미한다. 많은 사람들이 좋은 아이디어를 가지고 있지만 그것들을 실행에 옮기지는 않는다. 예를 들어, 내게 기업가의 정의는 그 새로운 아이디어를 실행할 수 있는 능력을 혁신 및 독창성과 결합시킬 수 있는 사람이다. 삶에 있어서 중심이 되는 이분법이란 당신에게 흥미를 주거나 심려를 끼치는 문제들에 대해 당신이 긍정적인지 부정적인지에 관한 것이라고 어떤 사람들은 생각한다. 낙관적인 시선을 가지는 것이 나은지 비관적인 시선을 가지는 것이 나은지에 대한 이 질문에 쏟아지는 관심은 많다. 내 생각에 더 나은 질문은 당신이 그것에 대해 뭔가를 할 것인지 아니면 인생이 그냥 지나치게 놔두길 묻는 것이다.

| 정답해설 | ③ 59% 밑줄 친 부분은 attention을 수식하는 분사구로 attention과 pay는 수동의 관계이다. 따라서 attention (which is) paid의 구조가 되도록 현재분사인 paying을 과거분사인 paid로 고쳐야 한다.

| 오답해설 | ① 4% means의 목적어로 동명사 getting이 사용되었고, 「get + 목적어(stuff) + 목적격 보어(done)」의 구조도 올바르다.

② 18% the issues를 선행사로 하는 주격 관계대명사 that이 사용되었다. interest와 concern은 타동사로 목적어로 you를 취했다.

④ 19% are going to에 이어지는 동사원형인 do와 let이 병렬 구조를 이루고 있다. 「let + 목적어(life) + 목적격 보어(pass)」의 쓰임도 알맞다.

| 더 알아보기 | 준사역동사 get의 문장 구조

> • get + 목적어 + to부정사/현재분사: ~이 …하도록 하다
> • get + 목적어 + 과거분사: ~이 …을 당하다

어휘

entrepreneur 기업가	ingenuity 독창성
execute 실행하다	dichotomy 양분, 이분

11 독해 > Logical Reading > 문맥상 다양한 추론 오답률 15% 답 ④

| 해석 | 대부분의 사람들은 말하기를 좋아하는 반면, 듣기를 좋아하는 사람은 거의 없다. 하지만 잘 듣는 것은 모든 사람들이 높이 평가해야 할 드문 재능이다. 뛰어난 경청가들은 더 많이 듣기 때문에 더 많이 알고 대부분의 사람들보다 그들 주변의 돌아가는 상황에 대해 더 민감한 경향이 있다. 게다가, 뛰어난 경청가들은 판단하고 비판하기보다는 수용하고 인내하는 경향이 있다. 그러므로, 그들은 대부분의 사람들보다 적이 더 적다. 실제로, 그들은 아마 가장 사랑받는 사람들일 것이다. 그러나, 그러한 일반론에도 예외는 있다. 예를 들어, John Steinbeck은 아주 뛰어난 경청가였다고 알려졌지만, 그는 그가 글의 소재로 쓴 몇몇 사람들로부터 미움을 받았다. 의심의 여지 없이 그의 듣기 능력은 그의 작문 실력에 기여했다. 그럼에도 불구하고 그의 경청의 결과는 그를 ④ 인기 없게(→ 인기 있게) 만들지 않았다.

| 정답해설 | ④ 85% 경청 능력이 뛰어나면 사랑을 받는 것이 일반론인데, 예외도 있다고 하면서 John Steinbeck을 예로 들고 있다. 그는 뛰어난 경청가로 알려졌지만, 그가 글의 소재로 쓴 몇몇 사람들로부터 미움을 받았다고 했다. 따라서 글의 흐름이 자연스러워지려면 unpopular를 popular로 바꾸어, '그의 경청의 결과는 그를 인기 있게 만들지 못했다'는 흐름이 되는 것이 자연스럽다. 이 문장은 부정문이므로 특히 문맥에 주의해야 한다.

| 오답해설 | ① 3% 듣기를 좋아하는 사람은 거의 없다고 했으므로 경청하는 것이 드문 능력임을 알 수 있다. 따라서 rare의 쓰임은 적절하다.

② 7% 뛰어난 경청가들은 판단하고 비판하기보다는 수용하고 인내하는 경향이 있다고 하였으므로 '적이 더 적다'고 하는 것이 알맞다.

③ 5% 이어지는 문장에서 뛰어난 듣기 능력을 지녔음에도 불구하고 미움을 받았던 예외의 인물을 예시하고 있으므로 exceptions는 적절하다.

| 더 알아보기 | 대조의 연결사

- however, yet 그러나
- unlike ～와 달리
- though, although, even though 비록 ～이긴 하지만
- nevertheless 그렇기는 하지만, 그럼에도 불구하고
- for all, with all, despite, in spite of ～임에도 불구하고

어휘

treasure 대단히 귀하게 여기다   sensitive 민감한, 예민한
be inclined to V ～하는 경향이 있다 tolerate 용인하다, 참다, 견디다
generality 일반론; 대부분, 대다수

12 독해 > Macro Reading > 주제 오답률 19% 답 ④

| 해석 | 걱정은 흔들 목마와 비슷하다. 당신이 얼마나 빨리 가든, 당신은 어디로도 전혀 움직이지 않는다. 걱정은 완전한 시간 낭비이며 당신의 마음에 너무 많은 잡념을 만들어 내어 당신은 어떤 것도 명확하게 생각할 수 없게 된다. 걱정을 멈추는 것을 배우는 방법은 무엇이든 관심이 집중되는 것에 에너지를 쏟아야 한다는 것을 먼저 이해하는 것을 통해서이다. 그러므로, 당신 스스로가 더 많이 걱정하도록 놔둘수록, 일이 잘못될 가능성이 더 크다! 걱정은 너무나도 깊이 몸에 밴 습관이 되어서, 그것을 피하기 위해 당신

은 그렇게 하지 않도록(걱정하지 않도록) 의식적으로 자기 자신을 훈련시켜야 한다. 당신이 걱정으로 졸도할 지경에 이르고 있음을 발견할 때마다, 생각을 멈추고 다른 생각을 하라. 당신이 일어나기를 원하는 일에 더 생산적으로 정신을 집중시키고 당신의 삶 속에 이미 있는 멋진 것들에 대해 생각하면 더 멋진 일들이 생겨날 것이다.
① 걱정은 삶에 어떤 영향을 미치는가?
② 걱정은 어디서부터 비롯되는가?
③ 우리는 언제 걱정해야 하는가?
④ 우리는 어떻게 걱정을 극복하는가?

| 정답해설 | ④ 81% 세 번째 문장까지는 걱정의 무용성을 말하고 네 번째 문장부터는 걱정을 멈추는 방법에 대해 서술하고 있다. 따라서 주제로 가장 적절한 것은 ④이다.

| 오답해설 | ① 17% 걱정이 끼치는 영향이 언급되기는 했으나 본문의 일부 내용에 국한된다.

어휘

clutter 잡동사니, 어수선함
energize 열정을 돋우다, 에너지를 쏟다
ingrained 뿌리 깊은, 깊이 몸에 밴
have a fit (심한 충격, 분노 등으로) 졸도할 지경이 되다
cope with ～을 극복하다

13 독해 > Micro Reading > 내용일치/불일치 오답률 13% 답 ②

| 해석 | MHC 학생들은 비싼 수업료로 인한 스트레스를 받지 않는다. 왜냐하면 그들의 수업료가 무료이기 때문이다. Macaulay와 소수의 다른 군 사관학교들, 직업 학교, 단과 대학, 예술 학교 들에서 전교생의 100퍼센트가 4년 내내 전액 장학금을 받는다. Macaulay 학생들은 또한 연구, 업무 경험, 유학과 인턴십을 계속해 나가기 위해 노트북과 "기회 자금" 7,500달러를 지원받는다. "가장 중요한 것은 공짜 수업료가 아니라 등에 지워진 빚의 부담에서 벗어나 공부할 수 있는 자유예요." MHC의 학장, Ann Kirschner는 말한다. 그녀는 빚 부담은 "정말로 학생들이 대학에서 하는 결정들을 위태롭게 만들어요. 그리고 우리는 그들에게 그것으로부터 자유로워질 기회를 주고 있습니다."라고 말한다. 모든 학생들에게 무료 수업을 제공하는 학교는 드물지만, 더 많은 교육 기관들이 성적이 우수한 등록자들에게 장학금을 제공한다. Indiana University Bloomington과 같은 기관들은 평점과 반 석차가 우수한 성취도 높은 학생들에게 자동으로 장학금을 지급한다.

| 정답해설 | ② 87% Macaulay students also ~ internships.에 의하면 학생들은 노트북 컴퓨터를 제공받고, 별도로 7,500달러를 받음을 알 수 있다. 따라서 컴퓨터 구입 비용과 교외 활동 비용을 '합하여' 7,500달러를 지급한다는 ②의 내용은 지문과 일치하지 않는다.

어휘

tuition 수업료   a handful of 소수의
service academy 군 사관학교   conservatory 예술[미술, 음악] 학교
pursue (논의, 조사, 관여 등을) 계속하다; 추구하다
dean 학장   compromise 위태롭게 하다
free of ～이 없는, 면제된   enrollee 등록자, 가입자
award 장학금; 상, 상금, 상패   stellar 뛰어난, 우수한

14 어휘 > 유의어 찾기 ｜ 오답률 36% ｜ 답 ①

| 해석 | 경찰은 그 범죄 사건 해결에 7개월을 보냈지만 그 범죄자의 신원을 결코 밝혀낼 수 없었다.

① 64% 범인; 미결수
② 10% 예술 애호가
③ 11% (사회에서) 버림받은 사람
④ 15% 선동 정치가

| 정답해설 | ① malefactor는 '범죄자'라는 뜻으로 '범인, 미결수'라는 의미의 culprit과 의미가 가장 가깝다.

| 더 알아보기 | 어원 'mal(악)'을 활용한 어휘

- malaria 말라리아
- maleficent 악행을 저지르는
- malnutrition 영양실조

어휘

determine 알아내다, 밝히다

15 어휘 > 유의어 찾기 ｜ 오답률 21% ｜ 답 ④

| 해석 | 언뜻 보기에 그의 친구들은 단지 거머리 같은 사람들처럼 보이지만, 그들은 어떤 고난이 있어도 그가 의지할 수 있는 친구들임을 입증한다.

① 5% 즉시, 당장에
② 12% 종종, 가끔
③ 4% 즐거운 때에
④ 79% 좋을 때나 나쁠 때나

| 정답해설 | ④ through thick and thin은 '좋을 때나 안 좋을 때나, 어떤 고난이 있어도'라는 의미로 in good times and bad times와 의미가 가장 가깝다.

어휘

at first glance 처음에는, 언뜻 보기에는
leech 거머리(같은 사람)
depend on ~에 의지하다

16 독해 > Logical Reading > 삽입 ｜ 오답률 31% ｜ 답 ④

| 해석 | 말하기에 대한 우리의 인식과 생산은 시간에 따라 변화한다. 만약 우리가 장기간 원래 살던 곳을 떠난다면, 우리 주위의 새로운 말투가 낯설다는 우리의 인식은 단지 일시적일 뿐일 것이다. 점차적으로, 우리는 다른 사람들이 (다른) 말투를 가지고 있다는 느낌을 잃을 것이고, 새로운 기준에 우리의 말투를 순응시키기 위해 맞추기 시작할 것이다. 모든 사람들이 같은 정도로 이것을 행하는 것은 아니다. ④ 어떤 사람들은 그들 고유의 말투와 방언, 어구와 몸짓에 강하게 자부심을 느낀 채로 남는 반면에, 다른 사람들은 더 이상 "사람들 사이에서 튀지" 않기 위해 그들의 말하는 습관을 바꿈으로써 새로운 환경에 빠르게 적응한다. 그들이 이것을 의식적으로 행하는지 아닌지의 여부는 논쟁의 여지가 있으며 개인에 따라 다를 수 있지만, 언어와 관계 있는 대부분의 과정들처럼, 변화는 아마 우리가 인지하기도 전에 일어날 것이며 우리가 인지한다면 발생하지 않을 수도 있다.

| 정답해설 | ④ 69% 주어진 문장은 새로운 환경에 따라 말투를 빠르게 바꾸는 사람과 그렇지 않은 사람을 대조하고 있다. ④ 이전의 문장에서 모든 사람들이 이것(새로운 기준에 맞춰 말투를 바꾸는 것)을 같은 정도로 행하는 것은 아니라고 하였으므로 주어진 문장은 ④에 삽입하는 것이 가장 자연스럽다.

어휘

intensely 강렬하게
dialect 방언, 사투리

accommodate 순응하다, 적응하다
perception 인식, 자각
accent 말씨, 말투; 억양
have to do with ~와 관계가 있다
stand out 두드러지다
extended period 장기간
debate 토론하다, 논의하다

17 독해 > Micro Reading > 내용일치/불일치 ｜ 오답률 28% ｜ 답 ②

| 해석 | 불면증은 일시적이거나, 급성, 혹은 만성적인 것으로 분류될 수 있다. 일시적인 불면증은 일주일 미만으로 지속된다. 그것은 또 다른 장애, 수면 환경의 변화, 수면 시기, 극심한 우울증 혹은 스트레스에 의해 생겨날 수 있다. 졸음, 정신적 운동 수행 능력 손상과 같은 결과는 수면 부족의 결과와 유사하다. 급성 불면증은 한 달 미만의 기간 동안 지속적으로 숙면을 취할 수 없는 것이다. 급성 불면증은 잠에 들거나 수면을 지속하는 데 어려움이 있을 때나 취한 잠이 상쾌하지 않을 때 발생한다. 이러한 문제들은 적절한 수면 기회나 환경에도 불구하고 발생하며, 그것들은 낮 시간 동안의 기능을 손상시킬 수 있다. 급성 불면증은 또한 단기 불면증 혹은 스트레스와 관련 있는 불면증으로 알려져 있다. 만성적인 불면증은 한 달 넘게 지속된다. 그것은 또 다른 질병에 의해 유발되거나 혹은 이것이 주요 질병이 될 수도 있다. 스트레스 호르몬 수치가 높거나 시토킨 수치에 변화가 있는 사람들은 남들보다 만성적인 불면증을 겪을 가능성이 높다. 그것의 영향은 원인에 따라 다양하다. 그것들은 근육의 피로, 환각, 그리고/또는 정신적 피로감을 포함할 수 있다. 만성적인 불면증은 또한 복시를 유발할 수도 있다.

* 시토킨: 면역 체계의 특정 세포에 의해 발생되는 분자 그룹

① 불면증은 그것의 지속 기간에 따라 분류될 수 있다.
② 일시적인 불면증은 단지 부적절한 수면 환경에 의해서만 발생한다.
③ 급성 불면증은 보통 스트레스와 관련 있는 것으로 알려져 있다.
④ 만성 불면증 환자들은 환각을 겪을 수 있다.

| 정답해설 | ② 72% 세 번째 문장에서 일시적인 불면증의 원인으로 수면 환경의 변화, 수면 시기, 우울증이나 스트레스 등 다양한 원인을 제시하였으므로 solely due to라는 표현은 틀리다.

| 오답해설 | ① 10% 일주일 미만의 불면증은 일시적인 불면증, 한 달 미만은 급성 불면증, 한 달이 넘으면 만성 불면증으로 분류하고 있다.

③ 10% 본문 중후반에서 Acute insomnia is also known as ~ stress related insomnia.라고 언급하고 있으므로 글의 내용과 일치한다.

④ 8% 끝에서 두 번째 문장에서 만성적인 불면증이 초래하는 영향 중 한 가지로 환각을 제시하고 있으므로 글의 내용과 일치한다.

어휘

insomnia 불면증
acute 급성의
psychomotor 정신 운동(성)의
initiate 시작하다
hallucination 환각, 환영, 환청
transient 일시적인, 순간적인
chronic 만성적인
deprivation 결핍, 부족
impair 손상시키다, 악화시키다
fatigue 피로

18 독해 > Reading for Writing > 빈칸 구 완성 ｜ 오답률 43% ｜ 답 ②

| 해석 | 뭄바이에 있는 Everonn Education의 설립자 Kisha Padbhan은 그의 사업을 국가 건설로 여긴다. 인도의 2억 3천만 명의 학생 연령 인구 수(유치원부터 대학교까지)는 세계에서 가장 큰 수치 중 하나이다. 정부는 교육에 830억 달러를 지출하지만, 심각한 격차가 있다. "교사들과 교사들을 훈련시킬 기관이 충분하지 않아요."라고 Kisha는 말한다. "인도의 외진 곳에 사는 아이들에게 부족한 것은 좋은 교사들에 대한 접촉 기회와 양질의 콘텐츠에 대한 노출입니다." Everonn의 해결책은? 그 기업은 ② 가상의 교

실을 통해 그 격차를 메우기 위해 양방향 비디오와 오디오를 갖춘 인공위성 네트워크를 사용한다. 그것은 인도의 28개 주들 중 24개 주에 걸쳐 1,800개의 대학교와 7,800개의 학교에 도달한다. 그것은 디지털화된 학교 수업들부터 미래의 엔지니어들을 위한 입학시험 준비까지 모든 것을 제공하며 구직자들을 위한 훈련 또한 갖추고 있다.
① 교사 양성 시설의 질을 향상시키기 위해
② 가상의 교실을 통해 그 격차를 메우기 위해
③ 학생들을 디지털 기술에 친숙하게 만들기 위해
④ 온 나라에 우수한 교사들을 배치하기 위해

| 정답해설 | ② 57% 빈칸 이전에서는 인도의 외진 곳에 사는 아이들에게 부족한 것(문제점)을 제시하였고, 빈칸 문장은 그에 대한 해결책에 해당한다. 즉, 양방향 비디오와 오디오를 갖춘 satellite network(인공위성 네트워크)를 사용한다고 하였고 마지막 문장에서는 디지털화된 학교 수업을 언급하였으므로 빈칸에 가장 적절한 것은 통신망을 이용한 학교 교육의 목적을 언급한 ②이다.

| 오답해설 | ① 17% 본문에서 교사 양성의 문제를 언급하기는 하였으나, 해당 문장은 교육의 격차를 겪고 있는 아이들을 위한 해결책을 설명하는 것이지, 교사 양성을 위한 대책을 논하는 것이 아니다.
③ 6% 인공위성 네트워크를 사용하는 것은 아이들을 디지털 기술에 친숙하게 만들기 위한 것이 아니라, 교육의 격차를 줄이기 위한 것이다.
④ 20% 인공위성 네트워크를 사용하고 있다고 한 것을 고려하면, 가상이 아닌 현실에서의 부족한 교사 배치에 대한 내용은 아니다.

어휘

founder 설립자
satellite 인공위성
aspiring 장래의, 미래의
content 내용, 콘텐츠
digitize 디지털화하다
exposure 체험하기; 노출

오답률 TOP 1

19 독해 > Logical Reading > 배열   오답률 46%   답 ③

| 해석 | 개인이 그러한 기능의 전자 장비를 이용한 측정치를 관찰함으로써 자율적이거나 비자율적인 신체 기능에 대해 어떤 자발적인 통제력을 얻도록 하는 기술은 생체 자기 제어라고 알려져 있다.
(B) 전자 센서들은 심장 박동 수, 혈압과 피부 온도 같은 변수들을 측정하기 위하여 신체의 다양한 부위에 부착된다.
(A) 그러한 변수들이 원하는 방향으로 이동할 때(예를 들어, 혈압이 내려가는 것), 그것은 텔레비전, 측정기, 불빛과 같은 장치에서 나타나는 반응인 시각적이거나 청각적인 출력 정보를 촉발시킨다.
(C) 생체 자기 제어 훈련은 그러한 출력 정보들을 촉발시켰던 사고 패턴이나 행동들을 재현함으로써 원하는 반응을 다시 만들어 내도록 가르친다.

| 정답해설 | ③ 54% '생체 자기 제어'의 원리에 대해서 단계적으로 설명하고 있다. 먼저 주어진 문장에서 by observing electronic measurements(전자 장비를 이용한 측정치를 관찰함으로써)라고 제시하고 있으며, (B)에서는 관찰하기 위한 방법으로 신체에 부착하는 eletronic sensors(전자 센서들)에 대해 설명하고 있으므로 가장 먼저 (B)가 오는 것이 옳다. 또한 (B)에서 such variables가 제시되었는데, 이것은 (A)의 such a variable과 연결 지어 생각하는 것이 가장 적절하다. such a variable은 (B)의 heart rate ~ temperature 등을 지칭한다. 마지막으로 (C)에서 thought

patterns ~ the displays는 (A)의 visual or audible displays를 가리키는 것으로, (C)가 마지막에 와서 생체 자기 제어 훈련에 대한 원리를 정리하며 글을 마무리하는 것이 적절하다.

어휘

enable 가능하게 하다
autonomic 자율적인, 자율 신경계의
biofeedback 생체 자기 제어
audible 잘 들리는
voluntary 자발적인
involuntary 무심결의, 본의 아닌
trigger 유발하다
reproduce 다시 만들다, 재현하다

20 문법 > 비교   오답률 42%   답 ④

| 정답해설 | ④ 58% '~만큼 …하지 않다'라는 의미는 「not so + 형용사 + as」의 원급 비교 구문으로 나타낼 수 있다. 따라서 비교급 stingier를 stingy로 바꾸어야 한다.

| 오답해설 | ① 14% be good at은 '~을 잘하다'라는 뜻의 관용표현으로 전치사 at 뒤의 동명사 getting은 적절하다. 또한 get A across B는 'A를 B에게 이해시키다, 전달하다'라는 표현으로 적절하게 사용되었다.
② 14% 주어는 The traffic jams로 복수형이다. '서울의 교통체증들'과 '다른 도시의 교통체증들'을 비교하고 있으므로 The traffic jams를 대신하는 지시대명사 또한 복수형 those로 적절하게 사용되었다. 비교 대상을 「any other + 단수 명사」로 표현한 것도 어법에 맞다.
③ 14% 주어는 동명사 형태인 Making ~ to이므로 동사는 3인칭 단수 동사인 is가 적절하게 사용되었다. the person과 you are speaking to 사이에는 목적격 관계대명사 whom이 생략되었다. 또한 생략된 관계대명사 whom이 이끄는 절은 반드시 불완전한 형태여야 한다. you are speaking to는 전치사 to의 목적어가 없는 불완전한 형태로 올바르게 쓰였다. 여기서 speak는 자동사로 전치사 to가 반드시 함께 쓰여야 목적어를 가질 수 있다는 점에 주의해야 한다.

합격예상 체크

〈국가직 연도별 합격선〉

2017 합격기준

| 맞힌 개수 | /20문항 | 점수 | /100점 |

➡ □ 합격　□ 불합격

취약영역 체크

문항	정답	영역	문항	정답	영역
①	③	어휘 > 유의어 찾기	11	②	어휘 > 유의어 찾기
2	①	어휘 > 유의어 찾기	12	④	어휘 > 문맥상 다양한 추론
3	①	생활영어 > 회화/관용표현	13	②	독해 > Macro Reading > 제목
4	③	생활영어 > 회화/관용표현	14	②	독해 > Macro Reading > 요지
5	①	문법 > 강조와 도치	15	④	문법 > 가정법
6	②	문법 > 시제	16	④	문법 > 부정사
7	②	독해 > Reading for Writing > 빈칸 구 완성	17	①	독해 > Reading for Writing > 빈칸 구 완성
8	④	독해 > Reading for Writing > 빈칸 절 완성	18	③	독해 > Logical Reading > 삭제
9	①	독해 > Reading for Writing > 빈칸 구 완성	19	④	독해 > Logical Reading > 삽입
10	③	독해 > Micro Reading > 내용일치/불일치	20	②	독해 > Logical Reading > 배열

⬇ 영역별 틀린 개수로 취약영역을 확인하세요!

| 어휘 | /4 | 문법 | /4 | 독해 | /10 | 생활영어 | /2 |

➡ 나의 취약영역: _____

※ [정답해설]과 [오답해설] 선지의 50% 표시는 〈1초 합격예측 서비스〉를 통해 수집된 선지 선택률을 나타냅니다.

오답률 TOP 2

1　어휘 > 유의어 찾기　오답률 50%　답 ③

| 해석 | 나는 밤늦게까지 잠을 자지 않는다는 생각을 극도로 싫어했다.

① 20% 포기했다　② 21% 확인했다
③ 50% 혐오했다　④ 9% 방어했다

| 정답해설 | ③ detest는 '몹시 싫어하다'의 의미를 가지며, abhor와 그 의미가 가장 유사하다.

2　어휘 > 유의어 찾기　오답률 16%　답 ①

| 해석 | 나는 전에 어디선가 이 장면을 본 적이 있었다는 이상한 느낌이 들었다.

① 84% 이상한, 특이한　② 3% 계속 진행 중인
③ 8% 명백한　④ 5% 불쾌한, 모욕적인

| 정답해설 | ① uncanny는 '이상한, 묘한'의 의미를 가지며, odd와 그 의미가 가장 유사하다.

3　생활영어 > 회화/관용표현　오답률 3%　답 ①

| 해석 | A: 도와 드릴까요?
B: 이틀 전에 이 드레스를 샀는데요. 저에겐 조금 크네요.
A: ① 죄송하지만, 더 작은 치수가 없어요.
B: 그렇다면 환불을 받고 싶어요.
A: 영수증 좀 볼 수 있을까요?

B: 여기요.
① 죄송하지만, 더 작은 치수가 없어요.
② 그런데 제 생각에는 그게 당신에게 딱 맞는 것 같아요.
③ 저 드레스는 우리 가게에서 정말 잘 팔려요.
④ 죄송하지만, 구매하신 이 제품은 환불해 드릴 수 없어요.

| 정답해설 | ① 97% B는 이틀 전에 산 드레스가 조금 크다고 A에게 말했고, 곧 A의 대답을 들은 B가 환불을 요구하고 있다. 따라서 A가 더 작은 치수로 교환을 해 줄 수 없는 상황임을 말했음을 유추할 수 있다. 여기서는 더 작은 사이즈가 없다고 말한 응답이 빈칸에 가장 알맞다.

어휘

refund 환불(하다)

4　생활영어 > 회화/관용표현　오답률 1%　답 ③

| 해석 | A: 제가 이 가정용 혈압기를 사용할 때마다 다른 측정값이 나와요. 제가 잘못 사용하고 있는 것 같아요. 올바르게 사용하는 법을 보여 줄 수 있나요?
B: 네, 물론이죠. 먼저, 고정끈을 팔에 둘러주셔야 해요.
A: 이렇게요? 제가 맞게 하고 있나요?
B: 조금 꽉 매신 것 같아요.
A: 아, 지금은 어떤가요?
B: 지금은 너무 헐거워 보이네요. 너무 꽉 매거나 헐거우면, 부정확한 측정값을 얻을 거예요.

A: ③ 아, 그렇군요. 그 다음엔 무엇을 해야 하죠?
B: 지금 버튼을 누르세요. 움직이거나 말하지 않으셔야 해요.
A: 알겠어요.
B: 조금 있다가 화면에서 혈압을 보실 수 있어요.
① 제가 그들의 웹사이트를 확인해야 하나요?
② 맞아요, 저는 그 책을 읽어야 해요.
③ 아, 그렇군요. 그 다음엔 무엇을 해야 하죠?
④ 저는 오늘 아무것도 못 봤어요.

| 정답해설 | ③ 99% B가 가정용 혈압기의 고정끈을 매는 방법을 말하고 나서 다음 단계에 대해 설명하고 있으므로, A는 ③과 같이 다음으로 해야 할 일을 묻는 것이 가장 적절하다.

어휘

blood pressure monitor 혈압기
reading (기기에 나타나는) 측정값

| 5 | 문법 > 강조와 도치 | 오답률 33% | 답 ① |

| 해석 | ① 그들은 그의 이야기를 믿지 않았고, 나도 믿지 않았다.
② 내가 가장 관심을 갖는 스포츠는 축구이다.
③ Jamie는 제1차 세계 대전이 1914년에 발발했다고 책에서 배웠다.
④ 두 가지 요인이 과학자들로 하여금 지구상에 있는 종의 수를 결정하는 것을 어렵게 만들었다.

| 정답해설 | ① 67% 부정문이 앞에 있을 경우, 이에 대한 동의 표현은 「(and) neither + (대)동사 + 주어」의 형태이므로 옳은 표현이다.

| 오답해설 | ② 6% 관계대명사 that이 이끄는 절을 목적어로 갖는 전치사는 that 앞에 올 수 없으므로, 전치사를 동반할 수 있는 which로 고쳐 사용하는 것이 옳다.
③ 11% 제1차 세계 대전과 같은 과거의 역사적 사실은 시제 일치와 상관 없이 단순 과거 시제로 표현하므로 had broken out은 broke out으로 고쳐야 한다.
④ 16% 옳은 문장은 Two factors have made it difficult for scientists to determine the number of species on Earth.이다. made의 진목적어는 to determine ~이므로 가목적어인 it을 made 뒤에 위치시켜야 하며 scientists는 의미상 주어이므로 전치사 for와 함께 「for + 의미상 주어」의 형태로 써야 한다.

| 더 알아보기 | 등위접속사 nor

- 부정의 의미를 갖는 등위접속사로 '또한 ~ 아니다'라는 의미이다.
- The gentleman neither smokes nor drinks.
  그 신사는 담배를 피우지도 술을 마시지도 않는다.
  → The gentleman does not either smoke or drink.
  → The gentleman doesn't smoke, and he does not drink either.
  → The gentleman doesn't smoke, and neither does he drink.
  → The gentleman doesn't smoke, nor does he drink.

오답률 TOP 1

| 6 | 문법 > 시제 | 오답률 58% | 답 ② |

| 해석 | ① 지나가면서 들은 몇몇 단어들이 나를 생각하게 만들었다.
② 그녀가 그 집에 들어가자마자 누군가 불을 켰다.
③ 우리는 호텔까지 차를 몰고 갔는데, 그곳의 발코니에서 우리는 마을을 내려다볼 수 있었다.
④ 노숙자는 대개 직업을 구하는 데 큰 어려움을 겪기 때문에, 그들은 희망을 잃고 있다.

| 정답해설 | ② 42% '~하자마자 …했다'는 「Hardly[Scarcely] had + 주어 + p.p. ~ when[before] + 주어 + 과거동사 …」로 표현한다. 따라서 Hardly had she entered the house when someone turned on the light.가 옳은 문장이다.

| 오답해설 |
① 13% A few words (caught in passing) set me thinking.
　　　　주어　　　　과거분사구　　　　동사 목적어 목적격 보어
③ 27% 선행사로 the hotel을 취하는 소유격 관계대명사 whose가 계속적 용법으로 옳게 사용되었다.
④ 18% 「the + 형용사(homeless)」는 복수 보통명사로 사용되므로 복수 동사 have는 옳게 사용되었다. 「have difficulty (in) -ing」는 '~하는 데 어려움을 겪다'라는 동명사 관용표현이다.

| 더 알아보기 | 「the + 형용사」의 쓰임

복수 보통명사를 의미한다.
- the wounded = wounded people
- the dying = dying people
- the rich = rich people
- the poor = poor people
- the young = young people
- the old = old people
- the wise = wise people
- the foolish = foolish people

어휘

in passing 지나가는 말로, (다른) ~을 하는 길에
look down at ~을 내려다보다

| 7 | 독해 > Reading for Writing > 빈칸 구 완성 | 오답률 18% | 답 ② |

| 해석 | 왜 빈곤선 근처를 맴도는 사람들이 그들의 동료를 도울 가능성이 더 클까? Keltner는 그 이유의 일부가 가난한 사람들이 힘든 시간을 헤쳐 나가기 위해 종종 뭉쳐야 하기 때문이라고 생각하는데, 이것이 아마도 그들을 더욱 사회적으로 기민하게 만드는 과정일 것이다. 그는 "불확실성에 직면하면, 다른 사람들에게 자신을 순응시키게 된다. 당신은 이러한 강력한 사회적 네트워크를 구축하게 되는 것이다."라고 말한다. 예를 들어, 가난한 젊은 어머니가 아이를 낳으면, 그녀는 음식, (육아) 용품, 육아 (시설)을 확보하는 데 도움이 필요할 수 있으며, 만약 그녀가 건강한 사회 생활을 해 왔다면, 그녀의 지역 사회 구성원들이 도와줄 것이다. 그러나 한정된 소득이 이러한 종류의 공감과 사회적 반응을 발전시키기 위한 전제 조건은 아니다. 우리의 은행 계좌에 들어 있는 돈의 액수와 관계없이, 고난은 우리 자신의 고통이 우리로 하여금 다른 사람들의 요구에 ② 더 관심을 기울이게 하고 우리가 매우 잘 알고 있는 그러한 종류의 고난을 쥐고 있는 누군가를 볼 때 개입하게 만드는 이타주의 또는 영웅주의로 가는 통로가 된다.
① ~에 더 무관심한　　　② ~에 더 관심을 기울이는
③ ~에 덜 집착하게 되는　　④ ~에 덜 관련되는

| 정답해설 | ② 82% 가난한 사람이 가난한 사람을 더 쉽게 도울 수 있는 이유에 대해서 분석하는 글이다. 가난한 젊은 어머니의 육아를 지역 사회 구성원들이 나서서 도와줄 거라고 했고 이런 공감과

사회적 반응은 소득과 상관 없이 이루어진다고 했으므로 전체 글의 흐름에 일치하려면 빈칸에는 ②가 가장 어울린다.

[어휘]

hover 맴돌다, 서성이다   astute 기민한

secure 확보하다; 안전한   pitch in 협력하다, 돕다

prerequisite 전제 조건   conduit 도관

altruism 이타주의, 이타심

---

8   독해 > Reading for Writing > 빈칸 절 완성   오답률 40%   답 ④

| 해석 | 상하이에 있는 Soleil 백화점 아웃렛은 현대의 중국 소매업계에서 성공하기 위해 필요한 모든 생활 편의 시설을 갖추고 있는 것으로 보인다. 즉, 고급 브랜드와 독점적 위치이다. 그러나 이러한 장점에도 불구하고, 매장 경영진은 고객을 유치할 만한 무언가가 여전히 빠져 있다고 생각했다. 그래서 다음 주에 그들은 쇼핑객들이 5층 고급 매장에서 1층 고급 매장에 이르기까지 엄청난 속도로 순식간에 내려가기 위해 이용할 수 있는 거대하고, 비비 꼬인 용 모양의 미끄럼틀을 공개할 것이다. 소셜 미디어 사용자들은 그 미끄럼틀이 누군가를 죽일지, 반쯤은 농담으로 궁금해하고 있다. 그러나 Soleil은 중국 쇼핑몰들이 완전히 사라질 것이라는 다른 걱정을 안고 있다. 한때 무한한 공급으로 보였던 중국 쇼핑객은, 온라인 쇼핑의 증가로 인해 더 이상 오프라인 아웃렛에 나타나지 않고 있으며, 그들은 명품을 사기 위해 여전히 해외로 나가고 있다. 그래서, 시간과 돈을 소비할 다른 방법을 가진 소비자들을 위해 이 거대한 공간의 용도를 변경하는 데는 많은 창의성이 필요할 것이다. ④ 5층짜리 용 미끄럼틀은 나쁜 시작점은 아닐지 모른다.

① 명품 브랜드들이 Soleil 백화점에서 번창하고 있다

② Soleil 백화점은 과감한 조치를 취하는 것에 반대 결정을 해 왔다

③ 온라인 소비자 기반을 증대시키는 것이 마지막 희망일지 모른다

④ 5층짜리 용 미끄럼틀은 나쁜 시작점은 아닐지 모른다

| 정답해설 | ④ 60% 중국에 있는 Soleil 백화점이 5층에서 1층까지 내려올 수 있는 용 모양의 미끄럼틀을 만든 이유는, 온라인 시장과 해외로 빠져나가는 소비자들을 유치하여 오프라인에서 살아남으려면 창의적인 생각이 필요했기 때문이다. 이 시작이 나쁘지 않다고 마무리하는 문장이 빈칸에 들어갈 말로 가장 적절하다.

[어휘]

amenity 생활 편의 시설   unveil 공개하다, 베일을 벗기다

gigantic 거대한   death-defying 아슬아슬한

brick-and-mortar 소매의, 오프라인 거래의

오답률 TOP 3

9   독해 > Reading for Writing > 빈칸 구 완성   오답률 49%   답 ①

| 해석 | 향후 개발에 대한 실현 가능한 수많은 시나리오를 고안하는 것은 쉽고 겉보기에 각각의 시나리오는 동일하게 가능성이 있어 보인다. 어려운 작업은 실제로 어떤 것이 일어날지 파악하는 것이다. 지나고 나서 보면, 그것은 보통 명백해 보인다. 시간이 흐른 후 돌아보면, 각 사건은 명확하게 그리고 논리적으로 이전 사건을 따르는 것 같아 보인다. 그러나 사건이 일어나기 전에는, 가능성의 수가 무한해 보인다. 성공적인 예측을 위한 방법은 존재하지 않는다. 특히 복잡한 사회·기술적 변화를 포함한 영역들이 그러한데, 그 영역들은 결정적인 요소 중 다수가 알려지지 않았고, 어떤 경우에는 확실히 단일 그룹의 통제 하에 있지도 않다. 그럼에도 불구하고 ① 미래를 위한 합리적인 시나리오를 찾아내는 것은 필수적이다. 우리는 신기술이 배당금과 문제 둘 다, 특히 인간적, 사회적 문제를 초래할 것임을 알고 있다. 우리가 이러한 문제를 더 많이 예상하려고 노력할수록 우리는 그것들을

더 잘 제어할 수 있다.

① 미래를 위한 합리적인 시나리오를 찾아내는

② 미래의 변화로 생기는 가능한 배당금을 정당화하는

③ 기술적 문제의 다양한 측면을 제외하는

④ 현재에 초점을 맞추는 것이 어떠할지 고려하는

| 정답해설 | ① 51% 미래에 대한 성공적인 예측을 하는 것은 불가능하나, 그럼에도 불구하고, 우리가 더 많이 예상하려고 노력할수록 미래에 생길 문제들을 더욱 잘 제어할 수 있다고 이야기하고 있다. 양보의 연결사 Nonetheless를 기준으로 앞 문장과 뒤 문장이 서로 반대 이야기를 하고 있으며, 빈칸의 내용을 그 다음 문장에서 뒷받침해 주고 있으므로 ①이 빈칸에 들어갈 말로 가장 적절하다.

[어휘]

on the face of it 겉보기에는, 표면적으로는

dividend 배당금   anticipate 예상하다, 예측하다

legitimize 정당화하다   leave out 생략하다, 빼다

---

10   독해 > Micro Reading > 내용일치/불일치   오답률 15%   답 ③

| 해석 | 미뢰(맛 봉오리)는 19세기 독일 과학자 Georg Meissner와 Rudolf Wagner가 이름을 지었는데, 그들은 꽃잎과 같이 겹쳐 있는 미각 세포로 구성된 더미들을 발견했다. 미뢰는 7~10일마다 소모되며, 45세가 넘어가면 그렇게 자주는 아니지만, 우리는 그것들을 교체한다. 즉, 우리의 미각은 나이가 들수록 실제로 둔화된다. 같은 수준의 감각을 내기 위해서는 더 강한 맛이 필요하며, 어린이들이 가장 예민한 미각을 갖는다. 아기의 입에는 성인의 미뢰보다 더 많은 미뢰가 있으며, 심지어 일부는 뺨에까지 흩어져 있다. 부분적으로는 당분에 더 예민한 아이들의 혀끝은 수프가 식기도 전에 뜨거운 수프를 먹으려는 시도에 의해 아직 감각이 둔화되지 않았기 때문에 아이들은 단것을 좋아한다.

① 미뢰는 19세기에 발명되었다.

② 미뢰의 교체는 세월이 지남에 따라 느려지지 않는다.

③ 어린이는 성인보다 더 민감한 미각을 가지고 있다.

④ 미각은 차가운 수프를 먹는 것에 의해 저하된다.

| 정답해설 | ③ 85% 두 번째 문장의 콜론(:) 뒤 our palates really do become jaded as we get older에서 우리의 미각은 나이가 들수록 실제로 둔화된다고 했으며, 세 번째 문장의 and 뒤 children have the keenest sense of taste에서 어린이들의 미각이 가장 예민하다고 했으므로 내용과 일치한다.

| 오답해설 | ① 5% 미뢰는 '발명된(invented)' 것이 아니라 Georg Meissner와 Rudolf Wagner에 의해 '발견되어(discovered)' 이름 붙여졌다.

② 5% 45세가 넘어가면 미뢰를 자주 교체하지는 않는다는 내용을 들며, 실제로 미각이 둔화됨을 제시하고 있으므로 나이가 들수록 미뢰의 대체가 느려진다는 것을 알 수 있다. 따라서 본문의 내용과 일치하지 않는다.

④ 5% 수프가 식기도 전에 뜨거운 상태에서 먹으려고 함으로써 감각이 둔화된다고 했으므로 틀리다.

[어휘]

taste bud 미뢰   mound 무더기, 더미

overlap 겹치다, 포개다   palate 구개, 미각

jaded 감퇴한   adore 아주 좋아하다

blunt 둔화시키다

11 어휘 > 유의어 찾기　　오답률 20%　답 ②

| 해석 | 이 회사에서, 우리는 그러한 행동을 용인하지 않을 것이다.
① 10% 평가하다　　　　　② 80% 용인하다, 참다
③ 3% 기록하다　　　　　④ 7% 바꾸다, 수정하다

| 정답해설 | ② put up with는 '~을 용인하다, 참다, 견디다'라는 뜻으로, tolerate와 가장 유사한 의미를 가진다.

12 어휘 > 문맥상 다양한 추론　　오답률 39%　답 ④

| 해석 | ① 13% 나는 그의 이전 직위를 인계받게 될 것이다.
② 15% 나는 지금 더 이상의 일을 맡을 수 없다.
③ 11% 그 비행기는 짙은 안개 때문에 이륙할 수 없었다.
④ 61% 나는 내 막내 여동생을 닮아야(→ 돌봐야) 하기 때문에 나갈 수 없다.

| 정답해설 | ④ take after(~을 닮다)를 take care of(~을 돌보다)로 변경하는 것이 의미상 옳다.

어휘
take over 인계받다　　　　　　take on (일 등을) 맡다. (책임을) 지다
take off 이륙하다, 떠나다　　　　take after ~을 닮다

13 독해 > Macro Reading > 제목　　오답률 6%　답 ②

| 해석 | 드라마는 행위이다. 드라마는 실재이다. 드라마는 아주 평범한 것이다. 그것은 어려운 상황에 처했을 때, 우리 모두가 매일 관여하고 있는 것이다. 당신은 심한 두통이나 걷잡을 수 없는 우울증에 시달리며 아침에 일어나지만, 아무런 문제가 없는 척 그날을 맞이하고 사람들을 대한다. 당신은 다가올 중요한 회의 또는 인터뷰가 있으며, 따라서 미리 자신에게 그 문제를 설명해 보고 어떻게 하면 자신감 있고 쾌활한 표정을 지을지, 무엇을 입을지, 손으로 무엇을 할지 등을 결정한다. 당신은 동료의 서류 위에 커피를 쏟은 다음, 즉시 정교한 변명을 준비한다. 당신의 파트너는 당신의 가장 친한 친구와 (눈이 맞아) 도망갔지만, 당신은 호기심 많은 학급 학생들을 가르치러 들어가는 일을 피할 수 없다. 만약 우리가 우리의 존엄성을 유지하고 다른 사람들과 조화롭게 살아가려면, 하루하루의 삶을 계속하는 것은 일련의 문명화된 가면을 필요로 한다.
① 드라마의 역기능　　　　② 우리의 일상생활에서의 드라마
③ 공연 예술로서의 드라마　④ 감정의 극적 변화

| 정답해설 | ② 94% 일상에서 겪고 있는 '드라마'들에 대한 예시를 나열하고 있다. 따라서 이 글의 제목으로는 ②가 가장 적절하다.

어휘
engage in ~에 관여하다, 참여하다　cope with ~에 대응하다, 대처하다
elaborate 정교한, 공들인
inquisitive 꼬치꼬치 묻는, 호기심 많은
get on with ~을 계속하다, 해 나가다
dignity 존엄성　　　　　　　dysfunction 역기능, 기능 장애

14 독해 > Macro Reading > 요지　　오답률 27%　답 ②

| 해석 | 정부가 세계 경제의 세 가지 요소인 무역, 정보 및 자본의 흐름을 막음으로써 세계화를 억압하려 한다면 정부는 도대체 어떻게 가난한 자들을 도울 것인가? 부자와 가난한 사람 사이의 격차가 여전히 아주 크다는 것은 부인할 수 없다. 그러나 세계화와 시장 경제에 반대하는 사람들이 우리가 믿도록 만든 것과 같이 경제 성장이 부유한 사람들에게만 이롭고 가난한 사람들은 배제한다는 것은 사실이 아니다. 최근 세계은행의 "성장은 가난한

사람들에게 유익하다"라는 제목의 연구는 인구의 하위 5%의 소득과 1인당 GDP 간의 일대일 관계를 보여 준다. 즉, 모든 부문의 소득은 동일한 비율로 비례하여 증가한다. 이 연구는 해외 무역에 대한 개방성이 전체 경제에 이로운 만큼 빈곤층에게도 이롭다고 지적한다.
① 정부는 경제를 회복시키기 위해 무역의 흐름을 통제해야 한다.
② 세계화는 경제적 지위와 관계없이 유익할 수 있다.
③ 세계 경제는 빈곤층을 희생시켜 성장한다.
④ 세계화는 빈부의 갈등을 심화시킨다.

| 정답해설 | ② 73% 본문 후반부 세계은행의 예시와 함께 마지막 문장의 세계 경제의 세 가지 요소 중 하나인 무역에 대한 해외 개방성이 전체 경제와 빈곤층에게 동일하게 혜택을 준다고 서술하고 있으므로 요지로 가장 적절한 것은 ②이다.

| 오답해설 | ① 3% 경제 회복과 무역의 상관성은 본문에 언급되지 않았으므로 오답이다.
③ ④ 17% 7% 글의 요지와 정반대되는 서술이다.

어휘
on earth (의문문 강조) 도대체　　strangle 교살하다; 억압하다
stem 저지하다, 막다　　　　　　disparity 차이, 불균형
undeniable 부인할 수 없는　　　　opponent 반대자
proportionately 비례해서　　　　at the expense of ~의 희생으로

15 문법 > 가정법　　오답률 28%　답 ④

| 정답해설 | ④ 72% 우리말이 '~ 얻지 못했을 것이다'이므로 should는 가능을 뜻하는 조동사의 부정형인 couldn't가 되어야 한다.

어휘
headquarter 본사　　　　　splendid 훌륭한

16 문법 > 부정사　　오답률 31%　답 ④

| 정답해설 | ④ 69% '너무 ~해서 …할 수 없다'의 의미를 만들기 위해, 「too ~ to …」 구문이나 「so ~ that …」 구문으로 고쳐야 한다. 다음의 두 방법으로 고칠 수 있다.

1) He was too distracted by a text message to know that he was going over the speed limit.

2) He was so distracted by a text message that he didn't know that he was going over the speed limit.

| 오답해설 | ① 6% 부정 부사구인 Only after the meeting이 문두로 강조되어 뒤따라오는 어순이 도치되었다. 따라서 did he recognize의 어순은 올바르다.
② 4% 주장을 나타내는 동사 insist의 목적어로 쓰인 that절이 당위의 의미를 가지면 that절의 동사는 「should + 동사원형」으로 쓴다. 이때 should는 생략할 수 있다. 따라서 a bridge 다음에 동사원형인 be constructed의 형태가 오게 되었다. to solve ~ 이하는 to부정사의 부사적 용법(목적)으로 사용되었다.
③ 21% 양보절에 as를 사용할 때는 문장의 보어(형용사/명사)를 도치하여 사용할 수 있다. 맨 앞에 오는 as는 부사의 역할이니 참고하자.

As difficult a task as it was,
부사　　　　　　　　보어　　　　　접속사 주어 동사

| 더 알아보기 | 부정어 도치

> 부정부사(구) not, never, no, little을 문두로 이동하면 주어와 동사가 의문문 어순으로 도치된다.
>
> • I never thought of studying.
> 　나는 공부할 생각을 전혀 하지 않았다.
> 　→ Never did I think of studying.
> • I have never dreamed of that.
> 　나는 그것에 대해서 꿈도 꿔 본 적이 없다.
> 　→ Never have I dreamed of that.
> • He little expected that a letter would come from the school.
> 　그는 그 학교로부터 편지가 올 것을 거의 기대하지 않았다.
> 　→ Little did he expect that a letter would come from the school.
> • I little dreamed that I should never see my sister again.
> 　나는 내 여동생을 다시 볼 수 없을 거라고 전혀 생각하지 않았다.
> 　→ Little did I dream that I should never see my sister again.
> • She was not only sad but she was depressed.
> 　그녀는 슬플 뿐만 아니라 우울했다.
> 　→ Not only was she sad but she was depressed.
> • She did not know the fact until this morning.
> 　그녀는 오늘 아침이 될 때까지 그 사실을 몰랐다.(그녀는 오늘 아침이 되어서야 그 사실을 알았다.)
> 　→ Not until this morning did she know the fact.
> • He had scarcely[hardly] entered the room when[before] he fell (down).
> 　그는 방에 들어서자마자 쓰러졌다.
> 　→ Scarcely[Hardly] had he entered the room when[before] he fell (down).

어휘

construct 건설하다　　　　　　　　distracted 정신이 팔린, 주의가 산만한

17　독해 > Reading for Writing > 빈칸 구 완성　오답률 40%　답 ①

| 해석 | 귀와 대조했을 때 눈에 의해 수집된 정보의 양은 정확하게 계산되지 않아 왔다. 그러한 계산은 번역 과정을 포함할 뿐만 아니라 과학자들은 무엇을 세어야 하는지에 대한 지식 부족으로 어려움을 겪었다. 그러나 두 시스템의 상대적 복잡성에 대한 일반적인 개념은 눈과 귀를 뇌의 중심부까지 연결하는 신경의 크기를 (A) 비교함으로써 얻을 수 있다. 시신경은 달팽이관 신경보다 약 18배 많은 뉴런을 포함하고 있기 때문에, 우리는 그것이 적어도 그만큼 더 많은 정보를 전달한다고 추정한다. 사실, 정상적으로 주의를 집중하는 실험 대상에게, 정보를 (B) 쓸어 담는 데 있어서 눈은 귀의 천 배만큼이나 효율적일 수도 있다.

	(A)	(B)
①	비교하는	쓸어 담는, 처리하는
②	비교하는	줄이는
③	첨가하는	전파하는
④	첨가하는	말끔히 치우는, 해결하는

| 정답해설 | ① 60% (A) 빈칸 이후의 문장을 통해서 시신경과 달팽이관 신경을 비교한 구체적 수치인 18배를 제시하고 있다. 따라서 해당 문장 이전의 빈칸에는 시신경과 달팽이관의 신경의 뉴런 수를 '비교하는 것'이 가장 적절하므로 comparing이 적절하다.

(B) 빈칸 이전에 시신경이 달팽이관 신경보다 약 18배 많은 정보를 전달한다고 추정하고 있다. 따라서 빈칸에는 눈이 귀의 천 배만큼이나 정보를 '취득하는 것'과 관련된 맥락으로 sweeping up이 적절하다.

어휘

precisely 정확하게
handicap 불리하게 만들다, 어려움을 겪게 하다
notion 개념, 생각　　　　　　　　optic nerve 시신경
neuron 뉴런　　　　　　　　　　transmit 전달하다
alert 주의를 집중하는, 정신이 초롱초롱한
probable 있음직한, 충분히 가능한

18　독해 > Logical Reading > 삭제　오답률 36%　답 ③

| 해석 | 최근 수년간 아동 도서상이 급증했다. 그래서 오늘날에는 다양한 기관에 의한 상과 상금이 족히 100가지가 넘는다. 상은 특정 장르의 책에 대해 주어지거나 또는 단순히 주어진 기간 내에 출판된 모든 아동 도서 중 최고의 작품에 주어진다. 상은 아동 문학계에 바친 평생의 공헌에 대해 특정 책이나 저자에게 수여될 수도 있다. 대부분의 아동 도서상은 성인에 의해 선정되지만, 현재는 어린이가 선정한 도서상도 점점 늘고 있다. 대부분의 국가에서 수여되는 규모가 더 큰 국가상은 가장 영향력이 크며, 어린 독자들을 위해 발간되는 양서에 대한 대중의 인식을 높이는 데 큰 도움을 주어 왔다. ③ 출판 산업에의 뛰어난 노고에 대한 시상식이 연기되었다. 물론, 독자는 수상 도서에 너무 많은 믿음을 두지 않는 것이 현명하다. 상이 꼭 좋은 독서 경험을 의미하는 것은 아니지만, 책을 선택할 때 분명히 시작점을 제공해 준다.

| 정답해설 | ③ 64% 도입부에서 최근 아동 도서상이 증가했다고 하며 중반부까지 이러한 도서상에 대한 정보를 제공하고 있다. 그리고 후반부로 넘어가면서 '수상이 가지는 의미'에 대해 서술하며 마무리하고 있는데, 갑자기 '시상식이 연기되었다'라고 하는 문장은 글의 자연스러운 흐름을 해친다.

어휘

proliferate 급증하다
put ~ on hold ~을 연기하다, 보류하다

19　독해 > Logical Reading > 삽입　오답률 36%　답 ④

| 해석 | 동물이 사냥에서 사살되었을 때 일어나는 것과 같은 간단한 분배 상황을 예를 들어 살펴보자. 어떤 사람은 각 사냥꾼이 그것을 얻기 위해 한 일의 양에 따라 동물이 분배될 것을 기대할 수 있다. 어느 정도 이 원칙은 지켜지지만, 다른 사람들 또한 권리를 가진다. 캠프에 있는 각각의 사람은 사냥꾼과의 관계에 따라 자신의 몫을 얻는다. 예를 들어, 캥거루가 사냥되면, 사냥꾼은 주요 부위를 친족에게 주어야 하며, 가장 안 좋은 부위들은 사냥꾼 자신이 가져갈 수도 있다. ④ 이 불평등은 다른 사람들이 잡은 사냥감들로부터 더 나은 몫을 그들 차례에서 얻었을 때 해결된다. 장기적인 면에서 최종적인 결과는 사실상 각 개인에게 동일한 것이지만, 이 시스템을 통해서, 친족 관계 의무 원칙과 음식 공유의 도덕이 강조되어 온 것이다.

| 정답해설 | ④ 64% 주어진 문장의 This inequality가 지칭하는 내용으로 가장 적절한 것은 ④ 앞에 나온 캥거루의 주요 부분을 친족에게 주고, 가장 안 좋은 부위를 사냥꾼 자신이 가진다는 것이므로, 주어진 문장은 ④에 삽입되는 것이 가장 적절하다.

어휘

kinfolk 친척, 친족   net 결국의, 최종적인
substantially 상당히, 사실상   kinship 친척 관계, 혈족 관계
morality 도덕성

---

20 독해 > Logical Reading > 배열 | 오답률 34% | 답 ②

| **해석** | 그룹 치료법의 가장 혁신적인 방법은 Jacob L. Moreno의 아이디어인 심리극이었다. 그룹 치료의 한 형태인 심리극은 정신병이 본질적으로 정신 또는 마음 속에서 발생한다는 프로이트 학설의 세계관과는 꽤 다른 전제에서 시작되었다.

(B) 주류 관점과의 그의 이론적인 차이에도 불구하고, 20세기의 심리적 의식 형성에 대한 Moreno의 영향력은 상당했다. 그는 인간의 본성은 창의적이 되는 것이며 그리고 창조적인 삶을 사는 것이 인간의 건강과 행복의 열쇠라고 생각했다.

(A) 그러나 그는 또한 창의성이 고독한 과정이 아니라 사회적 상호 작용에 의해 이끌어내어진 것이라고 생각했다. 그는 창의력과 일반적인 사회적 신뢰를 증진시키는 수단으로서 역할극과 즉흥 연극을 포함한 연극 기법에 크게 의존했다.

(C) 그의 가장 중요한 연극적 도구는 참가자들에게 다른 사람의 외적 인격을 맡도록 요청하는, 그가 역할 바꾸기라고 불렀던 것이었다. 다른 이의 가죽을 쓰고 있는 사람인 "척"하는 행위는 감정 이입의 충동을 불러일으키는 것을 돕고 그것을 더 높은 수준의 표현으로 발전시키도록 설계되었다.

| **정답해설** | ② 66% 주어진 문장 내의 that were quite alien to the Freudian world view라는 부분을 통해 Moreno의 전제가 주류와 다름을 알 수 있다. (B)의 첫 문장의 Despite his theoretical difference가 이를 가리키고 있으므로, 주어진 문장의 다음 순서로 (B)가 오는 것이 적절하다. (B)에서는 '창의적인 삶을 사는 것이 인간의 건강과 행복의 열쇠'라고 했는데, (A)에서 창의성은 사회적 상호 작용에 의한 것이라고 하며 이 두 가지 역량을 증진시키기 위한 수단으로 역할극과 즉흥극을 제안하고 있고, (C)에서 그러한 연극의 표현 방식을 설명하고 있다. 그러므로 (B) – (A) – (C)의 순서가 알맞다.

어휘

innovative 혁신적인   psychodrama 심리극
brainchild 아이디어, 발명품   solitary 혼자의, 고독한
improvisation 즉흥으로 하는 것(연기, 연주 등)
persona 외적 인격; 인물, 등장인물

합격예상 체크

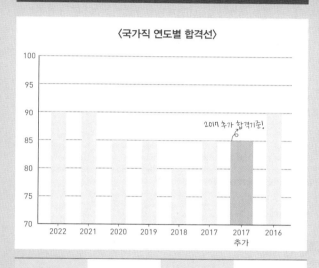

〈국가직 연도별 합격선〉

| 맞힌 개수 | /20문항 | 점수 | /100점 |

➡ ☐합격 ☐불합격

취약영역 체크

문항	정답	영역	문항	정답	영역
①	④	생활영어 > 회화/관용표현	11	④	어휘 > 빈칸 완성
2	②	생활영어 > 회화/관용표현	12	②	독해 > Logical Reading > 배열
3	③	문법 > 동사	13	③	문법 > 가정법
4	④	문법 > 일치	14	③	문법 > 부사
5	③	어휘 > 유의어 찾기	15	②	독해 > Reading for Writing > 빈칸 구 완성
6	②	어휘 > 유의어 찾기	16	④	독해 > Reading for Writing > 빈칸 절 완성
7	③	어휘 > 유의어 찾기	17	①	독해 > Reading for Writing > 빈칸 구 완성
8	③	독해 > Logical Reading > 삽입	18	④	독해 > Logical Reading > 삭제
9	④	독해 > Micro Reading > 내용 일치/불일치	19	④	독해 > Micro Reading > 내용 일치/불일치
10	①	독해 > Micro Reading > 내용 일치/불일치	20	①	독해 > Reading for Writing > 빈칸 절 완성

⬇ 영역별 틀린 개수로 취약영역을 확인하세요!

| 어휘 | /4 | 문법 | /4 | 독해 | /10 | 생활영어 | /2 |

➡ 나의 취약영역: _____

※ [정답해설]과 [오답해설] 선지의 50% 표시는 〈1초 합격예측 서비스〉를 통해 수집된 선지 선택률을 나타냅니다.

1 생활영어 > 회화/관용표현 　오답률 6%　답 ④

| 해석 | Mary: 안녕하세요, James. 어떻게 지내세요?
James: 안녕하세요, Mary. 오늘은 무엇을 도와드릴까요?
Mary: 이 소포를 배송하려면 어떻게 처리해야 하나요?
James: 고객 서비스 센터에 있는 Bob에게 말해 보는 게 어떠세요?
Mary: ④ 그의 번호로 전화를 해 봤지만, 아무도 받지 않아요.
① 물론이죠. 당신을 위해 제가 이 소포를 배송할게요.
② 알겠습니다. 제가 Bob의 고객을 맡을게요.
③ 세관 사무소에서 뵐게요.
④ 그의 번호로 전화를 해 봤지만, 아무도 받지 않아요.

| 정답해설 | ④ 94% Bob에게 문의해 보는 게 어떠냐는 James의 제안에 대한 답으로는 이미 그에게 전화를 해 봤지만 아무도 받지 않는다는 ④의 내용이 알맞다.

2 생활영어 > 회화/관용표현 　오답률 2%　답 ②

| 해석 | A: 우와! 저 긴 줄을 봐. 우린 적어도 30분은 기다려야 할 거야.
B: 네 말이 맞아. ② 다른 놀이기구를 찾아보자.
A: 그거 좋은 생각이다. 나는 롤러코스터를 타고 싶어.
B: 그건 내 취향이 아니야.
A: 그럼 후룸라이드는 어때? 재미도 있고 줄도 별로 안 길어.
B: 그거 괜찮다! 가자!
① 마술쇼 자리를 찾아보자.
② 다른 놀이기구를 찾아보자.
③ 퍼레이드 의상을 사자.
④ 분실물 보관소로 가 보자.

| 정답해설 | ② 98% 빈칸 B의 말에 A가 긍정적으로 동의한 후 롤러코스터를 타고 싶다고 말하는 것으로 보아 빈칸에는 줄이 긴 놀이기구 대신 다른 놀이기구를 찾아보자고 제안하는 말이 들어가는 것이 자연스럽다.

어휘

cup of tea (보통 부정문에 사용) 기호에 맞는 사람[물건]
ride 놀이기구

3 문법 > 동사 　오답률 34%　답 ③

| 정답해설 | ③ 66% promise는 '~을 약속하다'라는 의미로 주로 타동사로 쓰인다. 우리말의 '타협하다'는 compromise로 쓴다.

| 오답해설 | ① 10% by word of mouth는 '입에서 입으로, 입소문을 통해서'라는 뜻으로 알맞게 사용되었다.
② 10% must-see는 '꼭 보아야 할, 볼 만한'이라는 뜻으로 알맞게 사용되었다.
④ 14% on a tight budget은 '예산이 빠듯한, 돈이 없는'이라는 뜻의 관용구이고, 두 번째 문장에서 to spend는 명사 fifteen dollars를 수식하는 to부정사의 형용사적 용법으로 쓰였다.

| 4 | 문법 > 일치 | 오답률 30% | 답 ④ |

| 정답해설 | ④ 70% 해설이 3가지로 제시될 수 있다.

1) 주어에서 To control the process와 making improvement는 등위접속사 and에 의해 병렬 구조를 이루어야 한다. 따라서 To control the process and (to) make improvement 혹은 Controlling the process and making improvement로 바꿔야 한다. 또한 의미상 이 두 개의 개념을 하나의 개념으로 간주하고 있으므로 단수 동사 was로 쓴 것은 적절하나 보어 역시도 일치시켜 objective로 수정해야 한다. (단, 주어를 각각의 개념으로 볼 경우에는 were objectives가 옳다.)

2) 분사구문을 이용해서 To make improvement(부정사 주어), controlling the process(분사구문)로 표시하고 단수 동사 was로 나타낼 수 있다.

3) 주어진 문장의 어순을 그대로 활용한다면, 아래와 같은 경우도 가능하긴 하다. 분사구문을 활용해서 To control (Controlling) the process, making improvement를 주어로 우리말을 동시 상황으로 보고, '발전시키면서 과정을 관리하는 것'도 역시 가능하다.

| 오답해설 | ① 6% 부사절 When the dinner was ready를 분사구문으로 바꾼 것이다. 접속사 When은 생략하고, 주절과 종속절의 주어가 다르기 때문에 종속절의 주어 The dinner는 그대로 남아 있다. was는 주절의 동사 moved와 시제가 일치하기 때문에 being이 된다.

② 16% who that is over there은 동사 tell의 목적어 역할을 하고 있는 간접의문문에 해당한다. 따라서 「의문사 + 주어 + 동사」의 어순으로 왔다.

③ 8% rarely는 '거의 ~하지 않는'이라는 의미의 부정부사이다. 또한 prove는 불완전자동사로 사용되었으므로 형용사 fatal이 보어로 왔다.

| 더 알아보기 | 독립분사구문

> 주절의 주어와 분사구문의 주어가 다른 경우, 분사구문의 주어를 생략하지 않고 남겨두는데 이러한 분사구문을 독립분사구문이라고 한다.
> • After the sun had set, we started for home.
> 해가 져서, 우리는 집을 향해 출발했다.
> → The sun having set, we started for home.

오답률 TOP 2

| 5 | 어휘 > 유의어 찾기 | 오답률 55% | 답 ③ |

| 해석 | 요즘, 핼러윈은 이교도와 가톨릭 축제의 기원으로부터 많이 변화해 왔다. 그리고 우리가 달래는 영혼들은 더 이상 죽은 자들의 영혼이 아니다. 굶주린 영혼들은 의상을 입고 과자를 요구하는 아이들로 대체되었다.
① 13% 맡기다, 배정하다   ② 26% 체포하다, 이해하다
③ 45% 달래다, 진정시키다   ④ 16% 자극하다, 유발하다

| 정답해설 | ③ appease는 '~을 달래다'라는 뜻으로 선지 중 가장 가까운 의미를 지닌 것은 pacify이다.

어휘

drift 표류하다; 헤메다, (정처없이) 나아가다
pagan 이교도

| 6 | 어휘 > 유의어 찾기 | 오답률 33% | 답 ② |

| 해석 | 나는 주로 내 문제들을 가볍게 여긴다. 그리고 그것은 내 기분을 한결 낫게 만든다.
① 2% 어떤 것을 심각하게 여기다
② 67% 어떤 것을 중요하지 않은 것으로 취급하다
③ 14% 문제를 해결하기 위해 노력하다
④ 17% 수용할 만한 해결책을 찾다

| 정답해설 | ② make light of는 '~을 가볍게 여기다'라는 뜻으로 treat something as unimportant와 의미가 가장 가깝다.

| 더 알아보기 | '~을 중요시하다'를 뜻하는 표현

> • make much (account) of ~
> • make something of ~
> • attach importance to ~

어휘

make an effort 노력하다

| 7 | 어휘 > 유의어 찾기 | 오답률 20% | 답 ③ |

| 해석 | 패스트푸드 체인의 홍보 노력 덕택에, 햄버거와 감자튀김은 1950년대에 전형적인 미국 식사가 되었다.
① 1% 가장 건강한   ② 10% 입수 가능한, (가격 등이) 알맞은
③ 80% 전형적인, 일반적인   ④ 9% 비공식적인, 격식 차리지 않는

| 정답해설 | ③ quintessential은 '전형적인'이라는 뜻으로 typical과 의미가 가장 가깝다.

| 8 | 독해 > Logical Reading > 삽입 | 오답률 16% | 답 ③ |

| 해석 | Zealandia라고 불리는 길게 숨겨진 대륙이 뉴질랜드 아래에 숨어 있다고 지질학자들은 말한다. 그러나 아무도 새로운 대륙을 공식적으로 표기하는 일을 맡고 있지 않으므로, 각각의 과학자들은 결국 그들 스스로 판단해야 할 것이다. 지질학자로 구성된 한 팀은 그 새로운 대륙에 대해 과학적인 사례를 제시하는데, Zealandia가 대략 사백 구십만 평방킬로미터에 이르는 대륙 지각의 지속적인 팽창이라고 주장한다. 그것은 대략 인도 아대륙의 크기에 해당한다. 대체적으로 건조한 다른 대륙들과 달리, Zealandia의 94퍼센트가 대양 아래에 숨어 있다. ③ 오로지 뉴질랜드, 뉴칼레도니아 그리고 몇 개의 작은 섬들만이 파도 위로 살짝 보인다. 그러한 작은 지역들을 제외하고, Zealandia의 모든 부분은 대양 아래에 잠겨 있다. "만약 우리가 전 세계의 대양을 없앨 수 있다면, Zealandia가 주변 대양 지각의 약 3,000미터 위로 솟아 나와 있다는 점이 아주 명확해질 것입니다."라고 한 지질학자는 말한다. "만약 해수면이 없다면, 아주 오래 전에 우리는 Zealandia의 정체를, 즉 Zealandia가 대륙이라는 것을 알아봤을 것입니다."

| 정답해설 | ③ 84% 주어진 문장은 ③ 앞의 Zealandia의 94퍼센트가 대양 아래에 숨어 있다는 내용을 부연 설명한 것으로 보는 것이 가장 적절하다. 또한 ③ 뒤의 those tiny areas는 주어진 문장의 New Zealand, New Caledonia and a few small islands를 지칭하는 것이

다. 따라서 주어진 문장은 ③의 위치에 오는 것이 알맞다.

어휘

peek 살짝 보이다　　　　　　lurk 숨다, 잠복하다
designate 표기하다, 지명하다　　pitch 이야기하다; 던지다
expanse 팽창; 광활한 공간　　　continental crust 대륙 지각
subcontinent 아대륙　　　　　submerge 물에 잠기다
pull the plug on ～을 죽이다, 제거하다
ocean crust 대양 지각

오답률 TOP 3

9　독해 > Micro Reading > 내용일치/불일치　[오답률 54%]　답 ④

| 해석 | 17세기 초반의 수십 년은 보통 과학 혁명이라 일컬어지는 과정인 지구와 하늘에 대한 이해의 급격한 성장을 목격했다. 아리스토텔레스 철학에 대한 오래된 의존은 대학가에서 빠르게 약해지고 있었다. 자연 철학의 아리스토텔레스 체계에서, 물체의 움직임은 그들이 소유한 네 가지 원소(땅, 물, 공기, 불)의 양의 측면에서 '인과적으로' 설명되었고 물체는 그들을 구성하는 주어진 원소들의 우세함에 따라 그들의 '자연적인' 곳을 향해 위로 혹은 아래로 움직였다. 자연 철학은 광학, 유체 정역학, 그리고 화성학과 같은 '혼합 수학' 과목들과 늘상 대조되었는데, (이러한 과목들에서) 숫자는 길이 혹은 기간과 같은 측정 가능한 외부 수량에 적용될 수 있었다.
① 17세기 초반에 지구와 하늘에 대한 지식의 증가가 있었다.
② 아리스토텔레스 철학에의 의존은 17세기에 대학가에서 쇠퇴하고 있었다.
③ 자연 철학은 물체의 운동을 설명하기 위해 네 가지 원소를 제시하였다.
④ 자연 철학에서, 측정 가능한 외부 수량을 위해 늘상 숫자가 사용되었다.

| 정답해설 | ④ [46%] 마지막 문장에서 측정 가능한 외부 수량을 위해 숫자를 사용한 것은 자연 철학이 아니라 혼합 수학 과목이라고 했는데 자연 철학은 이와 대조를 이루었다고 하였으므로 ④는 본문과 일치하지 않는다.

| 더 알아보기 | Natural Philosophy (자연 철학)

> 만물의 생성 과정 또는 본질적인 자연 자체를 탐구하는 데 집중하는 철학 및 학문

어휘

exponential 기하급수적인; 급격한　　reliance 의존, 의지
wane 약해지다, 쇠약해지다　　　　causally 인과적으로, 원인이 되어
preponderance 우세함　　　　　routinely 일상적으로, 늘상
mathematical 수학의　　　　　　optics 광학
hydrostatics 유체 정역학, 정수 역학　harmonics 화성학
duration 기간

10　독해 > Micro Reading > 내용일치/불일치　[오답률 32%]　답 ①

| 해석 | 방치 혹은 학대와 같은 인생 초창기의 스트레스를 유발하는 사건들은 성인기에 접어들어서도 심리적인 영향을 미칠 수 있다. 새로운 연구는 이러한 영향들이 그들의 자녀와 심지어 그들의 손주들에게까지 지속될 수도 있다는 것을 보여 준다. Tufts 의과대학의 생화학자, Larry James와 Lorena Schmidt는 7주간에 걸쳐 규칙적으로 청소년기의 쥐들을 새로운 우리로 재배치함으로써 그들에게 만성적인 사회적 스트레스를 유발시켰다. 그런 뒤 그 연구원들은 쥐들이 얼마나 오래 미로의 트인 공간에서 시간을 보내는지 그리고 그들이 이전에 한 번도 본 적 없는 쥐들에게 얼마나 자주 다가가는지와 같은, 설치류의 불안 정도에 대한 일련의 표준 실험 척도들을 사용하여 이러한 스트레스를 겪은 성인 쥐들을 검사했다. 암컷 쥐들은 대조

군들과 비교했을 때 더 불안한 행동을 보였고, 반면 수컷들은 그렇지 않았다. 그러나 두 성별 모두의 새끼들은 더 불안한 행동을 보였고, 청소년기에 스트레스를 겪었던 수컷 쥐들은 심지어 이러한 행동 패턴을 그들의 손주들과 증손주들에게까지 물려주었다.
① 당신의 할아버지가 청소년이었을 때 겪었던 스트레스가 당신을 더 불안하게 만들 수도 있다.
② 어릴 적의 스트레스를 일으키는 경험들은 인생 후반부의 불안을 완화시킨다.
③ 한 장소에서 다른 장소로의 지속적인 이동은 자손들에게 이득을 줄 수 있다.
④ 만성적인 사회적 스트레스는 재배치로 인해 유발될 수 없다.

| 정답해설 | ① [68%] 두 번째 문장에서 어린 시절 받은 스트레스의 영향이 자신의 손주들에게까지 지속될 수 있다고 언급하고 있고, 마지막 문장에서도 쥐 실험을 통해 청소년기에 스트레스를 받은 수컷 쥐들의 불안한 행동 패턴이 손주들과 증손주들에게까지 전이되었다고 진술하고 있으므로 ①은 본문의 내용과 일치한다.

| 오답해설 | ② [18%] 청소년기에 받은 스트레스가 성인기의 불안한 행동 패턴에 영향을 준다는 내용은 있으나 인생 후반부의 불안을 완화시킨다는 내용은 찾아볼 수 없다.

③ [8%] 본문의 실험 내용에 의하면 규칙적인 우리의 재배치는 실험 쥐들의 스트레스를 유발했고, 이러한 스트레스는 실험쥐들의 자손들에게까지 영향을 미쳐 그들이 불안한 행동을 보이도록 만들었으므로 이득을 주었다고 할 수 없다.

④ [6%] 본문의 실험에서 연구원들은 장소의 재배치를 통해 실험쥐들의 스트레스를 유발했다.

어휘

biochemist 생화학자　　　　　chronic 만성적인
adolescent 청소년, 청년　　　　rodent 설치류의
offspring 새끼, 자손
transmit 전송하다; (자손에게) 물려주다, 유전시키다
alleviate 경감하다, 완화하다　　constant 지속적인

11　어휘 > 빈칸 완성　[오답률 26%]　답 ④

| 해석 | • 그녀는 그들의 최종 결정에 실망했지만, 결국 ④ 극복할 것이다.
• 내가 그녀의 죽음으로 인한 충격을 ④ 극복하는 것에는 아주 오랜 시간이 걸렸다.
① [12%] 도망치다, 벗어나다　　　② [5%] 내려가다, 엎드리다, 시작하다
③ [9%] 성공하다, 앞지르다　　　④ [74%] 극복하다, 이겨내다

| 정답해설 | ④ 문맥상 빈칸에 공통으로 들어가기에 가장 자연스러운 것은 '극복하다'의 의미를 지닌 get over이다.

12　독해 > Logical Reading > 배열　[오답률 6%]　답 ②

| 해석 | 대대로, 부지런한 사람들은 삶을 더 쉽게 만들기 위해 계속하여 편의 시설을 만들어 냈다. 바퀴에서 전구의 발명에 이르기까지, 발명품들은 사회가 앞으로 나아가게 했다.
(B) 한 가지 최근의 현대 발명품은 컴퓨터인데, 그것은 사람들의 삶의 많은 측면을 개선시켰다. 이는 특히 교육의 영역에 있어서 그러하다. 더 높은 수준의 교육에 관한 컴퓨터 기술의 중요한 한 가지 영향은 강의의 이용 가능성이다.

(C) 컴퓨터 네트워크 발전의 결과로, 학생들은 실시간으로 많은 대학의 강의를 들을 수 있다. 그들은 이제 디지털 스크린 앞에 앉아 다른 대학에서 제공되는 강의를 들을 수 있다.

(A) 게다가, 쌍방향 미디어는 강사에게 질문을 하거나 이메일을 통해 다른 학생들과 의견 교환을 하기 위해 사용될 수 있다. 그러한 컴퓨터화된 강의들은 학생들에게 이전에는 이용 불가능했던 지식으로의 접근을 제공한다.

| 정답해설 | ② 94% 주어진 글은 발명품이 사회를 발전하게 만들었다고 하며 마무리되었다. 따라서 그 예로 현대 발명품인 컴퓨터를 제시하고 있는 (B)가 이어지는 것이 자연스럽다. (B)의 마지막에서는 컴퓨터가 교육에 긍정적인 영향을 미치고 있다고 언급했고, 이를 (C)에서 온라인 강의의 예를 들며 구체적으로 설명하고 있다. (A)는 첨언의 연결사 In addition으로 시작하여 온라인으로 제공되는 강의의 이점에 대해 계속하여 설명하고 있으므로 (C) 다음에 오는 것이 자연스럽다. 따라서 적절한 순서는 (B) – (C) – (A)이다.

어휘

| industrious 부지런한, 근면한 | propel 나아가게 하다, 추진하다 |
| availability 유용성, 이용 가능성 | in real time 실시간으로 |

---

13 문법 > 가정법   오답률 32%   답 ③

| 해석 | ① 학부생들은 실험실에서 장비를 사용하도록 허용되지 않는다.
② 다양한 주제들에 대한 Mary의 지식의 범위는 나를 놀라게 한다.
③ 만약 그녀가 어제 집에 있었다면, 나는 그녀를 방문했을 텐데.
④ 당신의 대출 신청서가 승인되지 않았음을 알리게 되어 유감입니다.

| 정답해설 | ③ 68% 가정법 과거완료 구문으로 과거 사실과 반대되는 가정을 할 때 쓰인다. 「If + 주어 + had p.p. ~, 주어 + 조동사 과거형 + have p.p.」의 순서를 잘 따르고 있다.

| 오답해설 | ① 10% 「be allowed to + 동사원형」은 '~하는 것이 허용[허락]되다'라는 의미로 여기서 to는 전치사가 아니므로 using을 use로 바꿔야 한다. 또한 equipment는 불가산명사이므로 복수형이 불가능하다. 따라서 equipment로 고쳐야 한다.
② 10% 주어는 The extent로 3인칭 단수이다. 따라서 동사는 주어에 수 일치를 시켜 astounds가 되어야 한다.
④ 12% regret은 '유감스럽게 생각하다'라는 의미의 동사로, 목적어로 동명사가 오면 이미 지난 일에 대한 후회를, to부정사가 오면 앞으로 일어날 일에 대한 유감을 나타내므로 regret to inform you는 옳게 사용되었다. 「inform + 목적어 + that + 주어 + 동사」의 형태도 옳다. 단, approve는 타동사로 '~을 승인하다'의 뜻인데 여기서는 의미상 '승인되지 않다'라는 수동의 의미가 되도록 has not been approved가 되어야 옳다.

어휘

| laboratory 실험실 | loan 대출 |
| application 신청서, 지원 | approve 승인하다 |

오답률 TOP 1

14 문법 > 부사   오답률 65%   답 ③

| 해석 | ① 우리 아버지는 6주간 병원에 계셨다.
② 가족 모두가 독감으로 고생했다.
③ 그녀는 그것을 언급조차 하지 않았다.

④ 그녀는 경제적으로 독립하고 싶어 한다.

| 정답해설 | ③ 35% never so much as는 '~조차 하지 않는'이라는 의미의 부사구로 주어와 동사 사이에 삽입되었다. not so much as 형태에서 not 대신 never를 쓴 옳은 문장이다.

| 오답해설 | ① 15% 「기수 + 가산명사」 형태의 불특정 기간인 six weeks가 제시되었으므로 during six weeks는 for six weeks로 바뀌어야 하며, 이때는 과거시제와 현재완료시제 모두 사용 가능하다.
② 21% suffer가 전치사 from과 함께 사용되면, 자동사로 수동형이 불가하다. 따라서 are suffering from이나 suffer from이 옳다. suffer가 타동사로 쓰이는 경우에는 '~을 경험하다'라는 의미로 대개 수동형으로 사용하지는 않는다.
④ 29% financial은 뒤의 형용사 independent를 수식해야 하므로 부사 financially가 되어야 한다.

---

15 독해 > Reading for Writing > 빈칸 구 완성   오답률 45%   답 ②

| 해석 | 여러 민족이 섞여 있는 시카고 동네에서 자라는 중산층 유대인으로서, 나는 이미 매일 더 거친 노동자 계급의 사내아이들로부터 맞을 위험에 처해 있었다. 책벌레가 되는 것은 단지 그들에게 나를 때릴 결정적인 이유를 제공했을 뿐이다. 책을 읽고 공부를 하는 것이 여자아이들에게는 조금 더 허용적이었지만, 그들 역시 '건방지다'는 낙인을 얻지 않기 위해 너무 ② 똑똑해지지 않도록 주의해야만 했다.
① 운동 경기의, 건장한   ② 지적인, 똑똑한
③ 친절한, 환대하는   ④ 미숙한

| 정답해설 | ② 55% 빈칸 앞에서 독서와 공부가 여자아이들에게는 더 허용적이었다고 언급하고 있다. 그러나 뒤 문장은 역접 연결사 but으로 연결되고 빈칸 뒤에서는 건방지다고 낙인찍히지 않기 위해'라고 하였으므로 인과 관계를 고려하여 너무 '똑똑해지지 (intellectual)' 않도록 주의해야 한다고 하는 것이 문맥상 자연스럽다.

어휘

Jew 유대인	ethnically 민족[인종]적으로
permissible 허용되는, 무방한	lest ~하지 않도록
stigma 치욕, 오명, 낙인	stuck up 거만한, 건방진

---

16 독해 > Reading for Writing > 빈칸 절 완성   오답률 34%   답 ④

| 해석 | 당신은 우리에게 물었다. "무엇이 인공위성이 하늘로부터 떨어지지 않도록 유지시킵니까?" 지난 반세기 동안, 2,500개가 넘는 인공위성들이 첫 번째 인공위성을 따라 우주로 향했다. 무엇이 그것들 전부를 계속 떠 있게 하는가? 그것은 인공위성의 속도와 중력의 당김 사이의 미세한 균형이다. 인공위성들은 ④ 기본적으로 계속해서 떨어지고 있다. 말도 안 되지 않는가? 인공위성은 만약 그것들이 올바른 속도로 움직이고 있다면 지구의 만곡부가 그것들로부터 멀어지는 것과 같은 속도로 떨어지고 있다. 이는 우주의 더 먼 곳으로 질주하거나 지구로 나선형을 그리며 떨어지는 것 대신, 그것들이 행성(지구) 근처의 궤도에서 버틴다는 것을 의미한다. 인공위성을 바르게 유지하기 위해 종종 조정이 필요하다. 지구의 중력은 어떤 곳에서는 다른 곳들보다 더 강하다. 인공위성은 태양, 달 그리고 심지어 목성에 의해서도 이리저리 당겨질 수 있다.
① 일단 그것들이 궤도에 있으면 멈추도록 만들어진다

② 지구의 중력을 강화시키기 위해 고안된다
③ 이론적으로 다른 행성들을 당기고 있다
④ 기본적으로 계속해서 떨어지고 있다

| 정답해설 | ④ 66% 우주로 쏘아 올린 인공위성이 다시 떨어지지 않고 유지될 수 있는 원리에 대해 설명하는 글이다. "Crazy, right?"으로 보아 빈칸에는 언뜻 보기에 상식적으로 납득하기 어려운 내용이 들어갈 것임을 추측할 수 있다. 빈칸 앞에서 인공위성을 계속 떠 있게 만드는 것은 그것의 속도와 중력의 당김 사이의 미세한 균형이라고 하였고, 빈칸 다음 문장에서는 They fall ~이라고 하며 그것들은 떨어진다고 설명하고 있다. 따라서 빈칸에 들어가기에 가장 자연스러운 것은 인공위성이 계속해서 떨어지고 있다고 서술하는 ④이다.

어휘

afloat 떠돌아, 뜬　　　　　　race 질주하다
straight and narrow 바르게 사는 법, 정도(正道)
farther 더 멀리　　　　　　intensify 심해지다, 증대하다

17　독해 > Reading for Writing > 빈칸 구 완성　오답률 27%　답 ①

| 해석 | Rosberg는 무역 간행물 Industrial Marketing에서 컬러 광고가 흑백 광고보다 더 많은 관심을 불러일으킨다는 점을 관찰했다. Rosberg의 연구에서 컬러 광고가 그에 상응하는 흑백 광고보다 게재하기에 훨씬 더 비쌌다는 점은 주목할 만한 흥미로운 역사적 정보이다. 컬러 광고가 더 많은 관심을 불러일으켰음에도 불구하고, 그것들은 흑백 광고만큼의 달러당 구독자 수를 이끌어 내지는 못했다. 오늘날, 컬러 광고가 더 이상 희귀하지 않을 정도까지 기술, 경제, 그리고 인쇄의 효율성이 발달했다. 그 결과, 컬러 광고는 아마 더 이상 '이례적인 것'이 아닐 것이다. 총천연색의 화려한 잡지나 텔레비전에서 컬러 광고는 너무나 흔해서 드문 흑백 광고가 이제는 ① 대비로 인해 관심을 끈다.
① 대조, 대비　　　　　② 적대감
③ 수송, 이송　　　　　④ 자선, 자비심

| 정답해설 | ① 73% 본문 중반 Today 이후에는 오늘날에는 컬러 광고가 흔해져 상대적으로 흑백 광고가 드물어졌는데, 이것 때문에 더 관심을 끌게 되었다고 했다. 따라서 빈칸에 들어갈 원인으로 가장 적절한 것은 컬러 광고와 흑백 광고의 '대조(대비)'이다.

어휘

sidelight 측면으로부터의 빛; 부수적인 정보, 간접적인 설명
considerably 상당히, 많이　　　corresponding 해당[상응]하는
progress 발전하다, 진보하다

18　독해 > Logical Reading > 삭제　오답률 45%　답 ④

| 해석 | 연구원들은 자신들이 말하길 북방긴수염고래의 개체수에 대한 더 나은 추정치를 제공해 줄 새로운 모델을 개발했는데, 소식이 좋지 않다. 그 모델은 사망률이 높은 한 해를 보내고 있는 이 멸종 위기의 종을 구하려는 노력에 결정적으로 중요할 수도 있다고 국립해양대기국 북동해안 어업과학센터의 큰 고래 팀을 이끄는 Peter Corkeron은 말했다. 그 기관은 그 분석이 2010년 이래로 개체수가 줄어들었을 가능성이 거의 100퍼센트임을 보여 준다고 말했다. "한 가지 문제는, 그것들이 정말로 줄어들고 있는 것인가 아니면 우리가 그것들을 보지 못하고 있는 것인가? 하는 것이었다. 그것들은 실제로 줄어들었고, 그리고 그것이 요점이다."라고 Corkeron은 말했다. ④ 그 새로운 연구 모델은 수컷과 암컷의 개체수 격차가 벌어지고 있다는 우려에도 불구하고 북방긴수염고래의 수가 그대로임을 성공적으로 입증했다.

| 정답해설 | ④ 55% 글 전반에 걸쳐 북방긴수염고래의 개체수가 줄어들고 있다고 했는데, 개체수가 온전히 남아 있다고 한 ④는 글의 일관성을 해치고 있다.

어휘

North Atalantic right whale 북방긴수염고래
critically 결정적으로; 비판적으로
in the midst of ~의 한가운데에, ~가 한창일 때
the bottom line 요점　　　　intact 온전한, 손상되지 않은

19　독해 > Micro Reading > 내용일치/불일치　오답률 9%　답 ④

| 해석 | 징이 울리면, 베이징 레스토랑 Duck de Chine의 거의 모든 손님들은 몸을 돌린다. 바로 그 도시의 가장 위대한 요리 쇼인 북경오리고기 저미기가 시작될 참이기 때문이다. 종종 중국의 지역 가이드들 사이에서 그 도시의 최고의 북경오리고기로 꼽히는 Duck de Chine의 오리고기 껍질은 바삭하고 설탕으로 졸여지며, 고기는 부드럽고 육즙이 많다. "우리의 오리구이는 다른 곳과는 살짝 달라요." Duck de Chine의 매니저 An Ding은 말한다. "우리는 60년이 넘은, 강한 과일 향을 풍기는 대추나무를 사용하여 오리에 특히 바삭한 껍질과 풍미를 입혀 냅니다." 얇게 썬 봄양파와 오이 위에 뿌려지고 얇은 팬 케이크 안에서 오리 껍질에 싸여 있는, 달콤한 해선장 소스는 또 다른 하이라이트이다. "우리 서비스의 목적은 디테일에 집중하는 것입니다."라고 Ding은 말한다. "그것은 우리가 오리구이를 제공하는 방식과 고객을 위해 만드는 맞춤 소스 둘 다 포함합니다." 심지어 접시와 젓가락 받침까지도 오리 모양이다. Duck de Chine는 또한 중국 최초의 Bollinger 샴페인 바를 자랑한다. 북경오리가 최고 인기이긴 하지만, 메뉴에는 다른 훌륭한 음식들도 많다. 그 레스토랑은 프랑스식이 살짝 가미된 광동 요리와 베이징 요리를 둘 다 제공한다.
① 그 레스토랑은 요리 공연을 보여 준다.
② 그 레스토랑은 베이징에서 상당히 찬사를 받는다.
③ 그 레스토랑은 특별한 샴페인 바를 특징으로 한다.
④ 그 레스토랑은 오로지 베이징 지역의 음식만 제공한다.

| 정답해설 | ④ 91% 마지막 문장에서 Duck de Chine 레스토랑은 베이징 요리뿐만 아니라 광동 요리를 제공한다고 했다.

어휘

gong 징　　　　　　　　culinary 요리의
crispy 바삭바삭한　　　　　caramelize 설탕으로 졸이다
tender 연한, 부드러운　　　　jujube 대추(나무)
drizzle (액체를) 조금 붓다　　spring onion 봄양파
present 내놓다, 보여 주다　　　boast 자랑하다, 뽐내다

20　독해 > Reading for Writing > 빈칸 절 완성　오답률 31%　답 ①

| 해석 | 개를 목욕시키는 것은 엉망진창이 되고, 시간이 오래 소요되며, 관계된 모든 이에게 전혀 재미있지 않은 경향이 있기 때문에, "내 개를 얼마나 자주 목욕시켜야 할까?" 하고 의문을 가지는 것은 자연스러운 일이다. 흔히 그렇듯이, 정답은 ① "상황에 따라 다르다."이다. "개는 모낭의 성장을 용이하게 하고 피부 건강을 유지시키기 위해 스스로 털을 손질합니다."라고 Rhawnhurst 동물 병원의 Adam Denish 박사는 말한다. "그렇지만, 그 과정을 보완하기 위해 대부분의 개는 목욕이 필요합니다. 하지만 너무 자주 목욕시키는 것은 당신의 개에게 해로울 수도 있습니다. 그것은 피부에 염증을 일으키고, 모낭을 손상시키고 박테리아나 세균 감염의 위험성을 높일 수도 있습니다."라고 반려동물 의학 박사이자 수의학 지도 교수인, Jennifer Coates는 덧붙인다. "가장 적절한 목욕 빈도는 목욕의 이유에 따라 다릅니다. 대부분의 시간을 실내에서 보내는 건강한 개들은 자연스러운 '개 냄새'

를 통제하기 위해 1년에 몇 번만 목욕을 필요로 할 수 있습니다. 반면에, 목욕을 자주하는 것은 알러지성 피부 질환과 같은 몇몇 질병 관리에 있어 중요한 부분입니다."

① 상황에 따라 다르다
② 오로지 한 번
③ 목욕은 절대 필요하지 않다
④ 목욕이 당신의 개에게 해로울 때이다

| 정답해설 | ① 69% 목욕은 필요하지만 너무 자주 하는 것은 개에게 해로울 수도 있다고 했다. 또한 후반부에서 가장 적절한 목욕 빈도는 목욕의 이유에 따라 다르다고 설명하고 있다. 따라서 개를 목욕시키는 빈도는 상황에 따라 달라진다는 것을 알 수 있다. 그러므로 빈칸에는 ①이 알맞다.

어휘

as is often the case 흔히 있는 일이지만, 흔히 그렇듯이
groom 몸치장하다; (동물의 털을) 손질하다

detrimental 해로운, 불리한	irritate 염증을 일으키다
hair follicle 모낭	fungal 균성의, 균에 의한
veterinary 수의사; 수의의	advisor 고문; 지도 교수
odor 냄새, 악취, 향수	medical condition 질병

2016

4월 9일 시행
국가직 9급 (②책형)

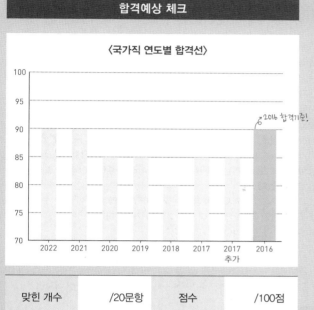

합격예상 체크

〈국가직 연도별 합격선〉

2016 합격기준

| 맞힌 개수 | /20문항 | 점수 | /100점 |

➡ □ 합격 □ 불합격

취약영역 체크

문항	정답	영역	문항	정답	영역
1	④	어휘 > 빈칸 완성	11	②	어휘 > 유의어 찾기
2	①	어휘 > 유의어 찾기	12	③	어휘 > 유의어 찾기
3	①	생활영어 > 회화/관용표현	13	③	문법 > 조동사
4	①	생활영어 > 회화/관용표현	14	④	독해 > Macro Reading > 제목
5	④	문법 > 접속사	15	③	독해 > Macro Reading > 주제
6	①	독해 > Macro Reading > 제목	16	①	독해 > Micro Reading > 내용 일치/불일치
7	④	독해 > Micro Reading > 내용 일치/불일치	17	①	독해 > Logical Reading > 배열
8	②	독해 > Logical Reading > 삭제	18	④	문법 > 동사
9	④	독해 > Logical Reading > 삽입	19	④	독해 > Reading for Writing > 빈칸 절 완성
10	②	독해 > Micro Reading > 내용 일치/불일치	20	③	독해 > Reading for Writing > 빈칸 구 완성

⬇ 영역별 틀린 개수로 취약영역을 확인하세요!

| 어휘 | /4 | 문법 | /3 | 독해 | /11 | 생활영어 | /2 |

➡ 나의 취약영역: _____

※ [정답해설]과 [오답해설] 선지의 50% 표시는 〈1초 합격예측 서비스〉를 통해 수집된 선지 선택률을 나타냅니다.

오답률 TOP 3

1 어휘 > 빈칸 완성   오답률 47%   답 ④

| 해석 | 공해를 없애자는 캠페인은 대중의 이해와 온전한 협조를 얻지 못한다면 ④ 무용지물로 판명될 것이다.

① 9% 유혹적인, 마음을 끄는   ② 22% 향상된, 강화된
③ 16% 풍부한, 비옥한   ④ 53% 무용지물인, 쓸데없는, 헛된

| 정답해설 | ④ 공해를 없애자는 캠페인이 대중의 협조를 얻지 못한다면 무용지물일 것이므로 futile이 정답이다.

어휘

eliminate 제거하다, 없애다   cooperation 협조, 협동

2 어휘 > 유의어 찾기   오답률 32%   답 ①

| 해석 | 지금까지, 신문기사들은 이 엄청나게 복잡한 문제를 오직 수박 겉핥기식으로 다뤄왔다.

① 68% ~을 피상적[표면적]으로 다루다
② 26% ~의 정곡을 찌르다, 적절한 말을 하다
③ 4% ~을 (붙)잡다
④ 2% ~을 긍정적으로 끝까지 하다

| 정답해설 | ① scratch the surface of는 '~을 수박 겉핥기식으로 다루다'라는 의미이므로, superficially dealt with와 의미가 가장 가깝다. superficially는 '표면적으로'라는 뜻의 부사이며 deal with는 '~을 다루다, 처리하다'라는 뜻의 동사구이다.

3 생활영어 > 회화/관용표현   오답률 4%   답 ①

| 해석 | A: 제가 어제 여기서 산 식탁보를 환불받고 싶은데요.
B: 식탁보에 문제가 있나요?
A: 저희 식탁에 맞지 않아서 반품하고 싶어요. 여기 영수증이요.
B: 죄송하지만 이 식탁보는 마지막 세일 품목이어서 환불이 안 됩니다.
A: ① 아무도 저에게 그걸 말해 주지 않았어요.
B: 그건 영수증 아래쪽에 쓰여 있어요.

① 아무도 저에게 그걸 말해 주지 않았어요.
② 가격표는 어디 있나요?
③ 그것에 무슨 문제가 있나요?
④ 저는 그것을 좋은 가격에 샀어요.

| 정답해설 | ① 96% 환불이 안 된다는 B의 말에 A가 빈칸의 대답을 하자, B는 '그것이 영수증 아래쪽에 쓰여 있다'라고 말하며 환불 불가 규정이 명시되어 있음을 설명하고 있다. 따라서 빈칸에서는 A가 환불이 되지 않는다는 것에 대해 몰랐다고 반박했음을 알 수 있으므로 빈칸에 가장 적절한 것은 ①이다.

| 더 알아보기 | 쇼핑과 관련된 표현

- rip-off 바가지 물품
- bargain 정상가보다 싸게 사는 물건
- cost an arm and a leg 큰돈이 들다

어휘

refund 환불; 환불하다   tablecloth 식탁보
fit 맞다, 적합하다, 어울리다

| **4** | 생활영어 〉 회화/관용표현 | 오답률 7% | 답 ① |

| **해석** | A: 여보세요? 안녕, Stephanie. 나는 사무실로 가는 길이야. 뭐 필요한 거라도 있니?
B: 안녕, Luke. 프린터에 쓸 여분의 종이 좀 사다 줄래?
A: 뭐라고 했어? 프린터에 쓸 잉크를 사다 달라고? 미안, ① 내 전화가 여기서 수신이 잘 안 돼.
B: 지금은 들려? 프린터에 쓸 종이가 더 필요하다고 말했어.
A: 다시 말해 줄래?
B: 됐어. 문자로 보낼게.
A: 그래. 고맙다, Stephanie. 조금 있다가 봐.
① 내 전화가 여기서 수신이 잘 안 돼.
② 나는 종이를 더 살 수 없었어.
③ 전화를 잘못 건 것 같아.
④ 이번엔 각 품목을 따로따로 살 거야.

| **정답해설** | ① 93% 빈칸 뒤에서 B가 지금은 잘 들리는지 묻고 있고, 이후에도 A가 알아듣지 못하자 B가 문자를 보낸다고 말하고 있으므로 빈칸에는 전화의 수신 상태가 나쁘다는 내용인 ①이 들어가는 것이 알맞다.

어휘

pick up (주로 가격이 싼 물건을) 사다, 얻다
reception (전화, 라디오 등) 수신 상태

| **5** | 문법 〉 접속사 | 오답률 31% | 답 ④ |

| **정답해설** | ④ 69% 의미상 「not A nor B but C」(A도 B도 아닌 C)의 구조가 되어야 하므로 or은 but으로 변경하는 것이 옳다. 즉, '끝까지 생존하는 생물은 가장 강한 생물(A)도, 가장 지적인 생물(B)도 아니고, 변화에 가장 잘 반응하는 생물(C)이다.'의 구조이다.

| **오답해설** | ① 2% 「remember -ing」는 '(과거에) ~했던 것을 기억하다'라는 의미로 올바르게 영작되었다. 참고로 「remember + to부정사」는 '(미래에) ~할 것을 기억하다'의 의미이다.
② 13% 「It takes + 목적어 + 시간 + to부정사 ~」는 '목적어가 to부정사 하는 데 ~만큼의 시간이 걸리다'라는 의미로 올바르게 사용되었다.
③ 16% as를 기준으로 주절과 부사절로 분리되어 있고, 과거시제로 두 절의 시제가 일치되어 있다.

| **더 알아보기** | 「not A but B」(A가 아니라 B)

| **6** | 독해 〉 Macro Reading 〉 제목 | 오답률 11% | 답 ① |

| **해석** | 구직 면접 결과에 대한 많은 양의 자료를 분석한 후에, 한 연구팀은 놀라운 사실을 발견했다. 채용될 가능성이 자격 조건에 달려 있었을까? 혹은 업무 경험이었을까? 사실, 둘 다 아니었다. 단 한 가지 중요한 요인은 지원자들이 호감 가는 사람으로 보였는지였다. 어떻게 해서든 환심을 산 지원자들은 일자리를 제공받을 가능성이 매우 높았고, 그들은 성공을 향한 자신들의 길을 매력으로 얻었다. 일부 지원자들은 미소를 짓고 눈 맞춤을 유지하려는 특별한 노력을 해 왔다. 다른 지원자들은 그 조직을 칭찬했다. 이러한 적극성은 그토록 호감이 가고 사회성이 뛰어난 지원자들이 직장에 잘 적응할 것이므로 (그러한 지원자들에게) 일자리가 주어져야 한다고 면접관들을 확신시켰다.
① 직업을 얻기 위해서는 호감 가는 사람이 되어라
② 더 많은 자격 조건들이 더 좋은 기회를 가져온다
③ 중요한 것은 성격이 아니라 능력이다
④ 면접에서 자신의 참모습을 보여 주어라

| **정답해설** | ① 89% 구직 면접 결과에 영향을 끼친 것은 '자격 조건'이나 '업무 경험'이 아니라 '호감 가는 사람'이었다는 내용이다.

어휘

likelihood 가능성, 기회   qualification 자격, 자질
ingratiate 환심을 사다   charm 매혹하다; 매력으로 얻다

| **7** | 독해 〉 Micro Reading 〉 내용일치/불일치 | 오답률 24% | 답 ④ |

| **해석** | 대부분의 작가들은 이중적인 삶을 산다. 그들은 합법적인 직업에서 상당한 수입을 얻고, 이른 아침, 늦은 밤, 주말, 휴가 기간과 같이 자신들의 글쓰기를 위한 시간을 그들이 할 수 있는 한 최선을 다해 할애한다. William Carlos Williams와 Louis-Ferdinand Céline은 의사였다. Wallace Stevens는 보험 회사에서 일했다. T.S. Elliot은 은행원이었다가, 후에는 출판업자가 되었다. Don DeLilo, Peter Carey, Salman Rushdie, 그리고 Elmore Leonard는 모두 오랫동안 광고업계에서 일했다. 다른 작가들은 가르치는 일을 한다. 오늘날 그것은(교직에 종사하는 것은) 아마도 가장 흔한 해결법일 것이다. 그리고 모든 주요 종합 대학과 단과 대학이 이른바 문예 창작 강좌들을 제공하기 때문에, 소설가들과 시인들은 이들 강좌 중 한 자리를 차지하기 위해 계속 서로 할퀴며 쟁탈전을 벌이고 있다. 누가 그들을 비난할 수 있겠는가? 월급은 많지 않을 수 있지만, 그 일은 안정적이고 시간도 적절하다.
① 일부 작가들은 문예 창작 강좌를 가르치는 강사직을 얻기 위해 고군분투한다.
② 의사로서, William Carlos Williams는 글을 쓸 시간을 마련하기 위해 노력했다.
③ 가르치는 것은 오늘날 작가들이 생계를 꾸리는 흔한 방법이다.
④ Salman Rushdie는 광고업계에서 잠시 일하며 큰 성공을 거두었다.

| **정답해설** | ④ 76% 본문 중반에서 Don DeLilo, Peter Carey, Salman Rushdie, 그리고 Elmore Leonard는 모두 오랫동안 광고업계에서 일을 했다고 언급하고 있다. 따라서 Salman Rushdie가 광고업계에서 잠시 일했다는 ④는 글의 내용과 일치하지 않는다.

| **오답해설** | ① 13% novelists and poets are continually scratching

~ themselves a spot을 통해 본문과 일치함을 알 수 있다.
② 5% (they) carve out time for their writing as best they can:
~ William Carlos Williams and Louis-Ferdinand Céline
were doctors를 통해 본문과 일치함을 알 수 있다.
③ 6% Other writers teach. ~ common solution today를 통해
본문과 일치함을 알 수 있다.

어휘

carve out 베어 내다, 잘라 내다	stretch 일련의 기간, (연속된) 길, 범위
so-called 이른바, 소위	course 수업, 강좌; 과정
scratch 긁다, 할퀴다	
scramble 서로 쟁탈하다, 앞을 다투어 빼앗다, 서로 다투다	

---

8 독해 > Logical Reading > 삭제　　오답률 18%　　답 ②

| 해석 | 어린 소녀들이 여성으로 성장하는 것을 축하하는 가장 큰 행사들 중 하나가 라틴 아메리카와 히스패닉 문화권에 존재한다. 이 행사는 La Quinceañera, 즉 열다섯 번째 해로 불리운다. 그것은 젊은 여성이 이제 결혼 가능한 나이라는 것을 인정해 준다. 그날은 보통 추수 감사절에 대한 미사로 시작된다. ② 한 문화의 통과 의례와 다른 문화의 통과 의례를 비교함으로써, 우리는 신분 계층의 차이를 가늠해 볼 수 있다. 그 젊은 여성은 발끝까지 오는 흰색 또는 파스텔톤 색의 드레스를 입고, 여성 들러리와 남성 수행원 역할을 하는 14명의 친구와 친지들의 시중을 받는다. 그녀의 부모와 대부모는 제단 아래에서 그녀를 둘러싼다. 미사가 끝날 때, Quinceañera가 직접 꽃다발을 성모의 제단에 바치는 동안 다른 젊은 친척들이 참석한 사람들에게 작은 선물을 준다. 미사에 이어 춤, 케이크, 그리고 축배가 있는 정성 들인 파티가 열린다. 마지막으로, 그날 저녁 시간을 마무리하기 위해 그 젊은 여성은 가장 맘에 드는 (남성) 수행원과 함께 왈츠 춤을 춘다.

| 정답해설 | ② 82% 이 글은 젊은 여성의 성인식인 라틴 아메리카의 La Quinceañera 풍습에 대한 내용이다. 문화 차이를 통해 (신분) 계층 차이를 알 수 있다는 내용의 ②는 앞뒤 문맥과 전혀 연관성이 없으므로 삭제해야 한다.

어휘

passage 변화; 통과	occur 발생하다; 존재하다
acknowledge 인정하다	Mass (가톨릭의) 미사
rites of passage 통과 의례	assess 가늠하다, 판단하다
maid of honor (미혼의 여성) 들러리	escort 수행원, 남성 동반자
the foot of something ~의 맨 아래 부분[발치/바닥]	
altar 제단	elaborate 정성 들인, 정교한
toast 축배, 건배	

오답률 TOP1
9 독해 > Logical Reading > 삽입　　오답률 56%　　답 ④

| 해석 | Disney의 작품은 과도하게 동화, 신화, 그리고 민간전승으로부터 나오는데 그것들은 전형적인 요소들에 많다. Pinoccio는 어떻게 이러한 요소들이 표면적인 현실주의 아래에 가려지는 것이 아니라 강조될 수 있는지에 대한 좋은 예이다. 영화 초반부에, 소년이자 인형인 Pinocchio는 "진짜 소년"이 되기 위해서는 그가 "용감하고, 진실되고, 이기적이지 않다"는 것을 보여 주어야 한다고 듣는다. 그 영화의 세 가지 주요 에피소드들은 의례적인 시련들을 나타내며, 그 소년의 도덕적 의연함을 시험한다. ④ 그는 처음 두 가지에서는 참담히 실패하지만, 마지막 고래 에피소드에서는 만회를 하는데, 거기에서 그는 정말로 용기, 정직, 그리고 비이기적임을 입증한다. 이처럼, 대부분 Disney의 작품들과 마찬가지로 Pinoccio가 지닌 가치관들은

전통적이고 보수적인데, 즉 그것들은 가족의 거룩함에 대한 확인, 우리의 운명을 이끄는 데 있어서 신의 중요성, 그리고 사회의 규율대로 행동해야 할 필요성이다.

| 정답해설 | ④ 44% Pinocchio의 도덕적 용기를 시험하는 세 가지(용기, 정직, 그리고 이기적이지 않음) 시련을 언급한 다음에 Pinocchio가 처음 두 가지에서 실패하게 된다는 주어진 문장이 들어가야 자연스럽게 이어진다. 또한 주어진 문장의 내용을 부연 설명하는 문장으로 가족의 신성함, 운명을 인도하는 초자연적 힘, 그리고 사회 규칙의 준수와 같은 첨언이 뒤로 이어짐으로써 이야기가 마무리된다. 따라서 주어진 문장이 들어갈 가장 적절한 곳은 ④이다.

| 오답해설 | ② 5% ③ 앞의 "brave, truthful, and unselfish"를 주어진 문장의 the first two로 지칭한다고 생각하면 ③의 위치에 주어진 문장이 들어갈 수 있는 가능성이 있다. 그러나 ③ 뒤의 문장은 ③ 앞의 문장을 부연 설명하고 있으므로 그 사이에 주어진 문장이 위치하여 이 두 문장의 유기성을 파괴할 수는 없다.

어휘

dismally 참담하게, 음침하게	redeem 만회하다, 회복하다
profuse 많은	archetypal 전형적인
submerge 물속에 가라앉히다, 잠기다	
realism 현실주의	ritualistic 의례적인, 관습적인
fortitude 의연함, 불굴의 정신	conservative 보수적인
affirmation 확언, 단언	sanctity 고결함, 거룩함

---

10 독해 > Micro Reading > 내용일치/불일치　　오답률 12%　　답 ②

| 해석 | Stanislavski는 여러 모로 운이 좋았다. 그는 폭넓은 교육의 혜택, 즉 국내외에서 가장 위대한 극예술계의 대표 인물들을 볼 수 있는 기회를 줄 수 있는 부유한 남자의 아들이었다. 그는 높은 목표를 설정하고 목표로 가는 어려운 길 도중에 결코 흔들리지 않기 때문에 굉장한 명성을 얻었다. 일에 대한 그의 개인적인 고결함과 고갈될 줄 모르는 능력은 그를 일류 전문 예술가로 만드는 데에 기여했다. Stanislavski는 또한 잘생긴 외모, 좋은 목소리 그리고 천재적인 재능을 선천적으로 풍부하게 부여받았다. 배우, 감독 그리고 교사로서, 그는 그와 함께 일하거나 그의 밑에서 일했던 또는 무대 위에 있는 그를 보는 특혜를 가졌던 많은 사람에게 영향과 영감을 줄 운명이었다.
① Stanislavski는 매력적인 외모를 가지고 태어났다.
② Stanislavski는 그의 일생 동안 동료들에게 영향력이 없는 상태였다.
③ Stanislavski의 아버지는 그의 교육을 지원해 줄 만큼 충분히 부유했다.
④ Stanislavski는 고결한 성격과 지치지 않는 능력 덕택으로 일류 예술가가 되었다.

| 정답해설 | ② 88% 마지막 문장 he was destined to influence ~ him on the stage.에 언급된 것처럼, Stanislavski는 그와 함께 일하거나 그의 밑에서 일했던 많은 사람에게 영향과 영감을 주었기 때문에 그의 동료들에게 일생 동안 영향력이 없었다는 내용은 본문과 일치하지 않는다.

어휘

theatre art 극예술	exponent 대표적 인물; 전형, 상징
falter (용기 · 결심 등이) 흔들리다	integrity 성실, 고결
inexhaustible 지칠 줄 모르는	endow 부여하다; 기부하다
exterior 외모, 겉모습, 외부	affluent 부유한
upright 고결한, (도덕적으로) 올바른	

11 어휘 > 유의어 찾기   오답률 29%   답 ②

| 해석 | 그건 개인적인 일이었어. 왜 너는 참견을 해야만 했니?
① 5% 서두르다
② 71% 참견하다, 간섭하다
③ 18% 코를 훌쩍거리다, 냄새 맡다
④ 6% 물러나다, 사임하다

| 정답해설 | ② stick one's nose in(~에 참견하다)은 interfere와 유사한 의미를 가지고 있다.

어휘

personal 개인적인

12 어휘 > 유의어 찾기   오답률 46%   답 ③

| 해석 | Newton은 수학, 광학, 역학 물리학에 전례 없는 공헌을 하였다.
① 7% 보통의, 평범한   ② 10% 시사하는, 암시적인, 도발적인
③ 54% 유례없는, 탁월한   ④ 29% 도발적인, 자극하는

| 정답해설 | ③ unprecedented는 '전례 없는, 비길 데 없는'을 의미하며, unsurpassed와 유의어 관계이다.

어휘

contribution 공헌, 기여   optics 광학
mechanical physics 역학 물리학

13 문법 > 조동사   오답률 31%   답 ③

| 해석 | ① Jessica는 자신의 지식을 향상시키기 위해서는 거의 노력을 하지 않는 아주 태평한 사람이다.
② 그가 올지 안 올지는 확실치 않다.
③ 경찰은 그녀가 당분간은 그 나라를 떠나지 말아야 한다고 요구했다.
④ 호텔이 더 비쌀수록, 호텔 서비스는 더 좋다.

| 정답해설 | ③ 69% demand는 요구 동사로 that절의 동사는 「should + 동사원형」으로 써야 한다. 이때 should는 생략이 가능하므로 not leave만 남아 있는 것은 어법상 적절하다.

| 오답해설 | ① 15% much는 비교급을 강조할 때 사용한다. 원급인 careless를 수식하는 부사는 very이다.
② 9% 주어는 명사여야 하며, 절을 사용할 경우 명사절을 이끄는 접속사가 필요하다. But은 명사절을 이끌 수 없으므로 틀리다. 여기서는 뒤의 or not으로 보아 Whether로 고치는 것이 적절하다.
④ 7% 「the + 비교급, the + 비교급」 구문이다. expensive는 3음절 형용사로 「more + 원급」의 형태로 비교급을 나타내므로 more expensive가 옳다. 또한 「the + 비교급, the + 비교급」 표현으로 '~할수록, 더…하다'의 의미를 나타내기 위해서, more expensive가 the와 함께 쓰여 문두에 위치하여야 한다. 따라서 The more expensive a hotel is가 옳은 표현이다.

어휘

careless 태평한, 걱정 없는; 부주의한; 경솔한
improve 개선하다   for the time being 당분간

14 독해 > Macro Reading > 제목   오답률 22%   답 ④

| 해석 | 인격이란 인간에 대한 존경이며, 경험을 다르게 해석할 권리이다. 인격은 이기심을 천성으로 인정하지만, 협력하려는 인간의 머뭇머뭇하면서도 용기를 북돋우는 본능을 굳게 믿는다. 인격은 독재에는 알레르기 반응을 보이며, 무지에 화를 내고 개선에 항상 열려 있다. 무엇보다도, 인격은 진실 앞의 거대한 겸손으로, 즉, 심지어 진실이 쓴 약일 때조차도 진실과의 자동적인 동맹이다.
① 진실에 대한 인격의 저항
② 인격과 협력하는 방법
③ 인격에 대한 무지
④ 인격이란 무엇을 의미하는가

| 정답해설 | ④ 78% 제시문은 '인격'에 대한 추상적인 정의를 내리고 있다.

어휘

tyranny 독재, 횡포   irritable 화를 잘 내는; 민감한
humility 겸손   alliance 동맹, 연합

15 독해 > Macro Reading > 주제   오답률 11%   답 ③

| 해석 | 학교에서 자기 능력보다 낮은 성적을 내는 아이들은 낮은 지능을 가졌다기보다는 그저 작업 기억력이 부진한 것인지도 모른다. 한 대학교의 연구진들은 3,000명이 넘는 모든 연령의 초등학생들을 조사했는데, 그들 중 10%가 학습을 심하게 방해하는 안 좋은 작업 기억력으로 고생한다는 것을 알아냈다. 전국적으로 이것은 거의 500,000명의 초등 교육을 받는 아이들이 영향을 받는 것과 같다. 그 연구진들은 또한 교사들이 안 좋은 작업 기억력을 좀처럼 알아채지 못하며, 종종 이러한 문제를 가진 아이들을 집중력이 없거나 덜 똑똑하다고 설명한다는 것을 발견했다.
① 학교에서 아이들의 교사와의 공감성
② 초등학생들의 낮은 지능
③ 안 좋은 작업 기억력이 초등학생들에게 미치는 영향
④ 아이들의 작업 기억력 문제를 해결하기 위한 교사들의 노력들

| 정답해설 | ③ 89% 자기 능력보다 낮은 성적을 내는 초등학생들이 사실 지능이 낮다기보다는 작업 기억력이 부진한 것일 수 있다는 연구 결과를 설명하는 글이므로 ③이 주제로 가장 적절하다.

어휘

underachieve 자기 능력보다 낮은 성적을 내다
working memory [심리] 작업 기억력
primary school 초등학교   impede 방해하다, 지연시키다
equate 동등하게 생각하다; 동일시하다
inattentive 부주의한, 태만한

16 독해 > Micro Reading > 내용일치/불일치   오답률 14%   답 ④

| 해석 | Harvard 연구진들에 의한 새로운 연구는 캔에 든 수프와 주스를 당신의 식탁에서 없앨 설득력 있는 이유를 제공할지도 모른다. 그 연구에 의하면, 5일 동안 매일 캔에 든 1인분 음식을 먹은 사람들은 상당히 높은 수치(10배가 넘는 증가)의 비스페놀 A, 즉 BPA를 가지고 있었는데, 이는 대부분의 음식과 음료 캔 안에 막을 형성하는 물질이다. 미국 보건관리국 관리자들은 그것을 규제하라는 압력을 점점 더 받고 있다. BPA에 관한 어떤 연구들은 그것이 암, 심장병, 그리고 비만의 높은 위험성과 관련이 있다는 것을 보여 준다. 그러나 일부 연구자들은 사람들에 대한 건강상의 위협으로서의 그것의 평판이 과장된 것이라고 반박한다. 「The Journal of the

American Medical Association」에 실린 새로운 연구는 사람이 캔에서 곧바로 나온 음식을 먹을 때 소화되는 BPA의 양을 처음으로 측정한 연구이다.

| 정답해설 | ④ 86% Public health officials ~ pressure to regulate it.을 통해 ④가 본문과 일치하는 내용을 서술하고 있음을 알 수 있다.

| 오답해설 | ① 3% 오히려 통조림 음식의 위험성을 입증할 이유를 제공할지도 모른다고 하였기에 본문과 일치하지 않는다.

② 4% 일부 연구자들이 비스페놀 A와 질병과의 연관성이 과장되었다고 반박한다고 했으므로 본문과 다르다.

③ 7% 「The Journal of the American Medical Association」에 실린 새로운 연구에서는 캔에서 바로 나온 음식을 먹고 소화되는 BPA의 양을 처음으로 측정했다고 서술했다.

어휘

compelling 설득력 있는, 강력한 serving 1인분
tenfold 10배의 line ~의 안에 막을 형성하다
come under (비난·공격 등을) 받다

오답률 TOP 2

17 독해 > Logical Reading > 배열 오답률 48% 답 ③

| 해석 | 모든 동물들은 자는 동안 인간과 같은 종류의 뇌 활동을 한다. 그들이 꿈을 꾸는지 안 꾸는지는 별개의 문제인데, 이것은 오직 또 다른 질문을 제기함으로써 풀릴 수 있다: 동물들은 자각을 가지고 있을까?

(B) 오늘날 많은 과학자들은 동물들이 언어와 명제적 또는 상징적 사고 능력이 부족하다는 점에서 아마도 우리의 것과는 꽤 다른 제한된 형태의 자각을 가지고 있다고 생각한다.

(C) 동물들은 꿈을 진짜 꾸더라도 당연히 꿈에 대해서 보고하지 못한다. 그러나 어떤 애완동물 주인이 그들이 가장 좋아하는 동물 친구가 자각과 기억 그리고 감정이 있다는 것에 대해 의심할까?

(A) 이것들이 자각의 세 가지 중요한 측면들이다. 그리고 그것들은 동물들이 우리들처럼 음성 언어를 가지고 있든 가지고 있지 않든 경험될 수 있다. 잠을 자는 동안 동물의 뇌가 활성화될 때, 동물들이 일종의 지각이 있고, 감정적인 기억의 경험을 한다고 가정하는 것은 어떨까?

| 정답해설 | ③ 52% 주어진 문장에서 던진 질문에 대한 대답으로 (B)가 오는 것이 적절하다. 또한 (A)의 three of the key aspects는 (C) 마지막의 perception, memory, and emotion을 가리키므로 (C) 다음에 (A)가 와야 적절하다.

어휘

pose 제기하다 consciousness 자각, 의식
perceptual 지각의
propositional 명제의, 명제로 이루어지는

---

18 문법 > 동사 오답률 23% 답 ④

| 해석 | 옛말에, 당신이 먹는 것이 곧 당신이라고 한다. 당신이 섭취하는 음식은 당신의 신체 활동에 분명하게 영향을 미친다. 그것들은 또한 당신의 뇌가 업무를 처리하는 방식에 영향을 끼칠지도 모른다. 만약 당신의 뇌가 그것들을 잘 처리한다면, 당신은 더 명확하게 사고하고, 당신은 정서적으로 더 안정된다. 적절한 음식은 당신이 집중할 수 있게 도움을 주며, 계속 동기 부여된 상태로 있게 해 주며, 기억이 선명해지도록 해 주며, 당신의 반응 시간을 빠르게 해 주며, 스트레스를 줄여 주며, 아마도 심지어는 당신의 뇌가 나이 들지 않도록 예방해 줄 것이다.

| 정답해설 | ④ 77% 「prevent + 목적어 + from -ing」 구문을 묻는 문제이다. '목적어가 ~하는 것을 예방[방해]하다'의 의미로, 출제 포인트는 prevent와 어울리는 전치사 및 동명사의 사용이다.

| 오답해설 | ① 4% 관용적으로 사용되는 부분으로, '옛말에'라는 표현이다. The old saying은 단수 주어이므로 go가 goes로 변경되어야 한다.

② 6% 문장의 주어는 The foods이며 동사는 affect이다. obvious는 동사 affect를 수식하는 부사 형태여야 하므로 obviously로 변경하여야 한다.

③ 13% help는 준사역동사로 목적어와 목적격 보어의 관계가 능동일 때는 원형부정사 또는 to부정사를 목적격 보어로 취한다. 또한 목적어와 목적격 보어의 관계가 수동일 때는 과거분사를 사용한다. 이 문장에서는 목적어와 목적격 보어의 관계가 능동이므로 being concentrated를 concentrate나 to concentrate로 변경해 주어야 한다.

| 더 알아보기 | 방해·금지의 타동사: 「주어 + 동사 + 목적어(사람) + from -ing」

- keep, prevent, hinder, prohibit, deter, stop, disable, dissuade, discourage
  We should discourage them from making a trip.
  우리는 그들이 여행을 가지 않도록 설득해야 한다.

---

19 독해 > Reading for Writing > 빈칸 절 완성 오답률 33% 답 ①

| 해석 | 당신의 문에 노크 소리가 난다. 당신 앞에 서 있는 것은 도움을 필요로 하는 젊은 남성이다. 그는 부상을 입었고 피를 흘리고 있다. 당신은 그를 안으로 데려와서 도와주고, 그가 편안하고 안전하다고 느끼도록 해 주고 구급차를 부른다. 이것은 분명히 해야 할 옳은 일이다. 그러나 Immanuel Kant에 의하면 만약 당신이 그가 안됐다는 기분이 들었기 때문에 그를 도왔다면, ① 그것은 도덕적인 행동이 전혀 아니다. 당신의 동정심은 당신의 행동의 도덕성과는 관련이 없다. 그것은 당신의 성격의 일부이지만, 옳거나 그른 것과는 관계가 없다. Kant에게 도덕성은 그저 당신이 무엇을 하느냐에 대한 것이 아니라, 당신이 그것을 왜 하는지에 대한 것이었다. 옳은 행동을 하는 사람들은 단순히 그들이 어떻게 느끼는지(감정) 때문에 그것을 하지 않는다. 그 결정은 이성, 즉 당신이 어떻게 느끼게 되는지에 관계없이 당신의 의무가 무엇인지 말해 주는 이성에 기반을 두어야 한다.

① 그것은 도덕적인 행동이 전혀 아니다
② 당신의 행동은 이성에 기반을 둔다
③ 그렇다면 당신은 도덕적인 행동을 보여 주고 있다
④ 당신은 그를 정직한 사람이 되도록 격려하고 있다

| 정답해설 | ① 67% 마지막 부분을 보면 Kant가 말하는 도덕적인 행동은 이성에 기반한 것이지 감정 때문에 하는 일이 아니라고 했다. 따라서 동정심(= 감정) 때문에 남성을 도운 것은 도덕적인 행동이 아니므로 빈칸에는 ①이 적절하다.

| 오답해설 | ② 26% 동정심에서 비롯된 행동은 이성이 아니라 감정 때문에 하는 일이다.

③ 5% Kant는 도덕성과 동정심(= 감정)이 서로 관계가 없다고 했으므로, 빈칸 앞의 행동을 도덕적 행동이라고 인정하지 않는다.

④ 2% 단순히 도움을 준 것이지, 정직한 사람이 되도록 동기 부여

를 한 것이 아니다. 본문과 관계없는 내용이다.

어휘

irrelevant 관련이 없는   morality 도덕성, 윤리성
character 성격, 특성   ethical 윤리적인, 도덕적인

---

20   독해 > Reading for Writing > 빈칸 구 완성   오답률 25%   답 ③

| 해석 | 공룡 유형의 소형 생명체인 두 발로 뛰어다니는 파충류 무리는 그들의 적과의 경쟁과 추적에 의해 멸종 혹은 높은 언덕 지대나 바닷가의 더 추운 환경에의 적응이라는 대안들로 밀려난 것처럼 보인다. 이러한 곤궁에 처한 종들 사이에서, 새로운 유형의 비늘이 발달했는데, 그 비늘은 깃 모양의 형태로 길어졌고 곧 깃털의 불완전한 시초로 분화되었다. 이러한 깃 모양의 비늘은 서로를 덮고 지금까지 존재했던 어떠한 파충류의 가죽보다 더 효율적인, 열을 유지하는 덮개를 만들어 냈다. 그래서 그것들은 그것이 없었다면 아무도 살지 않았을 더 추운 지역에 대한 침범을 가능케 했다. 아마도 이러한 변화들과 동시에 이러한 생명체들에게는 그들의 알에 대한 더 커다란 근심이 생겼다. 대부분의 파충류들은 그들의 알에 대해 꽤 부주의한데, 그것들은 부화를 위해 태양과 계절에 방치된다. 그러나 생명의 나무(생물의 진화 계통)의 새로 생겨난 가지 위의 그 변종들의 일부는 그들의 알을 지키고 ③ 그들의 체온의 온기로 그것들을 따뜻하게 유지하는 습관을 얻었다. 추위에 대한 이러한 적응으로, 이러한 생명체들, 즉 원시 새들을 온혈 동물로 만들고 햇볕을 쬐지 않아도 되게 하는 다른 내적 변이들이 진행되었다.
① 부화를 성공하지 못하게 하는
② 그것들을 태양 아래 혼자 두는
③ 그들의 체온의 온기로 그것들을 따뜻하게 유지하는
④ 그것들을 비늘이 있는 파충류들에게 나르는

| 정답해설 | ③ 75% 빈칸 바로 앞 부분에서 일부 변종들이 알을 지키는 습관을 얻었다고 하였으므로, 등위접속사로 연결된 빈칸의 내용역시 알을 지키는 습관에 대해서 설명할 것임을 유추할 수 있다. 따라서 정답은 ③이다.

어휘

tribe 종족, 부족
genus (동물 분류상의) 속(*pl.* genera)
distressed 곤궁에 처해 있는, 고민하고 있는
elongate 길게 하다, 연장하다   quill 깃, 가시
hitherto 지금까지   uninhabited 사람이 살지 않는
solicitude 염려, 근심   bask 쬐다, 일광욕하다

오늘의 내 기분은
행복으로 정할래.

지방직

해설 &
기출분석 REPORT

지방직 기출 POINT

Point 1 고난도 어휘보다는 필수 어휘 중심으로 출제되는 경향이 강하다.

Point 2 문법 영역은 기출과 동일한 포인트가 출제되었으나, 영작형 문법에서 우리말 해석과 불일치하는 선지가 종종 출제되고 있다.

Point 3 낯설고 생소한 소재보다는 보편타당한 독해 소재가 출제되고 있다.

2023년 지방직 시험 대비전략

"수험에서 가장 중요한 건 기출"

Point 1 전체 영역중 기존에 기출로 다뤄지지 않았던 영역은 없었다. 즉 기출문제를 정확하게 분석하는 훈련이 꼭 필요하다.

Point 2 선택지 소거법을 활용한 문제풀이가 키포인트가 될 수 있다. 독해 문제 풀이시 전체 선택지 상의 유사표현을 분류하는 전략적 훈련이 필요하다.

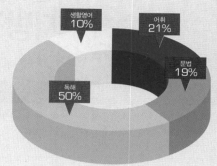

▲ 최근 7개년 평균 출제비중

생활영어 10%
어휘 21%
문법 19%
독해 50%

최근 7개년 출제경향 및 출제비중

연도	총평	어휘	문법	독해	생활영어
2022	**달라진 문항 비율, 난이도는 평이!** · 2021 지방직, 2022 국가직 시험보다 독해가 1문항 더 출제되었으나 크게 어려운 문항이 아니어서 체감 난이도는 높지 않았음 · 기출 문제의 핵심 요소가 반복 출제되어 기출을 정확히 분석했다면 고득점이 가능했음	20% (4문항)	20% (4문항)	50% (10문항)	10% (2문항)
2021	**정확하게, 빠르게!** · 같은 해 국가직 9급 시험에 비해 빈칸 문제가 다수 출제되어 논리적 사고를 묻는 것이 출제포인트 · 문장 간 분석에 정확성을 요하는 문장 출제로 수험생의 구분 실력에 따라 고득점 여부가 결정되는 유형	25% (5문항)	20% (4문항)	45% (9문항)	10% (2문항)
2020	**기본에 충실한, 성적에 충실한!** · 실제로 시험의 변별력은 실력보다는 생소한 소재나 어휘에서 결정되는 경우가 많은데, 2020년 지방직은 수험생들이 노력한 만큼 비례해서 성적이 나올 수 있는 시험이었음 · 문제 난이도가 평이한 만큼 훈련을 통해 실수를 줄이는 연습 필요	25% (5문항)	20% (4문항)	45% (9문항)	10% (2문항)
2019	**변별력이 확보된 고른 분포의 시험!** · 생활영어가 2문항 출제되어 시간 안배에 용이했음 · 독해 지문의 길이가 늘어나고 개수가 많아진 일치/불일치 문항으로 체감 난도 상승	20% (4문항)	15% (3문항)	55% (11문항)	10% (2문항)
2018	**기출문제에 대한 철저한 분석과 예상 필요!** · 기출문제의 응용이 계속 반복됨 · 어휘의 난도는 평이한 반면, 생활영어에서 관용표현의 범위가 넓어지고 있음	20% (4문항)	20% (4문항)	50% (10문항)	10% (2문항)
2017	**독해와 어휘가 다소 어려운 편!** · 고난도 어휘 다수 분포 · rack one's brain이라는 다소 넓은 범위의 관용표현 제시 · 기출문제에 기인한 문법 그대로 출제	20% (4문항)	20% (4문항)	50% (10문항)	10% (2문항)
2017 추가	**국가직에 비해 난이도 상승!** · 독해는 지문의 길이가 길지 않고 지문 내 단어와 구성도 평범함 · 문법과 어휘가 상대적으로 어렵게 출제됨 · convoluted, pass over라는 어휘가 매력적 오답으로 출제	20% (4문항)	20% (4문항)	50% (10문항)	10% (2문항)
2016	**실수만 하지 않는다면 고득점 가능!** · 전 영역 평이한 난이도 · put on은 대표 의미를 제외하고, 문맥상 필요한 어휘로 출제되었음 · 문맥상 어휘 추론 능력이 중요한 시험이었음	20% (4문항)	20% (4문항)	50% (10문항)	10% (2문항)

합격예상 체크

〈지방직 연도별 합격선〉

2022 합격기준!

맞힌 개수	/20문항	점수	/100점

➡ ☐ 합격 ☐ 불합격

취약영역 체크

문항	정답	영역	문항	정답	영역
①	②	어휘 > 유의어 찾기	11	③	독해 > Logical Reading > 배열
2	①	어휘 > 유의어 찾기	12	③	독해 > Logical Reading > 삽입
3	④	어휘 > 유의어 찾기	13	④	독해 > Macro Reading > 제목
4	④	어휘 > 빈칸 완성	14	③	독해 > Logical Reading > 삭제
5	②	문법 > 일치, 태	15	③	독해 > Micro Reading > 내용 일치/불일치
6	②	문법 > 일치	16	③	독해 > Micro Reading > 내용 일치/불일치
7	①	문법 > 부정사	17	①	독해 > Macro Reading > 요지
8	①	문법 > 시제	18	①	독해 > Logical Reading > 연결사
9	④	생활영어 > 회화/관용표현	19	②	독해 > Reading for Writing > 빈칸 구 완성
10	④	생활영어 > 회화/관용표현	20	②	독해 > Reading for Writing > 빈칸 구 완성

⬇ 영역별 틀린 개수로 취약영역을 확인하세요!

어휘	/4	문법	/4	독해	/10	생활영어	/2

➡ 나의 취약영역: _____

※ 해당 회차는 〈1초 합격예측 서비스〉의 데이터 누적 기간이 충분하지 않아 오답률, 선지 선택률 기재를 생략하였습니다.

---

1 어휘 > 유의어 찾기 답 ②

| 해석 | 학교 교사들은 학생들의 다른 능력 수준에 대처하기 위해 융통성이 있어야 한다.
① 강한
② 적응할 수 있는
③ 정직한
④ 열정적인

| 정답해설 | ② flexible은 '융통성 있는, 탄력적인'이라는 의미로, 선지 중에서는 adaptable(적응할 수 있는)과 의미가 가장 가깝다.

어휘
flexible 융통성 있는, 탄력적인   cope with ~에 대처[대응]하다
adaptable 적응할 수 있는

2 어휘 > 유의어 찾기 답 ①

| 해석 | 곡물 수확량은 달라지는데, 일부 지역에서는 향상되고 다른 곳에서는 감소한다.
① 변하다, 달라지다
② 감소하다
③ 확대되다
④ 포함하다

| 정답해설 | ① vary는 '다르다, 달라지다'라는 의미로, 가장 의미가 비슷한 것은 change(변하다, 달라지다)이다.

어휘
crop 곡물, 작물   yield 수확량, 산출량

3 어휘 > 유의어 찾기 답 ④

| 해석 | 나의 교육에 관하여 나는 누구에게도 열등하다고 느끼지 않는다.
① ~의 위험이 있는
② ~에도 불구하고
③ ~에 찬성하여
④ ~면에서는, ~에 관하여

| 정답해설 | ④ with respect to는 '~에 관하여'라는 의미이므로 문맥상 의미가 가장 가까운 것은 in terms of(~면에서는, ~에 관하여)이다.

어휘
inferior 열등한, 하위의   with respect to ~에 관하여
in terms of ~면에서는, ~에 관하여

4 어휘 > 빈칸 완성 답 ④

| 해석 | 때때로 우리는 다음 급여일 훨씬 이전에 돈을 ④ 다 써 버린다.
① ~로 변하다
② 다시 시작하다
③ ~을 참다, 견디다
④ ~을 다 써 버리다, ~이 바닥나다

| 정답해설 | ④ 문맥상 급여일 이전에 돈을 '다 써 버리는 것'이 가장 자연스러우므로, 정답은 run out of(~을 다 써 버리다, ~이 바닥나다)이다.

어휘

turn into ~로 변하다   put up with ~을 참다, 견디다
run out of ~을 다 써 버리다, ~이 바닥나다

---

5   문법 > 일치, 태   답 ②

| 해석 | ① 그는 나에게 왜 매일같이 계속해서 돌아오는지 물었다.
② 아이들이 일 년 내내 원했던 장난감들이 최근 버려졌다.
③ 그녀는 항상 도움을 줄 준비가 되어 있는 사람이다.
④ 곤충들은 종종 우리에게는 분명치 않은 냄새에 이끌린다.

| 정답해설 | ② 주어는 복수형 명사 Toys이고 children wanted all year long은 주어를 수식하는 목적격 관계대명사절이므로, has는 have가 되어야 하며, Toys는 discard(버리다, 포기하다, 폐기하다)되는 대상이므로 수동형이 되어야 알맞다. 따라서 ②는 Toys children wanted all year long have recently been discarded.가 되어야 옳다.

| 오답해설 | ① 의문사 why가 이끄는 명사절이 ask의 직접목적어로 왔으므로 간접의문 어순인 「의문사 + 주어 + 동사」가 올바르게 사용되었다. 또한 keep은 동명사를 목적어로 취하는 동사로 「keep -ing」는 '계속 ~하다'라는 표현이다.
③ 선행사가 사람일 때는 관계대명사 who를 사용한다. 「be ready to + 동사원형」은 '~할 준비가 되어 있다'라는 뜻이며 lend[give] a hand는 '도움을 주다'라는 표현으로 여기서 hand는 비유적으로 '도움, 도움의 손길'을 의미한다.
④ 곤충은 이끌리는 객체이므로 수동태가 알맞게 사용되었다. 또한 빈도부사 often은 be동사 뒤에 오는 것이 어법상 알맞다. scents는 사물 명사이므로 관계대명사 that 또는 which가 이끄는 관계사절로 수식할 수 있다.

| 더 알아보기 | **목적격 관계대명사의 생략**

> 문장의 주어를 수식하는 관계사절 중 목적격 관계대명사는 생략이 가능하다. 문장에서 「명사[선행사] + 명사[주어] + 동사[서술어] ~」의 형태가 제시되었을 때는 목적격 관계대명사가 생략되었을 수 있으므로 주의해서 해석해야 하며, 문장의 주어를 수식하는 경우 주어-동사의 수 일치에 주의해야 한다.

어휘

discard 버리다, 포기하다, 폐기하다   lend a hand 도움을 주다
scent 냄새, 향기   obvious 분명한, 명백한

---

6   문법 > 일치   답 ②

| 해석 | ① 당신은 종이의 양면에 써도 된다.
② 나의 집은 내게 안전함, 따뜻함, 그리고 사랑의 느낌을 준다.
③ 자동차 사고의 수가 증가하고 있다.
④ 네가 무슨 일을 하려는지 내가 알아차렸더라면, 나는 너를 말렸을 거야.

| 정답해설 | ② 등위접속사 and는 같은 품사의 단어를 연결해야 하므로 명사를 나열하는 중간에 형용사인 warm이 쓰인 것은 옳지 않다. 따라서 security, warmth, and love가 되어야 옳다.

| 오답해설 | ① both는 가산명사의 복수형 앞에 사용되므로, both sides는 알맞은 표현이다.
③ 주어가 the number로 단수이므로 동사는 단수형 is가 알맞게 사용되었다.
④ 가정법 과거완료는 「If + S + had p.p.~, S + 조동사 과거형 + have p.p. …」로 쓰는데, If가 생략되면 주어, 동사가 도치되어 「Had + S + p.p. ~」가 된다. 따라서 Had I realized ~는 옳게 사용된 것이다. 또한 what절이 realized의 목적어로 쓰인 간접의문문이므로 「의문사 + 주어 + 동사」의 어순으로 알맞게 쓰였다.

어휘

on the rise 증가하고 있는   intend 의도하다, 계획하다

---

7   문법 > 부정사   답 ①

| 정답해설 | ① afford는 '~할 여유가 있다, ~할 형편이 되다'라는 뜻으로, I can afford ~는 '나는 ~할 여유가 있다[형편이 된다]'라는 뜻이다. 주어진 우리말이 '~할 수 없다'라는 부정형이므로 I can't afford로 고쳐야 옳다.

| 오답해설 | ② 해당 문장에서 fade는 자동사로 쓰였으며 fade from은 '~에서 사라지다, ~에서 희미해지다'라는 의미로 옳게 쓰였다.
③ 「have no alternative but to + 동사원형」은 '~ 외에는 대안이 없다, ~할 수밖에 없다'라는 의미의 관용표현으로, 「have no choice but to + 동사원형」과 유사한 표현이다.
④ 「aim + to부정사」는 '~할 작정이다, ~하는 것을 목표로 하다'라는 의미의 표현이며, 시간의 경과를 나타내어 '~ 후에'라고 말할 때는 전치사 in을 쓸 수 있다.

어휘

afford ~할 여유가 있다, 형편이 되다
fade 사라지다, 흐려지다   alternative 대안
resign 사임하다   aim 목표하다, 작정이다

---

8   문법 > 시제   답 ①

| 정답해설 | ① 부정어가 문두에 사용되면 뒤따라오는 문장의 어순이 의문문 어순으로 도치된다. '~하자마자 …했다'는 「No sooner had + S + p.p. ~ than + S + 과거 동사 …」의 형태로 쓰며 시제와 어순에 유의해야 한다. 따라서 ①은 No sooner had I finished the meal than I started feeling hungry again.이 되어야 옳다.

| 오답해설 | ② '조만간'은 sooner or later라고 하며 미래의 일이므로 조동사 will을 사용했다.
③ 「A is to B what C is to D」는 'A와 B의 관계는 C와 D의 관계와 같다'라는 의미의 표현이다.
④ 「end up -ing」는 '결국 ~하게 되다'라는 표현으로 알맞게 사용되었다.

| **더 알아보기** | '～하자마자' 관용표현

～하자마자		～했다
주어 + had no sooner p.p. ～	than	주어 + 과거 동사 …
No sooner had + 주어 + p.p. ～		

1. 어순 주의: 부정부사 no sooner가 문두에 올 경우, 뒤따라오는 절은 의문문 어순으로 도치된다.
2. 접속사 주의: 주절과 종속절을 연결해 주는 접속사는 than을 사용해야 한다.
3. 시제 주의: no sooner를 포함한 주절의 시제가 과거완료이면, than이 이끄는 종속절의 시제는 과거시제이어야 한다.

어휘

sooner or later 조만간　　　　　end up -ing 결국 ～하게 되다

---

9 생활영어 > 회화/관용표현 답 ④

| **해석** | ① A: 나는 이 신문이 독선적이 아니어서 좋아.
　　 B: 그것이 그게 가장 발행 부수가 가장 많은 이유야.
② A: 그렇게 잘 차려입은 좋은 이유라도 있니?
　　 B: 응, 오늘 중요한 구직 면접이 있어.
③ A: 연습 중에는 공을 똑바로 칠 수 있는데, 게임 중에는 안돼.
　　 B: 나한테는 늘 일어나는 일이야.
④ A: 캔버스에 그리고 싶은 특별한 주제가 있니?
　　 B: 나는 고등학교에 다닐 때, 역사를 잘하지 못했어.

| **정답해설** | ④ 캔버스에 그리고 싶은 '주제(subject)'에 관해 묻는 질문에 고등학교 시절 역사를 잘하지 못했다고 '과목(subject)'에 대해 답하는 것은 대화의 흐름상 어색하다.

어휘

opinionated 독선적인, 독단적인　　　circulation 발행(부수); 유통

---

10 생활영어 > 회화/관용표현 답 ④

| **해석** | A: 야! 지리 시험 어땠어?
B: 그럭저럭, 고마워. 난 그저 끝난 것이 기쁠 따름이야! 너는 어때? 과학 시험 어땠어?
A: 오, 정말 잘 봤어. ④ 그것을 도와준 것에 대해서는 고맙다는 말로는 부족해. 내가 너에게 한턱내야겠어.
B: 괜찮아. 그러면, 다음 주에 예정된 수학 시험 준비하고 싶어?
A: 물론이지. 같이 공부하자.
B: 좋아. 나중에 봐.
① 이거 때문에 자책해도 소용없어
② 여기서 널 볼 줄은 전혀 생각 못 했어
③ 사실, 우린 매우 실망했어
④ 그것을 도와준 것에 대해서는 고맙다는 말로는 부족해

| **정답해설** | ④ 시험 결과에 관한 대화로, A가 빈칸의 말을 한 후, B에게 '한턱낸다'고 말하고 있으므로 A가 B에게 고마워하고 있음을 유추할 수 있다.

어휘

geography 지리(학)　　　　　owe 빚지다, 신세지다
treat 대접, 한턱　　　　　　beat oneself up 자책하다

---

11 독해 > Logical Reading > 배열 답 ③

| **해석** | 눈이 보이지 않는 분들에게, 우편물을 분류하거나 빨래 더미를 세탁하는 것과 같은 일상적인 일들은 도전 과제를 줍니다.
(B) 하지만 만약에 그분들이 볼 수 있는 누군가의 눈을 "빌릴" 수 있다면 어떨까요?
(A) 그것이 바로 수천 명의 사용자가 스마트폰이나 Aira 전매특허의 안경을 이용해 상시 대기 직원(on-demand agent)에게 자신들의 주변 환경에 대한 라이브 비디오 송출을 가능하게 해 주는 신규 서비스인 Aira가 지지하는 생각입니다.
(C) 연중무휴 연결 가능한 Aira의 직원들은, 그러면 질문에 답하거나, 물체에 관해 설명하거나, 한 장소로 사용자를 안내할 수 있습니다.

| **정답해설** | ③ (A)와 (C)에는 Aira가 공통적으로 언급되며, (A)의 내용을 통해 Aira는 안경을 이용해 도움을 제공하는 것임을 알 수 있다. 즉, Aira는 (B)에서 언급한 눈을 빌려주는 것에 대한 해결책이므로 (B)가 맨 먼저 와야 한다. (B)의 they는 주어진 문장의 people who are blind를 가리킨다. 이어서 (B)에서 언급한 '다른 사람들의 눈을 빌린다'는 개념을 That's the thinking ～이라고 구체적으로 설명해 주는 (A)가 연결되고, 마지막으로 (A)에서 직원과 연결되어 라이브 비디오를 송출한 후의 상황을 then으로 연결하여 설명하는 (C)가 오는 것이 옳다. 그리고 (A)에서 최초 제시된 정보인 an on-demand agent를(부정관사 사용) (C)에서는 정관사를 사용하여 The Aira agents로 구체화하고 있는 것을 통해서도 (A)가 (C) 앞에 오는 것이 적절함을 알 수 있다.

| **오답해설** | ①② (A)의 thinking이 주어진 문장 전체를 가리킨다고 볼 여지도 있으나, 그렇다면 (B)가 들어갈 위치가 어색해진다. (B)의 they는 주어진 문장의 people who are blind를 가리키고 있는 것이 명백하므로, 가장 적절한 위치는 (B)가 주어진 문장에 바로 이어지는 것이다.
④ (C)의 then은 선후 관계를 이어 주는 연결사인데, 주어진 글과 (C)는 선후 관계가 아니므로, (C)가 주어진 문장에 바로 이어지는 것은 부자연스럽다.

어휘

sort 분류하다, 구분하다　　　　　present 주다, 수여하다
surroundings 환경　　　　　　　on-demand 요구가 있으면 즉시
proprietary 전매특허의, 소유주의

---

12 독해 > Logical Reading > 삽입 답 ③

| **해석** | 비유는 두 사물이 꽤 근본적인 많은 면에서 유사하다고 주장되는 수사적 표현이다. 그것들의 구조, 그것들의 부분과의 관계, 또는 그것들이 수행하는 필수 목적은 유사하지만, 그 두 사물은 또한 전혀 다르다. 장미와 카네이션은 비유적이지 않다. 그것들은 둘 다 줄기와 잎이 있고 둘 다 붉은 색일 수도 있다. 그러나 그것들은 이러한 특징들을 같은 방식으로 보여 준다. 그것들은 동일한 속(屬)이다. ③ 하지만, 심장을 펌프에 비유하는 것은 진정한 비유이다. 이것들은 서로 전혀 다른 것들이지만, 중요한 특징들, 즉, 기계 장치, 판막(밸브) 소지, 압력 증감 능력, 그리고 액체를 흐르게 하는 능력을 공유한다. 그리고 심장과 펌프는 이러한 특징들을 다른 방식으로 그리고 다른 상황에서 보여 준다.

| 정답해설 | ③ 주어진 문장의 역접 연결사 however로 보아 주어진 문장과 대조되는 내용이 앞서 제시될 것임을 알 수 있다. ③ 이전에서는 구조도 같고 같은 속에 속하며 다른 구석이 전혀 없는 장미와 카네이션을 예로 들어 'analogy(비유)'가 아님을 서술하고 있는데, ③ 이후에서는 '이것들은 서로 전혀 다른 것들이지만 중요한 특징들을 공유한다'라고 설명하면서 다른 점도 있고 공통점도 있는 것들에 대해 언급하고 있다. 이를 통해서 앞서 서술하고 있는 '장미와 카네이션'의 경우와는 대조적인 흐름으로 글을 이어나가고 있음을 파악할 수 있다. 따라서 ③의 자리에 역접 연결사를 포함한 주어진 문장이 들어가 글의 흐름을 전환해 주는 것이 가장 적절하다.

| 오답해설 | ①② 장미와 카네이션에 관한 내용이 이어지므로 역접 연결사가 있는 주어진 문장이 빈칸에 들어가는 것은 부적절하다.
④ 전후 내용이 모두 심장과 펌프의 비유에 대한 설명이므로 중간에 역접 연결사로 이어지는 문장이 들어가는 것은 문맥상 부자연스럽다.

어휘

genuine 진정한, 진짜의
figure of speech 수사적 표현, 비유적 표현
assert 주장하다, 단언하다
fundamental 근본적인, 핵심적인
stem 줄기
quality 특징
disparate 서로 전혀 다른, 이질적인
apparatus 기관; 기구, 장치
fluid 액체

analogy 비유
respect 면, 점, 사항
analogous 유사한, 비유적인
exhibit 보이다, 드러내다
genus (생물의) 속(屬), 종류
possession 소유, 소지
context 전후 사정, 맥락

---

13 독해 > Macro Reading > 제목 　　　　답 ④

| 해석 | 효율성이 최적화될 수 있는 분야 중 하나는 노동계로, 주어진 시간에 한 직원이 처리하는 업무(생산되는 제품, 서비스를 받는 고객)의 양으로 정의되는, 개개인의 생산성 향상을 통해 그러할 수 있다. 최적의 성과를 보장하기 위해 당신이 반드시 적절한 설비, 환경, 그리고 훈련에 투자하는 것 외에도, 당신은 직원들이 '멀티태스킹'이라는 현대판 에너지 소모를 종식시키도록 격려함으로써 생산성을 향상시킬 수 있다. 연구들은 당신이 동시에 다른 프로젝트들을 작업하려고 할 때 한 가지 일을 끝마치는 데 25~40% 더 시간이 걸린다는 것을 보여 준다. 컨설팅 기업 The Energy Project의 사업 개발 부사장인 Andrew Deutscher는 더 생산적이 되려면 "중단하지 말고, 지속적인 기간 동안 한 가지 일을 하라"라고 말한다.
① 인생에서 더 많은 선택지를 만드는 방법
② 일상적 신체 능력을 향상시키는 방법
③ 멀티태스킹이 더 나은 효율성에 대한 답이다
④ 더 큰 효율성을 위해 한 번에 한 가지 일을 하라

| 정답해설 | ④ 효율성에 관한 글로, 마지막 문장 To be more productive, says Andrew Deutscher, ~ for a sustained period of time.에 언급된 컨설팅 기업 The Energy Project의 사업 개발 부사장인 Andrew Deutscher의 말, '더 생산적이 되려면 "중단하지 말고, 지속적인 기간 동안 한 가지 일을 하라"'를 통해 효율성을 위해서는 한 번에 한 가지 일을 하는 것을 권하고 있다는 것을 알 수 있다.

| 오답해설 | ① 업무에서 효율성을 높이는 법에 대한 내용이므로, 인생에서 더 많은 선택지를 만드는 방법은 제목으로 적절하지 않다.
② 신체적 능력에 관해서는 본문에서 언급되지 않는다.
③ 본문의 주장과 반대되는 내용이므로 오답이다.

어휘

efficiency 효율성
workforce 노동계; 노동력
define 정의하다
invest 투자하다
optimal 최적의
drain (많은 시간·돈 등을) 고갈시키는[잡아먹는] 것
multitasking 멀티태스킹, 동시에 여러 가지 일을 하는 것
simultaneously 동시에
vice president 부사장, 부회장
uninterrupted 연속된, 중단되지 않는
sustained 지속적인

optimize 최적화하다
productivity 생산성
in addition to ~에 더하여, ~ 외에
equipment 설비
staffer 직원

productive 생산적인
firm 회사, 기업

enhance 향상시키다, 강화하다

---

14 독해 > Logical Reading > 삭제 　　　　답 ③

| 해석 | 좋은 논쟁을 하는 기술은 인생에서 중요하다. 그러나 그것은 부모들이 자식들에게 거의 가르치지 않는 기술이다. 우리는 아이들에게 안정적인 가정을 제공하길 원하므로, 형제자매들의 다툼을 멈추게 하고, 우리 자신의 논쟁도 비밀리에 한다. 그러나 만일 아이들이 의견 불일치에 전혀 노출되지 않는다면, 우리는 결국 그들의 창의성을 제한하게 될지도 모른다. ③ <u>아이들은 그들이 평화로운 환경에서 많은 칭찬과 격려를 받으며 자유롭게 브레인스토밍을 할 때 가장 창의적이다.</u> 고도로 창의적인 사람들은 종종 긴장감이 가득한 집안에서 성장한 것으로 밝혀진다. 그들은 주먹다짐이나 개인적인 모욕이 아니라 진정한 의견 불일치에 둘러싸여 있다. 30대 초반의 성인이 상상한 이야기를 써 보라고 요청받았을 때, 가장 창의적인 이야기들은 25년 전 가장 심한 갈등을 겪은 부모를 가진 이들에게서 나왔다.

| 정답해설 | ③ 의견이 불일치하고 긴장감이 가득한 상황에서 자란 아이들이 더 창의적이 된다는 것이 글의 요지이다. 그런데 ③에서는 아이들이 평화로운 환경에서 칭찬과 격려에 많이 노출될 때 아이들이 가장 창의적이 된다고 진술하고 있으므로, 전체 글의 주장과는 다른 의견이다.

| 오답해설 | ①②④ 모두 문맥상 갈등이 창의성에 도움이 된다는 내용이므로 글의 흐름에 부합한다.

어휘

critical 중요한
sibling 형제자매
behind closed doors 비밀리에
disagreement 불화, 의견 불일치
fistfight 주먹다짐
imaginative 상상력이 풍부한, 창의적인
conflict 갈등

stable 안정적인
quarrel 다투다, 언쟁하다
expose 노출시키다
tension 긴장, 갈등
insult 모욕

---

15 독해 > Micro Reading > 내용일치/불일치 　　　　답 ③

| 해석 | Christopher Nolan은 영어권에서 꽤 유명한 아일랜드의 작가이다. 태어날 때부터 뇌 손상을 입은 Nolan은 신체 근육을 거의 통제할 수 없었는데, 음식을 삼키는 데 어려움을 겪을 정도였다. 그는 혼자서 똑바로 앉아 있을 수 없었기 때문에 휠체어에 고정끈으로 고정되어 있어야 했다. Nolan은

알아들을 수 있는 말소리를 낼 수 없었다. 그러나 다행히도, 그의 뇌 손상은 지능은 손상되지 않고 청각은 정상인 정도였다. 그 결과, 그는 어린아이일 때, 말을 이해하는 것을 배웠다. 그러나 그가 10살이 지난 후, 그리고 그가 읽는 것을 배운 후 여러 해가 지나서야 그의 첫 번째 말을 표현할 수 있는 수단이 그에게 주어졌다. 그는 글자를 가리킬 수 있도록 머리에 부착된 막대를 이용해 이것을 했다. 그가 아직 10대일 때 시와 단편 소설 전집인 『Dam-Burst of Dreams』를 낸 것은 바로 한 글자 한 글자 이 '유니콘' 방식을 통한 것이었다.

| 정답해설 | ③ 본문 중반 Fortunately, though, his brain damage was such that Nolan's intelligence was undamaged and his hearing was normal.에서 그의 뇌 손상은 지능은 손상되지 않고 청각은 정상인 정도였다고 했으므로 본문 내용과 일치하지 않는다.

| 오답해설 | ① 두 번째 문장 맨 앞 Brain damaged since birth, ~에서 태어날 때부터 뇌 손상을 입었다고 했으므로 본문 내용과 일치함을 알 수 있다.
② 두 번째 문장 뒷부분 even to the extent of having difficulty in swallowing food를 보면 Nolan의 뇌 손상이 음식을 삼키는 데 어려움을 겪을 정도였다고 했으므로 본문 내용과 일치함을 알 수 있다.
④ 마지막 문장에서 10대일 때 시와 단편 소설 전집을 냈다고 진술하고 있다.

어휘

renowned 유명한	to the extent of ~할 정도까지
swallow 삼키다	
strap (끈으로) 묶다, 고정끈으로 고정하다	
utter 말하다	recognizable 인식 가능한
means 수단	attach 붙이다, 부착하다

---

16 독해 > Micro Reading > 내용일치/불일치   답 ③

| 해석 | 많은 가톨릭 국가에서, 아이들은 종종 성인의 이름을 따서 이름이 지어진다. 실제로, 몇몇 신부들은 부모들이 아이들의 이름을 드라마 배우나 축구 선수 이름을 따라 짓도록 허락하지 않을 것이다. 개신교 국가들은 이에 대해 더 자유롭다. 그러나 노르웨이에서 Adolf와 같은 특정한 이름들은 완전히 금기된다. 아프리카와 같이 유아 사망률이 매우 높은 국가들에서 부족들은 아이들이 다섯 살이 될 때에서야 겨우 이름을 지어 주는데, 이는 그들의 생존율이 증가하는 나이이다. 그때까지, 그들은 연령으로 불려진다. 많은 극동 국가들은 아이들에게 아이의 탄생 상황이나 아이에 대한 부모의 기대와 희망을 어떤 방식으로 묘사하는 특이한 이름을 준다. 일부 호주 원주민들은 자신들의 지혜, 창의력 또는 결단을 어떻게든 증명하는 중요한 경험의 결과로서 일생 동안 자신들의 이름을 계속 바꿀 수 있다. 예를 들어, 만일 어느 날, 그들 중 한 명이 춤을 매우 잘 춘다면, 그 또는 그녀는 자신의 이름을 '최고의 춤꾼' 또는 '가벼운 발'로 개명할 결심을 할지도 모른다.
① 많은 가톨릭 국가에서 아이들은 자주 성인의 이름을 따 이름 지어진다.
② 일부 아프리카 아이들은 5살이 될 때까지 이름이 지어지지 않는다.
③ 호주 원주민 문화에서 이름을 바꾸는 것은 결코 용납되지 않는다.
④ 다양한 문화권들은 다른 방식으로 아이들의 이름을 짓는다.

| 정답해설 | ③ 본문 후반부 Some Australian aborigines can keep changing their name throughout their life ~에서 일부 호주 원주민들은 일생 동안 자신들의 이름을 계속 바꿀 수 있다고 언급했으므로, 본문 내용과 일치하지 않는다.

| 오답해설 | ① 첫 번째 문장에서 글의 내용과 일치함을 확인할 수 있다.
② 세 번째 문장에서 언급되는 내용이다.
④ 글 전체를 아우르는 내용이므로 글의 내용과 일치한다고 볼 수 있다.

어휘

saint 성인	soap opera 드라마
protestant 개신교	ban 금지하다
infant 유아	mortality 사망률
refer 칭하다, 부르다	circumstance 상황, 환경
aborigine (특히 호주의) 원주민, 토착민	
determination 결심, 투지	unacceptable 받아들일 수 없는
various 다양한	

---

17 독해 > Macro Reading > 요지   답 ①

| 해석 | 젊은이들이 "hippie(히피)" 아니면 "straight(단정한)" 패션으로 옷을 입는 경향이 있던 1970년대 초반에 실시된 한 연구에서, 실험자들은 히피 또는 단정한 복장을 한 후, 전화를 걸 1다임짜리 동전을 캠퍼스에 있는 대학생들에게 요청했다. 실험자가 학생과 동일한 방식의 옷을 입었을 때, 요청은 그 사례의 3분의 2가 넘게 받아들여졌다. 학생과 요청자가 다르게 옷을 입었을 때, 동전은 절반 미만으로 제공되었다. 또 다른 실험은 비슷한 타인에게 우리의 긍정적인 반응이 얼마나 자동적일 수 있는지를 보여 주었다. 반전 시위 행진 참가자들은 비슷하게 옷을 입은 요청자들의 탄원서에 서명하고, 그것을 먼저 읽지도 않고 그렇게 할 가능성이 높은 것으로 밝혀졌다.
① 사람들은 자신처럼 옷을 입은 사람들을 도와줄 가능성이 더 높다.
② 격식을 차려 입는 것은 탄원서에 서명할 가능성을 높인다.
③ 전화를 하는 것은 다른 학생들과 교제하는 효과적인 방식이다.
④ 1970년대 초반 일부 대학생들은 자신들의 독특한 패션으로 추앙받았다.

| 정답해설 | ① 본문 초반 전화를 걸 동전을 빌리는 실험과 본문 후반 탄원서에 서명을 받는 실험에서 자신과 비슷한 복장을 한 사람들에게 응답자들이 더욱 긍정적으로 반응했다는 결과를 제시하고 있다. 따라서 전체 글의 요지로 가장 적절한 것은 ①이다.

| 오답해설 | ② 탄원서에 서명하는 것에 대한 실험은 두 번째 실험에만 국한된 것이며, 결정적으로 격식을 차려 옷을 입는 것과 탄원서에 서명하는 것의 관련성에 대해서는 본문에서 언급되지 않았다.
③ 다른 학생들과 교제하는 방법에 관한 글이 아니므로 글의 요지로 적절하지 않다.
④ 본문 초반에서 1970년대의 패션에 관해 언급되기는 하지만, 그 패션에 대한 다른 이들의 평가는 언급되지 않았으므로 오답이다.

어휘

don 입다	attire 의복
dime 다임(미국·캐나다의 10센트짜리 동전)	
grant 승인하다	instance 예, 사례
dissimilarly 다르게	
marcher (시위를 위한) 가두 행진 참가자	
demonstration 시위, 데모	petition 탄원서
formally 예의 바르게; 형식상; 정식으로	
socialize 사회화하다, 사귀다	admire 존경하다, 찬양하다
unique 독특한, 특이한	

18 독해 > Logical Reading > 연결사　　답 ①

| 해석 | 지속 시간은 빈도와 반비례 관계를 공유한다. 만일 당신이 친구를 자주 본다면, 만남의 지속 시간은 더 짧아질 것이다. 반대로, 만일 당신이 친구를 그다지 자주 보지 않는다면, 당신의 방문 지속 시간은 보통 상당히 증가할 것이다. (A) 예를 들어, 만일 당신이 친구를 매일 만나면, 사건들이 전개됨에 따라 무슨 일이 일어나고 있는지 따라잡을 수 있기 때문에 당신의 방문 지속 시간은 줄 수 있다. 그러나 만일 당신이 친구를 1년에 2번 본다면, 방문 지속 시간은 더 늘 것이다. 오랜 기간 동안 보지 못한 친구와 식당에서 저녁 식사를 하던 때를 돌이켜 생각해 보라. 당신들은 아마도 서로의 삶을 따라잡는 데 몇 시간을 보냈을 것이다. 만일 당신이 그 사람을 정기적으로 만난다면, 그와 같은 저녁 식사의 지속 시간은 상당히 짧아질 것이다. (B) 반대로, 연인 관계에서는 빈도와 지속 시간이 매우 높은데, 커플, 특히 최근에 사귄 커플은 서로와 가능한 한 많은 시간을 보내고 싶어 하기 때문이다. 관계의 강도도 또한 매우 높을 것이다.

|　　　(A)　　　　　　(B)
① 　　예를 들어　　　　　반대로
② 　그럼에도 불구하고　　　게다가
③ 　　그러므로　　　　　결과적으로
④ 　같은 방법으로　　　　그래서

| 정답해설 | ① (A) 첫 번째 문장이 글 전체의 주제로서, '지속 시간'과 '빈도'의 관계가 반비례 관계임을 명시하고 있다. 이후 두 번째와 세 번째 문장에서 제시하고 있는 일반적인 frequency(빈도) 즉, frequently와 not ~ very often을 (A)의 빈칸 이후에 구체적으로 every day와 twice a year로 상세화하여 예시하고 있으므로, 빈칸에는 예시를 나타내는 For example(예를 들어)이 들어가는 것이 가장 적절하다.

(B) 빈칸 앞 부분에서 '지속 시간'과 '빈도'가 반비례하는 경우를 예시하고 있으나 빈칸 (B) 이후에는 연인 관계에서는 '빈도'와 '지속 시간'이 매우 높다고 서술하고 있다. 즉, 앞서 제시한 내용과 대조적인 상황인 것을 알 수 있으므로, 빈칸에는 역접 연결사 Conversely(반대로)가 가장 적절하다.

| 오답해설 | ② (A) 전후가 양보 관계가 아니므로 빈칸에 Nonetheless는 어색하다.
③④ (B) 이후 내용이 이전 내용의 결과가 아니므로 As a result, Thus는 빈칸에 부적절하다.

어휘

duration (지속) 기간	inverse 역의, 반대의
frequency 빈도	encounter 만남
conversely 역으로, 반대로	significantly 대단히, 상당히
keep up with ~을 따라잡다, 이해하다	
unfold 전개하다; 일어나다; 진행되다	
catch up on (밀린 일을) 보충하다[따라잡다]	
considerably 상당히	on a regular basis 정기적으로
mint 만들다	intensity 격렬함, 강렬함, 강도

19 독해 > Reading for Writing > 빈칸 구 완성　　답 ②

| 해석 | 가장 흔히 사용되는 선전 기술 중 하나는 선전자의 견해가 보통 사람의 견해를 반영하고 그 또는 그녀는 그들의 최상의 이익을 위해 일하고 있다고 대중을 설득하는 것이다. 육체 노동자 청중에게 연설하는 정치인은 소매를 걷고, 넥타이를 풀고, 그 무리의 특정한 관용구를 사용하려고 시도

할 것이다. 그는 심지어 자신이 "그저 그들 중 한 명"이라는 인상을 주기 위해 고의로 언어를 틀리게 사용할지도 모른다. 또한 이 기술은 보통 정치인의 견해가 연설을 듣는 군중의 견해와 동일하다는 인상을 주기 위해 미사여구를 사용한다. 노조 지도자들, 사업가들, 각료들, 교육자들, 그리고 광고업자들은 ② 우리 자신과 같은 그저 평범한 사람들로 보임으로써 우리의 신뢰를 얻기 위해 이 기술을 사용해 왔다.

① 미사여구를 넘어선
② 우리 자신과 같은 그저 평범한 사람들
③ 남들과는 다른 무언가
④ 대중들보다 더 교육받은

| 정답해설 | ② 지도자 집단의 선전 기술에 관한 글이다. 본문에서는 지도자 집단의 인물들이 그들이 대변하고자 하는 보통의 대중들과 같아 보이고자 하는 것이 가장 흔히 사용되는 선전 기술(propaganda technique) 중 하나라고 말한다. 본문 마지막 문장은 그들이 이러한 기술을 사용하는 목적을 다시 한 번 정리한 문장이므로 그들이 우리 자신과 같은 평범한 사람들로 보이기 위해 기술을 사용한다는 표현이 들어가는 것이 문맥상 가장 자연스럽다.

| 오답해설 | ① glittering generalities(미사여구)는 지도자 집단들이 선전 기술의 일환으로 사용하는 기법 중 하나일 뿐이며, 그 지도자 집단들이 자신들을 나타내고자 하는 표현들은 아니므로 오답이다.
③④ 본문 내용과 달리 자신들을 대중과는 다르게 혹은 더 낮게 보이게 한다는 내용이 되므로 문맥상 빈칸에 적절하지 않다.

| 더 알아보기 | Glittering Generality (미사여구)

> 어떤 인물, 제품, 또는 주장을 돋보이도록 하기 위해 대중으로부터 호의적인 반응을 얻어낼 수 있는 단어들을 사용하는 것으로 가장 보편적인 '선전 기술(Propaganda Technique)' 중 하나이다.

어휘

propaganda 선전	convince 설득하다
propagandist 선전자	reflect 반영하다; 반사하다
blue-collar 블루칼라[육체 노동자]의	
idiom 관용구	incorrectly 틀리게, 부정확하게
impression 인상	folk 사람들, 민중
employ 쓰다, 채택하다	
glittering generality 화려한 추상어, 미사여구	
address 연설하다	minister 각료, 장관; 성직자
confidence 신뢰	appear ~처럼 보이다
plain 보통의, 평범한	

20 독해 > Reading for Writing > 빈칸 구 완성　　답 ②

| 해석 | 롤러코스터는 트랙의 첫 번째 오르막 언덕을 올라가면서 위치 에너지를 축적하고 있다. 땅 위로 더 높이 올라갈수록, 중력의 인력은 더 강해질 것이다. 롤러코스터가 오르막 언덕의 꼭대기에 이르렀다. 하강을 시작할 때, 그것의 위치 에너지는 운동 에너지, 즉 움직임의 에너지가 된다. 흔한 오해는 롤러코스터가 트랙을 따라 가면서 에너지를 소실한다는 것이다. 그러나, 에너지 보존 법칙이라고 불리는 주요한 물리학 법칙은 에너지는 절대로 생성되거나 파괴될 수 없다는 것이다. 그것은 그저 하나의 형태에서 또 다른 것으로 바뀌는 것이다. 트랙이 오르막으로 바뀌어 다시 올라갈 때마다, 차체의 운동량 — 운동 에너지 — 은 그것을 위로 데려갈 것이고, 이것이 위치 에너지를 축적하고, 롤러코스터는 반복적으로 위치 에너지를 운동 에너

지로 전환하고 다시 반대로 한다. 탑승의 마지막 구간에서, 롤러코스터 차체는 두 개의 표면 사이에 ② 마찰 저항을 생성하는 브레이크 장치에 의해 속도를 줄인다. 이 운동이 그것들을 뜨겁게 만드는데, 이는 속도를 줄이는 동안 운동 에너지가 열 에너지로 전환된다는 것을 의미한다. 탑승객들은 롤러코스터가 트랙의 끝에서 에너지를 잃는다고 잘못 생각할지도 모르지만, 에너지는 단지 다른 형태에서 다른 형태로 바뀔 뿐이다.

① 중력   ② 마찰 저항
③ 진공   ④ 가속

| 정답해설 | ② 롤러코스터가 작동할 때 발생하는 에너지에 관해 설명하는 글이다. 빈칸에는 롤러코스터가 멈추는 단계에서 브레이크 장치가 작동할 때 두 개의 표면 사이에 발생하는 에너지를 설명하는 표현이 들어가야 한다. 빈칸 이후의 문장인 This motion makes them hot ~을 통해서 두 개의 표면 사이에 열 에너지를 만드는 것이 'friction(마찰 저항)'임을 유추할 수 있다.

어휘

potential energy 위치 에너지   pull 인력, 당기는 힘
gravity 중력
crest 꼭대기에 이르다, 최고조에 달하다
descent 하강, 내려오기   kinetic energy 운동 에너지
misperception 오해, 오인   conservation 보존
momentum 운동량   convert 전환하다
mechanism 기계 장치   surface 표면
motion 운동   mistakenly 잘못하여, 실수로
friction 마찰, 마찰 저항   vacuum 진공
acceleration 가속, 가속도

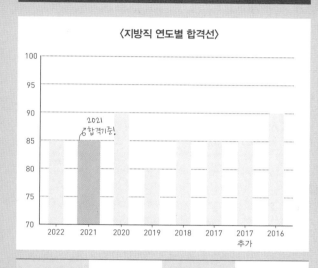

취약영역 체크

문항	정답	영역	문항	정답	영역
①	④	어휘 > 유의어 찾기	11	①	생활영어 > 회화/관용표현
2	③	어휘 > 빈칸 완성	12	③	생활영어 > 회화/관용표현
3	①	어휘 > 빈칸 완성	13	②	독해 > Micro Reading > 내용 일치/불일치
4	②	어휘 > 빈칸 완성	14	②	독해 > Logical Reading > 삭제
5	④	어휘 > 유의어 찾기	15	③	문법 > 동사
6	④	문법 > 동사	16	②	독해 > Reading for Writing > 빈칸 구 완성
7	②	문법 > 동사	17	④	독해 > Reading for Writing > 빈칸 구 완성
8	②	문법 > 부정사	18	①	독해 > Macro Reading > 요지
9	④	독해 > Macro Reading > 제목	19	③	독해 > Logical Reading > 연결사
10	①	독해 > Logical Reading > 배열	20	②	독해 > Logical Reading > 삽입

⬇ 영역별 틀린 개수로 취약영역을 확인하세요!

어휘	/5	문법	/4	독해	/9	생활영어	/2

➡ 나의 취약영역: _____

〈지방직 연도별 합격선〉

2021 ⑥합격기준!

맞힌 개수	/20문항	점수	/100점

➡ □ 합격 □ 불합격

※ [정답해설]과 [오답해설] 선지의 50% 표시는 〈1초 합격예측 서비스〉를 통해 수집된 선지 선택률을 나타냅니다.

1	어휘 > 유의어 찾기	오답률 11%	답 ④

| **해석** | 많은 충동 구매자들에게는 그들이 사는 물건이 아니라 구매하는 행위 자체가 만족을 가져오는 것이다.

① 3% 쾌활함 　　　　② 2% 자신감
③ 6% 평안 　　　　　④ 89% 만족

| **정답해설** | ④ gratification은 '만족, 희열'이라는 뜻이므로, 의미가 가장 유사한 것은 satisfaction(만족, 충족)이다.

어휘

compulsive buyer 충동 구매자　　gratification 만족, 희열
liveliness 쾌활함　　　　　　　　confidence 자신감, 확신
tranquility 평안, 고요　　　　　　satisfaction 만족, 충족

2	어휘 > 빈칸 완성	오답률 7%	답 ③

| **해석** | 세계화는 더 많은 국가들이 자신들의 시장을 개방하도록 하여, 그들이 더 큰 ③ 효율성과 더 적은 비용으로 자유롭게 재화와 서비스를 거래하도록 해 준다.

① 3% 멸종　　　　　　② 2% 불황, 우울
③ 93% 효율성　　　　④ 2% 주의

| **정답해설** | ③ 더 적은 비용으로 자유롭게 거래한다는 표현으로 보아 세계화의 장점에 대해 설명하는 글이므로, 빈칸에는 긍정적인 표현이 들어가는 것이 적절하다.

| **오답해설** | ①② 부정적 표현이며, 세계화의 장점이 아니므로 빈칸에 부적절하다.
④ 자유롭게(freely) 거래한다고 하였으므로, 더욱 주의(caution)를 기울인다고 하는 것은 문맥상 어색하다.

어휘

globalization 세계화　　　　　　extinction 멸종
depression 불황, 불경기; 우울, 우울증
efficiency 효율성, 능률, 효력　　　caution 주의, 조심, 신중

오답률 TOP2

3	어휘 > 빈칸 완성	오답률 64%	답 ①

| **해석** | 우리는 번아웃의 대가를 잘 알고 있다. 직장과 가정에서 에너지, 동기, 생산성, 참여, 그리고 책임이 모두 타격을 입을 수 있다. 그리고 ① 해결책들 중 많은 것들이 꽤 직관적이다. 즉, 정기적으로 전원을 뽑아라[휴식을 취하라]. 불필요한 회의를 줄여라. 운동하라. 하루 중 짧은 휴식 일정을 잡아라. 당신이 일터를 떠날 여유가 없다고 생각할지라도 휴가를 가라. 왜냐하면 당신은 때때로 떠나지 못하는 것을 감당할 수 없기 때문이다.

① 36% 해결책들　　　② 34% 손해 배상금
③ 12% 상들　　　　　④ 18% 문제들

| **정답해설** | ① 빈칸 이전 문장에서는 번아웃의 대가에 대해 언급하고, 빈칸 이후에서는 번아웃을 해결할 수 있는 여러 가지 방안을 제시하고 있으므로, 빈칸에는 '해결책들'이라는 의미의 fixes가 들어가는 것이 가장 적절하다.

engagement 참여, 관계
take a hit 타격을 입다
unplug 전원을 뽑다, 휴식을 취하다
now and then 때때로, 가끔

commitment 책임; 전념, 헌신; 약속
intuitive 직관적인
afford 여유[형편]가 되다, 감당하다

4　어휘 > 빈칸 완성　　오답률 36%　답 ②

| 해석 | 정부는 새로운 세액 조정 체계로부터 발생하는 증가한 세액 부담에 대해 급여를 받는 근로자들을 진정시킬 방안을 모색 중이다. 지난 월요일 대통령 보좌관과의 회의 중, 대통령은 출석한 사람들에게 대중과의 더 많은 소통 채널을 개방하도록 ② 요청했다.

① 3% 덤벼들었다　　　　② 64% 요청했다
③ 23% 집었다　　　　　④ 10% 거절했다

| 정답해설 | ② 정부가 문제 상황에 대한 해결 방안을 모색 중이라고 했으므로, 빈칸에는 '요청하다, 요구하다'라는 뜻의 call for가 가장 적절하다. 빈칸 뒤에 나온 those present ~는 those who are present ~에서 「관계대명사 + be동사」가 생략된 구조로, 형용사가 대명사를 후치 수식하고 있다. those가 '사람들'의 의미이고 present가 형용사임을 파악해야 한다.

soothe 진정시키다, 달래다
tax settlement 세액 조정
fall on ~에게 덤벼들다; ~로 쓰러지다
call for 요청하다; 촉구하다
turn down 거절하다

arise 생기다, 발생하다
presidential aide 대통령 보좌관

pick up 집어 들다; (차에) 태우다

5　어휘 > 유의어 찾기　　오답률 42%　답 ④

| 해석 | 중국어 서법을 공부할 때는 중국어의 기원과 그것들이 본래 어떻게 쓰였는지에 대한 것을 배워야 한다. 그러나, 그 국가의 예술적 전통 속에서 자란 사람들을 제외하고, 그것의 미적 의의는 파악하기 매우 어려운 것처럼 보인다.

① 17% 포함[망라]하다　　② 9% 침범하다, 방해하다
③ 16% 조사하다　　　　　④ 58% 파악하다

| 정답해설 | ④ apprehend는 '파악하다, 이해하다'라는 뜻이므로, grasp(파악하다, 이해하다)과 유의어이다. grasp은 '움켜잡다'라는 뜻 이외에도 '파악하다'라는 뜻을 지니고 있음에 유의한다.

calligraphy 서법, 서예
aesthetic 미의
apprehend 파악하다, 이해하다
intrude 침범하다, 방해하다
grasp 파악하다, 이해하다, 움켜잡다

bring up 양육하다, 기르다
significance 의의, 의미, 중요성
encompass 포함[망라]하다
inspect 조사하다

6　문법 > 동사　　오답률 36%　답 ④

| 정답해설 | ④ 64% see는 지각동사로, 목적어와 목적격 보어가 능동의 관계일 때는 현재분사 또는 원형부정사를, 수동의 관계일 때는 과거분사를 목적격 보어로 취한다. 이 문장에서는 가족이 이사를 오는 능동의 관계이므로, moved는 moving 또는 move가 되어

야 한다.

| 오답해설 | ① 4% to부정사가 난이형용사(hard, easy, difficult 등)를 후치 수식하면 '~하기에 …한'이라는 의미가 된다. 이때 to부정사는 형용사를 수식하는 부사적 용법이다.

② 18% 「It is no use -ing」는 '~해 봐야 소용없다'라는 의미의 동명사 관용표현이다.

③ 14% '매 ~마다'라는 표현은 「every + 기수 + 복수 명사」로 나타낼 수 있다.

| 더 알아보기 | '~해 봐야 소용없다' 표현

- It is no use (in) -ing
- It is no good (in) -ing
- There is no use (in) -ing
- There is no good (in) -ing

7　문법 > 동사　　오답률 62%　답 ②

| 정답해설 | ② 38% 사역동사 let은 목적격 보어로 과거분사를 취할 수 없고 원형부정사를 취한다. 따라서 목적격 보어가 수동의 의미를 갖는 경우에는 「be p.p.」 형태로 써야 한다. 따라서 distracted는 be distracted가 되어야 옳다. 또는 과거분사를 목적격 보어로 취할 수 있는 사역동사 make 또는 준사역동사 get을 이용해 Don't make[get] me distracted by the noise you make.로 고칠 수도 있다.

| 오답해설 | ① 25% 사역동사 have의 목적어와 목적격 보어가 수동의 관계이므로 과거분사 arrested가 알맞게 쓰였다.

③ 4% 사역동사 let은 원형부정사를 목적격 보어로 취한다. 이 문장에서는 원형부정사 know가 목적격 보어로 알맞게 쓰였다.

④ 33% 사역동사 have는 목적어가 행위의 주체일 때 목적격 보어로 원형부정사 또는 현재분사를 쓸 수 있다. 여기에서는 목적어가 전화를 거는 주체인 the students이므로 목적격 보어로 원형부정사 phone이 알맞게 쓰였다. 또한 등위접속사 and는 동일한 문장 성분을 연결하므로 ask는 원형부정사 phone과 병렬 구조를 이루며 적절하게 쓰였다. ask는 불완전타동사로 to부정사 to donate를 목적격 보어로 알맞게 취했다.

| 더 알아보기 | 사역동사의 문장 구조

		원형부정사(능동)
make		과거분사(수동)
		원형부정사(능동)
have	+ 목적어 +	현재분사(능동)
		과거분사(수동)
let		원형부정사(능동)

설명하고 있지만, 두 가지를 비교하는 내용은 아니다.

③ 6% 마지막 문장에서 SNS로 정보를 교환한다는 내용이 제시되어 있지만, 지엽적 내용이다.

어휘

cast 묘사[제시]하다	analytical 분석적인
digitalization 디지털화	perspective 관점
signify 의미하다, 나타내다	engage in ~에 참여하다
polydirectional 다방향의	

---

8 문법 > 부정사   오답률 58%   답 ②

| 해석 | ① 다정한 나의 딸이 갑자기 예측 불가능해졌다.
② 그녀는 새로운 방법을 시도했고, 말할 필요도 없이 다른 결과들을 얻었다.
③ 도착하자마자, 그는 새로운 환경을 충분히 이용했다.
④ 그는 그가 하고 싶어 하는 일에 대해 나에게 말할 정도로 충분히 편안함을 느꼈다.

| 정답해설 | ② 42% needless to say는 '말할 필요도 없이'라는 독립부정사 표현으로 등위접속사 and와 동사 had 사이에 삽입되었다. and 뒤에는 반복되는 주어 she가 생략되어 있다.

| 오답해설 | ① 7% become은 형용사를 보어로 취하는 불완전자동사이므로, 부사인 unpredictably는 형용사 unpredictable로 바뀌어야 한다.

③ 28% upon은 전치사로 명사 또는 동명사를 목적어로 취하며, 「upon -ing」는 '~하자마자'라는 뜻의 관용표현이다. 따라서 Upon arrived는 Upon arriving이 되어야 한다.

④ 23% enough는 형용사를 후치 수식하는 부사이다. 따라서 enough comfortable은 comfortable enough가 되어야 한다.

어휘

sweet-natured 상냥한	unpredictably 예측할 수 없게
needless to say 말할 필요도 없이	take advantage of ~을 이용하다

---

9 독해 > Macro Reading > 제목   오답률 29%   답 ④

| 해석 | '전환'의 정의는 디지털 전환을 사회적 현실 내에서의 디지털화의 역할에 우리가 집중할 수 있도록 해 주는 분석적 전략으로 묘사한다. 분석적 관점으로서, 디지털 전환은 디지털화의 사회적 의미를 분석하고 논의하는 것을 가능하게 해 준다. 그러므로 '디지털 전환'이라는 용어는 사회 내에서의 디지털화의 역할에 초점을 맞추는 분석적 접근을 의미한다. 만일 언어적 전환이 현실은 언어를 통해 구성된다는 인식론적 가정에 의해 정의된다면, 디지털 전환은 사회적 현실이 점점 더 디지털화에 의해 정의된다는 가정에 기반한다. 소셜 미디어는 사회적 관계의 디지털화를 상징한다. 개인들은 점점 더 소셜 네트워킹 사이트(SNS) 상에서의 정체성 관리에 참여한다. SNS는 다방향적인데, 이는 사용자들이 서로 연결되어 정보를 공유할 수 있다는 것을 의미한다.
① SNS에서의 정체성 재구축
② 언어적 전환 대 디지털 전환
③ 디지털 시대에 정보를 교환하는 방법
④ 사회적 현실이라는 맥락 내에서의 디지털화

| 정답해설 | ④ 71% turn이라는 용어의 정의와 언어적 전환이라는 방법론에 기초해 디지털 전환이라는 개념을 설명하는 글이다. 본문 초반에서 사회적 현실 내에서 디지털화의 역할에 집중할 수 있게 해 주는 전략으로서 디지털 전환을 설명하고 있으며, 본문 중반에서는 디지털 전환은 사회적 현실이 점점 더 디지털화에 의해 정의된다는 가정에 기반하는 것이라고 언급하고 있다. 따라서 전체 글의 제목으로 가장 적절한 것은 ④이다.

| 오답해설 | ① 4% 사회적 현실에서 디지털화가 이루어지는 상황을 개인의 SNS 사용 빈도 증가의 예로 설명하고 있을 뿐, SNS에서 새로운 정체성을 만든다는 내용은 아니다.

② 19% 언어적 전환의 정의에 비유하여 디지털 전환이라는 개념을

---

10 독해 > Logical Reading > 배열   오답률 25%   답 ①

| 해석 | 지구 기후 변화에 대한 증가하는 우려는 활동가들이 화석 연료 추출 소비에 반대하는 캠페인뿐만 아니라 재생 가능한 에너지를 지지하는 캠페인 또한 조직하도록 자극했다.

(C) 재생 가능한 에너지 산업의 성장을 빠르게 가속화하지 못하는 영국 정부의 무능함에 불만을 느낀 환경 운동가들은 1년에 2,500가구에 의해 사용되는 만큼의 전기를 생산하는 것으로 추정되는 육상 풍력 발전 단지를 갖고 있는, 2,000명이 넘는 회원을 보유한 공동체 소유의 조직인 Westmill Wind Farm Co-operative를 구성했다. Westmill Wind Farm Co-operative는 지역 시민들이 Westmill Solar Co-operative를 구성하도록 영감을 주었다.

(A) 이 태양열 협동조합은 1,400가구에 전력을 공급할 수 있는 충분한 에너지를 생산하는데, 이로써 그 조합은 국내에서 최초의 대규모 태양광 발전소 협동조합이 되었고, 회원들의 말에 의하면, 태양열 발전이 "일반인들이 그들의 지붕에서뿐만 아니라 공익 사업 규모로도 깨끗한 에너지를 생산할 수 있도록 해 주는 지속 가능하고 '민주적인' 에너지 공급의 새로운 시대"를 대표한다는 뚜렷한 신호가 된다.

(B) 유사하게, 미국의 재생 가능한 에너지 지지자들은 "참여하는 공익 설비 소비자들이 공동으로 소유한 중간 규모의 설비를 통한 청정 전력 발전 제공 모델"을 개척한 기업인 Clean Energy Collective를 설립했다.

| 정답해설 | ① 75% 주어진 글 후반부에서 기후 변화에 대한 우려가 재생 가능한 에너지를 지지하는 캠페인의 조직을 자극했다고 했으므로, 바로 이어질 내용으로 가장 적절한 것은 이러한 조직의 예인 영국 단체 Westmill Farm Co-operative를 소개하는 (C)이다. (C)의 마지막에서는 또 다른 조직인 Westmill Solar Co-operative가 제시되는데, (A)의 This solar cooperative가 이것을 지칭하므로, (A)가 (C) 뒤에 연결되는 것이 자연스럽다. 이어서 Similarly(유사하게)를 이용해 앞서 영국에서 설립된 단체와 유사한 미국의 단체에 대해 설명하는 (B)가 마지막에 오는 것이 자연스럽다. 따라서 (C)-(A)-(B)의 순서가 알맞다.

어휘

motivate 자극하다, 동기를 부여하다	fossil fuel 화석 연료
extraction 추출	renewable 재생 가능한
cooperative 협동조합	visible 뚜렷한, 눈에 보이는
reminder 신호, 암시	sustainable 지속 가능한
utility 공익 설비(전기·가스·상하수도·교통 기관 등); 공익 사업(체)	
pioneer 개척하다, 선구하다	facility 설비, 시설
collectively 공동으로, 집합적으로	accelerate 가속화하다
onshore wind farm 육상 풍력 발전 단지[발전소]	

| 해석 | A: 주말 잘 보냈니?
B: 응, 아주 좋았어. 우리는 영화 보러 갔어.
A: 오! 무엇을 봤니?
B: Interstellar. 정말 재미있었어.
A: 그래? ① 그것의 어떤 점이 가장 좋았니?
B: 특수 효과. 그것들은 아주 멋졌어. 난 그것을 또 봐도 괜찮을 것 같아.
① 그것의 어떤 점이 가장 좋았니?
② 네가 가장 좋아하는 영화 장르가 뭐니?
③ 그 영화는 전 세계적으로 홍보가 되었니?
④ 그 영화 매우 비쌌니?

| 정답해설 | ① 92% B는 영화가 재미있었다고 말한 후, A의 질문에 '특수 효과'라고 답하고 있으므로, (A)는 해당 영화에 대한 구체적인 B의 의견을 묻고 있음을 알 수 있다. 따라서 빈칸에는 영화에서 좋았던 점이 무엇인지 묻는 질문이 들어가는 것이 가장 적절하다.

어휘
costly 비싼

| 해석 | ① A: 나는 오늘 해야 하는 이 연설 때문에 너무 긴장돼.
  B: 가장 중요한 것은 침착함을 유지하는 거야.
② A: 그거 아니? 민수와 유진이가 결혼을 한대!
  B: 잘됐다! 언제 결혼한대?
③ A: 2개월의 방학이 마치 일주일처럼 지나갔어. 새 학기가 코앞이야.
  B: 맞아. 방학이 몇 주 동안 (시간을) 질질 끌었어.
④ A: 프랑스어로 '물'을 어떻게 말하니?
  B: 허끝에서 맴도는데, 기억을 못하겠어.

| 정답해설 | ③ 68% A는 방학이 빨리 지나갔다며 방학이 끝남을 아쉬워하고 있다. 이에 B는 That's the word.라고 맞장구치며 방학이 시간을 질질 끌었다며 불평하고 있으므로, 대화의 흐름상 어색하다.

| 더 알아보기 | 'tongue(혀)'과 관련된 표현

- hold one's tongue 묵묵부답하고 있다
- make a slip of the tongue 말실수하다
- on the tip of one's tongue 말이 혀끝에서 뱅뱅 도는, 기억이 날 듯 말 듯한

어휘
tie the knot 결혼하다
around the corner 코앞에 와 있는, 목전에 있는
drag on 질질 끌다
on the tip of one's tongue 말이 혀끝에서 뱅뱅 도는, 기억이 날 듯 말 듯한

| 해석 | 여성들은 뒷담화의 전문가들이며 그들은 항상 사소한 것들에 관해 이야기한다. 적어도 남성들은 그렇게 생각해 왔다. 그러나, 일부 새로운 연구는 여성들이 여성들과 말을 할 때, 그들의 대화는 시시한 것과는 거리가 멀고, 남성들이 다른 남성들과 말할 때보다 여러 가지 더 많은 주제(최대 40 가지의 주제)를 다룬다고 말한다. 여성들의 대화는 그 범위가 건강에서부터 그들의 집, 정치에서부터 패션, 영화에서부터 가족, 교육에서부터 인간관계의 문제점까지 이르지만 스포츠는 눈에 띌 정도로 없다. 남성들은 더 제한된 범위의 주제를 갖는 경향이 있는데, 가장 인기 있는 것들로는 일, 스포츠, 농담, 자동차, 그리고 여성이다. 1,000명이 넘는 여성을 인터뷰한 심리학자 Petra Boynton 교수에 따르면, 여성들은 또한 대화를 할 때 하나의 주제에서 다른 주제로 빨리 넘어가는 경향이 있는 반면, 남성은 대개 더 오랜 시간 동안 하나의 주제를 고수한다. 직장에서, 이러한 차이는 남성들에게 장점이 될 수 있는데, 그들이 다른 일은 제쳐두고 논의되고 있는 주제에만 온전히 집중할 수 있기 때문이다. 반면에, 그것은 또한 회의에서 동시에 여러 가지 일들이 논의되어야 할 때 그들이 때때로 집중하기 어려워한다는 것을 의미하기도 한다.

| 정답해설 | ② 85% 남녀 간의 대화 주제와 대화 방식의 차이에 관한 글이다. 본문 중반의 Women's conversations range from ~, but sports are notably absent.에서 여성들의 대화의 주제는 광범위하나 스포츠는 눈에 띌 정도로 없다고 했으므로, 본문의 내용과 일치하지 않는다.

| 오답해설 | ① 10% 첫 번째 문장 that's what men ~의 내용과 일치한다.
③ 1% 본문 중반 women also tend to move quickly from one subject to another in conversation에 언급된 내용이다.
④ 4% 마지막 문장의 they sometimes find it hard ~의 내용과 일치한다.

어휘
gossip 수다를 떨다, 뒷담화를 하다
trivial 사소한, 하찮은 frivolous 시시한, 하찮은
notably 눈에 띄게; 두드러지게 absent 없는, 부재의
stick to ~을 굳게 지키다, 고수하다

| 해석 | 15세기에는 과학, 철학, 그리고 마술에 구분이 없었다. 세 가지 모두는 '자연 철학'이라는 일반 주제 하에 포함되었다. 고전 작가들의 회복, 가장 중요하게는 아리스토텔레스의 작품이 자연 철학 발전의 중심에 있었다. ② 인문주의자들은 그들의 지식을 확산시키기 위한 인쇄기의 힘을 재빨리 깨달았다. 15세기 초에 아리스토텔레스는 철학과 과학에 대한 모든 학자적 견해의 토대였다. Averroes와 Avicenna의 아랍어 번역본과 논평에 생생히 살아 있는 아리스토텔레스는 인류와 자연 세계의 관계에 대한 체계적 시각을 제공했다. 「Physics」, 「Metaphysics」, 그리고 「Meteorology」와 같은 그의 남아 있는 문서들은 학자들에게 자연 세계를 창조한 힘을 이해할 수 있는 논리적인 도구를 제공했다.

| 정답해설 | ② 83% 아리스토텔레스의 작품이 15세기에 철학과 과학적 인식에 미친 영향에 대해 설명하는 글인데, 인쇄기의 힘을 깨달은 인문주의자들에 대해 언급하는 ②는 흐름상 알맞지 않다.

어휘
printing press 인쇄기 speculation 견해, 관점
commentary 주석, 주해 perspective 시각, 관점

15 문법 > 동사 | 오답률 58% | 답 ③

| 해석 | ① 지진에 따른 화재는 보험 회사에게 특별한 관심사이다.
② 워드프로세서는 과거에 타이피스트에게 궁극의 도구로 여겨졌다.
③ 현금 예측에서 소득의 요소는 회사의 상황에 따라 달라질 것이다.
④ 세계 최초의 디지털카메라는 1975년 Eastman Kodak사의 Steve Sasson에 의해 만들어졌다.

| 정답해설 | ③ 42% vary는 '(상황에 따라) 달라지다[다르다]'라는 뜻의 자동사이므로 be동사와 함께 사용하지 않고, 조동사 will 다음에 바로 위치해야 한다. 따라서 will be vary는 will vary가 되어야 한다.

| 오답해설 | ① 32% 해당 문장에서 following은 전치사와 현재분사로 볼 수 있다. 먼저 '~후에; (특정 결과)에 따라'를 뜻하는 전치사로 사용되어 전명구인 following an earthquake가 주어인 Fire를 수식한다고 볼 수 있다. 또는 현재분사로서 분사구 following an earthquake가 주어 Fire을 수식한다고 보아도 역시 옳다. 「of + 추상명사」는 형용사 역할을 하므로, of special interest가 주격 보어로 알맞게 쓰였다.

② 22% 「be considered to be + 명사/형용사」는 '~로 여겨지다'라는 뜻으로, 여기서는 「to be + 형용사 + 명사」 형태인 to be the ultimate tool이 보어로 알맞게 사용되었다.

④ 4% 디지털 카메라는 만들어진 대상이므로 수동태 was created가 알맞게 쓰였고, 행위자는 전치사 by를 이용해 적절하게 표시했다.

어휘

ultimate 궁극의, 최후의
vary 다르다
forecast 예측
circumstance 상황

오답률 TOP 1

16 독해 > Reading for Writing > 빈칸 구 완성 | 오답률 68% | 답 ②

| 해석 | 역사적으로 빠른 속도의 성장으로부터 중국 경제의 둔화는 다른 곳의 성장을 ② 압박할 것으로 오랫동안 예상되어 왔다. Yale대학교의 Stephen Roach는 "30년 동안 10%의 성장을 해 온 중국은 세계 경제를 앞으로 나아가게 한 많은 것들의 원동력의 강력한 원천이었다"라고 말했다. 성장률은 약 7%의 공식적 수치로 둔화되었다. Roach씨는 "그것은 명확한 감속이다"라고 덧붙였다.

① 속도를 높이다 ② ~을 압박하다
③ ~로 이어지다 ④ 결과적으로 ~이 되다

| 정답해설 | ② 32% 빠른 성장을 해 오던 중국 경제의 성장 속도 둔화가 세계 경제에 미치는 영향에 대해 설명하는 표현이 빈칸에 들어가야 한다. 빈칸 이후 문장에서 중국이 세계 경제를 앞으로 나아가게 한 원동력의 원천이었다고 했으므로, 중국 경제의 둔화는 세계 경제의 둔화로 이어짐을 유추할 수 있다. 따라서 빈칸에는 weigh on(~을 압박하다)이 가장 적절하다.

어휘

concrete 구체적인, 명확한
speed up 속도를 높이다
lead to ~로 이어지다
deceleration 감속
weigh on ~을 압박하다
result in 결과적으로 ~이 되다

---

17 독해 > Reading for Writing > 빈칸 구 완성 | 오답률 42% | 답 ④

| 해석 | 점점 더 많은 지도자들이 원격으로 일하거나, 컨설턴트와 프리랜서들뿐만 아니라 국가 전역 혹은 전 세계에 흩어져 있는 팀과 함께 일하게 됨에 따라, 당신은 그들에게 더 많은 ④ 자율성을 주어야 할 것이다. 당신이 더 많은 신뢰를 줄수록, 다른 사람들은 당신을 더 많이 신뢰한다. 나는 직업 만족도와 매 순간 그들을 그림자처럼 따라다니는 사람이 없이도 업무를 충분히 수행하도록 사람들이 얼마나 자율권을 부여받는지 사이에는 직접적인 연관성이 있다고 확신한다. 당신이 신뢰하는 사람들에게 책임을 주는 것은 당신의 조직이 더욱 매끄럽게 운영되도록 할 뿐만 아니라 당신이 더 큰 문제에 집중할 수 있도록 당신의 시간을 더 자유롭게 해 준다.

① 업무 ② 보상
③ 제한 ④ 자율성

| 정답해설 | ④ 58% 원격 업무에 있어서 빈칸이 포함된 문장 이후 직업 만족도와 자율권의 부여 정도 사이에 직접적인 연관성이 있다고 확신한다는 점을 서술하고 있다. 또한 마지막 문장에서는 신뢰하는 사람에게 책임을 주는 것의 장점에 대해서도 역시 서술하고 있다. 이 두 가지 점을 근거로, 전 세계에 흩어져 있는 팀원들에게 더 많은 '자율권'과 '책임'을 줘야 함을 알 수 있으므로 밑줄 친 부분에 들어갈 말로 가장 적절한 것은 ④ autonomy(자율성)이다.

| 오답해설 | ① 9% 업무량에 관한 내용은 본문에 없다.

② 28% 본문에서는 자율권과 책임을 부여하라고 했으며, 이것을 보상이라고 할 수는 없다.

③ 5% '제한'은 본문의 주장과는 대치된다.

어휘

remotely 원격으로, 멀리 떨어져
bestow 주다, 수여하다
execute 실행하다
autonomy 자율성, 자주성
scattered 산재한, 흩어진
empower 자율권[권한]을 주다
restriction 제한

---

18 독해 > Macro Reading > 요지 | 오답률 45% | 답 ①

| 해석 | "유대교에서, 우리는 주로 우리의 행위에 의해 정의된다"라고 몬트리올에 있는 Temple Emanu-El-Beth-Sholom의 수석 랍비 Lisa Grushcow는 말한다. "당신은 정말로 탁상공론뿐인 공상적 박애주의자가 될 수는 없다." 이 개념은 유대교의 tikkun olam이라는 생각과 관련이 있는데, 이는 "세상을 치료한다"라고 번역된다. 인간으로서 우리의 임무는 "망가진 것들을 고치는 것이다. 우리 자신과 서로를 돌보는 것뿐만이 아니라 우리 주변을 더 나은 세계로 만드는 것이 우리에게 지워진 의무이다"라고 그녀는 말한다. 이 철학은 선을 봉사에 기초한 무언가로 개념화한다. "내가 선한 사람인가?"라고 묻는 것 대신에, 당신은 "세상에서 나는 어떤 좋은 일을 행할 수 있는가?"라고 묻고 싶을 수도 있다. Grushcow의 사원은 그들의 공동체 안팎에서 이러한 믿음을 행동으로 옮긴다. 예를 들어, 그들은 1970년대에 캐나다에 오려고 하는 베트남 출신의 두 난민 가족을 후원했다.

① 우리는 세상을 치유하기 위해 노력해야 한다.
② 공동체는 피난처로서 기능해야 한다.
③ 우리는 선을 믿음으로 개념화해야 한다.
④ 사원은 공동체에 기여해야 한다.

| 정답해설 | ① 55% 유대교의 교리에 기초하여 우리가 행해야 할 의무를 설명하는 글로, 본문 중반의 Our job as human beings, ~에서 망가진 것들을 고치고 더 나은 세상을 만드는 것이 인간인 우

리의 의무라고 했다. 따라서 글의 요지로 가장 적절한 것은 ①이다.

| **오답해설** | ② 7% 공동체의 기능에 대해서 직접적으로 글에서 다루고 있지 않다.

③ 25% 선을 믿음으로 여기는 것보다는 선을 행동으로 행하는 것의 중요성을 강조하는 글이다.

④ 13% 마지막에 유대교 사원의 공헌의 한 가지 예를 제시하고는 있지만, 이는 인간이 행해야 할 선한 행위에 대한 예시이므로 글 전체의 요지로는 부적절하다.

어휘

Judaism 유대교	rabbi 랍비, 유대교 율법학자
armchair 탁상공론의, 이론뿐인	do-gooder 공상적 박애주의자
incumbent 의미로서 지워지는	conceptualize 개념화하다
refugee 난민	shelter 피난처
contribute 공헌하다, 기여하다	

---

19 독해 > Logical Reading > 연결사 | 오답률 47% | 답 ③

| **해석** | 고대 철학자들과 영적 스승들은 긍정적인 것과 부정적인 것, 낙관주의와 비관주의, 성공과 안정을 위한 노력과 실패와 불확실성에 대한 열린 마음의 균형이 필요하다는 것을 이해했다. 스토아학파는 "나쁜 것들에 대한 사전 계획", 즉 의도적으로 최악의 경우의 시나리오를 상상하는 것을 권고했다. 이것은 미래에 대한 불안을 줄여 주는 경향이 있다. 당신이 현실에서 일들이 얼마나 나쁘게 진행될 수 있는지 냉정하게 생각해 볼 때, 당신은 대개 당신이 극복할 수 있을 것이라고 결론짓는다. (A) 게다가, 당신이 현재 누리고 있는 인간관계와 소유물을 잃을 수도 있다고 상상하는 것은 지금 그것들을 가지고 있는 것에 대해 감사하는 마음을 증가시킨다고 그들은 말했다. (B) 대조적으로, 긍정적인 사고는 항상 미래에만 기대어 현재의 즐거움을 무시한다.

① 그럼에도 불구하고 – 게다가　② 더욱이 – 예를 들어
③ 게다가 – 대조적으로　　④ 그러나 – 결론적으로

| **정답해설** | ③ 53% (A) 이전 문장에서 부정적으로 사고하는 것에 대한 장점 한 가지(미래에 대한 불안 감소)를 설명했고, (A) 문장에서 부정적으로 사고하는 것의 또 다른 장점(현재 가진 것에 대해 감사하는 마음을 증가시킴)을 제시했으므로, 빈칸에는 첨언 연결사 Furthermore 또는 Besides가 적절하다.

(B) 이전 문장들에서는 부정적 사고의 장점을 설명하고 있는데, (B) 문장은 긍정적 사고의 단점을 설명하고 있다. 따라서 대조의 연결사 by contrast(대조적으로)가 가장 적절하다.

어휘

pessimism 비관주의	the Stoics 스토아학파
premeditation 사전 계획, 미리 사고하기	
deliberately 고의로, 의도적으로	soberly 침착하게
cope 극복하다, 해결하다, 견디다	

---

20 독해 > Logical Reading > 삽입 | 오답률 49% | 답 ②

| **해석** | 왜 일 중독자들은 그들의 일을 그렇게나 많이 좋아할까? 대개는 일하는 것이 몇몇 중요한 이점을 제공하기 때문이다. 그것은 사람들에게 생계를 유지하는 방법인 임금을 제공한다. ② 그리고 일하는 것은 재정적 안정성 이상의 것을 제공한다. 그것은 사람들에게 자신감을 준다. 그들은 자신들이 힘든 일을 하나 해내고 "내가 그것을 했어"라고 말할 수 있을 때 만족

감을 느낀다. 심리학자들은 일이 또한 사람들에게 정체성을 부여한다고 주장한다. 그들은 자아감과 개성을 얻기 위해 일한다. 게다가, 대부분의 일은 사람들에게 다른 사람을 만날 수 있는 사회적으로 용인된 방식을 제공한다. 일은 긍정적인 중독이라고 말할 수 있다. 아마도 일 중독자들은 그들의 일에 대해 강박적일지 모르지만, 그들의 중독은 안전하고, 심지어는 이로운 것처럼 보인다.

| **정답해설** | ② 51% 주어진 문장에서 more than financial security(재정적 안정성 이상의 것)라고 언급하고 있으므로, 이전 내용에 '재정'과 관련된 내용이 등장해야 함을 유추할 수 있다. ② 이전 문장에서 paychecks(임금)가 언급되므로, 주어진 문장은 이 문장 뒤에 이어지는 것이 자연스럽다.

어휘

earn a living 생계를 유지하다	self-confidence 자신감
identity 정체성	individualism 개성; 개인주의
addiction 중독	compulsive 강박적인

2020

합격예상 체크

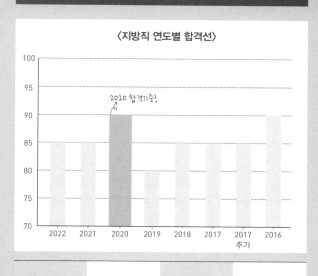

〈지방직 연도별 합격선〉

2020 합격기준

맞힌 개수	/20문항	점수	/100점

➡ □ 합격 □ 불합격

취약영역 체크

문항	정답	영역	문항	정답	영역
1	②	어휘 > 빈칸 완성	11	②	생활영어 > 회화/관용표현
2	②	어휘 > 유의어 찾기	12	②	생활영어 > 회화/관용표현
3	④	어휘 > 유의어 찾기	13	①	문법 > 동명사
4	①	어휘 > 유의어 찾기	14	④	독해 > Macro Reading > 제목
5	③	문법 > 시제	15	③	독해 > Logical Reading > 삭제
6	④	어휘 > 유의어 찾기	16	③	독해 > Reading for Writing > 빈칸 구 완성
7	②	문법 > 관계사	17	①	독해 > Macro Reading > 요지
8	③	문법 > 일치	18	③	독해 > Logical Reading > 배열
9	①	독해 > Logical Reading > 연결사	19	④	독해 > Logical Reading > 삽입
10	③	독해 > Macro Reading > 주제	20	④	독해 > Micro Reading > 내용 일치/불일치

⬇ 영역별 틀린 개수로 취약영역을 확인하세요!

어휘	/5	문법	/4	독해	/9	생활영어	/2

➡ 나의 취약영역: _____

※ [정답해설]과 [오답해설] 선지의 50% 표시는 〈1초 합격예측 서비스〉를 통해 수집된 선지 선택률을 나타냅니다.

---

1 어휘 > 빈칸 완성   오답률 40%   답 ②

| 해석 | 플라스틱 병의 문제는 그것들이 ② 단열 처리가 되지 않았다는 것이다. 따라서 온도가 올라가기 시작할 때, 당신의 물도 뜨거워질 것이다.
① 9% 위생적인
② 60% 단열 처리가 된
③ 26% 재활용할 수 있는
④ 5% 방수의

| 정답해설 | ② 온도가 올라갈 때, 병 안의 물이 함께 뜨거워지는 것은 단열이 되지 않기 때문이므로 빈칸에 가장 적절한 표현은 insulated(단열 처리가 된)이다.

| 어휘 |
heat up 뜨거워지다. 따뜻해지다

오답률 TOP 2

2 어휘 > 유의어 찾기   오답률 51%   답 ②

| 해석 | 그 잔인한 광경은 그렇지 않다면 그녀의 마음속으로 들어오지 않았을 생각들을 촉발했다.
① 8% ~을 돌보았다
② 49% ~을 촉발했다, 불러일으켰다
③ 11% ~을 보상했다, 보충했다
④ 32% ~와 접촉을 유지했다

| 정답해설 | ② 잔인한 광경(cruel sights)으로 인해 생각(thoughts)이 떠오른 것이므로 문맥상 touched off는 '촉발했다, 유발했다'라는 의미라는 것을 유추할 수 있다. 따라서 gave rise to(~을 불러일으켰다)와 의미가 가장 가깝다.

| 어휘 |
cruel 잔인한, 잔혹한   sight 광경, 모습

---

3 어휘 > 유의어 찾기   오답률 29%   답 ④

| 해석 | 작가가 집필 과정 중 채택하는 전략들은 주의력 과부하의 어려움을 완화해 줄 수도 있다.
① 10% 보완하다
② 14% 가속화하다
③ 5% 계산하다
④ 71% 완화하다

| 정답해설 | ④ alleviate는 '완화하다'라는 의미로, relieve(완화하다, 줄이다)와 의미가 가장 가깝다.

| 더 알아보기 | alleviate의 유의어

> ease(완화하다), relieve(완화하다, 경감하다), moderate(완화하다; 절제하다), allay(완화하다, 경감하다), assuage(완화하다, 진정시키다)

| 어휘 |
overload 과부하

---

4 어휘 > 유의어 찾기   오답률 30%   답 ①

| 해석 | 그 학교 불량배는 학급의 다른 학생들에 의해 꺼려지는[소외당하는] 것이 어떠한지 몰랐다.
① 70% 회피당하는
② 9% 경고받는
③ 12% 처벌받는
④ 9% 모방되는

| 정답해설 | ① shun은 '피하다, 멀리하다'라는 의미이므로, avoided와 의미가 가장 가깝다.

어휘

bully 불량배, 괴롭히는 사람

| **5** | 문법 > 시제 | 오답률 53% | 답 ③ |

| 해석 | ① 은하계에 있는 수십억 개의 별들 중, 얼마나 많은 것들이 생명체를 부화시킬 수 있는가?
② 크리스마스 파티는 정말 재미있었고 나는 시간 가는 것을 완전히 잊었다.
③ 나는 오늘 정오에 일을 시작할 것이기 때문에 지금 당장 떠나야만 한다.
④ 그들은 더 어렸을 때 책을 훨씬 더 많이 좋아하곤 했다.

| 정답해설 | ③ 47% 왕래발착동사 start의 현재진행시제(be -ing)는 현재 진행 중인 상황을 나타낼 때뿐만 아니라, 실현 가능성이 큰 미래의 약속, 계획 등에 대해 언급할 때 미래시제 대신 사용할 수 있다. 따라서 I am starting work at noon today(나는 오늘 정오에 일을 시작할 것이다)는 어법상 옳다.

I	must leave	right now	because	I	am starting	work
주어	동사	부사(구)	부사절 접속사	주어	동사	목적어

at noon	today.
전명구	부사

| 오답해설 | ① 21% much는 불가산명사를 대신하는 대명사이며, 선지에서는 가산명사인 stars를 대신해야 하므로, many로 고쳐야 한다.
② 20% 주어인 The Christmas party(크리스마스 파티)는 감정을 유발[제공]하는 대상이므로 -ing 형태의 현재분사가 와야 한다. 따라서 excited를 exciting으로 고쳐야 한다.
④ 12% used to는 '(과거에) ~이었다, ~했다'라는 의미로, 이때 to 뒤에는 동사원형이 와야 한다. 따라서 loving을 love로 고쳐야 한다.

| 더 알아보기 | **왕래발착동사**

- come, go, arrive, reach, leave, depart
  → 왕래발착동사는 가까운 미래를 나타내는 부사어구와 함께 쓰일 때 현재시제나 현재진행시제로 미래시제를 대신할 수 있다.

어휘

hatch 부화시키다   lose track of ~을 잊어버리다

| **6** | 어휘 > 유의어 찾기 | 오답률 38% | 답 ④ |

| 해석 | Francesca가 여름휴가 동안 집에 머무르는 것에 대해 옹호론을 편 후, 저녁 식탁에 불편한 침묵이 흘렀다. Robert는 지금이 그녀에게 자신의 거창한 계획에 대해 말할 적기인지 확신하지 못했다.
① 15% ~에 반대했다   ② 17% ~을 꿈꿨다
③ 6% 완전히 배제했다   ④ 62% 강력히 제안했다

| 정답해설 | ④ 두 번째 문장을 통해, Robert가 거창한 휴가 계획을 그녀에게 말하는 것을 망설인다는 것을 알 수 있다. 즉, Francesca는 여름휴가 동안 집에 머물기를 원하고 있다는 것을 유추할 수 있

어야 밑줄 친 부분의 뜻을 모르더라도 답을 고를 수 있다. made a case for는 '~의 옹호론을 펼쳤다, ~에 찬성하는 의견을 내다'라는 의미이며, 선지 중 이와 가까운 의미로 쓰일 수 있는 것은 strongly suggested(강력히 제안했다)이다.

어휘

grandiose 거창한

| **7** | 문법 > 관계사 | 오답률 49% | 답 ② |

| 정답해설 | ② 51% 복합관계대명사는 「관계대명사 + ever」의 형태로, 명사절을 이끌어 전치사의 목적어로 쓰일 수 있다. 특히, 사람을 나타내는 관계대명사 who의 경우 해당 절에서 관계대명사가 하는 역할에 따라, whoever(주격), whosever(소유격), whomever(목적격)로 그 형태가 달라진다. 해당 문장에서는 복합관계대명사절 내에 completes의 주어가 존재하지 않으므로, 복합관계대명사는 주격으로 사용되어야 한다. 따라서 whomever를 whoever로 고쳐야 한다.

A gift card	will be given	to	whoever	completes
주어	동사	전치사	복합관계대명사(주격)	동사

the questionnaire.
목적어

| 오답해설 | ① 13% 과거의 한 시점보다 더 이전에 발생한 사건을 언급할 때는 대과거(과거완료, 「had p.p.」)를 사용한다. '보증이 만료된 것'이 '수리를 한' 시점보다 더 이전에 발생한 일이므로 대과거(had expired)로 표현한 것은 적절하다.
③ 20% 휴가를 요청하지 않은 것은 과거의 일(지난달)이며 하와이에 있지 않은 것은 현재의 일(지금)이다. 서로 다른 시점의 반대 상황을 가정하여 말할 때는 혼합가정법을 사용하며 「If + 주어 + had p.p. ~(가정법 과거완료), 주어 + 조동사의 과거형 + 동사원형 …(가정법 과거).」 형태로 표현할 수 있다.
④ 16% what is worse는 '설상가상으로, 엎친 데 덮친 격으로'라는 의미의 관용표현이며, 전체적으로 과거시제를 사용하고 있으므로 시제 일치를 위해 what was worse로 사용한 것은 적절하다.

어휘

warranty 보증, 보증서   expire 만료되다
complete 완성하다   questionnaire 설문지
pass away 사망하다
what is worse 엎친 데 덮친 격으로, 설상가상으로

| **8** | 문법 > 일치 | 오답률 38% | 답 ③ |

| 해석 | Elizabeth Taylor는 아름다운 보석을 보는 안목이 있었고 수년 동안 몇몇 놀라운 보석들을 모았으며, 한 번은 "여자는 언제나 더 많은 다이아몬드를 가질 수 있죠."라고 단언했다. 2011년, 그녀의 최고급 보석들이 1억 1천 590만 달러의 수익을 낸 Christie's 주최 저녁 경매에서 판매되었다. 그 저녁 경매에서 팔린 그녀의 가장 소중한 소유물 중 하나는 Bulgari의 1961년작 보석 시계였다. 다이아몬드로 뒤덮인 머리와 꼬리, 그리고 측면을 거는 듯한 두 개의 에메랄드 눈을 가진 뱀이 손목 주위를 휘감도록 디자인된

잘 볼 수 없는 기계 장치가 작은 수정 시계를 드러내 보이기 위해 강렬한 틱을 벌린다.

| 정답해설 | ③ 62% 부사구가 문두로 나오면서 주어와 동사가 도치된 형태이다. 해당 문장의 주어는 her most prized possessions가 아니라 a 1961 bejeweled timepiece이므로, 주어-동사 수 일치 원칙에 따라 were는 was가 되어야 한다.

Among her most prized possessions sold during the evening sale
전명구(부사구)　　　　　과거분사　　　　　전명구

was a 1961 bejeweled timepiece by Bulgari.
동사　　　　주어　　　　　전명구

| 오답해설 | ① 15% 해당 문장의 declaring ~ diamonds는 동시상황을 나타내는 분사구문이다. a girl can always have more diamonds라고 말한 주체가 Elizabeth Taylor 자신이므로 능동의 의미를 가진 declaring이 오는 것은 적절하다.

② 11% 관계대명사 that이 이끄는 절은 사람과 사물을 둘 다 선행사로 취할 수 있으므로, 선행사 an evening auction(저녁 경매)을 수식하는 것은 적절하다.

④ 12% 「with + 목적어 + p.p.」 형태의 분사구문으로 수식받는 객체가 행위를 당하는 대상일 때는 수동의 의미를 지닌 과거분사가 쓰인다. its head and tail(그것의 머리와 꼬리)이 diamonds(다이아몬드)로 '뒤덮여 있는' 수동의 의미이므로, 과거분사 covered는 적절하게 쓰였다.

어휘

have an eye for ~을 보는 눈이 있다, 안목이 있다
amass 모으다, 축적하다　　　declare 단언하다, 주장하다
fine 질 좋은　　　　　　　auction 경매
bring in 들여오다, (이익, 이자를) 가져오다
prized 소중한　　　　　　possession 소유물
bejeweled 보석으로 장식한, 보석을 두른
timepiece 시계　　　　　serpent 뱀
coil 휘감다　　　　　　　hypnotic 최면을 거는 듯한
mechanism 기계 장치　　　fierce 강렬한
discreet 잘 볼 수 없는; 신중한　reveal 드러내 보이다
quartz 수정, 석영

---

9 독해 > Logical Reading > 연결사　오답률 23%　답 ①

| 해석 | 확신에 찬 행동은 당신의 권리를 옹호하고, 타인의 권리를 침해하지 않는 직접적이고 적절한 방식으로 당신의 생각과 느낌을 표현하는 것을 포함한다. 그것은 타인이 당신의 관점을 이해하도록 하는 일이다. 확신에 찬 행동 기술을 보여 주는 사람들은 좋은 대인관계를 유지하면서 확신을 갖고 쉽게 갈등 상황을 처리할 수 있다. (A) 그에 반해서, 공격적인 행동은 타인의 권리를 공공연히 침해하는 방식으로 당신의 생각과 느낌을 표현하고 당신의 권리를 옹호하는 것을 포함한다. 공격적인 행동을 보여 주는 사람들은 타인의 권리가 자신들의 것보다 덜 중요함에 틀림없다고 믿는 것 같다. (B) 그러므로, 그들은 좋은 대인관계를 유지하는 데 애를 먹는다. 그들은 통제권을 유지하기 위해 방해하고, 빨리 말하고, 타인을 무시하고, 비꼬는 말이나 다른 형태의 언어폭력을 사용할 가능성이 높다.
① 그에 반해서 – 그러므로　　② 유사하게 – 게다가
③ 그러나 – 한편으로는　　　④ 그에 따라 – 반면에

| 정답해설 | ① 77% (A) 확신에 찬 행동의 특징(긍정적)에 대해 언급한 후, 빈칸 이후에서는 확신에 찬 행동과는 대조적인 공격적인 행동의 특징(부정적)에 대해 언급하고 있으므로 빈칸에 가장 적절한 표현은 대조의 연결사 In contrast(그에 반해서)나 역접 연결사 However(그러나)이다.

(B) 빈칸 앞에서 공격적 행동을 보이는 사람들의 보편적인 생각에 대해 언급한 후, 빈칸 뒤에서 그러한 생각으로 인해 야기되는 결과(좋은 대인관계를 유지하는 것의 어려움)를 제시하고 있으므로, 빈칸에 가장 적절한 것은 인과 관계의 연결사 Thus이다.

| 오답해설 | ③ 8% (B) On one hand는 '한편으로는'이라는 의미로서 서로 대조적인 두 가지를 비교할 때 주로 사용되는데, (B) 이후에서는 앞과 마찬가지로 공격적인 행동을 보이는 사람들의 부정적 특징이 일관되게 제시되고 이와 대조적인 내용은 언급되지 않으므로 빈칸에 적절하지 않다.

어휘

assertive 확신에 찬, 적극적인　　stand up for ~을 옹호하다, 지지하다
viewpoint 관점　　　　　　　　exhibit 보이다, 드러내다
assurance 확신, 자신감　　　　　interpersonal 대인관계의
openly 솔직하게, 드러내 놓고　　subservient 덜 중요한, 부차적인
sarcasm 빈정댐, 비꼬는 말[행위]　verbal abuse 언어폭력, 폭언

---

10 독해 > Macro Reading > 주제　오답률 8%　답 ③

| 해석 | 태블릿 컴퓨터에서 이용 가능한 전자책 앱은 터치스크린 기술을 사용한다. 일부 터치스크린은 전자 충전된 두 개의 마주 보고 놓인 금속 표면을 덮고 있는 유리 패널을 특징으로 한다. 스크린이 터치되면, 두 개의 금속 표면이 압력을 감지하고 접촉한다. 이 압력이 컴퓨터로 전기 신호를 보내고, 이것이 터치를 명령으로 해석한다. 스크린이 손가락의 압력에 반응하기 때문에 이 버전의 터치스크린은 저항식 스크린이라고 알려져 있다. 다른 태블릿 컴퓨터는 유리 패널 아래의 전기가 통하는 단일 금속 막을 특징으로 한다. 사용자가 스크린을 터치하면, 일부 전류가 유리를 통해 사용자의 손가락으로 전달된다. 전하가 이동되면, 컴퓨터는 전력 손실을 명령으로 해석하고 사용자가 원하는 기능을 수행한다. 이 유형의 스크린은 정전식 스크린이라고 알려져 있다.
① 사용자가 신기술을 어떻게 학습하는가
② 태블릿 컴퓨터에서 전자책이 어떻게 작동하는가
③ 터치스크린 기술이 어떻게 작동하는가
④ 터치스크린은 어떻게 진화하였는가

| 정답해설 | ③ 92% 두 가지 터치스크린 기술(저항식 스크린과 정전식 스크린)의 작동 기제를 비교하는 글이므로, '터치스크린 기술이 어떻게 작동하는가'가 글의 주제로 가장 적절하다.

| 오답해설 | ② 4% 첫 문장에서 '전자책 앱(e-book applications)'이 제시되기는 하나, 이는 터치스크린 기술을 이용하는 앱의 한 종류로 언급되었을 뿐이고 태블릿 컴퓨터에서의 전자책 작동 원리는 본문에 언급되지 않았다.

④ 3% 대표적 터치스크린 기술 두 가지에 대해 언급하고 있으나, 터치스크린의 진화 과정에 대해서는 언급되지 않았다.

어휘

application 애플리케이션　　　employ 쓰다, 이용하다
feature 특징으로 삼다　　　　electronically 전자적으로, 컴퓨터로

charge 충전하다; 전하(電荷)   command 명령, 명령어
resistive 저항성의, 전기 저항의   electrified 전기가 통하는
current 전류   carry out 수행하다, 실시하다
function 기능, 작동   capacitive 전기 용량의

---

11   생활영어 > 회화/관용표현   오답률 10%   답 ②

| 해석 | A: 오, 또야! 스팸 메일이 너무 많아!
B: 나도 알아. 나는 하루에 10통이 넘는 스팸 메일을 받아.
A: 그것들이 오는 것을 막을 수 있을까?
B: 그것들을 완전히 차단하는 것은 불가능하다고 생각해.
A: ② 우리가 할 수 있는 것이 없을까?
B: 음, 너는 설정에서 필터를 설정할 수 있어.
A: 필터?
B: 그래. 필터는 일부 스팸 메일을 걸러낼 수 있어.
① 너는 이메일을 자주 쓰니
② 우리가 할 수 있는 것이 없을까
③ 너는 이렇게 굉장한 필터를 어떻게 만들었니
④ 내가 이메일 계정을 개설하는 것을 도와줄 수 있니

| 정답해설 | ② 90% 빈칸 이전의 대화에서 A가 B에게 스팸 메일이 오는 것을 막을 수 있는지 묻자 B가 완전히 막을 수는 없다고 답한다. 이후 A의 질문에 대해 B가 필터를 설정할 수 있다고 대답하며 어느 정도 효과가 있는 해결 방안을 A에게 제시해 주고 있다. 따라서 빈칸에는 해결 방안에 대해 묻는 표현이 들어가는 것이 가장 적절하다.

어휘
set up 설정하다; 개설하다   weed out 추려 내다, 제거하다

---

12   생활영어 > 회화/관용표현   오답률 15%   답 ②

| 해석 | ① A: 몇 시인지 아니?
     B: 미안해. 나는 요즘 바빠.
② A: 얘들아, 너희 어디 가니?
     B: 우리는 식료품점에 가려고 해.
③ A: 이것 좀 도와주겠니?
     B: 그래. 내가 너를 위해 박수를 칠게.
④ A: 내 지갑 본 사람 있니?
     B: 오랜만이야.

| 정답해설 | ② 85% A가 행선지를 묻고 있으므로 식료품점에 간다고 답하는 대화는 자연스럽다. be headed는 '(특정 방향으로) 가다, 향하다'라는 의미로 Where are you headed?는 Where are you going?과 같은 표현이다. 또한 be off to는 '~로 가다, 떠나다'라는 뜻으로 목적지, 행선지를 말할 때 자주 사용되는 표현이다.

| 오답해설 | ① 1% 시간을 묻는 질문에 바쁘다고 답하는 것은 어색하다.
③ 12% Can you give me a hand ~?는 도움을 요청하는 표현으로 박수를 치는 것(clap)과는 관계가 없다.
④ 2% Long time no see.(오랜만이야.)는 오랜만에 본 사이에서 하는 인사말로 지갑을 찾는 질문에 대한 대답으로는 부적절하다.

어휘
give a hand 거들어 주다, 돕다   clap 박수 치다

---

13   문법 > 동명사   오답률 32%   답 ①

| 정답해설 | ① 68% regret은 to부정사와 동명사를 둘 다 목적어로 취할 수 있지만, 동명사를 취하는 경우 '(과거 지향적) ~한 것을 후회하다'라는 의미가 되고 to부정사를 취하는 경우 '(미래 지향적) ~하게 되어 유감이다'라는 의미가 되므로 주의한다. 해당 문장의 우리말이 '~한 것을 후회한다'이므로 to tell을 telling으로 고쳐 써야 한다.

| 오답해설 | ② 5% 「소유격 + 명사」를 대신하기 위해 '~의 것'이라는 뜻의 소유대명사(mine, yours, his, hers, ours, theirs)를 사용할 수 있다. 해당 문장에서는 그의 경험(His experience)과 그녀의 경험(her experience)을 비교하고 있는데, '그녀의 경험' 대신 '그녀의 것(hers)'이라는 소유대명사를 사용했다.
③ 11% 「remind A of B」는 'A에게 B를 상기시키다'라는 표현이다.
④ 16% 선행사가 people(사람)이고 관계대명사절에서 관계대명사가 주어 역할을 하는 경우 주격 관계대명사 who를 사용한다. '~의 눈을 보다'는 「look + 목적격 + in the + 신체 부위」로, 해당 표현에서 신체 부위 앞에는 소유격이 아닌 정관사 the를 사용하여야 한다.

| 더 알아보기 | 목적어의 형태에 따라 의미가 달라지는 동사

- regret/forget/remember -ing: ~했음을 …하다
- regret/forget/remember + to부정사: ~할 것을 …하다

어휘
remind A of B A에게 B를 상기시키다

---

14   독해 > Macro Reading > 제목   오답률 8%   답 ④

| 해석 | Louis 14세는 자신의 위대함에 걸맞은 궁전이 필요했다. 그래서 그는 작은 사냥 오두막이 있는 Versailles에 웅장한 새집을 짓기로 결심했다. 거의 50년의 노동 이후, 이 자그마한 사냥 오두막은 4분의 1마일 길이의 거대한 궁전으로 탈바꿈하였다. 물을 강에서 끌어오고 습지의 물을 빼기 위해 수로를 팠다. Versailles는 17개의 커다란 창문 맞은편에 17개의 거대한 거울이 있는 유명한 Hall of Mirrors와 순은 왕좌가 있는 Salon of Apollo와 같은 정교한 방들로 가득했다. Apollo, Jupiter, 그리고 Neptune과 같은 그리스 신들의 조각상 수백 개가 정원에 있었는데, 각각의 신들은 Louis의 얼굴을 가지고 있었다!
① 그리스 신들의 진짜 얼굴
② Hall of Mirrors 대 Salon of Apollo
③ 수로가 단순히 물 이상의 것을 Versailles에 가져왔는가?
④ Versailles: 소박한 오두막에서 거대한 궁전으로

| 정답해설 | ④ 92% 본문 첫 문장에서 Versailles에는 본래 작은 오두막이 있었다고 했고 두 번째 문장에서는 작은 오두막이 거대한 궁전으로 탈바꿈했다고 했다. 이후에는 궁전의 모습을 자세히 묘사하는 내용이 이어지므로 글의 제목으로 가장 적절한 것은 ④이다.

| 오답해설 | ① 4% 마지막 문장에서 Versailles 정원에 세워진 그

리스 신들의 조각상 얼굴은 Louis 14세의 얼굴을 본따 만들어졌다고 했을 뿐, 본문의 내용은 그리스 신들의 진정한 얼굴과는 관계가 없다.

② 1% 본문에서 Hall of Mirrors와 Salon of Apollo는 Versailles 궁전의 정교한 방을 설명하기 위한 예시로 제시되었을 뿐, 이 둘을 서로 비교하는 내용은 언급되지 않는다.

③ 3% 본문에서 Canal(수로)을 판 목적이 언급되기는 하지만, 전체 글을 아우르는 내용은 아니다.

어휘

worthy of ~할 만한	lodge 오두막
transform 변형시키다, (더 좋게) 탈바꿈시키다	
canal 수로, 운하	dig(– dug – dug) 파다
drain 물을 빼내다, 흘려보내다	marshland 습지대
elaborate 정교한, 공들인	solid 순~, 순수한
throne 왕좌, 옥좌	humble 소박한, 변변찮은, 초라한

---

15 독해 > Logical Reading > 삭제   오답률 37%   답 ③

| 해석 | 철학자들은 인류학자들이 철학에 관심을 가진 것만큼 인류학에 관심을 갖지 않았다. 자신들의 연구에 인류학적 연구들을 참작하는 영향력 있는 현대 철학자들은 거의 없다. 사회과학 철학을 전공하는 사람들이 인류학 연구로부터 나온 사례를 고려하거나 분석할 수도 있으나, 주로 개념적인 요소나 인식론적 차이를 보여 주기 위해서, 아니면 인식론적 또는 윤리적 의미를 비판하기 위해 이것을 한다. ③ 사실, 우리 시대의 훌륭한 철학자들은 인류학과 심리학과 같은 다른 분야로부터 종종 영감을 얻었다. 철학과 학생들은 인류학을 공부하거나 (인류학에) 진지한 관심을 보이는 법이 거의 없다. 그들은 과학의 실험적 방법에 대해 배울지는 모르지만, 인류학적인 현장 연구에 대해서는 거의 배우지 않는다.

| 정답해설 | ③ 63% 철학자들은 인류학에 대해 거의 관심을 갖지 않는다는 내용의 글이다. 그런데 우리 시대의 훌륭한 철학자들이 인류학으로부터 영감을 얻었다고 언급하는 ③은 글의 요지와 상반되므로 글의 흐름상 어색하다.

| 오답해설 | ④ 28% 철학과 학생들(Philosophy students)이 인류학을 공부하지 않는다는 내용은 전체 주제와 부합되며 마지막 문장에서 They가 해당 문장의 Philosophy students를 가리키므로, 이전 문장에서 학생들에 대해 언급되는 것은 자연스럽다.

어휘

concerned with ~에 관심 있는	anthropology 인류학
influential 영향력 있는	contemporary 현대의
take ~ into account ~을 참작하다, 고려하다	
specialize in ~을 전문으로 하다	analyze 분석하다
illustrate 보여 주다, 실증하다	epistemological 인식론의
distinction 차이, 구분	implication 의미, 함축
draw inspiration from ~로부터 영감을 받다	
seldom 거의 ~않는	rarely 드물게, 좀처럼 ~하지 않는
fieldwork 현장 연구	

---

16 독해 > Reading for Writing > 빈칸 구 완성   오답률 48%   답 ③

| 해석 | 우리 모두는 무언가를 물려받는다. 어떤 경우에 그것은 돈, 재산 또는 어떤 물건, 즉 할머니의 웨딩드레스나 아버지의 공구 세트 같은 집안의 가보일 수도 있다. 그러나 그것 이외에, 우리 모두는 다른 어떤 것, ③ 훨씬

덜 구체적이고 덜 유형적인 어떤 것, 심지어 우리가 완전히 인지하지 못할지도 모르는 것을 물려받는다. 그것은 일상적인 일을 하는 방식일 수도 있고, 우리가 특정한 문제를 해결하거나 스스로 도덕적 사안을 결정하는 방식일 수도 있다. 그것은 휴일 또는 특정한 날짜에 소풍을 가는 전통을 지키는 특별한 방식일 수도 있다. 그것은 중요한 것이거나 우리의 사고의 중심인 어떤 것일 수도 있고, 우리가 매우 무심코 오랫동안 받아들여 왔던 사소한 것일 수도 있다.

① 우리의 일상과 아주 관계가 없는
② 우리의 도덕적 기준에 반하는
③ 훨씬 덜 구체적이고 덜 유형적인
④ 엄청난 금전적 가치가 있는

| 정답해설 | ③ 52% 빈칸 이전에서는 '유형의 유산' 즉, 형태가 있는 돈, 재산, 가보 등을 물려받는 경우에 대해 설명하고 있다. 그러나 빈칸 이후에서는 일상적인 일을 하는 방식, 문제 해결 방식, 휴일 또는 전통을 지키는 방식 등과 같은 '무형의 유산'에 대해 언급한다. 즉, 앞서 설명한 유산보다는 상대적으로 덜 구체적이고 실체가 없는 무형적인 유산이므로 빈칸에 가장 적절한 표현은 ③이다.

어휘

inherit 물려받다, 상속받다	heirloom (집안의) 가보
moral 도덕적인, 도덕상의	casually 무심코, 아무 생각 없이
concrete 구체적인	
tangible 유형적인, 실체가 있는, 만질 수 있는	
monetary 통화의, 화폐의	

---

17 독해 > Macro Reading > 요지   오답률 47%   답 ①

| 해석 | 진화론적으로, 생존하고자 하는 어떠한 종이든 자신들의 자원을 신중히 관리해야 한다. 그것은 식량과 다른 맛있는 것들에 관한 첫 번째 요구는 양육자, 전사, 사냥꾼, 농사꾼, 건축가 들과, 분명히 아이들에게 먼저 돌아가야 하며 기여하는 것보다 더 많이 소비하는 것처럼 보일지도 모르는 노인들에게는 그다지 많이 남겨지지 않는다는 것을 의미한다. 그러나 현대 의학이 기대 수명을 연장하기 전에도 보통의 가족들은 조부모, 심지어는 증조부모를 포함하고 있었다. 그것은 나이든 사람들이 종종 그들 주변을 맴도는 소동에 대해 균형 잡히고 이치에 맞는 중심을 잡아 줌으로써 그들이 물질적으로 소비한 것을 행동적으로 되돌려주었기 때문이다.

① 노인들은 가족에 기여를 해 오고 있다.
② 현대 의학은 노인의 역할에 초점을 맞추었다.
③ 가족 내에서 자원을 잘 할당하는 것이 가족의 번영을 결정짓는다.
④ 대가족에는 제한된 자원이라는 대가가 따른다.

| 정답해설 | ① 53% 진화론적 관점에서 노인들에게 자원이 적게 배분되는 것이 자연스러운 일임을 언급한 후, 그럼에도 불구하고 오래전부터 노인들이 가족의 일원으로 함께 살아왔다는 점을 강조하고 그 이유를 마지막 문장에서 제시하고 있다. 즉, 노인들이 가족에 기여한 바가 있음을 시사한다. 따라서 글의 요지로 가장 적절한 것은 '노인들은 가족에 기여를 해 오고 있다.'이다.

어휘

goodies 맛있는 것	breeder 양육자, 사육자
contribute 기부하다, 기여하다	old folk 노인들
behaviorally 행동으로	tumult 소동, 소란
swirl 소용돌이치다, 빙빙 돌다	allocate 할당하다
prosperity 번영	

18 독해 > Logical Reading > 배열 오답률 27% 답 ③

| 해석 | 요즘에 시계는 우리의 삶을 매우 많이 지배하고 있어서 그것 없는 삶을 상상하기는 어렵다. 산업화 이전에 대부분의 사회는 시간을 알기 위해 해나 달을 이용했다.

(B) 기계식 시계가 처음 등장했을 때, 그것들은 즉시 인기를 얻었다. 시계나 손목시계를 소유하는 것은 유행이었다. 사람들은 시간을 알려 주는 이 새로운 방식을 가리키기 위해 "of the clock"이나 "o'clock"과 같은 표현을 만들어 냈다.

(C) 이러한 시계들은 장식용이었으나, 항상 유용한 것은 아니었다. 이것은 도시, 지방, 그리고 심지어 이웃 마을조차도 시간을 알려 주는 방식이 달랐기 때문이다. 여행자들은 한 장소에서 다른 장소로 이동할 때마다 반복적으로 자신들의 시계를 다시 맞추어야 했다. 미국에는 1860년대에 약 70개의 다른 시간대가 있었다.

(A) 점점 늘어나는 철도망에 있어서 시간 기준이 없다는 사실은 재앙이었다. 종종, 겨우 몇 마일 떨어진 역들이 서로 다른 시간에 자신들의 시계를 맞추었다. 여행객들에게 혼란스러운 상황이 많았다.

| 정답해설 | ③ 73% 주어진 문장의 두 번째 문장에서는 산업화 이전에 시간을 알려 주는 방법에 대해 언급하고 있다. 이후 이어질 내용으로 가장 적절한 것은 기계식 시계가 최초로 등장한 때의 상황에 대해 설명하는 (B)이다. 이어 (B)에서 언급한 mechanical clocks를 (C)에서 These clocks로 대신하고 있으므로, (C)가 (B)에 연결되는 것이 적절하다. (C) 후반부에서는 서로 다른 시간대(different time zones)의 존재를 언급하였으므로 이러한 다른 시간대가 초래한 문제점을 설명하는 (A)가 (C) 뒤에 이어지는 것이 가장 자연스럽다.

어휘

industrialization 산업화 mechanical 기계로 작동되는
decorative 장식용의, 장식된 province 지방, 주(州)

19 독해 > Logical Reading > 삽입 오답률 45% 답 ④

| 해석 | 밀레니얼 세대(Millennials)는 종종 현대에서 가장 가난하고, 재정적 부담이 가장 큰 세대로 분류된다. 그들 중 다수가 대학을 졸업하면서, 충격적인 양의 학자금 대출과 함께 미국이 역대 목격한 최악의 노동 시장으로 진출했다. 놀랄 것도 없이, 밀레니얼 세대는 X세대가 인생의 비슷한 단계에서 모은 것보다 더 적은 부를 축적했는데, 이는 주로 그들 중 집을 소유한 사람이 더 적기 때문이다. 그러나 다른 세대의 미국인들이 무엇을 저축했는지에 대한 지금까지 가장 상세한 그림을 제공하는, 새롭게 이용 가능해진 데이터가 그 평가를 복잡하게 만든다. 그렇다. 1965년에서 1980년 사이에 태어난 사람들인 X세대들이 더 많은 순자산을 보유하고 있다. ④ 그러나 1981년에서 1996년 사이에 태어난 밀레니얼 세대가, X세대가 같은 나이인 22세~37세에 저축했던 것에 비해 은퇴에 대비하여 더 적극적으로 저축을 하고 있다는 분명한 증거가 또한 존재한다. 그리고 그것이 많은 사람들이 생각하는 것보다 그들을 더 나은 재정적 형편에 처하게 할지도 모른다.

| 정답해설 | ④ 55% 주어진 문장의 But으로 보아, 앞에서 이와 대조되는 내용이 나와야 한다는 것을 유추할 수 있다. 주어진 문장에서는 밀레니얼 세대가 X세대보다 은퇴에 대비하여 더 많은 저축을 하고 있다고 언급하며, 밀레니얼 세대가 X세대보다 재정적으로 더 우월할 수도 있음을 시사한다. 따라서 주어진 문장 이전에서는 X세대가 밀레니얼 세대보다 경제적으로 더 윤택하다는 취지의 대조적인 내용이 등장하는 것이 자연스럽다. ④ 이전 문장에서 1965년에서 1980년 사이에 태어난 사람들인 X세대들이 더 많은 순자산을 보

유하고 있다고 언급하고 있으므로 주어진 문장이 들어갈 가장 적절한 위치는 ④이다.

| 더 알아보기 | Millennials (밀레니얼 세대)

1980년대 초반~2000년대에 초반에 출생한 세대. 정보 기술에 능통하며 대학 진학률이 높다는 특징이 있다. 2008년 글로벌 금융 위기 이후 사회에 진출해 고용 감소, 일자리 질 저하 등의 어려움을 겪는 세대이기도 하다.

어휘

aggressively 적극적으로, 공격적으로
label 분류하다 staggering 충격적인; 비틀거리는
to boot 그것도(앞서 한 말에 대해 다른 말을 덧붙일 때)
accumulate 축적하다 to date 지금까지
assessment 평가 net worth 순자산

20 독해 > Micro Reading > 내용일치/불일치 오답률 22% 답 ④

| 해석 | 산호와 다른 암초 유기체의 붕괴로부터 수천 년 동안 축적된 탄산염 모래는 산호초 뼈대의 건축재이다. 그러나 이 모래는 바닷물의 화학적 구성에 민감하다. 바다가 이산화탄소를 흡수함에 따라, 그것들은 산성화되고, 특정 시점에 탄산염 모래는 그냥 용해되기 시작한다. 세계의 바다는 인간이 배출하는 이산화탄소의 약 3분의 1을 흡수해 왔다. 그 모래가 용해되는 속도는 위쪽에 있는 해수의 산성도와 크게 관련되어 있었고, 산호의 성장보다 해양의 산성화에 10배나 더 민감했다. 다시 말해, 바다의 산성화는 산호의 성장보다 산호초 모래의 용해에 더 많은 영향을 미칠 것이다. 이것은 아마도 자신들의 환경을 조정하고 부분적으로 바다의 산성화에 적응할 수 있는 산호의 능력을 반영하지만, 모래의 용해는 조정할 수 없는 지구화학적 과정이다.

① 산호초의 뼈대는 탄산염 모래로 만들어진다.
② 산호는 부분적으로 바다의 산성화에 적응할 수 있다.
③ 인간이 배출한 이산화탄소는 세계 바다의 산성화에 기여해 왔다.
④ 바다의 산성화는 산호초 모래의 용해보다 산호의 성장에 더 많은 영향을 미친다.

| 정답해설 | ④ 78% 본문 끝에서 두 번째 문장 In other words, ocean acidification will impact the dissolution of coral reef sands more than the growth of corals.에서 해양 산성화가 산호의 성장보다 모래의 용해에 더 많은 영향을 미친다고 했으므로 ④는 글의 내용과 반대된다.

어휘

carbonate 탄산염 breakdown 붕괴, 분해
coral 산호 reef 암초
acidify 산성화되다 dissolve 용해되다, 녹다
dissolution 용해, 소멸 geochemical 지구화학적

합격예상 체크

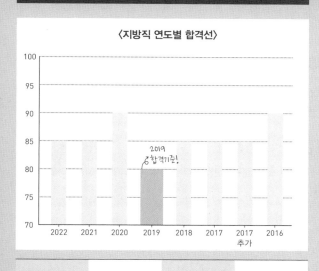

〈지방직 연도별 합격선〉

2019
ⓑ합격기준!

맞힌 개수	/20문항	점수	/100점

➡ ☐ 합격　☐ 불합격

취약영역 체크

문항	정답	영역	문항	정답	영역
①	①	어휘 > 유의어 찾기	11	④	어휘 > 유의어 찾기
2	①	어휘 > 유의어 찾기	12	①	어휘 > 유의어 찾기
3	④	생활영어 > 회화/관용표현	13	③	독해 > Reading for Writing > 빈칸 구 완성
4	③	생활영어 > 회화/관용표현	14	④	독해 > Logical Reading > 연결사
5	④	문법 > 태	15	④	독해 > Logical Reading > 삽입
6	②	문법 > 조동사	16	③	문법 > 동사
7	②	독해 > Logical Reading > 배열	17	①	독해 > Micro Reading > 내용 일치/불일치
8	②	독해 > Micro Reading > 내용 일치/불일치	18	①	독해 > Micro Reading > 내용 일치/불일치
9	②	독해 > Macro Reading > 주제	19	①	독해 > Reading for Writing > 빈칸 구 완성
10	④	독해 > Logical Reading > 삭제	20	②	독해 > Reading for Writing > 빈칸 구 완성

⬇ 영역별 틀린 개수로 취약영역을 확인하세요!

어휘	/4	문법	/3	독해	/11	생활영어	/2

➡ 나의 취약영역: ＿＿＿＿＿＿＿＿

※ [정답해설]과 [오답해설] 선지의 50% 표시는 〈1초 합격예측 서비스〉를 통해 수집된 선지 선택률을 나타냅니다.

---

1 어휘 > 유의어 찾기　　오답률 43%　답 ①

| 해석 | 나는 이 문헌들을 이제는 죽어서 묻혀 버렸지만 발굴되어져야 할 감수성의 유물로 여기게 되었다.

① 57% 파내지다
② 9% 포장되다, 꾸려지다
③ 30% 지워지다
④ 4% 축하받다

| 정답해설 | ① excavate는 '발굴하다, 파내다'라는 뜻을 가진 단어로, 유의어 관계에 있는 것은 exhume(파내다)이다.

어휘

relic 유물, 유적　　　　　sensibility 감성, 감수성
bury 매장하다

---

2 어휘 > 유의어 찾기　　오답률 32%　답 ①

| 해석 | 롤러코스터를 타는 것은 감정의 폭주 드라이브일 수 있다. 즉, 당신이 좌석에 안전띠를 맬 때의 긴장되는 기대, 당신이 위로, 위로, 위로 올라갈 때 생기는 의문과 후회, 그리고 그 차가 첫 하강할 때의 완전한 아드레날린의 분출이다.

① 68% 완전한
② 18% 무서운
③ 10% 가끔의
④ 4% 관리할 수 있는

| 정답해설 | ① sheer는 '완전한, 순수한'이란 뜻을 가진 단어이므로 유의어 관계인 것은 utter(완전한)이다.

어휘

joy ride 폭주 드라이브, 재미있는 드라이브　　questioning 의문, 질문

---

3 생활영어 > 회화/관용표현　　오답률 8%　답 ④

| 해석 | ① A: 우리 몇 시에 점심 먹을 거야?
　B: 정오 전에 준비될 거야.
② A: 너한테 몇 번이나 전화했어. 왜 안 받았어?
　B: 아, 내 휴대 전화가 꺼져 있었던 거 같아.
③ A: 이번 겨울에 휴가 갈 거야?
　B: 그럴지도. 아직 결정 못 했어.
④ A: 여보세요. 전화 못 받아서 죄송합니다.
　B: 메시지 남기시겠어요?

| 정답해설 | ④ 92% A가 상대방에게 전화를 못 받았다고 사과를 하고 있는데 B가 메시지를 남길 건지 묻는 것은 적절하지 않다.

어휘

turn off 끄다　　　　　leave a message 메시지를 남기다

---

4 생활영어 > 회화/관용표현　　오답률 35%　답 ③

| 해석 | A: 안녕하세요. 돈을 좀 환전해야 해요.
B: 네. 어떤 돈이 필요하세요?
A: 달러를 파운드로 바꿔야 해요. 환율이 어떻게 되나요?
B: 환율은 1달러당 0.73파운드입니다.
A: 좋아요. 수수료를 받나요?
B: 네, 저희는 소액의 수수료를 받는데 4달러예요.
A: ③ 역구매 정책은 무엇인가요?
B: 저희는 무료로 다시 환전을 해 드려요. 영수증만 가지고 오세요.
① 이것은 비용이 얼마나 드나요

② 제가 그것을 어떻게 지불해야 하나요
③ 역구매 정책은 무엇인가요
④ 신용카드를 받으시나요

| 정답해설 | ③ 65% 빈칸의 질문에 대한 답변으로 B가 무료로 다시 환전을 해 주며 영수증을 지참하라고 하는 것으로 보아, A는 환전한 돈을 다시 재환전할 때에 관한 질문을 했음을 유추할 수 있다. 따라서 역구매 정책에 관해 묻는 ③이 빈칸에 알맞다.

어휘

currency 통화, 화폐	convert 전환하다, 바꾸다
exchange rate 환율	commission 수수료
buy-back 역구매, 되사기	

---

5   문법 > 태   오답률 21%   답 ④

| 해석 | 매년, 27만 명이 넘는 보행자들이 전 세계의 도로에서 그들의 목숨을 잃는다. 많은 사람들이 어느 날 그러듯이 집을 떠났다가 결국 다시는 돌아오지 못한다. 전 세계적으로, 보행자들은 모든 도로 교통 사망자들의 22%를 차지하며, 어떤 국가들에서 이 비율은 모든 도로 교통 사망자들의 2/3에 해당할 만큼 높다. 수백만 명의 보행자들은 치명적이지 않은 부상을 당하는데, 그들 중 일부에게는 영구적 장애가 남는다. 이런 사고들은 경제적 어려움뿐만 아니라 많은 고통과 비통함을 야기한다.

| 정답해설 | ④ 79% 주어가 Millions of pedestrians이므로 수동태로 써야 '부상을 당하다'의 의미가 된다. 따라서 injuring은 injured로 바꿔야 한다. '부상당하다'는 be[get] injured라고 거의 관용적으로 쓰므로 숙지해 두는 것이 좋다.

| 오답해설 | ① 2% '매년 벌어지는 일'이므로 현재시제 동사 lose(잃는다)가 어법상 적절하고, 주어인 more than 270,000 pedestrians와도 수가 일치한다.
② 14% to부정사의 부사적 용법 중 결과를 의미하는 표현으로 '~했으나 결국 …하지 못했다'라는 의미이다.
③ 5% high는 be동사 is의 주격 보어 역할을 하는 형용사로 사용되었다. 해당 문장은 원급 비교 문장으로서 원급 형용사 high는 as에 의해서 수식받고 또한 수식 대상 as 이하 전명구와 함께 올바르게 사용되었다.

| 더 알아보기 | 주어-동사의 수 일치

(1) 단수 주어 → 단수 동사
(2) 복수 주어 → 복수 동사
   - 주어-동사의 수 일치는 수식어구(전명구, 분사구, to부정사, 관계사절, 동격 that)를 제외하고 주어와 동사를 수 일치시킨다.
- 전치사구
  One of the most important things in playing baseball **is** concentration.
  야구를 할 때 가장 중요한 것 중 하나가 집중이다.
- 현재분사(구)/과거분사(구)
  Citizens opposed to City Hall **were** demonstrating against the government policy.
  시청 건너편에 있던 시민들은 정부 정책에 반대하는 시위 중이었다.
- to부정사
  Her **proposal** to move **was** not accepted.
  이사를 가는 그녀의 제안은 받아들여지지 않았다.

- 관계사절
Most **people** who live in a big city **are** concerned about the yellow dust.
대도시에 살고 있는 대부분의 사람들이 황사에 대해 걱정한다.
- 동격절
The **idea** that we can produce many kinds of sports cars **was** accepted.
우리가 다양한 종류의 스포츠카를 생산할 수 있다는 생각은 받아들여졌다.

어휘

pedestrian 보행자	fatality 사망자
proportion 비율, 부분	permanent 영구적인
disability 장애	

---

6   문법 > 조동사   오답률 55%   답 ②

| 해석 | ① 그 신문은 자신의 목적을 위해 회사의 돈을 사용했다고 그녀를 비난했다.
② 의심이 생기지 않도록 그 조사는 극도로 주의하여 처리되어야 했다.
③ 해석 불가
④ 화석 연료를 연소시키는 것이 기후 변화의 가장 중요한 원인들 중 하나이다.

| 정답해설 | ② 45% 주어가 사물(The investigation)이므로 문맥상 동사가 수동태로 적절하게 쓰였다. 또한 접속사 lest가 이끄는 절에서 조동사 should는 생략할 수 있으므로 종속절의 동사 be aroused(생겨나다)는 올바르게 사용되었다. 또한 lest는 '~하지 않도록, ~하지 않으려고'라는 부정의 의미를 지니므로 부정부사를 사용하지 않은 것도 적절하다.

| 오답해설 | ① 8% 「charge A with B」는 'A를 B로 비난하다'를 뜻하며 with는 전치사이므로 목적어로 명사나 동명사를 취해야 한다. 해당 문장에서는 명사구 the company's money ~가 문맥상 use의 목적어 역할을 하고 있다. 따라서 전치사 with의 명사 목적어 기능과 동사로서 목적어를 갖는 역할을 동시에 할 수 있도록 동사와 명사의 기능을 함께하는 동명사가 필요하므로 use를 동명사 using으로 수정해야 옳다.
③ 22% 문맥상 2형식 동사인 would be 뒤에 주격 보어가 필요하므로 과거분사가 아닌 to부정사 또는 동명사가 나와야 한다.
④ 25% one of the 다음에는 복수 명사가 필요하다. 또한 '주요한'이라는 의미로 명사인 causes를 수식할 수 있는 것은 형용사이므로 lead를 분사 형태로 고쳐야 한다. 따라서 one of the leading causes가 어법에 맞는 표현이다.

| 더 알아보기 | 이중 부정 금지 접속사

- nor + 동사 + 주어: ~ 역시 아니다
- lest + 주어 + (should) + 동사원형: ~하지 않기 위해서
- for fear that + 주어 + (should) + 동사원형: ~하지 않기 위해서

어휘

charge A with B A를 B로 비난[고발, 고소]하다

utmost 극도의, 최대의	arouse 불러일으키다, 자극하다
shift 변화	fossil fuel 화석 연료

| **7** | 독해 > Logical Reading > 배열 | 오답률 59% | 답 ② |

| 해석 | 우리의 뇌리를 떠나지 않을 수도 있는 생각이 있다: 아마도 모든 것이 다른 모든 것에 영향을 줄 텐데, 도대체 어떻게 우리가 사회적 세계를 이해할 수가 있는가? 하지만, 만약 우리가 그 걱정에 짓눌리게 된다면, 우리는 결코 진보를 이루지 못할 것이다.

(A) 내게 익숙한 모든 학문 분야는 세상을 이해하기 위해 그것의 캐리커처를 그린다. 현대 경제학자들은 '모델들'을 만들어서 이것을 하는데, 이것들은 저 밖에 있는 현상에 대해 의도적으로 분해된 묘사들이다.

(C) 내가 "분해된"이라고 말할 때, 나는 정말 분해된 것을 의미한다. 그렇게 하는 것이 현실의 그러한 측면들이 어떻게 작동하고 상호 작용하는지를 우리가 이해할 수 있도록 해 줄 것이라고 희망하면서, 다른 모든 것을 배제하고 하나 또는 두 가지의 원인이 되는 요인들에 집중하는 것이 우리 경제학자들 사이에서는 드문 일은 아니다.

(B) 경제학자인 John Maynard Keynes는 우리의 주제를 이와 같이 설명했다. "경제학은 현대 세계와 관련된 모델들을 선택하는 기술과 결합된 모델들이라는 면에서 생각의 과학이다."

| 정답해설 | ② 41% 주어진 글에서는 '우리가 세상을 이해하는 방법'이라는 글의 소재를 제시하고 있다. (A), (B), (C) 모두 경제 혹은 경제학자들에 대해서 서술하고 있는데 첫 문단은 도입으로서 경제학자들의 모델들에 대해서 처음 언급하는 (A)가 가장 적합하다. 이어서 (A)의 후반부에서 언급된 '분해된 묘사들'에 대한 의미를 구체적으로 설명하는 (C)가 (A)에 이어 서술되는 것이 적합하다. 그리고 끝으로 글의 내용을 요약 정리하는 '경제학은 모델들을 선택하는 기술이다'라는 내용이 포함된 (B)가 마지막으로 서술되는 것이 적합하다. 따라서 글의 순서는 (A) – (C) – (B)가 가장 적절하다.

어휘

haunt 떠나지 않다, 계속 출몰하다	make sense of ~을 이해하다
weigh down 짓누르다	discipline 학문 분야
deliberately 의도적으로	strip down 분해하다, 벗겨내다
representation 묘사, 표현	phenomenon 현상 (pl. phenomena)
in terms of ~ 면에서, ~에 관하여	contemporary 현대의, 동시대의
causal 원인이 되는, 원인의	interact 상호 작용하다, 교류하다

| **8** | 독해 > Micro Reading > 내용일치/불일치 | 오답률 9% | 답 ② |

| 해석 | 대략 50만 년 전 선사 시대의 사회들은 정신적 장애와 신체적 장애를 뚜렷이 구별하지 않았다. 단순한 두통에서 발작 경련에 이르기까지, 비정상적인 행동들은 고통받는 사람의 몸속에 살고 있거나 그 사람을 통제하는 악령의 탓으로 돌려졌다. 역사학자들에 따르면, 이러한 고대인들은 많은 형태의 질병들을 악령 빙의, 마법, 또는 화가 난 조상 영혼의 명령 탓으로 돌렸다. 악마 연구라고 불리는 이러한 믿음 체계 내에서, 피해자는 보통 불운에 대해 적어도 부분적으로 책임이 지워졌다. 석기 시대 동굴 거주자들은 '두개골 수술'이라고 불리는 외과적 방법으로 행동 장애를 치료했을 수도 있음이 암시되었는데, 그 수술에서는 악령이 빠져나갈 수 있는 틈이 주어지도록 두개골의 일부가 잘려 나갔다. 사람들은 악령이 떠나면 그 사람이 정상적인 상태로 돌아올 것이라고 믿었을지도 모른다. 놀랍게도, 수술을 받은 두개골들이 치유된 것으로 밝혀졌는데, 이는 일부 환자들이 이렇게 극히 조잡한 수술에도 살아남았다는 것을 보여 준다.

① 정신적 장애는 신체적 장애와는 분명히 구분되었다.

② 비정상적인 행동은 사람에게 영향을 미치는 악령으로부터 비롯되었다고 믿어졌다.

③ 악령이 사람의 신체에 들어갈 수 있도록 두개골에 틈이 만들어졌다.

④ 두개골 수술에서 살아남은 동굴 거주자들은 없었다.

| 정답해설 | ② 91% 본문의 두 번째 문장에서 비정상적인 행동들은 병에 걸린 사람의 몸속에 살고 있거나 그 사람을 통제하는 악령의 탓으로 돌려졌다고 했으므로 ②가 본문과 일치하는 내용이다.

어휘

prehistoric 선사 시대의	disorder 장애, 이상
abnormal 비정상적인	evil spirit 악령
behest 명령, 지령	afflicted 고통받는, 괴로워하는
demonic 악령의	sorcery 마법
demonology 귀신론, 악마 연구	skull 두개골
chip away 깎아 내다, 잘라 내다	heal over 아물다, 치료하다
crude 조잡한, 거친, 대강의	differentiate 구별하다

| **9** | 독해 > Macro Reading > 주제 | 오답률 38% | 답 ② |

| 해석 | 디지털 혁명이 전국적으로 뉴스룸에 큰 영향을 주기 때문에, 여기 모든 기자들을 위한 나의 조언이 있다. 나는 25년 넘게 기자였기에, 6번의 기술적 수명 주기를 거치며 살아 왔다. 가장 급격한 변화는 마지막 6년 동안에 찾아왔다. 그것은 내가, 점점 더 잦은 빈도로, 일을 진행하면서 이야기들을 만들어 낸다는 것을 의미한다. 뉴스 업계에서 많은 시간을, 우리는 우리가 무엇을 하는지 모른다. 우리가 아침에 출근하면 누군가 "세금 정책/이민/기후 변화에 대해 (하나를 선택해서) 글을 써 줄래요?"라고 말한다. 신문이 하루에 한 번 마감 시간이 있을 때, 우리는 기자가 아침에 배워서 밤에 가르치는 거라고 말했다. 그 기자가 24시간 전에는 전혀 몰랐던 주제에 관해 내일의 독자들에게 알려 줄 수 있는 이야기를 쓰기에 말이다. 지금은 매시 정각에 배워서 매시 30분에 가르치는 것에 더 가깝다. 예를 들면, 나는 또한 정치 팟캐스트를 운영하고 있는데, 대선 후보 선정을 위한 전당 대회 동안, 우리는 어디서든 실시간 인터뷰를 하기 위해 그것을 이용할 수 있어야 한다. 나는 그냥 점점 더 대본 없이 일하고 있다.

① 교사로서의 기자
② 기자와 즉흥 (기사 작성)
③ 정치에서의 기술
④ 언론과 기술 분야

| 정답해설 | ② 62% 기자로서 필자는 24시간 전에는 알지 못했던 주제에 관해 내일의 독자에게 알려 주는 기사를 쓰곤 했지만 지금은 30분마다 기사를 쓰고 실시간 인터뷰를 위해 팟캐스트 이용법을 알아야 하는 등 점점 더 대본 없이 일하고 있다고 했으므로 ②가 이 글의 주제로 가장 적절하다.

어휘

upend 뒤집다, ~에 큰 영향을 미치다
at the top of the hour 매시 정각에
at the bottom of the hour (1시 30분, 2시 30분 등과 같이) 매시 30분에
presidential convention 대선 후보 선정을 위한 전당 대회
improvisation 즉흥, 즉석에서 하기

오답률 TOP3

| **10** | 독해 > Logical Reading > 삭제 | 오답률 63% | 답 ④ |

| 해석 | 역사를 통틀어 아이들의 놀이터는 시골의 황무지, 들판, 개울, 언덕, 그리고 마을, 소도시, 대도시의 도로, 거리, 그리고 비어 있는 장소들이었다. playground라는 용어는 아이들이 그들의 자유롭고 즉흥적인 놀이를 하기 위해 모이는 곳들 전부를 말한다. 오직 지난 몇 십 년 동안 아이들은 비디오 게임, 문자, 그리고 소셜 네트워킹에 대한 커지는 애정 때문에 이 자연의 놀이터들을 비워 두었다. 심지어 미국의 시골 지역에서도 어른의 동반 없이 여전히 마음대로 돌아다니는 아이들이 거의 없다. ④ 방과 후, 아이들이 동네에서 모래를 파고, 요새를 짓고, 전통적인 놀이를 하고, 기어오르거나, 공놀이를 하는 모습이 흔히 발견된다. 그들은 개울, 언덕, 그리고 들판과

같은 자연 지형에서 빠르게 사라지고 있으며, 도시의 그들의 비교 대상들처럼, 오락거리로 앉아서 하는 실내용 사이버 장난감에 의지하고 있다.

| **정답해설** | ④ 37% 과거에는 자연 속에서 아이들이 놀았던 반면, 현대의 아이들은 자연을 떠나 실내에서 사이버 장난감을 가지고 논다는 내용이다. ④는 실외에서 전통적인 놀이를 하는 아이들이 흔히 발견된다는 것으로 앞뒤 문장과 반대되는 내용이므로 글의 흐름상 어색하다.

어휘
wilderness 황무지 　　　　　　vacate 비우다, 떠나다
roam 돌아다니다, 배회하다
free-ranging 마음대로 돌아다니는, 방목의
fort 진지, 요새 　　　　　　　terrain 지형, 지역
counterpart 비교 대상, 상대방
sedentary 몸을 많이 움직이지 않는, 늘 앉아서 하는

---

11 어휘 > 유의어 찾기 　　　오답률 45% 　답 ④

| **해석** | 시간은 지루한 오후 수업 동안은 아주 느려지고, 뇌가 아주 재미있는 무언가에 열중할 때는 달려가는 것처럼 보인다.
① 25% ~의해 강화되다 　　② 11% ~에 무관심하다
③ 9% ~의해 안정되다 　　　④ 55% ~에 사로잡히다

| **정답해설** | ④ engrossed in은 '~에 열중하는'이라는 뜻으로 preoccupied with(~에 사로잡힌)와 유의어 관계이다.

어휘
slow to a trickle 아주 느려지다 　　race 급히 가다, 질주하다

---

12 어휘 > 유의어 찾기 　　　오답률 53% 　답 ①

| **해석** | 정부가 시장을 통제 하에 두려고 시도했기 때문에, 이 일일 업데이트는 독자들이 시장의 소식을 계속 접하는 것을 돕기 위해 만들어졌다.
① 47% ~을 알다 　　　　② 12% ~의해 영감을 얻다
③ 22% ~을 믿다 　　　　④ 19% ~을 멀리하다

| **정답해설** | ① keep abreast of는 '~의 소식을 계속 접하다, ~에 뒤지지 않게 하다'라는 뜻으로 be acquainted with(~을 알다)와 유의어 관계이다.

어휘
attempt 시도하다 　　　　keep under control ~을 통제하다

---

13 독해 > Reading for Writing > 빈칸 구 완성 　오답률 9% 　답 ③

| **해석** | 1840년대에, 아일랜드 섬은 기근을 겪었다. 아일랜드는 그 인구를 먹일 만큼 충분한 식량을 생산할 수 없었기 때문에, 대략 100만 명이 (A) 기아로 사망했는데, 단순히 생존하기 위해 먹을 것이 충분하지 않았기 때문이었다. 기근은 또 다른 125만 명의 사람들이 (B) 이민 가도록 만들었는데, 많은 이들이 그들의 고국 섬을 떠나 미국으로 갔고, 나머지는 캐나다, 호주, 칠레, 그리고 다른 국가들로 갔다. 기근 이전, 아일랜드의 인구는 대략 6백만 명이었다. 대기근 이후, 인구는 대략 4백만 명이었다.

　　　　(A) 　　　　　(B)
① 　탈수 　　　　　추방되다
② 　트라우마 　　　이민 오다
③ 　기아 　　　　　이민 가다
④ 　피로 　　　　　억류되다

| **정답해설** | ③ 91% (A) 빈칸 다음에 나온 '생존하기 위해 먹을 것이 충분하지 않았다'는 내용으로 보아 아일랜드 사람들의 사망 원인으로는 starvation(기아)이 적합하다.
(B) 빈칸 다음에 '많은 이들이 그들의 고국 섬을 떠나 미국으로 갔다'는 것으로 보아 빈칸에 들어갈 말로는 emigrate(이민 가다)가 적합하다.

어휘
famine 기근 　　　　　　　die of ~로 죽다
dehydration 탈수 　　　　　deport 강제 추방하다

---

14 독해 > Logical Reading > 연결사 　오답률 45% 　답 ④

| **해석** | 오늘날 가상 현실(VR) 체험의 시각적 요소를 만들어 내는 기술은 널리 접근이 가능하고 가격이 적정해지는 과정에 있다. 그러나 강력하게 기능하기 위해서, 가상 현실은 시각적인 것 이상에 관한 것이어야 할 필요가 있다. 당신이 듣고 있는 것이 시각적인 것들과 설득력 있게 일치하지 (A) 않는다면, 가상 체험은 실패로 돌아간다. 농구를 예를 들어 보자. 만약 선수들, 코치들, 아나운서들, 그리고 관중들이 코트 가운데 앉아 있는 것처럼 들린다면, 당신은 TV로 경기를 보는 것이 낫다. 당신은 당신이 "거기" 있는 만큼의 느낌만 받게 될 것이다. (B) 안타깝게도, 오늘날의 오디오 장비와 널리 사용되는 녹화 및 재생 포맷은 먼 행성의 전쟁터, 코트 사이드에서의 농구 경기, 또는 훌륭한 콘서트홀의 첫 줄에서 들리는 것 같은 심포니의 소리를 설득력 있게 재현하는 일에는 그저 불충분하다.

　　　　(A) 　　　　　　(B)
① 　만약 ~라면 　　　　대조적으로
② 　만약 ~하지 않다면 　결과적으로
③ 　만약 ~라면 　　　　비슷하게
④ 　만약 ~하지 않다면 　안타깝게도

| **정답해설** | ④ 55% (A) 가상 체험이 실패로 돌아가는 원인은 '당신이 듣고 있는 것이 시각적인 것들과 설득력 있게 일치하지 않는 경우'이므로 빈칸에는 Unless(그렇지 않다면)가 적합하다.
(B) 빈칸 뒤의 내용이 '오늘날의 오디오 장비, 녹화/재생 포맷이 실제 상황을 재현하기에 충분하지 않다'는 것을 지적하고 있으므로 빈칸에는 Unfortunately(안타깝게도)가 적합하다.

어휘
virtual-reality 가상 현실 　　　on one's way to ~로 가는 도중에
accessible 이용[출입, 접근] 가능한　affordable (가격이) 알맞은
convincingly 설득력 있게
break apart 실패로 돌아가다, 무너지다; 부서지다
may as well ~하는 편이 낫다 　　inadequate 불충분한, 부적절한

---

15 독해 > Logical Reading > 삽입 　오답률 34% 　답 ④

| **해석** | 행복한 뇌는 단기간에 집중하는 경향이 있다. 그렇다면, 결국에는 장기 목표들의 성취로 이어질 어떤 단기 목표들을 우리가 성취할 수 있는지를 고려하는 것은 좋은 생각이다. 예를 들어, 만약 당신이 6개월 후 30파운드를 감량하기를 원한다면, 당신은 어떤 단기 목표들을 당신이 거기에 도달하게 해 줄 더 적은 체중을 감량하는 것과 연관 지을 수 있는가? 아마 그것은 당신이 매주 2파운드를 감량하는 당신 자신에게 보상을 해 주는 것만큼 단순한 무언가일 것이다. ④ 동일한 생각이 직장에서 실적을 향상시키는 것과 같은, 많은 목표들에도 적용될 수 있다. 전체 목표를 더 작고 더 단기적인 부분들로 나눔으로써, 우리는 직업 목표의 엄청남에 압도되는 대신 서서히 증가하는 성취들에 집중할 수 있다.

| 정답해설 | ④ 66% 주어진 문장에서 '동일한 생각이 적용될 수 있다'라고 했으므로 언급된 생각과 유사한 것이 다음에 전개될 것임을 알 수 있다. ④ 이전까지는 몸무게 감량의 예시가 있고, ④ 이후에서는 직업에서의 목표 달성의 예시가 나오므로 주어진 문장은 ④에 위치하는 것이 가장 적절하다.

어휘

apply to ~에 적용하다 performance 실적, 성과
that being the case 사정이 그렇다면
associate A with B A와 B를 연관 짓다
incremental (서서히) 증가하는 enormity 엄청남, 막대함
profession 직업, 전문직

16 문법 > 동사 　오답률 27% 답 ③

| 정답해설 | ③ 73% 타동사 marry(결혼하다)는 '~와 결혼한 상태'를 표현할 때에는 「be married to + 목적어」를 써야 하며 결혼한 지 20년이 되었다고 했으므로 완료시제를 써야 한다. 따라서 has married는 has been married로 고쳐야 한다.

| 오답해설 | ① 6% 조건의 부사절 접속사 in case (that)가 문맥에 맞게 쓰였고, 「would like + to부정사」 역시 알맞게 사용되었다.
② 14% 동명사 관용표현 「be busy -ing(~하느라 바쁘다)」가 적절하게 사용되었다.
④ 7% to read가 to부정사의 형용사적 용법으로 명사인 a book을 수식하며 to부정사 앞의 for my son은 의미상의 주어로 「for + (대)명사」의 형태로 알맞게 쓰였다.

| 더 알아보기 | 동명사 관용표현

- be busy -ing: ~하느라 바쁘다
- cannot help -ing: ~하지 않을 수 없다
- It is no use -ing: ~해 봐야 소용없다
- feel like -ing: ~하고 싶은 심정이다
- be worth -ing: ~할 가치가 있다

어휘

in case (that) ~인 경우에 decade 10년

17 독해 > Micro Reading > 내용일치/불일치 　오답률 20% 답 ①

| 해석 | 19세기에는, 가장 존경받는 보건의학 전문가들 모두가 나쁜 공기를 위한 화려한 용어인 '독기'에 의해 질병이 유발된다고 주장했다. 서양의 보건 시스템은 이 가정에 근거했는데, 질병을 예방하려면, 방의 내부에 독기가 더 많은지 방의 외부에 독기가 더 많은지에 따라 창문을 열어 두거나 닫아 두었다. 귀족들은 나쁜 공기가 있는 주거지에서는 거주하지 않았기 때문에 의사들은 질병을 옮길 수 없다고 믿었다. 그러고 나서, 균이라는 개념이 등장했다. 어느 날, 나쁜 공기가 당신을 아프게 한다고 모두가 믿었다. 그러다가, 거의 하룻밤 만에 질병의 진짜 원인인 미생물과 박테리아라고 불리는 눈에 보이지 않는 것들이 있다고 사람들이 깨닫기 시작했다. 질병에 대한 이 새로운 시각은 의사들이 소독제를 채택하고 과학자들이 백신과 항생제를 발명하면서 의학에 전면적인 변화를 가져왔다. 그러나, 그만큼 중요하게도, 세균에 대한 생각은 일반인들에게 그들 자신의 삶에 영향을 줄 수 있는 힘을 부여했다. 이제, 만약 당신이 건강을 유지하기를 원한다면, 당신은 손을 씻고, 물을 끓이고, 음식을 완전히 익히며, 찰과상을 요오드로 소독할 수 있을 것이다.
① 19세기에, 창문을 여는 것은 독기의 농도와는 무관했다.
② 19세기에, 귀족들은 나쁜 공기가 있는 곳에서 살지 않는다고 믿어졌다.
③ 사람들이 미생물과 박테리아가 질병의 진짜 원인임을 깨달은 후 백신이 발명되었다.
④ 찰과상을 소독하는 것은 사람들이 건강을 유지하는 것을 도울 수 있을 것이다.

| 정답해설 | ① 80% 두 번째 문장에서 방의 내부나 외부 중 어디에 독기가 많은지에 따라 창문을 열어 두거나 닫아 둔다고 했으므로 ①은 본문과 일치하지 않는 내용이다.

어휘

miasma 나쁜 공기[분위기], 독기 pass along 넘기다, 전달하다
quarter 숙소 come along 나타나다, 생기다
microbe 미생물 sweeping 전면적인, 광범위한
antiseptic 소독약 antibiotic 항생제
momentously 중대하게 cuts and scrapes 찰과상
iodine 요오드 irrelevant 무관한

18 독해 > Micro Reading > 내용일치/불일치 　오답률 13% 답 ③

| 해석 | 추종자들은 리더십 방정식에서 중요한 부분이지만, 그들의 역할이 항상 인정받아 온 것은 아니다. 사실 오랫동안, "리더십에 대한 흔한 시각은 리더들이 적극적으로 이끌고, 나중에 추종자들이라고 불린, 종속된 이들은 수동적이고 고분고분히 따른다."는 것이었다. 시간이 지남에 따라, 특히 지난 세기에, 사회의 변화는 추종자들에 대한 사람들의 시각을 형성했고, 리더십에 관한 이론들은 리더십 과정에서 추종자들이 하는 능동적이고 중요한 역할을 점차 인정했다. 오늘날에는 추종자들이 하는 중요한 역할을 받아들이는 것이 자연스러워 보인다. 리더십의 한 측면은 이런 점에서 특히 리더십은 그룹 내 모든 구성원들 사이에서 공유되는 사회적 영향 과정이다. 리더십은 특정한 지위 또는 역할에 있는 누군가에 의해 행사되는 영향력에 국한되어 있지 않으며, 추종자들 역시 리더십 과정의 일부이다.
① 상당 기간 동안, 리더들은 적극적으로 이끌고, 추종자들은 수동적으로 따른다고 이해되었다.
② 종속된 사람들에 대한 사람들의 시각은 사회의 변화에 의해 영향을 받았다.
③ 추종자들의 중요한 역할은 오늘날 여전히 부인된다.
④ 리더들과 추종자들 둘 다 리더십 과정에 참여한다.

| 정답해설 | ③ 87% 본문 중반부에서 오늘날에는 추종자들이 하는 중요한 역할을 받아들이는 것이 자연스러워 보인다고 했으므로, ③은 본문과 일치하지 않는다.

어휘

follower 추종자 equation 방정식; 상황, 문제
subordinate 하급자, 종속된 사람 obediently 고분고분하게
exert 가하다, 행사하다 for a length of time 상당 기간 동안

오답률 TOP 1
19 독해 > Reading for Writing > 빈칸 구 완성 　오답률 66% 답 ①

| 해석 | 엄밀한 의미에서 언어는 그 자체가 2개의 층으로 되어 있다. 단일한 소리는 이따금만 의미가 있다. 대개 다양한 말소리들은, 서로 녹아드는 아이스크림의 다른 색들처럼, 오직 맞물리는 고리로 합쳐질 때만 일관성 있는 메시지를 전달한다. 새 울음에서도 또한, ① 개별적인 소리는 종종 거의 가치가 없는데, 연속적인 소리가 중요한 것이다. 인간과 새 둘 다에서, 이 전문화된 소리 체계의 조절은 뇌의 한쪽 절반, 보통은 왼쪽 절반에 의해 행하여지며, 그 체계는 살면서 상대적으로 일찍 학습된다. 그리고 많은 인간의

언어들이 방언을 가지는 것처럼, 일부 조류들도 마찬가지이다. 즉 캘리포니아에서, 노랑턱멧새는 지역마다 너무 다른 노랫소리를 가지고 있어서 캘리포니아 사람들은 이 참새들의 소리를 들음으로써 그들이 그 주의 어디에 있는지를 아마 구별할 수 있을 것이다.

① 개별적인 소리는 종종 거의 가치가 없다
② 리듬감 있는 소리가 중요하다
③ 방언이 중대한 역할을 한다
④ 어떤 소리 체계도 존재하지 않는다

| **정답해설** | ① 34% 빈칸 앞의 부사 also(또한)를 통해 빈칸에는 앞에 나온 문장과 유사한 내용이 이어짐을 알 수 있다. 앞에서 단일한 소리는 의미가 거의 없으며, 다양한 말소리들이 잘 결합되었을 때 일관성 있는 메시지를 전달한다고 했으므로, 빈칸에는 새들의 울음소리도 개별적인 소리이면 의미가 없다는 내용이 들어가는 것이 적절하다.

어휘

proper (명사 뒤에서) 엄밀한 의미의
double-layered 이중의
coherent 조리 있는, 일관성 있는
sequence 연속적인 것[사건, 행동, 소리 등]
exercise 행사하다, 발휘하다
white-crowned sparrow 노랑턱멧새

오답률 TOP 2

20 독해 > Reading for Writing > 빈칸 구 완성 오답률 64% 답 ②

| **해석** | 노벨상을 수상한 심리학자 Daniel Kahneman은 인간이 이성적인 의사 결정자라는 생각을 뒤집으며, 경제학에 대한 세상의 사고 방식을 바꾸었다. 그 과정에서, 여러 분야를 넘나드는 그의 영향은 의사들이 의학적 결정을 내리고 투자자들이 월 스트리트의 위험성을 평가하는 방식을 바꾸어 왔다. 한 논문에서, Kahneman과 그의 동료들은 중대한 전략적 결정을 내리기 위한 과정의 개요를 설명한다. "평가를 중재하는 규약", 즉 MAP라고 부르는 그들이 제안한 접근법은 단순한 목표를 가지고 있다. 즉 선택이 많은 개별적 요인들에 의해 정보를 제공받을 수 있을 때까지 감에 기반을 둔 의사 결정을 미루는 것이다. "MAP의 중대한 목표들 중 하나는 기본적으로 직감을 ② 미루는 것이다."라고 *The Post*와의 최근 인터뷰에서 Kahneman이 말했다. 조직된 과정은 6~7개의 이전에 선택된 특성들에 근거하여 결정을 분석하는 것을 필요로 하는데, 그것들 각각을 따로 논의하고, 그것들에 상대적 백분위의 점수를 할당하며, 마침내 그 점수들을 전체적 판단을 내리는 데 사용한다.

① 개선하다   ② 미루다
③ 소유하다   ④ 용이하게 하다

| **정답해설** | ② 36% 빈칸 앞 문장에서 선택이 많은 개별적 요인들에 의해 정보를 제공받을 수 있을 때까지 감에 기반을 둔 의사 결정을 미룬다고 했다. 즉, 직감을 미룬다는 것이다.

어휘

upend 뒤집다, 거꾸로 하다   along the way 그 과정에서
discipline-crossing 여러 분야를 넘나드는, 여러 분야를 통합하는
physician (내과) 의사   paper 논문, 신문, 서류
protocol 규약, 의례, 의식   gut-based 감에 기반한
intuition 직감, 직관력   call for ~을 필요로 하다
percentile 백분위의   holistic 전체론의

합격예상 체크

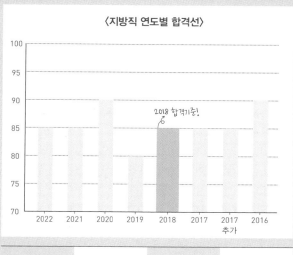

〈지방직 연도별 합격선〉

2018 합격기준

| 맞힌 개수 | /20문항 | 점수 | /100점 |

➡ ☐ 합격 ☐ 불합격

취약영역 체크

문항	정답	영역	문항	정답	영역
1	①	어휘 > 유의어 찾기	11	②	생활영어 > 회화/관용표현
2	②	어휘 > 유의어 찾기	12	①	독해 > Logical Reading > 문맥상 다양한 추론
3	④	문법 > 관계사	13	②	독해 > Logical Reading > 배열
4	④	문법 > 분사	14	①	생활영어 > 회화/관용표현
5	④	어휘 > 유의어 찾기	15	④	독해 > Reading for Writing > 빈칸 구 완성
6	③	어휘 > 빈칸 완성	16	③	독해 > Macro Reading > 제목
7	②	문법 > 가정법	17	①	독해 > Logical Reading > 연결사
8	①	문법 > 부정사	18	①	독해 > Micro Reading > 내용 일치/불일치
9	③	독해 > Logical Reading > 삭제	19	④	독해 > Logical Reading > 삽입
10	②	독해 > Macro Reading > 요지	20	①	독해 > Reading for Writing > 빈칸 절 완성

⬇ 영역별 틀린 개수로 취약영역을 확인하세요!

| 어휘 | /4 | 문법 | /4 | 독해 | /10 | 생활영어 | /2 |

➡ 나의 취약영역: _____

※ [정답해설]과 [오답해설] 선지의 50% 표시는 〈1초 합격예측 서비스〉를 통해 수집된 선지 선택률을 나타냅니다.

---

1 어휘 > 유의어 찾기   오답률 20%   답 ①

| 해석 | 의사의 가장 중요한 의무는 해를 끼치지 않는 것이다. 다른 모든 것 심지어 치유까지도 그 다음 일이어야 한다.
① 80% 주요한, 최고의
② 8% 선서한, 맹세한
③ 9% 성공적인
④ 3% 이해하기 힘든, 신비한, 비밀스러운

| 정답해설 | ① chief는 '주요한, 최고의'라는 뜻으로 paramount(가장 중요한, 최고의)와 의미가 가장 가깝다.

어휘
physician 의사, 내과 의사

---

2 어휘 > 유의어 찾기   오답률 20%   답 ②

| 해석 | 사람들이 북극으로 여행을 가는 것에 대해 겁을 먹는 것은 이상하지 않다.
① 7% 야망을 갖게 되다   ② 80% 두려워하다
③ 11% 지치다   ④ 2% 슬퍼지다

| 정답해설 | ② get[have] cold feet은 '무서워하다, 겁을 먹다'의 뜻으로 become afraid와 의미가 가장 가깝다.

| 더 알아보기 | '발'과 관련된 관용표현

- get[have] one's feet wet 새롭게 시작하다
- have one's feet on the ground 합리적이다, 이치에 맞다
- put one's foot in one's mouth 실언하다
- with both feet on the ground 현실적인, 합리적인

어휘
unusual 특이한, 흔치 않은, 드문, 이상한
ambitious 야심 있는, 야망을 가진   exhausted 지친, 기진맥진한
saddened 슬퍼진

---

3 문법 > 관계사   오답률 26%   답 ④

| 해석 | 저는 Ferrer 부인의 추천서에 대한 당신의 요청에 응하여 이 글을 쓰고 있습니다. 그녀는 지난 3년 간 제 비서로 근무했고, 뛰어난 직원이었습니다. 저는 그녀가 당신의 직무 기술서에 언급된 모든 자격 요건에 부합하며, 실제로 여러 방면에서 그 이상이라고 생각합니다. 저는 그녀의 완전한 진실성을 의심할 이유가 있던 적이 한 번도 없습니다. 그러므로 당신이 게재한 공고에 대해 Ferrer 부인을 추천하고 싶습니다.

| 정답해설 | ④ 74% 관계대명사 what은 선행사를 포함한 관계대명사로 뒤따라오는 문장은 불완전하며 선행사는 제시되지 않아야 한다. 주어진 문장에서 what 이후의 you advertise는 목적어가 없는 불완전한 형태이나 what 이전에 선행사 역할을 하는 post가 있으므로 옳지 않다. 따라서 밑줄 친 what은 목적격 관계대명사 which

또는 that으로 수정해야 한다.

| 오답해설 | ① 4% 「for the past/last + 숫자 + 단위 복수 명사」로 나타낸 시간의 부사구는 현재완료 시제와 함께 사용할 수 있다. 해당 문장에서는 '지난 3년 동안'이라는 의미로 for the last three years와 현재완료시제가 함께 쓰였으므로 옳은 표현이다.

② 9% requirements를 후치 수식하는 분사인데, 문맥상 수동의 의미이므로 과거분사가 옳게 사용되었다.

③ 13% to부정사의 형용사적 용법으로 앞의 명사 reason을 수식하고 있다.

어휘

in response to ~에 응하여　　　　reference 추천서, 보증서
requirement 필요 조건　　　　　　job description 직무 기술서
indeed 정말로, 사실은　　　　　　integrity 진실성; 고결함

4　　문법 > 분사　　　　오답률 30%　　답 ④

| 정답해설 | ④ 70% 원래 문장은 Because it was cold outside, I boiled some water to have tea.이다. 부사절을 분사구문으로 바꿀 때 주절의 주어와 부사절의 주어가 같지 않으면 생략할 수 없다. 따라서 해당 문장의 부사절의 비인칭 주어 it은 생략할 수 없으므로 분사구문으로 만들 경우에 Being cold outside는 It being cold outside가 되어야 한다. 이를 독립분사구문이라고 한다.

| 오답해설 | ① 11% information은 불가산명사이므로 이를 단수 취급하여 3인칭 단수 동사 was가 쓰였다.

② 10% 「should have p.p.」는 '~했어야 했다'라는 뜻으로 과거의 일에 대한 후회를 나타낸다.

③ 9% 영화가 시작한 것이 우리가 도착하기 이전에 일어난 일이므로 과거완료 동사 had already started가 쓰였다. 또한 부사인 already가 had와 과거분사 사이에 위치한 것도 옳다.

오답률 TOP 1

5　　어휘 > 유의어 찾기　　　　오답률 64%　　답 ④

| 해석 | 최신식 학습법을 두렵게 느끼는 학생은 그 또는 그녀가 예전 방식으로 배웠을 수도 있는 것보다는 덜 배운다.
① 5% 재미있는, 유머러스한　　② 37% 친절한, 친숙한
③ 22% 편리한　　　　　　　　　④ 36% 무서운, 겁을 주는

| 정답해설 | ④ 밑줄 친 intimidating은 '두렵게 하는, 겁을 주는'의 뜻으로 frightening(무서운, 겁을 주는)과 의미가 가장 가깝다.

어휘

state-of-the-art 최첨단의, 최신식의
approach (학문 · 문제로의) 접근법, 학습법, 연구법

6　　어휘 > 빈칸 완성　　　　오답률 42%　　답 ③

| 해석 | 에어컨이 지금 수리되고 있으므로, 사무실 직원들은 오늘 하루 선풍기로 ③ 견뎌야 한다.
① 23% ~을 제거하다, 처리하다
② 13% ~에서 손을 놓다

③ 58% (만족스럽지는 않지만) ~로 견디다, 때우다
④ 6% ~와 결별하다

| 정답해설 | ③ 에어컨이 수리 중이라는 원인에 따른 결과가 나와야 한다. 따라서 '(만족스럽지는 않지만) ~으로 견디다, 때우다'라는 뜻의 make do with를 이용하여 (에어컨 대신) 선풍기로 견뎌야 한다는 의미가 되는 것이 가장 적절하다.

7　　문법 > 가정법　　　　오답률 33%　　답 ②

| 해석 | ① 지난주 제가 드린 이메일 주소로 연락해 주세요.
② 물이 없다면, 지구상의 모든 살아 있는 생명들은 멸종될 것이다.
③ 노트북은 사무실 밖에 있는 사람들이 일을 계속해서 할 수 있게끔 한다.
④ 그들이 그들의 실수에 대해 설명하려고 시도할수록, 그들의 이야기는 더 나쁘게 들렸다.

| 정답해설 | ② 67% 현재 사실을 반대로 가정하는 가정법 과거의 「if it were not for ~((현재) ~이 없다면)」 구문에서 if가 생략되면 의문문 어순으로 바뀐다. 즉, 종속절의 동사 were가 주어 앞으로 도치되면서 Were it not for의 형태가 된다. 또한 가정법 과거이므로 주절에는 「would + 동사원형」이 알맞게 쓰였다.

| 오답해설 | ① 9% contact는 타동사이므로 전치사 없이 목적어를 취한다. 따라서 contact to me는 contact me로 바꾸는 것이 옳다. 또한 the email address와 I gave you 사이에는 목적격 관계대명사 which 혹은 that이 생략되어 있다.

③ 15% 「allow + 목적어 + to부정사」는 '목적어가 ~하게끔 허락하다'의 뜻으로 여기서는 목적격 보어로 to continue가 알맞게 쓰였다. 다만 주격 관계대명사 who가 이끄는 절의 동사는 선행사인 people과 수를 일치시켜야 하므로 is가 아닌 are가 되어야 한다.

④ 9% 「The + 비교급 ~, the + 비교급 …」은 '~할수록 더 …하다'라는 뜻이다. 따라서 최상급인 the worst를 비교급인 the worse로 바꾸어야 한다.

| 더 알아보기 | 「the + 비교급, the + 비교급」의 출제 포인트

- 비교급 앞에 반드시 'the'가 온다.
- 비교급의 형태에 주의한다.
- 비교급이 수식하는 명사, 형용사, 부사와 분리되어서는 안 된다.

8　　문법 > 부정사　　　　오답률 37%　　답 ①

| 정답해설 | ① 63% see off는 '~을 배웅하다'라는 뜻이다. 목적을 나타내는 to부정사의 용법으로 '배웅하기 위해'의 의미로 옳게 사용되었다.

| 오답해설 | ② 8% make believe (that)은 '~인 체하다'라는 관용적 표현으로 it을 삭제해야 한다.

③ 21% look forward to는 '~하기를 고대하다'라는 뜻으로, 여기서 to는 전치사이다. 따라서 뒤의 go를 동명사 going으로 바꾸어야 한다.

④ 8% interested의 수식 대상인 anything은 감정을 유발[제공]하

는 대상이므로 감정 유발 분사인 -ing 형태의 현재분사가 수식해야 한다. 따라서 interested는 현재분사 interesting(흥미로운, 흥미를 불러일으키는)으로 바꾸는 것이 옳다.

---

9   독해 > Logical Reading > 삭제   오답률 21%   답 ③

| **해석** | 르네상스 시대의 주방은 공들인 연회를 열기 위해 함께 일을 했던 일꾼들의 명확한 위계질서를 가지고 있었다. 우리가 봐 왔듯이 제일 높은 곳에는, 주방뿐 아니라 식당까지 맡아 관리하는 *scalco*, 즉 관리인이 있었다. 식당은 집사에 의해 감독되었는데, 그는 은식기류와 리넨 제품을 맡아 관리했으며, 연회를 시작하고 끝내는 음식(시작할 때에는 찬 음식, 샐러드, 치즈, 과일, 식사가 끝날 때에는 달달한 디저트와 설탕 절임)을 제공했다. ③ 이러한 공들인 장식과 서빙은 레스토랑에서 "접객 부서"라고 불리는 것이었다. 주방은 보조 주방장, 페이스트리 요리사, 주방 보조자들을 지휘하는 수석 주방장에 의해 감독되었다.

| **정답해설** | ③ 79% 르네상스 시대에 명확했던 주방 및 식당의 위계질서에 관한 글이다. ①에서 주방과 식당을 총괄하는 관리인, ②에서 식당을 관리하는 집사, ④에서 주방을 감독하는 수석 주방장에 대한 설명으로 이어진다. 그러나 ③의 This elaborate decoration and serving(이러한 정교한 장식과 서빙)이 가리키는 것을 앞에서 찾아볼 수 없을 뿐더러, 식당(dining room)과 주방(kitchen)이 아닌 레스토랑(restaurant)에 관한 내용이다. 따라서 글의 흐름상 가장 어색한 문장은 ③이다.

어휘

hierarchy 계급, 계층; 위계질서
elaborate 정교한, 공들인
banquet 연회
in charge of ~을 맡아서, 담당해서
steward 관리인, 집사
butler 집사(대저택의 남자 하인 중 책임자)
silverware 은식기류
confection 당과, 설탕 절임
the front of the house (FOH) 접객 부서

---

10   독해 > Macro Reading > 요지   오답률 35%   답 ②

| **해석** | 나의 학생들은 만약 그들이 단지 중요한 인물들을 더 많이 만난다면, 그들의 일이 향상될 것이라고 종종 믿는다. 그러나 당신이 이미 그 세계에 가치 있는 어떤 것들을 내어놓지 않는 이상 그러한 사람들과 관계를 맺는 것은 매우 어렵다. 그것은 조언자들과 후원자들의 호기심을 자극하는 것이다. 성과는 당신이 취하는 것만이 아니라, 줄 만한 것을 가지고 있다는 것을 보여 준다. 인생에서, 적임자를 아는 것은 확실히 도움이 된다. 그러나 그들이 당신을 얼마나 열심히 도와주는지, 그들이 당신을 위해 얼마나 큰 위험을 감수하는지는 당신이 제공하는 것에 달려 있다. 막강한 인맥을 구축하는 것은 당신이 인맥 쌓기의 전문가가 되기를 요구하지 않는다. 그것은 단지 당신이 어떤 것의 전문가가 되기를 요구할 뿐이다. 만약 당신이 대단한 연줄을 만든다면, 그것들은 당신을 출세시킬지도 모른다. 만약 당신이 일을 아주 잘하면, 그러한 인맥은 만들기가 더 쉬울 것이다. 당신의 명함이 아닌 당신의 통찰력과 일의 성과가 이야기를 하게 하라.
① 성공적인 커리어를 위해서 후원은 필수적이다.
② 좋은 인맥을 쌓는 것은 당신의 성과로부터 시작된다.
③ 막강한 인맥은 당신의 성공의 전제 조건이다.
④ 당신이 인맥 쌓기의 전문가가 됨에 따라 당신의 통찰력과 일의 성과도 향상된다.

| **정답해설** | ② 65% 중반부의 But 이후에 글의 요지가 나와 있다.

필자는 중요한 사람들과의 인맥을 형성하기 위해서는 그들에게 줄 것, 즉 성과가 있어야 한다고 주장한다. 따라서 글의 요지로 가장 적절한 것은 ②이다.

| **오답해설** | ① 3% 중요한 사람들과 인맥을 쌓는 방법에 대한 이야기이지, '후원(sponsorship)'에 대한 글이 아니다.

③ 11% 인맥을 구축하는 것이 인생에 도움이 된다는 내용은 있으나 그것이 성공의 전제 조건이라는 내용은 찾아볼 수 없다.

④ 21% 본문을 통해 네트워크 전문가가 되는 것과 개인의 통찰력 및 결과와의 관계를 추론해 낼 수 없다.

어휘

remarkably 두드러지게, 현저하게
engage 관계를 맺다; 종사하다, 관여하다
pique (흥미, 호기심 등을) 자극하다
go to bat for ~을 도와주다
stick one's neck out 위험을 자초하다, 무모한 짓을 하다
prerequisite 전제 조건

---

11   생활영어 > 회화/관용표현   오답률 3%   답 ②

| **해석** | A: 내 컴퓨터가 아무 이유 없이 꺼져 버렸어. 이걸 다시 켤 수도 없어.
B: 충전은 해 봤니? 그냥 배터리가 나간 것일지도 몰라.
A: 물론이지, 충전해 봤어.
B: ② 그럼 가장 가까운 서비스 센터에 가 봐.
A: 그래야 하긴 하는데, 내가 아주 게을러.
① 나는 네 컴퓨터를 어떻게 고치는지 몰라.
② 그럼 가장 가까운 서비스 센터에 가 봐
③ 음, 네 문제는 그만 생각하고 가서 잠을 자.
④ 내 동생이 컴퓨터 기사이니까, 네 컴퓨터를 고쳐 볼 거야.

| **정답해설** | ② 97% A의 컴퓨터가 고장 난 상황이다. B의 빈칸 이후에 A가 '그래야 하긴 하는데, 내가 아주 게을러.'라고 한 것으로 미루어 보아, B는 A에게 컴퓨터를 고치기 위해 B가 직접 해야 할 일을 조언했을 것임을 짐작할 수 있다. 그러므로 가장 적절한 것은 ②이다.

| **오답해설** | ③ 1% 가서 잠을 자라는 말에 A가 그래야 하긴 하는데, 내가 아주 게으르다고 대답하는 것은 어색하다.

---

12   독해 > Logical Reading > 문맥상 다양한 추론   답 ①
오답률 2%

| **해석** | 내 얼굴은 백지장처럼 하얘졌다. 나는 내 손목시계를 보았다. 시험은 지금이면 거의 끝났을 것이다. 나는 완전한 패닉 상태에서 시험장에 도착했다. 나는 자초지종을 설명하려고 시도했지만, 나의 문장과 설명하려는 몸짓은 너무 혼란스러워서 인간 토네이도의 아주 확실한 버전에 불과했다. 나의 산만한 설명을 관두게 하려는 시도로, 그 시험 감독관은 나를 빈자리로 데려가 시험 책자를 내 앞에 놓았다. 그는 의문스러운 듯이 나와 시계를 보다가 가 버렸다. 나는 필사적으로 잃어버린 시간을 보충하려고 노력했고, 미친 듯이 비유와 문장 완성 문제들을 간신히 풀었다. "15분 남았습니다." 운명의 목소리가 교실 앞에서 공표되었다. 대수 방정식, 산술 계산, 기하학 도형들이 내 눈 앞을 헤엄쳐 갔다. "그만! 연필을 내려놓으세요."
① 긴장하고 걱정되는   ② 흥분되고 기운찬
③ 차분하고 확고한   ④ 안전하고 느긋한

| **정답해설** | ① 98% 시험장에 늦어 당황한 상태로 허둥지둥 시험에

임하고 있는 화자의 상황을 묘사하고 있다. 따라서 ①이 화자의 심경으로 가장 적절하다. 본문의 in an absolute panic, got so confused, desperately 등을 통해서도 심경을 유추할 수 있다.

| 더 알아보기 | **심경을 나타내는 단어**

- ashamed 부끄러운, 창피한
- embarrassed 당황한
- depressed 우울한, 낙담한
- frustrated 좌절한
- pleased 기쁜
- humorous 재미있는, 익살스러운
- sympathetic 공감하는, 동정적인

어휘

white as a sheet 창백한, 핏기가 없는
panic 공황, 극심한 공포　　　　　descriptive 묘사하는
nothing more than ~에 불과한, ~에 지나지 않는
convincing 설득력 있는, 확실한　　tornado 회오리바람, 토네이도
in an effort to V ~해 보려는 노력으로
curb 억제하다, 제한하다　　　　　distracting 마음을 산란케 하는
proctor 시험 감독관　　　　　　　desperately 필사적으로
make up for ~을 보상하다, 만회하다
scramble through ~을 허둥지둥하다, 간신히 끝내다
analogy 비유; 유사점; 유추　　　　doom 죽음, 파멸, 비운
algebraic 대수의, 대수적인　　　　arithmetic 산수, 연산
geometric 기하학의, 기하학적인

13　독해 > Logical Reading > 배열　　오답률 51%　답 ②

| 해석 | 당신의 건강을 감시하고 추적하는 장치들은 모든 연령의 사람들 사이에서 점점 더 인기를 얻고 있다.
(B) 그러나, 자신의 집에서 나이 들어가는 고령자들에게 특히 집에 돌보미가 없는 이들에게 이러한 기술들은 생명을 구할 수도 있다.
(A) 예를 들어, 낙상은 65세 이상 성인들의 주요 사망 원인이다. 낙상 경보는 수년간 존재해 왔던 대중적인 양로 기술이지만 이제는 개선되었다.
(C) 이 단순한 기술은 노인이 낙상하는 바로 그 순간 자동적으로 911 혹은 가까운 가족에게 경보를 울릴 수 있다.

| 정답해설 | ② 49% 주어진 문장은 건강을 감시, 추적하는 장치들이 전 연령에서 인기가 있다는 내용인데, 이 뒤에는 However로 시작하며 이 기술이 특히 노인들에게 효과적이라는 내용인 (B)가 이어지는 것이 알맞다. (A)의 낙상 경보는 (B)의 예이므로 그 뒤에 오는데, 마지막에 낙상 경보 기술이 개선되었다고 말하고 있고 개선된 내용이 (C)에서 설명되므로 (C)는 (A) 뒤에 온다.

어휘

alert 경계 태세, 경계경보　　　　senior 연장자, 고령자
caretaker 경비원, 관리인; 돌보미　lifesaving 생명을 구하는

14　생활영어 > 회화/관용표현　　오답률 8%　답 ①

| 해석 | A: 당신은 우리 신혼여행을 어디로 가고 싶어요?
B: 우리 둘 다 가 본 적 없는 곳으로 가요.
A: 그렇다면 하와이는 어때요?
B: ① 그곳에 항상 가 보고 싶었어요.

① 그곳에 항상 가 보고 싶었어요.
② 한국은 살기 좋은 곳이 아닌가요?
③ 좋아요! 그곳에서의 제 마지막 여행은 엄청났어요!
④ 오, 당신은 이미 하와이에 다녀왔음이 틀림없군요.

| 정답해설 | ① 92% B는 신혼여행지를 둘 다 안 가 본 곳으로 가자고 했고 A가 하와이를 제안하고 있다. 이 제안에 대한 대답은 수락 또는 거절을 하는 표현이 가장 적절하다.

15　독해 > Reading for Writing > 빈칸 구 완성　오답률 23%　답 ④

| 해석 | 성공하는 사람들의 비결은 보통 그들이 한 가지 일에 온전히 집중할 수 있다는 것이다. 그들의 머릿속에 많은 것들이 들어 있을지라도, 그들은 그 많은 책무들이 서로를 방해하지 않고, 대신 좋은 내적 순서를 배당받는 방법을 찾아낸다. 그리고 이러한 순서는 꽤 단순하다. ④ 가장 중요한 일을 첫 번째로 하는 것이다. 이론상, 그것은 아주 명확해 보이지만 일상에서는 다소 달라 보인다. 당신은 아마 우선순위로 정하려고 노력했을지도 모르지만, 일상의 사소한 일들과 모든 예측 불가능한 방해물들로 인해 실패해 왔다. 예를 들어, 다른 사무실로 피해 들어가, 어떤 방해물들도 끼어들지 못하게 하여 어떠한 방해 요소도 방해가 되게 두지 마라. 당신이 우선순위의 한 가지 업무에 집중할 때, 당신은 심지어 당신이 가지고 있는지 알지도 못했던 에너지를 당신이 가지고 있다는 것을 알게 될 것이다.

① 더 빠를수록 낫다
② 늦더라도 하는 것이 안 하는 것보다 낫다
③ 눈에서 멀어지면, 마음에서도 멀어진다
④ 가장 중요한 일을 첫 번째로 하라

| 정답해설 | ④ 77% 성공한 사람들을 예로 들며 한 가지 일에 몰두하는 방법으로 우선순위를 정해 일을 하라고 조언하고 있다. 빈칸은 콜론(:) 앞의 And this order is quite simple을 부연 설명하는 내용, 즉 일의 순서와 관련된 내용이어야 하므로 ④가 알맞다.

어휘

commitment 전념, 헌신; 책무　　impede 지연시키다, 방해하다
priority 우선순위　　　　　　　　trivial 사소한, 하찮은
unforeseen 예측하지 못한, 뜻밖의
distraction 집중을 방해하는 것, 주의 산만
get in the way 방해되다

16　독해 > Macro Reading > 제목　　오답률 19%　답 ③

| 해석 | 그 과학자의 도움으로, 상업적인 어업은 그것이 계속되어야 한다면 어업이 과학적으로 행해져야 함을 깨달았다. 물고기 개체 수에 대한 어떠한 어업 압력이 없다면, 물고기의 수는 예상 가능한 풍부한 수준에 도달하여 유지될 것이다. 유일한 변동성은 먹이의 이용 가능성, 적절한 온도, 그 비슷한 것과 같은 자연 환경적인 요소들에 기인할 것이다. 만약 어장이 이러한 물고기들을 잡도록 발달된다면, 그것들의 개체 수는 어획량이 적을 경우 유지될 수 있다. 북해의 고등어가 좋은 예이다. 만약 우리가 어장을 늘려 매년 더 많은 물고기를 잡아들인다면, 우리는 우리가 매년 잡는 물고기 전체를 대체할 수 있는 이상적인 지점 아래로 개체 수를 감소시키지 않도록 주의해야만 한다. 우리가 최대 유지 생산량이라고 불리는 이 수준으로 포획한다면, 우리는 매년 가능한 최대 생산량을 유지할 수 있다. 만약 우리가 너무 많이 포획한다면, 물고기의 수는 매년 줄어 어업을 할 수 없을 수준이 될 것이다. 과도하게 남획된 동물의 예로는 남극의 대왕고래와 북대서양의 넙치가 있다. 최대 연간 생산량을 유지하기 위해 딱 맞는 양만 포획하는 것은 과학이자 기술이다. 우리가 물고기 개체 수를 더 잘 이해하고 어떻게 개체 수

의 고갈 없이 최대한으로 그것을 이용할지를 돕기 위해 연구는 계속해서 진행되고 있다.

① 상업적인 어업에 반대하라
② 어업으로 간주되는 바다 양식업
③ 왜 어업에 과학이 필요한가?
④ 남획된 동물들: 불법 어업의 사례들

| 정답해설 | ③ 81% 첫 문장에서 어업을 지속하기 위해서 과학의 도움이 필요하다고 했고, 이후 어업이 과학의 도움을 받아야 하는 이유가 나온다. 즉, 포획하는 물고기의 개체 수를 꼭 알맞게 유지해야 물고기 개체 수 고갈 없이 어업을 지속해 나갈 수 있으며, 이를 돕는 연구가 계속 진행되고 있다고 하였으므로 글의 제목으로 ③이 가장 적절하다.

어휘

predictable 예측할 수 있는	abundance 풍부
fluctuation 변동, 오르내림, 파동	fishery 어장
mackerel 고등어	sustainable 지속 가능한
yield 산출량, 생산량	severely 심각하게
overfish 물고기를 남획하다, 다 잡아 버리다	
Antarctic 남극의; 남극 지방	halibut 큰 넙치
deplete 고갈시키다, 대폭 감소시키다	

---

17 독해 > Logical Reading > 연결사   오답률 43%   답 ①

| 해석 | 테러리즘은 과연 효과가 있을까? 9/11 테러는 알카에다에게 막대한 전술적 성공이었는데, 부분적으로 그것은 전 세계 언론의 중심지이자 미국의 실질적인 수도에서 일어난 공격을 포함했고, (A) 그렇게 함으로써 그 사건의 가능한 가장 폭넓은 보도 범위를 확보했기 때문이다. 만약에 테러리즘이 당신이 많은 사람들이 보길 바라는 연극의 형태라면, 인류 역사에서 9/11 공격보다 더 많은 전 세계의 청중이 시청한 사건은 없었다. 당시에, 9/11 테러가 진주만 공격과 어떻게 유사했는지에 대한 논의가 많았다. 그것들은 둘 다 미국을 큰 전쟁으로 끌어들인 습격이라는 점에서 정말로 비슷했다. 그러나 그 둘은 다른 의미로 또한 유사했다. 진주만은 제국주의 일본의 크나큰 전술적 성공이었지만, 더 큰 전략적인 실패를 이끌었다. 진주만 공격 이후 4년 안에 일본 제국은 폐허가 되었고, 완전히 패배했다. (B) 유사하게, 9/11 공격은 알카에다에게는 크나큰 전술적 성공이었지만, 오사마 빈 라덴에게는 크나큰 전략적 실패로 드러나기도 했다.

(A)	(B)
① 그렇게 함으로써	유사하게
② 반면에	그러므로
③ 반면에	운이 좋게도
④ 그렇게 함으로써	대조적으로

| 정답해설 | ① 57% (A) 빈칸 이전의 '9/11 테러는 전 세계 언론의 중심지에서 일어난 공격을 포함했다'는 사실과 빈칸 이후의 '9/11 사건의 가능한 가장 폭넓은 보도 범위를 확보했다'는 사실은 서로 인과 관계에 있다. 따라서 thereby(그렇게 함으로써, 그로 인해)가 적절하다.

(B) 진주만 공격과 9/11 공격이 또 다른 의미에서 유사하다고 했고, 빈칸 앞뒤로 각각 진주만 공격과 9/11 공격이 어떻게 유사한지를 비교하고 있으므로 빈칸에 가장 알맞은 것은 Similarly(유사하게)이다.

어휘

enormous 막대한, 거대한	tactical 작전의, 전술의

---

take place (일이) 발생하다, 일어나다

coverage 보도, 범위	imperial 제국의
strategic 전략적인	utterly 완전히, 전적으로
defeat 패배시키다, 이기다	

---

18 독해 > Micro Reading > 내용일치/불일치   오답률 23%   답 ①

| 해석 | 중국 과학자들이 잠재적으로 치명적인 혈액 질환을 단지 그 아기에게서뿐만 아니라 이후 모든 후손으로부터 제거하기 위해 인간 배아를 변형하였을 때 우리는 인종으로서 새로운 국면에 진입했다. 연구자들은 이 과정을 "생식 계열 변형"이라고 일컫는다. 언론은 "designer babies"라는 어구를 좋아한다. 그러나 우리는 그것 그대로, "우생학"이라고 불러야 한다. 그리고 우리 인류는 우리가 그것을 사용하기 원하는지 아닌지를 결정할 필요가 있다. 지난달 미국에서, 과학 기관이 관여했다. 국립과학학회와 국립의학학회의 연합 위원회는 "합리적인 대안"이 없을 때, 심각한 질병을 유발하는 유전자를 겨냥한 배아 수정을 지지했다. 그러나 그 위원회는 이미 건강한 아이들을 더 강하고 더 키가 크게 만드는 것과 같은 "강화"를 위한 수정에 대해서는 더욱 경계했다. 그것은 공개 토론을 권했고, 의사들이 "현 시점에 진행해서는 안 된다"고 말했다. 위원회가 경계를 촉구하는 것에는 그럴 만한 이유가 있다. 우생학의 역사는 억압과 고통으로 가득하다.

① 의사들은 강화를 위한 배아 수정을 즉시 진행하도록 권고받았다.
② 최근에, 미국 내 과학 기관은 우생학 토론에 참여했다.
③ 중국 과학자들은 심각한 혈액 질환을 방지하기 위해 인간 배아를 수정했다.
④ "Designer babies"는 생식 계열 변형 과정에 대한 또 다른 용어이다.

| 정답해설 | ① 77% 후반부의 It recommended a public discussion, and said that doctors should "not proceed at this time."에서 미국의 국립의학학회가 참여한 연합 위원회는 강화를 위한 수정을 더욱 경계했고 의사들이 현 시점에서 배아 수정을 진행해서는 안 된다고 말했으므로 의사들이 강화를 위한 배아 수정을 즉시 진행하도록 권고받았다는 ①은 일치하지 않는다.

| 오답해설 | ② 5% Last month, in the United States, the scientific establishment weighed in.에서 미국 과학 기관이 관여했다고 하고 있으므로 본문 내용과 일치한다.

③ 11% 첫 번째 문장에서 언급된 내용이다.

④ 7% germline modification과 designer babies 그리고 engenics는 모두 같은 현상을 지칭하는 용어들로 소개되었다.

어휘

phase 국면, 양상	species (생물)종
alter 바꾸다, 고치다	embryo 배아
descendant 자손, 후손	germline 생식 계열
modification 수정, 변경	human race 인류
weigh in (논의, 언쟁, 활동 등에) 끼어들다, 관여하다	
endorse 지지하다, 보증하다, 홍보하다	
alternative 대안, 대체 수단	proceed 진행하다, 계속하다

---

19 독해 > Logical Reading > 삽입   오답률 13%   답 ④

| 해석 | 고대 올림픽은 마치 현대의 경기들과 같이 선수들에게 그들의 건강과 우월함을 증명할 기회를 제공했다. 고대 올림픽 경기들은 약자를 제거하고 강자를 찬양하기 위해 고안되었다. 우승자들은 벼랑 끝까지 내몰렸다. 현대와 마찬가지로, 사람들은 극한 스포츠를 좋아했다. 인기 있는 경기들 중 하나는 33번째 올림피아드에서 추가되었다. 이것은 판크라티온, 즉 레슬

링과 복싱이 극단적으로 섞인 것이었다. 그리스어 pakration은 "완전한 힘"을 뜻한다. 남자들은 금속 장신구가 박힌 가죽 끈을 착용했고, 그것은 상대방에게 끔찍한 상황을 만들어낼 수 있었다. 이러한 위험한 형식의 레슬링은 시간이나 무게 제한이 없었다. 이 경기에서는 오로지 두 가지 규칙만이 적용되었다. 첫 번째로, 레슬러들은 그들의 엄지 손가락으로 눈을 찌르는 것이 허용되지 않았다. 두 번째, 그들은 깨물 수 없었다. 이외의 것은 무엇이라도 공정한 경기로 여겨졌다. 경기는 복싱 경기와 같은 방식으로 판정되었다. 경쟁자들은 둘 중 하나가 쓰러질 때까지 경기를 계속했다. ④ 둘 중 아무도 항복하지 않으면, 둘은 하나가 쓰러질 때까지 주먹을 주고받았다. 오로지 가장 강한 자와 가장 결단력 있는 선수들만이 이 경기에 도전했다. 상대방의 손가락을 부러뜨려 별명을 얻은 "Mr. Fingertips"와 레슬링하는 것을 상상해 보라!

| 정답해설 | ④ 87% 강자와 약자를 가려내기 위한 고대 경기 중 극단적인 경기인 판크라티온에 대한 글이다. 주어진 문장은 게임의 규칙을 기술하며 neither과 the two를 제시하고 있으므로, 그 '둘'이 제시된 문장 뒤에 위치해야 한다. ④ 이전의 문장에서 Contenders continued until one of the two collapsed.로 경기를 하는 두 사람의 경기 방식이 처음 언급된다. 따라서 주어진 문장은 ④에 위치하는 것이 알맞다.

어휘

surrender 항복하다, 투항하다, 굴복하다
knock out 나가 떨어지게 하다   glorify 찬양하다
brink (벼랑, 강가 등의) 끝   strap 끈, 고정끈
stud 장식 못, 장식용 금속 단추   opponent 상대, 반대자
gouge 찌르다   contender 도전자, 경쟁자
collapse 쓰러지다, 붕괴되다, 무너지다

오답률 TOP 2

20 독해 > Reading for Writing > 빈칸 절 완성   오답률 58%   답 ①

| 해석 | 우리 시대에는, 인간에 대한 고유의 삶과 규칙을 가지는 것은 단지 시장의 법칙일 뿐만 아니라, 과학과 기술의 발전이기도 하다. 많은 이유로, 오늘날 과학의 문제점들과 구조는 과학자가 그의 문제들을 선택하지 않고 문제들이 과학자에게 문제를 받아들이도록 강요하는 그런 것이다. 그는 하나의 문제를 풀고, 그 결과는 그가 더 안심하거나 확신하는 것이 아니라, 다른 열 가지의 새로운 문제들이 해결된 하나의 문제가 있던 자리에 모습을 드러내는 것이다. 그것들은 그에게 해결하라고 강요한다. 그는 전에 없이 빨라지는 속도로 진행해야만 한다. 산업 기술에서도 동일하다. 과학의 속도는 기술의 속도를 강요한다. 이론 물리학은 원자 에너지를 우리에게 강요한다. 핵 폭탄의 성공적인 생산은 우리에게 수소 폭탄의 제조를 강요한다. 우리는 우리의 문제를 선택하지 않는다. 우리는 우리의 제품을 선택하지 않는다. 우리는 떠밀리고 우리는 강요당하는 것이다. 무엇에 의해서? 그것을 초월하는 목적과 목표가 없는, 그리고 ① 인간을 그것의 부속물로 만들어 버리는 시스템에 의해서이다.
① 인간을 그것의 부속물로 만들어 버리는
② 보안에 대한 잘못된 인식을 창출하는
③ 인간을 창의적인 도전들로 고무시키는
④ 시장의 법칙들을 통제하도록 과학자들에게 권한을 부여하는

| 정답해설 | ① 42% 오늘날 과학의 문제점은 인간이 문제들을 선택하는 것이 아니라, 문제들이 인간에게 문제를 해결하라고 강요하는 현상이라는 것이 이 글의 내용이다. 즉, 인간이 주체가 아니라 떠밀리고 강요받는 '부록, 부속물(appendix)'과도 같은 처지가 됨을 알 수 있다. 따라서 빈칸에는 ①이 가장 적절하다.

어휘

a number of 다수의, 얼마간의   force ~을 강요하다, ~하게 만들다
secure 안심하는, 안전한, 확실한
ever-quickening 전에 없이 빨라지는, 계속해서 빨라지는
theoretical 이론적인   physics 물리학
atomic 원자의   fission 핵 분열, (세포의) 분열
hydrogen 수소   transcend 초월하다
appendix 부록, 부속물   inspire 고무시키다, 영감을 주다
empower 권한을 부여하다

합격예상 체크

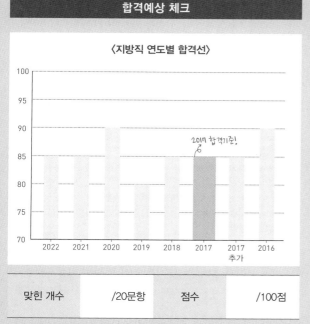

〈지방직 연도별 합격선〉

2017 합격기준!

| 맞힌 개수 | /20문항 | 점수 | /100점 |

➡ ☐ 합격 ☐ 불합격

취약영역 체크

문항	정답	영역	문항	정답	영역
1	②	생활영어 > 회화/관용표현	11	③	독해 > Logical Reading > 삽입
2	③	생활영어 > 회화/관용표현	12	②	독해 > Macro Reading > 제목
3	①	어휘 > 유의어 찾기	13	④	문법 > 비교
4	④	어휘 > 유의어 찾기	14	③	문법 > 관사
5	④	어휘 > 유의어 찾기	15	①	어휘 > 빈칸 완성
6	②	문법 > 동사, 관계사	16	③	독해 > Reading for Writing > 빈칸 구 완성
7	④	문법 > 강조와 도치	17	④	독해 > Logical Reading > 배열
8	①	독해 > Micro Reading > 내용 일치/불일치	18	④	독해 > Macro Reading > 요지
9	③	독해 > Logical Reading > 삭제	19	③	독해 > Reading for Writing > 빈칸 절 완성
10	④	독해 > Micro Reading > 내용 일치/불일치	20	②	독해 > Reading for Writing > 빈칸 절 완성

⬇ 영역별 틀린 개수로 취약영역을 확인하세요!

| 어휘 | /4 | 문법 | /4 | 독해 | /10 | 생활영어 | /2 |

➡ 나의 취약영역: _____

※ [정답해설]과 [오답해설] 선지의 50% 표시는 〈1초 합격예측 서비스〉를 통해 수집된 선지 선택률을 나타냅니다.

---

1   생활영어 > 회화/관용표현   오답률 19%   답 ②

| 해석 | A: 나 방금 옛 고등학교 친구들 중 한 명에게 편지를 받았어.
B: 잘됐다!
A: 그게, 사실 그에게서 소식을 들은 건 꽤 오랜만이야.
B: 솔직히 말하면, 나는 옛 친구들과 대부분 연락이 끊긴걸.
A: 나도 알지. 모두들 여기저기로 이사를 다니는 와중에 연락을 유지하기는 참 어려운 일이야.
B: 네 말이 맞아. ② 사람들은 멀어지기 마련이야. 그렇지만 너는 네 친구와 연락이 다시 닿아서 참 다행이야.

① 낮이 점점 길어지고 있어
② 사람들은 멀어지기 마련이야
③ 그 말은 내가 여태 들어본 말 중에 가장 웃겨
④ 나는 그의 이름을 듣기만 하면 화가 치밀어 오르기 시작해

| 정답해설 | ② 81% 밑줄 친 부분 앞에 나온 대화에서 A가 옛 친구들과 연락을 유지하기는 참 어렵다고 말하자 B가 이에 동의했다. 그러므로 '사람들은 멀어지기 마련이야.'라고 말하는 ②가 문맥상 가장 적절하다.

| 오답해설 | ① 15% 대화의 내용과 상관이 없으므로 적절하지 않다.
③ 1% B가 A의 말이 웃기다고 생각했다면, 앞서 You're right.이라고 하며 A의 말에 수긍하지 않았을 것이다.
④ 3% B는 그(A의 친구)와 아는 사이가 아니다.

어휘
out of touch with ~와 접촉[연락]하지 않는

drift apart 사이가 멀어지다   fume (화가 나서) 씩씩대다

---

2   생활영어 > 회화/관용표현   오답률 7%   답 ③

| 해석 | A: 넌 Ted에게 생일 선물로 무엇을 사 줄 거니? 나는 그에게 두 개의 야구 모자를 사 주려고 해.
B: 나는 적당한 선물을 생각해 내려고 ③ 머리를 쥐어짜고 있어. 그가 무엇이 필요한지 전혀 모르겠어.
A: 그에게 앨범을 사 주는 건 어때? 그는 사진이 많거든.
B: 완벽하다! 내가 왜 그 생각을 못 했을까? 제안해 줘서 고마워!

① 그에게 연락을 받고 있는   ② 하루 종일 자고 있는
③ 머리를 쥐어짜고 있는   ④ 사진 앨범을 수집하고 있는

| 정답해설 | ③ 93% B는 빈칸 다음에서 Ted가 무엇이 필요한지 모른다고 했으므로, 생일 선물을 생각해 내기 위해 고민하며 머리를 쥐어짠다고 말하는 것이 가장 적절하다.

어휘
have an inkling of ~을 짐작하다, 알아차리다
rack one's brain(s) 머리를 짜내다, 깊이 생각하다

---

3   어휘 > 유의어 찾기   오답률 50%   답 ①

| 해석 | 가장 최신 법률들 중 일부는 사람들이 필요할 때 그들 대신 의료 결정을 할 수 있는 대리인을 지정하는 것을 허가한다.

① 50% 대리인   ② 9% 보초[감시]병
③ 29% 전임자   ④ 12% 약탈자

| 정답해설 | ① surrogate는 '대리인'이라는 의미이며, proxy와 동일한 의미를 가진다.

---

4 어휘 > 유의어 찾기 오답률 27% 답 ④

| 해석 | A: 그는 그가 무엇이든 이룰 수 있다고 생각해.
B: 맞아, 그는 현실적일 필요가 있어.
① 9% 그 자신만의 세계에서 살다
② 5% 긴장을 풀고 마음껏 즐기다
③ 13% 용감하고 자신 있다
④ 73% 삶에 대해 분별 있고 현실적이다

| 정답해설 | ④ keep one's feet on the ground는 '~가 현실적이다, 들떠 있지 않다'라는 의미로, ④와 의미가 가장 유사하다.

| 더 알아보기 | '현실적인'을 뜻하는 표현

- down-to-earth 현실적인
- keep one's feet on the ground 현실적이다

---

^{오답률 TOP 2}
5 어휘 > 유의어 찾기 오답률 52% 답 ④

| 해석 | 그녀는 루브르 박물관에 있는 모나리자를 관람하러 가야 할지 결정을 못하고 있어.
① 6% 번민의, 고뇌에 찬 ② 37% 열광적인
③ 9% 불안한 ④ 48% 결정하지 못한

| 정답해설 | ④ on the fence는 '결정하지 못하여, 애매한 태도를 취하여'의 뜻으로, undecided와 의미가 가장 가깝다.

---

6 문법 > 동사, 관계사 오답률 38% 답 ②

| 해석 | ① 당신은 단지 야채를 많이 먹는 것이 당신을 완벽히 건강하게 유지시켜 줄 것이라고 생각할지도 모른다.
② 학문적 지식이 항상 당신이 올바른 결정을 내리도록 이끌지는 않는다.
③ 다칠지 모른다는 두려움이 그가 무모한 행동에 관여하는 것을 막지 못했다.
④ Julie의 담당의는 그녀에게 너무 많은 가공식품을 섭취하는 것을 중단하라고 말했다.

| 정답해설 | ② 62% lead를 that 이하의 관계대명사절의 동사로 본다면 그에 맞는 선행사를 찾을 수 없기 때문에 leads는 주절의 동사임을 알 수 있다. leads는 일반동사이므로 부정문을 사용할 때 be동사가 아닌 do동사를 사용해야 한다. 올바르게 고친 문장은 Academic knowledge doesn't always lead you to make right decisions.이다. 또한 is의 보어의 역할을 하는 명사가 없고 leads의 주어도 없으므로 선행사를 포함한 관계대명사로 바꿔 what leads you to make ~ 로 수정할 수도 있다.

| 오답해설 | ① 14% 해당 문장에서 주절인 you might think는 목적절로 that 이하를 갖는다. 목적절의 동사는 keep으로, keep은 불완전 타동사로 쓰일 때 「keep+목적어+목적격 보어」의 형태로 쓰인다. keep의 목적격 보어로 쓰인 healthy를 부사인 perfectly가 수식하고 있으므로 옳게 사용되었다.
③ 9% 「prevent A from B」는 'A가 B하는 것을 막다[방지하다]'라

는 뜻으로 B에는 명사나 동명사가 와야 한다.
④ 15% stop은 목적어로 오직 동명사만을 갖는다. 참고로 「stop + to부정사」의 to부정사는 목적어가 아니라, to부정사의 부사적 용법 중에 목적에 해당되는 것으로 '~하기 위해서'라는 의미로 해석된다. 즉, 「stop -ing」는 '~하는 것을 멈추다'라는 의미이고 「stop + to부정사」는 '~하기 위해 멈추다'라는 의미이다.

| 더 알아보기 | 목적어의 형태(동명사/to부정사)에 따른 동사의 의미 차이

(1) 「stop + to부정사」: ~하기 위해 멈추다(「자동사 + to부정사」의 부사적 용법)
「stop -ing」: ~하는 것을 그만두다(목적어 역할을 하는 동명사)
- The whale stops to breathe. 그 고래는 숨쉬기 위해서 멈춘다.
  → '숨쉬기 위해서'라는 의미로 '목적어'가 아닌 to부정사의 '목적'의 역할만 함
- The whale stops breathing. 그 고래는 숨쉬는 것을 멈춘다.
  → 동명사는 목적어 역할을 함
- I stopped to smoke. 나는 담배를 피우려고 멈췄다.
  → '담배를 피우기 위해서'라는 의미로 '목적어'가 아닌 to부정사의 '목적'의 역할만 함
- I stopped smoking. 나는 담배를 끊었다.
  → 목적어의 역할을 하는 동명사

(2) 「remember, forget, recall, regret -ing」: (과거) ~했던 것을 …하다
「remember, forget, recall, regret + to부정사」: (미래) ~해야 할 것을 …하다
- I remember seeing him last night. 나는 어젯밤에 그를 본 것을 기억한다.
- I remember to see him tomorrow. 나는 내일 그를 볼 것을 기억한다.

(3) 「mean + to부정사」: ~하는 것을 의도하다
「mean -ing」: ~하는 것을 의미하다
- He didn't mean to bother you. 그는 당신을 괴롭히려던 것이 아니었다.
- My new job will mean hiring employees. 내 새로운 일은 직원들을 고용하는 것을 의미할 것이다.

(4) 「try + to부정사」: ~하려고 노력하다
「try -ing」: 시험 삼아 ~하다
- He tried to move the piano. 그는 피아노를 움직이기 위해서 애썼다.
- He tried moving the piano. 그는 시험 삼아 피아노를 움직여 봤다.

어휘

engage in ~에 참여[관여]하다 reckless 무모한, 경솔한

---

7 문법 > 강조와 도치 오답률 46% 답 ④

| 해석 | ① 바다에는 아직 발견되지 않은 많은 생명체들이 있다.
② 지구에서 망원경 없이 관찰되기에 토성의 고리는 너무 멀리 있다.
③ Aswan High 댐은 주변 국가들의 기근으로부터 이집트를 보호해 오고 있다.
④ 이번 시리즈에는 다른 유명한 동화 중 하나인 "The Enchanted Horse"가 포함되어 있다.

| 정답해설 | ④ 54% 본래 문장은 "The Enchanted Horse," among other famous children's stories, is included in this series.이다. 보어인 included가 문장 맨 앞에 나와 주어와 동사가 도치되었다.

| 오답해설 | ① 12% that절의 선행사는 life가 아니라 forms이기 때문에 복수 동사 have가 와야 한다. 올바르게 고친 문장은 The

oceans contain many forms of life that have not yet been discovered.이다.

② 19% 문맥상 '…하기에 너무 ~한'이라는 의미의 「too ~ to」 구문이 쓰이는 것이 옳다. 올바르게 고친 문장은 The rings of Saturn are too distant to be seen from Earth without a telescope.이다.

③ 15% 댐이 이집트를 '보호한' 것이기 때문에 능동태 동사를 사용해야 하므로 has been protected가 아니라 has protected가 되어야 한다.

어휘

famine 기근, 기아　　　　　　　enchanted 마법에 걸린

8　독해 > Micro Reading > 내용일치/불일치　오답률 36%　답 ①

| 해석 | 농작물 재배를 위해 사용되는 농지의 토양은 토양이 형성되는 속도의 10~40배의 속도로, 그리고 삼림지에서는 500배~10,000배의 토양 침식 속도로 물과 풍식에 의해 휩쓸려 운반된다. 그러한 토양의 침식 속도는 토양의 형성 속도보다 훨씬 높기 때문에 그것은 흙의 순손실을 의미한다. 예를 들어, 미국에서 농작물 생산성이 가장 높은 주 중 하나인 아이오와의 표층 토양의 약 절반 가량이 지난 150년간 침식되어 왔다. 내가 아이오와에 가장 최근에 방문했을 때, 초청자들은 내게 그러한 토양 손실을 극적으로 볼 수 있는 예를 제공하는 교회 부지를 보여 주었다. 교회는 19세기에 농경지 한가운데에 지어졌고, 그 이후로 계속 교회로 유지되어 온 반면, 그곳 주변 땅에서는 농사가 지어졌다. 흙이 교회 부지에서보다 농지에서 훨씬 더 빠르게 침식된 결과, 그 교회 부지는 이제 주변의 농지라는 바다 위에 10피트 떠 있는 작은 섬처럼 서 있다.
① 아이오와에 있는 한 교회 부지는 주변 농지보다 더 높다.
② 아이오와의 농작물 생산성은 그곳의 토양의 형성을 가속화해 왔다.
③ 농지에서 토양의 형성 속도는 토양의 침식 속도보다 빠르다.
④ 아이오와는 지난 150년간 표층의 토양을 유지해 왔다.

| **정답해설** | ① 64% 맨 마지막 문장을 통해 아이오와의 교회 부지가 주변 농지보다 10피트 더 높다는 것을 알 수 있다.

| **오답해설** | ② 12% 농작물 생산성과 토양 형성 간의 관계는 언급되지 않았다.

③ 9% 첫 번째 문장과 두 번째 문장에서 토양의 침식 속도는 토양의 형성 속도보다 훨씬 빠르다고 했다.

④ 15% For instance ~ in the last 150 years.를 통해 아이오와는 지난 150년간 표층 토양이 절반 가량 침식되어 왔다는 것을 알 수 있다.

9　독해 > Logical Reading > 삭제　오답률 10%　답 ③

| 해석 | 당신이 여행을 해 오고 있든, 가족에게 집중하든, 또는 직장에서 바쁜 시즌을 보내고 있든, 운동을 14일간 거르는 것은 당신의 근육뿐 아니라, (업무) 성과, 뇌, 그리고 수면에도 타격을 끼친다. 대부분의 전문가는 만약 당신이 헬스장으로 돌아오지 않는다면, 2주 후에 곤경에 처할 것이라는 것에 동의한다. "운동을 하지 않은 지 2주가 된 시점에 건강 지수의 감소를 자연스럽게 나타내는 다수의 생리학적인 지표가 나타난다."라고 뉴욕을 기반으로 엘리트 운동선수들과 일하는 운동생리학자이자 트레이너인 Scott Weiss는 말한다. 결국에는, 이 모든 능력에도 불구하고, 인체(심지어 건강한 인체)는 아주 민감한 시스템이고 트레이닝을 통해 나타나는 생리학적인 변화들(근육의 강도 또는 더 뛰어난 유산소 베이스)은 당신의 운동량이 줄어

들면 간단하게 사라진다고 그는 언급한다. 훈련의 요구가 없기 때문에 당신의 몸은 간단하게 다시 기초선상으로 슬그머니 돌아가는 것이다. ③ 당신의 몸에서 빠른 속도로 근육을 만들기 위해서는 더 많은 단백질이 요구된다. 물론, 얼마나 많이 그리고 얼마나 빠르게 당신의 몸 컨디션을 망가뜨릴지는 당신이 얼마나 건강한지, 당신의 나이, 그리고 얼마나 오래 땀을 흘리는 습관을 가져왔는지와 같은 많은 요인에 달려 있다. "2~8개월 동안 운동을 아예 하지 않는 것은 당신의 건강 지수를 마치 운동을 한 번도 한 적이 없었던 것처럼 감소시킬 것이다."라고 Weiss는 언급한다.

| **정답해설** | ③ 91% 본문은 운동과 건강 지수의 관계에 관한 글인데, ③은 근육 형성과 단백질 섭취의 관계에 관한 내용이므로 ③은 글의 전체적인 흐름에서 벗어난다.

어휘

take a toll 피해[타격]을 주다　　　physiological 생리학적인
dwindle 줄어들다　　　　　　　slink 살금살금 움직이다
at a rapid pace 빠른 속도로　　　decondition 몸 컨디션을 망가뜨리다
a slew of 많은

10　독해 > Micro Reading > 내용일치/불일치　오답률 47%　답 ④

| 해석 | 15세기 이전에, 마녀의 네 가지 특징(야간 비행, 비밀 회동, 유해한 마법, 그리고 악마와의 계약 모두)은 교회에 의해 개별적으로 혹은 제한적으로 결합되어, 템플 기사단원, 이단자, 훈련받은 마법사, 그리고 기타 반체제 집단을 포함한 반대파들 탓으로 여겨졌다. 초자연적인 현상에 대한 민중의 믿음은 마녀 재판 동안 소작농들의 자백에서 부각되었다. 마법에 대한 대중적 견해와 학술적 견해 사이의 가장 두드러지는 차이점은 마녀는 악마로부터 나오지 않은 타고난 초자연적 힘을 가지고 있다는 민중의 믿음에 있다. 학자들에게 이것은 이단에 가까운 것이었다. 초자연적인 힘은 절대 인간이 타고 나지 않았을뿐더러, 마녀들은 그들의 기술을 당시에 남성의 전유물이었던 대학에서 학술적인 훈련을 요구하는 학습된 마법의 전통으로부터 얻을 수 없었다. 마녀의 힘은 필연적으로 그녀가 악마와 맺은 계약에서 나온 것이었다.
① 민중과 학자들은 마녀의 초자연적인 힘의 근원에 관하여 다른 견해를 가지고 있었다.
② 민중의 믿음에 의하면, 초자연적인 힘은 마녀의 본질적인 천성에 속했다.
③ 마녀의 네 가지 특징은 교회에 의해 그것의 반체제 집단의 탓으로 돌려졌다.
④ 학자들은 마녀의 힘이 대학의 학문적인 훈련을 통해 얻어진다고 믿었다.

| **정답해설** | ④ 53% 후반부의 For learned men 이하에서 학자들은 마녀의 힘은 대학의 학문적인 훈련을 통해 얻을 수 있는 것이 아니라고 믿었음을 알 수 있으므로 본문의 내용과 일치하지 않는다.

어휘

pact (개인 간의) 약속, 계약; (국가 간의) 협정, 조약
ascribe A to B A를 B의 탓으로 돌리다
adversary 상대방, 적수　　　　　heretic 이단자
dissident 반체제 인사　　　　　peasant 소작농
confession 자백, 고백　　　　　witchcraft 마법, 마술
innate 타고난
border on ~에 아주 가깝다, 거의 ~와 같다
heresy 이단　　　　　　　　　preserve 전유물

11 독해 > Logical Reading > 삽입   오답률 16%   답 ③

| 해석 | 내가 도착하자마자 다양한 의무들이 나를 기다리고 있었다. 소녀들의 공부 시간 동안 나는 그들과 함께 앉아 있어야만 했다. 그러고 나면 내가 기도문을 읽고 그들이 잠자리에 드는 것을 볼 차례였다. 그 후에 나는 다른 선생님들과 식사를 했다. 심지어 우리가 마침내 잠자리에 들 때조차도 껌딱지인 Gryce양은 여전히 나의 이야기 상대였다. 우리 촛대에는 끝이 짧은 초 하나만 있었고, 나는 그것이 전부 타 들어갈 때까지 그녀가 이야기를 할까 봐 두려웠다. ③ 그러나, 운이 좋게도, 그녀가 먹었던 성대한 저녁 때문에 그녀는 피곤해졌고 잠들 채비가 되었다. 그녀는 내가 옷을 다 벗기도 전에 이미 코를 골고 있었다. 아직 1인치 길이의 초가 남아 있었다. 나는 그때서야 내 편지를 꺼냈고, 이니셜 F의 직인이 있었다. 나는 봉투를 찢었다. 내용은 간략했다.

| 정답해설 | ③ 84% 앞에서 필자는 Gryce양이 이야기를 계속 할까 봐 두려웠다고 말하고 있다. 하지만 ③ 뒤에 그녀는 이미 코를 골고 있었다고 했으므로 그녀가 잠들었음을 알 수 있다. 그러므로 Gryce양이 잠들 채비가 되었다는 주어진 문장의 가장 적절한 위치는 ③이다.

| 오답해설 | ① ② 3% 10% 주어진 문장의 '그녀(Gryce양)'를 지칭할 만한 사람이 아직 언급되지 않았다.
④ 3% 앞의 She was already snoring before I had finished undressing.에서 이미 그녀가 잠에 빠진 것을 알 수 있다. 잠이 들고 난 다음에 또 '잠들 채비가 되었다'라고 하는 것은 문맥의 흐름상 적절하지 않다.

어휘
retire for the night 잠자리에 들다   inevitable 피할 수 없는, 반드시 있는
companion 말동무, 이야기 상대; 동료, 벗

12 독해 > Macro Reading > 제목   오답률 14%   답 ②

| 해석 | 두려움과 그것의 동료인 고통은 적절하게 사용된다면, 인간과 동물이 소유한 가장 유용한 것들 중 두 가지이다. 만약에 불에 데었을 때 아프지 않다면, 아이들은 그들의 손이 다 타버릴 때까지 불을 가지고 놀 것이다. 마찬가지로, 만약에 고통은 존재하지만 두려움은 존재하지 않는다면, 두려움은 그 아이에게 이전에 데인 적이 있는 불을 멀리하라고 경고하지 않을 것이기 때문에 아이는 반복해서 불에 데일 것이다. 정말로 두려움 없는 병사들은, 실제로 몇몇은 정말로 존재하는데, 좋은 병사가 아니다. 왜냐하면 그는 금방 죽을 것이고, 그리고 죽은 병사는 그의 군대에 아무 쓸모가 없기 때문이다. 그러므로 두려움과 고통은 인간과 동물이 가지고 있지 않으면 금방 죽어버릴지도 모르는 두 가지 보호 장비이다.
① 병사들에게 있어서의 두려움과 고통의 모호함
② 두려움과 고통의 필요성
③ 두려움과 고통에 대한 반감
④ 아이들과 두려움과 고통의 연관성

| 정답해설 | ② 86% 글의 도입부에서 두려움과 고통이 인간과 동물에게 유용한 두 가지임을 밝히고 있고, 이어지는 문장에서 이를 뒷받침하기 위해 아이와 불장난, 군인과 그들이 느끼는 두려움의 상관관계에 대한 예를 상세히 들고 있다. 그리고 마지막 문장을 통해 다시 한 번 '두려움과 고통의 필요성'에 대해 강조하고 있으므로 ②가 이 글의 제목으로 가장 적절하다.

| 오답해설 | ① 3% 병사들에 관한 내용은 두려움과 고통의 필요성을 설명하기 위한 예시로 언급되었으며, 아울러 두려움과 고통의 모호함에 대해서는 설명하고 있지도 않다.
③ 8% 반감이 아니라 필요성에 대해 강조하는 글이다.
④ 3% 두려움과 고통의 필요성에 대해 역설하기 위해 아이들과 불장난을 예로 들었을 뿐이다.

어휘
burn oneself 불에 데이다, 화상을 입다
obscurity 모호함, 잊혀짐   indispensability 필요, 긴요함
disapproval 반감

오답률 TOP 3
13 문법 > 비교   오답률 51%   답 ④

| 정답해설 | ④ 49% prefer를 이용한 비교급 문장에서는 비교 대상 앞에 than이 아니라 to를 쓰는 것에 주의해야 한다. 즉, 「prefer A to B」는 'B보다 A를 선호하다'라는 뜻이고, 이때 A와 B는 병렬 구조가 되어야 한다. 그러므로 바르게 고치면 I prefer staying home to going out on a snowy day.가 된다. 동명사 대신 to부정사를 사용하고 싶다면 I prefer to stay home rather than (to) go out on a snowy day.로 고쳐도 된다.

| 오답해설 | ① 13% '~하는 것을 규칙으로 세우다'라는 의미를 지닌 「make it a rule + to부정사」 관용표현이 사용되었다. 또한 부정관사가 기간을 나타내는 단어 앞에 오면 '~마다'라는 뜻으로 쓰이기도 한다. 여기에서 a month는 '매달'이라는 뜻으로 알맞게 쓰였다.
② 18% grab, catch, pull, take, seize, hold 등의 동사는 「목적격 + by + 정관사 + 신체 부위」로 쓴다. 이때 주의할 것은 by my arm이 아니라 정관사 the를 쓴다는 점이다.
③ 20% owing to는 전치사구이다. 그러므로 Owing to 뒤에 명사구인 the heavy rain이 온 것은 적절하다. 또한 문장의 마지막 전치사 by는 정도 혹은 차이를 나타내기 위해 사용된 것으로 적절하다.

| 더 알아보기 | **이유를 나타내는 구 전치사**

- due to: ~ 때문에
  = on account of
  = because of
  = on the ground of
  = owing to
- He cannot accept her invitation due to his illness.
  그는 아파서 그녀의 초대를 받아들일 수 없다.

14 문법 > 관사   오답률 41%   답 ③

| 정답해설 | ③ 59% tend는 '돌보다, 보살피다'라는 뜻의 타동사로 목적어가 필요하다. 형용사(sick and wounded)가 목적어가 되기 위해서는 명사로 바뀌어야 한다. 형용사 앞에 정관사를 붙여 「the + 형용사」의 형태로 쓰면 '~한 사람들'이라는 뜻의 복수 보통 명사가 된다. 따라서 sick and wounded는 the sick and the

wounded로 바꾸어야 알맞다.

| 오답해설 | ① 6% 「It ~ that」 강조 용법으로 not her refusal but her rudeness를 강조하고 있다. 또한 여기서 「not A but B」 구문이 사용되었는데, her refusal과 her rudeness는 병렬 구조를 이루고 있으므로 적절하다.

② 30% 「cannot be too + 형용사」의 형태로 '아무리 ~해도 지나치지 않다'라는 의미를 나타낼 수 있다.

④ 5% To make matters worse는 '설상가상으로'라는 의미의 관용표현이다. 또한 that절은 a report의 동격절이다.

| 더 알아보기 | 「cannot ~ too …」: 아무리 …해도 지나치지 않다

- 주어 + cannot + 동사원형 + too ~
  = 주어 + cannot + 동사원형 ~ enough
  = 주어 + cannot over동사원형
  = It is impossible ~ for + 의미상 주어 + to부정사 + too much
  = It is impossible ~ for + 의미상 주어 + to부정사 ~ enough
  = It is impossible ~ for + 의미상 주어 + to over동사원형
- We cannot praise her effort too much.
  우리는 그녀의 노력을 아무리 칭찬해도 지나치지 않다.
  = We cannot praise her effort enough.
  = We cannot overpraise her effort.
  = It is impossible for us to praise her effort too much.
  = It is impossible for us to praise her effort enough.
  = It is impossible for us to overpraise her effort.

어휘

perplex 당혹스럽게 하다   to make matters worse 설상가상으로

---

15 어휘 > 빈칸 완성   오답률 25%   답 ①

| 해석 | 우리의 주요리는 그다지 맛있지 않았지만 나는 조미료를 첨가하여 그것을 더 ① 맛있게 만들었다.

① 75% 맛있는, 맛 좋은   ② 4% 분해할 수 있는, 용해할 수 있는

③ 9% 마셔도 되는   ④ 12% 민감한; (~의) 여지가 있는

| 정답해설 | ① 접속사 but으로 보아 조미료를 첨가하여 '맛있게' 만들었다는 흐름이 알맞음을 유추할 수 있다. palatable은 '맛있는'이라는 의미이므로 빈칸에 알맞다.

어휘

condiment 조미료, 양념

오답률 TOP 1

16 독해 > Reading for Writing > 빈칸 구 완성   오답률 63%   답 ③

| 해석 | 런던의 택시 기사들은 25,000개가 넘는 도시의 도로 구획 배치를 배우는 것을 포함하여, 운행 허가증을 취득하기 위해 "the knowledge"라고 알려진 집중 훈련을 수년간 받아야 한다. 한 연구자와 그녀의 팀은 택시 기사들과 일반인들을 조사했다. 그 두 그룹은 아일랜드의 소도시를 통과하는, 그들에게 익숙하지 않은 노선 비디오를 시청하도록 요청받았다. 그 다음에는 노선을 대략적으로 그리고, 랜드마크를 식별하고, 장소들 간의 거리를 추정하는 것을 포함하여 비디오에 관한 시험을 치르도록 요청받았다. 두 그룹 모두 시험의 상당 부분을 잘 치렀지만, 택시 기사들은 새로운 노선을 파악하는 데에 있어서 확연히 더 잘했다. 이러한 결과는 택시 기사들의 숙달은 새롭고 잘 알려지지 않은 지역에서도 ③ 일반화될 수 있음을 암시한다. 계획적인 연습을 통한 몇 년 간에 걸친 훈련과 학습은 심지어 잘 모르거나 혹은 아예 모르는 장소에서도 그들이 유사한 도전을 받아들이도록 준비시킨다.

① 갇힌, 한정된   ② 헌신적인

③ 일반화된   ④ 기여된

| 정답해설 | ③ 37% 오랜 기간 받은 훈련으로 인해 런던의 택시 기사들은 익숙하지 않은 곳에서도 새로운 노선 파악을 뛰어나게 할 수 있을 정도로 그들의 능력이 '일반화'되어 발휘될 수 있었다는 내용이다.

어휘

undertake (일에) 착수하다   layout 배치

mastery 숙달, 통달

---

17 독해 > Logical Reading > 배열   오답률 14%   답 ④

| 해석 | 나는 Lewis가 그 폭포를 발견했던 날을 기억한다. 그들은 해가 뜰 때 야영지를 떠났고, 몇 시간 뒤에 그들은 아름다운 평원을 마주쳤다. 그리고 그 평원에는 그들이 이전에 어느 한 장소에서 봐 왔던 것보다도 많은 버팔로들이 있었다.

(C) 그들은 멀리 떨어진 폭포의 소리가 들릴 때까지 계속해서 전진했고, 멀리 떨어진 물보라 기둥이 솟아났다가 사라지는 것을 보았다. 그들은 그 소리가 점점 더 커질 때까지 그 소리를 따라갔다.

(B) 잠시 후에, 그 소리는 거대해졌고 그들은 미주리강의 큰 폭포에 있었다. 그들이 그곳에 도착했을 때는 정오쯤이었다.

(A) 그날 오후에 좋은 일이 생겼다. 그들은 폭포 아래로 낚시를 가서 송어를 6마리 잡았는데, 그것들은 길이가 16~23인치나 되는 좋은 것이기도 했다.

| 정답해설 | ④ 86% (A)의 A nice ~ that afternoon.과 (B)의 It was about noon ~ there. 문장을 통해 시간의 흐름상 (B)의 '정오' 다음에 (A)의 '오후'가 오는 것이 적절하다. 그리고 (B)의 첫 번째 문장에 있는 the sound는 (C)의 the faraway sound of a waterfall을 가리키므로 (C) 다음에 (B)가 와야 한다. 그러므로 (C) - (B) - (A)의 순서가 알맞다.

어휘

come upon 우연히 만나다   spray 물보라

---

18 독해 > Macro Reading > 요지   오답률 34%   답 ④

| 해석 | 새로움으로 인해 유발되는 시간의 확장은 실험실의 조건 하에서 연구될 수 있는 잘 특징지어진 현상이다. 단순히 사람들에게 일련의 자극에 노출되는 시간을 추정해 보라고 요청해 보는 것으로도 새로운 자극이 단순히 반복적이거나 평범한 자극들보다 더 오래 지속되는 것처럼 생각된다는 것을 보여 준다. 사실, 적당히 반복되는 일련의 것들 속에서 단지 첫 번째 자극이 되는 것만으로도 주관적인 시간 확장을 유발하기에는 충분해 보인다. 물론, 우리의 뇌가 왜 이러한 방식으로 작동하도록 진화해 왔는지 그 이유를 생각하기는 쉽다. 아마, 새롭고 색다른 자극은 익숙한 자극들보다 더 많은 생각과 숙고를 요구해서 뇌가 그것들에게 더 많은 주관적인 시간을 할당하는 것이 타당한 것이다.

① 자극에 대한 반응은 두뇌 훈련의 중요한 부산물이다.

② 자극의 강도는 반복과 함께 증가한다.

③ 자극에 대한 우리의 신체적 반응은 우리의 생각에 영향을 미친다.

④ 새로운 자극은 주관적인 시간의 확장을 유발한다.

| 정답해설 | ④ 66% 글의 첫 문장을 통해 이 글이 '새로움으로 인해 유발되는 시간의 확장'에 관한 것임을 알 수 있다. 첫 번째 자극이 되는 것만으로도 주관적인 시간 확장을 유발하는데, 그 이유는 익숙한 자극보다 더 많은 생각과 숙고를 해야 하기 때문이라고 설명한다. 그러므로 글의 요지로 가장 적절한 것은 ④이다.

어휘

a train of 일련의   unremarkable 평범한
presumably 아마   exotic 색다른, 이국적인, 외국의
give rise to ~을 낳다, 유발하다

---

19 독해 > Reading for Writing > 빈칸 절 완성   오답률 25%   답 ③

| 해석 | 우리의 마음이 부리는 속임수들 중 하나는 우리가 이미 믿고 있는 것이 사실임을 확인시켜 주는 증거를 더 강조하는 것이다. 만약에 우리가 라이벌에 대한 소문을 듣는다면, 우리는 "나는 그가 못된 사람이라는 것을 알고 있었어."라고 생각하는 경향이 있다. 만약에 우리가 가장 친한 친구에 대해 똑같은 소문을 들었다면, 우리는 "그건 단지 소문일 뿐이야."라고 말할 가능성이 더 크다. 당신이 확증 편향이라고 불리는 이러한 정신적인 습관에 대해 알게 된다면, 당신은 어디서든 그것을 보기 시작할 것이다. 이는 우리가 더 나은 결정을 내리고자 할 때 중요하다. 확증 편향은 우리가 옳다는 전제 하에서는 괜찮지만, 우리는 너무 자주 틀리고, 이미 너무 늦었을 때 결정적인 증거에 관심을 기울이게 할 뿐이다. 어떻게 ③ 우리가 확증 편향으로부터 우리의 결정을 보호할 수 있는지는 왜 심리학적으로 확증 편향이 일어나는가에 대한 우리의 인식에 달려 있다. 두 가지 가능한 원인이 있다. 하나는 우리의 상상 속에 사각지대가 있다는 점이고, 다른 하나는 우리가 새로운 정보에 대해 질문하는 것에 실패한다는 점이다.
① 우리가 라이벌이 우리를 믿도록 만드는지
② 우리의 사각지대는 우리가 더 나은 결정을 내릴 수 있도록 돕는지
③ 우리가 확증 편향으로부터 우리의 결정을 보호할 수 있는지
④ 우리에게 정확하게 같은 편견이 생기는지

| 정답해설 | ③ 75% 빈칸 앞은 우리의 믿음이 옳다는 전제 하에서는 확증 편향이 괜찮지만, 그렇지 않은 경우가 더 많기 때문에 우리는 옳지 않은 결정을 내리는 경우가 더 많다는 것을 지적하는 내용이다. 앞 문장의 내용에 근거하여 심리학적으로 확증 편향이 왜 일어나는가에 대해 아는 것으로 얻을 수 있는 결과로 가장 적절한 것은 ③이다.

| 오답해설 | ① 3% 라이벌은 확증 편향의 부정적 영향을 설명하기 위한 예시로 등장하였을 뿐, 라이벌이 우리를 어떻게 믿도록 만드는지에 관한 내용은 없다.

② 11% 맨 마지막의 One is ~ about new information.의 문장을 통해 사각지대는 확증 편향의 원인이 되는 것이고, 확증 편향은 우리가 옳은 결정을 내리는 것을 자주 막는다는 것을 알 수 있다.

④ 11% 본문을 통해 알 수 없는 내용이다.

어휘

nasty 못된, 고약한
piece of work (비꼬는 투로) 대단한 사람
deciding 결정적인   blind spot 사각지대, 약점

---

20 독해 > Reading for Writing > 빈칸 절 완성   오답률 39%   답 ②

| 해석 | 소비자 제품 브랜드들 중 많은 유명 브랜드들에게 현지 취향을 고려하여 현지의 노동력으로 해외 생산을 하고 수출을 하는 것은 해야 할 마땅한 것이라고 여겨져 왔다. 그렇게 하여, 기업들은 그들의 비용 구조를 개선하고, 신흥국에서 빠르게 확대되어 가는 소비자 시장에서 성장할 방법을 찾았다. 그러나, Sweets Co.는 국내 시장에 갇혀 있다. 그 기업의 제품들에는 방부제가 충분히 들어가, 먼 시장까지 장거리 이동을 견뎌낼 수 있음에도 불구하고, Sweets Co.는 해외 생산은 커녕, ② 거의 수출을 하지 않는다. 변화하는 세계에 대비하여 비즈니스 전략과 제품을 업데이트시키지 못하는 의지의 부족 혹은 무능함은 명백하게 그 기업에 손해를 입히고 있다.
① 수입에 여념이 없다
② 거의 수출을 하지 않는다
③ 운영을 간소화하기로 결정했다
④ 신흥 시장으로 발을 넓히고 있다

| 정답해설 | ② 61% 신흥국의 소비자 시장에서 성장하기 위해 현지의 노동력으로 해외 생산을 하고 수출을 하는 것은 해야할 마땅한 것이지만 Sweets Co.는 국내 시장에 갇혀 있으며 신흥국의 소비자 시장에서 성장할 수 있음에도 불구하고 비즈니스 전략과 제품을 업데이트시키지 못하고 있다고 서술하고 있다. 이를 통해서 Sweets Co.가 해외 생산은 커녕 '수출도 하지 않는다'는 것을 문맥상 유추할 수 있다. 따라서 정답은 ②이다.

어휘

let alone ~은 커녕   be intent on ~을 하는 데 여념이 없다
streamline 간소화하다

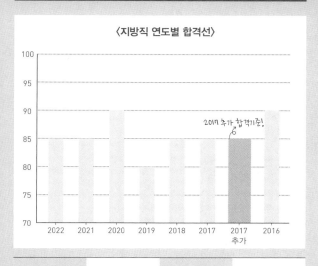

| 합격예상 체크 | 취약영역 체크 |

〈지방직 연도별 합격선〉

2017 추가 합격기준

| 2022 | 2021 | 2020 | 2019 | 2018 | 2017 | 2017 추가 | 2016 |

문항	정답	영역	문항	정답	영역
1	①	어휘 > 유의어 찾기	11	④	독해 > Logical Reading > 연결사
2	③	어휘 > 유의어 찾기	12	④	독해 > Logical Reading > 삭제
3	③	어휘 > 유의어 찾기	13	③	독해 > Micro Reading > 내용 일치/불일치
4	④	어휘 > 빈칸 완성	14	④	독해 > Micro Reading > 내용 일치/불일치
5	①	문법 > 동사	15	②	독해 > Logical Reading > 삽입
6	①	문법 > 형용사, 태	16	③	독해 > Macro Reading > 주제
7	③	생활영어 > 회화/관용표현	17	②	독해 > Reading for Writing > 빈칸 구 완성
8	②	생활영어 > 회화/관용표현	18	①	독해 > Reading for Writing > 빈칸 절 완성
9	④	문법 > 동사	19	④	독해 > Reading for Writing > 빈칸 구 완성
10	①	문법 > 분사	20	①	독해 > Macro Reading > 주장

⬇ 영역별 틀린 개수로 취약영역을 확인하세요!

| 맞힌 개수 | /20문항 | 점수 | /100점 |

| 어휘 | /4 | 문법 | /4 | 독해 | /10 | 생활영어 | /2 |

➡ ☐ 합격 ☐ 불합격   ➡ 나의 취약영역:

※ [정답해설]과 [오답해설] 선지의 50% 표시는 〈1초 합격예측 서비스〉를 통해 수집된 선지 선택률을 나타냅니다.

1 어휘 > 유의어 찾기   오답률 24%   답 ①

| 해석 | 두 차례의 세계 대전 동안, 새로운 항공기에 대한 정부 보조금과 수요가 그것들의 설계와 건조 기술을 대단히 발전시켰다.

① 76% 재정적 지원 ② 7% 장기 계획 수립
③ 9% 기술적 보조 ④ 8% 비제한적 정책

| 정답해설 | ① subsidies는 '보조금, 장려금'이라는 뜻의 subsidy의 복수형으로 financial support(재정적 지원)와 의미가 가장 가깝다.

어휘

subsidy 보조금   vastly 대단히, 막대하게
assistance 보조, 지원, 원조   non-restrictive 비제한적인

오답률 TOP 1

2 어휘 > 유의어 찾기   오답률 56%   답 ③

| 해석 | 화요일 밤의 그 TV 프로그램의 시즌 첫 방송은 그 프로그램의 복잡하게 얽힌 신화와 그것의 더 인간적이고 인물 중심적인 관점 사이에서 절충하려고 노력하고 있는 것으로 보였다.

① 30% 고대의 ② 10% 관계없는
③ 44% 복잡한 ④ 16% 저승의, 내세의

| 정답해설 | ③ 47% convoluted는 '복잡한, 뒤얽힌, 대단히 난해한'이라는 뜻으로 complicated(복잡한)와 의미가 가장 가깝다.

어휘

premiere 초연, 첫날

---

strike a balance between ~ 사이에서 절충하다, 균형을 유지하다
dimension 차원, 규모; 관점   character-driven 인물 중심의

3 어휘 > 유의어 찾기   오답률 38%   답 ③

| 해석 | 우리가 그 대화를 마무리 지을 때쯤, 나는 내가 제네바로 가지 않을 것임을 알았다.

① 16% 시작했다 ② 10% 재개했다
③ 62% 끝냈다, 종료했다 ④ 12% 방해했다, 간섭했다

| 정답해설 | ③ wound up은 wind up의 과거형으로 '마무리 짓다, 끝내다'라는 뜻이므로 terminated(끝냈다, 종료했다)와 의미가 가장 유사하다.

어휘

by the time ~할 때쯤[무렵]   wind up 마무리 짓다, 끝내다

오답률 TOP 3

4 어휘 > 빈칸 완성   오답률 52%   답 ④

| 해석 | 15년 경력의 경사는 젊은 경관에게 유리한 승진에서 ④ 제외된 이후 크게 실망했다.

① 9% (차에) 치이다 ② 15% (데이트를) 신청받다
③ 28% 이행되다 ④ 48% 제외되다, 누락되다

| 정답해설 | ④ 경사가 크게 실망했다는 내용으로 보아 승진에서 '제외되었다'고 하는 것이 문맥상 자연스럽다. 따라서 pass over(제외

시키다)의 수동태 표현이 빈칸에 가장 알맞다.

어휘

sergeant (경찰 계급) 경사
dismay 크게 실망시키다, 경악하게 하다, 낙담시키다
in favor of ~에 유리하게; ~에 찬성[지지]하여
pass over 제외하다, 누락시키다; 무시하다

| **5** | 문법 > 동사 | 오답률 42% | 답 ① |

| 해석 | 지난주 나는 독감으로 아팠다. 아버지가 내가 재채기와 기침을 하는 소리를 들었을 때, 그는 내가 필요한 것이 있는지 물어보려고 내 침실 문을 열었다. 나는 그의 친절하고 배려하는 얼굴을 보며 정말 행복했지만, 독감을 낫게 하기 위해 그가 할 수 있었던 것은 아무것도 없었다.

| 정답해설 | ① 58% 지각동사 heard는 목적격 보어로 원형부정사나 분사를 취할 수 있다. 문맥상 목적어인 me와 목적격 보어가 능동 관계이므로 현재분사 sneezing과 coughing은 어법상 적절하다.

| 오답해설 | ② 15% 의미상 '내가 무엇이 필요한지' 묻기 위해 방문을 연 것이므로 명사절 접속사 that은 '~인지'의 뜻을 갖는 명사절 접속사 if로 고쳐야 한다.

③ 13% anything과 he could do it 사이에 목적격 관계대명사가 생략된 anything (that) he could do it의 문장이다. 이때 목적격 관계대명사인 that이 동사 do의 목적어 역할을 하고 있으므로 it(= anything)은 중복 사용될 수 없기에 삭제해야 한다.

④ 14% 사역동사 make는 목적격 보어로 원형부정사나 과거분사를 취할 수 있다. 이 문장에서 목적어인 the flu와 go away가 능동의 관계이므로 목적격 보어로는 to go away가 아니라 원형부정사 go away가 와야 한다.

| **6** | 문법 > 형용사, 태 | 오답률 49% | 답 ① |

| 해석 | ① 일주일간의 휴가가 모든 사무직 근로자들에게 약속되었다.
② 그녀는 남을 돕는 삶을 살아갈 운명이었다.
③ 아이들 양육을 위해서라면 큰 도시보다는 작은 도시가 더 바람직한 것으로 보인다.
④ 최고의 소프트웨어 회사들은 앞서 나가는 것이 점점 더 힘들다는 것을 알아 가고 있다.

| 정답해설 | ① 51% A week's holiday는 '일주일간의 휴가'라는 의미로 시간을 나타내기 위해 소유격을 사용하였으므로 어법상 적절하다. 또한 A week's holiday가 직원들에게 '약속된' 것이므로 완료수동태인 has been promised도 어법상 적절히 쓰였다.

| 오답해설 | ② 21% destine은 '~을 예정해 두다'라는 의미의 타동사이며 수동태로 쓰여 '(운명으로) 정해지다, 운명 짓다'의 의미를 나타낸다. 따라서 능동태인 destined to live는 수동태인 is[was] destined to live로 고쳐져야 한다.

③ 20% 라틴어 비교급인 preferable, superior, inferior, senior, major, minor 등은 than 대신에 전치사 to를 동반하므로 preferable to가 되어야 한다.

④ 8% find는 3형식 완전타동사와 5형식 불완전타동사로 쓰인다. 그러나 주어진 문장처럼 「find + 형용사」 형태의 불완전자동사로

는 쓸 수 없으므로 목적어가 필요하다. 여기서는 to stay ahead가 진목적어이며 형용사 challenging을 동사 find의 목적격 보어로 보아야 한다. 따라서 가목적어 it을 써서 「find + 가목적어(it) + 목적격 보어 + 진목적어(to부정사)」 형태의 finding it increasingly challenging to stay ahead로 고쳐야 한다.

| 더 알아보기 | 「be + to부정사」 용법

to부정사의 형용사적 용법 중 서술적 역할에 해당되며, '예정, 의무, 가능, 운명, 의도'의 의미를 나타낸다.
(1) 예정
  • ~할 예정이다(be going to, be scheduled to)
  • 보통 미래 시간 부사구(next 등)와 주로 쓰임
    They **are to arrive** here at five.
    그들은 여기에 5시에 도착할 예정이다.
(2) 의무
  • ~해야 한다(should, must)
  • 규칙, 법규와 함께 쓰임
    You **are to obey** rules we made.
    너희는 우리가 만든 규칙을 따라야 한다.
(3) 가능
  • ~할 수 있다(can)
  • 뒤에 to부정사의 수동태가 나오는 경우가 많음
    It was too dark that night. Nothing **was to be** seen.
    그날 밤은 너무 어두웠다. 아무것도 보이지 않았다.
(4) 운명
  • ~할 운명이다(be destined[doomed] to)
    He **was to become** a hero during the war.
    그는 전쟁 동안 영웅이 될 운명이었다.
(5) 의도
  • ~할 작정이다(intend to)
  • 주로 if 조건절에 쓰임
    If you **are to succeed**, you must be diligent.
    성공하고자 한다면, 당신은 근면해야 한다.

어휘

destine 예정해 두다, 운명 짓다   raise 키우다, 양육하다
challenging 도전적인, 힘든, 어려운
stay ahead ~보다 앞쪽에 있다, (경쟁에서) 앞서다

| **7** | 생활영어 > 회화/관용표현 | 오답률 14% | 답 ③ |

| 해석 | A: 새로운 동네는 어때?
B: 대부분 좋아. 맑은 공기와 푸른 환경이 마음에 들어.
A: 참 살기 좋은 곳처럼 들려.
B: 응, 그렇지만 단점이 없는 것은 아니야.
A: 예를 들면?
B: 하나 말하자면, 상점이 다양하게 많지 않아. 예를 들어, 슈퍼마켓이 하나밖에 없어서 식재료가 정말 비싸.
A: ③ 그건 문제인 것 같다.
B: 네 말이 맞아. 그렇지만 다행이야. 그 도시에서 지금 새로운 쇼핑센터를 짓고 있거든. 내년이면 우린 더 많은 선택권을 가지게 될 거야.
① 그곳에 슈퍼마켓이 몇 개 있어?
② 그곳에 쇼핑을 할 곳이 많니?
③ 그건 문제인 것 같다.
④ 너희 동네로 이사 가고 싶어.

| 정답해설 | ③ 86% 빈칸 앞에서는 B가 새로운 동네의 단점을 말했고 빈칸 뒤에서는 B가 A의 말에 맞장구를 쳤다. 따라서 빈칸에서 A는 B가 한 말에 동조했음을 짐작할 수 있으므로 ③이 빈칸에 들어갈 말로 알맞다.

---

8 생활영어 > 회화/관용표현   오답률 14%   답 ②

| 해석 | A: 그래서 Wong씨, 뉴욕시에서는 얼마나 오래 거주하고 계시는 건가요?
B: 이곳에서 약 7년째 살고 있습니다.
A: 업무 경력에 대해 말씀해 주시겠어요?
B: 지난 3년간 피자 가게에서 일하고 있습니다.
A: 그곳에서 어떤 일을 하시죠?
B: 손님들에게 자리를 안내하고 서빙을 합니다.
A: 그 일에 대해 어떻게 생각하세요?
B: 좋습니다. 모두 정말 좋거든요.
A: ② 그렇다면, 왜 이 자리에 지원하시는 겁니까?
B: 저는 단지 조금 더 정규적인 환경에서 일을 하고 싶기 때문입니다.
A: 알겠습니다. 덧붙일 다른 말씀이 있나요?
B: 저는 사람들과 정말 잘 지냅니다. 그리고 이탈리어어와 중국어도 할 수 있습니다.
A: 알겠습니다. 감사합니다. 곧 연락드리겠습니다.
B: 얼른 소식을 듣게 되면 좋겠습니다.
① 그래서, 그곳 환경은 어떻습니까?
② 그렇다면, 왜 이 자리에 지원하시는 겁니까?
③ 그런데 능숙한 다른 외국어가 있습니까?
④ 그리고 이곳에서 일하려면 어떤 자질이 필요하다고 생각하십니까?

| 정답해설 | ② 86% 빈칸 이전에서 B는 현재 직장에서 만족하고 있다고 답했는데, 빈칸 바로 뒤에서 B는 정규적인 환경에서 일하고 싶다고 자신의 생각을 전하고 있다. 따라서 빈칸에는 현재 직장에 만족하는데 왜 이 자리에 지원하는지를 묻는 내용이 들어가는 것이 적절하다.

---

9 문법 > 동사   오답률 40%   답 ④

| 정답해설 | ④ 60% 동사 stop은 동명사만을 목적어로 취하는 동사로서, 「stop -ing」의 형태로 '~하는 것을 멈추다'라는 의미를 나타낼 수 있다. 참고로, 「stop + to부정사」에서 to부정사는 목적어로 쓰인 것이 아니며, '~하기 위해서 멈추다'라는 to부정사의 목적의 의미로 사용된 것이다. 해당 문장에서는 컴퓨터가 '작동하던 것을 멈추었다'는 내용이므로 동명사 목적어를 쓴 stopped working은 어법상 적절하다. 또한 사역동사 get의 목적어인 it(= computer)과 목적격 보어인 fix는 서로 수동 관계에 있으므로 과거분사 fixed는 어법상 올바르다.

| 오답해설 | ① 8% 과거 사실에 대한 반대의 상황을 가정하고 있으므로 「If +주어 + had p.p. ~, 주어 + 조동사의 과거형 + have p.p. …」의 가정법 과거완료를 사용해야 한다. 따라서 if절의 haven't는 hadn't로 고쳐야 한다.
② 15% 감정 유발 동사가 형용사처럼 쓰이는 경우, 사물이 주어가 되어 '감정을 제공'하면 현재분사 형태를 취해야 하고, 사람이 주

어가 되어 '감정의 상태'를 나타내면 과거분사 형태를 취해야 한다. 사물 주어인 The movie가 지루함을 유발하는 주체이므로 과거분사인 bored가 현재분사 boring으로 고쳐져야 어법에 맞다.
③ 17% 타동사 accompany는 '~와 동행하다'의 의미로 사용될 때, 전치사를 동반하지 않고 바로 목적어를 취하므로 with를 삭제해야 한다.

| 더 알아보기 | 감정형 분사

> • 감정 제공 형용사(현재분사): interesting, exciting, pleasing, amusing, boring 등
> • 감정 상태 형용사(과거분사): interested, excited, pleased, amused, bored 등

---

10 문법 > 분사   오답률 48%   답 ①

| 정답해설 | ① 52% 비교 대상을 나타내는 접속사 than 뒤에 주어와 be동사가 생략되어 있다. 따라서 예산이 '원래 기대되었던 것'보다 25퍼센트 더 높다고 하는 것이 적절하므로 수동의 의미를 가진 과거분사를 사용하는 것이 옳다. 따라서 expected로 고쳐야 한다. 원문은 ~ than it(= the budget) was originally expected이다.

| 오답해설 | ② 19% to be done은 명사 work를 수식하는 to부정사의 형용사적 용법으로 쓰였고, work는 의미상 '행하여지는' 대상이므로 to부정사의 수동태 to be done이 알맞게 쓰였다.
③ 18% 동사 take 다음에 시간 관련 명사가 오면 '(시간이) 걸리다'라는 의미로 「it takes + 시간 (for + 의미상 주어) + to부정사」의 구조로 쓰인다. 해당 문장은 to부정사의 의미상 주어가 생략된 형태의 문장이다. 또한 at least는 '최소한, 적어도'라는 의미의 부사구로 적절하게 사용되었다.
④ 11% 주격 관계대명사 who가 이끄는 절이 선행사 the head를 수식하고 있는 형태이다. 이 문장에서 the head는 '우두머리, 부서장'의 의미로 사람을 의미하므로 who를 사용하는 것이 옳다. 또한 문장의 동사는 has, 즉 3인칭 단수형으로 주어 The head of the department와 수가 일치되어 있다.

| 더 알아보기 | 「it takes + 시간 + to부정사」

> '시간이 걸리다'의 표현은 가주어 'it'을 사용하여 「it takes + 시간 + to부정사」로 표현한다.
> • It always takes a little time to tune in on a professor's style.
> 교수의 스타일에 적응하는 데는 항상 시간이 좀 걸린다.

---

11 독해 > Logical Reading > 연결사   오답률 42%   답 ④

| 해석 | 선진국에서의 국내 입양 횟수의 감소는 주로 국내로 입양 가능한 아이들의 공급이 감소한 결과이다. 대부분의 선진국에서의 합법적인 낙태에의 접근성뿐만 아니라 만연한 출산 연기 현상과 함께, 안전하고 믿을 만한 피임법의 광범위한 이용 가능성이 그 국가들에서 원치 않는 출산의 급격한 감소로 이어졌고, 결과적으로, 입양 가능한 아이들의 수의 감소로 이어졌다. (A) 게다가, 미혼모임이 더 이상 이전처럼 비난을 받지 않고, 미혼모들은 그들이 아이들을 양육할 수 있도록 도와주는 주 정부의 원조에 기댈 수

있다. (B) 그 결과, 입양을 희망하는 선진국 거주자들을 위한 입양이 가능한 선진국 내의 아이들이 충분히 없고, 장래의 양부모들은 외국에서 아이들을 입양하는 것에 점점 의지해 오고 있다.

	(A)	(B)
①	그러나	결과적으로
②	그러나	요약하면
③	게다가	그럼에도 불구하고
④	게다가	그 결과

| **정답해설** | ④ 58% (A) 이전 본문의 전반부에서 선진국에서 입양 가능한 아이들의 수가 줄어드는 원인을 합법적인 낙태, 만연한 출산 연기, 피임법의 광범위한 이용 가능성 등으로 열거하고 있으며, (A) 빈칸 이후에는 역시 입양 가능한 아이들의 수가 줄어드는 또 다른 원인으로 미혼모들이 아이를 양육할 수 있는 정부의 지원에 대해 서술하고 있다. 따라서 (A)의 빈칸에는 첨언을 나타내는 연결사 Furthermore가 들어가는 것이 적절하다. (B) 빈칸 앞에는 선진국에서 입양 가능한 아이들의 수가 감소하는 원인이 나오고, 빈칸 이후에는 선진국 내 입양 가능한 아이들의 감소로 인한 결과가 언급되므로 빈칸에는 결과의 연결사 As a consequence 혹은 Consequently가 적절하다.

어휘

adoption 입양
adoptable 양자로 삼을 수 있는; 채택할 수 있는

contraception 피임	pervasive 만연하는, 퍼지는
postponement 연기	childbearing 출산, 분만
abortion 낙태	stigmatize 낙인을 찍다, 비난하다
prospective 장래의, 유망한	adoptive parents 양부모
resort to ~에 기대다, 의지하다	

---

12 독해 > Logical Reading > 삭제 오답률 22% 답 ④

| **해석** | 현대 과학의 최첨단에 있는 한 이야기는 19세기 스웨덴 북부의 한 고립된 지역에서 시작되었다. 스웨덴의 이 지역은 19세기 첫 반세기에 걸쳐 예측할 수 없는 수확량을 거뒀다. 추수에 실패한 해에는 사람들이 굶주렸다. 그런데 좋은 해들은 아주 좋았다. 흉작 동안 굶주렸던 바로 그 사람들이 풍년에 상당히 과식을 했다. 한 스웨덴 과학자는 이러한 식습관의 장기적인 영향을 궁금하게 여겼다. 그는 그 지역의 수확량과 건강 기록을 연구했다. 그는 그가 발견한 것에 놀랐다. 풍년에 과식했던 소년들은 거의 먹을 것이 없던 소년들의 자녀와 손주들보다 약 6년 먼저 사망하는 자녀와 손자를 낳았다. 다른 과학자들은 소녀들에게서도 같은 결과를 알아냈다. ④ 소년과 소녀 모두 풍년의 수확들로부터 상당한 이득을 봤다. 그 과학자들은 단지 과식이라는 한 가지 원인이 여러 세대 동안 부정적인 영향을 미칠 수도 있다고 결론지어야만 했다.

| **정답해설** | ④ 78% 식사량과 수명의 상관관계의 연구에 관한 글로, 예측하기 힘든 수확량을 지닌 한 지역에서 수확량이 좋은 시기에 과식을 한 소년, 소녀들과 거의 먹을 것이 없던 소년, 소녀들을 비교하고 있다. 과식을 한 소년, 소녀들은 수명이 더 짧은 후손을 낳았는데 이는 과식이 후손에 부정적인 요인으로 작용했다는 내용에 해당된다. 따라서 '소년과 소녀 모두가 수확이 좋은 연도에 상당한 이득을 보았다'는 ④는 글의 흐름상 어색한 문장이다.

어휘

on the cutting edge of ~의 최첨단에, 선두에

---

unpredictable 예측 불가능한 harvest 수확
astonished 깜짝 놀란 be forced to ~하도록 강요받다

---

13 독해 > Micro Reading > 내용일치/불일치 오답률 5% 답 ③

| **해석** | 라디오와 같은 핫 미디어를 전화와 같은 쿨 미디어와, 혹은 영화와 같은 핫 미디어를 텔레비전과 같은 쿨 미디어와 구별하는 기본적인 원칙이 있다. 핫 미디어는 단일 감각을 "고선명도"에서 확장하는 것이다. 고선명도는 데이터로 잘 채워져 있는 상태이다. 사진은 시각적으로 "고선명도"에 해당한다. 만화는 단지 아주 조금의 시각적인 정보만 제공된다는 이유로 "저선명도"이다. 전화는 귀가 불충분한 양의 정보만을 받기 때문에 쿨 미디어, 혹은 저선명도이다. 그리고 말은 아주 적은 양이 주어지고 청자에 의해 많은 부분이 채워져야 하기 때문에 저선명도의 쿨 미디어이다. 반면에, 핫 미디어는 청중에 의해 채워지거나 완성되어야 할 여지를 많이 남겨두지 않는다.
① 미디어는 핫과 쿨로 분류될 수 있다.
② 핫 미디어는 데이터로 가득하다.
③ 전화는 고선명도로 여겨진다.
④ 쿨 미디어는 청중에 의해 채워져야 할 많은 부분을 남겨둔다.

| **정답해설** | ③ 95% 글 중반부에서 Telephone is a cool medium, or one of low definition이라고 했으므로 전화는 저선명도의 쿨 미디어에 해당한다.

어휘

distinguish A from B A를 B와 구별[구분]하다
definition (라디오 재생음·텔레비전 재생화의) 선명도, 명료도
be filled with ~로 가득 차다 meager 빈약한, 불충분한

---

14 독해 > Micro Reading > 내용일치/불일치 오답률 40% 답 ④

| **해석** | 12월은 주로 하와이에서 혹등고래 시즌의 시작을 나타내지만, 전문가들은 올해 그 동물들이 돌아오는 것이 늦어졌다고 말한다. 그 거대한 고래들은 그 섬에서 겨울의 상징적인 부분이며 패키지 투어 안내원들의 수입의 원천이다. 그러나 혹등고래 해양 보호 구역의 관리자들은 지금까지 혹등고래들을 발견하기가 어려워지고 있다는 보고를 받고 있다고 말했다. "한 가지 이론은 고래 수가 증가하여 이런 일이 발생한다는 것이었습니다. 이는 그들의 성공의 결과물입니다. 동물들이 더 많을수록, 그들은 먹이 자원을 위해 서로 경쟁하고, 돌아오는 긴 여행을 위해 비축한 에너지를 필요로 합니다." 마우이에 기반을 둔 자원 보호 매니저이자 보호구역의 대응 매니저인 Ed Lyman은 말했다. 그는 크리스마스이브에 고통받는 새끼 한 마리에 관한 (구조) 요청에 응하는 동안 얼마나 적은 수의 고래를 보았는지에 대해 놀랐고, "우리는 겨우 소수의 고래들만 봤어요."라고 말했다. 전임 보호 구역 공동 매니저인 Jeff Walters에 의하면, 매년 고래 수를 세는 것은 1월, 2월, 3월의 마지막 토요일이 되어서야 시작되기 때문에 관리자들이 구체적인 숫자를 알기까지는 시간이 좀 걸릴 것이다.
① 하와이에서 혹등고래 시즌은 보통 연말에 시작된다.
② 혹등고래들은 하와이의 패키지 투어 안내원들에게 이익이 된다.
③ 하와이에서 발견되는 혹등고래 수의 감소는 그들의 성공 때문일 수도 있다.
④ 이번 고래 시즌에 하와이로 돌아오는 혹등고래의 수가 공식적으로 집계되었다.

| **정답해설** | ④ 60% 마지막 문장을 보면, 매해 집계는 1월, 2월, 3월의 마지막 토요일이 되어서야 시작되며 구체적인 숫자를 알기까지는 시간이 걸린다고 언급되어 있으므로 하와이로 돌아오는 혹등고래의 수가 공식적으로 집계되었다는 ④는 글의 내용과 일치하지 않는다.

어휘

humpback whale 혹등고래
tour operator 패키지 투어 안내원
reserve 비축(물)
calf (코끼리, 고래 등의) 새끼
hard number 구체적 숫자

iconic ~의 상징[아이콘]이 되는
sanctuary 보호 구역, 피난처
distressed 괴로워하는, 아파하는
a handful of 소수의

---

15 | 독해 > Logical Reading > 삽입 | 오답률 50% | 답 ②

| 해석 | 사전은 단어 공부를 위한 당신의 가장 믿을 만한 자원이다. 그러나 그것들을 사용하는 습관은 길러져야 한다. 물론, 당신의 독서를 중단하고 단어를 찾아보는 것은 성가신 방해처럼 느껴질 수 있다. 당신은 스스로에게 만약 계속 읽다 보면, 결국 문맥에서 그 뜻을 이해할 것이라고 말할지도 모르겠다. 실제로, 독해 학습 안내서들은 종종 그렇게 조언한다. ② 그러나 이해가 되지 않는다면, 당신은 곧 졸게 될 자신을 발견할 것이다. 종종 발생하는 것은 잠에 대한 요구가 아니라 점진적인 의식의 상실이다. 여기에서 그 요령은 졸음이 지배하기 전에, 단어 공부를 위해 사전을 붙잡을 만한 충분한 의지를 발휘하기 더 쉬울 때 단어 혼동의 조기 신호를 인식하는 것이다. 이러한 특별한 노력이 요구될지라도, 일단 그 의미가 명확해지면, 지각할 수 있는 안도감이 그 노력을 가치 있게 만든다.

| 정답해설 | ② 50% 주어진 문장이 역접 연결사 However로 시작하므로 내용의 전환이 일어나는 곳을 찾아야 한다. ② 이전에는 잠이나 졸음에 대한 내용이 없으나 ② 바로 뒤에서 졸음이 쏟아지는 이유와 졸음을 예방하는 방법이 나온다. 따라서 이해가 안 되면 졸게 될 것이라는 내용의 주어진 문장이 ②에 위치해야 문맥이 자연스러워진다.

어휘

drowsy 졸리는, 나른한
cultivate (습관·품성 등을) 기르다, 계발하다
interruption 중단, 가로막음 | context 맥락
consciousness 의식, 자각 | knack 재주, 요령
perceptible 인지할 수 있는, 지각할 수 있는
worthwhile 가치 있는, 보람 있는

---

16 | 독해 > Macro Reading > 주제 | 오답률 24% | 답 ③

| 해석 | 사람들이 생산하는 다양한 것들을 보고 그것들의 차이점들을 묘사하는 것은 쉽다. 분명히 시는 수학 공식이 아니고, 소설은 유전학 실험이 아니다. 작곡가들은 분명히 시각 예술가들의 것과는 다른 언어를 사용하고, 화학자들은 극작가들이 하는 것보다 매우 다른 것들을 결합시킨다. 그러나 그들이 만들어 낸 다른 것들에 의해 사람들을 특징짓는 것은 그들이 창조하는 방식의 보편성을 놓치는 것이다. 왜냐하면 창의적인 과정의 단계에서, 과학자, 예술가, 수학자, 작곡가, 작가 그리고 조각가 들은 감정, 시각적 이미지, 육체적 감각, 재생 가능한 패턴과 비유를 포함하여 우리가 "사고의 도구"라고 부르는 공통적인 (도구) 세트를 사용하기 때문이다. 그리고 창의적으로 생각하는 모든 사람들은 이러한 주관적인 사고 도구들에 의해 생겨난 아이디어들을 그들의 통찰력을 표현할 대중 언어로 번역하는 것을 배우는데, 이것은 다른 이들의 마음 속에서 새로운 아이디어를 불러일으킬 수 있다.
① 창의적 사고의 장애물들
② 예술과 과학의 차이점
③ 창의적 과정의 공통점
④ 다양한 직종들의 뚜렷이 구별되는 특징

| 정답해설 | ③ 76% 전반부에서는 사람들이 만들어 낸 것들의 차이

점을 묘사하는 것은 쉽다고 하면서 이러한 차이점을 볼 수 있는 것들을 예시한다. 그러나 however가 있는 중반부 문장부터는 사람들이 만들어 낸 다른 것들에 의해 사람들을 특징짓는 행위는 그들의 창조 방식의 '보편성'을 놓치는 것이며, 그 사람들은 사고의 도구라고 불리는 a common set(공통적인 (도구) 세트)를 사용하고 있다고 했으므로 이 글의 주제로 가장 적절한 것은 ③이다.

어휘

mathematical 수학의, 수리적인 | formula 공식
chemist 화학자 | reproducible 재생 가능한
imaginative 창의적인, 상상력이 풍부한
give rise to ~을 불러일으키다, 낳다
distinctive 독특한, 특유한; 뚜렷이 구별되는

---

17 | 독해 > Reading for Writing > 빈칸 구 완성 | 오답률 41% | 답 ②

| 해석 | 과학에서 단순한 대답은 거의 없다. 겉보기에는 간단한 질문들조차도, 증거를 찾는 사람들에 의해 조사될 때, 더 많은 질문들을 낳는다. 그러한 질문들은 미묘한 차이들, 여러 겹의 복잡함, 그리고 우리가 예상했을지도 모르는 것보다 더 자주, ② 초기의 직관에 반하는 결론들을 낳는다. 1990년대에 "어떻게 우리는 산소에 굶주린 암세포들과 싸우는가?"라고 묻던 연구원들은 한 가지 분명한 해결책을 제공했다. 즉, 암세포들의 혈액 공급을 중단함으로써 그것들에게 산소의 결핍을 느끼게 하는 것이다. 그러나 Laura Beil이 "Deflating Cancer"에서 설명하듯이 산소 박탈은 실제로는 암이 커지고 퍼지게 만든다. 과학자들은 새로운 전략을 찾아냄으로써 응답해 왔다. 예를 들면, 콜라겐 고속도로의 형성을 차단하는 것, 혹은 심지어, Beil이 썼듯이, 암세포에 "더 적게가 아닌, 더 많은 피"를 주는 것이다.
① 실현되지 않은 채 끝나는 계획들
② 초기의 직관에 반하는 결론들
③ 조심스러운 관찰들로 시작되는 위대한 발명들
④ 과학의 발전을 거스르는 오해들

| 정답해설 | ② 59% 산소에 굶주린 암세포들과 싸우는 방법으로 연구원들은 혈액 공급 중단으로 산소 결핍을 느끼게 하자는 해결책을 제공했으나, 산소 박탈은 실제로는 암이 커지고 퍼지는 현상을 초래했다는 예시가 나온다. 즉, 직관적 해결책이 도움이 되지 않았음을 알 수 있으므로 빈칸에는 ②가 가장 적절하다.

어휘

seemingly 겉보기에는 | straightforward 간단한, 쉬운
probe 조사하다, 캐묻다 | nuance 뉘앙스; 미묘한 차이
layer 막, 층, 겹
starve A of B A에게 B의 결핍을 느끼게 하다, A에게 B를 갈망하게 하다
cut off ~을 잘라내다, 끊다
deflate 쪼그라들게 하다, 공기를 빼다
deprivation 박탈, 부족 | contradict 반박하다, 부정하다
intuition 직관력, 직감, 직관
go against ~에게 불리하다, ~에 반대하다

---

18 | 독해 > Reading for Writing > 빈칸 절 완성 | 오답률 26% | 답 ③

| 해석 | 강의가 시작되기 전에, 그날의 강연자는 청중 각자에게 그의 논문의 복사본을 나누어 주었는데, 나도 한 부 받아 그것을 대충 넘겨 보고는 그 논문의 주제를 파악했다. 그가 시작하기를 기다리며, 나는 그 연설자가 (논문을) 읽지 않고 대신 청중에게 그가 그 주제에 관해 알고 있는 것들을 그 자신의 말로 직접 말해 주기를 조용히 기도했다. 그러나 대단히 실망스럽게

도, 그는 ③ 그의 장황하고 잘 준비된 논문을 충실하게 읽어 나가기 시작했다. 곧 나는 내가 기계적으로 내 손에 있는 그 논문에 인쇄된 글자들을 따라 읽고 있음을 알아차렸다.
① 그의 강의를 너무 형식적으로 만들까 봐 걱정스러웠다
② 그의 논문을 보지 않고 그의 이론들을 상세히 설명했다
③ 그의 장황하고 잘 준비된 논문을 충실하게 읽어 나가기 시작했다
④ 청중의 매료시키기 위해 유머러스한 제스처를 많이 사용했다

| 정답해설 | ③ [74%] I prayed in silence ~ what he knew on the subject.에서 필자는 그 연설자가 논문을 그냥 읽어 내려가는 것이 아니라 자신의 언어로 직접 설명해 주기를 기대했음을 알 수 있다. 그러나 But to my great disappointment를 통해 그와는 반대되는 상황이 일어났음을 추측할 수 있으므로, 빈칸에는 ③이 들어가야 알맞다.

어휘
leaf through (책 등을) 대충 넘겨 보다
mechanically 기계적으로   elaborate 상세히 서술하다
faithfully 충실히   make use of ~을 이용하다

---

19   독해 > Reading for Writing > 빈칸 구 완성   오답률 51%   답 ③

| 해석 | Tolstoy에 관한 유명한 에세이에서, 진보적인 철학자 Isaiah Berlin 경은 그리스 서정 시인 Archilochus(기원전 7세기)의 말이라고 여겨지는 고대의 격언을 상기함으로써 두 종류의 사상가들을 구분했다. "여우는 많은 것을 알지만, 고슴도치는 중요한 한 가지를 안다." 고슴도치들은 하나의 중심적인 생각을 가지고 오로지 그 생각의 프리즘을 통해 세상을 바라본다. 그들은 복잡함과 예외들을 간과하거나 그들의 세계관에 어울리도록 그것들을 만든다. 모든 시대와 상황에 들어맞는 진실한 대답 한 가지가 존재한다. Berlin이 더 크게 공감했던 여우들은 세상에 대한 다양한 견해를 가지고 있는데, 그것은 그들이 ③ 하나의 중요한 구호를 조리 있게 말하는 것을 못하도록 한다. 그들은 세상의 복잡함이 일반화를 막는다고 느끼기 때문에 거창한 이론들에 대해 회의적이다. Berlin은 Shakespeare가 여우였던 반면 Dante는 고슴도치였다고 생각했다.
① 이성적으로 행동하는 것
② 다양한 해답을 찾아내는 것
③ 하나의 중요한 구호를 조리 있게 말하는 것
④ 세상의 복잡함을 이해하는 것

| 정답해설 | ③ [49%] Berlin이 구분한 두 종류의 사상가들을 각각 여우와 고슴도치에 비유해 설명하는 글이다. 빈칸에는 하나의 세계관으로 세상을 바라보는 고슴도치와 달리 다양한 견해를 가지고 있는 여우의 세계관과 일치하는 내용이 제시되어야 한다. 따라서 ③이 빈칸에 들어갈 말로 가장 적절하다.

어휘
attribute ~로 여기다; 원인을 ~에 돌리다
hark back to ~을 상기하다   lyric poet 서정 시인
hedgehog 고슴도치   exclusively 배타적으로; 오직
prism 프리즘, 각기둥   complication 복잡함; 문제; 합병증
have a take on ~에 대한 견해[의견]를 갖다
variegated 얼룩덜룩한; 갖가지의, 다양성이 많은
skeptical 회의적인, 의심 많은
articulate 분명히 표현하다, 조리 있게 말하다

오답률 TOP2
20   독해 > Macro Reading > 주장   오답률 54%   답 ①

| 해석 | Locke의 사유 재산 옹호론에서, 주요한 핵심은 우리가 우리의 노동을 신이 주신 토지와 조화시킬 때 발생하는 것이다. 우리는 일을 함으로써 그 토지에 가치를 부여한다. 우리는 한때 놀고 있던 땅을 비옥하게 만든다. 이러한 점에서 토지 가치의 근원 또는 부가된 가치는 바로 우리의 노동력인 것이다. 이러한 나의 노동력이 갖는 가치 창조의 힘은 그것을 개간함으로써 내가 가치 있게 만들었던 토지의 일부, 그것을 파서 내가 물을 가득 채웠던 우물, 내가 키우고 살 찌웠던 가축들을 내가 소유하는 것을 정당하게 만든다. Locke로 인해서 Homo faber(노동의 인간)는 정치사상사에서 최초로 지엽적 인물이 아닌 중심 인물이 된다. Locke의 세계에서, 지위와 명예는 여전히 귀족 계급으로 흘러갔는데, 그들은 광대한 토지를 소유할 권리를 부여받았으나 정확하게는 새로운 경제적인 현실이 노동에 의해 실제로 가치를 창출했던 중산층으로 부가 이행되는 과정에 있었기 때문에 역사가 그들을 그냥 스쳐 지나가게 놔 두었다. 시간이 지난 후 노동의 중요성에 대한 Locke의 부상은 떠오르는 중산층의 관심을 끌기 마련이었다.
① 사유 재산의 소유권은 노동으로부터 나온다.
② 노동은 귀족 사회에서 가장 중요한 이상이다.
③ 사유 재산의 축적은 행복의 원천이다.
④ 부르주아(중산층) 사회로의 순조로운 전환은 사회 진보에 있어 필수적이다.

| 정답해설 | ① [46%] '나의 노동력이 갖는 가치 창조적인 힘이 내가 개간한 토지, 내가 판 우물, 내가 키우고 살 찌운 가축들을 소유하는 것을 정당하게 만든다'는 Locke의 이론을 통해 그가 주장하는 바는 사유 재산의 소유권이 노동으로부터 나온다는 것임을 알 수 있다.

| 오답해설 | ② [38%] 글의 후반부에 부가 귀족 계급에서 중산층으로 이행되는 과정에서 노동을 중시하는 Locke의 사상은 중산층의 관심을 끌었다고 했으므로 노동은 귀족 사회가 아니라 부르주아 사회에서 중시되었음을 알 수 있다.
③ [4%] 본문에서 행복의 원천에 관해 언급한 적은 없다.
④ [12%] 중산층으로 부가 이행되는 과정이 언급되었지만 사회 발전과 연결시켜 설명하고 있지는 않다.

어휘
fertile 비옥한   fallow 사용하지 않는, 묵히고 있는
fatten 살찌우다, 살찌다   peripheral 주변적인, 지엽적인
landholding 소유하고 있는 토지, 토지 소유, 토지 임대
be bound to V ~하게 마련이다, ~할 수밖에 없다
bourgeois 중산 계급의 (시민); 상공업자; 자본가

<table>
<tr><th colspan="2">합격예상 체크</th></tr>
</table>

〈지방직 연도별 합격선〉

맞힌 개수	/20문항	점수	/100점

➡ □ 합격　□ 불합격

취약영역 체크

문항	정답	영역	문항	정답	영역
1	④	어휘 > 빈칸 완성	11	③	어휘 > 빈칸 완성
2	③	어휘 > 빈칸 완성	12	④	독해 > Logical Reading > 문맥상 다양한 추론
3	③	어휘 > 빈칸 완성	13	④	생활영어 > 회화/관용표현
4	①	문법 > 일치	14	④	생활영어 > 회화/관용표현
5	②	문법 > 일치	15	②	문법 > 동명사
6	③	독해 > Macro Reading > 제목	16	①	문법 > 부정사
7	④	독해 > Macro Reading > 제목	17	③	독해 > Logical Reading > 삭제
8	④	독해 > Micro Reading > 내용 일치/불일치	18	①	독해 > Logical Reading > 삽입
9	①	독해 > Micro Reading > 내용 일치/불일치	19	②	독해 > Reading for Writing > 빈칸 구 완성
10	④	독해 > Reading for Writing > 빈칸 절 완성	20	①	독해 > Reading for Writing > 빈칸 구 완성

⬇ 영역별 틀린 개수로 취약영역을 확인하세요!

어휘	/4	문법	/4	독해	/10	생활영어	/2

➡ 나의 취약영역: _____

※ [정답해설]과 [오답해설] 선지의 50% 표시는 〈1초 합격예측 서비스〉를 통해 수집된 선지 선택률을 나타냅니다.

1 어휘 > 빈칸 완성　오답률 16%　답 ④

| 해석 | 두 문화가 아주 완전히 ④ <u>달라서</u> 그녀는 한 문화에서 다른 문화로 적응하기가 힘들다는 것을 알았다.
① 6% 겹쳐진, 중복된　② 6% 동등한, 맞먹는
③ 4% 연합의, 결합하기 쉬운　④ 84% 다른, 공통점이 없는

| 정답해설 | ④ 그녀가 한 문화에서 다른 문화로 적응하기 힘들었던 이유로 적당한 것은 두 문화가 완전히 다르기 때문이라고 보는 것이 적절하므로 disparate가 들어가야 한다.

어휘
utterly 완전히, 철저히　adapt 적응[순응]하다

오답률 TOP 2

2 어휘 > 빈칸 완성　오답률 45%　답 ③

| 해석 | 페니실린은 그것에 알레르기 반응이 있는 사람에게는 ③ <u>부작용이</u> 있을 수 있다.
① 25% 긍정적인　② 7% 냉담한, 초연한
③ 55% 부정적인, 반대의, 불리한　④ 13% 암시하는, 넌지시 가리키는

| 정답해설 | ③ 페니실린에 알레르기 반응이 있는 사람에게는 페니실린이 adverse(부정적인, 불리한) 효과, 즉 부작용을 가져올 수 있을 것이다.

어휘
allergic 알레르기가 있는　effect (약의) 작용, 효능

3 어휘 > 빈칸 완성　오답률 25%　답 ③

| 해석 | 지난해에, 나는 극장에서 예술 행사를 ③ <u>상연하는</u> 것을 담당하는 직원들과 이 공연을 하는 좋은 기회를 가졌다.
① 19% ~으로 되다, 변하다　② 4% ~ 없이 지내다, 해내다
③ 75% 상연하다; (옷을) 입다　④ 2% 포기하다

| 정답해설 | ③ 직원들이 빈칸의 책임을 지닌다고 하였는데 빈칸의 힌트는 art events에 있다. 즉, 직원들이 art events를 진행하는 사람들이며, 그것을 목적어로 삼을 수 있는 동사는 '(연극 등을) 상연하다'라는 뜻을 갖는 put on이다.

어휘
responsible for ~에 책임이 있는, ~을 담당하는

4 문법 > 일치　오답률 27%　답 ①

| 정답해설 | ① 73% 병렬 구조가 제대로 이루어지지 않아서 틀렸다. 조동사 관용표현 would rather 뒤에는 동사원형이 와야 하고 이와 병렬 구조를 이루어야 하는 than 뒤의 동사 going도 원형인 go로 써야 한다.

| 오답해설 | ② 9% The police는 경찰 전체를 가리키는 집합명사로, 복수 취급하므로 복수 동사 are를 알맞게 썼다. 또한 「be unwilling to + 동사원형」은 '~하기를 꺼리다'라는 의미로 알맞게 옮겨졌다.

③ 11% '~해 봐야 소용없다'는 「It's no use -ing」로 나타내므로 옳다.
④ 7% 「so ~ that …」은 '너무 ~해서 …하다'의 의미를 가지며, 부정대명사 one은 선행하는 명사와 같은 종류의 것(또는 사람)을 가리킨다. 여기서의 ones는 my keys를 대신하는 부정대명사로 수를 일치시켰다.

| 더 알아보기 | use의 관용표현

- 「it is no use -ing」 = 「it is useless to + 동사원형」: ~해도 소용없다
- 「used to + 동사원형」: ~하곤 했다
- 「be used to + 동사원형」 = 「be used for + 명사」: ~(하는 데)에 사용되다
- 「be used to -ing/명사」: ~(하는 데)에 익숙하다

오답률 TOP3

| **5** | 문법 > 일치 | 오답률 41% | 답 ② |

| 정답해설 | ② 59% 양자 부정 표현으로 주절은 부정, than 종속절은 긍정으로 표현해야 한다. 따라서 don't가 대동사 do로 바뀌어야 옳다.

| 오답해설 | ① 15% 「talk ~ out of …」는 '~에게 …을 하지 않도록 설득하다'라는 뜻으로 알맞게 쓰였다.
③ 20% outnumber는 '~을 수로 압도하다'라는 뜻으로 수동태로 만들면 be outnumbered(수적으로 열세다)가 된다.
④ 6% of an age는 '같은 나이의'를 의미하며, 「of + 명사」는 형용사 역할을 할 수 있다.

어휘

outnumber ~을 수로 압도하다

| **6** | 독해 > Macro Reading > 제목 | 오답률 8% | 답 ③ |

| 해석 | 지구는 따뜻해지고 있다. 북극에서 남극까지, 그리고 그 사이에 있는 모든 곳이. 세계적으로, 수은주는 이미 화씨 1도가 넘게 올랐고 민감한 극지방에서는 훨씬 더 올랐다. 그리고 기온 상승의 결과들은 멀리 떨어진 미래를 기다리지 않는다(먼 미래의 이야기가 아니다). 그것들은 바로 지금 일어나고 있다. 징조들이 곳곳에서 나타나고 있고 그것들 중 일부는 놀랍다. 열은 빙하와 해빙을 녹이는 것뿐만 아니라 강수 패턴이 달라지고 동물들을 이동하게 만들고 있다.
① 기후 변화에 대한 예방책
② 북극 만년설의 해빙
③ 늘어나는 지구 온난화의 징조들
④ 온도 상승의 긍정적 효과

| 정답해설 | ③ 92% 온난화로 인한 기온의 변화와 기온 상승으로 인해 나타나는 징조들을 나열하는 글이다.

어휘

mercury 수은(주)	Fahrenheit 화씨
far-flung 광범위한, 멀리 떨어진	precipitation 강수량

| **7** | 독해 > Macro Reading > 제목 | 오답률 29% | 답 ④ |

| 해석 | 수익처럼 그렇게 많은 미묘한 넌센스와 혼란으로 얼룩져 있는 말은 거의 없다. 내 진보적인 친구들에게 그 단어는 근본적으로 인정받을 수 없고 가치가 없는 행동들에 대한 수익을 의미한다. 최소한으로는 탐욕과 이기심이고, 최대한으로는 수백 만의 무력한 피해자들에 대한 지독한 배신이

다. 수익은 가치 없는 성과에 대한 동기이다. 내 보수적인 친구들에게 그것은 가장 애정 어린 말이고 효율성과 분별을 의미한다. 그들에게 수익은 가치 있는 성과에 대한 궁극적인 보상책이다. 물론, 양쪽의 함축된 의미 모두 장점을 어느 정도 조금씩 가지고 있기는 하다. 수익이 탐욕스럽고 이기적인 행동들로부터 나올 수도 있고 분별 있고 효율적인 행동들로부터 나올 수도 있기 때문이다. 그러나 한쪽의 편견으로부터 지나치게 일반화하는 것은 수익과 인간의 능력 간의 관계를 이해하는 데 조금도 도움을 주지 않는다.
① 수익과 정당과의 관계
② 누가 수익으로부터 이득을 얻는가
③ 왜 수익을 내는 것이 바람직하지 않는가
④ 수익에 대한 양극화된 인식들

| 정답해설 | ④ 71% 수익에 대한 상반된 인식을 언급하고, 이러한 두 가지 인식 중 한쪽으로 편향되는 것은 결국 수익과 인간 능력 사이의 관계를 이해하는 데에 도움을 주지 않을 것이라고 결론 내렸다. 따라서 ④가 이 글의 제목으로 적절하다.

어휘

tainted 더럽혀진, 부패한	liberal 진보적인, 자유주의적인
connote 의미하다, 암시하다	royal screwing 지독한 배신
conservative 보수적인	endearment 사랑받음; 애정 어린 말
overgeneralization 과잉 일반화	

| **8** | 독해 > Micro Reading > 내용일치/불일치 | 오답률 38% | 답 ④ |

| 해석 | 전기차들은 항상 친환경적이고 조용하며 깨끗하지만 확실히 섹시하진 않다. Sesta사의 Speedking은 그 모든 것을 바꾸어 놓았다. 120,000달러에 팔리고 시속 125마일(시속 200km)의 최고 속력을 내는 배터리 구동식 스포츠카 Speedking은 처음 발표되었을 때부터 친환경 기술을 선호하는 사람들을 흥분시켰다. 일부 할리우드 연예인들 또한 Speedking의 긴 대기 줄에 동참했다. Wired와 같은 잡지들도 그것에 군침을 흘렸다. 수년간의 실패와 대개편 후에 올해 Sesta의 첫 Speedking이 고객들에게 배송되었다. 후기들은 열광적이었지만 Sesta Motors는 재정적 위기로 심한 타격을 받아 왔다. 저렴한 전기 세단을 개발하려는 계획들은 중단되었고 Sesta는 직원들을 일시 해고하고 있다. 그러나 비록 Speedking이 반짝하고 사라지는 제품이 되었을 지라도 그것은 흥미로운 전기차였다.
① Speedking은 새로운 전기 세단이다.
② Speedking은 부정적인 반응을 얻었다.
③ Sesta는 직원을 더 채용하고 있다.
④ Sesta는 신차 프로젝트를 중단시켰다.

| 정답해설 | ④ 62% Sesta사의 Speedking이라는 전기 스포츠카는 발표 때부터 사람들의 좋은 반응을 얻었고 출시 후 후기도 열광적이었지만, 재정적인 문제로 인해 전기 세단을 만들려는 계획이 중단되었으며, 직원들이 일시 해고되고 있다고 했다.

어휘

battery-powered 배터리로 동력을 얻는, 배터리 구동식의
clean-tech 친환경 기술적인
drool over ~에 군침을 흘리다, ~에 열중하다
setback 역행, 좌절, 실패
shake-up 대개편, 대정리, 흔들어 뒤섞기
turn out ~이 되다

9　독해 > Micro Reading > 내용일치/불일치　오답률 4%　답 ③

| 해석 | 콜라비는 주로 그것의 독특한 모양과 이상한 이름 때문에 많은 사람들이 피하는 채소들 중 하나이다. 그러나 콜라비는 맛있고 여러모로 쓸모 있으며 건강에 좋다. 콜라비는 브로콜리와 양배추를 포함하는 배추속의 일종이다. 배추속 식물은 항산화 물질 함량이 높고 콜라비도 예외가 아니다. 또한 콜라비는 섬유소, 비타민 B, 칼륨 및 칼슘과 더불어 유익한 양의 비타민 C를 함유하고 있다. 콜라비는 날로 먹을 수 있다. 얇게 썰어 샐러드와 섞으면 맛있다. 오븐에 덩어리 채로 굽거나 수프의 기본 재료로 사용할 수도 있다.

| 정답해설 | ③ [96%] 배추속 식물들은 항산화 물질 함량이 높다고 했고, 콜라비도 예외가 아니라고 했으므로, 콜라비 또한 항산화제를 풍부히 함유하고 있음을 알 수 있다.

어휘

versatile 다재다능한, 다방면의　brassica 배추속(屬) 식물
antioxidant 항산화제　potassium 칼륨, 포타슘
roast 굽다　chunk 큰 덩어리, 부분

10　독해 > Reading for Writing > 빈칸 절 완성　오답률 25%　답 ④

| 해석 | 단순 노출 효과의 초창기 시연에서, 실험에 참가한 사람들은 한 세트의 일본어 문자들에 노출되었다. 대부분의 사람들이 아는 것처럼, 일본어 문자들은 그림처럼 보이고 표의 문자로 불린다. 그 실험에서 각 표의 문자의 노출 지속 기간은 의도적으로 30밀리초로 짧게 유지됐다. 잠재적인 노출로 알려진 그런 짧은 노출 지속 기간에 사람들은 그 자극을 머릿속에 새길 수 없었고, 그렇기 때문에 실험 참가자들은 그 표의 문자들을 본 것을 상기할 것으로 예상되지 않았다. 그럼에도 불구하고 이전에 노출되었던 것과 노출되지 않았던 것의 두 세트의 문자가 참가자들에게 보여졌을 때, 참가자들은 전자에 대해 더 큰 호감을 보였다. 그들이 그것들(전자의 문자들)을 봤던 것을 상기할 수 없었는데도 말이다! 이러한 결과들은 수차례 다양한 종류의 자극 전체에 되풀이되어 왔으므로, 그것들은 확고하다. 단순 노출 결과들이 보여 주는 것은 ④ 사람들은 친숙한 자극을 좋아하게 된다는 것이다.
① 우리는 광범위한 노출을 통해 일본어를 배울 수 있다
② (노출) 지속 시간은 연구 전체의 확고한 결과에 대한 원인이 된다
③ 짧은 (노출) 지속 시간에 자극을 머릿속에 새기는 것은 불가능하다
④ 사람들은 친숙한 자극을 좋아하게 된다

| 정답해설 | ④ [75%] 30밀리초라는 짧은 시간 동안 노출되었던 문자와 전혀 노출된 적 없는 문자에 대한 호감도 측정 실험에서 참가자들은 전자에 더 큰 호감을 보였다고 했다. 이러한 실험 결과를 요약하는 것은 ④이다.

| 더 알아보기 | Mere Exposure Effect (단순 노출 효과)

> 수용자들에게 특정 메시지를 반복해서 들려주면 수용자들이 그 메시지를 특히 더 좋아하게 되고, 결국 그 메시지가 전하는 주장을 잘 받아들이게 되는 효과

어휘

exposure 노출, 드러남, 폭로　ideogram 표의 문자, 기호
millisecond 밀리초, 1/1000초　subliminal 잠재 의식의, 의식 하의
replicate 복제하다, 모사하다　robust 확고한, 강건한
develop a liking towards[for] ～을 좋아하게 되다

11　어휘 > 빈칸 완성　오답률 47%　답 ③

| 해석 | ・심리학자들은 학생들의 종합적인 성격 발달을 ③ 설명하기 위해 새로운 테스트를 이용했다.
・과자는 청소년들의 일상적인 에너지 섭취의 25~30%를 ③ 차지한다.
① [17%] 계속하다, 유지하다　② [26%] 알아내다, 해결하다
③ [53%] 설명하다, 차지하다　④ [4%] 의존하다

| 정답해설 | ③ account for는 여러 가지 뜻을 가지고 있다. 첫 번째 문장에서는 '설명하다'로, 두 번째 문장에서는 '차지하다'로 사용되었다.

12　독해 > Logical Reading > 문맥상 다양한 추론　오답률 4%　답 ④

| 해석 | 내가 너의 집에 처음 방문하러 왔을 때 나는 너의 아버지에 대해 아주 좋은 감정을 갖기 시작했다. 방문 전에 그는 나에게 나의 신체적 요구 사항에 대해 몇 가지 상세한 질문을 했다. 그가 무거운 나의 휠체어에 대해 알게 되자마자, 그는 현관문에 경사로를 설치할 방법을 계획하기 시작했다. 내가 그 집에 처음 간 날, 그가 직접 설치한 경사로가 준비되어 있었다. 후에, 네 아버지가 네 남동생의 자폐증에 대해 알았을 때, 그는 내가 절대 잊을 수 없는 말을 했다. "만약 Sam이 학교에서 배우지 못한다면, 나는 일을 2년 쉬고 우리는 세계를 향해할 거야. 나는 그 2년 동안 그가 알 필요가 있는 모든 것을 그에게 가르쳐 줄 거야."라고 그가 나에게 말했다. 그 말은 네 아빠의 성격에 대한 모든 것을 말해 준다.
① 엄격하고 근엄한　② 재미있고 유머러스한
③ 게으르고 느긋한　④ 배려심 있고 사려 깊은

| 정답해설 | ④ [96%] 친구 아버지의 친절함에 대해 진술하는 글이다. 내가 친구의 집에 방문하기 전에, 친구 아버지는 내가 신체적으로 필요한 것에 대해 물었고, 무거운 휠체어에 대해 알게 되자 휠체어가 올라갈 수 있도록 현관문에 경사로를 직접 설치했다. 또한 자폐증이 있는 아들 Sam의 교육과 관련한 그의 말로 보아 그는 사려 깊고 친절한 성격이라는 것을 알 수 있다.

어휘

ramp 경사로

13　생활영어 > 회화/관용표현　오답률 24%　답 ④

| 해석 | John: 실례합니다. 남대문 시장이 어디인지 말씀해 주실래요?
Mira: 그러죠. 앞으로 쭉 가시다가 저기에 있는 택시 정류장에서 오른쪽으로 도세요.
John: 오, 알겠습니다. 거기가 시장이 있는 곳인가요?
Mira: ④ 정확히는 아니에요. 당신은 두 블록은 더 내려가야 해요.
① 맞아요. 저쪽에서 시장으로 가는 버스를 타셔야 해요.
② 당신은 대개 전통 시장에서 물건을 좋은 가격에 살 수 있어요.
③ 정말 모르겠어요. 택시 운전기사에게 물어보세요.
④ 정확히는 아니에요. 당신은 두 블록은 더 내려가야 해요.

| 정답해설 | ④ [76%] Mira가 길을 안내해 주는 도중에 John이 '거기가 시장이 있는 곳인가요?'라고 물었다. 이에 대해 Mira는 '그렇다' 혹은 '아니다'라고 대답해야 하므로 선지 중 가장 적절한 것은 ④뿐이다.

14 생활영어 > 회화/관용표현 | 오답률 23% | 답 ④

| 해석 | ① A: 이번 주에 저랑 저녁 먹으러 가실래요?
  B: 네. 그런데 무슨 일인데요?
② A: 우리 언제 농구하러 가는 건 어때?
  B: 그러자. 언제 갈 건지 말만 해.
③ A: 여가 시간에 뭐 하세요?
  B: 그냥 집에서 쉬어요. 종종 TV도 보고요.
④ A: 무슨 일이라도 도와드릴까요?
  B: 네, 제가 그러고 싶어요. 그게 좋겠네요.

| 정답해설 | ④ 77% 돕겠다고 제안하는 사람에게 자신이 그렇게 하고 싶다고 대답하는 것은 어울리지 않는다. 이때는 Yes, please. 또는 That would be nice. 정도로 답할 수 있다.

15 문법 > 동명사 | 오답률 38% | 답 ②

| 해석 | ① 당신이 수영을 좋아하든 걷기를 좋아하든 그곳은 환상적이다.
② 그녀는 회의 후에 저녁을 먹으러 가자고 제안했다.
③ 내가 당신에게 말한 그 댄서가 시내로 오고 있다.
④ 만약 그녀가 지난밤에 약을 먹었다면, 그녀는 오늘 더 나아졌을 텐데.

| 정답해설 | ② 62% suggest는 목적어로 동명사를 취하므로 어법에 맞는 문장이다.

| 오답해설 | ① 4% like의 목적어인 swimming과 to walk는 병렬 구조를 취해야 한다. like는 목적어로 동명사, to부정사 둘 다 취할 수 있으니, 어느 것으로든 통일만 시키면 된다.
③ 19% about her에서 her는 목적격 관계대명사의 선행사인 The dancer를 지칭하므로 이중으로 쓸 수 없다. 따라서 The dancer that I told you about is coming to town.으로 써야 한다.
④ 15% 부사절인 if절에는 가정법 과거를, 주절에는 가정법 과거완료 형태를 사용했는데, 문제는 서로 시제가 바뀌었다는 것이다. 제시된 시간 부사에 따라 if절은 가정법 과거완료로, 주절은 가정법 과거를 쓰는 혼합가정법 문장이 되어야 한다. 따라서 If she had taken ~, she would be better ~.로 써야 한다.

16 문법 > 부정사 | 오답률 39% | 답 ①

| 해석 | ① 그 불쌍한 여자는 스마트폰을 살 형편이 되지 않았다.
② 나는 매일 일찍 일어나는 것에 익숙하다.
③ 그 도시에서 일어나는 화재 건수는 매년 증가하고 있다.
④ Bill은 Mary가 결혼했다고 생각해, 그렇지?

| 정답해설 | ① 61% afford는 목적어로 to부정사를 취한다. 보통 can과 같이 쓰여서 「can/can't afford + to부정사(~할 여유가 있다/없다)」로 쓰인다.

| 오답해설 | ② 14% '~하는 것에 익숙하다'는 「be used to -ing」로 표현한다. 따라서 get을 getting으로 바꿔야 한다.
③ 12% 주어는 The number이고 동사는 are로 서로 수 일치가 되지 않았다. 따라서 are를 is로 고쳐야 한다.
④ 13% 주절의 동사 suppose가 일반동사이므로 부가의문문의 동사는 isn't가 아니라 doesn't여야 한다.

| 더 알아보기 | 목적어로 to부정사를 취하는 동사

- want, hope, ask, threaten, choose, agree, need, decide, offer, afford

17 독해 > Logical Reading > 삭제 | 오답률 8% | 답 ③

| 해석 | 암과의 싸움에서 점차적으로 진전이 이뤄지고 있다. 1900년대 초에는 장기 생존의 희망을 가진 암 환자는 거의 없었다. 그러나 의학 기술의 발전으로 인해, 진전이 있어서 현재는 10명 중 4명의 암 환자가 살아남는다. ③ 흡연은 폐암의 직접적인 원인으로 밝혀졌다. 그러나, 그 전쟁은 아직 승리하지 못했다. 일부 암 형태에 대한 치료법은 밝혀졌지만 다른 암 형태는 여전히 증가하고 있다.

| 정답해설 | ③ 92% 이 글은 암과 관련된 의학 기술 발전에 대한 내용이다. ③은 특정 암의 발병 원인에 대한 내용으로 의학적 진보와는 상관없으므로 흐름상 어색한 문장이다.

18 독해 > Logical Reading > 삽입 | 오답률 16% | 답 ①

| 해석 | 어떤 사람들은 삶은 단순히 해결되어야 할 문제들의 연속이라고 확신한다. 그들이 맞닥뜨리고 있는 문제에서 더 빨리 벗어날수록, 그들은 더 빨리 행복해질 것이다. ① 그러나 진실은, 당신이 성공적으로 이 문제를 통과한 후에도, 맞닥뜨려야 할 또 다른 문제가 있을 것이라는 점이다. 그리고 그 장애물을 극복한 후에는 극복할 또 다른 것이 있을 것이고 올라야 할 산은 항상 존재할 것이다. 그것이 바로 목적지가 아니라 여정을 즐기는 것이 중요한 이유이다. 이러한 세계에서, 우리는 모든 것이 완벽하고 더 이상의 도전이 없는 곳에 절대 도달하지 못할 것이다. 목표를 설정하고 그것에 도달하는 것만큼 감탄할 만한 것도 없지만, 당신은 목표를 성취하는 데에 너무 몰두해서 당신이 현재 있는 곳을 즐기지 못하는 실수를 하지 말아야 한다.

| 정답해설 | ① 84% 주어진 문장은 문제를 성공적으로 통과한 후에도 또 다른 문제가 생길 것이라고 서술하고 있다. 주어진 문장이 역접의 접속사 But으로 시작하고 있으므로 이전에는 주어진 문장과 반대되는 내용이 서술되어야 함을 알 수 있다. 따라서 문제에서 빨리 벗어날수록 더 빨리 행복해질 것이라고 하는 두 번째 문장 뒤인 ①에 들어가는 것이 가장 적절하며, ① 뒤의 문장에서 주어진 문장의 problem을 that obstacle로 지칭하며 문제점[장애물]을 극복한 이후에도 극복할 또 다른 것이 있을 것이라고 서술하는 것이 자연스럽다. 따라서 주어진 문장이 들어갈 위치로 가장 적절한 곳은 ①이다.

19 독해 > Reading for Writing > 빈칸 구 완성 | 오답률 25% | 답 ②

| 해석 | 그것이 여성 또는 다른 남성들에게 어떻지는 잘 모르겠지만 내가 어렸을 때에, 나는 ② 결혼에 대한 두려움이 있었다. 나는 그것이 죽음으로 향하는 커다란 발걸음이라고 생각했다. 그래서, 나는 그것을 하지 않기 위해 할 수 있는 것을 모두 했다. 나에게 그 생각은 너무 무서웠기 때문이다. 그러던 어느 날 나는 첫 영화를 찍던 와중에 Jane을 만났다. 이것이 모든 것을 바꾸어 놓았다. Jane은 켄터키에서 왔는데 그 당시에 식당 종업원 일을 하고 있었고 나는 그녀를 바로 알아봤다. 그녀는 정말 아름다웠고 그녀에게 데이트 신청할 용기를 내는 데 꼬박 하루가 걸렸다. 바로 그때에, 영화의 메이크업 담당 직원이 우리 둘의 사진을 찍었다. 2년 전에 그가 나에게 그것을 보내면서 "여기 당신이 한 지역 여성에게 데이트 신청을 하고 있군

요."라고 말했다. 그는 그 "지역 여성"이 내 아내가 된 것을 몰랐다. 나는 여전히 그날을 생생히 기억하고 있다.
① 죽음　　② 결혼　　③ 영화 만들기　　④ 사진 찍기

| **정답해설** | ②　75%　자신의 아내 Jane을 운명적으로 만난 이야기를 하며 아내를 만난 일이 모든 것을 바꾸어 놓았다고 한 것으로 보아, 필자는 그 이전에 결혼에 대한 두려움이 있었음을 유추할 수 있다.

어휘
get up the nerve to V ∼할 용기를 내다

20　독해 > Reading for Writing > 빈칸 구 완성　오답률 33%　답 ①

| **해석** | 새로운 것들을 발견하는 데 있어서, 한 가지 잘 알려진 어려움은 인지 심리학자인 David Perkins에 의해 '오아시스의 함정'이라고 명명되었다. 지식은 풍부한 발견들의 '오아시스' 안에 집중되고, 여전히 생산적이고 물이 풍부한 구역을 벗어나기엔 그저 너무 위험하고 비용이 많이 든다. 그래서 사람들은 ① 그들이 알고 있는 것을 고수한다. 이것은 (바로) 수 세기에 걸쳐 중국에서 어느 정도 일어난 일이다. 중국에서 지식의 중심 간의 큰 물리적 거리 그리고 그 먼 중심들이 알고 보니 서로와 거의 다르지 않다고 밝혀졌다는 사실은 탐구를 좌절시켰다.
① 그들이 알고 있는 것　　　② 미지의 세상
③ 그들의 꿈과 상상　　　　④ 어떻게 상황이 변할지

| **정답해설** | ①　67%　빈칸 이전에 사람들이 새로운 것을 발견하기보다는 기존의 발견인 오아시스에 집중하며, 그곳을 빠져나가지 않는 것을 '오아시스의 함정'이라 서술하고 있다. 따라서 빈칸이 포함된 문장의 접속사인 So를 통해서 빈칸 이전과 이후가 원인과 결과임을 알 수 있다. 따라서 빈칸에는 '오아시스의 함정'에 빠진 사람들이 고수할 대상으로 '오아시스' 즉 '그들이 알고 있는 것'이 가장 적절하다.

어휘
cognitive 인지의, 인식의　　　　discourage 좌절시키다
exploration 탐구; 탐험, 탐사

서울시

해설 &
기출분석 REPORT

서울시 기출 POINT

2020년도 시험부터 서울시 출제처가 인사혁신처로
변경되어, 지방직과 동일한 시험지로 시행하게 됨

※ 단, 기술직 등 일부 직렬의 일부 과목은 서울시 자체 출제로 시행되었음

Point 1 기존 서울시 문제는 다양한 소재와 어휘를 사용하던 것이 특징이다. 따라서 9급 공무원 타 직렬의 고난도 문항을 대비할 수 있는 좋은 문제라는 점을 참고하여 학습하자.

Point 2 시험에는 직렬과 상관없이 빈출 개념이 반복하여 출제되고, 전체적인 문제 유형도 전 직렬이 유사하다. 따라서 이 교재에 수록된 과년도 서울시 9급 기출문제도 반드시 꼼꼼히 풀이해 보자.

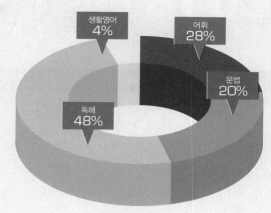

▲ 최근 4개년 평균 출제비중

최근 4개년 출제 경향 및 출제 비중

연도	총평	어휘	문법	독해	생활영어
2019	**예년에 비해 까다로운 문제 부재!** · 독해에서 9문항이 출제되어 시간 안배에 용이했음 · 영역별 고른 독해 소재로, 난이도가 전반적으로 평이	30% (6문항)	20% (4문항)	45% (9문항)	5% (1문항)
2018	**문법과 독해의 난이도 동반 상승!** · 어휘는 전 문항 밑줄형 유의어를 묻는 문제가 출제되어 난도가 상승 · 어법 또한 전 문항 밑줄형으로 출제 · 독해는 빈칸 완성 유형이 40%를 차지함	35% (7문항)	20% (4문항)	40% (8문항)	5% (1문항)
2018 기술직	**다소 높은 난도의 시험!** · 어휘와 문법은 그동안의 기출 범위를 벗어나지 않음 · 독해의 경우 어려운 단어와 추상적 내용으로 인해 어려움을 느꼈을 것으로 예상됨	20% (4문항)	20% (4문항)	55% (11문항)	5% (1문항)
2017	**대체로 평이한 수준!** · 기존에 보였던 영역별 문제 비율과는 아주 다른 비율로 출제 · head off라는 관용적 표현 출제	35% (7문항)	20% (4문항)	40% (8문항)	5% (1문항)
2016	**지문 길이, 소재 모두 대체적으로 평이!** · 생활영어 영역 미출제, 독해 문제 비율이 전체의 절반 이상 · 문법 영작 문제가 출제되지 않았음	20% (4문항)	20% (4문항)	60% (12문항)	0% (0문항)

합격예상 체크

〈서울시 연도별 합격선〉

2019 합격기준
6

	2019	2018	2018 기술직	2017	2016

맞힌 개수	/20문항	점수	/100점

➡ ☐ 합격 ☐ 불합격

취약영역 체크

문항	정답	영역	문항	정답	영역
①	④	어휘 > 유의어 찾기	11	②	독해 > Macro Reading > 제목
2	①	어휘 > 유의어 찾기	12	③	독해 > Logical Reading > 문맥상 다양한 추론
3	①	어휘 > 빈칸 완성	13	①	어휘+문법 > 빈칸 완성
4	②	어휘 > 빈칸 완성	14	③	독해 > Logical Reading > 연결사
5	②	어휘 > 빈칸 완성	15	④	독해 > Reading for Writing > 빈칸 구 완성
6	④	생활영어 > 회화/관용표현	16	②	독해 > Reading for Writing > 빈칸 구 완성
7	①	문법 > 동사	17	④	독해 > Reading for Writing > 빈칸 구 완성
8	①	문법 > 태	18	③	독해 > Logical Reading > 삭제
9	③	문법 > 일치	19	③	독해 > Logical Reading > 삽입
10	④	문법 > 비교	20	②	독해 > Logical Reading > 배열

⬇ 영역별 틀린 개수로 취약영역을 확인하세요!

어휘	/6	문법	/4	독해	/9	생활영어	/1

➡ 나의 취약영역: _____

※ [정답해설]과 [오답해설] 선지의 50% 표시는 〈1초 합격예측 서비스〉를 통해 수집된 선지 선택률을 나타냅니다.

---

1 어휘 > 유의어 찾기   오답률 24%   답 ④

| 해석 | 적어도 고등학교에서 그녀는 마침내 그녀의 부모와 일치하는 하나의 결정을 했다.

① 9% 다퉜다
② 10% 논쟁했다
③ 5% 헤어졌다
④ 76% 동의했다

| 정답해설 | ④ see eye to eye는 '(의견이) 일치하다'라는 의미를 갖는 관용표현이며 agree(동의하다)와 유의어 관계이다.

어휘

make a decision 결정하다

---

2 어휘 > 유의어 찾기   오답률 52%   답 ①

| 해석 | 정당화는 문제의 행위에 대한 책임을 인정하지만, 그것과 관련된 경멸적 자질을 부정하는 설명이다.

① 48% 경멸적인
② 12% 외향적인
③ 25% 의무적인
④ 15% 불필요한, 여분의

| 정답해설 | ① pejorative는 '경멸적인, 비난하는 의미의'를 뜻하는 단어로 유의어 관계에 있는 단어는 derogatory이다.

| 더 알아보기 | pejorative의 유의어

derogatory, contemptuous, slighting

어휘

justification 정당화
associate A with B A와 B를 연관 짓다

---

3 어휘 > 빈칸 완성   오답률 18%   답 ①

| 해석 | 검사들은 먼지와 열악한 위생 시설을 황열병의 원인에서 배제시켰고, 모기가 ① 의심되는 매개체였다.

① 82% 의심되는
② 9% 미개한, 야만적인
③ 3% 유쾌한, 기운찬
④ 6% 자원받은

| 정답해설 | ① 황열병의 원인에서 먼지와 위생은 배제되었으므로 모기가 '의심되는' 매개체임을 추론할 수 있다. 따라서 빈칸에 가장 적절한 표현은 '의심되는'이라는 뜻의 suspected이다.

어휘

rule out 배제하다, 제외하다   sanitation 위생 시설
yellow fever 황열병   carrier 매개체

---

4 어휘 > 빈칸 완성   오답률 45%   답 ②

| 해석 | 일반적으로 말해서, 현대를 인류 역사의 전체 규모와 비교했을 때 2018년에 살고 있는 사람들은 꽤 운이 좋다. 기대 수명은 약 72세에서 ② 맴돌고 있으며, 불과 1세기 전에 만연하고 치명적이었던 천연두나 디프테리아 같은 질병은 예방할 수 있거나 치료할 수 있거나 완전히 근절되었다.

① 14% 축소하다　　　　② 55% 맴돌다; 배회하다
③ 16% 시작하다　　　　④ 15% 악화시키다

| 정답해설 | ② 현재 기대 수명이 72세에서 맴돈다고 하는 것이 문맥상 적절하므로 빈칸에 알맞은 표현은 hovers(맴돌다)이다.

어휘

generally speaking 일반적으로 말하면
fortunate 운이 좋은　　　　　life expectancy 기대 수명
smallpox 천연두　　　　　　widespread 널리 퍼진
deadly 치명적인　　　　　　curable 치료할 수 있는
eradicate 뿌리 뽑다, 근절하다

---

5 어휘 > 빈칸 완성　　　오답률 49%　　답 ②

| 해석 | 과거의 사건들에 우리의 인생과 결정에 대한 ② 본보기들을 제공할 수 있는 구체적인 패턴이 있다고 상상하는 것은 역사에 그것이 실행시킬 수 없는 확실성의 희망을 투영시키는 것이다.

① 13% 환각들　　　　　② 51% 본보기들
③ 21% 질문들　　　　　④ 15% 소동

| 정답해설 | ② 만일 과거의 사건들에 구체적인 패턴이 있다면 그러한 패턴이 현재의 우리들에게는 하나의 예시 혹은 본보기가 될 수 있으므로, 빈칸에 알맞은 표현은 templates(본보기들)이다.

어휘

concrete 구체적인　　　　　project 투사하다
certainty 확실성　　　　　　fulfill 이행하다; 실행하다

---

6 생활영어 > 회화/관용표현　　오답률 11%　　답 ④

| 해석 | ① A: 토요일에 봤던 영화는 어땠어?
　　　 B: 훌륭했어. 정말 재미있게 봤어.
② A: 안녕하세요. 셔츠 몇 장을 다림질해 주셨으면 하는데요.
　　 B: 네, 그것들이 얼마나 빨리 필요하신데요?
③ A: 싱글 룸으로 하시겠습니까, 더블 룸으로 하시겠습니까?
　　 B: 오, 저만 사용할 거라서 싱글 룸이면 좋겠습니다.
④ A: 보스턴으로 가는 다음 비행기가 몇 시에 있나요?
　　 B: 보스턴까지 약 45분 정도 걸릴 거예요.

| 정답해설 | ④ 89% 보스턴으로 가는 다음 비행기가 몇 시에 있는지 물어보는 질문에 그곳까지 소요되는 시간을 답하는 것은 적절하지 않다.

어휘

press 다림질하다

---

7 문법 > 동사　　　오답률 49%　　답 ①

| 해석 | 발명가 Elias Howe는 재봉틀의 발견을 식인종에게 붙잡힌 꿈 덕분이라고 했다. 그는 그들이 그의 주위에서 춤을 출 때 창끝에 구멍이 있다는 것을 알아차렸고, 그는 이것이 그의 문제를 해결하기 위해 필요한 디자인적 특징이라는 것을 깨달았다.

| 정답해설 | ① 51% 「attribute A to B」는 'A를 B의 덕분[탓]으로 돌리다'라는 표현이다. 재봉틀의 발견이 꿈 덕분임을 문맥을 통해서 알 수 있으므로 for는 to로 고쳐야 한다.

| 오답해설 | ② 21% 선행사를 수식하는 「전치사 + 관계대명사」가 이끄는 절은 완전해야 한다. 따라서 주어진 문장의 밑줄 친 in which는 「전치사 + 관계대명사」의 형태로 관계사절이 이끄는 절 he was captured by cannibals가 완전한 문장이며 선행사 a dream을 수식하고 있으므로 어법상 알맞다.

③ 22% 동사 noticed의 목적어 역할을 하는 절을 이끄는 명사절 접속사 that이므로 어법상 적절하다.

④ 6% 밑줄 친 to solve는 목적을 나타내는 to부정사의 부사적 용법으로 어법상 적절하게 사용되었다. 주어진 문장의 he needed는 목적격 관계대명사가 생략된 관계사절로 선행사 the design feature를 수식하고 있다. 밑줄 친 to solve가 needed의 목적어로 쓰인 to부정사가 아님에 유의해야 한다.

어휘

attribute A to B A를 B의 탓으로 돌리다
sewing machine 재봉틀　　　　capture 잡다
cannibal 식인종　　　　　　　spear 창
feature 특징; 기능

---

8 문법 > 태　　　오답률 45%　　답 ①

| 해석 | 1955년 경 Nikita Khrushchev는 구소련에서 Stalin의 후계자로서 등장했으며, 그로써 동서양이 그들의 경쟁은 계속할 예정이지만 덜 대립적인 방법으로 하는 "평화 공존" 정책에 착수했다.

| 정답해설 | ① 55% emerge(나타나다, 등장하다)는 수동태로 사용할 수 없는 완전자동사이다. 따라서 had been emerged는 had emerged로 고쳐야 한다.

| 오답해설 | ② 10% embark on은 '~에 착수하다'라는 뜻이다. 1955년의 과거 사실을 서술하고 있고 주어와 능동 관계이므로 과거형인 embarked on은 어법상 옳은 표현이다.

③ 8% whereby는 '그로써 ~하는, 그것에 따라 ~하는)'이라는 의미의 격식체 관계부사로 사용되었으며, 뒤따라오는 절은 완전한 형태로 옳게 사용되었다.

④ 27% 주어가 복수 명사 East and West이므로 복수 동사 were가 오는 것은 어법상 적절하다. 또한 were to continue는 to부정사의 형용사적 용법 중 서술적 용법[be to 용법]으로 옳게 사용되었다.

| 더 알아보기 | 수동태로 쓸 수 없는 동사

• come 오다	• happen 발생하다
• occur 발생하다	• remain ~인 채로 남겨지다
• result in 결과적으로 ~이 되다	

어휘

emerge 나타나다, 등장하다　　　successor 후계자
embark on ~에 착수하다　　　　peaceful coexistence 평화 공존
whereby 그로써 ~하는, 그것에 따라 ~하는
confrontational 대립하는, 대결의　　manner 방법

9 　문법 > 일치　　오답률 28%　답 ③

| 해석 | 오징어, 문어, 갑오징어는 모두 두족류이다. 이 동물들 각각은 피부 아래에 색소, 즉 유색 액체가 들어 있는 특별한 세포를 가지고 있다. 두족류는 이 세포들을 피부 쪽으로 또는 피부로부터 멀어지게 이동시킬 수 있다. 이것은 그것이 자신의 외모의 무늬와 색을 바꿀 수 있게 한다.

| 정답해설 | ③ 72% 관계대명사 that의 선행사는 its skin이 아니라 special cells이다. 주격 관계대명사절의 동사는 선행사에 수를 일치시켜야 하므로 contains는 contain으로 고쳐야 한다.

| 오답해설 | ① 11% 주어가 squid, octopuses, and cuttlefish로 복수 명사이므로 보어로 복수 명사 types가 오는 것은 적절하다.

② 8% 문장의 동사가 3인칭 단수 형태인 has이므로 항상 단수 취급하는 대명사 Each가 주어로 쓰인 것은 옳다.

④ 9% 「allow + 목적어 + to부정사」 구문으로, '목적어가 ~하게 허용하다, 허락하다'라는 의미로 사용되어 적절하다.

어휘
cuttlefish 갑오징어　　　　cephalopod 두족류
pigment 색소, 안료　　　　appearance 외모, 외향

10 　문법 > 비교　　오답률 14%　답 ④

| 해석 | 도시를 유지하는 것보다 더 심각한 문제가 있다. 사람들이 혼자 일하는 것이 더 편안해질수록, 그들은 덜 사교적이 될 수도 있다. 한 번의 비즈니스 미팅을 위해 옷을 차려입는 것보다 편안한 운동복이나 목욕 가운을 입고 집에 있는 것이 더 쉽다!

| 정답해설 | ④ 86% 비교 대상이 동일한 품사 형태로 쓰여야 한다. 따라서 to stay와 병렬 구조를 이루도록, getting dressed는 to get dressed로 고쳐야 한다.

| 오답해설 | ① 2% '도시를 유지하는 것'이라는 의미로 동명사 maintaining은 올바른 표현이다.

② 6% 열등 비교는 「less + 형용사/부사의 원급」으로 표현한다. 따라서 less의 쓰임은 올바르다.

③ 6% 문장 후반부에 than이 있으므로 비교급 형용사 easier는 올바른 표현이다.

11 　독해 > Macro Reading > 제목　　오답률 7%　답 ②

| 해석 | 경제학자들은 정보재의 생산은 높은 고정 비용과 낮은 한계 비용을 수반한다고 말한다. 정보재의 첫 번째 사본 제작 비용은 상당할 수 있지만, 추가 사본을 제작(또는 복제)하는 비용은 무시할 수 있다. 이런 종류의 비용 구조는 많은 중요한 의미를 가지고 있다. 예를 들어, 가격에 바탕을 둔 가격 책정은 효과가 없다. 단가가 0일 때 10%나 20%의 가격 인상은 말이 되지 않는다. 당신은 당신의 생산 비용에 따라서가 아니라 소비자 가치에 따라 당신의 정보재의 가격을 책정해야 한다.
① 저작권 확보　　　　　② 정보재의 가격 책정
③ 지적 재산으로서의 정보　④ 기술 변화의 비용

| 정답해설 | ② 93% 정보재의 생산은 고정 비용은 높지만 한계 비용이 낮아서 생산 비용에 따라 값을 매기는 것이 아니라 소비자 가치에 따라 가격을 매겨야 한다고 설명하고 있으므로, 글의 제목으로 가장 적절한 것은 '정보재의 가격 책정'이다.

| 더 알아보기 | Information Goods (정보재)

책, 영화, 음악, 기술, 소프트웨어, 데이터 서비스 등 디지털화가 가능한 제품을 말한다. 초기에 원본을 생산하는 데는 막대한 비용이 소요되지만 추가적인 생산 비용이 거의 들지 않는다는 특징을 가지고 있다.

어휘
fixed cost 고정 비용　　　　marginal cost 한계 비용
substantial 상당한　　　　　negligible 무시할 수 있는
implication 의미, 암시　　　　markup 가격 인상
unit cost 단가　　　　　　　make no sense 말이 되지 않다
production cost 생산 비용　　intellectual property 지적 재산

12 　독해 > Logical Reading > 문맥상 다양한 추론　오답률 20%　답 ③

| 해석 | 드라큘라 개미는 때때로 자기 새끼의 피를 마시는 방식으로 이름을 날린다. 하지만 이번 주에, ① 그 곤충들은 명성을 떨칠 새로운 주장을 얻었다. 'Mystrium camillae' 종의 드라큘라 개미는 그들의 턱을 매우 빠르게 딱딱 소리를 내며 맞부딪힐 수 있어서, 당신은 5,000번의 딱딱거림을 우리가 눈을 깜박하는 데 걸리는 시간에 끼워 맞출 수 있을 것이다. 이번 주 Royal Society Open Science지에 발표된 한 연구에 따르면, 이것은 ② 그 흡혈 곤충들이 자연에서 가장 빠르다고 알려진 움직임을 행한다는 것을 의미한다. 흥미롭게도, 개미들은 단지 턱을 너무 세게 맞다물어서 ③ 그것들이 구부러지는 것만으로도 기록을 깨는 스냅을 만들어 낸다. 그것이 다른 쪽 턱을 미끄러지듯 지나 시속 200마일 이상의 최고 속도에 도달하면서 엄청난 속도와 힘으로 강타할 때까지 이것은 용수철처럼 한쪽 턱에 에너지를 저장한다. 그것은 당신이 손가락으로 딱딱 소리를 낼 때 벌어지는 일과 약간 비슷한데, 단지 1,000배 더 빠를 뿐이다. 드라큘라 개미는 ④ 그들이 나뭇잎 쓰레기 밑에서 또는 지하 터널에서 사냥하는 것을 선호하기 때문에 비밀스런 포식자들이다.

| 정답해설 | ③ 80% they는 their jaws(그들의 턱들)를 지칭하지만, 나머지 ①②④는 모두 드라큘라 개미를 가리킨다.

어휘
claim 주장; 요구, 청구; 권리　　fame 명성을 떨치다; 명성
snap 딱딱 소리를 내다　　　　blood-sucker 흡혈 동물
wield 사용하다, 휘두르다, 행사하다　slide 미끄러지다
lash out 후려갈기다, 강타하다　velocity 속도
secretive 비밀의, 숨기는　　　subterranean 지하의, 숨은

오답률 TOP 2
13 　어휘 + 문법 > 빈칸 완성　　오답률 67%　답 ①

| 해석 | 나는 바닥에 앉은 채로 독일의 한 기차에서 너에게 편지를 쓰고 있어. 기차는 사람들로 꽉 찼어. 그리고 좌석은 모두 만석이야. 하지만, 이미 자리에 앉아 있는 사람들에게 그들의 좌석을 ① 양보하게 하는 "comfort customers"라는 특별한 등급이 있어.

| 정답해설 | ① 33% comfort customers는 이미 자기 자리에 앉아 있는 사람들이 자기 자리를 '차지하는(take)' 것이 아니라 '양보하게(give up)' 만드는 특별한 등급의 승객임을 문맥을 통해서 파악할 수 있으므로 의미상 give up이 와야 하는데, 사역동사 make의 목적격 보어 자리이므로 원형부정사인 give up이 오는 것이 적절하다.

어휘
crowded 붐비는

14 독해 > Logical Reading > 연결사   오답률 15%   답 ③

| 해석 | 한 나라의 부는 교육에서 중심적인 역할을 수행하므로 민족 국가로부터 나오는 기금과 자원의 부족은 시스템을 약하게 할 수 있다. 사하라 이남 아프리카 정부들은 세계의 공공 자원의 2.4%만을 교육에 지출하지만 학령기 인구의 15%가 거기에 살고 있다. ③ 대조적으로, 미국은 전 세계에서 소비되는 전체 돈의 28%를 교육에 소비하지만 학령기 인구의 단지 4%만이 산다.

① 그럼에도 불구하고　　　② 게다가
③ 대조적으로　　　　　　④ 마찬가지로

| 정답해설 | ③ 85% 미국과 아프리카 지역이 각각 교육에 소비하는 기금, 그리고 자원과 학령기 인구의 수를 제시하는 글이다. 빈칸 이전에 사하라 이남 아프리카는 학령기 인구 15%에 세계의 공공 자원 2.4%를 지출하고 있으며, 빈칸 이후에 미국은 학령기 인구 4%에 세계에서 소비되는 전체 돈의 28%를 소비한다고 서술하고 있다. 즉 본문을 통해서 인구 대비 소비되는 교육 기금의 현저한 차이를 제시하고 있다. 따라서 학령기 인구 당 미국이 아프리카 지역과 비교해, 대조적으로 교육에 더 많이 투자하고 있다는 것을 알 수 있으므로 빈칸에는 역접, 대조를 나타내는 연결사 ③ Conversely가 들어가는 것이 적절하다.

어휘
central 중심적인
nation-state 민족 국가(민족을 단위로 하여 형성된 국가)
house 살다; 장소를 제공하다

오답률 TOP 1

15 독해 > Reading for Writing > 빈칸 구 완성   오답률 69%   답 ④

| 해석 | "매우 성실한 직원들은 나머지 우리들보다 일련의 일을 더 잘합니다."라고 성실성을 연구하는 Illinois대학의 심리학자인 Brent Roberts는 말한다. Roberts는 그들의 성공을 "위생" 요인에 돌린다. 성실한 사람들은 자신의 삶을 잘 정리하는 경향이 있다. 체계적이지 못하고 불성실한 사람은 올바른 문서를 찾기 위해 파일을 뒤지면서 20~30분을 낭비할지도 모르는데, 이는 성실한 사람들은 피하는 경향이 있는 비효율적인 경험이다. 기본적으로, 성실해짐으로써 사람들은 그렇지 않다면 그들이 스스로 만들어 낼 수 있는 ④ 스트레스를 회피한다.

① 좌절을 극복한다　　　　② 철저한 일을 한다
③ 표준을 따른다　　　　　④ 스트레스를 회피한다

| 정답해설 | ④ 31% 성실한 직원과 불성실한 직원의 차이를 위생 요인의 관점에서 설명한 글이다. 성실한 사람들은 자신의 삶을 잘 정리하지만 그렇지 않은 사람들은 성실한 사람들이 겪지 않는 비효율을 경험할 수도 있다고 말하고 있다. 따라서 성실하면 불성실로 인한 '스트레스를 회피할' 수 있다는 흐름이 되는 것이 적절하다.

어휘
conscientious 성실한　　　conscientiousness 성실함
hygiene 위생　　　　　　　tendency 경향
disorganized 체계적이지 못한　root 뒤지다, 파헤치다
folk 사람들　　　　　　　　setback 좌절
norm 표준, 기준　　　　　　sidestep 회피하다, 비켜 가다

16 독해 > Reading for Writing > 빈칸 구 완성   오답률 36%   답 ②

| 해석 | 기후 변화, 삼림 벌채, 널리 퍼진 오염, 그리고 생물다양성의 6번째 대량 멸종은 모두 오늘날 우리 세계에서의 삶, 즉 "인류세"로 알려지게 된 시대를 정의한다. 이러한 위기는 생산과 세계 생태계의 한계를 크게 초과하지만 비난은 균등하게 공유되는 것과 거리가 먼 소비에 의해 뒷받침된다. 세계에서 가장 부유한 42명이 가장 가난한 37억 명이 소유한 만큼의 재산을 소유하고 있으며, 그들은 훨씬 더 큰 환경적 영향을 초래한다. 따라서 일부에서는 끝없는 성장과 ② 소수의 주머니 안에 들어 있는 부의 축적이라는 자본주의의 논리를 반영하여 생태 파괴와 증가하는 불평등의 이 시대를 묘사하기 위해 "자본세"라는 용어를 사용할 것을 제안하였다.

① 여전히 우리의 손이 미치는 곳에 있는 더 나은 세상
② 소수의 주머니 안에 들어 있는 부의 축적
③ 기후 변화에 대한 효과적인 대응
④ 더 실행 가능한 미래를 위한 타오르는 욕구

| 정답해설 | ② 64% 빈칸 이전에 세계에서 가장 부유한 42명이 가장 가난한 37억 명이 소유한 만큼의 재산을 소유하는 것과 같이 부유한 사람에게 더 많은 자본이 몰리는 '부의 불평등' 문제를 지적하고 있다. 따라서 빈칸에는 '자본의 편중'을 지적하는 선지가 분명히 제시된 표현이 들어가는 것이 적절하므로 ② the accumulation of wealth in fewer pockets(소수의 주머니 안의 부의 축적)가 들어가는 것이 적절하다.

어휘
deforestation 삼림 벌채　　　mass extinction 대량 멸종
biodiversity 생물 다양성　　　Anthropocene 인류세
underpin 뒷받침하다　　　　　evenly 공평하게
generate 발생시키다　　　　　devastation 황폐, 파괴
inequality 불평등　　　　　　accumulation 축적
viable 실행 가능한

오답률 TOP 3

17 독해 > Reading for Writing > 빈칸 구 완성   오답률 55%   답 ④

| 해석 | 고대 그리스 비극 시대부터 서양 문화는 복수하는 사람에게 사로잡혀 있었다. 그 또는 그녀는 완전한 일련의 경계선 위에 서 있는데, 즉 문명과 야만 사이, ④ 그 혹은 그녀 자신의 양심에 대한 개인적 책임과 법치에 대한 공동체의 필요 사이, 그리고 정의와 자비의 상반되는 요구 사이에 서 있다. 우리가 사랑하는 사람을 죽인 자들에게 똑같이 복수할 권리가 우리에게 있는가? 아니면 복수심을 법이나 신에게 맡겨야 할까? 그리고 만약 우리가 우리 손으로 직접 행동을 취한다면, 우리는 살인을 한 원래 가해자와 같은 도덕적인 수준으로 우리 스스로를 낮추는 것은 아닌가?

① 복수하는 사람을 타락한 상태로부터 구원하는 것
② 인간의 잔혹 행위에 대한 성스러운 복수
③ 부패한 정치인들의 도덕적 타락
④ 그 혹은 그녀 자신의 양심에 대한 개인적 책임

| 정답해설 | ④ 45% 주어진 글은 개인적 복수의 정당성을 서술하고 있다. 빈칸이 포함된 문장은 이전에 서술된 내용인 '복수하는 사람이 서 있는 경계선'을 구체적으로 제시하고 있다. 다시 말해 빈칸 앞의 between civilization and barbarity(문명과 야만)와 빈칸 뒤의 between the conflicting demands of justice and mercy(정의와 자비)를 통해서 반대 의미인 두 개념을 제시한 것으로 보아, 빈칸에도 the community's need for the rule of law(법치에 대한 공동체

의 필요)와 반대되는 개념이 들어가야 함을 알 수 있다. 따라서 빈 칸에는 '공동체의 필요'와 반대 개념인 '개인적 책임'을 서술하는 ④ 가 가장 적절하다.

---

18 독해 > Logical Reading > 삭제   오답률 21%   답 ③

| 해석 | 각각 특징적인 방법과 목적이 있는 네 가지 종류의 읽기를 말하는 것은 나에게 가능한 것처럼 보인다. 첫 번째는 정보를 위한 읽기인데, 즉 무역이나 정치학, 또는 무언가를 성취하는 방법에 대해 배우기 위해 읽는 것이다. 우리는 이런 방법으로 신문, 대부분의 교과서들 혹은 자전거를 어떻게 조립하는지에 대한 설명서를 읽는다. 이 자료의 대부분으로 독자는 그가 필요한 것을 찾아내고 문장의 리듬 혹은 은유 작용처럼 그와 관련이 없는 것을 무시하면서 빠르게 페이지를 살펴보는 법을 배울 수 있다. ③ 우리는 또한 은유와 단어의 연관성을 통해 감정의 자취를 기록할 수 있다. 속독 과정은 눈이 빠르게 페이지를 이리저리 옮겨 다니는 것을 훈련하면서 우리가 이러한 목적을 위해 읽는 것을 도와줄 수 있다.

| 정답해설 | ③ 79% 네 가지 종류의 읽기 중 정보를 얻기 위한 읽기에 관한 글로, 그러한 읽기 유형이 필요한 자료와 읽기 방법, 그로 인한 효과가 설명되고 있다. 그러나 ③은 은유와 단어의 연관성을 이용한 기록 방법에 관한 내용으로 정보를 얻기 위한 읽기와 관련이 없다.

---

19 독해 > Logical Reading > 삽입   오답률 37%   답 ③

| 해석 | 일의 의미에서의 문화적 차이는 다른 측면에서도 나타날 수 있다. 예를 들어, 미국 문화에서, 일은 돈을 모으고 생계를 꾸리는 수단이라고 생각하기 쉽다. 다른 문화권, 특히 집단주의 문화권에서는 일이 더 큰 집단에 대한 의무를 이행하는 것으로 보일 수 있다. ③ 이러한 상황에서, 우리는 개인이 속한 조직과 그 조직을 구성하는 사람들에 대한 개인의 사회적 의무 때문에 한 직장에서 다른 직장으로의 개인들의 이동이 더 적다는 것을 알게 될 것이라고 예상한다. 개인주의 문화에서는, 자신으로부터 직업을 분리하는 것이 더 쉽기 때문에 한 직업을 버리고 다른 직업으로 가는 것을 고려하는 것이 더 쉽다. 다른 직장에서도 같은 목표를 쉽게 달성할 것이다.

| 정답해설 | ③ 63% 주어진 글은 집단주의 문화와 개인주의 문화에서의 일의 의미의 차이점을 서술하고 있다. 〈보기〉에서는 집단 구성원에 대한 사회적 의무로 개인의 이직이 적다고 서술하고 있는데, 이는 개인의 이직보다 집단 구성원에 대한 사회적 의무가 우선

시되는 것이므로 '집단주의 문화'와 관련된 것임을 유추 할 수 있다. 따라서 〈보기〉에서의 this situation은 '집단주의 문화'를 지칭하는 것이므로 〈보기〉의 문장은 '집단주의' 문화에 대한 서술이 처음으로 등장한 ② 이후 문장에 뒤이어 ③에 들어가는 것이 가장 적절하다. 또한 ③ 이후의 문장은 '개인주의' 문화에 대해서 서술하고 있으므로 〈보기〉의 문장이 ③에 들어가는 것이 옳다.

---

20 독해 > Logical Reading > 배열   오답률 15%   답 ②

| 해석 | ⓛ 북아메리카에서 발견되는 곤충을 잡아먹는 작은 박쥐인 마이크로박쥐는 어둠 속에서 길을 찾고 먹잇감을 포착하는 데 좋을 것 같지는 않아 보이는 작은 눈을 가지고 있다.

ⓔ 하지만 사실, 마이크로박쥐는 쥐와 다른 작은 포유동물들만큼 잘 볼 수 있다. 박쥐의 야행성 습관은 우리가 생각하는 것보다 밤에 먹이를 먹고 날아다니는 것을 훨씬 더 쉽게 해 주는 특별한 능력인 반향 위치 추적이라는 그들의 능력에 의해 도움을 받는다.

ⓖ 어둠 속에서 길을 찾기 위해 마이크로박쥐는 입을 벌리고 인간이 들을 수 없는 고음의 팩팩거리는 소리를 내지르며 날아다닌다. 이 소리들 중 일부는 앞에 있는 나뭇가지와 다른 장애물뿐만 아니라 날아다니는 곤충들에게 메아리친다. 박쥐는 메아리에 귀를 기울이고 그 앞에 있는 사물들의 순간적인 그림을 뇌 속에 넣는다.

ⓒ 반향 위치 측정, 즉 초음파라고도 불리는 것의 사용으로부터 마이크로박쥐는 모기나 다른 잠재적인 먹이에 대해 많은 것을 알 수 있다. 극도의 정확성으로, 반향 위치 측정은 마이크로박쥐가 동작, 거리, 속도, 움직임 및 모양을 인식할 수 있게 한다. 박쥐는 또한 인간의 머리카락보다 두껍지 않은 장애물을 감지하고 피할 수 있다.

| 정답해설 | ② 85% 먼저 마이크로박쥐가 무엇인지를 설명하는 ⓛ이 시작 문단으로 가장 적합하다. ⓛ에서 이 동물은 '밤에 돌아다니거나 먹이를 찾는 데 도움이 될 것 같지 않은 작은 눈을 가지고 있다'는 의문을 제시하고 있다. 이를 ⓔ에서는 역접의 접속사인 But으로 연결한 후, 실제로는 다른 포유동물만큼 잘 볼 수 있음을 제시하면서 반박하는 것이 자연스럽다. 그 이후 ⓔ에서 언급한 a special ability(특별한 능력)를 구체적으로 부연 설명하는 ⓖ을 통해서, 박쥐의 echolocation이 밤에 도움이 된다는 것을 언급하고 있다. 이어서 ⓖ에 제시된 능력을 통해, ⓒ에서는 '이것이 먹이를 찾는 데 도움'이 되는 것을 서술하는 것이 문맥상 가장 적절하다. 따라서 정답은 ② ⓛ – ⓔ – ⓖ – ⓒ 이다.

합격예상 체크

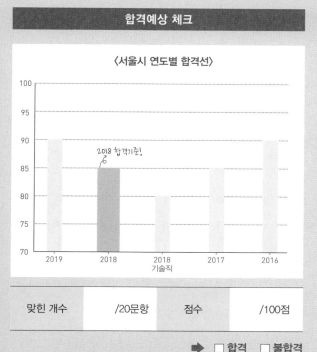

〈서울시 연도별 합격선〉

2018 합격기준!

| 연도 | 2019 | 2018 기술직 | 2018 | 2017 | 2016 |

| 맞힌 개수 | /20문항 | 점수 | /100점 |

➡ □합격 □불합격

취약영역 체크

문항	정답	영역	문항	정답	영역
1	④	독해 > Reading for Writing > 빈칸 구 완성	11	③	어휘 > 빈칸 완성
2	③	독해 > Micro Reading > 내용 일치/불일치	12	④	독해 > Micro Reading > 내용 일치/불일치
3	④	독해 > Logical Reading > 배열	13	①	독해 > Logical Reading > 연결사
4	③	어휘 > 유의어 찾기	14	④	어휘 > 반의어 찾기
5	①	어휘 > 유의어 찾기	15	④	어휘 > 빈칸 완성
6	②	어휘 > 유의어 찾기	16	③	문법 > 일치
7	③	생활영어 > 회화/관용표현	17	④	문법 > 동사
8	②	문법 > 부사	18	②	독해 > Logical Reading > 문맥상 다양한 추론
9	③	문법 > 형용사	19	①	어휘 > 빈칸 완성
10	①	독해 > Reading for Writing > 빈칸 절 완성	20	③	독해 > Reading for Writing > 빈칸 절 완성

⬇ 영역별 틀린 개수로 취약영역을 확인하세요!

| 어휘 | /7 | 문법 | /4 | 독해 | /8 | 생활영어 | /1 |

➡ 나의 취약영역: _____

※ [정답해설]과 [오답해설] 선지의 50% 표시는 〈1초 합격예측 서비스〉를 통해 수집된 선지 선택률을 나타냅니다.

1 　독해 > Reading for Writing > 빈칸 구 완성　 오답률 39%　　답 ④

| 해석 | 사회적 학습 이론가들은 가정에서 공격성을 경험하는 아이들에게서 보이는 반격에 대한 다른 설명을 제시한다. 공격적 행동과 강압적인 가정에 관한 광범위한 연구는 회피하는 결과가 공격적인 반응을 끌어내고 진행 중인 강압적인 행동을 가속화시킬 수도 있다고 결론짓는다. 이러한 공격적 행위의 희생자들은 결국 모델링을 통해 공격적인 (행동의) 교환을 ④ 시작하는 것을 학습하게 된다. 이러한 일들은 공격적 행동의 사용을 영속화하고 아이들이 성인처럼 행동하는 법을 훈련시킨다.

① 멈추다　　　　　　　　② 약화시키다
③ 혐오하다　　　　　　　④ 시작하다

| 정답해설 | ④ 61% 주어진 글은 가정에서 경험하는 공격적 행위가 어떻게 아이들에게 영향을 미치는지(어떻게 아이들이 배우게 되는지)를 사회적 학습 이론을 통해 설명한다. 빈칸 이전의 via modelling이라는 표현으로 보아 공격을 경험한 아이들은 결국 이를 배우게 된다는 흐름과, 빈칸 이후에 공격적 행동의 사용이 영속화되고 아이들이 성인처럼 행동하는 법을 훈련시킨다는 두 가지 점을 통해, 빈칸에는 공격적 행동의 교환을 시작한다(initiate)는 것이 내용상 가장 적절하다.

어휘

extensive 광범위한　　　　　　coercive 강압적인
aversive 회피적인, 혐오의　　　elicit 유도하다, 끌어내다
accelerate 가속화하다　　　　　via ~을 통하여, ~에 의해
interchange 교환　　　　　　　perpetuate 영속시키다

attenuate 약화시키다　　　　　　abhor 혐오하다

2 　독해 > Micro Reading > 내용일치/불일치　 오답률 19%　　답 ③

| 해석 | 프랑스 사회학자인 Marcel Mauss(1872~1950)는 Lorraine의 Épinal(Vosges)에서 태어났고, 긴밀하게 맺어진, 독실한 정통 유대인 가정 안에서 성장했다. Emile Durkheim은 그의 삼촌이었다. 18세 무렵, Mauss는 유대교 신앙에 반발했다. 즉, 그는 결코 신앙심이 깊은 사람이 아니었다. 그는 Bordeaux에서 Durkheim의 감독 하에서 철학을 공부했다. Durkheim은 그의 조카의 공부를 지도하는 데 수고를 아끼지 않았고 심지어 Mauss에게 가장 유용할 강의 주제들을 골라 주기까지 했다. 그리하여 Mauss는 처음에는 (초기 Durkheim 학파 사람들의 대다수처럼) 철학자였고, 철학에 대한 그의 이해는 무엇보다도 그가 항상 최고의 존경심을 가졌던 Durkheim 본인에게서 영향을 받았다.

① 그는 유대인 배경을 가지고 있었다.
② 그는 그의 삼촌의 감독을 받았다.
③ 그는 광신적인 믿음을 가지고 있었다.
④ 그는 철학적 배경을 가진 사회학자였다.

| 정답해설 | ③ 81% Mauss는 독실한 유대인 가정에서 자랐지만 유대교 신앙에 반발했고 결코 신앙심이 깊은 사람이 아니었다고 했으므로 ③은 본문 내용과 일치하지 않는다.

| 오답해설 | ① 4% 첫 문장에서 Mauss가 유대인 가정에서 태어났다고 했으므로 본문 내용과 일치한다.
② 5% 삼촌인 Emile Durkheim의 감독 하에 철학을 공부했다고

했으므로 본문 내용과 일치한다.

④ 10% 첫 문장에서 Mauss를 프랑스 사회학자라고 소개했고 본문 중반부에서는 삼촌의 감독 하에 철학을 공부했다고 했으므로 그가 철학적 배경을 가진 사회학자였다는 것은 본문과 일치한다.

어휘

sociologist 사회학자
pious 독실한
supervision 감독, 관리
doctrinaire 교조적인

close-knit 긴밀히 맺어진
orthodox 정통파의
retain 유지하다

---

3 독해 > Logical Reading > 배열   오답률 27%   답 ④

| 해석 | ⓓ 사람들이 벌목을 하는 데는 새로울 것이 없다. 고대에, 그리스, 이탈리아, 영국은 숲으로 뒤덮여 있었다. 수세기 동안 그 숲들은 점차 축소되었다. 지금은 남은 것이 거의 없다.
ⓐ 그러나 오늘날 나무는 훨씬 더 빨리 베어지고 있다. 매년, 대략 200만 에이커의 숲이 베어진다. 이것은 영국 전체의 면적보다 더 크다.
ⓒ 벌목을 하는 중요한 이유들이 있기는 하지만, 지구상의 생명체에 대한 위험한 영향 또한 있다. 현재 삼림 파괴의 주요 원인은 목재에 대한 전 세계적인 수요이다. 선진국에서는, 사람들이 종이를 위해 점점 더 많은 목재를 사용하고 있다.
ⓑ 이 국가들에서는 수요를 충족시킬 만큼 충분한 나무가 없다. 따라서 목재 회사들은 아시아, 아프리카, 남아메리카, 그리고 시베리아의 숲에서까지 목재를 가져가기 시작했다.

| 정답해설 | ④ 73% 과거의 울창했던 숲의 모습과 이후 헐벗게 된 유럽의 숲의 모습을 개괄적으로 정리한 ⓓ가 맨 앞에 오고 이 뒤에는 Today, however로 시작하며 오늘날의 벌목을 비교하는 ⓐ가 이어지는 것이 적절하다. 남은 것은 ⓑ와 ⓒ인데, ⓑ의 these countries가 가리키는 것은 ⓒ의 마지막 문장에 나온 industrialized countries로 보는 것이 가장 적절하므로 ⓒ 뒤에 ⓑ가 와야 한다. 따라서 ⓓ - ⓐ - ⓒ - ⓑ의 순서가 알맞다.

어휘

cut down 베어 쓰러뜨리다
industrialized country 선진국, 산업 국가
cut back 축소하다, 줄어들다

destruction 파괴

---

4 어휘 > 유의어 찾기   오답률 48%   답 ③

| 해석 | 인간은 새로운 생각을 억압하려고 시도했던 정부 당국, 그리고 변화는 터무니없는 것이라고 선언했던 이전부터 내려오는 견해의 권위에 대해 계속해서 반항해 왔다.
① 18% 표현하다   ② 11% 주장하다
③ 52% 억누르다   ④ 19% 펼치다, 퍼뜨리다

| 정답해설 | ③ muzzle은 '입막음하다, (말하는 것 등을) 억압하다'라는 의미로, suppress와 의미가 가장 유사하다.

어휘

disobedient 반항적인
authority 권위

authorities 정부, 당국
nonsense 허튼소리

오답률 TOP 3

5 어휘 > 유의어 찾기   오답률 53%   답 ①

| 해석 | 너무 과시하려고 하지 마라. 당신은 당신의 글이 너무 격식이 없고 구어체인 것을 원하지 않지만, 당신은 또한 당신의 말이 아닌 누군가처럼, 예를 들어 당신의 교수, 상관, 또는 Rhodes 장학생 교육 조교처럼 들리는 것도 원하지 않을 것이다.
① 47% 과시하는   ② 19% 평상시의, 우연한
③ 26% 공식적인   ④ 8% 진실된, 진짜의

| 정답해설 | ① pompous는 (글이나 문체가) '과시적인, 거만한'의 의미를 가지고 있다. 선지 중에서는 presumptuous(주제넘은, 건방진, 뻔뻔한)가 의미상 가장 가깝다.

어휘

colloquial 구어체의

---

6 어휘 > 유의어 찾기   오답률 48%   답 ②

| 해석 | 외과의들은 그 일에 적합한 도구들을 찾을 수 없었기 때문에 어쩔 수 없이 그만두게 되었다.
① 7% 시작하다   ② 52% 끝내다
③ 14% 기다리다   ④ 27% 취소하다

| 정답해설 | ② call it a day는 '~을 그만하기로 하다, 일과를 끝내다'라는 의미이므로 finish와 의미가 가장 유사하다.

---

7 생활영어 > 회화/관용표현   오답률 8%   답 ③

| 해석 | ① A: 내일 예약을 하고 싶어요.
　B: 네, 몇 시로요?
② A: 주문하시겠어요?
　B: 네, 그 수프로 할게요.
③ A: 당신의 리조또는 어때요?
　B: 네, 저희는 버섯과 치즈가 들어간 리조또가 있어요.
④ A: 디저트 드시겠어요?
　B: 저는 괜찮아요, 감사해요.

| 정답해설 | ③ 92% 리조또의 맛을 묻는 말에 yes 또는 no로 답하는 것은 알맞지 않으며, 뒤의 내용도 알맞은 응답이 아니다.

| 더 알아보기 | 식당에서 쓰는 생활영어 표현

- Here or to go? 여기서 드실 건가요, 아니면 가지고 가실 건가요?
- Can you give me a doggy bag? 남은 음식 좀 싸 주실 수 있나요?
- Can I have the check, please? 계산서 좀 가져다 주시겠어요?
- Let's go Dutch. 비용을 각자 부담하자, 더치페이하자.
- Keep the change. 잔돈은 됐습니다.

---

8 문법 > 부사   오답률 17%   답 ②

| 해석 | 1961년의 독립 이후 여러 해 동안 그의 생존은 진정한 정책 선택에 대한 논의가 공식적인 방식으로 거의 일어나지 않았다는 사실을 바꾸지 않는다. 사실, Nyerere가 NEC를 통해 논의해 왔어야 하는 많은 중요한 정책 이슈들이 항상 있었다.

| 정답해설 | ② 83% 부정부사 hardly와 never를 같이 쓰는 것은 이

중 부정이 되므로 never를 제거해야 한다.

| 오답해설 | ① 0% over는 '~동안'이라는 의미로 옳게 사용되었다.

③ 6% 가산명사 policy issues를 '많은 ~'이라는 뜻의 a number of가 수식하고 있다.

④ 11% policy issues를 선행사로 하는 목적격 관계대명사로 옳게 사용되었다.

| 더 알아보기 | 이중 부정에 주의해야 할 부정의 빈도부사

- never, seldom, scarcely, hardly, rarely, barely 등

어휘

alter 바꾸다　　　　　　hardly 거의 ~하지 않는

오답률 TOP 1

| 9 | 문법 > 형용사 | 오답률 57% | 답 ③ |

| 해석 | 150명이 넘는 사람들이 지난 3주간 주로 홍콩과 베트남에서 병에 걸렸다. 그리고 전문가들은 중국 광동의 또 다른 300명이 11월 중반에 시작된 같은 질병에 걸렸다고 의심한다.

| 정답해설 | ③ 43% another는 「another + 단수 명사」 형태로 직접적으로는 단수 명사를 수식하지만, 「another + 기수 + 복수 명사」의 형태로 쓰이면 '또 다른 ~들'이라는 의미가 된다.

| 오답해설 | ① 19% fall은 fall-fell-fallen으로 변화하는 불규칙 동사이므로 have fallen ill이 되어야 한다.

② 21% suspect는 타동사로 that절의 목적어를 가지려면 수동태가 아니라 능동태로 쓰여야 한다. 따라서 suspect that이 되어야 한다.

④ 17% 접속사 that이 이끄는 명사절에 had와 begin이 접속사 없이 나열되었으므로 옳지 않다. 문맥상 that 이하 문장의 주어는 another 300 hundred이고 동사는 had이다. 따라서 begin은 앞의 disease와 의미상 능동 관계이므로 현재분사 beginning in으로 수정하는 것이 옳다. 또한 disease를 수식하는 형용사절로서 관계사절로 쓰여 that began in으로도 수정 가능하다.

| 10 | 독해 > Reading for Writing > 빈칸 절 완성 | 오답률 43% | 답 ① |

| 해석 | 그러나 '500주년 기념일'을 위한 준비가 됨에 따라 1980년대까지 분명해진 것은 많은 미국인들이 불가능하지는 않을지라도, 그 기념일을 '기념일'로 보기가 어렵다는 것을 알아냈다는 것이었다. 콜럼버스의 유산을 축하할 것은 없었다. ① 콜럼버스의 많은 비판가들에 따르면, 그는 진보와 문명화가 아니라 노예제와 환경에 대한 무분별한 착취의 조짐이었다.

① 콜럼버스의 많은 비판가들에 따르면, 그는 진보와 문명화가 아니라 노예제와 환경에 대한 무분별한 착취의 조짐이었다.

② 1893년의 시카고 세계 박람회는 미국의 발견과 미국 진보의 힘 사이의 서술적 연관성을 강화시켰다.

③ 콜럼버스에 대한 19세기의 근거 없는 믿음의 이러한 역전은 흥미로운 사실을 보여 준다.

④ 따라서 콜럼버스는 미국의 진보가 신의 힘으로 정해졌다는 믿음인 명백한 사명으로 통합되었다.

| 정답해설 | ① 57% 빈칸 이전에 콜럼버스의 유산을 축하할 것은

없었다고 하며, 미대륙 발견을 부정적으로 평가했다. 빈칸에는 이렇게 부정적으로 평가하는 이유가 나와야 하므로, ①이 적절하다.

| 오답해설 | ③ 11% 콜럼버스에 대한 19세기의 근거 없는 믿음과 관련된 설명은 본문에 없으므로 빈칸에 적절하지 않다.

④ 27% 콜럼버스가 미국의 진보가 신의 힘으로 정해졌다는 믿음인 명백한 사명에 통합되었다는 것은 그에 대한 부정적 평가가 아니다.

어휘

Quincentenary Jubilee 500주년 기념일

harbinger 조짐	slavery 노예제
reckless 무모한, 무분별한	exploitation 착취
reinforce 강화하다	narrative 서술의, 이야기로 된
reversal 반전	revealing 흥미로운 사실을 보여 주는
integrate 통합하다; 완전하게 하다, 완성하다	
Manifest Destiny 명백한 사명(영토 확장론)	
divinely 신성하게, 신의 힘으로	
ordain (신이나 운명 등이) 정하다, 운명 짓다	

| 11 | 어휘 > 빈칸 완성 | 오답률 37% | 답 ③ |

| 해석 | 아버지의 투옥 후, 학교를 떠나 Charles Dickens는 Thames 강변의 구두약 공장에서 일할 수밖에 없었다. 황폐하고 쥐가 들끓는 공장에서, Dickens는 벽난로를 청소하는 데 사용되는 물질인 "검은색 구두약" 단지에 라벨을 붙이며 일주일에 6실링을 벌었다. 그것이 그가 가족을 부양하는 것을 돕기 위해 할 수 있는 최선이었다. 그 경험을 되돌아볼 때, Dickens는 "어떻게 그가 그렇게나 어린 나이에 너무나도 쉽게 내버려질 수 있었을까"가 궁금했다고 말하면서, 그것을 자신이 어린 순수함에 작별을 고했던 순간으로 여겼다. 그는 자신을 돌보기로 되어 있던 어른들에 의해 ③ 지지받는 (→ 버려진) 것처럼 느꼈다.

① 13% 버려진　　　　　② 17% 배신당한
③ 63% 지지받는　　　　④ 7% 무시된

| 정답해설 | ③ 빈칸 앞 문장에 어떻게 그가 그러한 어린 나이에 그렇게 쉽게 내버려질 수 있을까가 궁금했다고 했으므로 빈칸에는 '내버려지는' 것과 유사한 맥락의 abandoned(버려진), betrayed(배신당한), disregarded(무시된)는 알맞으나 buttressed(지지받는)는 적절하지 않다.

어휘

imprisonment 투옥

boot-blacking 구두닦기; (검은색) 구두약

run-down 황폐한	substance 실체, 본질
innocence 순수	cast away 버리다
buttress 지지하다	disregard 무시하다

| 12 | 독해 > Micro Reading > 내용일치/불일치 | 오답률 5% | 답 ④ |

| 해석 | 아이를 입양하기를 희망하는 가정은 우선 입양 기관을 선택해야 한다. 미국에서는 입양을 도와주는 두 가지 종류의 기관이 있다. 공공 기관들은 일반적으로 어느 정도 나이가 있는 아이들, 정신적 또는 신체적 장애가 있는 아이들, 혹은 학대나 방치를 당했던 아이들을 다룬다. 입양 희망 부모들은 공공 기관에서 아이를 입양할 때 보통 수수료를 지불하지 않는다. 위탁 양육, 즉 일시적인 형태의 입양도 공공 기관을 통해 가능하다. 사설 기관들은 인터넷에서 찾을 수 있다. 그들은 국내 및 국제 입양을 다룬다.

① 공공 입양 기관들이 사설 기관들보다 더 낫다.
② 부모들은 위탁 양육 가정으로부터 아이를 입양하기 위해 큰 비용을 지불한다.
③ 도움이 필요한 아이들은 공공 기관을 통해 입양될 수 없다.
④ 사설 기관들은 국제 입양을 위해 연락을 받을 수 있다.

| 정답해설 | ④ 95% 마지막 문장에서 사설 입양 기관은 국내 및 국제 입양을 다룬다고 했으므로 본문과 일치한다.

| 오답해설 | ① 1% 입양 기관의 우열 관계에 대해서는 언급되지 않았다.
② 1% 위탁 양육 가정으로부터의 입양 방법은 언급되어 있지 않다.
③ 3% children in need(도움이 필요한 아이들)는 본문의 children with mental or physical disabilities, or children who may have been abused or neglected를 말한 것이며, 이들은 공공 기관을 통해 입양이 가능하다.

어휘
adoption agency 입양 기관 　　　neglect 무시하다, 방임하다
prospective 장래의 　　　fee 수수료, 요금
foster (수양 부모로서) 아이를 맡아 기르다, 위탁 양육하다
domestic 국내의

---

13 독해 > Logical Reading > 연결사　　오답률 29%　답 ①

| 해석 | 현대 예술은 사실상 오늘날의 중산층 사회의 필수적인 부분이 되었다. 스튜디오에서 금방 나온 예술 작품들조차 열광을 받는다. 그것들은 꽤 빨리, 뿌루퉁한 문화 비평가들의 취향에는 너무 빨리 인정을 받는다. 물론, 모든 예술 작품들이 즉시 구입되는 것은 아니지만, 분명히 새로운 예술 작품들을 구입하는 것을 즐기는 사람들이 늘어나고 있다. 빠르고 비싼 자동차들 대신, 그들은 젊은 예술가들의 그림, 조각, 그리고 사진 작품 들을 구매한다. 그들은 또한 현대 예술이 그들의 사회적 위신을 높여 준다고 생각한다. 게다가, 예술은 자동차와 같은 정도로 마모되지 않기 때문에, 훨씬 더 좋은 투자이다.
① 물론 – 게다가　　　　② 그러므로 – 반면에
③ 그러므로 – 예를 들면　　④ 물론 – 예를 들면

| 정답해설 | ① 71% 첫 번째 빈칸 앞 문장에서, 예술 작품이 너무 빨리 인정을 받는다고 했고, 빈칸 뒤에는 모든 작품들이 빨리 팔리는 것은 아니라고 언급되어 있다. 빈칸 앞뒤 문장이 인과 관계는 아니므로 Of course가 알맞다. 두 번째 빈칸 앞에 예술품 구입의 구체적인 기능 중 하나인 사회적 위신의 향상이 언급되어 있고, 빈칸 뒤에 또다른 기능인 investment(투자)가 언급되기 때문에 추가의 의미를 가진 Furthermore가 적절하다. (단, 본문의 there is는 주어가 an increasing number of people이므로 is가 아니라 are가 올바르다.)

어휘
contemporary 동시대의, 현대의 　　enthusiasm 열광
recognition 인정 　　　surly 무뚝뚝한, 뿌루퉁한
undoubtedly 의심할 여지없이 　　prestige 위신, 명성

---

14 어휘 > 반의어 찾기　　오답률 41%　답 ④

| 해석 | 수정의 전제 조건으로서, 수분 작용은 과일과 씨앗 작물의 생산에 필수적이며, 번식으로 식물을 개량시키기 위해 고안된 프로그램에서 중요

한 역할을 한다.
① 10% 중요한 　　　　② 20% 필수적인
③ 11% 필요한, 필수의 　　④ 59% 어디에나 있는, 편재하는

| 정답해설 | ④ 밑줄 친 essential은 '필수적인'의 의미로 crucial(중요한), indispensable(필수적인), requisite(필요한, 필수의)와 의미가 유사하다. 반면에 omnipresent에서 접두어 omni는 all(全)에 해당하는 표현으로 '어디에나 있는'이라는 뜻이므로 essential과는 의미가 다르다.

어휘
prerequisite 필수 요건, 전제 조건 　　fertilization 수정
pollination (식물) 수분 작용 　　　breed 새끼를 낳다, 번식하다

---

15 어휘 > 빈칸 완성　　오답률 15%　답 ④

| 해석 | Johnson 씨는 그 제안이 잘못된 원칙 위에 기반을 두었고 또한 때로는 불편했기 때문에 그것에 반대했다.
① 4% 흠 있는 – 바람직한 　　② 9% 긴요한 – 합리적인
③ 2% 순응하는 – 비참한, 비통한　④ 85% 잘못된 – 불편한

| 정답해설 | ④ 빈칸은 제안에 반대하는 이유에 해당하므로 모두 부정적인 형용사가 적합하다. 부정적인 의미의 형용사로만 짝지어진 것은 ④뿐이다.

---

16 문법 > 일치　　오답률 13%　답 ③

| 해석 | 나는 내가 충분한 옷을 가지고 있어서 기쁘다. 미국 남성들은 일반적으로 일본 남성들보다 몸집이 크기 때문에, 시카고에서는 나에게 맞는 옷을 찾기가 매우 어렵다. 일본에서는 중간 사이즈인 것이 여기에서는 작은 사이즈이다.

| 정답해설 | ③ 87% 주격 관계대명사 that의 선행사는 Chicago가 아니라 복수 명사인 clothes이기 때문에 동사는 복수 명사 주어에 맞는 fit이 되어야 한다.

| 오답해설 | ① 3% 감정형 분사인 pleased가 I의 감정 상태를 서술하고 있으므로 옳다.
② 4% 진주어 to find를 대신하는 가주어 it이 적절하게 사용되었다.
④ 6% 선행사를 포함한 관계대명사 What이 주어로 쓰인 옳은 문장이다.

오답률 TOP 2
17 문법 > 동사　　오답률 54%　답 ④

| 해석 | BBC에 의해 제작된 자연 다큐멘터리 Blue Planet II는 플라스틱이 바다에 영향을 미치는 정도를 보여 준 후 시청자들을 상심하게 두었다.

| 정답해설 | ④ 46% affect(영향을 미치다)는 타동사이기 때문에 뒤에 전치사 없이 바로 목적어가 와야 한다. 따라서 affects가 옳은 표현이다.

| 오답해설 | ① 12% produced 뒤에 by the BBC가 나오고, 의미상으로도 documentary는 '제작되는' 것이므로 수동의 의미를 갖는 과거분사의 수식을 받는 것이 옳다.
② 10% viewers(시청자들)가 '상심한' 것이므로 감정 상태를 나타

내는 과거분사형 형용사 heartbroken은 옳게 쓰였다.
③ 32% showing the extent와 plastic affects the ocean to the extent에서 중복되는 명사 the extent를 선행사로 삼아 이후의 문장을 목적격 관계대명사절로 바꾸어서 연결하고, 전치사 to를 목적격 관계대명사 앞으로 옮겨 「전치사 + 관계대명사」 형태로 to which를 쓴 것은 알맞다.

| 더 알아보기 | **자동사로 착각하기 쉬운 타동사**

- resemble ~와 닮다
- marry ~와 결혼하다
- approach ~에 접근하다
- nerve ~에 용기를 북돋우다
- contact ~와 접촉하다

어휘

heartbroken 슬픔에 잠긴, 상심한   extent 정도, 범위

---

18 독해 > Logical Reading > 문맥상 다양한 추론   답 ②
오답률 50%

| 해석 | 우리의 민주주의 제도가 가장 좋은 것이라고 믿는 것과 그것을 다른 나라에게 강요하는 것은 별개의 일이다. 이것은 독립 국가의 내정 불간섭이라는 UN의 정책의 노골적인 위반이다. 서양의 시민들이 그들의 정치 제도를 위해 싸웠듯이, 우리는 다른 국가의 시민들도 그들이 원한다면 똑같이 할 것이라고 믿어야 한다. 민주주의는 또한 절대적인 용어가 아니다. 나폴레옹은 오늘날 서아프리카와 동남아시아의 지도자들이 그러는 것처럼 그의 권력에 대한 장악을 합법화하기 위해 선거와 국민 투표를 이용했다. 부분적인 민주주의 국가들은 국내에서의 질서를 유지하는 것을 지나치게 걱정하는, 선거 없이 권력을 잡은 독재 정부보다 종종 더 공격적이다. 상이한 형태들의 민주주의는 어느 기준을 부과할지를 선택하는 것을 불가능하게 만든다. 미국과 유럽 국가들은 정부의 규제 그리고 합의와 대립 사이의 균형이라는 측면에서 모두 다르다.
① 남의 떡이 더 커 보인다.
② 한 사람의 음식이 다른 사람에게는 독이다.
③ 예외 없는 법칙은 없다.
④ 로마에 가면 로마법을 따른다.

| 정답해설 | ② 50% 주제문인 첫 문장에서 우리의 민주주의 제도가 가장 좋은 것이라고 믿는 것과 그것을 다른 나라에게 강요하는 것은 별개의 일이라고 한 다음, 민주주의 제도가 각 국가별로 좋게 혹은 나쁘게 적용된 사례를 예시하고 있으므로 똑같은 것이라도 사람마다, 혹은 상황별로 다르게 해석될 수 있다는 의미의 속담인 ②가 본문 내용과 가장 잘 어울린다.

어휘

impose (의견을) 강요하다; (의무·벌금 등을) 지우다, 부과하다
blatant 노골적인, 뻔한   breach 위반; 위반하다
non-intervention 불간섭주의, 불개입
affairs 사건, 일   institution 기관
referenda 국민 투표, 총선거   legitimize 정당화하다, 합법화하다
hold on power 권력 장악   partial 부분의, 편파적인
unelected 선거로 뽑지 않은, 선거 없이 권력을 잡은
dictatorship 독재 정부   in terms of ~에 관하여
restraint 규제   consensus 합의, 의견 일치
confrontation 대립

---

19 어휘 > 빈칸 완성   오답률 18%   답 ①

| 해석 | 나방과 나비는 둘 다 인시목(目)에 속하지만 이 두 개의 곤충 종류 사이에는 수많은 신체적 그리고 행동적 차이들이 있다. 행동적인 측면에서, 나방은 ① 야행성이고 나비는 주행성(낮 동안에 활동적인)이다. 쉬고 있을 때, 나비는 대개 그들의 날개를 뒤로 접는 반면에 나방은 그들의 날개를 몸통에 붙여 납작하게 하거나 "제트기" 자세로 날개를 활짝 펼친다.
① 82% 야행성의   ② 2% 합리적인
③ 6% 영원한   ④ 10% 반원의

| 정답해설 | ① 나비와 나방의 차이를 설명하는 글이다. 빈칸 뒤에 나비는 낮에 활동적이라고 하였으므로 나방은 이와 반대되는 야행성인 것을 유추할 수 있다. 따라서 정답은 nocturnal(야행성)이다.

어휘

moth 나방   order (동식물 분류상의) 목(目)
diurnal 낮에 활동적인   flatten 납작하게 하다
position 자세   nocturnal 야행성의
eternal 영원한   semi-circular 반원의

---

20 독해 > Reading for Writing > 빈칸 절 완성   오답률 24%   답 ③

| 해석 | 광대가 사람들을 겁준다는 생각은 미국에서 힘을 얻기 시작했다. 예를 들면, 사우스 캐롤라이나에서 사람들은 밤에 숲이나 도시에서 광대 옷을 입은 사람들이 종종 숨어 있는 것을 봤다고 신고했다. 몇몇 사람들은 광대가 빈 집이나 숲으로 아이들을 꾀어내려는 시도를 하고 있었다고 말했다. 곧, 아이들과 어른들 둘 다를 겁주려고 하는 위협적인 모습을 한 광대에 대한 신고가 있었다. 비록 대개 폭력 사건 신고는 없었고, 신고된 목격의 대다수가 후에 거짓으로 밝혀졌지만, 이것은 ③ 전국적인 공포를 일으켰다.
① 서커스 산업에 이득이 됐다
② 광고에 광대의 사용을 촉진시켰다
③ 전국적인 공포를 일으켰다
④ 행복한 광대의 완벽한 이미지를 형성했다

| 정답해설 | ③ 76% 광대가 사람들을 겁준다는 생각이 미국에서 힘을 얻기 시작했다는 빈칸 앞의 내용들로 보아 빈칸에는 광대에 대한 부정적인 이미지로 인한 부정적인 결과가 와야 한다. 따라서 빈칸에는 ③이 알맞다.

| 오답해설 | ①②④ 2% 13% 9% 모두 광대에 대한 긍정적인 이미지와 영향에 대한 것이므로 알맞지 않다.

어휘

clown 광대   frighten 겁주다, 겁먹게 하다
individual 개인; 개별의   lure 꾀어내다
threaten 위협하다   violence 폭력
sighting 목격   nationwide 전국적인
panic 공포

합격예상 체크

〈서울시 연도별 합격선〉

2018 기술직
합격기준!

2019 2018 2018 기술직 2017 2016

맞힌 개수	/20문항	점수	/100점

➡ ☐ 합격 ☐ 불합격

취약영역 체크

문항	정답	영역	문항	정답	영역
①	①	어휘 > 유의어 찾기	11	②	독해 > Logical Reading > 삽입
2	④	어휘 > 유의어 찾기	12	②	독해 > Logical Reading > 삭제
3	④	어휘 > 빈칸 완성	13	④	독해 > Logical Reading > 연결사
4	①	어휘 > 빈칸 완성	14	③	독해 > Reading for Writing > 빈칸 구 완성
5	①	문법 > 동사	15	③	독해 > Macro Reading > 제목
6	④	문법 > 동사	16	②	독해 > Macro Reading > 요지
7	②	문법 > 분사	17	③	독해 > Logical Reading > 문맥상 다양한 추론
8	④	생활영어 > 회화/관용표현	18	①	독해 > Reading for Writing > 빈칸 구 완성
9	②	독해 > Reading for Writing > 빈칸 구 완성	19	②	독해 > Micro Reading > 내용 일치/불일치
10	①	문법 > 가정법	20	③	독해 > Logical Reading > 배열

⬇ 영역별 틀린 개수로 취약영역을 확인하세요!

어휘	/4	문법	/4	독해	/11	생활영어	/1

➡ 나의 취약영역: _____

※ [정답해설]과 [오답해설] 선지의 50% 표시는 〈1초 합격예측 서비스〉를 통해 수집된 선지 선택률을 나타냅니다.

---

1 어휘 > 유의어 찾기 |오답률 23%| 답 ①

| 해석 | 윤리적 고려는 생명 공학 규제의 <u>필수적인</u> 요소가 될 수 있다.
① 77% 주요한, 중요한
② 8% 우연한, 부차적인, 간접적인
③ 13% 상호적인
④ 2% 인기 있는, 유명한

| 정답해설 | ① integral은 '필수의, 완전한'이라는 의미이다. key는 형용사일 때 '중요한, 주요한'이라는 뜻이므로 의미가 가장 가깝다.

어휘

ethical 윤리적인   biotechnology 생명 공학

---

2 어휘 > 유의어 찾기 |오답률 45%| 답 ④

| 해석 | 만일 언어와 관련된 뇌의 영역이 손상된다면, 그 뇌는 손실된 세포를 보충하기 위한 하나의 방법으로 본래는 언어와 관련이 없는 뇌의 다른 부분들이 그 기술[말하기 기술]을 배우도록 하는 <u>유연성</u>을 사용할지도 모른다.
① 6% 정확성   ② 28% 체계성, 조직성
③ 11% 방해물, 장애물   ④ 55% 유순함, 유연함

| 정답해설 | ④ plasticity는 '유연성, 적응성'이라는 의미로 이와 유사한 의미를 지닌 어휘는 suppleness이다.

어휘

make up for ~을 보충하다, 만회하다

---

3 어휘 > 빈칸 완성 |오답률 27%| 답 ④

| 해석 | 메피스토는 서명과 계약을 요구한다. 단지 ④ <u>구두로만</u> 하는 계약은 진행되지 않을 것이다. 파우스트가 언급한 대로, 악마는 모든 것을 서면으로 원한다.
① 8% 진짜의, 진실된
② 8% 필수의, 본질적인
③ 11% 상호 간의; 상응하는; 보답의, 보복의
④ 73% 구두의, 말의

| 정답해설 | ④ 빈칸 앞뒤 문장에서 메피스토(=악마)는 서명과 계약을 요구하며 모든 것을 서면으로 하기를 원한다고 했다. 빈칸 문장의 맨 앞에 부정어 No가 제시되었기 때문에 빈칸에는 서면과 반대되는 어휘인 verbal이 들어가야 문맥이 자연스러워진다.

---

4 어휘 > 빈칸 완성 |오답률 50%| 답 ①

| 해석 | 회사와 노조는 양측이 비우호적인 사업 환경 속에서 회사의 ① <u>악화되는</u> 영업 이익을 심각하게 받아들였기 때문에 올해의 임금 협상에서 잠정적인 합의에 도달했다.
① 50% 악화되는   ② 31% 향상되는, 강화되는
③ 9% 개선되는, 좋아지는   ④ 10% 균일화된, 평등화된

| 정답해설 | ① 주어진 문장은 임금 협상에 대한 합의에 도달하는 결과에 따른 원인을 빈칸으로 서술하고 있다. 즉 빈칸 이전의 접속사 as가 문맥상 '~때문에'라고 해석되므로, 이후의 문장에는 임금

협상 합의에 이르게 한 원인이 제시되어야 한다. 따라서 빈칸에는 문맥상 '악화되는' 영업이익을 심각하게 받아들여 회사와 노조가 합의에 도달했다고 서술하는 것이 적절하다. 따라서 빈칸에 가장 적절한 것은 deteriorating이다.

어휘

operating profit 영업 이익
amid ~의 가운데에, ~이 한창일 때에

---

5 | 문법 > 동사 | 오답률 47% | 답 ①

| 해석 | 나는 처음부터 호박 케이크를 만드는 것이 (믹스) 상자로부터 케이크를 만드는 것보다 훨씬 쉬울 것이라고 확신했다.

| 정답해설 | ① 53% convince는 4형식으로 「convince + 사람(대상) + that ~」의 형태로 사용될 수 있다. 주어진 문장은 convince가 목적어 없이 바로 that절을 취했으므로 옳지 않으며, 밑줄 친 convinced는 '(주어)가 ~라고 설득되다'라는 의미로 수동형인 was convinced로 수정되어야 한다.

| 오답해설 | ② 18% from scratch는 '처음부터'라는 의미를 지닌다.
③ 21% even은 비교급을 강조하는 부사로 알맞게 쓰였다. much, even, far, still, a lot은 비교급을 강조한다.
④ 8% than 뒤의 making이 앞에 나온 that 뒤의 making과 병렬 구조를 이루며 올바르게 쓰였다.

| 더 알아보기 | 비교급/최상급 강조 부사

- 비교급 수식: still, a lot, much, even, (by) far
- 최상급 수식: much, very, (by) far

---

6 | 문법 > 동사 | 오답률 8% | 답 ④

| 해석 | 당신이 6살짜리 딸에게 TV에서 광고된 놀이공원에 왜 갈 수 없는지 설명할 이유를 찾으며 당신의 혀가 꼬이는 것을 깨닫게 될 때, 당신은 왜 우리가 기다리는 것을 어렵다고 생각하는지 이해할 것이다.

| 정답해설 | ④ 92% 의문사 why가 이끄는 절의 동사 find는 5형식으로 사용되었는데 가목적어 it이 있으므로 진목적어로 to부정사가 나와야 한다. 따라서 wait는 to wait가 되는 것이 적절하다.

| 오답해설 | ① 3% find가 5형식으로 사용되었는데 목적어인 tongue와 목적격 보어인 twisted가 수동의 관계이기 때문에 과거분사 형태로 알맞게 쓰였다.
② 2% six years old가 명사를 수식할 경우 six-year-old처럼 year를 단수형으로 쓰는 것이 옳다.
③ 3% 선행사 amusement park를 수식하는 형용사절을 이끄는 주격 관계대명사 that은 올바르게 쓰였다.

---

7 | 문법 > 분사 | 오답률 48% | 답 ②

| 해석 | 작은 회사의 소유자이면서 건설 현장 감독이었던 Lewis Alfred Ellison은, 호퍼에 실리던 도중에 떨어진 100파운드 무게의 얼음 덩어리에서 떨어져 나온 파편 조각이 그의 복부를 관통한 후에 입은 내상을 치료하는 수술 후 1916년에 사망했다.

| 정답해설 | ② 52% suffer는 '(상해를) 입다'라는 뜻의 타동사이다. suffer의 수식을 받는 명사 wounds는 suffer와 수동의 관계이므로 suffering은 과거분사인 suffered가 되어야 한다.

| 오답해설 | ① 7% 단수 명사 foreman을 한정하므로 a가 적절하다. 원래 동일인의 두 가지 직업을 나타낼 때 관사는 앞에 나오는 명사 앞에 한 번만 사용하는 것이 일반적이나, 각각의 직업을 강조하는 경우에는 별도로 표시해 주기도 한다.
③ 28% shards가 주어이고, penetrated가 동사로 알맞게 사용되었다.
④ 13% while it was loaded into a hopper가 분사구문으로 바뀐 것이다.

어휘

foreman 현장 주임[감독]	wound 부상
shard 파편	penetrate 관통하다
abdomen 복부, 배	load A into B A를 B에 싣다

---

8 | 생활영어 > 회화/관용표현 | 오답률 38% | 답 ④

| 해석 | A: 너는 중고차에 대해 잘 모르는구나, Ned. 휴! 70,000마일이야.
B: 오, 그게 많은 마일이구나! 우리는 엔진, 문, 타이어, 모든 것을 자세히 봐야 해.
A: 너무 비싸, Ned. ④ 나는 바가지를 쓰고 싶지 않아.
B: 너는 중고차 판매원들을 잘 지켜봐야 해.
① 그것을 사자.
② 나는 먼지를 털 거야.
③ 너는 무슨 모델을 원하니?
④ 나는 바가지를 쓰고 싶지 않아.

| 정답해설 | ④ 62% 중고차에 대하여 대화를 나누고 있다. A가 너무 비싸다고 이야기했으므로 바로 뒤의 빈칸에 적절한 것은 ④뿐이다. rip off는 '바가지를 씌우다'라는 의미이다.

---

9 | 독해 > Reading for Writing > 빈칸 구 완성 | 오답률 53% | 답 ②

| 해석 | 그 용어는 두 개의 개념을 결합시킨다. 생체 공학적인 팔처럼, 살아 있는 것에 인공적인 능력을 주는 것을 의미하는 "생체 공학", 그리고 살아 있는 것을 그것의 새로운 능력으로 가득 채우는 데 사용될 수 있는 100나노미터보다 작은 입자들을 ② 지칭하는 "나노"가 그것이다.
① 침입하다
② ~을 언급하다, 지칭하다
③ ~로부터 유래하다
④ (여정 중에 잠깐) 들르다, 머물다

| 정답해설 | ② 47% and 뒤는 "nano"가 100나노미터보다 작은 입자들이라고 설명하는 부분이므로 nano = particles라는 관계가 성립하도록 '언급하다, 지칭하다'라는 뜻의 refer to가 빈칸에 들어가는 것이 적절하다.

어휘

combine 결합하다　　　　　　　　capability 능력, 재능
particle 입자
imbue A with B A를 B로 가득 채우다[주입시키다]

오답률 TOP 2

| **10** | 문법 > 가정법 | 오답률 64% | 답 ① |

| 해석 | ① 만일 그 물건이 내일까지 배달되지 않는다면, 그들은 이것에 대하여 불평할 것이다.
② 그는 반에서 다른 어떤 야구 선수보다 더 능숙했다.
③ 그 바이올리니스트가 그의 연주를 끝내자마자 청중들은 일어나서 박수를 쳤다.
④ 제빵업자들은 밀 소비 장려를 요구하며 밖으로 나오도록 요구되어 왔다.

| 정답해설 | ① 36% 가정법 미래가 적절하게 쓰였는지 묻고 있다. 가정법 미래에서 if절은 「If + 주어 + should + 동사원형」이며, 주절의 형태는 다양하게 가능하다.

| 오답해설 | ② 31% 비교급을 이용한 최상급 표현이 적절하게 쓰였는지에 대해 묻고 있다. any other 뒤에는 단수 명사가 와야 하므로 any other baseball player로 고쳐야 한다.
③ 17% '~하자마자 …했다'는 「Hardly[Scarcely] + had + 주어 + 과거분사 ~ before[when] + 주어 + 과거 동사 …」로 표현한다. 따라서 Hardly has the violinist finished는 Hardly had the violinist finished가 되어야 한다.
④ 16% make가 사역동사일 때 수동태가 적절하게 쓰였는지에 대해 묻고 있다. make가 수동태가 되는 경우에 목적격 보어로 쓰였던 원형부정사는 준동사라는 것을 표현하기 위해 앞에 to를 붙여 주어야 한다. 따라서 Bakers have been made to come out ~의 형태가 되어야 한다.

| **11** | 독해 > Logical Reading > 삽입 | 오답률 58% | 답 ② |

| 해석 | 동물들은 그들이 건강하고 먹을 것이 충분하기만 하면 행복하다. 누구나 인간도 그래야 한다고 느끼지만, 현대 세계에서 그들은 적어도 대다수의 경우에 그렇지 않다. ② 만일 당신이 스스로 행복하지 않다면, 당신도 아마 이 점에서 예외적이지 않다는 것을 인정할 준비가 되어야 할 것이다. 만일 당신이 행복하다면, 당신의 친구들 중 몇 명이나 그러한지 자문해 보아라. 그리고 당신이 친구들을 관찰할 때 표정을 읽는 기술을 스스로 터득해라. 당신이 일상에서 만나는 사람들의 기분을 잘 받아들이도록 하라.

| 정답해설 | ② 42% ② 앞은 인간이 행복하지 않다는 내용이고 ② 뒤는 행복하다고 가정하는 경우가 나온다. 주어진 문장은 행복하지 않다고 가정하는 내용이므로 인간이 행복하지 않다고 주장한 내용 뒤, 그리고 행복하다고 가정하는 문장 앞에 오는 것이 적절하다. 따라서 주어진 문장은 ②에 오는 것이 알맞다.

어휘

receptive 잘 받아들이는, 수용하는

| **12** | 독해 > Logical Reading > 삭제 | 오답률 35% | 답 ② |

| 해석 | 담배 제품에 대한 더 엄격한 규제는 술, 탄산음료 및 기타 소비자 제품들로 번져 갔고, 그것은 고객의 선택을 제한하여 제품값이 더 비싸지게 했다. 국가들은 지난 40년 동안 과세, 그림을 이용한 유해 경고, 광고 및 홍보 금지를 포함하여 담배 제품에 반대하는 더 제한적인 조치를 취해 왔다. ② 규제 조치는 대중의 건강을 개선하지 못했고, 담배 밀수를 증가시켰다. 규제를 우선 담배에, 그리고 다른 소비자 제품들에 적용하는 것은 도미노 효과를 냈고, 다른 산업에서는 소위 "파멸에 이르는 길"을 만들어 냈다. 파멸에 이르는 길의 맨 끝에는 평범한 포장이 있는데, 여기서는 모든 상표와 로고, 브랜드 특유의 색깔이 사라졌고, 의도치 않은 결과와 지적 재산권의 심각한 침해를 초래했다.

| 정답해설 | ② 65% 주어진 글은 담배 산업에 대한 엄격한 규제가 다른 산업에 도미노처럼 영향을 미쳤다고 서술하고 있다. ①, ③, ④는 규제 조치에 대한 내용을 서술하고 있으나 ②는 규제 조치로 인한 부정적 영향을 서술하고 있으므로 흐름상 적절하지 않다. 따라서 정답은 ②이다.

어휘

tight 엄격한　　　　　　　　　　restrictive 제한하는, 한정적인
taxation 과세, 세금　　　　　　　pictorial 그림을 이용한, 그림의
regulatory 규제의, 단속의　　　　smuggling 밀수
a[the] slippery slope 파멸[전락]에 이르는 길
unintended 의도하지 않은　　　　infringement 위반, 침해
property right 재산권

| **13** | 독해 > Logical Reading > 연결사 | 오답률 61% | 답 ④ |

| 해석 | 한 언어를 사용하는 화자가 다른 언어를 사용하는 화자들과 접촉하게 될 때 언어는 변한다. 이것은 이주 때문일 수도 있다. 어쩌면 그들이 더 비옥한 땅으로 이주를 했기 때문에, 혹은 전쟁이나 가난, 질병으로 인해 쫓겨나기 때문일 수도 있다. 그것은 또한 그들이 침략당하기 때문일 수도 있다. 상황에 따라, 고국의 언어는 침략자의 언어에 의해 완전히 소멸할지도 모르는데, 우리는 이 경우에 대체에 대해 말한다. ④ 그 대신에, 고국의 언어는 침략자의 언어와 나란히 존속할 수도 있고 정치적인 상황에 따라 그것은 지배적인 언어가 될 수도 있다.
① 일반적으로, 전형적으로, 대체로
② 시종일관하여, 지속적으로
③ 비슷하게, 유사하게
④ 그 대신에, 선택적으로

| 정답해설 | ④ 39% 빈칸 전후 문장은 고국이 침략당했을 때 언어에 벌어지는 일을 나열하고 있다. 빈칸 이전에는 침략을 당하는 경우에 고국의 언어가 침입자의 언어로 대체될 수도 있다고 하고, 빈칸 뒤의 문장에서는 고국의 언어가 침략자의 언어와 공존하거나 지배적인 언어가 될 수도 있다고 언급하고 있다. 빈칸을 기준으로 대조되는 내용이기 때문에 연결사는 Alternatively가 들어가는 것이 가장 적절하다.

| 더 알아보기 | 대조·양보를 불러오는 연결사

• alternatively 그 대신에	• however 그러나
• unlike ~와 달리	• although 비록 ~일지라도
• nevertheless 그럼에도 불구하고	• in spite of ~임에도 불구하고
• on the other hand 반면에	

come into contact 접촉하다, 마주치다

migration 이주, 이동 　　　　　fertile 비옥한

displace 쫓아내다, 추방하다 　　　on account of ~ 때문에

invade 침략하다, 침입하다 　　　succumb 죽다, 양보하다

persist 존속하다, 지속하다 　　　side-by-side 나란히

dominant 지배적인, 우위의

---

14 독해 > Reading for Writing > 빈칸 구 완성　오답률 46%　답 ③

| 해석 | 상표를 붙이지 않고 테스트된 제품이 다소 더 객관적으로 평가된다는 개념은 완전히 ③ 잘못 인식된 것이다. 실제 세계에서 우리가 눈을 감고 코를 잡은 채로 어떤 것들을 평가할 수 없는 것처럼 우리는 우리가 구입하는 제품에 찍혀진 상표, 그것이 담긴 상자의 외형과 느낌, 요구되는 가격을 무시한 채로 평가할 수는 없다.

① 정확한 　　　　　　　　② 믿을 만한

③ 잘못 인식된 　　　　　　④ 편견 없는, 공정한

| 정답해설 | ③ 54% 빈칸 뒤의 문장에서 우리는 실제 세계에서 상표와 제품의 포장, 가격 등을 무시한 채 상품을 평가할 수 없다고 했으므로 상표를 붙이지 않고 테스트된 제품이 객관적으로 평가된다는 개념은 '잘못된' 것이라는 내용이 자연스럽다. 선지 중 이러한 의미를 나타낼 수 있는 것은 ③이다.

somehow 어쨌든 　　　　　　objectively 객관적으로

appraise 평가하다, 감정하다 　　entirely 완전히, 전적으로

---

15 독해 > Macro Reading > 제목　오답률 12%　답 ③

| 해석 | 미국에 가는 많은 방문객들은 미국인들은 운동과 여가 활동을 너무 진지하게 받아들인다고 생각한다. 미국인들은 마치 사업상 약속 일정을 잡는 것처럼 취미 활동 일정을 잡는다. 그들은 매일 같은 시간에 조깅을 하러 가거나, 일주일에 두세 번 테니스를 치거나, 매주 목요일마다 수영을 한다. 외국인들은 이러한 종류의 취미 활동은 휴식보다 일처럼 들린다고 생각한다. 그러나 많은 미국인들에게 그들의 취미 활동은 휴식이고 즐겁고 적어도 그럴 만한 가치가 있는데, 왜냐하면 그것들은 건강과 체력에 기여하기 때문이다.

① 건강과 운동

② 미국의 인기 있는 취미 활동들

③ 취미 활동에 대한 미국인들의 접근법

④ 취미 활동의 정의

| 정답해설 | ③ 88% 취미 활동을 진지하게 받아들이는 미국인들의 입장과 이를 바라보는 외국인들의 시선에 관한 글이므로 ③이 제목으로 가장 알맞다.

---

16 독해 > Macro Reading > 요지　오답률 50%　답 ③

| 해석 | 고통이나 기쁨, 또는 그 사이의 몇몇 속성에 대한 감정은 우리 마음의 기반이다. 우리는 종종 이 단순한 현실을 인지하는 것에 실패하는데, 이것이 우리를 둘러싼 사물과 사건에 대한 정신적인 이미지가 그것들을 묘사하는 단어와 문장의 이미지와 함께 우리의 과도한 관심을 아주 많이 소모시키기 때문이다. 그러나 그것들은 거기에 있고, 수많은 감정과 그와 관련된 상태, 지속적인 우리의 마음의 음악적인 노래가사, 우리가 잠을 때 사라지는 그만둘 수 없는 가장 보편적인 멜로디의 콧노래, 우리가 기쁨에 사로

잡혔을 때 완전히 노래로 변하는 콧노래, 혹은 슬픔이 장악할 때의 추모곡이다.

① 감정은 음악과 밀접하게 관련이 있다

② 감정은 고통과 기쁨으로 이루어진다.

③ 감정은 우리의 마음속 어디에나 존재한다.

④ 감정은 사물과 사건에 대한 정신적인 이미지와 관련되어 있다.

| 정답해설 | ③ 50% 우리를 둘러싼 사물과 사건에 대해 느끼는 수많은 감정을 음악적 상태와 비유하여 설명한 글이므로 ③이 요지로 가장 적절하다.

| 오답해설 | ① 23% 우리의 마음을 음악과 비유해서 설명했을 뿐 전체적인 요지로 보기에는 무리가 있다.

② 8% 고통이나 기쁨, 또는 그 사이의 몇몇 속성에 대한 감정이 우리 마음의 기반이라고 언급하였으나, 감정을 구성하는 종류를 지문의 요지로 볼 수 없다.

④ 19% 본문에 나온 어구 the mental images of objects and events를 이용한 오답으로 본문 내용과 관련이 없다.

bedrock 기반; 근본 원리 　　　myriad 무수한, 수많은

humming 콧노래 　　　　　　all-out 전력을 다한, 전면적인

requiem 진혼곡 　　　　　　take over 장악하다

---

17 독해 > Logical Reading > 문맥상 다양한 추론　오답률 7%　답 ③

| 해석 | 나는 게임에 참여하기를 바라면서, 동네의 학교 운동장에 간다. 그러나 거기에는 아무도 없다. 그물이 없는 농구 골대 아래에서 낙담한 채 모두 어디에 있는지 궁금해하며 근처에서 몇 분을 멍하니 서 있다가, 나를 기다리고 있을 것이라고 예상했던 사람들의 이름이 내 마음을 채우기 시작한다. 나는 수년 동안 이곳과 같은 장소에서 경기를 하지 않았다. 대체 그게 뭐였지? 나는 여기에 오면서 무슨 생각을 했던 것일까? 내가 어린아이, 소년이었을 때, 나는 놀기 위해 학교 운동장에 갔다. 그건 오래 전이었다. 여기에 있는 아이들은 알지도 못할 것이다. 내 주변의 콘크리트는 자갈들과 병들, 그리고 포장도로 밖으로 무서운 소음을 내면서, 내가 발길질을 하는 맥주 캔을 제외하고는 텅 비어 있다.

① 차분하고 평화로운 　　　　② 흥겹고 행복한

③ 황량하고 외로운 　　　　　④ 끔찍하고 무서운

| 정답해설 | ③ 93% 필자는 자신이 소년일 때 놀았던 운동장에 갔지만 아무도 없었고 콘크리트 위에는 자갈과 병, 맥주 캔만이 있을 뿐이다. 따라서 글의 분위기로 가장 적절한 것은 ③이다.

deject 낙담시키다, 풀이 죽게 하다　　claw 할퀴다

---

18 독해 > Reading for Writing > 빈칸 구 완성　오답률 65%　답 ①

| 해석 | 종종 전형적인 "가난뱅이에서 부자가 된" 이야기에서 묘사된 것처럼, 강철왕 Andrew Carnegie의 이야기는 1835년 Scotland의 Dunfermline에 있는 작은 원룸에서 시작된다. 빈곤한 노동자 가정에서 태어난 Carnegie는 그의 가족이 1848년에 미국으로 이주하기 전에는 학교 교육을 거의 받지 못했다. Pennsylvania주에 도착하자 그는 곧 직물 공장에서 일을 얻었고 거기에서 그는 1주에 겨우 1달러 20센트를 벌었다.

① 전형적인 - 빈곤한

② 예외적인 – 독실한
③ 흥미로운 – 꼼꼼한
④ 해로운 – 빈곤한

| 정답해설 | ① [35%] 선지 중 가난뱅이에서 부자가 되는 이야기의 성격으로 적당한 것은 quintessential(전형적인)과 interesting(흥미로운)이다. 두 번째 빈칸에서는 그의 가족에 대해 묘사하고 있는 것으로, 학교 교육도 거의 받지 못했다고 했으므로 destitute(빈곤한)나 impoverished(빈곤한, 헐벗은)가 알맞다.

어휘

rags to riches 가난뱅이에서 부자가 된, 출세한

steel magnate 철강왕　　　　　textile mill 직물 공장

19　독해 > Micro Reading > 내용일치/불일치　[오답률 49%]　답 ②

| 해석 | 이전에 멕시코 북부였던 미국의 남서부에서, Anglo-America는 Hispanic America와 충돌했다. 그 만남은 언어, 종교, 인종, 경제 그리고 정치 변수들과 관련되었다. Hispanic America와 Anglo-America의 경계는 시간이 지남에 따라 변화했으나 한 가지 사실은 변하지 않았다. 2개의 통치 권역 사이에 임의적인 지리적 경계를 그리는 것과 사람들을 설득하여 그것을 존중하게 하는 것은 별개의 이야기라는 것이다. 1848년 멕시코-미국 전쟁에서 승리하여 미국은 멕시코의 절반을 차지했다. 그 결과로 초래된 분열은 어떠한 자연의 계획도 승인하지 않았다. 국경 지방들은 생태학적으로 한 덩어리였다. 즉, 멕시코 북동부 사막은 미국의 남동부 사막에 민족주의의 형상화 없이 섞이게 되었다. 자연이 제공한 하나의 경계인 Rio Grande강은 그 사이를 흐르는 강이었지만, 실제로 연속적인 지형을 나눠 놓지는 않았다.
① 미국과 멕시코의 국경 지방은 긴 하나의 통치권 역사를 의미한다.
② 자연은 경계선을 그리지 않는 반면에, 인간 사회는 확실히 그렇게 했다.
③ 멕시코-미국 전쟁은 사람들이 국경을 존중하는 것을 가능하게 만들었다.
④ Rio Grande강은 임의의 지리학적인 경계로 여겨져 왔다.

| 정답해설 | ② [51%] 인간은 전쟁을 통해 국경이라는 임의적인 경계를 만들었지만, 멕시코와 미국의 국경 지방은 생태적으로 한 덩어리였다고 하면서 그 예로 멕시코 북동부 사막과 미국 남동부의 사막이 섞였고 Rio Grande강 또한 지형을 나누지 않고 두 나라를 흐른다고 했으므로 자연은 어떤 경계를 임의로 만들지 않아왔음을 알 수 있다. 따라서 ②가 본문 내용과 일치한다.

어휘

run into ~와 충돌하다, 우연히 만나다

border 국경, 경계　　　　　arbitrary 임의의, 제멋대로인

sphere 영역, 분야, 범위　　　sovereignty 주권, 영유권, 통치권

ratify 승인하다; 비준하다　　borderland 국경 지방, 경계지

prefigure 형상화하다, 예시하다, 예상하다

terrain 지형, 지세, 지역

오답률 TOP3

20　독해 > Logical Reading > 배열　[오답률 62%]　답 ③

| 해석 | ㉣ 난폭 운전은 너무 가깝게 따라가기, 과속, 안전하지 않은 차선 변경, 차선을 변경하려는 신호를 보내지 않기, 그리고 다른 형태의 부주의하거나 성급한 운전과 같은 하나의 교통 위반이나 복합적인 위반이다.
㉠ 공격적인 운전자의 도화선이 되는 것은 대개 거의 맞추기 불가능한 일정과 맞물리는 교통 혼잡이다.
㉢ 그 결과, 공격적인 운전자는 일반적으로 시간을 보충하려는 시도로 여러

개의 위반을 저지른다.
㉡ 불행하게도, 이러한 행동들은 우리들 모두를 위험에 빠뜨린다. 예를 들면, 지나가기 위해 도로 갓길을 사용하는 것에 의지하는 공격적인 운전자는 다른 운전자들을 깜짝 놀라게 하고 그들이 더 큰 위험이나 심지어 충돌을 유발하는 종잡을 수 없는 행동을 하게 한다.

| 정답해설 | ③ [38%] 난폭 운전을 하는 공격적인 운전자에 대한 설명글이다. ㉣은 난폭 운전의 정의와 예에 대해 나열하고 있으므로 가장 먼저 위치해야 한다. ㉣ 뒤에는 난폭 운전의 계기가 혼잡한 교통 속에서 일정을 맞춰야 하는 것이라는 ㉠이 이어지는 것이 알맞다. As a result로 시작되는 ㉢이 ㉠의 결과이므로 ㉢은 ㉠ 뒤에 온다. 마지막으로, 난폭 운전의 결과에 대해 서술하는 ㉡이 오는 것이 적절하다.

| 더 알아보기 | 인과 관계 연결어(구)

• therefore 그러므로	• thus 따라서
• as a result 결과적으로	• consequently 그 결과
• accordingly 따라서	

어휘

trigger (총포의) 방아쇠; (분쟁의) 계기, 도화선

aggressive 공격적인　　　　　　congestion 혼잡

couple with ~와 연결하다　　　　resort to ~에 의지하다

shoulder (도로의) 갓길　　　　　startle 깜짝 놀라게 하다

evasive 종잡을 수 없는; 회피적인　crash 충돌; 충돌하다

violation 위반　　　　　　　　　traffic offense 교통 위반

combination 조합　　　　　　　　negligent 태만한; 부주의한

inconsiderate 배려심 없는; 경솔한, 성급한

합격예상 체크

〈서울시 연도별 합격선〉

2017 합격기준

| 2019 | 2018 | 2018 기술직 | 2017 | 2016 |

| 맞힌 개수 | /20문항 | 점수 | /100점 |

➡ □ 합격 □ 불합격

취약영역 체크

문항	정답	영역	문항	정답	영역
1	②	어휘 > 빈칸 완성	11	③	어휘 > 빈칸 완성
2	②	어휘 > 빈칸 완성	12	②	독해 > Macro Reading > 주제
3	④	문법 > 분사	13	②	어휘 > 빈칸 완성
4	③	문법 > 동사	14	④	독해 > Logical Reading > 삽입
5	④	생활영어 > 회화/관용표현	15	④	독해 > Micro Reading > 내용 일치/불일치
6	①	독해 > Reading for Writing > 빈칸 구 완성	16	①	독해 > Macro Reading > 제목
7	①	어휘 > 유의어 찾기	17	④	독해 > Logical Reading > 배열
8	②	어휘 > 유의어 찾기	18	①	독해 > Logical Reading > 연결사
9	④	문법 > 일치	19	③	어휘 > 빈칸 완성
10	③	문법 > 분사	20	①	독해 > Reading for Writing > 빈칸 절 완성

⬇ 영역별 틀린 개수로 취약영역을 확인하세요!

| 어휘 | /7 | 문법 | /4 | 독해 | /8 | 생활영어 | /1 |

➡ 나의 취약영역: _____

※ [정답해설]과 [오답해설] 선지의 50% 표시는 〈1초 합격예측 서비스〉를 통해 수집된 선지 선택률을 나타냅니다.

오답률 TOP 2

1 어휘 > 빈칸 완성 오답률 58% 답 ②

| 해석 | 계속해서 우리는 한때 좋은 의미로 쓰였으나, 지금은 호의적이지 않은 의미로 쓰이는 단어들을 우연히 발견한다. 18세기 후반까지 이 단어는 남을 돕기 좋아하는, 우호적인, 매우 예의 바른, 친절한 의미로 사용되었다. 그러나 요즘 ② 참견 잘하는 사람은 그/그녀에게 속하지 않는 일에 참견하느라 바쁜 불청객을 의미한다.

① 17% 비굴한, 굽신거리는 ② 42% 참견 잘하는, 주제넘게 나서는
③ 24% 사교적인 ④ 17% 아부하는, 알랑거리는

| 정답해설 | ② 빈칸에 들어갈 단어는 자신과 관련 없는 일에 참견하느라 바쁜 사람을 의미하므로, officious가 가장 적절하다.

| 더 알아보기 | officious의 유의어

- self-important 자만심이 강한
- self-assertive 주제넘은, 자기 주장하는
- bumptious 잘난 체하는, 건방진
- condescending 거들먹거리는, 잘난 체하는

어휘

light on 우연히 발견하다
serviceable 친절한, 남을 돕기 좋아하는; 쓸모있는, 유용한
courteous 예의 바른, 공손한 obliging 친절한, 남을 잘 돕는
meddler 간섭[참견]하려는 사람

오답률 TOP 1

2 어휘 > 빈칸 완성 오답률 64% 답 ②

| 해석 | 암모니아나 식초의 희미한 냄새는 (생후) 일주일 된 아기들이 얼굴을 찡그리고 그들의 ② 고개를 돌리게 만든다.
① 21% 마구를 채우다 ② 36% 피하다, (고개를) 돌리다
③ 30% (소리를) 죽이다 ④ 13% (감정·기억을) 환기시키다

| 정답해설 | ② 빈칸 뒤에 나오는 목적어 their heads와 얼굴을 찡그렸다는 부분을 고려했을 때, 식초 냄새가 아기들이 고개를 돌리게 만든다는 내용이 자연스럽다. 따라서 avert가 가장 적절하다.

어휘

faint 희미한 odor 악취
grimace 얼굴을 찡그리다

3 문법 > 분사 오답률 20% 답 ④

| 해석 | 서유럽 최초의 카페는 무역 혹은 상업의 중심지가 아니라 옥스퍼드 대학 도시에서 문을 열었는데, 그곳에서 Jacob이라는 이름을 가진 레바논 남성이 1650년에 가게를 차렸다.

| 정답해설 | ④ 80% name은 '이름을 지어 주다, 명명하다'라는 의미의 타동사이다. 따라서 a Lebanese man은 Jacob이라는 '이름이 붙여지는' 것이므로 man (who was) named Jacob이 되어야 한다.

어휘

set up shop 사업을 시작하다, 가게를 내다

| **해석** | ① John은 그의 방을 청소할 것이라고 Mary에게 약속했다.
② John은 Mary에게 일찍 떠날 것이라고 말했다.
③ John은 Mary가 행복할 것이라고 믿었다.
④ John은 Mary에게 그녀가 그곳에 일찍 도착해야 한다는 점을 상기시켰다.

| **정답해설** | ③ 54% believe는 간접목적어를 취할 수 없으므로 John believed that Mary would be happy.로 고쳐야 한다. 「believe + 목적어 + 목적격 보어」의 5형식 형태로도 쓸 수 있는데, 이 경우에는 John believed Mary to be happy.라고 해야 한다.

| **해석** | A: 미스터 김, 제가 오늘 점심을 사는 게 어떨까요?
B: ④ 그럴 수 있다면 좋겠지만 저는 오늘 다른 약속이 있어요.
① 아뇨, 저는 아니에요. 그 시간이 저한테는 좋을 것 같아요
② 좋아요, 잊지 않도록 제 달력에 적어 둘게요
③ 네. 월요일에 다시 의논할게요
④ 그럴 수 있다면 좋겠지만 저는 오늘 다른 약속이 있어요

| **정답해설** | ④ 85% A는 B에게 오늘 점심 식사를 자신이 사겠다고 제안하고 있으므로, 빈칸에는 수락 또는 거절하는 응답이 와야 한다. ④는 A의 제안을 거절하는 내용으로 대화의 흐름에 적절하다.

| **오답해설** | ② 12% 달력에 적어 두겠다는 것은 오늘 일이 아니라 나중 일에 대한 제안의 대답으로 어울린다.

어휘
treat (식사를) 대접하다, 한턱 내다   commitment 약속

| **해석** | 수세기 동안, 해가 지고 나서 하늘을 바라보는 사람들은 수천 개의 선명하고 반짝이는 별들을 볼 수 있었다. 그러나 요즘은, 당신이 만약 북두칠성을 볼 수 있다면 운이 좋을 것이다. 가정집과 가로등에서 쏟아져 나오는 전기 불빛이 원인인데, 그 불빛의 밝음이 밤하늘을 흐리게 만든다. 미국에서는, 소위 광공해가 너무 심해져서, 한 추정치에 따르면, 오늘날 태어나는 아이들 10명 중 8명은 그들이 은하수를 볼 수 있을 정도의 충분히 어두운 하늘을 만날 수 없다고 한다. 하지만, 세상의 가장 어두운 장소에서 별을 관찰하는 것에 집중하는, 작지만 성장하는 산업들인 천문관광의 형태에 희망이 있다. 그중 다수가 국립공원에 있는데 이렇게 멀리 떨어진 장소들은 불과 야영지 비용으로 경관을 제공한다. 그리고 그것들을 운영하는 사람들은 종종 그 주변 지역 사회에서 광공해를 줄이기 위해 노력한다. 비록 천문관광은 일부 휴가들만큼 호화롭지 않을지라도 관광객들은 개의치 않는 듯하다.
① 어두운 – 비록 ~일지라도   ② 밝은 – ~이기 때문에
③ 어두운 – ~이기 때문에   ④ 밝은 – ~하다는 점에서

| **정답해설** | ① 58% 가정집과 가로등에서 나오는 전기 불빛으로 인해 발생하는 광공해 때문에, 어두운 밤하늘에서 선명한 별들을 제대로 보기가 어렵다고 말하고 있다. 그러므로 첫 번째 빈칸에는 dark를 넣어 은하수를 볼 수 있을 정도로 충분히 '어두운' 밤하늘을 만날 수 없다고 하는 것이 문맥의 흐름에 적절하다. 두 번째 빈칸에는 천문관광이 일부 휴가들만큼 호화스럽지는 않다는 내용과 '관광객들이 개의치 않는다'는 내용을 이어줄 수 있는 접속사를 찾아야

하는데 반대되는 내용이므로 역접 연결사나 양보 연결사가 필요하다. 따라서 Although가 가장 적절하다.

어휘
sunset 해 질 녘, 일몰   vibrant 진동하는; (색깔이) 선명한
the Big Dipper 북두칠성   culprit 범인, 원인
obscure 흐리게[어둡게] 만들다; 가리다
center on ~에 집중하다, 초점을 맞추다
astrotourism 천문관광
stargaze 별을 관찰하다, 별을 바라보다
surrounding 인근의, 주위의

| **해석** | 지도력과 힘은 불가분하게 한데 엮여 있다. 우리는 강한 사람들을 지도자로 보는데, 그들이 우리 그룹에게 닥친 위협으로부터 우리를 보호할 수 있기 때문이다.
① 90% 분리할 수 없이   ② 6% 생기 없이
③ 3% 헛되게, 무력하게   ④ 1% 경솔하게

| **정답해설** | ① '불가분하게'라는 뜻을 지닌 inextricably와 유의어 관계에 있는 것은 inseparably이다.

어휘
threat 위협, 위험

| **해석** | 신중함은 오랫동안 세워졌던 정부가 가볍고 일시적인 원인들 때문에 변해서는 안 된다는 점을 확실히 지시할 것이다.
① 21% 투명한, 명백한   ② 65% 순간적인
③ 2% 기억할 만한   ④ 12% 중요한

| **정답해설** | ② transient는 '일시적인, 순간적인'이라는 의미로 momentary와 유의어 관계에 있다.

| **더 알아보기** | transient의 유의어

• momentary 순간적인	• temporary 일시적인
• transitory 일시적인	• impermanent 일시적인

어휘
prudence 신중함, 사리분별   indeed 정말, 확실히
dictate 받아쓰게 하다; 지시[명령]하다

| **해석** | 대학교에의 입학을 할당하는 것에 있어서의 정당성이 대학교들이 철저히 추구하는 재화(재산)와 관련이 있다는 생각은 입학증을 판매하는 것이 왜 부당한지를 설명해 준다.

| **정답해설** | ④ 76% 주어는 The idea이기 때문에 동사 explain을 단수형인 explains로 바꿔야 한다.

| **더 알아보기** | 주어-동사 수 일치

뒤에서 명사를 수식할 수 있는 것에는 전명구, 분사구, to부정사구, 관계사절, 동격의 that절이 있는데, 구와 절로 명사의 수식을 받더라도 주어 역할을 하는 명사를 찾아낼 수 있어야 한다.

어휘

allocate 할당하다	access 접근, 입장
have something to do with ~와 관련이 있다	
goods 재화, 재산	properly (구어) 철저히, 매우
admission 가입, 입장, 입학	

---

10 문법 > 분사 　　　　오답률 15%　답 ③

| 해석 | 이상하게 보일지 모르지만, 사하라 사막은 한때 아프리카 평원과 관련된 종류의 동물의 삶을 지탱하는 광활한 초원이었다.

| 정답해설 | ③ 85% 의미상 동물의 삶을 '지탱하는' 초원이라는 흐름이 되어야 하므로, 능동의 의미를 가진 현재분사 supporting이 옳다.

어휘

expanse 넓은 공간	associate with ~와 관련시키다

오답률 TOP3

11 어휘 > 빈칸 완성 　　　　오답률 47%　답 ③

| 해석 | A: 당신은 우리가 대출을 받을 수 있을 것이라고 생각하세요?
B: 음, 상황에 따라 다르죠. 다른 재산을 소유하고 계세요? 주식이나 채권 같은?
A: 아니요.
B: 그렇군요. 그러면 당신은 어떤 ③ 담보물도 가지고 있지 않군요. 아마 당신을 위해 대출에 서명해 줄 사람인 보증인을 구해야 할 수도 있을 거예요.

① 40% 조사　　　　② 1% 동물들
③ 53% 담보물　　　④ 6% 영감, 자극

| 정답해설 | ③ 대화에서 B는 A에게 대출을 받을 때 필요한 주식이나 채권 같은 다른 재산의 소유 여부를 묻는다. 이에 A가 없다고 대답하자, B는 '빈칸'이 없으니 보증인이 필요하다고 했다. 따라서 빈칸에 알맞은 것은 '담보(물)'을 의미하는 collateral이다.

어휘

property 재산	stock 주식
bond 채권	loan 대출

---

12 독해 > Macro Reading > 주제 　　　　오답률 18%　답 ②

| 해석 | 1782년, 독립전쟁 동안 유럽으로 돌아가기 이전에 뉴욕에 정착했던 프랑스 이민자 J. Hector St. John De Crèvecoeur는 북아메리카 대륙의 영국 식민지에서의 삶에 대한 일련의 수필, 『Letters from an American Farmer』를 출간했다. 그 책은 영국, 프랑스, 미국에서 즉각적인 성공을 거두었다. 책의 가장 유명한 구절 중 하나에서, Crèvecoeur는 다른 배경과 나라에서 온 사람들이 식민지에서의 경험에 의해 변화하는 과정을 묘사하고, "그렇다면, 미국인은 누구인가?"라고 묻는다. 미국에서, Crèvecoeur는 "모든 국가의 사람들이 하나의 새로운 인종으로 융합되어, 그들의 노동과 후손들이 언젠가 세계에서 큰 변화를 일으킬 것이다."라고 제시한다. Crèvecoeur는 "melting pot"이라고 불려지게 된 미국에 대한 유명한 개념을 처음으로 개발한 사람들 중 한 명이다.
① Crèvecoeur의 책은 영국에서 즉각적인 성공작이 되었다.
② Crèvecoeur는 그의 책에서 'melting pot'의 개념을 발전시켰다.
③ Crèvecoeur는 미국의 개인주의에 대해 묘사하고 논했다.
④ Crèvecoeur는 그의 책에서 미국인들의 출신지를 설명했다.

| 정답해설 | ② 82% Crèvecoeur는 북미의 영국 식민지에서의 삶에 대한 수필을 썼고 그 책 속에서 미국인들의 정체성을 melting pot 이라는 개념으로 처음으로 설명하고 이 개념을 개발한 사람들 중 한 명이라고 했으므로 ②가 주제로 가장 알맞다.

어휘

immigrant 이민자	a series of 일련의, 시리즈의
posterity 후세, 후대; 자손, 후손	

---

13 어휘 > 빈칸 완성 　　　　오답률 35%　답 ②

| 해석 | 한국과 이집트와 같은 몇몇의 문화에서, 예의의 규범은 누군가 먹을 것이나 마실 것을 제안받으면, 처음에는 그 제안이 거절되어야 한다는 것을 요구한다. 하지만, 특히 거절에 대한 ② 이유가 만들어지지 않을 경우에는, 그와 같은 거절은 종종 다른 문화권에서 누군가의 환대에 대한 거절과 배려심이 없는 것으로 보이기도 한다. 예를 들어, 미국인과 캐나다인은 거절은 합당한 ② 이유가 동반될 것이라고 예상한다.

① 4% 역할　　　　② 65% 변명, 이유
③ 16% 선택　　　④ 15% 상황

| 정답해설 | ② '이것' 없이 거절하는 것은 몇몇 문화권에서 누군가의 환대를 거절하는 것, 배려심이 없는 것으로 비춰질 수 있다고 했다. 또한 거절을 할 경우에 합당한 '이것'이 필요하다고 했으므로 선지 중 가장 적절한 것은 excuse(변명, 이유)이다.

어휘

norm 규범, 기준	the first time around 처음에는
hospitality 환대	be accompanied by ~을 동반하다

---

14 독해 > Logical Reading > 삽입 　　　　오답률 13%　답 ④

| 해석 | 직업 만족도와 생산성 간에는 분명한 연관성이 존재한다. 하지만, 직업 만족도는 또한 조직의 서비스 문화에 따라 달라지기도 한다. 이러한 문화는 일을 특징적으로 만들고, 그곳에서 일하는 사람들이 그렇게 하도록 자긍심을 느끼게 만들어 주는 점들을 포함한다. "일하기 좋은 상위 10개의 기업"의 피고용자들이 *Fortune* 잡지로부터 왜 그들이 이 기업들을 위해 일하는 것을 사랑하는지에 대한 질문을 받았을 때, 그들이 임금, 보상 제도, 혹은 더 높은 직위로의 승진에 대해 언급하지 않았다는 점은 주목할 만했다. ④ 대신, 이 피고용자들은 우선 직장의 인간 관계의 진정성에 대해 이야기했는데, 즉 그들의 직장 문화는 마치 가정의 연장선처럼 느껴졌고, 그들의 동료들은 지원을 아끼지 않았다는 것이었다.

| 정답해설 | ④ 87% 주어진 문장의 these employees가 가리키는 것은 employees of the Top 10 Best Companies to Work For에 해당되며, 또한 ③ 이후의 문장에서 고용자들이 '자신의 회사에서 일하는 것이 왜 좋은지 질문'에 대한 대답으로 '임금, 보상 제도, 혹은 승진을 언급하지 않았다'고 서술하고 있다. 따라서 이후에는 앞선 질문에 대한 추가적인 대답으로 '임금, 보상 제도 등 대신에 인간관계의 진정성이 자신의 회사가 좋은 이유'라고 제시되는 것이 문맥상 적절하다. 따라서 주어진 문장이 들어갈 가장 적절한 곳은 ④이다.

어휘

organizatioin 조직, 단체	distinctive 특징적인, 특이한; 뚜렷한
notable 주목할 만한	scheme 계획, 설계

| 해석 | 그 많은 장소들 중 왜 Orkney일까? 어떻게 스코틀랜드의 북단에서 떨어져 나온 이 드문드문 흩어져 있는 섬들이 그토록 기술적, 문화적, 정신적 강국이 될 수 있었을까? 우선 첫째로, 당신은 Orkney가 멀리 있다는 생각을 그만둬야 한다. 역사의 대부분 동안, Orkney는 중요한 해상 중심지였고, 모든 곳으로 통하는 장소였다. 그곳은 또한 멕시코 만류 영향의 덕택으로, 영국에서 가장 비옥한 농토 중 일부와 놀랍도록 온화한 기후로 축복받았다.

① Orkney 사람들은 수많은 사회적, 자연적 난관들을 극복해야만 했다.
② 그 지역은 궁극적으로 그곳의 문명의 종말을 이끌었던 반란의 중심지 중 한 곳이었다.
③ 본토로부터 너무 멀었기 때문에 Orkney는 자원을 최대한으로 이용하지 않았다.
④ Orkney의 번영은 대체로 그곳의 지리학적 이점과 천연 자원 덕택이다.

| 정답해설 | ④ ｜91%｜ Orkney는 기술적, 문화적, 정신적 강국인데, 멕시코 만류의 영향으로 비옥한 농토와 온화한 기후로 축복받았다고 했으므로 ④가 본문 내용과 일치한다.

어휘

spiritual 정신적인, 영적인	powerhouse 유력 기관, 강국; 발전소
for starters 우선, 먼저	maritime 바다의, 해양의
Gulf Stream 멕시코 만류	rebellion 반란, 반역
annihilation 전멸, 소멸	
make the best of ~을 최대한 이용하다	

| 해석 | 초기에, 파피루스와 양피지는 본문의 방향에 따라서 수직으로 혹은 수평으로 펼칠 수 있는 두루마리로 보관되었다. 수평 형태가 더 흔했고, 두루마리가 꽤 길어질 수도 있었기 때문에, 서기는 보통 한 줄을 전체 길이에 걸쳐 쓰는 것을 삼갔고, 대신 적당한 너비의 열을 표시하곤 했다. 그러한 방식으로 독자는 읽는 동안 한 방향으로 펼 수도 있었고, 다른 방향으로 말 수도 있었다. 그럼에도 불구하고, 두루마리를 다시 말아야 하는, 끊임없이 계속되는 필요성은 이러한 형식에 있어서 주요 단점이었고, 우리가 책의 특정 페이지로 바로 건너뛰는 방식대로 두루마리에서 다른 곳으로 넘어가는 것이 불가능했다. 게다가, 독자는 두루마리를 계속 펼쳐 두기 위해 양손(혹은 무거운 것)이 필요했기 때문에 읽는 도중에 간신히 필기를 했다.

① 두루마리의 불편함
② 책의 발전
③ 쓰기와 읽기의 발전
④ 두루마리의 단점을 극복하는 방법들

| 정답해설 | ① ｜86%｜ 글의 초반부에는 파피루스와 양피지의 보관 형태인 두루마리의 특징을 서술하고 있으며 Nevertheless 이후에는 두루마리를 다시 말아야 하고, 특정 페이지로 건너 뛰어 읽을 수 없고, 두루마리를 읽기 위해 양손을 사용해야 하는 등 두루마리를 사용하는 것의 불편함을 연속해서 서술하고 있다. 따라서 글의 제목으로 가장 적절한 것은 ①이다.

| 오답해설 | ④ ｜12%｜ 두루마리의 단점이 언급되었으나 그것을 극복하는 방법에 대해서는 나와 있지 않다.

어휘

parchment 양피지	scroll 두루마리
scribe 서기, 대서인	mark off 구별하다, 표시하다

struggle to V 간신히 ~하다; ~하기 위해 고군분투하다

| 해석 | ⓔ 2013년에, 위험할 정도로 높은 수준의 오염으로 인한 베이징의 비상 사태는 낮은 가시성으로 인해 항공사가 어쩔 수 없이 비행을 취소시켜야 하는, 교통 체계의 혼란을 낳았다.
ⓒ 학교와 회사는 문을 닫았고, 베이징시 정부는 사람들에게 집 안에 머무르고, 공기 청정기를 작동시키며, 실내 활동을 줄이고, 가능한 한 비활동적인 상태를 유지하라고 경고했다.
ⓐ 눈물이 흐르고 따가운 눈, 지끈거리는 두통, 부비강 문제와 가려운 목구멍으로 고통받는 수백만 명의 사람들은 공기 여과기와 마스크를 찾아 가게를 샅샅이 뒤짐으로써 심신을 쇠약하게 하는 공기로부터 피신했다.
ⓑ 중국 거주민들의 분노와 세계 언론의 조사는 강제로 정부가 국가의 대기 오염의 문제에 대처하게 만들었다.

| 정답해설 | ④ ｜71%｜ 베이징의 대기 오염 문제를 언급한 ⓔ이 글의 도입부로 가장 적절하며, 이에 대한 베이징 시 정부의 상황 대처를 설명하는 ⓒ으로 이어지는 것이 적절하다. 다음으로 시민들의 증상을 설명하는 ⓐ이 오고, 이로 인한 자국민의 분노와 세계 언론의 압박이 중국 정부로 하여금 대기 오염 문제에 대처하게 만들었다는 ⓑ으로 글을 마무리 짓는 것이 문맥상 자연스럽다. 따라서 ⓔ - ⓒ - ⓐ - ⓑ의 순서가 알맞다.

어휘

stinging 찌르는, 쏘는	sinus 부비강
itchy 가려운	debilitate 심신을 쇠약하게 하다
scour 샅샅이 뒤지다	scrutiny 정밀 조사
impel 강제로 ~하게 하다	address 대처하다; 검토하다

| 해석 | 소설과 로맨스 둘 다 다수의 등장인물들이 있는 상상력이 풍부한 허구의 작업물이지만, 유사성은 그게 전부이다. 소설은 현실적이지만 로맨스는 그렇지 않다. 19세기에, 로맨스는 상징적이고, 상상력이 풍부하고, 비현실적인 방법으로 주제와 등장인물을 다루는 허구의 이야기를 했던 산문이었다. ① 전형적으로, 로맨스는 이국적이고 시공간이 독자들로부터 멀리 떨어진, 그리고 확실히 가공으로 만들어진 줄거리와 인물들을 다룬다.

① 전형적으로　　　② 반면에
③ 그럼에도 불구하고　　④ 어떤 경우에

| 정답해설 | ① ｜54%｜ 앞 문장에서 19세기 로맨스의 특징을 말하고, 뒷문장에서 로맨스의 전형적인 특징을 설명하고 있으므로 빈칸에는 Typically가 가장 적절하다. (단, 본문 다섯 번째 줄의 dealt with는 목적어가 뒤따라 오므로 과거분사 대신 dealing with가 더욱 자연스러운 표현이다.)

어휘

fictioin 허구, 소설	prose 산문
narrative 이야기, 서술	exotic 이국적인, 이색적인

| 해석 | 정의는 특히 아이들에게 ③ 도움이 되지 않는다. 자주 인용되는 1987년 연구가 있는데, 그 연구에서 5학년들은 사전적인 정의를 제공받았고, 정의된 그 단어들을 사용하여 그들 고유의 문장을 작문하도록 요청받았

다. 그 결과는 실망스러웠다. erode라는 단어를 받은 한 아이는 "우리 가족은 많이 침식시킨다(erode)."라고 적었다. 주어진 정의가 "eat out(외식하다), eat away(먹어치우다)"였기 때문이었다.

① 11% 이익이 되는   ② 6% 무례한
③ 79% 도움이 되지 않는   ④ 4% 잊기 쉬운

| **정답해설** | ③ 예시로 제시된 1987년 연구에 따르면, 한 아이는 erode의 사전적 정의를 받았지만 주어진 정의가 잘못되어 있어 그 단어를 포함하는 문장을 엉뚱하게 작문했다. 이를 통해 정의는 아이들에게 도움이 되지 않음을 알 수 있으므로 빈칸에는 unhelpful이 적절하다.

어휘

oft-cited 자주 인용되는(oft-often)

---

20   독해 > Reading for Writing > 빈칸 절 완성   오답률 25%   답 ①

| **해석** | 현대의 은행 업무는 고대 영국에 그 기원을 둔다. 그 당시에 그들의 금을 안전하게 지키기를 원했던 사람들에게는 두 가지 선택 사항이 있었다. 그것을 매트리스 아래에 숨기거나 안전한 보관을 위해 다른 사람에게 맡기는 것이었다. 보관을 위해 의지할 만큼 논리에 맞는 사람들은 지역 금세공인들이었는데, 그들이 가장 튼튼한 금고를 소유하고 있었기 때문이었다. 금세공인들은 금의 보관을 받아들였고, 후일에 그 금이 현금으로 교환될 수 있음을 명시하는 영수증을 주인에게 주었다. 상환일이 되면, 그 주인은 금세공인에게 가서, 금의 일부를 돈으로 교환받았고, 그것을 수취인에게 주었다. 그러고 나서, 그 수취인은 뒤돌아 안전한 보관을 위해 다시 금세공인에게로 돌아가 금을 맡겼을 가능성이 크다. 점차적으로, 물리적으로 금을 교환하기 위해 시간과 노력을 들이는 대신에, 사업가들은 ① 금세공인들의 영수증을 대금처럼 교환하기 시작했다.

① 금세공인들의 영수증을 대금처럼 교환하기 시작했다
② 이러한 제도에서 잠재적인 수익을 보았다
③ 그들의 금을 현금으로 교환하지 말라고 예금자들에게 경고했다
④ 수수료를 받고 다른 사람에게 금을 빌려주었다

| **정답해설** | ① 75% 빈칸에는 금을 교환하기 위해 시간과 노력을 들이는 대신에 할 수 있는 유사 은행 업무 행위를 제시해야 한다. 직접적이고 물리적인 교환 대신에 제시할 수 있는 방법은 선지 중 영수증을 대금처럼 교환하는 방법이 가장 적절하다.

어휘

turn A over to B B에게 A를 맡기다   safekeeping 안전한 보관
vault 금고   redeem 현금으로 교환하다
payee 수취인, 수령인   arrangement 제도; 장치; 타협, 조정
depositor 예금자

합격예상 체크

〈서울시 연도별 합격선〉

| 맞힌 개수 | /20문항 | 점수 | /100점 |

➡ □ 합격　□ 불합격

취약영역 체크

문항	정답	영역	문항	정답	영역
1	③	어휘 > 유의어 찾기	11	②	독해 > Logical Reading > 연결사
2	④	어휘 > 유의어 찾기	12	④	독해 > Reading for Writing > 빈칸 구 완성
3	①	어휘 > 유의어 찾기	13	②	독해 > Reading for Writing > 빈칸 구 완성
4	①	문법 > 일치	14	③	독해 > Reading for Writing > 빈칸 구 완성
5	③	문법 > 동사	15	③	독해 > Reading for Writing > 빈칸 구 완성
6	①	문법 > 일치	16	①	독해 > Reading for Writing > 빈칸 구 완성
7	④	문법 > 강조와 도치	17	③	독해 > Macro Reading > 주장
8	②	어휘 > 빈칸 완성	18	④	독해 > Logical Reading > 배열
9	①	독해 > Reading for Writing > 빈칸 구 완성	19	③	독해 > Logical Reading > 문맥상 다양한 추론
10	④	독해 > Reading for Writing > 빈칸 구 완성	20	②	독해 > Reading for Writing > 빈칸 절 완성

⬇ 영역별 틀린 개수로 취약영역을 확인하세요!

| 어휘 | /4 | 문법 | /4 | 독해 | /12 | 생활영어 | /0 |

➡ 나의 취약영역: _____

※ [정답해설]과 [오답해설] 선지의 50% 표시는 〈1초 합격예측 서비스〉를 통해 수집된 선지 선택률을 나타냅니다.

1　어휘 > 유의어 찾기　오답률 19%　답 ③

| 해석 | 부모들은 반항적으로 행동하거나, 사회적으로 서툴러 보이는 자녀를 포기해서는 안 된다. 이것은 대부분의 젊은이들이 경험하다가 나이가 들면서 결국 벗어나는 일반적인 단계이기 때문이다.
① 12% 수동적인　② 5% 정신 착란의, 매우 흥분한
③ 81% 반항적인, 복종하지 않는　④ 2% 산발적인, 드문드문한

| 정답해설 | ③ rebellious는 '반항적인'이라는 의미로 disobedient와 유사한 뜻을 가지고 있다.

어휘

awkward 어색한, 거북한, 서투른
outgrow 나이가 들면서 벗어나다; 자라서 못 입게 되다

2　어휘 > 유의어 찾기　오답률 30%　답 ④

| 해석 | 그는 1800년대에 New York의 부유한 가정에서 태어났다. 이러한 환경은 그가 그의 삶 중 많은 시간 동안 사치하는 생활을 누리도록 해 주었다.
① 12% 위증(죄)　② 6% 불안정한
③ 12% 치명적인, 유해한　④ 70% 사치하는, 낭비하는

| 정답해설 | ④ prodigal은 '사치하는, 낭비하는'의 의미로 lavish와 유사한 의미를 가지고 있다.

어휘

existence 생활 (양식), 생활상

오답률 TOP 1
3　어휘 > 유의어 찾기　오답률 60%　답 ①

| 해석 | 아마도 당시 미국의 고등 교육 상황에서 가장 밝은 부분은 학생들을 교정을 넘어 시민 생활에 관여시키는 것에 대한 관심의 부활이다.
① 40% 부활, 재개, 복귀, 회복　② 4% 실종, 소실
③ 46% 자극, 동기 부여　④ 10% 소량, 결핍, 부족

| 정답해설 | ① resurgence는 '부활, 재기'의 의미로 comeback과 유사한 의미를 가진다.

4　문법 > 일치　오답률 18%　답 ①

| 해석 | 그는 많은 한국인들이 1940년대에 일부 지역에서 혹독한 환경 하에 노동을 강요받았다는 것을 인정했다.

| 정답해설 | ① 82% that절의 주어는 the number of Koreans인데 동사인 were와 수가 일치하지 않는다. 문맥상 '한국인들의 수'가 강요를 받은 게 아니라 '많은 한국인들'이 강요를 받았다고 하는 것이 적절하므로 the number of를 a number of로 바꾸어야 한다.

| 오답해설 | ② 9% '~을 강요받다'는 be forced into로 표현한다.
③ 2% under harsh conditions는 '혹독한 환경 하에'라는 의미로 옳은 표현이다.
④ 7% during은 특정 기간과 함께 쓰이는 전치사로 특정 기간인 1940년대를 나타내므로 적절하다.

| 더 알아보기 | during vs. for

- during + 특정 기간[the/소유격/지시형용사 + 명사]
- for + 불특정 기간[기수 + 가산명사]

오답률 TOP 3

5 문법 > 동사 | 오답률 47% | 답 ③

| 해석 | Ann: 네 머리 스타일 괜찮네.
Tori: 카페테리아 옆에 새로 생긴 미용실에서 키 큰 헤어디자이너한테 자른 거야.
Ann: 내 머리가 드라이어에 끼었던 그 미용실은 아니지?
Tori: 아마 거기일 걸. 그래, 거기야.
Ann: 허, 아직도 영업을 하네.

| 정답해설 | ③ 53% 「get + 목적어 + 목적격 보어」의 형태에서 목적어 my head와 목적격 보어 stick이 수동 관계이므로 to stick을 stuck으로 변경하여야 옳다. 또한 해석상 드라이어에 머리가 끼는 것이 아니라 머리카락이 끼는 것이므로 head를 hair로 변경하여야 옳다.

| 오답해설 | ① 0% 불완전자동사인 look은 보어로 형용사를 취할 수 있다.

② 28% 사역동사 have는 목적어와 목적격 보어의 관계가 수동 관계일 때 목적격 보어를 과거분사로 취할 수 있으므로 옳은 문장이다.

④ 19% 「주어 + must be + 보어」는 '주어가 보어임에 틀림없다'로 무언가 확신할 때 쓰는 말이다. 보어는 Ann이 말한 그 헤어 살롱을 말한 것이기에 생략된 것이다.

| 더 알아보기 | 준사역동사의 문장 구조

help	+ 목적어 +	원형부정사/to부정사	~이 …하는 것을 돕다
get		to부정사/현재분사	~이 …하도록 하다
		과거분사	~이 …을 당하다

6 문법 > 일치 | 오답률 46% | 답 ①

| 해석 | 창의력은 독창적이고 실용적이며 의미 있는 문제 해결로 이끌거나 예술적 표현에 대한 새로운 생각이나 형식을 만들어 내는 방식으로의 사고이다.

| 정답해설 | ① 54% 선행사 ways를 수식하는 관계대명사절이 or에 의해 병렬 구조를 이루어야 하는 문장이다. 따라서 빈칸에는 that lead ~와 병렬 구조를 이루도록 that generate ~가 와야 한다.

7 문법 > 강조와 도치 | 오답률 30% | 답 ④

| 해석 | 내가 옳은 일을 했다는 것을 알았던 것은 바로 민주당원뿐만 아니라 공화당원들로부터도 정치적으로 전반에 걸쳐 지지를 받았을 때였다.

| 정답해설 | ④ 70% 「It + be동사 ~ that」 강조 용법이다. 「It + be동사」와 that 사이에는 강조하고 싶은 문장 요소가 들어가는데, 여기서는 부사절 when I got ~ Democrats가 들어갔다.

어휘
across the board 전반에 걸쳐, 전면적으로

8 어휘 > 빈칸 완성 | 오답률 8% | 답 ②

| 해석 | 대개 몇 마리의 스컹크가 모여 살지만, 성체가 된 수컷 줄무늬 스컹크들은 여름 동안 ② 혼자 있다.

① 4% 야행성의
② 92% 혼자의
③ 2% 약탈하는
④ 2% 잠자는, 휴면 중인

| 정답해설 | ② 역접 연결사 however로 연결되어 있으므로 빈칸에는 앞 절의 live together와 반대의 의미를 가진 solitary(혼자의, 고립의)가 적절하다.

9 독해 > Reading for Writing > 빈칸 구 완성 | 오답률 14% | 답 ①

| 해석 | 언어와 철자는 변한다. 영어권에서 가장 다작하는 작가 중 한 명인 Crystal은 그러한 진실을 많은 사람들에게 알리는 것을 도와 왔다. 만약, 인터넷 사용이 제안하는 것처럼, 사람들이 현재 "rhubarb"를 "rubarb"로 쓰기 시작하고 있다면, 그는, 그것이 언젠가 받아들여질 수 있는 ① 대체어가 될지도 모른다고 말한다.

① 대체하는 것, 대안
② 의무, 책무
③ 위험
④ 질서; 순서

| 정답해설 | ① 86% rhubarb를 rubarb로 쓰기 시작하고 있다면 언젠가는 rubarb가 받아들여질 수도 있다고 말한다. 따라서 '대체하는 것, 대안'을 의미하는 alternative가 빈칸에 들어갈 단어로 적절하다.

어휘
prolific 다작의
popularize 많은 사람들에게 알리다, 대중화하다; 보급시키다

10 독해 > Reading for Writing > 빈칸 구 완성 | 오답률 43% | 답 ④

| 해석 | ④ 완전히 무자비한 전사로서의 Genghis Khan의 명성은 실제보다 더 안 좋은 것일 수 있다. 우리 정보의 많은 부분은 종종 사실을 과장하는 당대의 연대기 기록자들로부터 나온다. 그들은 몽골인들이 그들의 적들에게 더 무섭게 보이도록 몽골의 고용인들에 의해 잔인함에 관한 이야기들을 과장하도록 권고받았을 수 있다.

① 과장하는 이야기 작가
② 용기 있는 왕
③ 영향력 있는 인물
④ 완전히 무자비한 전사

| 정답해설 | ④ 57% 주어진 빈칸의 내용에는 Genghis Khan이 어떤 명성을 얻었는지에 대한 내용이 들어가야 한다. 이후의 서술을 통해서 '몽골인들이 Genghis Khan의 잔인함에 관한 이야기들을 과장하도록 권고받았을 수도 있다'라는 문장을 제시하였으므로, 빈칸에는 '잔인함'에 관련된 표현이 적절하다. 따라서 빈칸에 들어갈 말로 가장 적절한 것은 ④이다.

어휘
chronicler 연대기 기록자   exaggerate 과장하다
utterly 완전히, 철저히

11 독해 > Logical Reading > 연결사 | 오답률 11% | 답 ②

| 해석 | 우리의 뇌는 여러 종류의 정보를 다양한 방식으로 처리하고 저장

한다. 사실에 기반을 둔 지식을 생각해 보자. 사실 기억은 이름, 얼굴, 글자, 날짜와 같은 명확한 정보를 배우는 것을 수반한다. 그것은 우리의 의식적인 생각 그리고 상징과 언어를 조작하는 능력과 관련이 있다. 사실 기억이 장기 기억으로 넘겨지면, 그것들은 보통 그들이 알게 된 전후 사정에 따라 정리하여 보관된다. ② 예를 들어, 당신이 새 친구인 Joe에 대하여 생각할 때, 아마도 당신은 그를 만났던 농구 경기장에서의 그를 상상할 것이다.

① 요약하면   ② 예를 들어
③ 무엇보다도   ④ 게다가

| 정답해설 | ② 89% 빈칸 이후의 내용은 사실 기억이 장기 기억으로 전환되는 경우의 예시에 해당하므로 빈칸에는 For instance가 들어가야 한다.

어휘

factual 사실에 기반을 둔; 사실의   entail 수반하다
explicit 명확한   conscious 의식적인
manipulate 조작하다
commit (기록·기억 등을) 넘기다, 맡기다

---

12   독해 > Reading for Writing > 빈칸 구 완성   오답률 20%   답 ④

| 해석 | 믿을 수 없게 들리겠지만 자신의 둥지를 보호하기 위해서 스스로를 ④ 희생하려고 하는 일부 곤충 종들이 있다. 침입자와 직면했을 때, Borneo의 Camponotus cylindricus 개미는 침입자에게 달라붙어 그것이 터질 때까지 꽉 누를 것이다. 그 개미의 복부는 파열되고, 방어자와 공격자 둘 다에게 치명적일 끈적이는 노란 물질을 방출한다. 그것은 영구적으로 그들을 붙여 놓아 공격자가 그 둥지에 다가오지 못하도록 막는다.

① 저지르다   ② 대체하다
③ 노출시키다   ④ 희생하다

| 정답해설 | ④ 80% 침입자를 막기 위해서 침입자가 터질 때까지 꽉 누르고 자신의 복부가 파열되어 치명적인 물질이 방출함으로써, 침입자와 자신의 몸을 영구적으로 붙여 놓아 공격자가 둥지로 못 다가오게 하는 것은 스스로를 '희생하는' 일이다.

어휘

squeeze 쥐어짜다, 꽉 누르다   explode 폭발하다
abdomen 복부, 배   rupture 터지다, 파열하다

---

13   독해 > Reading for Writing > 빈칸 구 완성   오답률 21%   답 ②

| 해석 | E-폐기물(전자 폐기물)은 이전에 본 적 없던 규모로 생산되고 있다. 컴퓨터와 다른 전자 기기들은 소비자들이 유행을 따르기 위해 새로운 것을 살 수 밖에 없도록 하여 불과 몇 년 후에는 쓸모없어지게 된다. 그래서, 수천 만대의 컴퓨터, TV, 그리고 핸드폰들은 매년 버려진다.

① 효율적인 - 문서로 기록된
② 쓸모없는 - 버려지는
③ 매혹적인 - 재사용되는
④ 동일한 - 던져진

| 정답해설 | ② 79% E-폐기물이란 버려지는 전자 기기들을 말하는데, 소비자들이 유행을 따르려고 새로운 것을 산다면 몇 년 후에는 '쓸모없어져' '버려질' 것이다.

어휘

electronic equipment 전자 기기
keep up (유행에) 뒤떨어지지 않도록 따라가다
tens of millions of 수천 만의

---

14   독해 > Reading for Writing > 빈칸 구 완성   오답률 35%   답 ③

| 해석 | 최근 20년 동안 미국인들이 그들의 직장에서 보낸 시간의 양은 꾸준히 증가하고 있다. 매년 그 변화는 적은데, 약 9시간, 즉 추가로 하루를 더 근무하는 것보다 약간 많다. 해당 연도에는 그러한 적은 증가가 아마도 ③ 감지되지 못했을 것이다. 그러나 20년이 넘는 동안 축적된 증가는 상당하다.

① 눈부신   ② 취약한, 영향 받기 쉬운
③ 근소한, 감지할 수 없는 ④ 의무적인

| 정답해설 | ③ 65% 빈칸 앞에서는 매년 근무 시간 증가의 변화가 적다고 했지만, 빈칸 뒤에서는 20년이 넘는 동안 축적된 근무 시간 증가는 상당하다고 말하고 있다. 역접 연결사 But이 나오기 전에 나오는 빈칸 문장은 해당 연도 한 해의 근무 시간 증가, 즉 매년 9시간의 근무 시간이 늘어나는 것에 대한 평가이므로 '근소한, 감지할 수 없는'이라는 뜻의 imperceptible이 빈칸에 알맞다.

오답률 TOP 2
15   독해 > Reading for Writing > 빈칸 구 완성   오답률 51%   답 ③

| 해석 | 세계에서 가장 높은 범죄율을 가진 나라는 거주자 한 명당 1.5건의 범죄를 저지르는 Vatican City이다. 그러나 이러한 높은 비율은 약 840명 정도인 그 나라의 적은 인구 때문이다. 대부분 소매치기와 가게 털이로 이루어지는 범죄의 대다수는 외부인에 의해 저질러질 가능성이 있다. Vatican에는 범죄 사실 조회, 출입국 관리, 교황의 경호를 담당하는 130명의 특수 경찰력이 있다. Vatican City에는 재판 이전에 범죄자들을 가두어 놓는 몇 개의 유치장을 제외하고는 감옥이 없다. 범죄자들의 대부분은 이탈리아 법원에 의해 재판받는다.

① 조작되는 - 밀봉되는   ② 지배되는 - 기각되는
③ 저질러지는 - 재판받는 ④ 수행되는 - 집행되는

| 정답해설 | ③ 49% 첫 번째 빈칸이 포함된 문장의 주어는 crimes로 외부인에 의해 범죄가 '저질러진다'는 문맥이 적절하므로 첫번째 빈칸에 가장 적절한 단어는 commit((범죄를) 행하다)의 과거분사 형태인 committed이다. 또한 두번째 빈칸이 포함된 문장의 주어는 The majority of criminals로 범죄자의 대부분은 이탈리아 법원에 의해 '재판받는다'는 문맥이 적절하다. 따라서 두번째 빈칸에 가장 적절한 단어는 try(재판을 받다)의 과거 분사 형태인 tried이다.

어휘

ratio 비율   pick-pocketing 소매치기
shop-lifting 가게 털이, (가게에서 하는) 좀도둑질
border control 출입국 관리

---

16   독해 > Reading for Writing > 빈칸 구 완성   오답률 32%   답 ①

| 해석 | Albert Einstein의 일반 상대성 이론은 막 100주년을 맞을 참이며 그의 혁명적인 가설은 결함을 찾아내려는 수많은 전문가들의 시도에도 불구하고, 세월의 시련을 견뎌내고 있다. Einstein은 우주와 시간이라는 가장 기본적인 것들에 대한 우리의 사고 방식을 바꾸어 놓았다. 그리고 그것은 우리가 우주 그리고 블랙홀과 같은 가장 흥미로운 것이 우주에서 어떻게 작동하는지에 대해 눈을 뜨게 했다.

① 견디다 - 결함들   ② 저항하다 - 증거들
③ 버리다 - 예시들   ④ 낭비하다 - 위험성들

| 정답해설 | ① 68% 수많은 전문가들의 '결함'을 찾아내려는 시도에도 불구하고 세월의 시련을 '견뎌냈다'는 흐름이 가장 알맞다.

17 독해 > Macro Reading > 주장 　오답률 11%　답 ③

| 해석 | Casa Heiwa는 사람들이 몇몇 중요한 삶의 기술과 새로운 환경에서 사는 것에 대처하는 방법을 배울 수 있는 아파트 건물이다. 그 건물의 관리자들은 그 건물에 거주하는 아이들과 성인들에게 많은 프로그램들을 제공하는 서비스를 운영한다. 아이들을 위해 아침 7시부터 저녁 6시까지 운영하는 놀이방이 있다. 또한 컴퓨터 처리 과정과 영어 회화 과정을 포함하는 성인을 위한 교육 프로그램도 있다.
① 교육적인 프로그램의 필요성을 주장하기 위해
② 아파트 건물 관리 직원을 모집하기 위해
③ 프로그램에 아파트 거주민을 유치하기 위해
④ 생활 수준을 향상시키기 위한 방법들을 추천하기 위해

| 정답해설 | ③ 89% 이 글은 Casa Heiwa라는 아파트에서 진행되는 프로그램을 홍보하는 글이다. 따라서 이 글의 목적으로 적절한 것은 ③이다.

| 오답해설 | ① 1% 교육적인 프로그램은 이미 만들어져 있고 그것에 대한 홍보를 하고 있는 것이지 프로그램에 대한 필요성을 주장하는 것이 아니므로 적절하지 않다.
② 5% 직원 채용에 관한 언급은 없으므로 적절하지 않다.
④ 5% 거주민들에게 도움을 줄지도 모르는 프로그램을 만든 것은 맞지만, 이 글의 목적이 생활 수준을 향상시킬 수 있는 방법을 추천하기 위한 것이라고 볼 수 없으므로 적절하지 않다.

어휘
cope with ~에 대처하다　　　recruit 모집하다

18 독해 > Logical Reading > 배열 　오답률 11%　답 ④

| 해석 | ⓔ 1955년 12월 1일에 Rosa Parks는 Alabama의 Montgomery 시내에 있는 가게인 자신의 직장에서 집으로 가는 시내버스를 탔다.
ⓛ 당시 인종 차별법에 따르면, 아프리카계 미국인인 Rosa Parks는 버스의 뒷자리에 앉도록 요구받았다. 그녀는 백인 전용 구역을 침범했다는 이유로 비난받았고, 그 버스 기사는 그녀를 설득하여 법을 따르게 하려고 했다.
ⓒ 대신에, Rosa Parks는 자신의 태도와 자신의 좌석을 지켰다. 끝내, 그 버스 기사는 그녀에게 경찰을 부르겠다고 경고했다. Parks는 "그러세요, 그들에게 전화하세요."라고 대답했다.
ⓐ Rosa Parks는 체포되었고, 수감되었으며, 유죄를 선고받고 벌금형에 처해졌다. 그녀는 벌금 지불을 거절했다. 그녀의 경험은 382일 동안의 Montgomery 시내버스 탑승 거부 운동을 유발시켰다.

| 정답해설 | ④ 89% 사건의 흐름대로 순서를 맞추면 되는 문제이다. Rosa Parks가 버스를 탔던 일(ⓔ)이 제일 먼저 와야 하고, 그 다음은 백인 전용 구역을 침범했다는 이유로 비난을 받았음에도(ⓛ), 자신의 자리를 지켰던 일(ⓒ)이 순서대로 와야 한다. 그 결과로, Rosa Parks가 결국 체포되었는데, 이것을 계기로 Montgomery 시내버스 탑승 거부 운동이 발발되었다(ⓐ)는 이야기가 나와야 한다.

어휘
convict 유죄를 선고하다　　　fine 벌금을 과하다
boycott 불매 운동, (사용·탑승 등의) 거부 운동
segregation law 인종 차별법　　be accused of ~로 비난받다
encroach 침입하다; (권리를) 침해하다
mien 태도, 처신

19 독해 > Logical Reading > 문맥상 다양한 추론 　오답률 7%　답 ③

| 해석 | Ryan Cox가 미국 Indiana주의 패스트푸드 드라이브 스루에서 자신이 주문한 커피값을 지불하려고 기다리고 있을 때, 그는 그가 TV 뉴스쇼에서 봤던 어떤 것을 시도해 보기로 했고 그는 자기 차 뒤에 있는 운전자의 커피 주문에 대한 돈을 지불했다. 그 작은 행동이 그 젊은 Indianapolis의 기업가의 기분을 좋게 만들었고, 그래서 그는 그의 경험을 페이스북에 공유했다. 한 나이 많은 친구는 사람들의 커피값을 대신 내주는 것보다 Ryan이 그 돈을 학생들의 연체된 점심 급식비 전액 지불을 돕는 것을 제안했다. 그래서 Ryan은 그 다음 주에 그의 조카의 학생 식당을 방문해서 그가 일부 연체금을 지불할 수 있는지 물었고 100달러를 건넸다.
① 우울한　　　　　　　② 고요한, 조용한
③ 감동적인　　　　　　④ 지루한

| 정답해설 | ③ 93% 낯선 사람이 대신 지불해 준 커피를 마신 사업가가 학생들의 연체된 점심 급식비를 내줌으로써 선행이 다른 선행을 낳았다는 내용이므로 '감동적인'이 이 글의 분위기로 가장 어울린다.

| 더 알아보기 | 분위기를 나타내는 표현

- festive 축제 분위기의　　　　· gloomy 우울한
- peaceful 평화로운　　　　　· cheerful 유쾌한
- instructive 교훈적인　　　　· tragic 비극적인
- urgent 긴박한

어휘
delinquent 비행을 저지른; 체납의　hand over 건네다

20 독해 > Reading for Writing > 빈칸 절 완성 　오답률 28%　답 ②

| 해석 | 달은 많은 면에서 지구와 다르다. 우선, 달에는 알려진 생명체가 없다. 그리고 크기 면에서, 그것은 지구보다 훨씬 더 작다. 당신은 그 둘 다 같은 둥근 모양을 가지고 있다고 생각할지 모른다. 그러나 엄격히 말하면, 그것들은 똑같지 않다. 달은 거의 완벽한 구 모양이다. 그것의 지름은 어떠한 방향에서든 겨우 1% 정도만 다를 뿐이다. 천체가 더 빨리 돌면 돌수록, 그것은 적도 쪽으로 더 불룩해지고 양극 쪽으로는 평평해진다. ② 달이 지구보다 더 느리게 돌기 때문에 그것은 거의 더 구 모양이다.
① 그래서 달과 지구를 제외하고 회전하는 물체는 형태의 변화를 겪는다.
② 달이 지구보다 더 느리게 돌기 때문에 그것은 거의 더 구 모양이다.
③ 게다가, 달의 직경은 지난 100년 동안 변해 왔다.
④ 사실, 달의 구 모양은 그것의 밀도와 중력을 고려할 때 다소 뜻밖이다.

| 정답해설 | ② 72% 천체가 빨리 돌면 적도 쪽으로 더 불룩해지고 양극 쪽으로는 평평해진다고 했으므로 구 모양에서 멀어진다. 그런데 달은 지구와는 달리 거의 완벽한 구 모양이라고 했는데, 이 말은 바꾸어 말하면 달이 지구보다 느리게 돈다는 뜻이다.

어휘
spherical 구형의, 둥근　　　strictly speaking 엄격히 말하면
bulge 불룩하게 하다, 부풀리다　equator 적도
flatten 납작해지다

포기하고 싶어질 때
왜 시작했는지를 기억하라.

법원직

해설 &
기출분석 REPORT

법원직 기출 POINT

Point 1 출제 문항 수가 다른 직렬보다 많은 25문항이며 독해 비율이 평균 20 문항 내외이므로, 시간 안배가 주요 관건이다.

Point 2 도표 및 문맥상 흐름, 요약문의 이해 등 수능형과 동일한 문제 유형으로 기존의 국가직, 지방직, 서울시 출제 유형과는 차이가 있으므로 이 부분에 대한 유형별 접근법을 반드시 숙지해야 한다.

Point 3 문법 영역은 기출 문항 위주로 주요 출제포인트에 가장 중점을 두고 학습하는 것이 효율적이다.

2023년 법원직 시험 대비 전략

"시간 안배와 독해력이 관건"

Point 1 시간 안배가 중요하므로 독해 영역에서 짧은 시간에 정확하게 문제풀이하는 Reading Techniques에 대한 사전 학습 및 충분한 훈련이 필수이다.

Point 2 해당 직렬 기출문제에 대한 소재 파악과 문제 유형 이해, 그리고 다양한 모의고사를 통한 문제 풀이 감각 훈련 등이 반드시 후행되어야 한다.

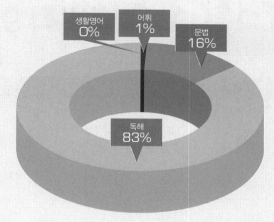

▲ 최근 7개년 평균 출제 비중

최근 7개년 출제 경향 및 출제 비중

연도	총평	어휘	문법	독해	생활영어
2022	**독해 비율 최대, 난이도 평이!** · 기존 출제 경향과 같이 독해 비율이 80% 이상에 해당 · 다양한 소재가 출제되어 문제 유형별 접근법뿐만 아니라 소재에 대한 폭넓은 이해가 사전에 대비되었다면 용이하였음	0% (0문항)	20% (5문항)	80% (20문항)	0% (0문항)
2021	**독해와 문법으로 승부** · 독해와 문법 문항으로 출제되니 시간 안배를 하면서 25문항을 빠르게 풀어 나가는 것이 관건임 · 수능에 가까운 독해 유형으로, 이에 적합한 문제풀이 전략이 반드시 필요함	0% (0문항)	16% (4문항)	84% (21문항)	0% (0문항)
2020	**빠른 독해, 바른 독해가 필수!** · 독해 문항에 대한 빠른 사고와 바른 접근이 관건 · 국가직과 다른 문제 유형에 대비해서, 평소에 법원직 기출문제 뿐만 아니라, 평가원에서 나온 수능 문제 등을 통한 다양성 연습이 반드시 필요	0% (0문항)	16% (4문항)	84% (21문항)	0% (0문항)
2019	**독해 문항 접근과 시간 안배가 관건!** · 다양한 독해 소재와 유형이 제시되어 시간 안배가 관건이었음 · 독해 유형 중 요약문 완성 등의 간접 글쓰기 영역에 대한 문제 풀이 접근법을 반드시 확보했어야 함	0% (0문항)	20% (5문항)	80% (20문항)	0% (0문항)
2018	**문맥상 어휘 흐름을 묻는 문제 2문항 출제!** · 요약문의 완성 중 선지 간의 위계 이해가 관건이었음 · 밑줄 친 부분 중 틀린 어법 찾기 문제와 짝지어진 단어 중 어법에 맞는 것 찾기 문제에 대한 접근법 확보가 필요했음 · 수능 유형인 지칭 추론 등에 대한 접근법 확보가 필요했음	4% (1문항)	20% (5문항)	76% (19문항)	0% (0문항)
2017	**새로운 유형 출제로 체감 난도 상승!** · 문맥상 어휘 추론 문제 중, 단순 어휘뿐 아니라 숙어를 묻는 문항 출제 · 요약문 완성 유형은 주제가 아니라 요약을 요구하여 체감 난도 상승 · 필자의 심경 변화를 묻는 문항 출제	4% (1문항)	12% (3문항)	84% (21문항)	0% (0문항)
2016	**다양한 소재의 독해로 인한 난도 상승!** · 인문, 자연 등의 고른 독해 소재 분포 · 필자의 주장 및 글의 목적을 묻는 수능형 문항 출제	0% (0문항)	8% (2문항)	92% (23문항)	0% (0문항)

합격예상 체크	

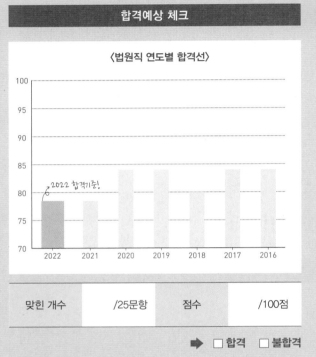

〈법원직 연도별 합격선〉

맞힌 개수	/25문항	점수	/100점

➡ ☐ 합격 ☐ 불합격

취약영역 체크	

문항	정답	영역	문항	정답	영역
1	①	문법 > 일치, 태, 관계사	14	②	독해 > Logical Reading > 삽입
2	①	독해 > Reading for Writing > 요약	15	④	문법 > 일치
3	①	독해 > Reading for Writing > 요약	16	②	독해 > Macro Reading > 요지
4	③	독해 > Logical Reading > 배열	17	③	독해 > Reading for Writing > 빈칸 구 완성
5	④	독해 > Micro Reading > 내용 일치/불일치	18	①	문법 > 시제
6	④	독해 > Reading for Writing > 빈칸 구 완성	19	①	문법 > 동사
7	①	독해 > Micro Reading > 내용 일치/불일치	20	②	독해 > Reading for Writing > 빈칸 구 완성
8	③	독해 > Logical Reading > 문맥상 다양한 추론	21	③	독해 > Logical Reading > 삽입
9	①	독해 > Reading for Writing > 요약	22	③	독해 > Macro Reading > 주제
10	④	독해 > Logical Reading > 배열	23	③	독해 > Macro Reading > 주제
11	①	문법 > 접속사, 시제, 태	24	②	독해 > Micro Reading > 내용 일치/불일치
12	③	독해 > Reading for Writing > 빈칸 구 완성	25	③	독해 > Micro Reading > 내용 일치/불일치
13	①	독해 > Logical Reading > 배열			

⬇ 영역별 틀린 개수로 취약영역을 확인하세요!

어휘	/0	문법	/5	독해	/20	생활영어	/0

➡ 나의 취약영역: _____

※ 해당 회차는 〈1초 합격예측 서비스〉의 데이터 누적 기간이 충분하지 않아 오답률, 선지 선택률 기재를 생략하였습니다.

1	문법 > 일치, 태, 관계사	답 ①

| 해석 | 어떠한 직업 또는 직무를 위한 적절한 보호복의 선택은 대개 주어진 위험에 대한 분석 또는 평가에 의해 좌우된다. 노출의 빈도와 유형뿐만 아니라 착용자의 예상되는 행위가 이러한 결정에 투입되는 전형적인 변수들이다. 예를 들어, 소방관은 다양한 연소재에 노출되어 있다. 따라서 주어진 열 관련 문제에 대응하기 위해 특화된 다층성 직물 계통이 사용된다. 이는 결과적으로 보통 꽤 무겁고 어느 화재 상황에 대해서도 본질적으로 가장 높은 수준의 보호를 제공하는 보호 장비가 된다. 대조적으로, 돌발성 화재가 존재할 가능성이 있는 곳에서 일해야 하는 산업 노동자는 매우 다른 세트의 위험과 요구 사항을 가지고 있을 것이다. 많은 경우에, 면 작업복 위에 착용된 내염성 커버롤이 그 위험을 적절히 해결한다.

| 정답해설 | ① (A) 주어는 The selection으로 단수 명사이고 of the appropriate protective clothing for any job or task는 주어를 수식하는 전명구이다. 따라서 동사는 단수 동사인 is가 옳다.
(B) 「be used + to부정사」는 '~하기 위해서 사용되다'라는 수동태 표현이다.
(C) 선행사가 장소를 나타내는 areas이고 관계사 이후 절이 the possibility of a flash fire exists로 주어, 동사가 모두 존재하는 완전한 문장 구조를 이루므로 빈칸에는 관계부사 where가 들어가는 것이 적절하다. (참고로, 지문의 2번째 문장에 제시된 input은 문맥상 were input이 더욱 적절하다.)

| 오답해설 | ② (B) be used 뒤에는 to부정사가 사용되어야 한다. 그리고 (C) 뒤에는 완전한 문장 구조가 왔으므로 관계대명사 which가 오는 것은 옳지 않다.
③④ (A) 주어 The selection이 단수 명사이므로 복수 동사 are가 오는 것은 옳지 않다.

| 더 알아보기 | used to를 활용한 관용표현

> 1) used to + 동사원형;(과거에) ~하곤 했었다, ~이었다
> 2) be used + to부정사: ~하기 위해서 사용되다(수동태)
> 3) be used to -ing[명사 계열 가능]: ~하는 것에 익숙하다

어휘

appropriate 적절한, 적합한	protective 보호하는
dictate ~을 좌우하다, ~에 영향을 주다	
analysis 분석	assessment 평가
hazard 위험	present 주다, 수여하다
exposure 노출	variable 변수
input 입력하다	determination 결심, 결정
specialize 특화하다, 전문화하다	gear 장비, 의복
flash fire 돌발적인 화재	resistant 저항하는
coverall 상하가 붙은 (소매가 있는) 작업복	
adequately 적절히	address 다루다; 착수하다; 해결하다

2 | 독해 〉 Reading for Writing 〉 요약 | 답 ①

| 해석 | 인도에서 인구의 1/3에 해당하는 약 3억 6천만 명의 사람들이 숲 속에서 또는 숲과 매우 가까이에 살고 있다. 이 사람들 중 절반이 넘는 이들이 공식 빈곤선 미만에 살고 있으며, 결과적으로 그들은 그들이 숲으로부터 얻는 자원에 결정적으로 의존하고 있다. 인도 정부는 현재 그들이 자신들의 숲의 상업적 관리에 참여하도록 하여 그들의 운이 나아지게 하는 것을 목표로 하는 프로그램들을 운영하는데, 이러한 방식으로 그들이 필요한 식량과 재료를 계속해서 얻을수 있도록 허용해 주지만 동시에 숲 작물을 파는 것도 허용해 준다. 만일 그 프로그램들이 성공한다면, 숲 거주자들은 더 부유해지겠지만, 그들은 자신들의 전통적 삶의 방식과 문화를 보존할 수 있을 것이며, 숲은 지속 가능하게 관리될 것이고, 따라서 야생 생물은 고갈되지 않을 것이다.
⇒ 인도 정부는 숲을 (B) 파괴하지 않고 숲 근처에 사는 빈곤한 사람들의 삶을 (A) 향상시키려고 노력하고 있다.

	(A)	(B)
①	향상시키다	파괴하는
②	통제하다	보존하는
③	향상시키다	제한하는
④	통제하다	확대하는

| 정답해설 | ① 인도 정부가 숲속 또는 숲 인근에 사는 사람들의 삶의 질을 향상시키기 위해 운영하는 프로그램에 대해 설명하는 글이다. 마지막 문장을 보면 숲을 상업적으로 관리하는 이 프로그램들이 성공한다면, 숲 거주자들은 자신들의 전통적 삶의 방식과 문화를 보존하면서도 더 부유해지고 숲은 지속 가능하게 관리될 것이고, 야생 생물은 고갈되지 않을 것이라고 했다. 따라서 빈칸에 가장 적절한 것은 ①이다.

| 오답해설 | ③ 인도 정부가 숲의 이용을 제한했다는 내용은 본문에 언급되지 않았으므로 오답이다.

어휘
consequently 결과적으로	crucially 결정적으로
resource 자원	obtain 얻다, 획득하다
lot 운, 운명	involve 관련시키다, 연루시키다
produce 생산물	dweller 거주자
prosperous 번영한; 부유한	preserve 보존하다
sustainably 지속 가능하게	deplete 고갈시키다
ruin 망치다, 파괴하다	enlarge 확대하다

3 | 독해 〉 Reading for Writing 〉 요약 | 답 ①

| 해석 | 팬데믹 중에는 얼굴 표정의 신호나 접촉이 없어서, 톤과 억양의 더 많은 강조, 속도 줄이기, 짜증스럽게 들리지 않으면서도 크게 소리내기를 포함하여, 대화의 다른 측면에 집중해야 할 필요성이 더 크다. 얼굴 표정이 없으면 구어의 많은 뉘앙스를 쉽게 놓치므로, 눈 맞춤이 훨씬 더 중요성을 지닐 것이다. 일부 병원 직원들은 이러한 문제를 해결하기 위해 혁신적인 방법을 개발해 왔다. 간호 전문가들 중 한 사람은 만성적으로 아픈 그녀의 어린 환자들이 그녀의 얼굴을 볼 수 없을 것을 매우 걱정해서, 어린이들이 가리킬 수 있도록 다양한 얼굴 모양 스티커를 프린트했다. 또한 어떤 병원들은 이제 그들의 환자들에게 직원들을 더 쉽게 식별하게 해 주는 '얼굴 표'를 제공하는데, 마스크를 쓰고 있을 때 당신 자신과 동료를 환자들에게 다시 소개하는 것은 언제나 유용하다.

일부 병원과 직원들은 팬데믹 동안 환자들과의 대화를 (B) <u>보완할</u> (A) <u>대안적인</u> 방법들을 찾고 있다.

	(A)	(B)
①	대안적인	보완할
②	성가신	분석할
③	효과적인	방해할
④	충격적인, 혼란 주는	개선시킬

| 정답해설 | ① 얼굴 표정을 보면서 대화할 수 없는 팬데믹 기간 중에 병원과 직원들이 환자들과 소통하기 위해 시도한 여러 대안적인 방법들을 소개하고 있으므로, 빈칸에 가장 적절한 표현은 ①이다.

| 오답해설 | ③ hinder는 '방해하다'라는 의미로, 본문 내용과 반대되므로 답과 거리가 멀다.

어휘
in the absence of ~이 없을 때에, ~이 없어서

emphasis 강조	inflection 억양
assume 맡다, 띠다	innovative 혁신적인, 획기적인
chronically 만성적으로	identification 신원 확인
alternative 대안적인	complement 보완하다
bothering 성가신	analyze 분석하다
hinder 방해하다	disturb 방해하다

4 | 독해 〉 Logical Reading 〉 배열 | 답 ③

| 해석 | 일단 그들이 어미를 떠나면, 영장류는 계속해서 그들이 맞닥뜨리는 새로운 식량이 안전한지 그리고 수집할 가치가 있는지에 대한 결정을 해야 한다.
(C) 자기 자신을 실험 도구로 사용하는 것이 하나의 선택지이지만, 사회적인 영장류들은 더 나은 방법을 찾아냈다. Kenneth Glander는 그것을 "샘플링"이라고 부른다. howler 원숭이들이 새로운 서식지로 이동할 때, 무리의 한 구성원이 나무로 가서 잎을 몇 개 먹어 보고 하루를 기다린다.
(B) 만일 그 식물이 특별히 강력한 독을 함유하고 있다면, 보통 도중에 그 원숭이를 아프게 만듦으로써 샘플러의 신체 체계가 그것을 분해하려고 할 것이다. "저는 이것이 발생하는 것을 본 적이 있습니다"라고 Glander가 말했다. "무리의 다른 구성원들이 큰 관심을 가지고 바라보고 있었습니다. 만일 그 동물이 아프게 된다면, 다른 동물들은 어느 누구도 그 나무로 가지 않을 것입니다. 주어지는 신호가, 그러니까 사회적 신호가 있습니다."
(A) 같은 이유로, 만일 샘플러가 괜찮다고 느끼면, 그것은 며칠 후에 나무로 다시 들어가서 조금 더 먹은 다음 다시 기다리는데, 천천히 더 많은 양으로 증가시킬 것이다. 마침내, 그 원숭이가 건강하다면 다른 구성원들은 이것이 괜찮다고 생각하고 그들은 새로운 식량을 받아들일 것이다.

| 정답해설 | ③ 주어진 글에서는 영장류가 식량의 안정성을 확인해야 한다는 내용이 제시된다. 글의 발단에 해당되며 새로운 정보를 처음 제시하는 단락은 (C)이다. (C)에서는 새로운 인물 Kenneth Glander가 등장하며, 또한 새로운 방법 sampling과 새로운 정보 a tree가 제시된다. 이어 (C) 뒤에 이어질 내용으로 가장 적절한 것은 나무가 독성을 지닌 상황을 먼저 가정하는 (B)이다. 이어서 By the same token이라는 연결사를 이용해 (B)에서 진술한 내용과 유사한 논조로 글을 이끌어가고자 하는 (A)가 이어지는 것이 글의 흐름상 가장 적절하다. 따라서 올바른 순서는 (C) – (B) – (A)이다.

| 오답해설 | ① (A)의 By the same token이 가리키는 내용이 주어진 글에 없으므로 (A)가 맨 앞에 오는 것은 부적절하다.
② the plant가 가리키는 내용이 주어진 글에 나와 있지 않다.

④ (A)에서 샘플러가 괜찮아서 새로운 식량을 받아들였다고 했는데 (B)에서 그 식물에 독이 있다고 다시 가정하는 것은 어색하다.

어휘

primate 영장류	encounter 만나다, 맞닥뜨리다
by the same token 같은 이유로	dose 양, 복용량
harbor 품다; 숨기다	toxin 독소
troop 무리	habitat 서식지

---

5 독해 > Micro Reading > 내용일치/불일치   답 ④

| 해석 | 제2차 세계대전에서의 일본의 패배에 이어 대부분의 한민족(100~140만)이 일본을 떠났다. 1948년 즈음 한민족의 인구는 약 60만 명이 되었다. 이 한국인들과 그들의 후손들은 흔히 Zainichi(문자 그대로 "일본에 거주하는")라고 칭해졌는데, 이는 전후 직후에 나온 용어이다. 일본에 남아 있던 한민족들은 다양한 이유로 그렇게 했다. 식민지 시대에 사업에서, 제국 관료 체제에서, 그리고 군대에서 성공적인 경력을 이루었거나 전쟁 직후 개방된 경제적 이득을 취했던 한국인들은 빈곤하고 정치적으로 불안정한 해방 후 한국으로 돌아가는 위험보다는 일본에서 상대적으로 특권을 가진 그들의 지위를 지키기로 결정한 것이다. 본국으로 송환된 일부 한국인들은 그들이 목격한 가난한 환경에 너무 혐오감을 느껴 일본으로 돌아가기로 결정했다. 일본에 사는 다른 한국인들은 출항 항구 중 한 곳으로 가는 기차 요금을 낼 여유가 없었고, 그들 중 일본인 배우자와 일본 태생으로 일본어를 하는 자녀들이 있는 사람들은 새로운 환경의 문화적, 언어적 어려움을 헤쳐 나가는 것보다는 일본에 머무르는 것이 더 이치에 맞았다.

| 정답해설 | ④ 마지막 문장 Other Koreans living in Japan ~ linguistic challenges of a new environment를 보면 출항 항구 중 한 곳으로 가는 기차 요금을 낼 여유가 없었던 사람들과 일본인 배우자가 있는 사람들이 일본에 살게 되었다고 했을 뿐 이들 간에 어떤 연결고리가 있는 것은 아니다. (참고로, 본문 6번째 문장의 repatriate는 문맥상 were repatriated가 더 적절하다.)

| 오답해설 | ① 세번째 문장에서 Zainichi는 일본에 거주하는 한국인들과 그 후손들을 일컫는다고 했다.
② 다섯 번째 문장에서 전쟁 직후 개방된 경제적 기회의 이득을 취한 한국인들은 일본에 남았다고 했다.
③ 여섯 번째 문장에서 한국으로 송환됐던 일부 한국인들이 가난한 환경에 혐오감을 느껴 일본으로 되돌아갔다고 했다.

어휘

ethnic 민족의	settle 정착하다
descendant 후손, 자손	refer 부르다, 칭하다
reside 거주하다, 살다	diverse 다양한
imperial 제국의	bureaucracy 관료, 관료 정치
colonial 식민지의	opt to V ~하기로 선택하다
relatively 상대적으로	privileged 특권이 있는
impoverished 가난한, 빈곤한	unstable 불안정한
post-liberation 해방 후	repulse 혐오감[불쾌감]을 주다
navigate (힘들거나 복잡한 상황을) 헤쳐 나가다, 뚫고 나가다	

---

6 독해 > Reading for Writing > 빈칸 구 완성   답 ④

| 해석 | 사람들이 ④ 자신들의 신호를 좀 더 충분히 발전시켜야 하는 몇몇 직업이 있다. 우리는 위로 향하는 손가락 하나가 타자는 아웃이고 삼주문에서 떠나야 한다는 것을 의미하는 크리켓에서처럼 심판들이 선수들에게 방

향을 신호하기 위해 팔과 손을 이용하는 것을 본다. 오케스트라 지휘자들은 자신들의 움직임을 통해 음악가들을 제어한다. 서로와 멀리서 일하는 사람들이 의사소통하고 싶다면 특별한 신호를 만들어야 한다. 기계들이 매우 시끄러운 공장이나 학생들로 가득한 수영장 주변의 인명 구조원과 같이 시끄러운 환경에서 일하는 사람들도 그러하다.
① 그들의 부모와 아이들을 지원하다
② 완전히 새로운 업무 스타일에 적응하다
③ 기본 인권을 위해 법정 싸움을 하다
④ 자신들의 신호를 좀 더 충분히 발전시키다

| 정답해설 | ④ 두 번째 문장 이후에 예시된 직업 종사자들의 공통점으로 빈칸을 채워야 한다. 심판, 지휘자, 서로와 멀리 떨어져 일하는 사람들, 시끄러운 공장에서 일하는 사람들과 학생으로 가득한 수영장 주변에서 일하는 인명 구조원들은 의사소통을 위해 손과 몸을 이용한 신호를 만들어야 한다고 했으므로 ④가 빈칸에 알맞다.

| 오답해설 | ① 부모와 아이들을 지원하는 것은 본문 내용과는 거리가 멀다.
② 새로운 업무 스타일에 적응하는 것에 관한 내용은 본문에 언급되지 않았다.
③ 인권이나 법정 싸움과 관련된 내용은 본문에 나오지 않았다.

어휘

referee (축구, 권투, 농구 등의) 심판, 주심	
umpire (야구, 크리켓, 테니스 등의) 심판	
conductor 지휘자	adapt to ~에 적응하다
fight in court 법정에서 싸우다	

---

7 독해 > Micro Reading > 내용일치/불일치   답 ①

| 해석 | 연구에서 동물 이용의 반대자들은 약물이나 다른 화합물의 안전성을 테스트하기 위해 동물을 이용하는 것 또한 반대한다. 제약산업 내에서, 복용했을 때 인간에게 암을 유발한다고 알려진 19개의 화학 물질 중 오직 7개만이 국립암연구소(National Cancer Institute)에서 설정한 기준을 사용하였을 때 쥐에서 암을 유발한다(Barnard and Koufman, 1997)는 것이 알려졌다. 예를 들어, 항우울제인 노미펜신은 쥐, 토끼, 개, 그리고 원숭이에게 아주 적은 독성을 보였지만, 인간에게는 간 독성과 빈혈을 유발했다. 이것과 다른 경우에, 일부 화합물은 동물 실험에 의해서는 예측되지 않았던 심각한 부작용이 인간에게는 있고 치료받은 인간이 장애 혹은 죽음에까지 이를 수도 있는 상태가 된다는 것을 보여 준다. 그리고 동물 실험을 끝낼 것을 요구하는 연구자들은 인간의 임상 실험, 부검 실험실의 지원을 받는 관찰과 같은 더 나은 이용 가능한 방법이 있다는 점을 명시한다.

| 정답해설 | ① 두 번째 문장 Within the pharmaceutical ~에서 인간에게 암을 유발한다고 알려진 19개의 발암 물질 중 7개만이 쥐에게서 암을 유발한다고 했으므로 본문과 일치하지 않는다. (참고로, 본문 3번째 문장의 For example, and는 문맥상 and를 an으로 수정하는 것이 더 적절하다.)

| 오답해설 | ② 세 번째 문장 For example, and antidepressant, ~ in humans에서 항우울제 노미펜신은 동물에게는 독성이 거의 없었지만 인간에게는 간 독성과 빈혈을 유발했다고 했으므로 본문과 일치한다.
③ 본문 후반 In these and other cases, ~ or even death에서 일부 화합물은 동물 실험에 의해서는 예측되지 않았던 심각한 부

작용을 인간에게 일으킨다고 했으므로 본문과 일치한다.

④ 마지막 문장 And researchers who ~ of autopsy tests에서 동물 실험의 대안으로 인간의 임상 실험, 부검을 통한 관찰을 제시했으므로 본문과 일치한다.

어휘

opponent 반대자	oppose 반대하다, 이의를 제기하다
compound 화합물, 합성물	pharmaceutical 제약의
antidepressant 항우울제	toxicity 유독성
adverse 반대의, 역의	disability 장애
call for 요구하다	laboratory 실험실
autopsy 부검	

---

8 독해 > Logical Reading > 문맥상 다양한 추론 답 ③

| 해석 | 찬물 샤워는 화씨 70° 미만의 수온으로 하는 모든 샤워이다. 그것은 건강상 이점을 지닐 수 있다. 우울증을 앓는 사람들에게 찬물 샤워는 일종의 가벼운 전기 충격 요법으로 작용할 수 있다. 찬물 샤워는 많은 전기 자극을 당신의 뇌로 보낸다. 그것들은 당신의 각성도, 명확성, 그리고 에너지 수준을 증가시키기 위해 당신의 (신체) 체계를 덜컥 움직인다. 때때로 행복 호르몬이라고도 불리는 엔도르핀 또한 배출된다. 이 효과는 행복감과 낙관적 기분으로 이어진다. 비만인 사람들에게 주당 2~3번 찬물 샤워를 하는 것은 증가된 신진대사에 도움이 될 수 있다. 시간이 지나면서 그것은 비만과의 싸움에 도움이 될 수 있다. 찬물 샤워가 정확히 어떻게 사람들이 체중을 줄이도록 돕는지에 대한 연구는 ③ 분명하다 (→ 불분명하다). 그러나, 그것(찬물 샤워)이 특정 호르몬 수치를 안정시키고 위장계를 치료할 수 있다는 점을 보여 준다. 이러한 효과들이 체중 감소로 이어지는 찬물 샤워의 능력으로 더해질 수도 있다. 게다가, 규칙적으로 할 때, 찬물 샤워는 우리의 순환계를 더욱 효율적으로 만들 수 있다. 몇몇 사람들은 또한 찬물 샤워의 결과로 그들의 피부가 더 좋아 보인다고 보고했는데, 아마도 더 나은 혈액 순환 때문일 것이다. 비록 우리는 운동으로 인한 부상을 입은 후 치료 차 하는 찬물 샤워를 지지하는 데이터를 오직 최근에서야 보았지만, 운동선수들은 수년 동안 이런 이점을 알고 있었다.

| 정답해설 | ③ 찬물 샤워가 비만인들의 체중 감소에 도움이 될 수 있음을 언급하였으나 이는 추측의 조동사 may를 썼으므로 아직은 필자의 태도가 명확하지 않은 상태이다. 이후에 역접의 연결사 However를 쓰면서 명백하게 찬물 샤워가 긍정적 영향을 미치고 있음을 제시하고 있다. 그러므로 however 이전에는 찬물 샤워가 비만에 미치는 영향에 대해서는 부정적 진술을 했다고 보는 것이 타당하다. 따라서 ③ clear(분명한)는 unclear(불분명한)가 되어야 적절하다.

| 오답해설 | ① 찬물 샤워가 뇌에 전기 자극을 준다고 했으므로, 각성도, 명확성, 에너지 수준을 '증가시키는(increase)' 것은 글의 흐름상 적절하다.

② 찬물 샤워의 긍정적 측면에 관해 진술하고 있으므로 optimism은 문맥에 어울린다.

④ 양보의 접속사 even if로 보아 주절의 for years와 대비되어 recently가 적절히 쓰인 것을 알 수 있다.

어휘

electroshock 전기 충격	impulse 자극, 충격
alertness 각성도, 기민함	clarity 명료성, 명확성
optimism 낙관주의, 낙천주의	obese 비만의

---

contribute to ~에 기여하다, 도움이 되다

metabolism 신진대사　　　　　　obesity 비만

even out ~을 균등하게 나누다; 안정되다

circulatory system 순환계

---

9 독해 > Reading for Writing > 요약 답 ③

| 해석 | 연구자들은 한 개인이 갈등이 발생할 때 그것에 대처하는 습관적인 방식에 관심을 가져 왔다. 그들은 이러한 접근법을 갈등 스타일이라고 불렀다. 몇 가지 분명한 갈등 스타일이 있는데, 각각은 장단점을 가지고 있다. 협력 스타일은 관련된 모든 사람에게 최상의 결과가 주어지는 가능성을 최대화하는 방식으로 문제를 해결하고자 하는 경향이 있다. 협력 스타일의 장점은 신뢰를 자아내고, 긍정적인 관계를 유지하고, 헌신을 구축하는 것이다. 그러나, 그것은 시간이 많이 소요되고 갈등 중 다른 사람과 협력하는 데 많은 에너지가 소비된다. 경쟁 스타일은 그들의 목표를 달성하지 않는 사람들에게 적대감이 생기게 할 수도 있다. 그러나, 경쟁 스타일은 갈등을 신속히 해결하는 경향이 있다.

> 협력 스타일은 (A) 상호 이해에 큰 가치를 부여하는 사람에게 사용될 수 있는 반면에, (B) 시간 효율성을 선호하는 사람은 경쟁 스타일을 선택할지 모른다.

	(A)	(B)
①	재정적 능력	상호 작용
②	시간 절약	평화
③	상호 이해	시간 효율성
④	효율성	일관성

| 정답해설 | ③ (A) 본문 중반 The pluses of a collaborating style include creating trust, maintaining positive relationship, and building commitment.에서 협력 스타일의 장점은 신뢰를 자아내고, 긍정적인 관계를 유지하고, 헌신을 구축하는 것이라고 언급했는데, 선지 중 협력 스타일을 가장 잘 묘사하는 것은 상호 이해에 가치를 부여한다는 것이다.

(B) 마지막 문장 However, the competing style tends to resolve a conflict quickly.에서 경쟁 스타일은 갈등을 신속히 해결하는 경향이 있다고 했으므로 시간 효율성을 중시하는 사람에게 적합한 스타일임을 알 수 있다.

| 오답해설 | ① (A) 재정적 요소에 관해서는 본문에 전혀 등장하지 않으므로 오답이다.

② (A) 시간 절약은 경쟁 스타일이 중시하는 요소이다. 반대로 (B) 평화는 상대적으로 협력 스타일이 추구하는 것이라고 볼 수 있다.

④ 본문의 내용과 관련이 없으므로 오답이다.

어휘

habitual 습관성의	cope with ~에 대처하다, 대항하다
conflict 갈등	apparent 분명한
pros and cons 장단점	collaborate 협력하다
involve 관련시키다, 연루시키다	plus 장점, 이점
commitment 헌신, 약속, 전념	
time consuming 많은 시간이 소요되는	
compete 경쟁하다	hostility 적의, 적대감
interaction 상호 작용	mutual 상호의, 공동의
efficiency 효율	consistency 일관성, 지속성

| 해석 | 분쟁해결학의 역사적 진화는 냉전의 정점이었던 1950년대와 1960년대에 탄력이 붙었는데, 이 시기에는 핵무기의 발달과 초강대국들 간의 갈등이 인간의 생존을 위협하는 것처럼 보였다.

(C) 다른 학문을 연구하는 한 무리의 선구자들이, 국제 관계에서, 국내 정치에서, 산업 관계에서, 공동체에서 발생하든 아니면 개인 간에 발생하든 간에, 유사한 특성을 지닌 일반적 현상으로서 갈등을 연구하는 것의 가치를 보았다.

(B) 그러나, 일부 사람들은 그들을 진지하게 생각하지 않았다. 국제 관계 전문직은 국제 갈등에 관한 자신들만의 이해를 가지고 있었고, 새로운 접근법의 가치를 제안한 대로 보지 않았다.

(A) 새로운 아이디어에 내포된 분석과 실천의 조합은 전통적 학문 기관 또는 외교관과 정치인 같은 현역들의 전통과 조화되기 쉽지 않았다.

| 정답해설 | ④ 주어진 글에서는 분쟁 해결학이 역사적으로 번성한 시기에 대해 언급하였다. 이에 이어질 내용으로 가장 적절한 것은 이 분쟁 해결이라는 학문의 최초 시작점에 대해 구체적으로 설명하는 (C)이다. 이어서 역접의 접속사 However가 포함된 (B)로, 그 다음 새로운 학문이 등장하였으나 일부 기존 학자들이 새로운 아이디어를 받아들이지 않았다는 내용의 (C)로 이어지는 것이 적절하다. (B)의 they는 (C)의 A group of pioneers from different disciplines를 의미한다. 마지막으로 (B)와 동일한 논조의 (A)가 연결되는 것이 전체 문맥상 자연스럽다. 따라서 올바른 순서는 ④ (C) – (B) – (A)이다.

| 오답해설 | ①② (B)의 they가 가리키는 대상이 주어진 글에 없으므로, 주어진 글에 (B)가 바로 이어지는 것은 문맥상 적절하지 않다. 또한 주어진 글과 (B)가 내용상 역접의 관계가 아니므로 서로 연결되는 것이 어색하다.

③ (A)와 (B)의 관계가 역접 관계가 아니므로, (A) 이후에 (B)가 연결되는 것은 문맥상 어색하다.

어휘

evolution 진화, 발전	Conflict Resolution 분쟁해결학
gain momentum 탄력이 붙다, 활기를 얻다	
at the height of ~의 절정에, ~이 한창일 때	
superpower 초강대국	practice 실행, 실천; 관행
implicit 내포된, 암시된	reconcile with ~와 조화를 이루다
scholarly 학문적인	
practitioner 현역(으로 일을 하는 사람); 개업자	
diplomat 외교관	profession 직종; 전문직
approach 접근(법)	pioneer 선구자
discipline 지식 분야, 학문	phenomenon 현상
property 특성	domestic 국내의

| 해석 | 경제를 이해하는 것의 비결은 항상 의도치 않은 결과가 있다는 점을 받아들이는 것이다. 사람들이 자신만의 타당한 이유로 취하는 행동은 그들이 상상하지 못한, 또는 의도하지 않은 결과를 낳는다. 지정학에도 동일한 것이 적용된다. BC 7세기에 확장을 시작했을 때 로마라는 마을이 500년 후에 지중해 지역을 정복할 종합 계획을 품고 있었을지는 의문이다. 그러나 그곳의 주민이 이웃 마을에 대항하여 취한 최초의 행위가 현실에 의해 속박당하면서도 의도하지 않을 결과로 가득한 과정에 시동을 건 것이다. 로마는 계획되지 않았지만 그렇다고 그냥 일어난 일도 아니다.

| 정답해설 | ① (A) 타동사 accept는 목적어로 명사절을 취할 수 있는데, 네모 뒤에 완전한 문장이 나오므로 that이 오는 것이 옳다.

(B) that절의 주어는 the village of Rome으로 단수이고 종속절인 when절의 동사 started가 과거형이다. 과거의 역사적 사실을 말할 때는 항상 과거시제를 사용하므로 had가 알맞다.

(C) 선행사는 a process이며 관계대명사 that절로 수식받고 있다. 해당 관계대명사의 동사는 등위상관접속사 both ~ and로 연결되는 구조로 수동태 was (both) constrained와, (C)에도 (was) filled로 수동으로 표현하는것이 문맥상 어법에 맞다.

| 오답해설 | ②③ (A) 뒤에 나오는 절이 완전한 문장 구조를 이루므로 what은 오답이다.

④ 과거의 역사적 사실은 항상 과거시제로 나타나며 주어와 동사의 수도 일치되지 않으므로 (B)에는 have가 올 수 없다. 또한 (C)의 fill은 타동사이므로 전치사 없이 목적어를 취해야 한다. 따라서 filling with는 어법에 맞지 않다.

어휘

unintended 의도하지 않은	consequence 결과
good 타당한, 사리에 맞는	envision 상상하다, 마음에 그리다
intend 의도하다	expansion 확장, 확대
conquer 정복하다	Mediterranean 지중해의
inhabitant 거주자	
set in motion ~에 시동을 걸다, ~을 움직이게 하다	
process 과정, 절차	constrain 구속하다, 속박하다

| 해석 | 물과 문명은 밀접한 관련이 있다. "수력학 문명"이라는 생각은 물이 역사를 통틀어 많은 대규모 문명의 통합적 배경이며 정당한 이유라고 주장한다. 예를 들어, 여러 세기의 다양한 중국 제국들은 어느 정도는 황하강의 홍수를 통제함으로써 할 수 있는 만큼 오래 살아남았다. 수력학 이론의 한 가지 해석은 대도시로의 인구 모집의 정당한 이유는 물을 관리하기 위한 것이라는 것이다. 또 다른 해석은 대규모 물 프로젝트가 대도시의 발전을 가능하게 한다는 것을 제안한다. 로마 제국이 그들이 통치했던 땅 전역에 송수로 망을 건설했던 것처럼 로마인들은 권력과 물의 관계를 이해했다. 로마 제국의 송수로 망들 중 다수가 여전히 온전히 남아 있다. 예를 들어, 남부 프랑스의 Pont du Gard는 오늘날 인류의 수도 시설에의 투자의 증거로 남아 있다. 로마의 총독들은 ③ 자신들의 권위를 집중시키고 강화하기 위한 방법으로 도로, 다리, 그리고 상수도를 건설했다.

① 젊은이들 교육에 집중하기

② 지역 시장에서의 자유 무역을 금지하기

③ 자신들의 권위를 집중시키고 강화하기

④ 자신들의 재산을 다른 나라에 넘겨주기

| 정답해설 | ③ 본문 후반 The Romans understood the connections ~ they controlled에서 로마 제국이 그들이 통치했던 땅 전역에 송수로 망을 건설했던 것처럼 로마인들은 권력과 물의 관계를 이해했다고 했으므로 물을 통제함으로써 통치자들이 권력을 강화하려고 했음을 유추할 수 있다. 따라서 빈칸에 가장 적절한 표현은 ③이다.

어휘

civilization 문명

go hand in hand 밀접한 관련이 있다, 떨어질 수 없는 관계이다

argue 주장하다

context 상황, 문맥   unify 통일하다, 결속하다

large-scale 대규모의   justification 타당한[정당한] 이유

interpretation 해석   empire 제국

intact 온전한, 전혀 다치지 않은   vast 막대한, 방대한

investment 투자   testament 증거

governor 통치자   infrastructure (기반) 시설

concentrate 집중시키다, 모으다   prohibit 금지하다

property 재산   authority 권위, 권한

    give up A to B A를 B에게 넘겨주다

---

13   독해 > Logical Reading > 배열   답 ①

| 해석 | 불명확함은 매우 불편해서 그것은 심지어 좋은 뉴스를 나쁜 것으로 바꿀 수도 있다. 당신은 지속적인 복통으로 병원에 간다. 의사는 이유가 무엇인지 알아낼 수 없어서, 검사를 하기 위해 당신을 검사실로 보낸다.

(B) 일주일 후 당신은 결과를 듣기 위해 호출된다. 당신이 마침내 그녀의 사무실로 들어가자 의사는 웃으며 모든 검사가 모두 음성이었다고 말한다.

(A) 그리고 무슨 일이 일어나는가? 당신의 즉각적인 안도는 이상한 불편감으로 바뀔지도 모른다. 당신은 여전히 그 고통이 무엇이었는지 모른다! 어딘가에 설명이 있어야 한다.

(C) 아마 그것은 암인데, 그들이 그것을 놓쳤을 것이다. 아마 그것은 더 나쁠 수도 있다. 분명히 그들은 원인을 찾을 수 있어야 한다. 당신은 확답이 없어 좌절을 느낀다.

| 정답해설 | ① 주어진 글에서는 불명확함의 불편함에 대해 언급하고 병원에서 검사를 받는 상황을 예로 들고 있다. 이어질 내용으로 가장 적절한 것은 검사 결과를 듣기 위해 호출되는 상황인 (B)이다. (B)에서 음성이라는 결과를 듣고서 생기는 일은 즉각적인 안도 후 찾아오는 불편감이라고 하는 (A)의 내용이다. (C)의 첫 두 문장은 (A)의 마지막 문장에 나온 an explanation의 예이므로 (A) 다음에 (C)가 와야 한다. 따라서 올바른 순서는 (B) – (A) – (C)이다.

| 오답해설 | ② (B)에서 음성의 결과를 듣고 안도를 한다는 내용이 먼저 등장하는 것이 글의 흐름상 조금 더 자연스럽다. 따라서 (B)와 (A)가 연속적으로 이어지는 것이 더 적절하다.

③④ 주어진 글에서는 아직 검사의 결과를 알지 못하는 상황이므로 (C)가 주어진 문장에 이어지는 것은 부적절하다.

어휘

ambiguity 불확실성, 모호함   persistent 지속되는, 반복되는

figure out 알아내다   relief 안도, 안심

replace 대신하다, 바꾸다   weird 이상한

discomfort 불편   negative 음성의

frustrated 좌절한, 불만스러워하는   definitive 확실한, 명확한

---

14   독해 > Logical Reading > 삽입   답 ②

| 해석 | 출근할 때 우리가 어떻게 옷을 입는지는 선택의 새로운 요소를 떠맡겼고, 그와 함께, 새로운 걱정거리도 떠맡았다. "약식 복장 근무일" 또는 "캐주얼 데이"를 갖는 관행은 10년 정도 전에 생겨나기 시작했는데, 그들이 돈을 절약하고 사무실에서 더 편안하게 느낄 수 있도록 하여 직원들의 삶을 더 편안하게 만들어 주고자 함이었다. ② 그러나 그 효과는 정반대였다. 평범한 직장용 의류에 더해, 직원들은 "직장용 캐주얼" 의류를 마련해야 했다. 그것은 사실 당신이 주말에 집에서 입는 추리닝이나 티셔츠가 될 수는 없었다. 그것은 편안하지만 동시에 진지한 어떤 이미지를 유지하는 일련의 의류여야만 했다.

| 정답해설 | ② 주어진 문장의 however로 보아, 주어진 문장의 전후로 대조적인 내용이 제시되어야 한다는 것을 알 수 있다. ② 이전에서는 직원들의 돈을 절약해 주고 직장에서 편안하게 느낄 수 있도록 "캐주얼 데이"라는 관행을 마련했다고 했으나, ② 이후에서는 그런 의도와는 반대로 직장에서 입을 또 다른 옷을 마련해야 했다는 내용이 제시되고 있다. 서로 대조적인 내용이 제시되고 있으므로, 주어진 문장은 ②에 들어가는 것이 가장 적절하다.

어휘

reverse 반대의, 역의   anxiety 걱정, 불안

practice 관습, 관례, 관행

dress-down day 약식 복장 근무일, 캐주얼 착용일

emerge 나타나다, 생기다   intend 의도하다

sustain 지탱하다, 유지하다

---

15   문법 > 일치   답 ④

| 해석 | 당신은 당신이 원하는 결과에 가장 적합한 연구 방법을 선택해야 한다. 당신은 많은 사람들에게 질문을 할 수 있게 해 주고 보고서 형식으로 완전한 분석을 제공해 주는 온라인 설문 조사를 진행할지도 모르고, 또는 일대일로 질문을 하는 것이 더 적은 범위의 선택된 사람들로부터 당신이 원하는 대답을 얻는 더 나은 방법이라고 생각할지도 모른다. 당신이 어떤 방법을 선택하든지, 같은 방법으로 비교해야 할 것이다. 사람들에게 같은 질문을 하고 답변을 비교하라. 유사점과 차이점을 둘 다 찾아보라. 패턴과 추세를 찾아보라. 기록 방식과 데이터 분석 방식을 결정하는 것이 중요하다. 간단히 스스로 만든 스프레드시트가 얼마간의 기초적인 연구 데이터를 기록하기에는 충분할 것이다.

| 정답해설 | ④ and로 연결된 동명사 주어가 긴밀히 연결된 관계일 때는 하나의 단위로 보아 단수로 취급할 수 있다. 따라서 Deciding on a way of recording and analysing the data를 하나의 묶음으로 보아 ④를 단수 동사 is로 쓰는 것이 바람직하다. deciding과 analysing을 동명사로서 2개의 주어인 복수로 볼 수 있으나, 해석상 recording과 analysing이 병렬 구조로 of의 목적어로 연결되었다고 보는 것이 문맥상 더욱 적절하다.

| 오답해설 | ① 선행사 the research method는 사물 명사이므로 주격 관계대명사로 that을 쓴 것은 어법에 맞다.

② 선행사는 a survey이고 주격 관계대명사 that절의 enables ~ people과 provides ~ format을 등위접속사 and가 병렬 구조로 연결하고 있으므로 어법상 옳다.

③ Whichever는 복합관계형용사로 명사와 결합하여 부사절을 이끌 수 있다.

어휘

outcome 결과   analysis 분석

format 형식, 포맷

like for like 비슷한 것끼리, 같은 방법으로, 비슷한 수단으로

spreadsheet 스프레드시트

terry 테리 직물(타월처럼 수분 흡수가 잘 되도록 짠 천)
overwhelmingly 압도적으로   significantly 상당히

---

16 독해 > Macro Reading > 요지   답 ②

| **해석** | 몇몇 범인들은 범죄가 제공할 수 있는 흥분과 전율을 좋아해서 불법 행동에 연루되었을 것이다. 그의 매우 영향력 있는 작품인 『Seductions of Crime』에서 사회학자인 Jack Katz는 범행에는 사람들을 범죄 생활로 "유혹하는" 즉각적인 이점이 있다고 주장한다. 어떤 사람들에게 상점 절도와 공공 기물 파손은 매력적인데, 왜냐하면 범죄에서 교묘히 빠져나가는 것은 개인적 능력의 스릴 넘치는 증명이기 때문이다. 흥분에 대한 욕구는 체포와 처벌의 두려움에 대항할 것이다. 실제로, 일부 범죄자들은 추가된 "전율" 때문에 특히 위험한 상황을 의도적으로 찾아낼 것이다. 흥분에 대한 욕구는 범죄 선택의 중요한 예측 변수이다.

| **정답해설** | ② 첫 번째 문장 Some criminal offenders may engage in illegal behavior because they love the excitement and thrills that crime can provide.에서 몇몇 범인들은 범죄가 제공할 수 있는 흥분과 전율을 좋아해서 불법 행위에 연루되었을 거라고 했고 이어지는 사회학자 Jack Katz의 주장에서도 흥분에 대한 욕구가 범죄 선택의 중요한 예측 변수라고 하였으므로 전체 글의 요지로 가장 적절한 것은 ②이다.

어휘

offender 범죄자, 범인   engage in ~에 관여하다, 연루되다
illegal 불법적인   seduction 유혹
argue 주장하다   immediate 즉각적인
criminality 범죄 행위, 범죄성, 범행   seduce 유혹하다
shoplift (가게 물건을) 슬쩍 훔치다, 들치기하다
get away with ~을 모면하다, 무사히 빠져나가다, 넘어가다
demonstration 증명; 증거   competence 능력, 자신감
counter ~에 대항하다, ~을 거역하다
apprehension 체포   deliberately 고의로, 의도적으로
significant 중요한   predictor 예측 변수

---

17 독해 > Reading for Writing > 빈칸 구 완성   답 ③

| **해석** | 애착의 중요성을 보여 주는 한 전형적인 연구에서, Wisconsin대학교의 심리학자 Harry Harlow와 Margaret Harlow는 새끼 원숭이들의 반응을 조사했다. 새끼들은 생물학적 어미들에게서 분리되었고 두 가지의 대리모들이 우리에 들여보내졌다. 하나는 철사 엄마였는데, 나무로 된 둥근 머리, 차가운 철사 뭉치, 그리고 새끼 원숭이가 빨 수 있는 젖병으로 구성되어 있었다. 두 번째 엄마는 발열되는 테리 직물 담요로 싸인 고무 스펀지 형태였다. 새끼 원숭이들은 젖을 먹으러 철사 엄마에게로 갔으나, 따스한 테리 직물 엄마를 압도적으로 선호하고 상당히 더 많은 시간을 그것과 함께 보냈다. 따스한 테리 직물 엄마는 젖을 주지 않았지만 ③ 편안함을 제공했다.
① 일자리   ② 약
③ 편안함   ④ 교육

| **정답해설** | ③ 새끼 원숭이의 대리모 실험에 관한 글이다. 새끼 원숭이는 젖은 주지만 차가운 철사 대리모보다는 젖은 주지 않지만 따스한 테리 직물 엄마와 더 많은 시간을 보냈다. 이러한 실험 결과를 바탕으로 빈칸에는 테리 직물 엄마가 새끼 원숭이에게 제공한 것이 무엇인지가 들어가야 하는데, 선지 중에서 빈칸에 가장 적절한 것은 comfort(편안함)이다.

어휘

attachment 애착   separate 분리하다, 떼어 놓다
biological 생물학적인   consist of ~로 구성되다
mesh 그물망, 철망   foam 발포고무, 스펀지

---

18 문법 > 시제   답 ①

| **해석** | 나의 생물학적 부모는 입양을 위해 (부모의 권리를) 포기했고 나는 생애 첫 10년을 고아원에서 보냈다. 나는 나한테 무슨 잘못이 있는 거라고 생각하며 여러 해를 보냈다. 내 부모가 나를 원하지 않는다면, 누가 그럴 수 있겠는가? 나는 내가 무엇을 잘못했는지 그리고 왜 그렇게 많은 사람들이 나를 떠나 보냈는지 알아내려고 노력했다. 이제 나는 그 누구에게도 가까이 갈 수 없다. 왜냐하면 만약 내가 그렇게 하면 그들은 나를 떠날지도 모르기 때문이다. 어릴 때 나는 살아남기 위해 감정적으로 나 자신을 고립시켜야 했고, 여전히 나는 내가 아이였을 때 가지고 있었던 가정대로 움직인다. 나는 버림받는 것이 너무 두려워서 모험을 하거나 최소한의 위험조차 감수하지 않을 것이다. 나는 지금 40살이지만 여전히 어린아이같다.

| **정답해설** | ① 등위접속사 and로 연결된 두 개의 절의 시제가 서로 상이하므로 어법상 적절하지 않다. 과거에 고아원에서 보냈던 10년에 관해 말하고 있으므로 과거형 spent가 되어야 옳다.

| **오답해설** | ② what 이하의 절이 불완전하므로 what이 figure out의 목적어 역할을 하는 명사절을 이끄는 것은 적절하다.
③ 주어의 동작이 자기 자신에게 미치고 있으므로 목적어로 재귀대명사 myself를 사용한 것은 옳다.
④ 「so + 형용사/부사 + that …」은 '매우 ~해서 …하다'라는 관용 표현으로, 해당 문장에서는 알맞게 사용되었다.

어휘

release (권리 등을) 포기하다; 양도하다
adoption 입양   biological 생물학적인
orphanage 고아원   figure out 알아내다
isolate 고립시키다   emotionally 감정적으로
operate 작동하다, 움직이다   assumption 추정, 가정, 명제, 가설
desert 버리다, 유기하다   venture out 무릅쓰다, 감수하다

---

19 문법 > 동사   답 ①

| **해석** | 음악은 일상생활로 이전될 수 있는 심리 요법 효과를 지닐 수 있다. 수많은 학자들은 사람들이 심리 요법 매개체로써 음악을 이용해야 한다고 제안했다. 음악 요법은 광의로 '그들의 심리적, 육체적, 인지적, 또는 사회적 기능을 향상시킬 수 있는 개인의 치료 또는 재활에의 보조 도구로서 음악의 사용'으로 정의될 수 있다. 음악으로부터의 긍정적인 감정적 경험은 치료 과정을 향상시킬 수 있고, 그리하여 전통적인 인지적/행동적 방법과 그것들의 일상적 목표로의 전이를 강화시킬 수 있다. 이는 부분적으로 음악과 일상적 행동에 의해 끌어내어진 감정적 경험이 긍정적인 감정과 동기 부여를 초래하는 중복되는 신경 경로를 공유하기 때문일지도 모른다.

| **정답해설** | ① suggest는 5형식 동사로 사용될 수 없으며, 동명사 또는 that절을 목적어로 취할 수 있다. 따라서 A number of scholars suggested that people (should) use music as psychotherapeutic agent.가 되어야 옳다.

| **오답해설** | ② functioning은 명사화된 동명사로 형용사의 수식을 받을 수 있다.
③ 등위접속사 and는 동일한 형태의 단어, 구, 절을 연결한다. 이 문장에서는 조동사 may 뒤에 오는 동사원형 improve와 병렬 구

조를 이루는 strengthen이 적절하게 사용되었다.

④ 부사절 접속사 because절의 주어 emotional experiences가 복수형이므로 동사도 복수형 share가 알맞게 쓰였다. 여기서 elicited by music and everyday behaviors는 주어 emotional experiences를 수식하는 과거분사구이다.

어휘

agent 매개물	broadly 광범위하게, 폭넓게; 광의로
define 정의하다	adjunct 부속물; 조수, 보조 도구
rehabilitation 재활	cognitive 인지의
functioning 기능	therapeutic 치료의
process 과정, 절차	partially 부분적으로
elicit 이끌어 내다, 유도하다	overlap 중복되다, 겹치다
neurological 신경학상의, 신경의	pathway 경로

---

20 독해 > Reading for Writing > 빈칸 구 완성　　답 ②

| 해석 | 문화적 이해는 보통 측정할 수 있는 증거보다는 ② 편견에 기초하여 이루어진다. 주장은 순환하는 경향이 있다. 사람들은 게으르기 때문에 가난하다. 우리가 그들이 게으른지 어떻게 "아는가"? 왜냐하면 그들이 가난하기 때문이다. 이러한 이해의 선동자들은 낮은 생산성이 게으름과 노력의 부족이 아니라 생산에의 자본 투입 부족으로부터 온다는 것을 이해하지 못한다. 아프리카의 농부들은 게으른 것이 아니라 토양, 영양분, 트랙터, 지선 도로, 관개된 토지, 저장 시설과 같은 것들이 부족한 것이다. 아프리카인들이 일을 거의 하지 않아서 가난하다는 고정 관념은 남녀를 불문하고 몹시 힘든 노동이 일상인 마을에서 하루를 보냄으로써 바로 잠재워진다.

① 통계　　　　　　② 편견
③ 외모　　　　　　④ 환경

| 정답해설 | ② 빈칸에는 '측정할 수 있는 증거'와는 대조되는 표현이 들어가는 것이 적절하다. 아프리카 농부들이 게을러서 가난하다는 것은 고정 관념이고 실제로는 농사에 필요한 토양, 도구, 시설이 부족하기 때문에 가난하다고 했는데 토양, 영양분, 트랙터, 지선 도로 등등이 '측정할 수 있는 증거'에 해당하므로 빈칸에는 '고정 관념'에 해당하는 단서가 들어가야 한다. 따라서 prejudice(편견)가 빈칸에 알맞다.

어휘

interpretation 해석, 이해	
on the basis of ~에 기초하여, ~을 기준으로	
measurable 측정 가능한	argument 주장
circular 순환하는	promoter 주장자, 선동자
productivity 생산성	input 투입, 입력
nutrient 영양	feeder road 지선 도로
irrigate 관개하다, 물을 대다	plot 작은 지면[땅], 구획된 터
storage 저장	facility 시설, 설비
like 동등한[같은] 것(들)	stereotype 고정 관념
put ~ to rest ~을 잠재우다[중단시키다]	
backbreaking 매우 힘든, 고된	norm 표준, 일반적인 것; 규범
statistics 통계	prejudice 편견
appearance 외모	circumstances 환경, 상황

---

21 독해 > Logical Reading > 삽입　　답 ③

| 해석 | 농업에서 자유 시장은 결코 작동한 적이 없고, 앞으로도 그러할 것이다. 가족 농장의 경제 원리는 기업의 그것과는 매우 다르다: 가격이 떨어지면 기업은 사람들을 정리 해고하고 일 없는 공장의 가동을 중단시킬 수 있다. 마침내 시장은 공급과 수요 사이의 새로운 균형을 찾는다. ③ 그러나 식품에 대한 수요는 탄력적이지 않다. 사람들은 식품이 단지 저렴하다고 하여 더 많이 먹지는 않는다. 그리고 농부들을 정리 해고하는 것이 공급을 줄이는 것에 도움이 되지 않는다. 당신은 나를 해고할 수 있지만 나의 땅을 해고할 수는 없다. 왜냐하면 더 많은 현금 유동성을 필요로 하거나 나보다 더 효율적이라고 생각하는 다른 농부 몇몇이 들어와서 그것을 경작할 것이기 때문이다.

| 정답해설 | ③ 주어진 문장에서는 But을 통해 이전 내용과는 대조적인 내용을 제시하고 있다. 주어진 문장에서는 식품의 수요가 탄력성 있지 않다고 설명하였으므로, 그 앞에는 탄력성 있게 변화하는 수요에 관한 진술이 나와야 함을 알 수 있다. ③ 앞에서 가격이 하락할 때 기업은 노동자와 공장을 해고함으로써 수요와 공급을 탄력적으로 조절하여 균형을 맞출 수 있다고 하였다. 그러나 ③ 뒤에는 순접의 접속사 and로 시작하면서 농부를 해고하는 것은 공급을 줄이는 데 도움이 되지 않아 탄력적이지 않은 경제 원리를 서술하고 있다. 즉 ③ 이전 내용과는 대조적인 내용이므로, 주어진 문장이 들어갈 가장 적절한 위치는 ③이다.

어휘

demand 수요	lay off 정리 해고하다
idle 한가한, 할 일이 없는	supply 공급
cash flow 현금 유동성, 현금 유출입	farm 경작하다, 농사짓다

---

22 독해 > Macro Reading > 주제　　답 ②

| 해석 | 일상적 훈련은 운동선수에게 특별한 영양학적 필요 사항을 만드는데, 특히 훈련 헌신도가 거의 상근직인 엘리트 선수일 경우 그러하다. 그러나 레크리에이션 스포츠조차도 영양학적 필요 사항을 만들어 낼 것이다. 그리고 스포츠에의 관여도가 어느 정도이든 간에 당신이 훈련으로부터 최대한의 성과를 얻으려면 이러한 도전 과제들을 충족시켜야만 한다. 잘 먹지 않는다면 당신의 훈련 목적의 많은 부분을 잃게 될 것이다. 최악의 경우의 시나리오에서는, 식이 문제와 (영양) 결핍이 훈련 성과를 직접적으로 손상시킬 것이다. 다른 상황에서, 당신은 나아질 수도 있지만 당신의 잠재력 이하의 속도로 또는 당신의 경쟁자보다 더 느리게 나아질 것이다. 그러나, 긍정적인 측면에서, 매일 올바른 식사 계획을 짠다면, 당신의 훈련에의 헌신은 충분히 보상받을 것이다.

① 신체 유연성을 향상시키는 방법
② 운동할 때 잘 먹는 것의 중요성
③ 과도한 다이어트에 의해 유발되는 건강 문제
④ 지속적인 훈련을 통해 기술을 향상시키기

| 정답해설 | ② 본문에 반복적으로 nutritional needs가 등장하므로, 본문은 영양 섭취에 관련된 내용이란 것을 유추할 수 있다. 중반부에 잘 먹지 않는다면 훈련 목적의 많은 부분을 잃게 될 거라고 한 다음, 식이 문제와 (영양) 결핍이 훈련 성과에 미치는 부정적인 영향을 언급했다. 마지막 문장에서 올바른 식사 계획을 짠다면 훈련을 열심히 한 것에 대해 보상받을 거라고 하여 운동할 때 잘 먹는 것의 중요성을 다시 강조했다. 따라서 글의 주제로 가장 적절한 것은 ②이다.

| 오답해설 | ① 유연성에 관해서는 본문에 언급되지 않는다.
③ 본문에서는 다이어트가 아니라 훈련 중 식이 요법에 관해 설명하고 있다.

④ 본문은 훈련에 관한 내용이기는 하지만 훈련 시 영양 섭취에 초점이 맞추어진 글이다.

어휘

nutritional 영양의	athlete 운동선수
commitment 헌신, 약속, 전념	recreational 레크리에이션의, 오락의
challenge 도전 과제; 문제	involvement 관여, 연루, 참가
meet 충족시키다	sound 충분한; 건강한
deficiency 결핍, 부족	impair 손상시키다, 해치다
flexibility 유연성	excessive 과도한

---

23   독해 > Macro Reading > 주제   답 ③

| 해석 | Ernst Gombrich라고 하는 매우 존경받는 미술사가가 "관람자의 몫"이라고 불리는 것에 대해 글을 썼다. 관람자가 예술 작품을 "완성시킨다"라는 것과 예술 작품의 의미의 일부는 바라보는 사람에서 나온다는 것이 Gombrich의 믿음이었다. 그러므로 당신이 바라본다. 잘못된 답은 없다. 왜냐하면 예술 작품을 완성시키는 관람자는 바로 당신이기 때문이다. 만일 당신이 갤러리에서 미술품을 본다면, 예술 작품 옆에 있는 벽에 쓰인 글을 읽어 보라. 만일 직원이 있다면, 질문을 하라. 함께 간 방문자들에게 그들의 생각을 물어보라. 질문을 하는 것이 더 잘 이해하는 것의 비결이다. 그리고 그것은 예술뿐만 아니라 인생의 어느 것에라도 적용된다. 하지만 무엇보다도 먼저, 예술 작품 앞에서 자신감을 가져라. 만일 당신이 예술 작품을 찬찬히 보고 있다면, 당신은 의도된 관람자이고 당신이 생각하는 것은 중요하다. 당신이 중요한 단 한 명의 비평가이다.

| 정답해설 | ③ 본문은 미술사가 Ernst Gombrich가 주장한 '관람자의 몫'에 관한 내용으로, 두 번째 줄 It was Gombrich's belief that ~ from the person viewing it.을 참고하면 그는 예술 작품을 완성시키는 것이 관람자라고 했다. 또한 필자는 예술 작품 감상에 잘못된 답은 없으며 당신이 생각하는 것이 중요하다고 말한다. 따라서 글의 주제로 가장 적절한 것은 ③이다.

어휘

well-respected 매우 존경받는	beholder 보는 사람
share 몫, 부담	fellow 동료
go for ~에 해당되다	above all 무엇보다도, 특히
contemplate 바라보다, 응시하다	intend 의도하다
matter 중요하다	critic 비평가
count 중요하다	

---

24   독해 > Micro Reading > 내용일치/불일치   답 ②

| 해석 | 아르헨티나는 세계에서 8번째로 큰 나라이고, 거의 남미의 남쪽 절반 전체를 이루고 있다. 스페인에 의한 식민 지배는 1500년대 초에 시작되었으나 1816년 Jose de San Martin이 아르헨티나의 독립운동을 이끌었다. 아르헨티나의 문화는 19세기 말과 20세기 초 대규모 유럽인 이주에 의해 영향을 크게 받았는데, 주로 스페인과 이탈리아로부터였다. 다수의 사람들은 적어도 명목상으로는 가톨릭 신자였고, 그 나라에는 남미에서 가장 많은 유대인 인구(약 30만 명)가 있다. 1880년부터 1930년까지 농업 발전 덕분에 아르헨티나는 세계 10대 부국 중 하나였다.

| 정답해설 | ② 세 번째 문장 The culture of Argentina has been ~ primarily from Spain and Italy.에서 아르헨티나의 문화는 19세기 말과 20세기 초 대규모 유럽인 이주에 의해 영향을 크게 받았는데, 주로 스페인과 이탈리아로부터였다고 했으므로 본문 내용과

일치하지 않는 것을 알 수 있다.

| 오답해설 | ① 두 번째 문장 Colonization by Spain ~ for Argentine independence.에서 1816년 Jose de San Martin이 스페인의 식민 지배로부터 아르헨티나의 독립운동을 이끌었다고 했으므로 본문 내용과 일치하는 것을 알 수 있다.
③ 끝에서 두 번째 문장 후반부에서 남미에서 가장 많은 유대인 인구를 가지고 있다고 했으므로 본문 내용과 일치함을 알 수 있다.
④ 마지막 문장 From 1880 to 1930, ~ wealthiest nations.에서 1880년부터 1930년까지 농업 발전 덕분에 아르헨티나는 세계 10대 부국 중 하나였다고 했으므로 본문 내용과 일치한다.

어휘

comprise 구성하다, 이루다	colonization 식민 지배
migration 이주	primarily 주로
nominally 명목상으로는	agricultural 농업의

---

25   독해 > Micro Reading > 내용일치/불일치   답 ③

| 해석 | Sonja Henie는 링크와 스크린에서 세계에서 가장 유명한 피겨 스케이팅 선수 중 한 명으로서 출세 가도를 달린 그녀의 기술로 유명하다. 3번의 올림픽 금메달과 노르웨이 챔피언과 유럽 챔피언을 거머쥔 Henie는 소름 돋게 극적이고 발랄한 스타일의 피겨 스케이팅을 개발했다. 그녀는 짧은 치마, 흰색 스케이트, 그리고 매력적인 동작을 도입했다. 그녀의 화려한 회전과 점프는 모든 경쟁자들에 대한 기대치를 높였다. 1936년에 21세기 폭스사는 그녀가 'One in a Million'에 출연하도록 계약했고, 그녀는 곧 할리우드의 주연 여배우들 중 한 명이 되었다. 1941년, 그녀가 여배우로 출연한 영화 'Sun Valley Serenade'는 3개의 아카데미상 후보에 올랐다. Henie의 나머지 영화들은 찬사를 덜 받았지만 그녀는 아이스 스케이팅계에서 인기가 급증했다. 1938년에 그녀는 Hollywood Ice Revues라고 하는 화려한 투어 쇼를 선보였다. 그녀의 많은 사업은 그녀에게 부를 가져다주었지만, 그녀의 가장 큰 유산은 어린 소녀들이 스케이트를 타도록 영감을 준 것이었다.

| 정답해설 | ③ 본문 중반 In 1941, the movie 'Sun Valley Serenade' received ~ as an actress.를 보면 Henie가 1941년에 출연한 영화 'Sun Valley Serenade'는 아카데미상 3개 부문의 후보로 올랐다고 했을 뿐 수상했다는 내용은 없다.

| 오답해설 | ① 첫 번째 문장에서 본문 내용과 일치함을 알 수 있다.
② 두 번째 문장에서 본문 내용과 일치함을 알 수 있다.
④ 마지막 문장에서 본문 내용과 일치함을 알 수 있다.

어휘

thrillingly 오싹하게, 소름 돋게	theatrical 극적인, 연극 같은, 과장된
athletic 운동 경기의; 활발한, 발랄한	
spectacular 화려한; 깜짝 놀라게 하는	
raise the bar 기대치를 높이다	star 주연을 맡다
leading 선두의, 가장 중요한	nomination 후보에 오름, (후보) 지명
acclaim 열렬히 환호하다, 갈채를 받다	
trigger (방아쇠를) 당기다, 유발하다, 촉발하다	
surge 급등, 급증	extravagant 사치하는; 화려한
revue 리뷰(촌극·노래·춤 등을 함께 섞어 만든 일종의 뮤지컬 코미디 같은 것으로 풍자극의 성격을 띰)	
venture 모험, 모험적 사업	make a fortune 큰돈을 벌다
legacy 유산	inspire 영감을 주다

합격예상 체크		**취약영역 체크**		

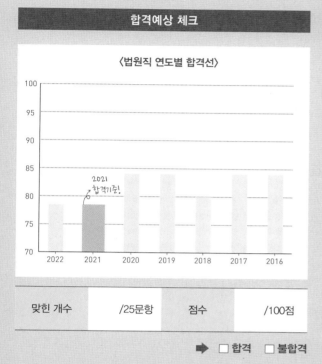

〈법원직 연도별 합격선〉

문항	정답	영역	문항	정답	영역
①	④	독해 > Reading for Writing > 요약	14	②	독해 > Macro Reading > 주장
2	④	독해 > Logical Reading > 문맥상 다양한 추론	15	①	독해 > Macro Reading > 주제
3	④	문법 > 태, 부사, 대명사	16	①	독해 > Macro Reading > 주제
4	②	독해 > Logical Reading > 배열	17	④	독해 > Logical Reading > 문맥상 다양한 추론
5	②	문법 > 동사	18	①	문법 > 접속사, 부정사, 동사
6	④	독해 > Logical Reading > 삽입	19	②	독해 > Logical Reading > 배열
7	①	독해 > Reading for Writing > 빈칸 구 완성	20	②	독해 > Logical Reading > 배열
8	②	독해 > Logical Reading > 삭제	21	②	독해 > Logical Reading > 삭제
9	①	독해 > Reading for Writing > 빈칸 절 완성	22	③	독해 > Logical Reading > 배열
10	③	독해 > Logical Reading > 문맥상 다양한 추론	23	②	독해 > Micro Reading > 내용일치/불일치
11	③	독해 > Macro Reading > 요지	24	②	독해 > Macro Reading > 심경
12	④	독해 > Macro Reading > 요지	25	②	독해 > Micro Reading > 내용일치/불일치
13	④	문법 > 분사			

⬇ 영역별 틀린 개수로 취약영역을 확인하세요!

맞힌 개수	/25문항	점수	/100점

어휘	/0	문법	/4	독해	/21	생활영어	/0

➡ □ 합격 □ 불합격

➡ 나의 취약영역: _____

※ [정답해설]과 [오답해설] 선지의 50% 표시는 〈1초 합격예측 서비스〉를 통해 수집된 선지 선택률을 나타냅니다.

---

1 독해 > Reading for Writing > 요약 | 오답률 38% | 답 ④

| 해석 | 미생물은 계산적인 존재가 아니다. 당신이 비누 샤워를 함으로써 수백만 마리의 그것들(미생물)을 도살할 때 당신이 어떠한 고통을 야기하는가에 대해 당신이 신경 쓰지 않는 것처럼, 그것들도 자신들이 당신에게 하는 일에 대해 신경 쓰지 않는다. 병원체가 당신에게 관심을 가지는 유일한 때는 그것이 당신을 너무 잘 죽일 때이다. 만일 그것들이 이동하기 전에 당신을 제거한다면, 그것들은 아마 스스로 사멸할 것이다. 사실 이것은 때때로 발생한다. 역사는 "한때 무시무시한 전염병을 일으킨 후 그것들이 생겨났을 때와 마찬가지로 불가사의하게 사라진" 질병들로 가득하다고 Jared Diamond는 지적한다. 그는 강력했지만 다행히도 일시적이었던 영국의 속립열(粟粒熱)을 인용하는데, 그것은 1485년부터 1552년까지 창궐하여, 소멸하기 전까지 그것이 가는 곳에서 수만 명의 사람들의 목숨을 빼앗았다. 너무 높은 효율성은 전염성이 있는 유기체 그 어떤 것에게나 좋은 것만은 아니다.

⬇

병원체가 더욱 (A) 전염성이 있을수록, 더 빨리 (B) 사라질 가능성이 있다.
① 더 약한 – 사라지다 ② 더 약한 – 퍼지다
③ 전염성이 있는 – 퍼지다 ④ 전염성이 있는 – 사라지다

| 정답해설 | ④ 62% 병원체가 이동하기도 전에 당신을 제거한다면, 스스로 사멸할 것이다. 한때 무시무시한 질병을 일으킨 후 그것들이 생겨났을 때와 마찬가지로 불가사의하게 사라진 질병들, 그리고 마지막 문장에서 너무 높은 효율성은 전염성이 있는 유기체 그 어떤 것에게나 좋은 것만은 아니라고 한 내용 등으로 미루어 보아 병

원체의 전염성이 높아 사람들을 더 빨리 죽게 한다면, 그것이 더 빨리 소멸될 수 있음을 알 수 있다. 따라서 빈칸에는 infectious와 disappear가 알맞다.(참고로, 빈칸 (B) 앞의 it is likely to be는 기출에 it is likely be to로 출제되었으나, 문법상 옳도록 it is likely to be로 수정하였다.)

| 더 알아보기 | infectious의 유의어

catching, contagious, communicable

어휘

microorganism 미생물 calculating 계산적인, 용의주도한
entity 존재, 실체
not A any more than B B가 아닌 것처럼 A도 아닌
distress 고통, 곤경 slaughter 도살하다
eliminate 제거하다
may well 아마도[틀림없이] ~할 것이다
epidemic 전염병, 유행병 cite 인용하다
robust 강력한, 강건한 mercifully 다행히도
transient 일시적인, 순간적인
rage 격심하게 계속되다, 맹위를 떨치다
burn oneself out 사력을 다하다, 과로로 일찍 죽다
efficiency 효율성 infectious 전염성의
organism 유기체; 생물, 미생물

2 독해 > Logical Reading > 문맥상 다양한 추론 답 ④

오답률 54%

| 해석 | 만약 글이 충실하고 좋으면, 작품을 희생시키지 않고 작가의 분위기와 기질이 결국 드러낼 것이다. 그러므로, 스타일을 얻기 위해서는, 아무것에도 영향을 주지 않는 것부터 시작하라. 즉, 독자의 관심을 글의 감각과 본질에 집중시켜라. 신중하고 정직한 작가는 스타일에 대해 걱정할 필요가 없다. 당신이 언어 사용에 능숙해질 때, 당신 자신이 나타날 것이기 때문에 당신의 스타일이 나타날 것이고, 이런 일이 일어나면 당신은 당신을 다른 마음으로부터 분리시키는 장벽을 깨고 마침내 당신을 글의 한가운데 서게 하는 것이 점점 더 쉬워짐을 알게 될 것이다. 다행히도, 작문, 즉 창조의 행위는 정신을 단련시킨다. 글쓰기는 계속해서 사고하는 한 가지 방법이며, 글쓰기의 실천과 습관은 <u>마음 속 생각을 배출시킨다</u>.

① 마음을 치료하기
② 세심해지도록 돕기
③ 그/그녀의 호기심을 충족시키기
④ 배경에 자신을 위치시키기

| 정답해설 | ④ 46% 본문은 글쓰기의 본질과 작가의 태도에 대해 구체적으로 언급하고 있다. 작가가 글쓰기 즉 언어 사용에 능숙해지면 창조와 정신 단련 또한 용이해짐을 이점으로 서술하고 있다. 밑줄 친 drains the mind는 '마음 속 생각을 배출시킨다'의 의미로 글쓰기 작업을 통한 장점에 해당된다. 이에 가장 가까운 의미로 창조 활동의 과정을 담는 표현으로는 ④ to place oneself in the background(배경에 스스로를 위치시키기)가 적절하다.

어휘

temper 성질	reveal 드러내다, 밝히다
at the expense of ~을 희생하여	affect 영향을 미치다
substance 본질	proficient 능숙한
emerge 나타나다	
break through ~을 돌파하다, 뚫고 나아가다	
barrier 장벽	composition 작문
discipline 단련시키다	go about 계속 ~하다
drain 빼내다, 비우다, 유출시키다	

3 문법 > 태, 부사, 대명사 답 ④

오답률 28%

| 해석 | 인생에서 자기 자신과 우리의 운명에 대한 우리의 불만족 중 일부는 실제 상황에 기반한 것이며, 일부는 사실이 아니고 그저 실제라고 (A) 인식되는 것이다. 그 인식된 것들은 선별되고 버려져야 한다. 현실은 바뀔 수 있거나 바뀔 수 없는 범주로 나뉘게 될 것이다. 그것이 후자에 있다면, 우리는 그것을 받아들이려고 노력해야 한다. 그것이 전자에 있다면, 우리는 그보다도 그것을 제거하거나, 교환하거나, 또는 수정하도록 노력할 대안을 가진 것이다. 우리 모두는 인생에서 고유한 목적이 있다. 그리고 우리 모두는 재능이 있는데, 단지 (B) 다르게 재능이 있는 것이다. 그것은 한 가지, 다섯 가지 또는 열 가지의 재능이 주어진 것이 공평한지 아니면 불공평한지에 대한 논쟁이 아니다. 그것은 우리의 재능을 가지고 우리가 무엇을 했느냐에 관한 것이다. 그것은 우리에게 주어진 (C) 것들에 우리가 얼마나 잘 투자해 왔느냐에 관한 것이다. 만일 누군가 자신들의 인생이 불공평하다는 관점을 고수한다면, 그것은 정말로 신에 대한 모욕을 하고 있는 것이다.

① 인식하다 – 다른 – 그것들을 ② 인식하다 – 다르게 – ~한 것들
③ 인식된 – 다른 – 그것들을 ④ 인식된 – 다르게 – ~한 것들

| 정답해설 | ④ (A) 주어 some이 가리키는 것은 dissatisfactions(불만족들)이며, 문맥상 '불만족'은 '인식되는' 수동의 관계이므로 과거분사 perceived가 적절하다. 등위접속사 and는 동일 문장 성분을 연결하는 병렬구조를 이끌기 때문에, 주어인 some을 수식하는 주격 보어인 형용사 false와 함께 and 이후에 형용사 역할을 하는 과거분사 perceived가 적절하다. 또한 등위 접속사 and가 절과 절을 연결하는 연결사로서 some are false and (some are) simply perceived ~로도 볼 수 있다.

(B) 형용사 gifted(재능이 있는)를 수식하고 있으므로, 부사 형태인 differently가 알맞다.

(C) 대명사 them과 those 모두 목적어 자리에 올 수 있으나, 뒤에 관계대명사가 생략된 목적격 관계대명사절(we have been given)의 수식을 받고 있으므로 them은 불가능하다. 따라서 those가 알맞다.

어휘

dissatisfaction 불만족	lot 운명, 운
circumstance 환경, 상황	perceive 인식하다, 인지하다
sort out 분류하다, 선별하다	discard 버리다
fall into ~로 나뉘다	classification 범주, 분류
strive 분투하다, 노력하다	alternative 대안
modify 수정하다	unique 고유의, 독특한
gifted 재능이 있는	invest 투자하다
hold on to ~을 고수하다	outlook 관점
offense 모욕, 무례	

4 독해 > Logical Reading > 배열 답 ②

오답률 33%

| 해석 | 사람들은 낮은 가격이나 경쟁사보다 낮은 가격을 부과함으로써 그들이 더 많은 고객을 얻을 것이라고 추측한다. 이것은 일반적인 오류이다.

(B) 그것은 경쟁사에 비해 인하된 가격을 부과하면, 당신은 고객 시장의 하위층을 유치하기 때문이다. 이러한 고객은 더 적은 비용으로 더 많은 것을 원하며 종종 당신의 비즈니스에서 더 많은 시간과 간접비를 차지한다. 그들은 또한 여러분이 상대하고 계속 만족시키기에 가장 어려운 고객일 수도 있다.

(C) 또한 아이러니하게도 더 좋은 고객이 더 높은 수준의 제품이나 서비스에 대해 더 높은 가격을 지불하기 때문에 당신은 더 좋은 고객을 쫓아 버리게 된다. 우리는 많은 경쟁사들이 시장에 나와 지속 가능하지 않은 일일 요금을 부과하는 것을 보아 왔다. 그들은 종종 그들의 할당량을 채우기 위해 고군분투하다가, 곧 포기하고 다른 일을 하는 것으로 넘어간다.

(A) 따라서, 당신은 시작할 때 더 적은 양, 더 높은 이윤의 제품 및 서비스를 갖는 것이 훨씬 좋다. 만일 부득이하다면, 당신은 가격을 낮추도록 언제든 협상할 수 있지만, 당신이 인상 협상을 할 수 있을 경우는 드물다.

| 정답해설 | ② 67% 주어진 글에서 낮은 가격을 제공하는 것이 더 많은 고객 유치에 도움이 될 것이라는 견해는 오류라고 주장하고 있다. 따라서 이러한 상황을 제시하며, 낮은 가격으로 유치된 고객의 단점에 대해 설명하고 있는 (B)가 주어진 글 이후에 바로 이어지는 것이 적절하다. 이후에는 also(또한)를 사용해 좋은 고객을 쫓아 버리는, 낮은 가격 제공의 단점을 부가적으로 설명하고 있는 (C)가 이어지는 것이 알맞다. 마지막으로, therefore(그러므로)를 이용해 이러한 이유로 높은 이윤의 제품 및 서비스를 책정하는 것이 더 낫다고 결론을 설명하고 있는 (A)가 오는 것이 흐름상 가장 적절하다. 따라서 (B) – (C) – (A)의 순서가 적절하다.

| 더 알아보기 | 결론을 유도하는 연결어(구)

- therefore 그러므로
- as a result 결과적으로
- accordingly 따라서
- thus 따라서
- consequently 그 결과
- finally 결국

어휘

competitor 경쟁자, 경쟁사	fallacy 오류, 틀린 생각
volume 양	margin 이윤, 마진
negotiate 협상하다	competition 경쟁; [집합적] 경쟁자
take up 차지하다	overhead(s) 간접비
sustainable 지속 가능한	quota 할당량

---

5 문법 > 동사　　오답률 28%　답 ②

| 해석 | 글쓰기를 즐기는 아이들은 종종 인쇄된 자신들의 작품을 보는 것에 관심이 있다. 한 가지 비격식적인 접근법은 그들의 시를 타이핑하고 인쇄하여 게시하는 것이다. 또는 많은 어린이 작가들의 시 선집 사본을 만들 수도 있다. 그러나 진정으로 열심이고 야심 있는 아이들에게는 출판을 위해 시를 제출하는 것이 훌륭한 목표이다. 그리고 아이들의 원본 시를 인쇄하는 몇몇 웹 및 인쇄 수단들이 있다. 어린이 시인들이 원고 제출 프로토콜(스타일, 형식 등등)에 익숙해지도록 도와라. 그들이 어떤 시를 가장 자랑스러워하는지 선택하고, 제출한 모든 것의 사본을 보유하며, 부모의 승낙을 받게 해 주어라. 그런 다음 그들의 작품이 받아들여지고 인쇄되어 나올 때 그들과 함께 축하하라. 그들을 축하하고, 그들의 성취를 공개적으로 보여 주고, 소문을 내라. 성공은 성공을 고무시킨다. 그리고 물론, 만일 그들의 작품이 거절된다면 지지와 격려를 해 주어라.

| 정답해설 | ② 72% 한 문장에는 본동사가 한 개만 존재해야 하는데, 문장 내에 이미 본동사 is가 있으므로 동사 형태인 submit은 알맞지 않다. 대신에 목적어(a poem)를 가지며 동시에 주어 역할을 할 수 있는 명사 상당어구가 필요하다. 따라서 submit은 준동사 submitting 또는 to submit으로 바뀌어야 옳다.

| 오답해설 | ① 0% 대명사 their가 가리키는 대상은 문장의 주어 Children으로 알맞다.

③ 7% 명사를 수식할 수 있는 의문형용사 which가 뒤의 명사 poems를 알맞게 수식하고 있다.

④ 21% 동사 showcase를 수식하는 자리이므로 부사인 publicly가 온 것은 어법상 옳다.

어휘

dedicated 열심인, 헌신하는	ambitious 야심에 찬, 야망 있는
submit 제출하다	worthy 훌륭한
resource 공급원, 수단	manuscript 원고
permission 허가, 승낙	showcase 보여주다, 소개하다
accomplishment 성취	inspire 영감을 주다, 고무하다
reject 거부하다, 거절하다	

---

6 독해 > Logical Reading > 삽입　　오답률 33%　답 ④

| 해석 | 푸에블로 인디언(Pueblo Indian) 문화에서, 옥수수는 사람들에게 생명의 상징이다. "태양과 빛의 할머니"인 Corn Maiden은 이 선물을 가져와 사람들에게 생명력을 가져다 주었다. 태양에 의해 옥수수가 생명을 얻으면, Corn Maiden은 인간의 몸에 태양의 불길을 가져다주며, 자연을 통해 그녀의 사랑과 힘의 여러 표상을 인간에게 보여 준다. 각각의 Maiden은 아

이에게 주어진 것과 같은 사랑으로 길러진 옥수수 씨앗 하나를 가져다주고, 이 한 개의 씨앗이 전체 부족을 영원히 살아가게 해 준다. ④ 그 부족으로부터의 사랑과 힘을 받아 그 작은 씨앗들은 무럭무럭 크게 자라 사람들을 위한 작물이 된다. Corn Maiden들의 영혼은 부족 사람들과 함께 영원히 존재한다.

| 정답해설 | ④ 67% 주어진 문장의 the tribe와 the tiny seeds를 통해, tribe와 seed가 이전에 먼저 언급되어야 함을 알 수 있다. ④ 이전 문장에서 the entire tribe와 one seed라는 새로운 정보가 제공되고 있으므로, ④에 주어진 문장이 위치해야 한다.(참고로, ③ 앞에 나오는 her love and power는 기출에 his love and power로 출제되었으나, Corn Maiden이 여성형이므로 문법상 his를 her로 수정하였다.)

어휘

mature 성숙하다	representation 표상, 표현(한 것); 묘사
nurture 기르다, 양육하다	sustain 지속하다; 유지하다; 부양하다
tribal 부족의	

---

7 독해 > Reading for Writing > 빈칸 구 완성　　오답률 50%　답 ①

| 해석 | 너도밤나무, 참나무, 가문비나무, 그리고 소나무는 항상 새로운 것(잎, 가지)들을 자라게 하며 오래된 것들을 제거해야 한다. 가장 분명한 변화는 매년 가을에 발생한다. 잎들은 제 역할들을 해 왔다: 그것들은 이제 시들고 충해로 구멍이 숭숭 나 있다. 나무들이 그것(잎)들에게 이별을 고하기 전에, 그것(나무)들은 노폐물을 그것(잎)들 속에 주입한다. 당신은 그것(나무)들이 배설의 기회를 잡고 있다고 말할 수 있을 것이다. 그러면 그것(나무)들은 잎이 자라고 있는 잔가지로부터 각각의 잎을 분리시키기 위해 약한 조직층을 자라게 하고, 잎들은 다음 미풍이 불 때 땅으로 떨어진다. 이제 땅을 뒤덮는 바스락거리는, 그리고 당신이 그것들 사이를 밟고 지날 때 매우 만족스러운 바스락바스락 소리를 내는, 잎들은 근본적으로 ① 나무의 화장실 휴지인 것이다.

① 나무의 화장실 휴지　　　② 식물의 부엌
③ 나무의 폐　　　　　　　④ 곤충의 부모

| 정답해설 | ① 50% 나무들이 잎들에게 이별을 고하기 전 노폐물을 그 속에 주입한다는 내용, 그리고 나무들이 배설의 기회를 잡고 있다고 한 내용 등을 통해 땅에 떨어진 나뭇잎들을 묘사할 가장 적절한 표현은 ①임을 유추할 수 있다.

어휘

beech 너도밤나무	oak 참나무
spruce 가문비나무	pine 소나무
get rid of ~을 없애다, 제거하다	worn out 낡은, 닳은
riddle with ~로 구멍이 숭숭 나다	bid ~ adieu ~에게 이별을 고하다
pump A into B A를 B에게 주입시키다	
relieve oneself 배설하다, 변을 보다	
tissue 조직	twig 잔가지
tumble 떨어지다	breeze 미풍, 산들바람
rustle 바스락거리다	
scrunch (자갈·눈 위를 밟을 때와 같은) 부스럭거리는[뽀드득뽀드득] 소리를 내다	
scuffle 발을 질질 끌며 걷다	

| **해석** | 소설(허구)은 많은 쓰임이 있는데, 그것(이용)들 중 하나는 공감을 구축하는 것이다. TV를 시청하거나 영화를 볼 때, 당신은 다른 사람에게 발생하는 일들을 보고 있는 것이다. 산문 소설은 당신이 26개의 글자와 몇 개의 구두점으로부터 구축하는 어떤 것이며, 당신, 오로지 당신만이 당신의 상상력을 이용하여 세계를 창조하고 그곳에 살며 다른 사람의 눈을 통해 본다. 당신은 사물을 느끼고 그게 아니라면 당신이 결코 알지 못할 장소와 세계를 방문한다. ② 다행히도, 지난 10년간 세계에서 가장 아름답고 알려지지 않은 많은 장소들이 각광을 받아 왔다. 당신은 그곳에 있는 모든 사람들이 나와 마찬가지라는 것을 알게 된다. 당신은 다른 사람이 되는 중이고, 당신이 자신의 세계로 돌아가면, 당신은 약간 달라질 것이다.

| **정답해설** | ② 93% 소설을 통해 허구의 장소에서 다른 사람의 눈으로 세상을 보는 것에 관한 글인데, 세계의 아름답고 알려지지 않은 장소들이 각광받고 있다는, 실제 세계의 장소에 대해 언급하고 있는 ②는 글 전체 흐름상 어색하다.

| **오답해설** | ① 0% 이전 문장에서 상상력을 통해 세계를 창조한다고 설명하고 있으므로, 이어서 (소설을 통해) 결코 알 수 없었던 장소와 세계를 방문하게 된다고 설명하는 것은 문맥상 적절하다.

③ 7% there는 ①의 문장에서 언급된 places and worlds you would never otherwise know를 가리키고 있으므로 문맥상 적절하다.

④ 0% 소설을 통해 다른 사람의 눈으로 본다고 했으므로, 다른 사람이 된다고 말하는 것은 문맥상 자연스럽다.

어휘

fiction 소설, 허구	empathy 공감, 감정 이입
prose fiction 산문 픽션[소설]	a handful of 소수의 ~
punctuation mark 구두점	otherwise 그렇지 않으면
in the spotlight 각광을 받아	

| **해석** | 버드나무와 포플러 나무의 씨앗은 너무 작아서 당신은 날아다니는 폭신폭신한 털에서 두 개의 작은 어두운 색깔의 점만을 판별할 수 있을 것이다. 이러한 씨앗들 중 한 개는 무게가 0.0001그램에 불과하다. 이렇게 빈약한 에너지를 비축하고 있기에 묘목은 원기가 다 고갈되기 전까지 겨우 1~2 밀리미터만 자랄 수 있으며, 어린 잎을 이용해 스스로 만드는 식량에 의존해야 한다. 그러나 그것은 오직 그 작은 싹을 위협하는 경쟁이 없는 장소에서나 유효하다. 그것 위에 그늘을 드리우는 다른 식물들은 즉시 그 새 생명을 소멸시킬 것이다. 그래서, 이와 같은 작은 솜털 씨앗 주머니가 가문비나무 또는 너도밤나무 숲에 떨어지면, 그 씨앗의 생명은 시작도 하기 전에 끝난다. 그것이 바로 버드나무와 포플러 나무가 ① 비어 있는 지역에 정착하는 것을 선호하는 이유이다.
① 비어 있는 지역에 정착하는 것을 선호하다
② 초식동물의 식량으로 선택되어 왔다
③ 사람의 개입을 피하도록 진화해 왔다
④ 늦겨울까지 죽은 잎을 가지고 있다

| **정답해설** | ① 55% 버드나무와 포플러 나무 씨앗의 성장 조건에 대한 글이다. 이 씨앗들은 스스로 만드는 식량에 의존해야 하는데, 이것은 그것을 위협하는 경쟁자가 없는 장소에서만 유효하다고 했다. 즉, 다른 경쟁자가 없는 빈 곳에 자리를 잡는 것이 씨앗들의 생

존 전략임을 유추할 수 있으므로 빈칸에는 ①이 들어가는 것이 적절하다.

어휘

willow 버드나무	poplar 포플러 나무
fluffy 솜털 같은, 폭신폭신한	meagre 빈약한
reserve 저장, 비축	seedling 묘목
run out of steam 기력이 다하다	for oneself 스스로, 자신을 위해
competition 경쟁(자)	sprout 새싹
extinguish 소멸시키다	spruce 가문비나무
beech 너도밤나무	settle 정착하다
unoccupied 비어 있는, 임자 없는	territory 구역, 지역
herbivore 초식동물	intervention 개입, 간섭

| **해석** | 좋은 워킹화는 중요하다. 대부분의 주요 스포츠 브랜드는 걷기용으로 특별히 고안된 신발을 제공한다. 착화감과 편안함이 스타일보다 더 중요하다. 당신의 신발은 지탱해 주는 듯한 느낌이 들어야 하며, 조이거나 갑갑해서는 안 된다. 갑피는 가볍고, 통기성 있으며, 유연해야 하고, 깔창은 방습이 되고, 밑창은 충격을 흡수해야 한다. 뒤꿈치 굽은 ③ 낮추어져(→ 높여져)야 한다. 그래서 신발의 뒤쪽 밑창은 앞쪽보다 두 배 더 두껍다. 마지막으로, 앞심은 당신이 스포츠 양말을 신고 있을 때조차도 공간이 충분해야 한다.
① 지탱하는, 지지하는　　② 충격을 흡수하는
③ 낮추어진　　　　　　④ 널찍한

| **정답해설** | ③ 67% the sole at the back of the shoe is two times thicker than at the front(신발의 뒤쪽 밑창은 앞쪽보다 두 배 더 두껍다)로 보아 뒷굽이 앞굽보다 더 높다는 사실을 알 수 있다. 따라서 뒷굽이 '낮추어져야(lowered)' 한다는 흐름은 문맥상 적절하지 않다. lowered(낮추어진)는 raised(높여진)가 되어야 흐름상 알맞다.

| **오답해설** | ① 10% 워킹화는 착화감과 편안함이 중요하다고 했으므로 신발이 supportive(지탱하는)하게 느껴진다는 흐름은 문맥상 적절하다.

② 10% absorbent는 '흡수력 있는'이라는 뜻의 형용사로, 하이픈(-)을 이용해 앞에 명사에 붙어 '~을 흡수하는'이라는 뜻으로 사용될 수 있다. 여기에서 shock-absorbent는 워킹화의 밑창이 '충격을 흡수하는'이라는 표현이 되며, 이는 문맥상 적절하다.

④ 13% (두꺼운) 스포츠 양말을 신고 있을 때조차도 앞심(toe box)은 spacious(널찍한, 공간이 충분한)해야 한다는 흐름은 적절하다.

어휘

athletic 운동의, 스포츠의	fit 맞음
constrict 조이다; 수축시키다	upper (신발의) 갑피
breathable 통기성 있는	insole 깔창
moisture-resistant 방습의	sole 밑창
toe box (신발 끝의 안쪽에 넣는) 앞심	

11 독해 > Macro Reading > 요지 오답률 5% 답 ③

| 해석 | 만일 당신의 아이들이 비디오 게임을 할 때마다 싸운다면, 그들이 게임을 하려고 앉을 때 당신이 그들의 소리를 들을 수 있을 만큼 충분히 가까이 있도록 하라. 그들이 사용하는 공격적인 특정 단어 또는 목소리의 톤을 들으려고 귀를 기울이고 있다가 그것이 발생하기 전에 개입하도록 노력하라. 일단 화가 가라앉으면, 아이들을 앉혀 놓고 비난 또는 힐난하지 않고 문제를 논의하게끔 해 보아라. 아이들 각자에게 방해받지 않고 말할 기회를 주고 그들 스스로 문제에 대한 해결책을 생각해 내게끔 하라. 아이들이 초등학생 나이가 되면, 그들은 그 해결책 중 어떤 것이 서로에게 이득이 되는 해결책인지, 그리고 어느 것이 가장 효과가 있고 시간이 지나면서 서로를 만족시킬 수 있을지 평가할 수 있다. 그들은 또한 해결책이 더 이상 효과가 없을 때 문제를 다시 논의하는 것도 배워야 한다.
① 아이들에게 자신들의 시험을 평가하도록 요구하라.
② 아이들이 서로 경쟁하게끔 하라.
③ 아이들이 갈등을 해결하는 것을 배우도록 도와라.
④ 아이들에게 논쟁에서 이기는 법을 가르쳐라.

| 정답해설 | ③ 95% 아이들이 비디오 게임을 할 때 싸우는 경우를 예로 들며, 아이들 간에 문제가 생기기 전에 부모가 어떻게 개입해야 하는지를 설명하는 글이다. 본문 중반 Give each kid a chance to talk, ~ have them try to come up with solutions to the problem themselves.라고 권하고 있으므로, 글의 요지로 가장 적절한 것은 Help your kids learn to resolve conflict.(아이들이 갈등을 해결하는 것을 배우도록 도와라.)이다. (해당 지문의 3번째 문장에서 seat your kids는 기출 문제에서 sit your kids로 출제되었지만, 어법상 seat your kids가 적절하므로 본 교재에는 옳게 수정하여 수록하였다.)

어휘

aggressive 공격적인
temper 화, 울화통; 성질
accuse 비난하다, 힐난하다, 고소하다
uninterrupted 방해받지 않는
evaluate 평가하다
intervene 개입하다
blame 책임을 전가하다, 비난하다
come up with ~을 생각해 내다
revisit 다시 논의하다

12 독해 > Macro Reading > 요지 오답률 5% 답 ④

| 해석 | 어떻게 해서든 세균을 피하려는 것이 현재의 추세이다. 우리는 화장실, 부엌, 그리고 공기를 살균한다. 우리는 세균을 죽이기 위해 손을 소독하고 구강 청결제로 가글한다. 일부 사람들은 가능한 한 많은 사람들과의 접촉을 피하고 심지어는 세균에 노출될까 봐 악수도 하지 않는다. 나는 일부 사람들은 그들의 마음을 빼고는 전부 정화할 것이라고 말해도 무방하다고 생각한다. "거품 속의 아이(the Boy in the Bubble)" 이야기를 기억하는가? 그는 면역 체계 없이 태어나 인간과의 접촉 없이 완전한 무균실에서 살아야만 했다. 물론, 모든 사람들은 청결과 개인 위생에 대한 합당한 기준을 유지하기 위해 세심한 조치를 취해야 한다. 그러나 많은 경우에 우리는 과도해지고 있지 않은가? 우리가 대부분의 세균과 접촉할 때, 우리의 몸은 그것들을 파괴하고, 그 결과 우리의 면역 체계 그리고 더 나아가 질병과 싸울 수 있는 능력을 강화시킨다. 그러므로, 이 "좋은 세균들"은 사실 우리를 더 건강하게 만든다. 모든 세균을 피하고 살균 환경에서 사는 것이 가능하더라도, 그렇다면 우리는 "거품 속의 아이"처럼 되지 않겠는가?

| 정답해설 | ④ 95% 모든 사람들은 청결과 개인 위생 기준 유지를 위해 세심한 조치를 취해야 하지만, 많은 경우에 우리는 과도해지고 있다고 한 후 세균은 우리를 더 건강하게 만들어 줄 수 있다고

주장한다. 따라서 글의 요지로 가장 적절한 것은 '과도하게 세균을 제거하려고 하는 것이 오히려 면역 능력을 해친다.'이다.

어휘

at all cost 어떻게 해서든, 무슨 수를 써서라도
disinfect 살균하다, 소독하다
sanitize (소독·청소·살균 등으로) 위생적이 되게 하다
for fear of ~할까 봐 (두려워서) purify 정화하다
immune system 면역 체계 prudent 세심한, 신중한
reasonable 합당한, 적당한 hygiene 위생
overboard 과도한, 너무 심한 sterile 균 없는, 살균한

오답률 TOP 3

13 문법 > 분사 오답률 51% 답 ④

| 해석 | 황금 도시로 알려진 Jaisalmer는 Khyber 고개로 가는 길에 있는 과거 캐러밴(대상 행렬)의 중심지였던 곳으로, 모래 바다 위에 솟아 있으며, 그곳의 30피트 높이의 성벽과 중세의 사암으로 된 요새는 사파이어 빛 하늘로 솟아오른 조각된 첨탑과 궁전을 보호한다. 좁고 구불구불한 길과 숨겨진 사원들이 있는 Jaisalmer는 『아라비안나이트(The Arabian Nights)』에서 곧바로 튀어나왔고, 이곳의 생활은 거의 변하지 않아서 13세기로 거슬러 올라가 있는 당신 자신을 상상하기가 쉽다. 그곳은 인구의 4분의 1이 성벽 안에 살면서 여전히 제 기능을 하는 인도 내의 유일한 요새 도시이고, 그곳은 (사람들이 많이 밟아) 다져진 길에서 벗어나 충분히 멀리 있어서 관광업으로 인한 최악의 파괴를 면했다. 그 도시의 부유함은 본래 지나가는 낙타 캐러밴들에게 부과한 상당한 통행료에서 비롯되었다.

| 정답해설 | ④ 49% 「with + 명사 + 분사」의 with 분사구문의 형태이다. 명사(one quarter of its population)와 live가 능동의 관계이므로, lived는 현재분사인 living으로 고쳐야 한다.

| 오답해설 | ① 2% 주어인 Jaisalmer와 know가 수동 관계이므로, Knowing을 과거분사 Known으로 고친 것은 적절하다.

② 40% 이 문장에서 본동사는 rises이고 its 30-foot-high walls 앞에 접속사가 없으므로 또 다른 동사인 shelters가 나오는 것은 올바르지 않다. 따라서 shelters는 its 30-foot-high walls and medieval sandstone fort를 주어로 하는 독립 분사구문이 되어야 하는데 주어와 shelter가 능동 관계이므로 sheltering으로 고친 것은 올바르다.

③ 9% 문맥상 '너무 ~해서 …하다'라는 뜻의 「so ~ that …」 결과 구문이 되는 것이 알맞다. 이때 부정어 so little이 앞으로 나가 조동사 has와 주어가 도치된 형태이다. 따라서 which를 명사절 접속사 that으로 바꾸는 것은 적절하다.

| 더 알아보기 | with 분사구문

동시에 일어나고 있는 상황을 묘사할 때 주로 쓰인다.
• with + 목적어 + 현재분사: 목적어와 분사의 관계가 능동일 때
• with + 목적어 + 과거분사: 목적어와 분사의 관계가 수동일 때

어휘

caravan 캐러밴, (특히 사막을 건너는) 대상 (행렬)
medieval 중세의 sandstone 사암
fort 요새 shelter 보호하다
carve 조각하다 soar 치솟다, 솟아오르다
winding 구불구불한 alter 변하다

fortress 요새, 성채　　　　　　　beaten 밟아 다져진
spare 피하게[면하게] 하다　　　ravage 파괴
substantial 상당한　　　　　　　toll 통행료

identity 정체성　　　　　　　　self-esteem 자존감
mother tongue 모국어

14　독해 > Macro Reading > 주장　　오답률 5%　답 ②

| 해석 | 학자들은 세계의 문제에 대해 냉담하지도 않고 무관심하지도 않다. 이러한 문제에 대한 책들이 그 어느 때보다 더 많이 출판되고 있지만, 일반 대중의 관심을 사로잡는 것은 거의 없다. 마찬가지로, 새로운 연구 발견들이 대학에서 끊임없이 이루어지고, 전 세계의 학회에서 공유되고 있다. 안타깝게도 이러한 활동의 대부분은 자기 잇속만을 차리는 일이다. 과학을 제외하고 — 그리고 여기에도, 마찬가지로 오직 선별적으로 — 새로운 식견들이 우리의 삶을 향상시키는 데 도움이 되는 방식으로 대중에게로 나아가지 않고 있다. 하지만, 이러한 발견들은 단순히 엘리트들의 자산이 아니며, 선택된 일부 전문가들의 소유로만 남아 있어서는 안 된다. 각각의 사람들은 그 또는 그녀 자신의 삶의 결정을 내려야 하며, 우리가 누구이며 우리에게 좋은 것이 무엇인가에 대한 현재 우리의 이해를 고려하여 그러한 선택들을 해야 한다. 그러한 점에서, 우리는 어떻게든 모든 사람이 새로운 발견에 접근할 수 있도록 하는 방법을 찾아내야만 한다.

| 정답해설 | ② 95% 본문의 마지막 문장에 필자의 주장이 담겨 있다. 새로운 발견들이 대중에게 스며들지 않고 특정 전문가들의 자산이나 소유로만 남아 있는데, 모두가 이것에 접근 가능해야 한다는 내용이므로, '새로운 연구 결과에 모든 사람이 접근할 수 있게 해야 한다.'가 필자의 주장으로 알맞다.

apathetic 무관심한, 심드렁한　　　indifferent 무관심한
self-serving 자기 잇속만을 차리는　selectively 선택적으로
insight 식견, 통찰　　　　　　　　property 자산, 재산
possession 소유　　　　　　　　　select 선택된
in light of ~을 고려하여, ~에 비추어
accessible 접근 가능한

15　독해 > Macro Reading > 주제　　오답률 40%　답 ①

| 해석 | 언어는 개인에게 정체성과 소속감을 준다. 아이들이 자랑스럽게 자신들의 언어를 배우고, 집과 이웃에서 그것을 말할 수 있을 때, 그 아이들은 높은 자존감을 갖게 될 것이다. 게다가, 모국어의 진정한 가치를 아는 아이들은 그들이 외국어를 말할 때 자신들이 성취자라고 느끼지 않을 것이다. 고양된 자아 정체성 및 자존감을 가지면, 아이의 학급 성적도 향상된다. 왜냐하면 그러한 아이는 언어적 소외감에 대한 걱정을 덜 하며 학교에 가기 때문이다.
① 아동 발달에 있어서 모국어의 중요성
② 아이들의 외국어 학습에 미치는 영향
③ 아이들의 자존감을 높이는 방법
④ 언어 분석의 효율성

| 정답해설 | ① 60% 언어, 특히 모국어가 아이에게 미치는 긍정적 영향을 서술한 글이다. 즉, 정체성과 소속감을 주고 자존감을 높이며 학습 성적이 향상된다고 했다. 따라서 전체 글의 주제로 가장 적절한 것은 '아동 발달에 있어서 모국어의 중요성'이다.

| 오답해설 | ③ 16% 모국어를 말하는 것이 자존감을 향상시킬 수 있다는 내용은 언급되나, 그 방법을 설명한 글은 아니다.
④ 8% 언어 분석에 관해서는 본문에 언급되지 않았다.

16　독해 > Macro Reading > 주제　　오답률 19%　답 ①

| 해석 | 많은 동물이 혼자 있기를 더 좋아하는 것은 아니다. 그들은 함께 살고 함께 일을 함으로써 더 효과적으로 세상과 교류할 수 있다는 것을 (스스로) 발견했거나 아니면 자연이 그들을 위해 발견해 주었다. 예를 들어, 어떤 동물이 혼자서 먹이를 사냥한다면, 그것은 단지 자신보다 훨씬 더 작은 동물을 잡아서 죽이고 먹을 수 있다. 하지만 동물들이 한 집단으로 무리를 이룬다면, 그것들은 자신들보다 더 큰 동물을 잡아서 죽일 수 있다. 한 무리의 늑대는 한 마리의 말을 죽일 수 있고, 그것은 그 집단을 매우 잘 먹일 수 있다. 따라서 동물들이 함께 일하면 혼자서 일하는 것보다 같은 숲속에서 같은 동물들이 먹을 수 있는 먹이가 더 많다. 협동에는 다른 이점들도 있다. 동물들은 위험에 대해 서로에게 알릴 수 있고, (만일 그들이 개별적으로 수색하고 먹이를 찾는 데 성공한 개체를 따라간다면) 더 많은 먹이를 찾을 수 있으며, 아프고 다친 동물들에게 얼마간의 돌봄을 제공할 수도 있다. 동물들이 집단을 이루어 살면 멀리 따로 떨어져 살 때보다 짝짓기와 번식도 또한 더 쉽다.
① 동물들이 사회적이 되는 것의 이점들
② 협력적인 행동의 결점들
③ 동물과 인간의 공통적인 특징들
④ 짝짓기와 번식에 있어서의 경쟁들

| 정답해설 | ① 81% 단독 생활을 하는 것보다 집단 생활을 할 때 동물들이 누릴 수 있는 장점을 제시하고 있는 글이므로 주제로 가장 적절한 것은 '동물들이 사회적이 되는 것의 이점들'이다.

loner 혼자 있기를 더 좋아하는 동물[사람]
effectively 효과적으로　　　　　band together 무리를 이루다
pack 무리, 떼　　　　　　　　　cooperation 협동, 협력
alert 알리다; 경보를 발하다; 주의를 환기시키다
mating 짝짓기　　　　　　　　　reproduction 번식
drawback 결점, 단점　　　　　　cooperative 협동의, 협력의

17　독해 > Logical Reading > 문맥상 다양한 추론　답 ④
　　　　　　　　　　　　　　　　　　　오답률 49%

| 해석 | 대학에서의 철학 공부가 나의 호기심을 유발했다. 그 수업은 우리가 공부해야 할 수많은 철학자들을 목록화했고, 나는 처음에 우리의 과제는 일종의 비종교적인 성서로서 그들의 연구를 배우고 흡수하는 것이라고 생각했다. 그러나 나는 나의 개인 교사가 내가 그들의 이론을 인용하는 것이 아니라 오직 내가 과거의 철학자들을 권위자들이 아니라 자극제로 활용하며 나 자신의 것을 발전시키도록 돕는 것에 관심이 있다는 것을 알게 되어서 기뻤다. 그것은 나의 지적 자유의 비결이었다. 이제 나는 스스로 생각하고 무엇이든 다 질문하고 오직 내가 그것이 옳다고 생각할 때에만 동의하는 공식적인 허가를 받은 것이었다. 훌륭한 교육은 내게 그러한 허가를 훨씬 더 빨리 제공해 주었다. 아아, 몇몇 사람들은 그것을 전혀 받은 적이 없고, 마치 그것들이 신성불가침인 것처럼 타인의 규칙을 계속해서 인용하고 있는 것 같다. 결과적으로 그들은 자신도 모르게 다른 사람들의 세계의 ④ 반대자들(→ 추종[지지]자들)이 된다. 이제 나는 철학이 전문적인 철학자들에게만 남겨지기에는 너무나도 중요하다고 생각한다. 우리 모두는 초등학교부터 시작하여 철학자들처럼 생각하는 법을 배워야 한다.

| 정답해설 | ④ 51% 과거 철학자들의 이론(규칙)을 계속적으로 인용하는 사람들에 대해 언급하고 있는데, 이러한 사람들은 다른 사람들

(과거 철학자들)의 세계에 동조하는 사람들임을 유추할 수 있다. 따라서 '반대자들'의 의미인 opponents는 followers(추종자들), supporters(지지자들), prisoners(포로들) 등의 어휘로 교체되어야 알맞다.

| **오답해설** | ① [26%] 과거 철학자들의 이론에 맹목적으로 동조하지 않고 나만의 의견을 발전시킬 수 있는 허가를 받은 것에 대한 장점을 설명하고 있으므로, 개인 교사가 이러한 방식으로 자신을 교육한 것에 대해 delighted했다(기뻤다)는 표현은 문맥상 적절하다.

② [9%] 이후 문장에서 스스로 생각하고 무엇이든 다 질문하고 내가 옳다고 생각할 때에만 동의하는 공식적인 허가를 받았다고 했으므로, freedom(자유)은 문맥상 적절하다.

③ [14%] 자신의 개인 교사의 방식에 대해 긍정적으로 평가하고 있으므로, 이를 good(훌륭한) 교육이라고 한 것은 문맥상 자연스럽다.

어휘

absorb 흡수하다	secular 비종교적인, 세속의
recite 인용하다, 암송하다, 나열하다	stimulant 자극제
authority 권위자	permission 허가, 허락
alas 아아(슬픔·유감을 나타내는 소리)	
opponent 반대자, 상대자	

18 문법 > 접속사, 부정사, 동사 오답률 44% 답 ①

| **해석** | 과거를 돌이켜 보면서, 과학자들은 마야의 지도자들이 강우에 대한 자신들의 불안정한 의존 상태에 대해 여러 세기 동안 알고 있었다는 산더미 같은 증거를 발견해 왔다. 물 부족은 이해되고 있었을 뿐만 아니라 기록도 되고 계획도 세워졌다. 마야인들은 강우량이 적은 해에는 재배할 작물의 종류, 공공 용수의 사용, 식량 배급을 엄격히 통제하면서 (물) 보존을 시행했다. 3천 년 통치의 전반부 동안 마야인들은 건기에 대비해 빗물을 저장하는 더 큰 규모의 지하 인공 호수와 수조를 계속 만들었다. 공들여 꾸민 그들의 신전들도 인상적이었지만, 물을 모으고 저장하기 위한 그들의 효율적인 체계는 설계와 공법에 있어서 걸작이었다.

| **정답해설** | ① [56%] (A) 뒤의 절이 완전한 문장 구조를 이루고 있으므로 명사 evidence의 동격의 명사절을 이끌 수 있는 접속사 that이 알맞다.

(B) larger underground artificial lakes and containers를 수식하면서 목적어 rainwater를 취할 수 있는 것은 준동사 중에 to부정사인 to store가 어법에 맞는 표현이다.

(C) 양보절의 보어가 형용사인 impressive이므로, 형용사 보어를 취할 수 있는 be동사가 오는 것이 적절하다. 따라서 알맞은 것은 were이다.

어휘

uncover 발견하다	dependence 의존
enforce 시행하다, 강요하다	conservation 보존, 보호
tightly 엄격하게	regulate 통제하다
reign 통치	artificial 인공의
drought 가뭄	elaborately 공들여, 정교하게
warehouse 저장하다	

19 독해 > Logical Reading > 배열 오답률 63% 답 ②

| **해석** | 종교는 분명 한 사람이 최선을 발휘하도록 할 수 있지만, 이것이 그 속성을 갖는 유일한 현상은 아니다.

(B) 아이를 갖는 것은 종종 사람에게 놀랄 만큼 성숙해지는 효과가 있다. 잘 알려진 바와 같이, 전시는 사람들에게 능력을 발휘할 많은 기회를 주며, 홍수, 허리케인과 같은 자연재해에도 마찬가지이다.

(C) 그러나 하루하루 계속되는 평생의 준비에는, 아마도 종교만큼 효과적인 것이 없을 것이다. 그것은 힘 있고 재능 있는 사람들을 더 겸손하고 인내하게 만들고, 평균적인 사람들을 그들 자신보다 성장하게 하며, 음주나 마약, 범죄로부터 벗어나는 데 절실하게 도움이 필요한 많은 사람들에게 견고한 지원을 제공한다.

(A) 그렇지 않은 경우에는 자기도취적이거나, 얕거나, 조잡하거나, 단순히 그만두는 사람들은 우리 모두가 자랑스러워할 어려운 결정을 내리는 데 그들에게 도움을 주는 삶에 대한 관점을 부여받을 때, 종종 그들의 종교에 의해 고귀해진다.

| **정답해설** | ② [37%] 주어진 글에서는 종교만이 사람이 최선을 발휘하도록 하는 것은 아니라고 했으므로, 종교 외에 사람이 최선을 발휘하도록 하는 여러 속성들을 제시하는 (B)가 첫 순서로 가장 적절하다. 이어서 역접 접속사 But(그러나)으로 시작하여 앞서 언급한 다른 속성들보다 종교의 효과가 크다는 내용을 제시하는 (C)가 이어지는 것이 자연스러우며, 마지막으로 otherwise를 이용해 앞서 설명한 종교의 긍정적 역할이 없는 상황을 가정하는 (A)가 오는 것이 옳다. 따라서 (B) – (C) – (A)의 순서가 알맞다.

어휘

bring out the best in somebody ~가 최선을 발휘하도록 하다

phenomenon 현상	property 속성, 특성
otherwise 그렇지 않으면	self-absorbed 자기도취의
shallow 얕은	crude 조잡한, 거친; 미숙한
ennoble 기품을 주다, 고귀하게 하다	
perspective 관점	mature 성숙하게 하다
an abundance of 풍부한, 많은 ~	occasion 기회, 때, 경우
rise to (예상 밖의 상황·문제 등에 직면하여) 능력을 발휘하다	
brace 대비[준비]하다	humble 겸손한
sturdy 튼튼한, 견고한	desperately 필사적으로

20 독해 > Logical Reading > 배열 오답률 9% 답 ②

| **해석** | 더 많은 사람들은 더 많은 자원을 필요로 하고, 이것은 인구가 증가함에 따라 지구의 자원이 더 빨리 고갈된다는 것을 의미한다.

(B) 이러한 고갈의 결과는 사람들이 증가하는 인구를 수용하기 위해 인류가 지구로부터 자원을 빼앗아 감에 따른 삼림 벌채와 생물 다양성의 손실이다.

(A) 인구 증가는 또한 주로 이산화탄소 배출로 인한 온실가스의 증가를 초래한다. 시각화하면, 4배의 인구 증가를 보였던 바로 그 20세기에 이산화탄소 배출은 12배 증가했다.

(C) 온실가스가 증가함에 따라 그러한 기후 패턴도 증가하며, 궁극적으로는 기후 변화라고 불리는 장기적인 패턴을 초래한다.

| **정답해설** | ② [91%] 주어진 문장은 인구 증가로 인해 자원 고갈이 빨라진다는 내용이다. 주어진 문장의 the Earth's resources deplete more rapidly(지구의 자원이 더 빨리 고갈된다)를 this depletion(이러한 고갈)으로 받아 지구 자원의 고갈로 생기는 결과

를 설명하고 있는 (B)가 첫 순서로 알맞다. 이어서 also(또한)를 이용해 인구 증가로 인한 또 다른 영향인 이산화탄소 배출로 인한 온실가스 증가를 설명하는 (A)가 오는 것이 알맞고, 마지막으로 (A)에서 설명한 이러한 온실가스 증가로 인한 결과, 즉 기후 변화를 제시하는 (C)가 오는 것이 자연스럽다. 따라서 (B) – (A) – (C)의 순서가 알맞다.

어휘

resource 자원	emission 배출
visualization 가시화, 시각화	-fold ~배
depletion 고갈	deforestation 삼림 벌채
biodiversity 생물 다양성	strip A of B A에게서 B를 빼앗다
accommodate 수용하다	ultimately 궁극적으로, 결국

21	독해 > Logical Reading > 삭제	오답률 35%	답 ②

| 해석 | 인간 생물학과 생리학을 광범위하게 교육받는 의학 인류학자들은 질병의 전염 패턴과 특정 집단이 말라리아와 수면병과 같은 질병의 존재에 어떻게 적응하는지 연구한다. 바이러스와 박테리아의 전염은 사람들의 식단, 위생, 그리고 다른 행동들에 의해 강하게 영향을 받기 때문에, 많은 의학 인류학자들은 질병의 확산에 영향을 미치는 문화적 관습을 확인하기 위해 전염병학자들과 팀을 이루어 일한다. ② 대부분의 학생들이 성공적인 의학 직종의 금전적 보상보다는 인도주의적인 이유로 의학계에 발을 들인다는 것이 일반적으로 갖는 믿음일지는 몰라도 선진국에서는 지위의 전망 및 보상이 아마도 하나의 유인일 것이다. 다른 문화들은 질병의 원인과 증상, 질병을 치료하는 최선의 방법, 전통적 치유사들과 의사들의 능력, 그리고 치료 과정에의 공동체 참여의 중요성에 대해 다른 생각을 가지고 있다. 인간 공동체가 그러한 것들을 어떻게 인식하는지를 연구함으로써, 의학 인류학자들은 병원과 다른 기관들이 건강 관리 서비스를 더욱 효과적으로 전달하도록 돕는다.

| 정답해설 | ② 65% 의학 인류학자들의 역할에 대해 설명하는 글인데, ②에서는 학생들이 의학계에 입문하는 원인에 대해 언급하고 있으므로 글 전체의 흐름과 관련이 없다.

어휘

anthropologist 인류학자	extensive 광범위한, 넓은
physiology 생리(학)	transmission 전염
sanitation 위생	humanitarian 인도주의적인
prospect 전망	incentive 유인(誘因); 자극; 장려책
perceive 인식하다	

22	독해 > Logical Reading > 배열	오답률 12%	답 ③

| 해석 | Sequoya(1760?~1843)는 Tennessee주 동부의 체로키(Cherokee) 부족의 전통과 종교에 대한 지식으로 높이 평가받는 명망 있는 가문에서 태어났다.

(C) 어렸을 때, Sequoya는 체로키어 구전 전통을 배웠으며, 어른이 되었을 때, 그는 유럽계 미국인 문화를 접하게 되었다. 그의 편지에서, Sequoya는 유럽계 미국인들이 소통하기 위해 사용하던 글쓰기 방법들에 그가 어떻게 매료되었는지 언급한다.

(A) 그의 부족민들을 위해 글쓰기가 가진 가능성을 인식한 Sequoya는 1821년에 체로키 문자를 발명했다. 이러한 작문 체계로, Sequoya는 고대 부족의 관습을 기록할 수 있었다.

(B) 더 중요한 것은, 그의 문자가 신문과 책을 인쇄할 수 있도록 체로키족이 출판 산업을 발전시키는 데 도움을 준 것이다. 그리하여, 취학 연령의

아이들은 체로키 문화와 전통에 대해 그들만의 언어로 배울 수 있었다.

| 정답해설 | ③ 88% 주어진 글은 Sequoya의 탄생에 대해 설명하고 있으므로, 이어질 내용으로 가장 적절한 것은 시간의 흐름에 따라 그의 어린 시절과 성인기에 대해 설명하는 (C)이다. 이어서 a Cherokee alphabet으로 부정관사를 이용해 체로키 문자에 대해 새로운 정보를 제공하는 (A)가 연결되고, 마지막으로 his alphabet을 통해 (A)에서 설명한 이 문자에 대해 부연하는 (B)가 이어지는 것이 자연스럽다. 따라서 (C)-(A)-(B)의 순서가 알맞다. (참고로 (B)의 More importantly는 기출에 More important로 출제되었으나, 문법상 옳도록 More importantly로 수정하였다.)

어휘

prestigious 명망 있는, 칭송받는	recognize 인식하다
nation 민족	fascinated 매료된

23	독해 > Micro Reading > 내용일치/불일치	오답률 7%	답 ②

| 해석 |
사랑을 퍼뜨리세요
땅콩버터 운동 기간에 굶주림에 맞서 싸우세요

약간의 도움을 필요로 하는 지역의 가족들을 도움으로써 우리의 지역 사회에 기여하세요. 우리는 굶주림에 직면한 Northeast Louisiana의 어린이, 가족, 노인 들을 돕기 위해 제4회 연례 전 지역 땅콩버터 운동을 시작합니다. 땅콩버터는 어린이와 어른이 좋아하는 단백질이 가득한 음식이므로 푸드뱅크에 많이 필요한 기본 식품입니다. 플라스틱 병에 든 땅콩버터나 기부금을 Monroe 푸드뱅크에 3월 29일 금요일 오후 4시까지 기부해 주세요. 땅콩버터 기부품들은 월요일부터 금요일까지, 오전 8시에서 오후 4시 사이에 Monroe의 Central Avenue 4600번지에 위치한 푸드뱅크의 배급 센터에 가져다 놓으시면 됩니다. 금전적 기부는 여기에서 하시거나 427-418-4581로 전화하시면 됩니다.
다른 기부 장소를 보시려면, 저희 웹사이트 https://www.foodbanknela.org를 방문해 주세요.

| 정답해설 | ② 93% 땅콩버터 기부품들을 월요일부터 금요일까지, 오전 8시에서 오후 4시 사이에 가져다 놓으면 된다고 했으므로, 안내문의 내용과 일치하지 않는다.

| 오답해설 | ① 5% 안내문의 첫 번째 문단에 땅콩버터 운동의 목적이 굶주림에 직면한 어린이, 가족, 노인 들을 돕는 것이라고 했다.

③ 2% 두 번째 문단의 마지막 문장 Monetary donations can be made here or by calling 427-418-4581을 통해 금전 기부는 전화로도 가능함을 알 수 있다.

④ 0% 마지막 문장 For other drop-off locations, visit our website at ~에 Monroe 푸드뱅크 외의 다른 기부 장소를 알아볼 수 있는 웹사이트를 소개하고 있다.

어휘

drive (조직적) 운동, 캠페인	contribution 공헌, 기여, 기부
kick off 시작하다	staple (기본) 식품; 주식
donate 기부하다	drop off 가져다 놓다
distribution 배급, 분배	

24 독해 > Macro Reading > 심경 　오답률 14% 　답 ②

| 해석 | 우리 가족 모두가 가난에 시달렸다. Garoghlanian 집안의 모든 분파는 세상에서 가장 기막히고 우스꽝스러울 정도의 가난한 생활을 하고 있었다. 우리가 어디에서 우리의 뱃속을 계속 채워 줄 음식값을 얻었는지는 아무도 알지 못했다. 하지만, 가장 중요한 것은 우리는 정직하기로 유명했다는 것이다. 우리는 약 11세기 동안 정직으로 유명했다. 우리가 세상이라고 생각하고자 했던 곳에서 가장 부유한 집안이었을 때마저도 말이다. 우리는 자부심을 첫째로 삼고, 정직을 다음으로 삼았으며, 그 다음으로 우리는 옳고 그름을 믿었다. 우리들 중 누구도 절대 세상의 그 누구도 이용하지 않았다.
① 평화롭고 침착한
② 만족스럽고 자랑스러운
③ 공포에 휩싸이고 두려워하는
④ 놀라고 경악하는

| 정답해설 | ② 86% 글의 초반에는 집안이 가난했음을 언급했지만 양보의 접속사 though로 시작하는 문장 이후에는 그럼에도 불구하고 집안이 정직하기로 유명했음을 강조하고 있다. 따라서 화자의 심경으로 가장 적절한 것은 ②이다.

어휘
tribe (대)가족　　　　　　　　　branch 분파
wealthy 부유한　　　　　　　　　take advantage of ~을 이용하다

25 독해 > Micro Reading > 내용일치/불일치 　오답률 10% 　답 ②

| 해석 | 생식의 증가하는 인기에도 불구하고, 당신은 여전히 조리된 채소에서 영양분을 얻을 수 있다. 예를 들어, 우리의 몸은 토마토가 조리되었을 때 더 효율적으로 리코펜을 흡수할 수 있다. (그러나, 생토마토도 여전히 좋은 리코펜의 공급원이라는 점을 기억하라.) 그러나, 조리된 토마토는 생토마토보다 더 낮은 수준의 비타민C를 함유하고 있으므로, 당신이 (비타민C) 수준을 높이고자 한다면, 생토마토를 고수하는 것이 더 나을 것이다. 그것들을 조리해서 먹기로 결정하든 생으로 먹기로 결정하든 토마토의 건강상의 이점을 약화시키지 않는 것이 중요하다. 당신이 토마토 소스나 페이스트를 구매할 거라면, 소금 또는 설탕이 첨가되지 않은 종류를 선택하라. 그러나 그보다 더 나은 것은 자신의 소스를 집에서 만드는 것이다. 그리고 만약 토마토를 생으로 먹는다면, 그것들에 소금을 아주 약간만 치고, 칼로리와 포화 지방이 적은 샐러드 드레싱을 선택하라.

| 정답해설 | ② 91% 본문 중반 Cooked tomatoes, however, have lower levels of vitamin C than raw tomatoes에서 조리된 토마토가 생토마토보다 비타민C를 덜 함유하고 있다고 설명하고 있으므로, 글의 내용과 일치하지 않는다.

| 오답해설 | ① 0% 두 번째 문장 For example, our body can absorb lycopene more effectively when tomatoes are에서 토마토를 조리하여 먹었을 때 리코펜을 더 효율적으로 흡수할 수 있음을 알 수 있다.
③ 2% 끝에서 두 번째 문장 If you're buying tomato sauce or paste, choose a variety with no salt or sugar added에서 토마토 소스를 구입할 때는 소금이나 설탕이 첨가되지 않은 것을 선택하라고 했다.
④ 7% 마지막 문장에서 토마토를 생으로 먹을 때는 소금을 아주 약간만 치고 칼로리와 포화 지방이 적은 샐러드 드레싱을 선택

하라고 했다.

어휘
consume 섭취하다　　　　　　　　nutrient 영양분, 영양소
absorb 흡수하다
lycopene 리코펜(토마토 등의 붉은색 색소)
be better off -ing ~하는 것이 더 낫다
stick with ~을 고수하다　　　　　dilute 희석하다, 묽게 하다
sparingly 조금만　　　　　　　　saturated fat 포화 지방

합격예상 체크		

〈법원직 연도별 합격선〉

맞힌 개수	/25문항	점수	/100점

➡ ☐ 합격 ☐ 불합격

취약영역 체크					
문항	정답	영역	문항	정답	영역
①	②	독해 > Logical Reading > 문맥상 다양한 추론	14	③	문법 > 접속사
2	①	독해 > Reading for Writing > 빈칸 구 완성	15	③	문법 > 일치
3	②	독해 > Logical Reading > 문맥상 다양한 추론	16	②	독해 > Reading for Writing > 빈칸 절 완성
4	④	독해 > Macro Reading > 제목	17	③	독해 > Macro Reading > 주제
5	①	독해 > Reading for Writing > 요약	18	④	독해 > Logical Reading > 문맥상 다양한 추론
6	①	독해 > Logical Reading > 배열	19	④	독해 > Micro Reading > 내용 일치/불일치
7	①	독해 > Logical Reading > 배열	20	④	독해 > Macro Reading > 주제
8	①	독해 > Logical Reading > 연결사	21	④	독해 > Logical Reading > 문맥상 다양한 추론
9	③	문법 > 분사	22	②	독해 > Logical Reading > 삽입
10	①	문법 > 분사	23	③	독해 > Logical Reading > 문맥상 다양한 추론
11	②	독해 > Logical Reading > 문맥상 다양한 추론	24	③	독해 > Reading for Writing > 요약
12	②	독해 > Reading for Writing > 빈칸 구 완성	25	④	독해 > Logical Reading > 삽입
13	①	독해 > Reading for Writing > 요약			

⬇ 영역별 틀린 개수로 취약영역을 확인하세요!

어휘	/0	문법	/4	독해	/21	생활영어	/0

➡ 나의 취약영역: _____

※ [정답해설]과 [오답해설] 선지의 50% 표시는 〈1초 합격예측 서비스〉를 통해 수집된 선지 선택률을 나타냅니다.

1	독해 > Logical Reading > 문맥상 다양한 추론
	오답률 44%

답 ②

| 해석 | 지식과 사실을 동일시하는 것은 솔깃하지만, 모든 사실이 지식의 항목은 아니다. 동전 한 개가 들어 있는 밀봉된 종이 상자를 흔드는 것을 상상해 보라. 당신이 상자를 아래로 내려놓을 때, 상자 안의 동전은 동전의 앞면 또는 뒷면 중 하나가 나오게 떨어졌다. 그것이 사실이라고 하자. 하지만 아무도 상자 안을 보지 않는 이상, 이 사실은 모른 채 남게 되고 그것은 아직 (A) 지식의 영역 안에 들어온 것이 아니다. 또는 단순히 기록된다고 해서 사실이 지식이 되지도 않는다. 만약 당신이 '그 동전은 앞면으로 떨어졌다'라는 문장을 종이 쪽지 한 장에 적고, '그 동전은 뒷면으로 떨어졌다'라고 다른 종이에 적었다면, 당신은 종이 쪽지 중 하나에 사실을 적게 된 것이지만, 당신은 여전히 동전 던지기 결과에 대한 지식을 얻게 된 것이 아니다. 지식은 어떤 살아 있는 주제의 일부분에 대한 사실에의 접근을 요구한다. 그것에 접근할 마음이 (B) 없다면, 도서관과 데이터베이스 안에 저장되어 있는 것이 무엇이든지 지식이 되는 것이 아니라 단지 잉크 자국과 전자적인 흔적에 불과하다. 어떤 주어진 지식의 경우에, 이러한 접근은 개인에게 특별할 수도 있고 아닐 수도 있다. 같은 사실은 아마 여러 다른 사람이 아니라 한 사람에 의해 알려질지도 모른다. 일반적인 지식은 많은 사람들에 의해 공유될지도 모른다. 하지만 어떠한 주제와 (C) 떨어진 채로 대롱대롱 매달려 있는 지식은 없다.

(A)	(B)	(C)
① 사실	있다면	떨어진
② 지식	없다면	떨어진
③ 지식	있다면	붙어 있는
④ 사실	없다면	붙어 있는

| 정답해설 | ② 56% (A) 본문에서 모든 사실(fact)이 지식(knowledge)의 항목은 아니라고 구분하였다. 상자 안의 동전이 앞면이나 뒷면 중에 하나인 것은 사실(fact)이지만, 상자 안 동전의 면을 확인하지 않으면 사실(fact)은 알려지지 않게 되고, 그것은 지식(knowledge)의 영역이 아직은 아님을 알 수 있다. 따라서 빈칸 (A)에는 knowledge(지식)가 알맞다. 빈칸이 포함된 문장이 부정문임에 주의해야 한다.

(B) 앞의 상자 속 동전의 예를 통해서, 동전이 앞면 또는 뒷면으로 떨어진 것은 사실(fact)로 보는 반면에 상자를 열어서 안의 내용을 확인하지 않으면 그것은 지식(knowledge)이 아니라고 하였다. 이어지는 예시로 도서관과 데이터베이스에 저장된 것은 '접근'이 되어야 지식이 된다고 언급하고 있다. 따라서 빈칸(B)에는 '접근할 마음이 없다면 지식이 될 수 없다'는 서술이 되어야 하므로 without(~이 없다면)이 적절하다.

(C) (B)의 연장선에서 주제가 없는 지식은 없다고 하는 것이 글의 흐름상 적절하므로 unattached(떨어진)가 적합하다.

어휘
tempting 솔깃한
identify A with B A와 B를 동일시하다
sealed 봉인된, 포장된   land 떨어지다, 도착하다
realm 영역, 범위   outcome 결과

toss 동전 던지기
common 공통의
attached 붙어 있는

access 접근; (컴퓨터) 액세스하다
dangle 대롱대롱 매달리다
unattached 떨어져 있는

오답률 TOP 1

| **2** | 독해 > Reading for Writing > 빈칸 구 완성 | 오답률 57% | 답 ① |

| 해석 | 쉽게 외부의 영향을 받는 젊은이들만이 ① 또래 압력의 영향을 받는 사람들인 것은 아니다. 우리들 대부분은 아마 판매원으로부터 압박을 받은 경험이 있을 것이다. 영업 사원에게 당신의 경쟁사의 70%가 자신들의 서비스를 이용하고 있는데 왜 당신은 그렇지 않나요?라고 말하면서 '사무용 솔루션'을 팔려고 해 본 적이 있는가? 하지만 경쟁사의 70%가 바보라면? 아니면 그 70%가 너무 많은 추가 대가를 받았거나, 너무 낮은 가격을 제안받아 그들이 그 기회를 거부할 수 없었던 거라면? 그 관행은 오직 한 가지 일을 하기 위해 고안된 것이다. 바로 당신이 구매하도록 압박하는 것이다. 당신이 뭔가 놓치고 있다고 느끼게 하거나 당신 빼고 다른 사람 모두가 알고 있다고 느끼게 하기 위해서이다.

① 또래 압력
② 충동 구매
③ 괴롭히기 작전
④ 치열한 경쟁

| 정답해설 | ① 43% 빈칸 이후에서 판매원이 어떤 서비스를 판매하려고 할 때, 경쟁사의 70%들이 그 서비스를 사용한다며 자신들의 것을 구매하도록 압박하는 사례를 들고 있으므로 빈칸에 가장 적절한 것은 ① '또래 압력'이다.

| 오답해설 | ② 48% 사는 사람이 '충동적'으로 산다는 것이 아니라 영업사원이 물건을 팔 때 사는 사람이 구매하도록 압박하는 것이라고 하였으므로 빈칸에 적절하지 않다.

| 더 알아보기 | Peer Pressure (또래 압력)

> 동료 집단에서 암묵적으로 정해진 규칙이나 지침에 따라 생각하고 행동하도록 요구하는 것을 말한다. 개인 간 상호 작용 방식뿐만 아니라 가치관, 태도, 행위 등에 영향을 미치는 보이지 않는 힘에 해당된다.

어휘

impressionable 쉽게 외부의 영향을 받는
subject to ~의 영향을 받는; ~을 받기[당하기] 쉬운
sales rep 영업사원
competitor 경쟁자
resist 저항하다, 참다
practice 관행, 습관
bullying tactics 괴롭히기 작전, 괴롭혀서 뭔가를 하게[그만두게] 만드는 작전

| **3** | 독해 > Logical Reading > 문맥상 다양한 추론 | 오답률 17% | 답 ② |

| 해석 | 자존감이 높은 사람들은 자신의 기술과 능력에 자신감을 가지고 있으며 삶이 그들에게 제공하는 도전에 직면하는 것을 즐긴다. 그들은 자신만만하고 기여할 기회를 갖는 것을 즐기기 때문에 (A) 기꺼이 팀으로 일을 한다. 그러나, 자존감이 낮은 사람들은 어색해하고 수줍어하며 자기 자신을 표현하지 못하는 경향이 있다. 종종 그들은 회피 전략을 선택함으로써 자신들의 문제를 악화시키는데, 왜냐하면 그들은 자신들이 하는 일이 무엇이든지 결과적으로 실패할 것이라는 믿음을 (B) 가지고 있기 때문이다. 반대로, 자신이 가치 없다는 느낌을 감추기 위해 젠체하고 거만한 행동을 보임으로써 자존감 결핍을 보충할 수도 있다. 게다가, 그러한 개인은 자기 밖에 있는 이유를 찾아냄으로써 자신의 성공을 설명하는 반면, 자존감이 높은 사람은 자신의 성공을 내면의 특성의 (C) 결과로 본다.

	(A)	(B)	(C)
①	기꺼이	부인하다	시도하다
②	기꺼이	가지고 있다	~의 결과로 보다
③	마지못해	가지고 있다	시도하다
④	마지못해	부인하다	~의 결과로 보다

| 정답해설 | ② 83% (A)의 They는 자존감이 높은 사람들(People with high self-esteem)을 가리킨다. because 이하의 내용을 볼 때, 그들은 '기꺼이' 팀으로 일한다고 하는 것이 적절하다. 따라서 (A)에 willingly가 알맞다.

(B)의 they는 자존감이 낮은 사람들(those who have low self-esteem)을 가리키며, 그들이 하는 것은 무엇이든지 결과적으로 실패할 것이라는 믿음을 '가지고 있다'라고 하는 것이 문맥상 적합하므로 hold가 적절하다.

(C)가 포함된 마지막 문장은 자존감이 낮은 사람과 자존감이 높은 사람을 대조하고 있다. 자존감이 낮은 사람이 그들의 성공을 자기 밖에 있는 이유를 찾아내어 설명한다고 서술하고 있으므로 이에 반해 자존감이 높은 사람은 외부에서 원인을 찾기보다는 그들의 성공을 내면 특성의 '결과'로 본다고 서술하는 것이 문맥상 적합하다. 따라서 (C)는 문맥상 attribute가 가장 적절하다.

| 오답해설 | ③④ 7% 1% (A) 글의 문맥상 자존감이 높은 사람들은 팀으로 일하는 것을 꺼리는 사람들이 아니므로 unwillingly는 정답이 될 수 없다.

어휘

self-esteem 자존감
competence 능력
willingly 기꺼이
unwillingly 마지못해
awkward 어색한
compound 악화시키다
opt for ~을 선택하다
avoidance 회피
hold (생각, 마음 등을) 품다, 가지고 있다
conversely 반대로
compensate 보충하다, 보상하다
boastful 뽐내는, 젠체하는
arrogant 거만한
unworthiness 가치 없음
account for ~을 설명하다
attribute A to B A를 B의 결과로 보다, A를 B의 덕분으로 돌리다

| **4** | 독해 > Macro Reading > 제목 | 오답률 16% | 답 ④ |

| 해석 | 확실히, 숭고한 것에서부터 완전히 터무니없는 것에 이르기까지, 새롭고 독창적인 것을 고안해 내는 우리의 능력에 대해 다른 어떤 종도 권리를 주장할 수 없다. 다른 동물들도 분명 무언가를 짓는다. 새들은 그들의 복잡한 둥지를 조립하고, 비버는 댐을 건설하며, 개미는 정교한 터널망을 판다. "그러나 비행기, 이상하게도 기울어진 고층빌딩과 Chia Pets는 매우 인상적이다"라고 Fuentes는 말하면서, 진화적인 관점에서 볼 때 "창조력은 두 다리로 걷는 것, 큰 두뇌와 사물을 조작하기에 정말 좋은 손을 가지고 있는 것만큼이나 우리의 도구 키트의 일부이다."라고 덧붙였다. 큰 송곳니나 발톱, 날개나 다른 명백한 신체적 이점이 없는, 물리적으로 매력이 없는 영장류에게 있어서, 창조력은 훌륭한 동등 요소였고, 게다가 적어도 지금까지는, 호모 사피엔스의 생존을 보장해 왔다.

① 인간의 창조성은 어디에서 오는가?
② 영장류의 신체적 특징들은 무엇인가?
③ 다른 종들을 넘어서는 호모 사피엔스의 신체적 이점
④ 창조력: 생존을 위해 인간이 가지는 독특한 특성

| 정답해설 | ④ 84% 본문 마지막에 글의 주제가 나와 있는데, 창조력

이 적어도 지금까지 호모 사피엔스의 생존을 보장해 왔다고 하였으므로, 글의 제목으로 가장 적절한 것은 '창조성: 생존을 위해 인간이 가지는 독특한 특성'이다.

어휘

lay claim to ~에 대한 권리를 주장하다

capacity 능력	devise 고안하다
sublime 숭고한, 고상한; 황당한	sublimely 완전히, 심하게
ridiculous 터무니없는	assemble 조립하다
intricate 복잡한	construct 건설하다
dig 파다	elaborate 정교한
tilt 기울이다	skyscraper 고층 건물
evolutionary 진화의	standpoint 관점, 견지
manipulate 조작하다, 다루다	unprepossessing 매력 없는
primate 영장류	fang 송곳니
equalizer 동등[평등]하게 하는 것	trait 특징

---

5 | 독해 > Reading for Writing > 요약 | 오답률 20% | 답 ①

| 해석 | "대부분의 조류 식별은 일종의 주관적인 인상, 즉 새가 움직이는 방식과, 다양한 각도에서 본 작은 순간적인 모습들과 연속적인 다양한 모습들에 기초하며 새가 머리를 돌리고 날고 방향을 바꿀 때, 당신은 다양한 형태와 각도의 연속성을 보게 된다."라고 Sibley는 말한다. "그 모든 것이 결합해서, 사실상 따로 떼어내 말로 표현할 수 없는 새의 독특한 인상을 만들어 낸다. 새를 보려고 들판에 있는 것에 대해 당신은 새를 분석하고 그것은 이것, 이것과 이것을 보여 주기 때문에 그것은 이 종류임에 틀림없다고 말하는 데는 시간이 걸리지 않는다. 그것은 더 자연스럽고 본능적이다. 많은 연습 후에, 당신이 새를 보면 당신의 뇌 속에 작은 스위치가 켜진다. 그것은 맞는 것처럼 보인다. 당신은 한눈에 그것이 무엇인지 알고 있다."

Sibley에 따르면, 조류 식별은 (B) 별개의 분석보다 (A) 본능적인 인상에 기초를 둔다.

① 본능적인 인상 – 별개의 분석
② 객관적인 조사 – 주관적인 판단
③ 신체적 외형 – 행동적인 특징
④ 자세한 관찰 – 거리를 둔 관찰

| 정답해설 | ① 80% 마지막 두 문장에 Sibley가 말하는 것의 핵심이 드러난다. 조류를 식별할 때, 자세한 분석과 관찰보다는 한눈에 새를 구별하게 된다는 것이다. 따라서 요약문에서 rather than 전후로 (B)에는 본문의 Sibley가 주장하는 반대의 내용이 (A)에는 Sibley가 언급한 내용이 들어가는 것이 적합하므로 (A)에는 instinctive impression(본능적인 인상)이, (B)에는 discrete analysis(별개의 분석)가 적절하다.

어휘

identification 식별	subjective 주관적인
instantaneous 즉각적인	appearance 외형, 외모
angle 각도	sequence 연속, 연쇄
instinctive 본능적인	trigger 촉발시키다, 작동시키다
at a glance 한눈에	discrete 별개의
behavioral 행동의, 행동에 관한	observation 관찰

---

6 | 독해 > Logical Reading > 배열 | 오답률 33% | 답 ①

| 해석 | 자동차가 사람에 덜 의존하게 됨에 따라, 소비자가 제품을 사용하

는 수단과 환경도 자동차 공유와 단기 리스 프로그램에 대한 참여율이 높아지면서 상당한 변화를 겪을 가능성이 있다.
(A) 멀지 않은 미래에, 필요한 경우 무인 자동차가 당신에게 올 수 있고, 당신이 그것을 다 사용하고 나면, 그것은 주차 공간에 대한 필요 없이 차가 운전해서 가 버릴 수 있다. 자동차 공유와 단기 임대의 증가는 이에 상응하는 자동차 외부 설계의 중요성 감소와도 관련될 가능성이 높다.
(C) 자동차 외부는 개인화 및 자기 정체성을 위한 매개체 역할을 하기보다는, 점점 더 Free Car Media가 제공하는 것과 같은 브랜드 홍보 대사 프로그램을 포함한 광고 및 기타 홍보 활동을 위한 채널을 대표하게 될 것이다.
(B) 그 결과, 자동차로부터 파생된 상징적인 의미들, 그리고 그것들과 소비자 스스로의 정체성 및 지위와의 관계도 결국 바뀌게 될 가능성이 있다.

| 정답해설 | ① 67% 주어진 글에서 큰 변화를 겪게 될 것이라고 (undergo significant changes) 했으므로 그 변화를 서술하는 내용이 다음에 이어져야 한다. 따라서 멀지 않은 미래에 자동차 공유와 단기 임대라는 변화가 생길 가능성이 있다고 서술하는 (A)가 먼저 와야 한다. (A)의 마지막에 decrease in the importance of exterior car design(자동차 외부 설계의 중요성 감소)과 상응하는 내용이 언급되는 (B)가 (A) 다음에 와야 하고 마지막으로 그 결과 자동차와 소비자의 관계도 결국 바뀌게 될 가능성이 있다는 (C)가 오는 것이 자연스럽다.

어휘

dependent 의존적인	circumstance 환경, 상황
undergo 겪다	significant 중요한
lease 임대하다	be associated with ~와 관련이 있다
corresponding 상응하는	derive from ~로부터 파생하다
in turn 결국	medium 매개체
personalization 개인화	exterior 외부
represent 대표하다	ambassador 대사

---

7 | 독해 > Logical Reading > 배열 | 오답률 26% | 답 ①

| 해석 | 일본의 조립 라인을 보러 일본에 간 미국 자동차 임원들의 멋진 사연이 있다. 조립 라인 끝에는 문에 경첩이 달려 있었는데, 이는 미국과 같았다.
(A) 그런데 뭔가 빠져 있었다. 미국에서는 (조립) 라인 노동자가 고무망치를 가지고 문 가장자리를 두드려서 그것이 완벽하게 맞는지 확인하곤 했다. 일본에서는 그런 업무가 존재하지 않는 것 같았다.
(B) 당황한 미국 자동차 임원들은 어느 시점에 문이 꼭 맞는지를 확인하는지 물었다. 그들의 일본인 안내원이 그들을 바라보며 수줍게 웃었다. "우리는 디자인할 때 그것이 꼭 맞는지 확인합니다."라고 말했다.
(C) 일본 자동차 공장에서, 그들은 최상의 해결책을 알아내기 위해 문제를 조사하고 데이터를 축적하지 않았다. 그들은 처음부터 그들이 원하는 결과를 설계했다. 만약 그들이 원하는 결과를 얻지 못했다면, 그들은 그것이 그 과정의 시작에서 내린 결정 때문이라고 이해했다.

| 정답해설 | ① 74% 주어진 글에서는 일본과 미국 자동차 공장 조립 라인에서의 공통점이 언급되었다. (A)에서 미국의 공장과 다른 점을 발견하고 미국 임원들이 당황하여 이유를 물어보는 내용의 (B)가 (A) 다음에 와야 하고, 마지막으로 일본 자동차 공장과 미국 자동차 공장의 차이를 설명하는 (C)가 오는 것이 자연스럽다.

| 오답해설 | ③ 12% 주어진 글에 미국 자동차 임원들이 당황할 만한 내용은 언급되지 않았으므로 (B)가 주어진 글 바로 다음에 오는

것은 문맥상 어색하다. 미국과 일본의 자동차 공장 조립 라인의 차이점을 알게 된 후 그들의 감정을 서술하는 것이 문맥상 더 적절하다.

| 더 알아보기 | 역접을 나타내는 연결어(구)

• but 그러나	• however 그러나
• on the contrary 반대로	• though 그러나

어휘

assembly line 조립 라인	hinge 경첩
mallet 망치	sheepishly 수줍게, 소심하게
plant 공장	accumulate 축적하다
figure out 알아내다; 이해하다	engineer 설계하다

---

8 독해 > Logical Reading > 연결사 [오답률 35%] 답 ①

| 해석 | Ekman의 논문과 누출이라는 그의 생각까지 거슬러 올라가는 속임수에 대한 비언어적 단서에 관해 많은 연구가 있었다. 사람들이 거짓말을 탐지하는 방법으로 타인의 비언어적 행동을 이용한다는 것은 잘 입증되어 있다. 나의 연구와 다른 많은 연구들은 정직성을 평가할 때 다른 사람들의 비언어적 행동 관찰에 대한 사람들의 의존을 강하게 지지해 왔다. (A) 그러나, 다양한 비언어적 행동과 거짓말을 하는 행위 사이의 연관성에 대한 사회과학 연구는 그 연관성이 전형적으로 매우 강하거나 일관되지 않다는 것을 시사한다. 내 연구에서, 나는 한 거짓말쟁이를 드러내는 것처럼 보이는 비언어적 신호들이 두 번째 거짓말쟁이가 주는 신호들과 다르다는 것을 관찰했다. (B) 더욱이, 비언어적 행동과 속임수를 연관 짓는 과학적 증거는 시간이 흐를수록 약해졌다. 사람들은 다른 사람들이 비언어적으로 자신을 표현하는 방법에 근거하여 정직함을 추론하지만, 그것은 매우 제한된 효용성과 타당성을 가지고 있다.

① 그러나 − 더욱이
② 그 결과 − 반면에
③ 그러나 − 그럼에도 불구하고
④ 그 결과 − 예를 들어

| 정답해설 | ① [65%] (A) 앞의 문장에서 비언어적 행동을 관찰하여 정직성을 평가하는 연구를 지지해 왔다고 언급하고 있다. 하지만 (A) 뒤에서는 다양한 비언어적 행동과 거짓말을 하는 행위 사이의 연관성은 매우 강하지 않고 일관성이 없다는 것을 시사한다는 내용이 나오므로 역접의 의미를 갖는 However가 알맞다.
(B) 뒤의 비언어적 행동과 거짓말 사이의 연관성에 대한 과학적 증거가 시간이 흐를수록 약해졌다는 내용은 앞 문장의 내용에 대해 부연 설명을 하는 부분이다. 따라서 What's more가 적절하다.

어휘

nonverbal 비언어적인	cue 단서, 신호
deception 속임수	date back to ~까지 거슬러 올라가다
leakage 누설, 누출	detect 발견하다
reliance 의존, 의지	assess 평가하다
consistent 일관된	give away 누설하다
utility 효용성	validity 타당성

---

9 문법 > 분사 [오답률 26%] 답 ③

| 해석 | 신생 기업이 설립되자마자 그것은 은행 계좌가 필요할 것이고, 급여 계좌에 대한 필요가 빠르게 뒤따를 것이다. 심지어 가장 작은 사업체들

과의 서비스에서부터 시작하여, 은행들은 급여 지불과 그에 관련된 세금 부기 서비스에 매우 경쟁적이다. 이것들은 기업이 최고 품질의 서비스와 얻을 수 있는 최고의 "무료" 회계 지원을 원하는 영역들이다. 급여 지불 세법 변경은 특히 50개 주의 많은 곳에서 판매 부서를 운영하려고 할 때, 따라잡기에 골칫거리이다. 그리고 요구되는 보고서들은 회사 관리 직원들의 부담이다. 그런 서비스들은 종종 은행원들에 의해 가장 잘 제공될 수 있다. 이 영역에서 은행의 증빙 서류는 ADP 같은 급여 서비스 대체제와 비교되어야 하지만, 결정할 때는 미래와 장기적 관계를 염두에 두어야 한다.

| 정답해설 | ③ [74%] 주어인 reports가 요구하는 것이 아니라 요구되어지는 것이므로 현재분사 requiring을 수동의 의미를 갖는 과거분사 required로 고쳐야 한다.

| 오답해설 | ① [13%] 분사구문의 주어는 The banks이고, 가장 작은 사업체들과 함께 시작을 하는 것이므로 능동의 의미를 갖는 현재분사 starting은 적절하다.
② [6%] 뒤에 나오는 절의 문장 구조가 완벽하므로 선행사로 areas를 갖는 관계부사 where는 적절하다.
④ [7%] when절의 주어인 a decision은 결정이 되는 것이므로 수동태가 오는 것이 적절하다. 현재진행시제의 수동태는 「be동사 + being p.p.」로 표현하므로 어법에 맞다.

| 더 알아보기 | 관계대명사 vs. 관계부사

뒤따라오는 절 구조의 완전성 여부로 관계대명사와 관계부사를 구분할 수 있다.
• 선행사 + 관계대명사[who/which/whom/that] + 불완전한 문장
• 선행사 + 관계부사[when/where/why/how] + 완전한 문장
* 관계부사 how는 선행사 the way와 함께 사용할 수 없으므로 둘 중 하나만 사용한다.

어휘

start-up 신생 기업	incorporate 설립하다
payroll 급여 지불 명부	account 계좌
competitive 경쟁적인	bookkeeping 부기, 장부 기입
legislation 입법, 법안	sales force 판매 부서
administrative 관리의, 행정의	alternative 대안, 대체

오답률 TOP 3
10 문법 > 분사 [오답률 51%] 답 ①

| 해석 | 많은 사람들은 동물 보호소를 방문하는 것이 너무 슬프거나 우울하다고 생각하기 때문에 그곳을 방문하는 것을 거부한다. 그들은 그렇게 안 좋게 느끼지 않아도 되는데, 왜냐하면 많은 운 좋은 동물들이 교통사고, 다른 동물들이나 인간들의 공격, 그리고 여러 요인에 영향을 받는 길 위의 위험한 삶으로부터 구조되기 때문이다. 마찬가지로 길을 잃은 많은 애완동물들이 그저 동물 보호소로 데려와지는 것만으로 당황한 주인들에 의해 발견되고 되찾아진다. 가장 중요한 것은, 입양이 가능한 동물들이 집을 찾고, 아프거나 위험한 동물들은 인도적으로 그들의 고통에서 벗어나게 된다.

| 정답해설 | ① [49%] they find it too sad or depressed라는 문장에서 it은 to visit animal shelters를 의미한다. 사물의 상태를 나타낼 때 감정분사형 형용사는 과거분사형이 아니라 현재분사형으로 사용해야 어법에 맞다. 그러므로 depressed가 아니라 depressing이 적절하다.

| 오답해설 | ② [17%] 뒤에 나오는 절의 문장 구조가 완벽하므로

streets를 선행사로 하는 관계부사 where는 적절하다.

③ 13% 동사 are found의 주어가 Many lost pets로 복수 명사이 므로 복수 동사를 사용한 것은 옳다. 또한 뒤에 행위자 by distraught owners가 나오므로 동사를 수동태로 쓴 것도 어법 에 맞다.

④ 21% '입양 가능한 동물'이라는 의미로 형용사 adoptable은 적절 한 표현이다.

오답률 TOP 2
11 독해 > Logical Reading > 문맥상 다양한 추론   답 ②
오답률 57%

| 해석 | EQ 테스트가 믿을 만한 테스트 방법으로 수행된다면, 당신에게 당 신 자신에 대해 매우 유용한 정보를 제공해 줄 수 있다. 수천 명의 사람들을 테스트해 오면서, 나는 많은 사람들이 그들의 결과에 약간 놀란다는 것을 알게 되었다. 예를 들어, 자신이 사회적으로 매우 책임감이 있고 종종 다른 사람들을 걱정한다고 믿었던 한 여성은 그 분야에서 (A) 평균 점수가 나왔 다. 그녀는 그녀의 점수에 꽤 실망했다. 그녀는 사회적 책임감에 대해 매우 높은 기준을 가지고 있어서 그녀를 평가할 때 그녀 자신에게 극도로 (B) 엄 격했던 것으로 드러났다. 실제로, 그녀는 대부분의 사람들보다 사회적으로 (C) 더 책임감이 있었지만, 그녀는 자신이 지금보다 훨씬 더 나아질 수 있다 고 믿었다.

	(A)	(B)	(C)
①	평균의	쉬운	덜
②	평균의	엄격한	더
③	놀라운	엄격한	덜
④	놀라운	쉬운	더

| 정답해설 | ② 43% (A) 앞에 EQ 테스트의 결과에 놀라는 사람들 이 많다고 하였으므로, 그 결과가 예상과는 다르게 나왔기 때문임 을 짐작할 수 있다. 따라서 사회적으로 매우 책임감이 있는 여성의 테스트 결과, 그 분야의 점수가 높지 않고 average(평균)로 나왔음 을 추론할 수 있다.

(B) 앞에서 그녀는 사회적 책임감에 대해 매우 높은 기준을 가지고 있다고 했으므로, 그녀가 자기 자신에 대한 테스트에서도 '엄격하 게' 했다고 추론할 수 있다. 따라서 hard(엄격한)가 적절하다.

(C) 필자가 예로 든 테스트 대상자가 사회적으로 책임감이 강한 사 람이라고 했으므로 대부분의 사람보다 더(more) 사회적으로 책임 감이 있다는 내용으로 연결되는 것이 적절하다.

12 독해 > Reading for Writing > 빈칸 구 완성   오답률 19%   답 ②

| 해석 | 사람은 자신에게 유리하게 증거를 사용함으로써 ② 특정한 믿음을 초래하려고 노력할지도 모른다. 한 어머니가 아들에게 "이번 학기에 영어는 잘하고 있니?"라고 묻는다. 그는 "아, 방금 쪽지 시험에서 95점을 받았어

요."라고 쾌활하게 대답한다. 이 진술은 그가 다른 모든 쪽지 시험에서 낙제 했다는 사실과 실제 평균이 55점이라는 사실을 은폐한다. 하지만, 만약 그 녀가 그 문제를 더 이상 추궁하지 않는다면, 어머니는 아들이 아주 잘하고 있다는 것에 기뻐할지도 모른다. Linda는 Susan에게 "Dickens를 많이 읽 었니?"라고 묻고, Susan은 "오, *Pickwick Papers*는 내가 가장 좋아하는 소 설 중 하나야."라고 대답한다. 이 진술은 *Pickwick Papers*가 그녀가 읽은 Dickens의 유일한 소설이라는 사실을 숨길 수 있으며, 그것은 Linda에게 Susan이 Dickens의 대단한 열성팬이라는 인상을 줄 수도 있다.

① 여분의 돈을 벌다
② 특정한 믿음을 초래하다
③ 기억력 문제를 숨기다
④ 다른 사람들이 죄책감을 느끼게 만들다

| 정답해설 | ② 81% 빈칸 뒤에 나온 예시를 통해 어떤 진술이 숨겨 진 다른 사실을 은폐할 수도 있고 그 진술을 어떻게 해석하느냐에 따라 상대방이 다른 사람에 대해 오해할 수 있다고 하였으므로 빈 칸에 적절한 것은 '특정한 믿음을 초래하다'이다.

13 독해 > Reading for Writing > 요약   오답률 11%   답 ①

| 해석 | 우리가 우리의 외모, 우리의 정원, 우리가 준비한 저녁 식사, 아니 면 사무실에서의 업무에 대해 칭찬을 받든 받지 않은 간에, 일을 잘 했다는 것에 대해 인정을 받는 것은 항상 만족스럽다. 확실히, 강화 이론은 가끔의 칭찬이 새로운 기술을 배우는 것에 도움이 된다고 본다. 그러나, 일부 증거 들은 성과 개선에 칭찬을 사용하는 것에 대해 광범위한 일반화를 하지 말라 고 경고한다. 칭찬은 어떤 일에서는 성과를 향상시키지만, 대신에 다른 일 에서는 해로운 것으로 판명될 수도 있다. 승리를 기대하는 고향 팬들의 열 띤 지지가 그들의 팀의 몰락을 불러오는 상황을 상상해 보라. 이런 상황에 서, 칭찬은 선수들에게 부담을 안겨 주고 경기를 방해하는 것으로 보인다.

↓

(A) 칭찬이 성과에 도움을 주는지 해를 입히는지는 (B) 일의 유형에 달려 있다.

	(A)	(B)
①	칭찬	일의 유형
②	경쟁	협동의 질
③	칭찬	협동의 질
④	경쟁	일의 유형

| 정답해설 | ① 89% 본문 중반부의 however 이하에서 칭찬을 성과 개선에 사용하는 것을 광범위하게 일반화하지 말라고 경고한 다음, 칭찬은 어떤 일에서는 성과를 향상시키지만 다른 일에서는 해로울 수 있는 것처럼 보인다고 했다. 그런 다음 승리를 기대하는 고향 팬 들의 열띤 지지가 부담이 되어 그들의 팀의 몰락을 불러오는 상황 을 예로 들어 칭찬이 항상 성과를 향상시키는 것만은 아니라는 내 용을 뒷받침하고 있으므로, 빈칸 (A)에는 praise(칭찬)이, (B)에는 task types(일의 유형)가 적절하다.

recognition 인정
occasional 가끔의
generalization 일반화
performance 성과, 실적
disrupt 방해하다, 피해를 주다

reinforcement 강화
sweeping 광범위한
regarding ~에 관하여, ~에 대해
downfall 몰락

---

14 문법 > 접속사 [오답률 19%] 답 ③

| 해석 | 미디어 소비를 익명의 사회적 관계의 맥락에서 고려할 때, 우리는 술집과 같은 공공장소에서 텔레비전을 보거나, 콘서트나 댄스 클럽에 가거나, 버스나 지하철에서 신문을 읽는 등 낯선 사람들이 있는 것과 관련된 모든 경우들을 의미한다. 전형적으로, 우리가 우리 주변의 사람들과 그리고 미디어 제품과 어떻게 상호 작용하는지를 지배하는 사회적 규칙들이 있다. 예를 들어, 우리 문화에서는 다른 사람의 어깨 너머로 책을 읽거나, 공공장소에서 일어나서 TV 채널을 바꾸는 것은 무례하거나, 적어도 공격적으로 여겨진다. 음악 팬이라면 누구나 특정한 종류의 콘서트에서 무엇이 적절한지 안다. 다른 사람들의 존재는 환경과 그에 따른 미디어 소비의 활동을 정의하는 데 종종 결정적인데, 비록 그 관계가 특정 개인과 완전히 상관없다는 사실에도 불구하고 그러하다.

| 정답해설 | ③ [81%] read가 포함된 문장의 주어 it은 가주어이며 read over ~ to get up and change TV channels in a public setting이 진주어이다. 따라서 진주어 형태인 to read가 와서 to get up and change와 병렬 구조를 이루어야 한다.

| 오답해설 | ① [1%] 밑줄 친 going은 앞의 viewing과 뒤의 reading과 함께 병렬 구조를 이루며 옳게 쓰였다.
② [9%] 주격 관계대명사절의 동사는 선행사의 수에 일치시킨다. 선행사인 social rules가 복수 명사이므로 복수 동사 govern은 알맞게 쓰였다.
④ [9%] despite는 전치사로 다음에 절이 아닌 명사구나 명사가 와야 한다. despite의 목적어는 명사 the fact이고 that절은 the fact의 동격절이므로 어법에 맞다.

어휘
consumption 소비
anonymous 익명의
presence 존재
interact 상호 작용하다, 교류하다
aggressive 공격적인
crucial 결정적인, 중요한

context 맥락
occasion 경우, 때
govern 지배하다, 통제하다
rude 무례한
setting 장소, 환경
impersonal 특정 개인과 상관없는

---

15 문법 > 일치 [오답률 6%] 답 ③

| 해석 | 우리들 중 다수는 건망증, 즉 갑작스런 기억 상실 때문에 사람의 이름과 신분을 상기할 수 없게 된다고 믿는다. 이러한 믿음은 보통 영화, 텔레비전, 문학에서 기억 상실증이 묘사되는 방법을 반영할 수 있다. 예를 들어, 영화 'The Bourne Identity'에서 Matt Damon의 캐릭터를 보면, 우리는 그가 누구인지, 그는 왜 자신이 펼치는 그 기술을 가지고 있는지, 혹은 자신이 어디 출신인지에 대한 기억이 없다는 것을 알게 된다. 그는 이 질문들에 답하려고 애쓰는 데 영화의 많은 부분을 쓴다. 하지만, 당신이 당신의 이름과 신분을 기억하지 못하는 것은 현실에서는 매우 드물다. 기억 상실증은 과거의 기억의 대부분은 손상되지 않은 채, 환자가 새로운 기억을 형성할 수 없게 하는 뇌손상으로 나타나는 경우가 가장 흔하다. 어떤 영화들은 더 흔한 이 증상을 정확하게 묘사한다. 바로 우리가 가장 좋아하는 'Memento'가 그

렇다.

| 정답해설 | ③ [94%] 동사 are의 주어는 the inability이고 to remember 이하는 the inability를 수식하는 to부정사이다. 따라서 동사는 단수 주어에 수를 일치시켜 단수 동사 is가 와야 어법상 적절하다.

| 오답해설 | ① [0%] amnesia는 묘사되는 대상이므로 과거분사인 portrayed는 어법상 알맞다.
② [2%] 「spend + 목적어[돈, 시간] + -ing」는 '~하는 데 (돈이나 시간을) 사용하다[쓰다]'라는 의미를 갖는 관용표현이다.
④ [4%] 「with + 목적어 + 분사」는 '목적어가 분사인 채로'라는 의미를 갖는 표현이다. with most memories of the past intact에서 분사 being이 생략된 표현이므로 형용사 intact가 온 것은 적절하다.

어휘
amnesia 기억 상실증
inability 무능, 불능
exceedingly 매우
intact 손상되지 않은, 그대로인

loss 손실
portray 묘사하다, 설명하다
victim 희생자; 환자
syndrome 증후군

---

16 독해 > Reading for Writing > 빈칸 절 완성 [오답률 27%] 답 ②

| 해석 | 현재 자연 재해와 그것이 사람과 그들의 재산에 미치는 부정적인 영향에 대해서는 많이 알려져 있다. 논리적인 사람이라면 누구나 그러한 잠재적 영향을 회피하거나 최소한 그러한 영향을 최소화하기 위해 그들의 행동이나 재산을 바꿀 것이 분명해 보인다. 그러나 인간이 항상 이성적인 것은 아니다. 어떤 사람이 개인적인 경험을 갖거나 그런 경험을 가진 사람을 알 때까지, 대부분의 사람들은 잠재의식적으로 "그런 일은 여기서는 일어나지 않을 거야." 또는 "나에게는 일어나지 않을 거야."라고 믿는다. 위험, 발생 확률, 사건 비용을 잘 알고 있는 박식한 과학자들조차도 ② 항상 적절하게 행동하는 것은 아니다.

① 침묵하기를 거부하다
② 항상 적절하게 행동하는 것은 아니다
③ 유전적 요인을 상위에 두다
④ 자연적 위험을 정의내리는 데 어려움을 겪다

| 정답해설 | ② [73%] 빈칸 앞에서 대부분의 사람들은 자연 재해에 대해 무의식적으로 "그런 일은 여기서는 일어나지 않을 거야." 또는 "나에게는 일어나지 않을 거야."라고 믿는다고 하면서, 인간이 항상 이성적인 것은 아니라고 했다. 따라서 빈칸이 포함된 문장의 주어인 knowledgeable scientists(박식한 과학자들)조차 비이성적으로 행동하기도 한다는 내용이 이어지는 것이 글의 흐름상 적절하므로 빈칸에는 '항상 적절하게 행동하지는 않는다'가 적절하다.

| 오답해설 | ④ [19%] 자연 재해에 대해 인간이 어떻게 생각하는지가 이 글의 주된 내용으로 자연적 위험을 정의내리는 것은 글에서 서술하고 있지 않다.

어휘
hazard 위험
property 재산, 소유물
rational 합리적인, 이성적인
knowledgeable 박식한
occurrence 발생

impact 충격, 영향
modify 바꾸다, 수정하다
subconsciously 잠재 의식적으로
odd 확률, 가능성
genetic 유전의, 유전학의

factor 요인

17 독해 > Macro Reading > 주제　　오답률 30%　답 ③

| 해석 | 도시와 왕국의 부흥과 교통 인프라의 향상은 특성화를 위한 새로운 기회를 가져왔다. 인구 밀도가 높은 도시들은 전문 구두닦이들과 의사들뿐만 아니라 목수, 사제, 군인, 변호사 들에게도 정규직 일자리를 제공했다. 정말 좋은 포도주, 올리브유, 도자기 등을 생산한다는 명성을 얻은 마을들은 거의 독점적으로 그 제품을 특화해서 그들이 필요로 하는 다른 모든 상품들과 그것을 다른 촌락들과 교환할 가치가 있다는 것을 발견했다. 이것은 매우 이치에 맞았다. 기후와 토양이 다르므로, 포도나무에 훨씬 더 적합한 토양과 기후의 장소에서 나온 더 부드러운 여러 종류(의 와인)를 살 수 있다면 왜 여러분의 뒤뜰에서 나온 평범한 와인을 마시겠는가? 만약 당신의 뒤뜰에 있는 점토가 더 튼튼하고 예쁜 항아리를 만들기에 적합하다면, 당신은 다른 것과 교환을 할 수 있다.
① 기후와 토양이 지역 제품에 어떻게 영향을 미치는가
② 지역 특산품에 대해 좋은 평판을 얻는 방법
③ 무엇이 사람들을 특성화와 무역에 종사하게 만들었는가
④ 도시의 부흥과 전문직들의 정규직 고용

| 정답해설 | ③ 70% 글 중반부에서 정말 좋은 포도주, 올리브유, 도자기 등을 생산한다는 명성을 얻은 마을들은 거의 독점적으로 그 제품을 특화해서 그들이 필요로 하는 다른 모든 상품들과 그것을 교환할 가치가 있다는 것을 발견했다고 한 다음, 글의 마지막까지 그 일의 타당함을 역설하고 있으므로 이 글의 주제로 가장 적절한 것은 '무엇이 사람들을 특성화와 무역에 종사하게 만들었는가'이다.

어휘
transport 교통
bring about 가져오다, 초래하다
densely 밀집하여
reputation 명성, 평판
exclusively 독점적으로
engage in ~에 종사하다
infrastructure 인프라, 사회 자본
specialization 특성화, 전문화
carpenter 목수
worth one's while ~할 가치가 있는
mediocre 평범한, 보통의

18 독해 > Logical Reading > 문맥상 다양한 추론　오답률 21%　답 ④

| 해석 | 9살의 Ryan Kyote는 캘리포니아주 Napa에 있는 집에서 아침을 먹고 있었는데, 그때 Indiana주의 한 학교가 점심 식사 계좌에 돈이 충분히 있지 않았던 6살짜리 아이의 밥을 빼앗았다는 뉴스를 보았다. Kyote는 그의 친구들에게 그런 일이 일어날 수 있는지 물었다. 그의 엄마가 학군에 알아보려고 연락했을 때, 그녀는 그들 학군 학교의 학생들이 점심 빚을 모두 합해서 2만 5천 달러나 지고 있다는 것을 알게 되었다. 비록 그 학군은 빚을 진 학생들을 처벌한 적이 없다고 말하지만, Kyote는 그가 저축한 용돈 약 74달러를 그의 학년의 빚을 갚기 위해 사용하기로 결정했는데, 그것은 점심 빚을 청산하려는 운동의 시작이 되었다. 10월에 Gavin Newsom 캘리포니아 주지사가 "점심시간에 창피 주기" 즉 빚진 학생들에게 더 안 좋은 음식을 주는 것을 금지하는 법안에 서명했을 때, 그는 이 문제에 대한 인식을 높이는 데 있어서 그의 "공감과 용기"에 대해 Kyote에게 감사했다. Kyote는 "영웅들은 모든 연령에서 나와요."라고 지적한다.
① 주지사는 점심 빚이 있는 학생들에게 점심 식사를 거부하는 법안에 서명했다.
② Kyote는 점심 식사 계좌에 돈이 다 떨어져서 점심을 빼앗겼다.
③ 재정적 부담이 있는 학군은 예산을 삭감했고 양질의 음식을 제공하는 데 실패했다.
④ 점심값을 낼 형편이 못 되는 학군 내의 많은 학생들이 점심 빚의 부담을 지고 있었다.

| 정답해설 | ④ 79% 본문 중반부에서 Kyote의 엄마가 학군에 알아보려고 연락했을 때, 그녀는 그들 학군 학교의 학생들의 점심 빚이 2만 5천 달러나 된다는 것을 알게 되었다고 했으며, Kyote는 자신이 모은 돈으로 그 빚 중 일부를 갚기로 결정했으므로 주지사가 언급한 the issue는 ④이다.

| 오답해설 | ① 7% 점심 식사를 거부하는 법안이 아니라 lunch shaming(점심시간에 창피 주기)이라는 것을 금지하는 법안에 서명했다.
② 5% Kyote가 겪은 일이 아니라 Indiana주의 한 학교에서 그런 일이 있었다고 언급되었다.
③ 9% 본문에서 언급되지 않은 내용이다.

어휘
school district 학군
debt 빚
allowance 용돈
lunch shaming 점심시간에 창피 주기
bill 법안
burden 부담; 부담을 지우다
all fold 모두 합해서, 총
penalize 벌칙을 주다
ban 금지하다
empathy 공감

19 독해 > Micro Reading > 내용일치/불일치　오답률 6%　답 ④

| 해석 | 세계에서 가장 큰 심장은 청고래 안에 있다. 그것의 무게는 7톤이 넘는다. 그것은 방 하나 크기다. 이 생물은 태어날 때, 몸길이는 20피트이고 몸무게는 4톤이다. 그것은 당신의 자동차보다 훨씬 크다. 그것은 매일 엄마 고래로부터 나오는 100갤런의 우유를 마시고, 하루에 200파운드씩 체중이 증가하고 7, 8세가 되면, 상상할 수 없는 사춘기를 견디고, 그 후 꼭 인간의 시야에서 사라지는데, 왜냐하면 짝짓기 습성, 이동 패턴, 식단, 무리 생활, 언어, 사회 구조 그리고 질병에 대해 거의 알려진 것이 없기 때문이다. 전 세계에 1만 마리 정도의 청고래가 있는데, 지구의 모든 대양에서 지금껏 살았던 가장 큰 동물이며, 우리가 거의 아는 것이 없는 동물이다. 하지만 우리는 이것은 알고 있다. 세계에서 가장 큰 심장을 가진 동물들은 보통 짝을 이루어 이동하고, 날카로운 갈망의 소리인 그들의 귀를 찌를 듯한 신음 소리는 물속에서 몇 마일이고 들릴 수 있다.

| 정답해설 | ④ 94% 마지막 문장의 the animals with the largest hearts in the world generally travel in pairs에서 세계에서 가장 큰 심장을 가진 동물들은 일반적으로 짝을 이루어 이동했으므로 혼자서 이동한다는 ④는 글의 내용과 일치하지 않는다.

| 오답해설 | ① 1% It drinks a hundred gallons of milk from its mama every day and gains 200 pounds a day.의 내용과 일치한다.
② 2% it endures an unimaginable puberty and then it essentially disappears from human ken의 내용과 일치한다.
③ 3% The biggest heart in the world is inside the blue whale.에서 세계에서 심장이 가장 큰 동물인 것을 알 수 있고, of the largest animal who ever lived를 통해 세계에서 가장 큰 동물이라는 것도 알 수 있다.

어휘

creature 창조물
puberty 사춘기
next to nothing 없는 것과 다름없는
mate 짝짓기를 하다
moan 신음 소리를 내다
yearning 갈망하는

endure 인내하다, 견디다
ken 은신처, 소굴; 시야
penetrating 귀를 찌를 듯한
piercing 날카로운

---

20 독해 > Macro Reading > 주제 　오답률 12%　 답 ④

| 해석 | 신선 제품을 다룰 때는 온도를 제어하는 것 외에도 공기의 제어가 중요하다. 보관 중 건조를 막기 위해 약간의 습기가 공기 중에 필요하지만, 너무 많은 습기는 곰팡이의 성장을 촉진시킬 수 있다. 일부 상업용 저장 장치는 이산화탄소와 습도의 수준을 둘 다 주의 깊게 조절하면서, 공기를 제어한다. 때때로 에틸렌 가스와 같은 다른 가스들이 바나나와 다른 신선 제품들의 최적의 품질을 이루는 데 도움을 주기 위해 통제된 수준에서 도입될 수 있다. 가스와 습기의 제어와 관련하여 저장된 음식들 사이에서 어느 정도 공기의 순환은 필요하다.
① 공기에서 해로운 가스들을 제어하는 것의 필요성
② 식물 및 과일 재배에서 습도의 수준을 제어하는 최고의 방법
③ 전 세계에서 매년 증가하는 탄소 발자국의 심각성
④ 저장 음식에서 일정 수준의 가스와 습도를 제어하는 것의 중요성

| 정답해설 | ④ 88% 글의 초반부에서 신선 제품을 다룰 때 온도를 제어하는 것 외에도 공기의 제어가 중요하다고 서술하며 제품을 보관할 때 건조를 막기 위해 약간의 습기가 필요하고 가스가 신선 제품의 최적의 품질에 도움을 준다고 서술하였으므로, 글의 주제로 가장 적절한 것은 ④이다.

| 오답해설 | ② 7% 식물이나 과일 재배 시의 습도 조절에 관한 내용은 본문에 제시되지 않는다.

어휘

atmosphere 공기
dehydration 건조; 탈수
mold 곰팡이
optimal 최적의

moisture 습기
storage 저장
regulate 조절하다; 통제하다
circulation 순환

---

21 독해 > Logical Reading > 문맥상 다양한 추론 답 ④
　오답률 25%　

| 해석 | 비록 거짓말이 특정한 경우에 어떤 해로운 영향을 끼치지 않더라도, 그것은 여전히 도덕적으로 잘못되었는데 왜냐하면 만약 그것이 밝혀지면, 거짓말은 인간의 의사소통이 의존하는 진실 말하기의 일반적인 관행을 약화시키기 때문이다. 예를 들어, 만약 내가 허영심 때문에 나의 나이에 대해 거짓말을 한다면, 그리고 나의 거짓말이 들통난다면, 비록 어떤 심각한 해는 끼치지 않았을지라도 나는 전반적으로 당신의 신뢰를 ① 약화시켰을 것이다. 그런 경우 당신은 내가 앞으로 말할 어떤 것도 믿기가 아주 쉽지 않을 것이다. 그래서 모든 거짓말은 그것이 들통났을 때, 간접적으로 ② 해로운 영향을 끼친다. 하지만, 아주 가끔, 이러한 해로운 영향은 아마 거짓말로 발생할 ③ 이득보다 더 적을지도 모른다. 예를 들어, 만약 누군가가 심각하게 아프다면 그들의 예상 수명에 대해 그들에게 거짓말을 하는 것이 어쩌면 그들에게 더 오래 살 기회를 줄 수도 있다. 반면에, 그들에게 진실을 말하는 것은 아마 그들의 신체적 쇠약을 가속화시키는 우울증을 ④ 막아줄(→ 악화시킬) 수도 있을 것이다.

| 정답해설 | ④ 75% 끝에서 두 번째 문장에서는 중병에 걸린 사람

에게 예상 수명에 대한 거짓말을 해서 오래 살 기회를 줄 수도 있다고 했다. 그런데 대조의 연결사 On the other hand로 이어진 마지막 문장에서 진실을 말해서 신체적 쇠약을 가속화시키는 우울증을 '막는다(prevent)'라고 하는 것은 글의 일관성을 해친다. 따라서 prevent를 '악화시키다'라는 의미의 aggravate로 바꿔야 문맥이 자연스러워진다.

| 오답해설 | ①②③ 10% 4% 11% 거짓말로 인해 신뢰가 약화(undermine)되고, 거짓말을 들키게 되었을 때 해로운(harmful) 영향을 미치게 되고, 아주 가끔은 거짓말로 인한 해로운 영향이 거짓말로 인해 생긴 이득(benefits) 보다 더 적다고 한 것은 모두 글의 흐름상 적절하다.

어휘

morally 도덕적으로
rely on ~에 의존하다
vanity 허영심
outweigh ~보다 더 크다, 더 무겁다
life expectancy 예상 수명
accelerate 가속화하다

weaken 약하게 하다
on grounds of ~의 이유로
undermine 약화시키다

depression 우울증

---

22 독해 > Logical Reading > 삽입 　오답률 38%　 답 ②

| 해석 | 바닷물의 몇 가지 공통된 특성들은 바다 생물들의 생존과 복지에 매우 중요하다. 물은 대부분의 해양 유기체 부피의 80~90퍼센트를 차지한다. 그것은 수영하고 떠다니는 유기체에게 부력과 몸을 지탱하는 힘을 주어 무거운 골격 구조에 대한 필요를 줄인다. ② 물은 또한 생명을 유지하기 위해 필요한 대부분의 화학 반응을 위한 매개물이다. 해양 유기체의 생명 과정은 투명성과 화학적 구성을 포함한 바닷물의 많은 기본적인 물리적, 화학적 특성을 차례로 변화시켜 유기체를 전체 해양 환경의 필수적인 부분으로 만든다. 유기체와 그들의 해양 환경 사이의 상호 작용을 이해하려면 바닷물의 더 중요한 물리적, 화학적 특성 중 일부에 대한 간단한 조사가 필요하다. 담수와 바닷물의 특성은 어떤 면에서 서로 다르므로, 우리는 우선 담수의 기본적 특성을 고려한 다음 그 성질들이 바닷물에서는 어떻게 다른지 조사한다.

| 정답해설 | ② 62% 주어진 문장은 물이 화학적 반응을 위한 매개물이라는 내용이다. 따라서 바닷물의 화학적 작용에 대해서 언급하기 전인 ②에 와야 글의 흐름상 적절하다.

어휘

medium 수단, 매개물
crucial 중대한, 결정적인
account for ~을 차지하다
in turn 차례로; 결국
transparency 투명도
attribute 속성, 자질

properties 성질, 특징
inhabitant 서식 동물
buoyancy 부력
alter 바꾸다
integral 필수적인

---

23 독해 > Logical Reading > 문맥상 다양한 추론 답 ③
　오답률 12%　

| 해석 | 여기 훨씬 더 놀라운 부분이 있다. AI의 도래는 인간 체스 선수의 성적을 전적으로 (A) 감소시킨 것만은 아니었다. 그와 정반대다. 값싸고, 매우 똑똑한 체스 프로그램은 그 어느 때보다도 더 많은 사람들이 어느 때보다도 더 많은 토너먼트에서 체스를 두도록 (B) 격려했고, 선수들은 그 어느 때보다도 더 잘하게 되었다. 지금은 Deep Blue가 Kasparov를 처음 이겼을

때보다 두 배 더 많은 그랜드 마스터들이 있다. 오늘날 인간 체스 랭킹 1위인 Magnus Carlsen은 AI로 훈련을 받았으며 모든 인간 체스 선수들 중에서 가장 컴퓨터 같은 존재로 여겨져 왔다. 그는 또한 역사상 (C) 가장 높은 인간 그랜드 마스터 등급을 가지고 있다.

	(A)	(B)	(C)
①	감소시키다	낙담한	가장 높은
②	증가시키다	낙담한	가장 낮은
③	감소시키다	격려하는	가장 높은
④	증가시키다	격려하는	가장 낮은

| 정답해설 | ③ 88% (A) 뒤에서 더 많은 사람들이 체스를 두게 하였다고 했다. (A) 앞에 부정어 didn't가 있으므로 '감소시키지 않았다'는 뜻이 되도록 diminish(감소시키다)가 빈칸에 알맞다.

(B) 어느 때보다 더 많은 사람들이 체스를 두었다고 했으므로 AI 체스 프로그램이 사람들을 격려하여 체스를 두게 했다는 의미가 되도록 빈칸에는 inspired가 알맞다.

(C) Magnus Carlsen은 가장 컴퓨터 같은 체스 선수이므로 등급이 매우 높은 선수일 것이라고 추론할 수 있다. 따라서 highest가 적절하다.

어휘

advent 도래, 출현 opposite 반대의
deem 여기다

---

24 독해 > Reading for Writing > 요약 오답률 15% 답 ③

| 해석 | 미술 오브젝트의 미적 가치와 마찬가지로 패션 오브젝트의 미적 가치는 자기 지향적이다. 소비자들은 매료되고자 하는 욕구와 매력적인 다른 사람들에게 둘러싸이고자 하는 욕구가 있다. 그러나 미술의 미적 가치와 달리 패션의 미적 가치는 타자 지향적이기도 하다. 외모의 매력은 다른 사람들의 반응을 끌어내고 사회적 상호 작용을 용이하게 하는 방법이다.

↓

패션의 미적 가치는 ③ 자기 지향적이기도 하고 타자 지향적이기도 하다.
① 본질적으로 단지 자기 지향적
② 다른 하나와 달리 단지 타자 지향적
③ 자기 지향적이기도 하고 타자 지향적
④ 그것의 본성에 상관없이 정의하기 어려운

| 정답해설 | ③ 85% 첫 문장에서 패션의 미적 가치는 자기 지향적(self-oriented)이라고 하였고 세 번째 문장에서는 패션의 미적 가치가 타자 지향적(other-oriented)이라고 했으므로 패션의 미적 가치는 두 가지 다라는 것을 알 수 있다. 따라서 요약문의 빈칸에 들어갈 정답은 ③이다.

어휘

aesthetic 미적의 fine art 미술, 예술
elicit 끌어내다 facilitate 용이하게 하다

---

25 독해 > Logical Reading > 삽입 오답률 45% 답 ④

| 해석 | 몇몇 사람들은 꿈에는 아무런 가치가 없다고 믿지만, 밤에 일어나는 이러한 드라마를 무관하다고 묵살하는 것은 잘못이다. 기억하는 것에서 얻어지는 것이 있다. 우리는 더 연결되어 있고, 더 완전하며 그리고 더 잘 진행되고 있다고 느낄 수 있다. 우리는 영감, 정보 그리고 위안을 얻을 수 있다. Albert Einstein은 그의 상대성 이론이 꿈에서 영감을 받았다고 말했다. 사실, 그는 꿈이 그의 많은 발견의 원인이 되었다고 주장했다. 왜 우리가

꿈을 꾸냐고 묻는 것은 왜 우리가 숨을 쉬냐고 묻는 것과 마찬가지의 의미이다. 꿈은 건강한 삶의 필수적인 부분이다. ④ 아주 좋은 소식은 우리가 꿈을 기억하든 못하든 간에 이것이 사실이라는 것이다. 많은 사람들이 비록 그들이 특정한 꿈을 기억 못한다 할지라도, 깨어나자마자 문제에 대한 새로운 접근법이 생각난다고 말한다.

| 정답해설 | ④ 55% 주어진 문장의 The great news가 무엇인지 알면 주어진 문장이 들어가야 할 위치도 금방 알 수 있다. 또한 this가 사실이라는 것이 the great news(아주 좋은 소식)라고 했으므로 꿈에 대한 긍정적인 내용을 this로 표현했음을 알 수 있다. 꿈을 긍정적으로 말한 것은 ④ 앞에 있는 문장뿐이므로 ④에 주어진 문장이 들어가는 것이 적절하다.

어휘

dismiss 묵살하다 nocturnal 밤에 일어나는
irrelevant 상관없는, 무관한 on track 제대로 진행되고 있는
inspiration 영감 theory of relativity 상대성 이론
integral 필수적

합격예상 체크

〈법원직 연도별 합격선〉

2022년부터 막대그래프: 2022, 2021, 2020, 2019(2019 합격기준), 2018, 2017, 2016

맞힌 개수	/25문항	점수	/100점

➡ ☐ 합격 ☐ 불합격

취약영역 체크					
문항	정답	영역	문항	정답	영역
①	③	문법 > 동사	14	②	독해 > Macro Reading > 주제
2	③	독해 > Logical Reading > 문맥상 다양한 추론	15	④	독해 > Reading for Writing > 빈칸 절 완성
3	③	독해 > Logical Reading > 삭제	16	④	독해 > Macro Reading > 주장
4	③	문법 > 동명사, 관계사, 일치	17	①	독해 > Macro Reading > 제목
5	②	독해 > Reading for Writing > 빈칸 절 완성	18	③	독해 > Logical Reading > 문맥상 다양한 추론
6	②	독해 > Micro Reading > 내용 일치/불일치	19	②	독해 > Reading for Writing > 요약
7	①	독해 > Reading for Writing > 요약	20	②	독해 > Logical Reading > 문맥상 다양한 추론
8	③	독해 > Logical Reading > 문맥상 다양한 추론	21	④	문법 > 태
9	②	독해 > Macro Reading > 요지	22	③	문법 > 관계사, 분사
10	④	독해 > Micro Reading > 내용 일치/불일치	23	③	문법 > 접속사
11	②	독해 > Logical Reading > 문맥상 다양한 추론	24	④	독해 > Logical Reading > 문맥상 다양한 추론
12	①	독해 > Reading for Writing > 빈칸 구 완성	25	②	독해 > Reading for Writing > 빈칸 절 완성
13	③	독해 > Logical Reading > 삽입			

⬇ 영역별 틀린 개수로 취약영역을 확인하세요!

어휘	/0	문법	/5	독해	/20	생활영어	/0

➡ 나의 취약영역: _____

※ [정답해설]과 [오답해설] 선지의 50% 표시는 〈1초 합격예측 서비스〉를 통해 수집된 선지 선택률을 나타냅니다.

1	문법 > 동사	오답률 32%	답 ③

| 해석 | 최근의 연구는 일부 사람들이 유전적으로 수줍음을 잘 타는 성향이 있다는 것을 보여 준다. 즉, 어떤 사람들은 수줍게 태어난다. 연구원들은 신생아의 15~20%가 수줍음의 징후를 보인다고 말한다. 즉, 그들은 더 조용하고 더 경계심이 강하다. 연구원들은 빠르면 두 달 안에 나타나는 사교적인 아기들과 수줍은 아기들 사이의 생리적인 차이를 확인했다. 한 연구에서, 나중에 수줍은 아이로 밝혀진 두 달 된 아이들은 움직이는 모빌들 그리고 녹음된 인간의 목소리 같은 자극에 심장 박동 수 증가, 팔과 다리의 경련적인 움직임들, 그리고 과도한 울음 같은 스트레스 징후로 반응했다. 수줍음의 유전적 근거에 대한 추가적인 증거는 수줍음이 많은 아이들의 부모나 조부모들이 그렇지 않은 아이들의 부모나 조부모보다 더 자주 그들이 어릴 때 수줍음을 탔다고 말한다는 사실이다.

| 정답해설 | ③ 68% 주어가 two-month-olds이고 who were later identified as shy children이 관계대명사절로 선행사인 two-month-olds를 수식하고 있다. 주어에 대한 동사가 없으므로 reacting은 reacted로 고쳐야 한다.

| 오답해설 | ① 6% 「be predisposed to + 명사」는 '~의 성향이 있다'라는 뜻으로 어법상 적절한 표현이다.

② 1% that은 differences를 선행사로 하는 주격 관계대명사로 알맞다.

④ 25% than은 more often과 연결되어 비교급을 이루므로 알맞다.

어휘

vigilant 경계하는
sociable 사교적인
jerky 경련하는
physiological 생리적인
stimulus 자극(pl. stimuli)

2	독해 > Logical Reading > 문맥상 다양한 추론		답 ③
		오답률 25%	

| 해석 | 한국은 세계 최고의 대중문화 수출국이 되겠다는 헌신적인 목표를 가진 유일한 나라 중 하나이다. 그것이 한국이 '소프트 파워'를 개발하는 길이다. 그것은 군사력이나 경제력을 통해서가 아니라 국가가 국가의 이미지를 통해서 휘두르는 (A) 무형의 힘을 가리킨다. 한류는 처음에는 중국과 일본으로, 나중에는 동남아와 전 세계 여러 나라로 퍼져 나갔다. 2000년에는, 50년간의 한일 대중문화 교류 금지가 일부 해제되었고, 이것은 일본인들 사이에서 한국 대중문화의 (B) 급증으로 개선되었다. 한국의 방송 당국은 여러 나라에 그들의 TV 프로그램과 문화 콘텐츠를 홍보하기 위해 대표단을 파견해 왔다. 한류는 한국, 한국 기업, 문화, 국가 이미지에 축복이었다. 1999년 초부터, 한류는 아시아 전역에서 가장 큰 문화 현상의 하나가 되었다. 한류 효과는 엄청나 2004년에는 한국의 GDP의 0.2%에 기여했는데, 이는 약 18억 7천만 달러에 달한다. 더 최근인 2014년에, 한류는 한국 경제에 추정가로 116억 달러라는 (C) 상승을 기록했다.

| 정답해설 | ③ 75% (A) 한류라는 문화적 현상을 설명하는 것이므로 intangible(무형의)이 적절한 표현이다.

(B) 앞에 improved(개선되었다)라는 동사가 있으므로 '급증'이라는

뜻의 surge가 적절한 표현이다.

(C) 한류로 인한 수익이 2004년에는 18억 7천만 달러였으나 2014년에는 116억 달러로 엄청나게 증가했으므로 boost(상승)가 적절한 표현이다.

어휘

tangible 유형의	intangible 무형의
wield 휘두르다	
lift (제재·금지령 등을) 해제하다, 철폐하다	
surge 급등	broadcast authority 방송 당국
delegate 대표단, 사절단	phenomenon 현상(*pl.* phenomena)
estimated 추정된	boost 증가, 상승
stagnation 침체	

---

3 독해 > Logical Reading > 삭제 오답률 3% 답 ③

| 해석 | 그룹 Queen이 부른 오페라 스타일의 불멸의 싱글 앨범 Bohemian Rhapsody는 1975년에 발매되어 9주간 영국 차트 1위를 차지했다. 독특한 스타일과 길이 때문에 이전에는 발표되지 않았지만 (사람들에게) 연주될 것이라고 Freddie가 주장했던 이 노래는 즉시 알아볼 수 있을 정도의 히트곡이 되었다. 이 무렵 Freddie의 독특한 개성은 명확해졌는데, Queen에게 다채롭고 예측 불가능하고 화려한 개성을 부여한 엄청난 음역대의 목소리와 무대에서의 존재감이었다. ③ Bomi와 Jer Bulsara의 아들인 Freddie는 어린 시절 대부분을 인도에서 보냈으며 그곳에 있는 St. Peter 기숙학교를 다녔다. 곧 Queen의 인기는 영국의 해안을 넘어 유럽 전역, 일본, 그리고 미국의 차트에 올라 승리를 거두었는데, 특히 미국에서 1979년에 그들은 Freddie의 노래 Crazy Little thing Called Love로 차트 1위를 차지했다.

| 정답해설 | ③ 97% 본문은 그룹 Queen과 Freddie가 어디에서 얼마만큼 인기를 얻었는가에 대한 것이 주된 내용이므로 Freddie의 어린 시절에 대한 내용인 ③은 글의 흐름과 관계없는 문장이다.

어휘

operatically 오페라 풍의	release 발매하다, 출시하다
recognizable 눈에 띄는, 알아챌 수 있는	
unpredictable 예측 불가능한	flamboyant 화려한

오답률 TOP 3

4 문법 > 동명사, 관계사, 일치 오답률 57% 답 ③

| 해석 | 많은 업계 전문가들에 의해 애니메이션 목소리 연기의 창시자로 생각되는 Mel Blanc은 한 지역 라디오 쇼의 성우로 1927년에 활동을 시작했다. 당시 제작자들은 여러 명의 배우를 고용할 돈이 없어서 Mel Blanc은 쇼에 필요한 다른 목소리와 페르소나를 (A) 만들어 내는 것에 의지했다. 그는 The Jack Benny Program에 고정 출연자가 되었는데, (B) 그 프로그램에서 그는 인간, 동물 그리고 엔진 정비가 필요한 자동차 같은 무생물까지 많은 등장인물의 목소리를 연기했다. Porky Pig를 위해 그가 만들어 낸 독특한 목소리는 Warner Bros.에서 큰 성공의 바탕이 되었다. 곧 Blanc은 Hanna-Barbera Studios의 등장인물들뿐만 아니라 그 스튜디오의 대형 만화 스타들 중 다수와 밀접한 관련을 맺었다. 그의 가장 오랜 목소리 연기는 Daffy Duck이었는데 약 52년간 계속되었다. Blanc은 자신의 작품을 극도로 지키려고 했는데 "Mel Blanc에 의한 목소리 연기"라고 쓰인 스크린 크레디트는 항상 그의 계약 조건에 (C) 있었다.

| 정답해설 | ③ 43% (A) resort to는 '~하는 것에 의지하다'라는 뜻으로 여기서 to는 전치사이므로 동사 create가 아니라 동명사 creating이 와야 한다.

(B) 뒤에 오는 문장이 완전한 형태의 절이므로 관계부사 where가 올바른 표현이다. 여기서 where는 계속적 용법으로 쓰여 '그런데 거기서 ~'라는 의미로 해석한다.

(C) 문장의 주어가 복수 명사인 screen credits이므로 수를 일치시켜 복수 동사 were가 와야 한다.

어휘

tune-up 엔진 정비가 필요한	distinctive 독특한
breakout success 큰 성공	
credits 크레디트(영화 등에 참여한 사람들의 이름을 언급하는 것)	
the terms of contract 계약 조건	

---

5 독해 > Reading for Writing > 빈칸 절 완성 오답률 29% 답 ②

| 해석 | 현재 사무용 건물에 대한 수요 시장이 폭락하여 많은 공실이 발생하고 있는 상황에서, 우리는 주거용과 상업용 또는 사무용 기능 사이에 어느 정도 교환할 수 있는 계획을 개발할 필요가 있다. 이 공실은 역사적인 수준에 도달했는데, 현재 네덜란드의 주요 도시들은 약 5백만 평방미터의 비어 있는 사무실 공간이 있는 반면, 16만 가구의 주택이 부족하다. 네덜란드 부동산 개발업자 협회에 따르면, 적어도 100만 평방미터는 공실로 남아 있을 것으로 예상된다고 한다. 주요 도시들 주변에 빈 사무용 건물들의 '유령 도시'들이 생겨날 것이라는 실질적인 두려움이 있다. 이러한 전망에도 불구하고, 수익률이 높은 기간 동안 계획되었기 때문에, 사무용 건물 활동은 전속력으로 계속되고 있다. 그러므로, 이제는 ② 사무용 건물들에 대한 많은 계획들이 주거용으로 다시 재개발되어야 하는 것이 필수적이다.

① 건물 유지 비용을 절감하기 위해 새로운 디자인이 채택되어야 한다
② 사무용 건물들에 대한 많은 계획들이 주거용으로 다시 재개발되어야 한다
③ 주거용 빌딩이 상업용 빌딩으로 전환되어야 한다
④ 가능한 많은 가게들을 만들어서 넘겨주어야 한다

| 정답해설 | ② 71% 주거용 건물은 모자라지만 사무용 건물은 수요 시장이 폭락하여 공실이 발생하고 있다고 했으므로 사무용 건물의 용도를 주거용으로 변경하는 것이 필요하다고 하는 것이 알맞다. 빈칸 앞에 인과관계를 나타내는 Therefore(그러므로)를 사용해 주장을 더 강조해서 언급하고 있으므로, 빈칸에 적절한 표현은 ②이다.

어휘

plummet 추락하다	vacant property 공실
property 부동산	spring up 발생하다
at full tilt 최고 속력의	

---

6 독해 > Micro Reading > 내용일치/불일치 오답률 46% 답 ②

| 해석 | 아동심리학자들은 출생에서 11세까지 개인에 대한 연구에 집중한다. 발달심리학자들은 태어나기 전 시기에서부터 성인기, 노년기에 이르는 행동 및 성장 유형을 연구한다. 많은 임상심리학자들은 아이들의 행동 문제들을 전문적으로 다룬다. 아동심리학의 연구는 근로 행동에 대한 설명을 돕기도 한다. 예를 들어, 아동 학대와 방임의 희생자들은 장기적인 영향을 겪게 될 수 있다. 그중에는 낮은 IQ와 읽기 능력, 더 많은 자살 시도, 더 높은 실업, 저임금 근로 등이 있다. 오늘날 많은 사람들이 인간발달에서 성년기에 대한 연구에 관심을 갖게 되었다. 발달심리학자들의 연구는 중년의 위기와 같은 중년의 문제에의 폭넓은 관심으로 이어졌다. 발달심리학자들의 직장과 관련된 관심사는 왜 많은 임원들이 은퇴 후 조기 사망하는지에 관한 것이다.

| **정답해설** | ② 54% 발달심리학자들은 태어나기 전 시기에서부터 성인기, 노년기에 이르는 행동, 성장 유형을 연구한다고 했으므로 본문과 일치한다.

| **오답해설** | ① 0% 아동심리학의 연구 대상은 출생부터 11세까지라고 했으므로 본문과 일치하지 않는 내용이다.

③ 13% 학대를 받은 아동들은 더 높은 실업과 저임금 근로 등의 장기적인 영향을 받을 수 있다고 했으므로 본문과 일치하지 않는 내용이다.

④ 33% 임원들의 은퇴 후 조기 사망은 임상심리학자들의 관심사가 아니라 발달심리학의 관심사이므로 본문과 일치하지 않는 내용이다.

어휘

developmental psychologist 발달심리학자
prenatal 태어나기 전의 maturity 성인기
clinical psychologist 임상심리학자 childhood abuse 아동 학대
neglect 방임 executive 임원

---

7 독해 > Reading for Writing > 요약 오답률 40% 답 ①

| **해석** | 의사 결정에 영향을 줄 수 있는 한 설명 요인은 대조 효과이다. 예를 들면, 70달러짜리 스웨터는 처음에는 저렴한 물건으로 보이지 않는다. 그러나 만약 이 스웨터가 200달러에서 할인되었음을 알게 되면, 갑자기 매우 저렴한 물건처럼 보인다. "거래를 성사시킨" 것은 바로 대조 효과이다. 이와 마찬가지로, Massachusetts주에 살고 있는 우리 가족은 추위에 매우 익숙하다. 추수감사절을 보내기 위해 Florida주에 있는 숙모를 방문할 때, 그들은 기온이 화씨 60도이니 모자를 쓸 것을 권하는데, 실질적으로, 아이들의 관점에서는 수영복을 입을 날씨이다. 한 연구는 사람들이 작은 접시에 음식을 먹을 때보다 큰 접시에 먹을 때 더 많이 먹는다는 것을 보여 주는데, 같은 양이라도 큰 접시보다 작은 접시에서 더 크게 보이는 것이다. 그리고 우리는 보이는 양의 크기를 우리가 배가 불렀다는 것을 알려주는 신호로 사용한다.

↓

대조 효과란 (B) 이전의 경험과의 두드러진 비교에 따라 다르게 (A) 인식하는 경향이다.

   (A)   (B)
① 인식하다 이전의 경험
② 제공하다 예견된 미래
③ 인식하다 예상하지 못한 사건
④ 제공하다 첫 인상

| **정답해설** | ① 60% 추운 날씨에 익숙한 아이들이 따뜻한 Florida에서 춥다고 느끼는 날씨가 그들에게는 수영할 수 있는 날씨라고 생각하듯이 이전의 익숙한 상황들과의 비교를 통해 현재의 상황을 인식하는 것이 대조 효과이므로 요약한 문장의 (A)에는 perceive(인식하다), (B)에는 previous experience(이전의 경험)가 들어가는 것이 적절하다.

| **더 알아보기** | Contrast Effect (대조 효과)

> 인간이 어떤 사람이나 사물에 대해 비교를 할 만한 그 무엇이 있을 때 판단을 내리기가 더 쉽다는 것을 의미한다. 즉, 뭔가 부족한 것을 뒤이어 보여 주면 앞에 본 것이 더 아름답다거나 더 값지다는 식으로 판단한다는 것에 해당된다.

어휘

contrast effect 대조 효과 seal the deal 거래를 성사시키다
salient 주요한, 두드러진

---

8 독해 > Logical Reading > 문맥상 다양한 추론 오답률 20% 답 ③

| **해석** | 대부분의 치명적인 사고는 과속 때문에 발생한다. 속도를 더 내려고 하는 것은 인간의 자연스러운 잠재의식이다. 만약 기회가 주어진다면, 인간은 무한한 속도를 달성하려고 할 것이다. 그러나 우리가 다른 사람들과 도로를 공유할 때, 우리는 항상 다른 차량의 뒤에 있을 것이다. 속도를 올리는 것은 사고 위험과 사고 중 부상을 입을 심각성을 배로 증가시킨다. 더 빠른 차량은 더 느린 차량보다 사고가 나기 더 쉽고 더 빠른 차량의 경우 사고의 심각성도 더 클 것이다. 속도를 더 올리면 위험도 더 커진다. 고속에서 차량은 제동 거리, 즉 정지하기 위해 더 많은 거리가 필요하다. 더 느린 차량은 즉시 정지하는 반면, 더 빠른 차량은 정지하기 위해 더 긴 거리를 필요로 하며 또한 운동의 제1법칙 때문에 ③ 짧은(→ 긴) 거리를 미끄러진다. 고속으로 이동하는 차량은 충돌 시 더 큰 충격을 받게 되며, 따라서 더 많은 부상을 입게 될 것이다. 앞으로 다가올 사건을 판단할 수 있는 능력도 더 빠른 속도로 운전하면 감소하여 판단 착오, 그리고 결국 충돌 사고의 원인이 된다.

| **정답해설** | ③ 80% '더 느린 차량은 즉시 정지하고, 더 빠른 차량은 정지하기 위해 더 긴 거리를 필요로 한다고 했으므로 속도가 빠를수록 운동의 제1법칙 때문에 제동 거리를 더 길게 필요로 한다는 것을 알 수 있다. 따라서 short가 아니라 long(긴)이 글의 흐름상 적절한 표현이다. (해당 지문의 7번째 문장은 기출 문제에서 Higher the speed, greater the risk.로 출제되었지만, 본 교재에는 어법상 옳게 수정하여 The higher the speed, the greater the risk.로 수록하였다.)

| **오답해설** | ① 3% 과속으로 인한 사고의 치명성과 위험성을 설명하는 것이 글의 주된 내용이다. 따라서 '속도를 올리는 것'은 사고의 위험과 사고 중 부상을 입을 심각성을 증가시키는 것이므로 적절한 표현이다.

② 3% 속도를 올리면 위험도 커지는 것이므로 The Higher는 적절한 표현이다.

④ 14% 과속을 하면 앞으로 다가올 사건을 판단할 수 있는 능력이 '감소하는' 것이므로 reduced는 문맥상 적절하다.

어휘

fatal 치명적인 subconscious 잠재의식의
infinity 무한함 multiply 곱하다
be prone to ～하기 쉽다 skid 미끄러지다

---

9 독해 > Macro Reading > 요지 오답률 37% 답 ②

| **해석** | 읽을 가치가 있는 것처럼 보이는 것에든 무엇이든 관심을 갖기 위해 노력하는 것이 먼저 필요하다. 학생은 다른 사람들이 그 책의 어디를 좋아하는지를 알아내려고 성실히 노력해야 한다. 모든 독자들은 걸작이라도 좋아하거나 싫어할 자유가 있지만, 그는 왜 그것이 칭찬받는지를 이해할 때까지 그것에 대한 의견을 가질 위치에 있지 않다. 그는 책에서 무엇이 나쁜지가 아니라 무엇이 좋은지 깨달으려고 노력해야 한다. 단점을 찾아내기 위해 정신을 단련함으로써 비평 능력이 가장 잘 개발된다는 일반적인 이론은 거짓말처럼 악랄하다. 어떤 혹평가라도 걸작에서 결점을 찾을 수 있으며, 그것의 모든 장점을 발견할 수 있는 것은 계몽된 사람뿐이다. 좋은 책을 감

상하려는 진지한 노력이 독자를 흥미 없게 하는 일은 거의 일어나지 않을 것이다.
① 책의 명성에 해가 될 수 있는 약점에 집중하라.
② 판단하기 전에 읽을 만한 책의 가치를 이해하기 위해 노력하라.
③ 당신이 관심 있는 책뿐만 아니라 관심 없는 책도 읽어라.
④ 책을 다 읽을 때까지 주제에 대해 비평적인 시각을 유지하라.

| 정답해설 | ② 63% 본문의 첫 번째 문장이 주제문으로, 책의 좋고 나쁜 것을 판단하는 것이 아니라 먼저 그것의 가치를 이해하기 위해 독자들이 관심을 가지려고 노력하는 것이 필요하다고 주장하고 있다. 따라서 글의 요지로 가장 적절한 것은 ② '판단하기 전에 읽을 만한 책의 가치를 이해하기 위해 노력하라.'이다. (해당 지문의 마지막 문장에서 a good book은 기출 문제에서 good book으로 출제되었지만, 어법상 a가 있는 것이 적절하므로 본 교재에는 옳게 수정하여 수록하였다. 또한 ②에서도 기출에서 출제된 while 대신 문맥상 옳은 worthwhile로 수정하여 수록하였다.)

어휘

endeavor 노력	worthwhile 가치가 있는
wherein 어디에서	be at liberty 자유이다
appreciate 감상하다; 감사하다	carper 혹평가
the enlightened 계몽된 사람	reputation 명성

---

10 독해 > Micro Reading > 내용일치/불일치 오답률 42% 답 ④

| 해석 | 대부분의 미국인들은 건강에 대한 우려 때문에 유기농 식품을 구입하고 있다. 국민의 절반 이상이 유기농 과일과 채소가 기존 방식으로 재배한 농산물보다 건강에 더 좋다고 말한다. 40%가 넘는 사람들은 유기농 농산물이 사람의 건강에 더 좋지도 나쁘지도 않다고 말하고, 가장 적은 수의 사람들은 유기농 생산물이 사람의 건강에 더 나쁘다고 말한다. 더 적은 수의 미국인들이 유기농 농산물이 전통적으로 재배한 과일과 채소보다 더 맛이 좋다고 말한다. ④ 미국 성인의 약 3분의 1이 유기농 농산물이 더 맛있다고 말하고, 3분의 2가 넘는 사람들이 유기농과 재래식 재배 농산물이 거의 같은 맛을 낸다고 말한다.

| 정답해설 | ④ 58% 유기농 농산물과 그렇지 않은 농산물의 맛이 비슷하다고 대답하는 사람이 59%로 전체의 3분의 2(약 67%)에는 못 미치므로 ④는 도표와 일치하지 않는 문장이다.

| 오답해설 | ① 2% 건강에 더 좋다고 생각하는 사람들의 비율은 55%이므로 More than half of the public은 도표의 내용과 일치한다.

② 4% 유기농 농산물이 건강에 더 좋지도 않고 나쁘지도 않다고 말한 사람의 비율이 41%이므로 일치한다.

③ 36% 더 맛이 좋다고 말한 사람들은 32%로 맛이 비슷하다(59%)고 답한 사람들보다 적은 수이므로 일치한다.

어휘

organic 유기농의	conventionally 전통적으로
produce 농산물	

---

11 독해 > Logical Reading > 문맥상 다양한 추론 오답률 21% 답 ②

| 해석 | 의사와 환자 사이의 의사소통의 대부분은 개인적인 것이다. 의사와 좋은 파트너십을 맺기 위해서는 당황스럽거나 불편하더라도 성이나 기억력 문제 같은 민감한 주제에 대해 이야기하는 것이 중요하다. 대부분의 의사들은 개인적인 문제에 대해 말하는 것에 익숙하고 여러분의 불편함을 덜어 주려고 노력할 것이다. 이 주제들은 많은 나이든 사람들과 관련이 있다는 것을 명심해라. 당신은 의사와 대화할 때 민감한 주제를 꺼내는 것을 도와주는 책자와 다른 자료들을 사용할 수 있다. 기억력, 우울증, 성 기능, 요실금 등의 문제가 반드시 노화의 정상적인 부분은 아니라는 것을 이해하는 것이 중요하다. 좋은 의사는 이 주제들에 대한 당신의 고민을 진지하게 받아들일 것이고 그것들을 무시하지 않을 것이다. 만약 의사가 여러분의 걱정을 심각하게 받아들이지 않는다고 생각한다면, 그나 그녀에게 여러분의 감정에 대해 말하거나 새로운 의사를 찾는 것을 고려해 보라.
① 당신과 민감한 주제를 토론하다
② 당신이 갖고 있는 몇 가지 고민을 무시하다
③ 당신이 말하는 것을 편안하게 느끼다
④ 불편한 주제를 심각하게 다루다

| 정답해설 | ② 79% 의사들은 개인적인 문제에 대해 이야기하는 것이 익숙하고 당신의 불편함을 덜어 주려고 할 것이라고 하였으므로 좋은 의사들은 환자의 고민을 함부로 간과하지 않는다는 것을 알 수 있다. brush off는 '~을 무시하다'라는 의미이므로, ②의 의미로 볼 수 있다.

| 더 알아보기 | '무시하다'를 뜻하는 구동사 표현

• brush off	• put aside
• brush aside	

어휘

discomfort 불편함	brush off ~을 무시하다

---

12 독해 > Reading for Writing > 빈칸 구 완성 오답률 19% 답 ①

| 해석 | 언어학자 Edward Sapir와 Benjamin Lee Whorf가 제안한 유명한 가설에 따르면, 우리 모두는 시각을 위한 눈, 청각을 위한 귀, 후각을 위한 코, 촉각을 위한 피부, 미각을 위한 입 등 세상을 감지하기 위해 같은 신체 기관을 가지고 있지만, 세계에 대한 우리의 인식은 우리가 말하는 언어에 크게 좌우된다고 한다. 그들은 그들의 언어가 우리가 특정한 방식으로 세상을 "보는" 안경과 같다고 가설을 세웠다. 언어와 인식의 관계에 대한 전형적인 예로는 눈이라는 단어가 있다. 에스키모어는 눈에 해당하는 32개의 다른 단어가 있다. 예를 들어, 에스키모인들은 내리고 있는 눈, 땅 위의 눈, 얼음처럼 단단하게 뭉쳐진 눈, 녹은 눈, 바람에 날리는 눈, 그리고 우리가 "옥수수 가루" 눈이라고 부르는 것에 대해 서로 다른 단어를 가지고 있다. 이와는 대조적으로, 멕시코의 고대 아즈텍어들은 눈, 추위, 얼음을 의미하기 위해 단 하나의 단어만을 사용했다. 따라서 만약 Sapir-Whorf 가설이 맞고 우리가 그것에 대응하는 단어를 가지고 있는 사물만 인식할 수 있다면, 아즈텍인들은 눈, 추위, 얼음을 ① 하나로 그리고 같은 현상으로 인식했다.
① 하나의 그리고 같은 현상
② 서로 구별되는 것
③ 독특한 특징들로 구별된 사물들
④ 특정한 신체 기관에 의해 감지된 것

| 정답해설 | ① 81% 빈칸 앞에서 에스키모어에는 '눈(snow)'에 해당하는 단어가 32개인 반면 아즈텍인들은 단어 하나가 눈, 추위, 그

리고 얼음을 모두 의미한다고 했으므로, 아즈텍인들의 눈, 추위, 얼음에 대한 인식을 나타내는 것으로 빈칸에 들어갈 적절한 표현은 ① '하나의 그리고 같은 현상'이다.

어휘

physical organ 신체 기관	to a great extent 상당하게
linguist 언어학자	slushy 눈이 녹아 진창이 된
cornmeal 옥수수 가루	hypothesis 가설

---

13 독해 > Logical Reading > 삽입   오답률 9%   답 ③

| 해석 | "소프트 파워"라는 개념은 미국 정치학자이자 클린턴 행정부의 국방부 차관이었던 Joseph Nye, Jr.에 의해 1990년대 초에 만들어졌다. 미국 J. Nye 교수의 사상은 "힘" 개념의 해석을 신선하게 볼 수 있게 해 주었고, 과학적 논쟁을 불러일으켰으며, 국제 정치의 실용적 측면을 자극했다. 그의 연구에서 그는 두 가지 유형의 힘을 입증하는데, "하드 파워"와 "소프트 파워"가 그것이다. 그는 "하드 파워"를 "다른 사람들이 그들의 초기의 선호도와 전략에 모순되는 방식으로 행동하게 하는 능력"이라고 정의한다. ③ 반면에 "소프트 파워"는 "강제나 돈이 아닌 끌림과 설득을 통해 목표를 달성할 수 있는 능력"이다. 국가의 "소프트 파워"는 세계 정치 과정에 있는 다른 참가자들에게 "매력"을 보일 수 있는 능력, 자기 문화의 매력(문맥상으로는 타인에게 매력적), 정치적 가치와 외교 정책(합법적이고 도덕적으로 정당하다고 판단될 경우)을 보여 줄 수 있는 능력이다. "소프트 파워"의 주요 구성 요소는 문화, 정치적 가치, 외교 정책이다.

| 정답해설 | ③ 91% 주어진 문장의 on the contrary(반면)를 통해 주어진 문장 앞에는 "소프트 파워"와 반대되는 내용에 대한 정의가 언급되어야 한다는 것을 알 수 있다. 따라서 "하드 파워"에 대한 정의를 내리는 내용 뒤인 ③에 주어진 문장이 오는 것이 적절하다.

어휘

coercion 강제, 강압	deputy defense 국방부 차관
interpretation 해석	identify 입증하다, 발견하다
contradict 반박하다	legitimate 합법적인
justified 정당화된	

---

14 독해 > Macro Reading > 주제   오답률 33%   답 ②

| 해석 | 다른 분야에서 AI 배치의 신속성은 몇 가지 중요한 요인에 달려 있다. 소매업은 몇 가지 이유로 특히 적합하다. 첫째는 테스트하고 측정하는 능력이다. 적절한 안전 장치를 갖추면, 거대 소매업체들은 AI를 배치하고 소비자 반응을 테스트하고 측정할 수 있다. 그들은 또한 그들의 수익률에 미치는 영향을 상당히 빠르게 직접 측정할 수 있다. 두 번째는 실수로 인한 비교적 작은 결과들이다. 승객을 착륙시키는 항공기의 인공 지능 에이전트는 자칫 인명 피해가 발생할 수 있어 실수를 할 수가 없다. 매일 수백만 건의 결정을 내리는 소매업계에 배치된 인공 지능 에이전트는 전반적인 효과가 긍정적인 한 약간의 실수를 할 수도 있다. 몇몇 똑똑한 로봇 기술이 이미 소매업에서 구현되고 있다. 하지만 가장 중요한 변화는 물리적 로봇이나 자율 주행차보다 AI의 배치에서 비롯될 것이다.

① 인공 지능 에이전트의 위험   ② 왜 소매업이 AI에 적합한가
③ 소매업 기술과 환대   ④ AI 개발의 중요한 요인들

| 정답해설 | ② 67% 소매업이 AI를 배치하기에 특히 적합하다고 한 다음, 그에 대한 이유를 몇 가지 들어 설명하고 있으므로, 글의 주제로 가장 적절한 것은 ② '왜 소매업이 AI에 적합한가'이다.

어휘

deployment 배치	retail 소매업(체)
bottom line 순이익	hospitality 환대

---

15 독해 > Reading for Writing > 빈칸 절 완성   오답률 22%   답 ④

| 해석 | "뿌린 대로 거둔다."라는 것은 카르마가 어떻게 작동하는가에 대한 기본적인 이해이다. 카르마라는 단어는 말 그대로 "행동"을 의미한다. 카르마는 몇 가지 단순한 영역으로 나뉠 수 있는데, 그것은 선과 악, 개인과 집단이다. 사람은 자신의 행동에 따라, 그 행동의 열매를 수확하게 될 것이다. 그 열매는 이미 행해진 행동에 따라 달콤할 수도 있고 시큼할 수도 있을 것이다. 만약 한 무리의 사람들이 어떤 행동 혹은 행동들을 했다면, 그 열매는 집단적인 방식으로 수확될 수 있다. 우리가 말하고 행동하는 것은 앞으로 우리의 미래에 무엇이 일어날지 결정한다. 우리가 정직하게 행동하든 정직하지 못하게 행동하든, 남을 도와주든, 해를 끼치든 간에 모든 것들은 기록되고 이번 생에서든 다음 생에서든 하나의 카르마 행동으로 나타난다. 모든 카르마의 기록은 다음 생의 영혼과 육체에 전달된다.

① 비가 오기만 하면 쏟아진다 (불운은 한꺼번에 닥친다)
② 호미로 막을 것을 가래로 막는다
③ 백지장도 맞들면 낫다
④ 뿌린 대로 거둔다

| 정답해설 | ④ 78% 사람은 자신의 행동에 따라, 그 행동의 열매를 얻게 될 것이라는 내용과 우리가 말하고 행동하는 것이 앞으로 우리의 미래에 무엇이 일어날지를 결정한다는 내용을 볼 때, 본인이 한 행동과 말이 그대로 돌아온다는 것이 카르마의 기본적인 의미이므로, 빈칸에는 '뿌린 대로 거둔다'가 들어가는 것이 가장 적절하다.

어휘

karma 카르마, 업보	category 범주, 영역
reap 수확하다	manifest 나타나다

---

16 독해 > Macro Reading > 주장   오답률 24%   답 ④

| 해석 | 틀을 깨는 생각을 하도록 영감을 주는 문화를 창조하는 것은 궁극적으로 사람들이 더 나아가도록 영감을 주는 것이며, 사람들이 변화를 주도하도록 권한을 주는 것이다. 리더로서, 당신은 변화가 힘든 그런 시기에 지원을 제공할 필요가 있는데, 이러한 지원은 당신이 설정한 본보기, 당신이 권장하는 행동 그리고 당신이 보상하려고 하는 성과에 대한 것이다. 먼저, 당신이 본보기를 보였던 것에 대해 생각해 보아라. 당신은 지속적으로 당신 스스로 틀을 깨는 행동의 모범을 보였는가? 당신은 한 단계 나아가서 책임을 지고, 해법에 집중하고, 호기심을 보였는가? 다음으로, 틀을 깨려는 단계가 준비된 사람들에게 권유하고 권한을 부여하는 방법을 찾아라. 당신은 그들의 노력을 알고 있고, 그들이 생각을 다듬는 것을 돕고 어떤 위험이 감수할 가치가 있는지를 결정한다는 것을 그들이 알게 하라. 그리고 무엇보다도, 어떤 성과에 보상을 해 줄지 깊이 생각하라. 당신은 안전하게 하려는 사람들만 인정하는가? 아니면 당신은 또한 기꺼이 멀리 나아가려는 사람들, 틀을 깨는 행동을 보여 줬지만 공격적인 목표는 이루지 못한 사람들 또한 보상할 것인가?

| 정답해설 | ④ 76% 이 글은 틀을 깨는 사고를 장려하는 리더의 역할에 관한 내용으로 ④가 필자의 주장으로 가장 적절하다.

어휘

out-of-box thinking 틀을 깨는 생각	stretch 연장하다, 확장하다
empower 권한을 주다	accountability 의무, 책임
curiosity 호기심	fall short of ~이 부족하다

aggressive 공격적인

| 해석 | 사전은 승리하는 것을 "경쟁에서 타인에 대한 승리를 달성하고, 성과에 대한 상이나 보상을 받는 것"이라고 정의하고 있다. 그러나, 내 생애에서 가장 의미 있는 승리들 중 일부는 다른 사람들에 대한 승리도 아니고, 수반된 상도 없었다. 내게 있어, 승리하는 것은 장애물을 극복하는 것을 의미한다.

나의 첫 승리 경험은 초등학교 체육관에서 일어났다. 거의 매일, 팔굽혀펴기와 스쿼트로 몸을 예열한 후, 우리는 릴레이 경주를 해야 했다. 비록 나는 어렸을 때 천식을 앓았지만, 우리 팀은 많은 경주에서 승리했다. 이런 레이스에 이어지는 몇 분 동안은 가슴이 아주 불타는 것처럼 느껴지곤 했지만, 내가 다른 사람을 이겼기 때문이 아니라 핸디캡을 이겨냈기 때문에 아주 자랑스러워 할 만한 가치가 있었다. 그러나저러나, 나는 11살에 나의 만성적인 상태를 "극복"했다.

고등학교 때, 나는 또 다른 승리를 경험했다. 비록 나는 생물학에 관한 책을 읽는 것을 좋아했지만, 실험실에서 개구리를 해부할 수는 없었다. 나는 죽은 것의 냄새도 싫었고, 개구리의 배를 갈라 연다는 생각이 나를 역겹게 했다. 메스를 개구리에게 가져가려 할 때마다, 손이 떨리고 배가 요동치곤 했다. 최악의 것은, 나의 생물 선생님이 나의 헛된 시도에 경멸의 반응을 보였다는 것이었다. (C) 재미있는(→ 고통스러운) 몇 주 후에, 나는 침착해지기로 결심했다. 나는 내가 과민반응하고 있다는 것을 깨달았다. 결연한 각오로, 나는 다음 실험 시간에 쏙 들어가 테이블로 걸어간 후, 한 번의 빠른 동작으로 개구리의 배를 길게 열어 젖혔다. 그 사건 이후, 나는 생물학을 뛰어나게 잘했다. 나는 미지의 것에 대한 두려움을 정복하고 내 자신에 대한 새로운 무언가를 발견했다. 나는 또 다시 승리했다.

이러한 경험을 통해, 나는 이러한 장애들을 극복하기 위해 희생해야 한다면 삶을 더욱 고맙게 여긴다는 것을 이제 알게 되었다. 이것은 내게는 긍정적인 추진력이다. 바로 승리하는 정신이다.

어휘

obstacle 장애	squat thrust 스쿼트
outgrow 극복하다	chronic 만성적인
dissect 해부하다	disgust 역겹게 하다
get hold of oneself 침착하다, 제정신이 들다	
scalpel 해부용 칼, 메스	swift stroke 빠른 동작
slit 길게 자르다	impediment 장애물

---

17 독해 > Macro Reading > 제목　　오답률 5%　답 ①

| 해석 | ① 나에게 승리란 무엇인가?　② 행복의 추구
③ 후반전의 승자(역전의 명수)　④ 긍정적 사고의 이야기

| 정답해설 | ① 95% 첫 문단 마지막 문장에서 필자에게 승리하는 것이란 장애물을 극복하는 것이라고 말한 뒤 그와 관련한 경험을 예시한다. 즉, 어린 시절 천식을 극복하고 릴레이 경주에서 이긴 것과 고등학교 시절 개구리를 해부하지 못했지만 다시 각오를 다지고 개구리 해부에 성공한 뒤 자신이 생물학을 매우 뛰어나게 잘했다고 말하면서 필자에게 승리란 무엇인지 설명하고 있으므로, 글의 제목으로는 ① '나에게 있어 승리란 무엇인가'가 가장 적절하다.

---

18 독해 > Logical Reading > 문맥상 다양한 추론　오답률 17%　답 ③

| 정답해설 | ③ 83% (C) 앞의 내용으로 보아 개구리 해부가 필자에게 즐거운 일이 아니었다는 것을 알 수 있다. 따라서 amusing은 painful(고통스러운)과 같은 부정적 의미의 단어로 고치는 것이 알맞다.

---

19 독해 > Reading for Writing > 요약　오답률 14%　답 ③

| 해석 | 한 고전 심리학 연구는 엄마와 그들의 12개월 된 아기들을 참여시켰다. 각각의 엄마는 연구 내내 그녀의 아기와 함께 있었지만, 엄마들은 A와 B라는 두 개의 그룹으로 나뉘었다. 그룹 A와 B는 모두 같은 상황에 노출되어 있었는데, 유일한 차이점은 그룹 B의 엄마들은 그들의 아기가 그들의 앞에 있는 무엇인가를 가지고 놀도록 긍정적으로 격려해야 했던 반면, 그룹 A의 엄마들은 단지 그들의 아기가 무엇을 가지고 놀고 있는지에 대한 반응으로 평소처럼 행동해야 했다.

이 아기들은 뭘 가지고 놀고 있었을까? 매우 크지만 길들여진 비단뱀이었다. 이 연구는 다음과 같이 진행되었다. 그룹 A의 아기를 바닥에 눕혀서 비단뱀이 그들 사이로 스르르 나아갈 수 있게 했다. 뱀에 대한 공포는 인간에게 선천적이지만 대략 두 살까지 활성화되지 않기 때문에, 이 아기들은 이 비단뱀을 커다란 장난감으로 보았다. 그룹 A의 아기들이 살아 있는 비단뱀을 가지고 놀기 시작했을 때, 그들은 그들의 엄마가 무엇을 하고 있는지 보기 위해 고개를 들었다. 평소처럼 행동하라는 말을 들은 엄마들은 당연히 겁먹은 것처럼 보였다. 엄마의 얼굴에 나타난 공포를 보고, 아기들은 울음을 터뜨렸다. 그룹 B의 차례가 되었을 때, 엄마들은 웃으면서 그들의 아기들에게 계속해서 비단뱀을 가지고 놀도록 격려했다. 그 결과 이 아기들은 비단뱀을 잡아서 씹고 있었는데, 모두 그들의 엄마가 그들의 새 장난감을 지지했기 때문이었다.

↓

아이들은 대개 특정한 것들에 대한 부모의 (B) 반응을 보는 것에 의해, (A) 모든 공포들이 학습된다.

	(A)	(B)
①	게임의 규칙들	지지
②	장난감에 대한 선호	참여
③	모든 공포들	반응
④	다양한 감정들	격려

| 정답해설 | ③ 86% 비단뱀을 가지고 노는 아기들을 보고 그룹 A의 엄마들이 공포에 질린 얼굴을 하자 아기들은 엄마의 얼굴을 보고 울음을 터뜨렸지만, 그룹 B의 엄마들은 아기들이 비단뱀을 가지고 놀도록 격려를 해 주자 아기들이 전혀 거부감 없이 비단뱀을 장난감처럼 잘 갖고 놀았다는 실험 내용이다. 요약문의 빈칸 (A)는 뱀에 대한 공포를 아기들이 어떻게 느끼는지에 대한 것이므로 All phobias(모든 공포들)가, (B)는 아기들의 행동이 엄마의 반응에 따라 학습되는 것이므로 reaction(반응)이 들어가야 적절하다.

어휘

positively 적극적으로
be themselves 평소의 모습을 유지하다

tame 길들여진	python 비단뱀
innate 선천적인	activate 활성화시키다
horrified 겁먹은	phobia 공포

오답률 TOP2

20 독해 > Logical Reading > 문맥상 다양한 추론   답 ②

오답률 64%

| 해석 | 고령화 근대화 이론에 따르면, 사회가 현대화됨에 따라 고령자의 위상은 낮아진다. 노년의 지위는 수렵 채집 사회에서는 낮았지만 노인들이 토지를 지배하는 안정된 농경 사회에서는 극적으로 높았다. 산업화의 도래와 함께 현대 사회는 노인을 ② 재평가하는(→ 평가 절하하는) 경향이 있다고 한다. 고령화 근대화 이론은 고령자의 역할과 지위가 기술 진보와 반비례 관계에 있다는 것을 시사한다. 도시화와 사회적 이동성 같은 요소들은 가족을 흩어지게 하는 경향이 있는 반면, 기술적 변화는 노인들의 지혜나 삶의 경험을 평가 절하하는 경향이 있다. 일부 조사자들은 현대화의 핵심 요소들이 사실, 다른 사회에서 나이든 사람의 지위 하락과 광범위하게 관련이 있다는 것을 발견했다.

| 정답해설 | ② 36% 기술적 변화는 노인들의 지혜나 삶의 경험을 평가 절하하는 경향이 있다고 했으므로, 현대 사회가 노인을 revalue(재평가하다)하는 것이 아니라 devalue(평가 절하하다)한다는 것을 알 수 있다.

| 오답해설 | ① 7% 역접 접속사 but 앞의 내용이 사냥과 수렵 사회에서 노인의 지위가 낮았다는 것이므로 but 뒤의 내용은 앞과 반대여야 하므로 rose는 적절한 표현이다.

③ 21% 이어지는 Factors such as urbanization and social mobility tend to disperse families, whereas technological change tends to devalue the wisdom or life experience of elders.에서 기술과 지위가 '반비례(inversely)' 관계에 있다는 것을 알 수 있다.

④ 36% 글의 주된 내용이 현대화에 따른 고령자의 낮아진 지위이므로 현대화로 인해 나이든 사람들의 지위가 '하락(declining)'한다는 것은 적절한 표현이다.

어휘

hunting-and-gathering society 수렵 채집 사회
revalue 재평가하다   devalue 평가 절하하다
inversely 반대로, 거꾸로   disperse 흩어지게 하다

21 문법 > 태   답 ④

오답률 40%

| 해석 | 벼 줄기는 성숙하면 고개를 숙이고 옥수수 알갱이는 익어도 새싹에 남는다. 이것은 이상하게 보이지 않을지 모르지만, 실제로는 이러한 종류의 쌀과 옥수수는 자연에서 살아남아서는 안 된다. 보통, 그것들이 성숙할 때, 씨앗은 발아하기 위해 땅으로 떨어져야 한다. 그러나 쌀과 옥수수는 변종이며, 편리하고 효율적인 수확을 목적으로 종자가 부착되도록 개량되었다. 인간은 이러한 현상이 발생하도록 품종 교배 기술을 통해 지속적으로 그러한 돌연변이를 선택하고 길러 왔다. 이러한 돌연변이 씨앗은 의도적으로 퍼져 나갔는데, 이는 식물이 씨앗을 온전히 유지하기 위해 번식하면서 자연에서 발견되지 않는 인위적인 종이 되었다는 것을 의미한다. 이러한 품종을 육성함으로써, 가장 선호되는 씨앗이 생산된다.

| 정답해설 | ④ 60% breed는 '~을 키우다'라는 뜻의 타동사로 목적어를 수반하는 동사이다. 그러나 having bred to keep에 목적어가 없으므로 수동태 분사구문이 되어야 한다. 따라서 having been bred로 고쳐야 한다.

| 오답해설 | ① 14% 목적어인 seeds와 목적격 보어 attach(부착하다)는 수동의 관계이므로 attached(부착된)는 알맞은 표현이다.

② 17% for these phenomena는 to부정사인 to occur의 의미상 주어로 적절한 표현이다.

③ 9% which는 계속적 용법의 관계대명사로 앞 절 These mutant seeds have been spread intentionally를 선행사로 하는 알맞은 표현이다.

어휘

rice stalk 벼 줄기   corn kernel 옥수수 낱알
on the shoots 새싹으로   ripe 무르익다, 성숙하다
mutant 돌연변이 종
breed (품종을) 개량하다, 교배하다; 번식시키다
intentionally 의도적으로   nurture 키우다

22 문법 > 관계사, 분사   답 ③

오답률 27%

| 해석 | 첫인상에 대한 편견이란 우리의 첫인상이 틀을 잡는 것을 의미하는데 이 틀에 의해 나중에 이 사람에 대해 우리가 수집하는 정보가 처리되고 기억되고 적절한 것으로 간주된다. 예를 들어, 수업 시간에 Ann-Chinn을 관찰한 것에 근거하여, Loern은 그녀를 전형적인 아시아 여성으로 보고, 그녀가 조용하고 열심히 일하며 내성적이라고 가정했을지도 모른다. 옳든 그르든 이러한 결론에 도달한 그는 이제 Ann-Chinn의 행동을 이해하고 해석하기 위한 일련의 초기 모델과 구조를 가지고 있다. 시간이 흐르면서, 그는 그의 초기 모델과 일치하는 행동에 맞추고 그가 이미 그녀에 대해 만들어 놓은 인상으로 구축해 간다. 그가 자신이 선택한 범퍼 스티커에 대해 그녀가 불신감을 표현하는 것을 발견했을 때, 그는 단순히 그것을 무시하거나 그의 기존의 초기 모델과 맞지 않기 때문에 그녀의 본성에 대한 이상한 예외로 볼 수도 있다.

| 정답해설 | ③ 73% (A) later information we gather about this person is processed, remembered, and viewed as relevant by the mold가 관계사절을 만들기 이전의 문장이다. 따라서 이전 문장에 포함된 the mold를 관계대명사 which로 대신하고 전치사 by를 관계대명사 which 앞으로 이동해야 한다. 결국 by the mold는 「전치사 + 관계대명사」 구조로 by which가 올바르며, 이후의 문장은 완전한 문장 형태이므로 어법상 옳다.

(B) reached 다음에 목적어가 있으므로 수동형 분사구문이 아닌 능동형 분사구문을 사용하는 것이 적절하다. 따라서 Having reached가 알맞은 표현이다.

(C) 관계대명사절 앞에 선행사 the impression이 있으므로 관계대명사 that을 쓰는 것이 적절하다.

어휘

mold 틀   stereotypical 전형적인
unassertive 내성적인   construct 구성하다, 구축하다
consistent 일치하는   dismiss 무시하다
prototype 원형, 견본

23 문법 > 접속사   답 ③

오답률 56%

| 해석 | 아동 언어 습득에 대한 연구의 물결은 언어 교사들과 교사 교육 담당자들로 하여금 제1언어 습득과 제2언어 습득 사이의 유사성을 도출하기 위해서 심지어 제1언어 학습 원리에 기초한 특정 교육 방법과 기법을 정당

화하기 위해서 그러한 연구의 일반적인 발견의 일부를 연구하도록 이끌었다. 표면적으로, 유추하는 것이 전적으로 타당하다. 모든 아이들은, 정상적인 발달 환경이 주어지면, 그들의 모국어를 유창하고 효율적으로 습득한다. 게다가, 비록 어느 정도의 노력과 언어에 대한 관심이 없다면 아니기는 하겠지만, 그들은 특별한 교육이 없이도 그것들[모국어]을 "자연적으로" 습득한다. 그러나 직접 비교는 주의 깊게 다루어져야 한다. 제1언어 학습과 제2언어 학습 사이에는 수십 가지의 두드러진 차이가 있다. 성인의 제2언어 학습의 경우, 가장 분명한 차이는 성인과 아동 사이의 엄청난 인지적, 정서적 차이이다.

| 정답해설 | ③ 44% despite는 전치사로서 다음에 명사나 명사구가 와야 하므로 despite 다음에 not without ~으로 시작하는 전치사구가 위치하는 것은 어법상 올바르지 않다. 원래 문장은 [al]though it is not without significant ~로 부사구의 주어와 be동사인 it is가 생략된 형태이다. 따라서 [al]though not without significant ~로 표현하는 것이 어법상 알맞다.

| 오답해설 | ① 36% with a view to ~에 연결되는 것으로 drawing과 병렬 구조를 이루어야 하므로 동명사 justifying은 적절한 표현이다.

② 12% given ~은 '~이 주어진다면'이라는 뜻으로 조건의 분사구문을 이끄므로 올바른 표현이다.

④ 8% is의 주어가 the most obvious difference라는 단수 명사이므로 올바른 표현이다.

| 더 알아보기 | 전치사 vs. 접속사

	접속사 + 주어 + 동사	전치사(구) + 명사(구)/동명사/대명사
양보	although, though, even if	despite, in spite of
이유	because	because of, owing to, due to
시간	while	during, for
비례	according as	according to

어휘

language acquisition 언어 습득
analogy 유추, 유사점
tremendous 엄청난

with a view to ~할 목적으로
salient 두드러지는
cognitive 인지적인

오답률 TOP 1

24 독해 > Logical Reading > 문맥상 다양한 추론
오답률 68%　답 ④

| 해석 | 미국의 생리학자인 Hudson Hoagland는 모든 곳에서 과학적 미스터리를 보았고 그것을 풀어야 할 그의 소명을 느꼈다. 한 번은, 그의 아내가 열이 있을 때 Hoagland는 아스피린을 사러 약국으로 차를 몰았다. 그는 그것에 대해 재빠르게 대처했지만, 그가 돌아왔을 때, 평상시에는 이성적인 그의 아내가 그가 당밀처럼 느렸다고 화를 내며 불평했다. Hoagland는 그녀의 열이 그녀의 내부 시계를 왜곡시켰는지 궁금해서 체온을 재고 그녀에게 1분간의 길이를 추정하게 하고 아스피린을 투여한 다음 체온이 떨어졌을 때 1분을 계속 추정해 보게 했다. 그녀의 체온이 정상으로 돌아왔을 때 그는 로그 그림을 그렸고 그것이 직선 모양이라는 것을 발견했다. 나중에, 그는 자신의 실험실에서 연구를 계속하면서, 그가 옳다고 확신할 때까지 실험 대상자들의 체온을 인위적으로 올리고 낮췄다. 즉, 체온이 더 높아지면

신체 시계를 더 빨리 가게 만드므로, 그의 아내가 ④ 정당하게(→ 부당하게) 짜증냈던 것은 아니었다.

| 정답해설 | ④ 32% 체온이 높아지면 신체 시계가 더 빨리 가게 된다는 것이 실험의 결론이므로 그의 아내가 짜증을 냈던 것은 정당하다고 볼 수 있다. 밑줄 친 justifiably 앞의 동사에 부정어 not이 포함되어 있으므로 '그의 아내가 부당하게 짜증내는 것은 아니었다'는 의미가 되도록 justifiably를 unjustifiably(부당하게)로 고치는 것이 문맥상 적절하다.

| 오답해설 | ① 21% normally(평상시에)라는 단어를 통해 아프지 않으면 짜증을 내지 않는다는 것을 알 수 있으므로 reasonable은 적절한 표현이다.

② 14% Hoagland는 재빠르게 대처했지만 평상시와 달리 아내가 느리다고 불평하자 열이 그녀의 내부 시계를 어떻게 '왜곡시켰는지' 궁금한 것이므로 distorted는 적절한 표현이다.

③ 33% 체온이 정상으로 돌아왔을 때 로그 그림이 직선 모양이라는 의미로 linear를 쓴 것은 적절하다.

어휘

calling 소명
distort 왜곡하다
justifiably 정당하게

slow as molasses 매우 느린
linear 직선 모양의
cranky 짜증 내는

25 독해 > Reading for Writing > 빈칸 절 완성　오답률 39%　답 ②

| 해석 | Saint Paul은 눈에 보이는 것에 의해 보이지 않는 것을 이해해야 한다고 말했다. 그것은 히브리인의 생각이 아니라 그리스의 것이었다. 고대 그리스에서만 사람들은 눈에 보이는 것에 몰두하고 있었는데, 그들은 그들 주위의 세계에 실제로 있는 것 속에서 욕망의 만족을 찾고 있었다. 그 조각가는 선수들이 경기에서 다투는 것을 지켜봤고 그가 상상할 수 있는 어떤 것도 그 강하고 젊은 몸들처럼 아름다울 수 없을 것이라고 느꼈다. 그래서 그는 그의 아폴로 동상을 만들었다. 그 이야기꾼은 길에서 지나가는 사람들 중에서 헤르메스를 발견했다. 그는 호머의 말대로 "청년이 가장 사랑스러웠던 그 시대의 젊은이들처럼" 그 신을 보았다. 그리스의 예술가들과 시인들은 직선적이고 빠르며 강한 인간이 얼마나 화려할 수 있는지를 깨달았다. 그는 아름다움을 찾는 그들의 성취였다. 그들은 그들 자신의 마음속에 형성된 어떤 환상을 창조하고 싶은 마음이 없었다. 그리스의 모든 예술과 모든 사상은 ② 인간을 중심에 놓았다.

① 현실과의 유사함이 전혀 없었다
② 인간을 중심에 두다
③ 전지전능한 신과 관련이 있었다
④ 초자연적인 힘에 대한 열망을 나타낸다

| 정답해설 | ② 61% 그리스의 예술가들과 시인들은 직선적이고 빠르며 강한 인간이 얼마나 화려할 수 있는지를 깨달았고 그들 자신의 마음속에 형성된 어떤 환상을 창조하고 싶은 마음이 없었다는 내용에서 보이지 않는 것들은 전혀 관심이 없고 인간들이 자신들의 주된 관심사이고 미의 형태라는 것을 알 수 있다.

어휘

the invisible 보이지 않는 것
be preoccupied with ~에 사로잡혀 있다
contend 싸우다, 경쟁하다
omnipotent 전지전능한

semblance 유사; 외관, 외형
supernatural 초자연적인

취약영역 체크

문항	정답	영역	문항	정답	영역
①	④	독해 > Macro Reading > 주제	14	④	독해 > Logical Reading > 문맥상 다양한 추론
2	②	어휘 > 빈칸 완성	15	②	문법 > 분사
3	③	독해 > Logical Reading > 문맥상 다양한 추론	16	③	문법 > 분사
4	④	독해 > Logical Reading > 연결사	17	④	독해 > Logical Reading > 문맥상 다양한 추론
5	①	독해 > Macro Reading > 제목	18	④	독해 > Logical Reading > 문맥상 다양한 추론
6	②	독해 > Micro Reading > 내용 일치/불일치	19	③	문법 > 동사
7	③	독해 > Logical Reading > 문맥상 다양한 추론	20	②	독해 > Logical Reading > 삽입
8	③	독해 > Reading for Writing > 빈칸 구 완성	21	④	독해 > Logical Reading > 삽입
9	④	독해 > Logical Reading > 삭제	22	②	독해 > Reading for Writing > 빈칸 구 완성
10	②	독해 > Macro Reading > 제목	23	③	독해 > Logical Reading > 삽입
11	④	문법 > 태	24	③	독해 > Reading for Writing > 빈칸 구 완성
12	④	독해 > Logical Reading > 문맥상 다양한 추론	25	③	문법 > 강조와 도치
13	④	독해 > Reading for Writing > 요약			

⬇ 영역별 틀린 개수로 취약영역을 확인하세요!

어휘	/1	문법	/5	독해	/19	생활영어	/0

➡ 나의 취약영역: _____

※ [정답해설]과 [오답해설] 선지의 `50%` 표시는 〈1초 합격예측 서비스〉를 통해 수집된 선지 선택률을 나타냅니다.

1　독해 > Macro Reading > 주제　`오답률 17%`　답 ④

| 해석 | 단기 스트레스는 생산성과 면역력을 높일 수 있다. 그러나 스트레스가 계속되면, 어려움을 겪을 수도 있다. 사람들은 건강할 때보다 더 많은 스트레스를 받을 때 어떤 징후를 보인다. 첫째로, 집중할 수가 없다. 스트레스를 받으면, 몸이 투쟁 또는 도피 모드로 들어가 위험으로부터 안전을 지키기 위해 노력한다. 그렇기 때문에 단일 작업에 집중하는 것이 어려울 수 있으며, 산만해질 가능성이 있다. "당신의 두뇌의 반응은 모두 생존을 위한 것이 된다."라고 「Stressaholic: 스트레스와의 관계를 변화시키는 5단계의 저자」인 Heidi Hanna는 말한다. "두려움에 대한 반응은 자신을 어떻게 보호해야 하는지에 두뇌의 모든 에너지를 소비한다." 둘째, 비관적이 되는 경향이 있다. 당신의 생존을 위해 준비가 되어 있기 때문에, 당신의 뇌는 긍정적인 것보다 부정적인 것에 주의를 기울이는 회로가 더 많다. "인생의 혼란에 압도당했을 때, 잘 되고 있는 모든 것에 감사할 시간을 가지세요. 당신은 의도적으로 긍정주의를 실천합니다."라고 Hanna는 말한다.

① 단기적인 스트레스의 장점　② 왜 사람들은 계속 산만해지는가
③ 비관주의의 위험　④ 과도한 스트레스의 징조

| 정답해설 | ④ `83%` 스트레스가 지속되었을 때 나타나는 징후들을, 집중할 수 없는 것과 비관적이 되는 경향이 있다는 두 가지로 말하고 있으므로 '과도한 스트레스의 징조'가 주제로 적절하다.

(참고로, 세 번째 문장에서 than when they are healthy는 기출문제에서 than is healthy로 출제되었지만, 어법상 than when they are이 적절하므로 본 교재에는 옳게 수정하여 수록하였다.)

| 오답해설 | ① `12%` Short-term stress can boost your productivity and immunity.라는 문장으로 글을 시작하고 있지만 but ~ 이하를 통해 스트레스의 단점을 말하고 있다.

②③ `3%` `2%` 왜 산만해지는지와 비관주의는 스트레스가 과도해질 때 나타나는 징후 중 하나이지 이 글의 주된 내용이 아니다.

어휘

boost 북돋우다　　　　　　immunity 면역력
linger 오래 머물다　　　　　struggle 투쟁하다
suffer from ~로 고통받다　　take up 소비하다
pessimistic 비관적인　　　　prime 준비하다

2　어휘 > 빈칸 완성　`오답률 17%`　답 ②

| 해석 | 때때로, 유추의 의미가 명확하지 않을 수도 있다. 예를 들어, "흰 코끼리" 또는 "검은 양"이라는 말을 들을 때 무엇이 생각나는가? "흰 코끼리"라는 표현은 태국에서 온 것이다. 오래 전 태국에서는, 흰 코끼리가 매우 드물었다. 흰 코끼리가 발견될 때마다, 그것은 왕에게 바쳐졌다. 그 아름다운 동물을 돌보는 데 많은 돈이 들기 때문에 왕은 자신이 좋아하지 않는 사람에게 그 코끼리를 왕실의 "선물"로 주곤 했다. 그 누구도 그런 선물을 거절할 수는 없었지만, 재정적으로 주인을 망하게 할 수 있었다. 게다가, 왕으로부터 받은 선물을 학대하는 것은 중대한 범죄였다. 심지어는 그것을 타는 것도 허용되지 않아서, 흰 코끼리는 거의 무용지물이었다. 이 표현은, 18세기에 영국에 소개되었는데, (A) 비용이 많이 들지만 (B) 가치 없는 공공건물

을 묘사하는 데 유용한 것으로 밝혀졌다. 오늘날, 이것은 (A) 비용이 많이 들고 (B) 가치 없는 것을 지칭하기 위해 사용된다.

	(A)	(B)
①	가치 있는	보호받지 못하는
②	비용이 많이 드는	가치 없는
③	낭비벽이 심한	적절한
④	대단히 귀중한	환경 친화적인

| 정답해설 | ② 83% It could financially ruin its owner. Moreover, it was a serious crime to mistreat a present from the king. Even riding it was not allowed, so a white elephant was almost useless.에서 흰 코끼리는 관리하는 데 돈은 많이 들지만, 탈 수도 없어서 무용지물이었음을 알 수 있다. (A)에는 costly, (B)에는 worthless가 들어가는 것이 가장 적절하다.

| 더 알아보기 | Analogy (유추)

두 개의 사물이 여러 면에서 비슷하다는 것을 근거로 다른 속성도 유사할 것이라고 추론하는 것을 의미한다.

어휘

analogy 비유
ruin 망치다
refer to ~을 언급하다
cost a fortune 많은 돈이 들다
mistreat 잘못 다루다

3	독해 > Logical Reading > 문맥상 다양한 추론	오답률 25%	답 ③

| 해석 | 질문을 받으면, 거의 모든 사람들이 칭찬에 대한 적절한 응답은 "감사합니다."라고 말한다. 그러나 연구자들은 실제로 칭찬을 받으면, 단지 3분의 1만이 그것을 단순하게 받아들인다는 것을 발견했다. 어려움은 모든 칭찬 ("스웨터 멋지다!")에는 두 가지 수준이 있다는 데 있다. 즉, 선물 구성 요소(승인 또는 거부)와 콘텐츠 구성 요소(동의 또는 불일치)의 두 가지이다. 칭찬을 받는 사람은 딜레마에 직면하게 된다. 이 두 가지에 어떻게 동시에 반응을 해야 하는지에 대한 딜레마이다. "나는 칭찬한 사람과 동의해야 하며, 자화자찬을 피하면서 칭찬이라는 선물에 감사해야 한다." 흥미롭게도, 여성과 남성 둘 다 여성보다 남성에게서 오는 칭찬을 수용할 가능성이 ③ 더 적다(→ 더 많다). 어떤 남성이 "좋은 스카프네요"라고 말하면, 여성은 "고마워요, 내 동생이 나를 위해 짜 줬어요."라고 긍정적으로 대답할 가능성이 크다. 그러나 한 여성이 다른 여성에게 "그것은 아름다운 스웨터네요."라고 말하면, 그 칭찬을 받는 사람은 동의하지 않거나 피하게 된다. "할인 판매를 해서 샀는데 심지어 내가 원했던 색깔도 없었어요."라고 대답한다.

| 정답해설 | ③ 75% 본문 후반의 예시로 보아 여성과 남성 둘 다 여성보다 남성에게서 오는 칭찬을 더 수용한다는 내용이 흐름상 적절하다. 따라서 less를 more로 바꾸어야 한다.

어휘

compliment 칭찬
simultaneously 동시에
affirmatively 긍정적으로
recipient 받는 사람
self-praise 자화자찬
deflect 피하다

4	독해 > Logical Reading > 연결사	오답률 15%	답 ④

| 해석 | 의장은 합의된 견해로 나아가는 점진적인 토론을 추구해야 한다. 토론이 진행됨에 따라, 의장은 회원들의 견해의 무게가 가리키는 방향을 찾으려고 노력해야 한다. (A) 예를 들어, 만약 5명의 회원이 있고, 그중 두 명

이 코스 A를 따르기를 원하고, 3번째 사람은 코스 B를 따르려고 하는 것을 의장이 감지했다면, 초점은 나머지 두 명의 회원으로 향해야 한다. 의장은 4번째 회원에게로 향한다. 만약 그 사람이 A 코스를 원할 경우, 의장은 먼저 다른 중립 회원(회원 5), 그 다음 반대하는 3번 회원에게 코스 A가 다수의 의견이라는 사실에 동의하도록 만드는 일을 해야 한다. (B) 반면에, 만약 4번 회원이 코스 B를 원한다면, 5번 회원의 의견이 중요하므로, 의장은 그 의견을 받아들여야 한다. 그리고 매우 빠르게, 의견의 균형이 어디를 가리키는지 감지할 수 있으며, 회의를 만장일치의 동의로 움직일 수 있다.

	(A)	(B)
①	반면에	마찬가지로
②	예를 들면	그러므로
③	반면에	예를 들면
④	예를 들면	반면에

| 정답해설 | ④ 85% (A) 빈칸 뒤에서 의장과 5명의 회원의 선택에 관한 예를 들고 있으므로 for example이 들어가야 한다.
(B) 빈칸 앞에는 4번 회원이 A 코스를 원하는 경우가 나오고 빈칸 뒤에서는 4번 회원이 B 코스를 원하는 경우가 나오므로 대조의 연결사 on the other hand가 들어가야 한다.

| 더 알아보기 | 예시의 연결사

- for example 예를 들어
- such as 예를 들어
- that is to say 즉, 다시 말해
- for instance 가령, 예를 들어
- namely 즉, 다시 말해

어휘

progressive 점진적인; 진보적인
dissent 반대하다
majority 대다수
neutral 중립적인
assent 동의하다
critical 중요한

5	독해 > Macro Reading > 제목	오답률 28%	답 ①

| 해석 | 기원전 525년, 남부 이탈리아에서 살았던 그리스인 Theagenes는 신화를 과학적 유추 또는 우화로 간주했는데, 그것은 사람들이 이해할 수 없는 자연 현상을 설명하기 위한 시도였다. 그에게, 예를 들면, 자기들끼리 싸우는 신들의 신화적 이야기는 물과 불같이 서로 반대되는 자연의 힘을 대표하는 하나의 우화였다. 이것은 모든 사회 또는 문명에서 발견될 수 있는 우주, 세계 및 인류의 창조를 설명하는 것으로 시작하는, 많은 설명을 하기 위한 또는 "인과 관계를 나타내는" 신화의 근원이다. 이 "과학적" 신화는 계절, 해가 뜨고 지는 것, 그리고 별들의 길까지 설명하려고 시도했다. 이와 같은 신화는 어떤 면에서는 과학의 선구자였다. 자연 현상에 대한 오랜 신화적 설명은 특히 기원전 500년경부터 시작된 그리스의 과학과 철학의 주목할 만한 시기에 세상을 이해하기 위한 합리적 시도로 대체되기 시작했다.

① 신화: 과학적 궁금증의 토대
② 과학에 대한 신화(통념)을 없애기
③ 어떻게 창조 신화는 보편적인가
④ 신화가 우리의 세계관에 얼마나 영향을 미치는가

| 정답해설 | ① 72% 우주, 세계 및 인류의 창조, 계절, 해가 뜨고 지는 것, 별들의 길 등 사람들이 이해할 수 없는 자연 현상을 과학적 신화를 통해 설명하려 시도했다고 하였으므로 신화가 세상을 이해하기 위한, 즉, 과학적 궁금증을 해소하기 위한 토대가 되었음을 알 수 있다. 따라서 글의 제목으로 가장 적절한 것은 ①이다.

| 오답해설 | ④ 9% 신화 창조가 우리의 세계관에 영향을 미친다는

것이 아니라 신화를 통해 자연 현상을 설명하려고 했다고 말하고 있다.

어휘

analogy 유추	allegory 우화
occurrence 발생	explanatory 설명하는
casual 인과 관계의, 원인을 나타내는	
civilization 문명	forerunner 선구자
era 시대	dispel 없애다

---

6 | 독해 > Micro Reading > 내용일치/불일치 | 오답률 10% | 답 ②

| 해석 | 매년 10월 초, 헬싱키의 항구는 1743년에 처음 열린 발트해 청어 축제로 활기차고 화려하게 변한다. 핀란드 전국에서 온 어부들은 핀란드에서 가장 오래된 축제 중 하나에 참가하기 위해 그들이 가장 최근에 잡은 청어를 갖고 헬싱키에 온다. 밝은 오렌지색 텐트 안의 판매자들은 항구에 줄을 이루어 상상할 수 있는 모든 형태의 청어를 판다. 튀김, 절임, 훈제, 병조림, 통조림, 수프, 피자 및 샌드위치. 선택할 수 있는 것들은 끝이 없다. 축제 첫날, 가장 맛있게 양념된 청어와 최고의 청어 서프라이즈를 뽑기 위한 대회가 열린다. 청어 서프라이즈는 청어, 치즈 그리고 양파로 만드는 전통적인 요리이다. 각 대회의 우승자에게 트로피가 주어진다.

① 축제는 1743년 이후 2년마다 열려 왔다.
② 판매자들은 항구를 따라 오렌지색 텐트를 설치하고 청어를 판다.
③ 축제의 경연 대회는 헬싱키 거주자들로 제한된다.
④ 트로피는 최고의 청어 서프라이즈 우승자에게만 주어진다.

| 정답해설 | ② 90% 세 번째 문장 Sellers in bright orange tents line the harbor and sell herring.을 통해 글의 내용과 일치함을 알 수 있다.

| 오답해설 | ① 1% 매년 개최된다고 했으므로 일치하지 않는다.
③ 3% 핀란드 전국에서 온 어부들이라고 했으므로 헬싱키 거주자들에게만 국한되지 않는다.
④ 6% 청어 서프라이즈 우승자뿐만 아니라 가장 맛있게 양념된 청어 요리 대회의 우승자도 트로피를 받는다고 했으므로 일치하지 않는다.

어휘

herring 청어	take part in ~에 참가하다
imaginable 상상할 수 있는	seasoned 양념된

---

7 | 독해 > Logical Reading > 문맥상 다양한 추론 | 오답률 40% | 답 ③

| 해석 | 어렸을 때 나는 언니와 침실을 같이 썼다. 비록 나이 차이는 적었지만, 지성과 성숙함에서 그녀는 나를 엄청난 차이가 있는 곳에서 온 사람으로 보았다. 그녀의 진지한 학문적, 문화적 탐구는 라디오 쇼를 꼼꼼하게 모니터링하는 나의 활동과 크게 대조되었다. 우리 사이의 이렇게 다른 관심사와 하나의 침실이라는 제한된 자원으로 인해, 우리는 자주 방해가 되고 배려 없는 행동에 대해 갈등이 있었다. 몇 달 동안, 우리의 다른 견해에 있어서 "절충을 하고" "모두 공평하게 나누는" 것을 실행함으로써 타협하려는 시도가 있었다. 종이에 적힌 스케줄과 합의 및 부모님의 중재가 있었지만, 논쟁은 계속되었다. 결국, 우리가 차후의 계산적인 타협을 위해 교묘하게 행동하고 제자리를 잡으면서, 상당한 시간과 에너지가 낭비되고 있다는 것을 인식했을 때 그 문제는 ③ 악화되었다(→ 해결되었다). 상호 이익을 위해 문제를 해결하려는 공통의 관심사를 인식하면서, 우리는 공간, 시간 및 자료의 물리적 자원을 넘어서 생각할 수 있었다. 우리 둘의 요구에 맞는 만족

스러운 해결책은 라디오용 이어폰 구입이었다.

| 정답해설 | ③ 60% 타협을 위해 상당한 시간과 에너지가 낭비되고 있다는 것을 인식하게 되었고, 이후 서로 만족스러운 해결책을 찾았다는 내용이 이어지므로, 문제가 악화되기보다는 '해결되었다'고 하는 것이 적절하다. 따라서 aggravated는 settled(해결된, 합의된)로 고치는 것이 글의 흐름상 적절하다.

어휘

maturity 성숙	dissimilar 같지 않은, 다른
constitute ~이 되다	inconsiderate 사려 깊지 못한
compromise 타협하다	
share and share alike 똑같이 공평하게 나누다	
controversy 논쟁	aggravate 악화되다
maneuver 연습시키다, 작전적으로 행동하게 하다	

---

8 | 독해 > Reading for Writing > 빈칸 구 완성 | 오답률 15% | 답 ③

| 해석 | 세계에서 가장 인기 있는 컴퓨터 게임 중 하나는 Age of Empires이다. 몇 달 동안 열 살 된 내 아들은 그 게임에 중독되었다는 말 외에 따로 표현할 말이 없었다. 그 게임의 바탕이 되는 전제는 세계의 역사가 제국 갈등의 역사라는 것이다. 경쟁하는 정치 단체들은 서로서로 제한된 자원 즉, 사람들, 비옥한 땅, 숲, 금광 및 수로를 두고 경쟁한다. 끝없는 투쟁 안에 경쟁하는 제국들은 경제 발전의 필요성과 전쟁이라는 긴급 사태 사이에서 균형을 유지해야 한다. 매우 공격적인 플레이어는 만약 그가 그의 기존 영토를 경작하고, 인구를 늘리고, 금을 축적하는 수고를 들이지 않으면 곧 자원이 바닥난다. 부유하게 되는 데 너무 집중하는 플레이어들은 만약 그가 당분간 그의 방어를 무시한다면 자신이 ③ 침략에 약하다는 것을 알게 될지 모른다.

① 병에 면역력이 있다는
② 변화에 관용적이라는
③ 침략에 약하다는
④ 오락에 중독되었다는

| 정답해설 | ③ 85% 공격적인 플레이어와 달리, 부의 축적에 집중하는 플레이어는 공격력을 높이지 않았으므로 방어를 등한시한다면 침략되기 쉽다는 것을 유추할 수 있다.

어휘

all but 거의	premise 전제
imperial 제국의	entity 단체
finite 유한한	vulnerable 취약한

---

9 | 독해 > Logical Reading > 삭제 | 오답률 17% | 답 ④

| 해석 | 오래된 핸드폰이 열대 우림을 구하는 데 도움을 줄 수 있을까? 사실, 그것은 가능하다. 열대 우림의 불법 벌목은 수년 동안 문제였지만, 불법 벌목꾼들을 잡는 것이 어렵기 때문에, 많은 것들이 행해지지 않았다. 이 문제를 해결하기 위해, 미국인 엔지니어, Topher White는 버려진 휴대폰으로 RFCx라는 장치를 개발했다. 나무에 부착된 장치가 전기톱 소리를 듣게 되었을 때, 관리인의 핸드폰으로 경보 메시지를 보낸다. 이 장치는 관리인들에게 벌목꾼의 위치와 불법 벌목을 중단시키는 데 필요한 정보를 제공하게 된다. ④ 열대 우림의 파괴는 벌목, 농업, 광업 그리고 다른 인간의 활동 때문이고, 이것들 중에 벌목이 자연 손실의 가장 주된 원인이다. 그 장치는 인도네시아에서 테스트를 받았고, 잘 작동된다는 것이 증명되었다. 그 결과, 그것은 현재 아프리카와 남미의 열대 우림에서 사용되고 있다.

| 정답해설 | ④ 83% 핸드폰과 열대 우림의 보호에 관한 글로, ①②③은 핸드폰을 사용해 불법 벌목꾼들을 단속하는 것에 관한 내용이다. 하지만 ④는 열대 우림 파괴의 원인을 나열하고 있으므로 글의

흐름과 관계없는 문장이다.

오답률 TOP3

10 독해 > Macro Reading > 제목 | 오답률 59% | 답 ②

| 해석 | 어떤 심포니이든, 작곡가와 지휘자는 다양한 책임을 지게 된다. 그들은 금관 악기 호른이 목관 악기와 합주가 잘 되고, 타악기가 비올라 소리를 막지 않도록 해야 한다. 그러나 그들의 관계를 완벽하게 하는 것은, 비록 그것이 중요할지라도, 그들의 노력의 궁극적인 목표는 아니다. 지휘자와 작곡가가 원하는 것은 그것의 웅장함이 여러 부분들의 합을 넘어서 이러한 관계들을 하나로 모으는 능력이다. 따라서 이러한 것들이 관객에게 폭넓은 호소력을 갖는 심포니의 특성이다. 경계를 오고 가는 사람, 발명가, 그리고 은유를 만드는 사람들 모두 관계의 중요성을 이해한다. 그러나 개념의 시대에는 관계 사이의 관계를 파악하는 능력을 요구한다. 이런 더 초월적인 능력은 많은 이름들, 시스템적 사고, 게슈탈트 사고, 전체론적 사고 등으로 흘러간다.
① 음악의 힘
② 큰 그림을 보는 것
③ 창조의 본질
④ 협업이 차이를 만든다

| 정답해설 | ② 41% 지휘자와 작곡가는 오케스트라 개개의 악기들의 능력보다 그것들이 합쳐져서 하나의 웅장함을 만들어 내는 것을 중요시한다는 내용이므로 ② '큰 그림을 보는 것'이 글의 제목으로 적절하다.

| 오답해설 | ① 2% '음악의 힘'은 이 글에서 언급하고 있지 않다.

③ 3% '창조의 본질'보다는 하나로 만들어 내는 것에 관해 언급하고 있다.

④ 54% '협업이 차이를 만들어 낸다.'는 지문에서 말하고자 하는 주된 내용이 아니다. 지휘자와 작곡가가 관계의 중요성을 인식하고 그것을 통해 더 큰 것을 만들어 내는 것이 주제이다.

---

11 문법 > 태 | 오답률 20% | 답 ④

| 해석 | 형사 소송에서, 입증 책임은 종종 기소된 범죄의 모든 구성 요소에 대한 합리적인 의심을 넘어서 피고가 유죄라는 것을 재판관(판사나 배심원들)에게 설득시키는 검사에게 있다. 만약 검사가 이를 입증하지 못하면, 무죄 판결이 내려진다. 이러한 증거의 기준은 민사 사건과는 대조되는데, 일반적으로 민사 사건에서는 피고가 개연성의 균형에 (50% 이상으로) 책임이 있다는 것을 원고가 입증해야 한다. 미국에서, 이것은 증거의 우세라고 지칭된다.

| 정답해설 | ④ 80% 「refer to A as B」는 'A를 B라고 지칭하다[일컫다]'라는 의미를 갖고 있는 숙어이다. 문장에 'A'에 해당하는 목적어가 없으므로 수동태가 되도록 referred로 고쳐야 한다.

| 오답해설 | ① 4% persuade는 4형식 동사로 「persuade + 간접목적어 + 직접목적어」의 어순을 취한다. that the accused is guilty는

persuade의 직접목적어 역할을 하는 목적절이다.

② 4% render는 '(판결을) 내리다, 언도하다'라는 뜻의 동사로, 주어인 a verdict of not guilty는 '판결 내려지는' 것이므로 수동태가 적절한 표현이다.

③ 12% 관계부사 where 다음에 「주어 + 동사 + 목적어」의 완전한 문장이 왔으므로 적절한 표현이다.

---

12 독해 > Logical Reading > 문맥상 다양한 추론 | 오답률 6% | 답 ④

| 해석 | 각각의 코스 수요를 맞추기 위해, Escoffier는 그의 주방을 다섯 개의 다른 구역으로 나누어 요리 준비를 현대화했다. 첫 번째 구역은 차가운 음식을 만들었고 전체 주방을 위한 재료들을 조직화했다. 두 번째 구역은 수프, 채소 그리고 디저트들을 관리했다. 세 번째 구역은 굽거나 그릴에 굽거나 튀기는 요리들을 다뤘다. 네 번째 구역은 오로지 소스에만 집중했고, 마지막 구역은 페스트리를 만들기 위한 곳이었다. 이는 레스토랑의 부엌에서 과거보다 그들의 요리를 더 빨리 만드는 것을 가능하게 했다. 예를 들어, 만약 고객이 에그 플로렌틴을 주문했다면, 한 구역에서는 계란을 요리할 것이고, 다른 구역에서는 소스를 만들 것이며, 또 다른 구역에서 페스트리를 만들 것이다. 그러고 나면, 총괄 요리사가 고객에게 음식이 나가기 전에 요리를 조합할 것이다. 이 시스템은 매우 효율적이었기 때문에 그것은 오늘날 많은 레스토랑에서 여전히 사용되고 있다.
① 주방의 여러 구역에서의 경쟁
② 필요한 재료들을 준비하기 위한 확장된 방
③ 총괄 요리사에 의해 고객들에게 다른 요리들이 분배되는 것
④ 음식을 준비하기 위해 다른 구역들로 나눠진 주방

| 정답해설 | ④ 94% 각각의 코스의 수요를 맞추기 위해, 주방을 다섯 개의 다른 구역으로 나누어 요리 과정을 분류하고 요리를 준비하는 것을 현대화했다고 하면서 그 구체적인 방법을 설명하고 있으므로, This system은 요리를 준비하기 위해 구역을 분리한 주방이라는 것을 유추할 수 있다.

---

13 독해 > Reading for Writing > 요약 | 오답률 28% | 답 ④

| 해석 | McAdams는 정체성에 대한 중요한 주장을 한다. 그것은 과거에 무슨 일이 일어났는지 지금 당신은 어떤 종류의 사람인지를 이해하기 위해 당신이 당신 자신에 대해 말하는 이야기이다. 이런 관점에서, 이야기가 사실인지는 본질적이지 않다. 나는 나 자신이 문화적으로 모험적(다시 말하면 굉장히 개방적이다)이라는 것을 안다. 나는 이것이 사실이라고 믿게 되었다. 다시 말하면, 다른 사람과 비교했을 때, 나는 상대적으로 메뉴에서 새로운 것을 시도하는 것과 새로운 활동들을 잘 받아들이고, 새로운 장소를 방문하는 것 등등에 개방적이다. 그러나 McAdams의 관점에서, 우리가 우리의 정

체성에 대해 이야기할 때, 우리 자신에 대한 믿음이 진실인지 아닌지는 크게 관계가 없다.

↓

McAdams에 따르면, 우리의 정체성은 우리가 만들어 낸 (A) 이야기이고, 그것은 본래 사실이거나 (B) 사실이 아닐 수 있다.

　(A)　　　(B)
① 모험　　흥미있는
② 이미지　볼 수 있는
③ 문　　이용할 수 있는
④ 이야기　사실인

| **정답해설** | ④ 72% It is a story you tell about yourself.에서 정체성을 '이야기'로 정의내린 것을 알 수 있으므로 (A)에는 narrative(이야기)가 적절하다. When we're talking about identity, whether our beliefs about ourselves are true or not is pretty much irrelevant.에서 이야기가 진실이냐 허구냐는 큰 의미가 없다고 했고 (B) 앞에 may not be가 있으므로 factual(사실인)이 적절하다.

어휘
identity 정체성　　make sense out of ~을 이해하다
irrelevant 관계없는　narrative 이야기
factual 사실인　　visible 볼 수 있는

---

14 독해 > Logical Reading > 문맥상 다양한 추론　오답률 17%　답 ④

| **해석** | Watson은 아침 식사 테이블에 앉은 이후로 ① 그의 동료를 골똘히 바라보고 있었다. Holmes가 우연히 고개를 들었다가 그의 시선을 붙잡았다. "저, Watson, 너 지금 무슨 생각하고 있니?" 그가 물었다.
"너에 대한 생각."
"② 나에 대해?"
"그래, Holmes. 나는 너의 속임수들 중 이런 것들이 얼마나 피상적인지 그리고 대중들이 그것들에 호기심을 보이는 것을 계속하는 것이 얼마나 훌륭한지 생각하고 있었어."
"나도 꽤 동의해." Holmes가 말했다. "사실, 나는 ③ 나 스스로 비슷한 발언을 했던 기억을 갖고 있어."
"너의 방법이라." Watson이 엄격하게 말했다. "그것들은 정말 쉽게 습득되는 것이야."
"맞아." Holmes는 미소를 지으며 대답했다. "아마 너도 ④ 너 스스로 이 추론 방법의 예를 말할 수 있을 거야."

| **정답해설** | ④ 83% Watson과 그의 동료 Holmes의 대화로, 문맥상 ①②③은 Holmes를 가리키지만 ④는 Watson을 가리킨다.

어휘
companion 동료　　intently 골똘하게
superficial 피상적인　recollection 기억
remark 발언　　reasoning 추론

---

15 문법 > 분사　오답률 33%　답 ②

| **해석** | 1860년대, Manhattan과 Brooklyn의 인구는 빠르게 증가하고 있었고, 두 지역 사이 통근자들의 수도 그러했다. 수천 명의 사람들이 매일 East River를 건너는 보트와 페리를 탔지만, 이러한 형태의 교통수단은 불안정했고 종종 나쁜 날씨로 인해 중단되었다. 많은 뉴욕 사람들은 Manhattan과 Brooklyn을 직통으로 연결하는 다리를 원했다. 왜냐하면 그것이 그들의 통근을 더 빠르고 더 안전하게 만들어 줄 것이기 때문이었다. 불행하게도, East River의 엄청난 너비와 거친 조류 때문에 그 위에 무엇을 짓기는 어려웠다. 그 당시 그것은 매우 혼잡한 강이어서, 수백 척의 배가 끊임없이 그 강을 항해하고 있었다.

| **정답해설** | ② 67% connected는 a bridge를 수식하는 분사이고 connect는 목적어가 필요한 타동사이다. connected의 목적어 역할을 하는 Manhattan and Brooklyn이 뒤에 나오므로 connected를 능동의 의미를 갖는 현재분사 connecting으로 바꾸어야 한다.

| **오답해설** | ① 15% '~도 역시 그렇다'라는 의미의 「so + 동사 + 주어」 도치 구문으로 주어가 the number of ~로 시작하는 단수형이기 때문에 was는 적절한 표현이다.
③ 5% to build anything on it이 진주어이므로 가주어 it을 사용한 것은 적절한 표현이다.
④ 13% 「with + 주어 + 분사」 형태의 with 분사구문으로, hundreds of ships가 '항해하는' 것이므로 능동의 의미를 갖는 현재분사 sailing은 적절한 표현이다.

어휘
commuter 통근자　　tide 조류

---

16 문법 > 분사　오답률 23%　답 ③

| **해석** | 최근에, P2P 대출은 대체 금융 산업의 전형이 되어 왔다. 2015년에, Morgan Stanley는 그러한 시장 대출이 2020년까지 세계적으로 1500억 달러에서 4900억 달러까지 장악할 것이라고 예측했었다. P2P 대출은 양 당사자들이 은행 같은 전통적인 대출 공급자들의 주변을 둘러보는 것을 가능하게 만들면서, 투자자들을 직접적으로 대출자와 연결해 주는 온라인 서비스를 통해 개인 혹은 기업들에게 돈을 빌려주는 관행이다. 대출 기관들은 전형적으로 수익률 개선을 이루려고 하는 반면에, 개인들과 SMEs(중소형 기업들)의 대출자들은 유연하고 경쟁력 있게 가격이 책정된 대출에 접근하고자 한다. 투자자들에게, 이익은 매력적이다. 대출자와 연결되는 것은 며칠에서 수 시간이 걸릴 수 있다. 그리고 은행이 전형적으로 개인 대출에서 2% 미만의 수익을 내는 곳에서, P2P의 수익은 그것의 세 배 이상이 될 수 있다.

| **정답해설** | ③ 77% enabled가 접속사 없이 연결되어 있으므로 분사구문이라는 것을 알 수 있다. 「enable + 목적어 + to부정사」는 '목적어가 ~을 가능하게 하다'라는 의미이다. enabled 다음에 목적어인 both parties가 나오므로 능동태 분사구문임을 알 수 있다. 따라서 enabled는 enabling으로 고쳐야 한다.

| **오답해설** | ① 10% in recent years는 과거의 어느 시점에서 현재까지를 나타내는 시간 부사구로 현재완료시제인 has become의 쓰임은 적절하다.
② 11% 주절에서 과거시제 predicted를 사용했으므로 종속절인 that절의 시제도 과거형이 되어야 한다. 따라서 would의 쓰임은 적절하다.
④ 2% 동명사구가 주어인 문장으로, match는 목적어가 필요한 타동사인데 with a borrower가 뒤에 오면서 목적어가 없는 수동태 동명사구(Being + p.p.)로 쓰였음을 알 수 있다.

어휘
P2P lending P2P 대출　　poster child 전형

flexible 유연한
competitively priced 경쟁력 있게 가격이 책정된
return 수익

---

17 독해 > Logical Reading > 문맥상 다양한 추론   오답률 50%   답 ④

| 해석 | 그래서 내가 Old Timers 경기에서 회색 머리의 투수를 노려보며 본루에 섰을 때, 그리고 과거에는 속구였지만 지금은 단지 내 가슴 쪽으로 뜨는 단순한 볼을 그가 던지고 나서, 내가 방망이를 휘두르고 공을 쳐서 탁(thwock)하는 익숙한 소리를 듣고, 내가 무언가 멋진 일을 해 냈다고 확신하며, 나의 늙은 체력은 잊고, 내 팔과 다리는 예전처럼 힘이 넘치지 않는다는 것도 잊고, 사람이 나이가 들고 벽은 더 멀어진다는 것도 잊은 채로, 나는 야구 방망이를 떨어뜨리고 달리기 시작했는데, 내가 위를 올려다 보고 처음에 강력한 타격이라고, 아마도 홈런이라고 생각했었던 것이 이제 내야 너머 2루수가 대기하고 있는 글러브 쪽으로 떨어지고 있는 것을 보았을 때, 그것은 단지 짧은 플라이볼, 젖은 폭죽, 쓸모없는 공에 지나지 않는 것이었으며, 내 머릿속의 목소리가 "놓쳐라! 놓쳐라!"라고 소리쳤는데, 그때 그 2루수가 이 화나게 하는 게임에 바친 나의 마지막 제물을 그의 글러브로 움켜 쥐었다.
① 질투하는   ② 기쁜
③ 열정적인   ④ 실망스러운

| 정답해설 | ④ 50% 처음에는 홈런이라 생각했지만 달리면서 아웃이 되는 공이었음을 알 수 있었을 때 'I'의 심경은 '실망스러웠을' 것이다.

어휘
plate 본루   pitcher 투수
fabulous 멋진   gauge 한계, 범위
infield 내야   pop-up 내야 플라이 (= pop fly)
dud 못 쓰는[제대로 작동하지 않는] 것
squeeze 꽉 쥐다   maddening 격노하게 하는, 화나는

---

18 독해 > Logical Reading > 문맥상 다양한 추론   오답률 14%   답 ②

| 해석 | 우리 매일의 의식적인 활동에서, 우리는 정신과 신체의 분리를 경험한다. 우리는 우리 몸과 신체 활동에 대해 생각한다. 동물들은 이런 분리를 경험하지 않는다. 우리가 신체적 구성 요소를 갖는 어떠한 기술을 배우기 시작할 때, 이런 분리는 훨씬 ② 덜(→ 더) 분명해지게 된다. 우리는 관련된 다양한 행동, 따라야 할 단계들에 대해 생각해야만 한다. 우리는 우리의 느린 속도와 어떻게 이상한 방향으로 우리의 신체가 반응하는지 인지한다. 특정한 시점에, 우리가 개선될 때, 우리는 이 과정이 어떻게 다르게 기능하는지, 정신이 신체의 길을 방해하지 않으면서 기술을 매끄럽게 수행하는 것을 어떻게 느끼는지 어렴풋이 이해할 수 있다. 그렇게 잠깐 보는 것으로, 우리는 무엇을 목표로 해야 하는지 알고 있다. 우리가 충분히 연습하면 기술은 자동적이 되고, 우리는 정신과 신체가 하나가 되어 작동한다는 느낌을 갖게 된다.

| 정답해설 | ② 86% 우리는 의식적으로 정신과 신체를 구별하면서 활동하는데 우리가 신체적 구성 요소를 갖는 어떠한 기술을 배우기 시작할 때, 이런 분리는 훨씬 '더' 분명해지게 된다는 것이 자연스러우므로, less는 더 명백해진다는 의미로 more가 되어야 한다.

| 오답해설 | ① 1% Animals do not experience this division.에서 '분리'는 인간만이 경험하는 것을 알 수 있다. 따라서 separation은 적절하다.

---

③ 4% 인간이 어떤 활동이 미숙하거나 아직 익숙하지 않을 때 신체가 반응을 이상하게 한다는 내용 뒤에 '특정한 시점에 우리가 개선될 때 ~'라는 표현이 오는 것이 자연스러우므로 improve는 적절하다.

④ 9% 미숙에서 개선 그리고 기술 습득이 충분해지면 '자동적으로' 기술을 실행할 수 있다는 뜻이므로 automatic은 적절하다.

어휘
conscious 의식적인   apparent 명백한
awkward 이상한
have a glimpse of 어렴풋이 이해하다
aim for ~을 목표로 하다   sensation 느낌

---

19 문법 > 동사   오답률 52%   답 ③

| 해석 | 2000년에, Harvard 대학교의 과학자들은 모나리자의 알아볼 수 없는 미소를 설명하는 신경학적인 방법을 제안했다. 관람객들이 그녀의 눈을 볼 때, 입은 흑백으로 보이는 주변부 시야에 있다. 이것은 미소를 더 넓게 보이게 만들면서, 입 주위의 그림자를 강조한다. 그러나 당신이 그것을 똑바로 바라볼 때, 미소는 줄어든다. 그녀의 미소를 매우 생동감 있고 매우 신비롭게 만드는 것은 바로 그녀 미소의 변동성, 즉 당신이 그것으로부터 눈길을 돌릴 때 변화한다는 사실이다.

| 정답해설 | ③ 48% 사역동사 make가 쓰인 분사구문으로, 목적격 보어 자리에는 원형부정사가 와야 하므로 seem으로 고쳐야 한다.

| 오답해설 | ① 4% 전치사 다음에 동명사를 쓰는 것은 문법상 적절하다.

② 10% which는 peripheral vision을 선행사로 하는 주격 관계대명사로 이때 peripheral vision은 사물에 해당하므로 which는 옳은 표현이다.

④ 38% 「It is ~ that …」 강조 구문으로 that은 문법상 적절하며 이때 the fact ~ from it은 삽입구이다.
The variability of her smile makes her smile so alive, so mysterious.
→ It is the variability of her smile that makes her smile so alive, so mysterious.

어휘
neurological 신경학적인   elusive 알아볼 수 없는
peripheral 주변부   accentuate 강조하다
diminish 줄어들다   variability 다양성
look away (from) (~로부터) 눈길을 돌리다
mysterious 신비롭게

오답률 TOP 2
20 독해 > Logical Reading > 삽입   오답률 70%   답 ②

| 해석 | 우리가 아기일 때, 우리의 두뇌는 최초의 양육자와의 관계 사이에서 발달한다. 그들이 우리에게 주는 감정과 사고 과정이 무엇이든지 간에 성장 중인 우리의 두뇌에 투영되며, 반응되고 규정된다. 상황이 잘 흘러갈 때, 우리의 부모들과 양육자들은 또한 우리가 느끼는 것을 인정하고 반응하면서, 우리의 기분과 정신 상태를 비추고 검증한다. ② 그래서 우리가 두 살 정도가 될 즈음에, 우리의 두뇌는 이미 뚜렷하고 개별적인 형태를 갖게 될 것이다. 그러면 우리의 좌뇌는 언어를 이해할 수 있을 만큼 충분히 성숙해

진다. 이러한 두 가지의 발달은 우리가 두 부분의 두뇌를 어느 정도 통합할 수 있게 해 준다. 우리는 우뇌의 감정을 언어로 표현하기 위해 좌뇌를 사용하는 것을 시작할 수 있게 된다.

| **정답해설** | ② 30% 이전 문장에서 아기일 때 부모 혹은 양육자와의 관계를 통해 감정을 느끼는 두뇌 부분이 발달하게 된다고 설명하고 있다. ② 이후에 그러면 우리의 좌뇌는 언어를 이해할 수 있을 만큼 충분히 성숙해진다며 단순한 감정을 관할하는 뇌가 아닌 언어를 이해하는 좌뇌 발달에 관한 내용이 나오고 있으므로 ②에 두뇌가 이미 뚜렷하고 개별적인 패턴을 가지고 있다는 주어진 문장이 들어가는 것이 적절하다.

어휘

distinct 뚜렷한
mirror 투영하다
validate 검증하다
to some extent 어느 정도

caregiver 양육자, 돌보는 사람
be laid down 규정되다
sufficiently 충분히

---

21 독해 > Logical Reading > 삽입 오답률 12% 답 ③

| **해석** | 수천 년 동안, 인간은 자신이 어디에 있었는지 알아내는 데 어려움을 겪었다. 그래서 그들은 이 문제를 해결하는 데 많은 시간과 노력을 기울였다. 그들은 복잡한 지도를 그렸고, 올바른 길을 추적하기 위해 커다란 랜드마크를 건설했으며 심지어 별을 쳐다보면서 항해하는 것을 배웠다. ③ 지금은 우리가 어디에 있는지 어느 방향으로 가야 하는지 쉽게 알아낼 수 있는데, 왜냐하면 당신은 당신의 손 끝에 세계에서 가장 위대한 발명품 중 하나를 갖고 있기 때문이다. 전 지구 위치 파악 시스템(GPS) 수신기를 사용하는 한 당신이 길을 잘못 들어서는 것에 대해서는 걱정할 필요가 없다. GPS는 정확한 위치를 알려주고 당신이 지구상 어디에 있든 간에, 당신이 가야 하는 어디든지 갈 수 있는 방향을 제시한다!

| **정답해설** | ③ 88% 이전 문장에서 복잡한 지도를 그리거나 커다란 랜드마크를 건설하거나 별을 쳐다보면서 항해하는 것을 배우는 것 등 GPS가 발명되기 이전에 길을 찾거나 위치를 파악했던 방법을 설명하고 있다. 주어진 문장은 Nowadays로 시작하고 예전 방법과 다른 방법을 설명하고 있으므로 ③에 들어가는 것이 가장 적절하다.

어휘

fingertips 손끝
have difficulty -ing ~ 하는 데 어려움을 겪다
figure out 파악하다, 이해하다
GPS(= Global Positioning System) 전 지구 위치 파악 시스템

---

22 독해 > Reading for Writing > 빈칸 구 완성 오답률 28% 답 ②

| **해석** | 훌륭한 광고는 멋지다. 그것이 바로 우리가 광고를 사랑하는 이유이다. 그러나 당신이 보고 있는 것은 거기 있는 것의 단지 절반에 지나지 않으며 당신이 보지 못하는 부분은 당신이 볼 수 있는 부분보다 광고의 성공에 더 크게 관련되어 있다. 이러한 표면적 특징들(훌륭한 헤드라인이나 시각적 효과 그리고 줄거리, 등장인물, 해설 소리 혹은 무엇이든 간에)이 효과를 내기 전에, 광고는 중요한 것을 말해야 한다. 진정한 소비자들의 동기와 문제를 다뤄야 한다. 그렇지 않으면 광고는 누구에게도 말한 게 아닌 것이다. 그래서 훌륭한 광고를 만들기 위해서 그들이 시작한 부분부터 시작해야 한다. ② 보이지 않는 부분부터.

① 효과적인 도구
② 보이지 않는 부분
③ 공동 요구 사항
④ 표면적 특징

| **정답해설** | ② 72% 마지막 문장이 주제문으로, 진정한 소비자들의 동기와 문제를 다뤄야 하며, 그렇지 않으면 광고는 누구에게도 말한 게 아니라는 내용을 통해 단순히 화려한 광고가 훌륭한 광고가 아니라 보이지 않는 소비자들에 대한 문제도 다루는 것이 중요함을 유추할 수 있다. the part you can't see has more to do with that ad's success than the part you can.이라는 문장으로 광고에서 보이지 않는 부분이 광고의 성공에 큰 영향을 미치는 것을 알 수 있다.

어휘

have to do with ~와 관련이 있다
voiceover 해설 소리
corporate needs 공동 요구 사항

terrific 훌륭한
invisible 보이지 않는

---

23 독해 > Logical Reading > 삽입 오답률 29% 답 ④

| **해석** | Walter Fredrick Morrison과 그의 여자친구 Lucile Nay는 그들이 캘리포니아 해변가에서 날리고 있던 금속 케이크 팬을 낯선 사람이 사겠다고 물어봤을 때 시장성이 있다는 것을 알았다. 1938년에, 그 커플은 5센트짜리 팬을 한 개당 25센트에 판매했다. 후에, Morrison은 비행 케이크 팬보다 더 좋은 비행 원반을 만들려고 시도했다. Franscioni와 함께, 그는 Pluto Platter를 만들었다. ④ 훌라후프로 유명한 선견지명이 있는 장난감 회사 Wham-O는 1년 후에 권리를 인수하고 비행 원반을 Frisbee라고 다시 이름을 지었다. 1960년대 중반 그것은 매우 유명해져서 당신은 거의 모든 집들의 지붕 위에 Frisbee가 걸려 있는 것을 볼 수 있었다.

| **정답해설** | ④ 71% 뒤에 거의 모든 집들의 지붕 위에 Frisbee가 걸려 있는 것을 볼 수 있었다고 하면서 비행 원반을 Frisbee라고 명명하고 있다. 따라서 Frisbee라고 이름을 바꿨다는 내용이 있는 주어진 문장은 그 앞인 ④에 위치하는 것이 적절하다.

어휘

visionary 선견지명이 있는
flying disc 비행 원반
flip 넘기다

rename 다시 이름을 짓다
marketable 시장성이 있는
try one's hand at ~을 시도하다

오답률 TOP 1
24 독해 > Reading for Writing > 빈칸 구 완성 오답률 72% 답 ③

| **해석** | 역설적으로, 어떤 관심의 초기 발견은 발견한 사람들에 의해 종종 간과되곤 한다. 다시 말하면, 당신이 무언가에 관심을 가지기 시작하면, 그 일이 무엇인지 깨닫지 못할 수도 있다. 지루하다고 느끼는 감정은 항상 자의식이다 ― 당신이 그것을 느낄 때 당신은 그것을 느끼고 있다는 것을 안다 ― 하지만 당신의 주의가 새로운 활동이나 경험에 끌릴 때, 당신은 아마 무슨 일이 일어나는지 거의 알 수 없을 것이다. 이것은 새로운 시도의 시작 단계에서, 당신 자신에게 초조하게 며칠에 한 번씩 열정을 찾았는지 물어보는 것은 ③ 너무 이르다는 뜻이다.

① 관련 있는
② 필요한
③ 너무 이른
④ 드문

| **정답해설** | ③ 28% 어떤 것에 관심을 보이기 시작할 때, 당신은 아마 무슨 일이 일어나고 있는지 깨닫지 못할 수도 있다는 내용에서 새로운 것을 시작하거나 경험할 때 잘 모를 수 있다는 것을 알 수 있다. 따라서 새로운 활동의 시작에 자신에게 초조하게 며칠에 한 번씩 열정을 찾았는지 물어보는 것은 너무 '이르다'고 유추할 수 있다.

| **25** | 문법 > 강조와 도치 | 오답률 44% | 답 ③ |

| 해석 | 많은 시행착오 후에, Richard는 마침내 태양 전지판에 의해 충전된 낡은 자동차 배터리에 의해 작동되는 반짝이는 LED 불빛 시스템을 완성했다. Richard는 울타리를 따라 조명들을 설치했다. 밤에는, 불빛을 외양간 바깥에서부터 볼 수 있었고 번갈아 가며 깜박거렸는데, 이는 마치 사람들이 횃불을 들고 돌아다니는 것처럼 보였다. 다시는 사자들이 Richard의 울타리를 건너지 못했다. Richard는 그의 시스템을 Lion Lights라고 불렀다. 이 간단하고 실용적인 장치는 사자들에게 어떠한 해도 끼치지 않았다. 그래서 인간들, 소떼들, 그리고 사자들이 마침내 서로서로 평화를 찾을 수 있었다.

| 정답해설 | ③ 56% 부정어인 never가 문두에 위치하면 주어와 동사가 도치된다. cross는 일반동사이고 문장의 시제는 과거이므로 대동사 do를 사용하여 did lions cross로 고쳐야 한다.

| 오답해설 | ① 1% powered 다음에 by an old car battery that was charged by a solar panel이 나오므로 수동의 의미를 가지는 과거분사 powered는 적절한 표현이다.

② 14% which는 앞 절을 선행사로 하는 계속적 용법의 주격 관계대명사이다.

④ 29% one another는 '(셋 이상에서) 서로'를 뜻하는 표현으로 적절하게 사용되었다.

| 더 알아보기 | 부정부사 도치

> 부정부사 'not, never, no, little' 등이 문두에 위치하면 이어지는 문장은 의문문 어순이 된다.
> • She was not only sad but she was depressed.
>   그녀는 슬플 뿐만 아니라 우울했다.
>   → Not only was she sad but she was depressed.

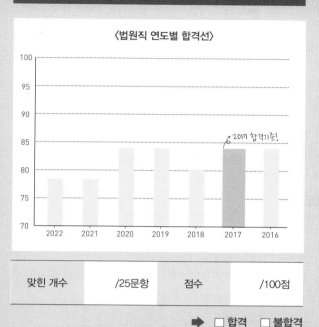

합격예상 체크

〈법원직 연도별 합격선〉

2017 합격기준!

| 2022 | 2021 | 2020 | 2019 | 2018 | 2017 | 2016 |

| 맞힌 개수 | /25문항 | 점수 | /100점 |

➡ □ 합격 □ 불합격

취약영역 체크

문항	정답	영역	문항	정답	영역
1	④	독해 > Logical Reading > 문맥상 다양한 추론	14	④	독해 > Logical Reading > 연결사
2	①	독해 > Reading for Writing > 빈칸 절 완성	15	②	독해 > Logical Reading > 문맥상 다양한 추론
3	③	독해 > Logical Reading > 문맥상 다양한 추론	16	③	독해 > Macro Reading > 제목
4	③	독해 > Logical Reading > 삽입	17	②	독해 > Logical Reading > 삽입
5	③	문법 > 동사, 관계사	18	②	독해 > Macro Reading > 제목
6	③	독해 > Reading for writing > 빈칸 절 완성	19	②	독해 > Logical Reading > 문맥상 다양한 추론
7	①	독해 > Reading for Writing > 빈칸 절 완성	20	③	어휘 > 빈칸 완성
8	①	독해 > Reading for Writing > 요약	21	④	독해 > Micro Reading > 내용 일치/불일치
9	②	문법 > 관계사	22	④	독해 > Macro Reading > 주제
10	③	독해 > Logical Reading > 문맥상 다양한 추론	23	③	독해 > Logical Reading > 삽입
11	②	독해 > Logical Reading > 삭제	24	③	문법 > 조동사
12	③	독해 > Logical Reading > 삭제	25	③	독해 > Reading for Writing > 빈칸 구 완성
13	④	독해 > Logical Reading > 연결사			

⬇ 영역별 틀린 개수로 취약영역을 확인하세요!

| 어휘 | /1 | 문법 | /3 | 독해 | /21 | 생활영어 | /0 |

➡ 나의 취약영역: _____

※ [정답해설]과 [오답해설] 선지의 50% 표시는 〈1초 합격예측 서비스〉를 통해 수집된 선지 선택률을 나타냅니다.

---

1 독해 > Logical Reading > 문맥상 다양한 추론
오답률 35% 답 ④

| 해석 | 모든 생물들은 기본적인 특성을 공유한다. 이러한 공통된 특징들은 공통 조상에서 내려온 후손으로 설명할 수 있다. 많은 종류의 증거들이 단일 세포로부터 생명이 시작되었다는 것과 현재 가지각색 유기체들이 이러한 공통 기원으로부터 수억 년 동안 진화되었다는 것을 암시한다. 바꾸어 말하면, 진화의 과정이 생물에서 우리가 관찰하는 단일성을 설명한다. 지구 상의 생명체에 대한 또 다른 놀라운 점은 그것의 다양성이다. 같은 산호초에는 다수의 동물 종들이 포함되어 있다. 그러나 각각의 신체 유형은 특정한 삶의 방식에 적합하다. 유전 물질의 변화와 다양한 환경에 적합한 물리적 변형을 포함하는 진화의 과정은 우리가 생물에서 보게 되는 ④ 단일성(→ 다양성)을 설명한다.

| 정답해설 | ④ 65% 이 글은 생물의 단일성과 생물의 다양성을 설명하고 있다. 후반부에는 다양성을 설명하고 있으므로 unity를 diversity로 변경하는 것이 적절하다.

어휘

thread (어떤 사물의 전체적) 특징, 요소
descent 후손
hundreds of millions 수억
rainbow 가지각색, 무지개
suit 적합하다

---

2 독해 > Reading for Writing > 빈칸 절 완성
오답률 30% 답 ①

| 해석 | 생물학 교사는 유기 화학의 기초를 이해하지 못하고 단백질, 탄수화물, 지방, 비타민을 가르칠 수 없다. 교사는 온도계 사용법을 가르치면서 온도 측정의 다양한 척도에 대해 토론할 수 있다. 만약 그나 그녀가 건강한 사람의 체온이 37℃라고 말하고 학생은 켈빈 또는 화씨로 온도를 알고 싶다고 말하면, 교사는 하나의 온도 측정 척도에서 다른 온도 측정 척도로 전환하는 법을 알고 있는 경우에만 학생을 만족시킬 수 있다. 마찬가지로, 단백질, 효소, 탄수화물, 지방 등을 가르치는 화학 선생님은 주제를 학습자의 삶의 경험과 관련시킴으로써 효과적으로 이러한 개념을 설명하기 위해서, 인간의 소화 시스템에 대해 어느 정도 이해해야 한다. 따라서 과학의 모든 분야는 ① 고립된 상태에서 가르쳐질 수 없고 배울 수 없다.

① 고립된 상태에서 가르쳐질 수 없고 배울 수 없다
② 유기 화학 지식으로 모여든다
③ 각 학습자의 경험과 상호 관련이 있다
④ 화학의 기초로 습득해야 한다

| 정답해설 | ① 70% 생물학 교사, 화학 교사 등 과학 분야의 교사들이 그 과목에 대한 지식만 가지고 학생들을 만족시킬 수 없다고 주장하고 있다. 예를 들어 단백질, 효소, 탄수화물, 지방 등을 가르칠 때, 이들이 실제 학습자의 삶과 경험과 관련시켜 소화 과정에서 어떻게 처리되는지에 대해 설명할 수 있어야 한다는 것이다. 따라서 과학의 모든 분야는 고립되지 않았으며 연관이 있음을 유추할 수 있다.

| 3 | 독해 > Logical Reading > 문맥상 다양한 추론 | 오답률 18% | 답 ③ |

| 해석 | 혼자 남겨진 Dodge는 불에 탄 토양에 빠르게 누웠다. 불길이 다가오자, 그는 연기를 들이마시지 않기 위해 젖은 손수건으로 입을 막았다. 불길이 그를 둘러싸고 있을 때, Dodge는 눈을 감고 지면 근처에 남아 있는 ③ 두꺼운(→ 얇은) 산소층에서 숨을 들이쉬려고 했다. 고통스러운 몇 분이 지났고, Dodge는 화재에서 살아남았고 무사했다. 슬프게도, 바위에 있는 작은 균열에 있는 쉼터를 발견한 두 사람을 제외하고, 다른 모든 사람들은 끔찍한 화재로 사망했다.

| 정답해설 | ③ 82% 불길에 휩싸인 상황에서는 산소층이 '두꺼운' 층으로 있는 것이 아니라 '얇은' 층으로 존재할 것이다. 따라서 글의 흐름상 thick를 thin으로 수정하는 것이 적절하다.

| 4 | 독해 > Logical Reading > 삽입 | 오답률 44% | 답 ③ |

| 해석 | 인간의 빛이 자연계로 흘러 들어갈 때마다, 생명 번식, 먹이기, 이주와 같은 삶의 일부 면이 영향을 받는다. 일부 조류 그중에서도 중 블랙 버드(blackbirds)와 나이팅게일(nightingales)은 인공 조명이 있는 곳에서 부자연스러운 시간에 노래한다. 과학자들은 긴 인공 낮과 인위적으로 짧은 밤이 광범위한 새들의 이른 번식을 유도한다고 결정했다. 그리고 긴 낮은 더 긴 먹이 주기를 허용하기 때문에, 이동(이주) 일정에도 영향을 줄 수 있다. ③ 영국에서 겨울을 보내고 있는 한 무리의 Berwick의 백조들이 평소보다 더 빨리 살이 쪘으며, 이것이 시베리아 이주를 일찍 시작할 준비를 하게 만들었다. 그들이 가진 그 이동(이주)과 관련된 문제는, 조류 행동의 다른 측면과 마찬가지로, 이주가 정확하게 시기적절한 생물학적 행동이라는 것이다. 일찍 이동하는 것은 둥지를 틀 조건으로는 너무 일러서 적절하지 않을 수도 있다는 의미이다.

| 정답해설 | ③ 56% 이전에 인공 조명으로 낮이 길어져 먹이 주기 시간이 길어졌으므로 주어진 문장의 'Berwick의 백조들이 평소보다 더 빨리 살이 쪘다'는 예시가 뒤로 수반되는 것이 가능하다. 또한 ③ 뒤에서 주어진 문장의 begin their Siberian migration early를 that migration(그 이주)으로 되받고 있으며, Berwick's swans를 them으로 되받고 있다. 따라서 주어진 문장은 ③에 오는 것이 가장 적절하다.

| 5 | 문법 > 동사, 관계사 | 오답률 31% | 답 ③ |

| 해석 | 일단 우리가 어린 시절에서 벗어나면, 실제로 눈을 마주치는 것은 속임수에 대한 믿을 수 없는 단서가 된다. 왜일까? 대답은 눈 맞춤이 제어하기 굉장히 쉽다는 것이다. 땀투성이의 손이나 입 안에 건조한 느낌과 같

이 긴장을 느낄 때 우리에게 일어나는 일의 대부분은 통제할 수 없다. 그러나, 우리 중 대부분은 우리가 보고 있는 것에 대해 많은 통제권을 가지고 있다. 그러므로, 많은 성인들이 거짓말을 하는 동안 다른 사람들을 눈으로 바라보는 데 거의 문제가 없다. 게다가, 숙련된 의사소통자는 사람들이 눈 맞춤의 부족을 속임수와 동일시한다는 것을 알고 있기 때문에, 상대방이 의심을 갖지 않도록, 거짓말을 할 때 의도적으로 보통의 눈 맞춤을 유지한다. 속담에서 말하듯, 눈은 영혼의 창문이 될 수 있지만, 눈 맞춤은 정직의 창문은 아니다!

| 정답해설 | ③ 69% (A) 주어는 Much of what happens to us이며, 문장에 동사가 없기 때문에 being이 아니라 is가 오는 것이 적절하다.

(B) 절과 절을 이어주는 관계대명사를 선택하여야 하는데, 선행사가 존재하지 않으므로 선행사를 포함하는 관계대명사인 what이 필요하다.

(C) know의 목적절인 that절에서 주어 people에 대한 동사가 없으므로 동사 형태인 equate가 오는 것이 적절하다.

| 6 | 독해 > Reading for Writing > 빈칸 절 완성 | 오답률 21% | 답 ③ |

| 해석 | 분쟁 해결을 위한 조언

(A)
논쟁에서 "이기는" 것이 아니라 관계를 유지하고 강화하는 것이 항상 최우선적이어야 한다. 상대방과 그 또는 그녀의 관점을 존중하라.

(B)
오래된 상처와 분노를 붙잡고 있다면, 현재 상황을 알 수 있는 능력이 약해질 것이다. 과거를 보고 (남의) 탓으로 돌리는 대신, 문제를 해결하기 위해 지금 할 수 있는 일에 집중하라.

(C)
갈등은 에너지와 시간을 소모하는 일일 수 있으므로, 문제가 당신의 시간과 에너지를 쓰기에 정말로 합당한지 여부를 고려하는 것이 중요하다. 만약 여러분이 (주차장을) 15분 동안 돌고 있다면 주차 공간을 양보하고 싶지 않을 수도 있다. 그러나 수십 개의 장소가 있다면, 하나의 공간에 대해 다투는 것은 가치가 없다.

(D)
합의에 도달할 수 없다면, 의견이 다르다는 것에 동의하라. 논쟁을 계속하려면 두 사람이 필요하다. 갈등이 해결되지 않는다면, 당신은 (그 일은) 잊고 다른 일을 하도록 선택할 수 있다.

① (A) 관계를 최우선으로 생각하라.
② (B) 현재에 집중하라.
③ (C) 말하기 전에 당신의 말을 따져 보라.
④ (D) 언제 포기해야 하는지를 알아라.

| 정답해설 | ③ 79% (C)는 논쟁하기 전에 가치가 있는 일인지 생각하라는 내용이므로 '말하기 전에 당신의 말을 따져 보라.'는 (C)의 내용과 전혀 어울리지 않는다.

7 독해 > Reading for Writing > 빈칸 절 완성 | 오답률 32% | 답 ①

| 해석 | "부족"이라는 단어는, 우리 대부분이 상품의 공급이 부족하다는 것을 의미한다. 즉, 주변을 둘러볼 물건이 충분하지 않다는 것이다. "충분한 것"을 구성하는 것에 대한 명확한 이해가 없는 경우도 있지만, 사실은 지구상의 모든 사람들을 지탱할 수 있는 충분한 음식 이상이 있다는 것은 단순한 사실이다. 육지와 재생 에너지에 대해서도 마찬가지이다. 따라서 중요한 질문은 왜 삶의 필수 요소가 너무 불균등하게 분배되느냐는 것이다. 예를 들어, 세계 인구의 5%를 약간 넘는 미국이 전 세계 자원의 약 40%를 사용하는 이유는 무엇인가? 부족의 문제로 보이는 것은, 정밀히 따지고 보면, 배포의 문제이다. 그러나 주류 경제학자들은 ① 이 문제에서 눈을 돌리고 있다. 그들은 주어진 시스템이 생산적인지 능률적인지에 대해서만 이야기하며, "누구를 위한 것인가?"라는 질문은 우리에게 달려 있다.

① 이 문제에서 눈을 돌리고 있다
② 불평등 감소에 관심을 두고 있다
③ 분배 문제 해결에 집착하고 있다
④ 효율성 향상에 관심이 없다

| 정답해설 | ① 68% 빈칸 뒤에서 they는 mainstream economists (주류 경제학자들)를 가리키는데 그들은 주어진 시스템이 생산적인지 능률적인지에 대해서만 이야기하며 "누구를 위한 것인가"는 우리에게 달려 있는 문제라고 하였다. 따라서 경제학자들은 이 문제[배포의 문제]를 회피하고 있는 것으로 볼 수 있다.

어휘

scarcity 부족, 결핍	clear-cut 명백한, 뚜렷한
constitute 구성하다, 조성하다	renewable 재생 가능한
staple 주요한	avert to ~에 눈을 돌리다
cling to ~을 고수하다	

8 독해 > Reading for Writing > 요약 | 오답률 33% | 답 ①

| 해석 | 사람들이 일상적인 활동에 충분한 주의를 기울이지 않으면 때로는 부상을 입는다. 그러한 부상은 순수한 부주의 또는 불행으로 인해 발생하지만, 다른 부상들은 사람들이 자신을 너무 조심스럽다고 인식하는 것을 원하지 않기 때문에 발생한다. 예를 들어, 지나친 조심성이라는 인상을 준다는 이유로, 많은 사람들이 자동차의 안전벨트, 자전거 및 오토바이의 헬멧, 보트의 구명 기구 착용을 피하는 것 같다. 게다가, 많은 사람들은 전동 공구 또는 위험한 기계를 작동할 때 긴장하거나 매우 조심스럽게 보일 수 있으므로 보호 장비(예: 안전 고글, 장갑 및 헬멧)를 착용하는 것을 꺼린다. 이러한 우려는 어린 나이에 나타난다. 일화로, 6~7세의 어린아이들은 다른 아이들이 그들에 대해 생각할 것 때문에, 롤러스케이트를 탈 때, 무릎 보호대와 안전모를 착용하지 않을 수도 있다.

⬇

왜 사람들이 부상을 입을까?
1. 사람들은 (A) 조심성이 부족하다.
2. 사람들은 (B) 지나치게 조심스럽게 보이는 것보다 위험을 감수하는 경향이 있다.

	(A)	(B)
①	경계, 조심	지나치게 조심하는
②	부주의	겁을 내는
③	신중	대담한
④	부주의함	취약한

| 정답해설 | ① 67% 사람들이 부상을 입는 이유를 본문에서 찾으면 된다. 부상은 첫째 철저히 부주의하기 때문에, 둘째 지나치게 조심스러운 인상을 주기 싫기 때문에 입는다고 했다.

어휘

misfortune 불운, 불행	life preserver 구명 기구
reluctant 꺼리는, 주저하는	anecdotally 일화(逸話)로

오답률 TOP 1

9 문법 > 관계사 | 오답률 61% | 답 ②

| 해석 | 암기하여 연주하는 것은 종종 음악성과 음악적 소통을 향상시키는 효과가 있는 것으로 보인다. 암기의 바로 그 행위가 음악에 대한 보다 철저한 지식과 친밀한 관계를 보장할 수 있다고 일반적으로 주장된다. 게다가, 암기는 관객과의 직접적인 시선 접촉을 가능하게 하는데, 그것은 악보를 참고하는 것보다 설득력이 있다. 이런 방식으로 음악을 "소유하는" 사람들은 종종 그들이 자연스럽고 진실하게 의사소통을 한다는 인상을 전달한다. 그리고 실제로 현대의 증거는 이 목표를 달성한 음악가가 청중에게 반응을 더 잘 받았다는 것을 시사한다. 또한, 공연자가 청중의 시각적 피드백을 받고 그것에 반응할 때, 공연은 당사자 일동 사이에서 진정한 의사소통을 포함하여, 진정으로 상호 작용을 하게 된다.

| 정답해설 | ② 39% 문장의 선행사가 바로 앞에 있는 an audience 가 아니라 direct eye contact이므로 관계대명사를 which로 고쳐야 한다.

| 오답해설 | ① 14% 앞에 있는 불완전타동사 see가 수동태로 쓰이면서, 목적격 보어로 사용되었던 원형부정사 have를 to부정사로 고쳐 사용한 옳은 표현이다.
③ 18% 해당 동사의 주어는 복수 명사 musicians이므로 복수 동사 are를 사용한 것은 옳다.
④ 29% 분사구문으로 쓰였으며 뒤에 목적어 genuine communication 이 따라오고 해석상 '~을 포함하여'가 적절하므로 현재분사 involving을 사용한 것은 옳다.

어휘

musicality 음악성	intimate 친밀한
memorization 기억, 암기	convey 전달하다, 전하다

10 독해 > Logical Reading > 문맥상 다양한 추론 | 오답률 34% | 답 ③

| 해석 | 사람들이 사회적 지위와 부유함 둘 다를 추구하긴 해도, 그들의 주요 목적은 사회적 지위를 얻는 것이다. 특히, 풍요의 추구가 도구가 될 수 있는 경우가 있다. 즉, 풍요 자체를 위해서가 아니라 증가된 풍요로움이 사회적 지위를 향상시킬 것이기 때문에 그것을 추구한다. 결국, 왜 그들은 옷, 차, 그리고 그들이 원하는 집을 원할까? 대부분이, 이러한 것들을 성취하면 다른 사람들에게 깊은 인상을 줄 수 있기 때문이다. 실제로, 주변에 인상을 줄 사람이 없다면, 사치스러운 것을 위해 일할 필요가 없이, 사치스러움을 얻을 수 있다 할지라도, ③ 검소한(→ 사치스러운 또는 풍요로운) 삶을 살아가도록 몰리는 느낌이 드는 이는 거의 없을 것이다. 마찬가지로 부유한 사람들이 사치스럽게 사는 사람들을 존경하기보다 경멸하는 문화에 살고 있는 자신들을 발견하면, 진입로에 오래된 차가 주차되어 있는 평범한 집을 좋아해서 저택과 최신 모델의 자동차를 버릴 것이라고 누구라도 상상할 것이다.

| 정답해설 | ③ 66% 실제로 인상을 줄 사람이 없다면, 사치스러운(풍요로운) 삶을 살도록 몰리는 느낌이 들지 않을 것이라는 이야기를 하고 있다. 따라서, '검소'가 아니라, '사치스러움' 또는 '풍요'로 단어를 변경하여야 한다. 따라서 frugality를 luxury 또는 affluence 정도로 고치는 것이 적절하다.

- 검소한: frugal, thrifty, prudent
- 사치스러운: luxurious, extravagant, lavish

어휘

affluence 풍족, 부, 부유   frugality 검소, 검약
despise 경멸하다, 멸시하다   driveway 진입로, 도로

---

11   독해 > Logical Reading > 삭제   오답률 46%   답 ②

| 해석 | 일반적으로 영장류는 약 8천만 년 전에 지구상에 처음으로 출현한 것으로 알려져 있다. 파충류와 달리, 그들은 매우 사교적인 동물이었고, 커다란 공동체 사회를 만들었다. 영장류가 사회적 지원의 네트워크를 구축한 여러 가지 방법 중 하나는 몸단장을 하는 것이었다. ② 대부분의 경우, 영장류는 그 부위를 가볍게 몸단장했더라면 없어질 수 있었던 눈에 띄는 주름이 있다. 예를 들어, 유인원들은 서로 몸단장해 주는 데 많은 시간을 보냈다. 흥미롭게도, 바바리 원숭이(Barbary macaque)의 경우, 몸단장의 제공은 몸단장을 받는 것보다 더 많은 스트레스 감소라는 결과를 가져왔다.

| 정답해설 | ② 54% 영장류의 네트워크 중 하나가 '몸단장'이었고, 바바리 원숭이의 경우 몸단장을 제공하는 것이 몸단장을 받는 것보다 스트레스 감소 효과를 가져온다는 내용이다. ②는 '몸단장하다(groom)'의 단어가 문장에 속해 있기는 하지만, '주름'과 관련된 외적 이야기만을 하고 있으므로, 본문 전체에서 언급하는 '사회적 지원 수단'으로서의 몸단장과 거리가 멀다.

어휘

primate 영장류   approximately 대략, 약
groom 손질하다, 다듬다   ape 유인원

---

12   독해 > Logical Reading > 삭제   오답률 24%   답 ③

| 해석 | 대부분의 사람들은 플라톤(Plato)이 꽤 훌륭한 교사라는 데 동의한다. 그는 사람들에게 생각하는 법을 가르치기 위해 자주 이야기를 사용했다. 플라톤이 민주주의의 한계에 대해 가르치기 위해 사용한 한 이야기는 바다 한가운데 있는 배에 관한 이야기였다. 이 배에는 다소 근시안적이고(선견지명이 없고) 약간 귀가 먹은 선장이 타고 있었다. 그와 그의 선원들은 항해 방향에 관한 결정에 다수결의 원칙을 따랐다. 그들은 항해 중에 별을 읽는 법을 알고 있는 매우 숙련된 항해사가 있었지만, 그 항해사는 인기가 없었고, 다소 내성적이었다. ③ 알다시피, 특히 배에서, 내향적인 사람들과 의사소통하는 것은 쉽지 않다. 길을 잃을까 봐 공포를 느끼는 선장과 선원들은 선원들 중에서 가장 카리스마가 있고 설득력 있는 사람을 따르기로 투표로 결정을 했다. 그들은 항해사의 제안을 무시하고 조롱했고, 길을 잃은 채 결국은 바다에서 굶어 죽었다.

| 정답해설 | ③ 76% 플라톤(Plato)이 민주주의의 한계를 설명하기 위해 바다에서 굶어 죽은 선장과 선원들의 이야기를 하였다. 선장과 선원들이 일방적으로 다수결의 원칙 및 투표로 생존에 중요한 정보를 가진 숙련된 항해사의 말을 무시한 것이지, 그 항해사가 내성적인 것이 소통에 문제가 되어서 결국 다 같이 바다에서 굶어 죽었다는 내용은 아니므로 ③은 글의 흐름상 무관하다.

고대 그리스의 대표 철학자이자 수학자이다. 소크라테스의 제자이자 아리스토텔레스의 스승으로도 알려져 있다. 마음의 눈으로 보는 사물의 순수하고 완전한 형태를 가리키는 '이데아'라는 개념을 구체적으로 정의했고, 우주는 물, 불, 공기, 흙 네 가지로 이루어져 있다고 주장했다.

어휘

shortsighted 근시(안)의   deaf 귀가 먹은, 청각 장애가 있는
introverted 내성적인   starve to death 굶어 죽다

---

13   독해 > Logical Reading > 연결사   오답률 21%   답 ④

| 해석 | 돈을 만들어 내기 전에, 사람들은 그들이 필요로 하는 것을 가지고 있는 것과 교환하곤 했다. 이러한 교환 시스템을 물물 교환이라고 한다. 사람들은 동물의 털, 조개껍질, 목걸이용 구슬, 옷감 등을 거래했다. 나중에, 사람들은 일부 상품이 다른 상품보다 쉽게 거래된다는 사실을 깨달았고 이러한 항목은 물물 교환에서 보다 보편화되었다. (A) 예를 들어, 사람들은 대부분의 사람들이 금이 가치가 있고 필요하다면 다시 교환할 수도 있다는 것을 알고 있었기 때문에 거의 모든 상품에 대해 금을 교환할 수 있었다. 얼마 후, 특정 상품이 교환의 표준 상품이 되었고, 모두가 동일한 상품으로 거래하기 시작했다. 결국, 그 표준 상품은 대부분의 사람들이 사업에서 그리고 일상생활에서 받아들여 사용하는 무역의 하나의 공통된 단위인 돈이 되었다. (B) 그럼에도 불구하고, 오늘날 일부 사람들은 여전히 물물 교환 제도를 사용하고 있다. 특히, 개발도상국에서 사람들은 생존을 위해 다양한 종류의 음식을 교환한다.

	(A)	(B)
①	게다가	예를 들어
②	다시 말해서	뿐만 아니라
③	그에 반해서	그러나
④	예를 들어	그럼에도 불구하고

| 정답해설 | ④ 79% (A) 빈칸 앞에서 언급한 '다른 상품보다 쉽게 거래되는 일부 상품'에 대한 예시로 '금'을 설명하고 있으므로 예시의 연결사 For example이 가장 적절하다.
(B) 무역의 하나의 공통 단위인 '돈'이 생겨난 이후에도 개발도상국에서는 물물 교환이 이루어지고 있는 것으로 보아, 양보의 연결사 Nevertheless가 가장 적절하다.

어휘

fur 모피, 털   bead 구슬, 염주, 묵주
barter 물물 교환하다

---

14   독해 > Logical Reading > 연결사   오답률 32%   답 ④

| 해석 | 많은 사람들이 신체 장애가 있는 사람을 이해하기가 어렵다고 생각하는데, 흔히 장애가 있는 사람과 개인적으로 상호 교류가 없었기 때문이다. (A) 예를 들어, 휠체어 사용자와 함께 한 번도 시간을 보내 본 적이 없기 때문에, 이동에 장애가 있고 휠체어를 사용하는 사람에게 무엇을 기대할지 잘 모를 수 있다. 이러한 이해 부족은 장애가 있는 사람들에게 추가적인 어려움을 초래할 수 있다. 만약 사회가 장애가 있는 사람들에게 보다 적절하게 대응한다면, 많은 도전과 한계를 거의 경험하지 않을 것이다. 휠체어를 사용하게 된 직장인을 생각해 보자. 단 한 개의 층만이 있거나 층 사이에 경사로 또는 승강기가 있는 경우, 그들은 직장에서 전혀 아무런 도움이 필요하지 않을 수 있다. (B) 즉, 개조된 작업 환경에서는 장애를 가지지 않는 것이다.

	(A)	(B)
①	그러나	그리하여
②	그에 반해서	마찬가지로, 유사하게
③	뿐만 아니라	게다가
④	예를 들어	즉, 다시 말해서

| **정답해설** | ④ 68% (A) 앞서 말한 '신체 장애가 있는 사람과의 관계를 어렵게 생각하는 이유'에 대해서 휠체어 사용자와의 관계로 예를 들고 있기 때문에, 예시의 연결사 For example이 적절하다.

(B) 앞서 말한, '휠체어를 사용하는 직장인이 경사로나 승강기가 있다면 도움을 필요로 하지 않을 수 있고, 따라서 이러한 작업 환경에서는 장애를 갖지 않는다고 부연 설명하고 있으므로, 환언의 연결사 In other words(즉, 다시 말해서)가 적절하다.

어휘

disability 장애 impairment 장애
adapted 개조된

| **15** | 독해 > Logical Reading > 문맥상 다양한 추론 | 오답률 16% | 답 ② |

| **해석** | 나를 화나게 하기 위해 Charles가 정확히 무엇을 했는지 확실히 지적하지 못했음에도 불구하고, 나는 항상 Charles에게 화가 났다. Charles는 그저 나를 불쾌하게 만드는 사람들 중 하나였다. 그러나, 나는 끊임없이 화가 났다. 우리가 이 수업에서 분노를 보기 시작했을 때, 나는 생각했다. "Charles에 대한 나의 주된 느낌은 무엇일까?" 나는 내가 실제로 느끼는 것보다 훨씬 불안정한 것처럼 보이게 하기 때문에 내가 발견한 것을 인정하는 것이 거의 싫었지만, 그러나 나의 주된 느낌은 두려움이었다. 나는 재기와 독설을 겸비한 Charles가 나를 다른 학생들 앞에서 바보처럼 보이게 할까 봐 걱정했다. 지난주에 나는 그에게 수업이 끝나고 남아주기를 부탁했고 나는 그에게 그가 사소한 부분에서 나를 꼼짝 못하게 했을 때 내가 얼마나 위협을 느꼈는지에 대해서 말해 주었다. 그는 다소 어안이 벙벙해 했고, 그는 나를 안 좋게 보이게 하려던 의도가 아니었으며, 그는 정말로 나에게 아첨 점수를 따려 했다고 말해 주었다. 우리는 그것에 대해 웃고 넘겼으며, 나는 그에게 더 이상 위협을 느끼지 않는다. 그가 잊어버리고 나를 꼼짝 못하게 할 때, 나는 그저 웃으면서, "어이, 너를 위한 또 다른 아첨 점수야."라고 말한다.

① 안도하는 → 화나는
② 불안한 → 안도하는
③ 침착한 → 부러워하는
④ 겁먹은 → 무관심한

| **정답해설** | ② 84% Charles의 의도를 오해했을 때 나는 심정이 불안하고(uneasy) 불쾌했지만, 오해를 풀고 나서는 웃고 넘길 정도로 안정되었다(relieved).

어휘

put one's finger on ~을 확실히 지적하다
rub 짜증나게 하다, 문지르다 insecure 위험한, 불안한
brilliance 재기, 광휘, 광명 sharp tongue 독설
pin somebody down ~을 꼼짝 못하게 하다

| **16** | 독해 > Macro Reading > 제목 | 오답률 41% | 답 ③ |

| **해석** | 자연환경의 혼돈과 혼란 속에서, 포식자들은 다른 모든 것을 무시하면서, 명백한 징후를 찾는 데 집중한다. 이것에는 큰 이점이 있다. 당신이 전문적으로 특정 세부 사항을 검색할 때, 심지어 아리송한 색의 먹이라도 명백하게 보일 수 있다. 그러나 다른 대안을 보지 못하게 한다는 점에서 너무 주의를 기울이면 대가가 따른다. 새가 작은 나뭇가지처럼 보이는 유충을

열심히 찾다 보면, 나무껍질처럼 보이는 근처의 나방을 놓친다. 천연색을 숨기는 이점은 생존의 확실한 보장을 제공하는 것이 아니라, 계속되는 위협적인 만남을 통해 계속 살아갈 기회에 작은 이점을 지속적으로 제공한다는 것이다. 최소한으로, 포식자의 접근과 후속 공격 사이의 작은 지연조차도 먹이가 도망가는 것을 도울 수 있다. 그리고 기껏해야, 먹이가 완전히 (포식자에게 보이지 않고) 지나쳐지는 것이다.

① 변장을 한 포식자
② 집중의 아름다움
③ 위장: 약간의 유리함
④ 전문화된 탐색의 장점

| **정답해설** | ③ 59% 먹이가 '위장'을 하는 것은 최소한 포식자의 접근과 후속 공격 사이에 지연을 가능하게 해 주는 정도이며, 확실한 생존 보장을 하는 것이 아니라고 했으므로, 이 글의 제목으로 가장 적절한 것은 ③ '위장: 약간의 유리함'이다.

어휘

amid ~ 중에 predator 포식자, 포식동물
telltale 숨길 수 없는 caterpillar 애벌레
moth 나방 bark 나무껍질

오답률 TOP 3

| **17** | 독해 > Logical Reading > 삽입 | 오답률 58% | 답 ② |

| **해석** | 애매모호한 용어는 하나 이상의 의미를 지니며 문맥에 의도된 의미가 명확하게 표시되어 있지 않은 용어이다. 예를 들어, 산길 갈림길에 게시된 "Bear to the Right"라는 표시판이 두 가지 방법으로 이해될 수 있다. 더 그럴 듯한 의미는 등산객에게 왼쪽이 아니라 오른쪽 산길을 선택하라고 지시한다는 것이다. ② 그러나, 표식을 칠한 삼림 관리원은 정반대로 말하려 했다고 해 보자. 그는 그 지역을 지나다니는 곰이 있기 때문에, 등산객들에게 오른쪽 산길을 선택하는 것을 경고하려고 했을 것이다. 그러므로, 삼림 관리원의 언어는 부주의하고 심각한 결과를 초래할 수 있는 잘못된 해석에 노출되어 있다. 모호성을 피할 수 있는 유일한 방법은 가능한 한 명확하게 설명하는 것이다. "계속 왼쪽으로 가시오. 오른쪽으로 나 있는 산길을 이용하지 마시오. 그 지역에 곰이 있음."

| **정답해설** | ② 42% 뒤에 나온 He가 가리키는 사람이 ② 앞의 문장에는 없다. 주어진 문장의 the ranger(삼림 관리원)를 가리키도록 주어진 문장은 ②에 들어가는 것이 가장 적절하다.

어휘

ranger 삼림 관리원 misinterpretation 오해
ambiguity 애매모호함 explicitly 명시적으로, 솔직하게

| **18** | 독해 > Macro Reading > 제목 | 오답률 58% | 답 ② |

| **해석** | 강 수달은 물갈퀴가 있는 발, 짧은 다리, 그리고 점점 가늘어지는 꼬리를 가지고 있다. 이런 이유로, 강 수달은 물속을 매우 쉽게 움직일 수 있는 유선형 몸체를 가지고 있다. 바다 수달은 대개 육상 생활보다 수중 생활이 훨씬 더 중요하기 때문에 근시안이다. 결과적으로, 수달은 수중 생활만큼 육상 생활에 적합하지 않다.

① 수상 생활과 육상 생활의 차이점은 무엇인가?
② 수달은 수생 동물인가 아니면 육상 동물인가?
③ 바다 수달의 신체적 특성
④ 수달: 완벽한 육상 생활

| **정답해설** | ② 42% 강 수달은 유선형 몸체와 근시안을 특징으로 가지고 있어, 육상 생활보다 수중 생활에 더 적합하다고 말하고 있다. 따라서 이 글의 제목으로 ② '수달은 수생 동물인가 아니면 육상 동물인가?'가 가장 적절하다.

| 19 | 독해 > Logical Reading > 문맥상 다양한 추론 | 오답률 13% | 답 ② |

| 해석 | 검은 후추는 세계에서 가장 널리 사용되는 향신료 중 하나이다. 처음에는, 요리의 기본 재료로 인도에서 재배되었다. 그러나, ① 그것은 고기가 상하지 않도록 하는 데 그것을 사용하는 일부 유럽인들에게 훨씬 더 중요해졌다. 15세기 전까지, 이탈리아의 몇몇 도시들은 검은 후추 무역의 중심지였다. 그러나 중동의 오스만 제국이 16세기에 더욱 강력해지자, ② 그것이 유럽 상인들로 하여금 높은 세금을 지불하게 했다. 이러한 사실은 검은 후추를 매우 비싸게 해서, 오직 부유한 사람들만이 ③ 그것을 살 수 있었다. 유럽의 일부 지역에서는, 검은 후추가 심지어 금처럼 귀중한 것으로 여겨졌다. ④ 그것에 대한 큰 수요는 유럽인들로 하여금 인도로 향하는 새로운 항로를 모색하게 만들었다.

| 정답해설 | ② 87% ①③④는 모두 black pepper(검은 후추)를 가리키지만, ②는 the Ottoman Empire를 가리키고 있다.

어휘

black pepper 후추   spice 양념, 향신료
cultivate 경작하다, 재배하다

| 20 | 어휘 > 빈칸 완성 | 오답률 37% | 답 ③ |

| 해석 | 개별 자원의 문제 외에도, 에너지, 식량 그리고 물 사이의 관계가 증가하고 있다. 결과적으로, 한 영역의 문제가 다른 영역으로 확산되어 (A) 파괴적인 순환이 생길 수 있다. 예를 들어, 우간다는 2004년과 2005년에 식량 공급을 위협하는 장기간의 가뭄을 겪었다. 이 나라는 거대한 빅토리아 호수에서 많은 양의 물을 사용하여 수위가 1미터까지 떨어졌으며 우간다는 호수에서 수력 발전을 줄였다. 전기 가격이 거의 두 배가 되었으므로, 우간다 사람들은 연료로 더 많은 목재를 사용하기 시작했다. 사람들은 숲을 대대적으로 베어 버렸으며, 이것이 토양을 (B) 훼손시켰다. 식량 공급원에 대한 위협으로 시작된 가뭄은 전기 문제가 되었고, 결국에는, 더욱 심각한 식량 문제가 되었다. 이러한 순환은 전체 인구에 대한 정치 불안과 재해로 끝날 수 있다.

| (A)   (B)
① 공격적인, 잔인한   비료를 주다
② 도덕적인, 고결한   악화되다
③   파괴적인   훼손시키다
④   건설적인   약화시키다

| 정답해설 | ③ 63% (A) 이어지는 예를 보면, 우간다 지역에서 가뭄으로 수력 발전을 줄이게 되자, 전기 가격이 두 배가 되었다. 따라서 목재를 연료로 사용하는 사람들이 늘었고 토양이 훼손되어 식량 문제가 발생했다는 것이므로 서로 '파괴적인' 효과를 가져왔음을 알 수 있다.
(B) 숲을 대대적으로 베어낼 결과는 토양의 훼손이다.

어휘

prolong 연장하다, 늘리다   drought 가뭄, 고갈
hydroelectric 수력 전기의   profound 심오한, 깊은, 지대한

| 21 | 독해 > Micro Reading > 내용일치/불일치 | 오답률 18% | 답 ④ |

| 해석 | 이 그래프는 15세에 다양한 수준의 읽기 능력을 갖춘 OECD 국가의 남녀 학생 비율을 비교한 것이다. ① '1b 수준 이하'에서 소녀의 비율은 소년의 비율보다 3배 이상이다. ② '5 수준'에서 소녀의 비율은 소년의 비율보다 2배 이상이다. ③ 남녀 비율의 차이는 '4 수준'에서 가장 작고 '6 수준'에서 가장 크다. ④ 소녀의 비율은 '3 수준 이상'에서 소년보다 항상 높고, 반면에 '2 수준 이하'에서 소년의 비율은 소녀의 비율보다 더 높다.

| 정답해설 | ④ 82% 소녀의 비율은 '3 수준'과 '그 이상 수준'에서 소년보다 항상 높고, 반면에 '2 수준'과 '그 이하 수준'에서 소년의 비율은 소녀의 비율보다 더 높게 나타났으므로 ④가 일치하는 내용이다.

| 오답해설 | ① 4% '1b 수준 이하'에서 소년의 비율은 1.8%, 소녀의 비율은 0.5%로 소년의 비율이 소녀의 비율보다 3배 이상이다.

② 8% '5 수준'에서 소녀의 비율은 8.8%이고 소년의 비율은 4.8%로, 4.8%의 2배 이상은 9.6% 이상이어야 하므로, 소녀의 비율이 소년의 비율의 2배까지는 되지 않는다.

③ 6% 남녀 비율의 차이는 '4 수준'에서 가장 크고(7.9%), '6 수준'에서 가장 작다(0.7%).

어휘

proficiency 숙달, 능숙

| 22 | 독해 > Macro Reading > 주제 | 오답률 20% | 답 ④ |

| 해석 | Béla Bartók의 'Duos for Two Violins'는 불협화음이 특징이다. 이 작품에서 불협화음을 사용함으로써, Bartók은 풍부한 소리의 다양성을 드러내려 한다. 그러나, 불협화음은 상대적인 개념이며, 협화음과 관련하여 이해되어야 할 필요가 있다. 게다가, 이 작품에서 만연하는 불협화음은 무질서를 나타내지 않는다. 오히려, 그것은 개별적인 소리들 사이의 미묘한 조화를 불러일으키려 한다. 이것은 불협화음이 주로 조화로운 개성의 표현으로 인식될 수 있기 때문이다.
① 소리의 다양성을 드러내는 방법
② 바이올린 연주에 있어 협화음의 역할
③ '두 개의 바이올린을 위한 2중주'에서 조화의 중요성
④ Béla Bartók의 작품에서 불협화음의 진정한 의미

| 정답해설 | ④ 80% Béla Bartók의 '두 개의 바이올린을 위한 2중주'는 불협화음이 오히려 무질서하지 않고 미묘한 조화를 이룬다고 말하고 있다. 따라서 글의 주제로 ④ 'Béla Bartók의 작품에서 불협화음의 진정한 의미'가 가장 적절하다.

어휘

characterize 특징을 나타내다   dissonance 불협화음
consonance 협화음   prevalent 널리 퍼진, 만연한
subtle 미묘한, 교묘한   harmonious 조화로운, 어울리는

| 23 | 독해 > Logical Reading > 삽입 | 오답률 42% | 답 ③ |

| 해석 | Charles Schulz가 만든 이 둔한 캐릭터는 만화 비평가도, 'Peanuts'를 사들이는 것을 원하지 않는 월트 디즈니의 사람들의 마음도 끌지 못했다. 그들은 캐릭터들이 사람들에게 꿈을 꾸게 하거나 희망을 갖도록 격려하도록 고무시키지 못했다고 말했다. 심지어 많은 신문에서 인기를 얻은 후에도, 여전히 비평가들은 만화가 재미없는 캐릭터를 가지고 있다고 비판하면서, 신문 연재 만화가 실패할 것이라고 생각했다. 어떤 사람들은 개

스누피를 (만화에서) 빼 버려야 된다고 말했다. ③ 그럼에도 불구하고, Schulz는 그의 작업을 믿었으며 Peanuts를 바꾸지 않았다. 그는 역사상 가장 사랑받는 만화 캐릭터 중 하나인 스누피를 오히려 지켰다.

| 정답해설 | ③ 58% 앞뒤로 스누피를 빼버려야 한다는 말과, Schulz가 스누피를 지켰고 현재까지 사랑받는 캐릭터가 되었다고 하는 상반된 내용이 서술되어 있다. 주어진 문장은 Schulz가 자신의 캐릭터를 믿고 'Peanuts'를 바꾸지 않았다고 했으므로, ③에 들어가 흐름을 유지하는 것이 가장 적절하다.

어휘

dull 둔한, 흐릿한   comic strip 연속 만화

---

24 문법 > 조동사   오답률 43%   답 ③

| 해석 | 대부분의 경우 저널리즘은 아마도 몹시 서둘러 수집된 사건의 순간적인 기록을 제공할 수 있을 것이다. 많은 뉴스 기사는 실제로는 일어난 일에 대한 가설이다. 과학은 물론 가설로 작동하며, 오류가 발견되었을 때에는 이를 버리고, 심지어 오류가 생명을 희생시키더라도 누구의 탓 없이 대체로 그렇게 한다. 과학적 정확성을 주장하지 않는 언론은 그 오류를 쉽게 용서받지 않는다. 틀림없이, 언론은 가끔씩 뉴스에 대한 굶주림의 반응으로, 정보가 충분하지 않은 상태에서 인쇄하려 몰려든다. 유토피아 사회는 언론이 절대 확실성에 도달할 때까지 아무것도 인쇄하지 말 것을 요구할 수 있다. 그러나 그러한 사회는 사건의 최종 형태를 기다리는 동안 루머, 경각, 거짓으로 가득 차서 우리의 저널리즘의 오류가 비교적 진실의 모형처럼 보일 것이다.

| 정답해설 | ③ 57% 요구동사 demand의 목적어로 쓰이는 that절이 당위성을 지니면 that절의 동사는 「should + 동사원형」으로 써야 하는데, 이때 should는 생략할 수 있다. 따라서 동사원형 print만 남은 옳은 표현이다.

| 오답해설 | ① 11% 동사 compile은 타동사로 '수집하다, 편집하다'의 의미를 가진다. compiling 뒤에 목적어가 없고 문맥상 '수집된 사건'으로 events와 compile이 수동 관계에 있으므로 compiling은 수동의 의미를 갖는 과거분사 compiled로 고쳐야 한다.
② 16% 관계대명사 that은 계속적 용법으로 쓸 수 없으므로 that을 which로 바꾸는 것이 적절하다.
④ 16% 관계대명사 which 이하의 절이 완전한 것으로 보아, 관계대명사 자리가 아니라 접속사나 관계부사 자리라는 것을 알 수 있다. 윗줄에 so가 존재하는 것으로 보아 의미상 '너무 ~해서 … 하다'라는 「so ~ that …」 구문임을 알 수 있으므로 which는 that으로 변경하는 것이 적절하다.

| 더 알아보기 | 당위의 조동사 should 생략

「S + 주장/요구/명령/제안 동사 + (that) + S + (should) + 동사원형」
• 주장, 제안: propose, insist, argue, suggest
• 요구, 명령: require, request, ask, demand, order, command
• 조언, 권고: advise, recommend

어휘

fleeting 순식간에   compile 수집하다, 모으다, 편집하다
at bottom 사실은   hypothesis 가설
discard 버리다, 폐기하다   accuracy 정확, 정확도
ultimate 궁극적인, 최종적인, 최후의

---

25 독해 > Reading for Writing > 빈칸 구 완성   오답률 60%   답 ③

| 해석 | 아이들은 종종 원하는 의미를 표현할 수 있는 새로운 방법을 만들어 낸다. 1995년 논문에서, 언어학자 Clark는 24개월 된 아이의 말 "쥐-남자가 온다."라는 말과 25개월 된 아이의 말 "엄마는 방금 이 작살-종이를 고쳤다."와 같은 예들을 인용했다. "쥐-남자"는 심리학 실험실에서 쥐를 연구하는 아버지의 동료였다. "작살-종이"는 그녀의 어머니가 테이프로 붙여 놓은 작살을 들고 있는 밀림 부족의 찢어진 그림이었다. Clark는 또한 28개월 된 아이의 말인 "당신은 검객이며 나는 사수다."라는 말을 인용했다. 이러한 예에서 알 수 있듯이, 아이들의 혁신적인 언어 사용은 ③ 무작위와는 거리가 멀다. 그것들은 새로운 단어를 형성하기 위한 규칙을 반영한다. 예를 들어, 단어를 조합할 때 자신에게 의미가 있고, 의미가 확실한 단어나 다른 구성 요소를 조합하는 것과 같이 새로운 단어를 형성할 때 규칙을 반영한다. 이러한 언어적 창의성은 아이들의 제한된 어휘가 허용하는 그 이상의 의미를 표현할 수 있게 해 준다.

① 즉흥적으로   ② 상당히 임의적인
③ 무작위와 거리가 먼   ④ 끝없는 훈련 결과

| 정답해설 | ③ 40% 빈칸 뒤에서 아이들이 새로운 단어를 형성할 때 규칙을 반영한다고 했으므로, 무작위와는 거리가 멀다는 선지가 본문의 내용과 가장 일치한다.

어휘

spear 창, 작살   tribe 부족, 종족
innovative 획기적인   unambiguous (뜻이) 모호하지 않은
linguistic 언어(학)의

합격예상 체크

〈법원직 연도별 합격선〉

| 맞힌 개수 | /25문항 | 점수 | /100점 |

➡ □ 합격 □ 불합격

취약영역 체크

문항	정답	영역	문항	정답	영역
1	②	독해 > Reading for Writing > 빈칸 구 완성	14	②	독해 > Reading for Writing > 빈칸 구 완성
2	③	독해 > Logical Reading > 배열	15	④	문법 > 일치, 분사, 동사
3	④	문법 > 태	16	④	독해 > Logical Reading > 삽입
4	③	독해 > Logical Reading > 문맥상 다양한 추론	17	②	독해 > Logical Reading > 연결사
5	④	독해 > Logical Reading > 문맥상 다양한 추론	18	④	독해 > Logical Reading > 문맥상 다양한 추론
6	④	독해 > Logical Reading > 문맥상 다양한 추론	19	③	독해 > Logical Reading > 삽입
7	④	독해 > Macro Reading > 제목	20	④	독해 > Logical Reading > 연결사
8	③	독해 > Logical Reading > 삭제	21	①	독해 > Reading for Writing > 빈칸 절 완성
9	④	독해 > Reading for Writing > 빈칸 구 완성	22	①	독해 > Reading for Writing > 빈칸 구 완성
10	③	독해 > Logical Reading > 배열	23	④	독해 > Macro Reading > 목적
11	②	독해 > Logical Reading > 배열	24	③	독해 > Macro Reading > 주장
12	③	독해 > Logical Reading > 배열	25	③	독해 > Logical Reading > 문맥상 다양한 추론
13	②	독해 > Reading for Writing > 요약			

➡ 영역별 틀린 개수로 취약영역을 확인하세요!

| 어휘 | /0 | 문법 | /2 | 독해 | /23 | 생활영어 | /0 |

➡ 나의 취약영역: _____

※ [정답해설]과 [오답해설] 선지의 50% 표시는 〈1초 합격예측 서비스〉를 통해 수집된 선지 선택률을 나타냅니다.

1 독해 > Reading for Writing > 빈칸 구 완성 | 오답률 22% | 답 ②

| 해석 | 인류학자들은 사랑니, 즉 세 번째 어금니가 씹는 힘을 더 많이 필요로 하고 과도한 치아 마모를 발생시킨 우리 조상들의 초기 식단인 나뭇잎, 뿌리, 견과류, 그리고 고기와 같은 거친 음식에 대한 진화론적인 해답이었다고 믿는다. 더 부드러운 음식으로 이루어진 현대의 식사는 포크, 숟가락, 그리고 칼과 같은 현대 기술의 경이와 함께 사랑니의 필요성이 존재하지 않도록 만들었다. 결과적으로, 진화 생물학자들은 이제 사랑니를 흔적 기관, 즉 ② 진화 때문에 기능이 없어진 신체의 일부로 분류한다.
① 충치
② 진화
③ 딱딱함
④ 그것들의 모양

| 정답해설 | ② 78% '사랑니(wisdom teeth)'는 초기 인류가 먹었던 거친 음식들 때문에 생긴 진화론적인 해답이었지만 현대 사회에서는 포크, 숟가락, 칼 등의 도구와 더 부드러운 음식으로 인해 사랑니가 크게 필요하지 않게 되었다는 내용이므로, 빈칸에 적절한 표현은 evolution(진화)이다.

| 오답해설 | ①③④ 8% 11% 3% 사랑니가 현대 사회에 왜 기능이 없는 신체의 일부나 흔적 기관이 되었는지 설명할 수 있는 표현들이 아니므로 빈칸에 적절하지 않다.

어휘

anthropologist 인류학자
molar 어금니
wisdom teeth 사랑니
evolutionary 진화(론)의
coarse 거친
excessive 지나친, 과도한
along with ~와 함께
vestigial 흔적의, 남아 있는
chew 씹다
wear 마모
marvel 경이
decay 부패

2 독해 > Logical Reading > 배열 | 오답률 28% | 답 ③

| 해석 | 오늘날의 기술 주도의 세상에서, 거의 모든 사람들은 그들의 인생의 어떤 시점에서 전자레인지를 사용했거나 어떤 형태로든 접촉을 해 왔다. 우리 과거의 훌륭한 발명품들 중 많은 것들처럼, 전자레인지 뒤에 숨겨진 아이디어는 1946년에 우연히 마주치게 되었다.

(B) Percy Spencer 박사는 당시, Raytheon Corporation에서 엔지니어로 일하던 중이었는데 레이더 관련 연구 프로젝트를 진행하고 있던 어느 날 그가 매우 특이한 것을 발견했다. 전자관으로 알려진 새로운 진공 튜브를 시험하던 동안, 그는 그의 주머니의 초코바가 녹았음을 발견했다.

(C) 호기심이 생겨서, Spencer는 추가적인 실험을 결심했다. 나중에, 팝콘 봉지와 계란에 그 튜브를 향하게 한 후, 각각의 케이스를 관찰한 결과 두 실험에서 비슷한 결과를 얻었다. (팝콘은 터지고 계란이 폭발했다.) 그는 모두 저밀도 마이크로파 에너지가 원인이라고 정확히 결론 내렸다.

(A) 우연한 발견 직후, Raytheon의 엔지니어들은 Spencer의 새로운 아이디어에 대해 작업을 했고, 실용적인 사용을 위해 그것을 발전시키고 개선시켰다.

| 정답해설 | ③ 72% 전자레인지가 어떻게 발명되었는지를 설명하는 글이다. 주어진 글에서 전자레인지에 대한 아이디어가 '우연히'

떠올랐다고 설명하고 있다. 따라서 누가 어떻게 그런 생각을 했는지가 다음에 이어질 내용으로 가장 적절하므로 Dr. Percy Spencer라고 시작하는 (B)가 오는 것이 흐름에 맞다. (C)에서 호기심이 생겨서, Spencer가 추가적인 실험을 결심했다고, (B)와 관련된 추가적인 실험 내용을 설명하고 있으므로 (C)가 (B) 다음에 와야 한다. (A)에서 엔지니어들이 Spencer의 아이디어를 실용적으로 발전시키고 개선했다고 했으므로 (A)가 가장 마지막에 오는 것이 적절하다. 따라서 (B) − (C) − (A) 순서가 알맞다.

어휘

technology-driven 기술 주도의	microwave oven 전자레인지
stumble upon 우연히 만나다	refine 정제하다
magnetron 전자관	melt 녹다
intrigue 호기심을 자극하다	kernel 알맹이
attribute ~의 결과로 보다	low-density 저밀도

---

3 문법 > 태 〔오답률 23%〕 답 ④

| 해석 | "쉽게 이기다" 혹은 "아주 적은 노력이나 노력 없이 이기다"라는 뜻의 "win hands down"이라는 표현은 경마에 그것의 유래가 있다. 근접한, 사진으로 판독이 가능한 경주에서, 기수는 전형적으로 막대나 고삐로 강제로 말의 속도를 유지하거나 올리기 위해 말을 때린다. 경주마가 어느 정도 차이가 나게 리드를 하고 승리가 확실할 때, 기수는 대개 경주마를 때리는 것을 멈추거나 고삐를 느슨하게 만든다. 사실상, 그는 그의 "손을 내려놓는" 것이다. 이 표현은 19세기 중반에 나타났다. 그 세기 말쯤에, 그것은 경마 밖에서도 "전혀 문제가 없다"라는 의미로 사용되는 중이었다.

| 정답해설 | ④ 〔77%〕 appear는 '나타나다, 발생하다'라는 뜻을 가진 목적어가 필요 없는 자동사이다. 따라서 수동태로 사용할 수 없으므로, was appeared를 appeared로 바꾸는 것이 문법상 적절한 표현이다.

| 오답해설 | ① 〔9%〕 To "win hands down" which means to "win easily" or "win with little or no effort"는 관계대명사절이 주어로 쓰인 to부정사구 To "win hands down"를 수식하는 구조이다. to부정사 주어는 단수 취급하므로 소유격 대명사 its는 알맞게 쓰였다.
② 〔5%〕 문장의 동사 strikes를 수식하는 부사 typically(전형적으로)는 문법상 적절하다.
③ 〔9%〕 사역동사 let은 목적격 보어로 원형부정사를 취하므로 go는 문법상 적절하다.

어휘

win hands down 쉽게 이기다	photo-finish 사진 판독이 가능한
jockey 기수	rein 고삐
assured 확실한, 보증된	in effect 사실

---

4 독해 > Logical Reading > 문맥상 다양한 추론 〔오답률 15%〕 답 ③

| 해석 | 많은 면에서, 운동화들 사이의 차이는 미미하다. Twitchell은 그것들을 대체가능한 것, "본질적으로 교환 가능한" 것들이라고 부른다. 그러나 연이은 요령 있는 광고 전략은 작은 Oregon의 스포츠 상점을 전 세계적으로 (A) 우세한 스포츠 거대 기업 Nike로 바꾸어 놓았다. 그들의 부메랑 로고는 실제 이름이 필요 없게, 현재 지구상에서 가장 많이 알아보는 이미지 중

하나이다. 그리고 Nike가 (B) 유명인 홍보를 추구하는 첫 번째 회사가 아니었을지 모르지만, Michael Jordan과의 회사의 관계는 역사상 거의 틀림없이 가장 성공적인 보증이다. 1988년에 Just Do It 모토 발표는 그들의 브랜드를, 겉으로 보기에는 영원히, 스포츠의 영감을 주고 극적인 육체적 능력과 함께 그들의 브랜드를 엮어냈던 회사를 위한 (C) 변화의 순간이었다.

| 정답해설 | ③ 〔85%〕 (A) Oregon의 작은 스포츠 상점이 세계적으로 거대 기업 나이키가 되었다는 의미이므로 dominant(우세한, 지배적인)가 알맞은 표현이다. dormant는 '휴면기의'라는 뜻이다.
(B) 다음에 its relationship with Michael Jordan이라는 표현으로 유명인을 이용한 마케팅에 대한 내용이라는 것을 유추할 수 있다. 따라서 빈칸에는 celebrity(유명인)가 적절하다. celebrator는 '축하자'라는 의미이다.
(C) Just Do It이라는 모토로 브랜드 이미지가 크게 변화하였으므로 빈칸에는 transformative(변화의, 변화를 일으키는)가 적절하다. transparent는 '투명한'이라는 의미이다.

어휘

marginal 미미한	fungible 대체 가능한
interchangeable 교환 가능한	successive 연속적인
savvy 요령 있는	swoosh logo Nike의 부메랑 로고
render 만들다	plug 홍보
arguably 거의 틀림없이	endorsement 보증
release 출시; 발표	weave 짜다
seemingly forever 겉으로 보기에는 영원히	
physicality 육체적 능력; 육체 중심주의	

〔오답률 TOP 3〕

5 독해 > Logical Reading > 문맥상 다양한 추론 〔오답률 43%〕 답 ④

| 해석 | "모든 나무 뒤에는 사악한 인디언이 있을 수 있다."라고 Goodman Brown은 혼잣말을 했다. 그리고 ① 그는 "악마가 내 바로 옆에 있다면 어떡하지!"라고 덧붙여 말하면서 두려워하며 뒤를 흘깃 봤다. 그는 고개를 뒤로 돌린 채, ② 그는 구부러진 길을 지나갔고, 다시 앞을 보면서, 오래된 나무 아래에 심각하고 품위 있는 옷을 입은 남자의 모습을 보았다. 그는 Goodman Brown이 접근할 때 일어났고 ③ 그와 함께 나란히 앞으로 걸었다. "늦었군요. Goodman Brown." 그 남자가 말했다. "내 아내가 잠시 나를 붙잡았습니다."라고 그가 말했다. 완전히 예상치 못하지는 않았지만, ④ 그의 갑작스런 등장에 그는 목소리를 떨면서 대답했다.

| 정답해설 | ④ 〔57%〕 본문 후반부의 "You are late, Goodman Brown," said the man.에서 Goodman Brown 외에 다른 남자가 등장한 것을 알 수 있다. ④의 him은 Goodman Brown이 아닌 Goodman Brown과 만난 상대 남자이다.

어휘

devilish 사악한	glance 흘깃 보다
at one's elbow ~ 바로 옆에	crook 굽이
behold 보다	decent 괜찮은, 품위 있는
attire 의복, 복장	at the foot of ~ 하단부에
onward 앞으로 나아가는	side by side 나란히, 함께
tremor 떨림	

| 오답률 34% | 답 ③ |

| 해석 | 우리의 "에고" 혹은 자아상은 부풀어진 상태로 머물기 위해 외부적인 사랑의 헬륨을 영원히 요구하고, 무시라는 가장 작은 구멍에도 영원히 취약한, 새고 있는 풍선으로 그려질 수 있다. 다른 사람들의 관심에 의해 우리가 고무되고 그들의 무시로 가라앉을 정도의 진지함과 동시에 터무니없는 무언가가 있다. 우리의 기분은 동료가 우리에게 산만하게 인사를 하거나 우리 전화에 답변이 없기 때문에 ③ 즐거워질(→ 우울해질) 수 있다. 그리고 우리는 누군가가 우리의 이름을 기억하거나 우리에게 과일 바구니를 보내기 때문에 인생을 살 만한 가치가 있다고 생각할 수 있다.

| 정답해설 | ③ 66% 동료들이 우리를 무시하는 상황을 설명하고 있으므로 기분이 '즐거워지는' 것이 아니라 '우울해지는' 것이 자연스러우므로 be depressing이 적절하다.

| 오답해설 | ① 12% 풍선으로 자아상을 비유했기 때문에 inflated(부풀어진)는 적절한 표현이다.

② 22% 문장 전후가 반대되는 내용이므로 attentions(관심)의 반의어인 disregard(무시)는 알맞은 표현이다.

④ 0% worthy 다음에 because someone remembers our name or sends us a fruit basket.라는 표현으로 보아 이 인생이 살 만한 '가치가 있다(worthy)'는 것은 알맞은 표현이다.

어휘

self-conception 자아상	leak 새다
inflate 부풀리다	vulnerable 취약한
pinprick 아주 작은 구멍	
sobering 정신이 번쩍 드는, 진지하게 하는	
absurd 터무니없는	distractedly 주의가 산만하게

| 오답률 22% | 답 ④ |

| 해석 | 만약 블랙홀이 아무리 작아도 0이 아닌 온도를 가지고 있다면 가장 기본적으로 안정된 물리 원칙들은 그것이 빛나고 있는 부지깽이처럼 방사능을 방출하도록 요구할 것이다. 그러나 모두가 알고 있듯이, 블랙홀은 검고 아마 어떤 것도 방출하지 않을 것이다. 이것은 1974년에 Hawking이 정말 놀라운 무언가를 발견하기 전까지의 경우였다. 블랙홀이 완전히 검은 것은 아니라고 Hawking은 발표했다. 만약 양자역학을 무시하고 오직 고전적인 일반 상대성 법칙만을 적용한다면, 60여 년 전에 원래 발견된 것처럼, 블랙홀은 틀림없이 어떤 것도, 심지어는 빛도, 그들의 중력을 벗어나도록 허용하지 않는다. 그러나 양자역학의 포함은 이 결론을 심오한 방식으로 변경시키고, Hawking은 블랙홀이 양자역학적으로 방사선을 방출한다는 것을 발견했다.

① 블랙홀 안에서는 무슨 일이 일어나는가?
② 양자 세계의 미스터리
③ 일반 상대성의 탄생
④ 블랙홀은 정말 검은가?

| 정답해설 | ④ 78% 블랙홀은 완전히 검고 중력으로 인해 아무것도 방출하지 않는다고 알려졌던 것이 Hawking의 발견 이후 뒤집혔다는 내용의 글이다. 즉, 과거에 일반 상대성 법칙을 적용하여 생각했던 블랙홀과 Hawking의 발견 이후 양자역학을 적용하여 알게 된 블랙홀의 차이점에 대해 설명하고 있으므로, '블랙홀은 정말 검은가?'가 제목으로 적절하다.

| 더 알아보기 | Black Hole (블랙홀)

우주에서 가장 빠른 빛조차 빠져나가지 못할 정도로 중력이 강한 천체이다. 1915년 아인슈타인이 발표한 '상대성 이론(Theory of relativity)'에서 개념화됐다.

어휘

well-established 확고한, 안정된	emit 방출하다
radiation 방사선	poker 부지깽이
quantum mechanics 양자역학	invoke 적용하다; 호소하다, 의지하다
gravitational grip 중력의 힘	inclusion 포함

| 오답률 12% | 답 ③ |

| 해석 | 전체 신세계에 있어서, Columbus의 도착 이후 1~2세기 동안의 인디언 인구의 감소가 95%에 이른다고 추정된다. 주요 사망 요인은 인디언들이 노출된 적이 없고 그래서 그들이 면역성도 없었고 유전적 내성도 없었던 구세계의 세균들이었다. 천연두, 홍역, 유행성 감기, 그리고 발진티푸스는 사망 요인들 중 1위 자리를 놓고 경쟁했다. 예를 들면, 1837년 대평원에서 가장 정교한 문화를 가졌던 Mandan 인디언 부족은 St.Louis에서 Missouri 강을 올라오던 증기선으로부터 천연두에 걸렸다. ③ Mandan 부족은 무역으로부터 얻는 음식도 일부 있었지만 주로 사냥, 농사, 야생 식물 수집으로 생존했다. 한 Mandan 마을의 인구는 2,000명에서 몇 주 안에 40명 미만으로 급락했다.

| 정답해설 | ③ 88% 본문의 주요 내용이 Columbus의 아메리카 대륙 발견 이후 인디언들의 주된 사망 요인에 대한 것이다. Mandan 부족이 식량을 어떻게 구했는지 설명하는 ③은 인디언의 사망과 관련 없는 내용으로 글의 흐름상 적절하지 않은 문장이다.

어휘

germ 세균	immune 면역
smallpox 천연두	measles 홍역
typhus 발진티푸스	tribe 부족
elaborate 정교한	contract (병에) 걸리다
plummet 급락하다	

| 오답률 14% | 답 ④ |

| 해석 | 세계의 대도시들 중 대다수는 그 순간의 필요에 대한 반응으로 조금씩 무작위로 성장해 왔다; 먼 미래를 위해 계획된 도시는 매우 드물다. 도시의 진화는 뇌의 진화와 같다: 그것은 작은 중심에서 발전하고 천천히 자라고 변화하여, 많은 예전 부분들이 여전히 기능하도록 놔둔다. 진화가 ④ 뇌의 오래된 내부를 제거하고 좀 더 현대적인 제조물인 무언가로 교체하는 방법은 없다. 뇌는 개조 동안에 기능해야 한다. 이것이 우리의 뇌간이 R 영역으로, 그리고 변연계 그리고 마침내 대뇌피질로 둘러싸여 있는 이유이다. 예전 부분들은 너무 많은 기본적인 기능들을 담당하고 있어 그것들이 모두 교체될 수는 없다. 따라서 그것들은 낡고 때로는 비생산적이지만, 우리 진화의 필요한 결과로 쌕쌕거리며 따라왔다.

① 신도시 거리의 배열
② 외계 물질의 침입
③ 자연선택의 장점
④ 뇌의 오래된 내부

| 정답해설 | ④ 86% 도시의 발전 과정을 뇌의 진화 과정에 비유하여 설명하는 글이다. 빈칸 앞뒤로 무언가를 제거하고 새로운 것으로 교체하는 방법은 진화에 없다고 설명하고 있으므로 정답은 '뇌의 오래된 내부'이다.

어휘

remote 먼	brain stem 뇌간
fundamental 기본적인	wheeze 쌕쌕거리다
out-of-date 낡은	counterproductive 비생산적인
arrangement 배열	invasion 침입
alien substance 외계 물질	

---

10 독해 > Logical Reading > 배열   오답률 25%   답 ③

| 해석 | 단어의 "명시적 의미"는 그 단어가 글자 그대로 의미하는 것이다. 예를 들면, 파랑은 "맑은 날의 하늘색"을 의미한다.

(C) 그러나 단어의 명시적 의미를 넘어서, 우리는 또한 색의 이름에서 많은 다른 의미들을 발견할 수 있다. 우리는 보통 우울함(blue)을 느끼고 싶어 하지 않지만, 우리는 훌륭한 블루스(blues) 가수를 듣는 것을 즐길 수 있다.

(A) 마찬가지로, 우리는 "충실한(true blue)" 친구를 가지고 싶어 하고, "최고상(blue ribbon)"을 얻고 싶어 하며, "블루칩 주식(blue-chip stocks)"을 가지고 싶어 한다. 그러나 우리는 "도덕군자(bluenose)"라고 불리는 것은 좋아하지 않을 수도 있다.

(B) 위에서 보듯, 색을 부르는 단순한 단어조차도 그것이 어떻게 사용되는지에 따라 아주 다양한 의미들을 가질 수 있다. 이것이 함축, 단어의 암시된(제시된) 의미에 의해 의도되는 것이다.

| 정답해설 | ③ 75% 주어진 글에서 denotation(명시적 의미)이 무엇인지 설명하고 있다. 따라서 denotation이 언급된 표현인 Beyond the denotation of the word로 시작하며 blue가 들어간 기본 표현이 예시되는 (C)가 다음에 와야 한다. 그 뒤에는 Likewise(마찬가지로)로 시작하면서 blue가 들어간 합성어의 예를 추가적으로 드는 (A)가 (C) 다음에 와야 한다. 마지막으로 모든 것을 종합하여 설명하는 표현인 As you see above가 있는 (B)가 오는 것이 적절하다. 따라서 (C) – (A) – (B)의 순서가 적절하다.

어휘

denotation 명시적 의미	true blue 충실한
blue ribbon 최고상	bluenose 도덕군자
a range of 다양한	connotation 함축, 내포
imply 암시하다	suggest 암시하다; 제안[제시]하다
feel blue 우울하다	blues 블루스

---

11 독해 > Logical Reading > 배열   오답률 8%   답 ②

| 해석 | "목표를 마음에 새기고 시작하라"는 모든 것들은 두 번 창조된다는 원칙에 기반하고 있다. 정신의, 즉 첫 번째 창조가 있고 실체적, 즉 두 번째 창조가 모든 것들에게 있다.

(B) 집의 건축을 예로 들어 보자. 당신은 당신이 첫 번째 못을 제자리에 박아 넣기 전까지 아주 상세하게 그것을 설계한다. 당신은 당신이 어떤 종류의 집을 원하는지 매우 분명하게 감지해 내려고 노력한다.

(A) 만약 당신이 가족이 중심이 된 집을 원한다면, 당신은 자연스러운 모임 장소가 될 가족실을 계획할 것이다. 당신은 미닫이문과 아이들이 밖에서 놀 테라스를 계획한다. 당신은 아이디어 작업을 한다. 당신은 당신이 짓고 싶어 하는 것의 명확한 이미지를 얻을 때까지 머리로 작업한다.

(C) 그런 다음 당신은 청사진으로 그것을 축소하고 건설 계획을 발전시킨다. 이 모든 것이 땅에 손을 대기 전에 이루어진다. 만약 그렇지 않으면, 실체적 창조인 두 번째 창조에서, 당신은 당신의 집의 비용을 두 배로 만들지도 모르는 값비싼 변화를 치러야만 한다.

| 정답해설 | ② 92% 주어진 글에서 설명하는 정신의 창조와 관련된 것으로 예를 (B)에서 들고 있으므로 주어진 글 다음에 (B)가 와야 한다. (B)의 후반부에 어떤 종류의 집을 원하는지 감지하려고 노력한다고 했으므로 이 문장 다음에 원하는 집의 유형을 설명하는 (A)가 와야 한다. (C)에서 Then으로 시작하면서 머릿속에 있는 아이디어, 즉 첫 번째 창조 과정을 청사진과 같은 구체적인 실체로 만드는 두 번째 창조 과정을 예시하는 (C)가 (A) 다음에 와야 한다. 따라서 (B) – (A) – (C)가 글의 순서로 가장 적절하다.

어휘

physical 실체적인	gathering 모으는
sliding door 미닫이문	patio 테라스
construction 건축	hammer 망치; 망치질을 하다
blueprint 청사진	

---

12 독해 > Logical Reading > 배열   오답률 6%   답 ③

| 해석 | 관찰이 무슨 데이터가 관련이 있는지에 대한 명확한 지각으로 항상 착수되는 것은 아니다. 1882년, 길고 거친 바다 여행에서 배의 승객들의 대다수가 배멀미로 고통을 받았다.

(C) 그러지 않았던 한 사람은 미국의 철학자이자 심리학자인 William James였다. James는 언어 장애인이었던 15명의 승객들이 전혀 영향을 받지 않았던 것을 알아채는 아주 좋은 행운을 가졌다.

(A) James는 언어 장애인들에게는 전혀 민감하지 않은 문제인 배멀미가 틀림없이 일시적인 내이의 어긋남 때문이라고 추측했다. James에 의해 실행되었던 몇 개의 실험을 포함한 후의 실험은 이러한 의심을 확인시켜 주었다.

(B) 배멀미의 원인에 대한 이 중요한 단서는 다른 사람들은 간과했던 흥미로운 사실의 중요성을 보는 James의 능력 덕분이었다.

| 정답해설 | ③ 94% 주어진 글에서는 관찰이 특정 데이터의 관련성을 명확히 지각한 상태에서만 이루어지지 않는다고 하면서 배멀미로 고통받는 승객들의 예시를 소개하고 있다. 이 다음에는 William James라는 사람이 관찰을 통해 언어 장애인들이 배멀미를 하지 않는 것을 우연히 알게 되었다는 것을 언급하는 (C)가 먼저 와야 한다. 그 다음에는 언어 장애인들이 배멀미를 하지 않은 이유를 설명하는 (A)가 (C) 다음으로 와야 한다. (A) 후반부에 실험으로 James의 추측을 확인했다고 하였고 이를 (B) This crucial clue로 받고 있으므로 (B)가 마지막에 와야 한다. 따라서 (C) – (A) – (B)가 글의 순서로 가장 적절하다.

어휘

undertake 착수하다, 시작하다	voyage 여행
be afflicted with 고통을 받다	seasickness 배멀미
speculate 추측하다; 투기하다	disturbance 어긋남
inner ear 내이	deaf mute 농아
experimentation 실험	suspicion 의심
crucial 중요한	overlook 간과하다

---

13 독해 > Reading for Writing > 요약   오답률 42%   답 ②

| 해석 | 심판과 다른 스포츠의 임원들은 그들의 말이 경기장에서의 법인, 결정을 내리는 사람들이고, 규칙을 집행하는 사람들이다. 그러한 권한은 상응하는 무거운 책임과 함께 한다. 스포츠 임원들은 규칙의 공정한 숙련자들

이어야 하며 쉽게 동요되지 않아야 한다. 그들은 항상 경기의 수행에 대한 제어력을 유지해야 하고, 좋은 의사소통자여야 하며, 빠르게 열기가 오를 수 있는 상황에서 침착해야 하는데, 경기장에서든 관람석에서든 말이다. 스포츠에서는 모든 승리자에 대해 패배자가 있기 마련이며, 물론 그 결과는 몇몇 중요한 판정에 달려 있을 수 있다. 투 스트라이크 쓰리 볼 상황에서 던진 공이 볼인가 스트라이크인가? 마지막 순간의 슛이 버저 비터인가 아닌가? 즉시 재생이 프로 스포츠와 중요한 대학 스포츠에서 대비책을 제공하는 반면에, 다른 경기에서는 경기 진행자들이 권한을 행사한다. 이해 관계는 단지 한 게임 그 이상일 수 있다. 고등학교 운동선수들은 대학교 장학금을 바랄 수 있고 그들에 반하는 치명적 판정은 스카우트가 가능할 때 그들의 기회에 해를 가할 수도 있다. 어느 고등학교의 노련한 심판이 말한 것처럼 "누가 관람석에 있는지 절대 모릅니다."

↓

심판들의 역할은 매우 (A) 폭넓어서 그들은 경기장의 플레이뿐만 아니라 선수들의 개인적 미래에도 (B) 중대한 영향을 미칠 수 있다.
① 전문적인 – 약간의
② 폭넓은 – 중대한
③ 모호한 – 가치 있는
④ 포괄적인 – 긍정적인

| 정답해설 | ② 58% (A) 스포츠에서 심판과 진행자들의 역할에 대해 설명하는 글이다. 그들은 결정을 내리고 규칙을 집행하는 사람들로 항상 경기 수행에 대한 제어력을 유지해야 하고, 좋은 의사소통자여야 하며, 빠르게 열기가 오를 수 있는 상황에서 침착해야 한다고 했으므로 그들의 역할이 매우 방대하다는 것을 알 수 있다. 따라서 (A)에는 expansive(폭넓은)가 가장 적절한 표현이다.

(B) 본문 후반부에 고등학교 운동선수를 예로 들며 심판의 치명적 판정이 그들의 대학교 장학금이나, 스카우트 기회에 해를 가할 수 있다고 서술하고 있으므로 선수들의 개인적 미래에 '중대한' 영향을 미칠 수 있음을 알 수 있다. 따라서 (B)에 들어갈 적절한 표현은 significant(중대한)이다.

| 오답해설 | ① 9% 심판의 '전문성(professional)'이 아니라 경기와 선수들에게 영향을 미치는 심판의 영향력에 대해 설명하고 있으므로 정답으로 적절하지 않다. 심판이 선수들에게 미치는 영향 또한 매우 중요하므로 'slight(약간의)'도 적절하지 않다.
③ 9% 본문에서 심판에 대해 'ambiguous(모호한)'하다고 설명하고 있지 않으므로 적절하지 않다.
④ 24% 심판이 선수들에게 항상 'positive(긍정적인)' 영향만을 미치는 것은 아니므로 적절하지 않다.

어휘
umpire 심판	rulebook 규칙서
enforcer 집행자	unbiased 공정한
thick skin 쉽게 동요하지 않음	ride on ~에 달려 있다
crucial 중대한	instant replay 즉시 재생
fallback 대비책	stake 이해 관계
on hand 편리한, 구할 수 있는	expansive 폭넓은
ambiguous 모호한	comprehensive 포괄적인

14 독해 > Reading for Writing > 빈칸 구 완성 오답률 26% 답 ②

| 해석 | 왜 누군가는 돈의 공급에 대해 논쟁할 만큼 어리석을까? 돈은 더 많을수록, 더 즐겁다. 그런가? 틀렸다. 슬랩스틱 영화에서, 갈팡질팡하는 갱스터들은 지폐로 가득한 가방을 떨어뜨리고, 구경꾼들은 몇 장 집으려고 서로 지나쳐 뛰어든다. 행인들은 항상 웃지만, 나쁜 사람들은 울부짖고 경

제학자들도 그러하다. 왜 경제학자들이 갱스터들과 울까? 문제는 몇 개의 가방이 벌컥 열린다고 발생하지 않는다. 그러나 많은 짐이 마을로 쏟아져 들어온다면, ② 인플레이션이 따를 수 있다. 만약 돈의 액수가 제품을 생산할 능력을 압도한다면, 쓸 돈이 더 많아진 소비자들은 가격을 올린다. 마을은 예전보다 더 부유하지 않으며, 더 많은 지폐가 만약 모두가 연봉에 0을 두 개 더 추가한다고 하는 것보다 더 높은 삶의 기준을 가져오지는 않는다.
① 불황
② 인플레이션
③ 파산
④ 실업

| 정답해설 | ② 74% 빈칸 다음 문장인 If the amount of money overwhelms the capacity to produce goods, consumers, with more money to spend, bid up prices.는 시중에 돈이 많이 풀리면서 화폐 가치가 하락하여 물가가 올라가는 inflation에 대한 내용이다. 따라서 빈칸에 알맞은 말은 '인플레이션'이다.

| 더 알아보기 | Inflation (인플레이션)

통화량이 팽창하여 화폐 가치가 떨어지고 물가가 계속적으로 올라 일반 대중의 실질적 소득이 감소하는 현상을 의미한다.

어휘
bumble 갈팡질팡하다	bystander 구경꾼
grab 쥐다	passer-by 행인
wail 울부짖다	burst 터지다
overwhelm 압도하다	bid up 값을 올리다

오답률 TOP 1

15 문법 > 일치, 분사, 동사 오답률 50% 답 ④

| 해석 | 정확하게 어떻게, 언제, 왜, 그리고 어디에서 첫 번째 지도들이 만들어지게 되었는지는 발견하기 힘들다. 선사 시대와 역사 초기에 그려진 것의 대다수가 남아 있지 않아서, 우리가 오늘날 발견하는 것은 한때 거기에 있었던 것을 전체적으로 대표하지 않을 수도 있다. 현대 관찰자에게 다른 문제들이 있다. 선사 시대에 만들어진 지도는 그림의 의미를 설명하거나 그 내용물을 묘사하는 타이틀이 동반될 수 없다. 그러나, 우리는 초창기에, 오늘날처럼, 지도가 다양한 목적으로 만들어졌고 다양한 형태들을 가지고 있었다는 것을 확신할 수 있다. 일반적인 믿음과는 반대로, 지도가 오랫동안 사용되었던 모든 목적들 중, 가장 덜 중요한 목적이 길을 찾는 것이라는 사실 또한 분명하다. 해도는 유럽의 중세 시대까지 존재하지 않았고, 지형도는 18세기가 되어서야 육로로 여행하는 사람들이 일반적으로 지니고 다니게 되었다.

| 정답해설 | ④ 50% (A) 주어는 Much of what was drawn이고 in prehistoric and early historical times는 주어를 수식하는 전명구이다. 전명구는 동사의 수에 전혀 영향을 미치지 않는다. 주어의 핵심인 Much는 셀 수 없는 명사로 단수 취급하는 것이 적절하므로 has가 알맞다.

(B) 주어인 Maps는 '만들어진' 것이므로 수동의 의미를 갖는 과거분사 made로 수식하는 것이 알맞다. Maps의 동사는 cannot be accompanied이다.

(C) take는 '가지다'라는 뜻으로 목적어를 취하는 타동사이다. 뒤에 a variety of forms라는 목적어가 있으므로 과거형 동사 took가 알맞다. taken은 앞의 be동사 were에 이어져 수동태를 이루게 되므로 적절하지 않다.

어휘

be representative of ~을 대표하다　contrary to ~에 반해서
put through ~을 겪게 하다　　　　sea chart 해도
topographical map 지형도

16　독해 > Logical Reading > 삽입　　오답률 21%　답 ④

| 해석 | 어떤 무대 극장에서든 커튼이 닫힐 때, 관중들은 갑자기 박수를 친다. 보통 주저하며 스스로 박수 치는 것을 시작하는 몇몇 사람들이 있고, 다른 사람들은 그 다음에 참여한다. 박수는 각자 공연자들을 인정하려고 하는 것이면서, 또한 군중 속으로 섞이려고 노력하기도 하는 우스운 것이다. 당신은 다른 사람들에 앞서 박수 치기를 원하지 않거나 다른 사람들이 멈춘 후 계속하기를 원치 않는다. 사실, 만약 당신이 그것을 살펴본다면, 당신은 관중들이 침묵에서 가장 힘찬 박수갈채로 이동해 가는 방식에 확연한 패턴이 있다는 것을 발견할 것이다. ㉣ 전 세계의 무대 녹음은 그 패턴이 다른 문화적 습관을 초월하고 다른 군중들이 모두 어떻게 소리가 수초 동안 커지는지를 보여 주는 하나의 통일적인 곡선을 따른다는 사실을 보여 준다. 더 두드러지게, 하나가 근처의 다른 사람들이 하는 것에 아주 강하게 의존하기 때문에, 이 곡선은 어떻게 원자 또는 분자의 그룹이 집단적으로 한 종류의 행동에서 다른 것으로 빠르고 갑자기 가는지를 묘사하는 물리학에서 알려진 곡선과 절대적으로 똑같다.

| 정답해설 | ④ 79% 주어진 문장의 the pattern에 관한 설명이 주어진 문장 전에 나와야 한다. ㉣ 전 문장의 a pronounced pattern이 주어진 문장에서 말하고 있는 the pattern이므로 주어진 문장은 ㉣에 위치하는 것이 글의 흐름상 적절하다.

어휘

transcend 초월하다　　　　　　universal 일반적인
curve 곡선　　　　　　　　　　burst into 갑자기 ~하다
applause 박수　　　　　　　　　hesitantly 머뭇거리며
give credit to 믿다　　　　　　pronounced 확연한
remarkably 현저하게, 두드러지게　identical 똑같은
molecule 분자　　　　　　　　　abruptly 갑자기

17　독해 > Logical Reading > 연결사　　오답률 19%　답 ②

| 해석 | 50년 전에, 벌들은 그들이 먹을 많은 꽃들이 있었고, 음식인 꽃을 오염시키는 살충제가 거의 없고 이국적인 질병과 해충도 거의 없어서, 우리 도시와 시골 지역에서 건강한 삶을 살았다. 야생벌들은 방해를 받지 않는 흙과 잔가지에 성공적으로 집을 지었다. (A) 그러나, 벌들은 농작물 그리고 도랑, 도로가 잔디에서 아주 많은 종자식물들을 죽이는 제초제의 광범위한 사용 때문에 꽃가루와 꿀의 원천을 찾는 데 어려움이 있다. 꽃은 벌들을 직접적으로 죽일 수 있거나 건강에 만성적이고 해로운 영향을 초래하는 살충제에 오염될 수 있다. (B) 게다가, 세계적인 무역과 운송의 증가와 함께, 피를 빨아먹는 기생충, 바이러스 그리고 다른 벌 병원균들은 전 세계적으로 무심코 벌들에게 전해져 왔다. 특히 농업 강도가 높고 살충제 사용이 많은 나라들에서, 꽃의 부족으로부터의 영양 실조의 영향을 더 쉽게 만드는 이 기생충과 병원균은 벌의 면역 체계를 약화시킨다.

　　(A)　　　　　　(B)
① 그러나　　　　　결과적으로
② 그러나　　　　　게다가
③ 그러므로　　　　대조적으로
④ 그러므로　　　　다른 한편으로

| 정답해설 | ② 81% (A) 빈칸 앞에서는 벌들이 건강한 삶을 살았다고 했지만 뒤에서는 제초제의 광범위한 사용 때문에 꽃가루와 꿀의

원천을 찾는 데 어려움이 있다고 하면서 서로 반대되는 내용을 서술하고 있으므로 역접 연결사 However가 알맞다.

(B) 빈칸 다음에 벌의 개체수를 줄이는 또 다른 원인을 추가적으로 설명하고 있으므로 첨가의 연결사 In addition이 알맞다.

어휘

feed on ~을 먹다　　　　　　insecticide 살충제
contaminate 오염시키다　　　floral 꽃의
exotic 이국적인　　　　　　　pest 해충
nectar 꿀　　　　　　　　　　herbicide 제초제
ditch 도랑　　　　　　　　　　chronic 만성적인
debilitating 쇠약하게 하는　　pathogen 병원균
inadvertently 무심코　　　　　immune system 면역 체계
susceptible 민감한　　　　　　agricultural 농업의
intensity 강도

오답률 TOP 2

18　독해 > Logical Reading > 문맥상 다양한 추론　답 ④
　　　　오답률 50%

| 해석 | 바다 거품은 바다가 바람과 파도에 의해 요동칠 때 만들어진다. 각각의 해안 지역은 바다 거품의 형성을 좌우하는 (A) 다른 조건을 가지고 있다. 녹조 현상은 두꺼운 바다 거품의 흔한 원인이다. 녹조가 앞바다에서 썩을 때, 많은 양의 썩은 해조가 해안으로 자주 씻겨 온다. 거품은 이 유기 물질이 (B) 파도에 의해 물가에 부딪쳤다가 물러갈 때 만들어진다. 대부분의 바다 거품은 인간에게 해가 없고, 종종 생산적인 바다 생태계를 나타내는 조짐이다. 그러나 많은 유해한 녹조 현상이 바닷가에서 썩을 때, 인간의 건강과 환경에 영향을 미칠 가능성이 있다. 예를 들면, Karenia brevis의 대증식 동안 걸프 해안가를 따라 터지는 바다 거품 방울은 조류 독소가 공기로 전파되는 하나의 방법이다. 그 결과로 발생한 연무제는 해수욕 하러 가는 사람들의 눈을 (C) 자극하고 천식이나 다른 호흡기 질환을 가진 사람에게 건강상의 위험을 제기한다.

| 정답해설 | ④ 50% (A) 각각의 해안 지역은 바다 거품의 형성을 좌우하는 '다른' 조건을 갖는 것이 문맥상 적절한 표현이다. 따라서 differing(다른)이 알맞다. diffusing은 '퍼지는'이라는 의미이다.

(B) 본문 첫 문장인 Sea foam forms when the ocean is agitated by wind and waves.에서 바다 거품을 만드는 것은 바람과 파도라고 했으므로 surf(파도)가 알맞다. surface는 '표면'이라는 뜻이다.

(C) 터지는 바다 거품 방울은 조류 독소가 공기로 전파되는 하나의 방법이라고 했으므로 독소가 공기 중에 있고 그로 인해 사람들에게 건강의 위험을 가할 수 있다는 것을 알 수 있다. 따라서 irritate(자극하다)가 알맞다. irrigate는 '물을 대다'라는 뜻이다.

어휘

agitate 불안하게 만들다; 요동치다　diffuse 퍼지다
govern 좌우하다; 지배하다　　　　algal bloom 녹조 현상(조류 대증식)
algae 조류　　　　　　　　　　　decay 부패하다
offshore 앞바다에서　　　　　　　ashore 해안으로
churn up (파도 등이) 거품을 생기게 하며 물가에 부딪쳤다가 물러가다
indication 조짐　　　　　　　　　airborne 공기로 전파되는
aerosol 연무제, 에어로졸　　　　　asthma 천식
respiratory 호흡의

19 　독해 > Logical Reading > 삽입 　오답률 14% 　답 ③

| 해석 | 다양한 대기 오염 물질은 인간의 건강과 환경에 해로운 영향으로 알려져 왔거나 그러한 영향을 초래한다고 의심되어 왔다. 유럽의 대부분의 지역에서, 이 오염 물질들은 주로 공간의 난방, 전기 생산 또는 자동차로부터 나오는 연소물이다. 이 원천들로부터 발생한 오염 물질들은 이 원천들과 바로 이웃한 곳의 문제를 증명할 뿐 아니라 먼 거리에 영향을 미칠 수도 있다. 일반적으로 만약 당신이 젊고 건강 상태가 좋다면, 보통의 대기 오염의 수준이 어떠한 심각한 단기적인 영향을 줄 것 같지는 않다. ⓒ 그러나 대기 오염의 높아진 수준과/또는 대기 오염에 대한 장기적인 노출은 인간의 건강에 영향을 주는 더 심각한 증상들과 질환들로 이끌 수 있다. 이것은 주로 호흡 시스템과 염증 시스템에 영향을 주지만, 또한 심장병과 암과 같은 더 심각한 질환들로 이어질 수 있다. 폐나 심장과 관련된 질환을 가진 사람들은 대기 오염의 영향에 더 민감할지도 모른다.

| 정답해설 | ③ 86% 주어진 문장의 more serious symptoms and conditions affecting human health(인간 건강에 영향을 주는 더 심각한 증상들과 질환들)가 무엇인지 설명하는 내용이 주어진 문장 다음에 나오는 것이 흐름상 적합하다. ⓒ 뒤에서 이것은 주로 호흡 시스템과 염증 시스템에 영향을 주지만, 또한 심장병과 암과 같은 더 심각한 질환들로 이끌 수 있다고 설명하고 있으므로 주어진 문장은 ⓒ에 오는 것이 가장 적절하다. (첫 번째 문장에서 have been known to be or suspected to cause는 기출 문제에서 have known or suspected로 출제되었지만, 어법상 옳도록 수정하여 수록하였다.)

어휘

elevate 올리다	long-term 장기간의
principally 주로	combustion 연소
vicinity 부근, 인근	short-term 단기간의
respiratory 호흡의	inflammatory 염증의
lung 폐	susceptible 민감한

20 　독해 > Logical Reading > 연결사 　오답률 17% 　답 ④

| 해석 | 바다뱀들은 지구상에서 가장 독성이 강한 생물들 중 일부이다. 이 독은 산호뱀, 방울뱀, 또는 심지어 킹코브라의 독보다 훨씬 더 치명적이다. 바다뱀은 그들의 독을 그들이 먹는 물고기를 죽이고 포식자들로부터 그들 자신을 보호하는 데 사용한다. 그러나 바다뱀이 자신을 보호하는 데 독을 사용하는 것이 반드시 좋은 것은 아니다. 독은 만드는 데 많은 에너지가 필요한데 이는 성장이나 사냥에 사용될 수 있는 에너지이기도 하다. (A) 또한, 바다뱀이나 다른 독을 가진 동물이 더 자주 공격을 받을수록, 자신을 보호할 수 있다고 하더라도 부상을 당하게 될 가능성이 더 많아진다. 산호뱀처럼, 많은 바다뱀들도 이 문제를 눈앞의 포식자들에게 경고함으로써 해결한다. (B) 예를 들면, yellow-bellied 바다뱀은 포식자들에게 어느 것도 시도하지 말라고 말하는 밝고, 눈에 확 띄는 색을 지닌다. 수백만 년 동안 포식자들은 이 경고에 주의를 기울이도록 진화되었다. 오직 일부 종류의 상어와 바다독수리만이 감히 바다뱀을 공격한다. 이것은 바다뱀들이 계속해서 자신들을 보호해야 하는 것을 막아 주고, 그들의 생존 기회를 높인다.

	(A)	(B)
①	그러나	다시 말해
②	또한	대조적으로
③	그러나	게다가
④	또한	예를 들면

| 정답해설 | ④ 83% (A) 빈칸 전후로 바다뱀이 독을 사용하는 것의

단점이 설명되고 있다. 빈칸 앞에서는 독을 만드는 데 많은 에너지가 필요하다고 말하고 있고, 뒤에서는 바다뱀이나 다른 독을 가진 동물이 더 자주 공격을 받을수록 부상을 당하게 될 가능성이 더 많아진다고 했으므로, 추가 설명을 나타내는 연결사 Also가 알맞다.

(B) 많은 바다뱀들이 이 문제를 포식자들에게 미리 경고함으로써 해결한다고 한 뒤 yellow-bellied 바다뱀이 포식자에게 보내는 경고를 예로 들고 있으므로, 예시의 연결사 for example이 알맞다.

어휘

sea snake 바다뱀	venomous 독이 있는
venom 독	coral snake 산호뱀
rattlesnake 방울뱀	
up front 앞줄의; 눈에 잘 띄는; 솔직한	
splashy 눈에 확 띄는	

21 　독해 > Reading for Writing > 빈칸 절 완성 　오답률 37% 　답 ①

| 해석 | 아마 당신이 생각하고 있는 것에도 불구하고, 심리학자인 Richard Wiseman의 연구에 따르면, ① 행운은 운명 혹은 숙명의 문제가 아니다. 대신에, 이것은 운이 좋은 사람들이 생각하고 행동하는 방식의 결과이다. 누구라도 운이 따르는 법을 배울 수 있다는 의미이다! 예를 들면, Wiseman은 운이 좋은 사람들은 항상 그들 주위에서 무슨 일이 일어나는지 알아채고, 새로운 경험들과 기회들에 항상 열려 있는 자세를 유지하는 것을 발견했다. 반면에, 불행한 사람들은 더 긴장하고 특정한 업무들에 지나치게 집중하는 경향이 있어서 그들이 분명하게 찾고 있지 않는 기회들을 알아채는 것을 막는다. 그래서 다음에 당신이 파티에 간다면, 마음속으로 목표를 세우고 가지 마라(비록 당신이 누군가를 얼마나 많이 매료시키기를 원할지라도). 대신에, 일의 흐름에 맡기고 당신은 무슨 일이 일어날지 결코 알려고 하지 마라. 당신은 오히려 아주 멋진 새로운 친구 몇 명을 사귈 수도 있다.
① 행운은 운명 혹은 숙명의 문제가 아니다
② 행운은 당신에게 더 친밀한 관계를 가져온다
③ 행운은 어떤 대가를 치러도 얻을 수 없다
④ 행운은 인간에게 가장 소중한 자산이다

| 정답해설 | ① 63% 빈칸 다음의 Instead, it's a result of the way lucky people think and act ~ which means that anyone can learn to be lucky!에서 행운이 따르는 법을 배울 수 있다고 했으므로 선지 중 이와 가장 관련 있는 '행운은 운명 혹은 숙명의 문제가 아니다'가 빈칸에 들어갈 말로 가장 적절하다.

어휘

take notice of ~을 알아채다	opportunity 기회
meanwhile 반면에	certain 특정한
task 업무	explicitly 명쾌하게, 분명히
attract 끌어들이다	
take things as they come 일의 흐름에 맡기다	

22 　독해 > Reading for Writing > 빈칸 구 완성 　오답률 18% 　답 ①

| 해석 | 산호초는 지구상에서 가장 다양하고 가치 있는 생태계들 중 일부이다. 산호초들은 어느 해양 환경보다 단위 면적당 더 많은 종들을, 대략 4,000종의 물고기들, 800종의 딱딱한 산호들과 수백 개의 다른 종들을 포함하여 살게 한다. 과학자들은 산호초 주변과 안에서 발견되지 않은 1백만~8백만에 이르는 또 다른 유기 생물체 종들이 존재할지 모른다고 예측한

다. ① <u>이러한 생물 다양성</u>은 21세기에 새로운 의약품을 찾는 데 매우 중요하다고 간주된다. 많은 약들은 암, 관절염, 인간의 박테리아 감염증, 바이러스, 그리고 기타 다른 병들에 대한 가능한 치료제로서 지금 산호초에 사는 동식물들로부터 개발되는 중이다. 거대한 생물학적인 풍부함의 보고인 산호초는 또한 수백만 명의 사람들에게 경제적이고 환경적인 서비스를 제공한다. 산호초는 매해 3,750억 달러의 가치를 지닌 상품과 서비스를 제공할지 모른다. 이것은 지구 표면의 1%조차 안되는 지역을 담당하는 환경에 비해서는 놀라운 수치이다.

① 이러한 생물 다양성　　② 그들의 아름다움
③ 산호초의 생존 기술　　④ 먹이 사슬

| 정답해설 | ① 82% 빈칸 앞에서 산호초들이 4,000종의 물고기들, 800종의 딱딱한 산호들, 수백 개의 다른 종들을 살게 하며, 과학자들은 산호초 주변과 안에서 발견되지 않은 1백만~8백만에 이르는 또 다른 유기 생물체 종들이 존재할지 모른다고 예측한다고 했으므로 산호초 안에 엄청나게 다양한 생물들이 서식하는 것을 알 수 있다. 따라서 빈칸에 적절한 표현은 '이러한 생물 다양성'이다.

어휘

coral reef 산호초	valuable 가치 있는
marine 해양의	estimate 예측하다, 어림짐작하다
cure 치료제	arthritis 관절염
storehouse 보고, 창고	immense 거대한
figure 수치	biodiversity 생물 다양성
food chain 먹이 사슬	

---

23 독해 > Macro Reading > 목적　오답률 5%　답 ④

| 해석 | Charlse 씨께,

어제 당신과 점심을 먹은 것은 즐거운 일이었습니다. 저는 당신이 언급한 새로운 가정용품에 매우 관심이 있고 그것을 개발하기 위해 당신과 함께 어떤 식으로 작업을 해야 할지에도 매우 관심이 있습니다. 저는 업계 잡지 중 어느 것에서도 그것과 비슷한 것이 광고된 것을 전혀 본 적이 없습니다. 그래서 그것은 어쩌면 독창적이고 유일한 제품이 될지도 모릅니다. 만약 그렇다면, 당신은 그것에 있는 당신의 지적 재산권을 보호하기 위해 그것을 등록하려고 빠르게 움직이길 원할 것입니다. 만약 당신이 이 일을 진행하기 원한다면 저에게 알려주십시오. 그러면 저는 우리 특허법 변호사가 제안서를 가지고 당신에게 연락하게 할 것입니다. 곧 다시 만납시다.

그때까지,
Frank

| 정답해설 | ④ 95% 본문 마지막의 you will want to move fast to register it to protect your intellectual property rights in it. Let me know if you want to pursue this and I will have our patent associate contact you with a proposal.에 편지를 쓴 목적이 나와 있다. 따라서 '새로 개발한 가정용품의 특허 등록을 제안하려고'가 글의 목적으로 적절하다.

어휘

household product 가정용품	one-of-a-kind 유일한
intellectual property 지적 재산권	patent associate 특허법 변호사

---

24 독해 > Macro Reading > 주장　오답률 14%　답 ③

| 해석 | 나는 내 아이들에게 예의바름, 배움, 그리고 질서는 좋은 것이라고 그리고 좋은 것은 그것 자체로 추구되고 발전되어져야 한다고 항상 가르쳐

왔다. 그러나 학교에서 아이들은 아주 빨리, 점심 시간 동안 1/4 마일 트랙을 달린 것에 대해 Nature Trail 표를 얻는 것을 배운다. 또는 운동장 위의 쓰레기를 줍거나 어린아이가 화장실을 찾는 것을 돕는 데 링컨이 새겨진 지폐를 받는다. 이런 것들은 '훌륭한 시민성'이라고 불렸던 행동들이다. 아이들의 최소한의 협조를 보상이나 선물로 사는 것이 왜 필요할까? 나를 불안하게 하는 것은 좋은 행동이 보상책으로 강화되어야 한다는 생각이다. 아이들은 스티커, 별, 그리고 초콜릿 바를 얻기 위해서가 아니라 그 자체로 좋은 행동을 해야 하는 것을 배워야 한다.

| 정답해설 | ③ 86% 본문의 Children must be taught to perform good deeds for their own sake, not in order to receive stickers, stars, and candy bars.가 필자가 주장하는 것이다. 즉, 보상을 얻기 위해 선행을 하는 것이 아니라 선행을 하는 것 자체가 올바른 행동이라는 것을 알고 선행을 해야 한다는 것이므로 ③ '아이들이 보상 없이도 선행하도록 교육시켜야 한다.'가 필자의 주장으로 적절하다.

어휘

for its own sake 그 자체를 위해　　deed 행동
treat 특별한 선물

---

25 독해 > Logical Reading > 문맥상 다양한 추론　오답률 13%　답 ③

| 해석 | 납은 지표에서 발견되는, 자연적으로 발생하는 유독성 금속이다. 그것의 만연한 사용은 광범위한 환경 오염, 인간의 노출, 그리고 세계의 많은 지역에서 대중의 중대한 건강 문제를 유발했다. 어린아이들은 특히 납의 유독한 영향에 취약하고, 특히 뇌와 신경 체계의 발달에 영향을 주는, 뿌리 깊고 영구적인 건강상의 악영향을 줄 수 있다. 납은 또한 고혈압과 신장 손상의 ③ <u>감소된(→ 증가된)</u> 위험을 포함하여 성인에게 장기적인 해를 끼친다. 임신한 여성의 높은 수준의 납에 대한 노출은 유산, 사산, 조산, 출생 시 저체중뿐만 아니라 심하지 않은 기형을 초래할 수 있다.

| 정답해설 | ③ 87% 납이 성인에게 장기적인 해를 끼친다고 한 것을 볼 때 질병의 발병을 '높인다'는 것이 문맥상 적절하므로 decreased(감소된)가 아니라 increased(증가된)가 알맞은 표현이다.

| 오답해설 | ① 5% result in은 '~ 결과를 유발하다'라는 표현으로 문장에서 Its widespread use(그것의 만연한 사용)가 extensive environmental contamination(광범위한 환경 오염)을 유발시키는 것이므로 result in은 적절한 표현이다. 참고로 result from은 '~이 원인이다'라는 뜻이다.

② 8% adverse는 '부정적인'이란 뜻으로 납이 건강에 악영향을 미친다는 것이므로 적절하게 사용되었다.

④ 0% 임신한 여성이 유산, 사산, 조산 등 여러 문제를 겪는 것은 납에 노출되었을 때이므로 exposure(노출)는 적절한 단어이다.

| 더 알아보기 | 감소하다 ↔ 증가하다

- 감소하다: decrease, diminish, decline
- 증가하다: increase, rise, swell

어휘

lead 납	contamination 오염
be vulnerable to ~에 취약하다	adverse 부정적인
nervous 신경의	kidney 신장
miscarriage 유산	stillbirth 사산
premature birth 조산	malformation 기형

교육행정직

교육행정직 기출 POINT

2019년도 시험부터 교육행정직 출제처가 인사혁신처로
변경되어, 지방직과 동일한 시험지로 시행하게 됨

Point 1 교육행정직의 경우 평가원의 수능 유형과 유사한 형태의 문항이 출제
되어서 기존에 수능을 치루었던 수험생들에게 유리했던 것이 사실이다.
그러나, 출제처가 2019년 이후로 변경되었으므로 수험생들은 국가직
및 지방직 기출문제를 통해서 수험 대비를 하는 것이 더 중요하겠다.

Point 2 시험에는 직렬과 상관없이 빈출 개념이 반복하여 출제되고, 전체적인
문제 유형도 전 직렬이 유사하다. 따라서, 이 교재에 수록된 과년도 교
육행정직 9급 기출문제도 반드시 학습 및 참고하자.

합격예상 체크

〈교육행정직 연도별 합격선〉

2018 합격기준!

맞힌 개수	/20문항	점수	/100점

➡ □ 합격 □ 불합격

취약영역 체크

문항	정답	영역	문항	정답	영역
1	②	어휘 > 빈칸 완성	11	①	독해 > Macro Reading > 주제
2	②	어휘 > 빈칸 완성	12	②	독해 > Reading for Writing > 빈칸 구 완성
3	④	어휘 > 빈칸 완성	13	①	독해 > Logical Reading > 연결사
4	②	독해 > Logical Reading > 문맥상 다양한 추론	14	③	독해 > Micro Reading > 내용 일치/불일치
5	④	문법 > 접속사, 분사	15	②	독해 > Micro Reading > 내용 일치/불일치
6	①	문법 > 형용사, 접속사	16	②	독해 > Macro Reading > 제목
7	④	독해 > Logical Reading > 문맥상 다양한 추론	17	①	독해 > Logical Reading > 배열
8	④	문법 > 동사	18	④	독해 > Logical Reading > 삽입
9	③	문법 > 분사	19	③	독해 > Logical Reading > 삭제
10	③	생활영어 > 회화/관용표현	20	③	독해 > Macro Reading > 요지

⬇ 영역별 틀린 개수로 취약영역을 확인하세요!

어휘	/3	문법	/4	독해	/12	생활영어	/1

➡ 나의 취약영역: _____

※ [정답해설]과 [오답해설] 선지의 50% 표시는 〈1초 합격예측 서비스〉를 통해 수집된 선지 선택률을 나타냅니다.

1 　어휘 > 빈칸 완성　　　오답률 22%　답 ②

| 해석 | 포스트모던은 어디에나 있기도 하고 아무데도 없기도 하다. 그것은 영점이 없고, 고정된 본질도 없다. 그것은 앞서 왔던 것들의 모든 흔적들을 포함하고 있다. 그것의 지배적인 논리는 절대 순수하지 않고, 항상 타협적이고, 양자택일이 아니라 둘 다 가능하다는 ② 잡종의 논리이다. 포스트모던 충동은 장난기 많고 역설적이다. 그것은 역사적인 형태들을 흉내 내고 흡수하며, 항상 양쪽을 다 가지며, 언제나 모던하면서 포스트모던하고, 아무것도 그것의 관심을 벗어날 수 없다.

① 10% 현실 　　　　　　② 78% 잡종
③ 5% 전문성 　　　　　　④ 7% 모의실험

| 정답해설 | ② 빈칸 다음에 나오는 절대 순수하지 않고, 항상 타협적이고, 양자택일이 아니라 둘 다 가능하다는 설명으로 보아 포스트모던은 '이것 아니면 저것'이라기보다 '타협과 모든 것이 가능하다'는 것을 유추할 수 있다. 따라서 빈칸에는 hybrid(잡종)가 적절하다.

어휘

essence 본질　　　　　　　　dominating 지배적인, 우세한
compromising 타협적인　　　　either-or 양자택일의
both-and 둘 다의　　　　　　　impulse 충동, 충격, 자극
paradoxical 역설의, 자기모순의　mock 조롱하다, 흉내 내다
have it both ways 양쪽을 다 원하다[가지다]
hybrid 잡종, 혼성체　　　　　　simulation 모의실험

2 　어휘 > 빈칸 완성　　　오답률 13%　답 ②

| 해석 | 다른 사람들과 이야기할 때, 당신이 의견을 달리하는 것들을 논의함으로써 시작하지 마라. 당신이 ② 동의하는 것들을 강조하고 계속 강조함으로써 시작하라. 가능하면, 당신들 둘 다 같은 목적을 위해 애쓰며, 당신들의 유일한 차이점은 목적이 아니라 방법이라고 계속 강조하라. 상대방이 처음부터 "네, 네"라고 말하게 만들어라. 가능하다면 당신의 상대방이 "아니오"라고 말하지 못하도록 하라.

① 3% 살다　　　　　　② 87% 동의하다
③ 3% 청구하다　　　　④ 7% 의심하다

| 정답해설 | ② 상대방에게 'No'가 아닌 'yes'를 말하게 하라며 둘 다 같은 목적을 갖고 있음을 강조하라고 했으므로 빈칸에는 agree(동의하다)가 오는 것이 알맞다.

| 더 알아보기 | agree의 반의어

- disagree 동의하지 않다　　　　· differ 동의하지 않다, 다르다
- stand off 동의하지 않다

어휘

keep on 계속하다
strive for ~을 위해 애쓰다, 노력하다, 분투하다
end 목적, 목표　　　　　　　at the outset 처음에, 처음부터
opponent 상대(방), 반대자
keep A from -ing A가 ~ 못하게 하다

| **3** | 어휘 > 빈칸 완성 | 오답률 44% | 답 ④ |

| **해석** | 평범한 상황에서, 개인은 자동차 도난이라는 큰 손실을 피하기 위해 상당한 조치들을 취할 것이다. 안전한 장소에 주차하기, 차 문 잠그기, 도난 방지 장치 사용하기 등 말이다. 그러나 일단 자동차가 거의 완전한 대비 가격 상당의 보험에 들어 있다면, 운전자는 그러한 ④ 예방 조치를 취하는 데 상당히 적은 동기를 가질 것이다.

① 2% 할인
② 8% 보상
③ 34% 위험
④ 56% 예방 조치

| **정답해설** | ④ 운전자가 도난 등에 대비한 완전한 보험에 가입해 있다면 상당히 적게 가지게 되는 동기는 예방 조치임을 유추할 수 있다.

오답률 TOP 1

| **4** | 독해 > Logical Reading > 문맥상 다양한 추론 | 오답률 82% | 답 ② |

| **해석** | 많은 미디어에서 예술 작품들을 만들고 그것들에 반응하는 것은 사회적 행위임을 기억하는 것이 중요하다. 이런 행위들이 어느 독특한 개인의 발명이라는 것은 생각할 수도 없다. 이미 진행 중인 예술적 생산과 반응의 행위들이 없다면, 예술을 만들려는 한 개인의 어떤 의도도 ② 의미 있을 (→ 의미 없을) 것이다. 만약 예술적 성공에 대한 공유된 기준들이 없다면, 예술이라는 단어는 서술적인 용어로서 객관적으로 사용될 수 없을 것이다. 만약 계속할 사람이 나 자신밖에 없다면, 내게 예술이라고 부르는 것이 맞는 것처럼 보이는 것은 무엇이든 맞는 것이다. 그리고 그것은 여기서 우리가 '맞는 것'에 대해 말할 수 없음을 의미할 뿐이다.

| **정답해설** | ② 18% 예술적 생산과 반응의 행위들이 없으면 예술을 만들려는 의도는 '의미 있는'이 아니라 '의미 없는'이 될 것이다. 따라서 meaningful은 반대의 뜻인 meaningless로 바꾸어야 한다.

| **오답해설** | ① 25% 예술 작품들을 만들고 그것들에 반응하는 것은 사회적 행위라고 했으므로 따라서 예술 행위들이 독특한 개인의 발명이 아니라는 흐름은 알맞다.

③ 30% 예술적 성공에 대한 공유된 기준이 없는 상황을 가정하고 있으므로 아마도 이때 예술이라는 단어는 '객관적으로' 사용될 수 없을 것이다.

④ 27% 앞서 ~ the word art cannot be used objectively로 '예술이라는 단어가 객관적으로 사용될 수 없다'고 제시하고 있으므로 결국 '주관적'임을 유추할 수 있다. 따라서 whatever is going to seem right to me to call art, 즉 '나에게 예술이라고 부르는 것이 맞는 것처럼 보이는 것은 무엇이든' 맞는 것이 될 수밖에 없다는 추론이 가능하다.

어휘

practice 관행, 행동, 실행
inconceivable 생각할 수 없는, 상상할 수 없는
distinct 뚜렷한, 독특한
on the part of ~으로서는, ~쪽에서는, ~쪽의
criterion 기준(pl. criteria)   descriptive 서술하는, 묘사하는
go on 계속하다

오답률 TOP 3

| **5** | 문법 > 접속사, 분사 | 오답률 55% | 답 ④ |

| **해석** | 1903년 12월 17일 Wright 형제들의 최초의 비행은 단 12초간 지속되었고 겨우 120피트를 갔 (A) 지라도 ("당신은 공을 더 멀리 던질 수도 있었다") 그것은 하늘 자체를 지배할 수 있는 가능성을 세계에 보여 줬다. 그 비행은 미국 정부에는 매우 (B) 당황스러운 것으로 드러났는데, 미 정부는 군대를 통해 Samuel P. Langley의 지시 하에서 비슷한 프로그램에 종잣돈을 지급했었다.

| **정답해설** | ④ 45% (A) 뒤에 주어(the Wright Brothers' maiden voyage)와 동사(lasted, covered)로 구성된 절이 온다. 따라서 접속사 Although가 알맞다.

(B) 주어 The flight는 사물이다. 사물의 상태를 나타내는 감정분사는 능동형으로 사용하므로 '당황스러운'의 뜻을 가진 embarrassing이 적절하다.

| **더 알아보기** | 감정형 분사

• 감정 제공 형용사 (현재분사): embarrassing, surprising, satisfying, exciting 등
• 감정 상태 형용사 (과거분사): embarrassed, surprised, satisfied, excited 등

어휘

maiden voyage 최초의 항해[비행]   last 지속되다
seed money 종잣돈
under the direction of ~의 지시 하에서

| **6** | 문법 > 형용사, 접속사 | 오답률 22% | 답 ① |

| **해석** | 현대 산업 사회들과 그들의 문제들은 점점 더 복잡해지고 있고, 오늘날 어떤 한 사람이 모든 사회과학에 통달할 수는 없기 때문에, 많은 사회 문제들에 대한 여러 분야가 관련된 접근법이 점점 더 강조된다. 여러 분야가 관련된 접근법은 다른 전문성을 가진 한 무리의 사회과학자들이 특정한 문제에 대해 함께 작업할 것임을 의미하는데, 그 집단의 어느 누구도 문제의 모든 측면들을 완전히 다 이해하지는 못한다.

| **정답해설** | ① 78% (A) 복잡해지는 사회와 문제들을 한 사람이 통달할 수 없다는 흐름이므로 부정어 no가 알맞다.

(B) 동사 means 이하는 목적어 역할을 하는 목적어절이다. 따라서 명사절 접속사 that이 알맞다.

어휘

place emphasis on ~을 강조하다
interdisciplinary 학제 간의, 여러 분야가 관련된
specialty 전문, 전문성, 전문 분야

| **7** | 독해 > Logical Reading > 문맥상 다양한 추론 | 오답률 37% | 답 ④ |

| **해석** | Alexander는 스포츠를 좋아했는데, 무엇보다 승마를 가장 좋아했다. 아무도 그보다 승마를 더 잘하지는 못했다. 한번은 그의 아버지가 아무도 길들일 수 없었던 아름다운 말을 샀다. 그의 이름은 Bucephalus였다. 누군가 ① 그를 타려고 시도할 때마다, 그들은 던져졌다. 그러나 Alexander는 왜 ② 그가 그렇게 했는지를 이해했다. 그 말은 자신의 그림자를 두려워했던 것이다. 그래서 Alexander는 그가 땅에 있는 ③ 그의 그림자를 볼 수 없

도록, 그의 고개를 태양 쪽으로 돌렸다. 그를 부드럽게 쓰다듬으면서 ④ 그는 자신을 그의 등 위쪽으로 휙 움직여 돌아서 탔고 경기장에 있던 모든 사람들의 박수를 받았다.

| 정답해설 | ④ 63% 지문 속에서 ①②③은 말인 Bucephalus를 지칭하며, ④는 그 말을 길들인 Alexander를 가리킨다.

어휘
riding 승마
mount 오르다
work out 이해하다
swing 휙 움직이다, 흔들다, 흔들리다
tame 길들이다
throw off 떨쳐 버리다, 던져 버리다
stroke 쓰다듬다

8　문법 > 동사　　　오답률 46%　답 ④

| 해석 | 이집트 최고 회의의 동의에 따라, Frank Goddio와 그의 팀은 그 부지에 건립될 가능성이 있는 수중 박물관에 관한 결정이 내려질 수 있을 때까지 그들의 탐사에서 발견된 유물들이 East Port에 남아 있을 것임을 확실히 했다. 그러나 일부 그들의 발견들의 중요성은, 미래의 학자들이 그것들을 상세히 연구할 수 있도록 해 줄 그것들의 모습에 대한 정확한 시각적 기록을 해 두지 않고는 해저에 그것들을 본래 그대로 남겨두고 싶어 하지 않을 정도였다. 주형을 가능하게 하기 위해 일부 물건들을 그것들이 있던 물속에서 일시적으로 꺼낸 후, 그것들을 다시 해저로 돌려보내는 것에 해결책이 있었다. 복제 작업은 주형 기술을 전문으로 하는 프랑스 예술가인 Georges Brocot에 의해 감독되었다.

| 정답해설 | ④ 54% by Georges Brocot로 보아 수동태 문장이어야 함을 알 수 있다. 이 문장에 동사가 없고 과거의 일이므로 과거시제를 사용하여 overseen은 was overseen이 되어야 한다.

| 오답해설 | ① 9% found는 명사 artifacts를 뒤에서 수식하는 수동의 의미를 가진 과거분사로 알맞게 쓰였다.
② 12% their finds(그들의 발견물들)라는 복수 명사를 대신하여야 하므로 them으로 알맞게 쓰였다.
③ 25% 전치사 in의 첫 번째 동명사 목적어 removing과 등위접속사 and로 연결된 또 다른 동명사 목적어 returning은 병렬 구조를 이루며 알맞게 쓰였다.

어휘
in agreement with ~에 따라서, ~와 일치하여
antiquity 유물, 골동품
find 발견물
be unwilling to V ~할 마음이 내키지 않다
untouched 훼손되지 않은, 본래 그대로의
seabed 해저
lie(-lay-lain) 놓여 있다
replication 복제
specialize in ~을 전문으로 하다
artifact 유물
in detail 상세히, 자세히
casting 주물
oversee 감독하다
molding 조형, 주형

9　문법 > 분사　　　오답률 33%　답 ③

| 해석 | 지속 가능성은 어렵고 복잡한 이슈이며, 달성하기 힘든 것이다. 그것은 다름 아닌 바로 이 행성에서 인류가 생존할 수 있는 가능성과 관계있기 때문에 엄청나게 중요하다. 인류가 부족하고 제한적인 자원을 사용하고 있는 속도로는 지금 조치가 취해지지 않는다면, 그리고 여전히 시간이 있다고 해도, 적어도 지금 우리가 이해하고 있는 것으로서의 문명의 미래는 조금도 과장하지 않고 불확실할 것으로 보인다. 그러한 복잡한 주제는, 특히

지속 가능성이 목표가 아니라 바로 과정이라는 것을 고려하면, 어떤 단순하고 쉬운 처리 방법은 없다는 결론이 나온다. 그것은 현재 세대를 위해 더 나은 삶과 앞으로의 세대를 위한 생존으로 이끌고, 그들이 물려받을 세계에 대처할 수 있는 그들의 능력을 향상시키게 된다.

| 정답해설 | ③ 67% 뒤에 목적어절에 해당되는 that절이 있으므로, considered는 '~을 고려해 보면'이라는 의미가 되도록 현재분사구문 considering이 되어야 한다.

| 오답해설 | ① 13% since는 전치사와 접속사 모두 가능하다. 여기서는 뒤에 절이 왔으므로 접속사로 쓰였고, 문맥상 '~ 때문에'라는 의미로 쓰였다.
② 8% 주어인 the future of civilization이 3인칭 단수이므로 단수 동사 is는 적절하게 쓰였다.
④ 12% 동시 동작을 나타내는 분사구문이다. enhancing 다음에 목적어가 있으므로 능동을 나타내는 현재분사 형태는 알맞다.

어휘
sustainability 지속 가능성
enormously 엄청나게, 어마어마하게
nothing less than 다름 아닌 바로, 그야말로
to say the least 조금도 과장하지 않고
it follows that ~라는 결론이 나오다
cope with ~에 대처하다, 대응하다
elusive 알기 어려운, 달성하기 어려운
have to do with ~와 관계가 있다
straightforward 쉬운, 단순한
inherit 물려받다, 상속받다

10　생활영어 > 회화/관용표현　　　오답률 3%　답 ③

| 해석 | A: Jenny, 다음 주 직무 교육 등록했어?
B: 아니, 안 했어. 너는?
A: 나는 벌써 다음 주 수요일 세션에 등록했어.
B: 잘했어. 그런데 나는 주중에는 참석을 못할 것 같아 걱정이야.
A: 걱정 마. 내가 듣기론 주말 프로그램들도 있어.
B: 정말?
A: 그래, 그런데 정원에 제한이 있을 거야.
B: 그러면, 바로 가서 등록하는 게 낫겠네.
A: 그래, 그래야 해. 알다시피 선착순이야.
① 넌 그들에게 갔었어야 했어
② 내가 너라면, 그것들에 등록할 거야
③ 바로 가서 등록하는 게 낫겠네
④ 이번에는 다음을 기약해야 해

| 정답해설 | ③ 97% A가 B에게 주중에 교육을 듣지 못하면 주말 프로그램도 있는데 수업 정원에 제한이 있다고 했으므로 빈칸에서 B는 ③과 같이 말하는 게 알맞다.

어휘
sign up for ~에 등록[신청]하다
in-service training 직무 연수, 현직 교육
good for you 잘했어
first come, first served 선착순
make it (모임 등에) 참여[참석]하다
take a rain check 다음을 기약하다

11　독해 > Macro Reading > 주제　　　오답률 6%　답 ①

| 해석 | 콜레스테롤을 낮추는 약들은 세계에서 가장 널리 사용되는 약품들 중 하나이다. 당신의 신체는 콜레스테롤을 만들어 내고, 그것은 많은 음식에서 발견된다. 그러나 왜 그럴까? 분명히, 당신의 간이 자연적으로 그것을 만들어 내기 때문에 콜레스테롤이 있는 것은 당연하지만, 왜 그럴까? 당

신은 당신의 신체가 여러 방식으로 좋은 건강의 기반으로서 콜레스테롤이 정말 필요하다는 것을 알면 놀랄 수도 있다. 예를 들면, 콜레스테롤은 당신의 신체가 신체적 그리고 정신적 스트레스에 반응하는 것을 돕는 호르몬을 만들기 위해 신체에 의해 사용된다. 그것은 또한 성 호르몬 생산의 기반이기도 한데, 생식 기능의 모든 측면을 포함하여 사춘기부터 임신에 이르기까지 신체 활동의 조절에 기여한다.

① 우리가 우리 몸 안에 콜레스테롤을 필요로 하는 이유
② 몸 안에서 콜레스테롤이 만들어지는 방식
③ 콜레스테롤을 낮추는 약의 작용 원리
④ 콜레스테롤의 생식 기능

| 정답해설 | ① 94% 중반부부터 콜레스테롤이 몸에 꼭 필요한 것이라고 하며 콜레스테롤이 우리 몸에 필요한 이유 두 가지를 제시하고 있다. 따라서 '우리가 우리 몸 안에 콜레스테롤을 필요로 하는 이유'가 글의 주제로 알맞다.

| 오답해설 | ② 3% 우리의 간이 그것을 자연적으로 만든다고 언급하고는 있지만 어떤 방식으로 만들어지는지는 구체적으로 언급하고 있지 않다.

③ 1% 콜레스테롤을 낮추는 약이 도입 문장에서 언급은 되었으나 그 약이 어떻게 작용하는지에 관한 내용은 없다.

④ 2% 콜레스테롤이 생식 기능에 필요하다고 했으나, 이것은 콜레스테롤이 우리 몸에 필요한 이유 중 하나로 언급되었을 뿐이다.

어휘

liver 간	foundation 근거, 기초
respond to ~에 반응하다	contribute to ~에 공헌하다
puberty 사춘기	pregnancy 임신
reproductive 생식의, 번식의	mechanism 작동 원리

오답률 TOP 2

12 독해 > Reading for Writing > 빈칸 구 완성　오답률 62%　답 ②

| 해석 | 영화는 가장 흔하게 문학과 비교되어 왔지만, 실제로는 건축과 훨씬 더 많은 공통점이 있다. 두 형태 모두 대중적이고 협력적이며, 무엇보다도 ② 비용이 많이 든다. 두 가지 예술에서, 경제적 제약은 언제나 제작되는 작품의 모습을 좌우한다. 그에 비해서, 문학(특히 "순수" 문학)은 거의 사제의 소명 의식처럼 보인다. 적어도 낭만주의 시대 이후로 소설가와 시인들은 (좋든 나쁘든) 독자나 비용을 고려하지 않고 대개 자신들을 즐겁게 해 주는 것은 무엇이든지 글로 쓸 수 있었다.

① 예술적인　　　② 비용이 많이 드는
③ 신성한, 종교적인　④ 생산적인

| 정답해설 | ② 38% 빈칸 다음 문장인 In both arts, economic constraints have always dictated the shape of the work produced.에서 영화와 건축의 경제적 제약은 언제나 제작되는 작품의 모습을 좌우한다고 했으므로 빈칸에는 '경제적 제약'과 가장 관련 있는 expensive(비용이 많이 드는)가 들어가야 함을 알 수 있다.

어휘

in common with ~와 비슷한	collaborative 협력적인
constraint 제약, 제한	dictate 명하다, 좌우하다
by comparison 그에 비해	serious literature 순수 문학
priestly 사제의, 사제 같은	calling 소명 (의식)
for better or worse 좋든 나쁘든	regard for ~에 대한 관심[배려, 고려]

sacred 신성한, 종교적인

13 독해 > Logical Reading > 연결사　오답률 30%　답 ①

| 해석 | 재난 관리, 즉 인명, 재산, 그리고 환경에 대한 피해 축소를 이끄는 동기 부여 개념은 전 세계적으로 대체로 동일하다. (A) 그러나, 이 사명을 수행하는 능력은 절대 같지 않다. 정치적이든, 문화적이든, 경제적이든, 혹은 다른 이유든 간에, 불행한 현실은 일부 국가들과 일부 지역들은 문제를 다루는 데 다른 나라들보다 더 유능하다는 것이다. 그러나 부나 영향력에 상관없이, 어떤 국가도 재난의 부정적 영향을 완전히 면할 정도로 발전하지는 않았다. (B) 게다가, 세계 경제의 등장은 어떤 재난의 결과를 한 국가의 국경 내에 두는 것을 점점 더 어렵게 만든다.

	(A)	(B)
①	그러나	게다가
②	그렇지 않으면	게다가
③	그러나	그에 반해서
④	그렇지 않으면	그에 반해서

| 정답해설 | ① 70% (A) 앞에는 동기 부여 개념이 전 세계적으로 동일하다는 내용이 나오고 빈칸 뒤에는 이 사명을 수행하는 능력은 절대 같지 않다고 했으므로 빈칸 전후 부분이 반대되는 내용임을 알 수 있다. 따라서 역접 연결사 However가 알맞다.

(B) 빈칸 앞은 부나 영향력에 상관없이, 어떤 국가도 재난의 부정적 영향을 완전히 면할 정도는 아니라고 했고, 빈칸 문장은 세계 경제의 등장으로 어떤 재난의 결과를 한 국가에 국한하는 것이 점점 어려워진다는 것으로 빈칸 앞의 문장 내용을 부연 설명하고 있는 것이므로 Furthermore(게다가)가 알맞다.

| 더 알아보기 | 역접을 나타내는 연결사

• but 그러나	• however 그러나
• on the contrary 반대로	• though 그러나

어휘

carry out 수행하다	by no means 절대 ~ 아닌
capable 능력 있는, 유능한	regardless of ~에 상관없이
immune from ~을 면한	emergence 등장, 도래

14 독해 > Micro Reading > 내용일치/불일치　오답률 8%　답 ③

| 해석 | Spencer Stanhope는 중산층 가정 출신이며, Oxford의 Rugby와 Christchurch에서 교육받았다. 그는 G. F. Watts와 함께 1850년에 예술을 공부하기 시작했고, 1853년에는 그와 함께 이탈리아를 방문했다. 그는 1850년대 중반에 라파엘 전파 주변의 젊은 예술가들의 예술계의 일원이 되었고, 특히 Burne-Jones와 친했는데, 그는 그의 그림에 영향을 주었고 평생 친구가 되었다. 그는 1859년 Royal Academy에서 처음으로, 나중에는 Grosvenor Gallery에서 전시했다. 그의 예술가 친구들처럼, 그는 보통 사람들에 공감했고, 종종 이상화된 방식이긴 했지만, 그들이 일하고 있는 모습을 보여 주는 주제를 자주 선택했다. 남자들이 낚시 작업을 하고 있는 동안 여자들은 빨래를 하는 "Washing Day"는 전형적인 Stanhope의 작품이다.

| 정답해설 | ③ 92% He first exhibited at the Royal Academy in 1859 and later at the Grosvenor Gallery.에서 그는 1859년에 Royal Academy에서 처음으로 전시회를 열었고 나중에 Grosvenor Gallery에서 전시했다고 했으므로 1859년에 열린 첫 전시회는

Royal Academy라는 것을 알 수 있다. 따라서 ③은 일치하지 않는다.

| **오답해설** | ① 1% He began to study art with G. F. Watts in 1850, visiting Italy with him in 1853.의 내용과 일치한다.

② 4% Burne-Jones, who influenced his painting이라고 했으므로 본문과 일치한다.

④ 3% 마지막 문장의 *Washing Day ~ is typical of Stanhope's work.*로 보아 ④는 본문과 일치한다.

어휘

middle-class 중산층의	circle ~계, 사회
Pre-Raphaelite 라파엘 전파	lifelong 평생의
sympathy 동정, 공감	get on with ~을 해 나가다

---

15   독해 > Micro Reading > 내용일치/불일치   오답률 8%   답 ②

| **해석** | 색이 선명한 나비와 나방은 그 수가 14만 종에 이르는데, 딱정벌레만이 그 수를 넘는다. 그 목의 학명인 "Lepidoptera"는 "비늘로 된 날개를 가진"이라는 뜻이며, 작은 비늘들이 대부분의 성체형의 날개와 몸통을 덮고 있다. 크기에 있어서, 나비와 나방은 다른 어떤 곤충군보다 더 다양하다. 남아메리카의 올빼미 새끼 나방은 가로로 1피트이다. Eriocranid 나방은 1/4인치의 날개폭을 가지고 있다. 어떤 종들은 훨씬 더 작다. 나비를 나방과 구별하기 위한 엄격한 규칙은 없다. 그러나 일반적으로, 나방은 고치를 짓고, 나비는 그렇게 하지 않는다. 휴식을 취할 때, 나비는 날개를 머리 위로 서로 밀착시키는 반면, 나방은 날개를 텐트처럼 접는 경향이 있다.

| **정답해설** | ② 92% In size, butterflies and moths vary more than any other insect group.(크기에 있어서, 나비와 나방은 다른 어떤 곤충군보다 더 다양하다.)에서 본문과 일치함을 알 수 있다.

| **오답해설** | ① 2% "Lepidoptera," the order's scientific name, means "scaly-winged," and tiny scales cover the wings and bodies of most adult forms.로 보아 Lepidoptera는 '모든' 성충이 아니라 '대부분의 성충'의 몸과 날개를 덮고 있다고 했다.

③ 2% the Eriocranid moth has a quarter-inch wingspan에서 Eriocranid 나방의 날개 폭은 1/2인치가 아니라 1/4인치라고 했다.

④ 4% 마지막 문장에서 나비는 날개를 머리 위로 서로 밀착시키고, 나방은 날개를 텐트처럼 접는다고 했으므로 날개를 접어서 쉬는 것은 나비가 아니라 나방이다.

어휘

moth 나방	beetle 딱정벌레
order (동식물 분류상의) 목	scientific name 학명
scaly 비늘로 덮인	scale 비늘
adult form [생물학] 성체형	owlet moth 올빼미 새끼 나방
foot [길이] 피트	wingspan 날개폭, 날개 길이
hard and fast rule 엄격한 규칙, 융통성 없는 표준	
tell A from B A와 B를 구별하다	
spin cocoons 고치를 짓다, 고치를 만들다	

---

16   독해 > Macro Reading > 제목   오답률 33%   답 ②

| **해석** | 고고학적 발견물들은 유물, 음식 찌꺼기, 집, 인간의 뼈, 기타 등등의 많은 형태로 나온다. 이 발견물들은 보통 실험실로 운송되기 위해 포장되기 전 현장에서 세척되고, 식별되고, 목록으로 작성된다. 현장에서 돌아오면, 발견물들뿐만 아니라 상세한 기록, 그림, 그리고 현장에서 얻어진 다른 기록된 데이터를 포함하는 이 데이터들은 분석의 대상이 된다. 이 단계에서 방사선 탄소 샘플과 꽃가루와 같은 일부 특정 자료들은 분석을 위해 전문가들에게 보내진다. 대부분의 실험실 분석은 상세한 유물 분류와 동물 뼈, 다른 음식 찌꺼기에 대한 연구를 포함한다. 이것은 추후 데이터 해석의 기반이 된다.

① 고고학적 발견물에 대한 다양한 실험실 분석들
② 고고학적 발견물의 처리와 분석
③ 인류 역사에서 고고학의 중요성
④ 다른 종류의 고고학적 발견물들

| **정답해설** | ② 67% 고고학적 발견물들이 실험실로 보내지기 전에 처리되는 단계, 그리고 실험실에서 분석되는 과정과 방법 등을 설명하는 글이다. 따라서 '고고학적 발견물의 처리와 분석'이 제목으로 알맞다.

| **오답해설** | ① 28% 실험실로 보내지기 전 단계에 대한 설명도 제목에 포함되어야 하므로 '고고학적 발견물에 대한 다양한 실험실 분석들'은 제목으로 부족하다.

③ 2% 고고학의 중요성은 본문에 언급되지 않았다.

④ 3% 첫 문장에서 다양한 형태의 발견물들이 나열되어 있으나 이것을 제목으로 볼 수는 없다.

어휘

archaeological 고고학의	and so on 기타 등등
catalog 목록을 작성하다; 분류하다	be subject to ~의 대상이 되다
radiocarbon 방사선 탄소	pollen grain 꽃가루
analysis 분석(*pl.* analyses)	

---

17   독해 > Logical Reading > 배열   오답률 55%   답 ①

| **해석** | 우리가 우리 자신에 대해 생각하기 위해 선택하는 은유나 비유는 우리의 이해와 행동에 다른 영향을 미칠 수 있다.

(A) 예를 들면, Michael White와 David Epston은 만약 우리가 사람들과의 관계가 복잡한 기계와 같다고 생각한다면, 우리는 아마 그들의 문제를 기계의 오작동으로 볼 것이고, 정비사가 그러하듯 해결책은 그것들을 수리하는 것이 될 것이라고 설명한다.

(C) 이것의 예는 압력솥의 증기처럼 우리 내부에 분노가 증가하고 있으며, 그 증기는 배출되어야 하며, 그렇지 않으면 솥이 폭발할 것이라고 우리가 말할 때이다.

(B) 이 은유에 유도되는 어떤 사람은 아마 증가하는 압력을 방출하기 위해 분노를 "배출하고" 표현하라고 그 사람에게 독려할 것이다.

| **정답해설** | ① 45% 주어진 문장에서 은유와 비유는 우리의 이해나 행동에 다른 영향을 미칠 수 있다고 했다. (A)는 For example로 시작하면서 인간을 복잡한 기계에 비유하는 예를 들고 있으므로 가장 먼저 온다. 이어서 인간을 구체적인 기계, 즉 압력솥에 비유하는 예시인 (C)가 오는 것이 적절하다. (C)의 like steam in a pressure cooker(압력 밥솥의 증기처럼)를 (B)에서 this metaphor(이런 은유)로 지칭하고 있으므로 (B)가 마지막에 오는 것이 알맞다. 따라서

적절한 순서는 (A) − (C) − (B)이다.

어휘

metaphor 은유, 비유	analogy 비유; 유사, 비슷함
malfunction 오작동	machinery 기계류
vent 배출시키다, 터뜨리다, 분출하다	build up 점점 커지다
pressure cooker 압력솥	let out 배출하다, 내뿜다

---

18 독해 > Logical Reading > 삽입　　　오답률 33%　　답 ④

| 해석 | 독일 영화들의 무언가는 분명이 "심미적인" 것으로 여겨졌지만, 그것이 무엇이었나? 미국에서, "독일 영화"라는 용어는 심미적인 공간을 그리게 되었는데, 말하자면, 관습적인 할리우드 스타일의 규범적 경계선 외부 어딘가였다. 할리우드 영화로부터의 이 심미적 거리가 얼마나 먼 외부에 있는지, 그리고 그 거리가 긍정적인 심미적 차이를 만들어 내는지 아니면 부정적인 심미적 차이를 만들어 내는지가 논쟁 중이었다. 개별 영화에 대한 토론은 세 가지 심미적인 기준들에 의해 만들어지는 경향이 있었는데, 이 각각의 기준은 긍정적인 관점과 부정적인 관점 둘 다 가지고 있었다. 극적인 / 과도한, 복합적인 / 엘리트적인, 그리고 예술적인 / 제멋대로인. ④ 개별 영화가 각 짝의 첫 번째 용어에 더 가깝게 묘사될수록, 할리우드 영화와의 차이는 더 "혁신적이고" 따라서 긍정적으로 여겨졌다. 그러나, 후자의 용어들로 정의된 영화는 너무 다르고 따라서 너무 "이상한" 것으로 여겨졌다.

| 정답해설 | ④ 67% 주어진 문장의 the first term in each pair(각 짝의 첫 번째 용어)를 통해 이 문장 앞에 짝으로 이루어진 용어에 대한 내용이 있다는 것을 유추할 수 있다. 따라서 each having both a positive and a negative dimension: spectacular / excessive, complex / elitist, and artistic / self-indulgent의 뒤인 ④에 위치하는 것이 가장 적절하다.

어휘

hence 따라서	aesthetic 심미적인, 미적인
mark out 표시하다, 그리다	normative 규범적인
at issue 논쟁 중인, 문제가 되는	
constitute 구성하다; (어떤 상태를) 만들어 내다	
criterion 기준(*pl.* criteria)	dimension 관점; 치수; 차원
spectacular 극적인, 장관의	artistic 예술적인
self-indulgent 방종한, 제멋대로 하는	latter 후자의

---

19 독해 > Logical Reading > 삭제　　　오답률 12%　　답 ③

| 해석 | 리더십은 리더의 독특한 자질들보다는, 리더들과 추종자들 간의 의사소통에 중점을 둔다. 관계로 여겨지는 리더십은 리더들과 추종자들 사이에서 일어나는 협력의 과정이 된다. 리더는 추종자들에게 영향을 주고, 추종자들에 의해 영향을 받으며, 리더와 추종자들 둘 다 결국 그들을 둘러싸고 있는 상황에 영향을 받는다. ③ 예를 들면, 모금 행사에서 리더는 모금 행사의 모든 단계와 절차를 알고 있고 이 지식을 효과적인 캠페인을 운영하는 데 사용할 수 있다. 이 접근법은 리더십이 직선 형태의 일방적인 일이 아니라, 오히려 상호 작용적인 일이라는 것을 강조한다.

| 정답해설 | ③ 88% 리더들과 추종자들 간의 의사소통의 관점에서 리더십을 설명하는 글이다. 그런데 ③은 모금 행사에서의 리더의 역할에 관한 내용이므로 전체 흐름에서 벗어난다.

어휘

center 중점을 두다	rather than ∼보다는
in turn 결국, 차례차례, 교대로	fund-raising campaign 모금 행사

---

procedure 절차	linear 직선 모양의
one-way 편도의, 일방적인	

---

20 독해 > Macro Reading > 요지　　　오답률 14%　　답 ③

| 해석 | 국가가 조세로 모은 돈을 쓸 때, 국가는 납세자들의 주머니에서 돈을 꺼내 국가가 돈을 쓰는 사람들의 주머니로 넣는 것이다. 지출은 정말로 투자일 수 있다. 예를 들면, 교육은 젊은 사람들에 대한 투자이며, 보편적으로 국가 책무의 일부로 여겨진다. 그러한 경우에, 만약 투자가 건전한 것이라면, 공공 지출은 분명히 정당화된다. 지역 사회는 그곳의 아이들을 교육시키는 것을 중단함으로써 그리고 항만, 도로, 공공 사업을 전반적으로 무시함으로써 궁극적으로 부유해지지는 않는다.

① 국가는 납세자들에게 국가의 투자 계획을 알려야 한다.
② 공공 지출을 줄이는 것은 지역 사회를 더 풍요롭게 만들 것이다.
③ 공공 지출은 적절한 투자를 통해서 정당화될 수 있다.
④ 국가는 교육보다 공공 사업에 더 많은 돈을 써야 한다.

| 정답해설 | ③ 86% The expenditure may be really an investment: education, for instance, is an investment in the young, and is universally recognised as part of the duty of the state. 등의 문장으로 보아 공공 부문의 지출은 단순히 소비가 아니라 교육처럼 지역 사회에 대한 투자라는 것이 이 글의 주제임을 알 수 있다. 따라서 정답은 Public expenditure can be justified through a proper investment.(공공 지출은 적절한 투자를 통해서 정당화될 수 있다.)이다.

| 오답해설 | ① 5% 국가가 납세자들에게 국가의 투자 계획을 알려야 한다는 내용은 나와 있지 않다.
② 3% 글의 내용과 상반된 내용이다.
④ 6% 교육과 공공 부문의 지출에 대한 경중은 언급되고 있지 않다.

어휘

raise 모으다; 올리다	taxpayer 납세자
expenditure 지출; 비용, 경비	provided 만약 ∼라면(if)
sound 건전한, 건강한, 상식적인	
enrich 질을 높이다, 풍요롭게 하다; 강화하다	
cease 멈추다	

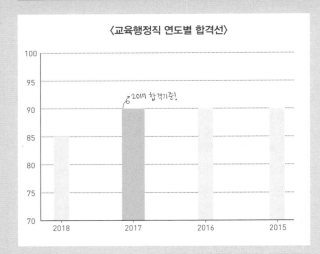

합격예상 체크			

〈교육행정직 연도별 합격선〉

2017 합격기준!

맞힌 개수	/20문항	점수	/100점

➡ ☐ 합격　☐ 불합격

취약영역 체크			

문항	정답	영역	문항	정답	영역
1	②	어휘 > 빈칸 완성	11	③	독해 > Logical Reading > 문맥상 다양한 추론
2	③	어휘 > 빈칸 완성	12	①	독해 > Reading for Writing > 빈칸 구 완성
3	④	어휘 > 빈칸 완성	13	①	독해 > Logical Reading > 연결사
4	①	독해 > Logical Reading > 문맥상 다양한 추론	14	④	독해 > Micro Reading > 내용일치/불일치
5	③	문법 > 전치사, 일치	15	④	독해 > Micro Reading > 내용일치/불일치
6	①	문법 > 동사, 비교	16	①	독해 > Macro Reading > 제목
7	②	독해 > Macro Reading > 주제	17	③	독해 > Logical Reading > 배열
8	③	문법 > 동사	18	②	독해 > Logical Reading > 삽입
9	②	문법 > 분사	19	③	독해 > Logical Reading > 삭제
10	②	생활영어 > 회화/관용표현	20	④	독해 > Macro Reading > 요지

⬇ **영역별 틀린 개수로 취약영역을 확인하세요!**

어휘	/3	문법	/4	독해	/12	생활영어	/1

➡ 나의 취약영역: _____

※ [정답해설]과 [오답해설] 선지의 50% 표시는 〈1초 합격예측 서비스〉를 통해 수집된 선지 선택률을 나타냅니다.

1　어휘 > 빈칸 완성　　오답률 14%　답 ②

| 해석 | 비가 내리기 시작할 때, 창문에 있는 빗방울들의 배열을 여러 차례 볼 수 있다. 비가 올 때마다 배열이 달라지지만, 우리는 그 배열들에서 어떠한 패턴도 볼 수 없으므로, (즉, 빗방울들의 모든 다른 배열처럼) 그것들은 여전히 모두 동일하게 보인다. 거기에는 찾을 수 있는 패턴이 없기에 우리의 사고방식은 그것에 대하여 ② 눈이 멀게[맹목적이게] 된다. 즉, 우리는 그것들을 알아채지 못한다.
① 5% 기민한
② 86% 눈이 먼, 맹목적인
③ 1% 날카로운
④ 8% 세심한

| 정답해설 | ② 빈칸 뒤에 있는 That is는 앞 문장을 재진술할 때 사용하므로, '그것들을 알아채지 못한다'는 의미에서 유추하면 blind가 알맞음을 알 수 있다.

어휘

arrangement 배열, 배치　　　visible 눈에 보이는, 가시적인
notice 의식하다, 알다; 알림

2　어휘 > 빈칸 완성　　오답률 25%　답 ③

| 해석 | 대화는 대개 ③ 즉흥적이다. 그러므로 화자들은 '일어선 채로 생각'하여야 한다. 그리하여 그들은 그들이 말하고 싶은 바를 계획할 시간이 없으며, 종종 바꾸어 말하기나 반복을 포함하여 그들의 문법은 필연적으로 느슨하게 구성된다.
① 8% 문법적인
② 9% 체계적인
③ 75% 즉흥적인
④ 8% 조종하는

| 정답해설 | ③ '말하고 싶은 바를 계획할 시간이 없음'과 '바꾸어 말하기'나 '반복', '문법이 느슨하게 구성됨'과 같은 단서들을 통해 대화가 즉흥적(spontaneous)이라는 것을 유추할 수 있다.

| 더 알아보기 | spontaneous의 유의어

impromptu, extempore, improvised

어휘

plan out 계획을 (면밀히) 세우다　　rephrase 바꾸어 말하다
manipulative 조종하는, 조작의

3　어휘 > 빈칸 완성　　오답률 22%　답 ④

| 해석 | 많은 시장들에서, 회사들은 동일한 소비자들을 위해 경쟁할 것이지만 단지 서로 다르기만 한 것이 아니라 직접적으로 ④ 반대되는 제품들을 제공할 것이다. 어떤 회사들은 담배를 판매하지만, 다른 회사들은 당신이 금연하도록 도와주는 제품들을 판매한다. 어떤 회사들은 패스트푸드를 판매하지만, 다른 회사들은 다이어트 보조 식품을 판매한다.
① 4% 승인하다
② 5% 광고하다
③ 13% 닮다
④ 78% 반대하다

| 정답해설 | ④ 주어진 빈칸 다음 문장에서 '담배를 파는 회사'와 '금연을 도와주는 제품을 판매하는 회사' 그리고 '패스트푸드를 판매하는 회사'와 '다이어트 보조 식품을 판매하는 회사'와 같이 서로 반대되는 제품을 판매하는 회사들의 구체적인 예시들이 제시되어 있다.

따라서 oppose가 빈칸에 가장 알맞다.

어휘

firm 회사, 상회 compete 경쟁하다, ~와 겨루다
not merely A but B 단지 A인 것이 아니라 B인

오답률 TOP 1

4 독해 > Logical Reading > 문맥상 다양한 추론 오답률 49% 답 ①

| 해석 | 집단들이 다양한 배경과 능력을 가지는 경우에 문제 해결은 더 잘되는 경향이 있다. 한 집단이 풍부하게 다양한 관점과 경험을 활용할 수 있을 때, 의사 결정은 집단의 구성원들에 의하여 공유되는 관점과 경험이 ① 다를(→ 같을) 때보다 더 좋은 품질을 가질 수 있다. 그러나 창의성과 혁신의 경우와 같이, 가장 효율적인 문제 해결은 다양성의 균형이 존재할 때 나타난다. 어떤 가치와 목표도 공유하지 않는 다양성은 집단을 분해시킬 가능성이 있다. 그러나, 공유된 가치와 목표는 Irving Janis가 '집단사고'라고 칭하는 것으로 이어질 수 있다. 집단 사고는 하나의 문제에 대해 하나의 답으로 의견을 모으고, 집단들이 비판적으로 해결책을 평가하기보다는 스스로와 서로에게 그들이 제시한 해결책이 최선이라고 납득시킬 때 일어나는 것을 말한다.

| 정답해설 | ① 51% 첫번째 문장은 '다양한 관점과 경험의 중요성'에 대해 서술하고, 두 번째 문장에서는 '의사 결정'을 예로 들어 이를 재서술하고 있다. 이때 첫번째 문장에서 서술한 '다양한 관점과 경험의 중요성'과 같은 맥락을 서술하기 위해서는 구성원들이 공유하는 관점들과 경험들이 '같을' 때보다 '다를' 때 의사 결정의 질이 높아진다고 서술하는 것이 옳다. 따라서 밑줄 친 different는 the same으로 수정하는 것이 문맥상 올바르다.

어휘

diverse 다양한 draw on ~을 이용[활용]하다
perspective 관점, 시각
converge on ~에 수렴하다, ~로 의견을 모으다
come up with (해답 등을) 제시하다

5 문법 > 전치사, 일치 오답률 16% 답 ③

| 해석 | 태초 (A) 이래로부터 인간과 동물의 삶은 밀접한 관계를 가지고 있으며, 이는 풍부한 상징성의 근원을 제공한다. 동물은 신으로서 숭배되어 왔으며, 행운 및 불운과 연관되었고, 힘과 지혜의 근원으로 (B) 여겨져 왔다. 많은 것은 상징적으로 인간성과 관련된다.

| 정답해설 | ③ 84% (A) Since는 전치사와 접속사 역할을 할 수 있으며, When은 접속사의 역할을 할 수 있다. 주어진 빈칸 이후에 명사구 earliest times가 있으므로 전치사의 기능을 할 수 있는 Since를 사용하는 것이 옳다. 또한 특정 시점을 나타내는 earliest times가 Since와 함께 '태초 이래로'라는 의미로 쓰였으며, 이에 따라 주절의 시제가 현재완료인 것도 문맥상 올바르다.
(B) 「A, B and C」 형태의 병렬 구조로, A, B, C의 형태가 동일해야 한다. 따라서 (have been) worshipped ~, linked ~, and seen ~으로 연결되는 것이 적절하다.

더 알아보기 | 현재완료와 함께 쓰이는 시간의 부사구

- lately
- recently (현재완료, 과거 시제 가능)
- in the past/last + 숫자 + 단위 복수
- for the past/last + 숫자 + 단위 복수
- during the past/last + 숫자 + 단위 복수

어휘

symbolism 상징주의 source 원천, 근원
worship 숭배하다, 예배하다 human quality 인간성

6 문법 > 동사, 비교 오답률 16% 답 ①

| 해석 | 프랑스인은 영국인이 (A) 그랬던 것과 거의 같은 시기에 북아메리카에 도착했다. 그러나 프랑스는 식민지화보다는 수익성 있는 모피 무역에 더욱 관심이 있었으므로 프랑스 정착민들을 거의 보내지 않았다. 그 결과, 뉴 프랑스의 인구는 남쪽에 있는 영국 식민지들의 (B) 그것과 비교하여 매우 적었다.

| 정답해설 | ① 84% (A) 일반동사인 arrived를 대신할 수 있는 대동사가 필요하므로 did가 빈칸에 적절하다.
(B) 비교 대상이 the population of New France와 the population of the English colonies to the south이다. the population이 이미 앞에서 언급되었고 단수 명사이므로 대명사 that으로 대신해야 한다.

어휘

colonization 식민지화 fur trade 모피 무역
settler 정착민 tiny 아주 작은

7 독해 > Macro Reading > 주제 오답률 9% 답 ②

| 해석 | 다른 언어를 흔히 구사하는 집단의 사람들의 성격은 나뉠 수 있다. 한 연구는 영어를 구사하는 미국인들과 스페인어를 구사하는 멕시코인들에 의해 행해진 성격 검사가 확실히 다르다는 것을 보여 주었다. 미국인들은 멕시코인들보다 훨씬 더 외향적이며, 쾌활하고, 양심적이었다. 그런데 왜 그런 것일까? 언어가 이러한 차이에서 한몫하는지를 알아보기 위하여, 연구원들이 그 후 텍사스, 캘리포니아 그리고 멕시코에서 스페인어와 영어의 이중 언어 구사자들을 찾아냈고, 그들에게 각 언어에서의 성격 등급을 제공했다. 그리고 실질적으로 언어가 정답이었다. 이중 언어를 구사하는 참여자들은 그들이 스페인어로 테스트를 수행했을 때보다 영어로 테스트를 수행했을 때 더 외향적이며, 쾌활하고, 양심적이었다.
① 성격 등급 발달의 절차
② 성격 차이에 대한 언어의 영향
③ 성격 테스트에서 이중 언어 구사자들의 시험 수행 전략
④ 언어 학습에서 환경의 역할

| 정답해설 | ② 91% 영어와 스페인어, 서로 다른 언어를 구사하는 사람들의 성격 검사를 시행했을 때 성격의 차이가 나타났다고 했고 후반부의 in fact 다음에 language was a key라는 문장을 통해 언어가 성격에 영향을 주었음을 확인시켜 주므로 ②가 글의 주제로 가장 적절하다.

어휘

agreeable 쾌활한, 기분 좋은 conscientious 양심적인
play a role 역할을 맡다, 한몫하다 scale 등급, 눈금, 저울

| **8** | 문법 > 동사 | 오답률 22% | 답 ③ |

| 해석 | 몇몇 연구자들은 공격적인 아이들이 단순히 폭력적인 TV를 좋아하는 것뿐이며 그런 노출이 없이도 폭력적으로 행동할 것이라고 주장한다. 그러나 그 주장은 아이들이 폭력적이거나 비폭력적인 비디오나 영화를 보도록 배정되었던 그 수많은 연구들의 결과를 설명하지 못한다. 이 연구의 대부분에서, 폭력에 노출된 이들은 나중에 즉시 더욱 공격적으로 행동했다. 예를 들면, 한 연구에서, 396명의 7~9세 소년들이 폭력적이거나 비폭력적인 영화 둘 중 하나를 시청하고 나서 실내 하키를 했다. 그 소년들이 어떤 영화를 시청했는지 알지 못하는 연구자들은 하키에서 금지된 행동들을 찾으면서, 경기 동안 그들의 공격적인 행동의 등급을 매겼다. 이것은 상대에게 엘보잉과 니잉 그리고 트리핑을 포함했다. 전반적으로, 폭력적인 영화를 본 소년들은 더욱 공격적이었다.

| 정답해설 | ③ 78% 주어는 Researchers이고 who did not know which film the boys had seen은 주어를 수식하고 있는 형용사절의 역할을 하는 주격 관계대명사절이므로 문장에 동사가 존재하지 않는다. 따라서 rating을 과거 동사의 형태인 rated로 고쳐야 한다.

| 오답해설 | ① 7% in which 이하의 절이 완벽하므로 「전치사 + which」가 적절하다.

어휘

aggressive 공격적인   argument 논쟁
numerous 많은   rate 등급을 매기다
elbowing 엘보잉, 팔꿈치로 상대방의 행동을 방해하는 행위
kneeing 니잉, 무릎으로 상대방의 행동을 방해하는 행위
tripping 트리핑, 무언가에 걸려 넘어지게 하는 행위

오답률 TOP 3

| **9** | 문법 > 분사 | 오답률 27% | 답 ② |

| 해석 | 신경학의 관점에서는, 당신이 새로운 것을 마주할 때마다 당신의 뇌는 가능한 한 많은 정보를 기록하려고 한다. 수천 개의 뉴런들이 자극을 받는데, 그것은 이 정보를 코드화하고 저장하는 것을 도우며, 최종적으로 당신이 많이 느끼고 알아차리게 한다. 그러나 시간이 지나면서, "새로운" 경험은 낡은 것이 되고, 당신의 뇌는 정보를 부호화하는 데 더 적은 에너지를 사용한다. 그저 당신의 뇌가 그것을 이미 알고 있기 때문이다. 만약 당신이 매일 직장을 왕복하여 운전하면, 그 운전 행위는 당신이 그 경로를 처음 운전했던 때만큼 뇌를 자극하지 못한다.

| 정답해설 | ② 73% Thousands of Thousands of neurons are stimulated, which help code and store this information과 ultimately ~ notice a lot 사이에 접속사가 없으므로 동사 caused가 분사의 형태로 사용되어야 한다. caused 뒤에 you라는 목적어가 있으므로 현재분사 형태인 causing이 되어야 한다.

어휘

neurological 신경학의   route 길, 경로
nearly 거의

| **10** | 생활영어 > 회화/관용표현 | 오답률 4% | 답 ② |

| 해석 | A: BW 프린트 숍에 오신 것을 환영합니다. 무엇을 도와드릴까요?
B: 안녕하세요. 제가 이 전단지를 복사하고 싶은데요.
A: 알겠습니다. 몇 부가 필요하신가요?
B: 250장의 복사본이 필요합니다.

A: 네, 배송해 드릴까요? 5,000원의 추가 비용이 있습니다.
B: 아니요, ② 복사가 끝나면 제가 그것들을 가지러 오겠습니다. 언제 준비가 될까요?
A: 약 한 시간 정도 후에요.
B: 좋습니다. 그때 다시 오겠습니다.
A: 네.
① 복사본의 장수를 알고 싶습니다
② 복사가 끝나면 제가 그것들을 가지러 오겠습니다
③ 제 사무실로 그것들을 보내 주세요
④ 저는 그것들을 합본하기를 원하지 않습니다

| 정답해설 | ② 96% 인쇄 매장에서 진행된 손님과 직원의 대화이다. 주어진 빈칸에 앞서 '배송해 드릴까요?'라는 직원의 물음에 거부의 의사를 밝혔으므로, 찾으러 오겠다고 답하는 ②가 B의 말로 적절하다.

| 오답해설 | ③ 2% B가 빈칸에 앞서 No라고 대답했으므로 사무실로 배달해 달라는 대답은 부적절하다.

어휘

flyer 전단지

| **11** | 독해 > Logical Reading > 문맥상 다양한 추론 | 오답률 17% | 답 ③ |

| 해석 | Nosipho가 처음으로 그들이 수업 시간에 노화에 관하여 토의할 것이라는 것을 들었을 때, 그녀는 약간 실망했다. 아마도 이 분야는 지금까지 수업에서 그들이 다뤄 왔던 자료보다 덜 흥미롭고 ① 그녀 자신의 인생과 덜 관련이 있을 것이다. 그러나 주제를 조금 읽은 이후 Nosipho는 그녀의 생각이 시골 지역에 살고 계시는 ② 그녀의 할머니에게로 향한다는 것을 알았다. 그녀는 대략 1년에 한 번씩 ③ 그녀를 만났으나 그녀의 할머니는 여전히 그녀 가족의 삶에서 매우 중요한 인물이었다. 나이 드신 분들께 존경심을 갖는 것은 ④ 그녀가 어렸을 적부터 그녀의 어머니가 그녀에게 강조하여 이해시켰던 것이다.

| 정답해설 | ③ 83% Nosipho의 할머니를 지칭한다.

| 오답해설 | ①②④ 1% 0% 16% Nosipho를 지칭한다.

어휘

rural area 시골 지역   figure 인물
impress (중요성을 강조하여) 이해시키다

오답률 TOP 2

| **12** | 독해 > Reading for Writing > 빈칸 구 완성 | 오답률 45% | 답 ① |

| 해석 | 인간들은 사자나 식량 자원의 갑작스러운 출현같이 급격한 변화와 눈에 띄는 사건들을 감지하도록 진화했다. 우리는 점진적인 변화를 훨씬 덜 감지할 수 있다. Ornstein과 Ehrlich는 사람들이 사냥꾼이나 채집가였을 때 생존을 도왔던 지각 능력이 지금은 ① 불리한 조건이 될 수 있다고 생각한다. 문명에 직면한 많은 위협들은 매우 느리게 발달한다. 그 예로는 환경 악화, 지구 온난화, 그리고 오존층의 파괴가 있다. Ornstein과 Ehrlich는 우리가 직면하는 대규모의 위협들을 그들이 "삶은 개구리 증후군"이라고 부르는 것과 관련 짓는다. 천천히 가열되는 물이 담긴 팬 속의 개구리는 서서히 상승하는 온도를 감지할 수 없다. 그들은 죽을 때까지 가만히 앉아 있을 것이다. 불운한 개구리처럼, 많은 사람들은 현대 문명에서 점진적이지만 위협적인 경향들을 감지할 수 없을 것처럼 보인다.

① 장애, 불리한 조건   ② 안도
③ 무기   ④ 치유

| **정답해설** | ① 55% 빈칸 뒤에 문명화가 직면한 많은 문제들이 매우 천천히 진행되며 사람들은 점진적인 변화를 감지하는 능력이 떨어진다는 내용이 서술되어 있으므로, 갑작스러운 출현을 감지하도록 진화되어 생존에 도움을 주는 지각 능력이 지금은 '불리한 조건'이 된다는 설명이 적절하다.

| **더 알아보기** | **Boiled Frog Syndrome (삶은 개구리 증후군)**

> 끓는 물에 집어넣은 개구리는 바로 뛰쳐나오지만, 서서히 데워지고 있는 찬물에 들어간 개구리는 조만간 직면할 위험을 인지하지 못해 결국 죽게 되는 현상을 나타낸다. 점진적으로 고조되는 위험을 미리 인지하지 못하거나, 그에 대한 적절한 조기 대응을 못해 결국 화를 당하게 됨을 비유하는 것을 지칭한다.

어휘

gatherer 채집가 civilization 문명
threat 위협 degradation 악화, 비하
doomed 운이 다한, 불운한

---

13 독해 > Logical Reading > 연결사 오답률 14% 답 ①

| **해석** | 또래들이 신체적 활동과 스포츠에 있어서의 능숙함을 중요하게 생각하는 것은 분명하다. 즉, 어린이와 청소년이 그들의 또래 사이에서 더 나은 지위를 얻을 수 있는 하나의 방법은 신체적으로 능숙한 것으로 여겨지는 것이다. ① 그러나, 체육 교육에서 지속되는 문제는 능숙하지 못한 어린이와 청소년들을 위해 공평한 학습 경험을 제공하지 못하는 것이다. 능숙하지 못한 학생들은 전형적으로 연습할 기회들을 적게 얻으며 그들의 능숙한 또래들보다 성공할 가능성이 적다. 게임이 진행될 때, 능숙하지 못한 학생들은 때때로 의미 있는 경기에 실제로 참가할 기회가 거의 없다.

① 그러나 ② 요컨대 ③ 예를 들면 ④ 다시 말해서

| **정답해설** | ① 86% 빈칸 앞은 또래 사이에서 신체적으로 능숙한 것이 중요하다는 내용이다. 그리고 빈칸 이후로는 신체 활동이 능숙하지 못한 학생들에 대한 불평등한 교육 경험에 대하여 서술하므로 역접의 연결사 However가 적절하다.

어휘

peer 또래 competence 능숙함, 능숙도
youth 청소년 perceive 여기다, 감지하다
equitable 공정한, 공평한

---

14 독해 > Micro Reading > 내용일치/불일치 오답률 2% 답 ④

| **해석** | 직업과 관련된 경력은 상당한 유동성에 의해 특징지어지므로, 직업에 자리잡는 것이 항상 영구적인 상황은 아니다. 미국의 노동통계국에 따르면, 2005년에는 3%가 넘는 노동자들이 매달 그들의 직장을 떠났고, 그들의 대부분이 다른 고용주가 있는 직장을 잡았다. 노동통계국은 또한 2004년 초에 임금과 봉급 노동자가 단 4년 정도만 현재의 고용주와 함께 근무했다는 것을 밝혔다. 기대했던 것과 같이, 나이 많은 노동자들이 젊은 노동자보다 동일한 직장에서 더 오래 머물렀다. 45세 이상의 노동자들 사이에서, 약 절반은 그들의 현재 고용주와 10년 이상을 함께 근무했다. 대조적으로, 35~44세 사이의 노동자들 중 단지 대략 1/4의 노동자들만이 같은 기간의 근무 기간을 가졌다.

| **정답해설** | ④ 98% 끝에서 두 번째 문장 Among workers 45 years of age and older, about half had been with their current employer for 10 years or more.에서 45세 이상 노동자의 약 절반이 현재 고용주와 10년 이상 근무했다고 했다.

| **오답해설** | ① 0% 3%가 넘는 피고용인이 직장을 옮겼다.
② 0% 2004년 초, 모든 임금 노동자는 그 당시 고용주와 단 4년 정도만 근무했다고 했다.
③ 2% 나이가 많은 노동자가 같은 직장에 더 오래 근무했다고 했다.

어휘

settle into ~에 자리잡다 permanent 영구적인
occupational 직업의 significant 중요한; 상당한
fluidity 유동성 tenure 재임 기간, 근무 기간

---

15 독해 > Micro Reading > 내용일치/불일치 오답률 4% 답 ④

| **해석** | Mark Young은 대형 병원의 페인팅 부서장이며 20명의 직원이 그에게 보고한다. 이 병원에 들어오기 전에, 그는 독립 계약자로 일했다. 병원이 어떻게 페인팅 서비스를 제공할지에 대한 변화가 필요하다고 믿었으므로, 그는 병원에서 새롭게 만든 지위를 맡았다. 업무를 시작하자마자, Mark는 페인팅 서비스의 직접 비용과 간접 비용에 대한 4개월 간의 분석을 수행했다. 그의 발견은 페인팅 서비스가 비효율적이고 비용이 많이 든다고 생각하는 관리자의 인식을 뒷받침했다. 그 결과, Mark는 부서를 완전히 재조직하고, 새로운 일정 절차를 계획하며, 기대 성과 기준을 다시 정의하였다.

| **정답해설** | ④ 96% Mark의 발견이 페인팅 서비스가 비효율적이고 비용이 많이 든다고 생각하는 관리자의 인식을 뒷받침했다는 것으로 보아, 비효율적인 페인팅 서비스를 발견하지 못했다는 선지는 글의 내용과 일치하지 않는다.

어휘

on board 합류한, 승선한 independent 독립된
costly 많은 비용이 드는 procedure 절차, 수순
redefined 다시 정의된 standard 수준, 기준

---

16 독해 > Macro Reading > 제목 오답률 8% 답 ①

| **해석** | 파인애플은 17세기 동안 초기 유럽 탐험가들에 의해 서인도 제도로부터 유입되었다. 그때부터 쭉, 파인애플은 유럽에서 경작되었고 왕족과 엘리트들에게 제공되는 인기 있는 과일이 되었다. 파인애플은 후에 북아메리카로 유입되었고 북아메리카의 환대의 일부가 되었다. 파인애플은 "배가 들어 왔어요! 와서 우리와 함께해요. 음식과 마실 것 전부!"라고 친구들과 지인들에게 알리면서 문이나 문기둥에 전시되었다. 그것이 도입된 이래로, 파인애플은 국제적으로 환대의 상징과 친근함, 따뜻함, 격려의 표시로 인식되어졌다.

① 파인애플: 환대의 상징
② 서양에서의 파인애플 경작
③ 서양의 파인애플 산업
④ 환대: 인간의 본질

| **정답해설** | ① 92% 파인애플이 국제적으로 환대의 상징으로 인식되게 된 경위를 설명하는 글이므로 ①이 글의 제목으로 가장 적절하다.

어휘

from that time on 그 후 favored 인기 있는
hospitality 환대, 접대 gatepost 문기둥
acquaintance 지인

17 독해 > Logical Reading > 배열   오답률 26%   답 ③

| 해석 | 일부 조직들은 남성들이나 여성들에게 아이를 돌보기 위해 경력상의 휴식을 취하는 것을 허락하는 정책들을 가지고 있다.

(C) 그러나, 아버지들은 실제로 그러한 기회를 거의 이용하지 않았을 뿐 아니라 그런 선택을 한 사례는 그들이 그렇게 하는 경우 그들의 경력을 평생 '망치는' 결과가 될 수 있음을 보여 준다.

(A) 정말로, 이러한 사실은 남성들의 해당 제도 이용 비율이 낮은 원인이 되는 것이 당연하다.

(B) 그래서, 조직들은 경력을 보다 유연하게 운영할 수 있는 구조를 갖추어야 할 뿐만 아니라, 전형적으로 철저하게 전통으로 남아 있는 태도들을 변화시켜야 한다.

| 정답해설 | ③ 74% (A)의 the knowledge of this(이러한 사실)는 (C)에 나오는 if they had done so, their careers would have been 'ruined' for life. 즉, '육아 휴직으로 인해 경력을 망치는 것'을 지칭하므로 (C) 다음 배치되는 것이 적절하다. (B)는 해결책을 제시하는 내용이므로 마지막이 알맞다. 따라서 (C) - (A) - (B) 순서가 옳다.

어휘
policy 정책, 방침   scheme 계획, 제도
anecdotal evidence 일화적 증거, 사례
avail oneself of ~을 이용하다

18 독해 > Logical Reading > 삽입   오답률 11%   답 ②

| 해석 | 성인 의뢰인들은 대개 가장 주된 수단으로서 말하는 것을 포함하는 치료법에 편안함을 느낀다. 소아 의뢰인들은 종종 놀이 치료가 가장 효과적인데, 이것은 그들의 언어적 표현을 보충하기 위한 장난감이나 다른 물건들을 이용하는 것이다. ② 그러나, 청소년 의뢰인들은 장난감을 가지고 놀기에는 너무 나이가 많고, 주로 언어적 형태가 편안하게 느껴지기에는 너무 어리다. 이것은 청소년을 치료하는 것은 그 의뢰인을 편안함을 느끼도록 도우며, 말하는 것과 자기표현, 그리고 문제 해결을 돕기 위해 다양한 종류의 구조의 창의적인 활용이 필요하다는 것을 의미한다. 이러한 종류의 구조는 더 많은 질문들, 치료사의 자기 개방, 많은 다양한 설정들을 제공하는 것 그리고 산책을 하는 것 또는 점심을 먹기 위해 식당에서 만나는 것과 같이 구조화된 상호적인 활동들을 포함한다. 연구는 청소년들에게는 "전통적인 장기적 개인 심리 치료는 더 간략하고 더 집중된 정신 요법의 개입보다 덜 효과적"이라는 사실을 알려준다.

| 정답해설 | ② 89% 주어진 문장은 청소년 의뢰인에 대한 내용이 제시된 부분이므로 청소년 의뢰인과 그 치료에 대한 내용이 시작되는 ②에 위치해야 한다.

어휘
primarily 주로   supplement 보충하다
psychotherapeutic 정신 요법의   intervention 조정, 중재, 개입

19 독해 > Logical Reading > 삭제   오답률 19%   답 ③

| 해석 | 기능주의 이론은 만약 사회가 그 사회의 가장 능력 있고, 열심히 일하는 구성원에게 사회의 가장 중요한 역할을 수행하기 위한 동기를 제공한다면 불평등은 반드시 필요하다는 입장을 취한다. 몇몇 역할들은 (직업을 포함하여) 다른 역할들이 하는 것보다 더 많은 기술과 훈련을 요구한다. 대개는, 역할을 수행하기 위해 더 많은 기술과 훈련이 요구될수록 더 적은 수의 사람들이 그 일을 할 수 있는 자격을 가지며, 다른 모든 것들과 동일하

게, 그들의 능력이 전체 집단에서 좀 더 가치가 있다. 기능주의자들은 동등하지 않은 보상이 가장 능력 있는 개인들을 가장 사회적으로 가치 있는 역할로 고용하는 효과적인 방법이라고 주장한다. ③ 불평등은 엘리트를 제외하고 아무에게도 혜택을 제공하지 않는다. 그리고 사실상, 그것이 만들어내는 불필요한 갈등으로 인하여 전체 사회에 해로운 영향을 끼친다. 우리 대부분에게 부족한 재능을 가지고 있는 사람들에 대한 보상이 없으면, 그들은 우리 모두에게 이익이 되는 행위들에 그들의 재능을 사용하기 위한 동기를 가지지 않을 것이다.

| 정답해설 | ③ 81% 이 글은 inequality is necessary 즉, 사회 전체의 이익을 위해 차별적인 보상이 필요함을 주장한다. 그런데 ③은 차별적인 보상이 '엘리트를 제외한 다른 사람에게는 혜택을 거의 주지 않고 전체 사회에 해가 된다'라면서 불평등의 부정적인 측면을 서술하고 있으므로 전체 흐름에 관계없는 내용이다.

어휘
functionalist 기능주의   incentive 동기 유발, 인센티브

20 독해 > Macro Reading > 요지   오답률 7%   답 ④

| 해석 | 불행하게도, 우리 뇌는 긍정적인 정보보다 부정적인 정보에 더 많은 영향을 받는다. 예를 들어, 두 가지 시나리오를 상상해 보자. 첫 번째 시나리오에서 당신은 Saks로부터 500달러의 상품권을 획득했다는 사실을 알게 된다. 당신은 그 사실에 대하여 매우 좋아할 것이다, 그렇지 않은가? 두 번째 시나리오에서, 당신은 500달러가 들어 있는 당신의 지갑을 잃어버린다. 당신은 그 사실에 대하여 얼마나 불행하다고 느낄까? 위험 부담 연구 결과에 따르면, 이러한 경험들에 대한 당신의 반응의 강도는 현저하게 다르다. 과학자들이 뇌의 부정적인 편견으로 언급하고 있는 것의 결과로, 500달러를 잃어버림으로써 당신이 겪은 정신적인 고통은 그 상품권을 획득했을 때 당신이 느낀 기쁨을 훨씬 초과할 것이다.

① 사람들은 부정적인 감정보다 기쁨을 더 쉽게 경험한다.
② 인간 뇌의 부정적인 편견은 긍정적인 경험에 의해 강화된다.
③ 긍정적인 감정과 부정적인 감정의 균형은 행복의 근원이다.
④ 사람들은 긍정적인 경험보다 부정적인 경험에 의해 더 영향을 받는다.

| 정답해설 | ④ 93% 첫 문장에서 '인간의 뇌는 긍정적인 정보보다 부정적인 정보에 의해 더 영향을 받는다'라는 내용이 제시되어 있고, 이후 구체적인 예시가 나오는 두괄식 지문이다. 따라서 ④가 이 글의 요지로 적절하다.

어휘
gift certificate 상품권   risk-taking 위험 부담
intensity 강도, 강렬함   markedly 현저하게, 뚜렷하게
refer to as ~라고 언급하다

합격예상 체크

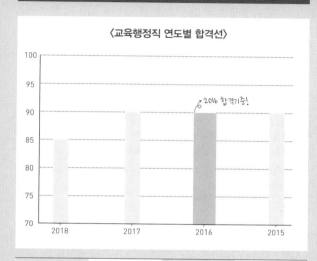

〈교육행정직 연도별 합격선〉

맞힌 개수	/20문항	점수	/100점

➡ □ 합격 □ 불합격

취약영역 체크

문항	정답	영역	문항	정답	영역
1	①	어휘 > 빈칸 완성	11	②	독해 > Logical Reading > 문맥상 다양한 추론
2	①	어휘 > 빈칸 완성	12	④	어휘 > 빈칸 완성
3	④	어휘 > 빈칸 완성	13	③	독해 > Micro Reading > 내용일치/불일치
4	③	독해 > Logical Reading > 문맥상 다양한 추론	14	②	독해 > Micro Reading > 내용일치/불일치
5	①	문법 > 전치사, 동사	15	①	독해 > Logical Reading > 연결사
6	③	문법 > 전치사, 일치	16	②	독해 > Macro Reading > 제목
7	④	생활영어 > 회화/관용표현	17	②	독해 > Logical Reading > 배열
8	②	문법 > 대명사	18	④	독해 > Reading for Writing > 요약
9	③	문법 > 관계사	19	④	독해 > Logical Reading > 삽입
10	③	문법 > 비교	20	④	독해 > Macro Reading > 요지

⬇ 영역별 틀린 개수로 취약영역을 확인하세요!

어휘	/4	문법	/5	독해	/10	생활영어	/1

➡ 나의 취약영역: _____

※ [정답해설]과 [오답해설] 선지의 50% 표시는 〈1초 합격예측 서비스〉를 통해 수집된 선지 선택률을 나타냅니다.

1   어휘 > 빈칸 완성   오답률 23%   답 ①

| 해석 | 농업은 생물 다양성 감소를 가속화시킨다. 농장을 만들기 위해 우리가 풀밭과 숲을 밀어 버렸기 때문에, 우리는 중요한 서식지를 잃었고, 이는 농업이 야생 동물 ① 멸종의 주요한 원인으로 작용하게 만든다.

① 77% 멸종   ② 10% 생식, 번식
③ 3% 분류   ④ 10% 다양화

| 정답해설 | ① 생물의 다양성을 감소시킨다는 것은 종의 개체수를 감소시킨다는 것이며, 선지 중 이와 관련된 것은 extinction(멸종)이다.

어휘
agriculture 농업
biodiversity 생물적 다양성
driver 추진 요인, 동인
accelerate 가속화시키다
habitat 서식지

2   어휘 > 빈칸 완성   오답률 19%   답 ①

| 해석 | 『To Free a Family』는 1848년 8월 그녀의 주인으로부터 떠나 북쪽으로 피난한 Mary Walker의 놀라운 이야기를 전한다. 그녀의 자유는 속박으로부터 ① 도망친 수천 명의 그것처럼, 한 마디 말도 없이 헤어진다는 것에 대한 후회, 그녀의 가족의 운명에 대한 두려움과 같은 큰 대가가 따랐다.

① 81% 도망친   ② 6% 달랐던
③ 3% 이득을 보았던   ④ 10% 비롯되었던

| 정답해설 | ① 『To Free a Family』는 Mary Walker가 주인으로부

터 도망쳐 피난 나온 이야기이다. 빈칸 앞의 '수천 명의 사람들'은 그녀와 비슷한 처지에 있는 사람들로 역시 속박으로부터 '도망친(escaped)' 사람들임을 유추할 수 있다.

어휘
remarkable 놀랄 만한, 놀라운
bondage 구속, 속박
remorse 죄책감, 회한
refuge 피난(처), 도피(처)
price 비용, 대가
part 떠나다

오답률 TOP 1
3   어휘 > 빈칸 완성   오답률 53%   답 ④

| 해석 | 달력이 1월에서부터 12월까지 계속되는 대부분의 우리와 다르게, 그리고 "회계 연도"가 회계 담당자가 생각하는 최고의 달이면 언제든지 시작하고 끝날 수 있는 기업과는 다르게, 콘서트 시즌은 대개 가을에서부터 봄까지로 ④ 여겨진다.

① 12% 위임받은   ② 24% 질문된
③ 17% 제정된   ④ 47% 여겨지는

| 정답해설 | ④ 주어는 concert seasons이며, 빈칸 뒤에 구체적인 기간이 나와 있으므로, 이에 어울리는 동사는 reckon(예상하다, 여기다)이다.

어휘
fiscal years 회계 연도
deem 여기다, 생각하다
treasurer 회계 담당자

| 해석 | 리더들은 능동적으로 자기계발의 일부 측면들을 이끌어 나간다. 자기 계발 목표를 그려내는 체계적인 계획은, 그것이 없다면 리더들이 간과해 버릴 수도 있는 기회를 이용하는 데에 도움을 줄 것이다. 또한 체계적인 계획을 발전시키는 것은 리더들이 다양한 목표의 중요성에 우선순위를 매기는 데에 도움을 준다. 어떤 세미나, 회의에 참석할지를 주의 깊게 선택하는 리더들은 개인적인 발전 관련 목표에 대한 그들의 기여를 ③ 줄이는(→ 늘리는) 데에 그들 자신에게 도움을 줄 수 있다. 리더들은 그들의 성장을 발전시킬 수 있는 책임감을 위해 직장이나 봉사 활동 내에서 기회를 찾는 것이 좋다.

| 정답해설 | ③ 81% 어떤 세미나, 회의에 참석할지를 신중하게 고르는 지도자는 목표에 대한 기여를 '줄이는' 것이 아니라 오히려 '늘리는'으로 생각하는 것이 알맞다. 따라서, lessen의 쓰임이 적절치 않으므로 increase(상승시키다) 등으로 수정하는 것이 옳다.

| 오답해설 | ① 9% 체계적인 계획이 없었다면 '간과해 버릴' 수도 있던 기회들을 살려 이용한다는 흐름은 적절하다.

② 7% 체계적인 계획을 세우는 것은 다양한 목표의 중요성에 '우선순위를 매기도록' 해 줄 것이다.

④ 3% 리더들이 기회를 찾는 것은 그들 자신의 성장을 위함이다. further는 이를 발전시키는 것으로 문맥상 옳다.

어휘

direct 지도하다, 이끌다
outline 윤곽을 나타내다, 개요를 서술하다
overlook 간과하다   further 발전시키다

| 해석 | 아이들과 간지럼은 우유와 쿠키(A)처럼 어울린다. 그런가? 그러나 갓 태어난 당신의 아기에게 간지럼을 태워 보라. 그러면 그녀는 미소조차 짓지 않을지도 모른다. 왜 그럴까? 아이를 (B) 웃게 만드는 것은 사실 간지럼을 당할 때의 그 감각이 아니다. 실제로, 연구들은 대부분의 사람들이 그 느낌을 실제로 즐기지 않는다는 것을 보여 준다.

| 정답해설 | ① 78% (A) 빈칸 뒤에 목적어가 왔으므로, '~처럼'이라는 의미를 지니며 목적어를 취할 수 있는 전치사 like가 알맞다.

(B) 앞의 사역동사 make의 목적격 보어 위치이다. 사역동사 make는 목적격 보어로 원형부정사를 취한다.

어휘

go together 어울리다   not so much as ~조차도 하지 않는
crack a smile 방긋 웃다

| 해석 | 스포츠가 우리 일상의 매우 중요한 부분이라는 사실에도 (A) 불구하고, 그것은 최근까지도 사회학자들에게 의해 진지하게 연구된 적이 거의 없다. 따라서, 사회 활동으로서의 스포츠의 명확하고 강렬한 정의 및 설명은 거의 없다.

| 정답해설 | ③ 65% (A) 뒤에 절이 아닌 명사구가 나오므로 양보의 전치사인 Despite가 와야 한다. (B) 주어는 복수인 definitions and descriptions이므로, 동사의 형태는 are가 적절하다.

어휘

salient 가장 중요한, 핵심의   sociologist 사회학자
compelling 강렬한

| 해석 | A: 지난주 포틀럭 파티에서 재밌었니?
B: 정말 재밌었어! 사람들이 맛있는 음식들을 많이 가져왔어.
A: 정말? 너는 어느 것이 가장 좋았어?
B: Brian의 것이 가장 좋았어. 그가 정말 맛있는 라자냐를 만들어 와서 하나도 남지 않았어.
A: 그걸 놓쳤다니, 안타깝네!
B: ④ 다음번에는 너도 오는 게 어때?
A: 글쎄, 나는 요리를 정말 못해. 나는 무얼 만들어야 할지도 모르겠어.
B: 걱정 마. 너는 대신에 과일이나 음료수 같은 것들을 가져와도 돼.
A: 다행이다. 그럼 너희들이 다시 모일 때 알려줘.
① 내가 한번 해 볼게.
② 조금 더 먹을래?
③ 그건 내가 말한 의미가 정확히 아니야.
④ 다음번에는 너도 오는 게 어때?

| 정답해설 | ④ 90% potluck 파티는 참석자 각자가 음식을 가지고 오는 파티이다. 빈칸의 B의 말에 대해 A는 자신이 음식을 잘 못한다고 말했고, 이에 B는 과일이나 음료수를 가져와도 된다고 했으므로 B는 다음에 A도 참석할 것을 제안했음을 알 수 있다.

어휘

give it a try 한번 해 보다

| 해석 | 실제로, 사람들이 이익을 발견할 때마다. 그들은 그것을 쫓기 마련이고, 그들이 손해를 발견할 때마다. 달아나는 것은 인간의 본성이다. 예를 들자면, 상인이 무역에 참여하고 하루에 일상적인 거리의 두 배를 이동하며, 하루를 연장하기 위해 밤을 이용하고(지새고), 너무 멀다 생각하지 않고 수천 마일을 이동할 때, 이것은 앞에 이익이 놓여 있기 때문이다.

| 정답해설 | ② 61% 문맥상 them은 앞에 나온 profit을 지칭하는 것이므로 단수 대명사 it으로 고쳐 써야 한다.

| 오답해설 | ① 14% 가주어 it, 진주어 that절로 알맞게 사용되었다.

③ 18% uses의 주어는 the merchant로, 3인칭 단수 동사가 옳게 사용되었다. 또한 engages, travels, covers와 병렬 관계에 있다.

④ 7% because는 명사절을 이끄는 접속사로 사용되고 있으며, 해당 문장에서 보어 역할을 하고 있다. because가 명사절을 이끄는 것은 주로 비격식체에서이다.

어휘

illustrate 설명하다, 예시를 들다   ordinary 일상적인

| 해석 | 나침판은 역사상 가장 중요한 발명품 중 하나였다. 그것은 엄청난 탐험 시대를 촉발시켰고 이것은 결과적으로 유럽에 엄청난 부를 가져왔다. 이러한 부는 훗날 계몽 운동과 산업 혁명과 같은 사건들이 일어나도록 만들었다. 그것은 세상에 알려진 이후로 사람들의 삶을 계속하여 간소화시키고

있다.

| 정답해설 | ③ 85% 관계대명사 that 이하에 동사 fuel의 주어 역할을 하는 명사가 없으므로 불완전한 형태이며, 선행사도 존재하지 않으므로, that은 선행사를 포함하는 관계대명사 what으로 고쳐야 한다.

| 오답해설 | ① 1% the most important는 최상급 표현으로, 「one of the + 최상급 + 복수 명사」의 형태는 적절하다.

② 9% which는 It sparked an enormous age of exploration을 선행사로 하는 계속적 용법의 주격 관계대명사이다.

④ 5% 주절에 현재완료가 쓰였으므로 since는 알맞다. 여기서 since는 '~ 이래로'라는 의미의 전치사로, 명사구를 이끌고 있다.

어휘

enormous 거대한, 막대한   fuel 연료를 공급하다, 부채질하다
Enlightenment 계몽 운동   Industrial Revolution 산업 혁명

오답률 TOP 2

10 문법 > 비교   오답률 50%   답 ③

| 해석 | 말하기에 대한 두려움, 혹은 의사소통의 불안감은 심지어 숙련된 연설자들에 의해서도 경험되는 흔한 증상이다. 그것의 원인들이 충분히 설명되지는 않지만, 그것은 연설자가 연설자의 의견을 수용하는 것에 높은 의구심을 가진 낯선 청중들 앞에서 익숙하지 않은 환경에서 익숙하지 않은 역할에 직면할 때 특히 잘 나타나는 것 같다. 의사소통의 불안감을 통제하는 것은 가능한 한 불확실하고 낯선 영역들을 많이 제거하는 것에 있다. 건강한 정신 자세를 동반한 철저한 준비와 연습은 의사소통의 불안감이라는 무능력을 예방하도록 도와줄 것이다.

| 정답해설 | ③ 50% 뒤의 as possible로 보아 「as + 형용사/부사의 원급 + as possible」의 구조가 되어야 한다. 단, 부정문의 경우 as 대신에 so를 사용할 수 있으나 해당 문장은 긍정문이므로 so를 as로 고쳐야 옳다.

| 오답해설 | ① 4% experienced는 a common condition을 후치 수식하고 있는 과거분사의 형태로 적절하다.

② 19% 소유격 관계대명사 whose는 an unfamiliar audience를 선행사로 취하며, 뒤에 나온 명사 reception을 수식하고 있으므로 적절하다.

④ 27% help의 목적어로 원형부정사가 올 수 있으므로 guard는 적절하다.

어휘

apprehension 불안, 걱정   seasoned 경험 많은, 노련한
surface 겉으로 드러나다   coupled with ~을 동반한, ~와 결부된

---

11 독해 > Logical Reading > 문맥상 다양한 추론   답 ②
오답률 6%

| 해석 | "전갈과 개구리"의 이야기를 들어본 적이 있는가?" 한 개구리가 전갈 앞에 와서 목숨을 구걸한다. 전갈은 개구리가 ① 그를 강을 건너게 해 주면 개구리를 죽이지 않겠다고 말한다. 그 개구리는 묻기를, "내가 당신을 실어다 주면 당신이 ② 나를 죽이지 않는다는 것을 어찌 아나요?" 그 전갈이 대답하기를, "내가 널 찌른다면, 우리는 분명 둘 다 죽을 것이다." 숙고하더니, 그 개구리가 동의하고 강을 반쯤 건널 때에 전갈이 개구리의 등을 찌른다. 둘 다 물에 빠지기 시작할 때, 그 개구리는 묻는다. "왜 ③ 당신은 나를

찔렀어요? 이제 우리 둘 다 죽게 됐잖아요." 그 전갈은 마지막 숨을 거두면서 대답한다. "그건 내가 통제할 수 없는 ④ 내 본능이기 때문이야."

| 정답해설 | ② 94% '개구리'를 지칭한다.

| 오답해설 | ① 2% ③ 2% ④ 2% 모두 '전갈'을 지칭한다.

어휘

plead 간청하다, 애원하다

---

12 어휘 > 빈칸 완성   오답률 18%   답 ④

| 해석 | 나는 연설자의 슬라이드인 북미 지도의 위아래가 뒤집어져 있었던 한 세미나에 참가한 적이 있다. 연설자가 재빨리 말했다. "북미를 남반구에서 보았을 때 이렇게 보이죠." 그리고 이것은 많은 웃음을 자아냈다. 그 후 일 년 정도가 지나, 나는 브라질의 지도가 거꾸로 놓인 상태에서 연설을 하고 있었다. 그래서 내가 말했다. "지구 중심에서 보았을 때 브라질이 이렇게 보이죠." 그들이 그것을 이해하는 데에 1분이 걸렸지만 그들도 이 말에 웃었다. 당신이 슬라이드를 바르게 놓으려고 조심했더라도, 가끔은 당신이 일을 그르칠 수도 있다. 그리고 만약 당신이 이러한 상투적인 ④ 농담들 중 하나를 준비해 놓는다면, 청중을 항상 당신 편에 서게 할 수 있다.

① 8% 지도들   ② 8% 슬라이드들
③ 2% 속담들   ④ 82% 농담들

| 정답해설 | ④ 실수를 농담으로 만회하고 청중을 웃게 한 일화를 말하는 글로, 빈칸이 있는 문장은 글 전체를 요약하고 있다. 즉, 어떤 일을 그르치더라도 상투적인 '농담(jokes)'을 준비하면 청중을 자신의 편에 서게 할 수 있다는 내용이 알맞다.

어휘

screw up (일을) 그르치다, 망치다   stock 진부한, 상투적인

---

13 독해 > Micro Reading > 내용일치/불일치   오답률 3%   답 ③

| 해석 | 2013년 세계 차(茶) 생산이 6퍼센트까지 상당히 올라 507만 톤으로 증가했다. 홍차 생산량은 계속적인 고정 가격으로 5.4퍼센트까지 증가했고, 녹차 생산량은 5.1퍼센트 증가했다. 세계 생산량의 증가는 주요 차 생산국가에서 증가가 컸기 때문이었다. 중국은 세계 시장의 38퍼센트 이상을 차지하며, 190만 톤의 생산량을 가진 최대의 차 생산국을 유지했다. 세계 두 번째 차 생산국인 인도의 생산 또한 120만 톤에 도달하며 증가했다. 또한 최대의 수출국인 두 나라에서의 생산량 또한 증가했는데, 케냐에서는 436,300톤, 스리랑카에서는 343,100톤에 달했다. 베트남에서 185,000톤으로 7.5퍼센트 감소한 것을 제외하고, 인도네시아, 방글라데시, 그리고 르완다와 같은 주요 생산 국가의 생산량은 증가했다.

| 정답해설 | ③ 97% Output also increased ~ in Sri Lanka.라는 문장을 통해 케냐와 스리랑카의 차 생산량이 증가하였음을 알 수 있다.

| 오답해설 | ① 0% 첫 문장 World tea producion increased significantly로 보아, 세계 차 생산량은 크게 증가하였음을 알 수 있다.

② 0% 최대의 차 생산국은 중국이고, 인도는 그 뒤를 잇고 있다.

④ 3% 마지막 문장 Apart from the 7.5 percent decline in Vietnam으로 보아 베트남의 차 생산량은 감소했음을 알 수 있다.

어휘

in response to ~에 응하여[답하여]   account for ~을 차지하다

| 해석 | Massachusetts주 Quaker 농장 가정에서 태어난 Abby Kelley Foster는 농부들이 아들을 갖기 위해 기도하던 시대에 (태어난) 일곱 번째 딸이었다. 그녀는 Worcester에서 자랐으며 중등학교를 마쳤고, Rhode Island의 Providence에 위치한 Quaker 학교에서 고등 교육에 진학한 몇 안 되는 소녀들 중 한 명이었다. 그녀는 자립하기 위해 학업과 아이들을 가르치는 일을 번갈아 가며 했다. William Lloyd Garrison의 노예 제도 강의를 들은 것이 그녀 삶의 방향을 바꿔 놓았다. Massachusetts주 Lynn에서 공부를 가르치는 동안 그녀는 지역의 반노예 제도 여성 단체에 가입했고, 곧 노예 폐지 운동을 위한 유급 강사가 되었다. 그녀는 1845년 Stephen S. Foster와 결혼하였으며, 그들은 종종 노예제 폐지 연설가로서 같이 다녔다. 그들은 Worcester의 농장에서 일했으며, 그곳을 도망 나온 노예들의 피난처로 만들었다.

| 정답해설 | ② 96% was one of the rare girls to go on to higher education(고등 교육에 진학한 몇 안 되는 소녀들 중 한 명이었다)이라고 했으므로 본문의 내용과 일치하지 않는다.

| 더 알아보기 | **내용일치/불일치 유형 문제풀이 TIP**

> 내용 일치/불일치 유형은 선지 내용의 일치 및 불일치 여부를 확인해야 하는 영역이다. '빠르고 정확한 독해 문제풀이'를 위해 이 영역은 본문 전체를 먼저 읽기보다는 선지의 내용을 지문에서 찾아봐야 한다. 특히 선지에서 고유명사, 숫자, 문장 부호 등이 본문 내용을 찾아가는 '지표'로 사용되기도 하니 이 점을 잘 활용한다면 효율적인 문제풀이를 할 수 있다.

어휘

alternate 교대로 하다, 번갈아하다　　spell 한 차례의 일; 교대
abolition 폐지　　haven 피난처, 안식처
fugitive 도망자, 탈주자

| 해석 | 기업들은 전통적으로 마케팅 노력의 성과로 고객과의 개별적인 거래에 초점을 맞추어 왔다. 그러나 세계 시장이 점점 경쟁이 과열되고, 불안해지자, 많은 기업들이 조직과 고객 사이의 지속적인 장기적 관계를 구축하는 것을 성공적인 마케팅 전략의 궁극적인 목적으로 관심을 돌렸다. 그들은 평생 고객 가치, 즉 긴 시간에 걸쳐 고객에 의해 생산될 수 있는 수익 흐름의 현재 가치를 늘리는 조치를 취하고 있다. ① 예를 들어, 자동차 제조업자에게 있어 제조업자에게 만족하고 충성도를 보일 생애 첫 자동차 구매자의 평생 가치, 즉 같은 회사에서 미래의 모든 신차를 구입하는 가치는 백만 달러가 족히 넘는 것이다.

① 예를 들어　　　　② 게다가
③ 그렇지 않으면　　④ 그럼에도 불구하고

| 정답해설 | ① 85% 빈칸 앞의 문장에서 기업들이 고객과 장기적 관계를 구축하는 것을 마케팅 전략의 목적으로 전환해 평생 고객의 가치를 늘리는 조치를 취하고 있다고 말하고 있고, 빈칸이 있는 문장에서는 자동차 제조업체의 평생 고객 가치의 예를 제시하고 있으므로 for instance가 알맞다.

어휘

transaction 거래　　　　　　fruition 성과, 결실
volatile 불안한, 변덕이 심한　　objective 목표
lifetime 평생, 생애; 일생의, 평생의

| 해석 | Uncle Walt는 디즈니랜드를 위해 필요한 땅을 모두 구입할 형편이 안 되었다. 그래서 모든 것이 들어갈 공간을 만들기 위해, 그는 영화 제작자의 속임수를 이용하여 모든 것을 더 크게 보이게 만들었다. 속임수 하나는 익숙한 것을 사용하되 정상 크기보다 작게 만드는 것이었다. 눈으로 유심히 보고 재 보지 않는 이상, 예를 들어, 당신은 디즈니랜드의 열차가 정상 크기라고 생각할 것이다. 그렇지 않은데 말이다. 그것은 5/8 크기로 만들어졌다. 많은 디즈니 건물들이 이와 같은 속임수를 사용하고 있으나, 이는 그저 시작에 불과하다. 일부 디즈니 건물들을 유심히 관찰해 보면, 당신은 조금 이상한 점을 발견할 수 있을 것이다. 그것들은 정상 크기보다 작을 뿐만 아니라 2층과 3층은 심지어 더 작다. 위층을 점점 가늘게 만듦으로써 디자이너는 그것들이 실제 크기보다 더 크고 높다고 믿도록 당신의 눈을 속이는 것이다.

① 디즈니랜드에서의 영화 제작
② 디즈니랜드: 착각의 땅
③ 속임수가 항상 먹히는 것은 아니다
④ 디즈니랜드의 안전 수칙

| 정답해설 | ② 82% Uncle Walt는 디즈니랜드를 위한 충분한 땅을 구입할 수 없어서, 대신 건물들의 크기를 줄이되 사람들이 눈치채지 못하도록 교묘한 속임수를 썼다고 하며 그 구체적인 방법을 설명했다. 따라서 글의 제목으로는 '디즈니랜드: 착각의 땅'이 가장 적절하다. (해당 지문의 9번째 문장에서 still smaller는 기출 문제에서 smaller still로 출제되었지만, 어법상 still smaller가 적절하므로 본 교재에는 옳게 수정하여 수록하였다.)

어휘

fit ~ in ~이 들어갈 공간을 만들다　　taper 점점 가늘게 만들다
fool 속이다, 기만하다

| 해석 | 특정 문화 체계의 정치 조직을 말할 때, 우리는 자주 정치적 경계와 문화적 경계가 같다는 인상을 받게 된다.
(B) 그러나 정치, 또는 정치적으로 조직된 단체의 그 경계는 삶의 특정 방식의 경계와 일치할 수도 일치하지 않을 수도 있다.
(C) 예를 들면, 대초원 지대의 Comanche 부족은 공통 언어, 관습, 그리고 민족 정체성을 공유했지만, 정치적으로, 그들은 절대 지역 집단을 넘어서게 조직되지 않았다.
(A) 따라서, Comanche 부족이라는 용어는 공통 언어와 문화를 같이하지만 결코 공통 정치 활동을 수행하도록 연합되지 않는 민족을 일컫는다.

| 정답해설 | ② 80% But으로 시작하는 (B)는 주어진 내용에 대한 반대의 가정이므로 처음 순서가 된다. For example로 시작해 Comanche 부족의 예를 들고 있는 (C)는 (B)의 예이므로 그 뒤에 와야 한다. 마지막으로 (A)는 (C)에 나온 Comanche 부족이라는 용어가 일컫는 바를 언급하며 글을 마무리하고 있다. 따라서 (B) – (C) – (A)의 순서가 알맞다.

어휘

correspond with ~와 상응하다, 일치하다
ethnic 민족의, 종족의　　　　carry out 수행하다, 이행하다

---

18 독해 > Reading for Writing > 요약 　오답률 28%　답 ④

| 해석 | 공유지의 딜레마는 다음의 우화에서 이름 붙여졌다. 당신은 작은 마을의 목동이다. 모두가 자유롭게 공유할 수 있는 공유지라 불리는 땅이 하나 있다. 대부분의 시간 동안, 당신의 양들은 당신의 땅에서 풀을 뜯어 먹지만, 몇몇 양들이 풀을 좀 더 먹어야 할 때, 당신은 공유지에 자유롭게 그 양들을 데려갈 수 있다. 그 마을에는 50명의 목동이 있는데, 공유지는 하루에 약 50마리의 양만 먹여 살릴 수 있다. 그래서 각각의 목동이 공유지로 평균적으로 하루에 한 마리의 양을 데려간다면, 모든 일은 잘 풀린다. 만약 일부 목동들이 그들의 땅의 풀을 아끼고자 하루에 몇 마리의 양을 공유지에 데려가기로 결정했다고 가정해 보자. 지지 않기 위해서, 다른 목동들도 똑같이 한다. 곧 공유지는 척박해지고 모두에게 쓸모가 없어진다. (A) 개인의 이익을 추구하는 것은 전체에는 오직 (B) 해로운 결과를 가져올 뿐이다.

	(A)	(B)
①	집단의, 공동의	해로운
②	집단의, 공동의	이로운
③	개인의	긍정적인
④	개인의	해로운

| 정답해설 | ④ 72% 주어진 우화에서 공유지는 모두가 자유롭게 이용할 수 있는 땅이지만, 50명의 목동이 함께 이용하려면 한 사람당 하루에 한 마리의 양만 데려갈 수 있다. 그러나 몇몇이 자기 땅의 풀을 아끼기 위해 이를 무시하고 그 이상의 양들을 공유지로 데려간다면, 결국 공유지는 쓸모가 없어져 모두에게 손해를 가져올 것이라고 했다. 이 글에서 필자가 주장하는 것은 '개인의' 이익 추구는 전체에 '해로운' 결과를 가져온다는 것이다.

| 더 알아보기 | The Commons Dilemma (공유지의 딜레마, 공유지의 비극)

> 누구나 자유롭게 사용할 수 있는 공공 자원은 사람들의 남용으로 쉽게 고갈될 수 있다는 이론이다. 개인의 사리사욕을 극대화하면 공동체나 사회 전체는 물론 자연까지 파괴할 수 있음을 경고하고 있다.

어휘
parable 우화　　　　　　　shepherd 목동
common 공유지　　　　　　outdo 능가하다, 이기다
barren 척박한, 황량한

19 독해 > Logical Reading > 삽입 　오답률 28%　답 ④

| 해석 | 혁신은 새로운 종교적 믿음에서부터 기술적 변화까지 아마도 사회 구성원에 의해 내부적으로 발생하는 무엇이든 될 수 있을 것이다. 사람들은 지속적으로 그들이 하는 일과 그들이 그것을 하는 방법을 변화시키고 있다. 대부분의 사례에서, 이러한 변화들은 사소하고, 너무 작아서 감지할 수 없고 무의식적이다. 신화를 이야기할 때, 사람은 다른 것은 자세하게 설명하면서도, 어떤 부분은 삭제하고 말할 수 있다. 개개인은 머리 길이를 다르게 하거나 새로운 디자인으로 얼굴을 색칠할지 모른다. 대부분의 혁신은 새로운 것을 만들어 내기 위해 존재하는 두 개 혹은 그 이상의 개념들과 물체들을 재결합하는 것으로 이루어진다. ④ 이러한 요인은 대부분의 기술적 발전이 그러한 재결합의 결과이기 때문에 기술적인 면에서 분명히 드러난다. 북미에서, Fulton은 외륜(paddle wheel), 증기 기관(steam engine), 그리고 배를 가져다 그것들을 한데 모아 증기선을 만들었다.

| 정답해설 | ④ 72% 주어진 문장의 such recombinations(그러한 재결합)는 ④ 앞에서 언급된 the recombining of two ~

something new의 '재결합'을 의미하고 있으므로 주어진 문장은 ④의 위치에 오는 것이 적절하다.

어휘
imperceptible 미세한, 근소한　　　elaborate 자세히 말하다[설명하다]
steamboat 증기선

20 독해 > Macro Reading > 요지 　오답률 21%　답 ④

| 해석 | 비록 곤경에 처한 사람이 낯선 사람일지라도 '유사성'은 같은 집단의 일부가 되는 것으로 구성될 수 있다. 한 연구에서, 학생들은 그들이 가장 선호하는 축구 팀에 대해 생각해 보기를 요청받았는데, 그렇게 함으로써 그 팀의 팬으로서의 그들의 정체성을 활성화시키는 것이었다. 각각의 참가자는 그런 다음 다른 건물로 걸어가도록 요청받았다. 가는 길에, 그는 가장 선호하는 팀의 셔츠 또는 경쟁 팀의 셔츠 또는 팀 이름이 없는 셔츠를 입은 한 학생이 부상을 당한 것을 발견한다. 그 부상 입은 학생은 다른 팀의 셔츠를 입었을 때보다 가장 선호하는 팀의 셔츠를 입었을 때 도움을 더 받았다. 같은 축구 팀의 팬인 사람은 내집단을 형성하며, 일반적으로 말해서, 우리는 외집단의 구성원보다는 내집단 구성원을 더 쉽게 도와주는 경향이 있다.

① 사회 정체성은 사람들의 취미와 깊은 관련이 있다.
② 외집단 구성원은 유사성을 우정의 핵심으로 간주한다.
③ 사람들은 도움을 얻기 위해서 서로를 흉내 내는 경향이 있다.
④ 유사성은 도움을 받을 가능성에 있어서 한몫한다.

| 정답해설 | ④ 79% 같은 축구 팀을 좋아하는 사람을 도울 가능성이 더 크다는 것을 확인했던 연구 결과를 소개하고 있다. 즉, 같은 축구 팀을 좋아하는 것은 '유사성'이 있는 것이다.

| 더 알아보기 | Ingroup & Outgroup

> • Ingroup (내집단): 한 개인이 그 집단에 속한다는 느낌을 가지며, 구성원 간에 우리라는 공동체 의식이 강한 집단
> • Outgroup (외집단): 내가 속한 집단이 아니며 이질감이나 적대 의식을 가지는 집단

어휘
in distress 곤경에 처한　　　　　ingroup 내집단
outgroup 외집단　　　　　　　play a role 역할을 맡다, 한몫하다

합격예상 체크

〈교육행정직 연도별 합격선〉

맞힌 개수	/20문항	점수	/100점

➡ ☐ 합격 ☐ 불합격

취약영역 체크

문항	정답	영역	문항	정답	영역
1	①	어휘 > 빈칸 완성	11	①	생활영어 > 회화/관용표현
2	①	어휘 > 유의어 찾기	12	③	독해 > Logical Reading > 배열
3	②	어휘 > 유의어 찾기	13	③	독해 > Logical Reading > 삭제
4	④	독해 > Logical Reading > 문맥상 다양한 추론	14	④	독해 > Logical Reading > 삽입
5	③	문법 > 동사	15	④	독해 > Logical Reading > 문맥상 다양한 추론
6	②	문법 > 시제, 태	16	④	독해 > Micro Reading > 내용일치/불일치
7	②	문법 > 관계사, 부사	17	②	독해 > Logical Reading > 연결사
8	④	문법 > 분사	18	①	독해 > Reading for Writing > 빈칸 구 완성
9	④	문법 > 분사	19	③	독해 > Macro Reading > 제목
10	①	생활영어 > 회화/관용표현	20	④	독해 > Macro Reading > 요지

⬇ 영역별 틀린 개수로 취약영역을 확인하세요!

어휘	/3	문법	/5	독해	/10	생활영어	/2

➡ 나의 취약영역: _____

※ [정답해설]과 [오답해설] 선지의 50% 표시는 〈1초 합격예측 서비스〉를 통해 수집된 선지 선택률을 나타냅니다.

---

1 어휘 > 빈칸 완성 오답률 22% 답 ①

| 해석 | 만약 당신이 누군가를 ① 이상한 사람으로 묘사한다면, 당신은 그 또는 그녀가 종종 유쾌하지 않은 방식으로 이상하거나 혹은 특이하다고 생각하는 것이다.

① 78% 이상한 ② 12% 외향적인
③ 3% 호응하는 ④ 7% 순종적인

| 정답해설 | ① strange or unusual로 미루어 보아 빈칸에는 이와 유사한 의미를 가지는 peculiar가 적절하다.

어휘
peculiar 이상한　　　　　　　extrovert 외향적인
submissive 순종적인

2 어휘 > 유의어 찾기 오답률 15% 답 ①

| 해석 | 역사를 통틀어서, 음식은 사회 변화, 정치 조직, 지정학적 경쟁, 산업 발전, 군사적 충돌 그리고 경제 확장의 ① 기폭제로서 문명에 커다란 영향을 주어 왔다.

① 85% 계기; 방아쇠 ② 2% 방해물
③ 6% 정당화 ④ 7% 결과

| 정답해설 | ① catalyst(기폭제, 촉매)는 '변화가 일어나는 계기'라는 뜻으로 사용되고, trigger(계기, 방아쇠) 역시 '사건이나 반응을 유발한 계기'라는 의미를 가지고 있다.

3 어휘 > 유의어 찾기 오답률 33% 답 ②

| 해석 | 초기 영장류들의 대부분의 특성들은 그들의 치아나 두개골의 화석들로부터 연구된다. '뼈 화석화'는 미네랄이 서서히 죽은 동물의 뼈의 유기물 함량을 대체하여, 그 결과 원래 뼈의 아주 상세한 석조 ② 복제품이 되는 과정을 말한다. 화석들은 매우 상세하여 현미경 아래에서 긁힌 자국까지 보여 준다.

① 5% 상징 ② 67% 복제품, 사본
③ 15% 남은 부분 ④ 13% 공예품

| 정답해설 | ② replica(복제품, 모형)는 duplicate(복제품, 사본)와 유사하다.

어휘
replica 복제품, 모형　　　　　　duplicate 복제품, 사본
remnant 남은 부분, 나머지

4 독해 > Logical Reading > 문맥상 다양한 추론 오답률 29% 답 ④

| 해석 | 전 세계에서, 에티오피아는 에티오피아 항공의 요하네스버그 사무소가 정기적으로, 음식이 있다 하더라도, 비행 중에 어떤 음식이 제공되는지에 관한 요령 있는 문의를 받을 정도로 사실상 기근 및 사망과 동의어이다. 가뭄과 변덕스러운 강우에 시달리는 대륙에 위치한 나라에 관한 이런 폭넓은 오해는 대중 매체의 작용들에 대해 많은 것을 말해 준다. 그것은 에티오피아에 대해서는 다소 덜 말해 준다. 서구의 잘못된 믿음과는 대조적으로, 에티오피아의 표면 영역의 절반을 포함하고 인구의 대다수를 부양하는

높은 중앙 고원은 아프리카 동쪽의 비옥한 땅에 인접한 가장 광범위한 지역이다. 사막들도 분명 존재하지만, 당신이 기대하는 것처럼 그곳들에는 인구가 ④ 빽빽하게(→ 희박하게) 거주한다. 그곳들은 대부분의 에티오피아인들의 삶에 거의 영향력을 미치지 못하며 관광객들에 의해 방문될 가능성이 거의 없다. 사실상, 비옥한 고랭지 고원이 에티오피아이다.

| 정답해설 | ④ [71%] 빈칸 뒤에 그 사막들은 에티오피아인의 삶에 거의 영향을 미치지 못한다는 내용이 나오므로 '희박하게 인구가 거주하는'이라는 뜻이 되도록 densely는 sparsely가 되어야 한다.

| 오답해설 | ① [6%] 에티오피아 항공기의 기내에서 식사가 제공되는지 문의를 받을 정도로 에티오피아가 기근 및 사막과 같은 의미로 사람들에게 인식된다는 의미이므로 synonymous(동의어인, 같은 의미를 가지는)는 적절하다.

② [10%] Contrary to Western myth ~ 이후의 문장을 통해 에티오피아가 가뭄과 불규칙한 강수량으로 고통을 겪는 나라라는 것은 오해임을 알 수 있다. 그러므로 myth(근거 없는 믿음)와 동의어인 misconception(오해, 잘못된 믿음)은 적절하게 쓰였다.

③ [13%] 비옥한 높은 중앙 고원에 대해 언급하며 앞서 제시된 에티오피아에 대한 일반적인 통념과 반대되는 내용이 이어지므로 대조를 나타내는 Contrary는 적절하다.

| 어휘 |

famine 기근	tactful 요령 있는
enquiry 문의	erratic 변덕스러운
contiguous 인접한, 근접한	to all intents and purposes 사실상

---

5 문법 > 동사 오답률 [23%] 답 ③

| 해석 | ① 나는 몇 년 만에 가장 인상적인 정부 정책들 중 하나를 보았다.
② 내가 만약 당신이라면, 나는 단지 경험을 위해서라도 그 자리에 지원할 것이다.
③ 내가 제주도에 온 후에 그 놀라운 생각이 갑자기 떠올랐다.
④ 나의 지난 편지에서 나는 그들이 그의 동료로서 대우받아야 한다고 촉구했다.

| 정답해설 | ③ [77%] occur는 완전자동사이므로 수동태로 쓸 수 없다. 따라서 was suddenly occurred를 suddenly occurred로 고쳐야 한다.

| 오답해설 | ① [5%] 「one of the + 최상급 + 복수 명사」의 형태가 올바르다.

② [10%] 현재 사실과 반대되는 것을 가정하는 가정법 과거 문장으로, 이때 be동사는 주어의 인칭과 상관없이 were를 사용한다.

④ [8%] 명령, 주장, 제안, 요구 등의 뜻을 나타내는 동사의 목적어로 쓰인 that절이 당위성을 가지면 that절의 동사는 「should + 동사원형」의 형태로 쓴다. 이때 should는 생략 가능하다.

| 더 알아보기 | 수동태로 쓸 수 없는 동사

• come 오다	• happen 발생하다
• occur 발생하다	• remain ~인 채로 남겨지다
• result in 결과적으로 ~이 되다	

---

6 문법 > 시제, 태 오답률 [36%] 답 ②

| 해석 | 미국의 양봉가들은 2006년에 처음 그들의 벌 무리가 죽어 가고 (A) 있다는 것을 알아챘다. 그 후로 과학자들이 무엇이 붕괴를 유발하고 있는가를 알아내기 위해 필사적으로 (B) 노력하고 있다.

| 정답해설 | ② [64%] (A) that절의 주어가 their bee colonies로 복수형이며 in 2006라는 시간 부사구가 있으므로 were가 적절하다.
(B) 주어 scientists(과학자들)와 try는 능동의 관계이므로 동사는 have been trying이 되어야 한다.

| 어휘 |

beekeeper 양봉가	collapse 붕괴, 몰락

---

7 문법 > 관계사, 부사 오답률 [23%] 답 ②

| 해석 | 우리는 우리가 감지 (A) 하는 것을 전체적이고 연속적인 형상으로 체계화하는 경향이 있다. 만약 자극 패턴이 불완전하다면, 우리는 대부분 누락된 요소를 채우려고 할 것이다. K..O.. ..E..A라는 글자들을 읽으면서, 한국인들은 KOREA라는 단어를 형성하기 위해 누락된 철자를 추가하기 쉽다. 그러나 다른 문화의 사람은 이 글자들을 (B) 다르게 읽을 것이고, 무의식적으로 글자 R을 넣지 않을 것이며, 따라서 완전히 다른 글자 해석에 도달할 수 있다.

| 정답해설 | ② [77%] (A) 뒤에 목적어가 없는 불완전한 문장이 오며 앞에 선행사가 없으므로 선행사를 포함한 관계대명사 what이 알맞다.
(B) 앞에 나온 동사 read를 수식하는 부사의 자리이므로 differently가 알맞다.

| 어휘 |

unconsciously 무의식적으로	interpretation 해석

---

8 문법 > 분사 오답률 [23%] 답 ④

| 해석 | 나는 그의 딸이 한 달 동안 그녀의 친구들에게 13,000건의 문자 메시지를 보냈다고 말하는 한 대학 교수를 만났다. 만약 각각의 메시지가 입력되는 데 15초가 걸린다고 한다면, 그 아버지는 딸이 하루에 몇 시간을 아직 나의 맞춤법 검사기가 인식하지도 못하는 단어로 문자 메시지를 보내는 데 소비한다고 계산했다. 문자 메시지를 보내는 것은 분명 중독성이 있고 강박적인 행동이다. 나의 아내와 나는 언젠가 손을 놓고 자전거를 타는 한 젊은 남자를 지나쳐 운전했다. 한 손으로 그는 문자 메시지를 엄지손가락으로 넘겨 보고 있었다. 다른 손에 그는 3~4개월 정도의 아기로 보이는 것을 들고 있었다.

| 정답해설 | ④ [77%] drove와 rode 총 2개의 동사가 연결사 없이 하나의 문장 내에서 사용되었으므로 문법상 옳지 않다. 본동사는 drove이므로 rode는 준동사로 쓰여야 한다. a young man과 ride의 관계가 능동이므로 riding이 되어야 한다.

| 오답해설 | ① [7%] 본동사 met보다 that절의 시제는 한 시제 앞서므로 대과거로 「had p.p.」 형태인 had sent가 적절하다.

② [12%] 「take + 시간 + to부정사」의 구조가 알맞게 쓰였다.

③ [4%] 주어는 동명사 Sending text messages로, 동명사 주어는 단수 취급하므로 be동사 is는 적절하다.

어휘

addictive 중독성이 있는   compulsive 강박적인

오답률 TOP 2

9 문법 > 분사   오답률 37%   답 ④

| 해석 | 감성 지능에 대한 우리의 지식이 계속하여 진화하듯이 정서적 그리고 사회적 지능에 대한 이 책 역시 마찬가지이다. 우리가 이 책의 초판을 쓴 이래로 겨우 10년이 지났다. 이전의 개정판들은 이러한 새로운 주제에 대하여 발생한 과학적이고 경험적인 지식 둘 다의 거대한 증가에 의해 주도되었다. 현재의 개정은 주로 세계에서 가장 널리 사용되는 감성 지능 테스트의 제1차 주요 개정이자, 지금은 Emotional Quotient Inventory 2.0이라고 언급되는 Emotional Quotient Inventory에 의해 주도된 것이다.

| 정답해설 | ④ 63% refer는 '언급하다, 지칭하다'의 의미로, 「refer to A as B(A를 B로 언급한다)」의 형태로 주로 사용된다. 여기서는 refer 뒤에 목적어 없이 to as가 바로 연결된 것으로 보아 수동태인 「A be referred to as B」 형태가 되어야 함을 알 수 있다. 의미상으로도 Emotional Quotient Inventory 2.0이라고 '언급되는'것이므로 referring은 referred로 고쳐져야 한다.

| 오답해설 | ① 2% 본동사가 일반동사 continues이고, so가 이끄는 절의 주어가 단수형인 this book이므로 '이 책도 그렇다'는 so does this book이 되어야 한다.

② 2% 시간, 거리, 가격, 무게 등은 통상적으로 단수 취급을 한다. 그러나 예외적으로 '몇 년이 지나갔다'라는 의미로 하나하나 셀 수 있을 때에는 복수 취급을 한다. 해당 문장에서는 10년이 각각 1년씩 10개가 지나갔다는 의미로 복수 취급을 했으므로 동사 have는 알맞다.

③ 33% 앞의 knowledge를 선행사로 갖는 주격 관계대명사 that으로, both scientific and experiential은 삽입구이다.

어휘

revise 개정하다. 변경하다

오답률 TOP 1

10 생활영어 > 회화/관용표현   오답률 38%   답 ①

| 해석 | A: 나 배고파 죽겠어.
B: 나도 그래. 무엇을 먹고 싶니?
A: 단연코 한식이지. 너도 알다시피 나는 불고기를 정말 좋아하잖아.
B: 오, 이 근처에 괜찮은 한식당이 있다고 들었어.
A: ① 그럼 우리 뭘 기다리는 거야?
B: 좋아! 지금 곧장 갈래?
A: 물론. 예약이 필요하지는 않을까?
B: 아마도, 내가 전화해서 물어볼게.
① 그럼 우리 뭘 기다리는 거야?
② 와, 믿을 수 없어! 거저나 마찬가지야!
③ 내가 고기 싫어하는 거 몰랐니?
④ 오늘은 정말 재수 없는 날인 것 같아.

| 정답해설 | ① 62% 빈칸 다음에 B가 좋다고 수긍하며 지금 곧장 갈지를 물었으므로 빈칸에서 그 한식당에 가자는 의미의 말을 했을 것으로 유추할 수 있다. 따라서 ①이 A의 말로 적절하다.

어휘

be in the mood for ~을 하고 싶은 기분이다
That's a steal. 공짜나 마찬가지야.

11 생활영어 > 회화/관용표현   오답률 14%   답 ①

| 해석 | A: 이봐, 너 늦었어.
B: 미안해. Jenny가 수학 숙제 하는 것을 돕느라 바빴어. 그녀가 몇 개의 문제로 고민하는 것처럼 보였거든.
A: 뭐라고? 곱슬머리 Jenny?
B: 응. 우리 반 Jenny Kim 말이야.
A: ① 너는 물고기에게 수영을 어떻게 하는지 가르친 거야.
B: 그게 무슨 의미야?
A: 그녀는 수학 천재야. 그녀는 사실상 수학에 관해서 모든 것을 알고 있어.
B: 오, 난 그건 몰랐어. 그녀가 도움이 필요 없다고 나에게 전혀 말하지 않았어.
A: Jenny가 아주 생각이 깊어. 그녀는 아마도 네 마음을 상하게 하고 싶지 않았을 거야.
① 너는 물고기에게 수영을 어떻게 하는지 가르친 거야.
② 너에게 먹이를 주는 손은 물지 마.
③ 그녀는 그저 대세를 따른 거야.
④ 말이 도망친 후에 마구간 문을 잠근 거야.

| 정답해설 | ① 86% A가 뒤에 Jenny가 수학 천재라고 말한 것으로 보아 B는 결국 수학 천재가 수학 숙제하는 것을 도운 셈이다. You taught a fish how to swim.은 B와 같이 오지랖이 넓은 사람에게 할 수 있는 비유적 표현으로 가장 적절하다.

| 오답해설 | ② 5% Don't bite the hand that feeds you.는 은혜를 입은 사람에게 배은망덕한 행동은 하지 않아야 한다는 의미이다.

③ 7% She just jumped on the bandwagon.(그녀가 대세를 따랐다.)는 대화 내용과는 관련이 없다.

④ 2% You locked the barn door after the horse escaped.는 '소 잃고 외양간 고친다.'라는 우리말 속담과 일맥상통한다.

| 더 알아보기 | fish를 활용한 관용표현

- a big[small] fish 대단한[하찮은] 인물
- a big fish in a little pond 정저지와(우물 안 개구리)
- a cold fish 냉혈한, 냉정한 사람
- a pretty kettle of fish 아수라장, 엉망진창
- fish in troubled waters 혼란을 타 자기 이익을 취하다

어휘

You taught a fish how to swim. 번데기 앞에서 주름잡다.
jump on the bandwagon 시류에 편승하다

12 독해 > Logical Reading > 배열   오답률 14%   답 ③

| 해석 | 포스트구조주의 이론에서 사회 조직, 사회 의미 그리고 권력과 개인 의식에 대한 분석의 공통 요인은 언어이다.
(C) 언어는 사회 조직의 실제적이며 가능한 형태들과 그들의 그럴싸한 사회적, 정치적 결과들이 정의되고 경쟁하게 되는 곳이다.
(A) 그러나 그것은 또한 우리 자신에 대한 우리의 감각, 즉 우리의 주관성이 구성되는 장소이다.
(B) 주관성이 구성된다는 추정은 그것이 타고난 것이 아니고, 유전학적으로

결정된 것도 아니며 사회적으로 생성된 것이라는 점을 시사한다.

| **정답해설** | ③ 86% (C)는 주어진 문장을 부연 설명하는 내용으로 주어진 문장 바로 다음에 와야 한다. (A)에서 대명사 it이 가리키는 것은 language이고 부사 also와 the place를 통해 (C)에 대한 부연 설명을 하고 있음을 알 수 있다. 그리고 (B)의 The assumption은 (A)에 언급된 내용을 가리키는 것이다. 따라서 (C) – (A) – (B) 순서가 적절하다.

어휘

consciousness 의식, 자각　　　subjectivity 주관성
imply 시사하다, 암시하다

---

13 독해 > Logical Reading > 삭제　　오답률 22%　답 ③

| **해석** | 그들이 1600년대 초반 대서양을 가로질러서 항해했을 때, 유럽 사람들은 그들 자신의 문화적 렌즈를 통해서 새로운 세상을 바라보았다. 그들은 외견상으로는 무한한 풍요로 채워져 있으나, 길들여지지 않았으며, 경작된 밭이나 울타리 또는 농가가 없는 황무지를 보았다. 그들이 만난 미국 원주민들은 유럽 문명의 특징들을 가지고 있지 않았고, 이러한 관점에 따르자면 진정한 종교도 가지고 있지 않은 야만적인 사람들로 여겨졌다. 그러나 그들은 문명화되지 않고, 자연계와 가깝게 살았으며, 그리고 몇몇 유럽 사람들은 이것이 그들에게 유럽 사람인 자신들에게는 없는 단순한 고귀함을 준다고 믿었다. ③ 미국 원주민들은 오랜 경험을 통해 외부인들이 전쟁과 죽음, 그리고 파괴를 가지고 온다고 이해했다. 그래서 그들은 미국 원주민들을 묘사하기 위해 "고결한 야만인"이라는 용어를 만들었다.

| **정답해설** | ③ 78% 본문은 유럽 사람들이 바라본 미국 원주민들에 대한 서술이다. 그런데 ③은 미국 원주민들이 외부인들에 대해 갖고 있었던 생각이므로 전체 글의 내용과 관련이 없다. 이 문장을 제거하고 보면 ②와 ④의 문장이 인과 관계로 자연스럽게 연결된다.

어휘

wilderness 황무지, 황야　　　abundance 풍요
untamed 길들여지지 않은　　　savage 야만인, 미개인
nobility 고귀함, 고결함　　　coin (새로운 어구를) 만들다

---

14 독해 > Logical Reading > 삽입　　오답률 23%　답 ④

| **해석** | Euathlos는 Protagoras로부터 자신의 첫 재판에서 승리할 때까지 그의 수업료에 대해 어떠한 것도 지불할 필요가 없다는, 매우 관대한 합의 하에 어떻게 변호사가 되는지를 배웠다. 그러나 Protagoras가 화가 나게도, Euathlos를 훈련시켰던 그의 시간들을 포기한 후, 그 학생은 음악가가 되기로 결심하고 어떠한 소송도 맡지 않았다. Protagoras는 Euathlos에게 그의 노고에 대한 돈을 지불할 것을 요구하고, 그 음악가가 거절하면, 그를 법정에 세울 것이라고 결심한다. Protagoras는 만약 Euathlos가 소송에서 진다면 그, 즉 Protagoras가 이길 것이고, 이 경우에 그는 그의 돈을 되찾아 올 수 있을 것이며, 그리고 더 나아가 심지어 그가 진다고 하더라도 Euathlos가 소송에 이기게 될 테니 그러므로 그는 여전히 빚을 다 갚아야 할 것이라고 판단한다. ④ 그러나 Euathlos는 다소 다르게 판단한다. 만약 내가 진다면, 그가 생각하기를, 그렇다면 나는 나의 첫 재판을 지는 것이고, 그 경우, 원래의 합의는 어떠한 수업료를 지불해야 하는 것으로부터 나를 해방시켜 줄 것이라고 말이다. 그리고 심지어 그가 이기더라도, Protagoras는 여전히 계약을 강요할 권리를 잃을 것이고, 그리하여 그가 아무것도 지불할 필요가 없을 것이다.

| **정답해설** | ④ 77% 주어진 문장에 역접의 연결사 however가 있고 Euathlos가 자신의 입장에서 소송의 결과를 예측하는 내용이 이어

지므로, 주어진 문장은 Protagoras가 자신의 입장에서 소송의 결과를 예측하는 문장 뒤인 ④ 자리에 들어가는 것이 적절하다. 또한 ④ 뒤에 나오는 문장 Protagoras will still have lost the right to enforce the contract(Protagoras는 여전히 계약을 강요할 권리를 잃을 것이다)에도 Euathlos의 소송 결과에 대한 예측임이 드러나 있다.

어휘

arrangement 합의, 협의　　　reason 판단하다

---

15 독해 > Logical Reading > 문맥상 다양한 추론　　오답률 23%　답 ④

| **해석** | 1984년 10월 21일 대통령 Ronald Reagan과 그의 도전자였던 전직 부통령 Walter Mondale이 대통령 선거 준비 기간에 전국적으로 TV에 방영되는 두 번의 2인 대선 후보 토론 중 하나를 개최했다. Reagan 대통령은 인기를 유지했지만 그의 지지는 ① 그의 나이(그는 토론 당시 73세였다)에 대한 염려가 증가함에 따라 약화되었다. 3주 앞선 이전 토론에서 그의 형편없는 토론은 ② 그의 정신 건강에 대한 의문으로 향하는 문을 열었다. 사회자가 그에게 나이가 선거에서 걱정거리인지를 물었을 때, 그는 ③ 그가 나이를 그 대선 캠페인의 이슈로 만들지 않겠다며 다음과 같이 유명한 말로 답했다. Reagan은 말했다. "저는 정치적인 목적을 위하여 저의 상대방의 젊음과 경험 부족을 부당하게 이용하지 않을 것입니다." 56세로 꼭 햇병아리만은 아니었던 Mondale은 후에 그는 바로 그 순간에 ④ 그가 선거에서 졌음을 알았다고 말했다.

| **정답해설** | 77% ④의 he는 Mondale을 가리키고 나머지 ①②③이 지칭하는 인물은 Reagan이다.

어휘

run-up 준비 (기간)
in light of ~을 고려하여, ~의 관점에서
moderator 조정자, 중재자　　　exploit (부당하게) 이용하다

---

16 독해 > Micro Reading > 내용일치/불일치　　오답률 5%　답 ④

| **해석** | 1982년 7월 2일, 별명이 'Lawnchair Larry'인 미국 트럭 운전사 Lawrence Richard Walters는 직접 비행선을 만들었다. 그의 접이식 의자, 45개의 기상 관측용 헬륨 기구들, 시민 밴드 라디오 및 공기총을 이용하여, 그는 로스앤젤레스 국제공항 근처의 통제된 영공의 위를 15,000피트의 높이로 비행했다. 45분 후, 그는 상업적 영공을 위반했다는 것을 깨달았고, 여러 개의 기구들을 총으로 쏘고 하강하기 시작했다. 그는 그의 공기총을 비행선 밖으로 잃어버렸고 그리고 결국 송전선에 걸려서 Long Beach에서 20분간 정전을 유발했다. 연방 항공법을 위반한 그의 행동과 이후에 진행된 체포는 매체에서 큰 인기를 끌었으며, 영화, 연극, 음악 그리고 심지어 비디오 게임에서까지 문화적인 재해석의 흐름을 낳았다.

| **정답해설** | ④ 95% His action and subsequent arrest for breaking federal aviation laws에서 그가 연방 항공법을 위반하여 체포되었음을 알 수 있다.

어휘

lawn chair 접이식 의자　　　weather balloon 기상 관측용 기구
pellet gun 공기총　　　breach 위반하다
overboard 선체 밖으로　　　spawn (어떤 결과, 상황을) 낳다

17 독해 > Logical Reading > 연결사 | 오답률 10% | 답 ②

| 해석 | 화학자들 또는 물리학자들과 같은 자연 과학자들은 일반적으로 "다른 모든 것들"이 사실은 고정된 (또는 가상으로라도 그러한) 곳에서 통제된 실험들을 수행할 수 있다. 그들은 대단히 정확하게 두 변수들 사이의 가정된 관계를 실험한다. (A) 예를 들어, 그들은 물체가 떨어지는 높이와 바닥과 충돌할 때까지 걸리는 시간의 길이를 측정할 것이다. 그러나 경제학은 실험실 과학이 아니다. 경제학자들은 그들의 이론을 현실 세계의 데이터를 이용하여 실험하고, 이것은 실제 경제 활동에 의해 생성된다. 이러한 다소 혼란스러운 환경에서, "다른 것들"은 변한다. 다른 것들을 동일하게 유지하도록 설계된 복잡한 통계 기술의 발달에도 불구하고, 통제가 완벽하지 않다. (B) 그 결과, 경제학 원리들은 실험실 과학의 원리들보다 덜 확실하고 덜 정확하다. 그것은 또한 그것들이 많은 과학 이론들보다 더 논란의 여지가 있을 것이라는 점을 의미한다.

	(A)	(B)
①	예를 들어	그럼에도 불구하고
②	예를 들어	그 결과
③	그에 반해서	반대로
④	그에 반해서	그러므로

| 정답해설 | ② 90% (A) 빈칸 뒤의 문장은 대단히 정확하게 두 변수들 사이의 가정된 관계를 실험한다는 앞 문장에 대한 구체적 예시이므로 For example이 알맞다.

(B) 빈칸 앞의 control is less than perfect(통제가 완벽하지 않다)라는 내용은 economic principles are less certain and less precise than those of laboratory sciences(경제학 원리들은 실험실 과학의 원리들보다 덜 확실하고 덜 정확하다)라는 빈칸 문장의 원인이다. 따라서 빈칸에는 인과 관계를 나타내는 연결사 As a result가 알맞다.

어휘
precision 정확성, 정밀성   bewildering 혼란스러운

18 독해 > Reading for Writing > 빈칸 구 완성 | 오답률 27% | 답 ①

| 해석 | 수세기 전, 철학자 Jeremy Bentham은 "고통과 기쁨은 우리가 하는 모든 일에서, 우리가 말하는 모든 것에서, 우리가 생각하는 모든 것에서 우리를 지배한다."라고 글을 썼다. 사회의 기관들과 보상 구조들은 대개 Bentham의 주장에 따라서 작동하고 그리하여 인간 행동의 가장 심오한 동기 부여 요소의 일부를 놓치고 있다. Bentham과 나머지 우리가 전형적으로 간과하고 있는 것은 인간이 물리적인 고통과 기쁨만큼이나 기본적인 또 다른 관심사들과 연결되어 있다는 것이다. 우리는 ① 사회적으로 연결되어 있다. 우리는 친구들 및 가족들과의 관계를 유지하고자 하는 깊은 동기들에 의해 움직인다. 우리는 자연스럽게 다른 사람의 마음에는 무슨 일이 일어나는지를 궁금하게 여긴다. 이러한 연결들은 이성적인 이기심에 대한 우리의 기대를 위반하는 행동으로 이어지며, 오직 우리의 ① 사회적 본성이 우리가 누군가에 대한 시작점으로서 받아들여질 때 설명이 된다.

① 사회적   ② 창의적
③ 직관적   ④ 이기적

| 정답해설 | ① 73% 첫 번째 빈칸 바로 다음 문장 We are driven by deep motivations to stay connected with friends and family. 에서 우리는 친구들 및 가족들과의 관계를 유지하고자 하는 깊은 동기들에 의해 움직인다고 하였는데, 이런 인간의 특징을 설명하는 말로 가장 적절한 것은 '사회적으로 연결되어 있다'는 것이다. 따라

서 빈칸에는 social이 가장 적절하다. 두 번째 빈칸에도 동일한 단어를 넣으면 our social nature로 문맥상 자연스러워짐을 알 수 있다.

| 더 알아보기 | Jeremy Bentham (제러미 벤담)

> 영국의 철학자이자 법학자로 영국의 법을 연구하며 엄격하고 통일되지 않은 법률 문제를 비판했다. '최대 다수의 최대 행복'을 추구하는 공리주의를 주장해 유럽 여러 나라에 큰 영향을 끼쳤다. 벤담의 공리주의는 오늘날 민주주의의 기초가 되었다.

어휘
govern 통치하다, 지배하다   miss out on ～을 놓치다
self-interest 이기심   egocentric 이기적인

19 독해 > Macro Reading > 제목 | 오답률 20% | 답 ③

| 해석 | 역사를 통틀어, 그리고 모든 문화에서, 감성적인 눈물들은 흐른다. 누구나, 어디서든, 언젠가는 운다. 예를 들어, 발리를 제외한 모든 문화에서 장례 의례 동안 사람들이 우는데, 심지어 그곳에서도 사람들은 애도하며 운다. 눈물 없는 장례식은 오직 이 의식이 죽음 이후 만 2년이 될 때까지 연기되어야만 가능하다. 전 세계에서, 유아들은 배가 고프거나 아플 때 울며 아이들은 좌절할 때 그리고 실망할 때 운다. 감정 표현을 지배하는 규칙이 시간과 장소에 따라 매우 다양하기는 하지만 성인들은 무수히 많은 이유로 울고 그리고 때때로 소수의 사람들이 주장하기를 아무 이유 없이 운다. 미국 문화에서, 심지어 자신들은 결단코 울지 않는다고 주장하는 보기 드문 사람들도 (대체적으로 남성인) 그들이 어렸을 때 그렇게 했던 것을 기억할 수 있다.

① 우는 것의 문화적 이점들
② 울음을 그치고 생활을 시작하라
③ 눈물 흘리기: 인간의 보편성
④ 감성적인 울음의 다양한 효과

| 정답해설 | ③ 80% everyone, everywhere, cries at some time (누구나, 어디서든, 언젠가는 운다)라는 문장으로 글을 시작하며 장례식장에서의 눈물, 아기와 아이, 성인들이 우는 이유를 언급하며 누구나 운다는 사실을 말하고 있다. 따라서 글의 제목으로는 Shedding Tears: A Human Universal(눈물 흘리기: 인간의 보편성)이 가장 적절하다.

| 오답해설 | ① 5% 본문에서 언급되지 않은 내용이다.
② 3% 울음을 부정적인 관점에서 바라보지 않았다.
④ 12% 울음의 효과들을 설명하고 있지 않다.

어휘
mourning 애도   myriad 무수히 많은
rare 드문, 진귀한, 희귀한

20 독해 > Macro Reading > 요지 | 오답률 21% | 답 ④

| 해석 | 수렵·채집은 자연 환경에서 야생으로 자라는 식물들을 수집하고 이용 가능한 동물들을 사냥하는 것에 기초한 최저 생계 전략이다. 어떤 경우에는 수렵·채집이 전혀 생산처럼 보이지 않을 수도 있다. 숲속을 걸으며, 열매가 나는 나무를 찾고, 그 열매를 따고, 그것을 먹는 것은 현대의 도시인들에게 생산이 아니라 에덴에서 사는 것 같은 느낌을 줄 수 있다. 자연과 직접 접촉하고 살며 식량 확보에 상대적으로 적은 기술을 이용하는 대부분의

사람들은 사실상 단순히 낮게 매달린 과일들을 따는 것보다 더 열심히 일하지만, 자연 환경에서 야생으로 자라는 것을 수집하는 것은 생산의 한 형태이다. 그것은 또한 수렵·채집가의 핵심적인 경제적 전략이다. 생산은 자연 환경의 자원들을 음식으로 바꾸기 위해 의도되는 인간의 어떠한 행위를 말한다. 덤불에서 자라는 딸기들은 식물의 재생산을 위한 단순한 씨앗 운반자이다. 그것들은 그들이 먹을 수 있는 것으로 식별되고 덤불에서 꺾여지기 전까지는 "음식"이 될 수 없다. 그래서 과일을 식별하고 따는 것은 생산 행동이다.

① 생산 활동들은 인간의 생존을 위해 가치가 있다.

② 야생에서 음식을 획득하기 위한 수렵·채집 전략들은 개발되어야 한다.

③ 인간의 생존을 지원하기 위해 환경을 개발하는 것이 필요하다.

④ 우리는 수렵·채집을 생산 행동으로서 이해해야 한다.

| **정답해설** | ④ 79% 수렵·채집은 현대의 도시인들에게 전혀 생산처럼 보이지 않을 수 있지만, 수렵·채집도 생산의 한 형태라고 하면서 수렵·채집이 생산 활동이라는 주장을 뒷받침하기 위한 근거를 제시하는 글이다. 따라서 이 글의 요지로 가장 적절한 것은 ④이다.

| **오답해설** | ① 9% 생산 활동의 가치를 역설하고 있는 글이 아니라 수렵·채집을 생산 활동으로 여겨야 한다는 요지의 글이다.

②③ 9% 3% 본문에서 언급된 바 없다.

어휘

foraging 수렵·채집	subsistence 최저 생활, 생존 수준
strike ~하다는 느낌을 주다	unbanity 도시 생활, 도시풍

편저자 **성정혜**

■ 약력
누적 수강생 43만여 명
(現) 에듀윌 공무원 영어 대표 교수
(現) EBS 영어 전임 강사
(前) 이투스 영어 전임 강사

2023 에듀윌 9급공무원 7개년 기출문제집 영어

발 행 일	2022년 9월 21일 초판
편 저 자	성정혜
펴 낸 이	권대호
펴 낸 곳	(주)에듀윌
등록번호	제25100-2002-000052호
주 소	08378 서울특별시 구로구 디지털로34길 55
	코오롱싸이언스밸리 2차 3층

ISBN 979-11-360-1909-7 (13350)

www.eduwill.net

대표전화 1600-6700

여러분의 작은 소리
에듀윌은 크게 듣겠습니다.

본 교재에 대한 여러분의 목소리를 들려주세요.
공부하시면서 어려웠던 점, 궁금한 점,
칭찬하고 싶은 점, 개선할 점, 어떤 것이라도 좋습니다.

에듀윌은 여러분께서 나누어 주신 의견을
통해 끊임없이 발전하고 있습니다.

에듀윌 도서몰 book.eduwill.net
• 부가학습자료 및 정오표: 에듀윌 도서몰 → 도서자료실
• 교재 문의: 에듀윌 도서몰 → 문의하기 → 교재(내용, 출간) / 주문 및 배송